PLANNING AND DEVELOPMENT LAW

(Second Edition)

AUSTRALIA
Law Book Co.
Sydney

CANADA and USA
Carswell
Toronto

HONG KONG
Sweet & Maxwell Asia

NEW ZEALAND
Brookers
Wellington

SINGAPORE and MALAYSIA
Sweet & Maxwell Asia
Singapore and Kuala Lumpur

Planning and Development Law

(SECOND EDITION)

Garrett Simons

Senior Counsel

THOMSON ROUND HALL
2007

Published in 2007 by
Thomson Round Hall
43 Fitzwilliam Place
Dublin 2
Ireland

Typeset by
Gough Typesetting Services
Dublin

Printed by
MPG Books, Cornwall

ISBN 978-1-85800-436-5

A catalogue record for this book
is available from the British Library

To My Parents

FOREWORD TO THE FIRST EDITION
(2004)

This work is the first major work on Irish Planning Law since the coming into force of the Planning and Development Act 2000. The work is a most welcome addition to the library of any practitioner interested in the field. Mr Simons has demonstrated considerable scholarship and has not been afraid to express opinions on areas of the law which have not been the subject of judicial decision or to question decisions which have been made in the past.

The book deals with all major areas of planning, commencing with development plans and local area plans, the latter of which arises in the context of the Planning and Development Act 2000. The author then deals with the concepts of development and exempted development, which are fundamental to an understanding of the need for planning permission. In the third chapter the author addresses applications for planning permission.

The book then deals with the various stages of applications for planning permission; grants of planning permission; and claims for compensation arising from decisions of planning authorities. The author sets out in a clear manner the procedures to be followed at the stages of application for planning permission and the making of claims for compensation.

Chapter seven of the work deals with the area of enforcement which has been modified by the new Act. This is an area which results in many court applications and will be of particular assistance to legal practitioners.

Chapter nine relates to the appeal procedure to An Bord Pleanála and the author addresses the many important changes in this area effected by the new Act.

Chapter eleven deals with the vexed area of the special judicial review procedure before the Superior Courts. Chapter twelve is related to this chapter insofar as it deals with grounds of challenge. This overall area is one in which the author has demonstrated particular insight and he presents many challenging opinions on the law in this area. Undoubtedly, his experience as a practising barrister will have assisted him in this chapter in which he shows his legal scholarship. This chapter is particularly well presented and will be of considerable assistance to other legal practitioners in the field. The area of judicial review in planning matters results in a huge volume of cases coming before the High Court which is required to deal with these applications as speedily as possible. The author highlights what he perceives to be the disadvantages of the requirement for applications on notice for leave to bring applications for judicial review, which often take many hearing days in the High Court and which may result in further delays before the substantial hearing is concluded in the High Court.

The author has addressed changes in the law since the passing of the Planning and Development Act 2000 and it is clear that this is an area which has been the subject of enormous change in recent years. The effect of this work will be to make a number of existing works redundant. I am sure that this work will prove to be an indispensable tool for many a practitioner as it is a most welcome addition at this time.

The author is to be commended and I wish him every success with the book as it is clear that a huge amount of time and energy has been devoted by him to bringing this work to fruition.

Aindrias Ó Caoimh.
Judge of the High Court,
Four Courts,
Dublin 7.

DISCLAIMER

The content of this book and the views and comments expressed herein are those of, and personal to, the author and are intended for general discussion purposes only. The content of this book is not intended to be, and should not be, relied upon by any party. No representation or warranty is given as to the accuracy or correctness of the content of this book, nor is same represented as containing (or as a substitute for) legal advice or assistance. In particular, given the difficulty in tracking amendments to the legislation and in obtaining up-to-date judgments, no representation or warranty is given that the law was ever correctly stated in respect of any issue or matter, still less that the law is now correctly stated in respect of any issue or matter. Readers must take professional legal advice and assistance in relation to any issue or query which they have in respect of planning law.

No liability whatsoever (whether in contract, negligence, negligent misstatement or otherwise at all) is accepted to any person arising out of any reliance on the content of this book.

PREFACE TO THE SECOND EDITION

It is less than four years since the first edition of *Planning and Development Law* was published. In publishing terms, such an interval is very short, indeed some might say unseemly. An explanation is, therefore, called for. The necessity for a second edition after such a short period arises for two reasons. First, the pace of change—both in terms of case law and legislation—is such that the first edition was in danger of becoming outdated. Secondly, and perhaps more importantly, the compass of the book has been extended so as to take in the implications of European law for town planning, both in terms of the Environmental Impact Assessment Directive ("the EIA Directive") and the European Convention on Human Rights. Each of these topics now has its own dedicated chapter.

The upshot of all of this is that the book has now grown to twice its original size. The curious thing, however, is that, despite the volume of recent case law, the actual contribution which planning law makes to town planning, and, in particular, the contribution which it makes to better decision-making, remains minimal. With the exception of a number of judgments delivered by Clarke J.—in particular, in *Sweetman v An Bord Pleanála* [2007] I.E.H.C. 153 and *Dun Laoghaire Rathdown County Council v Glenkerrin Homes*, unreported, July 19, 2007—most of the case law concerns narrow procedural points and has very little useful to say about town planning or the function of planning authorities and An Bord Pleanála. The courts remain notoriously reluctant to subject decision-making under the planning legislation to meaningful review. If anything, the trend is towards reducing the courts' involvement further. The attitude of the courts to *locus standi* (a person's standing to bring proceedings) and time-limits has hardened, with many more cases being dismissed on such procedural grounds. The judgment of *O'Keeffe v An Bord Pleanála* [1993] 1 I.R. 39 continues as a monolith blocking any evolution in merits-based review. The standard of reasons which a decision-maker is required to give remains minimal, notwithstanding the introduction of what appears to have been intended as a more exacting standard under s.34 of the Planning and Development Act 2000.

Recent legislative reforms also conspire to reduce the usefulness of the courts' role in the planning process. Stricter time-limits have been introduced under the Planning and Development (Strategic Infrastructure) Act 2006, thus placing further obstacles in the way of litigants. The requirement for the leave application in judicial review proceedings to be on notice, and for an applicant to demonstrate "substantial grounds" of challenge, remains. This leave procedure is indefensible, and in many instances simply adds to delay.

The interaction between law and town planning is thus an unhappy one, with the involvement of lawyers making very little positive contribution. This is unfortunate. The decisions of planning authorities and An Bord Pleanála can have a huge impact on the lives of many people, and in the circumstances the courts should be assiduous in ensuring that these powers are properly exercised.

The somewhat *laissez faire* attitude of the Irish courts may have to change in order to comply with the requirements of European law. The case law on Art.6 of the European Convention on Human Rights may well have implications for the procedural requirements governing planning decisions. Moreover, Art.10a of the EIA Directive requires that Member States make provision for a review procedure of the substantive and procedural legality of acts and decisions under the public participation provisions of that Directive. As the discussion in Chapters 13 and 14 demonstrates, the Irish courts have shown little enthusiasm to date for these reforms, but hopefully this will all change.

On a more cheerful note, it is my pleasant task to thank a number of people for their assistance in the completion of this second edition. Professor Yvonne Scannell of Trinity College, Dublin and Arthur Cox Solicitors provided me with inspiration (in the form of her wonderful *Environmental and Land Use Law* (Thomson Round Hall, Dublin, 2006)) and practical help (in the form of insightful comments and advice on a draft of Chapter 13). Yvonne has been a great friend and mentor since my time at Trinity College, Dublin and I am more grateful to her than she will ever know.

My father, Frank Simons, a former planning consultant, kindly read a number of draft chapters and saved me from a number of errors. Frank first sparked my interest in planning law, and has always taken a tremendous interest in my career at the bar.

Dr Áine Ryall of University College Cork and Rónán Kennedy of University College Galway both kindly took time out from their busy teaching and writing schedules to comment on draft chapters.

My colleagues at the Law Library, Niamh Hyland, B.L., Rory Mulcahy, B.L., Jarlath FitzSimons, B.L., and Declan McGrath, B.L., all generously lent of their extensive experience in planning and environmental law. Another colleague, Niall Handy, B.L., burned the midnight oil proofreading the final draft, making numerous suggestions for improvements. My former devil Fintan Valentine, B.L. also read a number of chapters. Fintan, together with another former devil, Nap Keeling, B.L., is writing the planning law section of the forthcoming *Construction Law Practitioner*, which will undoubtedly be a great success. Margaret Gray, B.L., who practices both here and in London, shared with me her expertise in Human Rights law and read a number of drafts of Chapter 14. I also want to thank Colm MacEochaidh, B.L. and Micheál D. O'Connell, B.L., for continually challenging me with their views on planning law.

In terms of the publication process, I am very grateful—again—to both Catherine Dolan and Martin McCann of Thomson Round Hall for the enthusiasm and professionalism with which they oversaw the production process. I had the pleasure of working with both Catherine and Martin on the first edition, and hope to do so again on the third (albeit not for at least five years). My secretary, Jackie Campbell, provided good-humoured assistance throughout. I also owe a debt of gratitude to Des Mulhere of the Law Library for his thoroughness in proofreading and cite-checking.

Finally, I want to thank Austin for putting up with me while I was working on this second edition; I would not have completed it without his love and encouragement.

Garrett Simons
Law Library Distillery Building,
145–151 Church Street,
Dublin 7.
July 24, 2007.

PREFACE TO THE FIRST EDITION

Planning enjoys an undeserved reputation as a dull and technical area of the law. This stems in large part from the fact that it is heavily codified and thus lacks the colour of the common law with its snails in bottles and precocious toddlers. I readily admit, however, that I am biased in this regard and that my interest in planning law owes more to the following two individuals than to any intellectual curiosity.

My initial interest in planning law was sparked by my father. Frank is a civil engineer by qualification but in the latter years of his professional life he had practised primarily as a planning consultant. His enthusiasm for planning law, and, in particular, his enjoyment of the cut and thrust of oral hearings, was infectious. Like many lawyers, I am unable to either add or subtract and accordingly I had to settle for studying law instead of engineering at college. At Trinity College Dublin I was lucky enough to be taught environmental and planning law by Yvonne Scannell. Yvonne was and is an inspirational lecturer. She has also shown me great kindness and given me encouragement throughout my career and for this I am very grateful.

My original intention had been to write a book which would deal principally with the procedural aspects of planning law. In particular, it had been intended to concentrate on the three areas of greatest relevance to legal practitioners, namely appeals and referrals to An Bord Pleanála; judicial review proceedings; and enforcement proceedings. It soon became apparent, however, that in order to put these in context, it would be necessary to extend the scope of the work to include an overview of the planning code as a whole. Thus whereas there is certainly still a bias in favour of procedural aspects (with detailed chapters on judicial review and enforcement), I hope that the book may be of interest to more than just legal practitioners and students. I am conscious, however, that I have yet to achieve the correct balance between procedural and substantive law content. This is something which will have to be addressed in any subsequent edition; in this regard, any comment or constructive criticism would be welcome.

The (altered) objective of this book is thus to attempt to provide a guide to the provisions of the Planning and Development Acts 2000 to 2002. That any guide is needed at all is a cause for regret: the consolidation and modification of the planning legislation under the Planning and Development Act 2000 represented a golden opportunity to provide a clear statement of planning law. The opportunity was not taken however and the Planning and Development Act 2000 is an unwieldy piece of legislation. The language used is often obscure and unnecessarily wordy. The Act is badly laid out, with some individual sections running on over several pages. Even the attempt at consolidation failed: the Planning and Development Act 2000 has already been amended on numerous occasions, in particular by the Local Government Act 2001; the Planning and Development (Amendment) Act 2002; and the Protection of the Environment Act 2003.

The lack of clarity is all the more disappointing given that planning is an issue which impacts on members of the public on a daily basis. The planning legislation should therefore be readily accessible and understandable, and it should not be necessary to have recourse to legal advice save in exceptional cases. In practice, however, it is often difficult to know what is intended by the legislation. Moreover, certain modifications introduced under the Planning and Development Act 2000 have given rise to traps for the unwary. To take just one example: in order to make an appeal against the decision on an application for planning permission, it is necessary for a third party appellant to ensure that the appeal is accompanied by an acknowledgment from the planning authority of the receipt of submissions or observations made by the appellant.

Many planning authorities fail to provide such written acknowledgment in good time, or issue same in an incorrect name. This may well result in the right of appeal being frustrated. Recent reports from An Bord Pleanála indicate that a greater proportion of appeals than ever before have been rejected as invalid since the coming into effect of the Planning and Development Act 2000 for this and other reasons.

The difficulty in knowing what the law says is not confined to lay people. I must frankly admit that I have found it very hard to identify what the legal requirements are in respect of particular aspects of the planning legislation. This difficulty stems not only from the obscure language used in the legislation but also from the fact that it is not always possible to track subsequent amendments to legislation given that same are often hidden in unrelated Acts or, worse still, in statutory instruments. There are also problems in relation to sourcing judgments in that same are not always circulated promptly. For this reason, I have only been able to attempt to state the law as of June 1, 2003. No representation or warranty is given that the text is accurate up to even this date.

Finally, it is my pleasant task to acknowledge a number of people who have assisted, whether directly or indirectly, in the production of this work. Mr. Justice Ó Caoimh has very kindly written a foreword for which I am very grateful. My father, Frank Simons, read the entire of the first draft and made numerous suggestions for amendment and improvement which I was pleased to take on board. My colleague Declan McGrath provided useful comment on a draft of the chapter on enforcement. My former devils Neil Steen and Nap Keeling both provided valuable assistance and support. Maryrose Fitzsimons prepared much of typescript with unfailing good humour. Mick and Rosaleen O'Connell generously put me up in their home in Valentia Island while I proofread the final draft. Catherine Dolan of Thomson Roundhall remained committed to the project in its various guises. Des Mulhere burnt the midnight oil proofreading.

Last but not least I wish to record my gratitude to Denis McDonald, S.C., for whom I devilled, and to Colm Allen, S.C., by whom I was led in my first planning case. Each, in his own way, taught me a great deal about the business of being a barrister. More than this, however, each gave me invaluable support and encouragement in my early years of practice for which I am genuinely grateful.

Garrett Simons
Law Library Distillery Building,
145–151 Church Street,
Dublin 7.
September 1, 2003.

TABLE OF CONTENTS

TABLE OF CASES

IRELAND

ENGLAND AND WALES

SCOTLAND

UNITED STATES OF AMERICA

EUROPEAN COURT OF JUSTICE

EUROPEAN COURT OF HUMAN RIGHTS

TABLE OF LEGISLATION

IRISH STATUTORY INSTRUMENTS

EC TREATY

EUROPEAN DIRECTIVES

THE EUROPEAN CONVENTION ON HUMAN RIGHTS

ENGLISH STATUTES

CHAPTER ONE

DEVELOPMENT PLANS AND LOCAL AREA PLANS DEVELOPMENT CONTRIBUTION SCHEMES

A. Introduction

Under Pt II of the Planning and Development Act 2000 (hereinafter referred to as the "PDA 2000" where convenient), each planning authority is required to make a plan indicating the development objectives for its area. More specifically, a development plan shall set out an overall strategy for the proper planning and sustainable development of the area of the development plan, and shall consist of a written statement and a plan or plans indicating the development objectives for the area in question.[1] A planning authority also has discretion to make any number of local area plans in respect of particular areas.[2] These local area plans are subservient to the development plan: a local area plan must be consistent with the objectives of the development plan[3] and, in the event of conflict, it is the development plan which prevails.[4]

1–01

---

[1] PDA 2000, s.10(1). The written statement and plans are to be read together: see *Aer Rianta v An Bord Pleanála*, unreported, High Court, Kelly J., June 25, 2002.
[2] PDA 2000, s.18.
[3] PDA 2000, s.19(2).
[4] PDA 2000, s.18(4).

1–02 The development plan lies at the heart of the planning legislation. The Supreme Court famously described the development plan as forming an "environmental contract" between the planning authority and the public.[5]

> "The plan is a statement of objectives; it informs the community, in its draft form, of the intended objectives and affords the community the opportunity of inspection, criticism, and, if thought proper, objection. When adopted it forms an environmental contract between the planning authority, the Council, and the community, embodying a promise by the Council that it will regulate private development in a manner consistent with the objectives stated in the plan and, further, that the Council itself shall not effect any development which contravenes the plan materially. The private citizen, refused permission for development on such grounds based upon such objectives, may console himself that it will be the same for others during the currency of the plan, and that the Council will not shirk from enforcing these objectives on itself."

B. Legal Effects of Development Plan

1–03 The legal effects of the development plan are manifold, and extend from representing a blueprint for the determination of applications for planning permission,[6] to operating as a fetter on the local authority's own development.[7] These various effects are considered next in further detail. The procedure for the making, amendment, and variation of a development plan and a local area plan are then examined.

1. General duty to secure objectives

1–04 A planning authority is under a general duty to secure the objectives of the development plan. More specifically, under s.15 of the PDA 2000 it shall be the duty of a planning authority to take such steps within its powers as may be necessary for securing the objectives of the development plan. In this regard, the manager of a planning authority shall, not more than two years after the making of a development plan, give a report to the elected members of the planning authority on the progress achieved in securing the objectives.[8] An additional monitoring requirement applies in the case of a development plan subject to environmental assessment under the Planning and Development (Strategic Environmental Assessment) Regulations 2004.[9]

---

[5] *Attorney General (McGarry) v Sligo County Council* [1991] 1 I.R. 99 at 113; [1989] I.L.R.M. 768 at 772. See, generally, J. Macken, "The Legal Status of the Development Plan: Environmental Contract or Development Guidelines?" (1995) 2 I.P.E.L.J. 11.

[6] *Tennyson v Dun Laoghaire Corporation* [1991] 2 I.R. 527 at 535.

[7] PDA 2000, s.178.

[8] PDA 2000, s.15(2).

[9] Under art.13J of the Planning and Development Regulations 2001 (as inserted by the 2004 Regulations), the planning authority is required to monitor the significant environmental effects of the implementation of the development plan in order, *inter alia*, to identify at an early stage unforeseen adverse effects and to be able to undertake appropriate remedial action and, for this purpose, existing monitoring arrangements may

It is unclear as to the extent to which the statutory duty under s.15 might be **1–05** enforced before the courts. As appears from the wording of the section, there is a very significant qualification on the duty in that a planning authority is only required to take such steps as are "within its powers". Moreover, development objectives will inevitably be expressed in broad terms, and thus it would be difficult to establish that a planning authority was, in fact, in breach of this duty. This is especially so where no date is specified in the development plan by which a particular objective is to be fulfilled. There is also the following practical consideration. Although a planning authority is empowered itself to develop or secure the development of land, and to acquire land,[10] the reality is that the successful implementation of a development plan depends to a large extent on private-sector investment and on government funding, matters over which a planning authority can exercise little control. Accordingly, it would seem to be difficult to enforce the duty as against the planning authority.

As against this, s.15 may nevertheless have some bite. Under the previous **1–06** legislation, the equivalent provision had been successfully invoked in conjunction with that provision prohibiting a local authority from effecting any development in its functional area which contravenes materially the development plan[11] so as to enjoin certain local authority development. (The case law in relation to the statutory prohibition is discussed immediately below at paras 1–10 to 1–20.) Whereas it would seem that the judgments were largely influenced by the statutory prohibition on local authority development in material contravention of the development plan, it may be that the general duty to secure the objectives of the development plan will come to the fore given certain legislative changes introduced since. In particular, the significance of the statutory prohibition on local authority development in material contravention of the development plan has been attenuated in certain contexts by subsequent statutory amendment: for example, in the context of the development of facilities for waste disposal or recovery.[12] In the circumstances, an ingenious objector may seek to invoke the provisions of s.15, which do not appear to have been by-passed.

In at least two cases under the previous legislation[13] an attempt had been made **1–07** to invoke the duty to secure the objectives of the development plan. In *Browne v Cashel UDC*,[14] the High Court held that one consequence of the duty was that the planning authority could not purport to give an undertaking or indication that planning permission for development in material contravention of the

---

be used, if appropriate, with a view to avoiding duplication of monitoring. The statutory report of the manager under s.15(2) shall include information in relation to progress on, and the results of, monitoring the significant environmental effects of the implementation of the development plan.

[10] Pt XIV of the PDA 2000.

[11] See now PDA 2000, s.178.

[12] See, generally, s.4 of the Waste Management (Amendment) Act 2001 amending the Waste Management Act 1996. See further paras 8–352 to 8–353.

[13] Local Government (Planning & Development) Act 1963, s.22.

[14] Unreported, High Court, Geoghegan J., March 26, 1993.

development plan would be granted. The judgment arose in the context of a claim for compensation: as under the PDA 2000, the previous legislation had allowed a planning authority to defer a claim for compensation by serving a notice indicating that, in the opinion of the planning authority, the land in question was capable of other (beneficial) development for which planning permission ought to be granted. The High Court in *Browne v Cashel UDC* suggested that the power to serve such a notice was limited to circumstances where the other development would not represent a material contravention of the development plan. This judgment has since been overruled by the Supreme Court in *Ballymac Designer Village Ltd. v Louth County Council.*[15]

1–08　In *Hynes v An Bord Pleanála*,[16] it was suggested that one instance of where the statutory duty to secure the objectives of the development plan operated to constrain a planning authority was in respect of the manner in which it could authorise the use of land in its functional area. More specifically, it was argued that a planning authority could not consent to the making of an application for planning permission by a private-sector developer over lands in its ownership in circumstances where the proposed development would represent a material contravention of the development plan. On the facts, the statutory prohibition on the effecting of such development would not appear to have been directly applicable in that the development was to be carried out by a private-sector developer.

1–09　Finally, reference is made to the judgment in *O'Mahony v An Bord Pleanála.*[17] The applicant sought leave to challenge a decision of An Bord Pleanála confirming a compulsory purchase order. One of the grounds advanced was to the effect that An Bord Pleanála had not had proper regard to an alleged breach of s.15. The applicant argued that the proposed road improvements made inadequate provision for access to his lands and that, as these lands were zoned for residential use, this represented a breach of the planning authority's obligations under s.15. O'Neill J. ruled that the decision as to whether there was such a breach was one which was within the competence of An Bord Pleanála to consider, and indicated that, in circumstances where the matter had been extensively canvassed at the oral hearing before An Bord Pleanála, its decision could only be disturbed if it was shown to be irrational. On the facts, O'Neill J. stated that there was "ample material" to support An Bord Pleanála's decision.

2. Local authority development

1–10　A local authority is prohibited from effecting any development in its functional area which contravenes materially the development plan.[18] This prohibition

---

[15] [2002] 3 I.R. 247; [2002] 2 I.L.R.M. 481.
[16] Unreported, High Court, Laffoy J., December 10, 1997 (leave application); unreported, High Court, McGuinness J., July 30, 1998 (full hearing).
[17] [2005] I.E.H.C. 39; unreported, O'Neill J., February 18, 2005.
[18] PDA 2000, s.178.

represents a significant fetter on a local authority: generally, local authority development in its own functional area is exempted development,[19] and thus free from the requirement to obtain planning permission.

The equivalent provision under the previous legislation had been invoked on a **1–11** number of occasions so as to enjoin local authority development.[20] This case law represents almost the only example of judicial activism in planning law. The approach of the courts in this regard can be contrasted dramatically with the very real self-restraint shown in respect of challenges to decisions on an application for planning permission.[21] Indeed, the case law in this area gave rise to one of the most celebrated conceits in environmental law, namely that of the "environmental contract". McCarthy J. sought to characterise a development plan as forming an environmental contract between the planning authority and the public in *Attorney General (McGarry) v Sligo County Council.*[22] The radical nature of the judgments in this area may be illustrated by reference to the following three points.

Actionable at the suit of any affected person

The first is the finding by the courts that a breach of the prohibition on local **1–12** authority development in material contravention of the development plan is actionable at the suit of any affected person. Although the relevant section had provided for a prohibition on such local authority development,[23] it had not indicated the consequence of any breach thereof: in particular, it had not indicated what remedy might be available. Presumably for this reason, in one of the early cases, that of *Attorney General (McGarry) v Sligo County Council* itself,[24] the applicants had taken the precaution of seeking the fiat (consent) of the Attorney General to the taking of the proceedings. McCarthy J. in the Supreme Court indicated that such caution was unnecessary.

> "The plaintiffs 'related' the allegations to the Attorney General and he, on 3rd November, 1983, authorised relator proceedings in which form the action proceeded with the Attorney General as plaintiff. The issue did not arise for discussion in the instant appeal, and is one that would require elaborate examination, but I am not to be taken as supporting or otherwise the apparent view of the High Court judge that it was necessary to bring these proceedings as a relator action."

In subsequent judgments it appears to have been taken as read that the statutory **1–13** prohibition was directly enforceable. This might be thought somewhat

---

[19] PDA 2000, s.4. See para.2–93 below.
[20] Local Government (Planning & Development) Act 1963, s.39.
[21] Exemplified by the decision in *O'Keeffe v An Bord Pleanála* [1993] 1 I.R. 39; [1992] I.L.R.M. 237.
[22] [1991] 1 I.R. 99 at 113; [1989] I.L.R.M. 768 at 772. See, generally, J. Macken, "The Legal Status of the Development Plan: Environmental Contract or Development Guidelines?" (1995) 2 I.P.E.L.J. 11.
[23] Local Government (Planning & Development) Act 1963, s.39.
[24] [1991] 1 I.R. 99; [1989] I.L.R.M. 768. *Cf. Attorney General (Martin) v Dublin Corporation*, unreported, High Court, Gannon J., February 13, 1979.

surprising: generally, it is a question of statutory interpretation as to whether or not breach of a statutory duty gives rise to a cause of action. At the very least, one might have expected that it would be necessary for an applicant to demonstrate that he or she had been personally affected by the alleged breach. Insofar as the matter has been discussed at all in subsequent decisions, it seems that the courts have latched onto the concept of an environmental contract as one allowing the statutory prohibition to be invoked by any person.[25]

Duty to disclose

1–14 The second aspect of the case law which is radical is the evolution of the concept of a material contravention. What is meant by "material contravention" is discussed in more detail at paras 1–46 to 1–55 below. It is sufficient for the purposes of the present discussion to make the following observations. The case law in relation to the statutory prohibition appears to have extended the concept of a material contravention from one involving a breach of a specific provision of the development plan, to one which amounts to the imposition of a duty to disclose on a planning authority.

1–15 The existence of such a duty to disclose was first tentatively suggested in the decision in *Keogh v Galway Corporation*.[26] The facts of the case briefly were these. The local authority had indicated a number of proposed locations for halting sites in the development plan. It was then sought to develop another, previously undisclosed, site. Carney J. held in the High Court that this would represent a material contravention of the development plan. In effect, the local authority, having indicated a number of sites, could not then proceed to develop an undisclosed site. Carney J. expressed no view as to the situation which would have prevailed had the development plan been silent as to halting sites. The judgment is of interest in that under the then legislation, objectives in relation to travellers' halting sites were not a mandatory development objective. In other words, there was no *express* requirement on a planning authority to include development objectives in this regard in the development plan. Notwithstanding this statutory position, Carney J. seemed to be suggesting that a planning authority was nevertheless required to give notice to a citizen of development which might affect him or her in a substantial way, in order that he or she might have the opportunity of stating his or her case in relation to what was projected.

1–16 This idea of a duty to disclose was expanded upon in subsequent decisions. In *Roughan v Clare County Council*,[27] Barron J. indicated that he did not accept that it was unnecessary for a local authority to include all its development objectives in its plan. In his opinion, if such a submission was to be accepted, it would enable the local authority, in perhaps only exceptional cases but

---

[25] See, for example, the decision in *Wicklow Heritage Trust Ltd. v Wicklow County Council*, unreported, High Court, McGuinness J., February 5, 1998.

[26] [1995] 3 I.R. 457.

[27] Unreported, High Court, Barron J., December 18, 1996.

certainly in some cases, to totally override not only the plan but the consultative procedures preceding the making of a development plan. In Barron J.'s view this could not be the law. Similar sentiments were expressed by McGuinness J. in *Wicklow Heritage Trust Ltd. v Wicklow County Council*.[28] Again, as in *Keogh v Galway Corporation*, the development was not of such a type as to be a mandatory development objective under the then legislation.

Private-sector comparator

The third example of judicial radicalism is to be found in a series of cases from the late 1980s, which put forward a test of a private-sector comparator. More specifically, these cases appeared to suggest that in determining whether or not there had been a material contravention of the development plan, it was appropriate to consider whether or not planning permission would have been granted to a private-sector developer (herein referred to as "the private-sector comparator"). This was a very bold stance in that under the then legislation,[29] as now, local authority development was exempted development and, therefore, any comparison with a private developer would seem to be misconceived. The private-sector comparator had first arisen in the decision in *O'Leary v Dublin County Council*.[30] It would seem, however, from a reading of the judgment that the private-sector comparator was a response to a specific argument put forward by the local authority. The case concerned a proposed development by the local authority of a travellers' halting site. The area in which the halting site was to be located was designated as an area of high amenity under the development plan. The local authority had sought to argue that as the extent of the proposed development was small in comparison with the very large area designated as high amenity, any contravention of the development plan was not material. O'Hanlon J. found it useful to draw a comparison between the local authority development and a hypothetical application for similar development by a private-sector developer, and concluded that a private developer would not be successful in relying on such a *de minimis* argument.

1–17

In the subsequent decision of *Wilkinson v Dublin County Council*,[31] Costello J. sought to extend the use of the private-sector comparator test. In particular, Costello J., having found that the proposed halting site in that case did not involve an infringement of the zoning provisions of the development plan, nevertheless went on to suggest that a development might still amount to a material contravention of the plan if it is one which was not consistent with the proper planning and development of the area. To this end, he sought to rely on the private-sector comparator test. With respect, Costello J.'s suggestion that a decision inconsistent with the proper planning and development of the area would represent a material contravention of the development plan is somewhat artificial. The real basis for review would appear to be that of administrative

1–18

---

[28] Unreported, High Court, McGuinness J., February 5, 1998.
[29] Local Government (Planning & Development) Act 1963, s.4.
[30] [1988] I.R. 150.
[31] [1991] I.L.R.M. 605.

unreasonableness[32]: the development plan is not the ultimate standard for what constitutes proper planning and development, as is evidenced by the fact that permission may be both refused or granted contrary to its terms.

1–19 The radical approach adopted in the decision in *Wilkinson v Dublin County Council* appears to have been disapproved of by the Supreme Court in its decision in *Ferris v Dublin County Council*.[33]

1–20 It is submitted that the entire episode illustrates the extent to which the courts were prepared to push back the boundaries in relation to the statutory prohibition on local authority development in material contravention of the development plan. The overstretched application of the private-sector comparator test came close to open defiance of the statutory provision which exempted local authority development from the requirement to obtain planning permission.

3. Application for planning permission

1–21 The development plan occupies a pivotal role in the determination of any application for planning permission. More specifically, under s.34(2)(a) of the PDA 2000, a planning authority, and An Bord Pleanála on appeal, are required to "have regard to" the provisions of the development plan in determining an application for planning permission. Similar provision is made in respect of a local area plan under s.18(3).

1–22 There is a presumption in favour of adhering to the development plan, in the sense that special procedures must be observed before planning permission may be granted for development which would represent a material contravention of the plan.[34]

1–23 In practice, consideration of the proper planning and sustainable development of an area, and of the development plan, are often inextricably linked; development objectives may be characterised as an attempt to articulate in general terms the proper planning and sustainable development of the area. Whereas in the context of many applications the subject-matter of these twin considerations will coincide, the key distinction is that the consideration of the proper planning and sustainable development of an area underpins the discretionary nature of the planning process. Each application must be considered on its own merits, and factors such as, for example, personal circumstances, may exceptionally be considered in the context of an individual planning application, notwithstanding the fact that such factors could not properly be made the subject of a general objective such as might be included in a development plan.[35]

---

[32] See, generally, paras 12–74 to 12–89.
[33] Unreported, Supreme Court, November 7, 1990.
[34] Paras 1–27 to 1–32 below.
[35] See, by analogy, *Great Portland Estates Ltd. v Westminster City Council* [1985] A.C. 661.

The terms of the development plan are not conclusive: the overriding   **1–24**
consideration must be the proper planning and sustainable development of the
area. The language of s.34 is noteworthy. A planning authority and An Bord
Pleanála are "restricted" to "considering" proper planning and sustainable
development, whereas they are only required to "have regard to" the provisions
of the development plan.[36] As discussed below at paras 1–27 to 1–32, express
provision is made under the legislation for planning permission to be granted
in breach (material contravention) of the development plan. The legislation,
therefore, prescribes a hierarchy of matters which are to be taken into account
in determining an application or an appeal. Thus, for example, an application
for a proposed development which would accord with the zoning objectives in
the plan, would nevertheless have to be refused if the proposed development
would be contrary to the proper planning and sustainable development of the
area.

The statutory formula "have regard to" was examined, albeit in the context of   **1–25**
regional planning guidelines, in *McEvoy v Meath County Council*.[37] Quirke J.
held that the requirement "to have regard to" obliged a planning authority to
inform itself fully of, and give reasonable consideration to, any regional planning
guidelines which are in force in the area which is the subject of the development
plan, with a view to accommodating the objectives and policies contained in
such guidelines. Quirke J. went on to state that whilst reason and good sense
would dictate that it was in the main desirable that planning authorities should,
when making and adopting development plans, seek to accommodate the
objectives and policies contained in relevant regional planning guidelines,
planning authorities were not bound to comply with the guidelines, and could
depart from them for bona fide reasons consistent with the proper planning
and development of the area for which the planning authority has planning
responsibilities.

It is submitted that a similar approach should apply in the context of an   **1–26**
application for planning permission. In particular, it is submitted that the
approach in *McEvoy v Meath County Council* is to be preferred to that of the
High Court in *Glencar Explorations plc v Mayo County Council*.[38] In this
latter judgment, Blayney J. had held that a local authority could not be said to
have had regard to the policy of the government in respect of mining when it
adopted as part of its development plan a policy which was totally opposed to
government policy. This is to impose too high a standard. Instead, the correct
balance will be achieved by insisting that a planning authority and An Bord

---

[36] See also PDA 2000, s.18(3) (have regard to local area plan).
[37] [2003] 1 I.R. 208; [2003] 1 I.L.R.M. 431. For an example of a case where a planning
authority was held to have failed to have regard to the provisions of the development
plan, see *Griffin v Galway City and County Manager*, unreported, High Court, Blayney
J., October 31, 1990.
[38] [1993] 2 I.R. 237. See also *Griffin v Galway City and County Manager*, unreported, High
Court, Blayney J., October 31, 1990.

Pleanála state reasons for not following the development plan. The formula in *McEvoy v Meath County Council* suggests that departure from the terms of a general policy is permissible for bona fide reasons consistent with the proper planning and sustainable development of the area. In order to police this limitation, however, it is essential that the decision-maker be required to state the reasons being relied upon for the departure.

Planning permission in material contravention of development plan

1–27 Express provision is made whereby a planning authority is entitled to grant planning permission for a development which would materially contravene the development plan.[39] A special statutory procedure must, however, be followed. The fact that a planning authority is expressly authorised to depart from the development plan confirms the point being made above to the effect that the provisions of the development plan are not binding, and as to the limitations on the statutory formula "have regard to".

1–28 The material contravention procedure is as follows. Notice must be given of the intention of the planning authority to consider granting planning permission in material contravention. This requires publication in at least one daily newspaper circulating in the functional area, and the giving of notice to the applicant and to any person who has submitted a submission or observation in writing in relation to the development to which the application relates. The planning authority must consider any submission or observation which is received by the planning authority not later than four weeks after the first publication of the notice. A resolution of the elected members requiring that a decision to grant permission be made must then be passed. The number of the members of the planning authority voting in favour of the resolution must be not less than three-quarters of the total number of the elected members of the planning authority.

1–29 It is to be noted that the requirement under s.34(6) that a special procedure be adopted before planning permission may be granted for development which would involve a material contravention of the development plan is disapplied in certain circumstances under the Waste Management Act 1996 (as amended by the Waste Management (Amendment) Act 2001, and by the Protection of the Environment Act 2003). See paras 3–140 to 3–143.

1–30 Different restrictions apply to An Bord Pleanála. Under the previous legislation, whereas An Bord Pleanála was required to have regard to the provisions of the development plan, no particular procedure had to be observed before the board could grant planning permission in material contravention of the development plan.[40] The position is more strict under the PDA 2000. In particular, where a planning authority has decided to refuse permission on the grounds that a

---

[39] PDA 2000, s.34(6).
[40] Local Government (Planning & Development) Act 1976, s.14(8).

proposed development materially contravenes the development plan, An Bord Pleanála may only grant planning permission where it considers that (i) the proposed development is of strategic or national importance; (ii) there are conflicting objectives in the development plan or the objectives are not clearly stated insofar as the proposed development is concerned; (iii) planning permission for the proposed development should be granted having regard to regional planning guidelines for the area, statutory guidelines, statutory policy directives, the statutory obligations of any local authority in the area, and any relevant policy of the Government, the Minister for the Environment, Heritage and Local Government or any Minister of the Government; or (iv) planning permission for the proposed development should be granted having regard to the pattern of development, and permissions granted, in the area since the making of the development plan.

Where An Bord Pleanála exercises its power to grant planning permission, there is a requirement under s.37(2)(c) to give additional reasons indicating the main reasons and considerations for contravening materially the development plan. **1–31**

It is to be noted that, somewhat surprisingly, these restrictions are only triggered where the planning authority has decided to refuse planning permission on the grounds that a proposed development materially contravenes the development plan. Thus if the planning authority mistakenly rules that a proposed development does not involve a material contravention of the development plan, and proceeds to grant planning permission without invoking the special material contravention procedure, then it seems that An Bord Pleanála is free from the restrictions. **1–32**

4. Application for strategic infrastructure development

In contrast to the position in respect of all other development, there are no restrictions on the circumstances in which An Bord Pleanála may decide to grant a permission for strategic infrastructure development, or any part thereof, which contravenes materially the development plan.[41] **1–33**

As discussed at para.10–49, the new strategic infrastructure procedure is only applicable to developments which meet certain qualifications: these include that the development be of strategic economic or social importance, or that the development would contribute significantly to the fulfilment of any of the objectives in the National Spatial Strategy or in any regional planning guidelines. In many cases, therefore, development of the type now subject to the new procedure would not, even under the unamended legislation, have had to be refused where it would involve a material contravention. **1–34**

---

[41] PDA 2000, s.37G(6) (as inserted by the 2006 Act).

5. Enforcement of planning control

1–35 Under the previous legislation, the development plan was a mandatory consideration to be taken into account by the planning authority in deciding whether or not to take certain types of enforcement action. In particular, a planning authority was required to have regard to the provisions of the development plan before deciding whether or not to serve an enforcement notice.[42]

1–36 The position under the PDA 2000 is less clear. There is no express requirement to have regard to the provisions of the development plan: under s.153(3) a planning authority in deciding whether to issue an enforcement notice shall consider any representations, submissions, or observations made to it, and any "other material considerations". It is submitted that this latter phrase is wide enough to include the provisions of the development plan. It would be anomalous were the planning authority to be at large to issue an enforcement notice in circumstances where the impugned development was consistent with the development plan.

1–37 From first principles, one might have thought that the same considerations which apply in relation to a decision on an application for planning permission should inform a decision on enforcement action. In a sense, the decision as to whether or not to serve an enforcement notice is the obverse of the decision to grant or refuse planning permission, in that given the Draconian effects of an enforcement notice it would seem inappropriate to issue an enforcement notice in circumstances where the development was not objectionable in planning terms, and planning permission would inevitably have been granted had an application in that regard been made.[43] The matter is complicated under the new legislation in that it is elsewhere provided that no enforcement action shall be stayed or withdrawn by reason of the fact that an application for retention planning permission has been made, or even granted.[44] This might be taken as suggesting that the two things are separate, and that the primary purpose of an enforcement notice is now regulatory, in the sense of penalising failure to apply for planning permission in a timely fashion.

---

[42] See s.31 of the Local Government (Planning & Development) Act 1963. See, generally, *Dublin Corporation v O'Callaghan*, unreported, High Court, Herbert J., February 13, 2001.

[43] In *R. v Leominster District Council, Ex p. Pothecary* [1998] J.P.L. 335, the Court of Appeal held that a planning authority was not merely entitled, but in practice bound, to take account of the existence of the unauthorised structure when determining an application for retrospective planning permission. Schiemann L.J. suggested that there would be situations where the planning authority would not have given permission for the development if asked for permission for precisely that which had been built, but the development would not so be objectionable that it would be reasonable to require it to be pulled down.

[44] PDA 2000, s.162(3) (as amended by the Local Government Act 2001, s.247(f)). See paras 7–08 to 7–11.

There is also an argument to be made that a planning authority should be required to state in the development plan its policy in relation to the taking of enforcement action.   **1–38**

6. Exempted development

The provisions of the development plan are also relevant in respect of exempted development. More specifically, the benefit of exempted development may be lost by reference to some (contrary) provision of the development plan. The most obvious example is that in relation to protected structures: under s.57(1) of the PDA 2000 it is provided that, notwithstanding s.4(1)(h), the carrying out of works to a protected structure, or a proposed protected structure, shall be exempted development only if those works would not materially affect the character of (a) the structure or (b) any element of the structure which contributes to its special architectural, historical, archaeological, artistic, cultural, scientific, social or technical interest.   **1–39**

In addition, it should be noted that certain of the qualifications on exempted development under the Planning and Development Regulations 2001 are triggered by provisions of the development plan. For example, the benefit of exempted development is lost where it is an objective of the planning authority to ensure that the building or other structure would remain available for continuance of an existing use and where such objective has been specified in the development plan, if the carrying out of such development would consist of the demolition or such alteration of a building or other structure as would preclude or restrict the use.[45] Other qualifications relate to views or prospects of special amenity value or special interest, the preservation of which is an objective of the development plan.[46] It should also be noted that many of these qualifications apply even in respect of a *draft* development plan.   **1–40**

Finally, it should be noted that the decision of the High Court in *Glencar Explorations plc v Mayo County Council*[47] appears to overstate the effect in that case of an objective of the development plan prohibiting mining. In particular, Blayney J. appears mistakenly to have considered that this would impact on exempted development: on the facts of the case, and given the wording of the relevant exemption, this does not appear to be correct.[48]   **1–41**

7. Compensation

The provisions of the development plan are of particular relevance in relation to compensation. The refusal of planning permission, or the grant of planning   **1–42**

---

[45] Planning and Development Regulations 2001, art.9(1)(a)(ix).
[46] Planning and Development Regulations 2001, art.9(1)(a)(vi).
[47] [1993] 2 I.R. 237.
[48] See comments of Keane C.J. in *Glencar Explorations plc v Mayo County Council* [2002] 1 I.R. 84; [2002] 1 I.L.R.M. 481.

permission subject to what might be described as onerous conditions, gives rise to a *prima facie* entitlement to compensation.[49] This is discussed in Chapter Six. This right to compensation is, however, lost in certain circumstances. In particular, the entitlement to compensation is lost where planning permission has been refused for a scheduled reason. These non-compensatable reasons for refusal are set out in the Fourth Schedule of the PDA 2000. Certain of these non-compensatable reasons relate back to the development plan. For example, compensation is excluded where planning permission is refused for the reason that a development of the kind proposed would be premature by reference to the order of priority, if any, for development indicated in the development plan, or pending the adoption of the local area plan in accordance with the development plan.[50]

1–43   Of particular significance is the fact that compensation is excluded where planning permission is refused for the reason that the proposed development would contravene materially a development objective indicated in the development plan for the zoning of land for the use solely or primarily of particular areas for particular purposes (whether residential, commercial, industrial, agricultural, recreational, as open space or otherwise or a mixture of such uses). Special provision is made in the case of a change in zoning by way of a variation in the development plan during the life of the plan.[51] The effect of all of this is to place a particular importance on the provisions of the development plan in relation to zoning. The fact that a proposed development would involve a material contravention of the zoning is not only sufficient to justify the refusal of planning permission but, further, generally will operate to exclude the payment of compensation for such a refusal.

1–44   The provisions in this regard are noteworthy in that they appear to confirm the general principle that a landowner is entitled to an opportunity to make submissions and representations in respect of any proposed decision which might impact on his property rights. The forging of a link between certain of the circumstances in which compensation is to be excluded, and the provisions of the development plan, affords the landowner the opportunity to participate in the statutory procedures leading up to the making of the development plan. For example, compensation is excluded where the proposed development would materially affect a protected structure,[52] or where planning permission is refused for the reason that the proposed development would adversely affect an architectural conservation area.[53] These are matters which must be included in the development plan, and thus an affected landowner may make submissions and observations before any final decision to make, vary or amend a development plan in this regard.

---

[49] PDA 2000, s.190.
[50] PDA 2000, Sch.4, para.3.
[51] PDA 2000, Sch.4, para.21.
[52] PDA 2000, Sch.3, para.3.
[53] PDA 2000, Sch.4, para.13.

The legislation is, however, open to the serious criticism that compensation is 1–45
also excluded in circumstances where there has been no advance notice to the
landowner. For example, compensation is excluded where the proposed
development would interfere with the character of the landscape or with a
view or prospect of special amenity value or of natural interest or beauty which
it is necessary to preserve.[54] There is no express requirement that these matters
should have been identified in the development plan, or, indeed, by way of
designation as a landscape conservation area. This would seem unfair, as the
landowner would thus appear to be precluded from arguing in advance that,
for example, a particular view was not of such amenity value or natural interest
or beauty as to defeat his *prima facie* right to compensation. It is further
submitted that given the fact that express provision is made for the designation
of an area as a landscape conservation area,[55] it is wrong that compensation
should be excluded by reference to the character of the landscape other than
where same has been designated for conservation.

C. Material Contravention

1. Introduction

As appears from the foregoing discussion in relation to the legal effects of the 1–46
development plan, the question of whether or not a proposed development will
involve a material contravention of the development plan can be of great
significance. This significance lies primarily in the context of the prohibition
under s.178 of the PDA 2000 on local authority development in material
contravention of the development plan,[56] and the imposition, in the context of
an application for planning permission, of special requirements and procedures
in case of material contravention.[57] The question is also of significance in
other areas: for example, in relation to claims for compensation.[58]

Accordingly, it is necessary to consider what is to be understood by the concept 1–47
of material contravention. It must be (unhelpfully) admitted from the outset
that the question of what is or is not a material contravention is a question of
degree and, for this reason, it is difficult to extract any general principles from
the case law. Nevertheless, an attempt to do this will be made. Before turning
to that task, however, a number of preliminary points should be noted as follows.

When one thinks of a material contravention, perhaps the clearest example 1–48
that comes to mind is that where the proposed development conflicts with the
zoning objectives of the development plan. Thus, for instance, one can readily
appreciate that the development of a travellers' halting site in an area zoned

---

[54] PDA 2000, Sch.4, para.8.
[55] PDA 2000, s.204.
[56] Paras 1–10 to 1–19 above.
[57] Paras 1–21 to 1–32 above.
[58] Paras 1–42 to 1–45 above.

high amenity,[59] or that development consisting of the erection of industrial buildings and other structures on lands zoned for agricultural use,[60] would involve a material contravention. Less obviously, however, there will be other objectives in a development plan of more general or universal application which might also be breached by a particular development. To illustrate by way of example, there is case law to the effect that breach of development objectives of the following types may also give rise to a material contravention: residential density[61]; traffic safety[62]; the preservation and protection of monuments[63]; an objective to the effect that no new development would be permitted which would give rise to concern as to the existence of fire hazards or potential fire hazards within the meaning of the Fire Services Act 1981[64]; an objective restricting development along a national primary route to the housing needs of farmholders' families[65]; a restriction on developments within a certain distance of a road in the interests of visual amenity and tourism[66]; and an objective to establish a linear park.[67]

1–49   As can be seen from these examples, a breach of a wide range of objectives of the development plan can represent a material contravention. It must be recognised, however, that there is some limit on the type of objective, breach of which can give rise to a material contravention. One such example is to be found in the decision in *Byrne v Fingal County Council*.[68] The applicant sought to prohibit the development of a travellers' halting site by the local authority. One of the grounds put forward in support of the application was that the proposed development involved a material contravention of the development plan. McKechnie J. ruled that as the use of the land as a halting site was expressly included as one of the acceptable uses under the relevant zoning, there was no question of a material contravention of the land-use provisions of the development plan. McKechnie J. then went on to consider whether or not a breach of an express obligation under the development plan to follow a consultation procedure with the local community in relation to the provision of a halting site could *per se* represent a material contravention of the development plan. McKechnie J. held that lack of consultation could not amount to a material contravention. In so holding, it appears that McKechnie J. considered that a material contravention would have to involve a (physical) breach of a planning objective or a planning policy.

---

[59] See, for example, the facts of *O'Leary v Dublin County Council* [1988] I.R. 150.
[60] See, for example, the facts of *Grange Developments Ltd. v Dublin County Council* [1986] I.R. 246 (especially at 255).
[61] *Tennyson v Dun Laoghaire Corporation* [1991] 2 I.R. 527.
[62] *P & F Sharpe Ltd. v Dublin City and County Manager* [1989] I.R. 701; [1989] I.L.R.M. 565.
[63] *Attorney General (McGarry) v Sligo County Council* [1991] 1 I.R. 99; [1989] I.L.R.M. 768; and *Dublin County Council v Marren* [1985] I.L.R.M. 593.
[64] *Calor Teoranta v Sligo County Council* [1991] 2 I.R. 267.
[65] *Griffin v Galway City and County Manager*, unreported, High Court, Blayney J., October 31, 1990.
[66] *Murray v Wicklow County Council* [1996] 2 I.R. 552; [1996] 2 I.L.R.M. 411.
[67] *Maye v Sligo Borough Council*, unreported, High Court, Clarke J., April 27, 2007.
[68] [2001] 4 I.R. 565; [2002] 2 I.L.R.M. 321.

2. Material contravention by omission?

Interestingly, it appears from a number of relatively recent cases that a material **1–50** contravention may arise, not only where there has been a breach of an objective contained in the development plan, but also where there has been an omission from the development plan. More specifically, in a series of cases relating to the development of travellers' halting sites, and, in one case relating to the development of a waste disposal facility, it was held that a failure by the planning authority to disclose in advance in its development plan its intention to carry out the impugned development gave rise to a material contravention.[69] The exact basis for these decisions is unclear. The judgments speak somewhat vaguely of a necessity for a local authority to include all its objectives in its plan. The difficulty with this analysis is that, under the then legislation, development objectives in relation to neither travellers' halting sites nor waste disposal facilities were mandatory objectives. Accordingly, it would seem on a literal reading of the then legislation that a local authority had a *discretion* as to whether or not to include such matters in its development plan.

It may be that justification for the earlier judgments is to be found in the fact **1–51** that, as local authority development is exempted development and there would, accordingly, be no application for planning permission (with the attendant rights of public participation), the development plan assumes a particular significance in relation to local authority development. The difficulty with this argument is that certain developments of the type involved might have been subject to control under the special form of public participation procedure prescribed under the then legislation (the former Pt X procedure under the Local Government (Planning & Development) Regulations 1994). Of course, if this point does provide the basis for the judgments, it would seem that a different standard might then apply in respect of the test for material contravention in the context of private-sector development which would be subject to an application for planning permission.

3. Formula in *Roughan v Clare County Council*

An attempt was made by Barron J. in *Roughan v Clare County Council* to **1–52** articulate what might be understood by the concept of a material contravention.[70]

> "What is material depends upon the grounds upon which the proposed development is being, or might reasonably be expected to be, opposed by local interests. If there are no real or substantial grounds in the context of planning law for opposing the development, then it is unlikely to be a material

---

[69] *Keogh v Galway Corporation (No. 1)* [1995] 3 I.R. 457; [1995] 1 I.L.R.M. 141; *Roughan v Clare County Council*, unreported, High Court, Barron J., December 18, 1996; and *Wicklow Heritage Trust Ltd. v Wicklow County Council*, unreported, High Court, McGuinness J., February 5, 1998.

[70] Unreported, High Court, Barron J., December 18, 1996. See also *Maye v Sligo Borough*

contravention. In the present case it seems clear that no [private-sector] development involving more than two units would be permitted by the local authority. It is also clear from previous applications for [planning] permission in special development zones that the local authority regards the exceptions laid down in the plan as being the only grounds upon which development may be permitted. I am satisfied that in the present case the proposed development is one which would be a material contravention of the development plan."

1–53 As appears from the foregoing quotation, there are two related peripheral matters which might provide some guidance as to whether or not there is a material contravention. The first of these is that the concept of a material contravention seems to allow for a *de minimis* argument. To put the matter another way, it may be possible to argue that a contravention of the development plan is nevertheless immaterial in circumstances where the proposed development is of a small scale. See, for example, *Duffy v Waterford Corporation*[71]; such an argument was unsuccessful on the facts in *O'Leary v Dublin County Council.*[72]

1–54 The second related issue, then, is the test of the private-sector comparator. It appears from some judgments that the courts have found it of assistance to consider whether or not planning permission would have been granted to a private-sector developer for development of the type at issue.[73] A note of caution needs to be sounded in relation to this test. First, obviously the test will only be of assistance in relation to material contravention in the context of local authority development: a comparison with a private-sector developer adds nothing in the context of an application for planning permission by a private-sector developer. Secondly, a material contravention of the development plan requires something more than that required to ground the refusal of planning permission. Thus the existence of matters which might justify the refusal of planning permission cannot necessarily be determinative of the issue as to whether or not there is a material contravention.

4. Draft Development Plan

1–55 Finally, it should be noted that a planning authority is not entitled to overcome what would otherwise be a material contravention by *anticipating* the coming into force and effect of a new or varied development plan. The question of whether or not there is a material contravention falls to be determined by reference to the provisions of the plan as it stands on the date of the decision,

---

Council, unreported, High Court, Clarke J., April 27, 2007 (if the extent of the deviation from what is specified in the development plan is such as might give rise to a reasonable expectation of opposition, then the deviation will be regarded as material) and *Wicklow County Council v Forest Fencing Ltd.*, unreported, Charleton J., July 13, 2007.

[71] Unreported, High Court, McGuinness J., July 21, 1999.

[72] [1988] I.R. 150.

[73] *O'Leary v Dublin County Council* [1988] I.R. 150; *Wilkinson v Dublin County Council* [1991] I.L.R.M. 605; *Roughan v Clare County Council*, unreported, High Court, Barron J., December 18, 1996; and *Wicklow Heritage Trust Ltd. v Wicklow County Council*, unreported, High Court, McGuinness J., February 5, 1998

not by reference to the draft, even where the draft has been adopted (but is not yet in effect).[74]

D. Interpretation of Development Plan

1. Introduction

Two issues arise as to the approach which should be adopted to the interpretation of the development plan. The first, and more straightforward, of these is as to the principles of interpretation which should apply. The second involves a consideration of the more complex question as to the extent, if any, to which the High Court should defer to the opinion or view of the planning authority on the interpretation of the development plan.   **1–56**

2. Principles of interpretation

Turning to the first issue, it is now well established that a court in interpreting a development plan should ask itself what a reasonably intelligent person, having no particular expertise in law or town planning, would make of the relevant provisions.[75] The development plan is not to be treated as if it were a piece of primary or secondary legislation emanating from skilled draftsmen and inviting the accepted canons of construction applicable to such material. Instead, a development plan falls to be construed in its ordinary meaning as it would be understood by members of the public without legal training, as well as by developers and their agents, unless the document, read as a whole, necessarily indicates some other meaning.[76]   **1–57**

The purpose of the development plan is to inform members of the public[77]; the plan should thus be interpreted as it would be understood by a reasonable intelligent person having no particular expertise in law or town planning.[78]   **1–58**

In all the circumstances, it is clear that the High Court possesses such expertise as may be necessary to engage in an assessment of the provisions of the   **1–59**

---

[74] *Moriarty v South Dublin County Council* [2006] I.E.H.C. 109.

[75] *Tennyson v Dun Laoghaire Corporation* [1991] 2 I.R. 527, *per* Barr J.

[76] *Tennyson v Dun Laoghaire Corporation* [1991] 2 I.R. 527 relying by analogy on the decision of the Supreme Court in *In Re XJS Investments Ltd.* [1986] I.R. 750.

[77] *Finn v Bray UDC* [1969] I.R. 169; *Attorney General (McGarry) v Sligo County Council* [1991] 1 I.R. 99; *Tennyson v Dun Laoghaire Corporation* [1991] 2 I.R. 527; *Tom Chawke Caravans Ltd. v Galway Corporation*, unreported, High Court, Flood J., December 20, 1991; and *Keogh v Galway Corporation (No. 1)* [1995] 3 I.R. 457; [1995] 1 I.L.R.M. 141.

[78] *Tennyson v Dun Laoghaire Corporation* [1991] 2 I.R. 527 at 535; *Roughan v Clare County Council*, unreported, High Court, Barron J., December 18, 1996; and *Wicklow Heritage Trust Ltd. v Wicklow County Council*, unreported, High Court, McGuinness J., February 5, 1998.

development plan. It is pre-eminently a question of law.[79] This is borne out by the decision of the Supreme Court in *Attorney General (McGarry) v Sligo County Council*,[80] where McCarthy J. distinguished *An Taisce v Dublin Corporation*[81] on the basis that the interpretation of a development plan did not require the resolution of any particular conflict of evidence, but rather turned on the inferences to be drawn. Accordingly, the courts are eminently qualified to interpret the development plan without deferring to the views of planning experts.[82]

1–60 It would also seem to follow that in interpreting the development plan, one is confined to the contents of the development plan *per se*. Accordingly, it is not normally permissible to have regard to documents outside the development plan (unless incorporated by express reference).[83]

3. Role of High Court

1–61 Turning now to the second issue identified at para.1–56 above, namely the respective roles of the planning authority and the High Court, with respect to the interpretation of the development plan, it is submitted that a consideration of this issue also leads to the conclusion that the interpretation of the development plan is ultimately a matter for the High Court.[84]

1–62 As indicated earlier, the significance of whether or not particular development would represent a material contravention of the development plan arises primarily in two contexts: first, in relation to the statutory prohibition on local authority development in material contravention of the development plan under s.178 of the PDA 2000; and secondly, in the context of an application for planning permission, given the restrictions (of varying degrees) imposed on a planning authority and An Bord Pleanála making a decision to grant planning permission for development which would involve a material contravention of the development plan.

1–63 One of the issues which will arise for determination in the event of legal proceedings being taken to challenge such development is, obviously, whether

---

[79] See *contra* J. Macken, "The Legal Status of the Development Plan: Environmental Contract or Development Guidelines?" (1995) 2 I.P.E.L.J. 11.

[80] [1991] 1 I.R. 99.

[81] High Court, *ex tempore*, January 31, 1973.

[82] *cf. Healy v Dublin County Council*, unreported, High Court, Barron J., April 29, 1993 (court must have evidence from those with expert knowledge of planning matters as to what is or is not material in the particular circumstances).

[83] *Ferris v Dublin County Council*, unreported, Supreme Court, November 7, 1990; see also *State (CIE) v An Bord Pleanála*, unreported, High Court, Carroll J., February 22, 1984 (at p. 11) (decided by Supreme Court on different grounds: December 12, 1984). *Cf. Hynes v An Bord Pleanála (No. 2)*, unreported, High Court, McGuinness J., July, 30, 1998.

[84] G. Simons, "The Unreasonable Planning Authority: Part I" (2000) 7 I.P.E.L.J. 164. See paras 12–74 to 12–109 below.

or not the proposed development does, in fact, constitute a material contravention of the development plan. The resolution of this issue necessitates the interpretation of the relevant provisions of the development plan. Invariably, the planning authority will argue that its interpretation of the development plan (to the effect that there is no material contravention involved) should prevail unless it is shown to be unreasonable or irrational in the *O'Keeffe* sense.[85] Such an approach is not supported by the legislation, however, in that a planning authority enjoys no statutory discretion in interpreting the development plan. In fact, the converse is true. In each of the two contexts identified above, the concept of material contravention is the litmus against which the legality of the planning authority's action is to be tested. A planning authority's power to carry out development is restricted to circumstances where there is no material contravention of the development plan. Similarly, the planning authority's power to grant planning permission is fettered by reference to the development plan: planning permission for such development may only be granted by adoption of the special voting procedure. To allow the planning authority to determine whether or not a material contravention is involved would undermine these two restraints on the planning authority's powers by, in effect, allowing the planning authority to determine its own competence.

In the case of the previous legislation, the application of these principles to the prohibition on local authority development in material contravention of the development plan was straightforward. The orthodox view seems to have been that the interpretation of the development plan is a question of law.[86] The High Court accordingly could determine this matter, at first instance, and no deference need be shown to the view of the planning authority. The most forthright expression of the principle is to be found in the decision in *Wicklow Heritage Trust Ltd. v Wicklow County Council.*[87] In that case, McGuinness J. declined to show any diffidence to the views of the planning authority, stating that the question was not whether the planning authority was unreasonable in thinking that the proposed development was not a material contravention, but that it was for the court to decide, as a question of law, whether or not there

1–64

---

[85] *O'Keeffe v An Bord Pleanála* [1993] 1 I.R. 39; [1992] I.L.R.M. 237. See, for example, *Keogh v Galway Corporation (No. 1)* [1995] 3 I.R. 457; [1995] 1 I.L.R.M. 141; and *Wicklow Heritage Trust Ltd. v Wicklow County Council*, unreported, High Court, McGuinness J., February 5, 1998.

[86] *Wicklow Heritage Trust Ltd. v Wicklow County Council*, unreported, High Court, McGuinness J., February 5, 1998 (at p. 35): "It is for the court and not for the local authority to decide as a matter of law whether a particular development is a material contravention of the local development plan." Followed in *Duffy v Waterford Corporation*, unreported, High Court, McGuinness J., July 21, 1999); *Keogh v Galway Corporation (No. 1)* [1995] 3 I.R. 457; [1995] 1 I.L.R.M. 141; and *Roughan v Clare County Council*, unreported, High Court, Barron J., December 18, 1996 (at p. 4) ("What is or is not a material contravention of the development plan is a matter to be determined by the court."). *Cf. O'Reilly v O'Sullivan*, unreported, High Court, Laffoy J., July 25, 1996 (disposed of by the Supreme Court on different grounds).

[87] Unreported, High Court, McGuinness J., February 5, 1998.

was a material contravention. A similar, albeit less cogent, approach had been adopted in a number of earlier cases.[88]

1-65 The position with respect to an application for planning permission under s.34 of the PDA 2000 may prove less clear-cut. The fact that the question of material contravention arises in the context of an adjudication on an application for planning permission can create the illusion that it is simply part and parcel of a wider determination, all of which is within the statutory discretion of the planning authority. The better view remains, however, that the development plan represents a statutory fetter on the planning authority's discretion; it is a prerequisite to the exercise of the planning authority's power to grant planning permission without the necessity for any special voting procedure that the proposed development does not involve a material contravention of the development plan. Although as a matter of practicality, a planning authority will have to make a preliminary assessment as to whether or not a material contravention is involved, the views of the planning authority on this threshold issue cannot be conclusive.[89] See, generally, paras 12–93 to 12–94.

E. Content of Development Plan

1. Mandatory objectives

1-66 A development plan shall consist of a written statement and a plan or plans indicating development objectives for the area in question.[90] There is no statutory definition provided for "development objective". Section 10(2) of the PDA 2000 prescribes a list of development objectives which must be included in a development plan. For ease of reference, these will be referred to as "mandatory development objectives".

(a) the zoning of land for the use solely or primarily of particular areas for particular purposes (whether residential, commercial, industrial, agricultural, recreational, as open space or otherwise, or a mixture of those uses), where and to such extent as the proper planning and sustainable development of the area, in the opinion of the planning authority, requires the uses to be indicated;

(b) the provision or facilitation of the provision of infrastructure including transport, energy and communication facilities, water supplies, waste recovery and disposal facilities (regard having been had to the waste management plan for the area made in accordance with the Waste Management Act 1996), waste water services, and ancillary facilities;

---

[88] See, for example, *Keogh v Galway Corporation (No. 1)* [1995] 3 I.R. 457; [1995] 1 I.L.R.M. 141; or *Roughan v Clare County Council*, unreported, High Court, Barron J., December 18, 1996.

[89] See *Tennyson v Dun Laoghaire Corporation* [1991] 2 I.R. 527. *Cf. Healy v Dublin City Council*, unreported, High Court, Barron J., April 29, 1993.

[90] PDA 2000, s.10(1).

(c) the conservation and protection of the environment including, in particular, the archaeological and natural heritage and the conservation and protection of European sites and any other sites which may be prescribed for the purposes of this paragraph;

(d) the integration of the planning and sustainable development of the area with the social, community and cultural requirements of the area and its population;

(e) the preservation of the character of the landscape where, and to the extent that, in the opinion of the planning authority, the proper planning and sustainable development of the area requires it, including the preservation of views and prospects and the amenities of places and features of natural beauty or interest;

(f) the protection of structures, or parts of structures, which are of special architectural, historical, archaeological, artistic, cultural, scientific, social or technical interest;

(g) the preservation of the character of architectural conservation areas;

(h) the development and renewal of areas in need of regeneration;

(i) the provision of accommodation for travellers, and the use of particular areas for that purpose;

(j) the preservation, improvement and extension of amenities and recreational amenities;

(k) the control, having regard to the provisions of the Major-Accident Hazards Directive and any Regulations, under any enactment, giving effect to that Directive, of—(i) siting of new establishments, (ii) modification of existing establishments, and (iii) development in the vicinity of such establishments, for the purposes of reducing the risk, or limiting the consequences, of a major accident;

(l) the provision, or facilitation of the provision, of services for the community including, in particular, schools, crèches and other education and childcare facilities; and

(m) the protection of the linguistic and cultural heritage of the Gaeltacht including the promotion of Irish as the community language, where there is a Gaeltacht area in the area of the development plan.

2. Discretionary objectives

In addition to the mandatory development objectives, a development plan may indicate objectives for any of the purposes referred to in the First Schedule of the PDA 2000 (hereinafter referred to as "discretionary development objectives"). The First Schedule is divided into five separate parts, each of which lists specific items under general headings. **1–67**

Part 1   Location and pattern of development

Part 2   Control of areas and structures

Part 3   Community facilities

Part 4   Environment and amenities

Part 5   Infrastructure and transport

3. Meaning of "development objective"

1–68   An examination of the mandatory development objectives, and the discretionary development objectives, suggests that the concept of "development objective" is a very broad one, capable of accommodating a wide range of matters. Given the breadth of the definition, it might be thought unnecessary and idle to elaborate upon it further. However, as the concept of a development objective would appear to determine what matters should or should not be included in a development plan, it may be that there is some benefit in embarking on this exercise. More specifically, the mapping of the contours of a development objective may be of assistance in relation to two issues. The foremost of these is in relation to what might be described as the duty to disclose. Case law in relation to the previous legislation had suggested that, in addition to the mandatory development objectives, a planning authority might also have to disclose other matters in the development plan.[91]

1–69   The leading judgments in this regard related to two types of development (namely travellers' halting sites, and waste disposal facilities) which have since been included as mandatory development objectives. Nevertheless, the case law appears to have established a principle that a planning authority may be under a duty to disclose even non-mandatory development objectives. If this is the case, it is important to know the scope of the concept of a development objective. For example, one matter in respect of which it is arguable that there is an obligation on a local authority to disclose its objectives is in relation to the use of compulsory purchase powers. Under the PDA 2000, there is no *express* obligation on a local authority to indicate, in advance, through the medium of the development plan, its intentions in relation to the use of compulsory purchase powers. Thus on a literal interpretation of the legislation, it would seem that even if the local authority had formulated a detailed policy in relation to compulsory purchase powers, it might not be necessary to include same in the development plan. Clearly, an understanding of the precise parameters of the concept of a development objective is crucial in this regard.

1–70   The second area in respect of which a working definition of development objective might be useful is in relation to determining the scope and effect of the development plan.

---

[91] See para.1–50.

The concept of a development objective has been considered in some detail in   **1–71**
two judgments, both arising out of the imposition of what has been described
as a mining ban by Mayo County Council. The background was as follows.
Mayo County Council had amended its development plan by the insertion of
the following provision:

> "[…] it is the *policy* of the council that no development and/or works shall take
> place in relation to minerals (as defined by the Minerals Act 1940, as amended)
> in the areas shown dotted on Map 10 A."
> *Emphasis supplied.

In effect, this amounted to a ban on mineral development in relation to an   **1–72**
extremely large area of land. A mineral development company sought to
challenge the legality of this ban by way of an application for judicial review.

The matter was dealt with in the following manner in the High Court.[92] Blayney   **1–73**
J. held that the inclusion of such a provision in the development plan was
illegal as it was *ultra vires* the local authority. The local authority was only
entitled to include in the plan development objectives within the meaning of
the legislation: development objectives must be objectives which have as their
aim the carrying out of works on, in, or under land, which meant that they must
be *positive* in character. Blayney J. indicated that it was not necessary for him
to decide whether or not a local authority is entitled to include matters of "policy"
in its plan: the terms "policy" and "objectives" are not mutually exclusive. The
correct test, however, was whether or not the contested provision could properly
be described as being a development objective.

The judgment is open to criticism on a number of levels. First, it is not at all   **1–74**
clear that a development objective must have as its aim the carrying out of
works on land. This aspect of the judgment has since been queried by the
Supreme Court in the context of a subsequent claim for damages brought by
the development company.[93] Keane C.J. expressly reserved for another occasion
the question as to whether the decision of the High Court on the substantive
issue was correct in point of law. In particular, Keane C.J. drew attention to the
fact that various other matters which a planning authority had discretion under
statute to include in its development plan did not require the carrying out of
works of any sort. Similar principles apply with respect to the PDA 2000. The
First Schedule of the PDA 2000 identifies objectives expressly "restricting",
"controlling", and "prohibiting" development.

The second principal criticism which may be directed towards the judgment is   **1–75**
of more immediate relevance to the present discussion. Blayney J. appears to
identify a possible distinction between development objectives and matters of

---

[92] *Glencar Explorations plc v Mayo County Council* [1992] 2 I.R. 237. See, generally, G.
Simons, "Development Plans – The Implications of Glencar" (1997) 3 I.P.E.L.J. 127.
[93] *Glencar Explorations plc v Mayo County Council* [2002] 1 I.R. 84; [2002] 1 I.L.R.M.
481.

policy, indicating that whereas the two are not mutually exclusive, only the former may properly be included in a development plan. This strict interpretation of "development objective" is unfortunate: planning authorities should be encouraged to include all their objectives and policies in their development plans, as inclusion of policies in development plans facilitates a debate on the merits of such policies, as part of a draft development plan, and allows for submissions and observations from the public.[94] The approach of Blayney J. in *Glencar Explorations plc* would also appear to be inconsistent with more recent judgments of the High Court. Reference is made in particular to the decision in *Wicklow Heritage Trust Ltd. v Wicklow County Council*.[95] McGuinness J. held that a local authority was required to disclose its objectives in the development plan. The case arose against the background of a proposed waste disposal site: under the then legislation, this was not a mandatory development objective.[96]

1–76   Reference is also made to the decision in *Keogh v Galway Corporation*.[97] Carney J. appears to have found that a local authority was required to disclose in the development plan its objectives in relation to travellers' halting sites: again, this was not a mandatory objective under the then applicable legislation.[98]

4. Zoning objectives

1–77   The aspect of development plans which has caught the popular imagination most, perhaps, is that of zoning. Reference is often made in the media to land being "rezoned" and to "rezoning" controversies. A change in zoning is often perceived as being extremely beneficial to the owners of the relevant lands.

1–78   The actual legal position is probably somewhat less dramatic. A restrictive zoning represents only one of a number of possible impediments to the grant of planning permission. As explained in the context of the discussion of material contravention (especially at para.1–48 above), a conflict with the zoning objectives is far from being the only circumstance which would result in a proposed development being in material contravention of the development plan. Thus the fact that the proposed development is of a type which is consistent with the zoning objective for the relevant lands does not necessarily mean that there is no material contravention involved, still less that planning permission must be granted.

1–79   In one important respect, however, a zoning objective is different from other types of development objectives. This arises in the context of a claim for

---

[94] *cf. Great Portland Estates v Westminster City Council* [1985] A.C. 661.

[95] Unreported, High Court, McGuinness J., February 5, 1998.

[96] See now PDA 2000, s.10(2)(b).

[97] [1995] 3 I.R. 457; [1995] 1 I.L.R.M. 141. *Cf. Malahide Community Council Ltd. v Fingal County Council* [1997] 3 I.R. 383, where Lynch J. suggested that a local authority was not required to include every knock-on effect in its development plan.

[98] See now PDA 2000, s.10(2)(i).

CONTENT OF DEVELOPMENT PLAN

compensation. Generally, an owner of land refused planning permission has a *prima facie* entitlement to the payment of compensation. One instance where the payment of compensation is excluded is where the development would contravene materially a development objective indicated in the development plan for the zoning of land for the use solely or primarily of particular areas for particular purposes (whether residential, commercial, industrial, agricultural, recreational, as open space or otherwise or a mixture of such uses).[99] See, generally, paras 6–32 to 6–41.

Compensation is thus not excluded by reason of a material contravention **1–80** *simpliciter*. For example, a material contravention of traffic standards, or of housing density standards, under the development plan would not come within the scope of the relevant zoning objectives of the plan under s.10(2)(a).[100]

Meaning of "zoning objective"

There is no definition provided under the PDA 2000 for "zoning objective". **1–81** The terms of s.10 do, however, indicate that zoned uses are in general terms, *i.e.* residential, commercial, industrial, agricultural, recreational, as open space or otherwise or a mixture of such uses. This point was taken up in *Abbeydrive Developments Ltd. v Kildare County Council (No.1)*.[101] Planning permission had been refused on the basis that the proposed development "would not integrate successfully with the existing village, would conflict with the provisions of the Development Plan and would seriously injure the amenities of the area". Counsel for the planning authority had argued that a reference in the development plan to "Special Village Status" and to the retention of the "special amenity character and quality of the village" constituted a land use zoning objective. Macken J. rejected this argument.

> "The reason given could only come within [the equivalent of para.20 of the Fourth Schedule of the PDA 2000] if it falls into the category of 'otherwise' after the words 'residential, commercial, industrial or agricultural'. I am not satisfied that 'otherwise' in the context in which it is found, is intended to cover, within any of those categories, a particular sort or character of one of these categories. The words 'residential commercial industrial or agricultural' all fall within the same genus of recognised types of development. The word 'otherwise' could of course cover, within the same genus, the development of, for example, sports arenas or similar facilities or many other types of development. But if the word is to cover something more, such as is contended for here by the respondent, it would have been necessary to adopt different and additional words to those used. As is clear from the decision of Denham, J. in *Hoburn Homes and another v An Bord Pleanala* (1993) I.L.R.M. 'compensation is a statutory right and should only be removed in clear, precise cases.'"

---

[99] PDA 2000, Sch.4, para.20. See also PDA 2000, s.190(2).
[100] It should be noted, however, that compensation is excluded under Sch.4, para.15 where the proposed development would materially contravene an objective indicated in a local area plan for the area.
[101] [2005] I.E.H.C. 209; unreported, Macken J., June 17, 2005.

1-82 In *Ebonwood Ltd. v Meath County Council*,[102] the High Court appears to have accepted that an objective to retain a route selection corridor (railway) represented a zoning objective for the purposes of compensation. This conclusion is surprising on two counts. First, the reservation of land for the purposes of a proposed railway route is not, to borrow the language of *Abbeydrive Developments Ltd.*, of the same "genus" as the uses identified in s.10. The designation of lands for the purposes of a proposed railway route is closer to the logically distinct concept of the reservation of land for a particular purpose than to a general zoning objective. In this regard, the judgment in *Ebonwood Ltd.* is somewhat inconsistent in that, having accepted that the route selection corridor represented a zoning objective, Peart J. nonetheless went on to say that the objective involved the "reservation of those lands for a particular purpose".

1-83 Secondly, there is an argument that before a designation can constitute a zoning objective it must apply to a sufficiently large area. A route selection corridor obviously only affects a small area of land. As against this, the judgment in *O'Connor v Clare County Council*[103] suggests that zoning might apply to even limited areas.

> "The limited area designated for development could hardly be described as being 'zoned' in the sense in which that is ordinarily understood. That term is generally used to describe a wider area where activities or developments having some measure of uniformity may be undertaken by a considerable number of owners or occupiers. However, there does not appear to be anything in [Paragraph 11 of the Third Schedule, Local Government (Planning & Development) Act 1990] aforesaid which would prevent a planning authority from indicating a specific development objective in relation to a *limited area* with a view to or as a consequence of formulating a development objective in relation to an adjoining larger area."
> *Emphasis supplied.

Is zoning a mandatory objective?

1-84 Although zoning is identified as a mandatory development objective under s.10 and, thus, must generally be included as part of the development plan, it is important to note that the planning authority retains significant discretion in this regard. Section 10(2)(a) is in the following terms.

> "the zoning of land for the use solely or primarily of particular areas for particular purposes (whether residential, commercial, industrial, agricultural, recreational, as open space or otherwise, or a mixture of those uses), where and to such extent as the proper planning and sustainable development of the area, in the opinion of the planning authority, requires the uses to be indicated"

1-85 As appears from the foregoing, the requirement to include zoning objectives

---

[102] [2004] 3 I.R. 34; [2004] 1 I.L.R.M. 305.
[103] Unreported, High Court, Murphy J., February 11, 1994 (at p.5).

only applies where in the "opinion" of the planning authority the proper planning and sustainable development of the area requires the uses to be indicated.

Matrix or table of uses

Many planning authorities employ a matrix or table which plots various types **1–86** of land use against the different zoning objectives.[104] A very simple matrix or table might employ the following three categories: "normally permissible", "open for consideration", or "not permissible". The appropriate category would then be indicated against the different zoning objectives for each type of land use. The types of land use would be listed on the vertical axis of the table, with the different zoning objectives being listed on the horizontal axis. By reading across the matrix or table, one could then determine the implications of each zoning objective for any particular land use.

No special voting required for rezoning

An attempt has been made elsewhere in the legislation to strengthen the role of **1–87** the development plan in the context of an application for planning permission by making it more difficult for a planning authority to grant planning permission in material contravention of the plan. As discussed above at paras 1–27 to 1–29, the number of the elected members voting in favour of a resolution to grant planning permission must be not less than three-quarters of the total number of the members of the planning authority. Somewhat anomalously, there is no special voting requirement in respect of the rezoning of lands. This is despite the fact that the wholesale rezoning of lands is, of course, more significant than a once-off grant of planning permission in material contravention of the existing zoning.

5. Record of protected structures

For the purpose of protecting structures, or parts of structures, which form part **1–88** of the architectural heritage and which are of special architectural, historical, archaeological, artistic, cultural, scientific, social or technical interest, every development plan shall include a record of protected structures, and shall include in that record every structure which is, in the opinion of the planning authority, of such interest within its functional area.[105] Subject to any additions or deletions made to the record, a record of protected structures shall continue to be part of that plan or any variation or replacement of the plan.

---

[104] For an example of a discussion of such a table or matrix see *McGovern v Dublin Corporation* [1999] 2 I.L.R.M. 314. The judgment appears to have limited the availability of a default planning permission to development which in the normal course of events is one which in principle is entitled to succeed ("normally permissible"). *Cf. Maye v Sligo Borough Council*, unreported, High Court, Clarke J., April 27, 2007 (*McGovern* explained as case involving a form of material contravention).

[105] PDA 2000, s.51.

1–89   The form of a record of protected structures is prescribed under the Planning and Development Regulations 2001.[106] A record of protected structures shall contain (a) in respect of each protected structure (i) an identifying number and (ii) an address; (b) one or more maps showing the location of each protected structure to a scale that enables clear identification of such structures; and (c) any other information that the planning authority considers necessary.

6. Architectural conservation areas

1–90   A development plan shall include an objective to preserve the character of a place, area, group of structures or townscape, taking account of building lines and heights, that (a) is of special architectural, historical, archaeological, artistic, cultural, scientific, social or technical interest or value, or (b) contributes to the appreciation of protected structures, if the planning authority is of the opinion that its inclusion is necessary for the preservation of the character of the place, area, group of structures or townscape concerned.[107]

Areas of special planning control

1–91   A planning authority may, if it considers that all or part of an architectural conservation area is of special importance to, or as respects, the civic life or the architectural, historical, cultural or social character of a city or town in which it is situated, prepare a scheme setting out development objectives for the preservation and enhancement of that area, or part of that area, and providing for matters connected therewith.[108]

1–92   The designation of an area of special planning control gives rise to a number of very significant legal effects. As an area of special planning control does not, strictly speaking, form part of the development plan, these matters are discussed separately at paras 8–68 to 8–69 below.

7. Housing strategy

1–93   A planning authority is required to include in its development plan a strategy for the purpose of ensuring the housing of the existing and future population of the area in the manner set out in the strategy.[109] A planning authority is also required to include objectives in the development plan in order to secure the implementation of the housing strategy.[110]

1–94   In conjunction with the inclusion of the housing strategy in its development plan, a planning authority shall ensure that sufficient and suitable land is zoned

---

[106] Planning and Development Regulations 2001, art.51.
[107] PDA 2000, s.81.
[108] PDA 2000, s.84.
[109] PDA 2000, s.94(1).
[110] PDA 2000, s.95(1)(b).

for residential use, or for a mixture of residential and other uses, to meet the requirements of the housing strategy and to ensure that a scarcity of such land does not occur at any time during the period of the development plan.

Social and affordable housing

Part V of the PDA 2000 (as amended by the Planning and Development   **1–95**
(Amendment) Act 2002) introduces a mechanism whereby a developer of residential development may be required to make provision for social and affordable housing. In this regard, a housing strategy shall provide that as a general policy a specified percentage, not being more than twenty per cent, of the land zoned for residential use, or for a mixture of residential and other uses, shall be reserved for the provision of social and affordable housing.

A planning authority is required to include in its development plan objectives   **1–96**
requiring that a specified percentage of land zoned solely for residential use, or for a mixture of residential and other uses, be made available for the provision of social and affordable housing.[111] Again, this is subject to a ceiling of twenty per cent.

Specific objectives may be indicated in respect of each area zoned for residential   **1–97**
use, or for a mixture of residential and other uses, and, where required by local circumstances relating to the amount of housing required as estimated in the housing strategy, different specific objectives may be indicated in respect of different areas, subject to the ceiling of twenty per cent not being exceeded.[112]

The default option is for the transfer of (undeveloped) land. Where this option   **1–98**
is not exercised, and one of the alternatives (such as, for example, the payment of monies to the planning authority) used instead, there is nevertheless a requirement that the aggregate monetary value of the property or amounts or both, as the case may be, transferred or paid under the alternative arrangement be equivalent to the monetary value of the land that the planning authority would otherwise have received. The effect of this is that whereas some flexibility is allowed as to how provision is to be made for social and affordable housing, the planning authority is entitled to a benefit equivalent to that which would have arisen on the transfer of land at a discount. The percentage of the land which the developer could have been required to transfer is fixed by the development plan, and thus this figure is relevant even in cases where there is to be no actual transfer of lands but simply a monetary payment.

In order to counteract undue segregation in housing between persons of different   **1–99**
social backgrounds, the planning authority may indicate in respect of any particular area that there is no requirement for social and affordable housing in respect of that area, or that a lower percentage than that specified in the housing strategy may instead be required.[113]

---

[111] PDA 2000, s.95(1)(b).
[112] PDA 2000, s.95(1)(c).
[113] PDA 2000, s.95(1)(d).

8. Waste management plan

1–100   The development plan for the time being in force in relation to the functional area of a local authority shall be deemed to include the objectives for the time being contained in the waste management plan in force in relation to that area.[114] In the event of a conflict, an objective introduced under the waste management plan prevails over a development objective *simpliciter*.[115]

9. Strategic development zones

1–101   A planning scheme made in respect of a strategic development zone shall be deemed to form part of any development plan in force in the area of the scheme until the scheme is revoked, and any contrary provisions of the development plan shall be superseded.[116]

F. Procedure for Making Development Plan

1. Timetable for development plan

1–102   Under s.9 of the PDA 2000, a planning authority is required every six years to make a development plan. Under s.11, a planning authority shall give notice of its intention to review its existing development plan and to prepare a new development plan for its area not later than four years after the making of a development plan. In the case of default by the elected members, the remedy provided for under the legislation is for the manager to make the development plan.[117]

Availability of mandamus

1–103   It is arguable that, in circumstances where a planning authority fails to comply with these timescales, an order of mandamus will lie against it to enforce the statutory duty. As against this, a decision of the High Court in relation to timescales under the previous legislation might suggest a different result. More specifically, in *Blessington Heritage Trust Ltd. v Wicklow County Council*,[118] the High Court quashed an amended development plan on the basis that same had been made out of time. This judgment is open to the very real criticism that such a finding of invalidity does not advance the mischief which the requirement for a periodic review of the development plan was presumably

---

[114] Waste Management Act 1996, s.22(10A) (as substituted by the Waste Management (Amendment) Act 2001 and the Protection of the Environment Act 2003).

[115] Waste Management Act 1996, s.22(10A) (as substituted by the Waste Management (Amendment) Act 2001 and the Protection of the Environment Act 2003).

[116] PDA 2000, s.169(9).

[117] PDA 2000, s.12(14). Moreover, the Minister for the Environment, Heritage and Local Government has certain limited powers under PDA 2000, s.31.

[118] [1999] 4 I.R. 571.

intended to address, namely the need for the development plan to reflect the current requirements of an area. It would seem from the decision in *Blessington Heritage Trust Ltd.* that the planning authority is *precluded* from reviewing its development plan out of time. On this interpretation, the duty to review is ephemeral: no sooner does it become enforceable, *i.e.* on the expiration of the statutory period, than it is spent. It is submitted that the judgment errs in regarding the planning authority as acting *ultra vires* in purporting to review the plan outside the statutory period when, in reality, the breach of duty is the failure to review the plan *within* the statutory period. The appropriate remedy for this breach is an order of mandamus directing the planning authority to review; in this regard, it is to be remembered that an order of mandamus will lie even in respect of a directory requirement. An order prohibiting such a review would be contrary to the purpose of the legislation in that it would, in effect, lock the planning authority into the previous (but now outdated) development plan.

Timetable not absolute

It should be noted that the various timescales provided for in relation to the various procedural steps in respect of the making of the development plan are not necessarily absolute. More specifically, it is expressly provided under s.12(16) (as amended)[119] that a person shall not question the validity of the development plan by reason only that the procedures as set out under subsections (3) to (5) of s.11, and subsections (1), (4), (5), (6), (7), (8), and (9) of s.12, were not completed within the time required under the relevant subsection.   **1–104**

Similarly, in the context of a variation of the development plan, a person shall not question the validity of a variation by reason only that the procedures as set out in s.13 were not completed within the time required.[120]   **1–105**

2. Environmental Assessment

The Planning and Development (Strategic Environmental Assessment) Regulations 2004 ("the 2004 Regulations") introduce a requirement that the making of certain development plans be subject to environmental assessment.[121] The 2004 Regulations are intended to ensure that the making of such plans complies with Directive 2001/42/EC on the assessment of the effects of certain plans and programmes on the environment.   **1–106**

---

[119] Planning and Development (Amendment) Act 2002, s.7.

[120] PDA 2000, s.13(10).

[121] See also the EC (Environmental Assessment of Certain Plans and Programmes) Regulations 2004. These latter Regulations make changes to ss.10, 13, 19, 23 and 168 of the PDA 2000. In effect, the amendments replace the previous requirement that the relevant plan or programme contain information on the likely significant effects on the environment of its implementation, with a power for the Minister to make Regulations.

Threshold: population of 10,000 persons or more

1–107   An environmental assessment is mandatory where the area of the development plan has a population of 10,000 persons or more.

Screening of sub-threshold development plans

1–108   Where the population is less than 10,000 persons, the planning authority is required to carry out a form of screening. The planning authority is required to consider whether or not the implementation of a new plan would be likely to have significant effects on the environment, taking account of relevant criteria set out in Sch.2A of the Regulations. Schedule 2A largely replicates Annex II of Directive 2001/42/EC on the assessment of the effects of certain plans and programmes on the environment.

1–109   Where the planning authority itself determines that the implementation of the relevant plan is not likely to have significant effects on the environment, it must give notice to and invite submissions from the Environmental Protection Agency ("the EPA"); the Minister for the Environment, Heritage and Local Government (where it appears that the plan might have significant effects in relation to the architectural or archaeological heritage or to nature conservation); and the Minister for Communications, Marine and Natural Resources (where it appears to the planning authority that the plan might have significant effects on fisheries or the marine environment).

1–110   The EPA and the Ministers, where notified, are entitled to make submissions within the period specified in the notice, which period shall not be less than four weeks from the date of the notice. The planning authority is then required to reconsider the question as to whether or not the implementation of a new plan would be likely to have significant effects on the environment, again taking account of the relevant criteria set out in Sch.2A, and any submission or observation received.

Screening decision to be available for public inspection

1–111   In all events, the planning authority is required to make a copy of its decision, including, as appropriate, the reasons for not requiring an environmental assessment, available for public inspection at its offices during office hours.

1–112   The planning authority is also required to notify its decision to the EPA, and to the Ministers where previously notified.

1–113   Where the making of a development plan is to be subject to environmental assessment—whether because the population of the area exceeds 10,000 persons or because the planning authority has determined that the implementation of the plan would be likely to have significant effects on the environment—additional public notice requirements apply. These additional requirements are described below, in the context of the discussion of the procedures governing the review of an existing development plan.

3. Review of existing development plan

Under the previous legislation, a planning authority had been required to prepare, and to put on public display, a draft of any proposed new development plan. Under the PDA 2000, the process of public consultation is pushed one step forward, and must now commence prior to the *preparation* of the draft development plan.

1–114

Notice requirements

Notice of the intention to review the existing development plan, and to prepare a new plan, is to be given to the Minister for the Environment, Heritage and Local Government; the prescribed authorities; any adjoining planning authorities; An Bord Pleanála; any relevant regional authority; and any town commissioners and city and county development boards within the functional area of the planning authority.[122] In addition, public notice must be published in one or more newspapers circulating in the area to which the development plan relates.[123]

1–115

The notice shall (a) state that the planning authority intends to review the existing development plan and to prepare a new development plan; (b) indicate that submissions or observations regarding the review of the existing plan and the preparation of a new development plan may be made in writing to the planning authority within a specified period (which shall not be less than eight weeks); and (c) indicate the time during which and the place or places where any background papers or draft proposals (if any) regarding the review of the existing plan and the preparation of the new development plan may be inspected.[124]

1–116

As soon as may be after giving notice of its intention to review a development plan and to prepare a new development plan, a planning authority shall take whatever additional measures it considers necessary to consult with the general public and other interested bodies. Without prejudice to the generality of this requirement, s.11(3) goes on to state that a planning authority shall hold public meetings and seek written submissions regarding all or any aspect of the proposed development plan and may invite oral submissions to be made to the planning authority regarding the plan.

1–117

A planning authority is also required to take whatever measures it considers necessary to consult with the providers of energy, telecommunications, transport and any other relevant infrastructure and of education, health, policing, and other services in order to ascertain any long-term plans for the provision of the infrastructure and services in the area of the planning authority.[125]

1–118

---

[122] PDA 2000, s.11(2). The prescribed bodies are enumerated at art.13 of the Planning and Development Regulations 2001 (as amended by the 2006 Regulations)
[123] PDA 2000, s.11(2).
[124] PDA 2000, s.11(2).
[125] PDA 2000, s.11(3)(c).

Additional notice requirements where plan subject to environmental assessment

1–119   Additional requirements apply where the plan is subject to environmental assessment. The notice shall state that the planning authority proposes to carry out an environmental assessment and that, for this purpose, the planning authority will prepare an environmental report of the likely significant effects on the environment of implementing the new plan. The public notice should also indicate that the special procedural requirements applicable to environmental assessment will apply.

Manager's report

1–120   Following on from the public consultation, the manager of the planning authority is required to prepare a report on any submissions or observations received and on the matters arising out of any consultation. Such a report shall be submitted to the elected members of the planning authority (or to a committee of the planning authority, as may be decided by the elected members of the planning authority), for their consideration. Following the consideration of the report, the elected members of the planning authority or of the committee, as the case may be, may issue directions to the manager regarding the preparation of the draft development plan. Any such directions must take account of the statutory obligations of any local authority in the area and any relevant policies or objectives for the time being of the Government or of any Minister of the Government.[126] In issuing directions, the elected members shall be restricted to considering the proper planning and sustainable development of the area to which the development plan relates.[127]

4. Draft development plan

1–121   The manager of the planning authority shall, not later than twelve weeks following the receipt of any directions from the elected members,[128] prepare a draft development plan and submit it to the elected members for their consideration.[129] The elected members of the planning authority are required, as soon as may be, to consider this draft. The default position is that this draft prepared by the manager shall be deemed to be the draft development plan, unless, within eight weeks of the submission of the draft, the elected members of the planning authority, by resolution,[130] amend the (manager's) draft.[131]

---

[126] PDA 2000, s.11(4)(d).
[127] PDA 2000, s.11(4)(f).
[128] See para.1–120 above.
[129] PDA 2000, s.11(5).
[130] Under PDA 2000, s.2(7) this is a reserved function.
[131] PDA 2000, s.11(5)(c).

Notice requirements

Once the draft development plan has been prepared, the draft must be put on public display for a period of not less than ten weeks.[132] Any written submissions or observations with respect to the draft made to the planning authority within the period stated in the statutory notices must be taken into consideration before the making of the plan. **1–122**

The planning authority is required to send notice and a copy of the draft development plan to the Minister for the Environment, Heritage and Local Government, An Bord Pleanála, the prescribed authorities,[133] any town commissioners in the area, and any city or county development boards in the area and any town commissioners and city and county development boards within the area.[134] The planning authority is also required to publish notice of the preparation of the draft in one or more newspapers circulating in its area.[135] **1–123**

Environmental report where environmental assessment applicable

Where the plan is subject to environmental assessment, the manager is required to prepare an environmental report.[136] The draft plan shall be accompanied by or include this environmental report. **1–124**

Provision is made for the scoping of an environmental report.[137] In this regard, the planning authority is required to invite submissions from the EPA; the Minister for the Environment, Heritage and Local Government (where it appears to the planning authority that the plan might have significant effects in relation to the architectural or archaeological heritage or to nature conservation); and the Minister for Communications, Marine and Natural Resources (where it appears to the planning authority that the plan might have significant effects on fisheries or the marine environment) as to the scope and level of detail to be included in the environmental report. The notice should indicate, *inter alia*, that a submission or observation may be made to the planning authority within a specified period, which shall be not less than four weeks from the date of the notice. **1–125**

An environmental report must identify, describe and evaluate the likely significant effects on the environment of implementing the plan, and reasonable alternatives taking into account the objectives and geographical scope of the **1–126**

---

[132] PDA 2000, s.12(2).
[133] Planning and Development Regulations 2001, art.13 (as amended by the 2006 Regulations).
[134] PDA 2000, s.12(1)(a).
[135] PDA 2000, s.12(1)(b).
[136] Planning and Development Regulations 2001, art.13C (as inserted by the 2004 Regulations).
[137] Planning and Development Regulations 2001, art.13D (as inserted by the 2004 Regulations).

plan.[138] The environmental report is required to contain the information specified in Sch.2B. It should also take account of any submission or observation received from the EPA or the relevant Minister(s) as to the scope and level of detail to be included in the environmental report. An environmental report must also be of sufficient quality to meet the requirements of the Regulations.

1–127 An environmental report shall include the information that may reasonably be required taking into account (a) current knowledge and methods of assessment; (b) the contents and level of detail in the plan; (c) the stage of the plan in the decision-making process and (d) the extent to which certain matters are more appropriately assessed at different levels in the decision-making process in order to avoid duplication of environmental assessment.

Protected structures

1–128 Where the draft includes any provision relating to any addition to or deletion from the record of protected structures, the planning authority shall serve on each person who is the owner or occupier of the proposed protected structure or the protected structure, as the case may be, a notice of the proposed addition or deletion, including the particulars.[139] The notice shall state (i) that a copy of the proposed addition or deletion may be inspected at a stated place or places and at stated times during a stated period of not less than ten weeks (and the copy shall be kept available for inspection accordingly); (ii) that written submissions or observations with respect to the proposed addition or deletion made to the planning authority within the stated period will be taken into consideration before the making of the addition or deletion; (iii) whether or not the proposed addition or deletion was recommended by the Minister for the Environment, Heritage and Local Government[140]; and (iv) that, if the proposed addition or deletion was recommended by the Minister for the Environment, Heritage and Local Government, the planning authority shall forward to that Minister for his or her observations a copy of any submission or observation made.

1–129 Where a planning authority proposes, at any time other than in the course of making its development plan, to make an addition to or a deletion from its record of protected structures, it is required to follow certain procedural steps.[141] In particular, it must serve notice of the proposed addition or deletion (including the particulars) on each person who is the owner or occupier of the proposed protected structure or the protected structure, as the case may be. See further para.8–17

---

[138] Planning and Development Regulations 2001, art.13E (as inserted by the 2004 Regulations).

[139] PDA 2000, s.12(3).

[140] The Minister for the Environment, Heritage and Local Government now exercises the functions previously exercised by the Minister for the Arts, Heritage, Gaeltacht and the Islands. See Heritage (Transfer of Departmental Administration and Ministerial Functions) Order 2002 (S.I. 356 of 2002).

[141] PDA 2000, s.55.

5. Manager's report

The manager of a planning authority shall prepare a report on any submissions **1–130** or observations received, and submit the report to the elected members of the planning authority for their consideration.[142] This report is to be prepared not later than twenty two weeks after the giving of notice of the publication of the draft plan.

The manager's report shall (i) list the persons or bodies who made submissions **1–131** or observations; (ii) summarise the issues raised by the persons or bodies in the submissions or observations; and (iii) give the response of the manager to the issues raised, taking account of any directions of the elected members, the proper planning and sustainable development of the area, the statutory obligations of any local authority in the area and any relevant policies or objectives of the Government or any Minister of the Government.[143] (Including, if appropriate, any observations made by the Minister for the Environment, Heritage and Local Government in relation to any addition to or deletion from the record of protected structure.)

6. Legal status of draft development plan

In determining an application for planning permission, both the planning **1–132** authority and An Bord Pleanála are required to have regard to the provisions of the development plan. A difficulty arises, however, in that a development plan has a relatively long life (up to six years) and towards the latter years the development plan may become less and less meaningful in that its objectives may well have been overtaken by events. For example, the pattern of development in the intervening period may be such as to render certain objectives of the plan out of date. In such circumstances, the argument might be made that it would be more meaningful to consider the provisions of any proposed draft development plan. In support of this argument, the additional point might be made that the lead time for the making of a new development plan is such that to ignore the provisions of the draft in the interim might well result in its objectives being hopelessly compromised before the draft development plan is formally made.

The PDA 2000 is largely silent on this question as to the extent to which it is **1–133** permissible to have regard to the provisions of a draft development plan in determining an application for planning permission.[144] Limited provision is made under the Act whereby the draft development plan is to have legal effect in specific contexts. For example, certain restrictions apply to even a *proposed*

---

[142] PDA 2000, s.12(4).
[143] PDA 2000, s.12(4).
[144] The position under the previous legislation was somewhat different in that transitional provisions had been enacted which regulated the interregnum between the coming into

protected structure. Further, under the Planning and Development Regulations 2001 certain restrictions in respect of exempted development are triggered even by the provisions of the draft development plan.

1–134   In *Ebonwood Ltd. v Meath County Council*,[145] the High Court considered, in general terms, the question as to whether it might ever be permissible to have regard to a draft development plan in determining a planning application. Peart J. indicated that, in his opinion, the public's right of participation in the planning process would effectively be set at nought if a planning authority could have regard to considerations not forming part of the adopted development plan. With respect, this approach is too strict. In particular, it is submitted that it is legitimate to refuse planning permission where the proposed development would be inconsistent with the current draft development plan: to do otherwise would compromise the draft and frustrate its ever being implemented. It is submitted that there are sufficient safeguards to prevent any prejudice arising as a result of such an approach. For example, the provisions of the draft development plan could not be relied upon for the purposes of excluding compensation (as in *Ebonwood Ltd. v Meath County Council* itself). Equally, the question as to whether or not the proposed development involved a material contravention of the development plan would fall to be determined against the provisions of the development plan alone, and not those of the draft development plan.[146]

7. Amendment of draft development plan

1–135   Following the consideration of the draft development plan and the manager's report, a planning authority may decide to amend the draft. However, in circumstances where the amendment to the draft would, if made, be a "material alteration" of the draft, it is necessary for there to be a further (truncated) period of public consultation. More specifically, the proposed amendment of the draft must be advertised, and the proposed amendment available for

---

force for the first time of a statutory requirement to make a development plan, and the actual making of such plans. These transitional provisions appeared to be spent once the first development plan was actually made. However, an amendment effected under the Local Government (Planning & Development) Act 1976 (which introduced the possibility of making a fresh development plan as an alternative to simply varying the existing plan) had, on one interpretation, the unexpected result of reviving these transitional provisions in that, once again, there was the possibility of the existence of an unmade development plan. Such an interpretation was rejected by the High Court in *Ebonwood Ltd. v Meath County Council* [2004] 3 I.R. 34; [2004] 1 I.L.R.M. 305. Peart J. held that the intention of the transitional provisions was to put in place some measures during the lead period prior to the making, for the first time, of a development plan, so as to enable the planning authorities to have some basis on which to control development while they completed their first plans. The transitional provisions were not intended to refer to any period of time between the publication of any second or subsequent development plan (in draft form) and its adoption.

[145]   [2004] 3 I.R. 34; [2004] 1 I.L.R.M. 305.
[146]   *Moriarty v South Dublin County Council* [2006] I.E.H.C. 109.

inspection for a period of not less than four weeks. Written submissions or observations with respect to the proposed amendment of the draft, made to the planning authority within the stated period, must be taken into consideration before the making of any amendment. The better view would seem to be that the determination of whether an alteration is "material" is a question of law subject to review by the High Court.[147]

A further report is to be prepared by the manager in relation to the submissions **1–136** and observations received in relation to the proposed amendment. The elected members of the planning authority shall, by resolution, having considered the amendment and the manager's report in this regard, make the plan with or without the proposed amendment. If the elected members of the planning authority decide to accept the amendment, they may do so subject to any "modifications" to the amendment as they consider appropriate. It is expressly provided that the (second) public consultation procedure does not apply in respect of such a modification to an amendment.[148] Given the importance which the courts attach to the right of public consultation, it is submitted that the term "modifications" must be interpreted narrowly so as to exclude any substantial change to the proposed amendment.[149]

Oral submissions

The former position where a ratepayer was entitled under the previous legislation **1–137** to request an opportunity to state his case before a person or persons appointed by the planning authority has been modified. There is no absolute entitlement to make such an oral presentation: however, under s.12(15), when considering the draft development plan or amendments thereto, a planning authority may invite such persons as it considers appropriate to make oral submissions regarding such plan or amendment.

Environmental assessment

In circumstances where the development plan is subject to environmental **1–138** assessment and the planning authority is engaging in a further round of public consultation, the public notice must additionally state that information on the likely significant effects on the environment of implementing the proposed amendment will also be available for inspection, and that a submission or observation in relation to such information made to the planning authority within the period stated in the notice will also be taken into consideration before the making of any amendment.[150]

---

[147] *cf. Keogh v Galway Corporation (No. 1)* [1995] 3 I.R. 457; [1995] 1 I.L.R.M. 141.
[148] The position was different under the previous legislation; see *Raggett v Athy UDC* [2000] 1 I.R. 469; [2000] 1 I.L.R.M. 375.
[149] See, by analogy, *Finn v Bray UDC* [1969] I.R. 16.
[150] Planning and Development Regulations 2001, art.13G (as inserted by the 2004 Regulations).

8. Making the development plan

Reserved function

1–139   The making of the development plan is a reserved function.[151] In broad terms, reserved functions may be regarded as functions which may only be exercised by the elected members of a local authority, in contrast to executive functions, which may be discharged by the manager or some other delegated person. One practical consequence of this is that a provision in a development plan which purports to empower the executive authority to disregard the development plan and, in effect, to rewrite it, will represent an illegal and invalid intrusion on the powers of elected members.[152]

Default power of manager to make development plan

1–140   Notwithstanding the fact that the making of the development plan is a reserved function, provision is made whereby, in the event of default on the part of the elected members, the manager shall make the plan. More specifically, s.12(14) provides that where a planning authority fails to make a development plan within two years of the giving of notice of its intention to review its existing development plan and to prepare a new development plan for its area, the manager shall make a plan subject to the proviso that so much of the plan that has been agreed by the elected members of the planning authority shall be included as part of the plan as made by the manager.[153]

Environmental assessment

1–141   A planning authority is expressly required to take account of (a) the environmental report; (b) any submission or observation made in this regard; and (c) any transboundary consultations, during the preparation of the plan and before its adoption.[154]

9. Notice of making of development plan

1–142   The planning authority is required to publish notice of the making of the plan in at least one newspaper circulating in the area. The notice must state that a copy of the plan is available for inspection at a stated place or places.[155]

---

[151] Under PDA 2000, s.2(7), the doing of anything that is required under the Planning and Development Act 2000 to be done by resolution shall be a reserved function.

[152] *Grange Developments Ltd. v Dublin County Council (No. 2)* [1989] I.R. 296 (claim for compensation). It is probable that the impugned provision was also invalid on the separate ground that it had rendered the provisions of the development plan ambulatory.

[153] Even more Draconian provision is made in case of a waste management plan as a result of the amendments introduced under the Waste Management (Amendment) Act 2001, and the Protection of the Environment Act 2003.

[154] Planning and Development Regulations 2001, art.13H (as inserted by the 2004 Regulations).

[155] PDA 2000, s.12.

Environmental assessment

Additional requirements apply where the making of the development plan was   **1–143**
subject to environmental assessment.[156] A statement is to be made available
which summarises (a) how environmental considerations have been integrated
into the plan; (b) how (i) the environmental report, (ii) submissions and
observations made and (iii) transboundary consultations have been taken into
account during the preparation of the plan; (c) the reasons for choosing the
plan, as adopted, in the light of other reasonable alternatives dealt with; and
(d) the measures decided upon to monitor the significant environmental effects
of the implementation of the plan.

10. Public right of way

A special procedure applies where a planning authority proposes to include,   **1–144**
for the first time, a provision in a development plan relating to the preservation
of a specific public right of way.[157] The inclusion of a public right of way in a
development plan shall be evidence of the existence of such a right unless the
contrary is shown.[158] These provisions do not affect the existence or validity
of any public right of way which is not included in the development plan.[159]

The planning authority shall serve notice (which shall include particulars of   **1–145**
the provision and a map indicating the right of way) on any owner and occupier
of the land over which the right of way exists. The notice shall state that (a) the
planning authority proposes to include a provision in the development plan
relating to the preservation of the public right of way; (b) written submissions
or observations regarding the proposal may be made to the planning authority
within a stated period of not less than six weeks and that the submissions or
observations will be taken into consideration by the planning authority; and
(c) where, following consideration of any submissions or observations received,
the planning authority considers that the provision should be adopted, or adopted
subject to modifications, a right of appeal to the Circuit Court exists in relation
to such provision.

The elected members of a planning authority, having considered the proposal   **1–146**
to include the right of way and any submissions or observations made in respect
of it, may, by resolution as they consider appropriate, recommend the inclusion
of the provision in the development plan, with or without modifications, or
may recommend against its inclusion. Any person on whom notice has

---

[156] Planning and Development Regulations 2001, art.13I (as inserted by the 2004
Regulations).
[157] PDA 2000, s.14. Where any existing development plan contains any provision relating
to the preservation of a public right of way, the provision may be included in any
subsequent development plan without the necessity to comply with this procedure: PDA
2000, s.14(6).
[158] PDA 2000, s.14(7)(b).
[159] PDA 2000, s.14(7)(a).

previously been served shall be notified of the recommendation accordingly and a copy of such notice shall be published in at least one newspaper circulating in the area.

1–147   There is a statutory right of appeal to the Circuit Court against the inclusion in the development plan of the proposed provision. The appeal must be taken before the expiration of the twenty one days next following the notification. The Circuit Court, if satisfied that no public right of way exists, shall so declare and the provision shall accordingly not be included in the development plan. The taking of an appeal does not prejudice the making of a development plan except in regard to the inclusion of the proposed right of way.[160] If the Circuit Court subsequently decides that the public right of way exists, same shall be deemed to be part of the development plan.

G. Variation of Development Plan

1–148   The general position is that a development plan is to be made every six years,[161] with the review process beginning after the fourth year.[162] An element of flexibility is provided for, however, in that provision is made for the "variation" of the (existing) development plan. It is expressly stated that a planning authority may at any time, for stated reasons, decide to make a variation of a development plan which for the time being is in force.[163]

1. Environmental assessment

1–149   A planning authority is required to engage in a screening process in order to determine whether the proposed variation would be likely to have significant effects on the environment.[164] As in the case of the making of a development plan, there is a requirement to notify the EPA, and the relevant Ministers in circumstances where the (initial) determination of the planning authority is not to require an environmental assessment. The scoping and the contents of the environmental report are similar to those for the making of a development plan. Similar procedural requirements also apply in relation to transboundary effects; the matters of which account is to be taken of during the making of the variation and before its adoption; the information on the decision; and monitoring.

---

[160] PDA 2000, s.14(5).
[161] PDA 2000, s.9(1).
[162] PDA 2000, s.11(1).
[163] PDA 2000, s.13(1).
[164] See Planning and Development Regulations 2001, arts 13K to 13R (as inserted by the 2004 Regulations).

2. Regional planning guidelines

A planning authority is required to review its existing development plan **1–150** following the making of regional planning guidelines for its area, and to consider whether any variation of the development plan is necessary in order to achieve the objectives of the regional planning guidelines.[165]

3. Procedure

The procedure for the variation of a development plan is prescribed under s.13 **1–151** of the PDA 2000. The procedure is largely similar to that which applies in relation to the making of the development plan: the most significant differences being that the timescale for the various procedural steps is truncated; and that, as indicated above, there is a requirement to state the reason for the variation.

The steps may be summarised as follows. Once the draft variation has been **1–152** prepared (again, there is a requirement for consultation in advance of the preparation of the draft), the planning authority must send notice and copies of the proposed variation of the development plan to the Minister for the Environment, Heritage and Local Government, An Bord Pleanála, and, where appropriate, to any adjoining planning authority, the prescribed authorities,[166] any town commissioners and the city and county development boards within the area of the development plan.[167] The planning authority is also required to publish notice of the proposed variation of the development plan in one or more newspapers circulating in that area.[168] The statutory notice must state the reason or reasons for the proposed variation.[169]

A copy of the proposed variation must be put on public display for a stated **1–153** period of not less than four weeks.[170] Any written submissions or observations with respect to the proposed variation made to the planning authority within the stated period are to be taken into consideration before the making of the variation.[171]

In *Sandyford Environmental Planning and Road Safety Group Ltd. v Dun* **1–154** *Laoghaire Rathdown County Council*,[172] a variation of a development plan was challenged on the basis that there had not been proper compliance with the requirements of s.13.

---

[165] PDA 2000, s.27(4).
[166] Planning and Development Regulations 2001, art.13 (as amended by the 2006 Regulations).
[167] PDA 2000, s.13(2)(a).
[168] PDA 2000, s.13(2)(b).
[169] PDA 2000, s.13(3)(a).
[170] PDA 2000, s.13(3)(b).
[171] PDA 2000, s.13(3)(c).
[172] [2004] I.E.H.C. 133; unreported, McKechnie J., June 30, 2004.

1–155 The first ground of challenge raised was that the public notice failed to state properly the reason or reasons for the proposed variation as required under s.13. The stated reason was in the following terms: "The draft of the proposed variations proposes the rezoning of four acres in the county from open space to residential use to provide for future residential development and the deletion of a long term roads proposal." It was argued on behalf of the applicant company, however, that the true justification for the proposed rezoning was to implement the planning authority's own housing strategy and to ensure compliance with the regional planning guidelines. The applicant company based this argument on the fact that the manager's report made express reference both to the housing strategy and the regional planning guidelines. McKechnie J. rejected this argument, holding that the manager's reference to the housing strategy and the regional planning guidelines was merely for the purposes of establishing the context of the proposed variation. McKechnie J. stated that given the complementary and interactive workings of a local authority, it would be quite proper that in reporting to his council the manager would establish the context and give the relevant background to any proposal contained within that report.

1–156 The High Court held that the stated reason for the variation was adequate.

> "The objective is to put the public on notice of matters likely to interest those concerned and to do so in such a way that any member, who informatively considers the notice, will recognise the essentials of the proposal, and depending on detail or complexity, will be alerted sufficiently to further evaluate the underlying reasons for that proposal. For any proposal there may be reasons, some of which are proximate, some of which are less so, and indeed, some of which are so remote that any connection with the subject matter is highly tenuous. What is required, in my view, in order to comply with the duty of the provision in question, is to meaningfully impart information, sufficiently intelligible to a reasonable person, who could, from such information, understand the said proposal."

> […]

> "What would a reasonable person take from the suggested future residential development of the land in question? In my view, this type of phrase would immediately convey an intention behind the proposal, to provide for those lands, if the variation was adopted, a scheme which resulted in the construction of a residential development with such associated and ancillary services which follow from such a development. What in broad terms that would have involved, not only for the existing use but also for its future direction, was or, with ease, could have been ascertained. In addition, having specified the exact location of the subject lands, one would have been able to immediately identify the adjacent location of Fitzsimons Wood. Again, an enquiring person would readily have been able to envisage, at least some consequences for that designated conservation area. As a result, I am quite satisfied that the notice served its intended statutory purpose and that it was far more meaningful than if there was simply a reference to a Housing Strategy or to the Strategic Planning Guidelines, even if either or both of these were the true reasons for the said proposal, a suggestion which, in fact, I reject."

Interestingly, in reaching his conclusion on this issue, McKechnie J. attached **1–157** significance to the nature of the decision being challenged, stating that the decision was simply a proposal emanating from a local authority, and not one which could have profound and immediate consequences for those affected. Nor was the court dealing with a statutory report from an inspector or other designated person, whether under the Planning Acts, the Housing Acts or otherwise. McKechnie J. also gave some weight to the fact that the public notice was to be given by way of newspaper notice, and that, by its very nature, it was not practical or feasible to give extensive reasons through the medium of a newspaper notice.

McKechnie J. did, however, sound the following note of caution. **1–158**

> "In saying this, however, I wish to emphasise that, in my view, a local authority should not have or adopt a minimalist standard to the contents of such a notice and, if anything, should err on the side of an expansive approach. If for example the true reasons for this proposal were the Council's Housing Strategy and or the Strategic Guidelines, then, whilst these would have to be referred to, I doubt strongly if a mere reference to such documents, and no more, would have conveyed in recognisable language the meaningful information which, in my opinion, the public are entitled to expect from such a notice. So, whilst I believe that the notice in this case did contain reasons which were 'proper, intelligible and adequate', I would caution strongly against any practice or policy, used or designed, directly or indirectly to limit, whether by omission, phraseology, or otherwise, information which should be supplied to the public."

4. Protected structures

Where a planning authority proposes, at any time other than in the course of **1–159** making its development plan, to make an addition to or a deletion from its record of protected structures, it is required to follow certain procedural steps.[173] See further para.8–17.

5. Manager's report

As in the case of the making of the development plan, the manager is required **1–160** to prepare a report on any submissions or observations received, and to submit the report to the elected members of the planning authority for their consideration. The contents of the report are similar to those in the case of the making of the development plan.[174]

The elected members of a planning authority are required to consider the **1–161** proposed variation and the report of the manager; the consideration of the variation and the manager's report is to be completed not later than six weeks

---

[173] PDA 2000, s.55.
[174] PDA 2000, s.13(4).

after the submission of the manager's report.[175] The elected members of a planning authority, having considered the proposed variation and the manager's report, may, by resolution,[176] as they consider appropriate, make the variation, with or without modifications, or they may refuse to make it.[177]

1–162   The public participation procedure does not have to be repeated in the case of any modification to the proposed variation.[178] However, as with a modification to a proposed alteration in the context of the making of the development plan, it is submitted that the term "modification" should be interpreted narrowly so as to exclude the making of any substantial changes to the proposed variations.[179]

1–163   The adequacy of a manager's report was challenged in *Sandyford Environmental Planning and Road Safety Group Ltd. v Dun Laoghaire Rathdown County Council*.[180] It was alleged by the applicant company that the manager's report had been defective in a number of respects, as follows. First, it was claimed that the entire submissions and observations made in response to the public notice should have been circulated to each of the elected members prior to the first of the relevant meetings. Secondly, it was suggested that the manner of summarising the content of those submissions was inadequate and, when taken against the manager's response, conveyed an incomplete and unfair representation of those observations and submissions. Thirdly, it was claimed that the objectors' names should have been assigned against their particular objection.

1–164   The High Court rejected the applicant company's arguments. McKechnie J. held that the duty upon the manager was but to summarise the submissions and observations received; this duty could not be interpreted as obliging the manager to circulate in full all the submissions and observations received. In any event, copies of the submissions and observations were available for inspection. In complying with his obligation to summarise the submissions and observations, the manager was not bound to use any formula or to follow any specific method. On the facts, McKechnie J. found that, although quite briefly dealt with, the issues raised, both in substance and in materiality, were adequately outlined in the manager's report.

6. Oral submissions

1–165   As in the case of the making of the development plan, there is no express entitlement to an oral hearing: under s.13(9), when considering a variation of a

---

[175] PDA 2000, s.12(5).
[176] Thus a reserved function; see PDA 2000, s.2(7).
[177] PDA 2000, s.12(6).
[178] PDA 2000, s.13(6)(b).
[179] *Finn v Bray UDC* [1969] I.R. 16. *Cf. Raggett v Athy UDC* [2000] 1 I.R. 469; [2000] 1 I.L.R.M. 375.
[180] [2004] I.E.H.C. 133; unreported, McKechnie J., June 30, 2004.

development plan, a planning authority may invite such persons as it considers appropriate to make oral submissions regarding the variation.

7. Date of effect

A variation made to a development plan shall have effect from the day the variation is made.[181] This may be contrasted with the position in relation to the making of the development plan where, under s.12(17) of the PDA 2000, a development plan shall have effect four weeks from the day that it is made.

1–166

H. Regional Planning Guidelines and Development Plans

1. Regional planning guidelines

Regional planning guidelines are drawn up by regional authorities. Regional authorities are established in accordance with s.43 of the Local Government Act 1991.[182]

1–167

The objective of regional planning guidelines is to provide a long-term strategic planning framework for the development of the region for which the guidelines are prepared. The planning framework shall consider the future development of the region for which the guidelines are prepared for a period of not less than twelve years and not more than twenty years.[183]

1–168

The guidelines shall address, for the whole of the region to which the guidelines relate, in accordance with the principles of proper planning and sustainable development, the following matters: (a) projected population trends and settlement and housing strategies; (b) economic and employment trends; (c) the location of industrial and commercial development; (d) transportation, including public transportation; (e) water supply and waste water facilities; (f) waste disposal; (g) energy and communications networks; (h) the provision of educational, health care, retail and other community facilities; (i) the preservation and protection of the environment and its amenities, including the archaeological, architectural and natural heritage; and (j) such other matters as may be prescribed.[184]

1–169

---

[181] PDA 2000, s.13(11).
[182] See definition PDA 2000, s.2.
[183] PDA 2000, s.23(1)(a).
[184] PDA 2000, s.23(2).

2. Environmental assessment

1–170   Draft regional planning guidelines prepared by the regional authority shall be accompanied by or include an environmental report.[185] Provision is made for the scoping of the contents of an environmental report. The regional authority is required to give notice to the EPA; to the Minister for the Environment, Heritage and Local Government (where it appears to the regional authority that the plan might have significant effects in relation to the architectural or archaeological heritage or to nature conservation); and to the Minister for Communications, Marine and Natural Resources (where it appears to the regional authority that the plan might have significant effects on fisheries or the marine environment).

1–171   An environmental report shall identify, describe and evaluate the likely significant effects on the environment of implementing the regional planning guidelines and reasonable alternatives taking account of the objectives and the geographical scope of the guidelines. The report shall (a) contain the information specified in Sch.2B; (b) take account of any submission or observation received; and (c) be of sufficient quality to meet the requirements of the Regulations. Special procedures apply where the regional authority considers that implementation of the guidelines is likely to have significant effects on the environment of another Member State or where a Member State, likely to be significantly affected, so requests.[186]

1–172   A statement is to be made available summarising (a) how environmental considerations have been integrated into the guidelines; (b) how (i) the environmental report prepared pursuant to art.15B, (ii) submissions and observations made to the regional authority in response to a notice under s.24(4) of the PDA 2000, and (iii) any consultations under art.15E have been taken into account during the preparation of the guidelines; (c) the reasons for choosing the guidelines, as adopted, in the light of the other reasonable alternatives dealt with; and (d) the measures decided upon to monitor, in accordance with art.15H, the significant environmental effects of implementation of the guidelines.[187]

3. Duty to have regard to regional planning guidelines

1–173   A planning authority shall have regard to any regional planning guidelines in force for its area when making and adopting a development plan.[188] This

---

[185] See, generally, Planning and Development Regulations 2001, arts 15A to 15H (as inserted by the Planning and Development (Strategic Environmental Assessment) Regulations 2004).

[186] Planning and Development Regulations 2001, art.15E (as inserted by the Planning and Development (Strategic Environmental Assessment) Regulations 2004, art.10).

[187] Planning and Development Regulations 2001, art.15G (as inserted by the Planning and Development (Strategic Environmental Assessment) Regulations 2004, art.10).

[188] PDA 2000, s.27.

requirement is not mandatory after six years from the making of such guidelines.[189]

A planning authority is required to review its existing development plan **1–174** following the making of regional planning guidelines for its area, and to consider whether any variation of the development plan is necessary in order to achieve the objectives of the regional planning guidelines.[190]

The nature of the statutory obligation "to have regard to" was considered in **1–175** *McEvoy v Meath County Council*.[191] Quirke J. held that the requirement "to have regard to" obliged a planning authority to inform itself fully of and give reasonable consideration to any regional planning guidelines which are in force in the area which is the subject of the development plan, with a view to accommodating the objectives and policies contained in such guidelines. Quirke J. went on to state that whilst reason and good sense would dictate that it was in the main desirable that planning authorities should, when making and adopting development plans, seek to accommodate the objectives and policies contained in relevant regional planning guidelines, planning authorities were not bound to comply with the guidelines and could depart from them for *bona fide* reasons consistent with the proper planning and development of the area for which the planning authority has planning responsibilities.

On the facts, Quirke J. held that the officials and elected members of the **1–176** planning authority were informed fully and repeatedly of the existence and nature of the regional guidelines, and of the significance of same, in the context of the making and adoption of the development plan.

In relation to the second requirement, namely to give reasonable consideration **1–177** to the regional planning guidelines, Quirke J. found the position to be less satisfactory. It is stated in the judgment that the evidence adduced at the hearing strongly suggested that, in a number of respects, the development plan did not comply with the regional guidelines and, indeed, that in some of its provisions, the development plan had substantially departed from the guidelines' policies and objectives. Quirke J. went on, however, to state that he was of the view that the regional guidelines themselves were flawed to an extent, in that they were incomplete in failing to identify and define the type of consideration which they expected the planning authorities to give to them. Accordingly, Quirke J. held that, although the nature and extent of the consideration given by the elected members to the regional guidelines in the zoning of land for residential purposes gave rise to concern (and indeed unease), he was not satisfied that the evidence adduced had established that the planning authority had failed to "have regard to" the regional guidelines.

---

[189] PDA 2000, s.27(5).
[190] PDA 2000, s.27(4).
[191] [2003] 1 I.R. 208; [2003] 1 I.L.R.M. 431.

1–178   The fact that Quirke J. applied the attenuated standard of review provided for under *O'Keeffe v An Bord Pleanála*[192] is discussed at paras 12–83 to 12–84. What is of more immediate relevance in the present context is the seeming lack of significance attached to alternative methods of enforcing the planning authority's obligations. The gravamen of the applicants' case was that the planning authority had failed to comply properly with the requirement to have regard to the regional planning guidelines when making and adopting its development plan. A mechanism by which this duty might be enforced is provided under s.27(2) of the PDA 2000. More specifically, the Minister for the Environment, Heritage and Local Government may, by order, determine that planning authorities shall comply with any regional planning guidelines in force for their area, or any part thereof, when preparing and making a development plan, or may require in accordance with s.31 that an existing development plan comply with any regional planning guidelines in force for the area. Such order may relate to regional planning guidelines generally, or one or more specified guidelines, or may relate to specific elements of those guidelines. Given the existence of such an alternative mechanism for policing the planning authority's duty, it is arguable that judicial review should not lie against the planning authority.

I. Ministerial Directions Regarding Development Plans

1–179   The Minister for the Environment, Heritage and Local Government has a supervisory role in relation to development plans.[193] Control is exercised by issuing directions to the offending planning authority. This power is available in advance of, or following, the making of a development plan.

1–180   More specifically, where the Minister considers that any draft development plan fails to set out an overall strategy for the proper planning and sustainable development of the area of a planning authority, or otherwise significantly fails to comply with the PDA 2000, the Minister may, for stated reasons, direct the planning authority to take such specified measures as he or she may require to ensure that the development plan, when made, is in compliance with the PDA 2000. In the case of an existing, as opposed to a draft, development plan, the Minister may direct the planning authority to take specified steps to "review or vary" the development plan. This indicates that the Minister is not confined to directing a planning authority to reconsider the content of the plan, *i.e.* requiring the planning authority to "review" the plan in light of his concerns, but may actually stipulate what that content is to be by directing the planning authority to "vary" the plan. The fact that the Minister can determine the content of the variation is confirmed by s.31(3), which indicates that the Minister can

---

[192] [1993] 1 I.R. 39; [1992] I.L.R.M. 237.
[193] PDA 2000, s.31.

by-pass the normal public consultation requirements in respect of the varying of a development plan.[194]

The planning authority is required to comply with any such direction. Moreover, **1–181** neither the manager nor the elected members of any planning authority shall exercise the powers conferred on them under the PDA 2000 in conflict with such a direction.[195]

The Minister has recently made directions in respect of the development plan **1–182** of Laois County Council.

J. Local Area Plans

1. Introduction

A planning authority may at any time, and for any particular area within its **1–183** functional area, prepare a local area plan in respect of that area.[196] A development plan may indicate that specified development in a particular area will be subject to the making of a local area plan.[197] A local area plan may be prepared in respect of any area—including a Gaeltacht area or an existing suburb of an urban area—which the planning authority considers suitable and, in particular, for those areas which require economic, physical and social renewal and for areas likely to be subject to large-scale development within the lifetime of the plan.[198]

A local area plan is required to be consistent with the objectives of the **1–184** development plan. A local area plan consists of a written statement and a plan or plans indicating objectives in such detail as may be determined by the planning authority for the proper planning and sustainable development of the area to which it applies, including detail on community facilities and amenities and on standards for the design of developments and structures.[199] As a result of an amendment introduced under the Planning and Development (Amendment) Act 2002,[200] it is now expressly provided that a local area plan may include objectives for the zoning of land for the use solely or primarily of particular areas for particular purposes.

---

[194] Under s.31(3), the Minister may specify any of the public consultation provisions which are to apply in respect of the specified measures and any other provisions shall be disregarded. This power will have to be read now in light of the requirement for environmental assessment of plans.

[195] PDA 2000, s.31(4).

[196] PDA 2000, s.18.

[197] PDA 2000, s.10(7).

[198] PDA 2000, s.19(1).

[199] PDA 2000, s.19(3) (as amended by the Planning and Development (Amendment) Act 2002).

[200] Planning and Development (Amendment) Act 2002, s.8.

Mandatory local area plan

1–185   It is mandatory for a planning authority to make a local area plan in respect of an area which (i) is designated as a town in the most recent census of population, other than a town designated as a suburb or environs in that census; (ii) has a population in excess of two thousand; and (iii) is situated within the functional area of a planning authority which is a county council.

2. Legal effects of local area plan

1–186   The two principal effects of a local area plan are as follows. First, a local area plan is a mandatory consideration on an application for planning permission: a planning authority, and An Bord Pleanála on appeal, shall have regard to the provisions of any local area plan prepared for the area to which the application relates.[201] Secondly, it has implications in terms of the availability of compensation for adverse planning decisions. More specifically, compensation is excluded where planning permission is refused for the reason that development of the kind proposed would be premature pending the adoption of a local area plan in accordance with the development plan.[202] Further, compensation is also excluded where planning permission is refused for the reason that the proposed development would materially contravene an objective indicated in a local area plan for the area.[203]

1–187   The fact that express provision is now made in respect of local area plans avoids a concern which had arisen under the previous legislation as to the legality of hiving off certain matters from the development plan proper to other plans. More specifically, certain planning authorities had adopted the practice of preparing non-statutory plans (often referred to as "action area plans"). The legality of this practice was open to question, especially in circumstances where the procedures in respect of the making of such plans differed considerably from those applicable in relation to the making of the development plan, both in respect of public participation and the involvement of the elected members.[204]

3. Relationship between local area plan and development plan

1–188   As indicated above, a local area plan is required to be consistent with the objectives of the development plan.[205] A local area plan may, however, remain in force notwithstanding the variation of a development plan or the making of a new development plan affecting the area to which the local area plan relates except that, where any provision of a local area plan conflicts with the provisions

---

[201] PDA 2000, s.18(3).

[202] PDA 2000, Sch.4, para.3.

[203] PDA 2000, Sch.4, para.15.

[204] See, by analogy, *Great Portland Estates Ltd. v Westminster City Council* [1985] A.C. 661.

[205] PDA 2000, s.19(2).

of the development plan as varied or the new development plan, the provision of the local area plan shall cease to have effect.[206]

The fact that a local area plan is subservient to the development plan is a **1–189** matter which needs to be taken into account in laying the ground for a local area plan. Typically, a local area plan will be made subsequent to the development plan proper. Thus steps should be taken to ensure that some leeway is left under the development plan in respect of the area the subject-matter of the local area plan. Otherwise the *raison d'être* of the local area plan will be defeated by the objectives of the development plan. For example, if the area the subject-matter of the local area plan is not excepted from the general zoning objectives under the development plan, it will not then be possible to include local zoning objectives under the local area plan.

4. Environmental assessment

The Planning and Development (Strategic Environmental Assessment) **1–190** Regulations 2004 ("the 2004 Regulations") introduce a requirement that the making of certain local area plans be subject to environmental assessment. The 2004 Regulations are intended to ensure that the making of such plans complies with Directive 2001/42/EC on the assessment of the effects of certain plans and programmes on the environment.

Threshold: population of 10,000 persons or more

An environmental assessment is mandatory where the area of the local area **1–191** plan has a population of 10,000 persons or more.[207]

Screening of sub-threshold local area plans

Where the population is less than 10,000 persons, the planning authority is **1–192** required to carry out a form of screening. The planning authority is required to consider whether or not the implementation of the local area plan or an amended plan would be likely to have significant effects on the environment, taking account of relevant criteria set out in Sch.2A of the Regulations. Schedule 2A largely replicates Annex II of Directive 2001/42/EC on the assessment of the effects of certain plans and programmes on the environment.

Where the planning authority itself determines that the implementation of the **1–193** local area plan or an amended plan is not likely to have significant effects on the environment, it must give notice to and invite submissions from the Environmental Protection Agency ("the EPA"); the Minister for the Environment, Heritage and Local Government (where it appears that the local area plan or an amended plan might have significant effects in relation to the

---

[206] PDA 2000, s.18(4).
[207] Planning and Development Regulations 2001, art.14B (as inserted by the Planning and Development (Strategic Environmental Assessment) Regulations 2004, art.8.

architectural or archaeological heritage or to nature conservation); and the Minister for Communications, Marine and Natural Resources (where it appears to the planning authority that the local area plan or an amended plan might have significant effects on fisheries or the marine environment).

1–194 The EPA and the Ministers, where notified, are entitled to make submissions within the period specified in the notice, which period shall not be less than four weeks from the date of the notice. The planning authority is then required to reconsider the question as to whether or not the implementation of the local area plan or an amended plan would be likely to have significant effects on the environment, again taking account of the relevant criteria set out in Sch.2A, and any submission or observation received.

Screening decision to be available for public inspection

1–195 In all events, the planning authority is required to make a copy of its decision, including, as appropriate, the reasons for not requiring an environmental assessment, available for public inspection at its offices during office hours.

1–196 The planning authority is also required to notify its decision to the EPA, and to the Ministers where previously notified.

1–197 Where the making of the local area plan or an amended plan is to be subject to environmental assessment—whether because the population of the area exceeds 10,000 persons or because the planning authority has determined that the implementation of the plan would be likely to have significant effects on the environment—additional procedural requirements apply. These additional requirements are described below, in the context of the discussion of the procedures governing the making of a local area plan or an amended plan.

5. Procedure

Timetable

1–198 A planning authority is required to put the draft of a proposed local area plan, or of an amendment or variation, on public display at least every six years after the making of the previous local area plan.[208] A local area plan should indicate the period for which the plan is to remain in force: however, a planning authority may at any time amend or revoke a local area plan.[209]

---

[208] PDA 2000, s.19(1)(c). There is a transitional provision whereby the draft of the first local area plan is to be put on public display within two years of the making of a development plan.
[209] PDA 2000, s.18(5).

Environmental assessment

Where the making of a local area plan is subject to environmental assessment, **1–199** the planning authority is required to prepare an environmental report.[210] The draft plan shall be accompanied by or include this environmental report.

Provision is made for the scoping of an environmental report.[211] In this regard, **1–200** the planning authority is required to invite submissions from the EPA; the Minister for the Environment, Heritage and Local Government (where it appears to the planning authority that the plan might have significant effects in relation to the architectural or archaeological heritage or to nature conservation); and the Minister for Communications, Marine and Natural Resources (where it appears to the planning authority that the plan might have significant effects on fisheries or the marine environment) as to the scope and level of detail to be included in the environmental report. The notice should indicate, *inter alia*, that a submission or observation may be made to the planning authority within a specified period, which shall be not less than four weeks from the date of the notice.

An environmental report must identify, describe and evaluate the likely **1–201** significant effects on the environment of implementing the plan or the amended plan, and reasonable alternatives taking into account the objectives and geographical scope of the plan or the amended plan.[212] The environmental report is required to contain the information specified in Sch.2B. It should also take account of any submission or observation received from the EPA or the relevant Minister(s) as to the scope and level of detail to be included in the environmental report. An environmental report must also be of sufficient quality to meet the requirements of the Regulations.

An environmental report shall include the information that may reasonably be **1–202** required taking into account (a) current knowledge and methods of assessment; (b) the contents and level of detail in the plan or the amended plan; (c) the stage of the plan or the amended plan in the decision-making process; and (d) the extent to which certain matters are more appropriately assessed at different levels in the decision-making process in order to avoid duplication of environmental assessment.

---

[210] Planning and Development Regulations 2001, art.14B (as inserted by the 2004 Regulations).

[211] Planning and Development Regulations 2001, art.14C (as inserted by the 2004 Regulations).

[212] Planning and Development Regulations 2001, art.14D (as inserted by the 2004 Regulations).

Notice requirements

1–203   A planning authority is required to take whatever steps it considers necessary to consult the public before preparing, amending or revoking a local area plan, including consultations with any local residents, public sector agencies, non-governmental agencies, local community groups and commercial and business interests within the area.[213] A planning authority shall consult Údarás na Gaeltacht before making, amending or revoking a local area plan for an area which includes a Gaeltacht area.[214]

1–204   Notice of the making of a proposal to make, amend, or revoke a local area plan must be sent to An Bord Pleanála and to the prescribed authorities[215] (and, where applicable, a copy of the proposed plan or amended plan enclosed). A planning authority is also required to publish a notice of the proposal in one or more newspapers circulating in its area.

1–205   A copy of the proposal to make, amend or revoke a local area plan and (where appropriate) the proposed local area plan, or proposed amended plan, is to be put on public display for a stated period (being a period of not less than six weeks). Submissions or observations (presumably in writing) may be made during this period.[216]

1–206   Where the making of the local area plan or amended plan is subject to environmental assessment, then the statutory notices should also indicate that an environmental report has been prepared, and that submissions and observations may be made in respect of the environmental report.[217]

Manager's report

1–207   The manager of the planning authority is required to prepare a report in the usual form.[218] More specifically, the report must (i) list the persons who made submissions or observations; (ii) summarise the issues raised by the persons in the submissions or observations; and (iii) contain the opinion of the manager in relation to the issues raised, and his or her recommendations in relation to the proposed local area plan, amendment to a local area plan or revocation of a local area plan, as the case may be, taking account of the proper planning and sustainable development of the area, the statutory obligations of any local authority in the area and any relevant policies or objectives for the time being of the Government or of any Minister of the Government.

---

[213] PDA 2000, s.20(1).
[214] PDA 2000, s.20(2).
[215] Planning and Development Regulations 2001, art.14 (as amended by the 2006 Regulations).
[216] PDA 2000, s.20(3).
[217] Planning and Development Regulations 2001, art.14E (as inserted by the 2004 Regulations).
[218] PDA 2000, s.20(3)(c).

The elected members of a planning authority are required to consider the **1–208** proposal to make, amend or revoke a local area plan, and the report of the manager.[219] The default procedure is somewhat different from that in relation to the making of the development plan: following consideration of the manager's report, the local area plan shall be deemed to be made, amended or revoked, as appropriate, in accordance with the recommendations of the manager as set out in his or her report, six weeks after the furnishing of the report to all the elected members of the planning authority *unless* the planning authority, by resolution,[220] varies or modifies the proposal, otherwise than as recommended in the manager's report, or where appropriate decides not to make, amend or revoke, as the case may be, the plan.

Amendment of draft local area plan

Following the consideration of the draft local area plan, and the manager's **1–209** report, a planning authority may decide to amend the draft.[221] However, in circumstances where the amendment to the draft would, if made, be a "material alteration" of the draft, it is necessary for there to be a further (truncated) period of public consultation. More specifically, the proposed amendment of the draft must be advertised, and the proposed amendment available for inspection for a period of not less than four weeks. Written submissions or observations with respect to the proposed amendment of the draft, made to the planning authority within the stated period, must be taken into consideration before the making of any amendment. Where the local area plan or amended plan is subject to environmental assessment, then the notices should also indicate that information on the likely significant effects on the environment of implementing the proposed variation or modification will also be available for inspection, and that a submission or observation in relation to such information made to the planning authority within the period stated in the notice will also be taken into consideration before the making of any variation or modification.[222]

A further report is to be prepared by the manager in relation to the submissions **1–210** and observations received in relation to the proposed amendment.

The default position is that the local area plan is deemed to be made or amended, **1–211** as appropriate, with the variation or modification as recommended in the manager's report. The elected members may, however, by resolution, decide to make or amend the plan otherwise than in accordance with that recommendation. It is expressly provided that the (second) public consultation procedure does not apply in respect of any such further amendment.

---

[219] PDA 2000, s.20(3)(d).
[220] Thus a reserved function; see PDA 2000, s.2(7).
[221] PDA 2000, s.20(3)(d) (as substituted by the Planning and Development (Amendment) Act 2002).
[222] Planning and Development Regulations 2001, art.14G (as inserted by the 2004 Regulations).

1–212   Where the local area plan or amended plan is subject to environmental assessment, the planning authority is required to take account of the following during the preparation or amendment of the plan, and before its adoption: (a) the environmental report; (b) any submission or observation made to the planning authority in response to a notice under s.20(3); and (c) any transboundary consultations under art.14F.[223]

Public notice where plan subject to environmental assessment

1–213   As soon as may be following the making or amending of a local area plan, the planning authority shall prepare a statement ("the summary") which summarises (a) how environmental considerations have been integrated into the plan; (b) how (i) the environmental report, (ii) submissions and observations made to the planning authority in response to a notice under s.20(3), and (iii) any transboundary consultations under art.14F have been taken into account during the preparation or amendment of the plan; (c) the reasons for choosing the plan or amendment, as adopted, in the light of the other reasonable alternatives dealt with; and (d) the measures decided upon to monitor, in accordance with art.14J, the significant environmental effects of implementation of the plan or amended plan.[224]

1–214   The planning authority is required, as soon as may be following the making or amending of a local area plan, to give notice of that fact in at least one newspaper with a sufficiently large circulation in the area covered by the local area plan. The newspaper notice must state that a copy of the local area plan and the summary are available for inspection at a stated place or places.

1–215   The planning authority is also required to send a copy of the summary to any bodies consulted during the course of making the plan. A copy of the plan itself, together with a copy of the summary, must be send to the EPA and the Minister for the Environment, Heritage and Local Government and the Minister for Communications, Marine and Natural Resources (where the Minister(s) had previously been notified of the draft plan).

K. Development Contribution Schemes

1–216   The procedure by which a developer can be required to contribute towards the costs of infrastructure and facilities benefiting development has been changed significantly from that obtaining under the previous legislation. In particular, an attempt has been made to make the system more transparent by the introduction of a requirement that a planning authority publish its intentions by way of a development contribution scheme, or a supplementary development contribution scheme.

---

[223] Planning and Development Regulations 2001, art.14H (as inserted by the 2004 Regulations).
[224] Planning and Development Regulations 2001, art.14I (as inserted by the 2004 Regulations).

A planning authority may facilitate the phased payment of contributions, and **1–217** may require the giving of security to ensure payment of contributions.[225] Where a contribution is not paid in accordance with the terms of the condition laid down by the planning authority, any outstanding amounts due to the planning authority shall be paid (together with interest that may have accrued over the period while withheld) by the person required to pay the contribution.[226] A planning authority may recover, as a simple contract debt in a court of competent jurisdiction, any contribution or interest due to the planning authority.[227]

1. Transitional provisions

A planning authority is required to make a development contribution scheme **1–218** or schemes within two years of the commencement of s.48 of the PDA 2000.[228] The relevant commencement date is March 11, 2002.

The new statutory procedure did not apply pending the making of a development **1–219** contribution scheme.[229] Instead, notwithstanding its repeal, the provisions of s.26 of the Local Government (Planning & Development) Act 1963 in relation to requiring contributions in respect of expenditure by local authorities on works which facilitate development continued to apply. These transitional provisions are, however, subject to a time-limit of two years from the commencement of s.48 of the PDA 2000. The relevant commencement date is March 11, 2002. Thus it would seem that if a planning authority had still not made a development contribution scheme by March 2004, it would have no statutory power to attach a condition requiring a contribution towards the costs of infrastructure and facilities benefiting the development. This would continue to be the position thereafter until the relevant planning authority made a development contribution scheme.

2. Definitions

An important distinction is drawn between "public infrastructure and facilities" **1–220** and "public infrastructure projects or services". The full definitions are set out at paras 1–221 to 1–222 below. The essence of the distinction seems to be this. In the case of "public infrastructure projects or services", the project or service must have been provided or carried out, and must benefit the development to which the planning permission relates when carried out.[230] Conversely, in the case of "public infrastructure and facilities", the nexus between the infrastructure and facilities, on the one hand, and the development the subject-matter of the planning permission, on the other, is less clear: provided that the matter is

---

[225] PDA 2000, s.48(15)(a).
[226] PDA 2000, s.48(15)(b).
[227] PDA 2000, s.48(15)(c).
[228] PDA 2000, s.48(16)(a).
[229] PDA 2000, s.48(16)(b).
[230] PDA 2000, s.49(1).

dealt with in a development contribution scheme, it seems sufficient that the infrastructure and facilities benefits development in the area.[231]

1–221 "Public infrastructure and facilities" is defined as (a) the acquisition of land; (b) the provision of open spaces, recreational and community facilities and amenities and landscaping works; (c) the provision of roads, car parks, car parking places, sewers, waste water and water treatment facilities, drains and water mains; (d) the provision of bus corridors and lanes, bus interchange facilities (including car parks for those facilities), infrastructure to facilitate public transport, cycle and pedestrian facilities, and traffic calming measures; (e) the refurbishment, upgrading, enlargement or replacement of roads, car parks, car parking places, sewers, waste water and water treatment facilities, drains or water mains; and (f) any ancillary matters.[232]

1–222 "Public infrastructure project or service" is defined as (a) the provision of particular rail, light rail or other public transport infrastructure, including car parks and other ancillary development; (b) the provision of particular new roads; and (c) the provision of particular new sewers, waste water and water treatment facilities, drains or watermains and ancillary infrastructure.[233]

3. Contents of development contribution scheme

1–223 The basis for the determination of a contribution in respect of public infrastructure and facilities benefiting development in the area shall be set out in a development contribution scheme. A planning authority may make one or more schemes in respect of different parts of its functional area. A scheme may make provision for payment of different contributions in respect of different classes or descriptions of development.[234]

1–224 A scheme shall state the basis for determining the contributions to be paid in respect of public infrastructure and facilities.[235] In this regard, the scheme shall indicate the contribution to be paid in respect of the different classes of public infrastructure and facilities which are provided or to be provided by any local authority and the planning authority shall have regard to the actual estimated cost of providing the classes of public infrastructure and facilities, except that any benefit which accrues in respect of existing development may not be included in any such determination. A scheme may allow for the payment of a reduced contribution or no contribution in certain circumstances, in accordance with the provisions of the scheme.

---

[231] PDA 2000, s.48(1).
[232] PDA 2000, s.48(17).
[233] PDA 2000, s.49(7) (as amended by the Planning and Development (Amendment) Act 2002).
[234] PDA 2000, s.48(2).
[235] PDA 2000, s.48(3).

The extent of the detail which must be included in a development contribution scheme was considered by the High Court in *Construction Industry Federation v Dublin City Council*.[236] The applicant argued before the High Court that it was necessary for a development contribution scheme to specify the public infrastructure and facilities which have been or are intended to be provided. The applicant argued that it was not sufficient merely to identify *classes* of infrastructure and facilities to be provided. According to the applicant, the scheme should provide a description of the works involved in the projects, the timeframe for commencement or completion of any project, together with the costs associated with particular projects. Gilligan J. rejected these arguments, holding that none of the provisions of s.48 required a draft scheme or a scheme to specify the individual projects which the planning authority intended to fund wholly or partly from money raised under the scheme, nor was the scheme required to set out detail as to cost or timing.

1–225

In making the argument that there was a requirement to identify and cost individual projects, the applicant had raised a concern as to the possibility of a double contribution, whereby an applicant for planning permission could be required to make both a general development contribution and also a special contribution. In the absence of information as to which particular projects were covered by the development contribution scheme, it was submitted that an applicant would never be able to ascertain precisely whether the general contribution included that particular project and therefore whether the special contribution was warranted. The High Court declined to engage with these arguments, describing same as "hypothetical" in circumstances where, to date, no applicant had been required to pay a special contribution nor had there been a supplementary development contribution scheme. The High Court also stated that it was to be presumed that the planning authority would exercise its powers fairly and reasonably.

1–226

With respect, the concern raised by the applicant in the proceedings does seem to be a valid and very practical one. Unless some level of detail is provided as to which projects the planning authority say come within the general development contribution scheme, it is very difficult to envisage how an applicant could ever successfully challenge the imposition of a further or special contribution on the basis of double-charging.

1–227

4. Preparation of development contribution scheme

Public notice

A planning authority is required to give public notice of a proposal to make a development contribution scheme in one or more newspapers circulating in

1–228

---

[236] [2005] 2 I.R. 496 (High Court and Supreme Court); [2005] 2 I.L.R.M. 262 (Supreme Court). The Supreme Court ultimately decided the case on the narrower ground that the applicant company did not have a "sufficient interest" to maintain the proceedings.

the area to which the scheme relates.[237] The planning authority is also required to give notice to the Minister for the Environment, Heritage and Local Government.[238]

Submissions and observations

1-229 The draft scheme must be available for public inspection for a period of not less than six weeks. Submissions or observations may be made in writing to the planning authority in relation to the draft scheme before the end of the period for inspection.

1-230 The Minister for the Environment, Heritage and Local Government may make recommendations to the planning authority regarding the terms of the draft scheme within six weeks of being sent the scheme. It is not entirely clear from the legislation as to the weight to be attached to such recommendations. The recommendations do not, however, appear to be binding on the planning authority.

1-231 In *Construction Industry Federation v Dublin City Council*,[239] it had been argued that the public consultation process was inadequate in that neither the draft scheme itself, nor a consultants' report made available as part of the public consultation, contained enough information to allow interested parties to make a proper or full submission or to engage in the consultation process in any meaningful way. Gilligan J. rejected these arguments, holding that there was no requirement under the legislation that the level of information sought by the applicant need be set out. Insofar as the relationship between the draft scheme and a separate consultants' report was concerned, Gilligan J. found that the consultants' report was clearly an integral part of the consultation process and was freely available to all interested persons.

Manager's report

1-232 The manager of a planning authority is required to prepare a report on any submissions or observations received, and submit the report to the elected members of the planning authority for their consideration not later than four weeks after the expiration of the period for making submissions or observations.[240] The report shall (i) list the persons or bodies who made submissions or observations; (ii) summarise the issues raised by the persons or bodies in the submissions or observations; and (iii) give the response of the manager to the issues raised, taking account of the proper planning and sustainable development of the area.

---

[237] PDA 2000, s.48(4).
[238] PDA 2000, s.48(5).
[239] [2005] 2 I.R. 496 (High Court and Supreme Court); [2005] 2 I.L.R.M. 262 (Supreme Court). The Supreme Court ultimately decided the case on the narrower ground that the applicant company did not have a "sufficient interest" to maintain the proceedings.
[240] PDA 2000, s.48(6).

Decision

The elected members of the planning authority are required to consider the   **1–233**
draft scheme and the report of the manager, and to have regard to any
recommendations made by the Minister for the Environment, Heritage and
Local Government.[241] Following the consideration of the manager's report,
and having had regard to any recommendations made by the Minister, the elected
members shall make the scheme, unless they decide, by resolution, to vary or
modify the scheme, otherwise than as recommended in the manager's report,
or otherwise decide not to make the scheme. Such a resolution must be passed
not later than six weeks after receipt of the manager's report.[242]

The judgment of the High Court in *Construction Industry Federation v Dublin*   **1–234**
City Council suggests that there is no obligation on the planning authority to
undertake any further public consultation even in the case of a *material* variation
to the draft scheme. The position in this regard is, therefore, to be contrasted
with that obtaining in relation to draft development plans, where there is a
requirement to undertake further public consultation in the case of a material
alteration to the draft. It should be noted, however, that the High Court in
Construction Industry Federation v Dublin City Council found on the facts
that the amendments made were no more than a variation of the scheme and
could not be construed as in any way affecting the underlying structure or the
basis of the scheme. It may well be that future cases will be distinguished on
this basis, and it may be that notwithstanding the absence of any express statutory
requirement on the planning authority to do so, a future court may hold that it
is necessary to undertake a further round of public consultation in the event of
a material amendment to the draft scheme.

5. Conditions requiring special contributions

Provision is made whereby a planning authority may, in addition to the terms   **1–235**
of a scheme, require the payment of a special contribution in respect of a
particular development where specific exceptional costs not covered by a
scheme are incurred by any local authority in respect of public infrastructure
and facilities which benefit the proposed development.[243]

In the case of such conditions, certain safeguards (analogous to those of general   **1–236**
application under the previous legislation)[244] are set out. For example, the
local authority is required to refund the contribution (together with interest) if
the works in question are not commenced within five years of, or completed
within seven years of, the date of payment of the contribution to the local
authority.[245]

---

[241] PDA 2000, s.48(7).
[242] PDA 2000, s.48(8).
[243] PDA 2000, s.48(2)(c).
[244] See, for example, Local Government (Planning & Development) Act 1963, s.26(2)(h).
[245] PDA 2000, s.48(12).

6. Limited right of appeal to An Bord Pleanála

1-237   There is only a limited right of appeal to An Bord Pleanála in relation to a condition requiring a contribution to be paid in accordance with a development contribution scheme. An appeal may only be brought against such a condition where an applicant for planning permission considers that the terms of the scheme have not been properly applied in respect of any condition laid down by the planning authority.[246] The extremely limited function of An Bord Pleanála in determining such an appeal was emphasised by the High Court in *Cork City Council v An Bord Pleanála*.[247] Kelly J. stated that An Bord Pleanála has no entitlement to consider or review the merits of the scheme under which the contribution is required. Its remit is confined solely to the question of whether or not the terms of the relevant scheme have been properly applied. Kelly J. also indicated that the correct interpretation of the scheme was a matter of law.

1-238   The applicant can ensure that the commencement of development is not held up by the bringing of such an appeal by furnishing to the planning authority security for payment of the full amount of the contribution as specified in the condition. Provided that there is no other appeal pending brought by any other person, the planning authority is then required to make the grant of planning permission as soon as may be after the expiration of the period for the taking of an appeal. Thus by agreeing to provide security on a contingency basis, the applicant can secure a working grant of planning permission.[248]

Power of An Bord Pleanála to impose conditions requiring contribution

1-239   Where an appeal is brought to An Bord Pleanála in respect of a refusal to grant planning permission, and where An Bord Pleanála decides to grant permission, it shall, where appropriate, apply as a condition to the permission the provisions of the contribution scheme for the time being in force in the area of the proposed development.[249]

L. Traveller Accommodation Programme

1-240   The development of a travellers' halting site is subject to the provisions of both the statutory development plan and the statutory traveller accommodation programme. In addition, where the development involves expenditure over a certain monetary threshold, it is subject to a form of public consultation (previously under Pt X of the Local Government (Planning & Development) Regulations 1994, now under Pt 8 of the Planning and Development Regulations 2001). The precise relationship between these various overlapping controls

---

[246] PDA 2000, s.48(10)(a).
[247] [2006] I.E.H.C. 192; unreported, Kelly J., June 1, 2006.
[248] PDA 2000, s.48(10)(c).
[249] PDA 2000, s.48(11).

fell for consideration by the High Court in *Jeffers v Louth County Council*.[250] In summary, the High Court found that the carrying out of the site-specific statutory public consultation procedure under Pt X of the 1994 Regulations did not absolve the local authority from engaging, in advance of any particular site having been selected, in a more general form of public consultation where this had been provided for under the terms of its traveller accommodation programme.

The local authority's traveller accommodation programme had included a **1–241** provision that the local authority, in implementing the programme, would endeavour to ensure that "all traveller families secure accommodation of a type, standard and location acceptable to them" and, furthermore, that "there is full and meaningful consultation with travellers themselves, traveller representative groups, statutory and voluntary agencies, the appropriate local traveller accommodation consultative committee, elected members, the public generally and any other interested persons or bodies". The applicant argued that the local authority had failed to comply with its (self-imposed) obligation to consult under the traveller accommodation programme. In response, the local authority argued that the fact that it had undertaken the public consultation procedure under Pt X of the 1994 Regulations was sufficient to meet its obligations under the traveller accommodation programme. Gilligan J. rejected this line of defence, holding that the Pt X procedure is site-specific and should only come into play when a preferred location for a halting site has been identified and has thus achieved the status of a proposed development. Gilligan J. held further that what was required under the terms of the traveller accommodation programme was that a full and meaningful consultation with various parties take place regarding all available options for traveller accommodation *prior* to the identification of the preferred location for a halting site.

The local authority thus found itself hamstrung by the terms of its own traveller **1–242** accommodation programme. By including in the traveller accommodation programme generous provisions in respect of public consultation, the local authority, in effect, submitted to a more exacting regime than that provided for under statute. There does not appear to be any statutory obligation under the Housing (Traveller Accommodation) Act 1998 to engage in the level of public consultation envisaged by the traveller accommodation programme. The provisions in respect of a local traveller accommodation consultative committee under s.21 are somewhat vague and do not appear to entail an obligation to consult in relation to the development of particular sites. The High Court decided to hold the local authority to its (volunteered) commitment under the traveller accommodation programme. This result is somewhat surprising in that there is nothing in the 1998 Act itself which suggests that development in breach of the traveller accommodation programme is unlawful; this can be contrasted with the express provisions under the planning legislation in respect of a material

---

[250] Unreported, High Court, Gilligan J., December 19, 2003.

contravention of the development plan. It is difficult to reconcile this aspect of the judgment with the statutory obligation imposed on the local authority *qua* housing authority to provide accommodation.

1–243   The judgment in *Jeffers v Louth County Council* is also of interest insofar as it addresses the effect of the exception provided under s.27(2) of the Housing (Traveller Accommodation) Act 1998. Section 26 of the 1998 Act introduced, for the first time, an *express* requirement that a local authority include objectives in its development plan for the provision of accommodation for travellers and the use of particular areas for that purpose. (See now s.10 of the PDA 2000.) Subsection 27(2) then went on to provide that any thing done or act carried out by a housing authority for the purpose of implementing an accommodation programme shall be deemed not to contravene a development plan in the period between the coming into operation of this new requirement and the inclusion of such objectives in the development plan. This transitional provision seems intended to cover the interregnum between the amendment or variation of a development plan (so as to comply with the statutory requirement to include objectives for the provision of accommodation for travellers) and the use of particular areas for that purpose.

1–244   On the facts of *Jeffers*, the development plan had not yet been amended so as to include such objectives. The High Court went on to hold that the transitional provision only applied where the material contravention arose as a result of a failure to include objectives in relation to travellers in the development plan. In other words, it was not every type of material contravention which was absolved by the subsection. The High Court also held that the transitional provision was only available where the material contravention of the development plan arose where same was done for the purpose of implementing the traveller accommodation programme: if an act does not comply with any requirements imposed under the traveller accommodation programme it is not an act for the purpose of "implementing" the traveller accommodation programme, and, therefore, cannot avail of the protection afforded under s.27(2) of the 1998 Act. The local authority in *Jeffers* was not, therefore, entitled to rely on the exception in circumstances where the material contravention involved a breach of junction design standards (the proposed sight distances and gradients were not in compliance with the standards prescribed under the development plan), and where the High Court had already found that there had been a failure to comply with the consultation requirements under the traveller accommodation programme.

CHAPTER TWO

DEVELOPMENT AND EXEMPTED DEVELOPMENT

A. Concept of "Development"

1. Introduction

The concept of development is central to the planning legislation. The various **2–01** elements of the planning legislation (for example, the requirement to obtain planning permission, and most of the enforcement mechanisms) are triggered by the act (whether actual or anticipated) of development. Accordingly, it is necessary to consider this issue in some detail.

The matter is somewhat convoluted, with a number of different technical **2–02** definitions to be considered. It may help an understanding of all of this to flag now, at this early stage, the following points. First, the requirement to obtain planning permission, in its modern form, was first introduced on October 1, 1964.[1] Generally the requirement to obtain planning permission only arises in respect of development which commenced subsequent to that date. This had been made explicit under the previous legislation; the principle is, however, less obvious under the Planning and Development Act 2000 (hereinafter referred to as "the PDA 2000" where convenient).

---

[1] This was the relevant commencement date for the Local Government (Planning & Development) Act 1963.

2–03   The second preliminary point to note is that planning permission is not required in respect of every act of development. Certain development (usually of a minor nature) is exempt from the requirement to obtain planning permission. It is important to bear this in mind in that the definition of development is a very broad one and certain acts which one would not ordinarily expect to require planning permission do, in fact, come within the definition, only to be exempted from the requirement to obtain planning permission elsewhere under the legislation.

2. Requirement to obtain planning permission

2–04   Under s.32 of the PDA 2000, there is a general requirement to obtain planning permission (a) in respect of any development of land, not being exempted development, and (b) in the case of development which is unauthorised, for the retention of that unauthorised development. This statement of the requirement to obtain planning permission is somewhat unsatisfactory in that, unlike the previous legislation, there is no express exception from the requirement to obtain planning permission in favour of development commenced prior to October 1, 1964. Instead, one has to cross-refer to the definition of "unauthorised development" under s.2 of the PDA 2000.

3. Section 3 definition of "development"

2–05   Under s.3 of the PDA 2000, "development" means, except where the context otherwise requires, the carrying out of any works on, in, over or under land or the making of any material change in use of any structures or other land. The concept of development, therefore, consists of two limbs: "works" and "material change in use".

2–06   "Works" is defined as including any act or operation of construction, excavation, demolition, extension, alteration, repair or renewal and, in relation to a protected structure or proposed protected structure, includes any act or operation involving the application or removal of plaster, paint, wallpaper, tiles or other material to or from the surfaces of the interior or exterior of a structure.[2]

2–07   The definition of "use" states that "use" in relation to land does not include the use of the land by the carrying out of any works thereon.[3]

2–08   As indicated above, the term "use" is defined as not including the use of the land by the carrying out of any works thereon. This artificial definition of the term "use" has given rise to some apparently inconsistent judgments. The better view would seem to be that the intention of the artificial definition was to make it clear that the right to use land for a particular purpose did not necessarily

---

[2] PDA 2000, s.2.
[3] PDA 2000, s.2.

mean that a person had the right to carry out works for that purpose.[4] This certainly seems to have been the approach adopted in a number of decisions in relation to exempted development.[5] Thus, for example, the fact that land had an authorised use for say, industrial purposes, did not mean that all manner of industrial buildings or structures could be erected without any further planning permission.

An alternative explanation of the rationale of the artificial definition of "use"   **2–09**
has recently been put forward by Keane J. (as he then was) in the judgment in *Kildare County Council v Goode*, as follows:

> "The reason for the latter provision can be made clear by an example. In ordinary parlance, putting up a building on farmland hitherto used for growing crops would be treated as changing the use of the land. Since, however, the construction of farm buildings is, to some extent, an exempted development, the draftsman found it necessary to provide that the carrying out of works on land, by itself and of itself, was not a use of land for the purposes of the Act of 1963."[6]

Exempted development is often defined in terms of either a material change in   **2–10**
use, or works. The concern highlighted by Keane J. in the quotation above is that but for the artificial definition of "use", there was a risk that an exempted development defined solely in terms of works might be of no actual benefit if those works entailed a change of use. The change of use would not be covered by the exemption, and thus but for the artificial definition it would still be necessary to obtain planning permission.

4. Distinction between "works" and "material change in use"

There are at least two circumstances in which it is still necessary to distinguish   **2–11**
between development by way of material change in use, and by works.

Compensation

The first, and most dramatic, of these is in relation to the payment of   **2–12**
compensation. As discussed in detail at para.6–12 and onwards, there is a general statutory right to the payment of compensation in respect of the refusal of planning permission. One of the circumstances in which this *prima facie*

---

[4]   The obverse position was catered for under s.28(6) of the Local Government (Planning & Development) Act 1963, which ensured that planning permission for works carried with it use rights. The relevant provision in this regard has been modified under s.39(2) of the PDA 2000.

[5]   *Cairnduff v O'Connell* [1986] I.R. 73; [1986] I.L.R.M. 465 (works alleged to have been intended to effect a change from a house consisting of bedsitting rooms to a house consisting of two flats); and *Irish Wildbird Conservancy v Clonakilty Golf & Country Club Ltd.*, unreported, High Court, Costello P., July 23, 1996 (works carried out on lands not exempted as development consisting of the use of any land for the purpose of agriculture). See also *Cork Corporation v O'Connell* [1982] I.L.R.M. 505 (exempted development only applies to works and does not extend to a material change in use).

[6]   [1999] 2 I.R. 495 at 498; [2000] 1 I.L.R.M. 346 at 349.

entitlement to compensation is lost is where the proposed development consists of or includes the making of any material change in the use of any structures or other lands.[7]

2–13   This exception was interpreted strictly by the High Court in *Re Viscount Securities Ltd.*[8] In that case, the developer had been refused planning permission for a proposed residential development. The developer made a claim for compensation: the local authority responded by arguing that compensation was not payable as the proposed development involved a material change in use. Finlay P. (as he then was) held that the effect of the artificial definition of "use" was that the proposed development did not, as a matter of law, involve a material change in use of the lands. This was so notwithstanding the fact that in the ordinary or common sense use of language it would seem that there would be a material change in use: from agricultural use to residential use. In making this decision, Finlay P. emphasised the fact that what was at issue was constitutionally protected property rights.

Exempted development

2–14   The second area in respect of which the distinction is still important is in relation to exempted development. This point has already been flagged in the text above and might be summarised thus: the various classes of exempted development are often defined in terms of either a material change in use, or works. The traditional view had been that the benefit of the exempted development did not extend to include an allied change in use, or works, as the case might be.[9]

Distinction has become less important

2–15   The importance of the distinction between the two limbs of the concept of development has been eroded in recent years. Whereas it had been suggested at one stage that the two definitions were mutually exclusive, and that the same act of development could not constitute both development by works, and by material change in use,[10] the better view now seems to be that the same act of development might consist of both limbs.[11]

2–16   One area in respect of which the distinction used to be important is now gone: more specifically, under the previous legislation, the calculation of the time-limits in respect of the taking of enforcement action differed according to whether the unauthorised development was by way of material change in use, or by works. This distinction does not exist in the context of enforcement action under the PDA 2000. There is now a (new) seven year time-limit which

---

[7]   PDA 2000, ss.190 and 191, and Sch.3, para.1.
[8]   (1976) 112 I.L.T.R. 17.
[9]   *cf. Kildare County Council v Goode* [1999] 2 I.R. 495; [2000] 1 I.L.R.M. 346.
[10]   *Irish Wildbird Conservancy v Clonakilty Golf & Country Club Ltd.*, unreported, High Court, Costello P., July 23, 1996 (at page 19).
[11]   *Re Viscount Securities* (1976) 112 I.L.T.R. 17; and *Kildare County Council v Goode* [1999] 2 I.R. 495; [2000] 1 I.L.R.M. 346.

is reckoned by reference to the omnibus concept of "unauthorised development".[12] See, generally, paras 7–31 to 7–39.

B. "Works"

The concept of works is relatively straightforward and has given rise to little   **2–17**
discussion in the case law. This probably stems in large measure from the fact
that the concept had been comprehensively defined under the previous
legislation, and is now defined under s.2 of the PDA 2000, as follows.

> "'Works' includes any act or operation of construction, excavation, demolition,
> extension, alteration, repair or renewal and, in relation to a protected structure or
> proposed protected structure, includes any act or operation involving the
> application or removal of plaster, paint, wallpaper, tiles or other material to or
> from the surfaces of the interior or exterior of a structure."

> "'Alteration'" includes (a) plastering or painting or the removal of plaster or
> stucco, or (b) the replacement of a door, window or roof, that materially alters
> the external appearance of a structure so as to render the appearance inconsistent
> with the character of the structure or neighbouring structures."[13]

Of particular interest is the fact that the definition expressly includes demolition.   **2–18**
It is also to be noted that the definition of works has an extended meaning in
relation to protected structures. The relevant provisions of the PDA 2000 in
respect of development and protected structures are considered in greater detail
later at paras 8–21 to 8–34. In the case of works commenced prior to October
1, 1964, it would seem that the continuation to completion of the particular
works, commenced before the appointed day at an identified location, is
permitted.[14]

C. "Material Change in Use"

As is apparent from the definition, in order for there to be a material change in   **2–19**
use two conditions must be satisfied: first, there must be an actual change in
use; the act of development is the *change*, not the *use* itself. Secondly, the
change must be *material*.

1. Materiality of change

It is the second of these two requirements, namely that the change be material,   **2–20**
which has given rise to the greatest difficulty. There would appear to be two

---

[12] PDA 2000, s.2.
[13] See, by analogy, *Dublin Corporation v Bentham* [1993] 2 I.R. 58; and *Cairnduff v O'Connell* [1986] I.R. 73; [1986] I.L.R.M. 465.
[14] *Waterford County Council v John A. Wood Ltd.* [1999] 1 I.R. 556; [1999] 1 I.L.R.M. 217.

schools of thought, as follows. The first is to consider whether or not the *character* of the existing use of the land will be substantially altered by the proposed change: it is the change *from* use A to use B which is important. The second approach is to examine the materiality of the proposed change as it impacts on the proper planning and sustainable development of the adjoining area.

2-21 The distinction between the two approaches appears to be this. Under the first test, one simply examines the character of the use of the land before and after the change. The second approach involves a wider ranging consideration of the external effects of the proposed change.

2-22 Support for the first test, focussing as it does on the character of the use, is to be found in certain *obiter dicta* in *Cusack v Minister for Local Government*,[15] where it was suggested that a change of use from a solicitor's office to a dentist's surgery involved a material change in use because of the differing nature of the professions. Similarly, in *McMahon v Dublin Corporation*,[16] it was held that the use of houses for commercial short-term lettings is a different use from that which the houses had been designed or intended, namely residential use. Although reference was made in the judgment to external effects, such as the fact that holiday-makers are more likely to cause noise or disturbance, the judgment ultimately appears to turn on this narrow issue of the character of the use.

2-23 As will be seen shortly at para.2–119, further support for this approach may be derived from the use classes of exempted development. The fact that a class of exempted development has been created in respect of a change within a broad class of use might be taken as implicitly recognising that changes within a class may well constitute a material change in use; thus, it is submitted, concentrating attention on the *character* of the use.[17]

2-24 More recently, it would seem that it is the second of the two tests identified above which generally prevails. This second test was summarised by Budd J. in *Westmeath County Council v Quirke & Sons*, as follows:

> "Many alterations in the activities carried out on land constitute a change of use; however, not all alterations will be material. Whether such changes amount to a material change in use is a question of fact as is explained in *Monaghan County*

[15] Unreported, High Court, McWilliam J., November 4, 1980. On the facts, a change of use from residential use to use as a solicitor's office was held to be a material change in use. Reference is also made to the decision in *Fusco v Aprile*, unreported, High Court, Morris J., June 6, 1997 (change from convenience store to fast food outlet involved material change in use).

[16] [1996] 3 I.R. 509; [1997] 1 I.L.R.M. 227.

[17] See, further, *Cusack v Minister for Local Government*, unreported, High Court, McWilliam J., November 4, 1980; and *London Residuary Body v Secretary of State for the Environment* [1988] J.P.L. 637 at 642.

Council v Brogan [1987] I.R. 339. Consideration of the materiality of a change in use means assessing not only the use itself but also its effects."[18]

As stated above, this test requires a wider ranging examination than the first. **2–25** More specifically, it is necessary to consider the impact of the proposed change on the adjoining area. For example, it may be that the subsequent use might generate more traffic or noise than the previous use. Other factors which might have to be considered would include the timing of the subsequent use: a shift from daytime to nighttime (or possibly even to evening) use might be regarded as material, especially in a residential area.[19]

Some concern has been expressed as to the extent to which a court should **2–26** enter into a detailed consideration of the external effects. In this regard, it is important to emphasise that the concept of development simply triggers the requirement to obtain planning permission: a finding that a particular act is development has nothing at all to say as to whether or not planning permission should ultimately be granted. There is a danger that were a court to enter into a detailed consideration of the external effects of a particular act, it might (inadvertently) trespass on the function of a planning authority and An Bord Pleanála in relation to the decision whether or not to grant planning permission. The fact that planning permission would inevitably be granted for a particular act does not absolve the developer from the requirement to apply for planning permission.[20] If a change of use is material, it is not for the court to anticipate what matters, including possible objections, might be forthcoming in the event of there being an application for planning permission.[21]

Accordingly, the better view would seem to be that the court should take a **2–27** common sense approach in attempting to identify the possible external effects of the proposed change but should not regard the absence of direct evidence as to the impact of, or as to the existence of objections to, the proposed use as being decisive.[22] Insofar as the decision in *Galway County Council v Lackagh Rock Ltd.*[23] suggests otherwise, it is submitted that the reasoning of Keane J. in *Monaghan County Council v Brogan*[24] is to be preferred.[25]

---

[18] Unreported, High Court, Budd J., May 23, 1996 (at p.91).

[19] See the decision of the High Court, at first instance, in *Mahon v Butler*, unreported, High Court, Costello P., July 28, 1997. Ultimately, the Supreme Court found that the use of the lands for the staging of pop concerts did not require planning permission: *Butler v Dublin Corporation* [1999] 1 I.R. 565; [1999] 1 I.L.R.M. 481.

[20] *Monaghan County Council v Brogan* [1987] I.R. 333.

[21] *ibid.*

[22] See, for example, *Esat Digifone Ltd. v South Dublin County Council* [2002] 3 I.R. 585; [2002] 2 I.L.R.M. 547 (question of materiality to be determined by court: views of planning authority simply matters to be taken into account). See also *Monaghan County Council v Brogan* [1987] I.R. 333.

[23] [1985] I.R. 120.

[24] [1987] I.R. 333.

[25] See comments of Morris P. in *Butler v Dublin Corporation* [1999] 1 I.R. 565 (High Court); [1998] 1 I.L.R.M. 533.

2. Transient use

2–28   It would appear from the judgment of Keane J. in *Butler v Dublin Corporation*[26] that one aspect of materiality in material change in use is materiality in terms of time. Thus a short term or transient event (such as a one or two day pop concert) does not involve a material change in use. (It should be noted that certain transient events are now dealt with by way of a special licensing regime under Pt XVI of the PDA 2000. This is discussed in detail at paras 8–262 to 8–288).

3. Primary and ancillary uses, and multiple uses

2–29   A planning unit may be used for several activities: a single primary use and any number of ancillary uses. Generally, it is necessary to compare any proposed change of use against the primary use in order to determine whether or not a material change in use is involved. An ancillary use is regarded as part of the primary use so that cesser of the ancillary use does not give rise to a material change in use.[27] For example, the use of the façade of premises to advertise the business of the company which owns the premises is a use ancillary to the primary (commercial) use of the premises.[28] If an ancillary use becomes a separate use, this may constitute a material change in use.[29]

2–30   This concept is best illustrated by way of example. In *Rehabilitation Institute v Dublin Corporation*,[30] the developer had used certain premises for the assessment, training and placement of the handicapped. In the main, the premises were used for administration, although some training was carried out there. It was proposed to discontinue all training and to use the premises for the sole purpose of an office. The High Court analysed the use of the lands as follows. In law, there was only one use of the premises: use as an office for any purpose. The training use was to be regarded as ancillary to the general administrative use. Thus a change to a pure office use did not involve a material change in use.

2–31   Alternatively, the facts could be analysed as involving multiple uses. Where there are two or more separate, as opposed to primary/ancillary, uses, then cesser of one such use may ultimately lead to a material change in use: this is a question of fact. The *Rehabilitation Institute* case could be analysed as a case involving substitution of an office use for the (separate) training use, in which event it would then be a question of fact as to whether or not a material change in use had occurred.

---

[26] [1999] 1 I.R. 565; [1999] 1 I.L.R.M. 481.
[27] *Rehabilitation Institute v Dublin Corporation*, unreported, High Court, Barron J., January 14, 1988.
[28] *Dublin Corporation v Regan Advertising Ltd.* [1989] I.R. 61; [1986] I.R. 171.
[29] *Rehabilitation Institute v Dublin Corporation*, unreported, High Court, Barron J., January 14, 1988.
[30] Unreported, High Court, Barron J., January 14, 1988.

In *Dublin Corporation v Regan Advertising Ltd.*,[31] it was held that whereas **2–32** the use of the façade of the premises to advertise the business carried on in the premises was an ancillary use, a change of use to advertise third party products or services represented a separate (primary) use and thus required planning permission.

Similarly, in *Esat Digifone Ltd. v South Dublin County Council*,[32] it was held **2–33** that the installation of telecommunications antennae and equipment gave rise to a material change in use in that this use was not ancillary or complementary in any way to the primary use of the premises for the purpose of a public house.

In *Westport UDC v Golden*,[33] premises had been put to use as a restaurant **2–34** with an ancillary takeaway element. Following certain works, the premises reopened as a takeaway. Morris P. held that the underlying planning permission had created three separate planning units: first, a residential unit; second, a restaurant unit; and third, a takeaway unit. There could be no swapping around of the uses. There had been a change in use (to takeaway use) of that part of the premises which formerly constituted the restaurant area; the artificial subdivision of the altered premises was not a reality. This change of use was material in planning terms in point of traffic, noise and disturbance.

4. Certain changes expressly stated to be material changes of use

Without prejudice to the generality of the definition of development, s.3 of the **2–35** PDA 2000 goes on to provide that the use of land shall be taken as having materially changed where the land becomes used for certain specified purposes. In effect, the section declares that a change in the use of land to certain specified uses is development.

(a) Where any structure or other land or any tree or other object on land becomes used for the exhibition of advertisements.

Under s.2, "advertisement" means any word, letter, model, balloon, inflatable **2–36** structure, kite, poster, notice, device or representation employed for the purpose of advertisement, announcement or direction.[34]

The combined effect of these provisions would seem to be that a change in use **2–37** to use for the exhibition of advertisements will, generally, constitute development. This would seem to be the case even where what is being advertised is the business which is being carried out on the lands: in other words, even an ancillary use of the lands for the exhibition of an advertisement

---

[31] [1989] I.R. 61; [1986] I.R. 171.
[32] [2002] 3 I.R. 585; [2002] 2 I.L.R.M. 547.
[33] [2002] 1 I.L.R.M. 439.
[34] "Advertisement structure" and "exhibit" are also defined.

would seem to involve development (provided, of course, it had commenced after October 1, 1964).

2–38 It should also be noted that the Supreme Court held in *Dublin Corporation v Regan Advertising Ltd.*[35] that it does not follow as a corollary of the fact that use for the exhibition of advertisements is declared to be development that once such a use has been established, all and any use for the purpose of the exhibition of advertisements is authorised. It would seem that a change from one *type* of advertisement to another, or a change in the *purpose* of the advertisement, might itself represent a material change in use. In particular, the Supreme Court in *Dublin Corporation v Regan Advertising Ltd.*[36] held that where the object of the advertisements had changed from that of advertising the business being carried on at the premises, to advertising a third party's goods and services, this represented a material change in use.

2–39 The application of planning control to advertisements has given rise to much confusion in the case law. In particular, the courts seem unsure whether to regard advertisements as development by way of works or by way of material change in use. The better view seems to be that advertisements should be treated as giving rise to a use of land: this follows from s.3 of the PDA 2000, which expressly declares there to be a material change in use where any structure or other land or any tree or other object on land becomes used for the exhibition of advertisements. Under s.2 of the PDA 2000, "advertisement" means any word, letter, model, balloon, inflatable structure, kite, poster, notice, device or representation employed for the purpose of advertisement, announcement or direction.

2–40 In *Dublin Corporation v Lowe,*[37] the Supreme Court treated advertisements as giving rise to development works. The gable end of premises was used, under agreement, for the display of advertisement hoardings. The trial judge had found as a fact that on the appointed day, namely October 1, 1964, an advertisement hoarding had been in existence on the gable wall of the premises. The trial judge had also found that hoardings had been renewed or replaced from time to time, with the time periods between the removal and replacement being no more than a few days on any occasion. In or about the end of December 1995, the owner of the premises entered into a new agreement with a different advertising company, which resulted in the removal of one advertising hoarding and its replacement a number of days later with another. The new hoarding was identical in its dimensions to that which immediately preceded it.

2–41 Notwithstanding the provisions of s.3 of the PDA 2000, the Supreme Court addressed the case as one involving development works. Thus, even though the use of the lands had clearly not changed since October 1964, the Supreme

---

[35] [1989] I.R. 61; [1986] I.R. 171.
[36] [1989] I.R. 61; [1986] I.R. 171.
[37] [2004] 4 I.R. 259.

Court nevertheless considered whether planning permission might have been required. The Supreme Court ultimately held that the works involved were exempted development under the equivalent provision to what is now s.4(1)(h) of the PDA 2000. The relevant parts of this subsection provide for an exemption in favour of alterations which do not materially alter the external appearance of the structure so as to render its appearance inconsistent with the character of the structure itself or of neighbouring structures. The Supreme Court held that the term "alteration" was not confined to a mere visual alteration. For the purposes of assessing the impact of the alteration, the relevant structure was that which had been in place since prior to October 1964, namely the building or gable wall of the building with an advertisement hoarding attached to it: it would be unreal to look at a hoarding of this nature as a structure in isolation from the rest of the building.

> "The Applicant also submits that in any event the advertisement hoarding did materially affect the external appearance of the premises so as to render its appearance inconsistent with the character of the premises itself or that of neighbouring structures. It is, of course, true that the building itself is an old Georgian building, and no doubt advertising hoardings such as the present one would not have been present or in contemplation of the owners of the original building in Georgian times. However, what this Court is concerned with is the alteration of the hoarding by the substitution of a new hoarding, and that in itself in my view cannot possibly be said to have materially affected the external appearance of the premises."

It should also be noted that the courts have adopted a somewhat harsh attitude **2–42** in determining whether or not advertisement development has been abandoned. Strictly speaking, it would seem to follow from the provisions of s.3 that advertisement development represents development by way of material change in use. Accordingly, the ordinary principles in relation to abandonment (discussed at paras 2–72 to 2–78) should apply. In particular, the intention of the parties would seem to be paramount. Somewhat surprisingly then, the High Court has, in a number of decisions, treated advertisement development as development by way of works and has held that relatively minor changes in the physical works were such as to give rise to a finding of abandonment. This was so even in circumstances where it had clearly remained the intention of the parties to exhibit advertisements.[38]

(b) Where land becomes used for any of the following purposes – (i) the placing or keeping of vans, tents or other objects, whether or not movable and whether or not collapsible, for the purpose of caravanning or camping or habitation or the sale of goods, (ii) the storage of caravans or tents, or (iii) the deposit of vehicles whether or not usable for the purpose for which

---

[38] See, for example, *Fingal County Council v Crean*, unreported, High Court, Ó Caoimh J., October 19, 2001. See also *Dublin Corporation v Lowe*, unreported, High Court, Morris P., February 4, 2000. It should be noted that this decision was appealed to the Supreme Court, and, on consent, remitted to the High Court for a rehearing and then returned to the Supreme Court: [2004] 4 I.R. 259.

they were constructed or last used, old metal, mining or industrial waste, builders' waste, rubbish or debris.

2–43 This category is significant in that it would seem to capture, *inter alia*, the use of land as a travellers' halting site, and the use of land as a waste disposal site. Insofar as the sale of goods is concerned, it would seem that same must be carried on at the particular land concerned.[39]

Subdivision of dwelling house

2–44 Section 3(3) of the PDA 2000 provides as follows.

> "For the avoidance of doubt, it is hereby declared that, for the purposes of this section, the use as two or more dwellings of any house previously used as a single dwelling involves a material change in the use of the structure and of each part thereof which is so used."

2–45 This provision appears to overcome the difficulties (apparent from the decision in *Dublin Corporation v Sullivan*[40]) in otherwise establishing a material change in use in this regard.

5. Waste disposal or recovery

2–46 It can be a difficult question as to whether a fresh planning permission is required in the case of a change of use to one involving waste disposal/recovery. The Court of Appeal in England and Wales has indicated that the use of land for waste disposal/recovery can, in principle, represent a substantive use of lands in its own right, even where it occurs as part of some other process (typically, manufacturing): see *R. v Durham County Council Ex p. Lowther*.[41] It is therefore a question of fact and degree as to whether the land is subject to a single use (waste disposal/recovery) or a dual use (waste disposal/recovery and some other use), or whether the waste disposal/recovery is simply ancillary or incidental to the principal use of the lands.

2–47 In *Glancré Teoranta v Cafferkey (No. 2)*,[42] the High Court found that a change in use from use for the purpose of drying peat and the manufacture of fuel, to use for the purpose of waste disposal/recovery, represented a material change in use. In reaching this conclusion, the High Court placed particular emphasis, first, on the fundamental difference in the purpose to which the two activities were directed: the proposed activity was primarily directed to waste disposal albeit that a by-product in the form of a granulated fertiliser would arise, whereas the use permitted under planning permission was directed to the manufacture of a fuel product, one of the components of which was dried peat; and, secondly,

---

[39] *Dublin Corporation v Moore* [1984] I.L.R.M. 339.
[40] Unreported, High Court, Finlay P., December 21, 1984.
[41] [2002] 1 P. & C.R. 22.
[42] [2004] 4 I.R. 22.

on the differences in process (in terms of quarantining, odour treatment, treatment of waste water, specialised storage of sludge and emissions) arising from the differences in the raw materials.

Exempted development: waste disposal

The fact that a particular activity may be subject to both the planning legislation and the waste management legislation can present practical difficulties. For example, the requirements of a waste licence in respect of works or structures might be different from those of the relevant planning permission. This issue is, to some extent, addressed under the Waste Management Act 1996. Specifically, ss.54(4) and (5) provide that works which are necessary to give effect to any conditions to be attached to a waste licence are to be exempted development. There is a procedural requirement for the Environmental Protection Agency to consult with the relevant planning authority in this regard. **2–48**

The wording of s.54(4) is somewhat unusual and refers to circumstances not only where planning permission has previously been granted for development comprising, or for the purposes of, a waste disposal activity, but also where "an application has been made for such permission". The possibility of exempted development occurs where the necessary works are "not the subject of a permission or an application" for planning permission. The meaning and effect of this exemption was considered in *Yellow Bins (Waste Disposal) Ltd. v Environmental Protection Agency.*[43] On the facts of the case, an application for planning permission in respect of works which were considered necessary by the Environmental Protection Agency had been refused by An Bord Pleanála. The sequence of events left it open to the developer to make the ingenious argument that the provisions of s.54(4) arose notwithstanding the fact that an application for planning permission had actually been refused for the necessary works. **2–49**

The High Court rejected this argument, holding that the provisions of s.54(4) were only triggered where there was either an existing planning permission or a *pending* application for planning permission. The High Court also accepted the submission made on behalf of the Environmental Protection Agency to the effect that the section applied only in the limited circumstances where a developer had been granted or was seeking land use permission for the *general* works required in connection with the activity requiring the waste licence, but had not been granted nor sought permission for the *particular* works necessary to give effect to the conditions which the Agency believed were appropriate. **2–50**

In *Mason v KTK Sand and Gravel Ltd.*,[44] a further limitation on the exemption under s.54(4)(a) was highlighted. The High Court held that the exemption only applied to development works, and did not extend to a material change in the use of lands. Thus, a change from use as a sand and gravel quarry to use as **2–51**

---

[43] Unreported, High Court, Ó Caoimh J., July 9, 2004.
[44] Unreported, High Court, Smyth J., May 7, 2004.

a landfill would not be covered by the exemption. (On the facts, s.54(4)(a) would appear not to have been applicable in any event, in that it seems that the developer held only a waste permit and not a waste licence.)

D. Intensification of Development

2–52   It is now well established that an intensification of use, or an intensification of works, may represent development requiring planning permission. To put the matter in somewhat simplistic terms, more of the same can, in certain circumstances, represent a fresh act of development. Reference is made in this regard to the judgment of Keane J. (as he then was) in *Butler v Dublin Corporation*.[45]

> "Although the expression 'intensification of use' is not to be found in our planning code or its English equivalent, the legislatures in both jurisdictions must have envisaged that a particular use could be so altered in character by the volume of activities or operations being carried on that the original use must be regarded as having been materially changed. One man digging up stones in a field and carrying them away in a wheelbarrow for a few hours each week may be succeeded by fleets of bulldozers, J.C.B.s and lorries extracting and carrying away huge volumes of rock from the same site. The use in both instances may properly be described as 'quarrying', but that its intensification to a particular degree may constitute a material change in the original use is, I think, not merely borne out by the authorities to which I have referred, but is consistent with the underlying policy of the Act of 1963 and the amending legislation of ensuring that significant changes in the physical characteristics of the environment are subjected to planning control."

2–53   Before turning to a more detailed consideration of this concept of intensification, the following preliminary point should be made. Some initial concern had been expressed as to whether or not the concept of intensification could properly apply at all to works. In particular, O'Sullivan & Sheperd had commented that given the distinction between works, and use, once works had commenced, it was difficult to understand the relevance of the intensity at which they were carried out. This issue also featured in the early case law. For example, Costello J. in *Patterson v Murphy*[46] appears to have felt constrained by the artificial definition of use. Gannon J. adopted a more robust approach in *Dublin County Council v Sellwood Quarries Ltd.*,[47] holding that "use" connoted the idea of winning or taking from the land what it can yield or give with or without cultivation.

2–54   This controversy would appear to have since been resolved, however, by the decision of the Supreme Court in *Kildare County Council v Goode*.[48] The

---

[45] [1999] 1 I.R. 565; [1999] 1 I.L.R.M. 481.
[46] [1978] I.L.R.M. 85 at 104.
[47] [1981] I.L.R.M. 23.
[48] [1999] 2 I.R. 495; [2000] 1 I.L.R.M. 346.

Supreme Court held that the concepts of abandonment, and intensification, are applicable to both development by way of material change in use, and development by works. Abandonment is the objective sign of a decision not to continue with the development, whereas intensification may be the objective sign of an intention to carry out a different development. In the former case, if the intention revives, planning permission will be required; whereas in the latter, it is required as soon as it is obvious that what is being carried out is a new and different development.

A second preliminary point is this. As appears from below, much of the case law in this area is related to quarries. It should be noted that whereas the principles to be derived from this case law probably remain good, the practical significance of same in the specific context of quarrying is now limited as a result of new controls on quarries introduced under s.261 of the PDA 2000. The provisions in this regard are considered at paras 8–118 to 8–220. **2–55**

Much of the case law in relation to intensification arose in circumstances where the developer sought to rely on what he alleged to be an established development. More specifically, the developer would argue that the activities now being carried out on the lands were merely the continuation of development which had commenced prior to October 1, 1964, and, accordingly, did not require planning permission. **2–56**

The reality, in many instances, however, was that the nature and extent of the activity now being carried out on the lands was vastly different from that which had obtained on October 1, 1964. In a number of cases, the High Court held that there had been an intensification of development. In reaching these decisions, the High Court attached significance to factors including the following. First, the object of the operations carried on. For example, in *Patterson v Murphy*,[49] Costello J. found that the object of the present operations was to produce a different product to that being produced in 1964: the four inch stone being produced was different to shale, it was used for a different purpose in the building industry, and it fetched a different price.[50] **2–57**

Secondly, the method of production. Relevant factors here would be the use of larger or more efficient equipment and machinery[51]; for example, in *Patterson v Murphy*, Costello J. referred to the fact that the raw material (rock) for the end product was now obtained by means of blasting and that this was done on a regular basis. Moreover, large crushing and screening plant was used to produce stones of the correct dimensions. Considerable ancillary equipment was also used and a considerable labour force employed. **2–58**

---

[49] [1978] I.L.R.M. 85.
[50] See also *Westmeath County Council v Quirke & Sons*, unreported, High Court, Budd J., May 23, 1996 (change from production of quarry run rock, to crushed stone); and *Dublin County Council v Sellwood Quarries Ltd.* [1981] I.L.R.M. 23 (sand and gravel to rock).
[51] *Westmeath County Council v Quirke & Sons*, unreported, High Court, Budd J., May 23, 1996.

2–59 Thirdly, the scale of operations as compared to those carried on prior to October 1, 1964. For example, in *Westmeath County Council v Quirke & Sons*,[52] Budd J. drew attention to the fact that the volume and size of the trucks and machinery traffic had considerably increased since October 1, 1964. Budd J. also found that the effect of the operations prior to October 1, 1964 on the local residents' amenities was miniscule as compared with the significant effects of the large scale operations since July, 1990: dust and noise levels had greatly increased; and the area of operations was much larger,[53] with massive stock piles and much machinery and equipment in the vicinity of the quarry. In *Molumby v Kearns*,[54] it was held that an increase in the volume of heavy commercial traffic at an industrial estate *per se* amounted to an intensification of use.

2–60 To an extent, there is a danger of overstating the importance of the early case law in relation to intensification. The principal focus of much of the early case law was directed towards the artificial definition of use (which excluded use of lands by the carrying on of works). Now that this issue has seemingly been resolved by the Supreme Court in *Kildare County Council v Goode*,[55] the case law might be seen as involving an unremarkable application of the concept of material change in use. In each of the cases, the primary purpose of the use had changed and, accordingly, there would appear to be no particular reason as to why it would be necessary to invoke any special principle of intensification in order to support the finding that there had been development.

2–61 It was probably not until the judgment in *Galway County Council v Lackagh Rock Ltd.*[56] that the principle of intensification proved to be critical.[57] Barron J. distinguished the earlier cases to the extent that in those cases the primary purpose of the use of the land had actually changed. Barron J. went on to hold that, even though the primary purpose in the present case had not changed, the production process had. Barron J. found that the fact that the purpose was being achieved by different means which were material in the context of the planning code was significant. Although generally the primary purpose of the use determines the character of the use, planning considerations cannot be ignored. Otherwise, Barron J. suggested, it was difficult to see how an intensification of use could ever amount, as it can do, to a material change in use.

---

[52] Unreported, High Court, Budd J., May 23, 1996. See also *Stafford v Roadstone Ltd.* [1980] I.L.R.M. 1 at 14; and *Dublin County Council v Tallaght Block Company Ltd.*, unreported, Supreme Court, May 17, 1983; [1982] I.L.R.M. 534 (High Court).

[53] See *Waterford County Council v John A. Wood Ltd.* [1999] 1 I.R. 556; [1999] 1 I.L.R.M. 217.

[54] Unreported, High Court, O'Sullivan J., January 19, 1999.

[55] [1999] 2 I.R. 495; [2000] 1 I.L.R.M. 346.

[56] [1985] I.R. 120.

[57] This issue is not discussed in any great detail in *Dublin County Council v Tallaght Block Company Ltd.*, unreported, Supreme Court, May 17, 1983; [1982] I.L.R.M. 534 (High Court).

The importance of the judgment in the *Lackagh Rock Ltd.* case is that it would **2–62** appear to be authority for the proposition that intensification *per se* cannot be a material change in use: it must also be established that the intensification has affected the proper planning and development of the area. Thus, for example, in *Dublin County Council v Carty Builders and Company Ltd.*,[58] it was held that neither the fact that lands used as a caravan park were used more extensively, nor that the business was operated more successfully, in the years following the acquisition of the lands by the respondent could constitute a material change in use.[59]

The doctrine of intensification has been criticised as being uncertain[60]: if the **2–63** planners are incapable of formulating what was the use after intensification, and what was the use before, then it is arguable that there has been no material change in use.[61] However, given that the test proposed in *Lackagh Rock Ltd.* requires the intensification to be significant from a planning viewpoint, the doctrine will only apply in justifiable circumstances.

E. Intensification of Development Under Planning Permission

Most of the cases discussed above involved intensification of an (alleged) **2–64** established development, *i.e.* pre-1964 development. It would seem however that, in principle, intensification of even a development subject to a planning permission might give rise to a material change in use.[62] To a large extent this turns on the nature of the development permitted under the planning permission, and in particular, as to whether or not a particular use has been specified under s.39(2) of the PDA 2000. Even if a use has not formally been specified, it may be that the documentation accompanying the application suggests the level or scale at which the development is to be carried on. In this regard, it is important to note that it is almost a universal condition of all planning permissions that the development be carried out in accordance with the plans and particulars lodged with the application, or as part of a response to any request for further information.

---

[58] [1987] I.R. 355.
[59] *cf. Carrick Hall Holdings Ltd. v Dublin Corporation* [1983] I.L.R.M. 268 (large increase in licensed trade following grant of ordinary seven day licence in place of hotel licence); and *Molumby v Kearns*, unreported, High Court, O'Sullivan J., January 19, 1999 (increase in level of heavy commercial traffic).
[60] See also comments of O'Flaherty J. in *Butler v Dublin Corporation* [1999] 1 I.R. 565; [1999] 1 I.L.R.M. 481 (tight rein).
[61] *Kensington and Chelsea Royal Borough v Secretary of State for the Environment* [1981] J.P.L. 50.
[62] See, by analogy, *Readymix (Éire) Ltd. v Dublin County Council*, unreported, Supreme Court, July 30, 1974.

F. Development and Planning Permission

2–65   The existence of a planning permission can give rise to certain conceptual difficulties in the application of the statutory definition of development. Much of the case law involves circumstances where there was no planning permission: in such cases, the determination of whether or not development had occurred simply required a consideration of that which had existed before the alleged development and that which existed afterwards. For instance, in relation to an alleged material change in use, one simply compared the subsequent use as against the previous use. The existence of a planning permission complicates matters in that the terms of the planning permission may be sufficiently broad so as to accommodate further acts of development. For example, lands may be being used for the purpose of a particular type of industry. The use permitted by the planning permission may, however, be for use as industry generally. If so, and subject to there being no other limitations (whether express or implied) on the planning permission,[63] it may well be that the planning permission would allow for a change of use to a different type of industrial use notwithstanding that this might involve a fresh act of development.

2–66   It would seem therefore that in order to determine whether or not there has been development in the context of a planning permission, a two-step process is involved. First, as in the ordinary course, it is necessary to consider whether or not an act of development has occurred. Secondly, one then has to consider the terms of the planning permission in order to decide whether or not this fresh act of development might not also be authorised by the planning permission.

1. Exempted development

2–67   A question which sometimes arises in relation to a planning permission is as to whether or not it is necessary to first implement the planning permission in strict accordance with its terms, before seeking to avail of an exempted development. The decision in *Horne v Freeney*[64] would appear to suggest that in the case of works, a planning permission is indivisible in that it authorises the carrying out of the totality of the works for which the permission has been granted and not some of them only. Apparently, a developer cannot, at his election, implement a part only of the approved plans as no approval is given for the part as distinct from the whole.[65] The decision in *Palmerlane Ltd. v An Bord Pleanála*[66] seems to suggest that, in the context of a material change in use, it might be possible to proceed directly to rely on an exempted development without the necessity of first having implemented the stated use in the planning permission.

---

[63] See para.5–03 below for discussion of the PDA 2000, s.39(2).
[64] Unreported, High Court, Murphy J., July 7, 1982.
[65] *cf. O'Connor v Downtown Properties Ltd.* [1993] 1 I.R. 1.
[66] [1999] 2 I.L.R.M. 514.

2. Intensification

The existence of a planning permission can also cause difficulties in relation **2–68** to the application of the concept of intensification. Under s.39(2) of the PDA 2000, where planning permission is granted for a structure, the grant may specify the purposes for which the structure may or may not be used.[67] If these purposes are defined so as to preclude substantial intensification (for example, by limiting the quantity of products which may be produced, or the method of production, or the volume of effluent to be discharged), then exceeding the limitation imposed could be a breach of a condition in a planning permission. A similar result might occur if the application for planning permission (as opposed to the grant of permission) specified the purposes for which the proposed development was to be used, or not to be used. If the grant of planning permission contains the standard condition that the development is to be carried out in accordance with the plans and particulars lodged, then it is the combined effect of the permission and the other documents which must be looked at in determining the proper scope of the planning permission.[68] The developer might thus find himself hamstrung by the terms of the application if he subsequently seeks to intensify the use of the land or structures beyond the level applied for.

G. Pre–1964 Established Development

The imposition, for the first time, of a general requirement to obtain planning **2–69** permission, on October 1, 1964, represented a dramatic change in the law and involved the introduction of a restriction on property rights.[69] Presumably for this reason, the requirement to obtain planning permission was not retrospective (in the sense that development commenced prior to October 1, 1964 did not require planning permission). There was an express statement to this effect under s.24 of the Local Government (Planning & Development) Act 1963.[70]

This principle of established development continues, and is recognised (albeit **2–70** in less forthright terms) under the PDA 2000. In particular, each of the definitions of "unauthorised structure", "unauthorised use" and "unauthorised works", under s.2, excepts development commenced prior to October 1, 1964.

---

[67] It is also the case that the availability of exempted development under the Planning and Development Regulations 2001 is qualified where the development would, *inter alia*, be inconsistent with any use specified in a planning permission: art.9(1)(a)(i).

[68] *Readymix (Éire) v Dublin County Council*, unreported, Supreme Court, July 30, 1974, *per* Henchy J.

[69] This has been recognised by the Supreme Court: see, in particular, *Waterford County Council v John A. Wood Ltd.* [1999] 1 I.R. 556; [1999] 1 I.L.R.M. 217. See also *Butler v Dublin Corporation* [1999] 1 I.R. 565; [1999] 1 I.L.R.M. 481.

[70] See, generally, *Waterford County Council v John A. Wood Ltd.* [1999] 1 I.R. 556; [1999] 1 I.L.R.M. 217.

2–71   Moreover, under s.39(4), the established occasional use of lands is expressly preserved. More specifically, s.39(4) provides, in summary, that planning permission shall not be required in the case of land which, on October 1, 1964, was normally used for one purpose and was also used on occasions, whether at regular intervals or not, for any other purpose, for the use of the land for that other purpose on similar occasions after October 1, 1964. The similarly worded provision under the previous legislation (s.40(b) of the Local Government (Planning & Development) Act 1963) had been successfully invoked in a number of cases so as to permit the holding, on an occasional basis, of non-sporting events (including pop concerts) on lands normally used for sporting purposes.[71]

H. Abandonment of Development

2–72   The concept of abandonment might, in very simplistic terms, be regarded as the obverse of that of intensification. Just as intensification of development may give rise to a situation where a fresh grant of planning permission is required, so too may discontinuance result in a situation where the former development is taken to have been abandoned and the land left with a nil use.

2–73   As in the case of intensification, it is now established that the concept of abandonment applies equally to development by way of material change of use, as to development by way of works.[72]

2–74   The concept of abandonment is significant in two contexts. First, in relation to established development. As noted at paras 2–69 to 2–71, there is generally no requirement to obtain planning permission in respect of development commenced prior to October 1, 1964. This is, of course, subject to the concepts of abandonment, and intensification. Secondly, in respect of the taking of enforcement action. In very general terms, there is a seven year time-limit on the taking of enforcement action. This is considered in more detail at paras 7–31 to 7–39. It has been established that a manifest interruption or abandonment of the development is sufficient to stop the limitation period running, and that this time will only commence to run again upon the recommencement of the unauthorised development.[73] See, generally, paras 7–43 to 7–49.

2–75   The mere suspension of development will not, generally, amount to abandonment. It has been held, however, that where a previous development has not merely been suspended for a temporary and determined period but has

---

[71] *Butler v Dublin Corporation* [1999] 1 I.R. 565; [1999] 1 I.L.R.M. 481; and *Grimes v Punchestown Developments Company Ltd.* [2002] 1 I.L.R.M. 409.

[72] *Kildare County Council v Goode* [1999] 2 I.R. 495; [2000] 1 I.L.R.M. 346.

[73] See the decision of the High Court in *Kildare County Council v Goode*, unreported, High Court, Morris J., June 13, 1997. See also the decision in *South Dublin County Council v Balfe*, unreported, High Court, Costello J., November 3, 1995.

ceased for a considerable time, with no evinced intention of resuming it at any particular time, it is a question of fact whether or not the former use has been abandoned.[74] It seems that the issue of an intention to resume the development is an important factor in determining whether or not there has been abandonment. Thus, where the use of premises as a general industrial building was suspended for a period of four years without any satisfactory explanation, it was held that the use had been abandoned.[75] It seems that the length of the period of the abandonment is also an important factor.[76] It has to be said, however, that in the case of a number of decisions in relation to advertisements, an interruption for a very short period of time indeed has been held to be sufficient to constitute abandonment. This appears to have been so notwithstanding the fact that there seems to have been a clear intention to continue to use the lands for the exhibition of advertisements.[77]

It is not entirely clear as to whether or not abandonment can be taken as having occurred in circumstances where, rather than all use of the lands being abandoned, a lawful use is replaced by an unlawful use. There is some authority to the effect, that, in certain circumstances, where a lawful use is replaced by an unlawful use, the resumption of the former (lawful) use would not constitute development.[78]   **2–76**

As against this, it was stated in *Cork County Council v Ardfert Quarries Product Ltd.*[79] that if, as is the case, an authorised use may be lost or abandoned by a non-user over a period of time so that the resumption of the original use would itself involve material change, *a fortiori* the commencement at that time of any other user would necessarily involve such a change.[80]   **2–77**

---

[74] *Dublin County Council v Tallaght Block Company Ltd.* [1982] I.L.R.M. 535 at 540; unreported, Supreme Court, May 17, 1983 (applying the test in *Hartley v Minister for Housing and Local Government* [1970] 1 Q.B. 413). See also *Cork County Council v Ardfert Quarry Product Ltd.*, unreported, High Court, Murphy J., December 7, 1982; and *Westmeath County Council v Quirke & Sons*, unreported, High Court, Budd J., May 23, 1996.

[75] *Cork County Council v Ardfert Quarry Product Ltd.*, unreported, High Court, Murphy J., December 7, 1982.

[76] *Cork County Council v Ardfert Quarry Product Ltd.*, unreported, High Court, Murphy J., December 7, 1982; and *Westmeath County Council v Quirke & Sons*, unreported, High Court, Budd J., May 23, 1996.

[77] See, for example, *Fingal County Council v Crean*, unreported, High Court, Ó Caoimh J., October 19, 2001. See also *Dublin Corporation v Lowe*, unreported, High Court, Morris P., February 4, 2000. It should be noted that this decision was appealed to the Supreme Court, and, on consent, remitted to the High Court for a rehearing and then returned to the Supreme Court: [2004] 4 I.R. 259.

[78] *Young v Secretary of State for the Environment* [1983] All E.R. 1105, cited with apparent approval in *Rehabilitation Institute v Dublin Corporation*, unreported, High Court, Barron J., January 14, 1988. See also *dicta* in *Lee v O'Riordan*, unreported, High Court, O'Hanlon J., February 10, 1995, where O'Hanlon J. appears to disregard an intervening unauthorised use.

[79] Unreported, High Court, Murphy J., December 7, 1982.

[80] See also *Meath County Council v Daly* [1988] I.L.R.M. 274 (abandonment where interruption by another use, as opposed to non-use).

2–78   Budd J., in *Westmeath County Council v Quirke & Sons*,[81] appears to set an objective test for abandonment: would a reasonable man looking at the converted cattle shed or farm supplies store in the disused-looking quarry have concluded that quarrying and limestone production had been abandoned?

I. Abandonment of Planning Permission

2–79   The question of whether or not a planning permission can be abandoned is one of considerable significance from a conveyancing viewpoint. The need for certainty, and to ensure the integrity of the statutory planning register, would appear to militate against the introduction of such a concept.[82] The issue arose for consideration on the facts of *Westmeath County Council v Quirke & Sons*[83]: the then operator of the quarry had applied in 1967 for planning permission for the erection of a ground limestone plant and the erection of a storage shed. It was urged on behalf of the respondent that the application did not relate to quarrying works, as quarrying was an existing user, and further, that the erection of the shed for the storage of lime was consistent with quarrying. Budd J. appears to have rejected this analysis of the effect of the planning permission, holding as follows.

> "When Roadstone Ltd. implemented its 1967 planning permission to erect plant and a building described as a ground limestone plant, and implemented its permission to use the quarry for the production of ground limestone, I think that this planning permission supplanted the pre-existing user as a quarry for the extraction of quarry run rock. [...] While I accept that an existing user is a hardy beast, nevertheless, I think that the existing user was superseded by the implementation of the Roadstone planning permission for a ground limestone plant as this involved the use of the quarry as an entity for the extraction of rock and the process of crushing and storage. This ceased in 1971. Thus the existing user as a quarry had been superseded and supplanted by the [planning permission for the] ground limestone plant which in its turn was abandoned."[84]

2–80   This finding that the use permitted under a planning permission may be abandoned is unfortunate as it introduces uncertainty into the law. It also appears to be inconsistent with the objective test for abandonment posited by Budd J. earlier in the judgment: it is hard to think of a more objective indication of the continued existence of development rights than the terms of the planning register.[85]

---

[81] Unreported, High Court, Budd J., May 23, 1996.

[82] *Pioneer Aggregates (UK) Ltd. v Secretary of State for the Environment* [1985] A.C. 135, referred to with seeming approval in *State (Kenny) v An Bord Pleanála*, unreported, Supreme Court, December 20, 1984 (albeit in a different context).

[83] Unreported, High Court, Budd J., May 23, 1996.

[84] Unreported, High Court, Budd J., May 23, 1996 (at p. 125).

[85] See, by loose analogy, the decision in *Readymix (Éire) Ltd. v Dublin County Council*, unreported, Supreme Court, July 30, 1974.

This aspect of the judgment also highlights the importance of determining **2–81** whether quarrying be categorised as development by works or by material change in use. If it be categorised as the former, then it would seem that the planning permission would have to be treated as ongoing as each shovelful extracted would seem to represent a fresh act of development works.[86] If treated as a material change in use, however, as Budd J. appears to have done, then it may be the case that the planning permission may be regarded as spent once the change of use is implemented: the development is the *change* in use, and not the use itself. This analysis must be contrasted with the wording of s.40(2)(b) of the PDA 2000, which provides that notwithstanding the time-limits on the life of a planning permission, the continuance of any use, in accordance with a permission, of land, is not affected. This confirms that a planning permission enures for the benefit of the land: it is difficult to reconcile this statutory intent with a concept of abandonment.

In addition to the obvious criticism that the judgment appears to allow for the **2–82** abandonment of planning permission with the associated adverse implications for conveyancing practice, the decision also is significant in that it seems to apply a somewhat loose test in determining the effect of the implementation of planning permission on existing use rights: it is difficult to understand on the facts as outlined in the judgment, how the planning permission for the erection of plant could affect the existing use right as a quarry.

In *Molloy v Minister for Justice Equality and Law Reform*,[87] the High Court **2–83** again had to consider whether a grant of planning permission can be "abandoned". Planning permission had been granted for the erection of a three storey residential hostel block. Initially the premises were used for the permitted use but, after a period of six years, the use changed to an unauthorised use for religious purposes. This unauthorised use continued for a period of in excess of twenty years. The position in England and Wales seems to be that a planning permission (works) capable of implementation cannot be abandoned, but that once a planning permission has been implemented, it is spent, with the result that if the permitted use is displaced by another use, then the resumption of the permitted use itself represents a *fresh* act of development requiring planning permission. Thus on the facts of the present case, the resumption of the hostel use would appear to require a further grant of planning permission. The High Court, seemingly, took a different view. It has to be said that the reasoning of the High Court in this regard is somewhat unclear. The key issue seems to have been what is meant by a planning permission "capable of implementation". In the case of development involving mining or quarrying, the planning permission may be implemented in various stages. Conversely, in the case of a material change in use, the planning permission is, arguably, implemented once the permitted use is first commenced: the development is the *change*, not the use *per se*.

---

[86] *cf. Waterford County Council v John A. Wood Ltd.* [1999] 1 I.R. 556; [1999] 1 I.L.R.M. 217.
[87] [2004] 2 I.R. 493; [2004] 2 I.L.R.M. 343.

2–84   The High Court seems to have taken the view that reversion to the permitted use is always available, even where the lands have been put to a different use for a lengthy period of time (on the facts, in excess of twenty years). Gilligan J. stated that what he meant by "capable of implementation" was that there has been no material structural alteration of the land or property which would render the original planning permission incapable of being implemented. The inconsistency between the position of the courts of England and Wales, and our own High Court, might be explicable by reference to the provisions of s.28(6) of the Local Government (Planning and Development) Act 1963, which allows a planning permission to specify the purposes for which a structure may or may not be used: this might be thought to be broader than simply permitting a once-off change in use.

J. Extinguishment

2–85   An established use may be lost if a planning permission inconsistent with that use is actually implemented: the mere fact that another planning permission has been obtained is not sufficient.[88] It is also clear that it is the development as carried out, and not necessarily the planning permission as granted, which determines the inconsistency with the existing use. Thus in *McGrath Limestone Works Ltd. v Galway County Council*,[89] where planning permission in respect of the growing of mushrooms was never implemented, and the lands actually used occupied only five per cent of the site, Egan J. held that this could not possibly bolster an argument to suggest that all quarrying rights had been abandoned.

2–86   Where land or a structure perish, planning permission to use the premises also perishes.[90] Furthermore, the use for ancillary purposes of any out-buildings etc. is also extinguished with the primary use.[91] Special provision is made in respect of compensation where planning permission is refused for development substantially replacing structures demolished or destroyed by fire or otherwise.[92] See, generally, paras 6–23 to 6–24.

K. Exempted Development Under Planning Legislation

2–87   As appears from the foregoing, the breadth of the concept of development is such as to capture even relatively minor works, and some unexceptionable changes of use. All of this is compensated for somewhat by the creation of

---

[88] *State (Kenny) v An Bord Pleanála*, unreported, Supreme Court, December 20, 1984.
[89] [1989] I.L.R.M. 602.
[90] *Galway County Council v Connacht Protein Ltd.*, unreported, High Court, Barrington J., March 28, 1980 (at p. 5).
[91] *Galway County Council v Connacht Protein Ltd.*, unreported, High Court, Barrington J., March 28, 1980.
[92] PDA 2000, s.193.

classes of exempted development. In short, certain types of development are *exempted* from the requirement to obtain planning permission. The principal classes of exempted development are to be found under s.4 of the PDA 2000, and under the Planning and Development Regulations 2001. It should be noted, however, that certain other development is constituted as exempted development under other pieces of legislation. An attempt will be made towards the end of this chapter to identify some of these other pieces of legislation; however, this listing is not intended to be comprehensive. In any event, as the categories of exempted development are being added to regularly, it is always necessary to consider any particular development afresh.

The rationale for allowing for exempted development is, to an extent, articulated in the provisions of s.4(2) of the PDA 2000. This subsection allows for the making of Regulations providing for any class of development to be exempted development. In short, the Minister for the Environment, Heritage and Local Government must be of the opinion either (i) that by reason of the size, nature or limited effect on its surroundings, of the development belonging to that class, the carrying out of such development would not offend against the principles of proper planning and sustainable development, or (ii) that the development is authorised, or is required to be authorised, by or under any enactment (whether the authorisation takes the form of the grant of a licence, consent, approval or any other type of authorisation) where the enactment concerned requires there to be consultation (howsoever described) with members of the public in relation to the proposed development prior to the granting of the authorisation (howsoever described). **2–88**

Thus it will be seen that the objective of exempted development is either to remove certain minor or insignificant development from the requirement to obtain planning permission, or to avoid unnecessary duplication of control where development is subject to authorisation and consultation under other legislation. **2–89**

1. Section 4 of the Planning and Development Act 2000

Section 4 provides for the following to be exempted development. **2–90**

(a) Development consisting of the use of any land for the purpose of agriculture and development consisting of the use for that purpose of any building occupied together with land so used;

"Agriculture" is defined under s. 2 as follows. **2–91**

> "'Agriculture'" includes horticulture, fruit growing, seed growing, dairy farming, the breeding and keeping of livestock (including any creature kept for the production of food, wool, skins or fur, or for the purpose of its use in the farming of land), the training of horses and the rearing of bloodstock, the use of land as grazing land, meadow land, osier land, market gardens and nursery grounds, and 'agricultural' shall be construed accordingly".

2–92 There are a number of aspects of the wording of this class of exempted development which require further consideration. First, the wording is somewhat curious in that it suggests that it is the use of land for the purpose of agriculture which is exempted development. Of course, it is the case that the statutory definition of development applies to a change in use, and not to the use *per se*. It is submitted therefore that the words of s.4(1)(a) must be construed as meaning a "change of use to agriculture use", otherwise the exemption would not make sense. It would therefore appear that planning permission is not necessary for the change of use of any land to agricultural use, or for the change of use of any buildings to agricultural use provided that they are "occupied together with the land so used". Secondly, it is to be noted that the exempted development extends only to the use, and not to the carrying out of works for such purposes.[93] Thirdly, it should be noted that the benefit of this class of exempted development may be lost where the proposed development is subject to environmental impact assessment ("EIA"). Under s.4(4), the Minister for the Environment Heritage and Local Government may, in connection with the EIA Directive, prescribe development or classes of development which, notwithstanding subsection (1)(a), shall not be exempted development. Finally, it should be noted that the definition of agriculture has been amended from the previous legislation. In particular, turbary has been omitted from the definition. This is significant in that it would seem to remove the benefit of this class of exempted development from development consisting of peat extraction and/or bog drainage.[94] Ireland had been criticised by the European Court of Justice for the fact that certain development of this type had not been subject to environmental impact assessment.[95]

2–93 (b) Development by the council of a county in its functional area, exclusive of any borough or urban district;

(c) Development by the corporation of a county or other borough in that borough;

(d) Development by the council of an urban district in that district;

(e) Development consisting of the carrying out by the corporation of a county or other borough or the council of a county or an urban district of any works required for the construction of a new road or the maintenance or improvement of a road;

(f) Development carried out on behalf of, or jointly or in partnership with, a local authority that is a planning authority, pursuant to a contract entered into by the local authority concerned, whether in its capacity as a planning authority or in any other capacity;

---

[93] *Irish Wildbird Conservancy Ltd. v Clonakilty Golf & Country Club Ltd.*, unreported, High Court, Costello P., July 23, 1996. *Cf. Kildare County Council v Goode* [1999] 2 I.R. 495; [2000] 1 I.L.R.M. 346.

[94] Some more limited exemptions are provided under the Planning and Development Regulations 2001.

[95] *Commission v Ireland* (Case 392/96) [1999] E.C.R. 5901.

Subsections (b), (c), (d), (e) and (f) of s.4 represent perhaps the single most significant category of exempted development, namely that in respect of local authority development. In general terms, development by a local authority in its own functional area is exempted development. The enormity of this exemption is lessened somewhat by the fact that certain local authority development is required to undergo a form of public consultation procedure under Pt XI of the PDA 2000.[96] The control over local authority development is discussed in detail at paras 8–299 to 8–355.

(g)   Development consisting of the carrying out by any local authority or   **2–94**
      statutory undertaker of any works for the purpose of inspecting, repairing,
      renewing, altering or removing any sewers, mains, pipes, cables, overhead
      wires, or other apparatus, including the excavation of any street or other
      land for that purpose;

"Statutory undertaker" is defined under s.2 as follows.

> "'Statutory undertaker'" means a person, for the time being, authorised by or under any enactment or instrument under an enactment to— (a) construct or operate a railway, canal, inland navigation, dock, harbour or airport, (b) provide, or carry out works for the provision of, gas, electricity or telecommunications services, or (c) provide services connected with, or carry out works for the purposes of the carrying on of the activities of, any public undertaking".

It should be noted that the exemption does not apply in respect of development consisting of the provision for the first time of sewers, mains, pipes, cables, overhead wires or other apparatus. Much development of this nature and other related (mostly minor) development is exempted under Sch.2 of the Planning and Development Regulations 2001.

(h)   Development consisting of the carrying out of works for the maintenance,   **2–95**
      improvement or other alteration of any structure, being works which affect
      only the interior of the structure or which do not materially affect the
      external appearance of the structure so as to render the appearance
      inconsistent with the character of the structure or of neighbouring structures;

The benefit of the exempted development applies only to works, and thus   **2–96**
planning permission may nevertheless be required for any proposed material
change in use which the works are intended to facilitate.[97]

The benefit of the exempted development is further qualified in the case of a   **2–97**
protected structure, or a proposed protected structure. More specifically, s.57
of the PDA 2000 provides that notwithstanding s.4(1)(h), the carrying out of

---

[96] A form of public participation was first introduced as part of the legislative amendments made subsequent to the decision in the Mullaghmore litigation: *Howard v Commissioners of Public Works in Ireland* [1994] 1 I.R. 101; [1993] I.L.R.M. 665.

[97] *Cork Corporation v O'Connell* [1982] I.L.R.M. 505; and *Cairnduff v O'Connell* [1986] I.R. 73; [1986] I.L.R.M. 465.

works to a protected structure, or a proposed protected structure, shall be exempted development only if those works would not materially affect the character of (a) the structure, or (b) any element of the structure which contributes to its special architectural, historical, archaeological, artistic, cultural, scientific, social or technical interest.[98] A procedure is then provided whereby an owner or occupier may seek a declaration to this effect from the local authority. See further paras 8–24 to 8–34.

2–98   The character of a structure relates to its shape, colour, design, ornamental features and layout; and not to its particular use.[99] In determining whether or not exterior works affect the character of a structure, regard should be had to the appearance of the structure prior to (although not necessarily immediately prior to) the works.[100] In *Cairnduff v O'Connell*, the Supreme Court held that the existence of a window eleven years ago (the window had since blocked up) would not render works involved in re-opening the window immaterial.[101]

2–99   The replacement of Georgian windows (with their strong horizontal line) with hinged aluminium ones affects the *exterior* appearance of a Georgian house so as to render the structure inconsistent with its own character (but not necessarily with the character of neighbouring structures).[102]

2–100   In *McCabe v Coras Iompair Éireann*,[103] it was held that the exemption under s.4(1)(h) covered the renewal and reconstruction of a railway bridge, where the extent of the renewal or reconstruction was not such as to amount to the total or substantial replacement or rebuilding of the original structure. The works involved did not result in the external appearance of the bridge becoming inconsistent with its character. The only really noticeable difference in the bridge was the replacement of a semicircular arch with an opening of rectangular appearance. Herbert J. held that shape, however, is only one of the features which contribute to the character of a structure, and there was no objective basis for considering that one particular type of opening rather than another should be regarded as establishing the character of this sort of bridge.

2–101   Finally, it should be noted that although works affecting the interior of a structure are exempted development, a planning permission is indivisible and a developer is apparently nevertheless required to adhere to the plans submitted with the planning application, even where the proposed departures from the plans would subsequently constitute exempted development.[104] To put the matter another

---

[98] Similar provision is made in respect of architectural conservation areas under PDA 2000, s.82. The provision in respect of areas of special planning control is different: PDA 2000, s.87.

[99] *Cairnduff v O'Connell* [1986] I.R. 73; [1986] I.L.R.M. 465.

[100] *Cairnduff v O'Connell* [1986] I.R. 73; [1986] I.L.R.M. 465.

[101] *Cairnduff v O'Connell* [1986] I.R. 73; [1986] I.L.R.M. 465.

[102] *Dublin Corporation v Bentham* [1993] 2 I.R. 58.

[103] [2006] I.E.H.C. 356; unreported, Herbert J., November 10, 2006.

[104] *Horne v Freeney*, unreported, High Court, Murphy J., July 7, 1982. *Cf. O'Connors*

way, it is seemingly necessary to first implement the planning permission in strict accordance with its terms, before seeking to avail of an exempted development.

(i) Development consisting of the thinning, felling and replanting of trees, **2–102** forests and woodlands, the construction, maintenance and improvement of non-public roads serving forests and woodlands and works ancillary to that development, not including the replacement of broadleaf high forest by conifer species;

The exclusion of the replacement of broadleaf high forest by conifer species seems intended to comply with the requirements of environmental impact assessment. It may be, however, that other development in this category might also be subject to environmental impact assessment, and, accordingly, it is somewhat surprising that there is no express mechanism whereby such development might be de-exempted: s.4(4) of the PDA 2000 appears to be confined to the agricultural exemption.

(j) Development consisting of the use of any structure or other land within **2–103** the curtilage of a house for any purpose incidental to the enjoyment of the house as such;

There is no definition of "curtilage" under the planning legislation; however, it has been interpreted in England and Wales as land which is used to serve the purposes of the house in some necessary or reasonably useful way.[105] Thus it would seem that there must be a reasonable nexus between the use and the house: the parking of a private car, for example, would clearly have such a nexus.[106] The situation as regards commercial vehicles is more difficult: one view would be that such a use would not be incidental to the house but rather to the commercial activity.[107] Such a view is, it is submitted, supported by the fact that an express exemption is provided for the keeping or storing of a caravan, camper van or boat within the curtilage of a house.[108]

It is to be noted that this class of exempted development is different from that **2–104** under the previous legislation in that there is a new definition of "house" which replaces that of "dwelling house". "House" means a building or part of a building which is being or has been occupied as a dwelling or was provided for use as a dwelling but has not been occupied, and where appropriate, includes a building which was designed for use as two or more dwellings or a flat, an apartment or other dwelling within such a building.[109] This new definition

---

Downtown Properties Ltd. v Nenagh UDC [1993] 1 I.R. 1 at 17. *Dublin Corporation v O'Dwyer Brothers Ltd.*, unreported, High Court, Kelly J., May 2, 1997.

[105] *Sinclair-Lockhart's Trust v Central Landboard* 1951 S.C. 258; 1951 S.L.T. 121.
[106] *Dublin Corporation v Moore* [1984] I.L.R.M. 339, *per* Griffin J. (dissenting).
[107] *cf. Dublin Corporation v Moore* [1984] I.L.R.M. 339.
[108] Planning and Development Regulations 2001, Sch.2, Class 8.
[109] PDA 2000, s.2.

resolves the issue which arose in *Smyth v Colgan*[110] as to whether it was necessary that a building have actually been put to use as a dwelling before constituting a dwelling house, so as to benefit from the class of exempted development.

2–105 (k) Development consisting of the use of land for the purposes of a casual trading area (within the meaning of the Casual Trading Act 1995);

(l) development consisting of the carrying out of any of the works referred to in the Land Reclamation Act 1949, not being works comprised in the fencing or enclosure of land which has been open to or used by the public within the ten years preceding the date on which the works are commenced.

It was held in *Tralee UDC v Stack*[111] that the land reclamation contemplated by the Land Reclamation Act 1949 is land reclamation carried out by the Minister either at the request of the occupier of the lands or on the Minister's own initiative. In determining whether or not land reclamation works are involved, it seems that regard can be had to the primary object in carrying out the works. Thus, in *Lennon v Kingdom Plant Hire Ltd.*,[112] it was held that works which materially defaced the landscape to an extent far beyond that which would be expected in land reclamation could not benefit from the exemption: the primary object in the carrying out of the works was not to improve the land but to gather boulders.

2–106 Although not directly on point in that the judgment concerns exempted development under the previous Regulations,[113] reference is also made to the decision of the Supreme Court in *Dolan v Cooke*.[114] The Supreme Court indicated that reclamation clearly meant that land, which was not otherwise available for significant agricultural use of any sort, was being put in a condition where it would be available for agriculture use by the carrying out of whatever works were necessary. Accordingly, the spreading of spoil, clay and earth so as to lay a rough path or road did not constitute land reclamation within Pt III, Class 9 of the Second Schedule of the Local Government (Planning & Development) Regulations 1994.

2. Development required pursuant to enforcement action

2–107 Compliance with enforcement notices or orders will often require the carrying out of development. In principle, such development might be subject to the requirement to obtain planning permission. The lead time for obtaining the grant of planning permission is such, however, that a requirement to obtain planning permission might well frustrate urgent enforcement action. Presumably

[110] [1999] 1 I.R. 548.
[111] Unreported, High Court, Barrington J., January 13, 1984.
[112] Unreported, High Court, Morris J., December 13, 1991.
[113] Local Government (Planning & Development) Regulations 1994.
[114] Unreported, Supreme Court, April 6, 2001.

to avoid this, development pursuant to enforcement action is usually stated to be exempted development. For example, under s.163 of the PDA 2000, planning permission is not required in respect of development required by an enforcement notice, or by an order under s.160 (planning injunction). Similarly, under s.68, the carrying out of works under a restoration notice, or an endangerment notice, is exempted development. Further exemptions are provided for under the Planning and Development Regulations 2001. For example, under the Sch.2, Pt 1, Class 41, the carrying out of development in compliance with enforcement notices under the water pollution, and air pollution, legislation, respectively, is exempted development.

3. Planning and Development Regulations 2001

Introduction

A detailed examination of the scope of the classes of exempted development provided for under Sch.2 of the Planning and Development Regulations 2001 is simply beyond the scope of this book. Instead, it is proposed to make some general points in relation to the availability of the classes of exempted development in the hope that this might be of some assistance.   **2–108**

The scheme of the Regulations is as follows. Schedule 2 of the Regulations consists of four Parts: Pt I: Exempted development – general; Pt II: Exempted development – advertisements; Pt III: Exempted development – rural; and Pt IV: Exempted development – classes of use.   **2–109**

With the exception of the classes of use, each of the other classes is divided into two columns: the description of the development, and the conditions and limitations thereon. The conditions and limitations must be met in full in order to qualify as exempted development.[115]   **2–110**

In addition to the class-specific conditions and limitations, there are a number of general qualifications on the availability of exempted development. These are, for the most part, set out at art.6, and art.9, of the Planning and Development Regulations 2001. Among the more important of these are the following.   **2–111**

(i) Conditioned out

The benefit of the exempted development is not available if the proposed development would contravene a condition attached to a planning permission, or be inconsistent with any use specified in a planning permission. It is to be noted that this provision does not appear to be confined to the contravention of a condition attached to a planning permission relating to the premises in respect of which the development is to be carried out.[116]   **2–112**

---

[115] *cf. Dublin Corporation v Langan*, unreported, High Court, Gannon J., May 14, 1982.
[116] *Doolan v Murray*, unreported, High Court, Keane J., December 21, 1993 (at pp. 28-29). *Cf. Murray v Buckley*, unreported, High Court, Barron J., December 5, 1990 (at p. 3).

(ii) Traffic hazard

2–113   The benefit of the exempted development is not available where the proposed development would endanger public safety by reason of traffic hazard or obstruction of road users.

(iii) View or prospect of special amenity value

2–114   There is no exempted development where the development would interfere with the character of a landscape, or a view or prospect of special amenity value or special interest, the preservation of which is an objective of the development plan or in the draft variation or draft development plan.

(iv) Unauthorised structure

2–115   The extension, alteration, repair or renewal of an unauthorised structure or a structure the use of which is an unauthorised use, is not exempted development. This qualification represents one instance of where unauthorised development which is immune from enforcement action by virtue of the fact that more than seven years have passed since the commencement of the development is, nevertheless, treated as unlawful. One practical consequence of this is that the benefit of exempted development is not available. See, generally, paras 7–50 to 7–51.

(v) Environmental impact assessment

2–116   Exempted development is generally not available in respect of development which is subject to environmental impact assessment.[117] This is entirely understandable in that Ireland has chosen to implement the EIA Directive primarily through the framework of the planning legislation. Where development is exempted from the requirement to obtain planning permission, it may well not trigger any other provision of domestic law which would impose an obligation to undergo environmental impact assessment.

Major-accident hazards Directive/Seveso Directive

2–117   The benefit of exempted development is not available in respect of development if it consists of the provision of, or modifications to, a major-accident establishment, and could have significant repercussions on major-accident hazards.[118] As with EIA Directive development, there are difficulties in that there is no clear scheme for screening.

Protected structures

2–118   There does not appear to be any express qualification under the Planning and Development Regulations 2001 which would remove the benefit of exempted development in respect of works to protected structures. As has already been

---

[117] Planning and Development Regulations 2001, art.10(1)(c).
[118] Planning and Development Regulations 2001, art.9(1)(d).

noted, however, the availability of the exempted development under s.4(1)(h) is limited in respect of a protected structure, or a proposed protected structure, under s.57. It is not entirely clear, however, whether or not this qualification only applies to the exempted development under s.4(1)(h) specifically, or if it delimits all exempted development, including the classes of exempted development under the Planning and Development Regulations 2001.[119] See, generally, paras 8–21 to 8–23.

Use classes

Special provision is made for exempted development in the case of certain **2–119** changes of use. Under Pt 4 of Sch.2 of the Planning and Development Regulations 2001, eleven classes of use are prescribed. Generally, development which consists of a change of use *within* any one of the classes of use specified shall be exempted development. There are, however, a series of qualifications. For example, the benefit of the exempted development is lost, *inter alia*, where the development would involve the carrying out of works other than works which are exempted development; or would contravene a condition attached to a planning permission or be inconsistent within the use specified or included in such a permission or be a development where the existing use is an unauthorised use, save where such change of use consists of the resumption of a use which is not unauthorised and which has not been abandoned.

L. Exempted Development Under Other Enactments

Certain development under other enactments is stated to be exempted **2–120** development under the Planning and Development Regulations 2001. For example, under art.7, development for the purpose of giving effect to a condition attached to an integrated pollution prevention and control licence or revised licence is exempted. Similarly, works consisting of or incidental to the carrying out of development for the purpose of giving effect to a condition attached to a waste licence or revised licence under the Waste Management Act 1996, is exempted. Under art.8, works specified in a confirmed drainage scheme under the arterial drainage legislation are exempted development.

1. Derelict Sites Act 1990

Section 11(6) of the Derelict Sites Act 1990 exempts works specified in a **2–121** notice or amended notice served under s.11 of that Act.

---

[119] *cf.* Planning and Development Regulations 2001, art.9(1)(a)(xii) (architectural conservation area).

2. Roads Acts 1993 to 1998

2–122   Under s.19(6) of the Roads Act 1993, development consisting of the carrying out of any works by or at the direction of, or on behalf of, the National Roads Authority in relation to the construction or maintenance of a national road shall be exempted development.

3. Waste Management Acts 1996 to 2001

2–123   Under s.54(5) of the Waste Management Act 1996, the following are exempted developments. First, works consisting of or incidental to the carrying out of development which is necessary to give effect to any conditions attached to a waste licence.[120] Secondly, the provision of waste collection receptacles in accordance with Regulations.

4. Environmental Protection Agency Act 1992

2–124   Under art.7 of the Planning and Development Regulations 2001, development for the purpose of giving effect to a condition attached to an integrated pollution prevention and control licence or revised licence is exempted development.

5. Dublin Docklands Development Authority Act 1997

2–125   Under s.25 of the Dublin Docklands Development Authority Act 1997, the following are exempted development in an area in respect of which a planning scheme has been prepared and approved: (i) the carrying out by the planning authority of any development in the area which is consistent with that planning scheme, and (ii) the carrying out of any development in the area by a person other than the planning authority which development is certified (by the planning authority) to be consistent with the planning scheme. Such development may be subject to environmental impact assessment under s.26 of the Dublin Docklands Development Authority Act 1997. Under s.25(1)(c), a planning scheme shall not include any development prescribed for the purpose of environmental impact assessment other than industrial-estate development projects; urban development projects; and sea water marinas.

6. Transport (Dublin Light Rail) Act 1996

2–126   Section 4 of the Transport (Dublin Light Rail) Act 1996 provides that certain light railway works are exempted development.

---

[120] See paras 2–48 to 2–51. See also art.7 of the Planning and Development Regulations 2001.

CHAPTER THREE

APPLICATION FOR PLANNING PERMISSION

A. Strategic Infrastructure

Generally, an application for planning permission is made in the first instance **3–01** to the relevant planning authority, with a right of appeal thereafter to An Bord Pleanála. In the case of certain specified categories of strategic infrastructure development, however, the planning application is made to An Bord Pleanála directly. This chapter is concerned only with the general procedure, and strategic infrastructure is dealt with separately in Chapter 10 at para.10–32.

B. Public Notice Requirements

1. Planning and Development Regulations 2006

3–02 The public notice requirements have been modified slightly under the Planning and Development Regulations 2006 ("the 2006 Regulations").[1] Article 8 of those Regulations replaces the entire of Pt 4 of the Planning and Development Regulations 2001 ("the 2001 Regulations").[2] It would have been preferable had a set of consolidated Regulations been published instead. The absence of same means that it is necessary for an applicant to consult both the 2001 and 2006 Regulations.

2. Form of public notice

3–03 An applicant is required to give public notice of the making of a planning application, by way of a newspaper notice and a site notice.[3]

Newspaper notice

3–04 The newspaper notice must be published in an approved newspaper within the period of two weeks before the making of the application.[4] For this purpose, each planning authority is required to approve a list of newspapers, including national newspapers, it considers have a sufficiently large circulation in its functional area; different newspapers may be approved in respect of different parts of such functional area.[5] This list must be reviewed by the planning authority as may be appropriate and at least once a year.[6] The list is to be displayed in or at the offices of the planning authority or at any other place or by any other means—including electronic form—that the planning authority considers appropriate. Copies shall be made available at the offices of the planning authority free of charge.

Site notice

3–05 Detailed provision is made in respect of site notices.[7] Generally, the site notice

---

[1] S.I. No. 685 of 2006.

[2] S.I. No. 600 of 2001.

[3] Planning and Development Regulations 2001, art.17 (as substituted by the 2006 Regulations).

[4] Planning and Development Regulations 2001, art.18(1) (as substituted by the 2006 Regulations). See *Lennon v Cork City Council* [2006] I.E.H.C. 438; unreported, Smyth J., December 19, 2006 for a discussion of the calculation of the two week period.

[5] Planning and Development Regulations 2001, art.18(2) (as substituted by the 2006 Regulations). See discussion as to risk of leaving off choice of newspaper to the applicant for planning permission in *Monaghan UDC v Alf-a-bet Promotions Ltd.* [1980] I.L.R.M. 64 at 74.

[6] Planning and Development Regulations 2001, art.18(2)(b) (as substituted by the 2006 Regulations).

[7] Planning and Development Regulations 2001, art.19 (as substituted by the 2006 Regulations).

should be securely erected or fixed in a conspicuous position on or near the main entrance to the land or structure concerned from a public road, or where there is more than one entrance from public roads, on or near *all* such entrances, or on any other part of the land or structure adjoining a public road. The site notice should be easily visible and legible by persons using the public road, and shall not be obscured or concealed at any time. It is sufficient that the site notice is visible to people on the footpath, and it is not necessary that it should be visible or legible to people who are driving by in a motor car.[8]

Where the land or structure to which a planning application relates does not **3–06** adjoin a public road, a site notice shall be erected or fixed in a conspicuous position on the land or structure so as to be easily visible and legible by persons outside the land or structure, and shall not be obscured or concealed at any time. The planning authority has a discretion to require an applicant to erect or fix such further site notice or notices in such a manner and in such terms as it may specify where a planning authority considers that the erection or fixing of a single site notice is not sufficient to comply with the requirements of the Regulations, or does not adequately inform the public.[9] Ultimately, however, it would seem that the adequacy of the site notice is a matter of law and, accordingly, one which the High Court can consider *de novo*.[10]

The site notice shall be maintained in position on the land or structure concerned **3–07** for a period of five weeks from the date of receipt of the planning application by the planning authority, and shall be renewed or replaced if it is removed or becomes defaced or illegible within that period.[11] (There is an exception where any site notice erected by the applicant has been maliciously defaced or destroyed by any person other than the applicant.)[12] The site notice must be removed by the applicant following the notification of the planning authority's decision.[13] This is a new requirement, introduced under the Planning and Development Regulations 2006.

It seems that a planning authority is under an implied obligation to inspect the **3–08** site notice within the five week period from the date of the receipt of the planning application, and, further, that a failure on the part of the planning authority to do so may render the application invalid. These propositions are based on the judgment of the High Court in *Marshall v Arklow Town Council*.[14] This case was decided prior to the Planning and Development Regulations 2006, and

---

[8] *Springview Management Ltd. v Cavan Developments Ltd.* [2000] 1 I.L.R.M. 437.
[9] Planning and Development Regulations 2001, art.19(3) (as substituted by the 2006 Regulations).
[10] *Springview Management Ltd. v Cavan Developments Ltd.* [2000] 1 I.L.R.M. 437.
[11] Planning and Development Regulations 2001, art.20 (as substituted by the 2006 Regulations).
[12] Planning and Development Regulations 2001, art.26(7) (as substituted by the 2006 Regulations).
[13] Planning and Development Regulations 2001, art.20 (as substituted by the 2006 Regulations).
[14] [2004] 4 I.R. 92.

involved an allegation that the site notice requirement under art.19 of the 2001 Regulations had not been complied with where, allegedly, no site notice had been erected at all. The applicants for judicial review complained that, as a result of this breach, they did not become aware of the application for planning permission until after the decision to grant had already been made by the planning authority.

3–09   Peart J. considered that the conflict of evidence arising between the parties regarding the existence, or non-existence, of the site notice was impossible to reconcile, and he could not, therefore, determine that factual issue with absolute certainty. To decide either way would be to say that either the notice parties' professional did not comply with planning requirements and was deliberately untruthful, or that the site notice, missed by the many passers-by living on that street, did not fulfil the requirement that it "be easily visible and legible" by persons using the road as mandated by art.19(1)(c).

3–10   Instead, Peart J. preferred to decide the case by reference to the failure of the planning authority to inspect the site notice within five weeks beginning on the date of the receipt of the application for planning permission. Peart J. ruled that there was an obligation on the planning authority to inspect the land to which the application relates within the five week period. There was no such express duty under the 2001 Regulations, nor is there under the 2006 Regulations. Peart J. was, however, prepared to infer an implied duty from the provisions of art.26(4) of the 2001 Regulations.

Subsequent application

3–11   Where a subsequent application for planning permission is made within six months from the date of the making of the previous application in respect of substantially the same site or part of the site, then the site notice must be on a yellow background.[15] The wording in this regard has been modified under the 2006 Regulations so as to make it clear that a yellow site notice is only required where the earlier application was valid.[16] Thus if an application is made, but subsequently rejected as invalid for whatever reason, notice of a renewed application should be given on a white site notice.

Overhead transmission or distribution lines

3–12   The requirement to erect or fix a site notice shall not apply in relation to a planning application for development consisting of the construction or erection

---

[15] Planning and Development Regulations 2001, art.19(4) (as substituted by the 2006 Regulations).

[16] As it happens, the High Court—notwithstanding the absence of any *express* requirement that the application have been valid—had interpreted the previous wording under the 2001 Regulations as similarly being applicable to valid applications only. See *Kelly v Roscommon County Council* [2006] I.E.H.C. 197; unreported, McGovern J., June 20, 2006; and *Dunne v An Bord Pleanála* [2006] I.E.H.C. 400; unreported, McGovern J., December 14, 2006.

by an electricity undertaking of overhead transmission or distribution lines for conducting electricity, or development consisting of the construction or erection by any statutory undertaker authorised to provide a telecommunication service of overhead telecommunication lines.[17]

3. Further public notice

There is a requirement to give further public notice in circumstances where the planning authority receives further information, evidence, revised plans, drawings or particulars in relation to an application which contain "significant additional data", including information in relation to effects on the environment.[18] This is discussed further at paras 3–119 to 3–127 below.   **3–13**

4. Effect of non-compliance with public notice requirements

A planning application shall be invalid for failure to comply with the requirements in relation to public notices.[19] Moreover, even in the case of technical compliance, a planning application shall be invalid where a planning authority considers that the notice in the newspaper or the site notice, because of its content or for any other reason, is misleading or inadequate for the information of the public,[20] or where the site notice has not been maintained in position for five weeks.[21] The importance of public notices is thus elevated in that the (former) discretion of the planning authority in circumstances where there was some defect in either a newspaper notice or a site notice has since removed under both the 2001 and 2006 Regulations.[22] Failure to comply with the requirements in relation to notice renders the application invalid; and the planning authority cannot rescue the application by a request for further information.[23] This is so even where the planning authority does not discover   **3–14**

---

[17] Planning and Development Regulations 2001, art.17(3) (as substituted by the 2006 Regulations).
[18] Planning and Development Regulations 2001, art.35 (as substituted by the 2006 Regulations).
[19] Planning and Development Regulations 2001, art.26(3) (as substituted by the 2006 Regulations).
[20] Planning and Development Regulations 2001, art.26(3)(b) (as substituted by the 2006 Regulations).
[21] Planning and Development Regulations 2001, art.26(4) (as substituted by the 2006 Regulations).
[22] Under the Local Government (Planning & Development) Regulations 1994, a planning authority had a discretion to allow a defect to be remedied by the giving of further notice of the application for planning permission.
[23] A planning authority was expressly precluded—under art.33(2) of the Planning and Development Regulations 2001—from addressing public notice issues in a request for further information. The express prohibition in this regard has been removed under the 2006 Regulations, but it is submitted that it would be inconsistent with the scheme of the 2006 Regulations to allow a planning authority to remedy deficient public notices by way of a request for further information.

the defect until subsequent to the receipt and (initial) acknowledgement of the application.[24]

5. Content of public notice

3–15   The content of a newspaper notice, and a site notice, respectively, is prescribed under art.18, and Form No. 1 of Sch.3 of the Planning and Development Regulations 2001 (as substituted under the 2006 Regulations). As the content of both notices is broadly similar, it is convenient to consider the two notices together.

3–16   The notice should contain as a heading the name of the planning authority to which the planning application will be made.

(a) Name of applicant

3–17   The name of the applicant (not his or her agent) should be stated in the public notice. A deliberate attempt to conceal the true identity of the applicant for planning permission by, for example, the use of a nominee company for the purpose of the planning application, would represent a breach of this requirement.[25] To an extent, this concern has been met by the requirement in the standard planning application form to state the names of the company directors, and the address and registration number of the company.[26]

3–18   The courts have, in general, adopted a flexible approach to the description of companies. Thus, for example, the omission of the word "limited" from a newspaper notice was held not to be a breach.[27] Similarly, an unintentional misdescription of the applicant company which did not have the effect of misleading anyone and which could not possibly have been in anyway to the disadvantage either of the planning authority or of the public was not fatal to an application for judicial review by the applicant for planning permission.[28]

3–19   The Supreme Court indicated *obiter* in *State (Finglas Industrial Estates Ltd.) v Dublin County Council*[29] that the naming of an as yet unincorporated company as the applicant for planning permission might be fatal. Henchy J. stated that

---

[24] Planning and Development Regulations 2001, art.26(4) (as substituted by the 2006 Regulations).

[25] *State (NCE Ltd.) v Dublin County Council*, unreported, Supreme Court, May 14, 1980.

[26] Planning and Development Regulations 2001, art.22(1) and Form No. 2 (as substituted by the 2006 Regulations).

[27] *Blessington & District Community Council Ltd. v Wicklow County Council* [1997] 1 I.R. 273 at 282. See also, by analogy, *Kenney Construction Ltd. v An Bord Pleanála* [2005] I.E.H.C. 30; unreported, O'Neill J., February 10, 2005 (misdescription of third party appellant).

[28] *Thomas McDonagh & Sons Ltd. v Galway Corporation* [1995] 1 I.R. 191. See also *State (Toft) v Galway Corporation* [1981] I.L.R.M. 439; and *State (Alf-a-bet) Promotions Ltd. v Bundoran UDC* (1978) 112 I.L.T.R. 9 at 15.

[29] Unreported, Supreme Court, February 17, 1983.

he did not think that any provision of the company's legislation validating acts done before incorporation could detract from the fact that it was inherent in the planning code that both the planning authority and the public should have an opportunity of vetting the planning application in the light of, amongst other matters, the identity of a named and a legally existing applicant.

It is unlikely that the judgment in *Frank Dunne Ltd. v Dublin City Council*[30] **3–20** still represents good law in light of the new requirement to state, as part of the application itself, the names and addresses of the directors. The High Court had held that the requirements of the then Regulations were complied with even though it had not been stated that the applicant was applying on behalf of an undisclosed principal, namely the company. Although there is no requirement to identify the directors in the public notice, it is submitted that the spirit of the new Regulations requires greater frankness.

(b) Location, townland or postal address

In *Crodaun Homes Ltd. v Kildare County Council*,[31] a majority of the Supreme **3–21** Court held that both the letter and the spirit of the then Regulations required that in the case of land, and in particular land which is not in an urban area, the site on which it is proposed that development should take place must be correctly and accurately described in relation to the district in which the land is situate (for example, by the estate of which it forms part, or the townland, or the neighbouring village), so as to be readily and reasonably identifiable. In that case, the majority of the Supreme Court held that an informal, local name was not sufficient description.

In *Dooley v Galway County Council*,[32] it was held that the use of the name of **3–22** the townland only to describe the location when there were eighteen townlands of the same name in the county did not give ready and reasonably identifiable notice to the public of the location of the land.

(c) Nature of the application

The public notice must state whether the application is for permission for **3–23** development, permission for retention of development, outline permission for development, or permission consequent to the grant of outline planning permission. In the last case, it is necessary to state the reference number on the register of the relevant outline permission.[33]

---

[30] [1974] I.R. 45.
[31] [1983] I.L.R.M. 1.
[32] [1992] 2 I.R. 136.
[33] *cf. Burke v Drogheda Corporation*, unreported, High Court, McWilliam J., June 11, 1982.

(d) Nature and extent of the development

3–24   The public notice must state "a brief description of the nature and extent of the development". Prior to the 2006 Regulations, the requirement had been to state the nature and extent of the development *simpliciter*. The introduction of the qualifying words "a brief description" was presumably intended to lessen the burden on an applicant. The case law discussed presently all predates the introduction of the qualifying words, and for this reason may now be distinguishable.

3–25   In the case of particular types of development, the following specific requirements apply.

> (i)   Where the application relates to development consisting of or comprising the provision of houses, the number of houses to be provided must be stated. It would appear to be sufficient that the number of houses may be reckoned from the statement of plot numbers.[34]

> (ii)   Where the application relates to retention of a structure, the nature of the proposed use of the structure and, where appropriate, the period for which it is proposed to retain the structure must be stated.

> (iii) Where the application relates to development which would consist of or comprise the carrying out of works to a protected structure or proposed protected structure, an indication of that fact.

> (iv)   Where the application relates to development which comprises or is for the purposes of an activity requiring an integrated pollution prevention and control licence or a waste licence, an indication of that fact.

> (v)   Where the application relates to development in a strategic development zone, an indication of that fact.

3–26   Where the proposed development is subject to environmental impact assessment, then the public notices must additionally state that an environmental impact statement will be submitted with the application, and, in the case of the newspaper only, that same will be available for inspection on purchase (at a fee not exceeding the reasonable cost of making a copy) during office hours at the offices of the relevant planning authority.[35]

3–27   Where the proposed development relates to the provision of, or modification to, an "establishment" within the meaning of the Major-Accident Hazards Directive, then the public notices must additionally indicate that fact.[36]

3–28   The general requirement to state the nature and extent of the development had been considered in a number of cases decided prior to the introduction of the

---

[34] *Springview Management Ltd. v Cavan Developments Ltd.* [2000] 1 I.L.R.M. 437 at 442.
[35] Planning and Development Regulations 2001, art.98.
[36] Planning and Development Regulations 2001, art.133 (newspaper notice), and Form No. 1 (site notice).

qualifying words "a brief description of" under the 2006 Regulations. This previous case law indicated that whereas the courts would strictly enforce the requirement to describe the (immediate) nature and extent of the development, in the sense of physical aspects of the development, there was no requirement to state the possible or even probable consequences of the development. Thus, for example, it was held in the case of development consisting of a bulk liquefied petroleum gas depot that there was no requirement to state that the completed development might have inherent dangers for those living in the vicinity.[37] Similarly, failure to make reference to the effect of a proposed development on an underlying aquifer did not involve a breach as this would, according to the High Court, otherwise introduce an element which went far beyond the description of the nature and extent of the development.[38]

A clear example of a failure to properly state the nature and extent of the proposed development is to be found in *Monaghan UDC v Alf-a-bet Promotions Ltd.*[39] On the facts, the Supreme Court held that no member of the public could have been expected to glean from the general words "alterations and improvements" that planning permission was sought for the conversion of what had been a drapery shop into a betting office and amusement arcade. See also *Readymix (Eire) Ltd. v Dublin County Council,*[40] where it was suggested by Griffin J. that the term "replacement concrete plant" did not properly describe the proposed development of a readymix plant.
3–29

Whether or not the public notice must address the issue of vehicular access to the proposed development has been the subject of a number of decisions. In *Keleghan v Corby*[41] it was suggested *obiter* that failure to state that a new access was to be constructed from a cul-de-sac to a school represented a breach of the requirement to state the nature and extent of the development. As against this, a more robust attitude was taken in *O'Donoghue v An Bord Pleanála*[42] where it was held that once a building, of whatever size or configuration, was to be erected on the site there must be access to it and every member of the public reading the advertisement would have been conscious of that fact.
3–30

In *Cunningham v An Bord Pleanála,*[43] Lavan J. ruled that a newspaper notice should have indicated that the proposed development involved the demolition of habitable houses.[44] But in *Molloy v Dublin County Council,*[45] Blayney J. upheld the validity of an application which did not indicate that the proposed development involved the demolition of habitable houses, because the planning
3–31

---

[37] *Calor Teoranta v Sligo County Council* [1991] 2 I.R. 267.
[38] *McNamara v An Bord Pleanála (No. 2)* [1996] 2 I.L.R.M. 339 at 362–363.
[39] [1980] I.L.R.M. 64.
[40] Unreported, Supreme Court, July 30, 1974.
[41] (1977) 111 I.L.T.R. 144.
[42] [1991] I.L.R.M. 750.
[43] Unreported, High Court, Lavan J., May 3, 1990.
[44] Relief was ultimately refused as a matter of discretion.
[45] [1990] I.R. 90; [1990] I.L.R.M. 663.

authority itself had been at fault in not requiring the applicant to apply for planning permission to demolish the houses. In *Dunne v An Bord Pleanála*, McGovern J. found that there was nothing in the 2001 Regulations which suggested that it was necessary to indicate in the public notices that habitable houses were to be demolished.[46]

3–32   Finally, an issue can arise as to how the existing use of the land should be described for the purposes of identifying any proposed material change in use. For example, in the case of an existing unauthorised use of lands, a question may arise as to whether it is this existing unauthorised use which should be stated or the (previous) lawful use. In *Blessington & District Community Council Ltd. v Wicklow County Council*,[47] the High Court held that, on the facts, it would be misleading to refer to the original use of the lands in that it would not be a fair or accurate reflection of the *de facto* situation which had obtained in excess of ten years.

(e) Submissions or observations

3–33   The public notices should state that the planning application may be inspected, or purchased at a fee not exceeding the reasonable cost of making a copy, at the offices of the planning authority during its public opening hours. The public notices should also state that a submission or observation may be made to the planning authority in writing on payment of the prescribed fee within a period of five weeks beginning on the date of the receipt by the planning authority of the application.[48]

3–34   Clearly, this requirement to state that submissions and observations may be made is of crucial importance. It gives expression to what is the objective of having a public notice in the first place.[49] It would seem that failure to comply with this requirement would render the application for planning permission invalid, and, further, that given the significance of the requirement there would be little scope for the application of a *de minimis* exception. See further para.11–191 and onwards as to whether a breach of this requirement might only be actionable by a person who had seen the (defective) public notice and had been misled thereby.

---

[46] [2006] I.E.H.C. 400; unreported, McGovern J., December 14, 2006.

[47] [1997] 1 I.R. 273.

[48] Planning and Development Regulations 2001, art.18(1)(e) (newspaper notice) and Form No. 1 (site notice) (as substituted by the 2006 Regulations).

[49] See, for example, *Crodaun Homes Ltd. v Kildare County Council* [1983] I.L.R.M. 1 at 3. See also *State (Stanford) v Dun Laoghaire Corporation*, unreported, Supreme Court, February 20, 1981.

C. Content of Application for Planning Permission

1. Standard planning application form

The required content of a planning application is specified in art.22 of the   **3–35**
Planning and Development Regulations 2001 (as substituted under the 2006
Regulations). A standard planning application form has been introduced under
the 2006 Regulations, and is to be found at Form No. 2 in Sch.3.

Certain of the information required under the standard planning application   **3–36**
form replicates matters to be stated in the public notices. For example, it must
be stated whether the application is for permission for development, permission
for retention of development, outline permission for development or permission
consequent to the grant of outline permission.

Additional requirements include a requirement to state the name and address,[50]   **3–37**
and telephone number, mobile number and e-mail address, if any, of the
applicant and of the person, if any, acting on behalf of the applicant. Where the
applicant is a registered company, there is a requirement to state the names of
the company directors and the address and registration number of the company.

In the case of an application subject to social and affordable housing under Pt   **3–38**
V of the PDA 2000 (as amended),[51] there is a requirement to specify how the
applicant proposes to comply with any condition in relation to social and
affordable housing.[52]

2. Legal interest

The legal interest of the applicant for planning permission in the land or structure   **3–39**
must be stated in the planning application form. If the applicant is not the
owner, the name and address of the owner must be stated, and the application
accompanied by the written consent of the owner to the making of the
application.[53]

In *Burke v Drogheda Corporation*,[54] an equivalent provision under the then   **3–40**
Regulations did not require a technical or conveyancing description of the
applicant's interest: on the facts, it was held that the use of the expression
"owner" was sufficient. A planning authority is, however, entitled to seek any

---

[50] In *Walsh v Kildare County Council* [2001] 1 I.R. 483, a claim for a default planning
permission was defeated because of the failure to state the applicant's address with sufficient
particularity.
[51] Planning and Development (Amendment) Act 2002.
[52] Planning and Development Regulations 2001, art.22(2)(e) (as substituted by the 2006
Regulations).
[53] Planning and Development Regulations 2001, art.22(2)(g) (as substituted by the 2006
Regulations).
[54] Unreported, High Court, McWilliam J., June 11, 1982.

information as to any estate or interest in or right over land which the planning authority considers necessary to enable it to deal with the application.[55] Apparently, this is so even where the planning authority has received such information already in relation to a previous application.[56] Griffin J. in *Monaghan UDC v Alf-a-bet Promotions Ltd*.[57] suggested that the necessity under the then Regulations to state particulars of the applicant's interest in the land would be mandatory. In practice, however, the courts have frequently excused applicants' failures to state their interests accurately where the applications were submitted by persons who genuinely intended to develop the land.[58]

3–41   More generally, there is no express requirement under the PDA 2000 that an applicant for planning permission have any estate or interest in or right over land the subject-matter of the application. Indeed, insofar as the legislation touches on the issue of ownership at all, it would seem to be to the effect that there is no requirement for ownership: s.33(2)(g) of the PDA 2000 allows for the Minister for the Environment Heritage and Local Government to make Regulations, *inter alia*, requiring any applicants to submit any further information with respect to their applications including any information as to *any* estate or interest in or right over land.[59] This subsection appears to envisage a situation where an applicant might have no such interest, as do the Regulations themselves.

3–42   Notwithstanding this, the courts had, until relatively recently, purported to detect a legislative intent that an application for planning permission, to be valid, must be made either by, or with the approval of, a person who is able to assert sufficient legal estate or interest to enable him to carry out the proposed development, or so much of the proposed development as relates to the property in question.[60] More recent decisions, however, had indicated a more flexible approach to the issue.[61] Subsequently, the Supreme Court in *Keane v An Bord Pleanála*[62] has queried whether any requirement to have an interest in lands extends beyond that which is necessary to avoid unnecessary or vexatious applications. This would appear to be a significantly lower standard than that previously imposed.

---

[55] Planning and Development Regulations 2001, art.33(1)(a) (as substituted by the 2006 Regulations). See, generally, *State (Conlon Construction Company Ltd.) v Cork County Council*, unreported, High Court, Butler J., July 31, 1975.

[56] *Murphy v Navan UDC*, unreported, High Court, Ó Caoimh J., July 31, 2001.

[57] [1980] I.L.R.M. 64 at 72.

[58] See, for example, *McCabe v Harding Investments* [1984] I.L.R.M. 105; and *Molloy v Dublin County Council* [1990] I.R. 90; [1990] I.L.R.M. 633. See also *Thomas McDonagh & Sons Ltd. v Galway Corporation* [1995] 1 I.R. 191.

[59] See, generally, *State (Conlon Construction Company Ltd.) v Cork County Council*, unreported, High Court, Butler J., July 31, 1975. *Cf. Murphy v Navan UDC*, unreported, High Court, Ó Caoimh J., July 31, 2001.

[60] *Frescati Estates Ltd. v Walker* [1975] I.R. 77. *Cf. Frank Dunne Ltd. v Dublin County Council* [1974] I.R. 45 at 50.

[61] See, for example, *Schwestermann v An Bord Pleanála* [1993] 3 I.R. 437; [1995] 1 I.L.R.M. 301. See also *Scott v An Bord Pleanála* [1995] 1 I.L.R.M. 424 (working of minerals).

[62] [1998] 2 I.L.R.M. 241.

It has to be said that the comments in *Keane v An Bord Pleanála* were probably, **3–43** strictly speaking, *obiter*. In *Arklow Holidays Ltd. v An Bord Pleanála*,[63] Clarke J. granted leave to apply for judicial review on the basis that the precise extent of the rule requires a definitive decision.

> "The position therefore remains that the precise extent of the exclusion is one which requires a definitive decision. It may, on the one hand, be that, as was suggested in *Keane*, the true position is one which requires the court to exclude only cases where the applicant for planning permission is engaged in a vexatious or spoiling exercise. It may, on the other hand, be that the clear wording of the judgment in *Frescati* will prevail. Between those poles there are a number of intermediate positions which might also find favour."

Finally, it should be noted that in some cases an applicant will have an interest **3–44** given by statute allowing him to carry out the proposed development.[64]

3. Copies of public notices

A planning application shall be accompanied by the relevant page of the **3–45** newspaper in which notice of the application has been published, and by a copy of the site notice. There is no longer a requirement that the application be accompanied by a separate plan showing the position of the site notice(s): instead, the position of the site notice(s) may be identified as part of the "location map".

4. Documents, particulars, plans, drawings and maps

Detailed provision is made under the Regulations as to the other documents, **3–46** particulars, plans, drawings and maps which should accompany an application for planning permission. Other than making the following general observations, consideration of these matters is beyond the scope of this book.

General observations

First, failure to comply with the requirements in this regard would appear to **3–47** invalidate the application.[65] It had been thought at one stage that the courts might display a more tolerant attitude to defects in the documents accompanying a planning application, as opposed to the requirements in relation to public notices. The thinking seemingly being that the prejudice caused to a member

---

[63] Unreported, High Court, Clarke J., January 18, 2006, [7.6].
[64] *Electricity Supply Board v Gormley* [1985] I.R. 129; and *Scott v An Bord Pleanála* [1995] 1 I.L.R.M. 424.
[65] Planning and Development Regulations 2001, art.26(3) (as substituted by the 2006 Regulations). The judgment in *PM Cantwell v McCarthy* [2005] I.E.H.C. 351; unreported, Murphy J. November 1, 2005—a case decided prior to the 2006 Regulations—is incorrect insofar as it suggests that a breach of the requirements of art.23 would not invalidate an application. Article 23 simply elaborates upon the requirements of art.22 and thus failure to comply with art.23 would give rise to a breach of art.22.

of the public by a defective public notice is greater than that which might be caused by a defect in the application for planning permission itself, in that a defective public notice might fail to alert a member of the public to the proposed development, with the result that he or she might fail to exercise his or her right to make submissions and observations.[66] The fact that the Regulations now expressly provide that the application for planning permission is to be invalid would appear to remove any such distinction.

3–48   Secondly, a number of recent cases suggest that in determining whether or not there has been compliance with the requirements in relation to documents accompanying the application for planning permission, the courts will not necessarily confine themselves to a consideration of whether or not there has been technical compliance. To put the matter another way, the courts may no longer restrict their role to one of examining whether or not there has been perfunctory compliance—in the sense of documents of the prescribed type actually having been submitted—leaving over to the planning authority an assessment of the adequacy of the content of same.[67] Instead, the decision in *Seery v An Bord Pleanála*[68] would appear to suggest that the High Court will consider whether or not there has been substantive, as opposed to procedural, compliance. On the facts of *Seery*, it was alleged by the applicants that the location map misstated or misrepresented the separation distance between an existing neighbouring premises and the proposed development. The High Court ultimately set aside the grant of planning permission on this basis.

3–49   Thirdly, it should be noted that the requirements in relation to accompanying documents are relaxed in relation to an application for outline planning permission. More specifically, it is provided under art.24 of the Planning and Development Regulations 2001 (as substituted by the 2006 Regulations) that an outline planning permission shall, in addition to the requirements of art.22(2), be accompanied only by such plans and particulars as are necessary to enable the planning authority to make a decision in relation to the siting, layout or other proposals for development in respect of which a decision is sought.

Red line and blue line

3–50   It is a requirement of art.23(1)(a) of the Planning and Development Regulations 2001 (as substituted by the 2006 Regulations) that the site boundary be delineated in red on a site or layout plan. This is sometimes referred to colloquially as the "red line". Under art.22(2)(b), any land which adjoins, abuts or is adjacent to the application site, and which is under the control of the applicant or owner, must be marked in blue on the location map.

---

[66] *McCabe v Harding Investments Ltd.* [1984] I.L.R.M. 105 at 109. *Cf. Dublin County Council v Marren* [1985] I.L.R.M. 593.

[67] See, by analogy, the approach suggested in relation to the adequacy of an environmental impact state in *Kenny v An Bord Pleanála (No. 1)* [2001] 1 I.R. 565.

[68] Unreported, High Court, Quirke J., November 26, 2003.

The significance of the red line was considered—prior to the 2006 **3–51**
Regulations—in *PM Cantwell v McCarthy*.[69] It had been alleged that the failure
to encompass the route of a storm water or surface water drain within the red
line of the planning application had the result that the development of the
drain or pipeline was not authorised. Murphy J. rejected this argument. In so
doing, Murphy J. attached significance to the fact that the planning authority
had validated the application for planning permission and had not requested
fresh plans indicating the drain outlined in red. Murphy J. also suggested that
the route of drains cannot require a site boundary in the same manner as the
boundaries of a housing site.

The judgment in *PM Cantwell v McCarthy* turns largely on its own particular **3–52**
facts, and it would not be safe to regard it as authority for any general principle.
In particular, it seems that—leaving aside the red line—it was relatively clear
from the terms of the planning permission and the accompanying documentation
what the actual route of the drain or pipeline was to be. The better view remains,
therefore, that all works in respect of which planning permission is sought
should be included within the red line.

D. Procedure on Receipt of Planning Application

1. Whether application in compliance with Regulations

The procedure on receipt of a planning application is prescribed under art.26 **3–53**
of the Planning and Development Regulations 2001 (as substituted by the 2006
Regulations). In effect, the planning authority has two opportunities to reject a
planning application as invalid. First, the planning authority is required, on
receipt of the application, to consider whether the applicant has complied with
the requirements of the Regulations in terms of public notices and the content
of planning applications. At that stage, the application should either be rejected
as invalid, or simply date stamped and an acknowledgment of receipt sent to
the applicant.[70] Secondly, the planning authority is entitled to revisit the question
of the validity of the application following its inspection of the application
site. If at that stage the planning authority considers that the requirements in
terms of public notices and the content of planning applications have not been
met, or that the information submitted in the planning application is substantially
incorrect or substantial information has been omitted, then the application
should be rejected an invalid.[71]

---

[69] [2005] I.E.H.C. 351; unreported, Murphy J., November 1, 2005.
[70] Planning and Development Regulations 2001, art.26(2) and (3) (as substituted by the
2006 Regulations).
[71] Planning and Development Regulations 2001, art.26(4) (as substituted by the 2006
Regulations).

3–54 An exception is made for cases where any site notice erected by an applicant has been maliciously defaced or destroyed by any person other than the applicant.[72]

3–55 It should be noted that the planning authority enjoys very little discretion in deciding whether or not to reject an application as invalid.[73] It is expressly provided that failure to comply with certain specified requirements of the Regulations will result in the planning application being invalid. This represents an advance on the previous legislation, where, generally, there was no such express statement of invalidity. Instead, it had been left to the courts to attempt to determine whether or not compliance with any particular requirement was directory or mandatory.[74] The distinction here being that in the case of a directory requirement, a breach of same did not necessarily result in the application for planning permission being invalid. The case law in relation to directory and mandatory requirements was somewhat confused and inconsistent. For example, a somewhat indulgent attitude had been shown by the High Court in *Frank Dunne Ltd. v Dublin County Council*[75]; this decision has been subsequently doubted but not expressly overruled in a number of Supreme Court decisions.[76] Much of this case law is now not strictly relevant given the express statement of invalidity under the Planning and Development Regulations 2001 (as substituted under the 2006 Regulations).

3–56 The position in relation to *de minimis* breaches probably still stands. In other words, the current position would appear to be that compliance with the various requirements is mandatory: the gloss on this, however, is that technical and trivial breaches may be overlooked. It should be noted that the nature of the requirements in some cases is such that partial or substantial compliance would not be possible: for example, a time-limit is either met or not, there is no room for a *de minimis* breach.[77]

3–57 It would seem that failure to comply with the requirements of the Regulations cannot be remedied by a request for further information, or, in the case of a defective public notice, put right at the direction of the planning authority by the giving of further public notice. This would seem to follow from the express

---

[72] Planning and Development Regulations 2001, art.26(7) (as substituted by the 2006 Regulations).

[73] *cf. Garden Village Construction Co. Ltd. v Wicklow County Council*, unreported, High Court, Morris P., February 16, 1998. In *PM Cantwell v McCarthy* [2005] I.E.H.C. 351; unreported, Murphy J. November 1, 2005, it seems to have been suggested *obiter* that the fact that the planning authority had deemed an application valid precluded judicial review in this regard. It is submitted that this cannot be correct, and that the validity of an application is ultimately a question of law.

[74] For a good example of this exercise, see *Monaghan UDC v Alf-a-bet Promotions Ltd.* [1980] I.L.R.M. 64.

[75] [1974] I.R. 45.

[76] *Monaghan UDC v Alf-a-bet Promotions Ltd.* [1980] I.L.R.M. 64; and *Crodaun Homes Ltd. v Kildare County Council* [1983] I.L.R.M. 1.

[77] *McCann v An Bord Pleanála* [1997] 1 I.R. 264; [1997] 1 I.L.R.M. 314.

wording of art.26, and from the fact that there is no equivalent to that provision under the previous Regulations which had allowed for the planning authority to direct further public notice in circumstances where, *inter alia*, the (original) public notice was defective.[78]

2. Procedure on rejection of application

Once a planning authority has decided that an application is invalid, it is required under art.26(5), as soon as may be, by notice in writing (i) to inform the applicant that the application is invalid and cannot be considered by the planning authority; (ii) to indicate which requirements of the regulations have not been complied with and (iii) to request the removal of the site notice or notices. The application should then be returned to the applicant, and an indication that an invalid application has been made entered on the planning register.[79] The planning authority must also return to the applicant any fee paid with the application.

3–58

Any person or body who has made a submission or observation, and any of the prescribed bodies, should be informed of the fact that the application has been returned as invalid, and any fee paid by that person or body returned.[80]

3–59

3. Notice to prescribed bodies under Article 28

In the case of a valid application, the planning authority must give notice to certain prescribed bodies of the application.[81] Such notice shall include a copy of the planning application and of the location map, and shall state (a) the date of receipt by the planning authority of the application, and (b) that any submission or observation made to the planning authority in relation to the application before the decision is made on the application will be taken into account by the planning authority in making its decision.

3–60

The minimum period for determining a planning application is a period of five weeks beginning on the date of the receipt by the planning authority of the application, and therefore if a prescribed body wishes to be certain that its

3–61

---

[78] See art.17(2) of the Local Government (Planning & Development) Regulations 1994. See also *Blessington & District Community Council Ltd. v Wicklow County Council* [1997] 1 I.R. 273 at 285. Under the 2001 Regulations, it had been expressly provided that a request for further information may not require the submission of any further information in respect of arts 18, 19(1)(a) or 22, save proposals in relation to social and affordable housing. This express prohibition has since been removed under the 2006 Regulations. It is doubtful as to whether this alters the legal position as set out at para.3–57 above.
[79] It is no longer necessary for the planning authority to enter *details* of the invalid application on the planning register.
[80] Planning and Development Regulations 2001, art.26(8) (as substituted by the 2006 Regulations).
[81] Planning and Development Regulations 2001, art.28 (as substituted by the 2006 Regulations).

submission or observations are taken into account, it should endeavour to send same to the planning authority within that five week period. It is not precluded from making submission or observations outside the five week period, but equally the planning authority is free to make its decision any time thereafter. In this regard, it is expressly provided under art.27(6) that where a prescribed body does not make a submission or observation within the five week period, the planning authority may determine the application without further notice to that body.

3–62 A planning authority is required to acknowledge any submission or observation made. Where a prescribed body requests a copy of some or all of the documentation accompanying a planning application, the planning authority is required to make that documentation available as soon as possible.

3–63 It would appear—by analogy with the decision in *Ó Nualláin v Dublin Corporation*[82]—that compliance with this requirement is mandatory, and, that failure to so comply will have the effect that any decision to grant planning permission would be voidable. It should be noted, however, that the potential harshness of this decision is probably tempered by the following two considerations. First, the High Court, on an application for judicial review, has discretion to refuse relief even in circumstances where there has been a breach of a mandatory requirement. Depending on the facts of the case, the High Court might be prepared to overlook a breach in this regard as being technical or procedural only. Secondly, in any event, an applicant for judicial review is required to demonstrate that there are substantial grounds of challenge, and that he or she has a substantial interest in the matter.[83] These procedural hurdles may be of particular relevance in this context, in what might otherwise be regarded as a procedural defect.

3–64 As discussed at paras 9–09 to 9–12, the failure of a planning authority to notify a prescribed body will not preclude that body from bringing an appeal to An Bord Pleanála, notwithstanding the fact that it will not have made submissions or observations at the planning authority stage.

E. Access to Information on Application

3–65 There is extensive provision in relation to the making available of information on an application for planning permission. In addition to the public notices already described in detail at paras 3–03 to 3–34 above, the following requirements apply.

---

[82] [1999] 4 I.R. 137.
[83] PDA 2000, ss.50 and 50A.

1. Weekly list

A planning authority is required, not later than the fifth working day following a particular week, to make available a weekly list of the planning applications received by it.[84] The list is to be made available, for a period of not less than eight weeks, for inspection and purchase in the offices of the planning authority, and for inspection in each public library and mobile library in the functional area of the planning authority, and at any other place, or by any other means, including in electronic form, that the planning authority considers appropriate. Copies of the list are to be made available free of charge or for a fee not exceeding the reasonable cost of making a copy (and cost of postage where applicable). The list is also to be made available to the elected members of the planning authority in such manner as they may, by resolution, direct.

3–66

The weekly list should also indicate any planning application (a) which the planning authority has rejected an invalid, or (b) in respect of which further information or evidence or revised plans, drawings or particulars have been received by the planning authority pursuant to a requirement under arts 33 or 34.[85] A planning authority may include any other information in respect of planning applications which it considers appropriate.[86]

3–67

In *O'Connor v Cork County Council*,[87] the planning authority provided the facility of a computer printout of applications received. Through error, a particular application for planning permission was entered as having been made in 2004, and not, as was in fact the case, 2005. Consequently, the application did not appear on the correct computer printout. The High Court held that the planning authority, in making the facility of a computer printout available to the public, was required to ensure its accuracy. Members of the public were not obliged to search the planning file when a computerised facility had been made available.

3–68

The planning authority sought to remedy the position by agreeing to require the applicant for planning permission to publish further public notices, which would have the effect of allowing a further period of time for submissions and objections to be made. Murphy J. ruled that the applicant for planning permission was entitled to his costs as against the planning authority.

3–69

---

[84] Planning and Development Regulations 2001, art.27 (as substituted by the 2006 Regulations).

[85] Planning and Development Regulations 2001, art.27(3) (as substituted by the 2006 Regulations).

[86] Planning and Development Regulations 2001, art.27(4) (as substituted by the 2006 Regulations).

[87] [2005] I.E.H.C. 352; unreported, Murphy J., November 1, 2005.

2. Inspection and purchase of application and any EIS

3–70   The planning application may be inspected or purchased at the office of the planning authority.[88] Any environmental impact statement ("EIS") will also be available for inspection and purchase, as will any request for further information or evidence (and any response thereto), and any revised plans, drawings or particulars submitted pursuant to art.34 of the Planning and Development Regulations 2001 (as substituted by the 2006 Regulations).[89] A copy of any submissions or observations in relation to the planning application which has been received by the planning authority is also to be available for inspection and purchase as soon as may be after receipt.[90]

3–71   In *Doyle v Canty*,[91] the High Court deprecated a situation whereby a member of the public, exercising the "lawful and most important right to consult a planning file", was left with the choice of spreading it over the papers and the computer terminal on the desk of a very busy senior local government officer while that officer is trying to work, or of using the office floor.

3. Availability of documents in case of appeal

3–72   Under s.38 of the PDA 2000, where a planning authority gives its decision in respect of a planning application the following documents shall be made available within three working days for inspection and purchase by members of the public during office hours at the offices of the planning authority: (a) a copy of the planning application and of any particulars, evidence, environmental impact statement, other written study or further information received or obtained by the planning authority from the applicant in accordance with the regulations; (b) a copy of any submissions or observations in relation to the planning application which have been received by the planning authority; (c) a copy of any report prepared by or for the planning authority in relation to the planning application; (d) a copy of the decision of the planning authority in respect of the planning application and a copy of the notification of the decision given to the applicant; and (e) a copy of any documents relating to a contribution or other matter referred to in s.34(5).

3–73   (It is to be noted that some of these documents will already have been available to the public during the currency of the application before the planning authority.)

3–74   The fact that the planning authority's reports are available is of considerable assistance in preparing for an appeal to An Bord Pleanála.

---

[88] PDA 2000, s.38(1), and (3). Also by necessary implication from the provisions in relation to public notices under Planning and Development Regulations 2001, art.18 and art.19 (as substituted by the 2006 Regulations).

[89] PDA 2000, s.38(3).

[90] PDA 2000, s.38(3).

[91] [2005] I.E.H.C. 234; unreported, Herbert J., June 24, 2005.

F. Submissions or Observations

1. Procedure

Article 29 of the Planning and Development Regulations 2001 (as substituted **3–75**
by the 2006 Regulations) provides that any person or body, on payment of the
prescribed fee, may make a submission or observation in writing to a planning
authority in relation to a planning application within a period of five weeks
beginning on the date of receipt by the planning authority of the application.
Where the planning authority so consents, a submission or observation may be
made in electronic form.

The submission or observation shall (i) state the name and address, and **3–76**
telephone number and e-mail address, if any, of the person or body making the
submission or observation, and (ii) indicate the address to which any
correspondence relating to the application should be sent.

Where a submission or observation is received by the planning authority after **3–77**
the period of five weeks beginning on the date of receipt of the application, the
planning authority shall return to the person or body concerned the submission
or observation received and the fee, and notify the person or body that the
submission or observation cannot be considered by the planning authority.[92]
As is the case in relation to other time-limits under the planning legislation,
this is probably an absolute time-limit. This would appear to be the case even
in circumstances where the reason a submission or observation was not made
within time is as a result of some defect in the public notices. This rule would
seem to be harsh in that, as explained immediately below, it is generally a
precondition to the bringing of an appeal to An Bord Pleanála that the appellant
have made a submission or observation to the planning authority. Thus it would
seem that a person who, as a result of a defect in the public notices, is not
properly alerted to the existence of a planning application may be precluded
from bringing an appeal to An Bord Pleanála, and only have a remedy by way
of judicial review.

2. Written acknowledgment

It is generally a precondition to a (third party) appeal that the appellant have **3–78**
previously made submissions or observations in writing in relation to the
planning application to the planning authority in accordance with the
regulations.[93] In this connection, it is an express requirement that an appeal be

---

[92] Planning and Development Regulations 2001, art.29(3) (as substituted by 2006
Regulations).
[93] PDA 2000, s.37. Under PDA 2000, s.37(6) there is an exception to this general requirement
in the case of a person who has an interest in land adjoining land in respect of which
planning permission is to be granted, in circumstances where the development will differ
materially from the development as set out in the application for planning permission by
reason of conditions imposed, and the imposition of such conditions will materially affect

accompanied by the acknowledgment by the planning authority of receipt of the submissions or observations.[94]

3–79   A standard form of acknowledgment is now provided for at Form No. 3 of Sch.3 of the Planning and Development Regulations 2001 (as substituted in 2006). This is a welcome innovation. Prior to the 2006 Regulations, there was some inconsistency in approach on the part of planning authorities. An example of the difficulties which this could create is provided by *Murphy v Cobh Town Council*.[95] On the facts, MacMenamin J. held that the planning authority had unwittingly created a trap for the unwary in that the various letters it had issued to the appellant—the acknowledgement, the notification of decision and the notification of an appeal—were all similar in layout and substance, and the date of each set out in miniscule print. The appellant had mistakenly submitted the third, rather than the first, in a series of three almost identical letters as part of its appeal, and the appeal had been rejected as invalid. The appellants were then put to the trouble and expense of having to challenge that rejection before the High Court. As discussed in great detail at para.9–30, they were ultimately successful in that regard.

3–80   In other instances, planning authorities may simply fail to provide any form of acknowledgment. The absence of such a written acknowledgment would preclude a third party objector from bringing an appeal to An Bord Pleanála. A question thus arises as to what remedy is available to that third party. The procedural defect involved is unusual in that it does not appear to impact on the *quality* of the decision of the planning authority. The position is thus to be contrasted with other procedural defects: for example, it is clear from the legislative scheme that the legislature think that it is conducive to good decision-making that the decision-maker have regard to submissions or observations made by third parties. If, for whatever reason, such a third party is wrongly prevented from making such a submission or observation, then there is at least a risk that the decision reached is flawed. Conversely, in the case of a failure to provide a written acknowledgement, the quality of the decision of the planning authority remains unaffected. Instead, the third party suffers a different prejudice in that his or her right to appeal has been compromised. One possible means of redress for the third party might be to analyse the position as follows. Although the defect alleged has not affected the quality of the decision of the planning authority, it nevertheless remains the position that under the legislative scheme any decision of a planning authority was always to be subject to the safeguard of an appeal to An Bord Pleanála. The consequence of a failure on the part of a planning authority to provide an acknowledgement in writing is to frustrate this safeguard of the appeal and to render the decision of the planning authority unimpeachable. Such an unimpeachable decision was never in the

---

the appellant's enjoyment of the land or reduce the value of the land. The misnomer in the section as originally enacted (mistaken reference to grant *simpliciter* instead of to a decision to grant) has been amended by the Planning and Development (Amendment) Act 2002.

[94] PDA 2000, s.127(1)(e).

[95] [2006] I.E.H.C. 324.

contemplation of the legislative scheme, and, accordingly, is invalid on that ground.

Reference is made in this regard to the judgment of the High Court in *McAnenley* **3–81** *v An Bord Pleanála*.[96] This case also related to a defect on the part of the planning authority which did not impact on the quality of its decision. Under the (then) legislation, there was a requirement that in the case of an appeal to An Bord Pleanála, the planning authority concerned, within a period of fourteen days beginning on the day on which a copy of the appeal is sent to it by the board, submit to An Bord Pleanála certain specified documents. Kelly J. held that this requirement was mandatory and that in circumstances where there had been non-compliance the appeal was not within jurisdiction or in accordance with law. The decision of An Bord Pleanála was quashed, and the matter remitted to An Bord Pleanála to be dealt with afresh.

A less satisfactory outcome occurred in *Lynch v Dublin City Council*.[97] The **3–82** applicant had made a written objection to an application for planning permission. The planning authority failed to issue the requisite acknowledgement in writing. Moreover, the planning authority failed to notify the objector of the making of the decision to grant planning permission. The objector did not learn of the making of the decision until after the four week period delimited for the making of an appeal had expired. Accordingly, the objector was not in a position to make an appeal to An Bord Pleanála because, first, she did not have the necessary written acknowledgement and, secondly, she was, in any event, out of time. Ó Caoimh J. held that the requirement to furnish a written acknowledgement was mandatory in nature, but that failure to do so would not invalidate any subsequent decision to grant planning permission.

> "I am conscious of the fact that I have indicated that the requirement in question was mandatory, but at the same time I am not inclined to hold that the failure to comply with that requirement necessarily results in an invalidity in the decision process itself.
>
> In the instant case, as I have already indicated, the passage of time has resulted in the construction of the extension to the property owned by the notice party. While some suggestion has been made that the notice party may have proceeded with works somewhat prematurely, in light of the decision that had been made, it is quite clear that any works that have been effected were effected in circumstances where a decision had been made to grant planning permission. No application was made to this court at any time to restrain the development in question pending the outcome of the proceedings."

Accordingly, the High Court refused to set aside the planning authority's **3–83** decision. Insofar as costs were concerned, the High Court ordered that the planning authority pay the costs of the applicant. An order for the notice party's costs was made as against the applicant, with an order over as against the planning authority.

---

[96] [2002] 2 I.R. 763.
[97] Unreported, High Court, Ó Caoimh J., July 25, 2003.

3. Requirement to pay fee

3–84 Much criticism has been made of the fact that since 2001 it has been necessary to pay a fee when making a submission or observation. As against this, the level of service provided to a person or body making a submission or observation in relation to an application is greatly enhanced. For example, such a person is entitled to an acknowledgement of the submission or observation; to notification in circumstances where an application is returned as invalid; to notification of the decision on the application[98]; and to notification of the fact of an appeal.[99] Furthermore, where further information or revised plans are submitted which contain "significant additional data" then an observer is entitled to notification of the fact of the submission.[100]

3–85 The legality of the fee was upheld, in the context of the EIA Directive, by the European Court of Justice ("the ECJ") in *Commission v Ireland*.[101] This is discussed further at paras 13–179 to 13–181.

3–86 In *Openneer v Donegal County Council*,[102] objectors purported to make a submission in respect of two applications. The submission referred to both applications for planning permission, but was accompanied by a fee (twenty euros) appropriate to a single application only. The planning authority returned the submission on the basis that the incorrect fee had been paid. In subsequent judicial review proceedings it was argued that the planning authority should have accepted at least one of the submissions, by allocating the fee to one or other of the submissions. There was a further suggestion that the planning authority should have notified the objector of the incorrect fee. Macken J. indicated that it was for the objector to ensure that the statutory or regulatory requirements, duly notified to him by means of the site notices, were complied with. While the respondent planning authority had made an attempt to bring the deficiency in fees to his attention, this did not exonerate the objector from the obligation to ensure that the appropriate fee was paid. The judicial review proceedings were dismissed because the application was made outside the eight-week statutory period; see para.3–86. Consequently, the foregoing comments might, strictly speaking, be *obiter*.

4. Defamation

3–87 The interesting question as to how the law of defamation might apply to planning matters was considered tangentially in *Doyle v Canty*.[103] Herbert J. stated that

---

[98] Planning and Development Regulations 2001, art.31 (as substituted by the 2006 Regulations).

[99] Planning and Development Regulations 2001, art.69.

[100] Planning and Development Regulations 2001, art.35(1)(d) (as substituted by the 2006 Regulations).

[101] (Case 216–05); November 9, 2006.

[102] [2005] 1 I.E.H.C. 156; [2006] 1 I.L.R.M. 150.

[103] [2005] I.E.H.C. 234; unreported, Herbert J., June 24, 2005.

it had long since been decided that the administration of local affairs by local authorities is a matter of public interest, and this public interest must clearly include the processing of an application for a grant of planning permission. On the particular facts of the case, Herbert J. held that the communication of certain allegations in respect of planning matters to the Minister for the Environment Heritage and Local Government and to a senior local authority official was an occasion of qualified privilege.

G. Natural and Constitutional Justice

It is a curious feature of the planning legislation that many of the *indicia* of natural and constitutional justice are absent from the planning authority stage of the process. For example, whereas there is provision made for the possibility of an oral hearing at the stage of an appeal to An Bord Pleanála, no equivalent provision is made in relation to the planning authority stage. There is certainly extensive provision made for third parties in the sense that they are entitled to make submissions and observations in relation to the application, and, to this end, are entitled to inspect and purchase the application for planning permission, but when viewed from the position of the *applicant* for planning permission, the process is less satisfactory. In this regard, it is important to bear in mind that, generally speaking, the applicant for planning permission will either be the owner of, or have some proprietary interest in, the lands the subject-matter of the planning application. In such circumstances, it might be thought that the applicant has an entitlement to a heightened level of fair procedures over that afforded to a member of the public.[104] In this regard, the procedures are particularly unsatisfactory in that there is little or no interaction between the applicant and the planning authority. More specifically, save with the possible exception of the procedure under art.34 of the Planning and Development Regulations 2001 (as substituted by the 2006 Regulations) whereby an applicant may be invited to submit modified proposals, the applicant does not know the thinking of the planning authority in relation to the proposed development.[105] For example, there may be a particular aspect of the proposed development which is concerning the planning authority and, if the applicant were alerted to this fact, he could allay or otherwise meet the concern.[106] Strictly speaking, a planning authority is not entitled to use a request for further information to bring its concerns to the attention of the applicant.

3–88

It has to be said that the provision made for natural and constitutional justice at the appeal stage before An Bord Pleanála is more ample (for example, allowing for the possibility of an oral hearing, the production of documents, and the taking of evidence on oath), and it may be that the apparent deficit of fair

3–89

---

[104] See, by analogy, *State (Haverty) v An Bord Pleanála* [1987] I.R. 485 at 493.

[105] *cf.* the possibility of pre-planning consultation under PDA 2000, s.247.

[106] See, by analogy, the decision in *Frenchurch Properties Ltd. v Wexford County Council* [1992] 2 I.R. 268; [1991] I.L.R.M. 769.

procedures at the planning authority stage is only acceptable because of the existence of such a right of appeal.[107] It may also be the case that the decision-making process should be regarded as a unified decision-making process with only effective decision: see, by analogy, *Gammell v Dublin Corporation*.[108]

3–90   In *Jerry Beades Construction Ltd. v Dublin Corporation*,[109] the High Court found that there had been a breach of fair procedures in that an application for retention planning permission had not been considered fairly or impartially. The allegations made in the case were unusual. It had been alleged that an official of the planning authority had indicated to the principal of the applicant company that any application for retention planning permission would be treated with contempt. This allegation was then raised by the developer with a more senior planning official, which official indicated that he personally would deal with the application. This official prepared a report, which recommended the grant of planning permission, and the report was then send forward to the "decisions' section" which would transmit a draft manager's order to the assistant city manager for his ultimate decision. Following a meeting in the interim between the two officials and the Deputy Dublin City Planner, a (second) report, this time recommending the refusal of planning permission, was sent to the assistant county manager: this report had been countersigned by the Deputy Dublin City Planner. The first report was at some stage removed from the file by a person who has never been identified. Ultimately, a decision to refuse planning permission was made. This decision was then appealed by the applicant to An Bord Pleanála.

3–91   McKechnie J. held that the process and the planning authority's decision "were reached in a manner contrary to fair procedures and involved a breach of natural and constitutional justice". In particular, the decision of the assistant city manager was, according to McKechnie J., based on an incomplete version of the true circumstances. McKechnie J. further ruled that the breaches in this regard tainted the decision on the appeal to An Bord Pleanála.

> "As a result of these matters I believe that though entirely blameless the Board acted under a misapprehension regarding the true situation. In my view before it could come to a fully informed decision it would have to have information about the entire background, insofar as that was directly or indirectly relevant to planning issues, as well as in this case the report of [the senior planner]. In these circumstances the decision arrived at was not in my view one reached in accordance with law."

3–92   The judgment in *Jerry Beades Construction Ltd.* was considered in *Harding v Cork County Council*.[110] Clarke J. concluded that that an appeal will be regarded as an adequate remedy in a two stage statutory or administrative process unless either (a) the matters complained of in respect of the first stage of the process

---

[107] *McCann v An Bord Pleanála* [1997] 1 I.R. 264; [1997] 1 I.L.R.M. 314.
[108] [1983] I.L.R.M. 413.
[109] [2005] I.E.H.C. 406; unreported, McKechnie J., September 7, 2005.
[110] [2006] I.E.H.C. 295; unreported, Clarke J., October 12, 2006.

are such that they can taint the second stage of the process or effect the overall jurisdiction; or (b) the process at the first stage is so flawed that it can reasonably be said that the person concerned had not been afforded his or her entitlement to a proper first stage of the process in any meaningful sense.

H. Requests for Further Information or Additional Information

1. Further information or evidence under Article 33

Article 33 of the Planning and Development Regulations 2001 (as substituted **3–93** by the 2006 Regulations) empowers a planning authority to require an applicant (a) to submit any further information (including any plans, maps or drawings, or any information as to any estate or interest in or right over land) which the planning authority considers necessary to enable it to deal with the application, or (b) to produce any evidence which the planning authority may reasonably require to verify any particulars or information given in or in relation to the application. Such a request must be by notice in writing.[111]

Under art.23, a planning authority is entitled to request the submission of the **3–94** following by an applicant. Where it considers it appropriate, a planning authority may require an applicant to submit an assessment of the impact of the proposed development on transport in the area, including impact on roads. A planning authority may, by notice in writing, require an applicant to provide *additional copies* of any plan, drawing, map, photograph or other particular which accompanies the planning application. A planning authority may request an applicant to provide a scale model of a proposed development including land and buildings in the vicinity, showing the elevations and perspective of the proposed development and any other photographs, plans, maps, drawing or other material particulars required by the planning authority to assess the application. Presumably these matters all come within the concept of "information" for the purposes of art.33, and thus should be dealt with by way of a request under that article. The significance of this is that it is only a request under art.33 which stops time running against the planning authority for the purposes of default planning permission.

Any request under art.33 must be made within eight weeks of the receipt of the **3–95** planning application. It is important to note that, even where an applicant agrees or consents—under s.34(9) of the PDA 2000—to an extension of time for the making of the decision on the planning application, a request for further information may only ever be validly served within the first eight weeks. To put the matter another way, a planning authority, having obtained an extension

---

[111] Planning and Development Regulations 2001, art.33(1) ("by notice in writing"). See also *Calor Teoranta v Sligo County Council* [1991] 2 I.R. 267.

of time by consent, cannot secure further time by subsequently serving a request for further information outside the first eight weeks.

3–96 The most obvious consequence of failure to comply with these time-limits is that the request for further information will not then operate so as to vary the appropriate period for determining the planning application: this is of crucial importance in relation to default planning permission.[112] See further para.3-186.

3–97 A planning authority only has one shot at seeking further information or evidence; thereafter, the planning authority is confined to seeking such further information or evidence as may be reasonably necessary to *clarify* matters dealt with in the applicant's response or to enable same to be considered or assessed. A planning authority is expressly prohibited under art.33(2) from requiring an applicant who has complied with a request for further information to submit any further information or evidence save (a) as may be reasonably necessary to clarify the matters dealt with in the applicant's response to a requirement to submit further information or evidence or to enable them to be considered or assessed, or (b) where the request for further information is made under art.108(2) (environmental impact assessment), or art.128(1) (transboundary pollution). Planning authorities should therefore take care to specify *all* the further information or documentation which they require in the initial request.

3–98 Where either a request for further information, or a request for clarification of further information, is not complied with, the planning application shall be declared to be withdrawn after the period of six months from the date of the requirement for further information or evidence has elapsed.[113] The planning authority may, however, agree to extend this six month period by up to three additional months.[114]

2. Necessary or reasonably required

3–99 The "information" requested under art.33(1)(a) must be necessary to enable the planning authority to deal with the application. Similarly, any "evidence" requested under art.33(1)(b) must be reasonably required to verify any particulars or information given in, or in relation to, the application. The wording of the sub-articles—"which the authority considers necessary" and "which the authority may reasonably require"—suggests that the test is subjective. This might suggest that the courts should show deference to the planning authority's assessment of what is necessary or reasonably required. With the exception of

---

[112] PDA 2000, s.34(8)(b).
[113] Planning and Development Regulations 2001, art.33(3) (as substituted by the 2006 Regulations).
[114] *ibid.*

the judgment of *Murphy v Navan UDC*,[115] however, the courts have to date allowed little discretion to the planning authority, but instead have subjected the contents of requests for further information to full-blooded review.

It is now well established that once a planning authority has all the information **3–100** or sufficient information necessary to decide on a planning application, it should not resort to the procedures under art.33 for the purpose of negotiating changes in the proposed development, or as a device for extending the statutory period for the determination of an application.[116] Reference is made to the following passage from *State (NCE Ltd.) v Dublin County Council*.[117]

> "It is quite clear from this letter that the Council was not seeking any elucidation from the developers of their plans or that it lacked any information, explanation or evidence necessary for it to decide upon the merits of the application on planning grounds. The letter states the features of the proposal which the Council disliked and asks the developer to alter his proposal to meet the objections. As Butler J. pointed out in the case referred to above [*State (Conlon Construction Ltd.) v Cork County Council*]
>
> > 'It is perhaps understandable that a planning authority may wish to avoid a formal refusal which would give rise to these rights and at the same time to indicate that they disapprove of an application but would be prepared to consider it in a modified form. That is all the letter of 18 May amounts to and the Act provides no such half-way house.'
>
> In my opinion the letter of 26th January 1979 did not amount to a valid notice requiring the developer to give further information or to produce evidence in respect of the application so as to stop the period of two months running."

More recently, in *Illium Properties Ltd. v Dublin City Council*,[118] the High **3–101** Court ruled that a request for further information had been made for an improper purpose. Towards the end of the statutory period allowed for the determination of an application for planning permission (two months under the previous legislation), the planning authority approached the applicant company with a view to its consenting to an extension of time for the determination of the application. This was refused. Thereafter, the planning authority purported to serve a request for further information. The request for further information was divided into five categories. The court ruled that four out of five of these categories were beyond the scope of a proper request for further information.

---

[115] Unreported, High Court, Ó Caoimh J., July 31, 2001. The High Court allowed the planning authority great leeway, especially as to the necessity for information with respect to ownership. *Cf. State (Conlon Construction Company Ltd.) v Cork County Council*, unreported, High Court, Butler J., July 31, 1975.

[116] *State (Conlon Construction Company Ltd.) v Cork County Council*, unreported, High Court, Butler J., July 31, 1975 (applicant told that application unacceptable regarding layout and proposal for disposal of effluents, enquiry also made as to title); *State (NCE Ltd.) v Dublin County Council* [1979] I.L.R.M. 249 (access; gradients; and surface water sewer system); and *O'Connors Downtown Properties Ltd. v Nenagh UDC* [1993] 1 I.R. 1 (internal layout and adequacy of car parking facilities).

[117] [1979] I.L.R.M. 249 at 251.

[118] [2004] I.E.H.C. 327; unreported, O'Leary J., October 15, 2004.

Insofar as the remaining category was concerned, the court held that, whereas it might have been legitimate in other circumstances, the surrounding facts rendered it likely that it was included as part of a document with a hidden and illegal purpose of gaining more time for the planning authority to do its work. The court also held that the planning authority already had enough information to refuse planning permission (and probably enough information to approve same with conditions) at the time of the serving of the request for further information. A declaration as to a default planning permission was, accordingly, made.

3–102 To the extent that the decision of the Supreme Court in *Burke v Westmeath County Council*[119] appears to suggest a greater flexibility in or about the use of a request for further information, it is submitted that it is inconsistent with the previous authorities and should not be followed.

3–103 A request for further information should be confined to planning matters. In *Illium Properties Ltd. v Dublin City Council*,[120] the High Court criticised a request for further information on the basis that certain items sought were in respect of conservation matters, rather than planning matters. The request should also be confined to the development the subject-matter of the application. Thus, it would be improper for a planning authority to attempt to use a request for further information to address the planning status of other related development. In *Illium Properties Ltd. v Dublin City Council*, the High Court held that it was not appropriate to attempt, by way of a request for further information, to use a current planning application to rectify alleged planning breaches.

3–104 As indicated at para.3–13, in the event that the request for further information contains significant additional data, there is a requirement for further public notice.[121]

3–105 Finally, it should be noted that a planning authority is never obliged to serve a request for further information, but is entitled to determine an application on the basis of the information submitted and, where appropriate, to refuse planning permission. In particular, a planning authority is not required to afford the developer an opportunity to mend his hand by requesting further information where it considers the initial application to be deficient.[122]

3. Additional information under Article 22A

3–106 Under art.22A of the Planning and Development Regulations 2001 (as

---

[119] Unreported, Supreme Court, June 18, 1998.
[120] [2004] I.E.H.C. 327; unreported, O'Leary J., October 15, 2004.
[121] Planning and Development Regulations 2001, art.35 (as amended by the 2006 Regulations).
[122] See, by analogy, *Kildare County Council v An Bord Pleanála* [2006] I.E.H.C. 173; unreported, MacMenamin J., March 10, 2006, [75] (road development and environmental impact assessment).

substituted by the 2006 Regulations), a planning authority may request an applicant to submit specified additional information beyond that strictly required of a planning application under art.22. Article 22A(2) provides that no planning application shall be invalidated for failure to submit with the (initial) application any information or particulars so requested. This sub-article serves to emphasise that what is being sought is *additional* information, beyond that strictly required under art.22. Thus, the making of a request under art.22A does not carry with it any suggestion that the initial planning application was deficient; rather the planning authority is seeking more information than is usually required.

It should be noted that the making of a request under art.22A does not affect **3–107** the running of time for the determination of a planning application, and thus the planning authority must observe the time-limits under s.34(8) lest a default planning permission arise.

I. Revised Plans, Drawings and Particulars

1. Procedure under Article 34

Article 34 of the Planning and Development Regulations 2001 (as substituted **3–108** by the 2006 Regulations) empowers a planning authority to invite an applicant to submit to it revised plans or other drawings modifying, or other particulars providing for the modification of, the development. Under the unamended 2001 Regulations, it had been expressly provided that where such plans, drawings or particulars were submitted, the planning authority may decide to grant a permission for the relevant development as modified by all or any such plans, drawings or particulars. This express provision has been omitted under the 2006 Regulations.

The entitlement to invite revised plans etc. is triggered where a planning **3–109** authority, having considered a planning application, is disposed to grant a permission subject to any modification of the development to which the application relates. The power must now be exercised within eight weeks of receipt of the planning application. This is part of a number of reforms introduced under the 2006 Regulations in order to ensure that the planning authority secures an extension of time for the determination of the application. The related reforms are as follows. An applicant who wishes to avail of the opportunity to submit revised plans etc. is required to indicate in writing that he intends to submit such plans, drawing or particulars. This must be done within such period as may be specified by the planning authority, not being later than eight weeks from receipt of the planning application. At the same time, the applicant must consent in writing to the extension of the period for the making of a decision on the application under s.34(8) of the PDA 2000.

The power to invite revised plans etc. is a wide ranging one, and one which **3–110** gives rise to a risk of prejudicing the right of public participation. More specifically, one can readily envisage a situation whereby the effect of the revised plans may be such as to render an otherwise unobjectionable development objectionable. For example, the impact of the proposed development on neighbouring lands may well change as a result of revised plans, with the result that a person who had previously not made any submission or observation might now very well wish to object to the development.

3–111 Some of the concerns in this regard are met by the requirement under art.35 that there be further public notice in the event that the revised plans, drawings or particulars contain significant additional data. The wording of art.35 is somewhat curious in that whereas the test posed—"significant additional data"—would seem appropriate in the context of further information or evidence received, one would have thought that in the case of revised plans, drawings, or particulars the real issue is not so much one of additional data or information, as the nature and extent of the modification of the development. The operation of art.35 is discussed in detail at para.3–119 and onwards.

2. "Modification"

3–112 It should be noted that the power under art.34 is restricted to "modification" of the development. It is submitted that the term "modification" would not allow for a complete or very substantial change in the development. Were the planning authority to grant planning permission for development substantially different from that applied for, same might be vulnerable to judicial review. More specifically, an argument might be made that substantial changes go beyond the tolerance allowed for under art.34. In this regard, the point might be made that art.34 should be interpreted narrowly so as not to prejudice rights of public participation.[123] In the circumstances, it could be argued that the planning authority had failed to adjudicate on the application before it.[124]

3–113 This question of the extent to which the proposed development may be modified by revised plans arose—albeit in the context of an appeal to An Bord Pleanála— in *Dietacaron Ltd. v An Bord Pleanála*.[125] An Bord Pleanála had exercised its power under the then regulations to invite an applicant for planning permission to submit revised plans. An Bord Pleanála indicated that the revised plans would be circulated to the parties to the appeal, and those parties would be given a further opportunity to make submissions and observations in relation thereto. One of the parties to the appeal argued that the nature and extent of the revisions sought by An Bord Pleanála went beyond mere modifications and, in fact, so radically altered the development as to comprise a new development requiring a fresh application for planning permission.

---

[123] *Bernard Wheatcroft Ltd. v Secretary of State for the Environment* (1980) 43 P. & C.R. 233.
[124] See, generally, *State (Abenglen Properties Ltd.) v Dublin Corporation* [1984] I.R. 381; [1982] I.L.R.M. 590.
[125] [2005] 2 I.L.R.M. 32.

One of the preliminary issues to be determined by the High Court was as to the standard of review to apply. Quirke J. held that the decision fell to be reviewed against the standard of administrative unreasonableness. On the facts, Quirke J. held that the decision of An Bord Pleanála to invite revisions of the type sought was not unreasonable. **3–114**

More generally, Quirke J. recognised that dialogue between an applicant and a decision-making body is expressly permitted by the planning legislation, provided that other participants (including members of the public) are notified of such dialogue and permitted to participate in the process. **3–115**

3. Disposed to grant planning permission

Finally, the power under art.34 is of interest in that it appears to allow for the taking of a preliminary position by a planning authority in relation to an application for planning permission. The wording of the article is such that it is only triggered where the planning authority is *disposed* to grant planning permission subject to modification. This would appear to involve a level of prejudgement which is unusual in the context of the exercise of a quasi-judicial function. **3–116**

In *Ballintubber Heights Ltd. v An Bord Pleanála*,[126] the applicant for judicial review sought to argue that the effect of the precursor to art.34 was that, whatever might be the position in relation to pre-application discussions, once an application for planning permission had been made, the officials of the planning authority could only make known to the applicant for planning permission their views of the application through the formal statutory process, including the precursor to art.34. The point here seems to have been that members of the public must be afforded an opportunity to make submissions or observations directed to the preliminary thinking of the officials of the planning authority. On the facts, however, the High Court ruled that the company seeking the application for judicial review did not have sufficient *locus standi*. **3–117**

The provisions of art.34 can be contrasted with those of s.247 of the PDA 2000, which allow for consultations in relation to a *proposed* application for planning permission. The implication appears to be that it is not possible to have such consultations once the application for planning permission has, in fact, been made. **3–118**

---

[126] Unreported, High Court, Ó Caoimh J., June 21, 2002.

J. Further Public Notice

1. Procedure under Article 35

3–119 A planning authority is obliged under art.35 of the Planning and Development Regulations 2001 (as substituted by the 2006 Regulations) to require an applicant to give further public notice where "significant additional data" is received in respect of a planning application. The planning authority itself must notify the prescribed bodies, and any person who made a submission or observation on the application, of the receipt of the "significant additional data".

3–120 These requirements are triggered where a planning authority receives—whether in response to a request for further information under art.33 or in response to an invitation to submit revised plans under art.34 or otherwise—further information, evidence, revised plans, drawings or other particulars in relation to a planning application and where it considers that same contain "significant additional data, including information in relation to the environment".

3–121 The further public notice must be by way of both a fresh newspaper notice and site notice. The newspaper notice should be published in an approved newspaper, containing as a heading the name of the planning authority, marked "Further Information" or "Revised Plans" as appropriate. The site notice must comply with most of the requirements of art.19. See further paras 3–05 and 3–06 above.

3–122 Both types of notice must state (i) the name of the applicant; (ii) the location, townland or postal address of the land or structure to which the application relates; (iii) the register reference number of the application; (iv) that significant further information or revised plans, as appropriate, in relation to the application has or have been furnished to the planning authority, and that same are available for public inspection or purchase at a fee not exceeding the reasonable cost of making a copy, at the offices of the planning authority during its public opening hours; and (v) that submissions or observations can be made to the planning authority not later than two weeks after the receipt of the newspaper notice and site notice (five weeks in the case of EIA development).

3–123 The planning authority must send notice and a copy of the further information, evidence, revised plans, drawings or particulars to the prescribed bodies. The notice should indicate that a submission or observation may be made to the planning authority not later than two weeks after receipt of the newspaper notice and site notice by the planning authority.

3–124 The planning authority must notify any person who made a submission or observation in relation to the application (i) that significant further information or revised plans, as appropriate, has or have been furnished to the planning authority and are available for inspection or purchase (at a fee not exceeding the reasonable cost of making a copy) at the offices of the planning authority, during its public opening hours; (ii) that a submission or observation may be made to the planning authority not later than two weeks after receipt of the newspaper notice and site notice by the planning authority; (iii) that no fee or further fee shall be payable on condition that any submission or observation is accompanied by a copy of the acknowledgment by the planning authority of receipt of the (earlier) submission or observation.

It is important to note that the right to make submissions or observations is not confined to persons who had previously made a submission or observation on the planning application, *i.e.* within the initial five week period. Rather, the receipt of "significant additional data" gives rise to a fresh round of public consultation which is open to all. Anyone who had made an earlier submission or observation does have the benefit of being notified directly by the planning authority of its receipt of the "significant additional data", and, moreover, is not required to pay an additional fee provided he or she produces a copy of the acknowledgment of receipt of the earlier submission or observation.   3–125

The planning authority is required to acknowledge receipt of any submissions or observations. The standard form at Form No. 3 of Sch.3 of the Planning and Development Regulations 2001 (as substituted by the 2006 Regulations) is to be used in this regard. The written acknowledgment will ensure that a person who makes submissions or observations for the first time following the further public notice will be able to appeal to An Bord Pleanála.   3–126

2. "Significant additional data"

It would appear from the decision of the High Court in *Kinsella v Dundalk Town Council*[127] that the decision as to whether material received by the planning authority contains "significant additional data" is a matter for the planning authority in the first instance, and is protected by the principles in *O'Keeffe v An Bord Pleanála*.[128] It had been alleged in *Kinsella* that the relevant planning authority should have required further public notice on receipt of a response to a request for further information, on the basis that the response contained "significant additional data" such as to trigger the statutory requirement for further public notice. Kelly J. rejected this argument. The officials of the planning authority had addressed their minds to the specific question of whether the response contained "significant additional data". Kelly J. ruled that the only remaining basis for challenging the decision could be that the decision was unreasonable or irrational, and held that this ground was not made out on the facts.   3–127

---

[127] Unreported, Kelly J., December 3, 2004.
[128] [1993] 1 I.R. 39; [1992] I.L.R.M. 237. The attenuated standard of review posited in *O'Keeffe v An Bord Pleanála* was also applied in *Irish Hardware Association Ltd. v South Dublin County Council*, unreported, High Court, Butler J., July 19, 2000. A more vigorous form of review was seemingly exercised in *White v Dublin Corporation*, unreported, High Court, Ó Caoimh J., June 21, 2002. The Supreme Court resolved the case on the narrower ground that the officials of the planning authority had asked themselves the incorrect question: [2004] 1 I.R. 545; [2004] 2 I.L.R.M. 509.

3–128   In summary, therefore, the High Court will only interfere with the assessment of the planning authority as to the "significance" of the material received where it can be demonstrated that the planning authority's assessment is unreasonable or irrational. See further para.12–103.

3–129   In *White v Dublin City Council*[129]—a case decided under the Local Government (Planning & Development) Regulations 1994—the Supreme Court held that the relevant official of the planning authority had, in effect, asked himself the wrong question in deciding whether to require further public notice. The proper test was whether, in the circumstances of the application before the planning authority, some members of the public might reasonably wish to object to the plans as modified. Instead, the relevant official had acted as if he was deciding whether or not planning permission should be granted. The Supreme Court held that not to require further public notice was, on the facts of the case, unreasonable and irrational.

K. Time-Limits and Public Holidays

3–130   In calculating the various time-limits under the Planning and Development Regulations 2001 (as substituted by the 2006 Regulations), allowance is made under art.29A for public holidays or for any other day when the offices of the planning authority are closed.[130] The submissions, observations or request or documents, particulars or other information (as the case may be) shall be regarded as having been received before the expiration of the applicable time period if received by the planning authority on the next following day on which the offices of the planning authority are open.

L. Material Contravention Procedure

1.   Section 34(6)

3–131   Express provision is made whereby a planning authority is entitled to grant planning permission for a development which would materially contravene the development plan.[131]

3–132   The procedure is as follows. Notice must be given in the prescribed form of the intention of the planning authority to consider granting planning permission in material contravention.[132] This requires publication in at least one daily

---

[129] [2004] 1 I.R. 545; [2004] 2 I.L.R.M. 509.

[130] Planning and Development Regulations 2001, art.29A (as substituted by the 2006 Regulations).

[131] PDA 2000, s.34(6).

[132] The form of notice is prescribed at Form No. 5 of Sch.3 of the Planning and Development Regulations 2001 (as substituted by the 2006 Regulations).

newspaper circulating in the functional area,[133] and the giving of notice to the applicant and to any person who has submitted a submission or observation in writing in relation to the development to which the application relates.[134]

It is important to note that the right to make submissions or observations is not confined to persons who had previously made a submission or observation on the planning application, *i.e.* within the initial five week period.[135] Rather, the material contravention procedure involves a fresh round of public consultation which is open to all. Anyone who had made an earlier submission or observation does have the benefit of being notified directly by the planning authority of its intention to consider granting planning permission in material contravention.
3–133

Submissions or observations must be made not later than four weeks after the first publication of notice of intention. Any submission or observation must (a) state the name and address, and telephone number and email address, if any, of the person or body making the submission or observation; and (b) indicate the address to which any correspondence relating to the application should be sent.[136] The planning authority is required to acknowledge receipt of any submissions or observations.[137] The written acknowledgment will ensure that a person who makes submissions or observations for the first time following the further public notice will be able to appeal to An Bord Pleanála.
3–134

The planning authority must consider any submission or observation which is received not later than four weeks after the first publication of the notice. A resolution of the elected members requiring that a decision to grant permission be made must be passed before planning permission can be granted. The number of the elected members of the planning authority voting in favour of the resolution must be not less than three-quarters of the total number of the elected members of the planning authority.[138]
3–135

2. Role of manager

Under s.140 of the Local Government Act 2001, the elected members of a local authority may, by resolution, direct that any particular act, matter or thing be done or effected. It was established under the previous planning legislation that the statutory predecessor of s.140 of the Local Government Act 2001 (the infamous "Section 4 motion" under the City and County Management (Amendment) Act 1955) applied to the decision to grant planning permission.[139]
3–136

---

[133] PDA 2000, s.34(6)(a)(i).

[134] PDA 2000, s.34(6)(a)(ii).

[135] See also Planning and Development Regulations 2001, art.36(2) (as substituted by 2006 Regulations).

[136] Planning and Development Regulations 2001, art.36(3) (as substituted by 2006 Regulations).

[137] Planning and Development Regulations 2001, art.36(4) (as substituted by 2006 Regulations).

[138] PDA 2000, s.34(6)(b).

[139] *P & F Sharpe Ltd. v Dublin City and County Manager* [1989] I.R. 701; [1989] I.L.R.M.

3–137 Where the manager is given notice of intention to propose a resolution which, if passed, would require the manager to decide to grant planning permission, the manager should address his or her mind to the question of whether or not the proposed development would represent a material contravention of the development plan. If the manager is of the opinion that the development concerned would contravene materially the development plan, he or she shall, within one week of receiving the notice, make, by order, a declaration stating his or her opinion.[140] A copy of this opinion must be furnished by the manager to each of the signatories of the notice of intention. The effect of this declaration is that the matter must thereafter be dealt with pursuant to the material contravention procedure.

3–138 The notice of intention with respect to the resolution under s.140 of the Local Government Act 2001 shall be of no further effect.[141] Instead, if a resolution is duly passed authorising the material contravention, the manager is required to make a decision to grant the relevant permission.[142]

3–139 It is submitted that the manager's opinion as to whether or not the proposed development does involve a material contravention of the development plan is open to full-blooded review in the event of legal challenge. The question as to whether or not there is a material contravention is a question of law. See, generally, paras 1–61 to 1–65. There is nothing in the legislation to suggest that the position should be any different in the present context of a resolution under s.140 of the Local Government Act 2001. Indeed, the opposite is true in that the existence of a material contravention is a condition precedent to the exercise by the manager of an exceptional power, namely that of nullifying the intended s.140 resolution. The reference to the "opinion" of the manager does not carry the implication that this opinion is conclusive or unreviewable. This interpretation is supported by reference to the judgment in *P & F Sharpe Ltd. v Dublin City and County Manager*,[143] which suggests that the question of material contravention in this context is capable of objective assessment.[144] Insofar as a different conclusion appears to have been reached in *Byrne v Wicklow County Council*,[145] it is submitted it should not be followed.[146]

---

565. *Cf. Kenny Homes and Company Ltd. v Galway City and County Manager* [1995] 1 I.R. 178; [1995] 2 I.L.R.M. 586, where Blayney J. suggested that it was very difficult to see what form a resolution could take which would leave the elected members free to consider all the options possible in determining a planning application (especially the imposition of conditions), and at the same time require a "particular act, matter or thing specifically mentioned in the resolution [...] to be done or effected".

[140] PDA 2000, s.34(6)(c).

[141] PDA 2000, s.34(6)(c).

[142] PDA 2000, s.34(6)(d).

[143] [1989] I.R. 701; [1989] I.L.R.M. 565.

[144] See also *Murray v Wicklow County Council* [1996] 2 I.R. 552 at 558; [1996] 2 I.L.R.M. 411 at 416–417.

[145] Unreported, High Court, Keane J., November, 3 1994. See also *Wicklow County Council v Wicklow County Manager*, unreported, High Court, Ó Caoimh J., February 26, 2003 (motion directing *refusal* of planning permission).

[146] See, generally, G. Simons, "The Unreasonable Planning Authority: Part I" (2000) 7 I.P.E.L.J. 164.

3. Waste management plan

The requirement under s.34(6) of the PDA 2000 that a special procedure be   **3–140**
adopted before planning permission may be granted for development which
would involve a material contravention of the development plan is disapplied
in certain circumstances under the Waste Management Act 1996 (as amended
by the Waste Management (Amendment) Act 2001).[147] More specifically, where
a planning authority proposes to grant planning permission for development
which is consistent with the provisions (including any objectives contained
therein) of, and is necessary for the proper implementation of, a waste
management plan in relation to the planning authority's functional area, s.34(6)
is disapplied. Instead, the following requirements must be met.

The manager shall publish notice of the intention of the planning authority to   **3–141**
grant planning permission in material contravention in one or more newspapers
circulating in that area; and give a copy of the notice to the applicant for planning
permission and to any other person who has made a submission or observation
in writing in relation to the development in accordance with the regulations.

Any submission or observation in writing received by the planning authority   **3–142**
not later than four weeks after the publication of the notice shall be considered
by the manager of the planning authority.

Somewhat surprisingly, perhaps, no special provision is made as to the manner   **3–143**
in which an appeal in relation to such development should be dealt with.
Whereas the express statutory restrictions imposed on An Bord Pleanála in
relation to a material contravention of the development plan appear only to be
triggered in circumstances where the planning authority had refused planning
permission on the basis of a material contravention, it nevertheless remains
the case that An Bord Pleanála is required to have regard to the provisions of
the development plan. Accordingly, it would seem that it might be open to An
Bord Pleanála to refuse planning permission for the very reason that the
proposed development would involve a material contravention of the
development plan.

M. Environmental Impact Assessment

In determining an application for planning permission where an environmental   **3–144**
impact statement has been submitted, a planning authority, and An Bord
Pleanála, shall have regard to the statement, any supplementary information
furnished relating to the statement, and any submissions or observations
furnished concerning the effects on the environment of the proposed
development.[148]

---

[147] Waste Management Act 1996, s.22(10)(B) (as substituted by s.4 of the Waste Management
(Amendment) Act 2001).
[148] PDA 2000, s.173.

3–145 The requirements in relation to public notice, and the time-limits for the determination of the application, are also modified. The public notice must additionally state that an environmental impact statement will be submitted with the application, and that same will be available for inspection or purchase (at a fee not exceeding the reasonable cost of making a copy) during office hours at the offices of the relevant planning authority.[149] In the case of an appeal to An Bord Pleanála, An Bord Pleanála is only required to publish a newspaper notice where it has requested and received an environmental impact statement.[150] The period for the determination of an application for planning permission is modified as follows: where a request for further information is made in respect of an application accompanied by an environmental impact statement, then the application must be decided within eight weeks of the notice being complied with.[151] (Ordinarily, the requirement is four weeks from the notice being complied with.)[152]

3–146 The EIA Directive is discussed in detail in Chapter 13.

N. Major-Accident Hazards Directive (Seveso Directive)

1. Additional procedural requirements

3–147 Additional procedural requirements apply where a proposed development is subject to the Major-Accident Hazards Directive (sometimes referred to colloquially as the "Seveso" or "Seveso II" Directive).[153] These additional procedural requirements are intended to ensure that the objectives of preventing major accidents, and limiting the consequences of such accidents, are taken into account in the decision-making process. Member States are obliged under the terms of the Major-Accident Hazards Directive to pursue those objectives through controls on (a) the siting of new establishments; (b) modifications to existing establishments; and (c) new developments such as transport links, locations frequented by the public and residential areas in the vicinity of existing establishments, where the siting or developments are such as to increase the risk or consequences of a major accident.[154] An "establishment" is defined for the purpose of the Directive by reference to the presence of prescribed quantities of "dangerous substances".

---

[149] Planning and Development Regulations 2001, art.98.
[150] Planning and Development Regulations 2001, art.112 (as amended by the 2006 Regulations).
[151] PDA 2000, s.34(8)(b).
[152] PDA 2000, s.34(8)(c).
[153] Council Directive 96/82/EC of 9 December 1996 on the control of major-accident hazards involving dangerous substances. This Directive has been amended a number of times, principally by Directive 2003/105/EC of the European Parliament and of the Council of 16 December 2003 amending Council Directive 96/82/EC on the control of major-accident hazards involving dangerous substances.
[154] See, generally, Y. Scannell, *Environmental and Land Use Law* (Thomson Round Hall, Dublin, 2006), paras 10–43 to 10–54.

Under Art.12 of the Directive, Member States shall ensure that their land-use **3–148** and/or other relevant policies and the procedures for implementing those policies take account of the need, in the long term, to maintain appropriate distances between establishments covered by the Directive and residential areas, buildings and areas of public use, major transport routes as far as possible, recreational areas and areas of particular natural sensitivity or interest and, in the case of existing establishments, of the need for additional technical measures in accordance with Art.5 so as not to increase the risks to people. See further paras 8–221 to 8–246.

The Major-Accident Hazards Directive thus applies not only to planning **3–149** applications which seek permission to construct or modify a major-accident establishment, but also applies to applications for other types of development within the *vicinity* of a major-accident establishment. Depending on the nature of the risk posed, it may be inappropriate to permit populous development— such as major retail developments or community or leisure facilities—within the vicinity of a major-accident establishment. Similarly it may be inappropriate to locate, within the vicinity of a major-accident establishment, development of a type which would be difficult to evacuate in the case of an emergency, *e.g.* schools or hospitals.

The assessment of the risk posed by a major-accident establishment is a **3–150** specialist skill, and one which is not necessarily within the expertise of town planners. For this reason, then, Member States are obliged to ensure that "all competent authorities and planning authorities" responsible for decisions in this area set up appropriate consultation procedures. These procedures must be designed to ensure that "technical advice" on the risks arising from the establishment is available, either on a case-by-case or on a generic basis, when decisions are taken.

The requirements of the Directive in this regard are implemented under Pt 11 **3–151** of the Planning and Development Regulations 2001. In particular, provision is made for the planning authorities and An Bord Pleanála to notify and to seek technical advice from the Health and Safety Authority ("the HSA")[155] on the risk or consequences of a major accident. This then allows the planning authority or An Bord Pleanála, as appropriate, to make an informed decision on whether to grant or refuse planning permission. This obligation to notify the HSA will be referred to hereinafter by the shorthand "the notification requirement".

The nature of the notification requirement has been amended under Planning **3–152** and Development Regulations 2006. Rather than simply request technical advice as had been the position under the 2001 Regulations, a planning authority first

---

[155] The previous reference to the "National Authority for Occupational Safety and Health" has been replaced under art.32 of the Planning and Development Regulations 2006, and "Health and Safety Authority" substituted therefor.

requests a determination as to whether the Major Accidents Regulations apply to the proposed development. It is only if the HSA determines that the said Regulations do apply, that technical advice as to the effects of the proposed development on the risk or consequences of a major accident are to be provided to the planning authority.

3–153   This amendment helps to clarify the respective roles of the planning authority and the HSA. In particular, it seems now that the determination of issues such as, for example, the physical extent of the major-accident establishment—which is obviously of critical importance in applying separation distances—is principally a matter within the competence of the HSA. The legal position prior to this amendment had been considered by the High Court in *Harrington v An Bord Pleanála (No. 1)*.[156] See further paras 8–229 to 8–240.

2. Notification requirement

3–154   The notification requirement arises in the following circumstances. First, where a planning authority receives a planning application relating to the provision of, or modifications to, an establishment and, in the planning authority's opinion, the development would be relevant to a major accident.

3–155   Secondly, where a planning application is made for certain prescribed development within the vicinity of an existing establishment. Categories of development are prescribed for this purpose under Sch.8 of the Planning and Development Regulations 2001, and include developments of a type likely to be frequented by the public in large numbers, such as hotels, retail developments greater than 250 square metres or community and leisure facilities greater than 100 square metres. Also prescribed are categories of development likely to be used by persons with limited mobility, such as hospitals or crèches. Whether or not these categories of development are subject to the notification requirement is determined by reference to separation distances from major-accident establishments prescribed under Table 2 of Sch.8. The separation distances are calculated by reference to the type of major-accident establishment. Thus, for example, in the case of an establishment where explosives are manufactured, the notification requirement applies to prescribed development within a distance of 1,000 metres from the establishment perimeter. Shorter distances are prescribed in other instances. Thus, for example, a distance of 300 metres from the establishment perimeter is prescribed in the case of an establishment where non-pressurised flammable substances are stored in bulk.

3–156   If the proposed development is within the prescribed distance of an establishment, then the notification requirement arises. The notification requirement will also arise where the proposed development is located within such distance from a particular establishment as has been specified by the

---

[156] [2005] I.E.H.C. 344; [2006] 1 I.R. 388.

HSA in technical advice provided under art.27 of the European Communities (Control of Major Accident Hazards Involving Dangerous Substances) Regulations 2006.[157] The obligation to notify the HSA only arises where the HSA has not previously provided, either in relation to the development to which the application relates or on a generic basis, relevant technical advice on the risk or consequences of a major accident.

The third circumstance in which the notification requirement arises, where the planning authority is of opinion that the proposed development would be (i) in the vicinity of an establishment, and (ii) relevant to the risk or consequences of a major accident. In forming the requisite opinion, the planning authority is required to have regard to the tables of Sch.8. Again, the obligation to notify the HSA only arises is where the HSA has not previously provided, either in relation to the development to which the application relates or on a generic basis, relevant technical advice on the risk or consequences of a major accident.

3–157

Form of notification

Where the notification procedure applies, the planning authority is required to notify the HSA within three weeks of receipt of the application for planning permission. The planning authority is required to request a determination as to whether the European Communities (Control of Major Accident Hazards Involving Dangerous Substances) Regulations 2006 apply to the proposed development,[158] and to request, where the HSA determines that the said Regulations do apply, technical advice on the effects of the proposed development on the risk or consequences of a major accident.[159]

3–158

The request should be accompanied by a copy of the relevant planning application, and any environmental impact statement submitted with the planning application. Where the planning application relates to development within the vicinity of an establishment, the notice should identify the relevant establishment(s). The notice should also indicate, if applicable, that the development comprises, or is for the purposes of, an activity requiring an integrated pollution prevention and control licence or a waste licence.

3–159

The corresponding duty of the HSA to provide advice on land use planning is found under art.27 of the European Communities (Control of Major Accident Hazards Involving Dangerous Substances) Regulations 2006.

3–160

---

[157] S.I. No. 74 of 2006.
[158] Planning and Development Regulations 2001, art.139(3)(f) (as substituted by 2006 Regulations, art.33).
[159] Planning and Development Regulations 2001, art.139(3)(g) (as substituted by 2006 Regulations, art.33).

3. Public notice

3–161 Where an application relates to the provision of, or modifications to, an existing establishment, this fact must be indicated in the newspaper notice in respect of the application,[160] and in the site notice.[161]

4. No outline planning permission

3–162 An application for outline planning permission may not be made in respect of the provision of, or modifications to, a major-accident establishment.[162]

O. Limited Involvement of Elected Members in Decision-Making

3–163 The decision to grant or refuse planning permission is an executive function (as opposed to a reserved function). Thus, the decision is generally made by the manager or by some officer to whom the function has been properly delegated.

3–164 There is, however, provision for the elected members to have a limited involvement in the decision-making process. This may arise in two circumstances. First, planning permission may only be granted for development in material contravention of the development plan by resolution of the elected members.[163] The procedure in this connection is set out at para.3-132 above.

3–165 Secondly, the elected members may seek to pass a resolution directing that planning permission either be granted or refused. Under s.140 of the Local Government Act 2001 the elected members of a local authority may, by resolution, direct that any particular act, matter or thing be done or effected. It was established under the previous planning legislation that the statutory predecessor of s.140 (the infamous "Section 4 motion" under the City and County Management (Amendment) Act 1955) applied to the decision to grant planning permission.[164] Under s.139 of the Local Government Act 2001, the elected members may direct that a particular act not be done.

---

[160] Planning and Development Regulations, 2001, art.133.
[161] Form No. 1 of Sch.3 of the Planning and Development Regulations 2001 (as substituted by the 2006 Regulations).
[162] Planning and Development Regulations, 2001, art.134.
[163] PDA 2000, s.34(6).
[164] *P & F Sharpe Ltd. v Dublin City and County Manager* [1989] I.R. 701; [1989] I.L.R.M. 565. *Cf. Kenny Homes and Company Ltd. v Galway City and County Manager* [1995] 1 I.R. 178; [1995] 2 I.L.R.M. 586, where Blayney J. stated that it was very difficult to see what form a resolution could take which would leave the elected members free to consider all the options possible in determining a planning application (especially the imposition of conditions), and at the same time require a "particular act, matter or thing specifically mentioned in the resolution [...] to be done or effected".

It is important to note that there are very real limitations on the exercise of   **3–166**
these statutory powers. The general power of the elected members under s.140
of the Local Government Act 2001 to direct that a particular thing not be done
is not available in circumstances where, *inter alia*, the resolution would prevent
the performance of any function which the local authority is required by law or
by order of a court to perform. Similarly the power under s.139 of the Local
Government Act 2001 to direct that particular works not proceed is not available
where those works are required by or under statute.

It has to be said that a meeting of elected members does not represent an ideal   **3–167**
forum for the discharge of the quasi-judicial function involved in deciding an
application for planning permission. The political and public nature of such a
meeting may mean that the desired level of decorum may be lacking. There is
also a very real risk that the elected members will not observe the limitations
imposed on the matters which may legitimately be taken into account in
determining an application for planning permission. For example, the elected
members may take into account irrelevant matters such as the personal
circumstances of the applicant.[165]

It would appear from the judgment of the High Court in *Wicklow County Council*   **3–168**
v Wicklow County Manager[166] that the manager retains some autonomy in the
face of a resolution or direction under ss.139 and 140, and is entitled to disregard
a direction in circumstances where same is unlawful. On the facts, the invalidity
of a resolution directing that planning permission be refused stemmed from
the elected members having taken into account considerations irrelevant to
proper planning.

It also seems that the elected members must have some basis (such as an opinion   **3–169**
or report from another expert) before they may lawfully reject the advice of the
planning authority's own officials.[167] The requirement to consider what
conditions should be attached to a planning permission may also cause
difficulties.[168]

---

[165] *Flanagan v Galway City and County Manager* [1990] 2 I.R. 66; and *Griffin v Galway City and County Manager*, unreported, High Court, Blayney J., October 31, 1990.

[166] Unreported, High Court, Ó Caoimh J., February 26, 2003. *Cf. Kenny Homes and Company Ltd. v Galway City and County Manager* [1995] 1 I.R. 178; [1995] 2 I.L.R.M. 586 (manager not entitled to exercise any independent discretion as to whether he will obey the direction or not).

[167] *Child v Wicklow County Council* [1995] 2 I.R. 452. See also *Wicklow County Council v Wicklow County Manager*, unreported, High Court, Ó Caoimh J., February 26, 2003.

[168] *Kenny Homes and Company Ltd. v Galway City and County Manager* [1995] 1 I.R. 178; [1995] 2 I.L.R.M. 586.

P. Form of Decision

3–170   The form in which notification of a decision on a planning application is to be given is prescribed under art.31 of the Planning and Development Regulations 2001 (as substituted by the 2006 Regulations). Notification of the decision shall be given to the applicant, and to any other person or body who made a submission or observation, within three working days of the day of the decision and shall specify, *inter alia*, (a) the reference number of the application in the register; (b) the development to which the decision relates; (c) the nature of the decision; (d) the date of the decision; (e) in the case of a decision to grant permission, any conditions attached thereto; (f) the main reasons and considerations on which the decision is based, and where conditions are imposed, the main reasons for the imposition of any such condition; (g) that in deciding a planning application the planning authority, in accordance with s.34(3) of the PDA 2000, has regard to submissions or observations received; (h) in the event that the planning authority exercises its discretion under s.39(2) of the PDA 2000 to specify the purpose for which a structure may or may not be used, this should also be included as part of the decision; and (i) if the planning authority exercises its power under s.41 to vary the appropriate period or "life" of the planning permission, this too should be stated as part of the decision.

3–171   In addition, the notification should specify that an appeal against the decision may be made to An Bord Pleanála within the period of four weeks beginning on the date of the decision of the planning authority.[169] It should also be specified that in the event that there is no appeal to An Bord Pleanála within the period for the making of an appeal, the grant of permission shall be issued as soon as may be, but not earlier than three working days after the expiration of the period for the making of an appeal.[170]

3–172   It is likely that the notification requirements will be regarded as mandatory by the courts because of the importance given by the legislation, and reaffirmed by the courts, to public participation in the planning process.[171]

---

[169] Planning and Development Regulations 2001, art.31(k) (as amended by the 2006 Regulations).

[170] Planning and Development Regulations 2001, art.31(j) (as amended by the 2006 Regulations).

[171] *cf. Lynch v Dublin City Council*, unreported, High Court, Ó Caoimh J., July 25, 2003, where it was suggested that the consequences of a failure to give notification of decision might be lessened because of availability of other means of communication. On the particular facts of the case, it was unnecessary for the High Court to decide whether the requirement was mandatory or directory.

Q. Duty to State Reasons for Decision

1. Introduction

This entire topic is discussed in detail at paras 12–119 to 12–163. What follows **3–173** below is a summary of the principal statutory requirements.

Under s.34(10) of the PDA 2000, a planning authority is required to state the **3–174** main reasons and considerations on which its decision is based. The statutory obligation in this regard is replicated under the Planning and Development Regulations 2001 (as substituted by the 2006 Regulations).[172] There is an additional requirement under the Regulations to specify that, in deciding a planning application, the planning authority in accordance with s.34(3) of the PDA 2000 "has regard to submissions or observations" received by it.

The obligation under s.34(10) is more exacting than that which had applied **3–175** under the Local Government (Planning & Development) Acts. The planning authority is now required to state the "main reasons and considerations" on which the decision is based, rather than simply the "reasons" for the decision. The new wording replicates that found under the EIA Directive: see para.13–238

Prior to the amendments, the reasons given for planning decisions tended to be **3–176** formulaic, and in many cases involved little more than a recital of stock phrases such as that the proposed development would be "in accordance with proper planning and development" or "would not seriously injure amenities". Whereas the standard set for reasons was notionally high, in practice the courts were prepared to accept as adequate the most perfunctory of reasons. The new wording should result in more informative decisions.

2. Additional reasons in subsequent decisions

In *State (Aprile) v Naas UDC*,[173] the High Court examined the extent to which **3–177** a planning authority was entitled to rely on additional grounds for refusing planning permission in the event of a fresh planning application. O'Hanlon J. held that the fact that planning permission was refused on particular grounds did not amount to a representation that these were the only grounds on which the proposed development conflicted with the proper planning and development of the area, and additional grounds might be advanced subsequently. O'Hanlon J. then stated as follows.

> "This may seem to be calculated to work hardship on developers who incur expense in meeting objections raised to their first application, only to be

---

[172] Planning and Development Regulations 2001, arts 31(f) and (l) (as substituted by the 2006 Regulations).

[173] Unreported, High Court, O'Hanlon J., November 22, 1983.

confronted with new grounds when they have done so and renewed their application for permission. This difficulty can be surmounted quite readily, however, by a process of consultation between developers and the officials of the planning authorities and I believe that this is the course which is usually adopted in such circumstances."

3–178   It is submitted that the decision in *State (Aprile) v Naas UDC* should be viewed with some caution, and, in particular, may no longer be good law following the recasting of the wording of the duty to give reasons. It is in principle unfair to applicants not to indicate all of the fundamental objections to their proposed development in the decision on the application.

3. Reasons for conditions

3–179   Where conditions are imposed, the decision must state the main reasons for the imposition of any such conditions, provided that where a condition imposed is of a type expressly provided for under s.34(4), a reference to the paragraph of subsection (4) in which the condition is described shall be sufficient.

3–180   In *Killiney and Ballybrack Development Association Ltd. v Minster for Local Government*,[174] the Supreme Court stated that if the reasons given cannot fairly and reasonably be held to be capable of justifying the condition, then the condition cannot be said to be a valid exercise of the statutory power.

R. Time-Limit for Decision

1. Minimum period

3–181   The minimum period for the determination of an application for planning permission is generally five weeks, beginning on the date of the receipt of the application.[175] This period is extended to a minimum period of eight weeks where the planning authority has, by notice, made a request for further information or sought the production of evidence in support of the application.[176]

3–182   The minimum period for the determination of an application is not *expressly* extended where revised plans are received under art.34 of the Planning and Development Regulations 2001 (as substituted by the 2006 Regulations). In cases where the receipt of revised plans triggers further public notice under art.35, however, the planning authority should defer making its decision until the time allowed for the making of submissions and observations has elapsed.

---

[174] [1978] I.L.R.M. 78.
[175] Planning and Development Regulations 2001, art.30 (as substituted by 2006 Regulations).
[176] PDA 2000, s.34(8)(b).

In the case of EIA development which is likely to have significant effects on a transboundary State, a planning authority shall not make its decision until after (a) the views, if any, of any relevant transboundary State have been received in response to consultations under art.126(1), or (b) the consultations are otherwise completed.[177]

3–183

2. Maximum period(s)

Different time periods apply in respect of the maximum period allowed for determination. Failure by the planning authority to comply with the relevant time-limit may result in a decision to grant planning permission arising by default. The provision for default planning permission is considered in detail at paras 3-199 to 3–227.

3–184

Generally, a planning authority is required to make its decision within eight weeks beginning on the date of receipt by the planning authority of the application.[178] There are, however, a number of exceptions to this requirement, as follows.

3–185

(i) Request for further information or evidence

Where the planning authority has, by notice, made a request for further information or sought the production of evidence in support of the application, the decision shall be made within four weeks of the notice being complied with, provided that the total period is not less than eight weeks.[179] Thus the service of a request for further information or evidence stops time running for the purpose of a default planning permission. Time only runs again once both the (initial) request, and (presumably) any genuine request for clarification, have been complied with. Thereafter the period for the making of a decision will usually be four weeks.

3–186

Where the response to the request for further information contains "significant additional data"—and the planning authority has accordingly required the applicant to give further public notice under art.35—the four week period shall not commence until the planning authority has received copies of the public notices.[180]

3–187

Prior to the 2006 Regulations, the position—as interpreted by the High Court in *Maye v Sligo Borough Council*—had been that time ran from the date of the receipt by the planning authority of the response to the request for further

3–188

---

[177] Planning and Development Regulations 2001, art.130 (as substituted by the 2006 Regulations).
[178] PDA 2000, s.34(8)(a).
[179] PDA 2000, s.34(8)(b). This represents a modification of the previous legislation, where the (then) two month period effectively started afresh from the date of compliance with the notice; Local Government (Planning & Development) Act 1963, s.26(4).
[180] Planning and Development Regulations 2001, art.35(4)(a) (as substituted by the 2006 Regulations).

information.[181] This was so even where the planning authority required the giving of further public notice under art.35. This was unsatisfactory in that the time involved in (a) the planning authority considering the response and deciding whether to require further public notice, and (b) the developer arranging the further public notice, ate into the four week time period. Thus the period within which submissions in response to the public notices could be made might be very short. An attempt has been made to remedy this under the 2006 Regulations, but question marks have already been raised as the legality of amending the operation of the time-limit under s.34(8) by way of secondary legislation.[182]

3–189   If the request for information is not complied with after the period of six months—or such additional period, not exceeding three months, as may be agreed by the planning authority—the application for planning permission shall be declared to be withdrawn.[183]

(ii) Environmental impact statement: request for further information or evidence

3–190   In cases where the application has been accompanied by an environmental impact statement, the decision shall be made within eight weeks of the notice for further information or evidence being complied with.[184]

3–191   Where the response to the request for further information contains "significant additional data"—and the planning authority has accordingly required the applicant to give further public notice under art.35—the eight week period shall not commence until the planning authority has received copies of the public notices.[185] As discussed above at para.3–188, a question mark has been raised as to the legality of amending the operation of the time-limit under s.34(8) by way of secondary legislation.[186] Of course, in the case of EIA development, it may be possible to overcome any difficulty in this regard by giving a sympathetic interpretation to national law so as to ensure compliance with the requirements of the EIA Directive.[187]

3–192   In the case of EIA development which is likely to have significant effects on a transboundary State, an attempt has been made under the Planning and Development Regulations 2001 (as substituted by the 2006 Regulations) to modify the statutory time-limits as follows. Article 130 provides that a planning

---

[181] Unreported, High Court, Clarke J., April 27, 2007.
[182] *Maye v Sligo Borough Council*, unreported, High Court, Clarke J., April 27, 2007.
[183] Planning and Development Regulations 2001, art.33(3) (as substituted by the 2006 Regulations).
[184] PDA 2000, s.34(8)(c).
[185] Planning and Development Regulations 2001, art.35(4)(b) (as substituted by the 2006 Regulations).
[186] *Maye v Sligo Borough Council*, unreported, High Court, Clarke J., April 27, 2007.
[187] Clarke J. in *Maye v Sligo Borough Council* expressly left over any question as to the implications of the public participation requirements of EC law.

authority shall, notwithstanding s.34(8) of the PDA 2000, not decide to grant or refuse permission in respect of such a planning application until after (a) the views, if any, of any relevant transboundary State have been received in response to consultations under art.126(1), or (b) the consultations are otherwise completed. Again, it must be open to question as to whether it is lawful to amend primary legislation by secondary legislation in this way.

(iii) Material contravention procedure invoked

The next exception to the general eight week time-limit occurs where the proposed development would contravene materially the development plan, and the planning authority has set in train the special procedure to grant planning permission in material contravention. In such cases, the planning authority shall make its decision within the period of eight weeks beginning on the day on which the public notice of the intention of the planning authority to consider deciding to grant planning permission is first published.[188]   **3–193**

(iv) Major-accident hazards Directive

The final exception occurs where the proposed development would be likely to increase the risk of a major accident, or is of such a nature as to be likely, if a major accident were to occur and having regard to all the circumstances, to cause there to be serious consequences. In such cases, where a planning authority consults with a prescribed authority, *i.e.* the HSA, for the purpose of obtaining technical advice, the planning authority shall make a decision within four weeks beginning on the day on which the technical advice is received.[189] See, generally, paras 3–147 to 3–160.   **3–194**

3. Consent to extension of time

Provision is made under s.34(9) whereby the applicant for planning permission may give a consent in writing to the extension of the period for the making of the decision. The wording of this provision is different from that under the previous legislation.[190] In particular, it would appear that the consent in writing must be given within the initial eight week period. It would also seem that the extension is a one-off and that it is not possible to consent to a further extension of time.[191]   **3–195**

Where an applicant indicates—in response to an invitation by the planning authority under art.33—that he or she intends to submit revised plans, drawings or particulars, he or she must at the same time consent in writing to an extension of the period for making a decision.   **3–196**

---

[188] PDA 2000, s.34(8)(d).
[189] PDA 2000, s.34(8)(e).
[190] Local Government (Planning & Development) Act 1963, s.26(4A) (as inserted by Local Government (Planning & Development) Act 1976).
[191] *cf. Flynn & O'Flaherty Properties Ltd. v Dublin Corporation* [1997] 2 I.R. 558.

4. Appeals to An Bord Pleanála

3–197   In the case of an appeal to An Bord Pleanála, there is a general obligation on the board to ensure that appeals are disposed of as expeditiously as may be and, for that purpose, to take all such steps as are open to it to ensure that, insofar as is practicable, there are no avoidable delays at any stage in the determination of appeals.[192] This general obligation is subject to a more specific objective to ensure that every appeal is determined within a period of eighteen weeks beginning on the date of the receipt by the board of the appeal.[193] Where it appears to An Bord Pleanála that it would not be possible or appropriate to determine the appeal within the prescribed period, the board is required to serve notice in writing on the parties before the expiration of that period informing the parties of the reasons why it would not be possible or appropriate to determine the appeal, and to specify the date before which the board intends to determine the appeal. The board is then required to take such steps as are open to it to ensure that the appeal is determined before the date specified in the notice.

3–198   It should be noted that, unlike the position obtaining in respect of a decision by the planning authority, there is no provision for planning permission to arise by default in the case of an appeal to An Bord Pleanála. In this regard, the time-limits would appear to be largely an aspiration, and it does not appear that same would be enforceable before the courts. This issue was briefly considered by the High Court in *Dietacaron Ltd. v An Bord Pleanála*.[194] Quirke J. suggested that whereas the provisions of s.126 would appear to have been enacted primarily for the benefit of the applicant for planning permission, it was unlikely that they were not actionable at the suit of any other party. On the particular facts of the case it was unnecessary for the court to make an express finding on the issue: there was no breach of s.126 involved in that the delay was not "avoidable" given the scale and proportions of the proposed development. Moreover, Quirke J. was satisfied that the third party objector had been in no way prejudiced by the delay, and would have ample opportunity to participate fully in all stages of the appeal.

S. Default Planning Permission

1. An indefensible procedure

3–199   Where a planning authority fails to make a decision within the relevant time period, a decision by the planning authority to grant planning permission shall be regarded as having been given on the last day of that period.[195] This is

---

[192] PDA 2000, s.126(1).
[193] PDA 2000, s.126(2).
[194] [2005] 2 I.L.R.M. 32.
[195] PDA 2000, s.34(8)(f).

colloquially referred to as "default planning permission". The form of the decision is to grant planning permission *simpliciter* without any conditions.[196]

The existence of this default mechanism is indefensible. There is nothing to be said in its favour: it is inherently unfair; unpopular with judges; disproportionate to the mischief which it is intended to remedy; and inconsistent with other aspects of the PDA 2000. **3–200**

The seeming purpose of the default mechanism is to compel, as far as possible, a planning authority to consider and decide an application within the appropriate period.[197] The means chosen, however, are disproportionate to this aim. It would have been sufficient to make provision for a deemed *refusal* of planning permission, subject to an express right of appeal; this would then allow the applicant for planning permission to progress the matter before An Bord Pleanála. A deemed grant of planning permission goes too far, and provides the applicant with an unjustified windfall, *i.e.* a planning permission without any conditions attached, irrespective of the planning merits of the proposed development or the adverse impact on third parties. This setting at naught of third party rights is entirely inconsistent with the general tenor of the planning legislation, and, indeed, as discussed in detail at paras 14–189 to 14–193 may well be contrary to the European Convention on Human Rights. The legislation is not even consistent insofar as the objective of timely decision-making is concerned: as noted at para.3–198, there is no provision for planning permission to arise by default in the case of an appeal to An Bord Pleanála.[198] **3–201**

The default mechanism is unpopular with judges, and has been criticised in a number of cases.[199] The concerns were eloquently put by Blayney J. in *Molloy v Dublin County Council*.[200] **3–202**

> "The purpose is to ensure that planning authorities make a decision on planning applications within a reasonable time of their being submitted. Nobody could take issue with that. But what seems both illogical and objectionable is the nature of the sanction imposed in the event of the failure of the planning authority to communicate its decision within two months. One would expect the planning authority to be penalised for its failure, but it is not. It is the community that is penalised because a permission, which there may have been good grounds for refusing in the public interest, is deemed to have been granted. It would seem to

---

[196] *Burke v Westmeath County Council*, unreported, Supreme Court, June 18, 1998 (at p. 14).
[197] *State (Abenglen Properties Ltd.) v An Bord Pleanála* [1984] I.R 381 at 398; [1982] I.L.R.M. 590 *per* Walsh J.
[198] See further *Dietacaron Ltd. v An Bord Pleanála* [2005] 2 I.L.R.M. 32.
[199] See, for example, *Molloy v Dublin County Council* [1990] 1 I.R. 90 (at 97); *Flynn & O'Flaherty Properties Ltd. v Dublin Corporation* [1997] 2 I.R. 558; and *Illium Properties Ltd. v Dublin City Council* [2004] I.E.H.C. 327; unreported, O'Leary J., October 15, 2004. For an example of a case where a declaration of default planning permission was refused see *Burke v Westmeath County Council*, unreported, Supreme Court, June 18, 1998.
[200] [1990] 1 I.R. 90 at 97.

be a relatively simple matter to devise some alternative sanction which would achieve the same desirable purpose of having planning applications expeditiously dealt with, but which would not have the same potentially serious consequence for the community in the event of a failure on the part of a planning authority through error or inadvertence to comply with the statutory time limit, and I would hope that the legislature might give serious consideration to this suggestion."

3–203 It is regrettable that such sentiments were not taken on board at the time of the consolidation and reform of the planning legislation in 2000.

2. Section 34(8)(f)

3–204 Section 34(8)(f) of the PDA 2000 provides, in summary, that where a planning authority fails to make a decision within the appropriate period, a decision by the planning authority to grant planning permission shall be regarded as having been given on the last day of that period.

3–205 A number of points arise on the wording of this provision. First, it is to be noted that the requirement is that the decision be made within the relevant period: it is not necessary that the decision actually be *notified* within that period.[201] This represents a modification from the previous legislation (which required notice to be given),[202] and thus much of the earlier case law is no longer applicable.[203] Generally, it would appear that the date stated upon the order which gives effect to the decision is to be regarded as the date of the making of the decision, unless the contrary can be proved.[204]

3–206 The decision need not be a decision on the *merits* of an application, provided that the decision is determinative or dispositive of the application. Thus a decision to reject an application on the basis that there is an appeal pending to An Bord Pleanála in respect of the same development (or development of a similar type) is sufficient to stop time running.[205] By the same token, a decision to reject an application as invalid should also be sufficient to stop time running.

---

[201] Under art.31 of the Planning and Development Regulations 2001 (as substituted by the 2006 Regulations), notification of the decision shall be given to the applicant, and to any other person or body who made a submission or observation, within three working days of the day of the decision. In *Lynch v Dublin City Council*, unreported, High Court, Ó Caoimh J., July 25, 2003 it was suggested that the consequences of a failure to give notification of decision might be lessened because of the availability of other means of communication. On the particular facts of the case, it was unnecessary for the High Court to decide whether the requirement was mandatory or directory.

[202] Local Government (Planning & Development) Act 1963, s.26(4).

[203] *Flynn & O'Flaherty Properties Ltd. v Dublin Corporation* [1997] 2 I.R. 558; and *Freeney v Bray UDC* [1982] I.L.R.M. 29.

[204] *Keelgrove Properties Ltd. v An Bord Pleanála* [2000] 1 I.R. 47; [2000] 2 I.L.R.M. 168.

[205] *Swords Cloghran Properties Ltd. v Fingal County Council*, unreported, High Court, Herbert J., June, 2006.

It is well established that even an invalid decision is sufficient to prevent a default planning permission arising.[206]   **3–207**

> "In my view, the default provisions were enacted for the purpose of compelling a planning authority to direct its mind to an application. They do not amount to a statutory decree that every decision must be one which is sustainable in law. In my view a decision which, when questioned, is found to be *ultra vires* or unsustainable in law for any reason is nonetheless a 'decision' for the purposes of the default provisions. It is not possible to attribute to the Oireachtas the intention that every decision which has been proved to be unsustainable in law for one reason or another shall have the effect of giving the applicant permission for his proposed development—however outrageous it might be and however contrary to both the spirit and letter of the planning laws. It would require quite clear affirmative language in the statute to evidence any such legislative intention. No such language appears in the present legislation. Therefore, I am of opinion that a decision (within the meaning of that term in the default provisions of the statute) was given and that, therefore, the default procedure does not apply."

The second point arising on the wording of s.34(8) is that it provides for a deemed decision to grant planning permission, not an actual grant of planning permission. This would appear to be significant on a number of levels. The fact of a decision would seem to allow for an appeal (presumably by a third party) to be taken against the decision to An Bord Pleanála. It would also suggest that some further step is required before the grant of planning permission issues.[207] The procedure in this regard is discussed further at paras 3–219 to 3–221.   **3–208**

3. Application must be in accordance with regulations

A default planning permission is only available where the planning application has been made in accordance with the planning regulations and the requirements of the regulations have been complied with. The courts will insist on strict compliance with the requirements of the regulations governing an application for planning permission. Even minor defects in the form of the application, and, in particular, in the public notices, will preclude a default planning permission arising.[208]   **3–209**

---

[206] *State (Abenglen Properties Ltd.) v Dublin Corporation* [1984] I.R. 381 at 397, *per* Walsh J. See also *Swords Cloghran Properties Ltd. v Fingal County Council*, unreported, High Court, Herbert J., June, 2006.

[207] *cf. Freeney v Bray UDC* [1982] I.L.R.M. 29.

[208] *State (NCE Ltd.) v Dublin County Council*, unreported, Supreme Court, May 14, 1980, reversing High Court [1979] I.L.R.M. 249; *Monaghan UDC v Alf-a-bet Promotions Ltd.* [1980] I.L.R.M. 64 (public notice inadequate: failure to state nature and extent of development and omission of heading of city town or county); *Crodaun Homes Ltd. v Kildare County Council* [1983] I.L.R.M. 1 (public notice inadequate); *Dublin County Council v Marren* [1985] I.L.R.M. 593 (application not accompanied by such plans and such other particulars as were necessary to identify the land and to describe the works or structure to which the application related); *Murray v Wicklow County Council* [1996] 2 I.R. 552; [1996] 2 I.L.R.M. 411 (failure to pay proper fee; application lapsed in any event); and *Walsh v Kildare County Council* [2001] 1 I.R. 483 (failure to state applicant's address with sufficient particularity); *cf. Burke v Drogheda Corporation*, unreported,

4. Grant of planning permission must not be *ultra vires*

3–210   A default planning permission cannot arise unless the planning authority would have been lawfully entitled to grant planning permission for the particular development. In each of the examples discussed in detail below—material contravention and EIA development—a planning authority is required to comply with a prescribed procedure before it can grant planning permission. In each case, there are enhanced public consultation requirements, and an obligation to have regard to submissions and observations received before reaching a decision. If the planning authority purported to grant planning permission without going through these prescribed procedures, its decision would be *ultra vires*. In the circumstances, default planning permission is not available. If it were otherwise, a planning authority could evade mandatory procedural requirements by the simple expedient of delay. An analogy can be drawn in this regard with estoppel or legitimate expectation: neither of these doctrines will allow a planning authority to act *ultra vires*.

Material contravention

3–211   Default planning permission cannot arise where the proposed development would involve a material contravention of the development plan.[209] The rationale advanced for this is that the planning authority cannot grant planning permission for development in contravention of the development plan without first going through a rigorous procedure (involving, *inter alia*, public consultation, and a vote of the elected members),[210] and that the capacity to grant default planning permissions should be subject to similar constraints.[211] These important procedural safeguards—discussed in detail at para.1–28— would be set at naught were default planning permission available in such circumstances. The failure—whether accidental or deliberate—of the planning authority to make a decision within time cannot produce a result, *i.e.* the grant of planning permission, which it would not otherwise have been entitled to bring about.

3–212   The decisions of the High Court in *McGovern v Dublin Corporation*[212] and *Abbeydrive Developments Ltd. v Kildare County Council (No. 2)*[213] appear to

---

High Court, McWilliam J., June 11, 1982 (entitled to default outline planning permission); *Molloy v Dublin County Council* [1990] 1 I.R. 90 (minor defects in maps and plans); and *Frank Dunne Ltd. v Dublin County Council* [1974] I.R. 45 (misdescription of applicant).

[209] *State (Pine Valley Developments Ltd.) v Dublin County Council* [1984] I.R. 407; *Dublin County Council v Marren* [1985] I.L.R.M. 593; *Calor Teoranta v Sligo County Council* [1991] 2 I.R. 267; *P & F Sharpe Ltd. v Dublin City and County Manager* [1989] I.R. 701; [1989] I.L.R.M. 565; *Murray v Wicklow County Council* [1996] 2 I.R. 552; [1996] 2 I.L.R.M. 411; *McGovern v Dublin Corporation* [1999] 2 I.L.R.M. 314; and *Walsh v Kildare County Council* [2001] 1 I.R. 483.

[210] PDA 2000, s.34(6).

[211] See especially *State (Pine Valley Developments Ltd.) v Dublin County Council* [1984] I.R. 407; *Dublin County Council v Marren* [1985] I.L.R.M. 593; and *Maye v Sligo Borough Council*, unreported, High Court, Clarke J., April 27, 2007.

[212] [1999] 2 I.L.R.M. 314.

[213] Unreported, High Court, Murphy J., November 29, 2005.

have extended the requirement even further so as to restrict a default planning permission to an application which in the normal course of events is one which in principle is entitled to succeed. On the facts of *McGovern*, the development in respect of which a default planning permission was claimed was one of a type which was listed as "open for consideration" (as opposed to "normally permissible") under the relevant development plan. It was held by Barr J. that it would be unreal and potentially unjust to others to allow not only planning permission by default for a development which is "normally permissible" under the development plan, but also for development which is not "normally permissible" and for which sanction is dependent on the planning authority being satisfied that the proposed development is consistent with the proper planning and development of the area in the special circumstances of the case. With respect, the standard imposed in *McGovern* would seem to be too exacting. The essence of default planning permission is that the planning authority, having failed to make a decision within time, forfeits the right to adjudicate on the merits of the planning application: the question of whether or not the planning authority would have granted planning permission is then irrelevant. It is only necessary to consider whether or not the development represents a material contravention of the development plan in order to ensure that the restrictions ordinarily applicable to the grant of planning permission for such development are not by-passed.

The approach adopted in *McGovern* was followed in *Abbeydrive Developments*   **3–213**
Ltd. v Kildare County Council (No. 2).[214] Murphy J. suggested that a default planning permission will only be available where an application is "within the development plan". According to Murphy J. the onus is on the applicant for planning permission, not the planning authority, to demonstrate that there is compliance with the development plan. Where the proposed development is of a type which was open for consideration only, the development will only be permissible where the planning authority has actually had an opportunity to consider the proposed development and to decide whether it is consistent with proper planning.

This trend in the case law may now be reversed following the judgment in   **3–214**
Maye v Sligo Borough Council.[215] In the view of Clarke J., it was not appropriate to extend the limitations on an entitlement to default planning permission beyond the material contravention circumstances identified in *P & F Sharpe Ltd.*, and that to go further and involve the court in deciding questions of planning judgment as to what sort of planning permission might properly be allowed in a particular area would be wrong in principle.

Material contravention limitation unsatisfactory

Although there are certainly sound reasons for saying that a *grant* of planning   **3–215**
permission should not arise by default in the case of a material contravention,

---

[214] Unreported, High Court, Murphy J., November 29, 2005.
[215] Unreported, Clarke J., April 27, 2007.

the current position is unsatisfactory. It leaves certain applicants without any remedy against a dilatory planning authority. It is not the case that a planning authority can never grant planning permission in material contravention of the development plan: the legislation simply provides that a special procedure must be gone through.[216] Moreover, An Bord Pleanála has an express power to grant planning permission even if the proposed development contravenes materially the development plan.[217] The mischief which the provision for default planning permission appears to be intended to remedy is the failure of a planning authority to determine an application promptly; this mischief would seem to apply equally to proposed development which would involve a material contravention of the development plan. Indeed, an applicant for such development may well be anxious to obtain even a refusal from the planning authority, in order that the matter might then be pursued before An Bord Pleanála, where planning permission in material contravention of the development plan might be more readily obtained. To deny the possibility of a default decision is to leave such an applicant without any remedy in the face of delay on the part of the planning authority.[218] The obvious solution would be to provide for a deemed *refusal* of planning permission.

Environmental impact assessment

3–216   A default planning permission is not available where the proposed development is subject to the EIA Directive. The essence of environmental impact assessment is that an informed decision, subject to mitigation measures where appropriate, is made following a public consultation process. A default decision is the antitheses of this. Just as a planning authority is precluded from making a decision to grant planning permission for EIA development without carrying out the requisite assessment,[219] it cannot produce the same result by its inactivity.[220]

5. The effect of a request for further information

3–217   The service of a valid request for further information has the effect of stopping time running against the planning authority: once the request has been complied with, the planning authority has a further four weeks thereafter within which to make its decision.[221]

---

[216] A similar argument arises in the context of a claim for compensation. More specifically, the Supreme Court has recently held that a planning authority can serve a statutory notice barring compensation notwithstanding that the notice refers to development which would involve a material contravention of the development plan: *Ballymac Designer Village Ltd. v Louth County Council* [2002] 3 I.R. 247; [2002] 2 I.L.R.M. 481.

[217] PDA 2000, s.37(2).

[218] *cf. O'Neill v Clare County Council* [1983] I.L.R.M. 141 (damages).

[219] *R. (On the application of Wells) v Secretary of State for Transport, Local Government and the Regions* (Case C–201/02) [2004] E.C.R. I–723.

[220] See further Y. Scannell, *Environmental and Land Use Law* (Thomson Round Hall, Dublin, 2006), para.2–343.

[221] PDA 2000, s.38(8)(b). The total period allowed is not less than eight weeks.

The courts have held on a number of occasions that an invalid request for further information is ineffective to stop time running.[222] In reaching this conclusion, it seems to have been accepted that an invalid request for further information must be regarded as void *ab initio*.[223] The position in this regard is to be contrasted with that obtaining in respect of an invalid decision on a planning application: it has been held that even an invalid decision is sufficient to stop time running, for the purposes of the default mechanism.[224] One possible explanation for this difference in approach—suggested by O'Leary J. in *Illium Properties Ltd. v Dublin City Council*[225]—is that if an invalid request for further information were enough to stop time running this would set at nought the statutory provisions in respect of default planning permission by enabling the planning authority to effectively get unlimited extensions by the means of *ultra vires* requests. **3–218**

6. Procedure to claim default planning permission

Section 34(8)(f) provides for a deemed "decision" to grant, not an actual grant. In the event that the planning authority refuses to make the grant in the ordinary way (following the expiration of the period for the taking of an appeal),[226] the more conservative approach would be for the developer then to seek some form of declaratory relief from the High Court. The applicant is not required to first exhaust his rights by appealing to An Bord Pleanála before seeking judicial review.[227] **3–219**

It is not clear from the case law in relation to the previous legislation as to whether or not such proceedings should be taken pursuant to the special judicial review procedure applicable to challenges to planning decisions (now provided for under ss.50 and 50A of the PDA 2000). Strictly speaking, such declaratory proceedings would appear to be outside ss.50 and 50A in that same would not involve a challenge to the "validity" of a decision on an application: rather it is the failure to make a decision which is being challenged.[228] **3–220**

---

[222] *State (Conlon Construction Company Ltd.) v Cork County Council*, unreported, High Court, Butler J., July 31, 1975; *State (NCE Ltd.) v Dublin County Council* [1979] I.L.R.M. 249; *O'Connors Downtown Properties Ltd. v Nenagh UDC* [1993] 1 I.R. 1; and *Illium Properties Ltd. v Dublin City Council* [2004] I.E.H.C. 327; unreported, O'Leary J., October 15, 2004.

[223] As discussed at para.3–221, any challenge to the validity of the request for further information is itself subject to the eight week time-limit under ss.50 and 50A of the PDA 2000 (as amended by the 2006 Act).

[224] *State (Abenglen Properties Ltd.) v An Bord Pleanála* [1984] I.R 381; [1982] I.L.R.M. 590. See also *Swords Cloghran Properties Ltd. v Fingal County Council*, unreported, High Court, Herbert J., June, 2006.

[225] [2004] I.E.H.C. 327; unreported, O'Leary J., October 15, 2004.

[226] PDA 2000, s.34(11).

[227] *State (NCE Ltd.) v Dublin County Council* [1979] I.L.R.M. 249; *Molloy v Dublin County Council* [1990] 1 I.R. 90; and *Flynn & O'Flaherty Properties Ltd. v Dublin Corporation* [1997] 2 I.R. 558.

[228] *State (Pine Valley Developments Ltd.) v Dublin County Council* [1984] I.R. 407; and *Freeney v Bray UDC* [1982] I.L.R.M. 29. See also *dicta* in *Inver Resources Ltd. v Limerick*

3–221   As a result of the amendments introduced under the Planning and Development (Strategic Infrastructure) Act 2006, it is probably safer to proceed by way of an application under s.50. This will certainly be the case where the claim for a default planning permission is based on an allegation that some earlier step in the decision-making process was flawed. Thus, for example, if it is argued that a request for further information is invalid, then that request should itself be challenged within eight weeks, by way of an application under ss.50 and 50A.

7. Grounds for resisting a default planning permission

3–222   In principle, there are a number of grounds on which a planning authority might seek to resist a claim for a default planning permission. First, it might be argued that a decision was, in fact, made within time. In this regard, it is to be reiterated that—unlike the position under the previous legislation—it is not necessary that the decision have been notified or communicated to the applicant within the appropriate period.

3–223   Secondly, it can be argued that the application was not in accordance with or in compliance with the requirements of the planning regulations.

3–224   Thirdly, it might be argued that the proposed development was one which should have been subject to environmental impact assessment, or that the proposed development would involve a material contravention of the development plan.

3–225   Finally, the planning authority might urge the court to refuse relief as a matter of discretion. Factors which might be relevant in this regard would include the conduct of the applicant for planning permission. For example, if some act on the part of the applicant had contributed to the failure to make a decision in time, this might justify the refusal of relief. Thus in *Maye v Sligo Borough Council*,[229] the High Court indicated *obiter* that it would have refused relief to the applicant on the basis that no indication had been given to the planning authority that the applicant was contesting its view as to the operation of the statutory time-limit. The planning authority's notice to the applicant had stated that time would not run until a copy of the further public notice had been submitted to the planning authority. The applicant did not contest this at the time.

Corporation [1987] I.R. 159 at 161. It should also be noted that the wording of the previous legislation allowed for a staggered effect in that a decision might have been made within time only for an issue then to arise as to whether or not it was notified in time: the judgment in *Colgan v Dublin Corporation*, unreported, High Court, Costello J., March 19, 1991 appears to suggest that such a decision enjoys some sort of contingent validity, and that same would have to be set aside before a default planning permission could be declared. Under s.34(8), such a staggered effect cannot, of course, arise in that it is sufficient that the decision be made within time.

[229] Unreported, High Court, Clarke J., April 27, 2007.

The extent to which a court might, in the exercise of its discretion, take into   **3–226**
account the adverse impact which the default planning permission would have
on third parties is unclear. The High Court in *Maye v Sligo Borough Council*[230]
suggested that this is not a relevant factor, and that to impose a regime, under
the guise of judicial discretion, which would exclude significant developments
from the benefit of a default planning permission would amount in practice to
legislation by the courts.

This finding might have to be reconsidered in light of the European Convention   **3–227**
on Human Rights. If the adverse impact on third parties would be severe, then
it would be disproportionate to find in favour of a default planning permission.

T. Duty of Planning Authority in Case of Appeal

1.   Submission of documents to An Bord Pleanála

Where an appeal is made to An Bord Pleanála, a planning authority is required   **3–228**
to submit the following documents to the board within a period of two weeks
beginning on the day on which a copy of the appeal is sent to the planning
authority by the board: (i) a copy of the planning application concerned and of
any drawings, maps, particulars, evidence, environmental impact statement,
other written study or further information received or obtained by it from the
applicant; (ii) a copy of any (valid) submission or observation in respect of the
planning application[231] ; (iii) a copy of any report prepared by or for the planning
authority in relation to the planning application; and (iv) a copy of the decision
of the planning authority and a copy of the notification of the decision given to
the applicant.[232] The planning authority must also notify An Bord Pleanála
where the development is subject to transboundary consultation under Pt 10 of
the Planning and Development Regulations 2001 (as amended in 2006).[233]

The legal consequences of a failure to comply with the equivalent obligation   **3–229**
under the Local Government (Planning & Development) Acts[234] were
considered by the High Court in *McAnenley v An Bord Pleanála*.[235] Kelly J.
held that the statutory requirements in this regard were mandatory, and, further,
that on the facts of the case there had been substantial non-compliance with

---

[230] Unreported, High Court, Clarke J., April 27, 2007.
[231] The requirement to furnish copies of any (valid) submission or observation in respect of
the planning application was introduced for the first time under the Planning and
Development (Strategic Infrastructure) Act 2006.
[232] PDA 2000, s.128(1)(a) (as substituted by s.21 of the 2006 Act).
[233] Planning and Development Regulations 2001, art.127 (as substituted by the 2006
Regulations).
[234] Local Government (Planning & Development) Act 1992, s.6.
[235] [2002] 2 I.R. 763. See also *Jerry Beades Construction Ltd. v Dublin Corporation* [2005]
I.E.H.C. 406; unreported, McKechnie J., September 7, 2005 (failure to transmit an earlier
report prepared by a planner).

the obligations imposed on the planning authority. Kelly J. further held that, given the lacunae identified, he was not satisfied that the appeal to An Bord Pleanála was dealt with within jurisdiction or in accordance with law, and, consequently, the determination of An Bord Pleanála was quashed. The matter was remitted to An Bord Pleanála to be dealt with afresh.

2. Availability of documents

3–230   Under s.38 of the PDA 2000, where a planning authority gives its decision in respect of a planning application the following documents shall be made available within three working days for inspection and purchase by members of the public during office hours at the offices of the planning authority: (a) a copy of the planning application and of any particulars, evidence, environmental impact statement, other written study or further information received or obtained by the planning authority from the applicant in accordance with the regulations; (b) a copy of any submissions or observations in relation to the planning application which have been received by the planning authority; (c) a copy of any report prepared by or for the planning authority in relation to the planning application; (d) a copy of the decision of the planning authority in respect of the planning application and a copy of the notification of the decision given to the applicant; and (e) a copy of any documents relating to a contribution or other matter referred to in s.34(5).

U. Refusal of Planning Permission for Past Failures to Comply

3–231   Under s.35 of the PDA 2000 (as amended under the 2006 Act), a planning authority has a discretion to refuse planning permission by reference to the previous—and anticipated—conduct of a developer. The power applies where the planning authority is of the opinion that there is a "real and substantial risk" that the development in respect of which permission is sought would not be completed in accordance with the permission or its conditions. It is a prerequisite to the exercise of the power that the planning authority be satisfied that the applicant—or those with whom the applicant is connected by way of partnership or through a company—is not in compliance with a previous planning permission or its conditions.[236]

3–232   Where the planning authority considers there are good grounds for its being able to form the requisite opinion, it is required to afford the applicant an opportunity to make submissions as to why the planning authority should not

---

[236] The section applies where (a) the applicant carried out the non-compliant development; (b) a partnership of which the applicant is or was a member carried out the non-compliant development during the membership of the applicant; (c) a company related to, or a company under the same control as, the applicant carried out the non-compliant development; or (d) the non-compliant development was carried out by a company controlled by the applicant.

exercise its power to refuse planning permission.[237] If, having considered any submissions made, the planning authority proceeds to form the opinion that there is a "real and substantial risk" that the development would not be completed in accordance with the permission or its conditions, the planning authority must refuse to grant planning permission. There is no right of appeal to An Bord Pleanála against such a decision to refuse.

The applicant may, within eight weeks from the receipt of notification of a **3–233** decision to refuse, apply to the High Court for an order annulling the planning authority's decision. On the hearing of such an application, the High Court may, as it considers appropriate, confirm the decision of the authority; annul the decision and direct the authority to consider the applicant's application for planning permission without reference to the provisions of s.35; or make such other order as it thinks fit. The application is to be made by motion on notice to the planning authority, rather than by way of an application for judicial review under ss.50 and 50A.[238]

The time-limits for the determination of the application for planning permission **3–234** under s.34(8) are modified where the High Court directs the planning authority to consider the application for planning permission. Thus, for the purposes of default planning permission, time runs only from the date of perfection of the High Court order.[239]

---

[237] PDA 2000, s.35(4) (as inserted by the 2006 Act).
[238] PDA 2000, s.35(6) (as inserted by the 2006 Act).
[239] PDA 2000, s.35(6B) (as inserted by the 2006 Act).

CHAPTER FOUR

DECISION ON APPLICATION FOR PLANNING PERMISSION

A. Proper Planning and Sustainable Development

1. Introduction

The primary consideration in adjudicating on an application for planning **4–01** permission is the "proper planning and sustainable development of the area". It is expressly provided under s.34(1) of the PDA 2000 that in making its decision in relation to an application for planning permission the planning authority (and An Bord Pleanála on appeal)[1] shall be restricted to considering the proper planning and sustainable development of the area, with regard being had to a number of other prescribed matters.

There is no definition of "proper planning and sustainable development" **4–02** provided under the PDA 2000, and it is necessary therefore to seek guidance elsewhere under the legislation. In this regard, the provisions of s.34(4) setting out types of conditions which may be attached to a planning permission are most immediately relevant. Part XII of the PDA 2000 in relation to compensation is also of some assistance. Specifically, the schedule of reasons for refusal of planning permission which exclude the payment of compensation, and of conditions which similarly may be imposed without the payment of compensation, respectively,[2] are indicative of matters which come within the rubric of "proper planning and sustainable development". If a matter is sufficient to exclude compensation, it must *a fortiori* be a legitimate planning consideration.[3]

---

[1] PDA 2000, s.37.
[2] PDA 2000, Schs 4 and 5.
[3] See *Maher v An Bord Pleanála* [1993] 1 I.R. 439 at 448.

167

4–03   The statutory provisions in respect of the contents of development plans are also relevant. The contents of a development plan will often coincide with matters within the rubric of "proper planning and sustainable development". Often, but not always, coincide: "proper planning and sustainable development" is a wider concept which admits of exceptional matters which could not properly be the subject-matter of a general policy as stated in a development plan.[4]

4–04   It would seem that in order for a consideration to come within the concept of proper planning and sustainable development it must be rooted in some factual basis. Thus, for example, it was held in the context of telecommunications development that fear, apprehension and opposition within the local community with regard to the proposed development would not *per se* represent proper planning considerations, although it might well be that those factors which provoked such alleged fear, apprehension and opposition within the local community might themselves be matters which were relevant.[5]

2. "Of the area"

4–05   The qualification that it is the proper planning and sustainable development "of the area" which a planning authority (and An Bord Pleanála) is required to consider appears to be somewhat elastic. Section 34(2)(b) of the PDA 2000 provides, *inter alia*, that a planning authority shall have regard to the effect a particular decision by it may have on any area outside its functional area (including areas outside the State). This modification of the previous legislation would appear to be largely declaratory of the Supreme Court decision in *Keane v An Bord Pleanála*.[6] In *Keane*, the Supreme Court had indicated that the term "area" under the previous legislation[7] was not co-extensive with the "area of the relevant planning authority": it may encompass areas larger or smaller, including, where appropriate, the entire territory of the State, and, it may be, having regard to the breadth of the language used, "areas" or "places" outside the territorial limits of the State. The decision in *Keane* would also appear to be authority for the proposition that consideration of the effect outside the relevant area is not confined to deleterious effects: there was no reason why a planning authority or An Bord Pleanála should be obliged to have regard to an artificially defined catchment area in assessing the possible *benefits* of a development.

4–06   Section 34(2)(b) also provides that a planning authority shall consult with any other planning authority where it considers that a particular decision by it may

---

[4] See, for example, the decision in *Great Portland Estates v Westminster City Council* [1985] A.C. 661. This decision appears to suggest that personal circumstances which would not be a proper matter for inclusion in a development plan might nevertheless be a relevant consideration on an application for planning permission.
[5] *Eircell Ltd. v Leitrim County Council* [2000] 1 I.R. 479; [2000] 2 I.L.R.M. 81.
[6] [1998] 2 I.L.R.M. 241.
[7] Local Government (Planning & Development) Act 1963, s.26(5)(c).

have a significant effect on the area of that authority, and the planning authority shall have regard to the views of that other authority.

B. Relevant Considerations

The following examples of matters which come within the definition of "proper planning and sustainable development" provide useful illustrations of the scope of the concept.   **4–07**

1. Amenity

Matters related to amenity are a legitimate planning consideration. Thus in **4–08** *Maher v An Bord Pleanála*[8] the High Court held that it was clear that depreciation in value of property in the vicinity was a valid reason for refusing planning permission. In so finding, significance was attached to the fact that same is expressly referred to as one of the reasons for the refusal of planning permission which does not give any right to compensation.[9] By the same token, it is to be noted that compensation is also excluded where, for example, the proposed development would interfere with the character of the landscape or with a view or prospect of special amenity value or natural interest or beauty, any of which it is necessary to preserve,[10] or where the proposed development would cause serious air pollution, water pollution, noise pollution or vibration, or pollution connected with the disposal of waste.[11]

2. Public health and safety

The concept of proper planning and sustainable development would seem to **4–09** extend to matters of public safety. Thus, it is legitimate to refuse planning permission where the proposed development would endanger public safety by reason of traffic hazard.[12] Similarly, it is legitimate to take into account the fact that the proposed development would endanger or interfere with the safety

---

[8] [1993] 1 I.R. 439.
[9] For the purpose of excluding compensation under s.191 of the PDA 2000, the amenities injured must be those of property in the vicinity, and not amenities generally: *Abbeydrive Developments Ltd. v Kildare County Council* [2005] I.E.H.C. 209; unreported, Macken J., June 17, 2005. The decision of the Court of Appeal of England and Wales in *Lough v First Secretary of State* [2004] E.W.C.A. Civ. 905; [2005] 1 P. & C.R. 5; [2005] J.P.L. 208, indicates that the reduction in the value of property *per se* and without reference to loss of amenities, is not protected under Art.8 of the European Convention on Human Rights; see further Chapter 14.
[10] PDA 2000, Sch.4, para.8.
[11] PDA 2000, Sch.4, para.9.
[12] Again, this is a non-compensatable reason for refusal: PDA 2000, Sch.4, para.4. For a case where it was indicated that a refusal would be justified on this ground, see, for example, *P & F Sharpe Ltd. v Dublin City and County Manager* [1989] I.R. 701; [1989] I.L.R.M. 565.

of aircraft or the safe and efficient navigation thereof; endanger the health or safety of persons occupying or employed in a structure or any adjoining structure; or would be prejudicial to public health.[13]

3. Common good

4–10 The common good is a relevant consideration on an application for planning permission.[14] The concept of proper planning and sustainable development is not confined to the consequences of the development on the physical environment but entitles the decision-maker to take into account its impact (whether deleterious or beneficial) on people.[15] Thus, for example, it was held in one case that the fact that a proposed development would form a significant element of an internationally agreed network for marine navigation could properly be taken into account in determining an application.[16]

4. Prematurity

4–11 It is implicit from the provisions of the PDA 2000 in respect of compensation that planning permission may be refused on the basis of prematurity. A proposed development may be premature either by reference to physical constraints, or pending the making of certain statutory plans (in particular, a local area plan). Examples of the former type of constraint include, *inter alia*, where there is an existing deficiency in the provision of water supplies or sewerage services, or an existing deficiency in the road network serving the proposed development. It should be noted that, in assessing capacity of infrastructure, it is permissible for the planning authority or An Bord Pleanála to have regard, *inter alia*, to the requirements of other prospective development in respect of which planning permission has been granted, or which is indicated in the development plan. To put the matter another way, a planning authority has some discretion as to the allocation of scarce infrastructural capacity and the fact that there may be some capacity available does not mean that same must be allocated to the development in respect of which the application for planning permission is made.

4–12 The position in respect of the latter type of constraint, namely where the proposed development might be considered premature pending the making of certain statutory plans, is more difficult to state. To take the example of a local area plan, it would seem that whereas a planning authority or An Bord Pleanála have a *discretion* to consider a draft local area plan,[17] they would equally be entitled simply to refuse planning permission on the basis that no plan has yet

---

[13] PDA 2000, Sch.4, para.10.
[14] *Keane v An Bord Pleanála* [1998] 2 I.L.R.M. 241 at 262.
[15] *Keane v An Bord Pleanála* [1998] 2 I.L.R.M. 241 at 260–261.
[16] *Keane v An Bord Pleanála* [1998] 2 I.L.R.M. 241 at 260–261.
[17] PDA 2000, s.18(3).

been formally made.[18] A distinction should be drawn between those cases where the proposed development would be inconsistent with the current draft of the statutory plan, and those where it would be compatible. If planning permission were granted in the former case this would compromise the draft, and frustrate its ever being implemented. The more conservative approach would be to refuse planning permission: if the draft was not adopted, the applicant might then re-apply for planning permission.[19] Conversely, if the development is consistent with the draft, it might be thought to be unduly formalistic to delay granting planning permission until such time as the draft is officially adopted. Reference is made in this regard to the Department of the Environment, *Development Control Advice and Guidelines* (October 1982).[20] There it was suggested that a planning authority should consider the provisions likely to be included in the relevant plan and satisfy itself that there is a real possibility that the proposed development will be likely to be incompatible with these provisions or to frustrate the implementation of the plan in some material respect. The guidelines go on to state that the absence of a plan, or the fact that a plan may not have been formally approved by the planning authority, should not be used to justify refusal based on prematurity in cases where, having regard to the situation on the ground, or previous planning decisions, the range of options available is so small as to enable an *ad hoc* assessment of the development proposal to be carried out without difficulty.

Finally it should be noted that in order for the statutory entitlement to compensation to be excluded where planning permission is refused for reasons of prematurity, it is necessary that there should be some prospect of the current constraints on development being resolved: the term "premature" intimates that the development may be carried out at a later (ascertainable) date but that as yet it is too early.[21]   **4–13**

5. Precedent

It would appear that previous decisions of the planning authority, and, in particular, of An Bord Pleanála, may, in principle, be relevant to a subsequent application. Various provisions of the PDA 2000 would appear to recognise, by implication, that the fact that planning permission has been granted for certain development may serve as a precedent for the grant of planning permission for other development in the same area. For example, one of the circumstances in which An Bord Pleanála is entitled to overturn a decision of   **4–14**

---

[18] PDA 2000, Sch.4, para.3.
[19] See the decision in *Myton v Minister of Housing & Local Government* (1963) 16 P. & C.R. 240.
[20] At para.4.8 of the guidelines.
[21] *Hoburn Homes Ltd. v An Bord Pleanála* [1993] I.L.R.M. 368. See also *O'Connor v Clare County Council*, unreported, High Court, Murphy J., February 11, 1994. For the position under the European Convention on Human Rights, see the discussion of *Skibinscy v Poland* Application No. 52589/99; November 14, 2006 at para.14–92.

the planning authority at first instance to refuse planning permission on the grounds that a proposed development materially contravenes the development plan, is where the board considers that permission for the proposed development should be granted having regard to the pattern of development, and permissions granted, in the area since the making of the development plan.[22] Somewhat surprisingly, however, the only *express* reference to the consideration of previous decisions is in the context of appeals against conditions.[23]

4–15 Whereas the decisions of An Bord Pleanála are generally available for public inspection,[24] the better view would be that it may be necessary on occasion for the board to give notice to an applicant of an intention to have regard to a previous decision, at least where that previous decision is to be treated as conclusive.[25]

4–16 Although, as appears from the foregoing, it would seem that the decision on an application may in general terms be *guided* by precedent, the extent to which such precedents are *determinative* of the application, or are binding, is uncertain. This is a matter of degree: it is one thing to say that the pattern of development permitted in an area is such as to justify the grant of planning permission for further development, it is quite another to say that planning permission must be granted.

4–17 It has been suggested recently by the High Court of England and Wales in *McCarthy v Secretary of State for Communities and Local Government*[26] that the fact that development may attract further *unauthorised* development is a relevant consideration in deciding whether to refuse planning permission. Planning permission had been refused for a caravan site on the basis that it would create a precedent for further development at the location in question, which would be undesirable given the adverse impact on the countryside of the existing lawful development. The High Court found that this was a relevant consideration.

---

[22] PDA 2000, s.37(2)(b)(iv). See also PDA 2000, Sch.4, para.7 "The proposed development, by itself or by the precedent which the grant of permission for it would set for other relevant development, would adversely affect the use of a national road or other major road by traffic." See also Sch.4, para.11 "The development would contravene materially a condition attached to an existing permission for development."

[23] PDA 2000, s.139(2). An Bord Pleanála is restricted to considering, *inter alia*, the terms of any previous permission considered by the board to be relevant. As to the considerations relevant to this type of appeal, see generally *MCD Management Services Ltd. v Kildare County Council* [1995] 2 I.L.R.M 532 at 542–543. *Cf. Ashbourne Holdings Ltd. v An Bord Pleanála* [2002] 1 I.L.R.M. 321 (High Court).

[24] PDA 2000, s.146.

[25] *Stack v An Bord Pleanála*, unreported, High Court, O'Neill J., July 11, 2000 (at pp. 9-10) (application for leave to apply for judicial review). *Cf. Stack v An Bord Pleanála (No. 2)*, unreported, High Court, Ó Caoimh J., March 7, 2003. See also, by analogy, *State (Irish Pharmaceutical Union) v Employment Appeals Tribunal* [1987] I.L.R.M. 36. *Cf. Fairyhouse Club Ltd. v An Bord Pleanála*, unreported, High Court, Finnegan J., July 18, 2001 (at pp.10–11) (application for leave to apply for judicial review).

[26] [2006] E.W.H.C. 3287 (Admin); December 20, 2006.

"The reason why the setting of a precedent is a potentially material consideration is because it may lead to events occurring which have effects which are of significance in planning terms, such as an effect on the appearance of the area, on its amenities, on the use of facilities, on highway safety or on other planning considerations. If such effects would be harmful, the decision maker is entitled to take them into account as material considerations, which could, in appropriate cases, justify refusal. Why must it be any different if such development were unauthorised? Unauthorised development can itself affect the appearance of an area, or the use of the local road network, or in the case of unauthorised residential development, the provision or take up of services in an area. It would be illogical if such potential consequences were prevented from being material even if the decision maker had concluded that such events and effects were likely. Of course there may be arguments to be made to the decision maker on whether the same weight should be attached to the potential for unauthorised development, because steps can be taken to seek its removal, but that is not to deprive it of potential relevance as a material consideration, and matters of weight are for the decision maker and not for this Court."

6. Res judicata

It has been held that the doctrine of *res judicata* may apply, in principle, to planning decisions.[27] In practice, the doctrine is of little significance in that the courts have indicated that primary consideration is to be given to the proper planning and (sustainable) development of the area,[28] and, accordingly, that a change in circumstances will justify departing from a previous decision.[29] The point is most dramatically illustrated by reference to the case law in relation to the old law of outline planning permissions.[30] If there was a change in the proper planning and (sustainable) development of the area in the interim between the grant of outline planning permission and the application for approval, then the planning authority or An Bord Pleanála were entitled to refuse the approval,[31] or to revise conditions already attached to the outline   **4–18**

---

[27] *Ashbourne Holdings Ltd. v An Bord Pleanála* [2003] 2 I.R. 114; [2003] 2 I.L.R.M. 446; and *Delgany Area Residents Association Ltd. v Wicklow County Council*, unreported, High Court, Barr J., May 28, 1998 (at p. 17). See also *obiter dicta* in *State (Kenny) v An Bord Pleanála*, unreported, Supreme Court, December 20, 1984 (at p. 8). See, more generally, *Athlone Woollen Mills (Company) Ltd. v Athlone UDC* [1950] I.R. 1.

[28] *State (Tern Houses (Brennanstown) Ltd.) v An Bord Pleanála*, unreported, High Court, Barron J., July 11, 1985.

[29] This is implicit in the decision in *State (Kenny) v An Bord Pleanála*, unreported, Supreme Court, December 20, 1984 (at p. 8) "I do not find it necessary to express a view as to the application of *res judicata* in respect of decisions although I find it difficult to see how a planning authority can be permitted to come to a new or different view when circumstances do not change."

[30] The status of an outline planning permission has since been enhanced under PDA 2000, s.36.

[31] *State (Tern Houses (Brennanstown)) Ltd. v An Bord Pleanála* [1985] I.R. 725: "Accordingly, if there was a conflict between the immediate implementation of an outline permission and the proper planning and development of the area, it is the latter which must prevail."

planning permission.[32] If it was possible, in effect, to retrench on the terms of an outline planning permission (which grant, by definition, must have been directly relevant to the decision in hand), then it would seem to follow *a fortiori* that it must also be possible to depart from lesser precedents.

4–19 In *Grealish v An Bord Pleanála (No. 1)*,[33] the applicant had sought to argue that the failure of An Bord Pleanála to grant a further planning permission in respect of an advertisement sign was inconsistent. An Bord Pleanála had granted, on two consecutive occasions, temporary planning permissions for development consisting of a tri-vision rotating advertising sign. In each instance, the reason for granting only temporary planning permission was stated in terms of allowing an assessment of the effects or impact of the development. Leave to apply to challenge the subsequent refusal was denied because the basic ingredients necessary to bring the doctrine of *res judicata* into play were missing. In particular, the second of the three planning permissions was not intended to be a final decision permitting the development to endure for all time, but rather only authorised the development for a temporary period.

4–20 The importance of the doctrine of *res judicata* is further undermined by the fact that an earlier grant of planning permission by An Bord Pleanála in material contravention of the development plan does not absolve the planning authority from the requirement to invoke the special material contravention procedure[34] in the event of a subsequent application. In other words, far from being bound by the earlier decision of An Bord Pleanála, the planning authority, in the absence of the requisite resolution, would be required to refuse planning permission. In such circumstances, it is difficult to regard there as being any meaningful system of precedent.

4–21 Finally, it should be noted that the only express reference in the PDA 2000 to applications for similar development is to be found in s.37(5). The effect of this provision is that no application for planning permission for the same development, or for development of the same description, may be made until any appeal to An Bord Pleanála is resolved (whether by decision, withdrawal or dismissal). The purpose of this provision is to assert the primacy of the decision of An Bord Pleanála as the appellate body and to prevent the altogether inappropriate circumstance of the same issue being considered simultaneously by the planning authority and An Bord Pleanála with the unacceptable possibility of divergent conclusions.[35] The section may also have the benefit of preventing a potential abuse whereby a number of applications might be made, in quick succession, for the same or similar development in the hope that third party objectors might fail to make submissions or representations in

---

[32] *Irish Asphalt Ltd. v An Bord Pleanála*, unreported, High Court, Costello P., July 28, 1995.

[33] [2006] 1 I.L.R.M. 140.

[34] PDA 2000, s.34(4).

[35] *Swords Cloghran Properties Ltd. v Fingal County Council*, unreported, High Court, Herbert J., June 2006.

respect of each individual application. Any dispute as to whether the application is for the same development or for development of the same description may be referred to An Bord Pleanála for determination.[36] In *Swords Cloghran Properties Ltd. v Fingal County Council*, it was indicated that if the only issue between the parties was whether the development was the same, or development of the same description, judicial review would have been refused as a matter of discretion on the basis that An Bord Pleanála was uniquely equipped to resolve this factual issue.[37]

7. Planning history of lands

The previous planning history of the lands is a relevant consideration. It would seem that representations made by the applicant in previous applications might also be a relevant consideration.[38]   **4–22**

There is a tension between the desire for consistency in decision-making and the requirement that each application for planning permission be considered on its own individual merits. Reference is made in this regard to *North Wiltshire District Council v Secretary of State for the Environment*.[39]   **4–23**

> "One important reason why previous decisions are capable of being material is that like cases should be decided in a like manner so that there is consistency in the appellate process. Consistency is self-evidently important to both developers and development control authorities. But it is also important for the purpose of securing public confidence in the operation of the development control system. I do not suggest and it would be wrong to do so, that like cases *must* be decided alike. An inspector must always exercise his own judgment. He is therefore free upon consideration to disagree with the judgment of another but before doing so he ought to have regard to the importance of consistency and to give his reasons for departure from the previous decision.
> To state that like cases should be decided alike presupposes that the earlier case is alike and is not distinguishable in some relevant respect. If it is distinguishable then it usually will lack materiality by reference to consistency although it may be material in some other way. Where it is indistinguishable then ordinarily it must be a material consideration. A practical test for the inspector is to ask himself whether, if I decide this case in a particular way am I necessarily agreeing or disagreeing with some critical aspect of the decision in a previous case? The areas for possible agreement or disagreement cannot be defined but they would include interpretation of policies, aesthetic judgments and assessment of need. Where there is disagreement then the inspector must weigh the previous decision and give his reasons for departure from it. These can on occasion be short, for example in the case of disagreement on aesthetics. On other occasions they may have to be elaborate."

---

[36] PDA 2000, s.37(5).
[37] Unreported, High Court, Herbert J., June, 2006.
[38] *Ashbourne Holdings Ltd. v An Bord Pleanála* [2002] 2 I.L.R.M. 321 (High Court). This matter was not considered in the same detail by the Supreme Court: [2003] 2 I.R. 114; [2003] 2 I.L.R.M. 446.
[39] (1992) 65 P. & C.R. 137.

4-24   If too great a weight is given to a previous decision, it may well leave the decision-maker open to the accusation that it has fettered its discretion. This issue arose for consideration in *FitzGerald v An Bord Pleanála*.[40] The case concerned the proposed development of a house. The inspector dealing with the appeal had, in the context of an earlier application, previously recommended the refusal of planning permission on grounds of traffic safety. An Bord Pleanála did not follow his recommendation on that occasion, and instead made a decision to grant planning permission. In his report on a subsequent application for similar development—the subject-matter of the judicial review proceedings—the inspector stated that while he had not changed his opinion that the safety of the road access to this site was questionable, he did not consider that any circumstances had changed since the last appeal to justify a refusal. An Bord Pleanála in its decision stated that, having regard to the planning history of the site, it considered that the proposed development would be in accordance with the proper planning and sustainable development of the area. Murphy J. refused leave to apply for judicial review. The judgment attaches some significance to the fact that the inspector in the context of the second appeal had placed reliance on a condition requiring that the vehicular entrance should be located at the western end of the site frontage.

Previous material contravention of development plan

4-25   The fact that development in material contravention of the development plan has already been permitted on the lands might be relevant as establishing a non-conforming use. As indicated above, however, at para.4-20, the fact that planning permission has previously been granted in material contravention of the development plan does not absolve the planning authority from the requirement to invoke the special material contravention procedure in the event of a subsequent application. The pattern of development, and permissions granted, in the area since the making of the development plan, are considerations which would justify An Bord Pleanála overturning a decision by the planning authority, at first instance, to refuse to grant planning permission in material contravention of the development plan.[41] Moreover, the fact that a development would contravene materially a condition attached to an existing permission for development is a reason for refusal which excludes the payment of compensation, and *a fortiori* would seem to be a legitimate planning consideration.[42]

---

[40] [2005] I.E.H.C. 372; unreported, Murphy J., November 11, 2005. See also *Dunne v An Bord Pleanála* [2006] I.E.H.C. 400; unreported, McGovern J., December 14, 2006, where an argument that the board had erred in law in placing too much weight on the previous planning history of the application site was rejected.

[41] PDA 2000, s.37(2).

[42] See PDA 2000, Sch.4, para.11.

8. Existing development rights

It is not open to use the occasion of the grant of planning permission to seek to **4–26** encroach on existing development rights.[43] Thus, for example, if a developer had an existing right to maintain twenty five gaming machines on the ground floor of his premises, a planning authority could not restrict that right to eight machines under the guise of the imposition of a condition upon the grant of a *further* planning permission.[44] It does seem, however, that in the case of an application to carry out additional development, for example, the extension of premises, it may be legitimate to have regard to the fact that the existing use of the lands is unauthorised. To put the matter another way, whereas it would be unlawful to attempt to curtail the existing use, the planning authority is entitled to say, in its discretion: "we cannot stop this use (except with compensation) but on planning considerations we do not like it and we do not wish to encourage or extend it either in nature or in duration; the applicant can go on exercising it in his existing buildings but we are not going to permit him to put up any new buildings".[45]

9. Alternative sites

In certain circumstances, the availability and suitability of alternative sites for **4–27** the location of the proposed development will be a valid consideration. This will generally occur where the proposed development will have adverse effects on the environment. An example of such a development might be the use of land as a travellers' halting site: the Supreme Court decision in *Ferris v Dublin Corporation*[46] appears to suggest that it is consistent with proper planning and (sustainable) development to allow such development on a temporary basis in a particular area pending the availability of a more suitable location. Furthermore, where a proposed development requires the submission of an environmental impact statement, one of the factors which must be included is an outline of the main alternatives studied by the developer and an indication of the main reasons for his or her choice, taking into account the effects on the environment.[47] Perhaps the most sophisticated requirement to consider alternative sites is to be found under the Retail Planning Guidelines,[48] which require the application of a sequential test.

---

[43] *State (O'Hara and McGuinness Ltd.) v An Bord Pleanála*, unreported, High Court, Barron J., May 8, 1986.
[44] *ibid*. On the facts, the argument failed.
[45] *Western Fish Products Ltd. v Penwith DC* [1981] 2 All E.R. 204 at 226.
[46] Unreported, Supreme Court, November 7, 1990.
[47] Planning and Development Regulations 2001, art.94.
[48] These guidelines were made pursuant to PDA 2000, s.28 and came into effect on January 2, 2001.

10. Private interests

4–28 It has been held that the express statutory statement that a person shall not be entitled solely by reason of a planning permission to carry out development[49] has the consequence that a planning authority (or An Bord Pleanála) cannot be said to have authorised the developer by the grant of a permission to commit an act which would be otherwise unlawful (because it interfered, for example, with the right to light of other property owners).[50] Private law remedies (whether in nuisance, trespass or otherwise) remain available to an aggrieved neighbour. This might be taken as suggesting that the decision on an application for planning permission should be informed by public law issues only. Certain *obiter dicta* in *State (Boyd) v Cork County Council*,[51] however, suggest that it may be permissible on occasion to have regard to private interests. Specifically, Murphy J. indicated that:

> "[W]hilst it is true that planning permission does not confer a licence on the grantee relieving him from the obligation which he owes in tort to his neighbour not to cause unlawful damage to the premises which he owns or occupies, that does not mean that the possibility of such damage takes the matter out of the sphere of planning considerations."

11. Planning gain

4–29 A public benefit or planning gain offered by a developer enjoys an anomalous status in the context of an application for planning permission.[52] Although the exacting of such a planning gain is not permissible save where expressly authorised by statute (for example, by way of development contribution),[53] it seems that where a developer *volunteers* a planning gain, same can be taken into account in determining the application.[54] There are two obvious criticisms which can be levelled at this position. First, the inconsistency in approach between matters which can be the subject of conditions or can justify the refusal of planning permission, and other matters which apparently may nevertheless be relevant considerations, would appear difficult to justify. The principles which govern the refusal of planning permission, and the attachment of conditions, are well established and include rules such as that same must be related to proper planning and sustainable development, or must be related to the permitted development. To allow consideration of matters which would

---

[49] PDA 2000, s.34(13).

[50] *Convery v Dublin County Council* [1996] 3 I.R. 153 at 173.

[51] *State (Boyd) v An Bord Pleanála*, unreported, High Court, Murphy J., February 18, 1983 (at p. 5).

[52] For an excellent discussion of planning gain, see Y. Scannell, *Environmental and Land Use Law* (Thomson Round Hall, Dublin, 2006), paras 2–313 to 2–321.

[53] See *Bord na Mona v An Bord Pleanála* [1985] I.R. 205 at 210. The requirements of Pt V of the PDA 2000 (as amended) (social and affordable housing) represent a dramatic example of an express requirement for a planning gain.

[54] See *Ashbourne Holdings Ltd. v An Bord Pleanála* [2002] 2 I.L.R.M. 321 (High Court). See, generally, G. Simons, "Planning conditions and planning gain" (1994) 1 I.P.E.L.J. 12.

otherwise represent an irrelevant consideration simply because same are introduced by the applicant smacks of expediency.

Secondly and more significantly, the system runs the risk of abuse. Developers **4–30** may feel obliged to offer some form of planning gain lest their failure to do so result in their application being refused (albeit that the statement of reasons for refusal may not make any express reference to planning gain).

The entire question of planning gain was considered by the Supreme Court in **4–31** *Ashbourne Holdings Ltd. v An Bord Pleanála.*[55] Hardiman J., having cited with approval certain passages in the first edition of Scannell, *Environmental and planning law in Ireland* (Round Hall Press, Dublin, 1995), went on to state as follows.

> "Two things, in particular, underlie the state of affairs summarised by Professor Scannell in the last paragraph. The first is that a local authority, like a court of limited jurisdiction or other decision-making bodies, may be concerned with matters which are hugely important to persons who come before it. In such circumstances those who must appear before or apply to such a tribunal may be prepared to offer or agree to payments or other conditions which would be wholly outside the tribunal's jurisdiction to impose.
>
> Secondly, if such a body accepts what is offered or takes advantage of the acquiescence of a person before it in conditions which it could not impose, that fact will become known to professional people in the relevant area. They, in turn, seeing that such offers or acquiescence had produced a successful outcome in previous cases, will advise clients with new business to consider similar offers or acquiescence. If this process continued, it may lead to the situation in which a body's apparent jurisdiction, conferred by law, is only a very imperfect guide to its actual practice. Only an insider or a shrewdly advised person would know the true position and only a wealthy applicant could take advantage of it."

These considerations appear to have informed the exercise of the court's **4–32** discretion. More specifically, the respondent decision-maker, An Bord Pleanála, had urged that relief by way of judicial review should be refused as a matter of discretion on account of what it alleged was the applicant company's acquiescence in the unlawful conditions. (It had been suggested that the applicant company had offered or volunteered some form of planning gain in terms of public access to its lands.) Hardiman J. ruled that relief should not be refused, and suggested that it is particularly important that the principle that estoppel, acquiescence or consent does not avail against an invalid substantive decision be maintained in the public interest, so as to assert the principle of fairness as between one applicant for an identical or analogous permission and another, and so as to safeguard the integrity and transparency of the planning code.

[55] [2003] 2 I.R. 114; [2003] 2 I.L.R.M. 446.

12. Compulsory purchase order

4–33   The High Court held in *State (Sweeney) v Minister for the Environment*[56] that a planning authority was entitled to refuse outline planning permission on the basis that the application was premature having regard to the service of a compulsory purchase order. The applicant was held not to be prejudiced in that the refusal would not prejudge a subsequent application for planning permission in the event that the compulsory purchase order was not to be confirmed; nor did the refusal prejudice compensation in the event of the compulsory purchase order being confirmed.

C. Irrelevant Considerations

4–34   The following are illustrative of matters which do not come within the concept of proper planning and sustainable development.

1. Compensation

4–35   The refusal of planning permission (or the grant of planning permission subject to onerous conditions) gives rise to a *prima facie* entitlement to the payment of compensation.[57] This entitlement to compensation is lost in certain circumstances; in particular, where planning permission is refused for certain prescribed reasons.[58] It is well established that a planning authority is not entitled to have regard to a desire to exclude a claim for compensation in adjudicating on a planning application.[59] Accordingly, it is unlawful both to grant planning permission which would otherwise be refused merely to forestall a claim for compensation,[60] or to insert a non-compensatable reason into the statement of reasons for refusal other than in circumstances where same is properly applicable.[61]

2. Pre-existing works in an application for retention planning permission

4–36   The fact that a structure would have to be demolished if retention planning permission were refused has been held not to be a relevant planning

---

[56] [1979] I.L.R.M. 35.

[57] PDA 2000, s.190.

[58] PDA 2000, s.191. The reasons for refusal of planning permission which exclude compensation are set out in the Fourth Schedule of the PDA 2000.

[59] *Grange Developments Ltd. v Dublin County Council* [1989] I.R. 296 at 317–318; and *Dublin County Council v Eighty Five Developments Ltd. (No. 2)* [1993] 2 I.R. 392; [1992] I.L.R.M. 815.

[60] Indirect support for this proposition is to be found in *Grange Developments Ltd. v Dublin County Council* [1989] I.R. 296 at 317–318.

[61] *Dublin County Council v Eighty Five Developments Ltd. (No. 2)* [1993] 2 I.R. 392; [1992] I.L.R.M. 815.

consideration.[62] This makes some sense: were the existence of the structure to be a relevant consideration, a developer would be in a position to benefit from his own wrongdoing, namely his failure to apply for planning permission in advance of carrying out the development.

A more pragmatic approach has been taken by the Courts of England and Wales, however. In *R. v Leominster District Council, Ex p. Pothecary*,[63] the Court of Appeal held that a planning authority was not merely entitled, but in practice bound, to take account of the existence of the unauthorised structure when determining an application for retrospective planning permission. Schiemann L.J. suggested that there would be situations where the planning authority would not have given permission for the development if asked for permission for precisely that which had been built, but the development would not so be objectionable that it would be reasonable to require it to be pulled down.

4–37

More recently, in *South Bucks District Council v Porter (No. 2)*,[64] the House of Lords indicated that the unlawfulness of development might well militate *against* the grant of retrospective planning permission. Lord Brown of Eaton-Under-Heywood suggested that where the applicant for planning permission sought to rely on his or her long use of the lands in support of the application, it must be material to recognise the unlawfulness (if such it was) of that use as a consideration operating to weaken the claim.

4–38

3. Personal circumstances

Planning permission enures for the benefit of the land,[65] and thus it might seem that it would be inappropriate to take into account the personal circumstances of any particular applicant for planning permission. The fact that the land might subsequently be sold on must lessen the significance of any characteristics peculiar to the initial applicant which might justify the grant of planning permission to him or her. For example, the fact that the personal circumstances of an applicant for planning permission are such that his use of the development will give rise to few traffic movements would not justify granting planning permission where there are concerns in relation to traffic safety: a subsequent purchaser of the lands might not have such limited demands.[66] The High Court had interpreted the concept of proper planning

4–39

---

[62] *State (FitzGerald) v An Bord Pleanála* [1985] I.L.R.M. 117. See also *Village Residents Association Ltd. v An Bord Pleanála (No. 2)* [2000] 4 I.R. 321; [2001] 2 I.L.R.M. 22.

[63] [1998] J.P.L. 335.

[64] [2004] U.K.H.L. 33, [52].

[65] PDA 2000, s.39(1). See also *State (Sweeney) v Minister for the Environment* [1979] I.L.R.M. 35; and *Furlong v AF & GW McConnell Ltd.* [1990] I.L.R.M. 48 at 57. See more generally, *Readymix (Éire) Ltd. v Dublin County Council*, unreported, Supreme Court, July 30, 1974.

[66] See the facts of *Griffin v Galway City and County Manager*, unreported, High Court, Blayney J., October 31, 1990.

and development under the previous legislation as excluding consideration of such personal circumstances.[67] It has to be said, however, that each of these cases arose in the context of an attempt by the elected members to direct the manager to grant planning permission against his will, and this may have coloured the attitude of the court.

4–40 Following the enactment of the European Convention on Human Rights Act 2003, however, it will be necessary to have regard to the personal circumstances of those affected by certain acts and decisions, especially in the context of enforcement action. One obvious example is in relation to travellers, given that enforcement action may result in the loss of their home.[68] This entire issue is examined in detail in Chapter 14.

D. Other Matters to Which Regard Must Be Had Under Section 34

4–41 The structure of s.34 of the PDA 2000 is as follows. A planning authority and An Bord Pleanála are "restricted" to "considering" proper planning and sustainable development. The section then goes on to list a number of matters which a planning authority and An Bord Pleanála are required to "have regard to". The legislation, therefore, prescribes a hierarchy of matters which are to be taken into account in determining an application or an appeal, with the greatest emphasis being placed on the concept of proper planning and sustainable development. Thus, for example, an application for a proposed development which would accord with the zoning objectives in the development plan, would nevertheless have to be refused if the proposed development would be contrary to the proper planning and sustainable development of the area.

4–42 The concept of "have regard to" was examined in the context of regional planning guidelines in *McEvoy v Meath County Council*.[69] Quirke J. held that the requirement "to have regard to" obliged a planning authority to inform itself fully of and give reasonable consideration to any regional planning guidelines which are in force in the area which is the subject of the development plan, with a view to accommodating the objectives and policies contained in such guidelines. Quirke J. went on to state that whilst reason and good sense would dictate that it was in the main desirable that planning authorities should, when making and adopting development plans, seek to accommodate the objectives and policies contained in relevant regional planning guidelines,

---

[67] *Flanagan v Galway City and County Manager* [1990] 2 I.R. 66; and *Griffin v Galway City and County Manager*, unreported, High Court, Blayney J., October 31, 1990. *Cf. Great Portland Estates v Westminster City Council* [1985] A.C. 661.
[68] See, by analogy, *Buckley v United Kingdom* (1997) 33 E.H.R.R. 101; and *Chapman v United Kingdom* (2001) 33 E.H.R.R. 18.
[69] [2003] 1 I.R. 208; [2003] 1 I.L.R.M. 431.

planning authorities were not bound to comply with the guidelines and could depart from them for *bona fide* reasons consistent with the proper planning and development of the area for which the planning authority has planning responsibilities.

It is submitted that a similar approach should apply in the context of an **4–43** application for planning permission. In particular, it is submitted that the approach in *McEvoy v Meath County Council* is to be preferred to that of the High Court in *Glencar Explorations plc v Mayo County Council*.[70] The formula in *McEvoy v Meath County Council* suggests that departure from the terms of a general policy is permissible for *bona fide* reasons consistent with the proper planning and development of the area. In order to police this limitation it is essential that the decision-maker be required to state the reasons being relied upon for the departure.

1. The provisions of the development plan

In making a decision in relation to an application for planning permission, **4–44** regard is to be had to the provisions of the development plan.[71] Although a planning authority is not strictly bound in its determination by the provisions of the development plan, and is entitled to grant planning permission for development which would involve a material contravention of the plan,[72] there is a presumption in favour of upholding the development plan to the following extent. In order to grant planning permission for a development which would materially contravene the development plan, it is necessary for the planning authority to invoke a special procedure. This entails, *inter alia*, public consultation, and requires that a resolution be passed by three quarters of the total number of the elected members.[73]

In the context of an appeal to An Bord Pleanála, any presumption in favour of **4–45** upholding the development plan is weaker. An Bord Pleanála is expressly empowered to decide to grant planning permission even if the proposed development contravenes materially the development plan.[74] If, however, the planning authority had refused planning permission, at first instance, on the grounds that a proposed development materially contravenes the development plan, An Bord Pleanála may only grant planning permission where it considers that (i) the proposed development is of strategic or national importance; (ii) there are conflicting objectives in the development plan or the objectives are not clearly stated insofar as the proposed development is concerned; (iii)

---

[70] [1993] 2 I.R. 237. See also *Griffin v Galway City and County Manager*, unreported, High Court, Blayney J., October 31, 1990.
[71] PDA 2000, s.34(2)(a)(i). For a discussion of the status of the draft development plan, see paras 1–32 to 1–134
[72] PDA 2000, s.34(6).
[73] PDA 2000, 34(6). The procedure is described in more detail at paras 1–27 to 1–29 above.
[74] PDA 2000, s.37(2).

planning permission for the proposed development should be granted having regard to regional planning guidelines for the area, statutory guidelines, statutory policy directives, the statutory obligations of any local authority in the area, and any relevant policy of the Government, the Minister for the Environment Heritage and Local Government, or any Minister of the Government, or (iv) planning permission for the proposed development should be granted having regard to the pattern of development, and permissions granted, in the area since the making of the development plan.[75]

4–46   In circumstances where An Bord Pleanála has overturned a decision of the planning authority, at first instance, to refuse planning permission on the grounds that a proposed development materially contravenes the development plan, there is an express requirement that it indicate in its decision the main reasons and considerations for contravening materially the development plan.[76] This requirement is in addition to the general duty to state the main reasons and considerations on which a decision is based.[77]

4–47   As stated above, any presumption in favour of upholding the development plan is weaker in the case of An Bord Pleanála. Any restriction on the power of An Bord Pleanála to grant planning permission in material contravention of the development plan is only triggered where An Bord Pleanála seeks to overturn a decision of the planning authority refusing planning permission on the basis of material contravention. Thus, where the planning authority allows a material contravention there is no restriction on An Bord Pleanála doing likewise.

4–48   More generally, the fact that the restriction on An Bord Pleanála's powers is primarily defined in terms of overturning the decision of the planning authority has the result that the question of whether or not the proposed development does or does not actually represent a material contravention is less important at the appeal stage. Once the planning authority has refused planning permission on the basis of an alleged material contravention, then it would seem that the restrictions on An Bord Pleanála's power to grant planning permission apply, even if the planning authority were incorrect in finding a material contravention. Moreover, all of the permitted exceptions bar one relate to matters other than the development plan; the wording of the one exception which does relate to the development plan appears to afford a margin of appreciation to An Bord Pleanála, namely in considering whether or not there are conflicting objectives in the development plan, or whether the objectives are not clearly stated, insofar as the proposed development is concerned. In the circumstances, the scope of any review would appear to be limited to the standard in *O'Keeffe v An Bord Pleanála*.[78]

---

[75] PDA 2000, s.37(2)(b).

[76] PDA 2000, s.37(2)(c). See also Planning and Development Regulations 2001, art.74(2)(l) (as amended by the 2006 Regulations). As to the position under the previous legislation, see *Village Residents Association Ltd. v An Bord Pleanála (No. 3)* [2001] 1 I.R. 441.

[77] PDA 2000, s.34(10).

[78] [1993] 1 I.R. 39; [1992] I.L.R.M. 237.

Notwithstanding the fact that there is a presumption in favour of upholding the **4–49** objectives of the development plan, each application for planning permission must be assessed on its individual merits, and that the development plan cannot be conclusive on the question of whether or not planning permission should be granted. The concept of proper planning and sustainable development is more specific than the objectives of the development plan, and requires the consideration of the merits of the individual development. The development plan does not descend to the particular. Thus neither the fact that the proposed development is in accordance with, nor in contravention of, the provisions of the development plan is *per se* conclusive of whether or not planning permission should be granted or refused.

Waste management plan

The requirement under s.34(6) that a special procedure be adopted before **4–50** planning permission may be granted for development which would involve a material contravention of the development plan is disapplied in certain circumstances under the Waste Management Act 1996 (as amended by the Waste Management (Amendment) Act 2001). See further paras 3–140 to 3–143.

Somewhat surprisingly, perhaps, no special provision is made as to the manner **4–51** in which an appeal in relation to such development should be dealt with. Whereas the express statutory restrictions imposed on An Bord Pleanála in relation to a material contravention of the development plan appear only to be triggered in circumstances where the planning authority had refused planning permission on the basis of a material contravention, it nevertheless remains the case that An Bord Pleanála is required to have regard to the provisions of the development plan. Accordingly, it would seem that it might be open to An Bord Pleanála to refuse planning permission for the very reason that the proposed development would involve a material contravention of the development plan.

Finally, the provisions of s.26 of the Protection of the Environment Act 2003 **4–52** should be noted. Under s.22(10AA) of the Waste Management Act 1996 (as substituted), planning permission shall not be refused solely on the ground that the development to which the application relates is not specifically referred to in the waste management plan if the planning authority or An Bord Pleanála considers the development will facilitate the achievement of the objectives of the waste management plan.

2. The provisions of any special amenity area order relating to the area

Regard must be had to the provisions of any special amenity area order relating **4–53** to the area.[79] Under ss.202 and 203 of the PDA 2000, a planning authority is

---

[79] PDA 2000, s.34(2)(a)(ii).

empowered to declare an area to be an area of special amenity. This power is exercisable where, in the opinion of the planning authority, by reason of (a) its outstanding natural beauty or (b) its special recreational value, and having regard to any benefits for nature conservation, an area should be declared to be an area of special amenity. The order may state the objective of the planning authority in relation to the preservation or enhancement of the character or special features of the area, including objectives for the prevention or limitation of development in the area. Although there is no express restriction on the grant of planning permission in material contravention of a special amenity area order, it is probable that if a planning authority was minded to make a special amenity area order, then, presumably, the sentiments underlying this will also have been reflected in the objectives of the development plan. Thus breach of a special amenity area order may, indirectly, represent a material contravention of the development plan.

3. Any European site or other area prescribed for the purposes of the conservation and protection of the environment

4–54   Regard must be had to any European site or other area prescribed for the purposes of the conservation and the protection of the environment.[80] Under s.10(2)(c) of the PDA 2000, a planning authority is required to include objectives in its development plan for the conservation and protection of the environment including, in particular, the archaeological and natural heritage and the conservation and protection of any European sites and other sites which may be prescribed for the purpose of that subsection. The fact that these matters are included in the development plan might have the result that the proposed development may involve a material contravention of the development plan.

4–55   Under the European Communities (Natural Habitats) Regulations 1997 (as amended), an appropriate assessment is to be undertaken in respect of an application for planning permission in respect of a proposed development which is not directly connected with, or necessary to the management of, a European site but likely to have a significant effect thereon either individually or in combination with other development. A decision to grant planning permission may only be made where it is ascertained that the proposed development will not adversely affect the integrity of the European site concerned. Planning permission may be granted, notwithstanding a negative assessment and in the absence of alternative solutions, where the development has to be carried out for imperative reasons of overriding public interest.

---

[80] PDA 2000, s.34(2)(a)(iii).

4. Where relevant, the policy of the Government, the Minister for the Environment Heritage and Local Government or any other Minister of the Government

Regard must be had, where relevant, to the policy of the Government, the Minister for the Environment Heritage and Local Government or any other Minister of the Government.[81]   **4–56**

The effect of a provision to like effect under s.7 of the Local Government Act 1991 had been considered by the High Court in *Glencar Explorations plc v Mayo County Council*.[82] On the facts, the relevant government policy was to the effect that mineral resources should be explored for and should be exploited where this could be done in an environmentally acceptable manner. Blayney J. stated that, without attempting to define precisely the meaning of the phrase "shall have regard to", he was satisfied that a local authority could not be said to have had regard to the policy of the government in respect of mining when it adopted as part of its development plan a policy which was totally opposed to that policy. Ultimately, however, the High Court resolved the case on other grounds.   **4–57**

As discussed above at paras 4–42 to 4–43, the correctness of the approach adopted by the High Court in *Glencar Explorations plc v Mayo County Council*[83] would appear to be in doubt following the more recent judgment in *McEvoy v Meath County Council*.[84]   **4–58**

5. Conditions under Section 34(4)

In making the decision on an application for planning permission, a planning authority and An Bord Pleanála are required to have regard to the matters referred to in s.34(4) of the PDA 2000. This subsection enumerates a list of conditions which may be attached to the grant of planning permission. This list is expressly stated to be without prejudice to the generality of s.34(1). Although subsection (4) is expressed to be without prejudice to the generality of the earlier subsection, it had been suggested in the context of the equivalent provision under the previous legislation[85] that notwithstanding the reference to the generality of subsection (1), conditions must be of the same nature indicated in the particulars set out in the equivalent of what is now subsection (4).[86]   **4–59**

---

[81] PDA 2000, s.34(2)(a)(iv).
[82] [1993] 2 I.R. 237.
[83] [1993] 2 I.R. 237.
[84] [2003] 1 I.R. 208; [2003] 1 I.L.R.M. 431.
[85] Local Government (Planning & Development) Act 1963, s.26(1) and (2).
[86] *State (Abenglen Properties Ltd.) v An Bord Pleanála* [1984] I.R 381 at 396; [1982] I.L.R.M. 590 at 600, *per* Walsh J.

4-60   The implications of the equivalent provision under the previous legislation were considered again by the Supreme Court in *Ashbourne Holdings Ltd. v An Bord Pleanála.*[87] Hardiman J. held that the general words under subsection (1) would permit the imposition of an otherwise proper condition even if it were outside the scope of any of the subparagraphs of enumerated conditions. But when a condition is within the scope of any part of subsection (4), then the planning authority or An Bord Pleanála must have regard to the relevant part. Hardiman J. seems to suggest therefore that if a particular condition is within the scope of one of the subparagraphs but does not meet its requirements, it would contradict the intendment of subsection (1) to permit the condition to be imposed under the authority of the general words.

4-61   Although the judgment in *Ashbourne Holdings Ltd. v An Bord Pleanála* is undoubtedly correct on its facts, the proposition referred to above may not be of universal application. In particular, it is submitted that it is only where a condition would breach a restriction or limitation which would otherwise apply under s.34(4) that reliance on the general power is excluded *in limine*. The point may be illustrated by reference to conditions relating to the development or use of lands outside the application site. It is not uncommon for a condition to be attached to a planning permission requiring that access be secured over lands not within the application site. In order to overcome any allegation that the condition might be unenforceable (in that it may relate to matters outside the control of the applicant), such conditions are phrased in the negative using the formula "no development shall commence" until the access has been attended to. The propriety of such conditions has been upheld by the House of Lords.[88] On a strict or literal reading of the judgment in *Ashbourne Holdings Ltd. v An Bord Pleanála* such conditions might be objectionable in that same do not necessarily meet the requirement under s.34(4)(a) (as amended) that the land be under the control of the applicant. The wording of the subparagraph insofar as relevant is as follows.

> "conditions for regulating the development or use of any land which adjoins, abuts or is adjacent to the land to be developed and which is *under the control of the applicant* [...]"
> *Emphasis supplied.

4-62   It is submitted that such conditions would nevertheless be authorised under the general power to attach conditions under s.34(1), provided always that the usual limitations on the general power were satisfied. The restriction or limitation imposed by subparagraph (a) is that the condition be expedient for the purposes of or in connection with the permitted development or appropriate for conserving a public amenity. The term "expedient" has been interpreted as requiring that the condition be of benefit or advantage to the permitted development and not to any wider area.[89] This is to be contrasted with the

---

[87] [2003] 2 I.R. 114; [2003] 2 I.L.R.M. 446.
[88] *Grampian Regional Council v City of Aberdeen District Council* (1983) 47 P. & C.R. 633. See, generally, E. Farrell, "Grampian Planning Conditions" (1999) 6 I.P.E.L.J. 22.
[89] *Ashbourne Holdings Ltd. v An Bord Pleanála* [2003] 2 I.R. 114; [2003] 2 I.L.R.M. 446.

more general requirement that a condition must be relevant to the permitted development. The subparagraph would thus appear to supplement the general power to attach conditions by allowing for the imposition of a condition on the basis of a lesser test, namely that the condition be of benefit or advantage to the permitted development or be appropriate for conserving a public amenity. The availability of this special power is limited to where the lands (outside the application site) are under the control of the applicant. It is submitted that the existence of this special power does not preclude other conditions relating to lands outside the control of the applicant (especially conditions with respect to access) where such conditions meet the higher test of being relevant to the permitted development.[90]

6. Any other relevant provision or requirement of the Planning and Development Act 2000, and any Regulations made thereunder

Local area plan

Under s.18(3), regard is to be had to the provisions of any local area plan.   **4–63**
There is a *discretion* to consider any relevant draft local area plan which has been prepared but not yet made. There is also a requirement to have regard to an integrated area plan (within the meaning of the Urban Renewal Act 1998).

Protected structures

It is an express requirement that, in considering any application for planning   **4–64**
permission in respect of a protected structure, a planning authority or An Bord Pleanála shall have regard to the protected status of the structure.[91] Similarly, in the case of a proposed protected structure, regard is to be had to the fact that it is proposed to add the structure to a record of protected structures.[92] It is further provided that a planning authority or An Bord Pleanála shall not grant planning permission for the demolition of a protected structure, or a proposed protected structure, save in exceptional circumstances.[93]

Place of worship

Special provision is made in respect of a protected structure which is regularly   **4–65**
used as a place of worship.[94] When considering an application for planning permission which relates to the interior of a protected structure which is regularly used as a place of public worship, the planning authority, and An Bord Pleanála on appeal, shall, in addition to any other requirements of the PDA 2000, respect liturgical requirements.

---

[90] *cf. Parolen Ltd. v Drogheda Corporation*, unreported, High Court, Finnegan P., May 14, 2003 (application for leave to apply for judicial review).
[91] PDA 2000, s.57 (10)(a)(i).
[92] PDA 2000, s.57(10)(a)(ii).
[93] PDA 2000, s.57(10)(b).
[94] PDA 2000, s.57(6).

Architectural conservation area

4–66   Under s.82(2) of the PDA 2000, in considering an application for planning permission in relation to land situated in an architectural conservation area, a planning authority, or An Bord Pleanála on appeal, shall take into account the material effect (if any) that the proposed development would be likely to have on the character of the architectural conservation area. Under s.87(2), when considering an application for planning permission in relation to land situated in an area of special planning control, a planning authority, or An Bord Pleanála on appeal, shall have regard to the provisions of an approved special planning control scheme.

Social and affordable housing

4–67   Section 93(4) provides as follows.

> "For the avoidance of doubt, it is hereby declared that, in respect of any planning application or appeal, compliance with the housing strategy and any related objective in the development plan shall be a consideration material to the proper planning and sustainable development of the area."

4–68   This would seem to apply to all applications for planning permission, and not just to those applications for residential development.

4–69   Additional considerations apply in the case of an application for planning permission which is subject to social and affordable housing under Pt V of the PDA 2000 (as amended by the Planning and Development (Amendment) Act 2002). The provisions of Pt V are triggered in case of an application for residential development where a development plan objective requires that a specified percentage of any land zoned solely for residential use (or for a mixture of residential and other uses) be made available for social and affordable housing.[95] The planning authority and An Bord Pleanála are required to have regard to the proposals specified in the application as to how it is proposed to comply with a condition requiring a Pt V agreement.[96] Furthermore, for the purposes of a Pt V agreement, a planning authority is required to have regard to the following matters: (i) the proper planning and sustainable development of the area to which the application relates; (ii) the housing strategy and the specific objectives of the development plan which relate to the implementation of the strategy; (iii) the need to ensure the overall coherence of the development to which the application relates; and (iv) the views of the applicant in relation to the impact of a housing condition on the development.[97]

---

[95] PDA 2000, s.96(1) (as substituted by the Planning and Development (Amendment) Act 2002).
[96] PDA 2000, s.96(4) (as substituted).
[97] PDA 2000, s.96(3)(h) (as substituted).

Environmental impact assessment

It is to be noted that there is a subtle distinction between the relevant **4–70** considerations applicable in the case of development involving an environmental impact statement, and other applications, in that (in the former case) a planning authority or An Bord Pleanála, in addition to the requirements of s.34, is required to have regard to the environmental impact statement, any supplementary information furnished relating to the statement and any submissions or observations furnished concerning the effects on the environment of the proposed development.[98]

Section 143

Under s.143 of the PDA 2000 (as substituted by the 2006 Act), An Bord Pleanála **4–71** shall, in performing its functions, have regard to (a) the policies and objectives for the time being of the Government, a State authority, the Minister for Environment Heritage and Local Government, planning authorities and any other body which is a public authority whose functions have, or may have, a bearing on the proper planning and sustainable development of cities, towns or other areas, whether urban or rural; (b) the national interest and any effect the performance of the board's functions may have on issues of strategic economic or social importance to the State; and (c) the National Spatial Strategy and any regional planning guidelines for the time being in force.[99] A similarly worded requirement under the previous legislation had been interpreted as being entirely meaningless unless An Bord Pleanála was not also entitled, and indeed obliged, to take those policies and objectives into account in discharging its own statutory functions.[100]

Section 143 also applies where An Bord Pleanála is carrying out other **4–72** functions,[101] such as under the Roads Acts, and thus incorporates the concept of proper planning and sustainable development into such decision-making.[102]

The onus of demonstrating that An Bord Pleanála failed to comply with its **4–73** obligations under s.143, seemingly, lies with the applicant for judicial review.[103]

---

[98] PDA 2000, s.173.
[99] "Public authority" is defined under PDA 2000, s.143(2) (as substituted by the 2006 Act) and means any body established by or under statute which is for the time being declared, by regulation made by the Minister for the Environment, Heritage and Local Government, to be a public authority for the purpose of s.143.
[100] *Keane v An Bord Pleanála* [1998] 2 I.L.R.M. 241. See also *State (Coras Iompair Éireann) v An Bord Pleanála*, unreported, Supreme Court, December 12, 1984 (statutory provisions postulate an informed liaison).
[101] PDA 2000, s.218(4)
[102] *Kildare County Council v An Bord Pleanála* [2006] I.E.H.C. 173; unreported, MacMenamin J., March 10, 2006, [75].
[103] *Glancré Teoranta v An Bord Pleanála*, unreported, High Court, MacMenamin J., May 2, 2006.

Integrated pollution prevention and control licence

4–74   Where an integrated pollution prevention and control licence or revised licence under the Environmental Protection Agency Act 1992 has been granted or is or will be required in relation to an activity, a planning authority or An Bord Pleanála may, in respect of any development comprising the activity or for the purposes of the activity, decide to refuse a grant of planning permission where the planning authority or An Bord Pleanála considers that the development, notwithstanding the licensing of the activity, is unacceptable on environmental grounds, having regard to the proper planning and sustainable development of the area in which the development is or will be situate.[104]

Waste licence

4–75   Where a waste licence has been granted under the Waste Management Acts 1996 to 2001, or is or will be required in relation to an activity, a planning authority or An Bord Pleanála may, in respect of any development comprising the activity or for the purposes of the activity, decide to refuse a grant of planning permission where the planning authority or An Bord Pleanála considers that the development, notwithstanding the licensing of the activity under the waste management legislation, is unacceptable on environmental grounds, having regard to the proper planning and sustainable development of the area in which the development is or will be situate.[105]

Strategic development zones

4–76   Where an application is made to a planning authority for planning permission for development in a strategic development zone, a planning authority shall grant permission where it is satisfied that the development, where carried out in accordance with the application or subject to any conditions which the planning authority may attach to a permission, would be consistent with any planning scheme in force for the land in question. No planning permission shall be granted for any development which would not be consistent with such a planning scheme.[106]

Ministerial guidelines and directives

4–77   The Minister for the Environment Heritage and Local Government may, at any time, issue guidelines to planning authorities regarding any of their functions under the PDA 2000 and planning authorities shall have regard to those guidelines in the performance of their functions.[107] Similarly, the Minister may also, from time to time, issue policy directives to planning authorities

---

[104] PDA 2000, s.256 (as amended by s.61 of the Protection of the Environment Act 2003). See s.99F of the Environmental Protection Agency Act 1992 (as substituted under the Protection of the Environment Act 2003).

[105] PDA 2000, s.257.

[106] PDA 2000, s.170.

[107] PDA 2000, s.28.

regarding any of their functions under the PDA 2000 and planning authorities shall comply with any such directives in the performance of their functions.[108]

The Minister is precluded from exercising any power or control in relation to any particular case with which a planning authority or An Bord Pleanála is or may be concerned.[109]   **4–78**

E. Planning Conditions

In adjudicating on an application for planning permission, a planning authority and An Bord Pleanála are required not only to consider whether to grant or refuse planning permission, but also to consider the question of what conditions, if any, should be attached to the grant of planning permission.[110] The better view would be that this requirement extends to an obligation to consider whether or not conditions might be attached which would save an application which would otherwise have to be refused.   **4–79**

Before turning to a consideration of the statutory conditions under s.34(4), the following more general points should be made as to the nature and extent of conditions which might properly be attached to a planning permission.[111] First, a condition should be relevant to planning, and, in particular, to the permitted development. Thus it would seem inappropriate to attach a condition in relation to a matter dealt with under another legislative code: for example, a condition requiring that the applicant obtain a water pollution licence. It would be equally wrong to attempt to regulate development which is not the subject of the application for planning permission: for example, it would be wrong to seek to retrench on (unrelated) existing use rights.[112]   **4–80**

In the case of adjacent land not under the *control* of the applicant and thus outside s.34(4)(a), it may be possible to impose a negative condition specifying that no development shall be carried out until certain matters are attended to on other land (in relation to, for example, access).[113] Conditions of this type should, however, be used sparingly and only in circumstances where there is a   **4–81**

---

[108] PDA 2000, s.29.

[109] PDA 2000, s.30.

[110] *Kenny Homes and Company Ltd. v Galway City and County Manager* [1995] 1 I.R. 178 at 187.

[111] Department of the Environment "Development Control Advice and Guidelines" (1982) suggest the following basic criteria in regard to the use of conditions: necessary; relevant to planning; relevant to the development to be permitted; enforceable; precise; and reasonable (para.5.6).

[112] *State (O'Hara and McGuinness Ltd.) v An Bord Pleanála*, unreported, High Court, Barron J., May 8, 1986. See also *Kelly v An Bord Pleanála*, unreported, High Court, Blayney J., April 6, 1992 *ex tempore*: see judgment of November 19, 1993.

[113] *Grampian Regional Council v City of Aberdeen UDC* (1983) 47 P. & C.R. 633. See, generally, E. Farrell, "Grampian Planning Conditions" (1999) 6 I.P.E.L.J. 22.

reasonable prospect of the condition being fulfilled.[114] If there is no such reasonable prospect, then it would seem fairer to refuse planning permission, rather than to prejudice any entitlement to compensation which might otherwise arise by granting a conditional planning permission. It should also be noted that insofar as conditions of this sort suggest that matters be attended to on land outside the control of the applicant, they represent a gloss on any requirement that the applicant have an interest in the lands the subject-matter of the application.[115]

4–82   Secondly, a condition must be precise. Breach of a condition creates a liability to enforcement action and thus it is only fair that a developer should know with certainty what it is that is required of him by the condition. In *Dun Laoghaire Corporation v Frescati Estates Ltd.*,[116] it was held that, in the absence of an express condition, the developer could not be required to maintain or preserve an existing structure on the basis of a reference in the application to retaining the structure. The courts take a pragmatic approach to the interpretation of conditions and it seems that a condition will only be void for uncertainty if it can be given no meaning or no sensible or ascertainable meaning, and not merely because it is ambiguous.[117] Similarly there is some onus on the developer to make some attempt to understand a condition, if necessary by raising queries with the planning authority.[118]

4–83   The decision in *Dublin City Council v Liffey Beat Ltd.*[119] contains a number of criticisms of the manner in which planning conditions are written.

> "That requirement imposes an obligation upon planning authorities (and An Bord Pleanála) to take reasonable steps to ensure that, insofar as is practicable the terms of documents granting or refusing planning permission will be comprehensible to members of the public.
>
> Obviously, some documents of a technical character must, of necessity, be couched in technical terms. However, where it is possible, reasonable care should be taken by planning authorities (and An Bord Pleanála) to make the terms and conditions which apply to planning permissions comprehensible to the parties who have an interest in the property to be developed and to the members of the public who have an interest in the proper planning and development of the area in which they reside."
>
> [...]
>
> "Where a restrictive condition is imposed confining the use of property in a particular manner, then some care should be exercised by the party which is imposing the condition to clarify the nature and extent of the restriction imposed by the condition."

---

[114]   *cf. British Railways Board v Secretary of State for the Environment* [1994] J.P.L. 32.
[115]   *cf. Keane v An Bord Pleanála* [1998] 2 I.L.R.M. 241.
[116]   [1982] I.L.R.M. 469.
[117]   *Irish Asphalt Ltd. v An Bord Pleanála*, unreported, High Court, Costello J., July 28, 1995. See also *Houlihan v An Bord Pleanála*, unreported, High Court, Murphy J., October 4, 1993.
[118]   *Donegal County Council v O'Donnell*, unreported, High Court, O'Hanlon J., July 25, 1982.
[119]   [2005] I.R. 478 at 494; [2005] I.E.H.C. 82.

Thirdly, a condition must not be unreasonable. The concept of reasonableness **4–84** is so broad as to be unwieldy at times: what is meant by reasonableness in this context is that a condition should not seek to extract an unauthorised "planning gain" from the developer. The concept of "planning gain" was considered by the Supreme Court in *Ashbourne Holdings Ltd. v An Bord Pleanála*.[120] See paras 4–29 to 4–32 above.

Fourthly, in practice a planning permission will often contain conditions **4–85** requiring certain matters to be attended to "prior to commencement of development". Unfortunately developers often overlook these conditions and assume that works can commence immediately once the grant of planning permission has issued. This is a dangerous misconception as it leaves the development open to enforcement action. See paras 7–19 to 7–30.

Integrated pollution prevention and control licence and waste management licence

Finally, it should be noted that where an activity is subject to licensing (whether **4–86** an integrated pollution prevention and control licence or a waste management licence) a planning authority and An Bord Pleanála are expressly precluded from imposing conditions which are for the purposes of (a) controlling emissions from the operation of an activity, including the prevention, elimination, limitation, abatement, or reduction of those emissions, or (b) controlling emissions related to or following the cessation of the operation of the activity.[121]

1. Statutory conditions under Section 34(4)

Subsection 34(4) enumerates 17 types of condition which may be attached to **4–87** the grant of planning permission. The relationship between the general power to attach conditions under subsection (1) and the specific instances under subsection (4) is unclear. Although subsection (4) is expressed to be without prejudice to the generality of the earlier subsection, it had been suggested in the context of the equivalent provision under the previous legislation[122] that notwithstanding the reference to the generality of subsection (1), conditions must be of the same nature indicated in the particulars set out in the equivalent of what is now subsection (4).[123]

---

[120] [2003] 2 I.R. 114; [2003] 2 I.L.R.M. 446.
[121] PDA 2000, s.256 (as amended by s.61 of the Protection of the Environment Act 2003). See s.99F of the Environmental Protection Agency Act 1992 (as substituted under the Protection of the Environment Act 2003). See also Waste Management Act 1996, s.54 (as amended by PDA 2000, s.257, and s.45 of the Protection of the Environment Act 2003).
[122] Local Government (Planning & Development) Act 1963, s.26(2).
[123] *State (Abenglen Properties Ltd.) v An Bord Pleanála* [1984] I.R 381 at 396; [1982] I.L.R.M. 590 at 600, *per* Walsh J.

4-88   The relationship under the previous legislation between the general power to attach conditions, and the specific instances, was also considered by the Supreme Court in *Ashbourne Holdings Ltd. v An Bord Pleanála.*[124] Hardiman J. held that the general words under subsection (1) would permit the imposition of an otherwise proper condition even if it were outside the scope of any of the subparagraphs of enumerated conditions. But when a condition is within the scope of any part of subsection (4), then the planning authority or An Bord Pleanála must have regard to the relevant part. Hardiman J. seems to suggest therefore that if a particular condition is within the scope of one of the subparagraphs but does not meet its requirements, it would contradict the intendment of subsection (1) to permit the condition to be imposed under the general words. This judgment is discussed further at paras 4–60 to 4–62.

4-89   Irrespective of whether or not subsection (4) qualifies the general power under subsection (1), it would seem clear that in at least some instances, the provisions of subsection (4) *supplement* the general power in that certain conditions, for example, those in relation to the sequence and timing of works;[125] the provision of works and open spaces in excess of the immediate needs of the proposed development[126]; and, possibly, those requiring measures to reduce or avoid intrusion of any noise or vibration,[127] might not be justified by invocation of the general power alone.

2. List of conditions under Section 34(4)

4-90   (a) conditions for regulating the development or use of any land which adjoins, abuts or is adjacent to the land to be developed and which is under the control of the applicant if the imposition of such conditions appears to the planning authority— (i) to be expedient for the purposes of or in connection with the development authorised by the permission, or to be appropriate, where any aspect or feature of that adjoining, abutting or adjacent land constitutes an amenity for the public or a section of the public, for the purposes of conserving that amenity for the public or that section of the public (and the effect of the imposition of conditions for that purpose would not be to burden unduly the person in whose favour the permission operates);

This subsection has been amended by the Planning and Development (Strategic Infrastructure) Act 2006. In its initial form, the power to attach conditions under the subsection had been confined to circumstances where the conditions

---

[124] [2003] 2 I.R. 114; [2003] 2 I.L.R.M. 446.

[125] See, by analogy, *obiter dicta* in *Bord na Mona v An Bord Pleanála* [1985] I.R. 205 at 210.

[126] See reference in *Thomas McDonagh & Sons Ltd. v Galway Corporation* [1995] 1 I.R. 191 at 201–202 to open spaces in excess of immediate needs of development. The difficulty arising from the wording of the previous legislation has since been addressed: see PDA 2000, s.34(4)(m).

[127] See the decision in *Frank Dunne Ltd. v Dublin County Council* [1974] I.R. 45 at 54.

were "expedient for the purposes of or in connection with the development". The term "expedient" had been interpreted as requiring that the condition be of benefit or advantage to the permitted development and not to any wider area.[128] Thus a condition requiring that the public be allowed access to a golf course was held not to be expedient for the permitted clubhouse development (the laying of the golf course had been carried out as exempted development).[129] Similarly, a condition which required the restoration of a historic house on adjacent lands was held not to be expedient to permitted residential development.[130]

In its amended form the subsection allows for conditions to be imposed additionally for the purpose of conserving an amenity for the public or a section of the public. The effect of this amendment is to overcome the limitations on the power to attach conditions identified by the Supreme Court in *Ashbourne Holdings Ltd. v An Bord Pleanála*.[131] It is no longer necessary that the regulation of the adjoining, abutting or adjacent land be for the benefit of, or of advantage to, the permitted development. Conditions under s.34(4)(a) are unique in that there is no requirement even that same be relevant to the permitted development. Rather, the power to regulate the adjoining, abutting or adjacent land arises from the fortuity of the applicant for the planning permission having control of other land. It seems somewhat arbitrary to impose a requirement for a planning gain on such a happenstance. The only express limitation on the power is that the imposition of the condition would not be to "burden unduly" the person in whose favour the permission operates. **4–91**

There must be a question mark over the constitutionality of this provision. Although the Supreme Court accepted in *In re Part V of the Planning and Development Bill, 1999*[132] that the State is entitled to recoup some part of the enhanced value of development land—whether deriving from its zoning or from the grant of planning permission—the circumstances of that case were very different from those contemplated under the amended s.34(4)(a). The Supreme Court was concerned with a legislative scheme which was directed to an objective, namely the provision of social and affordable housing, which was pressing and substantial and, further, was clearly defined. The extent of the planning gain required—which consisted of the transfer of land at less than its open market value—was also clearly defined, and subject to a ceiling by reference to the value of twenty per cent of the land within the application site. Finally, the most that a developer could be compelled to do was to transfer land in its undeveloped state. **4–92**

The power under s.34(4)(a), in contrast, is open-ended. The objective justifying the extraction of a planning gain, namely to conserve an amenity for the public **4–93**

---

[128] *Ashbourne Holdings Ltd. v An Bord Pleanála* [2003] 2 I.R. 114; [2003] 2 I.L.R.M. 446.
[129] *ibid.*
[130] *State (FPH Properties SA) v An Bord Pleanála* [1987] I.R. 698; [1989] I.L.R.M. 98.
[131] [2003] 2 I.R. 114; [2003] 2 I.L.R.M. 446.
[132] [2000] 2 I.R. 321; [2001] 1 I.L.R.M. 81.

or section of the public, could not be said to be as pressing or substantial as the provision of social and affordable housing. The extent of the planning gain is delimited only by reference to the imprecise standard that it not "unduly burden" the beneficiary of the planning permission. There is no requirement, for example, that there be any proportionality between the value of the planning gain and the benefit of the planning permission (or, more relevantly, the value of public infrastructure unlocking the development potential of the application site). In the absence of a clear statement of the principle or policy in this regard, it will be almost impossible for a developer to challenge the imposition of such a condition. This offends against legal certainty, and may well render the subsection unconstitutional.

4–94   (b) Conditions for requiring the carrying out of works (including the provision of facilities) which the planning authority considers are required for the purposes of the development authorised by the permission;

It would seem that the works must be works on the lands the subject of the application for planning permission.[133] The fact that the condition must relate to works "required for the purposes of" the proposed development is consistent with the general principle that a planning condition must relate to the permitted development.[134] This can be contrasted with the special provision made under subsection 34(4)(m), which allows for works in excess of the immediate needs of the development but with a requirement for a contribution from the local authority.

4–95   (c) Conditions for requiring the taking of measures to reduce or prevent – (i) the emission of any noise or vibration from any structure or site comprised in the development authorised by the permission which might give reasonable cause for annoyance either to persons in any premises in the neighbourhood of the development or to persons lawfully using any public place in that neighbourhood, or, (ii) the intrusion of any noise or vibration which might give reasonable cause for annoyance to any person lawfully occupying any such structure or site;

But for the express power to attach such conditions, it is arguable that same would not meet the requirement of being sufficiently connected with the proper planning and sustainable development, or the preservation of the amenities thereof.[135]

[133] *State (FPH Properties SA) v An Bord Pleanála* [1987] I.R. 698 at 710–711; [1989] I.L.R.M. 98 at 103.
[134] Indirect authority for this proposition is to found in the following decisions: *State (FPH Properties SA) v An Bord Pleanála* [1987] I.R. 698 at 710–711; [1989] I.L.R.M 98 at 103); and *State (O'Hara and McGuinness Ltd.) v An Bord Pleanála*, unreported, High Court, Barron J., May 8, 1986 (at p.6).
[135] See the decision in *Frank Dunne Ltd. v Dublin County Council* [1974] I.R. 45 at 54. The then legislation was subsequently amended; Local Government (Planning & Development) Act 1976, s.39(c).

(d) Conditions for requiring provision of open spaces;　　　　**4–96**

Special provision is made for the enforcement of conditions of this type under s.45 of the PDA 2000. In brief, in default of compliance by the owner with a written request to provide open space, the planning authority may seek to acquire the land compulsorily. Provision is made for the payment of limited compensation only.[136] See further paras 7–206 to 7–219.

(e) Conditions for requiring the planting, maintenance and replacement of　**4–97**
trees, shrubs or other plants or the landscaping of structures or other land;

(f) Conditions for requiring the satisfactory completion within a specified period, not being less than two years from the commencement of any works, of the proposed development (including any roads, open spaces, car parks, sewers, watermains or drains or other public facilities), where the development includes the construction of two or more houses;

The effect of this condition is that the developer of residential lands while retaining some discretion as to the date of the commencement of development, may be required to complete the development within a specified period. This would appear to represent an exception to the general principle that a planning permission may be implemented at any stage during its statutory life.[137]

(g) Conditions for requiring the giving of adequate security for satisfactory　**4–98**
completion of the proposed development;

Conditions of this type can prove controversial in practice, as a local authority will occasionally seek the payment of a cash bond even in circumstances where planning permission was granted on appeal, and An Bord Pleanála provided a choice as to the method of payment. It is submitted that this would be unlawful.

(h) Conditions for determining the sequence and timing in which and the time　**4–99**
at which works shall be carried out;

(i) Conditions for the maintenance or management of the proposed development (including the establishment or a company or the appointment of a person or body of persons to carry out such maintenance or management);

(j) Conditions for the maintenance, until taken in charge by the local authority concerned, of roads, open spaces, car parks, sewers, watermains or drains and other public facilities or, where there is an agreement with the local authority in relation to such maintenance, conditions for maintenance in accordance with the agreement;

---

[136] A similar provision under the previous legislation was held not to have retrospective effect: *Dublin County Council v Grealy* [1990] 1 I.R. 77; [1990] I.L.R.M. 641.

[137] It was held in *Bord na Móna v An Bord Pleanála* [1985] I.R. 205 (at 209) that the date of *commencement* of development should be at the election of the developer.

(k) Conditions for the requiring the provision of such facilities for the collection or storage of recyclable materials for the purposes of the proposed development;

(l) Conditions for requiring construction and demolition waste to be recovered or disposed of in such a manner and to such extent as may be specified by the planning authority;

(m) Conditions for requiring the provision of road, including traffic calming measures, open spaces, car parks, sewers, watermains or drains, facilities for the collection or storage of recyclable materials and other public facilities in excess of the immediate needs of the proposed development, subject to the local authority paying for the cost of the additional works and taking them in charge or otherwise entering into an agreement with the applicant with respect to the provision of those public facilities;

This provision takes account of the practical reality that, on occasion, it will be appropriate to require infrastructure in excess of the immediate needs of the proposed development to be provided at the time of the construction of the development, in order to avoid further disruption at a later stage. An attempt is made to maintain the principle that the developer should not be required to address problems not created by his development, by requiring the local authority to pay for the cost of the additional works. For example, a developer might be required to provide a larger car park than that necessitated by his development in order to facilitate subsequent development. The wording differs from the analogous provision under the previous legislation,[138] so as to avoid the lacuna identified in *Thomas McDonagh & Sons Ltd. v Galway Corporation*,[139] whereby the requirement to pay a contribution was avoided in circumstances where the local authority was not to be responsible for the maintenance of the excess works (in that case, the car park was to remain in the control and ownership of the developer; the local authority were not therefore to be responsible for its maintenance).

4–100   (n) Conditions for requiring the removal of any structures authorised by permission, or the discontinuance of any use of the land so authorised, at the expiration of a specified period, and the carrying out of works required for the reinstatement of land at the expiration of that period;

(o) Conditions in relation to appropriate naming and numbering of, and the provisions of appropriate signage for, the proposed development;

(p) Conditions for requiring in any case in which the development authorised by the permission would remove or alter any protected structure or any element or a protected structure which contributes to its special architectural, historical, archaeological, artistic, cultural, scientific, social or technical interest – (i) the preservation by a written and visual record (either measured architectural drawing or colour photographs and/or audio

---

[138] Local Government (Planning & Development) Act 1963, s.26(2)(h).
[139] [1995] 1 I.R. 191.

visual aids as considered appropriate) of that structure or element before the development authorised by the permission takes place, and (ii) where appropriate, the architectural salvaging of any element, or the re-instatement of any element in a manner specified by the authority;

(q) Conditions for regulating the hours and days during which a business premises may operate.

This provision makes express a power, namely to regulate the hours and days during which a business premises may operate, which is probably implicit in the general power to attach conditions in any event.[140]

F. Statutory Conditions Other Than Under Section 34(4)

1. Conditions specifying purposes for which a structure may be used

Under s.39(2) of the PDA 2000, a planning permission may specify the purpose for which a structure may or may not be used. The better view would seem to be that it is not necessary to specify the use by way of condition.[141] Indeed, it seems that no particular formula need be used and that a use may be specified by implication. In this connection it seems that regard may be had to the documents accompanying the application, and to the public notice. Under the previous legislation, it was further provided that in the event of no use being specified, the planning permission was to be construed as including permission to use the structure for the purpose for which it was designed. In this regard, "designed" had been interpreted narrowly as meaning "intended".[142] The absence of a similar provision under s.39(2) is troublesome.

4–101

2. Occupancy conditions

In the case of use as a dwelling, the permission may also be granted subject to a condition specifying that the use as a dwelling shall be restricted to use by persons of a particular class or description and that provision to that effect shall be made in a s.47 agreement. Conditions of this type are often referred to colloquially as "occupancy conditions". Even if one were to leave aside the express provisions of s.39(2), and to approach the matter from first principles, it would seem that a planning authority would, in theory, have power to attach occupancy conditions. The general test for the validity of a planning condition is that it must have a planning purpose.[143] In certain instances, an occupancy

4–102

---

[140] *Dublin Corporation v Raso* [1976–1977] I.L.R.M. 139.

[141] *Readymix (Éire) Ltd. v Dublin County Council*, unreported, Supreme Court, July 30, 1974; and *Wilson v West Sussex County Council* [1963] 2 Q.B. 764.

[142] *McMahon v Dublin Corporation* [1996] 3 I.R. 509; [1997] 1 I.L.R.M. 227 (subsequently approved of in *Palmerlane Ltd. v An Bord Pleanála* [1999] 2 I.L.R.M. 514).

[143] See, by analogy, *Brady v Environmental Protection Agency* [2007] I.E.H.C. 58; unreported, Charleton J., March 9, 2007 (condition under integrated pollution control

condition could meet this test. For example, an agricultural occupancy condition might have the purpose of restricting development in a rural area while nevertheless allowing for the employment needs of the area. Such a condition thus serves the purpose of allowing development, which would otherwise be refused, to proceed.[144]

4–103   In practice, certain planning authorities have sought to draw such conditions very narrowly, for example, by seeking to confine occupancy to the applicant, and his or her immediate family. It is submitted that such a condition would be invalid. First, such a narrow grouping would not constitute "persons of a particular class or description"; the terms "class" or "description" indicate a larger grouping. Secondly, it is difficult to understand what planning purpose is advanced by the restriction. Whereas a condition restricting occupation to persons employed in agriculture can be justified as balancing the need to protect the environment, with the need to accommodate agricultural workers, the *personal* attributes of an applicant are generally an irrelevant consideration.[145]

4–104   The validity of occupancy conditions has been examined in detail by the Law Society's Law Reform Committee. The committee, with the assistance of Oran Doyle, B.L. and Alan Keating, B.L., published a comprehensive report entitled "Discriminatory Planning Conditions: The case for reform" in February 2005. It is not possible for me to improve on the quality of this report, and readers are strongly encouraged to consult same. What follows below is merely a summary of some of the key conclusions of the report.

4–105   The report identifies six grounds of discrimination commonly used in occupancy conditions as follows: local residency; local employment; bloodline or pedigree; agricultural employment; ability to speak the Irish language; and status as a returning emigrant. The report then goes on to consider whether any or all of these grounds are incompatible with the Constitution; the European Convention on Human Rights or European Union law. The authors of the report summarise their principal conclusions as follows.

> "We concluded that bloodline conditions are invalid with respect to the Constitution, the European Convention on Human Rights and EU law. We concluded that local residency conditions and local employment conditions, if either is attached as an exhaustive enumeration of privileged persons, are invalid with respect to EU law. We concluded that agricultural worker conditions and language conditions are legally valid but that a rigid rule of imposing such conditions over a wide area might be problematic. Finally, we concluded that returning emigrant conditions are of questionable validity with reference to the European Convention on Human Rights, EU law and domestic equality legislation.

---

licence must be reasonably related to the activity that is to be permitted, and for the avoidance of the harm for which licensing of an activity is required by legislation).

[144] *Fawcett Properties Ltd. v Buckingham County Council* [1961] A.C. 636; and *Good v Epping Forest District Council* [1994] 1 W.L.R. 376.

[145] See, for example, *Flanagan v Galway City and County Manager* [1990] 2 I.R. 66.

Based on our reading of the case law, we believe that the Irish Courts, the European Court of Human Rights and the European Court of Justice would recognise the maintenance of a strong rural population, independent of the holiday sector, as a legitimate objective. For this reason, we recommend that, if planning authorities wish to impose discriminatory planning conditions that in some way favour 'local people', they should do so through the combination of a local residency and a local employment condition. That is, they should restrict occupancy of the dwelling to those who are either already local residents or local employees, although we suggest a specific definition of 'employee' to render such conditions consistent with EU laws on freedom of movement and establishment."

The recommendation that a local residence requirement only be used in conjunction with an alternative requirement of local employment is based on a conclusion that use of either requirement on its own would be disproportionate. **4–106**

"Bloodline conditions and local residency conditions are disproportionate to the public interest objective in that they exclude people who could contribute to the maintenance of a strong rural population and economic activity independent of the holiday sector. There is no reason to believe that one must have a bloodline connection to a local or already be a local resident in order to contribute to a strong rural, economically active community. A local employment condition on its own is also disproportionate in its exclusion of people who could contribute to the objective, i.e. local residents. However, we suggest that the combination of a local residency condition and a local employment condition (i.e. a condition which allows the dwelling to be occupied by either a local worker or a local resident) would proportionately serve the public interest objective of the maintenance of a strong rural population and economic activity independent of the holiday sector."

The "Sustainable Rural Housing" guidelines issued to planning authorities in April 2005 contain an indicative occupancy condition in the following terms. **4–107**

"(a) The proposed dwelling when completed shall be first occupied as the place of residence of the applicant, members of the applicant's immediate family or their heirs and shall remain so occupied for a period of seven years thereafter, unless consent is granted by the planning authority for its occupation by other persons who belong to the same category of housing need as the applicant.

(b) Before development commences, the applicant shall enter into an Agreement with the planning authority, pursuant to Section 47 of the 2000 Planning and Development Act providing for the terms of this occupancy requirement.

(c) Within two months of the occupation of the proposed dwelling, the applicant shall submit to the planning authority, a written statement of the confirmation of the first occupation of the dwelling in accordance with paragraph (a) and the date of such occupation.

(d) This condition shall not affect the sale of the dwelling by a mortgagee in possession or by any person deriving title from such a sale."

The Law Society has recommended that solicitors should not certify compliance with discriminatory planning conditions, as they have no special expertise or **4–108** knowledge to qualify them to do so, and a statutory declaration by the proposed occupant should be acceptable to planning authorities.[146]

3. Conditions requiring development contributions

4–109 As indicated at paras 4–29 to 4–32 above, the imposition of a levy or the exacting of a planning gain is not permissible save where expressly authorised by statute. In this regard, express provision is made under the PDA 2000 for the imposition of planning conditions requiring the payment of a contribution in respect of infrastructure and facilities.

4–110 "Public infrastructure and facilities" is defined as (a) the acquisition of land; (b) the provision of open spaces, recreational and community facilities and amenities and landscaping works; (c) the provision of roads, car parks, car parking places, sewers, waste water and water treatment facilities, drains and watermains; (d) the provision of bus corridors and lanes, bus interchange facilities (including car parks for those facilities), infrastructure to facilitate public transport, cycle and pedestrian facilities, and traffic calming measures; (e) the refurbishment, upgrading, enlargement or replacement of roads, car parks, car parking places, sewers, waste water and water treatment facilities, drains or watermains; and (f) any ancillary matters.[147]

4–111 "Public infrastructure project or service" is defined as (a) the provision of particular rail, light rail or other public transport infrastructure, including car parks and other ancillary development; (b) the provision of particular new roads; and (c) the provision of particular new sewers, waste water and water treatment facilities, drains or watermains and ancillary infrastructure.[148]

4–112 Section 48 states that a planning authority may, when granting a planning permission, include conditions for requiring the payment of a contribution in respect of public infrastructure and facilities benefiting development in the area of the planning authority and that is provided, or that it is intended will be provided, by or on behalf of a local authority (regardless of other sources of funding for the infrastructure and facilities). Section 49 further provides that a planning authority may attach conditions requiring the payment of a contribution in respect of any public infrastructure service or project. The qualifications for a condition under s.49 differ from those for a condition under s.48 in a number of important respects. First, the project or service must have been provided or carried out, as may be appropriate, and must benefit the development to which the planning permission relates when carried out. Secondly, the public infrastructure service or project must be specified in a scheme made by the

---

[146] Law Society Law Reform Committee, "Discriminatory Planning Conditions: The case for reform" (Dublin, February 2005).

[147] PDA 2000, s.48(17).

[148] PDA 2000, s.49(7) (as amended by the Planning and Development (Amendment) Act 2002).

planning authority (a "supplementary development scheme"). Finally, the definition of "public infrastructure service or project" is narrower than that of "public infrastructure and facilities".

A planning authority may facilitate the phased payment of contributions, and may require the giving of security to ensure payment of contributions. Where a contribution is not paid in accordance with the terms of the condition laid down by the planning authority, any outstanding amounts due to the planning authority shall be paid (together with interest that may have accrued over the period while withheld) by the person required to pay the contribution. A planning authority may recover, as a simple contract debt in a court of competent jurisdiction, any contribution or interest due to the planning authority.[149] **4–113**

A planning authority shall not require the payment of a contribution in respect of a public infrastructure project or service where the person concerned has made a contribution under s.48 in respect of public infrastructure and facilities of which the said public infrastructure project or service constituted a part.[150] **4–114**

The new statutory procedure did not apply pending the making of a development contribution scheme.[151] Instead, notwithstanding its repeal, the provisions of s.26 of the Local Government (Planning & Development) Act 1963, in relation to requiring contributions in respect of expenditure by local authorities on works which facilitate development continued to apply. These transitional provisions are, however, subject to a time-limit of two years from the commencement of s.48. The relevant commencement date is March 11, 2002. Thus it would seem that if a planning authority has still not made a development contribution scheme by March, 2004, it will have no statutory power to attach a condition requiring a contribution towards the costs of infrastructure and facilities benefiting the development. This will continue to be the position thereafter until the relevant planning authority makes a development contribution scheme. **4–115**

In the case of a condition imposed under s.48, there is only a limited right of appeal to An Bord Pleanála against the condition; specifically, an appeal may only be brought where an applicant for planning permission considers that the terms of the relevant development contribution scheme have not been properly applied.[152] There is further provision whereby, in the event that there are no other appeals, the grant of planning permission may issue in advance of the determination of the limited appeal, on the furnishing of security for payment of the full amount of the contribution as specified in the condition.[153] **4–116**

---

[149] PDA 2000, s.48(15).
[150] PDA 2000, s.49(5).
[151] PDA 2000, s.48(16)(b).
[152] PDA 2000, s.48(10)(a) and (b).
[153] PDA 2000, s.48(10)(c).

4–117   Where an appeal is brought to An Bord Pleanála in respect of a refusal to grant planning permission, and where An Bord Pleanála decides to grant permission, it shall, where appropriate, apply as a condition to the permission the provisions of the contribution scheme for the time being in force in the area of the proposed development.[154]

4. Conditions requiring special development contributions

4–118   Particular rules govern conditions requiring the payment of a special contribution. A planning authority may, in addition to the terms of a development contribution scheme, require the payment of a special contribution in respect of a particular development where specific exceptional costs not covered by the development contribution scheme are incurred by any local authority in respect of public infrastructure and facilities which benefit the proposed development.[155] In the case of such conditions, certain safeguards (analogous to those of general application under the previous legislation)[156] are set out. For example, the local authority is required to refund the contribution (together with interest) if the works in question are not commenced within five years of, or completed within seven years of, the date of payment of the contribution to the local authority.[157]

4–119   The general power whereby An Bord Pleanála can treat an appeal against a condition only as a full review is removed in the case of an appeal against a condition of this type.[158] There is also provision made (in the event of there being no other appeals) for the grant of planning permission to issue in advance of the determination of the limited appeal, on the furnishing of security for payment of the full amount of the contribution as specified in the condition.[159]

5. Conditions requiring housing agreements: social and affordable housing

4–120   Part V of the PDA 2000 (as amended)[160] establishes the provision of social and affordable housing as an objective of the planning legislation, and introduces a mechanism whereby the developers of residential development may be required either to cede land at its existing use value to the planning authority

---

[154] PDA 2000, s.48(11).
[155] PDA 2000, s.48(2)(c).
[156] See, for example, s.26(2)(h) of the Local Government (Planning & Development) Act 1963.
[157] PDA 2000, s.48(12).
[158] PDA 2000, s.48(13)(a).
[159] PDA 2000, s.48(13)(b).
[160] Part V of the PDA 2000 was significantly amended by the Planning and Development (Amendment) Act 2002. The commencement date for Pt V was November 1, 2000. (Planning and Development Act 2000 (Commencement) Order, 2000 (S.I. No. 349 of 2000)).

for the purposes of social and affordable housing, or to make alternative provision equivalent in monetary value to the value of the land that the planning authority would otherwise have received.

The provisions of Pt V are triggered in case of an application for residential development where a development plan objective requires that a specified percentage of any land zoned solely for residential use (or for a mixture of residential and other uses) be made available for social and affordable housing.[161] Section 96 (as substituted by the Planning and Development (Amendment) Act 2002) requires that a condition be attached to a planning permission requiring the applicant, or any other person with an interest in the land, to enter into an "agreement" for the transfer of land (hereinafter referred to as a "Part V agreement"). In the case of mixed zoning, the condition only applies to that *part* of the application which relates to the development of houses.[162]

4–121

In its mandatory form, a Part V agreement will simply involve the transfer of land in its undeveloped state. Some flexibility is allowed for, however, in that the developer may, as an alternative to this, volunteer to make provision for social and affordable housing in other ways. The potential options include the transfer to the planning authority of the ownership of any other land within the functional area of the planning authority; and the transfer of built houses and/ or serviced sites (again, not necessarily on the lands the subject-matter of the application for planning permission). Moreover, it seems that a Part V agreement might provide simply for the payment of monies to the planning authority.

4–122

As stated above, the default option is for the transfer of (undeveloped) lands. Where this option is not exercised, and one of the alternatives used instead, there is nevertheless a requirement that the aggregate monetary value of the property or amounts or both, as the case may be, transferred or paid under the alternative arrangement be equivalent to the monetary value of the land that the planning authority would otherwise have received if the agreement solely provided for a transfer of land.

4–123

In considering the entry into of a housing agreement, the planning authority shall have regard to (i) whether such an agreement will contribute effectively and efficiently to the achievement of the objectives of the housing strategy; (ii) whether such an agreement will constitute the best use of the resources available to it to ensure an adequate supply of housing and any financial implications of the agreement for its functions as a housing authority; (iii) the need to counteract undue segregation in housing between persons of different social background in the area of the planning authority; (iv) whether such an agreement is in

4–124

---

[161] PDA 2000, s.96(1) (as substituted by the Planning and Development (Amendment) Act 2002).
[162] PDA 2000, s.96(1) (as substituted). The definition of "house" includes a flat or apartment; PDA 2000, s.2.

accordance with the provisions of the development plan; and (v) the time within which housing is likely to be provided as a consequence of the agreement.[163]

4–125 The mechanics of s.96 are unusual in that matters of basic detail (including the very identity of the land to be transferred) are not specified by way of condition attached to the planning permission but rather are left over for "agreement". This has the effect that final decisions as to the logistics are postponed; planning permission is granted in principle, in the first instance, subject to a condition requiring that the developer enter into an agreement. It also has the result that the public are excluded: the agreement process is not subject to public scrutiny nor can a member of the public appeal the terms of an agreement to An Bord Pleanála. Finally, the fact that such a condition leaves over significant matters for agreement with the planning authority represents an exception to the principle that the decision of An Bord Pleanála, on appeal, determines conclusively all substantial issues raised on the application.[164]

6. Points of detail

4–126 Section 34(5) of the PDA 2000 (as amended under the 2006 Act) states that the conditions referred to under subsection (1)[165] may provide that points of detail relating to a grant of planning permission may be agreed between the planning authority and the person carrying out the development. To an extent, this subsection merely involves an express declaration of a power which the courts had found to be implicit under the previous legislation.[166]

4–127 The amended subsection goes on to state that if the planning authority and that person cannot agree on the matter the matter may be referred to An Bord Pleanála for determination. This latter provision overcomes a possible deficiency in the original wording, whereby it appeared that the right to refer the matter to An Bord Pleanála for determination was contingent on express provision to that effect being included in the condition.[167] The new wording ensures that An Bord Pleanála has jurisdiction in all cases.

---

[163] PDA 2000, s.96(3)(c) (as substituted).
[164] cf. PDA 2000, s.34(5); *Boland v An Bord Pleanála* [1996] 3 I.R. 435; *McNamara v An Bord Pleanála* [1996] 2 I.L.R.M. 339; and *Houlihan v An Bord Pleanála*, unreported, High Court, Murphy J., October 3, 1993.
[165] Note that, on the wording of the PDA 2000, s.34(4), this includes conditions enumerated under that subsection.
[166] *Boland v An Bord Pleanála* [1996] 3 I.R. 435; and *McNamara v An Bord Pleanála (No. 2)* [1996] I.L.R.M. 339.
[167] See comments of Blayney J. in *Boland v An Bord Pleanála* [1996] 3 I.R. 435 as to the difficulties which might arise if the condition did not provide for a reference to An Bord Pleanála. Blayney J. suggested that that it might be preferable that the condition include the words "and in default of agreement shall be determined by the board". See also *Mulholland v An Bord Pleanála (No. 2)* [2005] I.E.H.C. 306; [2006] 1 I.R. 453; [2006] 1 I.L.R.M. 287, where the possibility of a developer challenging a condition without such a provision is mentioned.

It is only points of detail which can properly be left over for agreement[168]; any **4–128** matters of importance must be dealt with with particularity.[169] Further, the condition must set forth the purpose of such details; the overall objective to be achieved by the matters which have been left for agreement; state clearly the reasons therefor; and lay down criteria by which the developer and the planning authority can reach agreement.[170]

The judgment in *Kenny v Dublin City Council*[171] involved the application of **4–129** these established principles to a particular set of facts. The High Court rejected a challenge that the decision of the planning authority to agree a compliance submission went beyond the scope of the conditions or represented a material alteration to the development.

> "The faithful implementation of the decision of An Bord Pleanála in relation to its conditions depends in the first instance on the degree of specificity of those conditions. The more specific, the less discretion there is regarding their implementation. The more general they are the more scope there is between the planning authority and the developer. There is clear evidence that there are several ways whereby a general condition such as that relating to the western arm of building number 3 could be reduced in height in the interest of visual amenity by the omission of the first floor."

The applicant in the judicial review proceedings had previously challenged **4–130** the decision of An Bord Pleanála to grant planning permission, arguing, *inter alia*, that the conditions imposed by An Bord Pleanála amounted to an unlawful delegation by the board of its decision-making power to the planning authority and was thus *ultra vires*. It had been argued that the developer and the planning authority were at large as to the appearance, nature and scale of the ultimate development, all of which matters, or so it was alleged, could subsequently be agreed in private without any input from, or access by, members of the public. In rejecting this earlier challenge, the High Court in *Kenny v An Bord Pleanála*[172] emphasised that the subsequent conduct of the planning authority in agreeing submissions under the impugned conditions could itself be subject to judicial review proceedings if necessary. The High Court also stated that it should not be assumed that the planning authority would seek to exceed the limited discretion allowed to it in agreeing points of detail under the conditions.

> "In addition I do not believe that it would be correct of me to assume that the Planning Authority, which as a matter of law ought to be aware of its functions and responsibilities including its limitations, when dealing with conditions of this nature, would exceed its role which is to further the faithful, true and core implementation of the permission. It would be wrong in my view to ascribe to it any ultra vires intention when none has or could be so identified."

---

[168] *Boland v An Bord Pleanála* [1996] 3 I.R. 435 at 466. See also *Mulholland v An Bord Pleanála (No. 2)* [2005] I.E.H.C. 306; [2006] 1 I.R. 453; [2006] 1 I.L.R.M. 287.
[169] *Houlihan v An Bord Pleanála*, unreported, High Court, Murphy J., October 4, 1993 (at p. 8).
[170] *Boland v An Bord Pleanála* [1996] 3 I.R. 435 at 467.
[171] Unreported, High Court, Murphy J., September 8, 2004.
[172] [2001] 1 I.R. 565.

4–131   The provisions of s.34(5) fell for direct consideration in *Ryanair Ltd. v An Bord Pleanála*.[173] The applicant for judicial review sought to make the argument that the express power to attach conditions leaving points of detail over for agreement was confined to the planning authority, and was not available to An Bord Pleanála on appeal. The argument in this regard appeared to be to the effect that because there is no express reference under s.37 to s.34(5), this power is available only in respect of a decision by the planning authority. The powers of An Bord Pleanála in relation to an appeal are set out under s.37 of the PDA 2000. It is expressly provided that subsections (1), (2), (3) and (4) of s.34 shall apply, subject to any necessary modifications, in relation to the determination of an application by the board on an appeal under s.37 as they apply in relation to the determination under that section of an application by a planning authority. The High Court rejected this argument.

> "While it has been submitted on behalf of the applicant that the power of a planning authority to impose such a condition derives from s. 34 (5) alone, it has to be recalled that this Court has previously decided in the case of *Kenny v. An Bord Pleanála (No. 1)* [2001] 1 I.R. 565 that the power enjoyed by the Board to impose a condition that matters should be agreed between a planning authority and the recipient of a permission is one arising under s. 26 of the Act of 1963. In this regard, the court was following the earlier decision in *Boland v. An Bord Pleanála* [1996] 3 I.R. 435. It has not been suggested that the principles outlined in Bennion on *Statutory Interpretation,* referred to by counsel for the Board on this application, do not represent a correct statement of the law such that any intended removal of the power previously enjoyed by the Board should be removed by measured and considered provisions and that the least alteration of the law should be presumed, all matters being equal. I am also inclined to the reasoning of counsel for the Board as to the purpose of s. 34 (5). I am further inclined to accept the submissions of counsel for the first notice party that subs. (5) does not in fact confer the power in question but rather identifies the existing power."

4–132   Conditions of this type are open to two possible criticisms. First, that the public rights of participation are reduced. Secondly, that same involve an abdication of the appellate function of An Bord Pleanála.[174]

4–133   The function of the planning authority in agreeing the points of detail is very limited, and is subject to judicial review by the High Court.[175] Specifically, the planning authority must implement what has already been decided in essence. Thus, the planning authority must ascertain what is the true or correct meaning of the conditions attached to the planning permission and to confine itself and the developer to such proposals as are in compliance with the conditions.[176] The planning authority does not enjoy a statutory discretion in

---

[173] [2004] 2 I.R. 334.

[174] *Houlihan v An Bord Pleanála*, unreported, High Court, Murphy J., October 4, 1993.

[175] *O'Connor v Dublin Corporation (No. 2)*, unreported, High Court, O'Neill J., October 3, 2000. See also *Kenny v An Bord Pleanála (No. 1)* [2001] 1 I.R. 565.

[176] *O'Connor v Dublin Corporation (No. 2)*, unreported, High Court, O'Neill J., October 3, 2000 (at p. 29).

this regard, and, accordingly, its decision is not subject to the attenuated form of review otherwise applicable[177] (under the decision in *O'Keeffe v An Bord Pleanála*).[178]

The availability of judicial review might suggest that an opportunity should be allowed for the public to make submissions and representations at the agreement stage. There is no formal mechanism under the legislation or regulations for such consultation, however. The decision of Blayney J. in *Boland* seems to suggest that having regard to the very detailed instructions set out in the conditions, and the purpose for which they were imposed, no member of the public could reasonably have objected to them and so An Bord Pleanála in imposing the conditions was not interfering with or prejudicing any right of the public. This might be taken as suggesting that once the principle of the development has been accepted, *i.e.* the objectors have been unsuccessful, it is then in the objectors' interest that the development be regulated to the greatest possible extent, and, possibly, that an objector would not be prejudiced by being precluded from objecting to the ultimate form of works agreed. Barr J. in his decision in *McNamara v An Bord Pleanála (No. 2)*,[179] considered, however, that third parties would be entitled to make representations with respect to matters left over for agreement.[180] In *Arklow Holidays Ltd. v An Bord Pleanála*,[181] Clarke J. suggested that members of the public would be entitled to challenge an agreement reached on foot of such a condition if the agreement did not comply with the criteria specified in the condition imposed by An Bord Pleanála.

4–134

7. Transboundary effects

A planning authority or An Bord Pleanála, as the case may be, may, following the consideration of any submissions or observations received or any consultations entered into by a planning authority or An Bord Pleanála, impose conditions on a grant of planning permission in order to reduce or eliminate potential transboundary effects of any proposed development.[182]

4–135

8. Public rights of way

The interaction of the planning legislation and the roads legislation fell to be considered in *Coll v Donegal County Council*.[183] A condition attached to a

4–136

---

[177] *O'Connor v Dublin Corporation (No. 2)*, unreported, High Court, O'Neill J., October 3, 2000.
[178] [1993] 1 I.R. 39; [1992] I.L.R.M 237.
[179] [1996] 2 I.L.R.M. 339.
[180] *cf. R. v Lichfield DC Ex p. Lichfield Securities Ltd.* [2000] P.C.L.R. 458.
[181] Unreported, High Court, Clarke J., January 18, 2006.
[182] PDA 2000, s.174(3).
[183] [2005] I.E.H.C. 231; unreported, Peart J., July 7, 2005.

planning permission required that a proposed road realignment be carried out prior to the commencement of development. The road realignment necessitated the extinguishment of the public right of way over a small portion of an existing road, thereby incorporating that area of roadway into the development site, and its replacement with a new section of road and junction. (It was urged on behalf of the applicant in the judicial review proceedings that the fact that the road might be closed and replaced by an alternative stretch of road adjacent to it was not something which was obvious from the public notices in respect of the application for planning permission.)

4–137   The local authority commenced the procedure under s.73 of the Roads Act 1993, and a decision was made in October 2003 not to extinguish the public right of way. The issue of principle in the proceedings was as to whether the local authority could subsequently, approximately one year later, decide to extinguish the public right of way and, in effect, reverse the earlier decision. The High Court ruled that the earlier decision of October 2003 was not binding for all time, and that local authority were entitled to revisit the matter.

> "It seems to me from a reading of s.73 of the Roads Act 1993, that a local authority is not prevented from considering as often as it chooses a proposal that a public right of way should be closed. One could envisage reasons why a Council might wish to vote again on such a motion. It is possible for example that some years later, perhaps even following the election of a new Council, made up of different councillors from the out-going Council, there would be a majority in favour of extinguishment. It seems perfectly reasonable that such a new Council should be able to have another debate on the matter and take another vote. There could be other reasons why another attempt to extinguish the right of way might be considered. To take another example, which comes to mind, I could envisage a situation where because over a number of years traffic volumes might have increased over a road to such an extent that for safety reasons the road should be closed and perhaps put to a different use. The fact that a couple of years previously the Council, even composed of the same personnel, voted against extinguishment, could not prevent for all time that matter being voted on again."

4–138   Peart J. further held that any legitimate expectation the applicant might enjoy was confined to an expectation that the statutory procedures would be followed and that she would therefore be consulted in the way provided for whenever there is a proposal by the local authority to extinguish any public right of way.

9. Restoration conditions

4–139   A planning permission will sometimes contain conditions requiring the restoration of the land after permitted development, such as quarrying, is completed. Although a planning permission will generally only have a "life" of five years, certain conditions survive the expiration of the planning permission. In particular, the obligation of any person to comply with any condition whereby something is required either to be done or not to be done survives. In *Mason v KTK Sand and Gravel Ltd.*,[184] the somewhat ingenious argument was put forward that certain conditions under a long since expired planning permission allowed a disused sand and gravel quarry to be filled with inert waste. A waste permit had been granted under the Waste Management Acts, but no fresh grant of planning permission had been obtained. The developer argued that the backfilling of the excavated quarry with inert waste was authorised by a restoration condition under the planning permission. The relevant condition was in the following terms.

> "The whole of the surface area, including slopes and sections containing deposits accruing from the working of the pit shall be reinstated as closely as possible to the contours of the original ground. The date of commencement of restoration works, the phasing of such works, the sections to be reinstated and the final contours and levels to which the restoration shall be carried out shall be agreed with the Planning Authority."

Smyth J. appeared to accept that, in principle, a condition requiring restoration works to be carried out could implicitly include permission for those works. The scope of the planning permission, however, was a mater for construction, subject to the principle that the planning permission could not go beyond the scope of the initial application. Smyth J. held that the test to be applied was as to whether or not the operation of a landfill site was a different development from that which was originally intended in the way of restoration works under the planning permission. In applying this test, Smyth J. emphasised that in determining the nature and extent of development permitted under a planning permission regard had to be had to the description of the development in the application for planning permission. The purpose of the requirement to state the nature and extent of the proposed development was to ensure that both the planning authority and members of the public could evaluate or come to an appreciation of what development was intended. On the facts, Smyth J. held that the proposed and existing use of the land (as a landfill site) was not the subject of the original planning permission, and was not reasonably incidental either to the primary purpose of such use, for which permission was obtained, or incidental to the conditions attached thereto. The fact that one or more conditions in a planning permission left outstanding obligations did not *per se* permit of the carrying out of development of a radically different character (both as to its nature and extent) in purported discharge of such obligations. The operations, works, use and effects of the intended landfill site were a radically different development both in nature and extent than that which could be reasonably foreseen or envisaged from the description "extend existing sandpit into adjoining field" stated in the original planning permission. **4–140**

In reaching his conclusions, Smyth J. rejected a submission that particular weight should be attached to the (favourable) interpretation by the planning authority of the planning permission, holding that the interpretation of a planning permission was ultimately a matter for the courts. **4–141**

---

[184] Unreported, High Court, Smyth J., May 7, 2004.

CHAPTER FIVE

THE GRANT OF PLANNING PERMISSION

A. Effect of Grant of Planning Permission

1. Planning permission *per se* does not authorise carrying out of development

The grant of planning permission merely confirms that the provisions of the   **5–01**
planning legislation have been complied with and does not *per se* authorise
the development to proceed. It is expressly provided under s.34(13) of the
PDA 2000 that a person shall not be entitled solely by reason of a permission
to carry out development.[1] For example, it may be necessary to obtain further
licences or permits (such as a water pollution licence perhaps). It may also be
the case that the development is inhibited by private law requirements. For
example, the developer may not have the necessary legal title over all of the
relevant lands. Similarly, the fact that planning permission has been granted
does not forestall the development from giving rise to tortious liability under
the law of nuisance.

Reference is made in this regard to the decision of the Supreme Court in *Convery*   **5–02**
v Dublin County Council.[2] The Supreme Court stated that it was clear from
the equivalent provision to s.34(13) under the previous legislation that a planning
authority (or an Bord Pleanála on appeal) cannot be said to have authorised the
developer by the grant of a permission to commit an act which would be
otherwise unlawful, whether because it interfered, for example, with the right
to light of other property owners or created an unacceptable hazard for others
or otherwise.

---

[1] See *Keane v An Bord Pleanála* [1998] 2 I.L.R.M. 241 for a discussion of the equivalent
provision of the previous legislation: Local Government (Planning & Development) Act
1963, s.26(11). See also *Cablelink Ltd. v An Bord Pleanála* [1999] 1 I.R. 596.
[2] [1996] 3 I.R. 153 at 173.

2. Specified purpose

5–03   Under s.39(2), a planning permission may specify the purpose for which a structure may or may not be used. The better view would seem to be that it is not necessary to specify the use by way of condition.[3] Indeed, it seems that no particular formula need be used and that a use may be specified by implication. In this connection it seems that regard may be had to the documents accompanying the application, and to the public notice.

3. Planning permission as derogation from grant

5–04   An important point of conveyancing law fell for consideration by the Supreme Court in *William Bennett Construction Ltd. v Greene.*[4] Outline planning permission had been obtained for certain residential development. On the site layout plan accompanying the application for planning permission, a drain for the disposal of sewage was shown running in a south-easterly direction to connect with a foul water sewer in the road adjoining the site. Part of the lands were sold on, conditional on the purchaser obtaining an approval pursuant to the outline planning permission. The part of the lands sold excluded the lands on which the drain for the disposal of sewage was to run. The purchaser brought proceedings claiming that it had a way-leave in this regard, arguing that where land had been sold for a specific purpose known to both parties, *i.e.* the development of the land as shown on the site layout plan on the basis of which the outline permission had been granted, and the uncontradicted evidence established that it would be prohibitively expensive for the purchaser to develop the land in any other way so far as the disposal of the sewage was concerned, the conduct of the vendor in refusing to allow the development proceed in that manner constituted a derogation from the grant of the land. The Supreme Court rejected this argument, holding that at the time of the sale, there was not in existence an easement in the nature of a way-leave which, when part of the land was sold, remained in existence as a quasi-easement for the benefit of the lands sold.

> "The defendants in this case had never at any stage used any part of their land for the disposal of sewage by means of a pipe connecting with the main sewers of the local authority. They did no more than indicate in the site layout plan lodged with the application for permission that that was how they would propose to dispose of the sewage, in the event of permission being granted for the development and the development proceeding. There was, accordingly, no easement in existence being used at the time of the grant by the grantor for the benefit of the property granted over the property retained and hence no room for the application of the doctrine that the grantor cannot derogate from his grant."

---

[3] See the facts of *Glancré Teoranta v Cafferkey (No. 2)* [2004] 4 I.R. 22. See also *Readymix (Éire) Ltd. v Dublin County Council*, unreported, Supreme Court, July 30, 1974; and *Wilson v West Sussex County Council* [1963] 2 Q.B. 764.

[4] [2004] 2 I.L.R.M. 96.

The Supreme Court also made the point that a purchaser of the land becomes **5–05** entitled to the benefit of a planning permission, not by virtue of the conveyance, but because of the general principle that a grant of permission to develop land enures for the benefit of the land and of all persons for the time being interested therein.

B. Interpretation of Planning Permission

1. Objective interpretation

A planning permission is a public document; it is not personal to the applicant, **5–06** but rather enures for the benefit of the land. It follows as a consequence that a planning permission is to be interpreted objectively, and not in light of subjective considerations peculiar to the applicant or those responsible for the grant of planning permission.[5]

A planning permission is to be given its ordinary meaning as it would be **5–07** understood by members of the public without legal training, as well as by developers and their agents, unless such documents, read as a whole, necessarily indicate some other meaning.[6]

A planning authority is required to enter on the planning register the complete **5–08** decision—whether of the planning authority itself or of An Bord Pleanála— on an application for planning permission.[7] In principle, therefore, the planning register should contain full details of the terms of a planning permission, and it should not be necessary to go beyond the contents of the planning register when interpreting the planning permission. Where the permission contained in the planning register is self-contained, it will not be permissible to go outside in when construing it.[8] Extrinsic evidence will, however, be admissible in the following two circumstances.

---

[5] *Readymix (Éire) Ltd. v Dublin County Council*, unreported, Supreme Court, July 30, 1974, cited with approval in, *inter alia, Grianán An Aileach Interpretative Centre Company Ltd. v Donegal County Council (No. 1)* [2003] 2 I.R. 572; *Glancré Teoranta v Cafferkey (No. 2)* [2004] 4 I.R. 22; *Altara Developments Ltd. v Ventola Ltd.* [2005] I.E.H.C. 312; unreported, O'Sullivan J., October 6, 2005; and *Ryan v Roadstone Ltd.* [2006] I.E.H.C. 53; unreported, O'Donovan J., March 6, 2006.

[6] *In Re XJS Investments Ltd.* [1986] I.R. 750 at 756. See also *Carter Commercial Developments Ltd. (In administration) v Secretary of State for Transport, Local Government and the Regions* [2002] E.W.C.A. Civ 1914; [2003] J.P.L. 1048 (planning permission not to be construed like a commercial document, but is to be given the meaning that a reasonable reader would give to it, having available to him only the permission and the application form).

[7] PDA 2000, s.7(2)(e) and (f).

[8] *Readymix (Éire) Ltd. v Dublin County Council*, unreported, Supreme Court, July 30, 1974, *per* Henchy J.

(i) Planning permission incorporates other documents by reference

5–09   Where the planning permission incorporates other documents, it is the combined effect of the permission and such documents which must be looked at in determining the proper scope of the permission.[9] In practice, most planning permissions include a condition requiring that the development be carried out in accordance with the plans and particulars lodged as part of the application.[10]

(ii) Planning permission is ambiguous

5–10   Extrinsic evidence may be admissible where the planning permission is ambiguous.[11] It appears that the courts will also admit extrinsic evidence to resolve ambiguities as to the nature and extent of a developer's obligations under planning permission when a dispute as to the true construction of the permission arises between the planning authority and the original grantee.[12]

2. Double construction rule

5–11   There is a presumption that a planning permission is valid.[13] This would seem to follow, in part, from the fact that a challenge to the validity of a decision on an application for planning permission is expressly confined to an application for judicial review, and that such an application for judicial review must, generally, be made within eight weeks of the date of the decision.[14] One consequence of this would seem to be that an attempt should be made—where two or more interpretations are open—to favour the interpretation which would hold the planning permission valid. In other words, where the choice is open to it, a court should prefer the interpretation which means that the planning permission would be valid, *i.e.* the court should apply a form of double construction rule.

---

[9] *Readymix (Éire) Ltd. v Dublin County Council*, unreported, Supreme Court, July 30, 1974. See also *Jack Barrett Builders Ltd. v Dublin County Council*, unreported, Supreme Court, July 28, 1983 (link road indicated in maps and plans accompanying application); and *Coffey v Hebron Homes Ltd.*, unreported, High Court, O'Hanlon J., July 27, 1984 (breach where failure to build in accordance with plans and specifications).

[10] In *R. v Ashford Borough Council Ex p. Shepway DC* (1999) P.L.C.R. 12, it was suggested that for incorporation of the application to be achieved, more is required than a mere reference to the application on the face of the permission. Rather, words sufficient to inform a reasonable reader that the application forms part of the permission are needed.

[11] See *R. v Ashford Borough Council Ex p. Shepway DC* (1999) P.L.C.R. 12. For an example of a case where the High Court of England and Wales ruled that there was no ambiguity, see *R. (On the application of Sevenoaks District Council) v First Secretary of State* [2005] J.P.L. 116.

[12] See *Jack Barrett Builders Ltd. v Dublin County Council*, unreported, Supreme Court, July 28, 1983 (link road indicated in maps and plans accompanying application).

[13] See, for example, *Lancefort Ltd. v An Bord Pleanála*, unreported, High Court, McGuinness J., March 12, 1998.

[14] PDA 2000, s.50 (as amended).

3. Immaterial deviations

It seems that planning permissions are to be interpreted flexibly so as to allow for a tolerance in respect of what have been described as "immaterial deviations". Reference is made to the decision in *O'Connell v Dungarvan Energy Ltd.*[15] Finnegan J. appeared to approve of the following passage from the decision in *Lever (Finance) Ltd. v Westminster Corporation.*[16] **5–12**

> "In my opinion a planning permission covers work which is specified in the detailed plans and any immaterial variation therein. I do not use the words *de minimis* because that would be misleading. It is obvious that, as the developer proceeds with the work there will necessarily be variations from time to time. Things may arise which were not foreseen. It should not be necessary for the developers to go back to the planning authority for every immaterial variation. The permission covers any variation which is not material."

Reference is also made to the decision in *Cork County Council v Cliftonhall Ltd.*[17] In that decision Finnegan J. again had regard to the materiality of the deviation. **5–13**

4. Content of environmental impact statement

In the case of development subject to environmental impact assessment, it is legitimate to have regard to the content of the environmental impact statement in determining the nature and extent of the development permitted. For example, the assessment contained in the environmental impact statement will, in many instances, be based on assumptions as to the intensity at which the development will be carried out. One obvious example is in relation to traffic. It would undermine the objective of the environmental impact statement process were a planning permission to be subsequently interpreted as allowing a level of activity—with consequent environmental effect—which had not been anticipated or assessed at the time of the environmental impact statement. **5–14**

Obviously, if a particular aspect is not dealt with in the environmental impact statement at all, then there is a strong argument to say that the planning permission does not extend to cover that particular activity. Reference is made in this regard to the decision in *Derrybrien Cooperative Society Ltd. v Saorgus Energy Ltd.*[18] **5–15**

> "As the environmental impact statements in this case were furnished as part of the planning applications I have no doubt whatsoever that they must be considered as part of the documentation that must be looked at in determining the proper scope of the permission; it then becomes necessary to consider whether viewed objectively the documents as a whole could be said to make it clear that the

---

[15] Unreported, High Court, Finnegan J., February 27, 2001.
[16] [1972] All E.R. 496.
[17] Unreported, High Court, Finnegan J., April 6, 2001.
[18] Unreported, High Court, Dunne, J., June 3, 2005.

proposed development involved the removal of all the forestry at the Derrybrien site in respect of the relevant applications. I should just note at this point that reference was also made to the various plans and drawings in this regard but I do not place any particular reliance on the plans and drawings as they did not appear to me to be of great assistance in determining this issue. Having considered the matter carefully and in particular in the light of the matters set out in the environmental impact statements I have come to the conclusion that on a reading of the environmental impact statements attached to the various permissions it was quite clear that the proposed development envisaged the removal of the forestry thereon and the change of use on the lands from forestry to use as a wind farm. I can come to no other conclusion."

5–16   Reference is also made to the judgment of the High Court of England and Wales in *R. (On the application of Gregan) v Hartlepool Borough Council*[19] where it was suggested that if an activity is not described or assessed in an environmental impact statement, then the proper inference to be drawn (absent any indication to the contrary) must be that it does not form part of the permitted development.

5. Interpretation of planning conditions

5–17   The rules of interpretation discussed above apply equally to the interpretation of planning conditions. The High Court in *Altara Developments Ltd. v Ventola Ltd.*[20] rejected an argument that planning conditions fell to be interpreted, in cases of ambiguity, in favour of the developer by reference to a principle of *contra proferentem* or any extension thereof.[21]

5–18   In practice, the wording employed in many planning conditions leaves much to be desired. The judgment of the High Court in *Dublin City Council v Liffey Beat Ltd.*[22] should serve as a cautionary tale to planning authority officials to take more care in this regard. The planning authority sought to enforce a condition attached to a planning permission which permitted use of premises for public entertainment. The planning authority alleged that the premises were being used—in breach of condition—for the purposes of a night club. The relevant condition provided that no part of the permission entitled the use of any part of the premises as a night club or similar function type of premises other than those stated in two identified sub-paragraphs. Quirke J. stated that the conditions applying in respect of the relevant planning permissions had been drafted so poorly that their construction, for practical purposes, had proved very difficult. In all the circumstances, Quirke J. held that the planning authority had failed to discharge the onus upon it, as applicant under s.160, to establish that there had been an unauthorised use of the premises.

---

[19] [2003] E.W.H.C. 3278; [2004] J.P.L. 1088, [76].

[20] [2005] I.E.H.C. 312; unreported, O'Sullivan J., October 6, 2005.

[21] *cf. Cork County Council v Cliftonhall Ltd*, unreported, High Court, Finnegan J., April 6, 2001. For a detailed discussion see E. Galligan, "Onus of proof in section 160 applications" (2006) 13 I.P.E.L.J. 104.

[22] [2005] 1 I.R. 478; [2005] I.E.H.C. 82.

The decision is *Liffey Beat Ltd.* also contains criticism of the failure of the **5–19** planning authority to interact with or to respond to requests from the developer as to what a particular condition might mean.

> "In particular where clarification is sought from the planning authority (or An Bord Pleanála) by a party having an interest in the property as to the nature and extent of the restriction imposed by a condition within a planning permission, then reasonable steps should be taken by the planning authority (or the Board) to provide the clarification sought. The planning process is intended to be substantively consultative in nature subject to the application of the principles of natural and constitutional justice."

A further example of the practical difficulties which can arise if conditions are **5–20** not carefully drafted is provided by the English case of *R. (On the application of Sevenoaks DC) v First Secretary of State.*[23] The condition sought to be enforced against was in the following terms.

> "Prior to the commencement of the development hereby permitted details of all proposed engineering works associated with the laying out of golf courses including the creation of greens, bunkers, tees, ponds or lakes shall be submitted to and approved in writing by the District Planning Authority."

Unlike other conditions under the planning permission, this condition did not **5–21** expressly require that the works be carried out in accordance with the approved details. The local authority sought to argue that it was possible to imply such an implementation clause into the condition. This argument was rejected by the High Court of England and Wales, holding that it was essential that any obligation by way of a condition is clearly and explicitly imposed. The court attached great significance to the contrast between the wording of the relevant condition, and other conditions under the planning permission, observing that when the local authority wanted not merely that details be submitted and approved, but also that the works should be constructed in accordance with the approved details, it had expressly said so. In the circumstances, there was no basis for implying such an obligation if the local authority failed for whatever reason to impose it by express words. Attention was also drawn to the advice, and wording of a model condition, provided in a departmental circular.

> "The framing of conditions requires care, not least to ensure that a condition is enforceable. A condition, for example, requiring only that 'a landscape scheme shall be submitted for the approval of the local planning authority' is incomplete, since if the applicant were to submit the scheme, even if it is approved, the local planning authority is unlikely to be able to require the scheme to be implemented. In such a case the requirement that needs to be imposed is that landscape work shall be carried out in accordance with a scheme to be approved in writing by the local planning authority; and the wording of the condition must clearly require this."

---

[23] [2004] E.W.H.C. 771 (Admin); [2005] J.P.L. 116; [2005] 1 P. & C.R. 186.

5–22   The model condition was in the following terms.

> "No development shall take place until full details of both hard and soft landscape works have been submitted to and approved in writing by the local planning authority and these works shall be carried out as approved."

6. High Court declarations as to meaning of planning permission

5–23   Given that the interpretation of a planning permission is a question of law,[24] rather than one of fact and degree, one would have thought that the High Court should have jurisdiction to give a declaration as to the true meaning of a planning permission where it relates to the legal rights and entitlements of the parties. This was the approach adopted by Kelly J. in the High Court in *Grianán An Aileach Interpretative Centre Company Ltd. v Donegal County Council*.[25] The Supreme Court decided—on the basis of an argument not made before the High Court—that the existence of the Section 5 reference procedure precluded the High Court from determining such issues.[26] See further para.10–29 and onwards.

C. Amendment of Planning Permission

5–24   A planning permission may be amended in certain circumstances under s.146A of the PDA 2000.[27] The power of amendment resides with the relevant planning authority, or An Bord Pleanála, depending on which body granted the planning permission. The power of amendment may be exercised for the purposes of: (i) correcting any clerical error in the planning permission; (ii) facilitating the doing of any thing pursuant to the planning permission where the doing of that thing may reasonably be regarded as having been contemplated by a particular provision of the permission or the terms of the permission taken as a whole, but which was not expressly provided for; or (iii) otherwise facilitating the operation of the permission.

5–25   A planning authority, or An Bord Pleanála, before it decides whether to exercise its powers of amendment in a particular case, may invite submissions in relation to the matter to be made to it by any person who made submissions or observations to the planning authority or the board in relation to the permission.[28] The planning authority or An Bord Pleanála must have regard to any submissions made to it on foot of such an invitation.

---

[24] See, for example, *R. (On the application of Gregan) v Hartlepool Borough Council* [2003] E.W.H.C. 3278; [2004] J.P.L. 1088, [17].

[25] *Grianán an Aileach v Donegal County Council (No. 1)* [2003] 2 I.R. 572.

[26] [2004] 2 I.R. 625; [2005] 1 I.L.R.M. 106.

[27] PDA 2000, s.146A (as inserted by s.30 of the 2006 Act). The power is not confined to strategic infrastructure developments.

[28] PDA 2000, s.146A(3) (as inserted s.30 of the 2006 Act).

An amendment cannot be made if it would, in the opinion of the planning **5–26** authority or An Bord Pleanála, result in a "material alteration" of the terms of the permitted development.[29] No guidance is given under the section as to what is meant by a "material alteration". The phrase must, however, be interpreted consistently with the objective of ensuring effective public participation in the planning process. An amendment would not be appropriate therefore if it gives rise to a new planning issue, on which members of the public did not have an opportunity to make submissions or observations prior to the decision to grant planning permission.

It should be noted that the test is whether the amendment would result in a **5–27** material alteration of the terms of the development, the subject of the planning permission, rather than of the terms of the permission itself. This suggests that significant amendments may be introduced in respect of aspects of the planning permission which do not alter the terms of the development *per se*. Thus, for example, where as a result of a clerical error a condition requiring a financial contribution, or the entry into of an agreement under Part V in respect of social and affordable housing, has been omitted from a planning permission, it seems that this might be corrected by way of an amendment under s.146A.

D. Types of Planning Permission

In addition to a conventional grant of planning permission, there is provision **5–28** for the grant of outline planning permission, and retention planning permission.

1. Outline planning permission

Provision is made under s.36 of the PDA 2000 for the grant of an outline **5–29** planning permission. The mechanics in this regard are quite different from those that had existed under the previous legislation: indeed, many of the concerns voiced as to the utility of outline planning permission under the previous legislation (where it appeared that matters of principle might be revisited or retrenched upon in a subsequent application for approval), seem to have been resolved.[30]

---

[29] PDA 2000, s.146A(2) (as inserted by s.30 of the 2006 Act). In the case of strategic infrastructure development, an application may be made under s.146B to alter the terms of the permitted development, even where the alteration would be material, and even where it might have significant effects on the environment. See further paras 10–108 to 10–116.

[30] The principal difficulty under the previous legislation is that in a series of decisions the courts had indicated that it would be possible to revisit matters on an application for approval. Reference is made in particular to the decisions in *State (Tern Houses (Brennanstown) Ltd.) v An Bord Pleanála* [1985] I.R. 725; and *Irish Asphalt Ltd. v An Bord Pleanála*, unreported, High Court, Costello P., July 28, 1995.

5–30 An application for an outline planning permission may not be made in respect of the following types of development. Under art.21 of the Planning and Development Regulations 2001 (as substituted by the 2006 Regulations), an outline application may not be made in respect of (a) retention planning permission; (b) development which would consist of or comprise the carrying out of works to a protected structure or a proposed protected structure; or (c) development which comprises, or is for the purposes of, an activity requiring an integrated pollution prevention and control licence or a waste licence. Under art.96 of the Regulations an outline application may not be made in respect of development which is prescribed for the purposes of environmental impact assessment. Under art.134 of the Regulations, an outline application may not be made in respect of the provision of, or modifications to, an establishment which is subject to the European Communities (Control of Major Accident Hazards Involving Dangerous Substances) Regulations 2006.

Two planning permissions

5–31 An outline planning permission now involves, in effect, two planning permissions. First, an outline permission which establishes that the proposed development is acceptable in principle. Secondly, a subsequent planning permission. This second planning permission differs from a typical planning permission in two key respects. First, where an application for permission is made to a planning authority consequent on the grant of outline permission, the planning authority shall not refuse to grant permission on the basis of any matter which had been decided in the grant of outline permission, provided that the planning authority is satisfied that the proposed development is within the terms of the outline permission. The second respect in which a subsequent planning permission differs is that there is no appeal to An Bord Pleanála against a decision of a planning authority to grant permission consequent on the grant of outline permission in respect of any aspect of the proposed development which was decided in the grant of outline permission.

5–32 The application for the (second) planning permission must be made not later than three years beginning on the date of the grant of outline permission, or such longer period, not exceeding five years, as may be specified by the planning authority. It is expressly provided that the ordinary rules in relation to the appropriate period or "life" of a planning permission do not apply to outline planning permissions. Presumably, however, these rules do apply to the grant of the second planning permission. To put the matter another way, it would seem that, typically, the relevant cumulative time period here would be eight years: three years in which to make the application for the second planning permission, and a further five years representing the "life" of that second planning permission. In this regard, it would seem that the "life" of the second planning permission is not parasitic or dependent on that of the outline planning permission (subject always to the requirement to make the application for the second planning permission within the statutory three years or longer period).

Extent to which matters determined by outline planning permission

It is not entirely clear from the wording of s.36 as to the extent, if any, to which 　**5–33**
the planning authority can raise matters in relation to the second planning
permission in circumstances where such matters could have, and arguably
should have, been raised at the outline planning permission stage.

In relation to the previous legislation, with its different regime in relation to 　**5–34**
outline planning permission, Barron J. had suggested in *State (Tern Houses
(Brennanstown) Ltd.) v An Bord Pleanála*[31] that there was nothing in the (then)
legislation to support the argument that, because any particular condition *might*
have been imposed when the planning authority granted outline planning
permission, such condition cannot be imposed when the same planning authority
grants an approval based upon such outline planning permission. To put the
matter another way, Barron J. appears to be suggesting that it may be the case
that certain matters of principle relating to the development may have
nevertheless been left open by the outline planning permission and, further,
that it may be possible to refuse approval subsequently.

It remains to be seen as to whether or not this aspect of the decision in *State* 　**5–35**
(Tern Houses (Brennanstown) Ltd.) v An Bord Pleanála survives the reforms
introduced under s.36. The better view must be that it does not. It would
undermine the credibility of an outline planning permission were it to be the
case that the planning authority could, on the occasion of the application for
the (second) planning permission, raise matters of principle which could have
been addressed at the outline application stage. The planning authority should
have sufficient information before it at the time of the application for outline
planning permission to determine all matters of principle. It is submitted that
in granting an outline planning permission, the planning authority should be
taken as having decided those matters within the meaning of s.36(4). This
appears to be the view which was taken by Barrington J. in the High Court in
Pine Valley Developments Ltd. v An Bord Pleanála[32] in the context of the
previous legislation (which was less forthright in its wording).

At all events, cautious developers should be advised to expressly raise all matters 　**5–36**
of principle relating to their proposed developments in applications for outline
planning permission, and to seek a subsequent planning permission as soon as
possible after receiving outline planning permission.

It is submitted, by analogy with the previous legislation, that an application for 　**5–37**
a subsequent planning permission must relate to the same planning unit as that
referred to in the application for outline planning permission, but that piece-
meal applications within the same area are also acceptable.[33]

---

[31] [1985] I.R. 725.
[32] [1984] I.R. 407 (overruled by the Supreme Court on other grounds).
[33] *State (Silverhill Development Co. Ltd.) v An Bord Pleanála*, unreported, High Court,
O'Hanlon J., March 16, 1984 (approval on outline planning permission held to have been
properly refused).

2. Retention planning permission

5–38   Generally, planning permission represents a prior authorisation of development. In other words, it is necessary to apply for, and to obtain the grant of, planning permission prior to the commencement of development (other than exempted development). Indeed, to do otherwise represents a criminal offence under s.32. However, under s.34(12) an application may be made for the retention of unauthorised development and s.34 shall apply to such an application, subject to any necessary modifications.

5–39   A number of points need to be made in relation to this provision. First, the Supreme Court have made it clear that in adjudicating on an application for retention planning permission, neither a planning authority nor An Bord Pleanála is to have regard to the fact that the unauthorised development is (by definition) in place.[34] Thus, for example, it would be improper for a planning authority or An Bord Pleanála to have regard to the fact that the refusal of planning permission would cause hardship to the developer in that it might necessitate the removal of an unauthorised structure. Secondly, it does not appear that the grant of retention planning permission has retrospective effect. Certainly, in the specific context of enforcement actions, it is expressly provided under s.162(3) that no enforcement action shall be stayed or withdrawn by reason of an application for retention planning permission,[35] or the grant of that permission. Presumably, similar considerations apply in respect of matters such as compensation,[36] and the availability of exempted development: both of which are qualified in the case of unauthorised development.

5–40   It is probably not possible to apply for planning permission for the retention of the demolition of buildings.

5–41   Finally, compensation is excluded where planning permission is refused for the retention of any unauthorised structures.[37]

5–42   The dual role of a planning authority as decision-maker on applications for planning permission and as the body with principal responsibility for enforcement may present potential conflicts. In particular, it is arguable that, before deciding to take enforcement action, a planning authority must form the view that the development is objectionable in planning terms. To do otherwise, and to require the removal or demolition of innocuous development simply because the regulatory requirement of obtaining planning permission in advance was not complied with, would seem to be disproportionate, and, possibly, contrary to sustainable development. To the extent, then, that a

---

[34] *State (Fitzgerald) v An Bord Pleanála* [1985] I.L.R.M. 117. See also *Village Residents Association Ltd. v An Bord Pleanála* [2000] 1 I.R. 65; [2000] 2 I.L.R.M. 59.
[35] As amended by the Local Government Act 2001, s.247(f).
[36] The reduction in value is calculated by reference to value immediately before and after the relevant decision.
[37] PDA 2000, s.191(4).

planning authority considers these issues in the context of a decision whether or not to pursue enforcement action, it might be taken to have prejudged any subsequent application for retention planning permission. This issue arose tangentially in *Jerry Beades Construction Ltd. v Dublin City Council*.[38] The nature of the allegations made in that case were unusual and are summarised briefly elsewhere at paras 12–59 to 12–60.

> "As a matter of certainty some unauthorised works or uses must pre-exist a planning retention application and very often these come about in the context of an earlier planning permission which has not being fully adhered to. Therefore it must frequently be the case that some conflict exists between what is built and what is authorised. If a planning authority could legitimately have the view, as expressed in the aforesaid note, at a time when a planning retention application had not even been submitted and therefore the details not even outlined, there would in fact be no point in this statutory entitlement being afforded to a member of the public. Such a position could clearly circumvent the will of the Oireachtas and would be contrary to the duty imposed on planning authorities to consider and determine, on its merits, such an application and to do so in the same way as any other planning application. Any contrary position is in my view untenable."

Ultimately, McKechnie J. decided the case by reference to fair procedures, rather than by reference to bias or pre-judgment.   **5–43**

E. Limit of Duration of Planning Permission

1.   Introduction

A planning permission generally has a duration or, more colloquially, a life, of five years beginning on the date of the grant of planning permission.[39] Accordingly, a developer will, again generally, have a period of five years within which to implement the planning permission.[40] It is, however, possible to apply to have the duration or life of a planning permission extended where substantial works were carried out pursuant to the planning permission before the expiration of the life of the planning permission, and where the development will be completed within a reasonable time.   **5–44**

The foregoing represents only a very brief sketch of the provisions in this regard, and it is now necessary to turn to a more detailed consideration of the provisions.   **5–45**

---

[38] [2005] I.E.H.C. 406; unreported, McKechnie J., September 7, 2005.
[39] PDA 2000, s.40.
[40] See, generally, the decision in *Bord na Móna v An Bord Pleanála* [1985] I.R. 205, for a discussion as to the effect of this on the timing of conditions in relation to the making of contributions.

2. Five years

5–46   Generally, the duration or life of a planning permission will be five years beginning on the date of the grant of the planning permission. A planning authority or An Bord Pleanála are, however, empowered to vary the duration. More specifically, under s.41 a planning authority, or An Bord Pleanála, may, having regard to the nature and extent of the relevant development and any other material consideration, specify a period of more than five years. Where the duration of the planning permission is varied, this must be stated in the decision on the application or appeal.[41]

Exceptions

5–47   The general rules in relation to the duration or life of a planning permission do not apply in the following cases[42]: (i) a retention planning permission; (ii) a planning permission granted either for a limited period or a temporary planning permission under s.34(4)(n) of the PDA 2000.[43]

5–48   The rationale for the respective exceptions in this regard would appear to be as follows. In the case of a retention planning permission, the development will, by definition, have already been carried out and, therefore, no issue arises as to the time period within which the planning permission is to be implemented. In the case of a limited or temporary planning permission, it would be entirely inconsistent with its temporary or limited nature to apply the general life or duration of five years and, in particular, it is submitted that it would frustrate the temporary or limited nature of the planning permission to allow for an application to extend the life of the planning permission under s.42.

3. Effect of expiration of planning permission

5–49   On the expiration of the appropriate period (but without prejudice to the validity of anything done pursuant thereto prior to the expiration of that period), a planning permission shall cease to have effect as regards (a) in case the development to which the permission relates is not commenced during that period, the entire development; (b) in case the development is commenced during that period, so much of the development as is not completed within that period. It is expressly provided, however, that this shall not affect (i) the continuance of any use, in accordance with a planning permission, of land; and (ii) where a development has been completed, the obligation of any person to comply with any condition attached to the relevant planning permission whereby something is required either to be done or not to be done.[44]

---

[41] See Planning and Development Regulations 2001, art.31(i) and art.74(2)(i) (as amended by the 2006 Regulations).
[42] PDA 2000, s.40(2)(a).
[43] PDA 2000, s.40(2)(a)(i), and (ii).
[44] PDA 2000, s.40(2)(b).

In the case of a house, shop, office or other building which itself has been **5–50** completed, the obligation to provide any structure or works included in the relevant planning permission which are either necessary for or ancillary or incidental to the use of the completed building remains. In the case of a development comprising a number of buildings of which only some have been completed, the obligation to provide roads, services and open spaces included in the relevant planning permission which are necessary for or ancillary or incidental to the completed building remains.[45]

It would seem that the thinking here is that where development has been partly **5–51** carried out, it would be wrong to absolve the developer from the requirement to complete works (including infrastructural works) which are either necessary for or ancillary or incidental to the development already carried out.

4. Application to extend appropriate period

Under s.42 of the PDA 2000, a planning authority may extend the life or duration **5–52** of a planning permission, provided certain specified conditions are met. The application to extend must be made prior to the end of the life of the planning permission.[46] The application cannot, however, be made earlier than one year before the expiration of the period sought to be extended or extended further.[47] The conditions for the extension of a life of a planning permission are as follows. The planning authority must be satisfied that (i) the development to which the permission relates commenced before the expiration of the period sought to be extended; (ii) substantial works were carried out pursuant to the planning permission during that period; and (iii) the development will be completed within a reasonable time.

"Substantial works"

The term "substantial works" is a term of art and has been considered in a **5–53** number of decisions by the courts. In each case, whether "substantial works" have been carried out must be determined on the basis of the particular facts of the case and not by reference to any predetermined formula or rule of thumb.[48] In *Garden Village Construction Ltd. v Wicklow County Council*,[49] Geoghegan J. held that it would be wholly inappropriate to apply some mathematical formula as to either quantity of work or of expenditure in determining whether substantial works had been carried out, and that "substantial" should be given its ordinary meaning which is the opposite of insubstantial.

---

[45] PDA 2000, s.40(2)(a)(iii), and (iv).
[46] PDA 2000, s.42(1)(d).
[47] Planning and Development Regulations 2001, art.41 (as substituted by the 2006 Regulations).
[48] *Littondale Ltd. v Wicklow County Council* [1996] 2 I.L.R.M. 519 at 533.
[49] [1994] 1 I.L.R.M. 354. This decision was reversed on other grounds by the Supreme Court [1994] 3 I.R. 413; [1994] 2 I.L.R.M. 527, but it is submitted that the aspect of the judgment referred to above in the text remains unaffected.

5–54 The courts have attached particular significance to the statutory requirement that the substantial works were carried out "pursuant to" the planning permission. For example, in *Garden Village Construction Ltd. v Wicklow County Council*[50] the Supreme Court held that, in the context of a major housing scheme covered by several planning permissions, works "designed to benefit" the particular development covered by the expiring planning permission could not be taken into account. Thus it appears that infrastructural works such as roads and waterpipes provided to facilitate adjoining development and which will also facilitate the development proposed in the expiring planning permission cannot be taken into account in determining whether substantial works have been carried out under the expiring planning permission. Normally only works carried out in order to implement the planning permission to be extended and carried out pursuant to that permission, and no other permission, may be taken into account.[51]

5–55 It appears from the decision in *Garden Village Construction Ltd. v Wicklow County Council* that a distinction is to be drawn between the manufacture of building materials off-site for ultimate use on-site, and infrastructural works off-site. In the case of the former, the manufacture can properly be said to be pursuant to the (expiring) planning permission, whereas the latter represents "development" in its own right and must be authorised pursuant to another planning permission. On this basis the Supreme Court were able to distinguish the earlier decision in *Frenchurch Properties Ltd. v Wexford County Council.*[52] There, Lynch J. had held that in considering whether "substantial works" were carried out, the planning authority ought to have taken into account expenditure on floor slabs and steel works specially designed for the development and, further, that materials manufactured off the site could be counted as works.[53]

5–56 The requirement that substantial works have been carried out "pursuant to" the planning permission to be extended fell for further consideration in *McDowell v Roscommon County Council.*[54] The applicant challenged a decision to refuse an extension. The planning authority had, seemingly, taken the view that the development as actually carried out was not in compliance with the planning permission and was, therefore, unauthorised. The allegation was that the house was being built some two metres or more lower than permitted.

5–57 The High Court held that the planning authority had acted unlawfully in purporting to have regard to the alleged unauthorised nature of the development.

---

[50] [1994] 3 I.R. 413; [1994] 2 I.L.R.M. 527; [1994] 1 I.L.R.M. 354.

[51] *State (McCoy) v Dun Laoghaire Corporation* [1985] I.L.R.M. 533.

[52] [1992] 2 I.R. 268; [1991] I.L.R.M. 769 (approved by the Supreme Court in *Garden Village Construction Ltd. v Wicklow County Council* [1994] 3 I.R. 413; [1994] 2 I.L.R.M. 527).

[53] This aspect of the judgment in *Frenchurch Properties Ltd. v Wexford County Council* was subsequently approved of by Finnegan J., in the context of judicial review proceedings relating to a revocation of planning permission: *Electricity Supply Board v Cork County Council*, unreported, High Court, Finnegan J., June 28, 2000.

[54] [2004] I.E.H.C. 396; unreported, Finnegan P., December 21, 2004.

Two principal reasons were put forward for this conclusion. First, it was suggested that the function of the planning authority on an application to extend was a narrow one, that the planning authority was confined to a consideration of the statutory criteria set out under s.42 and did not enjoy some form of residual discretion to take into account whether the development was authorised or not.

"The Respondent further concluded that as it has concluded that the development does not comply with the planning permission it cannot be said that the planning permission relates to the development in fact being undertaken. In any particular set of circumstances the position may be that the development is fully in compliance with the planning permission or the development relates to the planning permission but is not fully in compliance with it. In the latter case it will be clear that the development although not in compliance therewith relates to a particular planning permission rather than to some other planning permission or to no planning permission at all. The reasons stated for the refusal recognise a relationship between the development and this particular planning permission. I am satisfied from a perusal of the plans that the development is that contemplated by the planning permission. I am further satisfied that the true effect of section 42 is that the Planning Authority must therefore consider the application in that light having regard to the matters enumerated in the section and those matters only. This it has failed to do by taking into account a matter not specified in the section that is compliance with the planning permission."

Secondly, in circumstances where the planning authority had available to it a range of enforcement mechanisms under Pt VIII of the PDA 2000 it was improper to use the occasion of an application for an extension to prevent the completion of what the planning authority regarded as an unauthorised development.   **5–58**

"In this case I am satisfied that the primary object of section 42 of the Act of 2000 is to enable a development already commenced to which a planning permission relates to be completed: it is not permissible to use the section to prevent the completion of a development to which the planning permission relates which the Planning Authority has concluded does not comply fully with that permission. What the Planning Authority must consider is whether the development relates to the permission and not whether it is in full compliance with the same. It is not permissible to use a statutory power conferred for a particular purpose for some other purpose."

It is respectfully submitted that the reasoning on neither count is convincing.   **5–59**
Insofar as the discretion of the planning authority is concerned, it is submitted that the requirement that the planning authority address its mind to the question as to whether substantial works have been carried out "pursuant to" the planning permission will, in some cases, require the planning authority to consider the issue of compliance. It is further submitted that it is incorrect for the court to suggest that it is sufficient that the development carried out to date "relates" to the planning permission: s.42 expressly requires that the works have been carried out "pursuant to" the planning permission. The two phrases are not synonymous. It is a question of fact and degree as to whether works can fairly be said to be pursuant to the planning permission. Whereas it may well be that on the

particular facts of *McDowell* any deviation from the terms of the planning permission was immaterial, and thus the works could properly be said to have been carried on pursuant to the planning permission, it is submitted that it is incorrect to suggest that the planning authority is not entitled to address its mind to this question.

5–60   The position obtaining in this jurisdiction as a result of the judgment in *McDowell v Roscommon County Council* is to be contrasted with that applying in England and Wales. There, provision is made for the expiry of planning permissions not implemented within a certain time. Development must be begun within a certain period: development is taken to begin on the earliest possible date on which any material operation comprised in the development begins to be carried out. It is well established that in order for operations to amount to the commencement of development under a planning permission, those operations must be authorised by the permission in question, read together with its conditions.[55] In general, operations carried out in breach of a condition cannot be relied upon. If the operations do not comply with the planning permission, they constitute a breach of planning control and for planning purposes will be unauthorised and thus unlawful.

5–61   Turning now to the second ground put forward in the judgment, namely that the refusal of an extension was for an improper purpose, *i.e.* to prevent the completion of an unauthorised development, it is submitted that this analysis simply begs the question at issue. Either the planning authority is entitled to take into account the fact that development may be in breach of the terms of the planning permission—and for the reasons set out above, it is submitted that the planning authority is so entitled—or it is not. This turns on the meaning to be attached to the phrase "pursuant to" the planning permission. If the planning authority is entitled to take into account the fact that development may be in breach of the terms of the planning permission, then there is no improper purpose.

5–62   In any event, it is artificial to characterise the refusal of an extension as the action which prevents the completion of the development: if the development truly is unauthorised then it has been unauthorised since the outset and the refusal of an extension does not change its status.

5–63   The concepts of "development" and "unauthorised development" are central to the planning legislation and a planning authority will often have to address its mind to whether a development is unauthorised in contexts other than enforcement proceedings. For example, in adjudicating on an application for planning permission, a planning authority is entitled to consider whether the development in respect of which planning permission is being sought is in aid of other unauthorised development. Moreover, the planning authority has an

---

[55] *Henry Boot Homes Ltd. v Bassetlaw DC* [2002] E.W.C.A. Civ 983, [37]; [2003] 1 P. & C.R. 23, citing *Whitley and Sons v Secretary of State for Wales* (1992) 64 P. & C.R. 296.

express power under s.5 to make a determination on the question of whether an act is or is not development (this is subject to an appeal to An Bord Pleanála). The Supreme Court in *Grianán An Aileach Interpretative Centre Company Ltd. v Donegal County Council*[56] suggests that the planning authorities are particularly well qualified to assess this. There is nothing inconsistent, therefore, with allowing the planning authority to address its mind to this question in the context of an application to extend the life of a planning permission.

Limited discretion of planning authority

The wording of s.42 suggests that a planning authority has very little discretion in relation to its decision as to whether or not to extend the life of a planning permission. In particular, it would seem—by analogy with judgments in respect of the equivalent provisions of the previous legislation[57]—that once the relevant statutory conditions have been fulfilled, the planning authority has no choice but to grant the extension. The judgment in *McDowell v Roscommon County Council*[58] seeks to restrict this discretion further. In particular, the judgment suggests that the planning authority is not entitled to take into account whether the development carried out to date is authorised or not. For the reasons set out at para.5–59, it is submitted that this aspect of the judgment is incorrect. The planning authority is required to consider whether substantial works have been carried out "pursuant to" the planning permission, and this must involve consideration of whether the development is authorised. A planning authority could only truly be said to have gone beyond the limits of its discretion if it took into account matters—such as the desirability or otherwise of the development being completed—which were not relevant to the question as to whether substantial works had been carried out pursuant to the planning permission.

5–64

It is submitted that the determination of compliance with the various statutory conditions is a question of law and, accordingly, one that the High Court is in a position to consider *de novo* in the event of judicial review proceedings being brought.[59]

5–65

No public participation; no appeal

There is no provision for public participation in the context of the decision to extend the life of a planning permission. Nor is there any provision for an appeal to An Bord Pleanála. These factors serve simply to highlight the administrative or ministerial nature (as opposed to quasi-judicial nature) of the function being exercised by a planning authority on an application to extend the life of a planning permission.

5–66

---

[56] [2004] 2 I.R. 625; [2005] 1 I.L.R.M. 106.
[57] *State (McCoy) v Dun Laoghaire Corporation* [1985] I.L.R.M. 533. See also *John A. Woods Ltd. v Kerry County Council*, unreported, High Court, Smyth J., October 31, 1997; and *Littondale Ltd. v Wicklow County Council* [1996] 2 I.L.R.M. 519 at 531-2.
[58] [2004] I.E.H.C. 396; unreported, Finnegan P., December 21, 2004.
[59] *cf. Littondale Ltd. v Wicklow County Council* [1996] 2 I.L.R.M. 519.

5–67   The judgment in *Coll v Donegal County Council*[60] appears to suggest that it follows, as a consequence of there being no formal public participation, that the availability of judicial review may also be limited. The applicant had sought to challenge a decision to extend the duration of a planning permission, arguing that the development was not likely to be completed with a "reasonable time". Peart J. ruled, on the facts, that the applicant did not have *locus standi* to challenge the decision.

> "In my view, firstly, the applicant enjoys no locus standi to seek the relief she seeks under this heading. Firstly, she did not participate in the planning process at all, but secondly and critically, the power of the planning authority to exercise a discretion to extend the duration of a planning permission is one which may be exercised appropriately without consultation with the public. It is not necessary under the statutory scheme to publish any notice of intention to apply for an extension, and neither is it necessary to erect any notice at the site of the development indicating an intention to apply for an extension. Under that scheme, as provided by s. 42 of the 2000 Act, a planning authority shall on application being made to it, extend the appropriate period for such additional period as it considers requisite to enable the development to be completed provided certain requirements are complied with, one of which is that referred to already, namely that the planning authority is satisfied that the development will be completed within a reasonable time. *The applicant has no entitlement to be consulted in the making of that decision and therefore in my view cannot be heard to raise objections to the decision made.* It is a matter within the discretion of the planning authority, and provided that the discretion is exercised in a judicial manner it is a decision which then planning authority may make in its discretion."
> *Emphasis supplied.

5–68   With respect, this reasoning is suspect. The grounds on which an administrative decision can be challenged are numerous, and are in no sense confined to allegations of a breach of fair procedures. Thus, even if the process leading up to a particular decision allows for *no* public participation, a person affected by the decision should be entitled to challenge the legality of that decision by reference to other judicial review grounds. Here the ground of challenge was a classic jurisdictional ground: the applicant was alleging that one of the prerequisites to an extension of planning permission, namely that the development would be completed within a "reasonable time", had not been satisfied. The entitlement of a person affected by the decision could in no way be contingent on the existence of a general right of public participation at an earlier stage.

5–69   As it happens, Peart J. was better than his word, and went on, in any event, to address the applicant's complaint that the planning authority could not have concluded that the development would be completed within a reasonable period of time as required under s.42. Peart J. ruled against the applicant, stating that the planning authority was entitled to revisit an earlier decision not to extinguish a right of way, and that, if the relevant right of way was extinguished, then in

---

[60] [2005] I.E.H.C. 231; unreported, Peart J., July 7, 2005.

those circumstances the planning authority could reasonably have formed the view that the development would be completed in a "reasonable time".

5. Default decision

In the event that a planning authority does not give notice to the applicant of its decision as regards an application to extend, within the period of eight weeks beginning on either the day of receipt by the planning authority of the application, or in any case where the requirements of the Regulations (including a request for further information) are only complied with subsequently, the day on which all of those requirements stand complied with, the planning authority is deemed to have made a decision to extend.[61] The wording of the provisions in this regard is noteworthy in that, unlike the position obtaining to a default planning permission, what the planning authority must do within the eight week period is to *notify* the decision. In relation to the (then) similarly worded provision under the previous legislation in respect of default planning permissions, O'Hanlon J. held that notice is only given by post when the letter is received.

    5–70

> "[…] time continues to run against the planning authority until the notice has been physically delivered to or brought to the notice of the applicant or left at some premises where it may reasonably be regarded as having come into his possession and control."[62]

6. Further extension of period

The planning authority may further extend the life of a planning permission which has already been extended provided, *inter alia*, a properly completed application is received for such further extension and the planning authority is satisfied that the relevant development had not been completed due to circumstances beyond the control of the person carrying out the development.[63] It seems from the wording of s.42(3) that this requirement is an alternative to, and not in addition to, the requirements which govern a first application to extend time. In other words, it is probably not necessary in the context of an application to further extend time to demonstrate that (further) substantial works were carried out during the period of the first extension, or that the development will be completed within a reasonable time. (Of course, it follows by definition from the fact that a first extension was granted that substantial works will have been carried out during the unextended life of the planning permission.)

    5–71

---

[61] Planning and Development Regulations 2001, art.45 (as substituted by the 2006 Regulations) allows a planning authority to serve a request for further information or evidence. Where an applicant does not comply with any requirement under this article within four weeks of such requirement, the planning authority shall refuse the application.

[62] *Freeney v Bray UDC* [1982] I.L.R.M. 29 at 35; and *Flynn & O'Flaherty Properties Ltd. v Dublin Corporation* [1997] 2 I.R. 558.

[63] PDA 2000, s.42(3).

5–72 It is not clear what is meant by "circumstances beyond the control" of the developer. For example, it is uncertain as to whether there must have been some physical impediment to the completion of the development, or whether financial constraints might be sufficient. It is also unclear as to the extent, if any, to which delays caused by poor design might be said to be within the control of the developer.

5–73 The duration of the planning permission shall be further extended only for such period as the planning authority considers requisite to enable the relevant development to be completed.

7. Social and affordable housing

5–74 Under the PDA 2000 as initially enacted, withering provisions had applied to planning permissions granted in respect of an application made after August 25, 1999.[64] The wording of these withering provisions was tortuous but what seems to have been intended under the initial legislation is this: there seems to have been a concern on the part of the legislature that there might be a rash of applications for planning permission made in the interregnum between the publishing of the Bill and the implementation of the provisions in respect of social and affordable housing. More specifically, given the lead time involved both in the enactment of the Bill itself, and subsequently in the preparation and implementation of housing strategies, it would have been obvious to developers for some considerable period of time in advance that there might be a requirement for social and affordable housing. The withering provisions appear to have been intended to prevent opportunistic developers exploiting this information. Thus, it seemed that where a planning permission was granted in respect of an application which had been made after August 25, 1999, but which avoided a requirement to provide social and affordable housing because the housing strategy was not yet in effect, such a planning permission would only have a duration or life of two years.

5–75 The legal position has been changed radically under the Planning and Development (Amendment) Act 2002. The amendments in this regard are achieved in a somewhat awkward manner. First, the ordinary provisions as to the life of a planning permission (in particular, as to the entitlement of a developer to apply to have the life of a planning permission extended in circumstances where he had carried out "substantial works" within the life of the planning permission) are expressly applied to applications made after August 25, 1999, to which the provisions in respect of social and affordable housing would have otherwise applied if the application for planning permission had been made after the inclusion of a housing strategy in the development plan. Thus the very real difficulties as to interpretation which had arisen in respect of s.96(15) of the PDA 2000 are recreated. See paras 5–83 to 5–86 below.

---

[64] PDA 2000, s.96(15) (as unamended).

Secondly, and as a *quid pro quo* for this release from the withering provisions, **5–76** the amendments go on then to impose a requirement for the payment of a levy. More specifically, a condition is deemed to be attached to the planning permission providing for the payment of a levy.[65]

In very broad terms, the levy is to be based on either the actual consideration **5–77** paid (in the case of a sale at arm's length) or otherwise on the market value. If the market value/consideration paid exceeds €270,000, then the levy is to be one per cent; if less than the figure of €270,000, one half per cent.

The payment of the levy is to be made at such time as the planning authority **5–78** specifies. It is important to note that the planning authority may specify that the payment be made *before* the date on which the disposal/sale concerned of the relevant house is effected. In other words, it would seem that a developer might be required to make a payment in advance of the actual sale.

Finally in this regard, there are comprehensive anti-avoidance provisions which **5–79** are designed to prevent the developer passing on the cost of the levy to the purchaser. Various transactions in this regard are stated to be void. Furthermore, provision is made whereby any monies paid in this regard by the purchaser (or other person obtaining the house) are to be paid back by the developer.

Levy does not necessarily apply to all houses

The requirement to pay the levy does not necessarily apply to all of the houses **5–80** under the planning permission. Again, the legislative provisions in this regard are cumbersome, and require consideration of the repealed s.96(15). Under s.96(15), a withering planning permission would, on its expiration, cease to have effect as regards any portion of the development consisting of buildings the external walls of which have not been completed. The requirement to pay a levy under s.96B only applies to those (individual) houses permission for which would have ceased to have effect or expired but for s.4 of the Planning and Development (Amendment) Act 2002. Thus it would seem that the requirement to pay the levy only applies to those (individual) houses the external walls of which had not been completed by the date on which the planning permission would otherwise have expired under the withering provisions. To put the matter another way, the levy only applies to those houses which are completed (external walls) more than two years from the date of the grant of the planning permission (or after December 31, 2002 if later).

Which planning permissions are affected?

Under s.96A, the requirement to pay a levy applies to planning permissions **5–81** granted pursuant to an application made after August 25, 1999 to which Part V:

---

[65] PDA s.96B(2) (as inserted by s.4 of the Planning and Development (Amendment) Act 2002).

"would have applied if the application for permission had been made after the inclusion of a housing strategy in the development plan under section 94(1)".

5–82   Section 96(1) provides, *inter alia*, that this section shall apply to an application for planning permission for the development of houses, or where an application relates to a mixture of developments, to that *part* of the application which relates to the development of houses. In other words, it would seem that Part V applies to any application in respect of residential development. Of course, given the fact that a housing strategy may specify different percentages for different areas of land zoned residential, and, indeed, may indicate in respect of a particular area that there is *no* requirement for social and affordable housing, it does not necessarily follow that every application for planning permission in respect of residential development will be subject to social and affordable housing. Section 96A is not sufficiently flexible, however, to tolerate this fact. Accordingly, it would seem that the withering provisions might apply to an application for planning permission in respect of land which would not, in any event, have been subject to a requirement to provide social and affordable housing under Part V (because of the contents of the housing strategy). This would produce the anomalous result that notwithstanding the fact that no benefit arose from the timing of the application for planning permission in such circumstances (in that the contents of the housing strategy had the effect that no requirement for social and affordable housing would have been imposed in any event), such a planning permission is nevertheless subject to the withering provisions.

Criticisms

5–83   The legislative provisions determining which planning permissions were affected by the withering provisions initially, and are now affected by the requirement to pay a levy, are amongst the most poorly drafted in the planning legislation. In particular, the provisions entirely fail to deal with the case of a planning permission which, although granted prior to there being a statutory requirement to provide social and affordable housing, is nevertheless subject to social and affordable housing.

5–84   Approaching the matter from first principles, one would have thought that the following would have to be attended to in drafting the anti-avoidance provisions. First, the type of planning permission affected would be identified precisely. Secondly, provision would then have been made to disapply the requirement to pay the levy in the event that, for whatever reason, a condition requiring social and affordable housing was, in fact, applied to a planning permission notwithstanding the fact that the application had been made in the interim period. Unfortunately the provisions of s.96A do not succeed in either of these respects.

5–85   The type of planning permission to which the levy applies is defined only in terms of the timing of the making of the application for planning permission. More specifically, s.96A refers to an application made after August 25, 1999 and to which Part V would have applied if the application for planning permission had been made after the inclusion of a housing strategy in the development plan. The most obvious criticism of this aspect of the provision is, of course, that on a literal interpretation the levy applies not only to those applications which took free of any requirement to provide social and affordable housing (on account of their being applied for prior to the coming into full force and effect of Part V), but also to all planning permissions since which were, in fact, subject to a requirement to make provision for social and affordable housing. If the seeming objective of the levy, namely to target opportunistic planning permissions, is to be achieved, a more appropriate form of wording would be as follows:

> "to which Part V would *otherwise* have applied if the application for planning permission had been made after the inclusion of a housing strategy in the development plan *but did not apply*".

On a literal interpretation of s.96A the levy applies even to those planning **5–86** permissions in respect of which a condition was attached under s.96 (following the coming into full force and effect of the requirement to make provision for social and affordable housing). Even were the courts to steer away from such a literal interpretation, and instead were to interpret the section in such a way as not to apply to planning permissions of this type, a difficulty may nevertheless still remain in relation to other (earlier) planning permissions. In particular, it seems that even prior to the coming into full force and effect of Part V it was open to an applicant for planning permission to *volunteer* to provide social and affordable housing. In practice, therefore, there will be certain planning permissions which, notwithstanding the fact that they were granted prior to the coming into full force and effect of s.96, will nevertheless provide for social and affordable housing. It would seem quite unfair, and entirely inconsistent with the apparent rationale, to require the payment of a levy in respect of such a planning permission. Yet this is what the effect of s.96A appears to be.

F. Revocation of Planning Permission

Limited provision is made under s.44 of the PDA 2000 for the revocation or **5–87** modification of planning permission. Given the fact that a grant of planning permission represents a vested right,[66] certain procedural safeguards must be observed in relation to the exercise of such a power of revocation or modification. Moreover, the circumstances in which the power may be exercised are expressly limited as follows. Under s.44(2), a planning authority shall neither revoke nor modify a planning permission unless the development to which the permission relates no longer conforms with the provisions of the development plan. It should be noted that the restriction in this regard represents a

---

[66] See *Electricity Supply Board v Cork County Council*, unreported, High Court, Finnegan J., June 28, 2000.

modification of that which had applied under the previous legislation.[67] Indeed, there was an argument to be made that under the previous legislation the power to revoke or modify only applied in cases where there had been a change in the physical proper planning and development of the area.[68]

5–88   There is also a restriction on the time at which the power to revoke or modify may be exercised. Where the planning permission relates to the carrying out of works, the power may be exercised at any time before those works have been commenced or, in the case of works which have commenced and which, consequent on the making of a variation in the development plan, will contravene the development plan, at any time before those works have been completed. The nature of the works required in this regard had been considered, albeit in the context of the differently worded provisions of the previous legislation, by the High Court in *Electricity Supply Board v Cork County Council*.[69] Finnegan J. held that the manufacture of site specific steel constituted "works" for the purpose of the previous legislation.

1. Procedure

5–89   The following are the procedural requirements in respect of the revocation or modification of a planning permission. The planning authority must serve a notice on the applicant and on any other person who, in its opinion, will be materially affected by the revocation or modification. The notice shall (a) refer to the planning permission concerned; (b) specify the provisions of the development plan to which the planning permission no longer conforms; (c) invite the person or persons served with the notice to make written submissions or observations to the planning authority within the period specified in the notice (being not less than four weeks from the service of the notice) concerning the proposed revocation or modification.

5–90   A planning authority is required to have regard to any such submissions or observations in making its decision to revoke or modify the planning permission.

5–91   The legislation thus envisages that the procedure before the planning authority will involve a two-stage process. First, the service of a notice. Secondly, the making of a decision as to whether or not to revoke or modify the planning permission. Somewhat surprisingly, there is no express requirement that the planning authority indicate in the *notice* the reasons for which it is said that the planning permission no longer conforms with the provisions of the development

---

[67] Local Government (Planning & Development) Act 1963, s.30 (as amended).

[68] In this regard, an analogy might have been drawn with cases in relation to outline planning permission. It seems to have been implicit in judgments such as that in *Irish Asphalt Ltd. v An Bord Pleanála*, unreported, High Court, Costello J., July 28, 1995, that there had to be a physical change before a planning authority could retrench on an outline planning permission.

[69] Unreported, High Court, Finnegan J., June 28, 2000.

plan. Under s.44(5), however, there is an express requirement that the planning authority specifies in the *decision* the provisions of the development plan to which the permission no longer conforms, and the main reasons and considerations on which the decision is based.

The better view would seem to be that a planning authority should, in fact, also state in the notice the main reasons and considerations for which it is proposed to revoke or modify the planning permission.[70] The point should also be made that the requirement that the development no longer conform with the provisions of the development plan is merely a condition precedent to the exercise of the power to revoke or modify: accordingly, the fact of non-conformity *per se* does not necessarily mean that there are good reasons for revoking the planning permission.[71] In the circumstances it is submitted that the duty to state reasons extends beyond a mere recital of the requisite non-conformity.   **5–92**

Under the previous legislation, there was no express requirement to allow submissions or observations be made in respect of a proposal to revoke or modify a planning permission. Notwithstanding this, it had been held that, as the decision to revoke a planning permission is a quasi-judicial function, same attracts the rules of natural and constitutional justice.[72] It is submitted, therefore, that the new statutory procedures should be read in this regard; in particular, it is submitted that the beneficiary of the planning permission is entitled either to have sight of the materials on which the proposed decision to revoke or modify the planning permission is to be made, or, at the very least, to have a sufficiently detailed statement of the contents of this material so as to enable him or her to make informed submissions or observations.[73]   **5–93**

2. Appeal to An Bord Pleanála

There is a statutory right of appeal from the decision of the planning authority to An Bord Pleanála. This right of appeal may be exercised by any person served with notice under s.44(1), namely the applicant for planning permission and any other person who, in the opinion of the planning authority, will be materially affected by the revocation or modification. Somewhat surprisingly, it seems that the right of appeal might extend even to a decision *not* to revoke or modify the planning permission. An appeal must be made within four weeks of the date of the decision of the planning authority.   **5–94**

---

[70] See, by analogy, *Hughes v An Bord Pleanála* [2000] 1 I.L.R.M. 452.

[71] *Hughes v An Bord Pleanála* [2000] 1 I.L.R.M. 452.

[72] *Eircell Ltd. v Leitrim County Council* [2000] 1 I.R. 479; [2000] 2 I.L.R.M. 81; and *Electricity Supply Board v Cork County Council*, unreported, High Court, Finnegan J., June 28, 2000.

[73] See, by analogy, *Electricity Supply Board v Cork County Council*, unreported, High Court, Finnegan J., June 28, 2000.

5–95   An Bord Pleanála may confirm the decision with or without modifications, or annul the decision. As in the case of the planning authority, An Bord Pleanála must specify the main reasons and considerations for its decision.

5–96   In practice, an issue may arise as to whether or not a person adversely affected by a decision to revoke or modify planning permission should pursue this statutory right of appeal, or, instead, bring an application for judicial review before the High Court. Approached as a matter of first principle, one might have thought that a person would be required to first exhaust his statutory right of appeal before moving before the High Court: this is certainly the position usually applying in respect of the decision of a planning authority on an application for planning permission.[74] A number of judgments under the previous legislation, however, suggest that where one of the complaints made against the decision of the planning authority is that it is invalid for having been reached in breach of fair procedures, then it is appropriate to proceed directly to the High Court and it is not necessary to first exhaust the statutory right of appeal.[75] It would also seem that judicial review may be the appropriate remedy where a question of law arises on the decision of the planning authority.[76] This issue of exhaustion of rights is discussed, more generally, at paras 11–214 to 11–229.

5–97   A planning authority may at any time before decision, for stated reasons, by notice in writing withdraw a revocation or modification notice.[77] Particulars of a decision to revoke or modify planning permission shall be entered in the register.[78] The revocation or modification is a reserved function.[79]

---

[74] See, generally, *State (Abenglen Properties Ltd.) v Dublin Corporation* [1984] I.R. 381; [1982] I.L.R.M. 590.

[75] *Eircell Ltd. v Leitrim County Council* [2000] 1 I.R. 479; [2000] 2 I.L.R.M. 81; and *Electricity Supply Board v Cork County Council*, unreported, High Court, Finnegan J., June 28, 2000.

[76] *Eircell Ltd. v Leitrim County Council* [2000] 1 I.R. 479; [2000] 2 I.L.R.M. 81; *cf. Electricity Supply Board v Cork County Council*, unreported, High Court, Finnegan J., June 28, 2000.

[77] PDA 2000, s.44(9).

[78] PDA 2000, s.44(10).

[79] PDA 2000, s.44(11).

CHAPTER SIX

CLAIMS FOR COMPENSATION

A. General Principles

1. Constitutional property rights

Under the Irish Constitution, the property rights of landowners are expressly protected.[1] The nature and extent of these rights is a matter of constitutional law, and a discussion of same is beyond the competence of this book. This present chapter is confined to the more mundane task of outlining the procedural aspects of making a claim for compensation under the planning legislation. **6–01**

It is sufficient for this limited purpose to identify in somewhat simplistic terms three principles of constitutional law which inform the statutory provisions in this regard. First, property rights are not absolute and the State may as occasion requires delimit the exercise of those rights with a view to reconciling their exercise with the common good.[2] The making of provision in the common good for proper planning and development is a legitimate objective and one which may justify interference with property rights.[3] Secondly, in certain **6–02**

---

[1] Art.40.3, and Art.43 of the Constitution.
[2] Art.43 of the Constitution.
[3] *Central Dublin Development Association v Attorney General* (1969) 109 I.L.T.R. 69.

circumstances the failure to make provision for the payment of compensation in respect of interference with property rights will represent an unjust attack on property rights.[4] Whether or not there is a requirement to pay compensation will depend to some extent on the nature of the interference. Where the interference amounts to a taking of property, compensation will normally be payable. A person who is compulsorily deprived of his or her property in the interests of the common good should normally be fully compensated at a level equivalent to at least the market value of the acquired property.[5] Thirdly, in addition to protecting substantive property rights, the Constitution also requires that landowners be afforded procedural rights.[6]

6–03 A landowner is generally entitled to advance notice that his or her property rights are to be restricted (for example, by the exclusion of compensation).[7] This entitlement to notice is provided for under many of the provisions of the planning legislation. For example, a landowner is entitled to specific notice of the fact that his building is intended to be added to the record of protected structures under the development plan.[8] Furthermore, compensation is excluded in certain circumstances by reference to the development plan. For example, compensation is excluded where the proposed development would materially affect a protected structure,[9] or where planning permission is refused for the reason that the proposed development would adversely affect an architectural conservation area.[10] However, compensation is also excluded in circumstances where there has been no advance notice to the landowner. For example, compensation is excluded where the proposed development would interfere with the character of the landscape or with a view or prospect of special amenity value, or natural interest or beauty, which it is necessary to preserve.[11] There is no express requirement that these matters should have been identified in the development plan, or, indeed, by way of designation as a landscape conservation area. This would seem unfair as the landowner would thus appear to be precluded from arguing in advance that, for example, a particular view was not of such amenity value or of natural interest or beauty as to defeat his *prima facie* right to compensation. It is further submitted that given the fact that express provision is made for the designation of an area as a landscape conservation area,[12] it is wrong that compensation should be excluded by reference to the character of the landscape other than where same has been designated for preservation.

---

[4] See, for example, *Blake v Attorney General* [1982] I.L.R.M. 117.
[5] *In the matter of Part V of the Planning and Development Bill, 1999* [2000] 2 I.R. 321; [2001] 1 I.L.R.M. 81. See also *Dreher v Irish Land Commission* [1984] I.L.R.M. 94.
[6] See, generally, *MacPharthalain v Commissioners of Public Works in Ireland* [1994] 3 I.R. 353; [1992] 1 I.R. 111.
[7] See, generally, *MacPharthalain v Commissioners of Public Works in Ireland* [1994] 3 I.R. 353; [1992] 1 I.R. 111.
[8] PDA 2000, s.55(1)(a).
[9] PDA 2000, Sch.3, para.3.
[10] PDA 2000, Sch.4, para.13.
[11] PDA 2000, Sch.4, para.8.
[12] PDA 2000, s.204.

2. European Convention on Human Rights

The provisions of Art.1 of the First Protocol of the European Convention on **6–04** Human Rights may also be relevant in determining whether compensation is payable in respect of planning decisions adversely affecting property rights. The European Court of Human Rights ("ECtHR") has emphasised that the requirement for proportionality applies similarly to the regulation of the use of land as it does to its expropriation. See, generally, Chapter 14, paras 14–68 to 14–97.

3. Principal circumstances where compensation arises under planning legislation

A statutory right to make a claim for compensation will be triggered under the **6–05** PDA 2000 in three principal circumstances. First, where land is acquired by way of compulsory acquisition. For example, a planning authority has a power to compulsorily acquire a protected structure,[13] or, more generally, to compulsorily acquire lands to facilitate the assembly of sites for the purposes of the orderly development of land.[14] Strictly speaking, the right to compensation does not always arise under the planning legislation directly: in certain cases, the formal right to compensation arises elsewhere under other legislation. Secondly, where land is transferred to a planning authority for the purposes of social and affordable housing. This represents somewhat of a hybrid category in that, although it involves an actual taking of lands, it is treated differently from the more usual forms of compulsory acquisition on account of the transfer arising in the context of the grant of a planning permission. Thirdly, where the use or other development of lands is restricted under the planning legislation. The most obvious instance of this is where planning permission is refused for development, or granted subject to onerous conditions. Other examples include where an owner of lands is required to take specified measures to comply with a special planning control scheme (such as the removal or alteration of a structure),[15] or where a public right of way is created compulsorily.[16]

4. Planning permission: an enhancement of property rights?

The traditional view was to regard the requirement to obtain planning permission **6–06** as representing an interference with, or restriction of, constitutional property rights.[17] The refusal of planning permission, accordingly, must be justified in

---

[13] PDA 2000, s.71.
[14] PDA 2000, s.212(4).
[15] PDA 2000, s.88.
[16] PDA 2000, s.200, and s.207.
[17] *Butler v Dublin Corporation* [1999] 1 I.R. 565 at 588; [1999] 1 I.L.R.M. 481 at 490-1; *Waterford County Council v John A. Wood Ltd.* [1999] 1 I.R. 556 at 561; [1999] 1 I.L.R.M. 217 at 222; and *Ashbourne Holdings Ltd. v An Bord Pleanála* [2002] 1 I.L.R.M. 321 (High Court).

the common good and generally attracts the payment of compensation. In certain circumstances compensation may be excluded, either by reference to the type of development applied for, or to the reasons given for the refusal. This approach was reflected in the previous legislation, and with the exception of the special provisions introduced in respect of social and affordable housing, and zoning, respectively, is continued under the PDA 2000. The right to compensation is pared down somewhat under Pt XII of the PDA 2000. For example, a number of new non-compensatable reasons for refusal have been introduced.

6–07   The decision of the Supreme Court in *In the matter of Part V of the Planning and Development Bill, 1999*[18] intrudes, however, to upset the traditional view by suggesting that a grant of planning permission may, in law, represent an enhancement of property rights, and that every person who acquires or inherits land takes it subject to any restrictions which the general law of planning imposes on the use of property in the public interest.[19]

6–08   The Supreme Court held that, whereas a person who is compulsorily deprived of his or her property in the interests of the common good should normally be compensated at a level equivalent to at least the market value of the acquired property, special considerations were applicable in the case of restrictions on the use of land imposed under the planning legislation, as follows.[20]

> "Every person who acquires or inherits land takes it subject to any restrictions which the general law of planning imposes on the use of the property in the public interest. Inevitably, the fact that permission for a particular type of development may not be available for the land will, in certain circumstances, depreciate the value in the open market of that land. Conversely, where the person obtains a permission for a particular development the value of the land in the open market may be enhanced."
>
> [...]
>
> "In the present case, as a condition of obtaining a planning permission for the development of lands for residential purposes, the owner may be required to cede some part of the enhanced value of the land deriving both from its zoning for residential purposes and the grant of permission in order to meet what is considered by the Oireachtas to be a desirable social objective, namely the provision of affordable housing and housing for persons in special categories

---

[18] [2000] 2 I.R. 321; [2001] 1 I.L.R.M. 81. See also *Cooper v Cork City Council* [2006] I.E.H.C. 353; unreported, Murphy J., November 8, 2006 and December 19, 2006, where the High Court took the view that the grant of planning permission represented an enhancement of property rights, and that it was legitimate to lessen the enhanced value by the imposition of conditions.

[19] [2000] 2 I.R. 321; [2001] 1 I.L.R.M. 81. *Cf.* United States Supreme Court in *Lucas v South Carolina Coastal Council* 120 L Ed. 2d 798 at 820 ("Where the State seeks to sustain regulation that deprives land of all economically beneficial use, we think that it may resist compensation only if the logically antecedent inquiry into the nature of the owner's estate shows that the proscribed use interests were not part of his title to begin with.").

[20] [2000] 2 I.R. 321; [2001] 1 I.L.R.M. 81.

and of integrated housing. [...] [The provisions] are rationally connected to an objective of sufficient importance to warrant interference with a constitutionally protected right and, given the serious social problems which they are designed to meet, they undoubtedly relate to concerns which, in a free and democratic society, should be regarded as pressing and substantial."

This proposition is somewhat baldly stated in the judgment and thus, on a **6–09** literal reading, would appear to support the radical argument that there is no constitutional entitlement to compensation in the case of the refusal of planning permission. The statement in the judgment was probably not intended to go that far. At the very least, the general principle against retrospective effect of legislation would probably operate so as to limit its effect. It is one thing to say that a person acquiring property does so subject to the *existing* planning legislation—with the result that the bundle of rights acquired on obtaining title excluded any "right" to carry on particular activities—it is quite another to suggest that further limitations, especially on the right to obtain compensation, could be imposed subsequently. In this regard, it is important to emphasise that the reduced measure of compensation under the (then) Planning and Development Bill 1999 did not apply retrospectively, insofar as special provision was made in respect of land acquired for value prior to the date of the publication of the Bill.

The Supreme Court judgment also suggests that the right to recoup some of **6–10** the enhanced value of the lands is not necessarily predicated on the State, through the relevant local authority, having contributed to the enhanced value of the lands by dint of physical infrastructural works.

"In the present case, as a condition of obtaining a planning permission for the development of lands for residential purposes, the owner may be required to cede some part of the *enhanced value* of the land deriving both from its *zoning* for residential purposes and the *grant of permission* in order to meet what is considered by the Oireachtas to be a desirable social objective, namely the provision of affordable housing and housing for persons in the special categories and of integrated housing. Applying the tests proposed by Costello J. in *Heaney v. Ireland* [1994] 3 I.R. 593 and subsequently endorsed by this court, the court in the case of the present Bill is satisfied that the scheme passes those tests. They are rationally connected to an objective of sufficient importance to warrant interference with a constitutionally protected right and, given the serious social problems which they are designed to meet, they undoubtedly relate to concerns which, in a free and democratic society, should be regarded as pressing and substantial. At the same time, the court is satisfied that they impair those rights as little as possible and their effects on those rights are proportionate to the objectives sought to be attained."
*Emphasis supplied.

The judgment of the Supreme Court related to conditions attached to the *grant* **6–11** of planning permission, and thus the interference with property rights involved was not as immediately apparent as in the case of a refusal of planning permission. The principles underlying the judgment, however, if pursued to their logical conclusion might suggest that the provision made for the payment of compensation (even in the pared down form prescribed under Pt XII) may be more than constitutional imperatives demand. The provisions of Pt V are at odds with the provisions of Pt XII in relation to compensation, in that the rationale of the former is that planning gain may be a *quid pro quo* for the granting of planning permission, whereas a presumption in favour of planning permission underlies the compensation provisions under Pt XII.

B. Compensation for Adverse Planning Decision

1. Entitlement to compensation

6–12   There is a statutory right to compensation under s.190 of the PDA 2000 where planning permission has been refused on appeal by An Bord Pleanála. Compensation is also payable under s.190 where planning permission has been granted subject to onerous conditions on appeal by An Bord Pleanála. It is important to emphasise that the matter must be pursued on appeal to An Bord Pleanála: it does not seem that a claim for compensation lies where the matter rests with, and the final decision is made by, the planning authority.

2. Restriction of compensation

6–13   This *prima facie* right to compensation is excluded in a number of circumstances.[21] In the case of the refusal of planning permission, compensation is excluded if the development is of a class or description set out under the Third Schedule of the PDA 2000, or if the reason or one of the reasons stated for the refusal is a reason set out in the Fourth Schedule. Reasons of this type will be referred to by the shorthand "non-compensatable reasons" where convenient.

6–14   In the case of conditions, compensation is excluded if the condition is of a class or description set out in the Fifth Schedule. In *Cooper v Cork City Council*,[22] the High Court expressed the view that the words "of a class or description" under the previous legislation, which govern the circumstances in which planning conditions do not attract the payment of compensation, were wider and more flexible than the words "a reason as set out in", which govern the reasons for refusal.[23]

6–15   It is expressly provided that compensation shall not be payable in respect of the refusal of planning permission based on any change of the zoning of any land as a result of the making of a new development plan.[24] The full extent to

---

[21] PDA 2000, s.191.
[22] [2006] I.E.H.C. 353; unreported, Murphy J., November 8, 2006 and December 19, 2006.
[23] See further para.6–50.
[24] PDA 2000, s.191(2).

which compensation is excluded by reference to zoning is discussed in greater detail at paras 6–32 to 6–41.

Retention planning permission

Compensation is excluded where planning permission is refused for the retention of any unauthorised structures, or where conditions are imposed on the grant of planning permission for the retention of any unauthorised structures.[25]   **6–16**

3. Exclusion of compensation not a legitimate planning consideration

It should be emphasised that a desire to exclude compensation is not a legitimate planning consideration. Reference is made in this regard to the judgment of the Supreme Court in *Dublin County Council v Eighty Five Developments Ltd. (No. 2).*[26]   **6–17**

> "It would be an abuse of that power and function for either [a planning authority or An Bord Pleanála] to refuse an application for planning permission, giving as a reason for refusal not the true planning consideration involved, but rather a reason which would be exclusionary [...] for the purposes of avoiding the payment of compensation."

4. Form of wording required to exclude compensation

As indicated above, one of the principal circumstances in which compensation is excluded is where the reason or one of the reasons stated for the refusal is a reason set out in the Fourth Schedule of the PDA 2000.[27] A question immediately arises therefore as to the extent to which the wording of the stated reason must match or mirror that set out in the Fourth Schedule.   **6–18**

The Supreme Court in its judgment in *Dublin County Council v Eighty Five Developments Ltd. (No. 2)*[28] has indicated that it is desirable where compensation is to be excluded that this be done by expressing the reason for refusal as closely as possible in accordance with the wording of the legislation. This requirement would seem to follow from the constitutional implications: a landowner is entitled to know with certainty whether or not his or her right to compensation is excluded. Failure to use the precise form of wording is, however, apparently not fatal, as the courts will undertake a common sense appraisal of the real reason. McCarthy J. went so far as to suggest that An Bord Pleanála might be reluctant to use the precise words of the relevant   **6–19**

---

[25] PDA 2000, s.191(4).
[26] [1993] 2 I.R. 392; [1992] I.L.R.M. 815.
[27] PDA 2000, s.191(1)(b).
[28] [1993] 2 I.R. 392; [1992] I.L.R.M. 815. See, generally, G. Simons, "Compensation under the Planning Acts" (1993) 87 *Incorporated Law Society of Ireland Gazette* 103.

exclusionary provision lest it might be thought that the reason was being advanced in order to defeat a claim for compensation. With respect, it is hopelessly unrealistic to expect that An Bord Pleanála would be unaware of the consequences of the reasons for refusal. Legal certainty demands that the words of the legislation be followed, and this should prevail over the sensibilities of An Bord Pleanála.

6–20 In the event, subsequent judgments have indicated that care should be taken to mirror the statutory wording. Examples of the wording of reasons for refusal which failed to trigger the exclusion of compensation are as follows. The statutory wording is indicated in parentheses. "Awkward alignment and restricted sightlines" ("endanger public safety by reason of traffic hazard"); "inadequate setting" for a national monument ("injure or interfere with a national monument"); and "visually sensitive location" ("a view or prospect of special amenity value").[29]

5. Prohibition on double compensation

6–21 Under s.186, where a person would otherwise be entitled to compensation under Pt XII in respect of any matter or thing, and also to compensation under any other enactment in respect of the same matter or thing, he or she is not entitled to compensation under both enactments. Further, such a person shall not be entitled to any greater amount of compensation under Pt XII than the amount of compensation to which he or she would be entitled under the other enactment.

6. Recovery of compensation

6–22 Provision is made under s.189 for the recovery of compensation in circumstances where land is subsequently developed for development of a significant nature, *i.e.* development of a residential, commercial or industrial character, consisting wholly or mainly of the construction of houses, shops or office premises, hotels, garages and petrol filling stations, theatres or structures for the purpose of entertainment, or industrial buildings (including warehouses), or any combination thereof.[30] Where the land developed forms part only of the land in respect of which compensation had been paid, the amount recoverable is confined to that attributable to the land falling within the development area.

---

[29] *J. Wood and Co. Ltd. v Wicklow County Council* [1995] I.L.R.M. 51.
[30] Defined under PDA 2000, s.192(2).

7. Replacement of structures demolished or destroyed by fire or otherwise

Special provision is made under s.193 in respect of structures substantially replacing structures demolished or destroyed by fire or otherwise. Subject to certain exceptions in the case of unauthorised structures and unlawful acts on the part of the owner, compensation is not to be excluded for the refusal of planning permission or the grant of planning permission subject to certain (onerous) conditions.   **6–23**

Every dispute and question as to whether a new structure would or does replace substantially a demolished or destroyed structure shall be referred to An Bord Pleanála for determination.   **6–24**

C. Overview of Circumstances in which Compensation is Excluded

In order for compensation to be excluded, there must be an *additional* factor, over and above the proper planning and sustainable development of the area, which justifies an exception to the general rule requiring the payment of compensation. Part XII of the PDA 2000 represents an attempt to articulate circumstances where not only is the refusal of planning permission justified by reference to proper planning and sustainable development, but further where there is no requirement to pay compensation.   **6–25**

Some attempt can be made to rationalise the exclusion of compensation in the varied circumstances identified under Pt XII (and the schedules) by reference to concepts such as the noxious use of land, and the generality of the regulation.   **6–26**

1. Noxious use of land

The restriction of property rights without the payment of compensation may be justified where it is necessary to prevent the injurious or noxious use of land. Examples under the Fourth Schedule include where the proposed development would endanger public safety by reason of traffic hazard[31]; would cause serious air pollution, water pollution, or pollution connected with the disposal of waste[32]; or would seriously injure the amenities, or depreciate the value, of property in the vicinity.[33] Such proposed development may be analysed as giving rise to a conflict between the exercise of the developer's property rights and the common good. Article 43 of the Constitution expressly allows   **6–27**

---

[31] PDA 2000, Sch.4, para.4.

[32] PDA 2000, Sch.4, para.9.

[33] PDA 2000, Sch.4, para.10. The amenities injured must be those of *property* in the vicinity, and not amenities generally: *Abbeydrive Developments Ltd. v Kildare County Council* [2005] I.E.H.C. 209; unreported, Macken J., June 17, 2005.

for the State to delimit property rights with a view to *reconciling* their exercise with the exigencies of the common good.

6–28   The weakness with the concept of noxious use is that certain development may be analysed either as the prohibition of an *injurious* use of land which does not require the payment of compensation, or as the conferring of a *benefit* on the public without just compensation to the landowner. For example, the exclusion of compensation where permission is refused for development which would injure or interfere with a historic monument may be regarded as the prohibition of a noxious use, *i.e.* the injury or interference to the historic monument, or, alternatively, as imposing the cost of preservation on an individual landowner, when in fairness the burden should be borne by the public.[34]

2. Generality of regulation

6–29   Even a non-injurious use of land may be prohibited if the regulation applies generally. An obvious example would be the zoning objectives of a development plan: while zoning at times reduces individual property values, the burden is shared relatively evenly and it is reasonable to conclude that on the whole an individual who is harmed by one aspect of the zoning will be benefited by another. A requirement that the regulation be of general application may explain why, in assessing compensation, regard may only be had to general zoning under the development plan, and not to the reservation of any land for *particular* purposes.[35] See further para.6–72.

6–30   A variation on this question as to how general the application of the regulation must be arises in the context of the legislative requirements for social and affordable housing under Pt V of the PDA 2000. In very basic terms, s.96 (as substituted by the Planning and Development (Amendment) Act 2002) requires, in the context of certain residential development, that a condition be attached to a planning permission requiring the applicant, or any other person with an interest in the land, to enter into an "agreement" for the transfer of land. In its mandatory form, an agreement will simply involve the transfer of land in its undeveloped state. Some flexibility is allowed for, however, in that the developer may, as an alternative to this, volunteer to make provision for social and affordable housing in other ways. The range of potential options includes the transfer to the planning authority of the ownership of any other land within the functional area of the planning authority; and the transfer of built houses and/ or serviced sites (again, not necessarily on the lands the subject-matter of the application for planning permission). Moreover, it seems that a housing agreement might provide simply for the payment of monies to the planning authority. In all cases, however, the developer is required to confer a planning

---

[34] *cf. In the matter of the Employment Equality Bill, 1996* [1997] 2 I.R. 321 at 387–388.
[35] *Dublin County Council v Shortt* [1983] I.L.R.M. 377.

gain on the planning authority. The measure of this planning gain is calculated by reference to the equivalent monetary value formula. See further Chapter 15.

It is submitted that a requirement which is confined to residential development **6–31** only lacks the generality of regulation which underpins the exclusion of compensation on general zoning grounds. This aspect was considered by the Supreme Court in its decision in *In the matter of Part V of the Planning and Development Bill, 1999*.[36] It is respectfully submitted that the judgment does not advance any convincing reason for rejecting the argument that the legislation unfairly and invidiously discriminated against landowners who propose to develop their land for residential development as opposed to other types of profitable development, *e.g.* commercial or industrial.

D. Exclusion of Compensation by Reference to Zoning Objectives

1. Position under previous legislation

The exclusion of compensation by reference to zoning objectives was first **6–32** introduced under the Local Government (Planning & Development) Act 1990, and was subject to a number of safeguards. In particular, a five year period of grace applied whereby compensation remained payable in circumstances where the proposed development would not have contravened the *previous* zoning objective of the land, notwithstanding that it did contravene the current zoning objective. Thus, a landowner was effectively entitled to rely, for compensation purposes only, on the previous zoning objective for a period of five years after its amendment. This period of grace was lost, however, where the land was sold on after the amendment of the zoning objective, or after the amendment of the zoning objective had first been indicated in the *draft* development plan.

These safeguards are largely removed under the PDA 2000. The Act proceeds **6–33** on the stated principle that there shall be no presumption in law that any land zoned in a particular development plan shall remain so zoned in any subsequent development plan.[37] The five year period of grace for a change in zoning is removed, and save where the change in zoning occurs as a "variation" during the currency of the development plan,[38] compensation is assessed by reference to the current zoning.[39]

---

[36] [2000] 2 I.R. 321; [2001] 1 I.L.R.M. 81.
[37] PDA 2000, s.10(8).
[38] The availability of this concession is discussed further at para.6-35.
[39] The transitional provisions are elliptical but it appears that an attempt was made to introduce a three year lead-in time from the date of commencement before this change is brought into effect: PDA 2000, s.268(1)(d) and (3). The reference to para.5 of the Fourth Schedule of the PDA 2000 appears to be incorrect. It remains to be seen whether the wording of the legislation is sufficient to achieve this purpose.

2. Present position

6–34 The refusal of planning permission for zoning reasons excludes the payment of compensation. The structure of the legislation is cumbersome in this regard in that the matter is dealt with at two separate points, and the wording used is different in each case. First, s.190(2) of the PDA 2000 provides that compensation shall not be payable in respect of the refusal of planning permission based on any change of the zoning of any land as a result of the making of a new development plan. Secondly, para.20 of the Fourth Schedule provides that compensation is excluded where:

> "[t]he development would contravene materially a development objective indicated in the development plan for the zoning of land for the use solely or primarily of particular areas for particular purposes (whether residential, commercial, industrial, agricultural, recreational, as open space or otherwise or a mixture of such uses)."

6–35 Although these two provisions would appear, broadly, to be to the same effect, the following points of distinction should be noted. First, under para.20 compensation is only excluded where the development would contravene materially the zoning objective; s.190(2) is arguably wider in that compensation is excluded where planning permission is refused on the basis of any change in zoning.[40] In principle, planning permission might be said to have been refused on the "basis" of a zoning objective even in circumstances where the proposed development did not materially contravene that objective. Secondly, the only express temporal qualification on the exclusion under s.190(2) is that the change in zoning objective have occurred on the occasion of the making of a new development plan, *i.e.* the exclusion does not apply where the change arises as a result of a "variation" during the life of the development plan. Conversely, the qualifications on the application of para.20 are much more complicated. It would appear from para.21 (and the wording is Delphic) that it is necessary that an application for planning permission actually have been made prior to the change in zoning[41] and that the proposed development would not have contravened materially the then zoning, in order for the entitlement to compensation to survive. Moreover, under para.22, the entitlement to compensation is lost, *inter alia*, where a person acquired his or her interest in the land with notice of either the change, or proposed change, in zoning.

6–36 It is to be noted that para.20 replicates the terms of s.10(2)(a). Compensation is thus not excluded by reason of a material contravention *simpliciter*; for example, a material contravention of traffic standards or of housing density standards under the development plan would not come within the scope of the

---

[40] There is no express requirement that this basis actually be stated as a reason for refusal.
[41] Admittedly this interpretation requires that the clause "and the development objective of which was changed as a result of the variation during such period" be read as if in parentheses.

relevant zoning objectives of the plan under s.10(2)(a).[42] The terms of s.190(2) are expressly limited to the zoning of the land.

3. "Zoning objective"

There is no definition of what constitutes a "zoning objective" provided for under the PDA 2000. The case law in this regard has been discussed briefly at paras 1–81 to 1–83. In the context of statutory compensation, one point which is of particular relevance is as to extent of the area which must be affected before a designation—to use a neutral term—can be said to represent a zoning objective. It can be argued that in order to legitimately exclude compensation, a zoning objective must be of general application. If this is the position, then the correctness of the High Court decision in *O'Connor v Clare County Council*[43] may be open to doubt. Murphy J. had held in that case that zoning could apply to even limited areas:

> "The limited area designated for development could hardly be described as being 'zoned' in the sense in which that is ordinarily understood. That term is generally used to describe a wider area where activities or development having some measure of uniformity may be undertaken by a considerable number of owners or occupiers. However, there does not appear to be anything in [para.11 of the Third Schedule, Local Government (Planning & Development) Act 1990] aforesaid which would prevent a planning authority from indicating a specific development objective in relation to a *limited area* with a view to or as a consequence of formulating a development objective in relation to an adjoining larger area."
> *Emphasis supplied.

The circumstances in which compensation is excluded by reference to zoning objectives were also considered in *Ebonwood Ltd. v Meath County Council.*[44] The facts might be summarised thus. It was an objective of the *draft* development plan to retain a route selection corridor along a disused railway line in order to facilitate its possible future reinstatement. Planning permission for an extension to an existing hotel was refused by reference, *inter alia*, to this objective. A claim for compensation was made under the (then) legislation. As in the case of the PDA 2000, compensation was excluded under the Local Government (Planning & Development) Act 1990 where the proposed development would contravene materially a development objective indicated in the development plan for the use solely or primarily of particular areas for particular purposes.

The actual issue for determination by the High Court was very narrow. Specifically, the High Court had to consider whether or not a reason for refusal

6–37

6–38

6–39

---

[42] It should be noted, however, that compensation is excluded under para.15 of the Fourth Schedule where the proposed development would materially contravene an objective indicated in a local area plan for the area.

[43] Unreported, High Court, Murphy J., February 11, 1994 (at p.5).

[44] [2004] 3 I.R. 34; [2004] 1 I.L.R.M. 305.

which cited the provisions of the *draft* development plan operated to exclude compensation. The High Court held that the reference under the 1990 Act to the development plan did not extend to a draft development plan.

6–40   The court went further, however, and considered the wider question as to whether compensation would have been excluded by reference to the objective. In this regard, Peart J. appears to have accepted that the objective to retain a route selection corridor (railway) represented a zoning objective for the purposes of compensation. It is submitted that this finding fails to attach proper weight to the requirement that a zoning objective be of general application. The designation of lands for the purposes of a proposed railway route is, at most, a form of spot zoning, and is closer to the logically distinct concept of the reservation of land for a particular purpose, than to a general zoning objective. The judgment is somewhat inconsistent in that, having accepted that the route selection corridor represented a zoning objective, Peart J. nonetheless went on to say that the objective involved the "reservation of those lands for a particular purpose". The concepts of zoning and reservation for a particular purpose will, generally, be mutually exclusive. It is to be noted in this regard that any depreciation or increase in the value of land attributable to the land or any land in the vicinity being reserved for a particular purpose in a development plan is to be disregarded in assessing compensation. It would seem anomalous for the legislature, having recognised that it would be unfair to reduce the quantum of compensation by reference to the reservation of land, to go on then to exclude the payment of compensation entirely by reference to the reservation of land.

6–41   The judgment is also open to the criticism that the court, incorrectly, sought to give a *broad* interpretation to the statutory provisions excluding compensation. It is submitted that a narrow interpretation of zoning objectives would exclude route reservations. Moreover, the essence of the reason for refusal was that the proposed development was premature pending the completion of a route selection process. Express provision is made to exclude compensation where a development is premature pending the determination of a road layout: the absence of a similar provision in the case of a railway indicates that compensation is not to be excluded.

E. Other Circumstances in which Compensation is Excluded

6–42   The following examples provide a flavour of the type of circumstances in which compensation is also excluded under the Third and Fourth Schedules of the PDA 2000.

1. Public health and safety

Compensation is excluded, *inter alia*, where the proposed development would endanger public safety by reason of traffic hazard[45]; endanger or interfere with the safety of aircraft or their navigation[46]; cause serious air pollution, water pollution, noise pollution or vibration or pollution connected with the disposal of waste[47]; or the proposed development is in an area which is at risk of flooding.[48]

6–43

2. Amenity reasons

Compensation is excluded where the proposed development would interfere with the character of the landscape or with a view or prospect of special amenity value or of natural interest or beauty which it is necessary to preserve.[49] Compensation is also excluded where any structure, addition or extension to a structure, would seriously injure the amenities, or depreciate the value, of property in the vicinity,[50] or where development is proposed in an area to which a special amenity area order relates.

6–44

3. Premature development

Compensation is excluded where development is premature by reference to matters such as, for example, a deficiency in the provision of water supplies or sewerage facilities (known colloquially as "piped services"); or a deficiency in the road network. Development may also be premature by reference to non-physical constraints. For example, development may be premature by reference to the order of priority for development indicated in the development plan, or pending the adoption of a local area plan in accordance with the development plan. It should be noted that there must be some prospect of the current constraints on development being resolved; the term "premature" intimates that the development may be carried out at a later (ascertainable) date, but that as yet it is too early.[51]

6–45

A useful analogy may be drawn with the case law in respect of the European Convention on Human Rights. For example, in *Skibinscy v Poland*,[52] the ECtHR

6–46

---

[45] PDA 2000, Sch.4, para.4. See *Liddy v Minister for Public Enterprise* [2004] 1 I.L.R.M. 9.

[46] PDA 2000, Sch.4, para.10.

[47] PDA 2000, Sch.4, para.9.

[48] PDA 2000, Sch.4, para.6.

[49] Seemingly, these do not have to be identified for preservation under the development plan.

[50] The amenities injured must be those of *property* in the vicinity, and not amenities generally: *Abbeydrive Developments Ltd. v Kildare County Council* [2005] I.E.H.C. 209; unreported, Macken J., June 17, 2005.

[51] *Hoburn Homes Ltd. v An Bord Pleanála* [1993] I.L.R.M. 368; and *O'Connor v Clare County Council*, unreported, High Court, Murphy J., February 11, 1994.

[52] Application No. 52589/99; November 14, 2006.

ruled that the prolonged designation of land for expropriation at some undetermined future date gave rise to a breach of the first sentence of Art.1. Part of the applicants' lands had been designated under a land-development plan for use for the construction of a major roadway. This resulted in the applicants being denied the opportunity to develop their lands for a period of approximately ten years, between 1994 and 2003. This was so notwithstanding that the local investment plan did not provide for the construction of the road to begin before 2010. The designation eventually expired at the end of 2003, and was not renewed. See further Chapter 14, paras 14–87 to 14–95.

4. Material change in use

6–47 Compensation is excluded in respect of any development which consists of, or includes, the making of any material change in the use of any structures or other lands. The term "use" in "material change in use" bears an artificial meaning in this context: use in relation to land does not include the use of land by the carrying out of any works thereon.[53] Thus, planning permission for the construction of houses on agricultural land does not, as a matter of law, involve any material change in use.[54]

F. Conditions Resolving Planning Difficulties of the Proposed Development

6–48 The imposition of an onerous condition gives rise to a *prima facie* entitlement to the payment of compensation.[55] However, a number of conditions which may be imposed without compensation are prescribed in the Fifth Schedule of the PDA 2000. A number of these conditions relate to the resolution of planning difficulties given rise to by the immediate needs of the proposed development. For example, conditions may be imposed (without the payment of compensation) relating to the extent of parking spaces required, or the facilities for the parking, loading, unloading or fuelling of vehicles. Where a condition relates to a planning difficulty not created by the proposed development, the payment of compensation may be required. This is expressly recognised under s.34(4)(m) where there is provision for the local authority to pay for the cost of additional works in the case of works in excess of the "immediate needs" of the proposed development.[56]

6–49 It must be borne in mind that the imposition of onerous conditions is subject to the same constitutional requirements as to the payment of compensation, as is

---

[53] PDA 2000, s.2.

[54] *Re Viscount Securities* (1978) 112 I.L.T.R. 17.

[55] PDA 2000, s.190.

[56] For a discussion of the position under the differently worded provisions of the Local Government (Planning & Development) Act 1963, see *Thomas McDonagh & Sons Ltd. v Galway Corporation* [1995] 1 I.R. 191.

the refusal of planning permission. This is not always obvious, as the grant of planning permission *per se* appears to vindicate the developer's property rights. It is only where the reasons underlying the imposition of an uncompensated onerous condition are similar to those which would justify the refusal of planning permission without compensation that the exclusion of compensation is constitutional.

In *Cooper v Cork City Council*,[57] the High Court held—in the context of the similarly worded provisions of the Local Government (Planning & Development) Act 1990—that there is a distinction between compensation for the refusal of permission and compensation in respect of the imposition of a condition. Murphy J. expressed the view that the words "of a class or description" under the previous legislation were wider and more flexible then the words "a reason as set out in". The High Court also indicated, somewhat surprisingly, that a purposive approach had to be taken to the interpretation of the various sub-paragraphs of what is now the Fifth Schedule. Murphy J. took the view that the grant of planning permission represented an enhancement of property rights, and that it was legitimate to lessen the enhanced value by the imposition of conditions.

6–50

The relevant condition in *Cooper* had prohibited development on a particular part of the application site, and required that this area instead be retained in its natural undeveloped state. Murphy J. held that this condition related to the "preservation and protection of trees, shrubs, plants and flowers", and, as such, was a non-compensatable condition.

6–51

G. Procedure for Making Claim

1. Time-limit

Generally, a claim for compensation should be made not later than six months after the decision of An Bord Pleanála.[58] (Again, it is to be noted that the matter must be pursued, on appeal, to An Bord Pleanála.) The High Court may, however, where it considers that the interests of justice so require, extend the period within which a claim may be brought.

6–52

2. Transitional

Article 178 of the Planning and Development Regulations 2001 provides, in summary, as follows. Where a compensation claim has been made in accordance with the Local Government (Planning & Development) Regulations 1994 prior

6–53

---

[57] [2006] I.E.H.C. 353; unreported, Murphy J., November 8, 2006 and December 19, 2006.
[58] PDA 2000, s.183. The date of the decision is not necessarily the same as the date of notification. *Cf. Keelgrove Properties Ltd. v An Bord Pleanála* [2000] 1 I.R. 47; [2000] 2 I.L.R.M. 168.

to the coming into force of these (2001) Regulations, the claim shall be determined in accordance with those (earlier) Regulations.

3. Form and content of application

6–54 Under the Planning and Development Regulations 2001, a compensation claim shall be made in writing to the planning authority and include, *inter alia*, details as to the claimant and a statement of his interest in the land; the amount of compensation claimed and the basis on which it has been calculated; and details as to any other person having an interest in the land.

6–55 It seems from the judgment in *Abbeydrive Developments Ltd. v Kildare County Council (No. 1)*[59] that it is not necessary that the claimant identify, in his initial claim, the exact nature of the legal interest under which he holds the lands, *i.e.* whether as freeholder, leaseholder, charge holder or so forth. The planning authority in that case had sought to argue that time should not start running for the purpose of serving a notice under s.13 of the 1990 Act (now s.192 of the PDA 2000) until the claimant had responded to a request for copies of the relevant conveyances.

4. Nature of interest

6–56 Compensation is payable in respect of the reduction in the value of an "interest" of any person existing in the land to which the decision relates at the time of the decision. It is not necessary that a claimant have retained an interest in the lands subsequent to the decision: it would be unfair were the claimant to be prevented, in order to acquire his compensation, from subsequently disposing of the lands.[60]

6–57 It seems clear that a claimant must have a proprietary interest in the land; thus, a licensee, for example, would probably not be entitled to claim compensation.[61] It should also be noted that the interest necessary to ground a planning application is less than that required to found a claim for compensation.[62]

6–58 Under s.194, there is a prohibition on the assignment to any person of all or any part of any prospective compensation, and every purported assignment or promise, express or implied, to pay any other person any money in respect of any such compensation is void.

---

[59] [2005] I.E.H.C. 209; unreported, Macken J., June 17, 2005.
[60] *Dublin Corporation v Smithwick* [1976-7] I.L.R.M. 280.
[61] *Frank Warr & Co. Ltd. v London County Council* [1904] 1 K.B. 713; *cf. Pennine Raceway v Kirkless Council* [1983] Q.B. 382.
[62] *Grange Developments Ltd. v Dublin County Council* [1989] I.R. 296

5. Reference to property arbitrator

A claim for compensation shall, in default of agreement, be determined by **6–59** arbitration under the Acquisition of Land (Assessment of Compensation) Act 1919. Thus in the event that the planning authority disputes the claim for compensation, it will be necessary to refer the matter to the property arbitrator. This is a relatively straightforward process involving the making of a request to the Reference Committee to nominate a property arbitrator.[63]

6. Supervisory jurisdiction of the High Court

It is important to note that the manner in which the supervisory jurisdiction of **6–60** the High Court may be invoked in the context of a statutory arbitration is unusual. In most other contexts under the planning legislation, legal challenges are brought before the High Court by way of an application for judicial review (whether conventional judicial review or the special judicial review under ss.50 and 50A (as amended in 2006)). In the case of a statutory arbitration, however, the better view is that judicial review does not lie and instead the jurisdiction of the High Court may only be invoked by way of the case stated procedure.[64]

One of the most significant differences between judicial review and the case **6–61** stated procedure is that in the case of the latter any legal proceedings must, in effect, be taken before the final decision or award is made by the arbitrator. This is because once a final decision or award has been made, same is generally unimpeachable.[65] Thus an applicant does not have the indulgence of awaiting sight of the decision or award of the arbitrator before committing himself to legal proceedings. Once the decision or award is made, it is then too late to take legal proceedings.

Case stated procedure

Either party to the statutory arbitration may request the arbitrator to state a **6–62** case to the High Court. The case stated must raise a point or question of law. The arbitrator has discretion as to whether or not to state a case, subject to the exceptional power of the High Court to direct the arbitrator to state a case. In practice, the High Court appears to be reluctant to direct a case to be stated.[66]

---

[63] See McDermott and Woulfe, *Compulsory Purchase and Compensation in Ireland: Law and Practice* (Butterworths, Dublin, 1992), p.285.

[64] See, generally, G. Simons, "The review of arbitration awards by the courts" (1997) 15 *Irish Law Times* 74. *Cf. Manning v Shackleton* [1996] 3 I.R. 85, where a property arbitrator's award was subject to judicial review without any discussion of the appropriateness of the remedy.

[65] Acquisition of Land (Assessment of Compensation) Act 1919, s.6, provides that the decision of a property arbitrator upon any question of fact shall be final and binding on the parties. A special case may be stated to the High Court on any question of law arising "at any stage of the proceedings", *i.e.* before a final decision has been made.

[66] See, for example, *Hogan v St. Kevin's Company* [1986] I.R. 80.

6–63 One type of question which often forms the subject-matter of a case stated is as to whether the *prima facie* right to compensation has successfully been excluded. In particular, a question may arise as to whether the wording of the reason stated for refusal is sufficiently close to the statutory language. This issue is discussed further at paras 6–18 to 6–20 above.

H. Determination of Amount of Compensation

1. Antecedent and subsequent values of land

6–64 Compensation is payable in respect of the reduction in the claimant's interest in the land. The reduction in value is calculated by reference to the difference between the open market value of the land prior to the relevant decision, and the subsequent open market value of the land after that decision. The rules for the determination of the amount of compensation are set out in the Second Schedule of the PDA 2000.

6–65 The reduction in value shall, subject to the other provisions of the Second Schedule, be determined by reference to the difference between the antecedent and subsequent values of the land. The "antecedent value" of the land is defined as the amount which the land, if sold in the open market by a willing seller immediately prior to the relevant decision (and assuming that the relevant application for permission had not been made), might have been expected to realise. The "subsequent value" of the land is defined as the amount which the land, if sold in the open market by a willing seller immediately after that decision, might be expected to realise.

2. "Regard shall be had to"

6–66 A series of matters are set out at para.2(a) of the Second Schedule to which regard is to be had in determining the antecedent value and subsequent value of the land, as follows.

   (i) Any contribution which a planning authority might have required or might require as a condition precedent to development of the land.
   (ii) Any restriction on the development of the land which, without conferring a right to compensation, could have been or could be imposed under any Act or under any order, regulations, rule or bye-law made under any Act.
   (iii) The fact that exempted development might have been or may be carried out on the land.
   (iv) The open market value of comparable land, if any, in the vicinity of the land whose values are being determined.

3. "No account shall be taken of"

6–67 A further series of matters of which no account shall be taken in determining the antecedent value and subsequent value of the land are set out at para.2(b), as follows.

(i) Value attributable to subsidies or grants

The property arbitrator is to disregard any part of the value of the land **6–68** attributable to subsidies or grants available from public moneys, or to any tax or rating allowances in respect of development, from which development of the land might benefit.

(ii) Special suitability or adaptability of the land

The property arbitrator is to disregard the special suitability or adaptability of **6–69** the land for any purpose if that purpose is a purpose to which it could be applied only in pursuance of statutory powers, or for which there is no market apart from the special needs of a particular purchaser or the requirements of any statutory body as defined. It is provided that any *bona fide* offer for the purchase of the land which may be brought to the notice of the arbitrator shall be taken into consideration.

The meaning and effect of an equivalent rule has recently been considered by **6–70** the House of Lords in *Waters v Welsh Development Agency*.[67] In a minority speech, Lord Scott of Foscote suggested that the rule envisaged a particular suitability which only the acquiring authority, or an authority with statutory powers, is able to exploit. It was not necessary that the land have a unique suitability not shared with any other land. The majority of the House of the Lords, however, considered that it was too late to disturb the long line of case law which had given a narrower interpretation to the rule. In these earlier cases "special suitability" had been held to require something exceptional in character, quality or degree. On this narrow interpretation, in most cases the statutory purpose will not be excluded by reference to this rule. It may, however, be excluded on the basis of the "no scheme world": see paras 6–76 above and onwards.

(iii) Unlawful use and structures

The property arbitrator is to disregard any increase in the value of land **6–71** attributable to the use thereof or of any structure thereon in a manner which could be restrained by any court, or is contrary to law, or detrimental to the health of the inmates of the structure, or to public health or safety, or to the environment. This suggests that the amount of compensation may be restricted by reference to unauthorised development which is immune from enforcement action under the seven year time-limits. Notwithstanding its immunity such development remains illegal.[68]

---

[67] [2004] U.K.H.L. 19; [2004] 2 P. & C.R. 29.
[68] See *obiter dicta* in *O'Connor v Nenagh UDC*, unreported, High Court, Geoghegan J., July 16, 1996. *Cf. Hughes v Doncaster Metropolitan Borough Council* [1991] 05 E.G. 133.

(iv) Reservation for a particular purpose in a development plan

6–72   The property arbitrator is to disregard any depreciation or increase in value attributable to the land, or any land in the vicinity, being reserved for a particular purpose in a development plan. It has been held that the reservation of land for a particular purpose is a different concept than the "zoning" of land; the term "reserved" means set apart, and the term "particular purpose" means a purpose distinct from the purpose for which the other land in the area is zoned.[69] The intention of the rule is to protect the owner from the detrimental effect on the value of his land of the reservation of the land for the particular purpose for the *benefit of the community* and to ensure that owners of other land do not profit from it.[70] It appears that the question as to whether or not land is reserved for a particular purpose is one of degree; there may be a point when an area is large enough in its own right so as not to be considered as set apart from other lands adjoining.[71]

6–73   An interesting question arises as to whether designation as a "protected structure" should be regarded as a form of reservation under the development plan. It is certainly arguable that designation involves "spot zoning". If designation as a protected structure is to be regarded as a reservation for a particular purpose, then the designation must be disregarded for the purpose of determining the antecedent value of the land. This will result in a higher level for the antecedent value; in particular, the likelihood of obtaining planning permission will fall to be considered without reference to the status as a protected structure. Conversely, if designation as a protected structure does not involve a reservation, then the likelihood of obtaining planning permission will have to be considered in light of designation under the development plan.[72]

6–74   It is to be noted that Part V of the PDA 2000 (as amended) refers to land being "reserved" for the purpose of social and affordable housing. This leaves it open for an ingenious developer to argue that a claim for compensation under Pt XII lies against a decision to impose a condition requiring social and affordable housing. Such an argument would involve exploiting the following two potential loopholes in the legislation. First, nowhere in the schedule of conditions which may be imposed without compensation is there reference to a condition with respect to social and affordable housing.[73] Secondly, the fact that land is "reserved" for social and affordable housing suggests that designation for that purpose under the development plan must be disregarded in assessing the antecedent value of the land in determining the amount of compensation payable.[74]

---

[69] *Shortt v Dublin County Council* [1982] I.L.R.M. 117.
[70] *Shortt v Dublin County Council* [1982] I.L.R.M. 117.
[71] *Monastra Developments Ltd. v Dublin County Council* [1992] 2 I.R. 468.
[72] PDA 2000, Sch.2, para.3(2).
[73] PDA 2000, Sch.5.
[74] PDA 2000, Sch.2, para.2(b)(iii).

(v) Value attributable to any unauthorised structure or use

Rule (v) is similar to Rule (iii)—discussed above at para.6–71—and requires **6–75** the property arbitrator to disregard any value attributable to any unauthorised structure or unauthorised use. Again, this suggests that the amount of compensation may be restricted by reference to even unauthorised development which is immune from enforcement action under the seven year time-limits. Notwithstanding its immunity such development remains illegal.[75]

(vi) Proposals of statutory body and scheme of development

(vii) Scheme of development undertaken by a statutory body

The property arbitrator is required to disregard the existence of proposals for **6–76** development of the land or any other land by a statutory body; or the possibility or probability of the land or other land becoming subject to a scheme of development undertaken by a statutory body. The objective of these last two rules appears to be to exclude any increase in the value of the lands arising from the proposed scheme, or from any statutory scheme of development.[76] This principle is sometimes referred to as the "no scheme world". The principle has been stated thus by the Privy Council.[77]

> "A landowner cannot claim compensation to the extent that the value of his land is increased by the very scheme of which (the compulsory acquisition) forms an integral part. A loss in value attributable to the scheme is not to enure to the detriment of a claimant ... The underlying reasoning is that if the landowner is to be fairly compensated, scheme losses should attract compensation but scheme gains should not. Had there been no scheme those losses and gains would not have arisen."

The extent to which matters consequential to a statutory scheme of development **6–77** fall to be considered as part of that scheme is unclear. On the narrowest interpretation, one might simply say that all that the above rules require is that the existence of the statutory powers of compulsory acquisition *simpliciter* be disregarded. In practice, however, any increase in the value of the lands does not derive so much from the exercise of the statutory powers of compulsory acquisition but from the fact that the acquiring authority is often in a position to unlock the development potential of the lands (for example, by the provision of services, or by rezoning the lands). The question then arises as to what extent the landowner is entitled to rely on these matters for the purpose of valuing the lands.

---

[75] See *obiter dicta* in *O'Connor v Nenagh UDC,* unreported, High Court, Geoghegan J., July 16, 1996.
[76] See, generally, McDermott and Woulfe, *Compulsory Purchase and Compensation in Ireland: Law and Practice* (Butterworths, Dublin, 1992), pp. 226-228.
[77] *Director of Buildings and Land v Shun Fung Ironworks Ltd.* [1995] 2 A.C. 111 at 136. This decision is discussed in *Waters v Welsh Development Agency* [2004] U.K.H.L. 19; [2004] 2 P. & C.R. 29.

6–78 In *Re Deansrath Investments Ltd.*,[78] the Supreme Court held that the provision of services to the land is not part of the scheme. In the later decision of *Re Murphy*,[79] however, it seems to have been suggested that a proposed change in the zoning objective of the land had to be disregarded. The proposal was to change the zoning objective so as to enable that statutory scheme; thus the proposed change only arose in the context of the statutory scheme and, seemingly, was therefore to be disregarded under the rule.

Capital value for taxation may be considered

6–79 Under rule 2(c), all returns and assessments of capital value for taxation made or acquiesced in by the claimant may be considered.[80]

Possibilities for developing land

6–80 In determining the antecedent value of the land, it will be necessary to consider the reasonable possibilities for its development. A number of material considerations are prescribed under the Second Schedule including the likelihood of obtaining planning permission in the light of the provisions of the development plan.

> "3.(1) In assessing the possibilities, if any, for developing the land, for the purposes of determining its antecedent value, regard shall be had only to such reasonable possibilities as, having regard to all material considerations, could be judged to have existed immediately prior to the relevant decision under Part III.
>
> (2) Material considerations for the purposes of subparagraph (1) shall, without prejudice to the generality thereof, include—
>
> (a) the nature and location of the land,
>
> (b) the likelihood or unlikelihood, as the case may be, of obtaining permission or further permission, to develop the land in the light of the provisions of the development plan,
>
> (c) the assumption that, if any permission to develop the land were to be granted, any conditions which might reasonably be imposed in relation to matters referred to in the Fifth Schedule (but no other conditions) would be imposed, and
>
> (d) any permission to develop the land, not being permission for the development of a kind specified in section 192(2), already existing at the time of the relevant decision under Part III."

6–81 The relationship between this provision and other provisions in connection with the development plan is unclear. This provision brings zoning objectives into play again. As the arbitrator is thus entitled to have regard to zoning in determining the value of the land, this may have the effect that even in circumstances where compensation is not excluded outright by reference to the zoning objectives (for example, in the case of a variation during the currency of the development plan), the *measure* of compensation may, in practice, be affected by the zoning objectives of the development plan.

---

[78] [1974] I.R. 228.

[79] [1977] I.R. 243.

[80] PDA 2000, Sch.2.

In determining the subsequent value of the land in a case in which there has **6–82** been a refusal of permission, the arbitrator is generally required to assume that, after the refusal, planning permission would not be granted for any development of a residential, commercial or industrial character, consisting wholly or mainly of the construction of houses, shops or office premises, hotels, garages and petrol filling stations, theatres or structures for the purpose of entertainment, or industrial buildings (including warehouses), or any combination thereof.[81]

(There is an exception to this where an "undertaking" under the previous **6–83** legislation is in force: in such circumstances, the assumption then becomes that planning permission would not be granted for any development *other* than development to which the undertaking relates.)

In determining the subsequent value of the land in a case in which there has **6–84** been a refusal of planning permission, the arbitrator shall also have regard to any conditions in relation to matters referred to in the Fifth Schedule (but no other conditions) which might reasonably be imposed in the grant of permission to develop the land.

I. Notices Excluding Compensation

Section 192 of the PDA 2000 allows a planning authority, having refused a **6–85** particular planning application, to serve a notice stating that the land in question is capable of *other* specified development for which planning permission ought to be granted.[82] In other words, the planning authority may indicate that, notwithstanding the refusal of planning permission for a particular development, planning permission will, in principle, be available for other (profitable) development. The other development must be of a residential, commercial or industrial character, consisting wholly or mainly of the construction of houses (the definition of which includes apartments and flats), shops or office premises, hotels, garages and petrol filling stations, theatres or structures for the purpose of entertainment, or industrial buildings (including warehouses), or any combination thereof.

Special care must be taken, in drafting such notices, to state the beneficial **6–86** development with precision: the broader the terms of the notice, the greater the permutations of application which will be consistent with the other development specified in the notice, and thus the greater the risk that planning permission will be refused and the notice annulled. To put the matter another way, it should be easier for the planning authority to anticipate the outcome of an application

---

[81] PDA 2000, Sch.2, rule 4.
[82] The form of notice is prescribed under art.177 of the Planning and Development Regulations 2001. Note that the nature and extent of the development must be indicated in outline.

(and appeal to An Bord Pleanála) in respect of a specific development, than for it (the planning authority) to say, for example, that residential or industrial development *simpliciter* would be granted planning permission.

6–87   One of the curious features of section 192 is that there is no suggestion that the scale of the development indicated in the notice be similar to that for which planning permission has been refused. Rather, it seems that the claim for compensation can be deferred by serving a notice indicating that the land is capable of development of a type indicated above at para.6–85, even on a small scale. This might give rise to unfairness in certain cases. For example, it would seem unjust were a claim in respect of the refusal of planning permission for, say, one hundred houses to be met with a section 192 notice specifying development of ten houses.

6–88   The notice must be served within twelve weeks of the receipt of the claim for compensation, and generally continues in force for a period of five years unless planning permission is, in fact, granted or refused for the other development specified in the notice. Where planning permission is refused,[83] the planning authority will not normally be permitted to serve a second section 192 notice, as the original claim for compensation will revive on the annulment of the first notice,[84] and the twelve week period in respect of the date of the original claim will usually have expired.

6–89   Where a claimant fails to apply, within five years, for planning permission for development of the type specified in the notice, it appears that his claim for compensation is permanently barred.[85]

6–90   In deciding to issue a section 192 notice, a planning authority is subject to the same constraints as it would be in deciding to grant planning permission. It would be unreasonable for a planning authority to form an opinion that the land in question is capable of other development for which planning permission ought to be granted, if such development would, for example, be contrary to the proper planning and sustainable development of the area. Accordingly, it would seem that a notice should not be served with the sole intention of defeating a claim for compensation.[86] Perhaps somewhat surprisingly, it seems that a notice can be served even where the other development specified in the notice would constitute a material contravention of the development plan. The Supreme Court so held in the context of the previous legislation in *Ballymac Designer Village Ltd. v Louth County Council*,[87] overruling an earlier decision of the

---

[83] No separate claim lies in respect of this fresh refusal: PDA 2000, s.192(6).

[84] *Arthur v Kerry County Council* [2000] 3 I.R. 407; [2000] 2 I.L.R.M. 414.

[85] PDA 2000, s.192(4)(b).

[86] See, by analogy, *Grange Developments Ltd. v Dublin County Council* [1989] I.R. 296 at 317–318; and *Dublin County Council v Eighty Five Developments Ltd. (No. 2)* [1993] 2 I.R. 392; [1992] I.L.R.M. 815.

[87] [2002] 3 I.R. 247; [2002] 2 I.L.R.M. 481.

High Court to opposite effect.[88] The Supreme Court attached particular significance to the fact that a planning authority may, by invoking a special procedure, grant planning permission even where the proposed development involves a material contravention of the development plan: seemingly, the requisite opinion for the statutory notice acts provisionally on the hypothesis that planning permission can be granted and does not require a prediction that planning permission will be granted, still less does it impose an obligation to grant planning permission or even to initiate the material contravention procedure.

J. Compensation for Revocation of Planning Permission

Special provisions[89] apply in circumstances where planning permission has been revoked under s.44 of the PDA 2000.[90] The revocation is to be treated as a refusal of planning permission for the purposes of compensation. In addition, the planning authority is required to pay compensation in respect of expenditure incurred in carrying out works which were rendered abortive by the revocation. Any expenditure reasonably incurred in the preparation of plans for the purpose of any works or upon other similar matters preparatory thereto is also to be compensated. **6–91**

K. Area of Special Planning Control

Where an area is subject to a special planning control scheme, a planning authority is empowered to serve a notice on the owner or occupier of land requiring that specified measures be undertaken including, as appropriate, measures for (i) the restoration, demolition, removal, alteration, replacement, maintenance, repair or cleaning of any structure; or (ii) the discontinuance of any use or the continuance of any use subject to conditions.[91] There is provision made for the payment of compensation in circumstances where an interest in land has been reduced, or a person having an interest in the land has suffered damage by disturbance, as a result of complying with such a special planning control notice.[92] **6–92**

A planning authority is required, by way of compensation, to pay to any person who shows that as a result of complying with the notice (i) the value of an interest he or she has in the land or part thereof existing at the time of the notice has been reduced, or (ii) he or she, having an interest in the land at that **6–93**

---

[88] *Browne v Cashel UDC*, unreported, High Court, Geoghegan J., March 26, 1993.
[89] PDA 2000, s.195.
[90] See *Hughes v An Bord Pleanála* [2000] 1 I.L.R.M. 452 for a discussion of the formal requirements as to service of a notice under the equivalent section of the previous legislation.
[91] PDA 2000, s.88.
[92] PDA 2000, s.198.

time, has suffered damage by being disturbed in his or her enjoyment of the structure or other land, a sum equal to the amount of such reduction in value or a sum in respect of the damage suffered.[93]

6–94   The planning authority is also required to pay any expenses that are reasonably incurred by the owner or occupier in carrying out the steps specified in the notice, other than expenses that relate to unauthorised development carried out not more than seven years prior to the service of the notice.[94]

6–95   Although not strictly speaking "compensation", it should be noted that there is also the prospect of the provision by the planning authority of advice, materials, equipment, the services of the planning authority's staff or other assistance required to carry out the measures specified in the notice.[95]

6–96   In determining the amount of compensation payable (by reference to the rules under the Second Schedule of the PDA 2000), it is important to note that an area of special planning control does not, strictly speaking, form part of the development plan. The significance of this lies in the fact that in assessing the possibilities, if any, for developing the land (for the purposes of determining its antecedent value), the development plan has a particular importance. More specifically, it seems that the likelihood or unlikelihood, as the case may be, of obtaining planning permission or further permission, to develop the land is to be considered in the light of the provisions of the development plan.[96] In circumstances where an area of special planning control does not, strictly speaking, form part of the development plan, it is submitted that no regard can be had to this designation when determining the antecedent value of the lands. This will result in the antecedent value being reckoned at an artificially high level, with a knock-on effect in terms of an increased award of compensation.

L. Protected Structures

6–97   Although not strictly speaking "compensation", it should be noted that there is also a requirement for a planning authority to provide financial assistance in relation to a restoration notice in respect of a protected structure under s.60.

M. Removal of Structure or Discontinuance of Use

6–98   If a planning authority decides, in exceptional circumstances, that (a) any structure should be demolished, removed, altered or replaced; (b) any use should be discontinued; or (c) any condition should be imposed on the continuance of

---

[93] PDA 2000, s.198(b).
[94] By necessary implication from the terms of the PDA 2000, s.88(2)(g).
[95] By necessary implication from the terms of the PDA 2000, s.88(2)(e).
[96] PDA 2000, Sch.2, para.3(2).

a use, the planning authority may serve a notice on the owner and on the occupier of the structure or land concerned and on any other person who, in its opinion, will be affected by the notice. The planning authority must, *inter alia*, invite any person served with a notice to make written submissions or observations in respect of the matters referred to in the notice within a specified period (being not less than four weeks from the date of the service of the notice). In deciding whether to confirm a notice, the planning authority must have regard to any submissions or observations received, and, to the following considerations (a) the proper planning and sustainable development of the area; (b) the provisions of the development plan; (c) the provisions of any special amenity area order, any European site or other area designated for the purposes of s.10(2)(c) relating to the area; and (d) any other relevant provision of the PDA 2000 and any Regulations made thereunder.

Provision is made under ss.196 and 197, for the payment of compensation. In this regard, an important distinction is drawn between the removal of a structure, and the discontinuance of a use. In particular, there are two exclusions which apply to the latter only. First, no compensation is payable in relation to the imposition of conditions on the continuance of the use of land where those conditions are imposed in order to avoid or reduce serious water pollution or the danger of such pollution. Secondly, no compensation is payable where the use of land is for the exhibition of advertising unless at the time of the discontinuance or compliance, the land has been used for the exhibition of advertising for less than five years, whether the use was continuous or intermittent or whether or not, while the land was being so used, advertising was exhibited at the same place on the land. The effect of this exclusion is that unless the land has only relatively recently (five years) been used for the exhibition of advertisements, any right to compensation is lost. **6–99**

Otherwise, there is a general right to the payment of compensation in respect of any reduction in the value of an interest of any person in the land existing at the time of the confirmation of the notice, or where any person having an interest in the land at that time has suffered damage by being disturbed in his or her enjoyment of the land. Such a person is entitled to be paid by the planning authority by way of compensation the amount of the reduction in value, or the amount of the damage. **6–100**

N. Compensation Regarding Cables, Wires and Pipelines

If, on a claim made to the local authority, it is shown that, as a result of the action of the planning authority pursuant to s.182 in placing, renewing or removing any cable, wire or pipeline, attaching any bracket or fixture or affixing any notice, the value of an interest of any person in the land or structure existing at the time of the action of the planning authority is reduced, or that any person having an interest in the land or structure at that time has suffered damage by being disturbed in his or her enjoyment of the land or structure, that person **6–101** shall be entitled to be paid by the local authority by way of compensation the amount of the reduction in value or the amount of the damage.[97]

O. Compensation Regarding Creation of Public Rights of Way

6–102 If, on a claim made to the planning authority, it is shown that the value of an interest of any person in land, being land over which a public right of way has been created by an order under s.207 of the PDA 2000 is reduced, or that any person having an interest in the land has suffered damage by being disturbed in his or her enjoyment of the land, in consequence of the creation of the public right of way, that person shall be entitled to be paid by the planning authority by way of compensation the amount of the reduction in value or the amount of the damage.[98]

P. Compensation Regarding Entry on Land

6–103 Compensation is payable where it is shown that as a result of anything done in exercise of the statutory powers of entry and inspection under ss.252 or 253 of the PDA 2000, any person has suffered damage.[99] Section 252 allows an authorised person to enter on any land at all reasonable times between the hours of 9 a.m. and 6 p.m., or during business hours in respect of premises which is normally open outside those hours, for any purpose connected with the PDA 2000. An authorised person entering on land under this section may do all things reasonably necessary for the purpose for which the entry is made and, in particular, may survey, carry out inspections, make plans, take photographs, take levels, make excavations, and examine the depth and nature of the subsoil. Section 253 allows an authorised person to enter lands at all reasonable times for the purposes of enforcement, or at any time if he or she has reasonable grounds for believing that an unauthorised development has been, is being or is likely to be carried out, enter any premises and to bring thereon such other persons (including members of the Garda Síochána) or equipment as he or she may consider necessary for the purpose.

---

[97] PDA 2000, s.199.
[98] PDA 2000, s.200.
[99] PDA 2000, s.201.

CHAPTER SEVEN

ENFORCEMENT PROCEEDINGS

A. General Introduction

Each of the different types of enforcement mechanism will be discussed in greater detail below. There are, however, a number of general principles which are common to two or more of the enforcement mechanisms: to avoid unnecessary duplication these will be considered first.   **7–01**

1. Special controls

This chapter is principally concerned with enforcement of the requirement to obtain planning permission. Other enforcement mechanisms are provided for elsewhere under the PDA 2000; for example, in respect of protected structures; areas of special planning control; tree preservation; and licensing of events and funfairs. These enforcement mechanisms are dealt with in Chapter 8, and will not be discussed further here.   **7–02**

2. Removal or alteration of structure or discontinuance of use

The PDA 2000 provides for a number of different types of enforcement mechanisms, both civil and criminal. Generally these are triggered where development has been, is being, or is likely to be, carried out other than in compliance with the terms and conditions of a planning permission. It should be noted that even where there has been no unauthorised development, a planning authority has an exceptional power to require that (a) any structure should be demolished, removed, altered or replaced; (b) any use should be discontinued; or (c) any condition should be imposed on the continuance of a use.[1] This power is truly exceptional, and generally attracts the payment of   **7–03**

---

[1] PDA 2000, s.44.

compensation. Strictly speaking this power is not an enforcement mechanism and for this reason it is dealt with in the chapter on special controls at paras 8–210 to 8–220. Brief mention is being made of it here only so as to indicate a possible remedy of last resort where a planning authority desires to bring a particular development to an end but is unable to rely on any of the traditional enforcement mechanisms because the development is not unauthorised (or is immune under the seven year time-limit).

3. Objective of enforcement

7–04   The effectiveness of the planning legislation in controlling development is dependent on there being a proper system of enforcement in existence. If the planning legislation is to have any real teeth, it is necessary that breaches of planning control can be enforced against rapidly and decisively. There is little point otherwise in imposing an elaborate system requiring permissions and consents to be obtained.

7–05   It is submitted that enforcement serves three separate objectives. First and foremost, it should ensure that objectionable development is discontinued, and that all necessary steps are taken to restore the position to that obtaining before the unauthorised development was carried out. This might necessitate, for example, the removal of structures and the carrying out of reinstatement works. Secondly, it should ensure that the terms and conditions of planning permissions are observed. Thirdly, it should police the regulatory requirement to obtain a grant of planning permission *prior* to the commencement of development. In the absence of an effective deterrent, developers might not observe the requirement to obtain planning permission in advance, and instead content themselves with making a subsequent application for retention planning permission.

7–06   The means by which this third objective is to be achieved is a matter of controversy. In particular, a question arises as to whether any consideration should be had to the qualitative nature of the unauthorised development. If the development is not objectionable in terms of proper planning and sustainable development, and if planning permission would have been granted had same been applied for in advance, then it would seem that enforcement should be directed only to the regulatory breach involved in failing to obtain planning permission in advance. On this view, the unauthorised development itself should not be enforced against directly: the development is unexceptionable in planning terms and, accordingly, it would be disproportionate to require its discontinuance or removal. Instead, some other form of penalty should be imposed on the developer so as to serve as a deterrent to others. There is, however, an alternative, stricter approach. This would require that the unauthorised development be discontinued or removed. The thinking here being that the most effective way to secure compliance with the requirement to obtain planning permission in advance is to deprive the developer of the benefit of the unauthorised development, even in cases where the development itself is not objectionable in terms of proper planning and sustainable development.

It is unclear as to which of these two approaches underlies Pt VIII of the PDA **7–07** 2000. Under the previous legislation, the fact that the unauthorised development might not be objectionable in planning terms had always been relevant. Thus, for example, the considerations informing the decision whether or not to serve an enforcement notice were the same as those applicable to a decision to grant or refuse planning permission. The implication of this being that if the planning authority would have been minded to grant planning permission had an application been made in the proper way, it would not be appropriate to serve an enforcement notice. The regulatory breach might instead be censured by way of a criminal prosecution. Similarly, the fact that planning permission might be granted was relevant to the exercise of the court's discretion on an application for an injunction. Conversely, the manner in which the PDA 2000 treats of retention planning permission suggests that a different result might be intended under the new legislation. This is discussed immediately below.

4. Retention planning permission

The grant of retention planning permission carries with it the clear implication **7–08** that the (previously unauthorised) development is not objectionable in planning terms. This being so, it is arguable that the only legitimate objective of enforcement is that of ensuring compliance with the regulatory requirement to obtain a prior grant of planning permission. The question arises as to whether this limited objective is adequately met by a prosecution for the offence of having carried out unauthorised development,[2] or whether it is still necessary to enforce against the development itself.

The interaction of retention planning permission and enforcement is addressed **7–09** under s.162 of the PDA 2000. Two aspects are treated separately. First, it is provided under s.162(2) that it shall not be a defence to a prosecution under Pt VIII for a defendant to prove that he or she has applied for, or has been granted, retention planning permission, if this occurred after (i) the initiation of proceedings; (ii) the sending of a warning letter; or (iii) the service of an enforcement notice in a case of urgency. It is submitted that this subsection is overbroad in its effect. Whereas it makes sense that it should not be a defence to the regulatory offence of having failed to obtain a grant of planning permission prior to the commencement of development for a person to say that he or she has since obtained planning permission, the position in respect of other offences under Pt VIII is different. The subsequent grant of retention planning permission indicates that it is not now necessary that the (previously unauthorised) development be removed or discontinued. In such circumstances, it would seem inconsistent to exclude the defence being raised to a prosecution

---

[2] PDA 2000, s.151. *Cf.* PDA 2000, s.32(2).

for an offence such as, for example, failing to comply with an enforcement notice.

7–10   The second aspect is more controversial. Under the previous legislation, a respondent would often seek to have enforcement proceedings adjourned, or any order made stayed, pending the making of, and determination of, an application for retention planning permission. An attempt has been made under the PDA 2000 to do away with the practice. Unfortunately, it seems that the amendment has gone too far.

7–11   Section 162(3) provides that no enforcement action under Pt VIII shall be stayed or withdrawn by reason of an application for retention planning permission, or the grant of retention planning permission.[3] The wording of this subsection is clumsy. For example, it is not clear whether a warning letter represents "enforcement action" for the purposes of the subsection. Of greater concern, however, is the fact that the subsection suggests that enforcement action must be pursued even where there has been a *grant* of retention planning permission. Surely the mischief to be remedied was that of an applicant putting in a retention application purely for the purposes of delay in circumstances where there was little or no prospect of retention planning permission actually being granted. It would have been sufficient for this purpose to confine the operation of the subsection to circumstances where an application for retention planning permission had been made, but not yet adjudicated upon. If retention planning permission has actually been granted, it seems absurd that the planning authority is compelled to press on with enforcement action even in circumstances where the object of that enforcement action may be to remove the works for which planning permission has now been granted. Once retention planning permission has been granted, all that remains to be addressed is the regulatory breach involved in the failure to obtain a prior grant of planning permission. This could be achieved by way of a criminal prosecution for the offence of carrying out development except under and in accordance with a planning permission.[4] It would seem disproportionate to require positive steps to be taken to remove the development or to discontinue the use.

5. Multiple proceedings

7–12   It would appear from the provisions of s.160(7) that the seeking of a planning injunction does not prejudice any other enforcement action: it is expressly provided that any other enforcement action may be commenced or continued. Under s.153(5), failure to issue a warning letter does not prejudice the issue of an enforcement notice or any other proceedings that may be initiated by the planning authority.

---

[3]   As amended by the Local Government Act 2001, s.247(f).
[4]   PDA 2000, s.32.

The fact that a planning authority may have served an enforcement notice **7–13** might preclude the making of an application for a planning injunction, until such time as the period specified in the enforcement notice for compliance has expired.[5] It would also seem that the fact that criminal proceedings have been dismissed does not preclude other enforcement proceedings.[6]

6. No estoppel

The Supreme Court in *Fingal County Council v William P Keeling & Sons* **7–14** *Ltd.*[7] has, finally, given the *quietus* to the illogical proposition that the making of an application for planning permission should preclude a party from arguing thereafter that planning permission was not, as a matter of law, required (whether because the development was exempted or otherwise). Fennelly J. put the matter thus.

> "If a proposed development is, in fact and in law, an exempted development, no principle has been identified whereby the owner of land should be estopped from asserting the exemption merely by reason of the fact, and by nothing more, that he or she has made a perfectly proper and lawful application for planning permission. That would be to deprive him of a right at law by reason of his exercise of a different right, which would require cogent justification. There could be many perfectly good and even laudable reasons for taking the course of applying for a planning permission, where there is an arguable case for exemption. It might be done through oversight or mistake or merely through an abundance of caution or to ensure that the planning situation was very clear on the sale of a property. It is perhaps better, at this stage, to say nothing more, as Mr Gallagher [counsel for the planning authority] reserves the right to assert the right of a planning authority to rely on the doctrine of estoppel based on a more extensive factual basis."

Prior to this judgment, it had been accepted in a number of cases that if a **7–15** person had applied for retention planning permission, he could not then be heard to argue in enforcement proceedings that planning permission is not, in fact, required.[8] This principle was founded on certain *obiter dicta* in *Dublin*

---

[5] *Blainroe Estate Management Co. Ltd. v IRG Blainroe Ltd.*, unreported, High Court, Geoghegan J., March 18, 1994.

[6] *Clare County Council v Floyd* [2007] I.E.H.C. 48; unreported, Charleton J., January 19, 2007. See also *Meath County Council v Daly* [1988] I.L.R.M. 274 at 278.

[7] [2005] I.E.S.C. 55; [2005] 2 I.R. 108. See also *Illium Properties Ltd. v An Bord Pleanála* [2004] I.E.H.C. 403; unreported, Smyth J., December 16, 2004. An Bord Pleanála had argued that the making of an application for planning permission in respect of a protected structure entailed an acknowledgement by the applicant that retention planning permission was required and that the works undertaken would "materially affect" the character of the structure. Smyth J. distinguished the decision in *Tallaght Block Ltd.* on the facts, emphasising that the proceedings were judicial review proceedings as opposed to proceedings for a planning injunction, and that the application for planning permission had been made under protest or without prejudice and clearly out of a sense of frustration with the applicant's perception of delays in the planning system.

[8] *Dublin County Council v Tallaght Block Company Ltd.* [1982] I.L.R.M. 534; unreported, Supreme Court, May 17, 1983; and *Molumby v Kearns*, unreported, High Court, O'Sullivan

County Council v Tallaght Block Company.[9] The principle had been criticised as being both unfair and illogical: unfair, because a respondent should not be penalised for taking the precaution of seeking planning permission for an activity which might not require same, and, illogical, in that a particular activity either requires planning permission or does not, and any mistaken view of the law which a respondent might take on this issue is irrelevant.

7. Enforcement and environmental impact assessment

7–16   As discussed presently, it is, seemingly, not mandatory for a planning authority to take enforcement action, but rather it enjoys a discretion to do so. The courts also enjoy a discretion in the context of the planning injunction under s.160. The nature of the respective discretions is discussed further, at para.7–56 and paras 7–166 to 7–195. An interesting question, which has not yet been considered by the Irish courts, is as to whether the discretion is lost in circumstances where the development being enforced against should have been—but was not—subject to environmental impact assessment. This might arise, for example, where an existing project was intensified or, more obviously, where there was a failure to apply for planning permission in respect of a new project. Scannell suggests that the courts have an obligation to ensure that EC law is properly applied when exercising their discretion under s.160.[10]

7–17   The ECJ has consistently held that the competent authorities of a Member State—which in the present context would include planning authorities and the courts—are to take, within the sphere of their competence, all the general or particular measures necessary to ensure that projects which are likely to have significant effects on the environment are subject to an impact assessment.[11] It is at least arguable that it would be inconsistent with this obligation were either a planning authority or a court to condone unauthorised development which involved a failure to comply with the EIA Directive. A further question arises as to how far it is necessary to go in order to achieve compliance with the EIA Directive. On one view, it would be legitimate to allow the developer an opportunity to apply for retention planning permission, and not to proceed to enforce against the development until such time, if any, as that application is refused. An alternative, more purist approach would be to say that as the EIA Directive envisages that the decision on the development consent be made in *advance* of the commencement of development, the development cannot be made compliant retrospectively. The European Commission has taken infringement proceedings against Ireland, arguing that

---

J., January 19, 1999. For a cogent criticism of this rule, see Walsh, *Planning and Development Law* (2nd ed., Incorporated Law Society, Dublin), para.4.07.

[9] [1982] I.L.R.M. 534.

[10] Y. Scannell, *Environmental and Land Use Law* (Thomson Round Hall, Dublin, 2006), para.2–466.

[11] *Aannemersbedrijf P.K. Kraaijeveld BV v Gedeputeerde Staten van Zuid-Holland* (Case C–72/95); [1996] E.C.R. I–5403; and *R. (On the application of Wells) v Secretary of State for Transport, Local Government and the Regions* (Case C–201/02) [2004] E.C.R. I–723.

the Irish planning legislation by allowing an application for retention planning permission to be made after a development has been executed, in whole or in part, without consent undermines the preventive objectives of the EIA Directive.[12] As of June 2007 those proceedings have yet to be heard.

8. Enforcement and European Convention on Human Rights

The taking of enforcement action is capable of engaging rights—in particular property rights and the right to respect for a person's home—under the European Convention on Human Rights. This topic is dealt with in detail in Chapter 14, especially at paras 14–194 to 14–245. In addition, reference is made to the Convention at appropriate points in this chapter.[13]

7–18

9. Conditions precedent: "prior to commencement of development"

To date, the Irish courts have not squarely addressed the question as to whether or not failure to comply with a condition which requires matters to be attended to *prior* to the commencement of development renders the entire development unauthorised. Strictly speaking, breach of such a condition is not capable of being remedied subsequently: once the development has commenced, the developer cannot turn back the clock and attend to the matters prior to the commencement of development. Notwithstanding this difficulty, the High Court has, on a number of occasions, taken a pragmatic approach and has refused injunctive relief in circumstances where there was belated compliance. Thus, for example, in *Mountbrook Homes Ltd. v Oldcourt Developments Ltd.*[14] Peart J. suggested that the court ought not to be concerned to punish a respondent by way of an order under s.160 for what the court may consider to have been a delay in proper compliance with a condition prior to commencement of development. (The condition had required certain drawings to be submitted for the written agreement of the planning authority prior to commencement of development.) In this regard, Peart J. cited *dicta* in *Dublin Corporation v McGowan*[15] to the effect that the planning injunction was intended as a fire brigade section to deal with an urgent situation requiring immediate action to stop clear breaches of the planning legislation.

7–19

Reference is also made to *Eircell Ltd. v Bernstoff*.[16] Proceedings had been brought under the (then) s.27 of the Local Government (Planning & Development) Act 1976 (as amended) alleging, *inter alia*, that certain conditions which required various matters to be attended to prior to the commencement of development had not been complied with in time. The applicants argued (i) that the requirements in question were conditions precedent to the

7–20

---

[12] (Case C–216/05); [2006] O.J. C/178/20.
[13] See, in particular, paras 14–217 to 14–245 (enforcement notices).
[14] [2005] I.E.H.C. 171; unreported, Peart J., April 22, 2005.
[15] [1993] I I.R. 405 at 411.
[16] Unreported, High Court, Barr J., February 18, 2000.

commencement of development; (ii) that they should be strictly interpreted; and (iii) that subsequent compliance did not render legal what was already an unlawful development. Barr J. refused the relief sought, stating that no court should make an order which is potentially futile, and if the development were to be declared unlawful, there was no doubt that application would be made to the planning authority for a retention planning permission, and in the circumstances would be granted for the asking.[17]

7–21 Although the pragmatic approach adopted by the Irish courts to date has much to recommend it, it may be difficult to reconcile with the actual wording of the legislation. In particular, a distinction is drawn under the legislation between development without planning permission, and development otherwise than in conformity with planning permission or in breach of a condition. It is at least arguable that failure to comply with a condition requiring matters to be attended to prior to the commencement of development renders the development unauthorised for all time. Although it is tempting to treat the action of the developer as simply giving rise to development in breach of condition (as opposed to unauthorised development), such an analysis can be criticised for failing to attach significance to the literal wording of the condition.

7–22 This question is not merely one of academic interest. It has particular relevance in relation to enforcement. Although, as a result of the amendments introduced under the PDA 2000, it is no longer strictly necessary to identify, in the context of an application for a planning injunction, whether the unauthorised development alleged consists of a failure to obtain planning permission, or of development in breach of planning permission, this distinction does remain significant in the context of an enforcement notice. Specifically, the contents of an enforcement notice as prescribed under s.154 appear to require the identification of which category of breach is alleged. The point is also relevant in the context of the calculation of time-limits. The limitation period for enforcement action against development without planning permission is seven years from the date of the commencement of development. In the case of development not in conformity with planning permission, however, the limitation period is significantly longer: seven years from the date of the expiration of the life of the planning permission. Moreover, it is only where a planning permission has been implemented that conditions can be said to bite. There is no limitation period for proceedings in respect of any condition concerning the use of land to which planning permission is subject. Accordingly, it may—perhaps ironically—be in a developer's interest to argue that a particular development was not carried out by reference to *any* planning permission, as unauthorised development of this type will be immune from enforcement action in a much shorter period of time.

---

[17] It is submitted that as the wording of subs.160(1)(c) suggests that the relief under that part of s.160 is intended to be prospective, the same result would be achieved by adopting a purposive approach to interpretation and that the primary objective should be to seek to ensure compliance, even if belatedly. *Cf.* PDA 2000, s.162(3) (as amended by the Local Government Act 2001, s.247(f)).

The question of the effect of non-compliance with such conditions has been considered in a number of cases in England and Wales. As discussed later at para.7–28, most recently the High Court there has sought to steer a middle course, looking to the substance of the matters to be agreed before deciding the effect of non-compliance. Before looking at that case, however, it is proposed to consider briefly the earlier case law. **7–23**

The legislative context in which the matter comes before the courts of England and Wales is as follows. Planning permissions there are generally subject to a deemed condition to the effect that the development must be begun not later than a particular date. The planning permission is controlled by and subject to the conditions. If works contravene the conditions, they cannot properly be described as commencing the development authorised by the permission.[18] Strictly speaking, if development works commence before the developer has obtained the agreement of the planning authority to all matters requiring agreement, then the development is unauthorised. The Court of Appeal in the leading case of *Whitley & Sons Ltd. v Secretary of State for Wales*[19] had to consider whether, in such circumstances, the developer had lost the benefit of the planning permission. On the facts, the developer had made application for approval in advance of the commencement of works and in advance of the expiration of the time-limit for the commencement of works. The Court of Appeal in *Whitley & Sons Ltd.* found that it was not necessarily fatal if approval was obtained *subsequent* to the commencement of development, or, indeed if approval was not obtained until after the time-limit for the commencement of works had expired (although the application for approval should have been made in advance of the expiry of the time-limit). **7–24**

> "However, if the approval which covered the operations had been given after the operations but prior to the expiry of the time limit it would be technical in the extreme to treat what had gone before as not complying with the time limit. As long as the approval had been obtained and the operations complied with that approval, it would be of no practical significance whatsoever which came first, the approval or the operations from the planning point of view. It is true that until the approval was obtained, technically enforcement action could be taken but once the approval had been obtained, there would be no practical possibility of enforcement proceedings succeeding, since the results that the conditions were designed to achieve would in fact have been achieved within the intended time scale."

The situation where approval had been given in fact, although no formal notice has been issued, is dealt with in *R. v Flintshire CC Ex p. Somerfield Stores Ltd.*[20] **7–25**

---

[18] *Whitley & Sons Ltd. v Secretary of State for Wales* (1992) 64 P. & C.R. 296; [1992] J.P.L. 856; [1992] 3 P.L.R. 72
[19] (1992) 64 P. & C.R. 296; [1992] J.P.L. 856; [1992] 3 P.L.R. 72
[20] (1998) 75 P. & C.R. 359.

7-26   It appeared to be accepted in *Whitley & Sons Ltd.*[21] that enforcement action could not be rationally contemplated in circumstances where the material required under the relevant conditions had been supplied *within* time, even if ultimately approved out of time.

> "I should also make it clear that the approach which I have sought to identify is not intended to be a charter to developers to ignore conditions which are intended to be complied with before a planning permission is implemented. If it is not already clear, I make it absolutely clear now, that if a developer does not comply with a condition he can have enforcement action or any other available action taken against him. The only consequence of the approach indicated in this judgment is that when the merits of the enforcement proceedings come to be considered, it is necessary to take into account the situation as it exists at the time and in particular whether or not at that time any approval required by the condition has been obtained."

7-27   The Court of Appeal in *Whitley & Sons Ltd.* took the pragmatic approach that a technical breach of planning permission—in terms of the timing of the commencement of works vis-à-vis the giving of the approval—should not result in the loss of the planning permission. To an extent, however, this represents the exception to the general principle that development works which do not comply with planning permission constitute a breach of planning control and for planning purposes are unauthorised. Woolf L.J. referred to the possibility that some conditions might be regarded as conditions precedent but went on reserve an opinion on the question for a case in which it was necessary to decide it.

7-28   The High Court of England and Wales in *R. (On the application of Hart Aggregates Ltd.) v Hartlepool BC* has recently returned to this question of conditions precedent, and has sought to steer a middle course by looking to the substance of the condition, and recognising that the mere fact that the literal wording of a condition requires matters to be attended to prior to the commencement of development should not necessarily be conclusive in deciding that the condition is truly a condition precedent.[22]

> "For the reasons set out above, I believe that the statutory purpose is better served by drawing a distinction between those cases where there is only a permission in principle because no details whatsoever have been submitted, and those cases where the failure has been limited to a failure to obtain approval for one particular aspect of the development. In the former case, common sense suggests that the planning permission has not been implemented at all. In the latter case, common sense suggests that the planning permission has been implemented, but there has been a breach of condition which can be enforced against. I appreciate that these are two opposite ends of a spectrum. Each case will have to be considered upon its own particular facts, and the outcome may well depend upon the number and the significance of the conditions that have not been complied with."

---

[21] [1992] 3 P.L.R. 72

[22] [2005] E.W.H.C. 840 (Admin), [67]. See note at [2005] J.P.L. 1263.

An earlier passage in the judgment of the High Court of England and Wales in **7–29** *Hart Aggregates Ltd.* provides examples of the range of matters which might be left over for agreement under planning conditions, and indicates the anomalies which might result if all conditions were treated as conditions precedent.[23]

> "Take the case where planning permission has been granted for the construction of a large industrial building, subject to a number of conditions relating to such matters as, for example, hours of operation, maximum noise emissions, arrangements for carparking etc. The permission is also subject to a landscaping condition, which provides that a landscaping scheme must be submitted to and approved by the local planning authority before development commences. No such scheme is submitted and approved, but nevertheless the development commences and the industrial building is completed. After four years it will have become immune from enforcement action. Since the planning permission will not, on the defendant's submission, have been implemented it will lapse, and with it the obligation to comply with the conditions relating to, for example, hours of operation, maximum noise emissions, carparking et cetera."

It is respectfully submitted that the approach ultimately adopted by the court— **7–30** which looks to the substance of the matters to be agreed—has much to recommend it. The implications of a finding that development is entirely unauthorised are such that it would be inappropriate that this should turn on a matter of form, *i.e.* the fact that a condition fortuitously leaves over matters for agreement. This is especially so where, as the above passage from the judgment in *Hart Aggregates Ltd.* illustrates, the nature of matters left over for agreement can range from the peripheral to those that go to the essence of the development. In applying this test, it will be necessary to consider what precisely has been left over for agreement under any particular condition, with a view to deciding whether the condition should properly be regarded as a condition precedent.

B. Time-Limits

1. Seven year time-limit

In very general terms, a seven year time-limit now applies to the taking of **7–31** enforcement action.[24] Prior to the PDA 2000, the time-limit had been five years. It should be emphasised at once, however, that the dates from which the time-limit is to be reckoned are not the same for all of the enforcement mechanisms. It should also be noted that certain proceedings may be commenced at any time in respect of any condition concerning the (ongoing) use of land to which planning permission is subject.[25]

---

[23] *ibid.*, [55].
[24] The decision in *Ellis v Nolan*, unreported, High Court, McWilliam J., May 6, 1983 is persuasive authority, if authority were needed, for the proposition that the Statute of Limitations does not apply to an application under s.160.
[25] See PDA 2000, s.157(4)(b) and s.160(6)(b).

7–32 In the case of a warning letter or enforcement notice, it is sufficient that same "issue" within the seven years; this might suggest that it may not be necessary to effect service within the seven years. In the case of proceedings for an offence, same must "commence" within the seven years. However, in the case of the planning injunction under s.160, it is the "application" which must be made within the seven year period. It is submitted, by analogy with the previous case law in relation to judicial review,[26] and in the interests of legal certainty, that s.160 proceedings should be issued and served within the seven years. The relevant time-limits are set out with greater particularity below.

Criminal offences under Part VIII of the PDA 2000

7–33 In the case of criminal proceedings under Pt VIII there may, in fact, be two different time-limits applicable. This is because in addition to the general seven year time-limit, there is a further time-limit in respect of summary proceedings before the District Court. The general seven year time-limit runs either from the date of the commencement of development (in respect of development without planning permission), or for seven years beginning on the expiration of the life of the planning permission.[27] It is expressly provided under s.157(4)(c) that it shall be presumed until the contrary is proved that proceedings were commenced within the appropriate period.[28]

7–34 If the offence is to be prosecuted summarily before the District Court, then this seven year limit represents the absolute outer time-limit. A special time-limit of six months applies to such summary proceedings. This six month time-limit is to be reckoned from the later of (i) the date on which the offence was committed, or (ii) the date on which evidence sufficient, in the opinion of the person by whom the proceedings are initiated, to justify proceedings comes to that person's knowledge. Obviously, this latter date is subject to the outer time-limit of seven years.

7–35 It is important to note that (unlike the six month time-limit) the seven year time-limit is not linked to the date of the offence but rather relates back to either the date of the commencement of the unauthorised development (in respect of development without planning permission), or the date of the expiration of the planning permission. The date of the offence (such as, for example, failure to comply with an enforcement notice) may well be much later and thus even a relatively recent offence might be protected by the seven year time-limit.

---

[26] See, especially, *KSK Enterprises Ltd. v An Bord Pleanála* [1994] 2 I.R. 128; [1994] 2 I.L.R.M. 1.

[27] PDA 2000, s.157(4).

[28] The wording of the PDA 2000, s.157(4) has the effect that the presumption is confined to criminal proceedings for an offence under Pt VIII. It does not apply to proceedings under PDA 2000, s.160.

Section 160 injunction

The seven year time-limit runs from the date of the commencement of the development (in respect of a development without planning permission), or from the date of the expiration of the life of the planning permission. Again, an exception is made in the case of any condition to which the development is subject concerning the ongoing use of the land: an application in this regard may be made at any time.

7–36

Enforcement notice

The seven year time-limit runs either from the date of the commencement of development (in respect of development without planning permission), or for seven years beginning on the expiration of the life of the planning permission.[29] There is no exception in the case of a breach of a condition concerning the ongoing use of land: the provisions of s.157(4)(b) apply only to the commencement of proceedings and not to the "issue" of an enforcement notice. Thus an enforcement notice cannot be issued outside the seven years even in the case of a breach of a condition concerning the ongoing use of the land; although criminal proceedings for the offence of failing to comply with an *earlier* enforcement notice might possibly be commenced outside the seven years.

7–37

Warning letter

A seven year time-limit on the issue of a warning letter runs either from the date of the commencement of development (in respect of development without planning permission), or for seven years beginning on the expiration of the life of the planning permission.[30] A warning letter cannot be issued outside the seven years even in the case of a breach of a condition concerning the ongoing use of the land: the provisions of s.157(4)(b) apply only to the commencement of proceedings and not to the "issue" of a warning letter.

7–38

It is important to note that the mere issue of a warning letter does not lay down a marker in respect of other enforcement mechanisms. Thus a planning authority cannot rely on the issue of a warning letter within the seven year time-limit in order to ground the subsequent issue of an enforcement notice outside the seven years. The issue of a warning letter does not stop time running.

7–39

2. Retrospective effect?

The fact that the limitation period has been extended from five years to seven years presents the possibility that certain unauthorised development which had achieved immunity under the previous legislation might now be subject to enforcement under the PDA 2000. This might arise in two situations, as follows.

7–40

---

[29] PDA 2000, s.157(4).
[30] PDA 2000, s.157(4).

First, as of the date of the commencement of Pt VIII of the PDA 2000[31] there would have been a category of unauthorised development in the bracket five to seven years. Unauthorised development of this vintage would have been immune under the previous legislation. Secondly, as a result of amendments introduced under Pt VIII, development in breach of an ongoing use condition is now open to certain types of enforcement action without any limitation period.[32]

7–41 The transitional provisions are silent as to whether the possibility of enforcement action has revived in respect of such development which would otherwise have been immune under the previous legislation. On one view, the fact that such development had always retained its status as unlawful development would appear to suggest that no "right" had been conferred and thus that there would be no impediment to the subsequent extension of the limitation period. As against this, the fact that the amendments result in a renewed exposure to *criminal* liability might be thought to trespass against the constitutional prohibition on retrospective criminal legislation.[33] There is also the judgment of the High Court in *Kenny v An Bord Pleanála (No. 1)*[34] which might be taken as suggesting that there is at least a presumption against retrospective effect in planning matters even in relation to non-criminal matters.

3. Transitional provisions

7–42 Only limited provision is made under Pt VIII to legislate for the changeover from the previous legislation. As discussed at para.7–41 above, there is no provision at all made in respect of the change giving rise to the most obvious difficulties, namely the change in the limitation period from five years to seven years. Provision is made under s.164 for what is to happen in the case of enforcement procedures which had been invoked under the previous legislation and were still pending on the commencement date,[35] as follows. Where (criminal) proceedings had been initiated in respect of any offence under the previous legislation; an enforcement notice or a warning notice had issued; or an application to court had been made pursuant to s.27 of the Local Government (Planning & Development) Act 1976 (as amended),[36] the relevant provision which applied before the repeal shall continue to so apply until the proceedings have been finalised; the notices complied with or withdrawn; or the application determined, as the case may be.

---

[31] March 11, 2002.

[32] PDA 2000, s.157(4)(b), and s.160(6)(b).

[33] Article 15 of the Constitution. Devoy suggests that if immunity had been gained under the five year rule before the commencement of the PDA 2000, it will not be possible for a prosecution to be brought under the seven year rule. M. Devoy, "Enforcement—are the extended time limits retrospective in effect?" (2004) 11 I.P.E.L.J. 147.

[34] [2001] 1 I.R. 565.

[35] March 11, 2002.

[36] Local Government (Planning & Development) Act 1992, s.19.

4. Application of time-limits in practice

Generally, the application of the seven year time-limit should be relatively **7–43**
straightforward. Difficulties can arise, however, where there has been a break
in the continuity of an unauthorised use, and a respondent seeks to link a chain
of dates in order to achieve seven years. The seven year limitation period on
enforcement action is intended to give the planning authority that length of
time within which to bring proceedings to restrain an unauthorised use. Where
the planning authority takes steps within the period (for example, by serving a
warning letter) and those steps bring about a cesser of the use, then the seven
year period should cease to run, and will only run afresh from the date, if any,
on which the use begins once more.[37]

Under the previous legislation, the High Court had held that a manifest **7–44**
interruption or abandonment of the development was sufficient to stop the
time running. It is a question of degree as to whether or not an interruption
represents a mere temporary suspension (which does not stop time running),
or a manifest interruption or abandonment (which does). Relevant factors
include the length of the interruption, and the intention of the parties. It may
also be relevant to consider whether or not any facilitating works have been
retained. The fact that the interruption is in response to the threat of, or the
taking of, enforcement action would appear to stop time running.[38] Reference
is made to the following passage from the judgment in *South Dublin County
Council v Balfe*.[39]

> "In my opinion when a use has been abandoned and then recommenced nearly
> four years later an occupant cannot rely on an earlier use to support a claim that
> the limitation period in the section should run from the earlier date and not from
> the date of recommencement. If construed in the way urged by the respondents it
> would be a simple matter to drive a coach-and-four through the section by
> discontinuing an unauthorised use after a warning notice had been served and
> then recommence it again after several years when a limitation period based on
> the discontinued unauthorised user had expired, and I consider that the section
> cannot be so construed.
>
> Secondly, when a wrongful continuous act (such as an unauthorised user of
> land) has been discontinued and abandoned then the wrong has ceased. When it
> is recommenced a new wrongful act occurs, and it is from the date of the
> recommencement that the time limit in the section begins to run in respect of this
> new unauthorised use."

---

[37] *Kildare County Council v Goode*, unreported, High Court, Morris P., June 13, 1997 (at p.
12) (disposed of on other grounds by the Supreme Court [1999] 2 I.R. 495; [2000] 1
I.L.R.M. 346).
[38] *Kildare County Council v Goode*, unreported, High Court, Morris P., June 13, 1997 (at p.
12) (disposed of on other grounds by the Supreme Court [1999] 2 I.R. 495; [2000] 1
I.L.R.M. 346); and *South Dublin County Council v Balfe*, unreported, High Court, Costello
P., unreported, November 3, 1995.
[39] Unreported, High Court, Costello P., November 3, 1995.

Multiple uses of land

7–45   The application of the seven year limitation period may cause difficulties where land has a number of uses. The fact that the established use of lands may include more than one use is expressly recognised under s.39(4) of the PDA 2000.[40] The application of the limitation period requires a consideration of the established use of the land at either end of the seven year period. The *established* use of land may consist of more than one use: for example, land may have as part of its established use both a *normal* and an *occasional* use, or, indeed, two *normal* uses. Insofar as the decision in *Earl of Mountcharles v Meath County Council*[41] appears to suggest that the changeover from one constituent use of the established use to another represents a fresh act of development, it is submitted that it is incorrect and should not be followed. Once a change to a dual use has occurred, that dual use represents the established use of the land, unless a (further) change to a single use occurs.

Partial breaches

7–46   The manner in which time-limits should be calculated in the context of a partial breach of a planning condition was considered by the High Court of England and Wales in *R. (On the application of St Anselm Development Company Ltd.) v First Secretary of State*.[42] A condition attached to a planning permission required that nineteen car parking spaces be provided and retained permanently for the accommodation of vehicles of the occupiers and users of the remainder of the building. In breach of this condition, fourteen of the nineteen spaces had been leased to, and used by, non-occupiers of the building. No enforcement action had been taken at the time this breach first occurred, and the relevant limitation period had since expired. The question before the court was as to whether the local authority was entitled to take enforcement action in respect of the use of the balance of the car parking spaces.

7–47   The respondent was arguing, in effect, that once any breach of the condition occurred, time began running against the local authority for the purposes of the limitation period. On this analysis, once the limitation period had expired, no enforcement action could be taken even though there had been partial compliance with the condition, *i.e.* five spaces had been confined to use by occupiers.

7–48   The court took a more pragmatic approach to the application of the time-limit, stating that the focus should be upon the *terms* of the enforcement notice which had been issued. The question was not whether an enforcement notice alleging a failure to comply with this condition could have been issued ten years ago (the relevant limitation period under English law), but whether an enforcement notice alleging this particular failure to comply with the condition, and requiring

---

[40]   See also *Hawes v Thornton Cleveleys UDC* (1965) 17 P. & C.R. 22 at 28

[41]   [1996] 3 I.R. 417; [1997] 1 I.L.R.M. 446.

[42]   [2003] E.W.H.C. 1592 (Admin); [2004] 1 P. & C.R. 404; [2004] J.P.L. 33.

this failure to be remedied by taking these steps, could have been issued ten years ago. If the answer to the latter question was yes, then the local authority should have lost its right to take enforcement action. In respect of those spaces where the local authority could not have required any remedial steps to be taken—because they were being retained for the use of occupiers/users of the building—there was no sensible reason why it should have lost its right to take enforcement action. Sullivan J. acknowledged that his decision was influenced by a desire to avoid the unfortunate consequences which an alternative interpretation might have. Commonsense suggested that merely because one car parking space has been used in breach of a condition, it cannot have been intended that the obligation to use the remaining spaces in accordance with the condition should cease merely because that one space has been used in breach of condition for a period of ten years.

With respect, the approach taken in R. *(On the application of St Anselm*   **7–49**
Development Company Ltd.) has much to recommend it. Time should only run in favour of unauthorised development where it is possible to enforce against the exact breach involved. The legislation provides a window of time within which enforcement action must be taken. In order for time to run, therefore, the development must be in peril of being enforced against. If for whatever reason—whether as the result of an interruption or the fact that unauthorised development is being carried on at only a particular intensity —enforcement action of the type now contemplated could not have been brought previously, time should not be taken as running.

5. Unlawful but immune

The fact that the limitation period has expired without enforcement action   **7–50**
having been taken does not have the effect of making the unauthorised development lawful.[43] It is not, for example, equivalent to planning permission having been granted by operation of law. Rather the development enjoys a hybrid status as unlawful but immune. It is important to bear in mind that although the development is immune from enforcement, it continues to be afflicted by certain adverse consequences because of its unlawful status. These include but are not limited to the following. First, the benefit of certain classes or categories of exempted development is lost.[44] Secondly, the calculation of market value for the purpose of compensation may be affected.[45] Thirdly, it may impact on an application for a liquor licence.[46] Fourthly, it may be relevant in the context of the landlord and tenant legislation, especially the

---

[43] *Dublin Corporation v Mulligan*, unreported, High Court, Finlay P., May 6, 1980.
[44] Planning and Development Regulations 2001, art.9(1)(a)(viii) and art.10(1)(d). See also *Fingal County Council v Crean*, unreported, High Court, Ó Caoimh J., October 19, 2001.
[45] PDA 2000, Sch.2, para.2(b)(v). See also *O'Connor v Nenagh UDC*, unreported, High Court, Geoghegan J., July 16, 1996. *Cf. Hughes v Doncaster Metropolitan Borough Council* [1991] 05 E.G. 133.
[46] *O'Connor v Nenagh UDC,* unreported, High Court, Geoghegan J., July 16, 1996.

reasonableness of a landlord withholding his consent for a change of user.[47] Finally, it is a matter which might be taken into account on any application for further development.[48]

7–51   Conroy argues that there is no legitimate rationale for treating development which is immune from enforcement as unlawful, suggesting that it undermines the objective of the seven year limitation period to leave such development in a legal twilight zone.[49]

C. Warning Letter Procedure

1. Duty to investigate

7–52   Under the previous legislation, a planning authority was under no express obligation to investigate, still less to take action against, any alleged unauthorised development. A new procedure has now been introduced under ss.152 and 153 of the PDA 2000 whereby a planning authority is under a general obligation to respond to, and to investigate, complaints made to it alleging unauthorised development (including anticipated development). More specifically, where a representation is made in writing to a planning authority by any person alleging unauthorised development, the planning authority is generally required to issue a warning letter.[50] A planning authority shall issue the warning letter as soon as may be, but not later than six weeks after receipt of the representation. Having served a warning letter, the planning authority must then make a decision as to whether or not to issue an enforcement notice. This decision is to be taken as expeditiously as possible, and, without prejudice to the foregoing, it shall be an objective of the planning authority to ensure that the decision shall be taken within twelve weeks of the issue of the warning letter. The person making the (initial) representation is entitled to notice of this decision within two weeks of the date of the decision not to serve an enforcement notice, or within two weeks of the date of service of an enforcement notice, as the case may be.[51] The planning authority is required to enter its decision, including the reasons for it, in the statutory register.[52] Failure to issue a warning letter shall not prejudice the issue of an enforcement notice or any other proceedings that may be initiated by the planning authority.[53]

---

[47] *Terry v Stokes* [1993] 1 I.R. 204; and *Dursley v Watters* [1993] 1 I.R. 224.

[48] *Western Fish Products Ltd. v Penwith DC* [1981] 2 All E.R. 204.

[49] B. Conroy, "Unlawful but not against the law? The planning code and 'Illegal but Immune' developments" (2005) 12 I.P.E.L.J. 12.

[50] The exceptions are where the representation appears to be "vexatious, frivolous or without substance or foundation", or where the alleged unauthorised development is "trivial or minor in nature". It is also the case that the issue of a warning letter is subject to the general seven year limitation period.

[51] PDA 2000, s.154(1), and (2). See also PDA 2000, s.155(2).

[52] PDA 2000, s.153(4).

[53] PDA 2000, s.153(5).

2. Legal effect of warning letter

The actual legal effect of a warning letter is minimal.[54] First, a warning letter **7–53** *per se* does not impose any liability or obligation on the developer. Secondly, the issue of a warning letter does not stop time running for the purpose of the seven year limitation period:[55] for example, the fact that a warning letter may have been issued within the seven years cannot be relied upon to ground the subsequent issue of an enforcement notice. (The date of issue of a warning letter does, however, have a relevance in the context of an application for retention planning permission in that if the application is made after the issue of the warning letter, it will not constitute a defence to a prosecution.)[56] Thirdly, the issue of a warning letter is not always a prerequisite to the issue of an enforcement notice:[57] for example, the requirement is expressly dispensed with in the case of urgency.[58] Finally, in circumstances where the discretion of the planning authority as to whether or not to issue a warning letter is severely limited, it would seem that the issue of the warning letter does not even carry with it an element of stigma: the issue of a warning letter does not involve any meaningful adjudication on the allegation of unauthorised development.

3. Discretion of planning authority

The discretion of the planning authority falls to be examined at two stages. **7–54** First, the planning authority has a very limited discretion as to whether or not to issue a warning letter: a planning authority may only refuse to issue a warning letter where the representation appears to be "vexatious, frivolous or without substance or foundation",[59] or where the alleged unauthorised development is "trivial or minor in nature".[60] Presumably, the planning authority is also required to consider whether or not the issue of a warning letter is barred under the seven year limitation period.[61] Secondly, a planning authority enjoys a far greater discretion in deciding whether to issue an enforcement notice: this latter discretion is discussed presently at para.7–56 and onwards.

4. Content of warning letter

A warning letter shall refer to the land concerned and shall (a) state that it has **7–55** come to the attention of the planning authority that unauthorised development may have been, is being or may be carried out; (b) state that any person served

---

[54] It would appear to attract a liability for costs and expenses in the event of an enforcement notice subsequently being issued: PDA 2000, s.154(5)(d).
[55] The time-limits under PDA 2000, s.157(4) are not reckoned by reference to the date of the issue of a warning letter.
[56] PDA 2000, s.162(2).
[57] PDA 2000, s.153(5).
[58] PDA 2000, s.155.
[59] PDA 2000, s.152(1)(a).
[60] PDA 2000, s.152(2).
[61] PDA 2000, s.157(4).

with the letter may make submissions or observations in writing to the planning authority regarding the purported offence not later than four weeks from the date of the service of the warning letter; (c) state that when a planning authority considers that unauthorised development has been, is being or may be carried out, an enforcement notice may be issued; (d) state that officials of the planning authority may at all reasonable times enter on the land for the purposes of inspection; and (e) explain the possible penalties involved where there is an offence, and explain that any costs reasonably incurred by the planning authority in relation to enforcement proceedings may be recovered from a person on whom an enforcement notice is served or where court action is taken.

D. Enforcement Notice

1. Discretion of planning authority

7–56   The terms of s.153 of the PDA 2000 indicate that a planning authority has a discretion as to whether or not to serve an enforcement notice. Regrettably, there are no principles and policies set out under the PDA 2000 as to in what circumstances enforcement action is justified, nor as to what considerations a planning authority is to take into account in deciding whether to issue an enforcement notice. The most that the legislation says is that the planning authority shall consider any representations made to it under s.152(1)(a), or submissions or observations made under s.152(4)(b), and any other material considerations. No definition is given to the phrase "other material considerations".

7–57   An attempt will be made in the discussion which follows to make some sense of the legislative scheme by suggesting what matters should inform a decision as to whether or not to serve an enforcement notice. It has to be said, however, that this aspect of the legislation may well be unconstitutional: this is discussed further at para.7–91 and onwards.

2. Relevant considerations

7–58   No guidance is given under Pt VIII of the PDA 2000 as to what considerations are relevant to a decision whether or not to issue an enforcement notice. Approaching the matter from first principles, one might have thought that the same considerations which apply in relation to a decision on an application for planning permission should operate. In a sense, the decision as to whether or not to serve an enforcement notice is the obverse of the decision to grant or refuse planning permission in that, given the Draconian effects of an enforcement notice, it would seem inappropriate to issue an enforcement notice in circumstances where the development was not objectionable in planning terms, and planning permission would inevitably have been granted had an application in that regard been made. On this analysis, then, the planning authority should have regard both to the statutory concept of "proper planning and sustainable development of the area", and to the development plan. The phrase "other material considerations" might be read accordingly.

Unfortunately, however, the matter may not be as clear-cut under the new legislation in that it is elsewhere provided that no enforcement action shall be stayed or withdrawn by reason of the fact that an application for retention planning permission has been made, or planning permission even granted.[62] One effect of s.162(3) would seem to be that, *once issued*, an enforcement notice may not be withdrawn by reason of the fact that retention planning permission has been granted. This might be taken as suggesting that the two things are separate, and that the primary purpose of an enforcement notice is now regulatory, in the sense of penalising failure to apply for planning permission in a timely fashion. If this is the case, then it would be unnecessary for the planning authority to consider the planning merits of the development being enforced against when deciding on whether or not to serve an enforcement notice. **7–59**

It is submitted that the better view is that the legislation should be interpreted in such a way as to confine the issuance of enforcement notices to circumstances where the development being enforced against is objectionable in planning terms. First, it would be contrary to the concept of "sustainable" development— which underlies the PDA 2000—to require the removal of structures which were acceptable in planning terms. Secondly, the removal of structures in such circumstances is likely to be seen as involving a disproportionate interference with rights under the European Convention on Human Rights. This is discussed in greater detail in Chapter 14. **7–60**

3. Reasons for decision whether or not to issue an enforcement notice

A planning authority is required to provide reasons for its decision whether or not to issue an enforcement notice. Under s.153(4), the decision, together with the reasons for it, are to be entered on the statutory register. Reference is made in this regard to the judgment in *Dublin Corporation v O'Callaghan*.[63] Although this judgment is in relation to the requirements of the previous legislation, it is submitted that at least some of the comments therein may be relevant to enforcement notices under the PDA 2000, and, in particular, to the duty to give reasons. *O'Callaghan* represents a robust defence of the rights of a person affected by an enforcement notice. Herbert J. held that it must clearly have been intended that the making of a decision by a planning authority that it was expedient to serve an enforcement notice must be attended by some formality, by some recording of the fact that a decision to serve a notice had been taken, and of the basis upon which it had been determined that it was expedient so to do. In the absence of such a record, the High Court would find **7–61**

---

[62] PDA 2000, s.162(3) (as amended by the Local Government Act 2001, s.247(f)). See para.7–08 onwards above.
[63] Unreported, High Court, Herbert J., February 13, 2001.

it difficult, if not entirely impossible, to review a decision of a planning authority to serve an enforcement notice. Herbert J. further held that this formal record must have come into existence prior to the enforcement notice being signed or served on the relevant owner and occupier: the enforcement notice cannot itself constitute this record which must both antedate, and be entirely separate from it.

4. Can planning authority be compelled to enforce?

7–62 A question which arises occasionally in practice is as to the extent, if any, to which a planning authority may be compelled to take enforcement action. This question will typically arise in circumstances where, a complaint having been made to it, the planning authority decides not to take enforcement action, or fails to respond to the complaint at all. The short answer seems to be that, absent some procedural breach on the part of the planning authority, a decision not to take enforcement action will generally not be reviewable. This is because the decision of the planning authority involves the exercise of a statutory discretion, and thus is generally only subject to review on the basis of administrative unreasonableness or irrationality. It is also significant in this regard that an alternative remedy is open in the form of the planning injunction under s.160. The existence of this alternative remedy—which is open to any person—suggests that a decision on the part of a planning authority not to take enforcement action does not determine the "rights or liabilities" of the complainant, and, as such, the decision may not be amenable to judicial review. It is always open to the complainant to seek a planning injunction in his or her own name, and thus effective enforcement action is not contingent on any particular step being taken by the planning authority.

7–63 The position where the planning authority fails to make any decision on whether or not to issue an enforcement notice is different. Once a warning letter has been issued, the planning authority is under a statutory duty to make a decision one way or another as to whether or not to proceed to issue an enforcement notice.[64] In the event that the planning authority fails to make a decision, it may well be that a mandatory order will lie against the planning authority requiring it to make a decision. Such an order may provide only limited practical benefit to a third party, however, in that the *content* of the decision will remain a matter for the planning authority. In other words, the order of the court will simply direct the planning authority to take a decision one way or another as to whether or not to proceed to issue an enforcement notice; the court is unlikely to dictate the outcome of the decision.

---

[64] PDA 2000, s.153.

5. Service

Generally, an enforcement notice will have been preceded by the issuance of a warning letter. The prerequisite of a warning letter is dispensed with, however, where, in the opinion of the planning authority, due to the nature of the unauthorised development and to any other material considerations, it is necessary to take urgent action with regard to the unauthorised development.[65]

7–64

An enforcement notice shall be served on the person carrying out the development and, where the planning authority considers it necessary, on the owner or the occupier of the land or any other person who, in the opinion of the planning authority, may be concerned with the matters to which the notice relates.[66]

7–65

A person shall not question the validity of an enforcement notice by reason only that the person or any other person, not being the person on whom the enforcement notice was served, was not notified of the service of the enforcement notice.[67] Provision is made for the service of other persons if, subsequent to the service of the enforcement notice, the planning authority becomes aware that any other person may be carrying out development or is an owner or occupier of the land, or may be affected by the notice.[68] The effect of these provisions is to remove technical defences which might otherwise have been open on the wording of the previous legislation.

7–66

6. Content of enforcement notice

An enforcement notice shall refer to the land concerned and shall (a) in respect of a development where no planning permission has been granted, require that development to cease or not to commence, as appropriate, or in respect of a development for which planning permission has been granted, require that the development will proceed in conformity with the permission, or with any condition to which the permission is subject; (b) require such steps as may be specified in the notice to be taken within a specified period, including, where appropriate, the removal, demolition or alteration of any structure and the discontinuance of any use and, insofar as is practicable, the restoration of the land to its condition prior to the commencement of the development[69]; (c) warn the person or persons served with the enforcement notice that, if within the period specified or within such extended period (not being more than six months) as the planning authority may allow, the steps specified in the notice to be taken are not taken, the planning authority may enter on the land and take

7–67

---

[65] PDA 2000, s.155. See also PDA 2000, s.153(5).
[66] PDA 2000, s.154(2).
[67] PDA 2000, s.154(13).
[68] PDA 2000, s.154(3)(b).
[69] As to this discretion, see *Garland v Minister of Housing and Local Government* (1968) 20 P. & C.R. 93.

such steps, including the removal, demolition or alteration of any structure, and may recover any expenses reasonably incurred by it in that behalf; (d) require the person or persons served with the notice to refund to the planning authority the costs and expenses reasonably incurred by the planning authority in relation to the investigation, detection and issue of the enforcement notice concerned and any warning letter (including costs incurred in respect of the remuneration and other expenses of employees, consultants and advisers), and the planning authority may recover these costs and expenses incurred by it in that behalf, and (e) warn the person or persons served with the enforcement notice that if within the period specified by the notice or such extended period, not being more than six months, as the planning authority may allow, the steps specified in the notice to be taken are not taken, the person or persons may be guilty of an offence.

7–68   It appears that it is still necessary to identify which category of breach is being alleged, *i.e.* development without planning permission or in breach of planning permission.[70] This is to be contrasted with the position obtaining in respect of the planning injunction under s.160 where there is an omnibus category of unauthorised development *simpliciter*.

7–69   The content of an enforcement notice was considered in *Dundalk Town Council v Lawlor*[71] in the context of a case stated from the District Court. The planning authority had served an enforcement notice on the defendant. The specified steps under the enforcement notice were as follows: cease all excavation site clearance works and return site to its previous condition. The enforcement notice purported to require the defendant to take the steps "within a period of immediately commencing on the date of the service of this notice".

7–70   O'Neill J. held that the enforcement notice did not properly specify the period within which the steps were to be taken. A specified period must be capable of having its beginning and end clearly ascertained. The use of the word "immediately" provided a beginning to a period, but did not indicate when the period ended. It did not create a period, it simply defined a point at which or from which something must be done, but it entirely failed to describe or limit a time within which the step is to be accomplished. O'Neill J. went on to say that, even if there were not an express statutory requirement to specify the period, the enforcement notice was lacking in sufficient precision as to the time permitted for the required steps to be taken to be the proper subject-matter of a criminal offence. A person served with an enforcement notice in this form could not know, even though steps had been taken, that there had been compliance with the notice in terms of time.

---

[70] See, by analogy, *Eldon Garages v Kingston upon Hull CBC* [1974] 1 All E.R. 358; [1974] 1 W.L.R. 276.
[71] [2005] 2 I.L.R.M. 106.

The second aspect of the case concerned whether the enforcement notice had **7–71** properly specified the steps required to be taken. The High Court ruled that it had not. It was not sufficient for the purposes of the enforcement notice merely to recite the phrases used in s.154(5)(b). The phrase "return site to its previous condition" failed to clearly and precisely indicate to the person served what exactly had to be done to comply. For example, insofar as the unauthorised development complained of involved the removal of topsoil and the stripping off of sod, it was not clear whether the notice required that the topsoil be restored and the sod be restored, or merely that the topsoil be reseeded.

7. Challenging an enforcement notice

There is no right of appeal in respect of the service of an enforcement notice. It **7–72** seems that the only method of challenging an enforcement notice is by way of judicial review before the High Court.[72] This is most unsatisfactory in that the costs and delay involved in judicial review proceedings mean that this is not an effective remedy. Moreover, as discussed presently, the grounds on which judicial review are available are severely limited.

It had been suggested under the previous legislation that where it was sought **7–73** to challenge an enforcement notice the appropriate procedure was by way of a Section 5 reference.[73] Under the previous legislation, the reference had been made in the first instance to An Bord Pleanála, with an appeal thereafter to the High Court. Whatever the previous position may have been, it is submitted that the reference procedure under s.5 of the PDA 2000 does not provide a viable alternative to judicial review proceedings.[74] The jurisdiction under s.5 is confined to the narrow question of whether a particular activity is or is not development, or is or is not exempted development. It does not allow for the consideration of other issues—relevant to the validity of an enforcement notice—such as whether the development being enforced against is immune under the seven year rule. More fundamentally, the outcome of a reference under s.5 is confined to the making of a declaration; there is simply no provision for granting relief setting aside an enforcement notice or staying enforcement proceedings. Thus judicial review remains the only avenue of challenge.

In order to appraise the value of judicial review as a remedy it is necessary, **7–74** first, to identify the grounds on which the recipient of an enforcement notice may wish to challenge that notice. These might include the following. First, that the development is not unauthorised: it might be argued, for example, that the use complained of was an established use or came within a class of exempted development. Secondly, that any unauthorised development is immune from

---

[72] Since October 17, 2006 any such challenge is now subject to the statutory judicial review procedure prescribed under ss.50 and 50A of the PDA 2000 (as substituted by the Strategic Infrastructure (Planning and Development) Act 2006, s.13).

[73] *O'Connor v Kerry County Council* [1988] I.L.R.M. 660.

[74] As to the Section 5 reference procedure generally, see para.10–01 and onwards.

enforcement action under the seven year rule. Thirdly, that the steps specified in the enforcement notice go beyond what is necessary, and encroach on established use rights. Fourthly, that the steps specified are disproportionate in all the circumstances.

7–75 The traditional grounds of judicial review involve the courts policing specialist decision-makers by ensuring that, in reaching their decisions, they confine themselves to the relevant statutory considerations. The absence of any clear statement of principles and policies under Pt VIII of the PDA 2000 means that this basis of review is meaningless in the present context.

7–76 Therefore, if judicial review is to have any role, it will be necessary to identify some other jurisdictional basis for the courts' intervention. Certain conditions must be satisfied before an enforcement notice is issued, and it is submitted that the courts should regard these as conditions precedent. If this is done, then the courts would be entitled to intervene to set aside an enforcement notice issued without the conditions precedent having been satisfied: by issuing an enforcement notice in such circumstances the planning authority would have been acting *ultra vires*.

7–77 What then are the conditions precedent? It is submitted that the two principal ones are as follows. First, there must be unauthorised development. Although there is no explicit requirement to this effect under Pt VIII, it is submitted that it follows from the tenor of the legislation. In particular, there is nothing which suggests that the planning authority has any statutory discretion or adjudicatory function in this regard, but rather the question of whether there is unauthorised development is one capable of objective assessment.[75] The question is a mixed one of fact and law, and therefore capable of resolution by the court on an application for judicial review.

7–78 The second condition precedent is that the unauthorised development must not be immune under the seven year rule. This follows from the terms of s.157(4) which, in summary, provides that no enforcement notice shall issue after various time periods have elapsed. The peremptory wording of the subsection indicates that the planning authority does not have jurisdiction to issue an enforcement notice out of time.

7–79 It will be seen, therefore, that the approach required of the courts in reviewing an enforcement notice is different from that in most other contexts. In particular,

---

[75] *cf. Jeary v Chailey Rural District Council* (1973) 26 P. & C.R. 280. One of the arguments advanced before the Court of Appeal was that an error as to whether the development had, as a matter of fact, taken place would mean that the local authority did not have jurisdiction to serve an enforcement notice. The Court of Appeal rejected this argument, drawing attention to the use, under the relevant legislation, of the formula "where it appears to the local planning authority". The absence of such words in the PDA 2000 might suggest that a contrary result should follow here.

the court must itself decide whether the conditions precedent have been satisfied, and it would not be appropriate to show any particular deference to the views of the planning authority on these points. There may be some reluctance on the part of some judges to engage in such a searching review. Although most judges would probably accept that the determination of whether an activity is or is not development, or exempted development, has a legal aspect and is therefore something which a court is equipped to decide, many would baulk at having to undertake the fact-finding role necessary to decide whether a particular activity is immune under the seven year rule.

8. European Convention on Human Rights Act 2003

There must be very real doubts as to whether the enforcement notice procedure is compliant with the European Convention on Human Rights. The effect of the service of an enforcement notice is to authorise a planning authority—following the expiration of the specified period—to enter onto land and take such steps as are specified in the notice. This may involve the demolition of structures and the restoration of land. Thus, a planning authority is afforded Draconian powers, without there being any necessity for court approval. It is only if the planning authority wishes to pursue a criminal prosecution for failure to comply with the notice that it is necessary to bring the matter before the court: the power to enter onto land and carry out works is self-executing. **7–80**

The foregoing scheme arguably offends against various provisions of the Convention. This is discussed in greater detail in Chapter 14, but for present purposes the concerns can be summarised as follows. First, the absence of any right of appeal from the planning authority's decision to serve an enforcement notice would appear to breach Art.6(1) of the Convention. The effects of an enforcement notice are so serious that there can be no doubt but that the decision to issue one involves a "determination" of the affected landowner's rights. Given its role in policy-making—in particular, as author of the development plan—a planning authority does not meet the Art.6(1) requirement of independence and impartiality. Moreover, the procedural safeguards leading up to a decision to issue an enforcement notice are deficient. There is only a limited opportunity for the owner or occupier to make submissions, and there is no provision for an oral hearing. There is no statutory appeal against an enforcement notice and thus judicial review is the only other "stage" of the decision-making process. The limited grounds on which judicial review is available under Irish law mean that the judicial review "stage" of the decision-making process cannot realistically be said to make good the deficiencies at the administrative stage of the process. **7–81**

Secondly, the fact that the service of an enforcement notice can, in principle, empower a planning authority to enter onto land and carry out the demolition of valuable structures gives rise to a potential breach of property rights under Art.1 of the First Protocol and, in some cases, may involve an interference with the right to respect for a person's home under Art.8. In order to be compliant **7–82** with the Convention, the interference must be proportionate: this ordinarily requires the carrying out of a balancing exercise wherein the individual's rights are weighed against the public interest. The difficulty with the enforcement notice procedure, of course, is that the planning authority is not required to carry out such a balancing exercise, and is not, in any event, independent or impartial.

7–83 Moreover, it is arguable that the demolition of structures would only ever be justified where the development being enforced against was objectionable in planning terms. Yet, on one reading of the PDA 2000, the enforcement notice procedure may be used to penalise a regulatory breach, *i.e.* the failure to apply for planning permission in advance of development, by requiring the removal of development which is not objectionable *per se*.

9. Effects of enforcement notice

7–84 The principal effects of an enforcement notice might be summarised as follows. First, it is an offence to fail to comply with the requirements of an enforcement notice.[76] (It shall be a defence to a prosecution if the defendant proves that he or she took all reasonable steps to secure compliance with the enforcement notice.)[77] It is also an offence to knowingly assist or permit the failure by another to comply with an enforcement notice.[78] On conviction, the court may, in addition to imposing the penalties specified, order the person convicted to take the steps specified in the enforcement order [*sic*].[79]

7–85 The second principal effect of an enforcement notice is this. If the steps specified in the notice are not taken within the period specified in the notice (or within such extended period, not being more than six months, as the planning authority may allow), the planning authority may enter on the land and take such steps itself. This power extends to taking steps including the demolition of any structure and the restoration of land. The planning authority may recover any expenses reasonably incurred by it in that behalf from the person served with the notice.

7–86 Particulars of an enforcement notice shall be entered in the statutory register.[80] Where an enforcement notice has been complied with the fact that it was complied with shall be recorded by the planning authority in the register.[81]

---

[76] PDA 2000, s.154(8).
[77] PDA 2000, s.154(7).
[78] PDA 2000, s.154(9).
[79] PDA 2000, s.156(8).
[80] PDA 2000, s.154(10).
[81] PDA 2000, s.154(11).

An enforcement notice shall cease to have effect ten years from the date of service. If service had been effected on another person subsequent to the initial service, the relevant time period is ten years from the date of that latter service.[82]   **7–87**

10. Withdrawal of enforcement notice

A planning authority may withdraw an enforcement notice.[83] The circumstances in which it would be appropriate to do so are not, however, clear from the legislation. The only guidance is negative: it would seem that neither the fact that retention planning permission has been applied for, or actually obtained, is a valid basis for withdrawing an enforcement notice.[84] This suggests that an enforcement notice must be complied with even where there has been a grant of retention planning permission: for a criticism of this approach see para.7–11.   **7–88**

Where an enforcement notice is withdrawn, the person served with the enforcement notice, and the person, if any, having made the initial complaint, are to be notified in writing of the stated reasons.[85] The fact that the enforcement notice was withdrawn, and the reason for the withdrawal, shall be recorded by the planning authority in the register.[86]   **7–89**

11. Second or subsequent enforcement notice

In *Clare County Council v Floyd*,[87] the District Court stated a case to the High Court as to whether it was open to a planning authority to serve, and prosecute a beach of, a second enforcement notice in circumstances where a prosecution in respect of an alleged breach of an earlier enforcement notice had resulted in an acquittal. Charleton J. held that it was not the law that a person was entitled to maintain an unauthorised development merely by reason of his acquittal in respect of a summons issued for an offence on one particular day (or a continuation thereafter) on one particular occasion. Once the dates as between the two enforcement notices were different, then two separate offences were alleged and the principle of *autrefois acquit* had no application.   **7–90**

12. Constitutional issues

There is a very real question mark over the constitutionality of the enforcement notice procedure. It is a well established principle of administrative law that statutory powers are to be exercised only in a manner that would be in conformity   **7–91**

---

[82] PDA 2000, s.154(12).
[83] PDA 2000, s.154(11).
[84] PDA 2000, s.162(3) (as amended by the Local Government Act 2001, s.247(f)). This is assuming that an enforcement notice is to be taken as representing "enforcement action".
[85] PDA 2000, s.154(11).
[86] PDA 2000, s.154(11).
[87] [2007] I.E.H.C. 48; unreported, High Court, Charleton J., January 19, 2007.

with the Constitution and within the limitations of the power as they are to be gathered from the statutory scheme or design.[88] Yet, the failure under Pt VIII of the PDA 2000 to state principles and policies renders a decision whether or not to take enforcement action unreviewable.

7–92   To illustrate by example, it is not clear whether an enforcement notice may only be served where the development is objectionable in planning terms and any application for planning permission would inevitably be refused, or whether the planning authority may decide to penalise a regulatory breach, *i.e.* the failure to apply for planning permission in advance of development, by requiring the removal of development which is not objectionable *per se*. In the absence of any statement of principles and policies it is simply not possible to say what are relevant, and what are irrelevant, considerations.

7–93   An analogy can be drawn here with the requirement, inferred from under Art.15 of the Constitution, that primary legislation identify the principles and policies governing the making of delegated legislation.[89] In each instance, the principles and policies must be laid down in the statute, leaving only matters of detail to be filled in or completed. Just as it is unlawful to confer a power to make delegated legislation without indicating the manner in which that power is to be exercised, so too, it is submitted, it is unlawful to leave over too broad a discretion to an administrative decision-maker.

E. Criminal Offences

1. List of offences

7–94   A number of criminal offences have been created in respect of breaches of planning control. First, it would seem that the carrying out of development (other than exempted development, or development carried out prior to October 1, 1964) other than in compliance with a planning permission and conditions, is an offence. The matter is somewhat confused in that it seems that two very similar offences have been created. Under s.151, any person who has carried out or is carrying out unauthorised development shall be guilty of an offence. "Unauthorised development" is defined under s.2 in terms which exclude exempted development; development carried out prior to October 1, 1964; and development carried out in compliance with planning permission and any condition to which that permission is subject. A separate offence appears to have been created under s.32, which provides that a person shall not carry out any development except under and in accordance with a permission granted under Pt III of the PDA 2000. The exceptions under s.32 are narrower than under s.151; in particular, there is no express exception for development carried

---

[88] See *State (Lynch) v Cooney* [1982] I.R. 337 at 380.
[89] See, for example, *Laurentiu v Minister for Justice Equality and Law Reform* [1999] 4 I.R. 26.

out prior to October 1, 1964. It is important to note that if a separate offence has been created under s.32, it is not an offence under Pt VIII; the significance of this being that certain provisions (for example, those in relation to time-limits, and retention planning permission) are stated to apply only to offences under Pt VIII.

The second, and third, offences relate to enforcement notices. Under s.154(8), **7–95** any person on whom an enforcement notice is served who fails to comply with the requirements of the notice (other than a notice which has been withdrawn or which has ceased to have effect) within the specified period or within such extended period as the planning authority may allow, not exceeding six months, shall be guilty of an offence. Under s.154(9), any person who knowingly assists or permits the failure by another to comply with an enforcement notice shall be guilty of an offence.

The fourth offence relates to protected structures. Under s.58(4), any person **7–96** who, without lawful authority, causes damage to a protected structure or a proposed protected structure shall be guilty of an offence.

2. Time-limits

A planning authority is empowered to bring summary proceedings, whether or **7–97** not the offence is committed in the planning authority's functional area.[90] The usual (six month) time-limit on the taking of summary proceedings under the Petty Sessions (Ireland) Act 1851 is altered: proceedings may be commenced at any time within six months from the date on which the offence was committed, or at any time within six months from the date on which evidence sufficient, in the opinion of the person by whom the proceedings are initiated, to justify proceedings comes to that person's knowledge.[91] For this purpose, a certificate signed by or on behalf of the person initiating the proceedings as to the date or dates on which evidence came to his or her knowledge shall be evidence of the date or dates and in any legal proceedings a document purporting to be a certificate and to be so signed shall be deemed to be so signed and shall be admitted as evidence without proof of the signature of the person purporting to sign the certificate, unless the contrary is shown.[92]

It should be noted that the outer time-limit of seven years applies only to offences **7–98** under Pt VIII.[93] Thus, for example, if a separate offence is created under s.32 there is no such outer time-limit. There may not be a time-limit on an offence under s.58(4).

---

[90] PDA 2000, s.157(1). *Cf. TDI Metro Ltd. v Delap (No.2)* [2000] 4 I.R. 520.
[91] PDA 2000, s.157(2).
[92] PDA 2000, s.157(3).
[93] PDA 2000, s.157(4).

3. Penalties

7–99   Under s.156, the following penalties are prescribed for, *inter alia*, the offences under s.151, s.154 and s.58. On conviction on indictment, a fine not exceeding £10,000,000, or imprisonment for a term not exceeding two years, or both. On summary conviction, a fine not exceeding £1,500, or imprisonment for a term not exceeding six months, or both.

7–100   A further offence is committed where a person having been convicted of an offence continues the offence after his or her conviction. The penalties for this further offence are as follows. On conviction on indictment, a fine not exceeding £10,000 for each day on which the offence is so continued, or imprisonment for a term not exceeding two years, or both, provided that if a person is convicted in the same proceedings of two or more such further offences the aggregate term of imprisonment to which he or she shall be liable shall not exceed two years. On summary conviction, a fine not exceeding £400 for each day on which the offence is so continued or to imprisonment for a term not exceeding six months, or both, provided that if a person is convicted in the same proceedings of two or more such further offences the aggregate term of imprisonment to which he or she shall be liable shall not exceed six months.

Minimum fines

7–101   Certain minimum fines are prescribed where the offence involved the construction of an unauthorised structure, as follows. On conviction on indictment, the estimated cost of the construction of the structure or £10,000, whichever is less, or, on summary conviction, the estimated cost of the construction of the structure or £500, whichever is less. There is an exception where the person convicted can show to the court's satisfaction that he or she does not have the necessary financial means to pay the minimum fine.

Other offences

7–102   Any person who is guilty of an offence under the PDA 2000 other than an offence referred to in s.156(1) or (2) shall be liable, on summary conviction, to a fine not exceeding £1,500 or, at the discretion of the court, to imprisonment for a term not exceeding six months or to both.

4. Offences by bodies corporate

7–103   Provision is made under s.158 of the PDA 2000 whereby an officer (or a person purporting to act in such a capacity) of a body corporate will also be guilty of an offence and liable to be proceeded against and punished as if he were guilty of an offence committed by the body corporate, in circumstances where it is proved that the offence committed by the body corporate was committed with the consent, connivance, or approval of, or facilitated by any neglect on the part of, that person. Where the affairs of a body corporate are managed by its members, the acts and defaults of a member in connection with his or her functions of management are to be treated as if he or she were a director.[94]

5. Payment of fines

Under s.159 of the PDA 2000, where a court imposes a fine (or affirms or varies a fine imposed by another court), it shall provide by order for the payment of the amount of the fine to the planning authority. Payment may be enforced as if due on foot of a decree or order made by a court in civil proceedings.

7–104

6. Costs

Where a person is convicted of an offence under Pt III, the court shall, unless it is satisfied that there are special and substantial reasons for not so doing, order the person to pay to the planning authority the costs and expenses of the action, measured by the court.[95]

7–105

The costs or expenses to be paid to the planning authority include any such costs or expenses reasonably incurred by the planning authority in relation to the investigation, detection and prosecution of the offence or order, as appropriate, including costs incurred in respect of the remuneration and other expenses of employees, consultants and advisers.[96]

7–106

7. Reverse onus of proof

The onus of proving the existence of a planning permission is on the defendant in any such prosecution.[97] Further, it shall not be necessary for the prosecution to show, and it shall be assumed unless the contrary is shown by the defendant, that the subject-matter of the prosecution was development and was not exempted development.[98]

7–107

It is not a defence to a criminal prosecution to prove that retention planning permission has been applied for, or granted, since the happening of any of the following events: the initiation of proceedings; the sending of a warning letter; or the service of an enforcement notice in a case of urgency under s.155.[99]

7–108

---

[94] See, by analogy, G. Simons, "Criminal Liability for Environmental Pollution" (1998) 3 *Bar Review* 458.
[95] PDA 2000, s.161(1).
[96] PDA 2000, s.161(2).
[97] PDA 2000, s.162(1).
[98] PDA 2000, s.156(6).
[99] PDA 2000, s.162(2).

F. Injunction in Respect of Unauthorised Development

1. Introduction

7–109 Section 160 of the PDA 2000 provides a procedure whereby an application may be made to either the High Court or the Circuit Court for orders in respect of unauthorised development. The section is widely drafted, and a variety of orders may be made. For example, orders may be made requiring the discontinuance of unauthorised development, or the restoration of any land so far as practicable to its condition prior to the commencement of any unauthorised development. The side note to the section refers to an "injunction" in relation to unauthorised development: this is somewhat of an understatement given the breadth of the orders which may be made.[100] The most notable feature of the procedure is that there is no *locus standi* or standing requirement: it is expressly provided under s.160(1) that an application may be made by the planning authority or any other person, whether or not the person has an interest in the land. For this reason, the courts had indicated that the grant of relief under the equivalent section of the previous legislation was discretionary.[101] The manner in which this discretion is to be exercised represents the subject-matter of much of the case law in this area.

7–110 The equivalent section of the previous legislation had been described as a "fire brigade" section intended to deal with clear and urgent breaches of the planning legislation.[102] As discussed at para.7–114 below, one consequence of this would appear to be that the procedure is not appropriate where novel questions of law and complex questions of fact are involved.

2. Previous legislation

7–111 Section 160 is the successor of s.27 of the Local Government (Planning & Development) Act 1976 (as amended by s.19(g) of the Local Government (Planning & Development) Act 1992). A number of significant amendments have been made, however. First, the procedure has been streamlined: under the previous legislation a distinction had been drawn between development in breach of planning permission, and unauthorised development, *i.e.* development without the benefit of any planning permission. Secondly, *quia timet* or anticipatory relief is now available; thus the lacuna identified in *Mahon v*

---

[100] See comments of Barrington J. in *Stafford v Roadstone Ltd.*[1980] 1 I.L.R.M. 1 at 19 "While the word 'injunction' is not used in this section it is clear that the section confers on the High Court jurisdiction to issue both restraining and mandatory injunctions." See also *Avenue Properties Ltd. v Farrell Homes Ltd.* [1982] I.L.R.M. 21 at 26.

[101] Local Government (Planning & Development) Act 1976, s.27 (as amended by s.19(g) of the Local Government (Planning & Development) Act 1992). See, for example, *Stafford v Roadstone Ltd.* [1980] 1 I.L.R.M. 1 at 19. See also *Avenue Properties Ltd. v Farrell Homes Ltd.* [1982] I.L.R.M. 21 at 26. See, generally, G. Simons, "Judicial enforcement of planning law?" (2002) 9 I.P.E.L.J. 143.

[102] *Dublin Corporation v McGowan* [1993] 1 I.R. 405 at 411.

Butler[103] has been legislated for. Thirdly, the basis of the division of jurisdiction between the High Court and Circuit Court has been partially clarified. Fourthly, the time-limit with respect to the taking of enforcement proceedings has been increased from five years to seven years. Finally, it is now expressly provided that planning permission shall not be required in respect of development required by an order under s.160.[104]

3. Jurisdiction of Circuit Court

The basis for the division of function between the Circuit Court and the High Court is not made clear. Under the previous legislation, the jurisdiction of the Circuit Court and the High Court was co-extensive. Under s.160, conversely, it seems that the Circuit Court's jurisdiction is confined to cases where the rateable valuation of the land the subject-matter of the application does not exceed IR£200.[105] Thus in cases involving lands with a greater rateable valuation, the proceedings may only be brought in the High Court. The question which remains unanswered, however, is as to whether an applicant may *choose* to proceed in the High Court even in those cases where the Circuit Court would have jurisdiction. Further, if the applicant does choose to proceed in the High Court, should he or she be limited in terms of any costs award to Circuit Court costs? In the absence of any express provision in this regard, it would seem that an applicant will in certain cases have a choice as to court, but will be on hazard as to costs pursuant to the provisions of s.17 of the Courts Act 1981.

7–112

4. Procedure

Proceedings under s.160 are instituted by way of originating notice of motion.[106] The procedure under s.160 is thus a summary procedure. In *Dublin Corporation v Garland*,[107] Finlay P. relied, *inter alia*, on the summary nature of the previous procedure in holding that the court had no function, on an application for a planning injunction, in any way to review, alter or set aside a decision of the planning authority with regard to the granting or withholding of planning permission. Instead, it would seem that in certain cases it would be more appropriate to, in effect, remit the matter to the planning authority by allowing time for an application for retention planning permission to be made.[108] As

7–113

---

[103] [1997] 3 I.R. 360; [1998] 1 I.L.R.M. 284, cited with approval in *Birmingham v Birr UDC* [1998] 2 I.L.R.M. 136; *Westport UDC v Golden* [2002] 1 I.L.R.M. 439; and *O'Connell v Dungarvan Energy Ltd.*, unreported, High Court, Finnegan J., February, 27, 2001.

[104] PDA 2000, s.163.

[105] PDA 2000, s.160(5). *Cf.* Civil Liability and Courts Act 2004, s.53.

[106] PDA 2000, s.160(3). See also Ord.103, Rules of the Superior Courts 1986; Ord.56, Circuit Court Rules, 2001.

[107] [1982] I.L.R.M. 104 at 106.

[108] *Furlong v AF & GW McConnell Ltd.* [1990] I.L.R.M. 48 at 57. See more generally *Dublin County Council v Kirby* [1985] I.L.R.M. 325. *Cf.* PDA 2000, s.162(3) (as amended by the Local Government Act 2001, s.247(f)).

discussed presently at para.7–197 and onwards, the provisions of s.162(3) may prevent such a course of action.

7–114   Although both the Rules of the Superior Courts and the Circuit Court Rules appear to envisage the possibility of oral evidence, the better view had been that the matter should generally proceed by way of affidavit evidence only.[109] Indeed, the procedural limitations of the equivalent provision of the previous legislation had been emphasised in a number of decisions. In particular, the Supreme Court had indicated in its decisions in *Mahon v Butler*[110] and *Waterford County Council v John A. Wood Ltd.*[111] that summary proceedings under the (then) s.27 of the Local Government (Planning & Development) Act 1976 were not appropriate where novel questions of law and complex questions of fact were involved. Subsequently, in *Dublin Corporation v Lowe*,[112] Morris P. had indicated, *obiter*, that proceedings under the then s.27 would have been inappropriate where there was an issue to be tried as to a pre-1964 use of lands: this issue could only be tried on full plenary hearing. Reference is also made to the decision in *Fingal County Council v RFS Ltd.*[113] Morris P. found that there were a variety of issues of a factual nature which remained to be resolved as to a pre-1964 use, and that given that the onus of proof rested with the applicant to establish facts from which the High Court could raise a probable inference that the premises had been used at and immediately prior to October 1, 1964 otherwise than in the manner in which they were now used, the applicant had failed to discharge the onus.

7–115   Pursued to its logical conclusion, the above case law gives rise to the following very practical problem: injunctive relief will never be available where there is a complex factual or legal background to the alleged unauthorised development. This is because there is no obvious alternative form of proceedings available. The PDA 2000 criminalises unauthorised development and provides a range of enforcement mechanisms: against such a statutory background it would be very difficult to persuade a court that it would be legitimate to infer a general right to pursue another, undisclosed form of proceedings. In particular, it must be very doubtful as to whether a planning authority has standing (*locus standi*) to bring proceedings by way of plenary summons seeking an injunction. Absent express statutory authority, it is normally only the Attorney General who has an entitlement to seek a civil injunction in aid of a breach of the criminal law, and only then in exceptional circumstances.[114]

---

[109] *cf. Cork Corporation v O'Connell* [1982] I.L.R.M. 505; *Galway Corporation v Lackagh Rock Ltd.* [1985] I.R. 120; *Monaghan County Council v Brogan* [1987] I.R. 333; *Dublin County Council v Tallaght Block Company Ltd.* [1982] I.L.R.M. 534; unreported, Supreme Court May 17, 1983; *Furlong v AF & GW McConnell Ltd.* [1990] I.L.R.M. 48; and *Dublin Corporation v Moore* [1984] I.L.R.M. 339.

[110] [1997] 3 I.R. 369; [1998] 1 I.L.R.M. 284.

[111] [1999] 1 I.R. 556; [1999] 1 I.L.R.M. 217.

[112] Unreported, High Court, Morris P., February 4, 2000. On appeal to the Supreme Court, the matter was remitted for other reasons, on consent, to the High Court for rehearing, and returned to the Supreme Court; [2004] 4 I.R. 259.

[113] Unreported, High Court, Morris P., February 6, 2000.

[114] In *Mahon v Butler* [1997] 3 I.R. 369; [1998] 1 I.L.R.M. 284, the Supreme Court relied

Thus, if a planning authority sought to circumvent the procedural limitations **7–116** of s.160 by proceeding by way of plenary summons, the respondent would have strong grounds for seeking to strike out those proceedings.

No exchange of pleadings

There is no provision made under s.160 for the exchange of pleadings between **7–117** the parties.[115] The only formal pleading is the originating notice of motion. The absence of pleadings serves to emphasise the summary nature of the procedure, and indicates that the procedure is not appropriate where novel questions of law and complex questions of fact are involved.[116]

Notwithstanding this, in a very recent judgment, *Limerick County Council v* **7–118** *Tobin (No. 1)*,[117] the High Court indicated that directions as to the exchange of pleadings could be given where appropriate.

> "Of course even in plenary proceedings, relief by way of interim injunction is available, and at short notice, but in planning matters the legislature has specifically provided the procedure under s.160, and it is reasonable that the planning authority in such circumstances would avail of that in the first instance. If, upon the interlocutory hearing, it appears that a Defence put forward by the respondent is one where oral evidence, and even pleadings and discovery are necessary or desirable, there does not seem to be any reason why the Court cannot order such directions as to pleadings and mode of trial as may be appropriate, and certainly there could in my view be no question that the planning authority could be non-suited as it were, having commenced its application by the method provided for in s.160, merely because the respondent raises a matter by way of defence which for its determination requires either pleadings or oral evidence."

Although this ruling has the benefit of pragmatism, and would overcome the **7–119** procedural problems discussed at paras 7–114 and 7–116, it is submitted that it should be treated with caution. The judgment was delivered in the context of an interlocutory application, and appears difficult to reconcile with the earlier Supréme Court judgments.

At all events, in most cases there will still be no formal exchange of pleadings. **7–120** It does seem, however, that a respondent should disclose the nature of any

---

on this principle in rejecting an argument that—in the context of the previous legislation— there was a general equitable jurisdiction to enforce planning control: "It must also be pointed out that the making of an order of this nature, except where expressly authorised by the terms of s. 27, runs counter to a fundamental legal principle, *i.e.* that an injunction should not normally issue to restrain the commission of an offence, which the holding of this event without planning permission would amount to, save at the instance of the Attorney General and even in that case only in exceptional circumstances."

[115] *cf. Drogheda Corporation v Gantley*, unreported, High Court, Gannon J., July 28, 1983 (at p.7).

[116] *Mahon v Butler* [1997] 3 I.R. 369; [1998] 1 I.L.R.M. 284.

[117] [2005] I.E.H.C. 281; unreported, Peart J., August 15, 2005. Judgment on the full hearing was delivered on March 1, 2006.

defence on which he proposes to rely in any replying affidavits filed.[118] A respondent may not be entitled to raise at the hearing of the motion a point by way of defence not raised on affidavit.[119]

5. Parties to application

Applicants

7–121 Section 160(1) provides that an application may be brought by the planning authority or any other person, whether or not that person has an interest in the land. Thus, there is no *locus standi* or standing requirement.[120] It is not a precondition to the bringing of an application that the applicant should have suffered or anticipated any loss peculiar to himself.[121] It has to be said, however, that the courts have been alive to the risk of vexatious or meddlesome litigants, and, for this reason, have retained a discretion to refuse relief on this ground.[122] It is also the case that the courts have recognised the special position of the planning authority (described as its "watch dog role"), and for this reason attach significant weight to its attitude to the development complained of, even in proceedings in which it is not joined as a party.[123] See further para.7–192 and onwards.

7–122 Although there is no express provision for same in either the Rules of the Superior Courts, or the Circuit Court Rules, the possibility of joining co-applicants after proceedings have been issued has been recognised.[124]

---

[118] See *South Dublin County Council v Balfe*, unreported, High Court, Costello J., November 3, 1995. See also *Kildare County Council v Goode*, unreported, High Court, Morris J., June 13, 1997 (at p. 13) (applicant planning authority permitted to adduce further evidence in circumstances where counsel for respondent had failed to identify, at the commencement of the case, the existence of a managerial order as an issue in the case).

[119] *South Dublin County Council v Balfe*, unreported, High Court, Costello J., November 3, 1995.

[120] See *Leen v Aer Rianta cpt* [2003] 4 I.R. 394 (possible political motive of applicant did not go to standing).

[121] *Avenue Properties Ltd. v Farrell Homes Ltd.* [1982] I.L.R.M. 21 at 26. See also *O'Connor v Frank Hetherington Ltd.*, unreported, High Court, Barr J., May 28, 1987 (at p.12).

[122] See especially *Stafford v Roadstone Ltd.* [1980] 1 I.L.R.M. 1 at 19.

[123] *Mahon v Butler* [1997] 3 I.R. 369; [1998] 1 I.L.R.M. 284. See also *Grimes v Punchestown Developments Company Ltd.* [2002] 1 I.L.R.M. 409. In *Cavan County Council v Eircell Ltd.*, unreported, High Court, Geoghegan J., March 10, 1999, the High Court had indicated that a court should be slow to adjourn such enforcement proceedings pending an application for retention planning permission if such an adjournment is opposed by the planning authority vested with the important statutory function to enforce the planning legislation. *Cf. Avenue Properties Ltd. v Farrell Homes Ltd.* [1982] I.L.R.M. 21 at 26 ("The section does not distinguish on its face between an application by a planning authority and an application by 'any other person'").

[124] *Irish Wildbird Conservancy v Clonakilty Golf & Country Club Ltd.*, unreported, High Court, Costello P., July, 23, 1996.

Respondents

The wording of s.160(1) is very wide and provides for the making of an order **7–123** requiring "any person" to do or not to do, or to cease to do, as the case may be, anything that the court considers necessary and specifies for the purposes prescribed in the section. In the ordinary course, any person against whom orders are sought should be joined in the proceedings as a respondent, served with the proceedings, and afforded an opportunity to be heard on the application. Special provision had been made under the previous legislation for the making of orders against persons whose identity was unknown.[125]

Generally, it would seem that the appropriate respondents to an application **7–124** should be the owner and occupier of the relevant land. This would seem to stem from the fact that compliance with any order under the section will require control over the relevant land, or at least a right of entry thereon. This would also be consistent with the provisions with respect to enforcement notices,[126] which indicate that an enforcement notice should be served on the person carrying out the development and, where the planning authority considers it necessary, the owner or the occupier of the land, or any other person who, in the opinion of the planning authority, may be concerned with the matters to which the notice relates.

Difficulties can arise where the breach of planning control alleged is historic, **7–125** as opposed to an ongoing unauthorised use. It may be that neither the (present) owner nor occupier of the land was the author of the unauthorised development. For example, the present owner may have purchased the land with an unauthorised structure already erected thereon. The present owner may wish to argue that it would be unconscionable to require him to make good the default of the previous owner.[127] However, the better view is that the objective of s.160 is remedial rather than punitive, and accordingly the issue of fault is not directly relevant; this is more properly an issue for any criminal prosecution. The former owner might equally well argue that without a legal right of entry or access to the relevant land, his ability to comply with the order would be entirely dependent on the co-operation of the present owner.[128] As to the position as between lessor and lessee, see *Patterson v Murphy*.[129]

Third party procedure

It would seem to follow, by analogy, from the decision in *Wicklow County* **7–126** *Council v Fenton*[130] that the third party procedure under the Civil Liability

---

[125] Rules of the Superior Courts (No. 1), 1996 (S.I. No. 5 of 1996); Ord.56, r.3, Circuit Court Rules, 2001 (S.I. 510 of 2001).

[126] PDA 2000, s.154.

[127] See, for example, *Dublin Corporation v McGowan* [1993] 1 I.R. 405.

[128] See *Dublin Corporation v Browne*, unreported, High Court, Gannon J., October 10, 1987. Gannon J. appears to have accepted an argument to this effect by counsel for the respondent developer (at p.18).

[129] [1978] I.L.R.M. 85 at 94 *et seq.*

[130] [2002] 2 I.R. 583; [2002] 2 I.L.R.M. 469. *Cf. County Meath VEC v Joyce* [1997] 3 I.R.

Act 1961 is not available in the context of an application under s.160. This would seem to stem from the following considerations: the summary nature of the procedure under s.160 is intended as a fast track procedure to provide urgent relief; there is no provision for the exchange of pleadings as between the parties; and the definition of a "wrong" under the Civil Liability Act 1961 does not seem apt to capture the statutory relief under s.160 of the PDA 2000.

Personal liability of directors

7–127   A number of decisions in relation to the previous legislation indicated that the wording was sufficiently wide to allow orders to be made against the directors of development companies personally.[131] It is submitted that the limits identified in these cases remain good law under s.160, especially in circumstances where the opportunity was not taken under s.158 to extend personal liability of officers of a company to include other than criminal liability. Barrington J. had suggested in *Dublin County Council v Elton Homes Ltd.*[132] that, particularly in the case of small companies, the most effective way of ensuring that the (solvent) company complies with its obligations would be to make an order against the directors as well as the company itself.[133] In order to pierce the corporate veil, however, it appears necessary to establish some evidence of impropriety (such as, for example, by way of fraud, or the siphoning off of large sums of money out of the company).[134] The fact that the affairs of the company may have been carried out with scant regard to the formalities of, or the requirements of, the companies legislation is not *per se* a good ground for visiting on the directors of a company a liability to conform with a planning permission at their own expense.[135] Nor is the fact that an application for planning permission was made in the personal name of a director.[136]

7–128   Again, the summary nature of the proceedings may tell against the making of such orders. Murphy J. in *Dublin County Council v O'Riordan* stated as follows.[137]

---

402. See also *Drogheda Corporation v Gantley*, unreported, High Court, Gannon J., July 28, 1983.
[131] *Dublin County Council v Elton Homes Ltd.* [1984] I.L.R.M. 297; *Dublin County Council v O'Riordan* [1985] I.R. 159; [1986] I.L.R.M. 104; *Dun Laoghaire Corporation v Parkhill Developments Ltd.* [1989] I.R. 447; [1989] I.L.R.M. 235; *Coffey v Hebron Homes Ltd.*, unreported, High Court, O'Hanlon J., July, 27, 1984; and *Sligo County Council v Cartron Bay Construction Ltd.*, unreported, High Court, Ó Caoimh J., May 25, 2001.
[132] [1984] I.L.R.M. 297 at 300.
[133] See also *Coffey v Hebron Homes Ltd.*, unreported, High Court, O'Hanlon J., July 27, 1984 (respondents fairly joined to ensure any order against company carried into effect).
[134] *Dublin County Council v Elton Homes Ltd.* [1984] I.L.R.M. 297.
[135] *Dublin County Council v O'Riordan* [1985] I.R. 159; [1986] I.L.R.M. 104. See also *Dun Laoghaire Corporation v Parkhill Developments Ltd.* [1989] I.R. 447; [1989] I.L.R.M. 235.
[136] *Ellis v Nolan*, unreported, High Court, McWilliam J., May 6, 1983.
[137] [1985] I.R. 159 at 166; [1986] I.L.R.M. 104 at 110. See also *Ellis v Nolan*, unreported, High Court, McWilliam J., May 6, 1983. Ó Caoimh J. distinguished *Dublin County Council v O'Riordan* in *Sligo County Council v Cartron Bay Construction Ltd.*, unreported, High Court, Ó Caoimh J., May 25, 2001.

"Similarly, where the application turns upon the relationship between a director or shareholder and a company in which he is interested I would anticipate that in most cases it would be necessary that the relationship be investigated in the first instance by a liquidator in accordance with procedures provided in the Companies Act for that purpose rather than seeking to establish all of the relevant facts on proceedings designed to be heard on affidavit."

For a recent example of a case where personal liability was imposed on the directors, reference is made to the decision in *Sligo County Council v Cartron Bay Construction Ltd.*[138] There had been a failure by a company to comply with the terms of an order made by the High Court under the (then) s.27 of the Local Government (Planning & Development) Act 1976 (as amended). Ó Caoimh J. held that insofar as the affairs of the respondent company were inextricably linked to the actions of the two director respondents, if the company had been in wilful default it had been through the medium of the actions of the directors. Insofar as a company can have a will, it must be by those in control of the company. In this connection, Ó Caoimh J. held that whereas the failure of a corporate entity will not necessarily give rise to a conclusion of wilful default on its part or on the part of its directors, on the facts, the directors were guilty of a substantial wilful failure to account to the company in respect of rent. **7–129**

6. Onus of proof

Unlike the position in respect of criminal prosecutions, there is no express statutory provision made in the case of a planning injunction as to where the onus of proof in respect of certain matters lies.[139] In *South Dublin County Council v Fallowvale Ltd.*,[140] the question arose as to where the onus of proof lay in circumstances where there was a dispute as to whether or not particular development was exempted development. McKechnie J. rejected a suggestion that reverse-onus provisions similar to those expressly provided for in the case of criminal prosecutions should be inferred. Ultimately, McKechnie J. ruled, from first principles, that the onus of establishing that the development was exempted development is upon he who asserts, *i.e.* the respondent developer. This point is discussed further at para.7–132. **7–130**

In the absence of express statutory provisions, it is submitted that the applicant under s.160 bears the onus of establishing that the matter complained of constitutes development, and, further, is not exempted development. This would seem to stem from the wording of the section which is predicated on there **7–131**

---

[138] Unreported, High Court, Ó Caoimh J., May 25, 2001.
[139] Under s.162(1) of the PDA 2000, the onus of proving the existence of a planning permission is on the defendant in a criminal prosecution. Further, under s.156(6) it shall not be necessary for the prosecution to show, and it shall be assumed unless the contrary is shown by the defendant, that the subject-matter of the prosecution was development and was not exempted development.
[140] [2005] I.E.H.C. 408; unreported, McKechnie J., April 28, 2005.

being unauthorised development. "Unauthorised development" is defined under s.2 in terms which exclude, *inter alia*, development commenced prior to October 1, 1964; development which is the subject of planning permission; and exempted development. Further support for this proposition is to be derived from the fact that it is only in the case of (criminal) proceedings for an offence that express provision is made to the effect that the onus of proving the existence of a planning permission is on the defendant. Reference is also made to the statement in *Dublin Corporation v Sullivan*[141] to the effect that in the absence of an express provision to the contrary, the onus of proof rests with the applicant to prove the case which he is making.[142]

Exempted development

7–132 Insofar as the decision of the Supreme Court in *Dillon v Irish Cement Ltd.*[143] and that of the High Court in *South Dublin County Council v Fallowvale Ltd.*[144] suggest that the onus to establish exempted development lies with the respondent, it is submitted that they are incorrect and that the approach in *Westport UDC v Golden*[145] is to be preferred. In particular, it is submitted that it is incorrect to regard the existence of exempted development as conferring a benefit or privilege: it is the requirement to obtain planning permission which represents the interference, and where the benefit of exempted development is available, it simply restores the *status quo*.

7. Hearsay

7–133 There are no grounds for admitting hearsay evidence in support of an application for final orders, such as would be appropriate in the exercise of a discretion as to whether or not to grant an interlocutory application.[146] One of the exceptions to the rule against hearsay is in respect of declarations against interest. Accordingly, a special condition in the contract for sale of the lands which disclosed the existence of unauthorised development was held to be admissible as evidence of the fact that certain structures had not, in fact, been erected prior to October 1, 1964.[147]

---

[141] Unreported, High Court, Finlay P., December 21, 1984.
[142] *Furlong v AF & GW McConnell Ltd.* [1990] I.L.R.M. 48 at 52.
[143] Unreported, Supreme Court, November 26, 1984.
[144] [2005] I.E.H.C. 408; unreported, McKechnie J., April 28, 2005.
[145] [2002] 1 I.L.R.M. 439. See also *Carroll v Brushfield*, unreported, High Court, Lynch J., October 9, 1995 (see O'Sullivan & Sheperd, *Irish Planning Law and Practice,* Butterworths, Dublin). *Cf. Lambert v Lewis*, unreported, High Court, Gannon J., November 24, 1982; and *Fingal County Council v Crean*, unreported, High Court, Ó Caoimh J., October 19, 2001.
[146] *Dublin Corporation v Sullivan*, unreported, High Court, Finlay P., December 21, 1984 (at p. 3).
[147] *South Dublin County Council v Balfe*, unreported, High Court, Costello J., November 3, 1995.

8. Undertaking as to damages

It is submitted that—save with the possible exception of circumstances where 7–134
interim or interlocutory orders are sought—there is no requirement on an
applicant for relief under s.160 to provide an undertaking as to damages.[148]
The purpose of an undertaking as to damages in plenary proceedings is to
allow the court to make *interlocutory* orders safely on the basis of the limited
information then before the court, by ensuring that the other side will be
compensated if it subsequently transpires that an interlocutory order was made
which the moving party was not entitled to. In the case of s.160, conversely,
the court generally will have made a *final* determination on the issues in advance
of the making of any order, and the question of an undertaking as to damages
will thus not normally arise.

Some confusion had arisen as to whether or not an undertaking as to damages 7–135
was required under the equivalent provision of the previous legislation.[149] It is
submitted that the confusion had arisen from the fact that the application
proceeded by way of originating notice of motion, grounded on affidavit.
Accordingly, the application partook of some of the characteristics of an
application for an interlocutory injunction in plenary proceedings. This might
suggest that, as in the case of an interlocutory application, an undertaking as to
damages should be a *quid pro quo* for the granting of an injunction. This would,
of course, be to miss the vital distinction between such a summary application
and plenary proceedings. As is the position under s.160, final orders were
made under the previous legislation on the basis of the originating notice of
motion and the affidavit evidence; generally, there would be no plenary
hearing.[150] Thus the court would have determined the issues between the parties
definitively on the basis of affidavit evidence. This is to be contrasted with the
grant of an interlocutory injunction where the court will only have made a
preliminary finding that there is a serious issue to be tried: the final resolution
of the issue must await the full hearing.

Undertaking where interim or interlocutory relief sought

Matters are slightly complicated by the fact that there is the possibility (under 7–136
s.160(3)) of obtaining interim or interlocutory relief in the context of s.160
proceedings, *i.e.* a holding order can be made even before the s.160 proceedings
are finally determined. It seems from the judgment in *Limerick County Council
v Tobin (No. 1)*[151] that relief of this type will require the giving of an undertaking
as to damages for the same reasons as an undertaking as to damages is required

---

[148] *cf.* Walsh, *Planning and Development Law* (2nd ed., Incorporated Law Society, Dublin)
para.12.46.
[149] See, for example, the judgment of the High Court in *Grimes v Punchestown Developments
Company Ltd.* [2002] 1 I.L.R.M. 409, which suggests that, in an appropriate case, the
court could require an undertaking as to damages under s.27 of the Local Government
(Planning & Development) Act 1976.
[150] *Mahon v Butler* [1997] 3 I.R. 369; [1998] 1 I.L.R.M. 284.
[151] [2005] I.E.H.C. 281; unreported, High Court, Peart J., August 15, 2005.

in any interim or interlocutory injunction. It also seems that the requirement to give an undertaking as to damages remains even where the application under s.160 is made by a planning authority. In the absence of express provision to the contrary, there does not appear to be any basis for treating a planning authority differently from any other applicant. If the planning authority insists on seeking relief on an interlocutory or interim basis, then it must be prepared to assume the risk inherent in an undertaking as to damages. This issue is discussed further immediately below.

9. Interlocutory injunction

7–137   There is little case law on the considerations to be taken into account by the court in determining an application pursuant to s.160(3) for an interlocutory injunction. In particular, it is unclear as to the extent, if any, to which the ordinary principles governing the grant of interlocutory injunctions (the *Campus Oil* principles) require to be modified. The usual approach is to consider, first, whether there is a serious issue to be tried; secondly, the adequacy of damages; and thirdly, the balance of convenience. The difficulty lies with the second and third of these considerations. It is arguable that the adequacy of damages is of only limited relevance. This is because—unlike other proceedings—there is no provision for the recovery of damages from either side. Damages cannot be claimed as a substantive or final relief in s.160 proceedings, and it would, therefore, seem anomalous were damages to be available on a temporary basis for the duration of any interlocutory orders.

7–138   This issue of the relevance of the adequacy of damages was touched on briefly in *Limerick County Council v Tobin (No. 1)*.[152] There, Peart J. seemed to take the view that damages would not be an adequate remedy for the planning authority.

> "As far as the question of irreparable harm and the adequacy of damages in the present case are concerned, it is not something which arises for consideration in an application of this kind, where the applicant is acting in the public interest rather than in order to protect some private commercial or other interest."

7–139   Perhaps surprisingly, Peart J. went on to find that damages would be an adequate remedy for the respondent.

> "If the respondent is restrained there may be a claim for damages against the applicant in the event that the injunction ought not to have been granted. The assessment of those damages, given the nature of the business and the length of time that the respondent has carried on that business means that damages should be easily capable of assessment, and it must be presumed that the applicant would be capable of discharging any award of damages which might be made in due course."

---

[152] [2005] I.E.H.C. 281; unreported, High Court, Peart J., August 15, 2005.

Peart J. did not, however, explain the basis on which any such claim for damages might be advanced.

7–140

Insofar as the third limb of the test is concerned, namely the balance of convenience, the planning authority will have a natural advantage in that it will usually be asserting a public interest in restraining the alleged unauthorised development. Countervailing considerations which might be relied upon by the developer to resist the application for an interlocutory injunction might include hardship (especially to innocent parties such as employees, customers or suppliers who would be adversely affected by the order).

7–141

> "I consider that even though the respondent may well, and in all probability will, suffer some losses by the granting of interlocutory relief pending the hearing of this case, it is a loss which will be quantifiable in the event that the respondent is correct and can prove his case. That prospect of losses does not in my view trump the need to maintain the status quo from this point onwards as far as the integrity of these sites is concerned. Once that integrity is destroyed, even partially, it cannot be restored adequately thereafter, in much the same way as in Dunne, the integrity of the alleged national monument could not be restored in the event that the development was not halted pending the hearing of the case. Not to allow the relief sought in a case such as this would be to permit or at least encourage those intent on breaking the law in this way from taking their chances, so to speak, in the hope, if not the expectation, that by the time matters reach Court for the substantive hearing they will have been able to benefit significantly by their own misdeeds. That would set at nought the intention of the Oireachtas in enacting legislation such as this."

One relevant consideration is obviously the power of the court to make restoration orders. On the facts of *Tobin*, the High Court considered that even with the possibility of making a restoration order, the balance of convenience lay in favour of granting an interlocutory injunction.

7–142

> "There is of course power under the section for the Court to order the restoration of the lands in due course, should the use and development turn out to be unauthorised and requiring planning permission. But the problem about relying on the power to order restoration of the land in those circumstances is that the Court would be entitled to assume that these lands would be worked to their maximum potential by the respondents during whatever period of time elapses between now and the full hearing. If that be the case, there would be very considerable destruction of the landscape by the quarrying which would take place, perhaps over a period of six months or even twelve months. The prospect of these lands, after such excavation and quarrying, being restored to anything reasonably comparing to its present state is remote in my view. The best that could be hoped for would be that the large excavated area would be filled in some fashion, but its present character would be destroyed permanently."

10. Costs

Section 161 provides that the court shall, unless it is satisfied there are special and substantial reasons for not so doing, order a person the subject of an order

7–143

under s.160 to pay the costs and expenses as measured by the court. Thus, a successful applicant is generally entitled to his costs and expenses.

7–144 It remains to be seen as to how the term "special and substantial reasons" will be interpreted. The court's discretion in this regard is similar to that obtaining under the previous legislation,[153] and that case law may provide some guidance. The conduct of the applicant, and, in particular, the fact that the applicant may have contributed to the need for the proceedings should, on occasion, tell against an award of costs even in favour of a successful applicant. For example, an applicant may succeed in obtaining orders on some only of the grounds, and it might be appropriate to allow the respondent to set off any costs unnecessarily incurred. In *Donegal County Council v O'Donnell*[154] O'Hanlon J. held that having regard to a number of unsatisfactory features in the way the planning authority had dealt with the application for planning permission (which planning permission was the subject-matter of the enforcement proceedings), no order as to costs should be made. Conversely, costs were awarded on a solicitor and own client basis against a planning authority, *as respondent*, in *Curley v Galway Corporation*.[155]

7–145 An applicant planning authority was required to pay the respondent's costs in circumstances where although the planning authority was granted certain orders, the respondent had succeeded in defeating a point raised as a test case by the applicant.[156]

7–146 Although the legislation is silent on the point, it would seem only fair that a respondent who has successfully resisted enforcement proceedings should generally be entitled to his costs. There may, of course, be exceptions where no order as to costs should be made, or even where the respondent might be required to pay the costs of the applicant.[157] For example, the fact that a respondent only makes a concession at a very late stage of the proceedings might well justify the costs to that date being awarded against him.[158] Similarly, a respondent may be required to pay costs where that respondent seeks to rely on a subsequent grant of (retention) planning permission.[159]

---

[153] Under Ord.99, r.1, Rules of the Superior Courts 1986, costs generally follow the event. See *Grimes v Punchestown Developments Company Ltd.*, unreported, Supreme Court, December 20, 2002.

[154] Unreported, High Court, O'Hanlon J., June 25, 1982.

[155] Unreported, High Court, Kelly J., March 30, 2001.

[156] *Dublin Corporation v Bentham* [1993] 2 I.R. 58.

[157] See, for example, *Cork County Council v Cliftonhall Ltd*, unreported, High Court, Finnegan J., April 6, 2001 (cavalier disregard for the planning process justified the institution of proceedings).

[158] The costs of bringing the proceedings, up to and including the first day, were awarded against a respondent who subsequently made a concession in respect of part of the development in respect of which relief had been claimed; *Fingal County Council v RFS Ltd.*, unreported, High Court, Morris P., February 6, 2000.

[159] *cf.* PDA 2000, s.162(3) (as amended by the Local Government Act 2001, s.247(f)). *Marray v Connaughton*, unreported, High Court, O'Hanlon J., January 25, 1984.

11. Nature and extent of orders

Under the previous legislation, a distinction was drawn between what might, **7–147** in broad terms, be described as development in breach of planning permission, and development without the benefit of any planning permission. More specifically, s.27(1) of the Local Government (Planning & Development) Act 1976 (as amended)[160] applied where development of land, for which a planning permission was required, had been carried out, or was being carried out, without such planning permission, and where an unauthorised use was being made of land. An "unauthorised use" was defined as a material change in use commenced after October 1, 1964, being development other than a development the subject of planning permission, or exempted development. Section 27(2) applied where any development authorised under planning permission had been commenced but had not been, and was not being, carried out in conformity with the permission because of non-compliance with the requirements of a condition or for any other reason.

In terms of the relief available, the court regarded the subdivision of the section **7–148** as intended to give effect to a vital and justified distinction in terms of the orders which might be made as between development in breach of planning permission, and development without the benefit of any planning permission. The case law in this regard is somewhat unsatisfactory in that the effect of certain amendments introduced under the Local Government (Planning & Development) Act 1992 does not appear to have been expressly considered in the subsequent case law: instead, at least some of the later judgments appear to have proceeded on the assumption that the limitations survived notwithstanding the amendments. As the matter is important in understanding the scope of the provisions of s.160 of the PDA 2000 it is proposed to chart briefly the progress of the case law in this area.

Under the provisions of s.27 of the Local Government (Planning & **7–149** Development) Act 1976 as originally enacted, the powers of the High Court in the case of development without the benefit of planning permission were to "prohibit the continuance of the development or unauthorised use". In the case of development not in conformity with planning permission, there was a more general power to "require any person specified in the order to do or not to do, or cease to do, as the case may be, anything which the court considers necessary to ensure the development is carried out in conformity with the permission and specifies in the order".

These provisions were interpreted as allowing for only limited relief in the **7–150** case of development without the benefit of planning permission. Specifically, it had been held that orders of a prohibitory nature only might be made: accordingly, it was not open to make orders requiring demolition,[161] or

---

[160] Local Government (Planning & Development) Act 1992, s.19.
[161] *Morris v Garvey* [1983] I.R. 319 at 322; and *Loughnane v Hogan* [1987] I.R. 322 at 328.

reinstatement.[162] Such orders might, however, be available in principle in respect of development not in conformity with planning permission.[163] The justification for this distinction in terms of the relief available was said to stem from the summary nature of the proceedings under s.27, and was explained thus in *Dublin County Council v Kirby*.[164]

> "In relation to the development and use of land within the scope of the Planning Acts when a permission has been granted, with or without conditions, obligations are created which are enforceable under statutory procedures which might be found deficient for want of expedition in some circumstances. In such circumstances there would be little risk of injustice in invoking the authority of the court by a summary procedure to enforce performance or to restrain abuse of the obligations imposed. On the other hand where a development of land is commenced without any previous defining or limiting circumstances, from which obligations or rights can be unequivocally asserted or inferred, any intervention, other than by restraint to prevent change, without full enquiry might or could result in an injustice."

7–151   Gannon J. went on to say that in the case of development without the benefit of planning permission.

> "It would be exceptional if in those circumstances either the planning authority or any member of the public could, save with great difficulty, assert or hope to prove any significant factor other than the absence of a planning permission."

7–152   Gannon J. concluded by stating that:

> "The distinction between the extent of the intervention by the High Court which may be invoked in a summary manner under s.27(1) as compared with sub-section (2) of the section is clearly evident from the wording of the two sub-sections, is very significant, and is in accordance with procedures founded upon principles of justice. There cannot be any doubt but that such distinction was intentional on the part of the Legislature. It leaves no room for inferring that the High Court may in such summary proceedings be moved to make orders of the mandatory nature which are made only after full and fair investigation in the course of proceedings instituted in the ordinary way."

7–153   The legislation was subsequently amended by the Local Government (Planning & Development) Act 1992. For the purpose of the present discussion, the effect of the amendment can be somewhat simplistically stated as follows: the powers were recast in terms broadly similar to the wording now found at subsections (1)(a) and (b) of s.160 of the PDA 2000. More specifically, the court was empowered to order any person to do or not to do, or to cease to do, as the case may be, anything that the court considers necessary and specifies in the order to ensure, as appropriate (i) that the development or unauthorised use is not

---

[162] *Dublin County Council v Kirby* [1985] I.L.R.M. 325; and *Dublin Corporation v Bentham* [1993] 2 I.R. 58 at 62.

[163] *Morris v Garvey* [1983] I.R. 319 at 323.

[164] [1985] I.L.R.M. 325 at 329. See also *Loughnane v Hogan* [1987] I.R. 322 at 327; and *Dublin Corporation v Maiden Poster Sites Ltd.* [1983] I.L.R.M. 48 at 49.

continued, and (ii) insofar as is practicable, that the land is restored to its condition prior to the commencement of the development or unauthorised use. This latter element appeared to extend the power of the court from one limited to the making of prohibitory orders, to include mandatory orders in respect of the restoration of the lands.[165] It was also the case that the temporal limitation on the availability of relief under the subsection ("is being carried out") was extended.[166]

Although the impediment to the granting of mandatory relief on the literal wording of the section had thus been removed, the principled objections identified in *Dublin Corporation v Kirby*,[167] which were rooted in the summary nature of the proceedings, remained. In the much later decision of *Dublin Corporation v Lowe*,[168] Morris P. refused to grant mandatory relief in an application under the amended s.27(1) of the Local Government (Planning & Development) Act 1976, citing with approval the above *dicta* of Gannon J. in *Dublin Corporation v Kirby*. At first blush, it would seem difficult to reconcile such a finding with the amendments introduced by the Local Government (Planning & Development) Act 1992.   **7–154**

Under the wording of s.160 of the PDA 2000, the former subdivision has been undermined. Specifically, the introductory subsections have been removed, and have been replaced instead with an omnibus concept of "unauthorised development". This term has been newly defined under s.2 as meaning, in relation to land, the carrying out of any unauthorised works (including the construction, erection or making of any unauthorised structure), or the making of any unauthorised use. "Unauthorised works" and "unauthorised use" are in turn defined negatively so as to capture any works, or material change in use, respectively, commenced on or after October 1, 1964 other than exempted development, or development the subject of a planning permission and which is carried out in compliance with that permission or any condition to which that permission is subject. (There is a saver in the case of pre-October 1, 1964 occasional uses.)[169]   **7–155**

Thus, the previously distinct concepts of development with, and without, planning permission have been subsumed under the omnibus concept of "unauthorised development". This, then, represents the threshold to relief under the section. The range of relief open is not expressly limited by reference to   **7–156**

---

[165] This appears to have been the understanding of academic commentators. See, for example, B. Grist, "The Planning Injunction" 1993 *Irish Law Times* 79.

[166] The temporal restriction was emphasised in the judgments in *Loughnane v Hogan* [1987] I.R. 322 at 327, and *Dublin Corporation v Bentham* [1993] 2 I.R. 58 at 62.

[167] [1985] I.L.R.M. 325. See, by analogy, *Dublin Corporation v Garland* [1982] I.L.R.M. 104 at 106.

[168] Unreported, High Court, Morris P., February 4, 2000: on appeal to the Supreme Court, the case was, on consent, remitted to the High Court for rehearing, and then returned to the Supreme Court: [2004] 4 I.R. 259. See also *Dublin Corporation v McGowan* [1993] 1 I.R. 405 at 411.

[169] PDA 2000, s.39(4).

the existence or otherwise of planning permission. A curious result of this might be that the courts now have a discretion to over-enforce in the following sense. Under the previous legislation, the admissible order in the case of development being carried out in breach of planning permission was that the development be carried out in conformity with the permission. The wording of s.160, however, would appear to admit of the possibility of a cross-over in the nature of the relief, and the court might be empowered instead to make an order requiring that any land be restored to its condition prior to the commencement of the unauthorised development. In other words, the court might decide to deprive the respondent of the benefit of the planning permission by requiring the entire development to be removed.

7–157   It remains to be seen, however, the extent to which the distinction between development with, and without, planning permission might resurrect itself. This might be done under the cloak of the discretionary nature of the remedies. It would certainly seem that the discretion enjoyed is sufficiently wide so as to allow discrimination in terms of relief available.

7–158   Turning now to the three categories of order expressly identified under s.160, the following very brief observations may be made.

Unauthorised development is not carried out or continued

7–159   Under s.160(1)(a), an order may be made that the unauthorised development is not carried out or continued. This category would appear to present little difficulty, the only concern being that the order should not encroach on established use rights. In the case of creeping intensification, it may be perplexing to identify the precise point at which the unauthorised development occurred.[170] It should be noted that this subsection expressly allows for *quia timet* or anticipatory relief.[171]

7–160   In *PM Cantwell v McCarthy*,[172] Murphy J. suggested that a court might not be allowed to restrict the *user* of an existing development, even if the development proved to be unauthorised. The facts of the case were unusual in that the applicant sought to restrain the use of a surface or storm water drainage system which, it was alleged, had been constructed without planning permission. Against this background, then, and where the construction works had been completed in full, the court naturally had concerns as to the utility of any order it might make. It is respectfully submitted that whereas on the particular facts the court would be entitled to exercise its discretion to withhold relief, it goes too far to say that the court would not have had jurisdiction to restrain the use of the drainage system. It is not correct to say that relief under s.160 is confined to ordering the carrying out of works (including works of demolition) or that a

---

[170] For an excellent discussion of this issue, see D. McGrath, "Planning Injunction under Section 27" [1996] D.U.L.J. 1
[171] *cf. Mahon v Butler* [1997] 3 I.R. 369; [1998] 1 I.L.R.M. 284.
[172] [2005] I.E.H.C. 351; unreported, Murphy J. November 1, 2005.

court cannot prohibit the continuation of a particular use but must instead the require the removal of the unauthorised structure. In certain circumstances a court might legitimately consider that it would be disproportionate to require the physical removal of an unauthorised structure, but it would not follow that there would then be an entitlement to use the structure as intended. For example, a developer might have erected, without planning permission, a structure with the intention of using it as a nightclub. The court might decide not to require the removal of the structure, but could quite properly prohibit its use as a nightclub.

Restoration of any land

Under s.160(1)(b), an order may be made that in so far as is practicable, any   **7–161**
land is restored to its condition prior to the commencement of any unauthorised development. As discussed at para.7–156 above, the literal wording of this provision might create a risk of over-enforcement. It should also be noted that the subsection refers to the restoration of *any* land: this is to be contrasted with the wording of the previous legislation which was confined to "the land".[173] The power to order the restoration of land is subject to the express qualification "in so far as is practicable".

Conformity with planning permission or any condition

The third form of order is to ensure that any development is carried out in   **7–162**
conformity with the planning permission pertaining to that development or any condition to which the permission is subject. The wording differs from the previous legislation in two respects. First, it is now expressly provided that conformity with a condition may be ordered. In other words, it would appear that breach of a condition is enforceable *per se*. Secondly, the planning permission must be one "pertaining to" that development. Difficulties can sometimes arise in categorising a breach of planning control as development without planning permission, or development in breach of planning permission. A developer will occasionally seek to avoid a condition biting by arguing that the development is entirely unauthorised. Under the previous legislation, the test used to be whether or not the planning permission had been implemented.[174] Arguably the concept of "pertaining to" is wider and might, for example, capture a situation (and thus allow a condition to be enforced against) where the proposed development deviated from that permitted in a relatively minor way.

The courts had interpreted the previous legislation as not being intended to   **7–163**
secure a partial compliance with the planning permission after the development to which it relates has been completed,[175] or a partial completion of a

---

[173] Local Government (Planning & Development) Act 1976, s.27(1)(b) (as amended by the Local Government (Planning & Development) Act 1992).

[174] See, by analogy, *McGrath Limestone Works Ltd. v Galway County Council* [1989] I.L.R.M. 602. See also *Kerrier DC v Secretary of State for the Environment* (1980) 41 P. & C.R. 284; and *Hilliard v Secretary of State for the Environment* (1979) P. & C.R. 129.

[175] *Dublin County Council v Browne*, unreported, High Court, Gannon J., October 6, 1987.

development.[176] Thus, the High Court declined to grant mandatory orders in circumstances where a development had been completed some nine years previously, and title and possession of the property had passed to the owners of the individual houses,[177] or to enforce a passive condition requiring that a premises continue in what was assumed to be its existing use in circumstances where there was no suggestion that the building of the premises was not completed to the entire satisfaction of the planning authority.[178]

7–164   Certain conditions attached to a planning permission are not necessarily directly related to the carrying on of the development *per se*. For example, a condition may require certain plans or particulars to be submitted, or may require the provision of adequate security.[179] In such circumstances, an issue might have emerged under the previous legislation as to how it could be said that the fact that such a condition had not been complied with meant that the *development* was not being carried out in conformity with the planning permission.[180] The fact that the wording of s.160 now appears to make a breach of condition enforceable *per se* may resolve this problem.

No damages

7–165   Finally it would seem that there is no provision for the payment of damages under s.160.[181]

12. Discretionary nature of remedy

7–166   As stated above, the courts had emphasised, on numerous occasions, the discretionary nature of the remedy under the equivalent provisions of the previous legislation.[182] That similar principles apply to relief under s.160 of the PDA 2000 has been confirmed by the decision of the High Court in *Leen v Aer Rianta cpt*.[183] In particular, this judgment emphasises that the court is entitled to consider the wider public interest in deciding whether or not to withhold relief. The judgment also confirms that the conduct and *bona fides* of the respondent are a relevant consideration too. The case concerned the development of a passenger terminal facility at Shannon airport. McKechnie

---

[176] *Dublin Corporation v McGowan* [1993] 1 I.R. 405 at 411.
[177] *Dublin County Council v Browne*, unreported, High Court, Gannon J., October 6, 1987.
[178] *Dublin Corporation v McGowan* [1993] 1 I.R. 405 at 411.
[179] Under the previous legislation, failure to comply with such a financial condition rendered the entire planning permission invalid: see Local Government (Planning & Development) Act 1963, s.26(10)(a), and *John A. Woods Ltd. v Kerry County Council*, unreported, High Court, Smyth J., October 31, 1997.
[180] *Meath County Council v Thornton*, unreported, High Court, O'Hanlon J., February 14, 1994 (insurance bonds).
[181] See, by analogy, *Ellis v Nolan*, unreported, High Court, McWilliam J., May 6, 1983. See also *Dublin Corporation v Gantley*, unreported, High Court, Gannon J., July 28, 1983.
[182] See, generally, G. Simons, "Judicial enforcement of planning law?" (2002) 9 I.P.E.L.J. 143.
[183] [2003] 4 I.R. 394.

J. ruled that the development had been carried out in breach of a condition precedent, namely that the matter of effluent treatment be resolved. In declining to grant injunctive relief however, McKechnie J. had regard, *inter alia*, to the public interest in ensuring that the airport was not closed down, and the *bona fides* of the respondent in its negotiations and dealings with the planning authority.

The Supreme Court had sought to define and delimit the scope of the discretion under the previous legislation in its decision in *Morris v Garvey*.[184] The Supreme Court had suggested a need for exceptional circumstances before relief would be withheld to an applicant; a consideration of the subsequent case law suggests perhaps that this decision represented the high water mark,[185] and that any requirement for there to be exceptional circumstances has been loosely interpreted. Henchy J. in *Morris v Garvey* had described the function of the court thus. **7–167**

> "[…] the High Court becomes the guardian and supervisor of the carrying out of the permitted development according to its limitations. In carrying out that function the High Court must balance the duty and benefit of the developer under the permission, as granted, against the environmental and ecological rights and amenities of the public, present and future, particularly those closely or immediately affected by the contravention of the permission. It would require exceptional circumstances (such as genuine mistake, acquiescence over a long period, the triviality or mere technicality of the infraction, gross or disproportionate hardship, or suchlike extenuating or excusing factors) before the court should refrain from making whatever order (including an order of attachment for contempt in default of compliance) as is 'necessary to ensure that the development is carried out in conformity with the permission'."

Although the cases turn largely on their own particular facts, a number of broad themes emerge and these are discussed under various sub-headings presently. Before turning to that task, however, it is necessary to examine briefly the implications, if any, of the European Convention on Human Rights Act 2003 ("the ECHR Act 2003"). In certain instances the effect of an order under s.160 will be to require the discontinuance of the use (and possibly the removal) of an existing home, and thus may engage Art.8 rights.[186] Even where an existing home is not involved, an order may affect the property rights of the landowner—for example, by requiring the demolition of existing buildings— and thus engage Art.1 of the First Protocol. A question arises, therefore, as to whether the previous practice of the Irish courts needs to be modified, in light of s.2 of the ECHR Act 2003, so as to ensure that the application of s.160 is **7–168**

---

[184] [1983] I.R. 319; [1983] I.L.R.M. 177.
[185] See, in particular, *White v McInerney Construction Ltd.* [1995] 1 I.L.R.M. 374. See also *Furlong v AF & GW McConnell Ltd.* [1990] I.L.R.M. 48 (purpose is essentially a matter of assisting and enforcing the proper use and development of lands in accordance with the planning objectives and regulation of the relevant planning authority).
[186] See, generally, paras 14–194 to 14–216.

compatible with the Convention. As discussed in Chapter 14, at paras 14–194 to 14–216, some minor changes will be required, and, in particular, the courts will need to make express reference to the concept of "proportionality" where applicable.[187]

Conduct of applicant

7–169   Given the absence of a *locus standi* or standing requirement, the courts in the exercise of their discretion will have regard to the effect of the development complained of on the applicant. For example, the fact that the applicant may not be resident in the area, and would not in any way suffer any injury from the events complained of, may well be relevant, especially in circumstances where there was no evidence of any concern by persons closely connected with the area.[188] The High Court in *PM Cantwell v McCarthy*,[189] while acknowledging that there was no statutory requirement on a person seeking relief to show prejudice, indicated that the absence of prejudice was a matter which the court could take into account. In this connection, the threshold of any requirement for personal prejudice would appear to be relatively low, and even the assertion of an applicant's own selfish interests may be sufficient. Moreover, neither the fact that an applicant is seeking to protect the privacy of his or her own dwelling house,[190] nor the fact that an applicant is a trade competitor of the respondent,[191] are necessarily bars to relief. The fact that an applicant may have a commercial interest in ensuring that a planning permission for a particular piece of infrastructure is complied is likewise not a bar.[192]

7–170   Similarly, the fact that an applicant is himself in breach of planning control does not *per se* disentitle him to relief, at least in circumstances where the applicant has placed this fact fairly before the court.[193]

7–171   It seems that an applicant is required to put before the court fairly and with candour all facts known to him which are relevant to the exercise of the court's discretion, and that he should satisfy the court of his *bona fides* and the true purpose of his application.[194] Thus relief was refused to an applicant who had

---

[187] See, for example, *Coates v South Buckinghamshire District Council* [2004] EWCA 1378; [2005] J.P.L. 668, [7].

[188] *Grimes v Punchestown Developments Company Ltd.* [2002] 1 I.L.R.M. 409. The order for costs was upheld on appeal: unreported, Supreme Court, December 20, 2002.

[189] [2005] I.E.H.C. 351; unreported, Murphy J., November 1, 2005.

[190] *Cairnduff v O'Connell* [1986] I.R. 73; [1986] I.L.R.M. 465.

[191] See, for example, *National Federation of Drapers and Allied Trades Ltd. v Allied Wholesale Warehouses, Irish Times*, November 29, 1979, cited in Walsh, *Planning and Development Law* (2nd ed., Incorporated Law Society, Dublin), para.12.43.

[192] *Mountbrook Homes Ltd. v Oldcourt Developments Ltd.* [2005] I.E.H.C. 171; unreported, Peart J., April 22, 2005 (neighbouring landowner had a "legitimate collateral motive" in ensuring as far as it could that a distributor road was constructed strictly in accordance with its permission).

[193] *Fusco v Aprile*, unreported, High Court, Morris P., June 6, 1997.

[194] *O'Connor v Frank Hetherington Ltd.*, unreported, High Court, Barr J., May 28, 1987. Cf. *Leen v Aer Rianta cpt* [2003] 4 I.R. 394 (applicant failed to disclose initially an additional political motive for making application).

failed to disclose the fact that his proceedings were being financed by a competitor of the respondent.[195]

In *Altara Developments Ltd. v Ventola Ltd*,[196] the High Court in deciding to refuse to grant an injunction attached some weight to the fact that the application was incorrectly presented on the basis that one of the applicants was a local resident who lived in the immediate vicinity of the site. This proved to be incorrect. **7–172**

Special considerations may apply where the applicant is a local authority, as the court may take into consideration the manner in which it has exercised its other statutory functions: for example, in the case of enforcement proceedings against travellers, it would seem that the court may properly take into account any alleged breach of the local authority's statutory duty to provide halting sites in deciding whether or not to grant relief against travellers,[197] even, apparently, where this might prejudice third party landowners.[198] **7–173**

The fact that a planning authority may have served an enforcement notice might preclude the making of an application for a planning injunction until such time as the period specified in the enforcement notice for compliance has expired.[199] **7–174**

Conduct of respondent

The state of a respondent's knowledge as to the existence of a breach of planning control may be a relevant factor. If the respondent acted in a *bona fide* belief that the development was authorised (for example, in a mistaken assumption that same constituted exempted development or did not otherwise require planning permission), this may be a factor in favour of withholding relief.[200] **7–175**

---

[195] *O'Connor v Frank Hetherington Ltd.*, unreported, High Court, Barr J., May 28, 1987.

[196] [2005] I.E.H.C. 312; unreported, O'Sullivan J., October 6, 2005.

[197] See, by analogy, *South Buckinghamshire District Council v Porter* [2002] 2 P. & C.R. 218. See, generally, G. Simons, "Unauthorised travellers' halting sites" (1997) 4 I.P.E.L.J. 53.

[198] See *County Meath VEC v Joyce* [1997] 3 I.R. 402; [1994] 2 I.L.R.M. 210. It should be noted that in that case the applicant was a neighbouring landowner but the planning authority had been joined in as a third party. As to the appropriateness of the use of the third party procedure see para.7–126 above.

[199] *Blainroe Estate Management Co. Ltd. v IRG Blainroe Ltd.*, unreported, High Court, Geoghegan J., March 18, 1994.

[200] *Dublin Corporation v McGowan* [1993] 1 I.R. 405 (respondent unaware of planning permission affecting lands as a result of inaccurate planning searches held to have acted in good faith); *Grimes v Punchestown Developments Company Ltd.* [2002] 1 I.L.R.M. 409 (*bona fide* belief that planning permission not required); *Stafford v Roadstone Ltd.* [1980] 1 I.L.R.M. 1 (material change in use by intensification); *Dublin County Council v Sellwood Quarries Ltd.* [1981] I.L.R.M. 23 (*bona fide* belief that planning permission not required); *Leech v Reilly*, unreported, High Court, O'Hanlon J., April 26, 1983 (rebuilding of previously existing workshop); and *O'Connor v Frank Hetherington Ltd.*, unreported, High Court, Barr J., May 28, 1987 (reliance on representation by planning authority that planning permission not required).

Keane J. stated in *Dublin Corporation v McGowan*[201] that it would be manifestly unjust to have the Draconian machinery brought into force against a person who behaved in good faith throughout.[202] Conversely, if a respondent proceeded with actual knowledge of the breach of planning control, or with a reckless disregard as to whether or not planning permission was required, then he can expect little sympathy from the court.[203] The fact that unauthorised development had been carried out with a view to deriving a profit is also relevant.[204]

7–176 The court should not exercise its discretion in favour of the respondent when to do so would lend support to unco-operative conduct.[205] In this connection, it would seem that the court is entitled to have regard to the conduct of the respondent both prior to, and during the course of, the legal proceedings. Thus, the High Court declined to exercise its discretion in circumstances where the respondent deliberately set out to disregard the planning procedures and had sought to avoid the service of a warning letter;[206] and in a case where an unauthorised use continued down to the day of the hearing.[207] It would also seem that the fact that a respondent fully contests proceedings, and succeeds in delaying same, would tell against a respondent.[208] A respondent's record in relation to planning matters may also be of some significance.[209]

7–177 The extent to which a developer can rely on the fact of his having had professional advice to the effect that development was in compliance with planning permission was considered in *Altara Developments Ltd. v Ventola Ltd.*[210] An application was brought under s.160 seeking to restrain what was

---

[201] [1993] 1 I.R. 405 at 412.

[202] See also *Leen v Aer Rianta cpt* [2003] 4 I.R. 394 (respondent had acted *bona fide* in its dealings with planning authority).

[203] *Dublin Corporation v Maiden Poster Sites Ltd.* [1983] I.L.R.M. 48 at 49 (respondents assumed to have known or ought to have known of the need to obtain a planning permission); *Dublin Corporation v O'Dwyer Brothers (Mount Street) Ltd.*, unreported, High Court, Kelly J., May 2, 1997 (respondent held to be fully alert to the need to apply for retention planning permission); *Curley v Galway Corporation*, unreported, High Court, Kelly J., December 11, 1998 (deliberate and conscious violation of terms of planning permission); *Mahon v Butler*, unreported, High Court, Costello P., July 28, 1997 (reversed by the Supreme Court on jurisdictional grounds: [1999] 3 I.R. 369; [1998] 1 I.L.R.M. 284) (respondent aware of significant risk of challenge); and *Cavan County Council v Eircell Ltd.*, unreported, High Court, Geoghegan J., March 10, 1999 (would have been reckless to proceed without legal advice on planning implications).

[204] *Dublin Corporation v Maiden Poster Sites Ltd.* [1983] I.L.R.M. 48; and *Dublin Corporation v O'Dwyer Brothers (Mount Street) Ltd.*, unreported, High Court, Kelly J., May 2, 1997 (at p. 11).

[205] *Westport UDC v Golden* [2002] 1 I.L.R.M. 439, *per* Morris P.

[206] *Westport UDC v Golden* [2002] 1 I.L.R.M. 439.

[207] *Galway County Council v Connacht Proteins Ltd.*, unreported, High Court, Barrington J., March 28, 1980.

[208] *Dublin Corporation v O'Dwyer Brothers (Mount Street) Ltd.*, unreported, High Court, Kelly J., May 2, 1997 (at p.9 *et seq.*).

[209] *Galway County Council v Connacht Proteins Ltd.*, unreported, High Court, Barrington J., March 28, 1980.

[210] [2005] I.E.H.C. 312; unreported, O'Sullivan J., October 6, 2005.

alleged to be development in breach of a condition attached to a planning permission. The relevant condition restricted the number of houses which could be constructed before a specified by-pass road had been "commissioned". The applicant argued that the condition required that the relevant road be operational; whereas the respondent argued conversely that it was sufficient that the developer had entered into an agreement with the planning authority with a view to the acquisition of the land necessary for the construction of the road, and to its construction thereafter. O'Sullivan J. held that the condition was concerned with traffic safety and that the phasing of house construction was related to actual road works on the ground and not merely to the putting in place of legal and contractual arrangements. The term "commissioned" should be interpreted as requiring that the road had become operational. O'Sullivan J. went on to say that even if he was incorrect in this, and that all that was meant was that the legal and contractual arrangements must have been put in place so as to ensure that the road would be constructed, the actual terms of the agreement were not sufficient in that the agreement provided that in the event that the planning authority had not acquired the adjoining lands and constructed the road within a period of four years, the agreement would be at an end and the obligations of either party would forthwith cease.

Notwithstanding the fact that a breach of the condition had been established, O'Sullivan J. refused to grant an injunction as a matter of discretion. In this regard, in addition to citing the conduct of the applicants in creating the misleading impression that one of the applicants lived in the vicinity of the site, and the financial hardship arising in terms of the sales of houses, O'Sullivan J. attached weight to the fact that the developer had received professional advice to the effect that the entry into of the agreement with the planning authority constituted compliance with the terms of the condition. **7–178**

> "Most of all I am taking into account that the respondent has proceeded with caution and care in dealing with this development. It had been advised that it was in compliance condition 2(3) even before the serving of the warning notice by the county council and in response to the service of that warning notice entered negotiations with the local authority.
> This is not a case of a developer pushing ahead regardless. On the contrary it has proceeded since November 2004 with the active support and blessing of the planning authority and in the reasonably held opinion that it was not in breach of the planning permission. In the circumstances I decline to make any order curtailing the respondent's construction works as requested by the applicant."

With respect, the effect of this judgment is to place too great a premium on professional advice. It is expressly stated in the judgment that the court had not been furnished with the advices received by the developer and thus did not know whether they were unqualified or the factual basis on which they were proffered. The interpretation of a planning permission and conditions is a matter of law for the court. The fact that a developer may have received advice with a contrary view cannot alter this, nor should it be a factor in the exercise of the court's discretion. If the approach adopted in *Altara Developments Ltd. v Ventola Ltd.* were to be followed, then there must be a risk that less scrupulous developers might put pressure on their advisers to provide favourable opinions. **7–179**

Prejudice and hardship to respondent

7–180   It has been accepted that relief may be withheld where an order would cause gross or disproportionate hardship to the respondent.[211] Hardship will carry little weight, however, if it is brought about as the result of a deliberate and conscious breach of planning control.[212]

7–181   In *Westport UDC v Golden*,[213] Morris P. held that in the exercise of its discretion under the equivalent provisions of the previous legislation, the court was entitled to take into account the extent to which the respondent contributed towards the situation upon which the court is asked to exercise its discretion. If through no fault of his or her own, a respondent stumbles upon a situation where the Fire Safety Regulations require that certain works be maintained notwithstanding the fact that such works are not authorised by planning permission, then in those circumstances the discretion might be exercised in favour of refusing the relief sought in the interests of doing justice between the parties.

7–182   The extent to which the effect of an order on the ability of a respondent to comply with the requirements of *other* environmental legislation should inform the exercise of the discretion to withhold relief was considered in *Curley v Galway Corporation*.[214] Enforcement proceedings had been taken against the local authority in connection with the operation of a landfill site at lands outside its functional area. Kelly J. had found that the respondent local authority was in deliberate and conscious violation of terms of the relevant planning permission, and refused to exercise a discretion in its favour. Kelly J. rejected a submission that the court should withhold its order, *inter alia*, on the basis of the statutory obligations of the respondent local authority, as follows.

> "Secondly, it is said to me that an order made today will give rise to very considerable difficulties for the Corporation in complying with its statutory obligations under, for example, the waste management legislation. In my view the Corporation has nobody but itself to blame if such difficulties are created. I cannot conceive of a situation where the Court can, in order to enable Galway Corporation to comply with its statutory obligations under one piece of legislation, permit it to breach obligations imposed upon it by another piece of legislation. In particular the Court cannot permit the fulfillment of a statutory obligation, for example, under the Waste Management Act by the commission of criminal offences under the planning legislation."

---

[211] *Avenue Properties Ltd. v Farrell Homes Ltd.* [1982] I.L.R.M. 21; and *Dublin County Council v Sellwood Quarries Ltd.* [1981] I.L.R.M. 23.

[212] See, for example, *Curley v Galway Corporation*, unreported, High Court, Kelly J., December 11, 1998 (at p.10); and *Mahon v Butler*, unreported, High Court, Costello P., July 28, 1997.

[213] [2002] 1 I.L.R.M. 439.

[214] Unreported, High Court, Kelly J., December 11, 1998.

Delay

The fact that a limitation period is prescribed for the institution of proceedings **7–183** under s.160 might be taken as indicating that there is no room for the implication of some sort of equitable concept of laches. In this connection, the fact that a statutory time-limit was only introduced for the first time to the statutory injunctive procedure in 1992 would indicate that earlier authorities should be treated with caution.[215] The question of whether or not delay could constitute a discretionary factor notwithstanding the statutory time-limits was considered in *Dublin Corporation v Lowe*.[216] Morris P. appeared to accept, in principle, a submission that notwithstanding a statutory outer time-limit of (then) five years, unreasonable delay on the part of the applicant planning authority could be interpreted as acquiescence. On the facts, however, Morris P. found that the applicant planning authority had acted entirely reasonably in holding off the institution of proceedings pending the determination of an application for planning permission.

In *Grimes v Punchestown Developments Company Ltd*,[217] Herbert J. (in the **7–184** context of an application to enjoin the holding of a pop concert) had regard in the exercise of his discretion to evidence to the effect that the event sought be to enjoined had been widely publicised for a very considerable period, and that the applicant did not take any steps to institute proceedings (or to notify the promoters) until shortly before the event was to take place. The facts of this case where somewhat unusual in that the primary finding was that a transient event of this type did not require the grant of planning permission.[218]

In *Mason v KTK Sand and Gravel Ltd*,[219] the High Court granted relief **7–185** notwithstanding an objection on the part of the respondent developer that the applicants had delayed. Smyth J. found that the applicants' solicitors had written to the respondent before the use complained of was first undertaken, and that the applicants had not waited until expenditure was incurred by the respondent before making their concerns known.

Although delay may not necessarily be a ground for withholding relief, it may **7–186** inform the exercise of the court's discretion as to the length of any stay on the order. For example, in *Dublin Corporation v Kevans*,[220] Finlay P. held that the respondent was entitled to a substantial period during which to make alternative

---

[215] *Dublin County Council v Matra Investments Ltd.* (1980) 114 I.L.T.R. 102; *Dublin Corporation v Mulligan*, unreported, High Court, Finlay P., May 6, 1980; and *Furlong v AF & GW McConnell Ltd.* [1990] I.L.R.M. 48. *Cf. Dublin Corporation v O'Dwyer Brothers (Mount Street) Ltd.*, unreported, High Court, Kelly J. May 2, 1997 (at p.6).

[216] Unreported, High Court, Morris P., February 4, 2000. On appeal to the Supreme Court, the matter was, on consent, remitted to the High Court for rehearing, and then returned to the Supreme Court; [2004] 4 I.R. 259.

[217] [2002] 1 I.L.R.M. 409. See also, unreported, Supreme Court, December 20, 2002 (costs).

[218] Events of this type are now subject to special control under Pt XVI of the PDA 2000.

[219] Unreported, High Court, Smyth J., May 7, 2004.

[220] Unreported, High Court, Finlay P., July 14, 1980.

arrangements with regard to the user of premises, where enforcement action by the planning authority had not been pursued with urgency.[221]

Trivial or technical breach

7–187   A court enjoys a discretion to withhold relief where the unauthorised development involves a trivial or technical breach.[222] It appears from the decisions in *O'Connell v Dungarvan Energy Ltd.*[223] and *Cork County Council v Cliftonhall Ltd.*[224] that the nature of the breach of a planning permission may also be relevant to the question as to whether there has, in fact, been any unauthorised development at all, in that it seems that planning permissions are to be interpreted flexibly so as to allow for a tolerance in respect of what has been described as "immaterial deviations".

7–188   The judgment in *Mountbrook Homes Ltd. v Oldcourt Developments Ltd.*[225] suggests that the courts will take a pragmatic approach to the enforcement of "prior to commencement" conditions. Peart J. indicated that the court ought not to be concerned to punish the respondent by way of an order under s.160 for delay in proper compliance with a condition requiring the submission of revised drawings prior to the commencement of development. Peart J. was satisfied that the condition had been belatedly complied with. No order as to costs was made in the case.

Public interest

7–189   In exercising its discretion under s.160, it would seem that the court is entitled to look not only at the convenience of the parties but also at the convenience of the public.[226] Thus the court is entitled to have regard to the fact that the respondent is operating an important factory, or to the interests of employees.[227] Conversely, there were no grounds for refusing relief where premises were conducted in such a manner as to constitute a health hazard and an appalling nuisance to local residents.[228]

7–190   In *Leen v Aer Rianta cpt.,*[229] the High Court had regard to the public interest in ensuring that the international airport at Shannon was not closed down. In this

---

[221] See also *Dublin County Council v Matra Investments Ltd.* (1980) 114 I.L.T.R. 102; and *Dublin Corporation v Garland* [1982] I.L.R.M. 104 (respondent allowed a period of twelve months within which to find alternative accommodation for office purposes).

[222] *Morris v Garvey* [1982] I.R. 319; [1983] I.L.R.M. 177. See also *Dublin County Council v Matra Investments Ltd.* (1980) 114 I.L.T.R. 102.

[223] Unreported, High Court, Finnegan J., February 27, 2001.

[224] Unreported, High Court, Finnegan J., April 6, 2001.

[225] [2005] I.E.H.C. 171; unreported, Peart J., April 22, 2005.

[226] *Stafford v Roadstone Ltd.* [1980] 1 I.L.R.M. 1.

[227] *Stafford v Roadstone Ltd.* [1980] 1 I.L.R.M. 1. See also *Dublin County Council v Sellwood Quarries Ltd.* [1981] I.L.R.M. 23 (very damaging consequences for the respondents and for those in their employment and for those to whom they are bound in contracts).

[228] *Galway County Council v Connacht Proteins Ltd.*, unreported, High Court, Barrington J., March 28, 1980 (at p. 15).

[229] [2003] 4 I.R. 394.

regard, McKechnie J. emphasised that it was the public interest, and not the commercial interests of the airport operator, which was informing the exercise of the court's discretion.

In *PM Cantwell v McCarthy*,[230] the High Court indicated that, had it been **7–191** necessary to do so, it would have withheld relief under s.160 on discretionary grounds by reference to the practical difficulties which would be caused by the grant of relief. The case concerned surface and storm water outflow, and Murphy J. expressed the view that to block the outfall in relation to the surface water would be tantamount to perverting the course of nature, and, in the case of storm water, would create a nuisance.

Attitude of planning authority

In a few cases, the courts have attached some weight to the attitude of the **7–192** planning authority to the development being enforced against. Thus in *Grimes v Punchestown Developments Company Ltd*,[231] Herbert J., in exercising his discretion to refuse an injunction under the previous legislation, had regard, *inter alia*, to the fact that the planning authority, as "official watchdog", was aware of the matters complained of and had not pursued enforcement action.[232]

The attitude of the planning authority was also considered significant in *Altara* **7–193** *Developments Ltd. v Ventola Ltd.*[233] There, O'Sullivan J. in refusing to grant an injunction at the suit of a third party stated that this was not a case of a developer pushing ahead regardless, but on the contrary, the developer had proceeded from a particular date with the active support and blessing of the planning authority and in the reasonably held belief that it was not in breach of planning permission.

The approach in *Altara Developments Ltd. v Ventola Ltd.* is open to the criticism **7–194** that undue weight was attached to the views of the planning authority. On the facts, both the developer and the planning authority had misunderstood the requirements of a planning condition which had been imposed by An Bord Pleanála. There is a risk that if the courts give too much weight to the views of the planning authority, this will undermine legal certainty and the role of An Bord Pleanála. As discussed at para.12–164 and onwards, the general view is that the doctrine of estoppel has no place in planning law. It would be most unfortunate if a result similar to estoppel were to be achieved by a sidewind by the courts giving too great a role to the planning authorities.

---

[230] [2005] I.E.H.C. 351; unreported, Murphy J., November 1, 2005.
[231] [2002] 1 I.L.R.M. 409. See also unreported, Supreme Court, December 20, 2002 (costs).
[232] See also *Mahon v Butler* [1997] 3 I.R. 369; [1998] 1 I.L.R.M. 284.
[233] [2005] I.E.H.C. 312; unreported, O'Sullivan J., October 6, 2005.

Would predetermine matter

7–195   It is inappropriate to grant relief by way of a statutory injunction where the effect of same would be to predetermine some other matter of substance.[234]

13. Pending application for retention planning permission

7–196   Under the equivalent provisions of the previous legislation, a respondent would very often seek an adjournment in order to allow an application for retention planning permission to be adjudicated upon. Factors to be taken into account in this regard included the attitude of the planning authority,[235] and the culpability of the developer. For example, in *Dublin Corporation v Maiden Poster Sites Ltd.*,[236] a stay was refused in that the court would not facilitate the respondent in continuing to derive a substantial income from an unauthorised development: it was indicated, however, that if an appeal to An Bord Pleanála was successful, the injunction should be lifted.

7–197   The provisions of s.162(3) of the PDA 2000 appear to intrude on the exercise of this discretion to adjourn enforcement proceedings. See, generally, paras 7–08 to 7–11 above. More specifically, s.162(3) provides,[237] in brief, that no enforcement action, including an application under s.160, shall be stayed or withdrawn by reason of an application for retention planning permission, or the grant of that permission. The wording of the subsection is unsatisfactory in that the use of the word "shall" might be taken as suggesting that there is no discretion to adjourn the proceedings. There is little benefit in forcing on proceedings in circumstances where planning permission might well be granted, and this is a matter in respect of which the court must be allowed some flexibility. Moreover, the latter suggestion that the fact of the *grant* of retention planning permission is not a reason to stay or withdraw enforcement proceedings might well prove meaningless in circumstances where as a result of the grant of planning permission there is no ongoing unauthorised development, nor any remedial orders required.[238]

7–198   Even after the proceedings have been heard and decided against the respondent, the court has a discretion to put a temporary stay on its order pending the determination of an application for retention planning permission. The exercise

---

[234] *Scarriff v Commissioners of Public Works in Ireland*, unreported, High Court, Flood J., March 15, 1995 (dispute as to right of way); and *Mahon v Butler* [1997] 3 I.R. 369; [1998] 1 I.L.R.M. 284 (judicial review proceedings outstanding).
[235] *Cavan County Council v Eircell Ltd.*, unreported, High Court, Geoghegan J., March 10, 1999; and *O'Connor v Frank Hetherington Ltd.*, unreported, High Court, Barr J., May 28, 1987.
[236] [1983] I.L.R.M. 48.
[237] As amended by the Local Government Act 2001, s.247(f).
[238] *cf. Marray v Connaughton*, unreported, High Court, O'Hanlon J., January 25, 1984 (at p. 5) (retention planning permission intended to relate to the houses as they have been erected and is effective to remove the taint of illegality from the development as it has actually been carried out).

of this discretion appears to be informed by two primary considerations. First, the conduct of the respondent. For example, the court will be very reluctant to grant a stay in circumstances where the effect of same would be to allow the respondent to continue to derive a profit from the unauthorised development.[239] The attitude of the respondent to the enforcement proceedings, and, in particular, whether or not the respondent has sought to contest fully the proceedings, has also been regarded as relevant.[240] Secondly, the wider public interest. For example, in *Curley v Galway Corporation*[241] the High Court reluctantly permitted the continued use of an unauthorised development for a period of one month, solely and exclusively for the purpose of receiving refuse, out of concern for the local residents who might otherwise have found themselves confronted with great difficulties over the Christmas period if their refuse could not be disposed of.

14. Section 5 reference

On occasion, the procedure under s.5 of the PDA 2000 may have been invoked in parallel with proceedings under s.160. In brief, s.5 allows for the referral of a question of what is or is not development, or is or is not exempted development, to the planning authority, and on review, to An Bord Pleanála, with provision for a planning authority to refer the matter directly to An Bord Pleanála. Thus, a situation might arise whereby a developer, in response to the threat of enforcement action, might seek to refer the matter for a determination under s.5. For example, it would seem that where it is sought to challenge an enforcement notice, the appropriate procedure may be a reference under s.5, rather than judicial review.[242]   **7–199**

It was well established under the previous legislation that the court had original jurisdiction to determine any question as to development or exempted development on the hearing of the enforcement proceedings, and that it was not necessary to adjourn those proceedings pending the outcome of a Section 5 reference. In particular, the Supreme Court had indicated that the injunction procedure represented a summary and self-contained procedure,[243] and that the jurisdiction was not ousted by the institution of a reference.[244] This reasoning   **7–200**

---

[239] *Dublin Corporation v Maiden Site Posters Ltd.* [1983] I.L.R.M. 48; and *Dublin Corporation v O'Dwyer Brothers (Mount Street) Ltd.*, unreported, High Court, Kelly J., May 2, 1997.

[240] *O'Dwyer Brothers (Mount Street) Ltd.*, unreported, High Court, Kelly J., May 2, 1997.

[241] Unreported, High Court, Kelly J., December 11, 1998.

[242] *O'Connor v Kerry County Council* [1988] I.L.R.M. 660.

[243] *Cork Corporation v O'Connell* [1982] I.L.R.M. 505 at 511, *per* Henchy J. See also *Patterson v Murphy* [1978] I.L.R.M. 85 at 103; *Dublin County Council v Tallaght Block Company Ltd.*, unreported, Supreme Court, May 17, 1983; [1982] I.L.R.M. 534 (High Court); *Dublin Corporation v Regan Advertising Ltd.* [1989] I.R. 61; [1986] I.R. 171 (delay by applicant); *Stafford v Roadstone Ltd.* [1980] I.L.R.M. 1 at 12–13; *Clarke v Brady*, unreported, High Court, Hamilton P., October 30, 1990; and *Cork County Council v Ardfert Quarry Product Ltd.*, unreported, High Court, Murphy J., December 7, 1982.

[244] *Cork Corporation v O'Connell* [1982] I.L.R.M. 505 at 510, *per* Griffin J.

applies *a fortiori* to the newly constituted reference procedure. Under the previous legislation, there was a statutory right of appeal to the High Court in relation to a reference, with the determination of first instance being made by An Bord Pleanála. The legislation now provides for the appeal to be to An Bord Pleanála. In the circumstances, it is submitted that whatever argument there may have been for suggesting that the enforcement proceedings should await the outcome of the hearing of an appeal to the High Court, there is little reason to suggest that such diffidence be shown to An Bord Pleanála.

15. Contempt of court

7–201   Breach of an order or failure to comply with an undertaking would appear to represent a contempt of court.[245] The House of Lords has suggested in *South Bucks District Council v Porter (No. 1)* that a court should not grant injunctive relief unless prepared, if necessary, to contemplate committing the respondent to prison for breach of the order.[246]

7–202   The decision in *Curley v Galway Corporation*[247] provides a dramatic example of the teeth of the planning injunction. The facts were unusual in that the respondent was itself a local authority: the development was being carried on outside its functional area, and, accordingly, subject to the requirement to obtain planning permission in the ordinary way. Various orders had previously been made under s.27 of the Local Government (Planning & Development) Act 1976 (as amended). An application to attach and commit the manager, and for the sequestration of the local authority's assets, had been brought arising out of breaches of those orders. Kelly J. held that the object of the contempt proceedings was coercive. In the light of undertakings received on oath, and subject to conditions, Kelly J. ruled that it was not necessary or appropriate to make orders of committal or sequestration at that juncture. Kelly J. instead adjourned the application for sequestration on terms and directed the appointment of an independent engineer, at the expense of the respondent local authority, to report to the High Court as to the level of compliance with its obligations under the terms of the existing court order. Kelly J. also imposed a fine of IR£50,000 and directed that the respondent local authority pay costs on a solicitor and own client basis.

7–203   By contrast, in the decision in *Leech v Reilly*,[248] the High Court was prepared to overlook the failure of a respondent to apply to be released formally from his undertaking, in circumstances where such release would have been forthcoming, and where the respondent was attempting to keep an established business in operation, while at the same time coping with legal proceedings and the intervention of the planning authority.

---

[245] *Morris v Garvey* [1982] I.R. 319; [1983] I.L.R.M. 177.
[246] [2003] U.K.H.L. 26; [2003] A.C. 558; [2003] J.P.L. 1412.
[247] Unreported, High Court, Kelly J., March 30, 2001.
[248] Unreported, High Court, O'Hanlon J., April 26, 1983.

It is submitted that a court should not grant injunction under s.160 unless it **7–204** would be prepared to enforce it by the exercise of its contempt jurisdiction where necessary. Reference is made in this regard to the approach adopted by the House of Lords in *South Bucks District Council v Porter*.[249]

> "When granting an injunction the court does not contemplate that it will be disobeyed: *In re Liddell's Settlement Trusts* [1936] Ch 365, 373-374; *Castanho v Brown & Root (UK) Ltd* [1981] AC 557, 574. Apprehension that a party may disobey an order should not deter the court from making an order otherwise appropriate: there is not one law for the law-abiding and another for the lawless and truculent. When making an order, the court should ordinarily be willing to enforce it if necessary. The rule of law is not well served if orders are made and disobeyed with impunity. These propositions however rest on the assumption that the order made by the court is just in all the circumstances and one with which the defendant can and reasonably ought to comply, an assumption which ordinarily applies both when the order is made and when the time for enforcement arises. Since a severe financial penalty may be imposed for failure to comply with an enforcement notice, the main additional sanction provided by the grant of an injunction is that of imprisonment. The court should ordinarily be slow to make an order which it would not at that time be willing, if need be, to enforce by imprisonment. But imprisonment in this context is intended not to punish but to induce compliance, reinforcing the requirement that the order be one with which the defendant can and reasonably ought to comply. […]"

It is submitted that similar considerations should apply before the Irish courts. **7–205**

G. Acquisition of Land for Open Spaces

A special enforcement mechanism is prescribed in respect of a breach of an **7–206** obligation under planning permission to provide or maintain open space.[250] In summary, a planning authority is empowered to acquire the open space land compulsorily. Special rules apply in respect of the amount of compensation payable. In particular, a nil award will generally have to be made on the assumption that the owner will recover, as a result of the development and the disposal of the balance of the lands, an amount equal to the value of the open space land at the time when the application for the planning permission was made.

1. Obligation to provide or maintain open space

The power to acquire land for open space applies where development is being **7–207** or has been carried out pursuant to a planning permission, and one or other of the following two qualifications is met.

---

[249] [2003] U.K.H.L. 26, [32]; [2003] 2 A.C. 558.
[250] PDA 2000, s.45.

(i) A condition requiring the provision or maintenance of land as open space was attached to the permission, or

(ii) It was either explicit or implicit in the application for planning permission that land would be provided or maintained as open space.

7–208 The power to acquire applies to any form of open space (whether referred to as open space or by any other description in the relevant application for planning permission or in a condition attached to the relevant permission), being land which is not described in the application or condition either as private open space or in terms indicating that it is not intended that members of the public are to have resort thereto without restriction.[251]

2. Procedure to enforce obligation to provide or maintain open space

Written request

7–209 As a precursor to the compulsory acquisition of the open space land, the planning authority must first serve on the owner of the land a written request that, within a period specified in the request (being a period of not less than eight weeks commencing on the date of the request), he or she will provide, level, plant or otherwise adapt or maintain the land in a manner so specified, being a manner which in its opinion would make it suitable for the purpose for which the open space was to be provided.[252]

7–210 If the owner fails to comply with, or to secure compliance with, the request within the period so specified, the planning authority may, if it thinks fit, decide to acquire the open space land.

Acquisition notice

7–211 An acquisition notice shall then be published in a newspaper circulating in the district. The acquisition notice shall indicate the planning authority's intention to acquire the land by order, and shall specify a period (being a period of not less than four weeks commencing on the date on which the notice is published) within which an appeal may be made to An Bord Pleanála.

7–212 Where a planning authority publishes an acquisition notice, it shall serve a copy of the notice on the owner of the land to which the notice relates not later than ten days after the date of the publication.[253]

Appeal to An Bord Pleanála

7–213 Any person having an interest in the land to which an acquisition notice relates may within the period specified in the notice appeal to An Bord Pleanála.[254]

---

[251] PDA 2000, s.45(10).
[252] PDA 2000, s.45(1)(c).
[253] PDA 2000, s.45(2).
[254] PDA 2000, s.45(3).

An Bord Pleanála may (a) annul the acquisition notice to which the appeal relates, or (b) confirm the acquisition notice, with or without modification, in respect of all or such part of the relevant land as An Bord Pleanála considers reasonable.

Vesting order

If an acquisition notice becomes effective (whether as a result of no appeal being taken; an appeal being withdrawn; or the acquisition notice being confirmed by An Bord Pleanála), the planning authority may make an order in the prescribed form which order shall be expressed and shall operate to vest the land to which the acquisition notice, or, where appropriate, the acquisition notice as confirmed, relates in the planning authority on a specified date for all the estate, term or interest for which immediately before the date of the order the land was held by the owner, together with all rights and liabilities which, immediately before that date, were enjoyed or incurred in connection therewith by the owner together with an obligation to provide or maintain the open space.[255]

7–214

Entry in planning register

A planning authority shall enter in the register (a) particulars of any acquisition notice published by it; (b) the date and effect of any decision on appeal in relation to any such notice; and (c) particulars of any vesting order made, and every entry shall be made within the period of seven days commencing on the day of publication, receipt of notification of the decision or the making of the order, as may be appropriate.[256]

7–215

Compensation

There is a statutory entitlement to claim compensation in respect of the compulsory acquisition of the open space land.[257] In default of agreement, the claim shall be determined by arbitration under the Acquisition of Land (Assessment of Compensation) Act 1919, in the like manner in all respects as if such claim arose in relation to the compulsory acquisition of land, but subject to the proviso that the arbitrator shall have jurisdiction to make a nil award. Special rules apply to the calculation of the amount of compensation, as follows.

7–216

First, the arbitrator is required to make a nil award, unless it is shown by or on behalf of the owner that an amount equal to the value (as of the date of the making of application for planning permission) of the land to which the relevant planning permission relates (i) has not been recovered as a result of the development, and (ii) will not in the future be recoverable as a result of the development by disposing of the balance of the lands to which the planning permission relates.

7–217

---

[255] PDA 2000, s.45(5).
[256] PDA 2000, s.45(9).
[257] PDA 2000, s.45(8).

7–218   It seems that this rule proceeds on the rebuttable presumption that the value of the lands will have increased as a result of the implementation of the planning permission. By definition, the power to acquire compulsorily the open space land will only ever be available where the obligation to provide and maintain open space land arises under a planning permission. The assumption is that the balance of the lands the subject-matter of the planning permission, *i.e.* the lands other than the open space land, will have increased in value as a result of the development. Unless the owner can show that he has not, and will not, recover an amount equal to the value (as of the date of the making of application for planning permission) of the (entire) land to which the relevant planning permission relates, he will receive no compensation.

7–219   The second special rule is that in the assessment of the value of the land no regard shall be had to its value for use other than as open space. Further a deduction shall be made in respect of the cost of carrying out such works (such as levelling or planting) as may be necessary to make the land suitable for the purpose for which the open space was to be provided.

H. Enforcement of Agreements

1. Section 47 agreements

7–220   Although not strictly speaking an enforcement mechanism, it may be appropriate to make brief reference here to the remedies in respect of statutory planning agreements. This form of statutory agreement is discussed in detail at paras 8–247 to 8–261. In short, a planning authority may enter into an agreement with any person interested in land in its area, for the purpose of restricting or regulating the development or use of the land, either permanently or during such period as may be specified by the agreement. Any such agreement may contain such incidental and consequential provisions (including provisions of a financial character) as appear to the planning authority to be necessary or expedient for the purposes of the agreement.[258]

7–221   The unusual feature of these agreements is that they are to run with the land in the sense of their binding subsequent owners. To this extent then, the ordinary rules in relation to privity of contract are disapplied. To achieve this result the legal fiction of a statutory restrictive covenant is employed. It is expressly provided that the agreement may be enforced by the planning authority, or any body joined with it, against persons deriving title under the other party to the agreement as if the planning authority or body, as may be appropriate, was possessed of adjacent land, and as if the agreement had been expressed to be made for the benefit of that land.

---

[258] PDA 2000, s.47.

2. Social and affordable housing

In the ordinary course of events, an applicant is not required to implement a **7–222** planning permission, and, indeed, a number of inconsistent planning permissions may exist in respect of the same lands.[259] The quasi-contractual nature of an agreement in relation to social and affordable housing complicates matters somewhat. As discussed in Chapter 15, a condition may be imposed in respect of certain residential development requiring the applicant to enter into an agreement with respect to the provision of social and affordable housing.

The radical argument might be made that such an agreement has a life of its **7–223** own, and that the developer is bound by same as a matter of contract law. Whereas the condition requiring the agreement can be expected to employ the "prior to commencement of development" formula (that is, to stipulate that the agreement must be finalised before the development commences),[260] and thus leave open the possibility of non-implementation of the planning permission,[261] were a developer to proceed as far as the execution of an agreement, it might be argued that he was obliged to comply with same, and to implement the planning permission. Certainly, it would seem that if a developer were not satisfied with the terms of any proposed agreement, he would be well advised to refuse to execute same. The fact that any dispute as to an agreement may be referred to An Bord Pleanála for determination at the instance of the *planning authority*,[262] and not just at the instance of the developer, suggests that there may be an element of coercion.

---

[259] See, for example, *State (Kenny) v An Bord Pleanála*, unreported, Supreme Court, December 20, 1984.

[260] The *Guidelines for Planning Authorities* provide that "The condition must require that the agreement be finalised before development commences", para.10.4.

[261] *Grampian Regional Council v City of Aberdeen District Council* (1983) 47 P. & C.R. 633.

[262] PDA 2000, s.96(5) (as substituted by the Planning and Development (Amendment) Act 2002).

CHAPTER EIGHT

SPECIAL CONTROLS AND COMPULSORY ACQUISITION OF LAND

A. Protected Structures

1. Introduction

A planning authority is required to include in its development plan a record of **8–01** protected structures.[1] The principal effect of designation as a protected structure is, first, to limit the availability of exempted development,[2] and, secondly, to restrict the discretion of a planning authority and An Bord Pleanála when determining an application for planning permission involving a protected structure.[3] Other consequences of designation as a protected structure include restrictions on the availability of compensation for the refusal of planning permission which would materially affect a protected structure,[4] or for the imposition of conditions relating to protection[5]; and the imposition of a duty on owners and occupiers to ensure that the structure, or any element of it which

---

[1] PDA 2000, s.51.
[2] PDA 2000, s.57(1).
[3] PDA 2000, s.57(10).
[4] PDA 2000, Sch.3, para.3.
[5] PDA 2000, Sch.5, para.34.

contributes to its special architectural, historical, archaeological, artistic, cultural, scientific, social or technical interest, is not endangered.[6] Finally, provision is made for the acquisition of a protected structure,[7] and for notices requiring restoration of the character of protected structures.[8]

8–02 One of the unusual features of the legislation in this regard is that many of the provisions apply equally to a *proposed* protected structure, as to a protected structure.[9] The provisions in this regard thus provide an example of a situation where the terms of a draft development plan have immediate legal effect.

2. Definition of "protected structure"

8–03 "Structure" is defined as any building, structure, excavation, or other thing constructed or made on, in or under any land, or any part of a structure so defined, and (a) where the context so admits, includes the land on, in or under which the structure is situate, and (b) in relation to a protected structure or proposed protected structure includes (i) the interior of the structure; (ii) the land lying within the curtilage of the structure; (iii) any other structures lying within that curtilage and their interiors; and (iv) all fixtures and features which form part of the interior or exterior of any structure or structures referred to in sub-paragraph (i) or (iii).[10]

8–04 At first blush, this definition might suggest that where any part of a structure is included in the record of protected structures, then the entire of the structure (as artificially defined) is included. That this is not so, however, is made clear on a reading of the definition of "protected structure" itself. "Protected structure" means (a) a structure, or (b) a *specified part* of a structure, which is included in a record of protected structures, and, where that record so indicates, includes any specified feature which is within the attendant grounds of the structure and which would not otherwise be included in this definition.[11] This definition confirms that the designation as a protected structure extends only to that part of a structure which is in the opinion of the planning authority of interest under one of the heads set out earlier above, and, so specified in the record of protected structures.[12]

---

[6] PDA 2000, s.58.

[7] PDA 2000, s.71.

[8] PDA 2000, s.60.

[9] The following are not applicable to a *proposed* protected structure: (i) the declaration procedure under s.57; (ii) endangerment and restoration notices under ss.59 and 60; and (iii) the powers of compulsory acquisition under s.71.

[10] PDA 2000, s.2.

[11] PDA 2000, s.2.

[12] cf. *Begley v An Bord Pleanála*, unreported, High Court, Ó Caoimh J., January 14, 2003. The extent of the judgment was clarified in a subsequent ruling on an application for leave to appeal to the Supreme Court: unreported, High Court, Ó Caoimh J., May 23, 2003. In this latter judgment, Ó Caoimh J. disavowed any suggestion that the earlier judgment entailed a finding that "a specified part of a structure" necessarily included the curtilage of the structure, such that the curtilage could not be excluded from the "protected structure".

This interpretation is borne out by the Ministerial guidelines of 2005, which **8–05** recognise that it is possible to protect part only of a structure. The guidelines go on, however, to recommend that consideration be given to extending protection to the entire structure.[13]

> "Although it is possible to give protection to part only of a structure, the initial assessment should include the whole of the structure including the interior and rear of the structure, the land within its curtilage and any structures in the curtilage before it is established that only a specified part of the structure is worthy of protection. Where only a part of a structure is currently listed for protection, consideration should be given to extending protection to the entire structure. For example, where the protected structure is a plaque, a shopfront or a façade, the entire structure of which the element is part may also be of interest and worthy of protection. The protection of a façade alone should generally only be considered where there is no surviving interior of any interest, for example where the building has previously been gutted and the façade is the only remaining feature of the original historic building. Generally a façade relates integrally to its building, which may retain interior detail of note including, for example, the original spatial plan, shop-fittings or decorative elements such as chimneypieces, staircases, window shutters or cornices. Elements of the external envelope and/or within the curtilage may also be of intrinsic interest and worthy of protection; these might include the roof, the rear elevation, outbuildings or other site features."

3. Record of protected structures

For the purpose of protecting structures, or parts of structures, which form part **8–06** of the architectural heritage and which are of special architectural, historical, archaeological, artistic, cultural, scientific, social or technical interest, every development plan shall include a record of protected structures, and shall include in that record every structure which is, in the opinion of the planning authority, of such interest within its functional area.[14] Subject to any additions or deletions made to the record, a record of protected structures shall continue to be part of that plan or any variation or replacement of the plan.

The form of a record of protected structures is prescribed under the Planning **8–07** and Development Regulations 2001.[15] A record of protected structures shall contain (a) in respect of each protected structure (i) an identifying number and (ii) an address; (b) one or more maps showing the location of each protected structure to a scale that enables clear identification of such structures; and (c) any other information that the planning authority considers necessary. The Ministerial guidelines make the following recommendations as to the form of the record of protected structures.[16]

> "The RPS should be clear and comprehensible. All protected structures within the functional area of a planning authority should be referred to in a single

---

[13] Architectural Heritage Protection – Guidelines for Planning Authorities (2005), §2.5.2.
[14] PDA 2000, s.51.
[15] Planning and Development Regulations 2001, art.51.
[16] Architectural Heritage Protection – Guidelines for Planning Authorities (2005), §2.8.2.

numbered list, ordered alphabetically by postal address, with each structure given a reference number unique in that planning authority area. For the sake of clarity there should be no organisational subdivision of the RPS into separate lists, for example of industrial heritage, houses, bridges, or for different geographical areas, or by perceived importance like 'national', 'regional' or 'local' (even if these are indicated by the NIAH), as this could lead to misunderstandings. Such categorisations or typologies, may, of course, be referred to, but should not be used to organise the list."

4. Criteria for including structures in record of protected structures

8–08   There is little guidance provided under the PDA 2000 as to the criteria to be taken into account in deciding whether or not to include a particular structure in the record of protected structures. It is *implicit* from the terms of s.51 that the structure must be of special architectural, historical, archaeological, artistic, cultural, scientific, social or technical interest, but beyond that no guidance is provided under the primary legislation. Instead, it is necessary to resort to the guidelines issued by the Minister for the Environment, Heritage and Local Government in 2005.

8–09   The legitimacy of leaving over the criteria to be dealt with by Ministerial guidelines must be in doubt. First, there is a question mark over the circumstances in which the guidelines came to be issued by the Minister for the Environment, Heritage and Local Government. Section 52 of the PDA 2000 indicates that guidelines identifying the criteria to be applied when selecting proposed protected structures for inclusion in the record of protected structures were to be issued by the Minister for Arts, Heritage, Gaeltacht and the Islands, following consultation with what was then known as the Minister for the Environment and Local Government. Heritage functions were transferred to the Minister for the Environment, Heritage and Local Government in 2002.[17] The fact that the separate functions of issuing the guidelines and consultation now reside in the one person, namely the Minister for the Environment, Heritage and Local Government, might be thought to offend against the principle confirmed in *Mulcreevy v Minister for the Environment, Heritage and Local Government*[18] that procedural safeguards provided for under primary legislation cannot be amended by way of secondary or delegated legislation. The safeguard of a requirement that there be consultation with a separate Minister before guidelines be issued has, in effect, been removed as a result of secondary legislation transferring Ministerial functions.

8–10   This first objection is somewhat technical, and it might well be argued that the objective of requiring consultation with the (then) Minister for the Environment and Local Government was simply to ensure that that Minister had an input in the drawing up of the guidelines. Such an objective is, arguably, now spent

---

[17] Heritage (Transfer of Departmental Administration and Ministerial Functions) Order 2002 (S.I. 356 of 2002).

[18] [2004] 1 I.R. 72; [2004] 1 I.L.R.M. 419.

given that the Minister for the Environment, Heritage and Local Government issues the guidelines himself. A much more substantial objection to the use of guidelines to set out the criteria for designating protected structures is as follows.

There are strong grounds for saying that the provisions of the legislation in this regard offend against the constitutional requirement under Art.15 that the Oireachtas be the sole law making body. Whereas it is permissible to allow matters of detail to be left over to be dealt with by secondary or delegated legislation, it is well established that the parent Act must specify the underlying policy and principles.[19] The language used under Pt IV of the PDA 2000 is very vague, and thus leaves a largely unreviewable discretion to the Minister in drawing up the guidelines. **8–11**

The point may be illustrated by the notion of a structure being designated by reference to its "social" interest. The primary legislation simply uses the word "social" without any guidance as to what this might involve. Thus, it is, in effect, left to the Ministerial guidelines to define the term. **8–12**

> "The characteristic of special social interest embraces those qualities for which a structure, a complex or an area has become a focus of spiritual, political, symbolic or other sentiment to any group of people. A community may have an attachment to a place because it is an essential reference point for that community's identity, whether as a meeting place or a place of tradition, ritual or ceremony. The configuration, disposition or layout of a space or group of structures, where they facilitate behaviour that would otherwise be difficult or impossible, may be of social interest. This category of special interest may sometimes not be directly related to the physical fabric of a particular structure or structures and may survive physical alteration. Care should be taken to recognise the pattern or internal relations of the parts of the structure that constitute its special interest, in order to ensure that they be conserved."

In addition to including in guidelines the criteria to be applied when selecting proposed protected structures, the Minister is also required to give guidelines concerning development objectives (a) for protecting structures, or parts of structures which are of special architectural, historical, archaeological, artistic, cultural, scientific, social or technical interest and (b) for preserving the character of architectural conservation areas. **8–13**

5. Recommendations by Minister for Environment Heritage and Local Government

Under s.53 of the PDA 2000,[20] the Minister for the Environment, Heritage and Local Government may make recommendations to a planning authority **8–14**

---

[19] *Cityview Press v An Comhairle Oiliúna* [1980] I.R. 381. Recent examples of the application of this precedent include *O'Neill v Minister for Agriculture* [1998] 1 I.R. 539; *Laurentiu v Minister for Justice Equality and Law Reform* [1999] 4 I.R. 26; and *Leontjava v Director of Public Prosecutions* [2004] 1 I.R. 591.

[20] See also Heritage (Transfer of Departmental Administration and Ministerial Functions) Order 2002 (S.I. 356 of 2002).

concerning the inclusion in its record of protected structures of any of the following (a) particular structures; (b) specific parts of particular structures; or (c) specific features within the attendant grounds of particular structures.

8–15 A planning authority is required to have regard to any recommendations made to it in this regard. It is important to emphasise, however, that the ultimate decision as to whether or not to include a particular structure in the record of protected structures lies with the planning authority, and not with the Minister. If a planning authority decides not to comply with a recommendation from the Minister, then the planning authority is required under s.53(3) to inform the Minister in writing of the reasons for its decision.

6. Additions or deletions to record of protected structures

New development plan

8–16 An addition to or deletion from the record of protected structures may be made either as part of the making of a new development plan under Pt II of the PDA 2000, or at any other time. If the addition or deletion is made as part of the making of the development plan, then the procedure provided in that regard is to be followed. This procedure is discussed generally at paras 1–121 to 1–139. In particular, it will be necessary under s.12(3) to give notice to the owner or occupier of the proposed protected structure or the protected structure, as the case may be.

Addition or deletion made at any other time

8–17 In the case of an addition or deletion made at any other time, the procedure prescribed under s.55 is to be followed. There is extensive provision in this regard for public participation. In addition to notifying the owner and occupier, the planning authority must send particulars of the proposed addition or deletion to the Minister for the Environment, Heritage and Local Government and to the prescribed bodies.[21] Notice must be published in at least one newspaper circulating in the planning authority's functional area.

8–18 The particulars of the proposed addition or deletion are to be put on public display for a specified period of not less than six weeks. Any person may make written submissions or observations with respect to the proposed addition or deletion to the planning authority within the specified period. Before making the proposed addition or deletion, the planning authority shall (a) consider any written submissions or observations received, and (b) have regard to any observations received from the Minister. The planning authority must decide whether or not the proposed addition or deletion should be made within twelve weeks after the end of the period allowed for public inspection.

---

[21] Planning and Development Regulations 2001, art.52 (as amended in 2006). The prescribed bodies include the Heritage Council; An Taisce; An Comhairle Ealaíon; Fáilte Ireland; and the appropriate chamber of commerce.

It is to be noted that, in contrast to the position obtaining in relation to the 8–19 procedure for the making or variation of a development plan (including the record of protected structures), there is no express provision to the effect that a person shall not question the validity of an addition or deletion by reason only that the specified procedures were not completed within the time required. Accordingly, it would seem, in theory at least, that the decision to add or delete might be vulnerable to judicial review on the basis that the time-limits were not complied with.

7. Registration as burden

Provision is made under s.56 for the registration of the fact of inclusion in the 8–20 record of protected structures as a burden affecting registered land. This would seem to be a sensible precaution in that it ensures that any subsequent purchaser of the land is on constructive notice of the designation as a protected structure.

8. Exempted development

The principal effect of designation as a protected structure is that certain types 8–21 of exempted development may not be carried out in respect of the structure. Section 57(1) provides as follows.

> "Notwithstanding section 4(1)(h), the carrying out of works to a protected structure, or a proposed protected structure, shall be exempted development only if those works would not materially affect the character of—
> (a) the structure, or
> (b) any element of the structure which contributes to its special architectural, historical, archaeological, artistic, cultural, scientific, social or technical interest."

On a literal reading of the section, it is submitted that the opening words 8–22 "notwithstanding section 4(1)(h)" govern the entire of what follows and, accordingly, the qualification on the availability of exempted development is confined to that class of exempted development. If this literal interpretation is correct, then it produces the anomalous result that, whereas one particular form of exempted development is heavily qualified, the full gamut of the classes of exempted development under the Planning and Development Regulations 2001 is nevertheless open. This is because, unlike the position obtaining in relation to a structure located in an architectural conservation area,[22] there is no qualification imposed under the Regulations themselves in respect of works to a protected structure or a proposed protected structure.

Under s.2 of the PDA 2000, "works" includes any act or operation of 8–23 construction, excavation, demolition, extension, alteration, repair or renewal and, in relation to a protected structure or proposed protected structure, includes

---

[22] Planning and Development Regulations 2001, art.9(1)(a)(xii).

any act or operation involving the application or removal of plaster, paint, wallpaper, tiles or other material to or from the surfaces of the interior or exterior of a structure.

9. Declaration as to works not materially affecting character of structure

8–24   The terms of s.57 are subjective, and the owner or occupier of a protected structure may well find it difficult to assess whether or not proposed works will materially affect the character of any element of the structure which contributes to its special architectural, historical, archaeological, artistic, cultural, scientific, social or technical interest. Presumably in recognition of this difficulty, and in ease of developers, an owner or occupier may make a written request to a planning authority to issue a "declaration" as to the type of works which it considers would or would not materially affect the character of the structure or any element of the structure.

8–25   The procedure in this regard is as follows. A planning authority is required to issue a declaration within twelve weeks after receiving a request, or within such other period as may be prescribed. Before issuing a declaration, a planning authority shall have regard to (a) the guidelines issued by the Minister under s.52, and (b) any recommendations made to the planning authority by the Minister.

8–26   The Ministerial guidelines indicate that it is not necessary for the applicant to have any specific works in mind when applying for a declaration, and go on to suggest that if the owner or occupier is contemplating major works to a protected structure, pre-planning discussions with the planning authority may be advisable and, depending on the outcome, the submission of a planning application may be required.[23]

Referral to An Bord Pleanála

8–27   A right of referral to An Bord Pleanála against both an initial declaration, and against any review of a declaration, is introduced under the Planning and Development (Amendment) Act 2002.[24] More specifically, any person to whom a declaration or a reviewed declaration has been issued may refer the declaration for review by An Bord Pleanála within four weeks from the date of the issuing of the declaration, or the declaration as reviewed, as the case may be.[25]

Places of worship

8–28   If the declaration relates to a protected structure that is regularly used as a place of public worship, the planning authority and An Bord Pleanála, in

---

[23] Architectural Heritage Protection – Guidelines for Planning Authorities, §4.15.

[24] Planning and Development (Amendment) Act 2002, s.13.

[25] PDA 2000, s.57(8) (as amended).

addition to having regard to the guidelines and recommendations referred to at para.8–25 above, shall respect liturgical requirements, and for the purpose of ascertaining those requirements shall comply with the guidelines concerning consultation issued by the Minister.

The Ministerial guidelines contain the following advice on declarations in respect of places of worship.[26] **8–29**

> "Many factors should be considered by a planning authority before issuing a declaration as to the type of works it considers would or would not materially affect the character of a protected structure that is regularly used as a place of public worship. The basic considerations are the effects, if any, of proposed works on the special interest of the structure, including its interior, and whether proposed alterations are necessitated by the liturgical requirements of worship. Planning authorities should consider whether any substantial structural changes or alterations to the existing plan-form are required for the proposed alterations, for example, the subdivision of important existing spaces, as well as any consequential effects in other parts of the building. Any proposed removal or alteration/ destruction of important fixtures and fittings, for example galleries, box pews or fixed seating will require careful consideration. The age, rarity and craftsmanship of the internal fixtures and fittings can contribute to the architectural coherence of the whole building and, even where not original to the building, the internal fixtures and fittings can be an important part of a later remodelling of the interior. Impact on decoration, for example any interesting decorative schemes such as stencilled decoration, tiling or panelling, should be taken into account. It would also be appropriate to consider any proposals to minimise the impact of proposed changes. Any proposals to store or salvage fixtures and fittings proposed for removal should also be assessed carefully."

Legal effect of a declaration

It is expressly provided that development consisting only of works of a type in respect of which a declaration has issued shall not be considered to be a breach of the statutory duty imposed on an owner and occupier to ensure that a protected structure, or any element thereof, is not endangered.[27] The precise legal effect of a declaration under s.57 is otherwise unclear. **8–30**

Although the fact that the planning authority has issued a declaration indicating that particular works would not fall foul of the qualification on exempted development under s.57(1) would presumably create an estoppel precluding the planning authority from taking any enforcement action in this regard, there would appear to be no express provision which would prevent a third party from taking enforcement action. **8–31**

---

[26] Architectural Heritage Protection – Guidelines for Planning Authorities, §5.2.4.
[27] It is expressly provided under PDA 2000, s.58(3) that, *inter alia*, development consisting only of works of a type in respect of which a declaration has issued shall not be considered to be a breach of the duty imposed on an owner and occupier to ensure that a protected structure, or any element thereof, is not endangered.

8–32 It should also be noted that a declaration under s.57 may be short-lived. More specifically, a planning authority may at any time review a declaration issued under s.57, but the review shall not affect any works carried out in reliance on the declaration prior to the review.[28] Although a review of a declaration does not have retrospective effect in the sense of condemning works already carried out, in practice the fact that a declaration is open to review may cause difficulties for conveyancing. More particularly, it may be that a prospective purchaser can take little comfort from the existence of a declaration that certain intended works would not require planning permission and, accordingly, may be unwilling to expend monies in this regard.

Section 5 reference

8–33 As a result of amendments introduced under the Planning and Development (Amendment) Act 2002, it seems now that the declaration procedure prevails over the more general reference procedure under s.5 of the PDA 2000. Section 5 establishes a procedure whereby questions as to development, and exempted development, may be referred, in the first instance, to the planning authority for determination, subject to an appeal to An Bord Pleanála. The procedure in this regard is discussed at para.10–01 and onwards.

8–34 Prior to the amendments introduced under the Planning and Development (Amendment) Act 2002, it had been expressly provided that a declaration shall not prejudice the application of s.5 to any question that arises as to what, in a particular case, is or is not exempted development.[29] This gave rise to a concern that a declaration under s.57 was liable to be upset by a determination on a Section 5 reference. As a result of the amendments, a right of referral against a declaration (or reviewed declaration) has since been introduced, and the proviso that a declaration shall not prejudice the application of s.5 has been deleted. The present position would therefore seem to be that the Section 5 reference procedure does not apply to any question involving the carrying out of works to a protected structure.

10. Relevant considerations on application for planning permission

8–35 The protected status of a structure (whether a protected structure or a proposed protected structure) is expressly stated to be a matter to which a planning authority or An Bord Pleanála shall have regard. Moreover, it is also provided that a planning authority, or An Bord Pleanála on appeal, shall not grant planning permission for the demolition of a protected structure or a proposed protected structure, save in exceptional circumstances.[30]

---

[28] PDA 2000, s.57(7).

[29] PDA 2000, s.57(9), as originally enacted.

[30] PDA 2000, s.57(10). In *Illium Properties Ltd. v Dublin City Council* [2004] I.E.H.C. 327; unreported, O'Leary J., October 15, 2004, the High Court criticised the use of a request for further information in this regard. The High Court held that if the information

Special provision is made in respect of a protected structure which is regularly **8–36** used as a place of worship.[31] When considering an application for planning permission for the development of land which (a) relates to the interior of a protected structure, and (b) is regularly used as a place of public worship, the planning authority, and An Bord Pleanála on appeal, shall, in addition to any other requirements of the PDA 2000, respect liturgical requirements.

11. Duty to ensure protected structure or proposed protected structure not endangered

There is a general obligation imposed under s.58 on an owner and occupier to **8–37** ensure that a protected structure is not endangered. More specifically, each owner and each occupier shall, to the extent consistent with the rights and obligations arising out of their respective interests in a protected structure or a proposed protected structure, ensure that the structure, or any element of it which contributes to its special architectural, historical, archaeological, artistic, cultural, scientific, social or technical interest, is not endangered.

It is expressly provided under s.58(3) that neither of the following shall be **8–38** considered to be a breach of this duty: (a) development in respect of which planning permission has been granted; and (b) development consisting only of works of a type in respect of which a declaration under s.57 has been made.

Under s.58(4) any person, who, without lawful authority, causes damage to a **8–39** protected structure or a proposed protected structure shall be guilty of an offence. It is expressly provided that, without prejudice to any other defence that may be available, it shall be a good defence to prove that the damage to the structure resulted from works which were (a) urgently required in order to secure the preservation of the structure or any part of it; (b) undertaken in good faith solely for the purpose of temporarily safeguarding the structure; and (c) unlikely to permanently alter the structure or any (contributing) element of it.

12. Endangerment notice and restoration notice

Detailed provision is made under Pt IV of the PDA 2000 for two distinct types **8–40** of notice. The first, under s.59, is a notice specifying the works which the planning authority considers necessary in order to prevent the protected structure becoming or continuing to be endangered (hereinafter referred to in shorthand as an "endangerment notice"). The second, under s.60, is in relation to works

---

as submitted with the application did not demonstrate "exceptional circumstances" then planning permission should have been refused, rather than further information sought. The judgment in *O'Brien v Dun Laoghaire Rathdown County Council* [2006] I.E.H.C. 177; unreported, O'Neill J., June 1, 2006, suggests that express reference should be made to any exceptional grounds in the planning reports: the case was ultimately dismissed on the basis that the applicant had not demonstrated a "substantial interest".

[31] PDA 2000, s.57(6).

required to be carried out for the purposes of restoring a structure or any of its elements, which, in the opinion of the planning authority, ought to be restored (hereinafter referred to in shorthand as a "restoration notice").

8–41   The single most significant point of distinction between the two types of notice seems to be that, in the case of a restoration notice, the planning authority shall pay any expenses that are reasonably incurred in carrying out the works other than works that relate to an unauthorised structure which has been constructed, erected or made seven years or less prior to the service of the notice.[32] In the case of an endangerment notice, the planning authority has a *discretion* to provide assistance in any form it considers appropriate, including advice, financial aid, materials, equipment and the services of the planning authority's staff.[33] It should be noted, however, that one of the prescribed grounds of appeal against an endangerment notice is that compliance with the requirements of same would involve unreasonable expense and that the person had stated in representations made to the planning authority that he or she did not have the means to pay.[34]

Resisting an endangerment notice or restoration notice

8–42   A person served with either a restoration notice or an endangerment notice has, in effect, two opportunities to resist same. First, there is provision for making representations to the planning authority before a notice becomes effective. More specifically, a planning authority is required to serve what amounts in practice to notice of an intention to serve a notice, prior to the notice becoming effective. Having served a notice, a planning authority must allow a period for the making of representations, and it is only after considering any representations made that the planning authority may confirm, amend or revoke the notice. The time for appealing to the District Court runs from the date of notification of confirmation or amendment of a notice. Accordingly, it would seem that it is only when a notice has been confirmed or amended by a planning authority that it first has legal effect: even then, a notice is not fully effective until either the period allowed for an appeal has expired without an appeal having been taken, or in the event that an appeal has been taken, until the date on which the decision of the District Court is pronounced, or the date on which that order is expressed to take effect, whichever is later.

8–43   The second opportunity to resist the notice is by way of an appeal to the District Court. Notice of an appeal shall be given to the planning authority, and it shall be entitled to appear, be heard and adduce evidence on the hearing of the appeal. The grounds of appeal are set out under s.61 as follows.

---

[32] By necessary implication from PDA 2000, s.60(3)(e).
[33] By necessary implication from PDA 2000, s.59(2).
[34] PDA 2000, s.61(1)(b).

(a) That the person is not the owner or occupier of the structure in respect of which the notice has been served;

(b) That, in the case of an endangerment notice, compliance with the requirements of the notice would involve unreasonable expense, and that the person had stated in representations made to the planning authority that he or she did not have the means to pay;

(c) That the person has already taken all reasonable steps to (i) in the case of an endangerment notice, prevent the structure from becoming or continuing to be endangered; (ii) in the case of a restoration notice, restore the character of the structure or the element; or (iii) in the case of a restoration notice in relation to a structure that forms a place, area, group of structures or townscape, assist in restoring the character of that place, area, group of structures or townscape as the case may be;

(d) That the time for complying with the notice is unreasonably short.

On the hearing of the appeal, the District Court may, as it thinks proper (a) **8–44** confirm the notice unconditionally; (b) confirm the notice subject to such modifications or additions as the District Court thinks reasonable; or (c) annul the notice.

13. Enforcement

It is an offence to fail to comply with an endangerment notice.[35] **8–45**

In the event of a failure to comply with either an endangerment notice or a **8–46** restoration notice, the planning authority has an option to carry out itself works to the protected structure. More specifically, where a person on whom a planning authority has served a notice fails to comply with the notice, the planning authority may take such steps as it considers reasonable and necessary to give effect to the terms of the notice including (a) entry on land by authorised persons, and (b) the carrying out, or the arranging of the carrying out, of the works specified in the notice.[36] The planning authority can recover (whether as a simple contract debt in a court of competent jurisdiction or otherwise) any expenses reasonably incurred by the planning authority from the owner or occupier.[37]

14. Access to lands

Detailed provision is made to ensure that the requirement to comply with either **8–47** an endangerment, or a restoration, notice is not frustrated by a denial of access or entry to the lands. For example, under s.64 it is expressly provided that any

---

[35] PDA 2000, s.63.
[36] PDA 2000, s.69.
[37] PDA 2000, s.70.

person who is the owner of the land or structure in respect of which a notice has been served, and his or her servants or agents, may enter that land or structure and carry out the works required under the notice. This is, presumably, intended to meet any difficulties which might otherwise arise as a result of the land being in the occupation of a person other than the owner (for example, a lessee). Under s.65, provision is made whereby an application can be made to the District Court where a person served with a notice is unable, without the consent of another person, to carry out the works required under the notice and that other person withholds consent. The District Court may, at its discretion, deem that consent to have been given, and, in that case, the person making the application shall be entitled to carry out the works required under the notice.

8–48   Under s.67, a person who has been served with an endangerment notice, and who has carried out the works required under the notice, may apply to a court of competent jurisdiction for an order directing that all, or such part as may be specified in the order, of the cost of those works be borne by some other person who has an interest in the structure concerned.

15. Compulsory acquisition of protected structure

8–49   A planning authority may acquire, by agreement or compulsorily, any protected structure situated within its functional area if it appears to the planning authority that it is necessary to do so for the protection of the structure.[38] It should be noted that the power to acquire a structure compulsorily (as opposed to by agreement) is confined to where the structure is not lawfully occupied as a dwelling house by any person other than a person employed as a caretaker.[39]

8–50   For the purposes of the statutory provisions concerning acquisition, the concept of a "protected structure" bears an extended meaning. More specifically, in this context, a reference to a "protected structure" shall be construed to include a reference to any land which (a) forms part of the attendant ground of that structure, and (b) is, in the planning authority's opinion, necessary to secure the protection of that structure, whether or not the land lies within the curtilage of the structure or is specified as a feature in the record of protected structures.[40]

Notice of intention to acquire protected structure compulsorily

8–51   A planning authority is required to serve notice of an intention to acquire a protected structure compulsorily on every owner, lessee and occupier (except tenants for one month or a period less than one month) of the structure.[41] In this context "owner" in relation to a protected structure means (a) a person, other than a mortgagee not in possession, who is for the time being entitled to

---

[38] PDA 2000, s.71(1).
[39] PDA 2000, s.71(1)(b).
[40] PDA 2000, s.71(2).
[41] PDA 2000, s.72(1)(b).

dispose (whether in possession or reversion) of the fee simple of the protected structure, and (b) a person who, under a lease or agreement the unexpired term of which exceeds five years, holds or is entitled to the rents or profits of the protected structure.[42]

The planning authority is also required to give public notice in one or more newspapers circulating in its functional area.[43]   **8–52**

A period of not less than four weeks is to be allowed for the making of objections to the acquisition of the structure.   **8–53**

Objection to compulsory acquisition of protected structure

The right to object to a proposed compulsory acquisition appears to be confined to a person on whom a notice of the proposed compulsory acquisition has been served. This would thus seem to limit the right of objection to an owner, lessee or occupier (as defined). See para.8–51 above.   **8–54**

Where an objection is submitted, and is not withdrawn, it is necessary for the planning authority to obtain the consent of An Bord Pleanála to the compulsory acquisition. An Bord Pleanála may, as it thinks fit, grant or refuse to grant consent to the compulsory acquisition of all or part of a protected structure. Again, as in the case of a conventional compulsory purchase order (see para.8–419 and onwards, the legislation is silent as to the precise considerations which An Bord Pleanála is to have regard to in making its decision.   **8–55**

An application for such consent shall be made within four weeks after the expiry of the time allowed by the planning authority for submitting an objection to that acquisition. The planning authority is entitled to submit its comments (if any) on the objection to An Bord Pleanála. On receipt of the planning authority's comments (if any) on the objection, An Bord Pleanála shall, by notice served on the person who made the objection, send a copy of the comments to that person who may, within three weeks from the date of the service of the notice, make observations to An Bord Pleanála in relation to the comments.   **8–56**

16. Order under sanitary services legislation

The fact of designation as a protected structure or a proposed protected structure has implications for the exercise of the powers of a sanitary authority under the Local Government (Sanitary Services) Act 1964. Under s.3(1), a sanitary authority is empowered to serve a notice in relation to dangerous structures. The notice may require works (including demolition works) to be carried out.   **8–57**

---

[42] PDA 2000, s.72(2).
[43] PDA 2000, s.72(1)(a).

The use of this power in relation to buildings which were, in the lexicon of the previous legislation, "listed buildings" had proved controversial. Perhaps the most dramatic example is that of the demolition of Turvey House.

8–58   Section 79 of the PDA 2000 requires that before issuing a notice under s.3(1) of the Local Government (Sanitary Services) Act 1964 in respect of a protected structure or a proposed protected structure, a sanitary authority shall consider (a) the protected status of the structure, and (b) whether, instead of a notice under s.3(1) of that Act, an endangerment notice should be issued or a notice issued under s.11 of the Derelict Sites Act 1990.

8–59   Under s.79(3) of the PDA 2000, a sanitary authority which carries out works on a protected structure, or a proposed protected structure, under s.3(2) of the Local Government (Sanitary Services) Act 1964, shall as far as possible preserve that structure in as much as the preservation of that structure is not likely to cause a danger to any person or property.

8–60   There are also requirements under s.79 to keep the Minister for Arts, Heritage, Gaeltacht and the Islands informed if he or she had recommended that the structure be protected.

B. Architectural Conservation Areas

8–61   The preservation of an architectural conservation area may be included as an objective of a development plan. More specifically, a planning authority is required to designate an architectural conservation area if of the opinion that the inclusion of an objective to preserve same is necessary for the preservation of the character of the place, area, group of structures or townscape concerned.[44]

8–62   The principal effects of such designation are as follows. First, the availability of exempted development is qualified where the development would consist of the carrying out of works to the exterior of a structure located in an architectural conservation area. More specifically, under s.82 it is provided that notwithstanding s.4(1)(h) the carrying out of works to the exterior of a structure in an architectural conservation area shall be exempted development only if those works would not materially affect the character of the area. The wording of this provision gives rise to the same concerns as those identified at paras 8–21 to 8–22 in relation to the equivalent provision with respect to protected structures. In particular, it is unclear as to whether or not the qualification on the availability of exempted development applies only in respect of the category of exempted development provided for under s.4(1)(h).[45]

---

[44] PDA 2000, s.81.

[45] This is perhaps less important given the express provision of Planning and Development Regulations 2001, art.9(1)(a)(xii).

Secondly, designation as an architectural conservation area is to be a relevant consideration on an application for planning permission.[46] More specifically, in considering an application for planning permission in relation to land situated in an architectural conservation area, a planning authority, or An Bord Pleanála on appeal, shall take into account the material effect (if any) that the proposed development would be likely to have on the character of the architectural conservation area. Thirdly, a planning authority is empowered to acquire (whether by agreement or compulsorily) any land situated within an architectural conservation area provided certain conditions are met.[47] Finally, the payment of compensation is excluded in circumstances where a reason for the refusal of planning permission is that the proposed development would adversely affect an architectural conservation area.[48]

Criteria for an architectural conservation area

The criteria for an architectural conservation area are as follows.[49] The character of a place, area, group of structures or townscapes is of special architectural, historical, archaeological, artistic, cultural, scientific, social or technical interest or value, or contributes to the appreciation of protected structures. **8–63**

It would seem to follow from these criteria that it is not necessary that any particular structure within an architectural conservation area be a protected structure. In other words, whereas none of the individual structures might be of sufficient special architectural, historical, archaeological, artistic, cultural, scientific, social or technical interest as to justify designation, in its own right, as a protected structure, the importance of the sum may be greater than the individual parts and, accordingly, a group of structures might properly be designated as an architectural conservation area. **8–64**

Compulsory acquisition

Under s.83, a planning authority is empowered to acquire (whether by agreement or compulsorily) any land situated within an architectural conservation area provided the following conditions are met. The planning authority must be of the opinion that it is necessary to so do in order to preserve the character of the architectural conservation area, and (i) the condition of the land, or the use to which the land or any structure on the land is being put, detracts, or is likely to detract, to a material degree from the character or appearance of the architectural conservation area, or (ii) the acquisition of land is necessary for the development or renewal of the architectural conservation area or the provision of amenities in the area. It should be noted that the power to acquire a structure compulsorily (as opposed to by agreement) is confined to where the structure is not lawfully **8–65**

---

[46] PDA 2000, s.82(2).
[47] PDA 2000, s.83.
[48] PDA 2000, Sch.4, para.13.
[49] PDA 2000, s.81.

occupied as a dwelling house by any person other than a person employed as a caretaker.[50]

8–66 For the purposes of the statutory provisions concerning acquisition, the concept of a "protected structure" bears an extended meaning. More specifically, in this context, a reference to a "protected structure" shall be construed to include a reference to any land which (a) forms part of the attendant ground of that structure, and (b) is, in the planning authority's opinion, necessary to secure the protection of that structure, whether or not the land lies within the curtilage of the structure or is specified as a feature in the record of protected structures.[51]

8–67 The procedure is as in the case of the compulsory acquisition of a protected structure.[52] See paras 8–51 to 8–56 above.

C. Special Planning Control Scheme
Area of Special Planning Control

1. Introduction

Special planning control scheme

8–68 An enhanced level of protection and control may be achieved over an architectural conservation area by the making of a "special planning control scheme".[53] A special planning control scheme may be made where a planning authority considers that all or part of an architectural conservation area is of special importance to, or as respects, the civic life or the architectural, historical, cultural, or social character of a city or town in which it is situated.[54]

8–69 A scheme shall indicate the period for which the scheme is to remain in force. A scheme may indicate the order in which it is proposed that the objectives of the scheme or provisions for their furtherance or attainment will be implemented.[55]

Area of special planning control

8–70 An architectural conservation area, or that part of an architectural conservation area, to which a special planning control scheme applies is referred to under the legislation as an "area of special planning control".[56]

---

[50] PDA 2000, s.83(2).
[51] PDA 2000, s.71(2) as applied by PDA 2000, s.83(3).
[52] PDA 2000, s.83(3).
[53] PDA 2000, s.85.
[54] PDA 2000, s.84(1).
[55] PDA 2000, s.84(4).
[56] PDA 2000, s.85(8).

2. Legal effects of special planning control

The principal effects of special planning control are as follows. First, any **8–71** development within an area of special planning control shall not be exempted development where it contravenes an approved special planning control scheme applying to that area.[57] Secondly, designation is expressly stated to be a relevant consideration on an application for planning permission. More specifically, when considering an application for planning permission in relation to land situated in an area of special planning control, a planning authority, or An Bord Pleanála on appeal, shall have regard to the provisions of an approved special planning control scheme.[58] The third, and possibly the most radical, effect is this. A planning authority may serve a notice on the owner or occupier of land requiring that specified measures be undertaken for either (i) the restoration, demolition, removal, alteration, replacement, maintenance, repair or cleaning of any structure; or (ii) the discontinuance of any use or the continuance of any use subject to conditions.[59] There is a right of appeal against such a notice to An Bord Pleanála.

3. Relationship between special planning control and development plan

It is an express requirement of the legislation that a special planning control **8–72** scheme be consistent with the objectives of the relevant development plan, any local area plan, or any integrated area plan (within the meaning of the Urban Renewal Act 1998) in force relating to the area to which the scheme relates.[60]

4. Procedure

The procedure for the preparation of a special planning control scheme is **8–73** somewhat similar to that which applies in respect of the preparation of a development plan. Thus, for example, there is provision for public advertisement of the preparation of the scheme; the placing of a draft of the scheme on public display; an entitlement to make submissions or observations on the draft within a specified period; and the preparation by the manger of a report on any submissions or observations received, such report to include the response of the manager to the submissions or observations.

Notice requirements

The planning authority is required to notify, and send copies of the scheme to, **8–74** the Minister for the Environment Heritage and Local Government, An Bord

---

[57] PDA 2000, s.87(1).
[58] PDA 2000, s.87(2).
[59] PDA 2000, s.88.
[60] PDA 2000, s.84(3).

Pleanála and any prescribed persons of the preparation of the scheme.[61] The planning authority is also required to publish notice of the preparation of the scheme in one or more newspapers circulating in the city or town concerned.[62]

Owners and occupiers

8–75   A planning authority is required to notify in writing each person who is the owner or occupier of land thereby affected, where the scheme includes an objective or provision relating to (i) the co-ordination, upgrading or changing of specified shop frontages; (ii) the control of the layout of specified areas, the density, building lines and height of specified structures and the treatment of spaces around and between specified structures; (iii) the control of the design, colour and materials of specified structures; (iv) the promotion of the maintenance, repair or cleaning of specified structures; (v) the control of the use or uses of any specified structure or other land in the area; (vi) the discontinuance of the existing use of any specified structure or other land; (vii) the development or redevelopment of specified derelict or vacant sites; or (viii) the control of specified advertisement structures or of the exhibition of specified advertisements.[63]

8–76   The notice shall specify, *inter alia*, the measures that are required to be undertaken in respect of the structure or other land to ensure compliance with the proposed objective or objectives.[64]

Submissions and observations

8–77   A copy of the scheme is to be kept available for inspection for a period of not less than eight weeks. Submissions or observations may be made in relation to the scheme within the period specified in the notice.

Manager's report

8–78   Not later than twelve weeks after giving notice and, where appropriate, the notification of the owner and occupier, whichever occurs later, the manager of a planning authority shall prepare a report on any submissions or observations received in relation to a scheme prepared and shall submit the report to the elected members of the planning authority for their consideration.[65] The report shall (i) list the persons who made submissions or observations in relation to the scheme; (ii) give a summary of the matters raised in those submissions or observations; and (iii) include the response of the manager to the submissions or observations. In responding to submissions or observations, the manager shall take account of the proper planning and sustainable development of the

---

[61] PDA 2000, s.85(2)(a). As to the requirement to send copies, see *Ó Nualláin v Dublin Corporation* [1999] 4 I.R. 137.

[62] PDA 2000, s.85(2)(b).

[63] PDA 2000, s.85(4).

[64] PDA 2000, s.85(4)(b).

[65] PDA 2000, s.85(5).

area, the statutory obligations of any local authority in the area and any relevant policies or objectives of the Government or of any Minister of the Government.

A planning authority may, after considering a scheme and the report of the manager, by resolution, approve the scheme with or without modifications, or refuse to so approve. Where a planning authority approves a scheme, it shall publish notice thereof in one or more newspapers circulating in the city or town concerned.[66] This notice shall indicate the place or places at which, and times during which, an approved scheme may be inspected (and a copy thereof shall be kept available for inspection accordingly).[67] A planning authority shall send a copy of the scheme to the Minister for the Environment, Heritage and Local Government, An Bord Pleanála and such other persons as may be prescribed. **8–79**

5. Section 88 notices

As indicated above, a planning authority may serve a notice on the owner or occupier of land requiring that specified measures be undertaken for either (i) the restoration, demolition, removal, alteration, replacement, maintenance, repair or cleaning of any structure; or (ii) the discontinuance of any use or the continuance of any use subject to conditions. There is a right of appeal against such a notice to An Bord Pleanála. These notices will be referred to by the shorthand "Section 88 notices". A Section 88 notice may by notice in writing be withdrawn for stated reasons. **8–80**

Procedure

A planning authority is required to serve notice of an intended Section 88 notice on the owner and occupier of land to which an objective or provision of an approved special planning control scheme applies. **8–81**

Contents of notice

A notice shall: **8–82**

(a) refer to the structure or land concerned;

(b) specify the date on which the notice shall come into force;

(c) specify the measures required to be undertaken on the coming into force of the notice including, as appropriate, measures for (i) the restoration, demolition, removal, alteration, replacement, maintenance, repair or cleaning of any structure, or (ii) the discontinuance of any use or the continuance of any use subject to conditions;

(d) invite the person on whom the notice is served, within such period as is specified in the notice (being not less than eight weeks from the date of

---

[66] PDA 2000, s.85(7).
[67] PDA 2000, s.85(9).

service of the notice) to make written representations to the planning authority concerning the notice;

(e) invite the person to enter into discussions with the planning authority, within such period as is specified in the notice (being not less than eight weeks from the date of service of the notice) concerning the matters to which the notice refers and in particular concerning (i) the period within which the measures specified in the notice are to be carried out, and (ii) the provision by the planning authority of advice, materials, equipment, the services of the planning authority's staff or other assistance required to carry out the measures specified in the notice;

(f) specify the period within which, unless otherwise agreed in the discussions entered into pursuant to an invitation in the notice in accordance with paragraph (e), the measures specified in the notice shall be carried out, being a period of not less than eight weeks from the date of the coming into force of the notice;

(g) state that the planning authority shall pay any expenses that are reasonably incurred by that person in carrying out the steps specified in the notice, other than expenses that relate to unauthorised development carried out not more than seven years prior to the service of the notice; and

(h) state that the planning authority shall, by way of compensation, pay to any person who shows that as a result of complying with the notice (i) the value of an interest he or she has in the land or part thereof existing at the time of the notice has been reduced, or (ii) he or she, having an interest in the land at that time, has suffered damage by being disturbed in his or her enjoyment of the structure or other land, a sum equal to the amount of such reduction in value or a sum in respect of the damage suffered.

8–83 If the invitation to enter into discussions is accepted, the planning authority shall take all such measures as may be necessary to enable the discussions concerned to take place.[68]

8–84 After considering any representations made and any discussions held, the planning authority may confirm, amend or revoke the notice and shall notify in writing the person to whom the notice is addressed.[69]

Appeal to An Bord Pleanála

8–85 There is a right of appeal to An Bord Pleanála from a decision to confirm or amend a Section 88 notice. Any person served with a notice may within eight weeks from the date of notification of the confirmation or amendment of the notice appeal to An Bord Pleanála against the notice.[70]

---

[68] PDA 2000, s.88(3).
[69] PDA 2000, s.88(4).
[70] PDA 2000, s.88(5).

In determining an appeal, An Bord Pleanála is required to take into account (a) the proper planning and sustainable development of the area; (b) the provisions of the development plan for the area; (c) any local area plan or integrated area plan (within the meaning of the Urban Renewal Act 1998) in force relating to the area to which the scheme relates, and (d) the provisions of the approved special planning control scheme.

8–86

6. Enforcement of Section 88 notices

Failure to comply with a Section 88 notice has the following consequences. First, under s.91 failure to comply with the requirements of the notice, or causing or permitting (another) person to fail to comply with such a requirement, is an offence.

8–87

Secondly, there is an element of self-help in that under s.89 the planning authority may enter the structure or land and may effect such restoration, demolition, removal, alteration, replacement, maintenance, repair or cleaning as is specified in the notice.

8–88

Thirdly, provision is made under s.90 for the bringing of an application to either the High Court or the Circuit Court for an order directing any person to comply with the notice or to do, or refrain from doing or continuing to do, anything that the court considers necessary or expedient to ensure compliance with the terms of the notice. To an extent, an application under s.90 is somewhat similar to an application for a planning injunction under s.160. For example, the application is to be brought by motion, and the court when considering the matter may make such interim or interlocutory orders, if any, as it considers appropriate. See, generally, para.7–109 and onwards.

8–89

It is submitted that the court would, however, enjoy an even greater discretion under s.90 than it would in the case of the planning injunction under s.160. The primary reason for this is that the requirement to carry out the works specified in the notice, or to discontinue the use or to continue it subject to conditions, would seem always to be contingent on the right of the owner or the occupier to the payment of compensation. The service of a notice in this regard represents a significant interference with property rights and under the Constitution it would seem that just compensation would have to be paid. The situation can, thus, be contrasted with that obtaining in respect of the planning injunction where, by definition, the respondent will be in default in the sense that unauthorised development is involved. The case law makes it clear that even in such circumstances the court has a discretion to withhold relief: see, generally, paras 7–166 to 7–195. This discretion must apply with even greater force in the present context where there is no suggestion of culpability on the part of the owner or occupier of the land. At the very least, it would seem that the court should make its order conditional on the payment of compensation by the planning authority.

8–90

Exempted development

8–91   Under s.92, it is expressly provided that planning permission shall not be required in respect of development required by a notice under s.88, or an order under s.90.

D. Area of Special Amenity

8–92   Under ss.202 and 203 of the PDA 2000, a planning authority is empowered to declare an area to be an area of special amenity. This power is exercisable where, in the opinion of the planning authority, an area should be declared to be an area of special amenity by reason of (a) its outstanding natural beauty or (b) its special recreational value. The Minister for the Environment, Heritage and Local Government may also, if he or she considers it necessary, direct a planning authority to make a special amenity area order.

8–93   The order may state the objective of the planning authority in relation to the preservation or enhancement of the character or special features of the area, including objectives for the prevention or limitation of development in the area. Any order may be revoked or varied by subsequent order. A planning authority may, from time to time, review a special amenity area order for the purpose of deciding whether it is desirable to revoke or amend the order. An order made pursuant to a direction of the Minister for the Environment, Heritage and Local Government shall be revoked or amended only with the consent of the Minister.

1. Effect of special amenity area order

8–94   The principal effects of designation as an area of special amenity are as follows. First, a planning authority, and An Bord Pleanála, are required to have regard to the provisions of any special amenity area order relating to the area in determining an application for planning permission.[71] It had been the position under the previous legislation that the restrictions on granting planning permission in material contravention of the development plan (comprising primarily a requirement to undertake a special procedure involving the passing of a special resolution by three-quarters of the total number of elected members)[72] applied equally to development which would contravene materially a special amenity area order. Although there is no such express requirement under the PDA 2000, it is probable that a similar result is achieved insofar as a development plan is required to include, *inter alia*, objectives for the preservation of amenities: if a planning authority is minded to make a special amenity area order, then presumably the sentiments underlying this should, in

---

[71] PDA 2000, s.34(2)(a)(ii).
[72] Local Government (Planning & Development) Act 1963, s.26(3) (as amended by s.45 of the Local Government Act 1991).

any event, be reflected in the objectives of the development plan. Moreover, under the Roads Act 1993, the National Roads Authority must comply with special requirements before issuing a direction in relation to any works which would, in the opinion of the National Roads Authority, if carried out require a road authority to contravene materially a special amenity area order.[73] See further para.8–351 below.

Secondly, the benefit of certain classes of exempted development is not available where the development would be in an area to which a special amenity area order relates.[74] The classes of exempted development involved include, *inter alia*, the construction, erection, lowering, repair or replacement of any fence or any wall of brick, stone, blocks with decorative finish, other concrete blocks or mass concrete; certain development for industrial purposes; certain development by statutory undertakers; and the exhibition of certain types of advertisement. In addition to the loss of the particular classes of exempted development prescribed under the Planning and Development Regulations 2001,[75] it is open to the planning authority, when making the special amenity area order, to state that any other class of exempted development shall be prevented or limited.[76]   **8–95**

Thirdly, there is a requirement to notify the following bodies of an application for planning permission where it appears to the planning authority that the land or structure is situated in an area of special amenity (whether or not an order has been confirmed): An Chomhairle Ealaíon; Fáilte Ireland; and An Taisce – The National Trust for Ireland.[77]   **8–96**

Fourthly, compensation is not payable where planning permission is refused in respect of development in an area to which a special amenity area order relates.[78]   **8–97**

Local authority development

Curiously, there is no statutory obligation on a local authority itself not to effect development which would materially contravene a special amenity area order.[79]   **8–98**

National Roads Authority

The Roads Act 1993[80] obliges the National Roads Authority to have regard to the provisions of any special amenity area order relating to the area in which a road is, or is to be, situated when performing any function in relation to the   **8–99**

---

[73] Roads Act 1993, s.20(2).
[74] Planning and Development Regulations 2001, art.9(1)(b).
[75] See, in particular, art.9(1)(b).
[76] Planning and Development Regulations 2001, art.9(1)(b)(iv).
[77] Planning and Development Regulations 2001, art.28(1)(a) (as amended by the 2006 Regulations).
[78] PDA 2000, Sch.3, para.6.
[79] *cf.* PDA 2000, s.178.
[80] Roads Act 1993, s.22.

construction or maintenance of a national road, including preparing a draft plan for the construction and maintenance of national roads under s.18.[81] The National Roads Authority also has power, under s.20 of the Roads Act 1993, subject to the procedures described at para.8–351 below, to direct a road authority to carry out specified works in relation to a national road even though the works would constitute a material contravention of a special amenity area order.

2. Special amenity area order procedure

8–100　As appears from the foregoing, it is clear that designation as a special amenity area will have implications for the property rights of the landowners concerned. In this regard, it is to be noted that certain procedural protections are built into the procedure whereby an area becomes designated as a special amenity area.

8–101　There is a requirement under s.203 that a planning authority publish notice of the making of a special amenity area order. This notice should state the fact of the order having been made, and describe the area to which it relates.

8–102　A copy of the order must be put on public display for a period of not less than four weeks. The order is subject to confirmation by An Bord Pleanála (even in cases where no formal objections have been made). Where any objections are duly made to the order and not withdrawn, an oral hearing must be held and the objections considered before the order can be confirmed. An Bord Pleanála may confirm the order, with or without modifications, or refuse to confirm it.

8–103　Perhaps somewhat surprisingly, there does not appear to be any express requirement on a planning authority to give individual notice to landowners affected by a special amenity area order. Nor, indeed, does it appear that there is an express requirement to state the reasons for why it is that the planning authority is of the opinion that the area should be declared to be an area of special amenity. It is submitted, however, by reference to general principles of natural and constitutional justice that an objector is entitled to a statement of reasons from the planning authority, and to know the materials on which the decision is based.[82] Accordingly, it is suggested that an objector should write to the planning authority seeking these reasons and information and, further, in the event that same are not forthcoming, An Bord Pleanála should exercise its powers insofar as it can to compel the planning authority to do so.

---

[81] To date no plan under s.18 of the Roads Act 1993 has been prepared. See, generally, *Condon v Tipperary South Riding County Council*; unreported, High Court, Murphy J., April 2, 2004.

[82] See, for example, *MacPharthalain v Commissioners of Public Works in Ireland* [1994] 3 I.R. 353; [1992] 1 I.R. 111.

E. Landscape Conservation Area

Under s.204 of the PDA 2000, a planning authority may, by order, for the purposes of the preservation of the landscape, designate any area or place within the functional area of the planning authority as a landscape conservation area. **8–104**

The effects of such designation are less dramatic than those applicable to, for example, designation as an architectural conservation area or as a special amenity area. The principal effect is the potential loss of exempted development: notwithstanding any exemption granted under s.4 or under any Regulations, the Minister for the Environment, Heritage and Local Government may prescribe development for the purpose of landscape conservation areas which shall not be exempted development. The planning authority then can, when making a landscape conservation area order, specify in relation to all or any part of the landscape conservation area that any development prescribed by the Minister shall be considered not to be exempted development in that area. **8–105**

The second principal effect would seem to be this: the statutory entitlement to compensation is excluded where a reason for the refusal of planning permission was that the proposed development would adversely affect a landscape conservation area.[83] **8–106**

Perhaps somewhat surprisingly, the payment of compensation is also excluded where a reason for the refusal of planning permission is that the proposed development would interfere with the character of the landscape or with a view or prospect of special amenity value or natural interest or beauty, any of which it is necessary to preserve.[84] One might be forgiven for thinking that, in circumstances where a planning authority has an express power to designate an area as a landscape conservation area, the exclusion of compensation by reference to matters related to the character of the landscape should be confined to those cases where the necessity for the preservation of the landscape has been identified under a landscape conservation area order. **8–107**

Procedure for making landscape conservation area order

The procedure whereby a landscape conservation area order is made is less stringent than that applicable, for example, to a special amenity area order. A landscape conservation area order is not subject to confirmation by An Bord Pleanála. Instead, the planning authority is required to give notice of a proposal to make a landscape conservation area order. The elected members of a planning authority, having considered the proposed order and any submissions or observations made in respect of it, may, as they consider appropriate, by resolution, make the order, with or without modifications, or refuse to make **8–108**

---

[83] PDA 2000, Sch.4, para.17.
[84] PDA 2000, Sch.4, para.8.

the order. A similar procedure applies in circumstances where a planning authority wishes to amend or revoke an order previously made.

F. Tree Preservation Orders

8–109   Under s.4(1)(i) of the PDA 2000, development consisting of, *inter alia*, the thinning, felling and replanting of trees, forests and woodlands is exempted development. Notwithstanding this, a planning authority may, under s.205, make a tree preservation order. The effect of a tree preservation order is somewhat unusual in that rather than simply removing the exemption otherwise available in respect of forestry development, the legislation instead makes it a criminal offence to contravene a tree preservation order, or, pending the decision of a planning authority, a proposed tree preservation order.[85]

8–110   The criteria for making a tree preservation order are that it appears to the planning authority that it is expedient, in the interests of amenity or the environment, to make provision for the preservation of any tree, trees, group of trees or woodlands. A tree preservation order may (a) prohibit (subject to any conditions or exemptions for which provision may be made by the order) the cutting down, topping, lopping or wilful destruction of trees, and (b) require the owner and occupier of the land affected by the order to enter into an agreement with the planning authority to ensure the proper management of any trees, group of trees or woodlands (including the replanting of trees), subject to the planning authority providing assistance, including financial assistance, towards such management as may be agreed. A tree preservation order shall not apply to the cutting down, topping or lopping of trees which are dying or dead or have become dangerous, or the cutting down, topping or lopping of any trees in compliance with any obligation imposed by or under any enactment or so far as may be necessary for the prevention or abatement of a nuisance or hazard.

Procedure for making tree preservation order

8–111   Presumably because the contravention of even a proposed tree preservation order (pending the decision of a planning authority) is a criminal offence, there is a requirement to serve notice of an intention to make a tree preservation order on the owner and the occupier of the land affected by the order. There is also a requirement to give public notice of the intention to make the order. Submissions or observations regarding the proposed order may be made to the planning authority within a stated period of not less than six weeks.

8–112   The planning authority, having considered the proposal and any submissions or observations made in respect of it, may by resolution, as it considers appropriate, make the order, with or without modification, or refuse to make

---

[85] PDA 2000, s.205(10).

the order. A similar procedure applies where a planning authority intends to amend or revoke an order already made.

It is clear from the wording of s.205(1) that the only relevant consideration in deciding to make a tree preservation order is the interests of amenity or the environment. Accordingly, a tree preservation order cannot be made solely on grounds of, for example, ecological, botanical or other similar interest or value unless the amenity aspect is also present.[86] Under the previous legislation,[87] provision was made whereby a tree preservation order might provide for an application for consent to the planning authority in respect of the cutting down, topping, lopping or wilful destruction of trees. Moreover, provision was made for the payment of compensation in the event that such consent was refused.[88] It has to be said, however, that the *prima facie* entitlement to payment of compensation was excluded in a number of specified circumstances under the previous legislation. So comprehensive were these exclusions that one might be forgiven for wondering if a claim for compensation would ever properly arise. **8–113**

In the circumstances, it may be that the omission of any express right to compensation from s.205 is not as dramatic a change as might first appear. As against this, one can readily envisage circumstances where the effect of the making of a tree preservation order would be to sterilise at least part of the lands and to make further development difficult. In the circumstances, there might be an argument to be made that to impose such a restriction on property rights, without the payment of compensation, represents an unlawful attack on those property rights. The argument being that it would be unfair to single out a particular individual to shoulder the burden of preserving amenity (in this context trees or woodlands) merely because that amenity fortuitously is located on his or her land.[89] **8–114**

The omission of provision for the payment of compensation is all the more worrying in circumstances where the right of appeal against the making of a tree preservation order which had existed under the previous legislation has been omitted from s.205. To this extent, the owner or occupier of land is thrown on the mercy of the planning authority. **8–115**

---

[86] See, generally, *Tree Preservation – Guidelines for Planning Authorities*, Department of the Environment (1994).
[87] Local Government (Planning & Development) Act 1963, s.45 (as amended by the Local Government (Planning & Development) Act 1990).
[88] Local Government (Planning & Development) Act 1990, s.21.
[89] *cf.* the decision of the Supreme Court in *O'Callaghan v Commissioners of Public Works in Ireland* [1985] I.L.R.M. 364, where a similar argument, in the context of the national monuments legislation, was unsuccessful.

G. Repair and Tidying of Advertising Structures and Advertisements

8–116 Under s.209, provision is made for a planning authority to serve a notice on a person having control of an advertisement structure or advertisement requiring that person to repair or tidy same within a specified period. The power to serve such a notice is exercisable where it appears to a planning authority that, having regard to the interest of public safety or amenity, an advertisement structure or advertisement should be repaired or tidied.

8–117 Similarly, where it appears to a planning authority that any advertisement structure or advertisement is derelict, the planning authority may serve on the person having control of the structure or advertisement a notice requiring that person to remove the advertisement structure or advertisement within a specified period.

H. Control of Quarries

1. Introduction

8–118 The use of planning legislation to control quarries presents certain conceptual difficulties. First, there is often a difficulty in defining the extent of a quarry. This is especially so in the case of excavation works commenced prior to October 1, 1964. Such works were not subject to the requirement to obtain planning permission, but obviously some limit on the extension of those works to other lands needs to be imposed.[90] Secondly, excavation works are sometimes intensified in a gradual way ("creeping intensification"), with the result that it is difficult to identify the precise point at which the development becomes unauthorised. A planning authority may delay taking enforcement proceedings until such time as it is clear that this point has been reached, *i.e.* that there has been a material change of use by way of intensification. There is a risk, however, that, by holding off taking enforcement action, the planning authority will leave it open for the developer to argue that the quarry had become unauthorised at a much earlier date, and thus avail of the seven year limitation period on enforcement action. Thirdly, even where a quarry was subject to planning permission, the inability of a planning authority to revise the planning conditions meant that it was unable to exercise ongoing control over the quarry or to impose more rigorous conditions in the light of technical advances. The rigid nature of a planning permission compares unfavourably with consents under the Environmental Protection Agency Act 1992, where integrated pollution prevention and control licences are subject to regular revision. Finally, as discussed in detail under the next heading, there is a tension between national law and the EIA Directive.

---

[90] *Waterford County Council v John A. Wood Ltd.* [1999] 1 I.R. 556. See further para.8–123.

An attempt has been made under s.261 of the PDA 2000 to address some of **8–119** these difficulties.[91] The wording of the section is far from satisfactory, however, and there are a number of discrepancies. In particular the section does not clearly distinguish between authorised and unauthorised quarries, with the result that a right to statutory compensation might extend even to unauthorised development. Moreover, there is no specific enforcement mechanism to give effect to the requirements of the section, nor is it clear what are the consequences, if any, of a planning authority failing to comply with the various time-limits prescribed in the section.

It may be possible to overcome some of these shortcomings by reliance on the **8–120** EIA Directive. A planning authority, as an emanation of the State, is required to give effect to the EIA Directive and, if necessary, to disapply any contrary provisions of national law.[92] This possibility will be examined in context in the discussion which follows.

2. Quarries and environmental impact assessment

Environmental impact assessment is mandatory in respect of all quarries **8–121** which—by reference to their characteristics, location or impact—are likely to have significant effects on the environment. Under the Planning and Development Regulations 2001, assessment is mandatory, in any event, where the surface area of a quarry site exceeds 25 hectares or, in the case of the extraction of stone, gravel, sand or clay, where the area of extraction would be greater than 5 hectares. These thresholds apply not only to new development projects, but also to any *extension* to an existing development project. Moreover, any extension which would result in an increase in size greater than 25 per cent, or greater than an amount equal to 50 per cent of the appropriate threshold, also triggers the requirement for an assessment. Thus, for example, the extension of an existing sand and gravel quarry by an area of greater than 2.5 hectares must be subject to environmental impact assessment, unless authorised under an existing planning permission.

---

[91] Section 261 was commenced on April 28, 2004, see S.I. No. 152 of 2004. Ministerial guidelines entitled "Quarries and ancillary activities" were issued pursuant to s.28 of the PDA 2000 in April, 2004. The necessity for renewed controls over quarries is stated thus in the guidelines. "Many of the quarries operating today have a history of operation from before the introduction of the Local Government (Planning and Development) Act, 1963 on 1 October 1964, whether permanently or on a seasonal or occasional basis. The recent growth in the economy has led to a rise in the number of quarries being worked on a permanent basis and an expansion in the size and activity of these quarries. Local concerns about the impact of quarries' operations on communities have as a consequence increased. In addition, quarries which never received planning permission or which received permission many years ago may be operating to older standards of environmental control than modern quarries, other than through voluntary compliance with the industry's codes of practice. However, given their authorised status, it has been difficult to require such quarries to seek consent for any expansion in their activities."

[92] See further para.13–259.

8–122 There is a tension between national law and the requirements of the EIA Directive insofar as pre-1964 quarries are concerned. The obligation under the Directive is to subject any quarry project to environmental impact assessment where that project is likely to have significant effects on the environment. This obligation applies where the project commenced subsequent to July 3, 1988, or where there has been a change or extension of the project which may have significant adverse effects on the environment subsequent to that date. The only possible exception to this was in the case of so-called "pipeline projects", *i.e.* projects in respect of which the consent procedure was initiated before the deadline for the implementation of the Directive of July 3, 1988. See para. 13–26.

8–123 Under national law, conversely, there is a long standing exception in favour of any development—the definition of which includes any act or operation of excavation—commenced prior to October 1, 1964.[93] The exception has been interpreted by the Supreme Court in *Waterford County Council v John A. Woods Ltd.*[94] as permitting the continuation to completion of excavation works commenced before October 1, 1964. Excavation works could be carried out, without any necessity for planning permission, on whatever area might reasonably have been anticipated as of October 1, 1964 as having been involved in the works then taking place. Relevant factors in this regard would include the extent of the landholding as of October 1, 1964. Murphy J. suggested that if a quarry operator had acquired the ownership of a large area of land for the purpose of extraction before the relevant date and had commenced work on part of those lands, the acquisition of the lands would have been of decisive importance in determining what might have been reasonably anticipated as the consequence of continuing the works commenced before October 1, 1964.[95]

8–124 Prior to the PDA 2000, therefore, the position under national law was that there was no requirement for planning permission, still less for an environmental impact assessment, in respect of the "completion" of quarrying works commenced prior to October 1, 1964. This was so irrespective of whether the excavation works were likely to have a significant effect on the environment.

---

[93] Under s.24 of the Local Government (Planning & Development) Act 1963, planning permission was not required in respect of development commenced before the appointed day, *i.e.* October 1, 1964. Under the PDA 2000, there is no express exception from the requirement to obtain planning permission in favour of development commenced prior to October 1, 1964. There is a general requirement under s.32 of the PDA 2000 to obtain planning permission (a) in respect of any development of land, not being exempted development, and (b) in the case of development which is unauthorised, for the retention of that unauthorised development. The definition of "unauthorised development" under s.2 of the PDA 2000 excludes development commenced prior to October 1, 1964.

[94] [1999] 1 I.R. 556.

[95] *cf. Limerick County Council v Tobin (No. 2)* unreported, High Court, Peart J., March 1, 2006, where the quarry operator acquired lands subsequent to 1964. Peart J. emphasised that excavation works cannot continue outwards in ever widening circles, like ripples from a lake, simply because there was evidence that some excavation works had commenced in a small area prior to October 1, 1964.

Section 261(7) restores the obligation to obtain development consent—in the form of planning permission—in limited circumstances. The detail of the subsection is discussed at para.8–157 and onwards. On its own, however, it does not go far enough to ensure compliance with the EIA Directive. This is because the obligation to apply for planning permission is only triggered where certain thresholds are met. The quarry must have either an "extracted area"[96] which is greater than five hectares, or be situated on a European site or any other area prescribed for the purpose of s.10(2)(c) of the PDA 2000 or on land to which an order under ss.15, 16 or 17 of the Wildlife Act 1976 applies. The use of a threshold of five hectares was, presumably, intended to ensure consistency with the classes of development prescribed for environmental impact assessment under the Planning and Development Regulations 2001.

8–125

It is well established that a Member State is not normally entitled to rely on criteria or thresholds which only take account of the size of projects, without also taking their nature and location into consideration. See para.13–51. The reference under s.261(7) to European sites and to sites designated under the Wildlife Act 1976 goes some way to ensuring that smaller quarries in sensitive locations will be subject to assessment. It is nevertheless quite possible that a quarry project of less than five hectares located in other areas might, because of its particular location or characteristics, have significant effects on the environment.[97] It is only if such a quarry would be subject to the requirement to obtain planning permission in the ordinary way, without the necessity to invoke or rely on s.261(7), that national law can pass muster.

8–126

It is submitted, therefore, that the exception in favour of pre-1964 quarries must now be read in light of the requirements of the EIA Directive, and that any extension of an existing quarry which is likely to have significant adverse effects, or exceeds the thresholds prescribed under the Planning and Development Regulations 2001, should trigger a requirement to obtain planning permission.

8–127

3. Quarries to which Section 261 applies

Section 261 allows a planning authority to regulate existing quarries notwithstanding the fact that the continued operation of such quarries would not normally require planning permission. What appears to have been intended is that two distinct categories of quarry development be subject to renewed control. The first category consists of quarries the excavation of which had

8–128

---

[96] The reference to an "extracted area" would appear to be a mistake, and should instead read "area of extraction". The impact of quarrying development depends not on the extent of the area already extracted, but rather on the area remaining to be extracted.

[97] See, by analogy, *Commission v Spain* (Case C–474/99) [2002] E.C.R. I–5293 (restriction of environmental impact assessment to Annex II projects affecting special areas of conservation established under the Habitats Directive was considered by the ECJ to have the impermissible effect of excluding a considerable number of projects, situated outside those areas, which were likely to have significant effects on the environment).

commenced prior to October 1, 1964. Such quarries had been regarded as having an established use, and did not require planning permission under the Local Government (Planning & Development) Act 1963. The second category consists of quarries with the benefit of what might be described as "old planning permissions", *i.e.* planning permissions granted more than five years before the coming into operation of s.261 on April 28, 2004.

8–129   Unfortunately, the wording of s.261(11) appears to go beyond what was intended, and the first category is not confined to authorised pre-1964 quarries but includes any quarry in operation on or after the coming into operation of s.261 on April 28, 2004 "being a quarry in respect of which planning permission was not granted". On a literal reading, this suggests that the provisions of s.261 are equally applicable to unauthorised quarries. If this is correct, then the owner of an unauthorised quarry may have a right to statutory compensation.

8–130   "Quarry" is defined by way of a cross-reference to the Mines and Quarries Act 1965. There, a quarry is defined in terms of an excavation or system of excavations for the getting of minerals. The definition of "quarry" includes any place on the surface surrounding or adjacent to the shafts of the quarry occupied together with the quarry for the storage or removal of minerals or for the purposes of a process ancillary to the getting of minerals, including the breaking, crushing, grinding, screening, washing or dressing of such minerals, but does not include any place at which any manufacturing process is carried on.

4. Obligation to register quarries

8–131   The owner or operator of a quarry to which s.261 applies was required, not later than one year from the coming into operation of the section on April 28, 2004, to register the quarry with the relevant planning authority. The registration process consisted of the owner or operator of the quarry providing the planning authority with certain information relating to the operation of the quarry. The planning authority was then required to enter the information on the planning register.

8–132   A non-exhaustive list of the type of information which was to be supplied is prescribed under s.261(2) as follows: (a) the area of the quarry, including the extracted area delineated on a map; (b) the material being extracted and processed (if at all); (c) the date when quarrying operations commenced on the land (where known); (d) the hours of the day during which the quarry is in operation; (e) the traffic generated by the operation of the quarry including the type and frequency of vehicles entering and leaving the quarry; (f) the levels of noise and dust generated by the operations in the quarry; (g) any material changes in the particulars referred to in paragraphs (a) to (f) during the period commencing on the commencement of s.261 and the date on which the information is provided; (h) whether planning permission under Pt IV of the Act of 1963 was granted in respect of the quarry and if so, the conditions, if any, to which the permission is subject, or the operation of the quarry commenced before October 1, 1964; and (i) such other matters in relation to the operations of the quarry as may be prescribed.

Further information

A planning authority may require a person who has submitted information in accordance with the section to submit such further information as it may specify, within such period as it may specify, relating to the operation of the quarry concerned. The legislation is silent as to what effect, if any, the service of such a request for further information has on the date of registration. The registration date is a matter of some importance because the planning authority is expected to take certain steps within various time-limits, all of which run from the date of registration of the quarry. There is a discrepancy in the wording of the section, however, in that the obligation on the planning authority is to register the "information", not to register the "quarry" *per se*.   **8–133**

One solution would be to say that a quarry cannot be regarded as being registered until such time as the information prescribed under s.261(2) has been provided in full. Thus, if the initial submission by the quarry owner or operator does not contain that information, then the planning authority may request the missing information to be submitted, and the quarry should not be regarded as being registered until the request has been complied with. If, conversely, the initial submission does provide all the prescribed information, but the planning authority seek *additional* information, then the date of registration of the quarry should be taken as the date of the initial submission.   **8–134**

Area of the quarry

An issue has arisen in practice as to the extent to which surrounding unworked lands may properly be registered as part of the area of a quarry. The section itself is silent on the point and it is, therefore, necessary to decide the question by reference to first principles. The objective of s.261 is to allow for the regulation of quarries which would not otherwise be subject to planning control. It seems to follow from this that registration should not be extended to any area the excavation of which would require planning permission in any event. Thus, registration should be confined to such an area as is either delimited under the existing planning permission, or the excavation of which can genuinely have been said to have been anticipated or contemplated as of October 1, 1964. A planning authority should refuse to register any larger area. The saver under the Local Government (Planning & Development) Act 1963 for existing quarries merely permits the continuation to completion of the particular works commenced before October 1, 1964 at an identified location. In this regard, it is necessary to ascertain what was or might reasonably have been anticipated at the relevant date as having been involved in the works then taking place.[98] This saver must be read now in light of the EIA Directive, and   **8–135**

---

[98] *Waterford County Council v John A. Wood Limited* [1999] 1 I.R. 556.

thus cannot apply where the extension of excavation works would be likely to have significant effects on the environment: see para.8–121.

Effect of registration

8–136   The effect of registration is simply to ensure that the planning authority, and members of the public, have sufficient information to allow the question of what renewed controls, if any, should be imposed to be addressed.

8–137   Some developers are of the mistaken belief that the registration of a quarry, in some way, confers the benefit of exempted development, or that enforcement proceedings cannot be taken once an existing quarry has been registered. Neither of these assumptions is correct, and s.261 simply supplements the normal controls. The controls under s.261 are in addition to—as opposed to in substitution for—the normal controls under the planning legislation. Thus, for example, the creation of a new quarry or the extension of an existing quarry is unaffected by s.261, and will require planning permission in the ordinary way.

Failure to register within one year or to submit further information

8–138   Where the owner or operator of a quarry to which s.261 applies fails to provide information in relation to the operations of the quarry in accordance with s.261(1) the quarry is deemed to be "unauthorised development".[99] Similarly, failure to provide information in response to a request for further information under s.261(3) will also result in the quarry being deemed to be "unauthorised development".[100]

8–139   Section 261(10) is silent as to how the seven year time-limit on the taking of enforcement action is to apply to a quarry deemed to be unauthorised development. On one view, the seven year time-limit applies in the ordinary way, and thus notwithstanding s.261(10) a quarry would be immune from enforcement action where it had first commenced more than seven years previously. Such an interpretation would, however, entirely undermine the effectiveness of s.261. The section is directed principally to long established quarries where development had either commenced pre-1964 or pursuant to an old planning permission, *i.e.* one granted more than five years before the coming into operation of s.261 on April 28, 2004. Quarries of this type will by definition have commenced more than seven years previously, and thus—save in cases of abandonment or intensification—would be immune from enforcement were the time-limits to apply. The penalty prescribed for failure to comply with the requirements of s.261, *i.e.* deeming the development unauthorised, would be pointless if the seven year time-limit applied. Such an absurd result cannot have been what the legislature intended. Rather, it is submitted that time only begins to run for the purpose of the seven year time-limit from the date that the development is *deemed* to be unauthorised. Prior to that date, the quarry development will, in most cases, have been authorised,

---

[99]   PDA 2000, s.261(10)(a).
[100]   *ibid.*

and time cannot be said to have run for the purpose of the seven year time-limit.

Section 261(10) should therefore be given a purposive interpretation in accordance with the Interpretation Act 2005. Where the quarry development is subject to a requirement for assessment under the EIA Directive, there is an added impetus to interpret the legislation in such a way as accords with the requirements of the Directive. **8–140**

5. Procedure following registration

Under s.261(4), a planning authority is required to engage in a form of public consultation within six months of the date of registration of the quarry. There is also an implicit requirement that the planning authority take a preliminary view as to whether it proposes to regulate the continued operation of the quarry by way of condition, or whether it proposes to require a planning application to be made and accompanied by an environmental impact statement. The public notice, in brief, should state that the quarry has been registered; indicate whether there is an existing planning permission; indicate what proposals the planning authority is considering; indicate the place or places and times at which the planning register may be inspected; and state that submissions or observations regarding the operation of the quarry may be made to the planning authority within four weeks from the date of the publication of the notice. **8–141**

The planning authority is required under s.261(5) to notify the owner or operator of the quarry—as soon as may be after the expiration of the public consultation period—if it proposes to impose, restate, modify or add to conditions on the operation of the quarry, or to require a planning application to be made and an environmental impact statement submitted. The notification must state (i) the reasons for the proposals and (ii) that submissions or observations regarding the proposals may be made by the owner or operator of the quarry to the planning authority within such period as may be specified in the notice, being not less than six weeks from the service of the notice. **8–142**

Thereafter, the planning authority must decide whether to impose renewed controls on the operation of the quarry, and, if so, to decide whether this is to be done by way of condition(s), or by requiring a planning application to be made and accompanied by an environmental impact statement. **8–143**

6. Renewed control by way of condition(s): Section 261(6)

Established pre-1964 use

In the case of a quarry which commenced operation before October 1, 1964, a planning authority may impose conditions on the operation of the quarry. The imposition of the conditions must be in the interests of proper planning and sustainable development. In deciding whether to impose conditions, the **8–144** planning authority must have regard to the development plan and any submissions or observations made. There is a right of appeal to An Bord Pleanála against the imposition of conditions.[101] The appeal must be made within four weeks from the date of receipt of notification. An Bord Pleanála may confirm, with or without modifications, the decision of the planning authority, or annul that decision.

8–145 Where an integrated pollution prevention and control licence has been granted in relation to a quarry, it is impermissible for either a planning authority or An Bord Pleanála to impose conditions relating to (i) the control (including the prevention, limitation, elimination, abatement or reduction) of emissions from the quarry, or (ii) the control of emissions related to or following the cessation of the operation of the quarry.[102]

8–146 It is not clear as to how any breach of an imposed condition is to be policed. Unlike the position in respect of the restatement, modification or addition of conditions to an existing planning permission, there is no provision *deeming* the conditions to have been imposed on the grant of a planning permission.

8–147 There does not appear to be any statutory obligation on a planning authority to pay compensation where conditions are imposed on a pre-1964 quarry pursuant to a notice under s.261(6). This is again to be contrasted with the position where an existing planning permission is modified. It is not entirely clear from the legislation as to why there is this difference in treatment. It may stem, however, from the fact that a planning permission is perceived to be a more valuable right than an existing pre-1964 use. The distinction may not be that important in practice in that it is unlikely that there are many pre-1964 quarries remaining to be worked out.

Old planning permission

8–148 In the case of a quarry in respect of which planning permission had been granted under the Local Government (Planning & Development) Act 1963 more than five years before the coming into operation of s.261 on April 28, 2004, a planning authority may restate, modify or add to conditions imposed on the operation of the quarry. The conditions must be in the interests of proper planning and sustainable development. In deciding whether to restate, modify or add to conditions, the planning authority must have regard to the development plan and any submissions or observations made.

8–149 There is a right of appeal to An Bord Pleanála.[103] The appeal must be made within four weeks from the date of receipt of notification. An Bord Pleanála may confirm, with or without modifications, the decision of the planning authority, or annul that decision. Scannell suggests that, as the conditions are

---

[101] PDA 2000, s.261(9).
[102] PDA 2000, s.261(6)(c).
[103] PDA 2000, s.261(9).

deemed to have been imposed pursuant to s.34, the general right of appeal to An Bord Pleanála under s.37 might arise in any event.[104]

Where an integrated pollution prevention and control licence has been granted in relation to a quarry, it is impermissible for either a planning authority or An Bord Pleanála to restate, modify, add to conditions relating to (i) the control (including the prevention, limitation, elimination, abatement or reduction) of emissions from the quarry, or (ii) the control of emissions related to or following the cessation of the operation of the quarry.[105]   **8–150**

The conditions are policed as if they were conditions attached to a grant of planning permission under s.34 of the PDA 2000. Under s.261(6)(b), the old planning permission is deemed, for the purposes of the PDA 2000, to have been granted under s.34, and any condition so restated, modified or added shall have effect as if imposed under s.34.   **8–151**

In cases where the new conditions are more restrictive than the conditions applicable under the old planning permission, the owner or operator of the quarry may claim compensation, in effect, on the same basis as if conditions had been imposed on the discontinuance of a use pursuant to s.46. This is subject, however, to the exception that no such claim may be made in respect of any condition relating to a matter specified in subparagraphs (a), (b), or (c) of s.34(4) of the PDA 2000 (as amended), *i.e.* conditions regulating the development or use of any land which adjoins, abuts or is adjacent to the land to be developed; conditions for requiring the carrying out of works which the planning authority considers are required for the purposes of the development; and conditions in respect of noise or vibration. Nor is compensation payable in respect of a condition relating to the prevention, limitation or control of emissions from the quarry, or the reinstatement of land on which the quarry is situated.   **8–152**

Nature of conditions

On a literal reading, the power to impose conditions under s.261(7) is unlimited in that the statutory power is expressed in the most general terms. In practice, however, the power will be construed as being confined to the objective of proper planning and sustainable development.[106] Specific examples of conditions which may be imposed are set out, then, under s.261(8)(a). These include conditions of the type set out at subparagraph (a), (b), or (c) of s.34(4) of the PDA 2000 (as amended), *i.e.* conditions regulating the development or use of any land which adjoins, abuts or is adjacent to the land to be developed;   **8–153**

---

[104] Y. Scannell, *Environmental and Land Use Law* (Thomson Round Hall, Dublin, 2006), para.2–427.

[105] PDA 2000, s.261(6)(c).

[106] See, by analogy, *Brady v Environmental Protection Agency* [2007] I.E.H.C. 58; unreported, Charleton J., March 9, 2007; and *Hanrahan Farms Ltd. v Environmental Protection Agency*, unreported, High Court, Smyth J., July 21, 2005.

conditions for requiring the carrying out of works which the planning authority considers are required for the purposes of the development; and conditions in respect of noise or vibration. It also follows from s.261(8)(a) that conditions may be imposed relating to the prevention, limitation or control of emissions from the quarry, or for the reinstatement of land on which the quarry is situated (provided the quarry is not subject to an integrated pollution prevention and control licence).

8–154 It is not entirely clear as to whether conditions may require the payment of development contributions. Section 261(6)(b) provides that where conditions have been restated, modified or added to an old planning permission, the planning permission shall be deemed for the purposes of the PDA 2000 to have been granted under s.34, and any condition so restated, modified or added shall have effect as if imposed under s.34. On one view, therefore, the power to restate, modify or impose conditions might be thought to be confined to conditions of a type enumerated under s.34. As the power to attach conditions requiring development contributions arises elsewhere, *i.e.* under ss.48 and 49, it might be argued that such conditions cannot be imposed in the context of a s.261(6) notice. As against this, however, the following counter-arguments can be made. First, the power to attach conditions under s.261(6)(a) is stated in the very widest terms, and is not expressly limited to conditions under s.34. Secondly, as an old planning permission is deemed to have been granted under s.34, it, arguably, should have all the same incidences of such a planning permission, and these include development contributions.

Environmental impact assessment

8–155 The scheme of s.261 appears to be that an environmental impact assessment will only be required in the context of s.261(7). As discussed presently, under s.261(7) a planning authority may require the owner or operator of the quarry to apply for planning permission and to submit an environmental impact statement. It should be noted, however, that the procedure under s.261(7) appears to be confined to pre-1964 development which does not have the benefit of planning permission. A quarry which is authorised under an old planning permission can, seemingly, only be subject to renewed control under s.261(6). In any case where the continued operation of such a quarry is likely to have significant effects on the environment, a planning authority may be required to undertake an assessment for the purposes of the EIA Directive prior to making any decision under s.261(6). In such cases, the registration process constitutes an application for a "development consent" within the meaning of the Directive. Failure to apply within the one year period stipulated results in the quarry being deemed to be unauthorised development under s.261(10). By analogy with *R. (On the application of Wells) v Secretary of State for Transport, Local Government and the Regions*,[107] an assessment is required in such circumstances.

---

[107] (Case C–201/02); [2004] E.C.R. I-723, [46] ("It would undermine the effectiveness of that directive to regard as mere modification of an existing "consent" the adoption of

No procedure is prescribed under national law for the carrying out of such an **8–156**
assessment. The planning authority must, therefore, improvise. It should rely
on its statutory power to request further information to require the submission
of an environmental impact statement, and modify the public consultation
procedure so as to replicate that provided for in the case of environmental
impact assessment in other contexts.

7. Requirement to apply for planning permission: Section 261(7)

Under s.261(7), a planning authority may require, by notice in writing, the **8–157**
owner or operator of the quarry to apply for planning permission and to submit
an environmental impact statement to the planning authority not later than six
months from the date of service of the notice (or such other period as may be
agreed with the planning authority). A notice requiring such an application for
planning permission must be served not later than one year after the date of
registration of the quarry.

A number of prerequisites must be met before the requirement to apply for **8–158**
planning permission is triggered. First, the continued operation of the quarry
must be likely to have significant effects on the environment. Secondly, the
quarry must have either an "extracted area"[108] which is greater than five
hectares, or be situated on a European site or any other area prescribed for the
purpose of s.10(2)(c) of the PDA 2000 or on land to which an order under
ss.15, 16 or 17 of the Wildlife Act 1976 applies. As discussed at paras 8–121
to 8–127, the legality of restricting the possibility of assessment by reference
to the latter thresholds or criteria is open to doubt.

Section 261(7) only applies to quarries which "commenced operation" before **8–159**
October 1, 1964. Presumably what was intended is that the subsection would
apply to quarries which are authorised by virtue of development works having
commenced prior to October 1, 1964, and those works not having been
abandoned or intensified in the interim. The actual wording used is, however,
ambiguous and, on one view, could also include quarries which subsequently
obtained planning permission, and unauthorised quarries, provided always that
the initial excavation commenced prior to October 1, 1964.

Payment of compensation

Where the owner or operator of a quarry is required to apply for planning **8–160**
permission and to submit an environmental impact statement, then compensation
is payable as if a notice had been served under s.46. No such claim may be

---

decisions which, in circumstances such as those of the main proceedings, replace not
only the terms but the very substance of a prior consent, such as the old mining
permission.").
[108] The reference to an "extracted area" would appear to be a mistake, and should instead
read "area of extraction". The impact of quarrying development depends not on the
extent of the area already extracted, but rather on the area remaining to be extracted.

made, however, in respect of any condition relating to a matter specified in subparagraph (a), (b), or (c) of s.34(4) of the PDA 2000 (as amended), *i.e.* conditions regulating the development or use of any land which adjoins, abuts or is adjacent to the land to be developed; conditions for requiring the carrying out of works which the planning authority considers are required for the purposes of the development; and conditions in respect of noise or vibration. Nor is compensation payable in respect of a condition relating to the prevention, limitation or control of emissions from the quarry, or the reinstatement of land on which the quarry is situated.

Status of quarry pending determination of planning application

8–161   Section 261(7) is silent as to what the status of a quarry is pending the determination of the application for planning permission. This constitutes a potential loophole in the legislation. The requirement to apply for planning permission can only be imposed where the continued operation and/or extension of the quarry is likely to have significant effects on the environment. Yet the determination of an application for planning permission can—allowing for the possibility of an appeal to An Bord Pleanála—take many months. If excavation works are allowed to continue in the interim, then the very environmental impacts which the planning application is intended to assess may have occurred in advance of the final decision to grant or refuse planning permission. Obviously, this would render the entire assessment procedure nugatory. It is possible that by the time a decision is made refusing planning permission, much of that very development will have been carried out.

8–162   The shortcomings in the national legislation may have to be supplemented—again—by reliance on the EIA Directive. National legislation which allows the administration to take no action and allow a project awaiting consent and assessment of its effects on the environment to be implemented without those assessments being made infringes arts 2(1) and 4 of the Directive.[109] Section 261 must be read, therefore, as precluding the continuation of development pending the grant of planning permission.

Failure to apply for planning permission

8–163   Section 261(10)(b) provides that, unless a planning application is submitted within the period specified in a s.261(7) notice, the quarry shall be unauthorised development. Presumably, the quarry should also be deemed to be unauthorised where a planning application is made within time, but subsequently withdrawn or allowed lapse. It would defeat the legislative intent were it sufficient simply to make the application, without there being an implicit requirement to progress the application, for example, by complying fully with a request for further information.

---

[109] See opinion of the Advocate General in *Commission v United Kingdom* (Case C–98/04) May 4, 2006, [34].

The question as to how the seven year time-limit on the taking of enforcement action is to apply to a quarry deemed to be unauthorised development under s.261(10) is discussed at paras 8–139 to 8–140.

8–164

8. Failure to comply with time-limits under Sections 261(6) or 261(7)

An interesting question arises as to what are the consequences, if any, of a failure on the part of a planning authority to give notice under either s.261(6) or s.261(7) within the time periods prescribed. Section 261(6) provides that the planning authority "may" notify the owner or operator of the conditions "not later than 2 years" from the registration of the quarry. Under s.261(7), the planning authority "shall", where the statutory prerequisites are met, require the owner or operator to apply for planning permission and to submit an environmental impact statement "not later than one year" after the date of the registration of the quarry.

8–165

Both subsections are silent as to whether the time-limits are mandatory or merely directory. Whether a provision in a statute, which on the face of it is obligatory, should be treated by the courts as truly mandatory or merely directory depends on the statutory scheme as a whole and the part played in that scheme by the provision in question.[110] One of the principal objectives of s.261 is to allow for renewed control to be exerted over established quarries, in the interest of proper planning and sustainable development. The section is also intended to ensure compliance with the requirements of the EIA Directive. There is a strong public interest in the achievement of each of these objectives, and it is submitted that neither should be frustrated merely because of delay on the part of the planning authority, at least not in circumstances where the delay is slight.

8–166

Moving beyond s.261, to a consideration of the scheme of the PDA 2000 as a whole, it is to be noted that elsewhere in the Act express provision has been made for "default decisions" in circumstances where a planning authority has not complied with certain time-limits. Thus, for example, a decision to grant planning permission will arise by default where a planning authority fails to make a decision on a planning application within time.[111] The absence of such a provision in the context of s.261 is *prima facie* evidence that the legislature did not intend the time-limits under that section to be mandatory. Such a difference in approach is entirely consistent with the exceptional nature of the

8–167

---

[110] *State (Elm Developments Ltd.) v An Bord Pleanála* [1981] I.L.R.M. 108 at 110. In *Director of Consumer Affairs v Governor and Company of the Bank of Ireland* [2003] 2 I.R. 217, Kelly J. held that a direction given out of time is not void, but at most voidable, citing *James v Minister for Housing and Local Government* [1966] 1 W.L.R. 135. The judgment in *Blessington Heritage Trust Ltd. v Wicklow County Council* [1999] 4 I.R. 571 is distinguishable on the basis that the statute prescribed the procedure to be adopted in cases where time for the making of a development plan was to be extended.

[111] PDA 2000, s.34(8). Other examples of default decisions arise in the context of an application to extend the duration of a planning permission under s.42, and an application for an exemption certificate under s.97.

jurisdiction under s.261. The section allows for the renewed regulation of ongoing development, and thus—in contrast with an application for planning permission—development is not put on-hold pending action on the part of the planning authority. In conclusion, therefore, it is submitted that neither the one year, nor the two year, time period should be regarded as mandatory.

8–168   The case for saying that the time periods are not mandatory is even stronger in respect of quarry projects subject to the EIA Directive. The requirement for an assessment cannot be defeated by reference to the time periods. To do so would undermine the effectiveness of the EIA Directive.[112] A planning authority, as an emanation of the State, is obliged to set aside or discard any provision of national law which prevents Community rules from having full force and effect.[113] The time periods under s.261 cannot be regarded as mere procedural rules within the competence of a Member State—subject only to the requirements of effectiveness and equivalence—because they affect the very substance of the obligation to carry out the assessment.

9. Enforcement against unauthorised quarries

8–169   Section 261 merely supplements the normal range of enforcement mechanisms, and, accordingly, there is nothing in s.261 which prevents enforcement action being taken against an unauthorised quarry under Pt VIII of the PDA 2000. This is so even if the quarry has been purportedly registered under s.261.

8–170   In this regard, the Ministerial guidelines state as follows.

> "It should be noted that the registration of quarries under section 261 does not confer planning consent for a quarry that is an unauthorised development. Therefore, an unauthorised development remains unauthorised even after registering with the planning authority. In the event of a planning authority becoming aware of an operating quarry which is unauthorised development, through the registration process or otherwise, or which has failed to comply with a request for further information or a requirement to apply for planning permission, the planning authority must consider taking enforcement action in accordance with Part VIII of the Planning and Development Act, 2000. It is not necessary to defer the enforcement proceedings until after the registration process is completed. The enforcement action could lead to an end to quarrying activities at the site as well as penalties for persons who carried out the unauthorised development."

8–171   In deciding whether a particular quarry involves unauthorised development, it is necessary to distinguish between excavation works commenced before and

---

[112] See, by analogy, *R. v Durham County Council Ex p. Huddlestone* [2000] J.P.L. 1125, where the Court of Appeal in England and Wales disapplied a provision of national law which allowed for a deemed decision on an application for a development consent.

[113] The jurisdiction to disapply national law which is inconsistent with EC law is well established, see, for example, *Simmenthal* (Case 106/77); [1978] E.C.R. 629. For an example of the application of this jurisdiction in the specific context of the EIA Directive, see *Aannemersbedrijf P.K. Kraaijeveld BV v Gedeputeerde Staten van Zuid-Holland* (Case C–72/95); [1996] E.C.R. I–5403.

after October 1, 1964. As discussed at para.8–123, excavation works commenced prior to that date may be continued to completion without any necessity for planning permission. There is no such entitlement in the case of excavation works commenced for the first time after October 1, 1964. Nor does the fact that excavation works have been ongoing for more than seven years—the general limitation period for enforcement action—confer an equivalent right to complete those works. The fact that excavation works first commenced more than seven years ago does not mean that the quarry can be extended laterally or vertically without limit. Such an extension represents further development, not merely the continuation of the development first commenced seven years previously.[114]

Even in the case of a pre-1964 quarry, if quarrying extends beyond the excavation area as anticipated or contemplated as of October 1, 1964, same represents unauthorised development. In *Limerick County Council v Tobin (No. 2)*,[115] Peart J. emphasised that excavation works cannot continue outwards in ever widening circles, like ripples from a lake, simply because there was evidence that some excavation works had commenced in a small area prior to October 1, 1964.   **8–172**

Given that more than forty years have elapsed from October 1, 1964, it is most unlikely that the material extension of any quarry into an extended area can be said to be authorised as an established pre-1964 use. This is because it is difficult to conceive how works reasonably contemplated as of October 1, 1964 could remain to be completed some forty years later. In this regard, it is worth emphasising that any interruption of the quarrying use in the intervening period would give rise to an abandonment of that use, with the result that the resumption of same thereafter would constitute a fresh act of development and require planning permission in the ordinary way.   **8–173**

Similarly, if what would otherwise have represented the continuation of a pre-1964 use is intensified, this will also represent a fresh act of "development" and, unless planning permission is granted for same, will be unauthorised.   **8–174**

Seven year time-limit and EIA development

It is arguable that a planning authority is required to disapply the national law time-limit in circumstances where the extension of the quarry is likely to have a significant effect on the environment. As flagged earlier, a planning authority, as an emanation of the State, is required to give effect to the EIA Directive. If the only thing preventing proper implementation of the Directive is a conflicting provision of national law, then there is a strong argument to be made that national law must be disapplied.   **8–175**

---

[114] See *Thomas David (Porthcrawl) Ltd. v Penybont Rural District Council* [1972] 1 W.L.R. 1526, cited with approval in *Westmeath County Council v Michael F. Quirke & Sons*, unreported, High Court, Budd J., May 23, 1996.
[115] Unreported, High Court, Peart J., March 1, 2006.

I. Strategic Development Zone

1. Introduction

8–176 The Minister for the Environment, Heritage and Local Government may propose land for designation as a strategic development zone under Pt IX of the PDA 2000.[116] Before making such a proposal, the Minister is required to consult with any relevant development agency or planning authority on the proposed designation. A "development agency" is defined as meaning the Industrial Development Agency (Ireland), Enterprise Ireland, the Shannon Free Airport Development Company Limited, Údarás na Gaeltacht, the National Building Agency Limited, a local authority or such other person as may be prescribed by the Minister for the Environment, Heritage and Local Government.[117]

8–177 Where, in the opinion of the Government, specified development is of economic or social importance to the State, the Government may by order designate one or more sites for the establishment of a strategic development zone to facilitate such development.[118]

8–178 The designation of lands as a strategic development zone appears to have three principal effects, as follows. First, it enables the relevant planning authority to acquire (possibly compulsorily) the lands, or to enter into an agreement with the owner of the lands. Secondly, once a planning scheme has been made, planning permission may only be granted for development consistent with the planning scheme, and, further, the decision on any particular application for planning permission cannot be appealed to An Bord Pleanála. Thirdly, there is what might be described as a presumption in favour of the grant of planning permission for development which is consistent with the planning scheme.

8–179 The provisions of Pt IX of the PDA 2000 might be contrasted with those of other legislation which establish similar planning schemes. For example, under the Dublin Docklands Development Authority Act 1997, the effect of a planning scheme is to create a new category of exempted development. Specifically, development which is certified to be consistent with the planning scheme is exempted from the requirement to obtain planning permission in the ordinary way. In contrast, there is still a requirement to obtain planning permission in a strategic development zone albeit that the procedure is expedited in the sense that there is no right of appeal to An Bord Pleanála.

2. Environmental assessment

8–180 Environmental assessment is mandatory in the case of the preparation of a draft planning scheme in respect of a strategic development zone as a result of amendments introduced under the Planning and Development (Strategic

---

[116] PDA 2000, ss.166(1) and (2).
[117] PDA 2000, s.165.
[118] PDA 2000, s.166(1).

Environmental Assessment) Regulations 2004. The usual provision is made for scoping.

Where an appeal is taken to An Bord Pleanála, the board shall, additionally, **8–181** take account of (a) the environmental report prepared; (b) any submission or observation made to the planning authority in response to public notice; and (c) any transboundary consultations, during the board's consideration of the scheme. The monitoring obligation in respect of a planning scheme in respect of a strategic development zone applies to the relevant development agency and any person who is a party to the agreement. Same shall monitor the significant environmental effects of the implementation of the planning scheme in order, *inter alia*, to identify at an early stage unforeseen adverse effects and to be able to undertake appropriate remedial action and, for this purpose, existing monitoring arrangements may be used, if appropriate, with a view to avoiding duplication of monitoring.

3. Designation as strategic development zone

An order designating one or more sites for the establishment of a strategic **8–182** development zone shall (a) specify the development agency or development agencies for the purposes of preparing a planning scheme; (b) specify the type or types of development that may be established in the strategic development zone; and (c) state the reasons for specifying the development and for designating the site or sites.[119] Development that is specified in an order shall be deemed to include development that is ancillary to, or required for, the purposes of development so specified, and may include any necessary infrastructural and community facilities and services.[120]

The Minister for the Environment, Heritage and Local Government is required **8–183** to send a copy of any order to any relevant development agency, planning authority and regional authority and to An Bord Pleanála.[121]

The Government may revoke or amend an order.[122] **8–184**

4. Acquisition of sites or lands for strategic development zones

A planning authority is entitled to use any of its statutory powers of land **8–185** acquisition (including any powers in relation to the compulsory acquisition of land) for the purposes of providing, securing, or facilitating the provision of, a site for a strategic development zone.[123]

---

[119] PDA 2000, s.166(3).
[120] PDA 2000, s.166(5).
[121] PDA 2000, s.166(4).
[122] PDA 2000, s.166(6).
[123] PDA 2000, s.167(1).

8–186   A development agency (as defined) may enter into an agreement with any person who has an interest in land, or any part of land, for the purpose of facilitating the development of the land. Such an agreement may be enforced by the relevant development agency against persons deriving title under that person in respect of that land.[124]

5. Planning scheme for strategic development zones

8–187   There is a requirement that a planning scheme be prepared in respect of all or any part of a strategic development zone.[125] A draft of such a planning scheme is to be prepared not later than two years after the making of the designation order. The draft is to be submitted to the relevant planning authority.

8–188   A planning scheme shall consist of a written statement and a plan indicating the manner in which it is intended that the site is to be developed. A planning scheme should in particular indicate:

(a)   the type or types of development which may be permitted to establish on the site (subject to the order of the Government under s.166);

(b)   the extent of any such proposed development;

(c)   proposals in relation to the overall design of the proposed development, including the maximum heights, the external finishes of structures and the general appearance and design;

(d)   proposals relating to transportation, including public transportation, the roads layout, the provision of parking spaces and traffic management;

(e)   proposals relating to the provision of services on the site, including the provision of waste and sewerage facilities and water, electricity and telecommunications services, oil and gas pipelines, including storage facilities for oil or gas;

(f)   proposals relating to minimising any adverse effects on the environment, including the natural and built environment, and on the amenities of the area; and

(g)   where the scheme provides for residential development, proposals relating to the provision of amenities, facilities and services for the community, including schools, crèches and other education and childcare services.

8–189   A planning scheme shall also contain information on any likely significant impacts on the environment of implementing the planning scheme.

Social and affordable housing

8–190   A planning scheme for residential development shall be consistent with the

---

[124] PDA 2000, s.167(2).
[125] PDA 2000, s.168.

housing strategy prepared by the planning authority in accordance with Pt V of the PDA 2000 (as amended).[126] Where land in a strategic development zone is to be used for residential development, an objective to secure the implementation of the housing strategy shall be included in the draft planning scheme as if it were a specific objective under s.95(1)(b).

6. Planning permission for development in a strategic development zone

The ordinary rules in relation to applications for planning permission are significantly modified for development in a strategic development zone.[127] First, a planning authority is required to grant planning permission in respect of an application for a development in a strategic development zone where it is satisfied that the development, where carried out in accordance with the application or subject to any conditions which the planning authority may attach to a permission, would be consistent with any planning scheme in force for the land in question. Secondly, no planning permission shall be granted for any development which would not be consistent with such a planning scheme. Thirdly, there is no right of appeal to An Bord Pleanála against a decision of a planning authority on an application for permission in respect of a development in a strategic development zone. **8–191**

Where the planning authority decides to grant permission for a development in a strategic development zone, the grant shall be deemed to be given on the date of the decision. **8–192**

The ordinary rules as to the "life" or duration of a planning permission apply to a planning permission in a strategic development zone.[128] See para.5–44 and onwards. **8–193**

7. Making of planning scheme

Public notice and display

Once a draft planning scheme has been prepared and submitted to the planning authority, the planning authority is required to give notice of the preparation of the scheme as soon as may be.[129] A public notice is to be published in one or more newspapers circulating in the planning authority's area. The planning authority is also required to send notice and copies of the draft scheme to the Minister for the Environment, Heritage and Local Government, An Bord Pleanála, and the prescribed authorities. **8–194**

A copy of the draft scheme, and the environmental report required under the 2004 Regulations, is to be kept available for public inspection during a stated **8–195**

---

[126] PDA 2000, s.168(4).
[127] PDA 2000, s.170.
[128] PDA 2000, s.171(5).
[129] PDA 2000, s.169(1).

period of not less than six weeks. Written submissions or observations with respect to the draft scheme and environmental report may be made to the planning authority within the stated period.

Manager's report

8–196   Not longer than twelve weeks after the giving of public notice, the manager of a planning authority shall prepare a report on any submissions or observations received and submit the report to the elected members of the planning authority for their consideration.[130] This report shall (i) list the persons or bodies who made submissions or observations; (ii) summarise the issues raised by the persons or bodies in the submissions or observations; (iii) give the response of the manager to the issues raised, taking account of the proper planning and sustainable development of the area, the statutory obligations of any local authority in the area and any relevant policies or objectives for the time being of the Government or of any Minister of the Government.

8–197   The elected members of a planning authority are required to consider the draft planning scheme and the report of the manager.[131] They must also consider the environmental report.

8–198   The default position is that the draft planning scheme shall be deemed to be made six weeks after the submission of that draft planning scheme and report to the elected members. The elected members may, however, within this six week period, resolve to (i) make, subject to variations and modifications, the draft planning scheme, or (ii) decide not to make the draft planning scheme.[132]

8–199   The planning authority is required to give notice of its decision (whether actual or deemed) as soon as may be, and in any case not later than six working days following the making of the decision.[133] Public notice is to be published in one or more newspapers circulating in its area. Notice of the decision is also to be given to the Minister for the Environment, Heritage and Local Government, An Bord Pleanála, the prescribed authorities and any person who made written submissions or observations on the draft scheme. A copy of the planning scheme is to be kept available for inspection at a stated place or places.

Right of appeal

8–200   There is a right of appeal against the decision of the elected members (whether an actual decision or a deemed decision) to An Bord Pleanála.[134] This right of appeal is confined to (i) the development agency, and (ii) any person who made submissions or observations in respect of the draft planning scheme. The reasons for the appeal must be stated.

---

[130] PDA 2000, s.169(3).
[131] PDA 2000, s.169(4).
[132] PDA 2000, s.169(4)(b).
[133] PDA 2000, s.169(5). See also Planning and Development Regulations, 2001, art.179G.
[134] PDA 2000, s.169(6).

An Bord Pleanála may, following the consideration of an appeal, approve the **8–201** making of the planning scheme, with or without modifications, or it may refuse to approve it.

Where An Bord Pleanála approves the making of a planning scheme, the **8–202** planning authority shall, as soon as practicable, publish notice of the approval of the scheme in at least one newspaper circulating in its area, and shall state that a copy of the planning scheme is available for inspection at a stated place or places (and a copy shall be kept available for inspection accordingly).

Relevant considerations

In considering a draft planning scheme a planning authority or An Bord **8–203** Pleanála, as the case may be, shall, in addition to the environmental report, consider the proper planning and sustainable development of the area and consider the provisions of the development plan, the provisions of the housing strategy, the provisions of any special amenity area order or the conservation and preservation of any European site and, where appropriate (a) the effect the scheme would have on any neighbouring land to the land concerned; (b) the effect the scheme would have on any place which is outside the area of the planning authority; and (c) any other consideration relating to development outside the area of the planning authority, including any area outside the State.[135]

Revocation of planning scheme

The consent of the relevant development agency is required for the amendment **8–204** of a planning scheme.[136]

Notice of the revocation of a planning scheme shall be given in at least one **8–205** newspaper circulating in the area of the planning authority.[137]

The revocation of a planning scheme shall not prejudice the validity of any **8–206** planning permission granted or anything done in accordance with the terms of the scheme before it was amended or revoked except in accordance with the terms of the PDA 2000.[138]

Amendment of planning scheme

The consent of the relevant development agency is required for the amendment **8–207** of a planning scheme.[139] Where a planning authority proposes to amend a planning scheme it shall comply with the procedure laid down in s.169 (described at paras 8–194 to 8–203 above) and that section shall be construed accordingly.[140]

---

[135] PDA 2000, s.169(8).
[136] PDA 2000, s.171.
[137] PDA 2000, s.171(3).
[138] PDA 2000, s.171(4).
[139] PDA 2000, s.171(1).
[140] PDA 2000, s.171(2).

8–208 The amendment of a planning scheme shall not prejudice the validity of any planning permission granted or anything done in accordance with the terms of the scheme before it was amended except in accordance with the terms of the PDA 2000.[141]

8. Relationship between planning scheme and development plan

8–209 A planning scheme shall be deemed to form part of any development plan in force in the area of the scheme until the scheme is revoked, and any contrary provisions of the development plan shall be superseded.[142]

J. Removal or Alteration of Structure or Discontinuance of Use

8–210 A planning authority has an express power to require the removal or alteration of a structure or the discontinuance of a use.[143] It is important to note that this power is available even where there is no unauthorised development involved.

8–211 More specifically, if a planning authority decides, in exceptional circumstances, that (a) any structure should be demolished, removed, altered or replaced; (b) any use should be discontinued; or (c) any condition should be imposed on the continuance of a use, the planning authority may serve a notice on the owner and on the occupier of the structure or land concerned and on any other person who, in its opinion, will be affected by the notice. The planning authority must, *inter alia*, invite any person served with a notice to make written submissions or observations in respect of the matters referred to in the notice within a specified period (being not less than four weeks from the date of the service of the notice).

8–212 In deciding whether to confirm a notice, the planning authority must have regard to any submissions or observations received, and, the following considerations (a) the proper planning and sustainable development of the area; (b) the provisions of the development plan; (c) the provisions of any special amenity area order, any European site or other area designated for the purposes of s.10(2)(c) relating to the area; and (d) any other relevant provision of the PDA 2000 and any Regulations made thereunder.

8–213 Particulars of both the service of, and confirmation of, a notice shall be entered in the statutory register. A planning authority may, for stated reasons, by notice in writing withdraw a notice. Where a notice is withdrawn, the fact that the notice was withdrawn shall be recorded by the planning authority in the register.

---

[141] PDA 2000, s.171(4).
[142] PDA 2000, s.169(9).
[143] PDA 2000, s.46.

1. Enforcement

Offence

It is an offence for any person served with a notice under s.46 to fail to comply **8–214** with the requirements of the notice, or to cause or permit a failure to comply with the requirements. Any person who is guilty of this offence shall be liable, on summary conviction, to a fine not exceeding £1,500 or, at the discretion of the court, to imprisonment for a term not exceeding six months or to both.[144] In the case of the offence continuing after conviction, that person shall be guilty of a further offence on every day on which the contravention continues and for each such offence he or she shall be liable on summary conviction to a fine not exceeding £400.[145]

Steps by planning authority

There is an element of self-help provided for in that the planning authority **8–215** may take steps itself to ensure compliance with the notice. More specifically, if, within the period specified in the notice, or within such extended period as the planning authority may allow, any demolition, removal, alteration or replacement required by the notice has not been effected, the planning authority may enter the structure and may effect such demolition, removal, alteration or replacement as is specified in the notice.[146]

2. Appeal to An Bord Pleanála

There is a statutory right of appeal to An Bord Pleanála against a notice **8–216** confirmed by the planning authority. Any person served with a confirmed notice may, within eight weeks of the date of service of the notice, appeal to An Bord Pleanála against the notice.

An Bord Pleanála may confirm the notice with or without modifications or **8–217** annul the notice. An Bord Pleanála is required to consider the same matters as the planning authority is, namely (a) the proper planning and sustainable development of the area; (b) the provisions of the development plan; (c) the provisions of any special amenity area order, any European site or other area designated for the purposes of s.10(2)(c) relating to the area; and (d) any other relevant provision of the PDA 2000 and any Regulations made thereunder.

3. Compensation

Compensation is payable under s.197 where it is shown that, as a result of the **8–218** discontinuance, or the compliance with conditions on the continuance, of any use of land consequent on a notice under s.46, the value of an interest of any

---

[144] PDA 2000, s.156(4).
[145] PDA 2000, s.156(5).
[146] PDA 2000, s.46(9).

person in the land existing at the time of the confirmation of the notice is reduced, or that any person having an interest in the land at that time has suffered damage by being disturbed in his or her enjoyment of the land.

8–219 Under s.196, there is a similar entitlement to compensation in circumstances where there has been a reduction in the value of an interest in land, or a person has suffered damage by being disturbed in his or her enjoyment of the structure, as a result of the removal or alteration of any structure consequent upon a notice under s.46.

Expenses reasonably incurred

8–220 The planning authority shall pay to the person complying with the notice the expenses reasonably incurred by the person in carrying out the demolition, removal, alteration or replacement specified in the notice, less the value of any salvageable materials.[147]

K. Major-Accident Hazards Directive
(Seveso Directive)

1. Land-use and major-accident establishments

8–221 The EC Major-Accident Hazards Directive (sometimes referred to colloquially as the "Seveso" or "Seveso II" Directive) requires Member States to take measures for the prevention of major accidents which might result from certain industrial activities, and for the limitation of the consequences of such accidents for man and the environment.[148] The Directive has been transposed into Irish law principally through the European Communities (Control of Major Accident Hazards Involving Dangerous Substances) Regulations 2006.[149] The Directive is also implemented, in part, under the PDA 2000.

8–222 In broad terms, it might be said that those aspects of the Directive which relate to the regulation and operation of prescribed establishments are dealt with under the 2006 Regulations, whereas the "land-use" aspects are dealt with under the planning legislation. The former are dealt with in detail by Scannell and readers are referred to that work.[150] The present chapter is concerned only with the land-use aspects.

---

[147] PDA 2000, s.46(10).
[148] Council Directive 96/82/EC of December 9, 1996 on the control of major-accident hazards involving dangerous substances. This Directive has been amended a number of times, principally by Directive 2003/105/EC of the European Parliament and of the Council of December 16, 2003 amending Council Directive 96/82/EC on the control of major-accident hazards involving dangerous substances.
[149] S.I. No. 74 of 2006.
[150] Y. Scannell, *Environmental and Land Use Law* (Thomson Round Hall, Dublin, 2006).

The recitals to the Directive include—at paragraph 22—one to the effect that **8–223** in order to provide greater protection for residential areas, areas of substantial public use and areas of particular natural interest or sensitivity it is necessary for land-use and/or other relevant policies applied in the Member State to take account of the need, in the long term, to keep a suitable distance between such areas and establishments presenting such hazards. Where existing establishments are concerned, land-use policies should take into account additional technical measures so that the risk to persons is not increased.

The Directive applies to establishments where dangerous substances are present **8–224** in quantities equal to or in excess of quantities described under Annex I of the Directive. "Establishment" is defined under the 2006 Regulations as meaning the whole area under the control of an operator where "dangerous substances" are present in one or more installations, including common or related infrastructures or activities, and includes new, existing and other establishments. The term "dangerous substance" is defined under the 2006 Regulations by way of cross-reference to Annex I of the Directive itself.

Article 12 of the Directive relates to what is described as "land-use planning". **8–225** Member States are required to ensure that the objectives of preventing major accidents and limiting the consequences of such accidents are taken into account in their land-use policies and/or other relevant policies. Those objectives are to be pursued through controls on (a) the siting of new establishments; (b) modifications to existing establishments; and (c) new developments such as transport links, locations frequented by the public and residential areas in the vicinity of existing establishments, where the siting or developments are such as to increase the risk or consequences of a major accident.[151]

Article 12 further provides that Member States shall ensure that their land-use **8–226** and/or other relevant policies, and the procedures for implementing those policies, take account of the need, in the long term, to maintain appropriate distances between establishments covered by the Directive and residential areas, buildings and areas of public use, major transport routes as far as possible, recreational areas and areas of particular natural sensitivity or interest and, in the case of existing establishments, of the need for additional technical measures in accordance with Art.5 so as not to increase the risks to people.

Member States are also required to ensure that all competent authorities and **8–227** planning authorities responsible for decisions in this area set up appropriate consultation procedures to facilitate the implementation of the policies. The procedures are to be designed to ensure that technical advice on the risks arising from the establishment are available, either on a case-by-case or on a generic basis, when decisions are taken. The procedure in this regard is discussed in detail at paras 3–147 to 3–162.

---

[151] See, generally, Y. Scannell, *Environmental and Land Use Law* (Thomson Round Hall, Dublin, 2006), paras 10–43 to 10–54.

8–228 The wording of the Directive is not entirely clear and, in particular, it is not certain as to whether the obligation to take these matters into account occurs at the stage of the formulation of policy only, or whether it descends to decisions on individual planning applications. Notwithstanding the lack of clarity in the wording of the Directive, the approach which appears to have been taken by Ireland under the relevant provisions of the PDA 2000 is to require that major-accident considerations be taken into account both at the stage of the making of the development plan, and in the determination of individual applications for planning permission. (Special procedures apply in the case of local authority and State authority development.)

2. Definition of "establishment"

8–229 The case of *Harrington v An Bord Pleanála (No. 1)*[152] concerned the definition of an "establishment" for the purposes of the Major-Accident Hazards Directive. Planning permission had been granted for the development of a gas terminal for the reception and separation of gas from off the Mayo coast (the so-called Corrib gas field). The planning permission related to the terminal building itself, together with some ancillary buildings and so much of the area immediately surrounding as was enclosed by a perimeter or security fence. As the proposed development came within the scope of the Directive, the planning authority had invoked the procedure then applicable under Pt 11 of the Planning and Development Regulations 2001[153] and had referred the application to the National Authority for Occupational Safety and Health (hereinafter referred to as "the HSA"). In giving its advice, the HSA considered the establishment to be confined to the area within the perimeter fence. The planning authority subsequently made a decision to grant, which decision was then appealed to An Bord Pleanála. In determining the appeal, An Bord Pleanála had before it the initial advice provided by the HSA to the planning authority. In addition, An Bord Pleanála had sought, and obtained, further advices or comment from the HSA during the course of the appeal proceedings. An Bord Pleanála ultimately made a decision to grant planning permission.

8–230 Under the Directive, an "establishment" is defined as the whole area under the control of an operator where dangerous substances are present in one or more installations, including common or related infrastructures or activities. "Installation" in turn is defined as meaning a technical unit within an establishment in which dangerous substances are produced, used, handled or stored. The definition of "installation" includes, *inter alia*, "pipework".

8–231 Mr Harrington, the applicant in the judicial review proceedings, sought to challenge An Bord Pleanála's decision to grant planning permission. Mr Harrington argued that An Bord Pleanála had erred in its understanding of what constituted the "establishment" for the purposes of the Major-Accident

---

[152] [2005] I.E.H.C. 344; [2006] 1 I.R. 388.
[153] The procedure has since been amended under the 2006 Regulations.

Hazards Directive. Mr Harrington further argued that the perimeter fence did not represent the limit of the establishment, but that, on the contrary, the *entire* site under the control of the operator represented the establishment. This argument was based on the submission that at least part of the pipeline came within the definition of "establishment" in that dangerous substances, *i.e.* the gases, were used or stored in it.

The High Court rejected these arguments. Macken J. did not accept that gas was being "stored" in the upstream pipeline. Macken J. held that there was a very clear distinction under the Directive between a "pipeline" on the one hand, and "pipework" on the other, with a "pipeline" intended to refer to a pipeline for the transportation of gas (or other hazardous or dangerous substances) whether to or from the terminal. There was, in her view, nothing inconsistent in regarding as part of the establishment that portion of the pipework which forms part of the terminal footprint, while excluding from the definition the upstream pipeline. In this regard, attention was drawn to the fact that the transport of dangerous substances in pipelines *outside* establishments was expressly excluded from the scope of the Directive under Art.4.   **8–232**

In holding that the transport of gas from the gas field to the terminal did not involve storage within the meaning of the Directive, Macken J. placed emphasis on the fact that the definition of "storage" under the Directive referred to the presence of a quantity of dangerous substances for the purposes of warehousing, depositing in safe custody or keeping in stock.   **8–233**

The approach adopted by the court to the question of the interpretation of the Directive is noteworthy. Notwithstanding that the application before the court was an application for leave only, and not the full hearing, the court was prepared to embark upon a detailed analysis of the provisions of the Directive. Thus, the court was seemingly content to deliver a ruling on the interpretation of an EC Directive under the guise of assessing whether the applicant had demonstrated "substantial grounds" of challenge. This is perhaps surprising given that there would appear to be at least some ambiguity as to the extent of the "establishment". In a subsequent ruling on an application for a certificate for leave to appeal to the Supreme Court,[154] Macken J. emphasised the limited *ratio* of her earlier decision. Mr Harrington was said to have failed to adduce any evidence of a technical or expert nature which could or might establish a context in support of his mere assertion that "establishment" had the particular meaning contended for him.   **8–234**

> "[…] far from concluding that the Directive must be interpreted in a particular way as to the meaning of 'establishment' or any obligation on the respondent pursuant to it, the decision, so far as any finding goes, was to the effect only that the applicant had failed to discharge the burden imposed on him to satisfy the court that his application was weighty in regard to his assertions, and that he had failed thereby to meet the statutory requirement, namely, 'substantial grounds'."

---

[154] Unreported, High Court, Macken J., March 16, 2006.

8–235 In addition to addressing the arguments as to the definition of "establishment", the judgment in *Harrington (No. 1)* also examines the nature of the respective roles of the HSA and An Bord Pleanála. Mr Harrington had argued that the interpretation of "establishment" involved a question of law, and, accordingly, the views of the HSA could not be conclusive. In this regard, it was argued that An Bord Pleanála—as an emanation of the State—should have exercised its own independent discretion as to what was the extent of the establishment, and that it had erred in considering itself to be bound by the HSA's view.

8–236 To be frank, the debate in this regard was probably unnecessarily complicated. The significance of the issue lay in the fact that An Bord Pleanála and the developer sought to elevate the HSA's view of what was meant by "establishment" to the status of a formal decision, so as to allow certain procedural arguments to be made. More specifically, it was sought to suggest that the HSA's view constituted a "decision" which could only be set aside on judicial review, and that this could not be done in the present proceedings in that the HSA had not been joined as a party. It was also argued that it was, in any event, now too late to challenge the HSA's decision. Although these arguments are superficially attractive, the fact remains that the interpretation of legislation—including EC legislation in the form of Directives—is ultimately a matter for the courts. Whereas weight might well be given to the views of expert bodies, the court remains the final arbiter.

8–237 The arguments made were also not necessarily in accordance with the division of function indicated under the then national implementing Regulations. As discussed at para.8–241, the law has since been amended under the Planning and Development Regulations 2006. Under the Directive, there is a distinction drawn between "competent authorities" and "planning authorities", with the latter having responsibility for land-use policies and decisions. This distinction had been observed under Irish law, with the HSA being designated as the central competent authority, with An Bord Pleanála/planning authorities bringing major-accident considerations to bear in planning decisions. It runs counter to this legislative scheme to suggest that the technical advice provided by the HSA to An Bord Pleanála/planning authorities has a particular legal status or that it is conclusive. Rather, the duty to correctly apply EC law applies equally to the HSA and An Bord Pleanála as emanations of the State. Accordingly, if the HSA had misinterpreted the terms of the Directive, then it would be open to An Bord Pleanála to remedy that mistake by substituting the correct interpretation for that of the HSA.

8–238 The matter is dealt with in the judgment as follows. Macken J. stated that there was nothing in Art.12 of the Directive which prohibited An Bord Pleanála/planning authorities from assessing land-use issues by reference to technical advice provided by the HSA as competent authority. There was no express obligation on An Bord Pleanála/planning authorities to determine the extent of an establishment under Art.12; their obligations were simply to assess the risks arising. In the circumstances, the court found that the approach of An Bord Pleanála—in following the HSA's interpretation—to be unexceptionable.

It is not entirely clear whether the judgment might not, in fact, go further: at **8–239** one point Macken J. seems to suggest that the views of the HSA might be binding, subject only to their being challenged in judicial review proceedings. It will be recalled that the argument being made on behalf of An Bord Pleanála and the developer was that the proceedings were flawed in that the HSA was not a party thereto.

To the extent to which this issue is dealt with in the judgment, the comments **8–240** would appear, strictly speaking, to be *obiter dicta* in that the High Court had already found that the interpretation of "establishment" actually applied was the correct one. In the circumstances, it was unnecessary to consider the division of function as, in the events that transpired, the interpretation relied upon by the HSA and An Bord Pleanála happened to be the right one.

Planning and Development Regulations 2006

The legal position in this regard has since been amended by the Planning and **8–241** Development Regulations 2006.[155] Rather than simply request technical advice as had been the position under the 2001 Regulations, a planning authority first requests a determination as to whether the Major Accidents Regulations apply to the proposed development. It is only if the HSA determines that the said Regulations do apply that technical advice as to the effects of the proposed development on the risk or consequences of a major accident are to be provided to the planning authority.

This amendment helps to clarify the respective roles of the planning authority **8–242** and the HSA. In particular, it seems now that the determination of issues such as, for example, the physical extent of the major-accident establishment—which is obviously of critical importance in applying separation distances—is principally a matter within the competence of the HSA.

3. Development plan objectives

Major-accident considerations are a mandatory objective for a development **8–243** plan. Specifically, under s.10(2)(k) a development plan shall include objectives for the control, having regard to the provisions of the Major-Accident Hazards Directive, of (i) siting of new establishments; (ii) modification of existing establishments; and (iii) development in the vicinity of such establishments, for the purposes of reducing the risk, or limiting the consequences, of a major accident.

In order to properly implement this provision, it will be necessary for each **8–244** planning authority to identify *existing* establishments within its functional area, and to provide guidance as what restrictions will be imposed on new development within the vicinity of such establishments. This might, for example,

---

[155] Planning and Development Regulations, art.33 (planning authorities) and art.34 (An Bord Pleanála).

take the form of a series of buffer zones. The more populous the proposed use, the greater the separation distance which will be required between it and the major-accident establishment.

8–245 The planning authority should, equally, identify sites where it would be appropriate to develop *new* major-accident establishments. A planning authority should also indicate the extent to which existing establishments will be permitted to modify (and, in particular, to expand).

8–246 Obviously, the objectives of the development plan in this connection are something which a planning authority and An Bord Pleanála are required to have regard to in determining any individual application for planning permission.

L. Statutory Planning Agreements

8–247 A special form of control over the development and use of land may be achieved by the entry into of a statutory planning agreement. Under s.47 of the PDA 2000, a planning authority may enter into an agreement with any person interested in land in its area for the purpose of restricting or regulating the development or use of the land, either permanently or during such period as may be specified by the agreement. Any such agreement may contain such incidental and consequential provisions (including provisions of a financial character) as appear to the planning authority to be necessary or expedient for the purposes of the agreement.

1. "Restricting or regulating"

8–248 An agreement under s.47 must be for the purpose of restricting or regulating the development or use of land. In *McHugh v Kildare County Council*,[156] the High Court had to consider—in the context of the similarly worded provisions of the previous legislation—whether an agreement to dedicate a certain percentage of lands to the planning authority, for the use by the planning authority for its statutory purposes, came within the ambit of "restricting or regulating" the development or use of land. Gilligan J. held that it did. It appears that the court had regard not only to the narrow purpose of the agreement—which was, in effect, an agreement to transfer land—but also to the wider objective which was to allow the transferred land to be developed for small industry independently of the adjoining private industrial development.

8–249 The background to the case was as follows. During the course of the statutory procedures in respect of the making of a new development plan, a landowner proposed that up to twenty per cent of his land, if rezoned, would be dedicated

---

[156] [2005] I.E.H.C. 356; [2006] 1 I.R. 100.

to the planning authority and that the dedication would be on a pro rata basis subject to an agreement on zoning. Prior to the adoption of the new plan, an agreement was entered into which declared that the landowner would dedicate twenty per cent of his lands to Kildare County Council, for the use of the planning authority for its statutory purposes, if the remainder of his lands were re-zoned. This agreement was stated to be in accordance with the provisions of s.38 of the Local Government (Planning & Development) Act 1963.

The landowner subsequently sought a declaration that the agreement was *ultra vires*, arguing, *inter alia*, that there was no lawful or proper consideration for the transfer of the lands as, in making a development plan, the planning authority was merely discharging an existing statutory duty. The High Court rejected these arguments, holding that there had been good consideration and that the agreement was for the purpose of "restricting or regulating" the use of land. **8–250**

The approach in *McHugh v Kildare County Council* is to be contrasted with that adopted by the courts of England and Wales in respect of an equivalent statutory provision. In *Wimpey Homes Holding Ltd. v Secretary of State for the Environment*,[157] the High Court of England and Wales held that an undertaking to transfer lands to another person, whether or not that person was a planning authority, was not in itself to enter into an obligation restricting the development or use of land. The transfer of title pursuant to the undertaking does not impose a restriction on development or uses; the transfer is only a first step towards imposing such a restriction on the subject land. **8–251**

The decision in *Wimpey Homes* was distinguished by the Court of Appeal in *R. v South North Hamptonshire District Council Ex p. Crest Homes*.[158] The Court of Appeal had to consider, *inter alia*, the legality of an obligation imposed under a planning agreement requiring the developer to transfer certain land to the planning authority for community purposes, such as an open space or for a school. The wording of the planning agreement was unusual in that the obligation was framed negatively. More specifically, the owner had covenanted with the planning authority that he would not commence any development of the land whatsoever without taking all necessary steps, including entering into any necessary additional legal agreements and bonding arrangements, to bring all the terms of the agreement into effect.[159] **8–252**

One further point which emerges from the decision in *McHugh v Kildare County Council* is that the validity of a planning agreement and that of any concomitant action on the part of the planning authority have to be considered separately. In particular, it seems that a planning agreement may nevertheless be enforceable on its own terms, notwithstanding the fact that there may be grounds for saying that the taking into account of the existence of the agreement may have been **8–253**

---

[157] [1993] 2 P.L.R. 54; [1993] J.P.L. 919.
[158] [1995] J.P.L. 200.
[159] See, generally, D. Brock, "Planning Obligations – Ideas for Reform" [2002] J.P.L. 12.

an improper consideration for the planning authority in exercising some other statutory discretion. Thus, for example, it may well be that a decision to grant planning permission is vitiated by the fact that the planning authority placed improper reliance on a planning agreement. The planning agreement itself may, however, survive the invalidity of the decision to grant planning permission. The point is illustrated by *JA Pye (Oxford Ltd.) v South Gloucestershire District Council*.[160] There, the developer sought to avoid its obligations under a planning agreement, arguing that, as the agreement was not connected to the permitted development, the planning authority had taken into account an irrelevant or immaterial consideration in determining an application for planning permission. The Court of Appeal held that it did not follow from the fact that the planning authority might have taken into account an irrelevant or immaterial consideration in determining the application for planning permission, that the agreement itself was in any way infected. The underlying planning application provided an opportunity to obtain a perfectly proper benefit for the locality (in terms of road development). If there was any vice, it was in granting the planning permission, not in determining to enter into the agreement.

8–254 Another issue which arises is as to whether or not a developer who has obtained the benefit of a favourable planning decision—whether in terms of planning permission or under the terms of a development plan—is estopped from seeking to avoid his obligations under the planning agreement.

2. "Agreement"

8–255 It is important to note that, save with one exception, a person cannot be obliged to enter into a statutory planning agreement. This follows from the use of the term "agreement" which clearly connotes a consensual arrangement, and from the more general principle that a planning authority is not entitled to employ its statutory powers to extract a planning gain or to impose an obligation on a third party, save where express provision is made to this effect.[161] In particular, it would be unlawful for a planning authority to attach a condition to a planning permission purporting to require the applicant to enter into a statutory agreement (save in the case of an occupancy condition, discussed immediately below).

Occupancy conditions

8–256 The one exception to the general rule that the agreement must be consensual is in respect of occupancy conditions. See, generally, para.4–102. It is expressly provided that where a grant of planning permission specifies use as a dwelling, the permission may also be granted subject to a condition specifying that the use as a dwelling shall be restricted to use by persons of a particular class or

---

[160] [2001] E.W.C.A. Civ. 450.

[161] See, by analogy, *Ashbourne Holdings Ltd. v An Bord Pleanála* [2003] 2 I.R. 114; [2003] 2 I.L.R.M. 446.

description and that provision to that effect shall be embodied in a statutory agreement under s.47.[162]

3. Agreement binding on subsequent owners

One unusual feature of s.47 agreements is that they are to run with the land in the sense of their binding subsequent owners. To this extent then, the ordinary rules in relation to privity of contract are disapplied. To achieve this result the legal fiction of a statutory restrictive covenant is employed. It is expressly provided that the agreement may be enforced by the planning authority, or any body joined with it, against persons deriving title under the other party to the agreement as if the planning authority or body, as may be appropriate, was possessed of adjacent land, and as if the agreement had been expressed to be made for the benefit of that land.[163]

8–257

4. Fetter on discretion?

A question arises as to the extent to which the entry into of a statutory agreement might impose a fetter on the exercise of a planning authority's discretion. For example, is the planning authority to be taken as indicating that it would be prepared to grant planning permission for a particular development on the strength of the applicant entering into a s.47 agreement?

8–258

It is expressly provided in s.47(4) that nothing in the section, or any agreement made thereunder, shall be construed as restricting the exercise of statutory powers so long as those powers are not exercised to materially contravene the provisions of the development plan. The implication of this seems to be that by entering into such an agreement, a planning authority is allowed to fetter its discretion, subject only to the proviso that the development plan must be complied with.

8–259

5. Amendment of agreement

A serious drawback of s.47 agreements is that there is no mechanism expressly provided whereby an application might be made to be released from the agreement where, for example, there was subsequently a change in the proper planning and development of the area.

8–260

The decision in *Langarth Properties Ltd. v Bray Urban District Council*[164] may resolve these concerns in at least some situations. On the facts, the planning authority had refused planning permission on the basis of a statutory agreement

8–261

---

[162] PDA 2000, s.39(2).
[163] For an excellent discussion of agreements under the previous legislation, see Stevenson, "Negotiated Planning: Circumventing the planning system" (1984) *The Irish Jurist* 15.
[164] Unreported, High Court, Morris P., June 25, 2001.

under the previous legislation[165] which prohibited further development of the lands. An Bord Pleanála subsequently granted planning permission, on appeal, and the planning authority then sought to enforce the statutory agreement as a restrictive covenant. Morris P. held that the planning authority when considering applications for future development of the land was limited to considering the proper planning and development of the area. It was not open to the planning authority to rely solely upon the fact that there was a statutory agreement in existence. To prevent or inhibit the development of lands for any reason other than the proper planning and development of the area would be an unconstitutional interference with the rights of private ownership of land. It followed that the limitation and restrictions imposed by the agreement remained valid only for so long as the proper planning of the area required that the restriction be maintained. The fact that An Bord Pleanála had granted planning permission authorising development which would otherwise be in direct conflict with the agreement was a clear indication that the proper planning and development of the area no longer required observance of the covenant.

M. Licensing of Events and Funfairs

1. Introduction

8–262   There had been some controversy under the previous legislation as to whether planning permission was required for transient events such as pop concerts. Earlier judgments such as that in *Earl of Mountcharles v Meath County Council*[166] appeared to have proceeded on the assumption that the use of the land for public events such as pop concerts might well represent a material change in the use of the lands, notwithstanding the very short duration involved. The subsequent judgment of the Supreme Court in *Butler v Dublin Corporation*[167] indicated that a fleeting change in use of lands (such as that involved in a one or two day pop concert) would not represent a material change in use such as to trigger a requirement to obtain planning permission.

8–263   This issue is now academic in view of the change in control introduced under the PDA 2000. The general position now is that the holding of an "event", as defined, is not to be construed as "development" within the meaning of the PDA 2000.[168] Accordingly, there is no requirement to obtain a grant of planning permission in respect of same. This privilege extends to works directly or solely relating to the holding of such an event. Instead, there is a requirement in the case of certain events to obtain a licence from the local authority under Pt XVI of the PDA 2000.[169]

---

[165] Local Government (Planning & Development) Act 1963, s.38.
[166] [1996] 3 I.R. 417; [1997] 1 I.L.R.M. 446.
[167] [1999] 1 I.R. 565; [1999] 1 I.L.R.M. 481. See also *Grimes v Punchestown Developments Company Ltd.* [2002] 1 I.L.R.M. 409.
[168] PDA 2000, s.240.
[169] PDA 2000, s.230. The events are prescribed under the Planning and Development Regulations 2001, art.183.

Existing planning permission

Special rules apply in the case of land with the benefit of an existing planning permission in respect of events. (Somewhat anomalously, certain planning authorities had purported to grant planning permission for such events, notwithstanding that strictly speaking same did not constitute "development".) The present legal position is that the requirement to obtain a licence only applies to any additional event over and above those permitted under the planning permission.[170]   **8–264**

2. Definition of "event"

An "event" is defined as (a) a public performance which takes place wholly or mainly in the open air or in a structure with no roof or a partial, temporary or retractable roof, a tent or similar temporary structure, and which is comprised of music, dancing, displays of public entertainment or any activity of a like kind, and (b) any other event as prescribed by the Minister for the Environment, Heritage and Local Government.   **8–265**

3. Obligation to obtain a licence for holding of an event

The obligation to obtain a licence applies to an event prescribed by the Minister for the Environment, Heritage and Local Government.[171] Under the Planning and Development Regulations 2001, the following type of event has been prescribed for this purpose: an event at which the audience comprises five thousand or more people.[172] "Audience" is defined as meaning persons attending an event on a particular day, other than persons working or performing at the event, and includes persons attending by invitation. Where an event comprises more than one performance at one or more locations at the venue on a particular day, the audience shall mean the total number of persons attending all such performances.[173]   **8–266**

Any person who (a) organises, promotes, holds or is otherwise materially involved in the organisation of a prescribed event, or (b) is in control of land on which an event is held, other than under and in accordance with a licence, shall be guilty of an offence.[174]   **8–267**

---

[170] PDA 2000, s.240(2).
[171] PDA 2000, s.230.
[172] Planning and Development Regulations 2001, art.183.
[173] Planning and Development Regulations 2001, art.182 (as amended by the 2006 Regulations).
[174] PDA 2000, s.230(3).

4. Application for a licence

8–268 The procedure for the making of an application for a licence is set out at Pt 15 of the Planning and Development Regulations 2001. The key aspects of the procedure are summarised below.

Pre-application consultation

8–269 A person intending to make an application for a licence may seek to enter into pre-application consultation with the local authority, and the prescribed bodies (principally, the Garda Síochána, and the Health Service Executive). In particular, the intended applicant may seek to discuss the submission of the application, including the draft plan for the management of the event. The local authority, and the prescribed bodies (principally, the Garda Síochána, and the Health Service Executive) cannot unreasonably refuse to agree to such pre-application consultation.[175]

Timing of application, and of decision

8–270 The application is to be made at least sixteen weeks prior to the date of the holding of the (first) event to which the application relates.[176]

8–271 A local authority shall make a decision not earlier than five weeks after receiving the application.

Public notice

8–272 Within the period of two weeks before applying for a licence, an applicant is required to give public notice of his or her intention to submit an application. The application is to be published in one local and one national newspaper.[177]

8–273 Any person may make a submission or observation in writing to the local authority in respect of the application within five weeks of the receipt of the application by the local authority.[178]

Availability of documents

8–274 The local authority shall make the application, any accompanying documents, maps and drawings and any submission or observation made in relation to it, available for public inspection during office hours at the offices of the local authority and such other places as it considers appropriate, for a period of five weeks from the date of receipt of the application.

---

[175] Planning and Development Regulations 2001, art.182 (as amended by the 2006 Regulations).
[176] Planning and Development Regulations 2001, art.186.
[177] Planning and Development Regulations 2001, art.185.
[178] Planning and Development Regulations 2001, art.190.

The local authority shall, on request, make a copy of the application and **8–275** accompanying documents available for purchase by any person on payment of a sum not exceeding the reasonable costs of making such a copy.

Consultation with prescribed bodies

The local authority is required to consult with the prescribed bodies.[179] The **8–276** prescribed bodies are the Garda Síochána; the Health Service Executive; and any county council, county borough corporation, borough corporation or urban district council (other than the local authority to whom the application is made), the area of which will be affected by the event.[180]

Further information, submissions, and observations

The local authority may request such further information from the applicant as **8–277** it considers necessary to enable it to make a decision. The local authority may request such further information from a prescribed body or any person who made a submission or observation as it considers necessary to enable it to make a decision. The local authority may, at its discretion, invite any other person to make a submission or observation to it in respect of an application. The local authority may take whatever measures it considers necessary, including the convening of meetings or the taking of oral submissions, to seek the views of any person in regard to the application.[181]

5. Decision on application for licence

In considering an application for a licence, the local authority shall have regard **8–278** to (i) any information relating to the application furnished to it by the applicant; (ii) any consultations held; (iii) any submissions or observations made to it; (iv) whether events have previously been held on the land concerned; (v) the types of conditions which may be attached to a licence; and (vi) any guidelines or codes of practice issued by the Minister for the Environment, Heritage and Local Government or by any other Minister of the Government.[182] Where an application for a licence is made in accordance with the regulations, the local authority may decide to grant the licence, grant the licence subject to such conditions as it considers appropriate or refuse the licence.

Without prejudice to the general power, conditions subject to which a licence **8–279** is granted may relate to all or any of the following (a) compliance with any guidelines or codes of practice issued by the Minister for the Environment, Heritage and Local Government or any other Minister of the Government, or with any provisions of those guidelines or codes of practice; (b) securing the safety of persons at the place in connection with the event; (c) the provision of

---

[179] Planning and Development Regulations 2001, art.189.
[180] Planning and Development Regulations 2001, art.182.
[181] Planning and Development Regulations 2001, art.191.
[182] PDA 2000, s.231(3).

adequate facilities for the health and welfare of persons at the place in connection with the event, including the provision of sanitary facilities; (d) the protection of the environment in which the event is to be held, including the control of litter; (e) the maintenance of public order; (f) the avoidance or minimisation of disruption to the neighbourhood in which the event is to take place; (g) ensuring the provision of adequate means of transport to and from the place in which the event is to be held; (h) the number of events which are permitted at a venue within a specified period not exceeding one year; (i) the payment of a financial contribution to the local authority of a specified amount or an amount calculated on a specified basis towards the estimated cost to the local authority of measures taken by the planning authority in connection with the event; (j) the payment of a financial contribution to a person or body consulted of a specified amount or an amount calculated on a specified basis towards the estimated cost to that person or body of measures taken by the person or body in connection with the event; (k) maintaining public liability insurance; (l) the display of notices for persons attending the event as to their obligations and conduct at the event.[183]

8–280   Conditions requiring the payment of a financial contribution may only relate to an event which is held wholly or mainly for profit.

8–281   A person shall not be entitled solely by reason of a licence to hold an event.

6. Codes of practice in relation to events

8–282   The Minister for the Environment, Heritage and Local Government or any Minister of the Government may draw up and issue codes of practice for the purpose of providing practical guidance with respect to the statutory requirements in relation to events. The Minister or any Minister of the Government, as appropriate, shall, before issuing a code of practice, consult any other Minister of the Government or other person or body that appears to that Minister to be appropriate. The Minister or any Minister of the Government, as appropriate, may amend or revoke any code of practice, following consultation with any other Minister of the Government or any other person or body that appears to the Minister to be appropriate.[184]

7. Enforcement of licensing

8–283   Where a local authority has reason to believe that an event in respect of which a licence is required is occurring or is likely to occur (a) without such a licence, or (b) in contravention of the terms of such a licence, the local authority may serve a form of enforcement notice. The notice may require, as appropriate (a) the immediate cessation of any event or the discontinuation or alteration of any preparations which are being made in relation to an event; (b) the removal

---

[183] PDA 2000, s.231(4).
[184] PDA 2000, s.232.

of any temporary buildings, structures, plant, machinery or the like from land which the planning authority believes is intended to be used as the location of an event; and (c) the restoration of the land to its prior condition. Failure to comply with a notice constitutes an offence.[185]

Proceedings for an offence may be brought by the local authority in whose area the offence is committed.[186] Conviction of an offence under Pt XVI is a ground for revocation of a licence.[187] This provision is not necessarily limited to the commission of an offence in connection with the same event. This, arguably, means that if a promoter of several events is convicted of an offence in respect of any one of them, this may provide a reason for the revocation (perhaps by entirely different local authorities) of licences in respect of the others. **8–284**

8. General obligations with regard to safety at events

A person to whom a licence is granted shall take such care as is reasonable in all the circumstances, having regard to the care which a person attending the event may reasonably be expected to take for his or her own safety and, if the person is at the event in the company of another person, the extent of the supervision and control the latter person may be expected to exercise over the former person's activities, to ensure that persons on the land in connection with the event do not suffer injury or damage by reason of any danger arising out of the licensed event or associated activities. It shall be the duty of every person, being on land in connection with a licensed event, to conduct himself or herself in such a way as to ensure that as far as reasonably practicable any person on the land is not exposed to danger as a consequence of any act or omission of his or hers.[188] **8–285**

9. Holding of an event by a local authority

A licence is not required for the holding of an event by a local authority.[189] A local authority is, however, required to undertake a form of public consultation under s.238 of the PDA 2000, and under Pt 15 of the Planning and Development Regulations 2001. **8–286**

The manager of a local authority shall, after the expiration of the period prescribed for the making of submissions or observations, prepare a written report in relation to the proposed event and submit the report to the elected members of the local authority. The report shall (i) specify the proposed event; **8–287**

---

[185] PDA 2000, s.233.
[186] PDA 2000, s.237.
[187] PDA 2000, s.237.
[188] PDA 2000, s.234.
[189] PDA 2000, s.230(4).

(ii) specify the type of "conditions" to which the holding of the proposed event will be subject; (iii) list the persons or bodies who made submissions or observations with respect to the proposed event; (iv) summarise the issues raised in any such submissions or observations and state the response of the manager to them; and (v) recommend whether or not the proposed event should be held.

8–288 The elected members of the local authority are required, as soon as may be, to consider the proposed event and the report of the manager. The default position is that the proposed event may be carried out as recommended in the manager's report, unless the elected members not later than six weeks after receipt of the manager's report pass a resolution deciding to vary or modify the event, otherwise than as recommended in the manager's report, or deciding not to proceed with the event.

10. Control of funfairs

8–289 The status under planning law of funfairs is not entirely clear. Insofar as a special scheme of control is provided for under s.239 (involving such matters as the imposition of a general statutory duty of care, and a requirement to hold a valid certificate of safety) it would seem that it is intended that funfairs are to be regulated other than by way of planning permission. Unfortunately, this is nowhere expressly stated under the PDA 2000. Although there is reference in the side note of s.240 to the exclusion of both events and funfairs from planning control, there is no reference to funfairs in the actual text of the section. Thus it would seem that s.240 is not competent to exclude funfairs from the ordinary requirement to obtain planning permission. It is to be noted that a limited exemption is provided under the Planning and Development Regulations 2001 for funfair use not exceeding fifteen days continuously or thirty days in aggregate in any year.[190]

8–290 Matters are further complicated by the imposition of a requirement to notify a local authority two weeks in advance of an intention to hold or organise a funfair, other than at a place where the operation of funfair equipment has been authorised by a planning permission or is not otherwise an unauthorised use. Again this would seem to suggest that the holding of a funfair is a matter capable of representing an act of development such as to require planning permission.

8–291 It would seem therefore that unlike an "event", as defined, where the provisions of Pt XVI of the PDA 2000 impose a substitute scheme of control, in the case of a "funfair", it is necessary to comply with the requirements of s.239 in addition to complying with the general requirement to obtain planning permission.

---

[190] Planning and Development Regulations 2001, Sch.2, Pt I, Class 37.

11. Definition of "funfair"

"Funfair" is defined as meaning an entertainment where "fairground equipment"   **8–292**
is used. "Fairground equipment" is defined as including any fairground ride or
any similar equipment which is designed to be in motion for entertainment
purposes with members of the public on or inside it, any equipment which is
designed to be used by members of the public for entertainment purposes either
as a slide or for bouncing upon, and any swings, dodgems and other equipment
which is designed to be in motion wholly or partly under the control of, or to
be put in motion by, a member of the public, or any equipment which may be
prescribed, in the interests of public safety, for the purposes of s.239.[191]

The organiser of a funfair and the owner of fairground equipment used at a   **8–293**
funfair are under a statutory duty to take such care as is reasonable in the
circumstances, having regard to the care which a person attending the funfair
may reasonably be expected to take for his or her own safety, and, if the person
is at the event in the company of another person, the extent of the supervision
and control the latter person may be expected to exercise over the former
person's activities to ensure that persons on the land in connection with the
funfair do not suffer injury or damage by reason of any danger arising out of
the funfair or associated activities.

It is the duty of every person being on land in connection with a funfair to   **8–294**
conduct himself or herself in such a way as to ensure that as far as is reasonably
practicable any person on the land is not exposed to danger as a consequence
of any act or omission of his or hers.

It is an offence for an organiser of a funfair or an owner of fairground equipment   **8–295**
to make available for use by the public any fairground equipment unless such
equipment has a valid certificate of safety in accordance with regulations, or is
exempted from such a requirement.

12. Requirement to give notice

A person who intends to hold or organise a funfair, other than at a place where   **8–296**
the operation of funfair equipment has been authorised by a planning permission
or is not otherwise an unauthorised use, shall give two weeks' notice (or such
other period of notice as may be prescribed) in writing to the local authority in
whose functional area the funfair is to be held. The notice shall be accompanied
by a valid certificate of safety for the fairground equipment to be used at the
funfair and shall give details of the names of the organiser of the funfair, the
owner or owners of the fairground equipment to be used at the funfair and the
location and dates on which the funfair is to be held.

---

[191] PDA 2000, s.239.

13.   Enforcement against funfairs

8–297   Where a local authority has reason to believe that a funfair is taking place, or is likely to take place, which is not in compliance with either the requirement to hold a valid certificate of safety, or the requirement to give notice of an intention to hold or organise a funfair, the local authority may serve a notice on any person it believes to be holding, organising or otherwise materially involved in the organisation of the funfair. The notice may require, as appropriate (i) the immediate cessation of any activity or any preparations which are being made in relation to the funfair within a specified time; (ii) the immediate cessation of the use of any fairground equipment without a valid certificate of safety; (iii) the removal, within a specified time, of any fairground equipment, temporary buildings or structures, plant, machinery or similar equipment which the planning authority believes is intended to be used in relation to the funfair; and (iv) the restoration of the land to its prior condition within a specified time. Failure to comply with a notice is an offence.

8–298   Where a person served with a notice fails to comply with it, the local authority concerned may, through its employees or agents, give effect to the terms of the notice, and where necessary for that purpose, enter on the land concerned. The local authority may recover the expenditure reasonably incurred by it in so doing from the person as a simple contract debt in any court of competent jurisdiction. A person who obstructs or impedes the local authority in the performance of these functions shall be guilty of an offence.

N. Local Authority Development

8–299   Under s.4 of the PDA 2000, local authority development in its own functional area is exempted development and as such does not require a grant of planning permission. See para.2–93. Notwithstanding this, local authority development is not entirely free from control under the planning legislation. Certain categories of local authority development are expressly subject to other types of control under the PDA 2000. The three principal forms of control are as follows.

8–300   First, under s.179 of the PDA 2000, and Pt 8 of the Planning and Development Regulations 2001, specified development by a local authority is required to undergo a form of public consultation. This is discussed at paras 8–303 to 8–315 below.

8–301   Secondly, certain local authority development is subject to environmental impact assessment. More specifically, where local authority development belongs to a class of development prescribed for the purposes of environmental impact assessment under s.176 of the PDA 2000 that development is subject to assessment by An Bord Pleanála. The law in respect of environmental impact assessment is discussed in detail in Chapter 13. Those procedural aspects peculiar to local authority development will be considered, in summary form, at paras 8–316 to 8–344 below.

Finally, in addition to these express statutory controls, there is also a prohibition under s.178 of the PDA 2000 on a local authority effecting any development in its functional area which contravenes materially its own development plan. This has been discussed earlier, at paras 1–10 to 1–19. This statutory prohibition is disapplied in the case of certain development and this is considered further at paras 8–349 to 8–355 below.

8–302

1. Public consultation procedure

As indicated above, certain prescribed local authority development is required to undergo a form of public consultation procedure.[192] The relevant development is prescribed under Pt 8 of the Planning and Development Regulations 2001.[193] A wide range of developments are affected, such as, for example, the construction or erection of a house; or the construction of a bridge or tunnel. There is also a general category based on the estimated cost of the proposed development exceeding $126,000.

8–303

In the case of local authority development not subject to environmental impact assessment, the requirements of the Major-Accident Hazards Directive are achieved by, in effect, deeming the relevant development to be development for the purposes of s.179 of the PDA 2000. The effect of this is to apply the provisions of Pt 8 of the Planning and Development Regulations 2001 to the development.

8–304

Major-accident hazards Directive/Seveso Directive

Local authority development which relates to the provision of, or modifications to, a major-accident establishment, and which could have significant repercussions on major-accident hazards is subject to the procedure under s.179 of the PDA 2000 and Pt 8 of the Planning and Development Regulations 2001.[194] There is a requirement to notify the HSA and request technical advice on the effects of the proposed development on the risk or consequences of a major accident. The manager's report prepared under s.179(3) is required to include a copy of any relevant technical advice received from the HSA.[195] Notice of the outcome of the Pt 8 procedure is to be sent to the HSA.

8–305

As in the case of development subject to planning permission, the obligations in this regard apply not only to development which consists of the provision of, or modifications to, a major-accident establishment, but also to development within the vicinity of an existing establishment. The separation distances under Sch.8 of the Planning and Development Regulations 2001 apply.

8–306

---

[192] PDA 2000, s.179.
[193] Planning and Development Regulations 2001, art.80.
[194] Planning and Development Regulations 2001, art.145.
[195] Planning and Development Regulations 2001, art.148.

8–307   If, however, the development is subject to environmental impact assessment, then the requirements of the Major-Accident Hazards Directive will be met as part of that assessment procedure, and s.179 of the PDA 2000 and Pt 8 of the Planning and Development Regulations 2001 will not apply.

Exceptions

8–308   Under s.179(6) of the PDA 2000, it is provided that the public consultation procedure shall not apply to development which (a) consists of works of maintenance or repair, other than works which would materially affect the character of a protected structure or proposed protected structure; (b) is necessary for dealing urgently with any situation which the manager considers is an emergency situation calling for immediate action; (c) consists of works which a local authority is required by or under statute or by order of a court to undertake; or (d) is development in respect of which an environmental impact statement is required.

8–309   Different rationales appear to underlie the various elements of this mixture of exceptions. The first and fourth are relatively straightforward: the public consultation is directed to new development and thus is generally unnecessary in the case of works of maintenance or repair; there is extensive provision made for public participation under the environmental impact assessment procedure and thus it would involve an unnecessary duplication of control to superimpose further requirements. The second and third are more significant. As discussed further at para.8–313 below, it seems that the purpose of the public consultation procedure is to introduce political accountability in respect of local authority development. This objective is reined in, however, by a concern that a local authority not be frustrated in the discharge of its statutory duties. Thus, the public consultation procedure may be by-passed where urgent action is required, or where a local authority is required by or under statute or by order of a court to undertake works.

Procedure

8–310   The procedure, to a large extent, mirrors that applicable to the making of an application for planning permission. Thus, for example, a local authority is required to give notice of the proposed development in an approved newspaper, and to erect or fix a site notice(s) on the land on which the proposed development will be situated. The public notices must state, *inter alia*, the nature and extent of the proposed development and indicate that submissions or observations with respect to the proposed development, dealing with the proper planning and sustainable development of the area, may be made in writing to the local authority. There is also a requirement to give notice to certain prescribed bodies, according to the nature and extent of the development.

Manager's report

The manager of the planning authority is required to prepare a report for the **8–311** elected members.[196] The report should include, *inter alia*, (i) a description of the nature and extent of the proposed development and the principal features thereof (including an appropriate plan of the development and appropriate map of the relevant area); (ii) an evaluation of whether or not the proposed development would be consistent with the proper planning and sustainable development of the area to which the development relates, having regard to the provisions of the development plan, giving the reasons and the considerations for the evaluation; (iii) a list of the persons or bodies who made submissions or observations with respect to the proposed development; (iv) a summary of the issues, with respect to the proper planning and sustainable development of the area in which the proposed development would be situated, raised in any such submissions or observations, and the response of the manager thereto; and (v) a recommendation whether or not the proposed development should be proceeded with as proposed, or as varied or modified as recommended in the report, or should not be proceeded with, as the case may be.

There is, in effect, a default acceptance of the proposed development, subject **8–312** to any resolution to the contrary by the elected members.[197]

Limited role of elected members

Although it is not expressly stated under the PDA 2000, the thinking behind **8–313** the procedure seems to be to allow a measure of political accountability in respect of local authority development. The procedure ensures that the elected members will have an opportunity to evaluate the proposed development, and, in particular, will have been made aware of the submissions and observations made by members of the public. In principle, the elected members have a form of veto over the proposed development. This then is the form of control substituted for the requirement to obtain a grant of planning permission.

In practice, the efficacy of this public consultation procedure is undermined by **8–314** the following two matters. First, the powers of a local authority are limited in a general way under s.179 of the PDA 2000 and under the Local Government Act 2001. Secondly, a local authority is prohibited from resolving that works not be proceeded with where such resolution would be contrary to, or inconsistent with, any provision of a waste management plan.[198] This latter restriction is self-explanatory. The first restriction requires further elaboration, as follows.

The general power of the elected members under s.139 of the Local Government **8–315** Act 2001 to direct that certain works not be proceeded with is not available in

---

[196] PDA 2000, s.179(3).
[197] PDA 2000, s.179(4)(b).
[198] Waste Management Act 1996, s.22(10)(g) (as inserted by s.4 of the Waste Management (Amendment) Act 2001, as amended by the Protection of the Environment Act 2003).

circumstances where the works are works which the local authority is required by or under statute or order of court to undertake. This provision seems intended to prevent the elected members from using their powers to frustrate development (especially unpopular development). It is unclear as to what, if any, discretion this leaves over to the elected members. On a generous interpretation, one might argue that whereas the statutory provision does not allow the elected members to frustrate the carrying out of the development, the elected members are still entitled to have a say in relation to where the development should be located and, to this end, to veto particular sites. As against this, similar wording was interpreted very narrowly by the Supreme Court in *East Wicklow Conservation Community Ltd. v Wicklow County Council*[199] so as to limit the discretion of a local authority even as to the selection of a particular site. The interpretation of the Supreme Court appeared to suggest that once a local authority was required to undertake particular works (in that case, a waste disposal facility), the elected members could not interfere with the choice made by the executive as to the location of same.

2. Environmental impact assessment by An Bord Pleanála

8–316   Certain local authority development is subject to environmental impact assessment by An Bord Pleanála.[200] There is a requirement under s.175 of the PDA 2000 (as amended by the 2006 Act) to prepare an environmental impact statement, and to submit it for approval to An Bord Pleanála. This requirement applies to development which is prescribed for the purposes of environmental impact assessment,[201] but which is not subject to the requirement to obtain planning permission, on account of its being exempted development under s.4 of the PDA 2000.[202] The development includes not just development carried out by the local authority itself, but extends to development carried out by some other person on behalf of, or jointly or in partnership with, a local authority, pursuant to a contract entered into by that local authority.[203]

8–317   There is a prohibition on carrying out development to which s.175 (as amended) applies unless An Bord Pleanála has approved it.[204] A person who contravenes a condition imposed by An Bord Pleanála on an approval shall be guilty of an offence.[205]

---

[199] [1996] 3 I.R. 175; [1997] 2 I.L.R.M. 72.
[200] PDA 2000, s.175 (as amended by the 2006 Act); and Pt 10 of the Planning and Development Regulations 2001 (as amended by the 2006 Regulations).
[201] PDA 2000, s.176; and the Planning and Development Regulations 2001, art.93 and Sch.5.
[202] The requirements of the PDA 2000, s.175 do not apply to proposed road development within the meaning of the Roads Act 1993 by or on behalf of a road authority.
[203] Note that PDA 2000, s.175(1) identifies development in terms similar to those under PDA 2000, s.4(1)(b), (c), (d), (e) and (f).
[204] PDA 2000, s.175(2).
[205] PDA 2000, s.175(13).

Sub-threshold development and screening

As in the case of private-sector development, one of the most obvious weaknesses of the environmental impact assessment procedure lies in the treatment of sub-threshold development.

8–318

Under art.120 of the Planning and Development Regulations 2001 (as amended under the 2006 Regulations), a local authority is under an *express* duty to "decide" whether sub-threshold development would be likely to have significant effects on the environment in the case of European sites and land subject to specified designations under the Wildlife (Amendment) Act 2000.[206] Where it decides that the proposed development would *not* be likely to have significant effects, the local authority must make its decision, including the main reasons and considerations on which it is based, available for inspection or purchase.[207]

8–319

In all other cases, an environmental impact statement is to be prepared where the local authority "considers" that the development would be likely to have significant effects on the environment. Presumably, this carries with it an *implied* duty to address its mind to, and reach a conclusion on, this question.[208] There is, however, no requirement to publish its decision or state the main reasons or considerations therefore.

8–320

It is not at all clear why an *express* obligation to consider the question of whether sub-threshold development would be likely to have significant effects, and to give reasons, was not imposed in all cases.

8–321

Of course, this *ad hoc* screening procedure is open to the criticism that the local authority, as promoter of the proposed development, is not a disinterested party and therefore may well be anxious to avoid the delays and uncertainties inherent in making an application to An Bord Pleanála for approval under s.175 (as amended). For this reason, the local authority may lean against imposing any requirement for an environmental impact assessment. At the very least, there may be a perception of the local authority being a judge in its own cause.

8–322

As it happens, art.120 of the Planning and Development Regulations 2001 goes on to state that An Bord Pleanála may require an environmental impact statement in the case of a sub-threshold project where it considers that the development would be likely to have significant effects on the environment.[209] The difficulty, however, is that there is no obvious procedure whereby such development would come to the attention of An Bord Pleanála. There is no

8–323

---

[206] Planning and Development Regulations 2001, art.120(2).
[207] Planning and Development Regulations 2001, art.120(7) (as amended by art.28 of the 2006 Regulations).
[208] See, by analogy, *Berkeley v Secretary of State for the Environment* [2001] 2 A.C. 603; (2001) P. & C.R. 492.
[209] Planning and Development Regulations 2001, art.120(3).

express obligation on a local authority to seek a screening decision from An Bord Pleanála, nor does there appear to be any procedure by which a third party could refer the matter to the board.

8–324 By contrast, in the context of private-sector development, most sub-threshold development will be subject to the requirement to apply for planning permission *simpliciter*, and thus the relevant planning authority, and An Bord Pleanála on appeal, will have an opportunity during the course of the planning application procedure to address its mind to the question whether or not there should be environmental impact assessment. In the case of local authority development, it is an all or nothing situation: the development is either subject to the full rigours of the EIA procedure under s.175 or it is not. There is no lesser form of application involved, which would bring sub-threshold development to the attention of An Bord Pleanála.

Procedural requirements governing application for approval

8–325 A planning authority may, before making its application, request An Bord Pleanála to provide a written opinion on the information to be contained in the environmental impact statement, *i.e.* a scoping opinion.[210]

8–326 Prior to making the application for approval to An Bord Pleanála, the local authority is required to give public notice of the proposed development.[211] Notice is to be published in one or more newspapers circulating in the area. The notice should indicate the nature and location of the proposed development; that an environmental impact statement has been prepared in respect of the proposed development; and that submissions or observations may be made to An Bord Pleanála relating to the implications of the proposed development for proper planning and sustainable development in the area concerned and its likely effects on the environment. If the proposed development is, in the opinion of the local authority, likely to have significant effects on the environment of a transboundary State, the notice should additionally indicate that the local authority is notifying the relevant State.[212]

8–327 The environmental impact statement is to be available for public inspection (and for purchase) for a specified period of not less than six weeks.

8–328 The local authority is also required to send a copy of the application and the environmental impact statement to the prescribed authorities,[213] together with a notice stating that submissions or observations may be made in writing to An Bord Pleanála.

---

[210] Planning and Development Regulations 2001, art.117.

[211] PDA 2000, s.175(4) (as amended by the EC (Environmental Impact Assessment) (Amendment) Regulations 2006 (S.I. No. 659 of 2006), art.6(1)).

[212] This amendment was introduced under the EC (Environmental Impact Assessment) (Amendment) Regulations 2006 (S.I. No. 659 of 2006), art.6(1).

[213] The bodies are prescribed under Planning and Development Regulations 2001, art. 121 (as amended by art.29 of the 2006 Regulations).

An Bord Pleanála has discretion to require the local authority to furnish to the board such further information in relation to (i) the effects on the environment of the proposed development, or (ii) the consequences for proper planning and sustainable development in the area in which it is proposed to situate the said development of such development, as the board may specify.[214]   **8–329**

An Bord Pleanála must require the local authority to give further public notice, and give notice to the prescribed bodies, where it considers that any further information received contains "significant additional data" relating to (i) the likely effects on the environment of the proposed development, and (ii) the likely consequences for the proper planning and sustainable development in the area in which it is proposed to situate the development of such development.[215] A period of at least three weeks must be allowed for the making of submissions and observations.   **8–330**

Where An Bord Pleanála is provisionally of the view that it would be appropriate to approve the proposed development with certain alterations, it may invite the local authority to make specified alterations to the proposed development, and to furnish such information, if any, as the board may specify or, where necessary, to furnish a revised environmental impact statement.[216] If a local authority accepts an invitation to make the specified alterations, then the proposed development shall be deemed to be the development as so altered.[217] In such circumstances, An Bord Pleanála must require the local authority to give further public notice, and give notice to the prescribed bodies, of the nature of the alterations to the proposed development and, if it be the case, that information in relation to the terms of the development as so altered, or a revised environmental impact statement, has been furnished to the board. A period of a minimum of three weeks must be allowed for inspection and purchase, and for the making of submissions and observations.[218]   **8–331**

Parallel compulsory acquisition procedures

In certain instances, the local authority will have invoked its compulsory acquisition powers in support of the proposed development. This will result in there being parallel proceedings in respect of the proposed compulsory purchase order. It is expressly provided under s.175(7) of the PDA 2000 that the person conducting an oral hearing in relation to the compulsory purchase of land which relates wholly or partly to a development subject to environmental impact assessment by An Bord Pleanála shall be entitled to hear evidence relating to the likely effects on the environment of the proposed development, and its likely consequences for proper planning and sustainable development in the area.[219]   **8–332**

---

[214] PDA 2000, s.175(5)(a)(i) (as substituted by the 2006 Act).
[215] PDA 2000, s.175(5)(c)(i) (as substituted by the 2006 Act).
[216] PDA 2000, s.175(5)(a)(ii) (as substituted by the 2006 Act).
[217] PDA 2000, s.175(5)(b) (as substituted by the 2006 Act).
[218] PDA 2000, s.175(5)(c)(ii) (as substituted by the 2006 Act).
[219] Similar provision is made under PDA 2000, s.220(1).

8–333 An Bord Pleanála should make any decision on the confirmation of the compulsory purchase order at the same time as its decision on the environmental impact assessment.[220]

Decision on environmental impact assessment

8–334 In deciding whether or not to approve the proposed development (with or without modifications), An Bord Pleanála shall have regard to the following considerations (a) the environmental impact statement itself, any submissions or observations made and any other information furnished relating to (i) the likely effects on the environment of the proposed development and (ii) the likely consequences for proper planning and sustainable development in the area in which it is proposed to situate the said development of such development; (b) the views of any other Member State of the European Communities or a State which is a party to the Transboundary Convention to which a copy of the environmental impact statement was sent; and (c) where there is an oral hearing, the report and any recommendations of the person holding the oral hearing.

8–335 In considering information furnished relating to the likely consequences for proper planning and sustainable development of a proposed development in the area in which it is proposed to situate such development, An Bord Pleanála shall have regard to (a) the provisions of the development plan for the area; (b) the provisions of any special amenity area order relating to the area; (c) if the area or part of the area is a European site or an area prescribed for the purposes of s.10(2)(c), that fact; (d) where relevant, the policies of the Government, the Minister for the Environment, Heritage and Local Government or any other Minister of the Government; and (e) the provisions of the PDA 2000 and Regulations thereunder where relevant.

8–336 An Bord Pleanála is required to state the main reasons and considerations on which its decision is based.[221] An Bord Pleanála has a wide discretion as to the type of decision it may make.[222] In particular, the board is not restricted to approving development in the form proposed by the local authority, but may instead grant approval for a modified form of development. An Bord Pleanála may also grant approval for the development in part only (with or without specified modifications). An Bord Pleanála may, of course, also refuse to grant approval. Where approval is granted, An Bord Pleanála may impose conditions.

8–337 An Bord Pleanála is required, as soon as may be following the making of its decision, to notify the local authority concerned, and any person who made a (valid) submission or observation.[223]

---

[220] PDA 2000, s.220(2).
[221] Planning and Development Regulations 2001, art. 122. For a general discussion of the duty to give reasons, see paras 12–119 to 12–163.
[222] PDA 2000, s.175(9) (as substituted by the 2006 Act).
[223] Planning and Development Regulations 2001, art.123 (as substituted by the 2006 Regulations).

Planning gain

Without prejudice to the generality of its power to attach conditions, An Bord **8–338** Pleanála is expressly empowered to attach a condition obliging the local authority to provide a planning gain in the form of a "facility or service" which would, in the opinion of the board, constitute a substantial gain to the community. The condition may require either the construction, provision or financing—in whole or in part—of such a facility or service. This power is subject to the following limitation: such a condition shall not require such an amount of financial resources to be committed as would substantially deprive the person in whose favour the approval operates of the benefits likely to accrue from the grant of the approval.

The concerns raised at paras 10–88 to 10–90—in the context of private-sector **8–339** development—as to the legality of the extraction of such a planning gain do not apply with the same force where the developer is a State body.

Costs and expenses

An Bord Pleanála shall direct the payment of such sum as it considers reasonable **8–340** by the local authority concerned to the board towards the costs and expenses incurred by the board in determining an application for approval, including (i) the costs of holding any oral hearing in relation to the application; (ii) the fees of any consultants or advisers engaged in the matter; and (iii) an amount equal to such portion of the remuneration and any allowances for expenses paid to the members and employees of the board as the board determines to be attributable to the performance of duties by the members and employees in relation to the application.[224]

If a local authority fails to pay the sum directed to be paid, An Bord Pleanála **8–341** may recover the sum from the authority as a simple contract debt in any court of competent jurisdiction.

Licensing by Environmental Protection Agency

Where the development subject to environmental impact assessment is also **8–342** subject to licensing by the Environmental Protection Agency (whether a waste management licence or an integrated pollution prevention and control licence), the powers of An Bord Pleanála to attach conditions are restricted.[225] More specifically, An Bord Pleanála is not entitled to subject any approval to conditions which are for the purposes of (i) controlling emissions from the operation of the activity, including the prevention, limitation, elimination, abatement or reduction of those emissions, or (ii) controlling emissions related to or following the cessation of the operation of the activity.

---

[224] PDA 2000, s.175(9A) (as inserted by the 2006 Act).
[225] PDA 2000, s.175(10)(a).

8–343 An Bord Pleanála may, however, still decide to refuse approval for the proposed development, where the board considers that the development, notwithstanding the licensing of the activity, is unacceptable on environmental grounds, having regard to the proper planning and sustainable development of the area in which the development is or will be situate.[226]

8–344 An Bord Pleanála may request the Environmental Protection Agency to make observations within such period (which period shall not in any case be less than three weeks from the date of the request) as may be specified in relation to the proposed development. An Bord Pleanála is required to have regard to any observations received from the Environmental Protection Agency.

Major-accident hazards Directive/Seveso Directive

8–345 An application for approval under s.175 must include a copy of any relevant technical advice provided by the HSA in circumstances where the Major-Accident Hazards Directive applies.[227] The obligation to seek such advice lies not with An Bord Pleanála, as confirming authority, but rather with the local authority as applicant for approval. As in the case of development requiring planning permission, the requirement to notify and to seek advice from the HSA can arise in a number of different circumstances.

Exemption from requirement for environmental impact assessment

8–346 In cases other than those where a transboundary State has indicated that it wishes to furnish views on the effects on the environment of the proposed development, An Bord Pleanála may, where it is satisfied that exceptional circumstances so warrant, exempt proposed local authority development from the requirement for environmental impact assessment.[228]

8–347 The board shall, in granting an exemption (i) consider whether the effects, if any, of the proposed development on the environment should be assessed in some other form, and (ii) make available to members of the public the information relating to the exemption decision, the reasons for granting such exemption and the information obtained under any other form of assessment.[229]

8–348 Notice of the grant of an exemption must be published in *Iris Oifigiúil* and in at least one daily newspaper published in the State. The Commission of the European Communities must also be notified of the grant of the exemption, and provided with a copy of any information made available to members of the public pursuant to any alternative procedure imposed by An Bord Pleanála.[230]

---

[226] PDA 2000, s.175(10)(b).
[227] Planning and Development Regulations 2001, art.144.
[228] PDA 2000, s.175(8)(a).
[229] PDA 2000, s.175(8)(b) (as substituted by the EC (Environmental Impact Assessment) Regulations 2006 (S.I. No. 659 of 2006), art.6(2)).
[230] PDA 2000, s.175(8)(c).

3. Material contravention of development plan

Section 178 of the PDA 2000 prohibits a local authority from effecting any **8–349**
development in its functional area which contravenes materially the
development plan. As discussed previously at para.1–10 and onwards, the
equivalent prohibition under the previous legislation had been interpreted by
the courts in such a way so as to impose a very effective control over local
authority development. In particular, the prohibition had been successfully
invoked on a number of occasions by objectors seeking to enjoin certain local
authority developments. The relevant case law in this regard has already been
considered, and it is not proposed to address the matter further here. The only
new or additional point that needs to be made is that the statutory prohibition
on local authority development in material contravention of the development
plan is disapplied in certain contexts, under other legislation, as follows.

Roads Act 1993

Under s.20 of the Roads Act 1993, the National Roads Authority may direct a **8–350**
roads authority to attend to certain matters. It is expressly provided that a road
authority shall, notwithstanding the (then) prohibition on local authority
development in material contravention of the development plan or any other
enactment, take all such measures as are necessary to comply with such a
direction.

The concept of material contravention does, however, retain some significance **8–351**
in that a special procedure is required to be followed in the event of a material
contravention. More specifically, under s.20(2) of the Roads Act 1993, the
National Roads Authority must comply with the following requirements before
issuing a direction in relation to any works which would, in the opinion of the
National Roads Authority, if carried out, require a road authority to contravene
materially a development plan or a special amenity area order.

(i) Publish in one or more newspapers circulating in the area where the
proposed works would be carried out a notice stating that it proposes to
issue such direction and that objections or representations may be made in
writing to the National Roads Authority in relation to such a proposed
direction before a specified date (which shall be not less than one month
after the date of first publication of the notice);

(ii) Serve a notice on the road authority and, where the road authority is not
the planning authority, on the planning authority, stating that it proposes
to issue such direction and that objections or representations may be made
in writing to the National Roads Authority in relation to such proposed
direction before a specified date (which shall be not less than one month
after the date on which the notice was served);

(iii) Consider any objections or representations made to it, and not withdrawn.

Waste Management Acts 1996 to 2001

8–352 The material contravention procedure is disapplied under the Waste Management Acts 1996 to 2001 (as amended by the Protection of the Environment Act 2003) in circumstances where the development is consistent with provisions (including any objectives contained therein) of, and is necessary for the proper implementation of, a waste management plan in force in relation to the area concerned. More specifically, s.4 of the Waste Management (Amendment) Act 2001 inserts a new s.22(10)(C) into s.22 of the Waste Management Act 1996. This subsection provides, *inter alia*, that notwithstanding the fact that the proposed development would materially contravene the development plan, the manager may decide to proceed with proposed development of the type referred to above. Again, there is a requirement for public consultation. The manager shall publish notice of the intention of the planning authority to carry out the proposed development in one or more newspapers circulating in that functional area. Any submission or observation in writing in relation to the proposed development which is received by the planning authority not later than four weeks after the publication of the notice shall be considered by the manager.

8–353 It is to be noted that this exception to the material contravention prohibition applies to works proposed to be carried out either by a local authority that is a planning authority, or some other person on behalf of, or jointly or in partnership with such a local authority, pursuant to a contract entered into by that local authority.

Housing (Traveller Accommodation) Act 1998

8–354 Perhaps somewhat surprisingly, only very limited provision is made under the Housing (Traveller Accommodation) Act 1998 to disapply the prohibition on local authority development in material contravention of the development plan. Specifically, the Act of 1998 had introduced for the first time an *express* requirement that a housing authority include, in its development plan, objectives in relation to the provision of accommodation for travellers. (Similar provision is now made under s.10(2)(i) of the PDA 2000.) The transitional provisions stipulated that anything done, or any act carried out, by a housing authority for the purpose of implementing a traveller accommodation program shall be deemed *not* to contravene a development plan in the period between the coming into operation of this (at the time, new) obligation, and compliance with same.[231] Thereafter, it would seem that the development of a halting site at a location not identified in the development plan would represent a material contravention.[232]

---

[231] *cf. Ward v Donegal County Council*, unreported, High Court, Ó Caoimh J., November 30, 2000, where it seems to have been intimated that the prohibition on material contravention might be disapplied in wider circumstances.

[232] *cf.* the provision made in respect of waste disposal facilities under the Waste Management Acts 1996 to 2001 (as amended by the Protection of the Environment Act 2003).

Interestingly, it would seem from the decision in *Byrne v Fingal County Council*[233] that the prohibition on the carrying out of development in material contravention of the development plan remains intact even in circumstances where the manager seeks to invoke the deemed "emergency situation" provisions. More specifically, the requirement which otherwise applies to inform the elected members of intention to carry out work, and the related power of the elected members to direct by resolution that such works not proceed,[234] do not apply in the case of an emergency situation. In this regard, "emergency situation" has an artificial definition and an emergency situation is deemed to exist where, in the opinion of the manager, the works concerned are urgent and necessary in order to provide a reasonable standard of accommodation for any person. The High Court in *Byrne v Fingal County Council* held that the equivalent provision to s.178 was not affected by the deemed emergency provisions. McKechnie J. held that the relevant provisions regulated the internal affairs of the local authority and defined the relationship between the manager and the elected members. The provisions did not, however, by-pass the statutory prohibition on works in material contravention of the development plan.

8–355

O. State Authority Development

There is no presumption—whether deriving from the provisions of the Constitution or from the common law—that a general statute does not apply to the State or State agencies unless it is either expressly so applied or must so apply by necessary implication.[235] In principle, therefore, development by a State authority is subject to the requirement to obtain planning permission in the ordinary way.

8–356

Under s.181 of the PDA 2000, however, the Minister for the Environment, Heritage and Local Government may provide that the provisions of the PDA 2000 shall not apply to any specified class or classes of development by or on behalf of a State authority where the development is, in the opinion of the Minister, in connection with or for the purposes of public safety or order, the administration of justice or national security or defence. The Minister then has a further discretion to require that any class of development so specified be subject to a form of public consultation. There is a separate requirement for environmental impact assessment where the development is likely to have significant effects on the environment.[236]

8–357

Thus, insofar as development by a State authority is concerned, there are four possible scenarios as follows. First, the development might be subject to the

8–358

---

[233] [2001] 4 I.R. 565; [2002] 2 I.L.R.M. 321.
[234] See now Local Government Act 2001, ss.138; 139; and 140.
[235] See, generally, *Howard v Commissioners of Public Works* [1994] 1 I.R. 101; [1993] I.L.R.M. 665.
[236] PDA 2000, ss.181A to 181C (as inserted by the 2006 Act).

requirement to obtain planning permission in the ordinary way. Secondly, the development might be free entirely from the provisions of the PDA 2000. Thirdly, the development might be free from the requirement to obtain planning permission, but nevertheless be subject to a form of public consultation under s.181(1)(b). Finally, the development might be free from the requirement to obtain planning permission, but nevertheless be subject to environmental impact assessment.

1. Development specified under Section 181

8–359   The Minister for the Environment, Heritage and Local Government has prescribed development for the purposes of s.181 under Pt 9 of the Planning and Development Regulations 2001.[237] The classes of development include, for example, Garda stations or other buildings or facilities used for the operations of the Garda Síochána; prisons or other places of detention; courthouses; and buildings or other premises used for the purposes of or in connection with the business of certain government departments (for example, those of Defence, Foreign Affairs, and Justice). Also included are development works carried out for reasons of national security within or bounding the curtilage of any building, premises or other installation occupied by, or under the control of, a State authority.

8–360   Development of these types are, therefore, excepted from the requirement to obtain planning permission. Such development will be referred to by the shorthand "specified development" where convenient.

2. Public consultation procedure under Section 181(1)(b)

8–361   Subject to an exception in favour of development consisting of the construction or erection of temporary structures urgently required for reasons of national security for the purposes of or in connection with the operations of the Defence Forces or An Garda Síochána, all classes of specified development are required to undergo a public consultation procedure under s.181(1)(b).[238]

8–362   The State authority is required to give public notice of the proposed development, by way of newspaper and site notices.[239] The notices must state (a) the location, townland or postal address of the proposed development; (b) the nature and extent of the proposed development; (c) where applicable, that the development would materially affect the character of a protected structure or proposed protected structure, or that the development would materially alter the character of an architectural conservation area; (d) that drawings and

---

[237] Planning and Development Regulations 2001, art.86.
[238] See art.87 of the Planning and Development Regulations 2001 (as amended by the 2006 Regulations).
[239] Planning and Development Regulations 2001, art.87(2) and (3) (as amended by the 2006 Regulations).

particulars of the proposed development are available for inspection; and (e) that submissions or observations may be made within a period of six weeks beginning on the date of the publication of the notice.[240]

Notice of the proposed development is also to be sent to the planning authority for the area in which the proposed development would be situated.[241] Notice must also be given to the Minister for the Environment, Heritage and Local Government in cases where the development would materially affect the character of a protected structure or proposed protected structure, or where the development would materially alter the character of an architectural conservation area.   **8–363**

The State authority is required to make the following documentation available for inspection for a period of six weeks beginning on the date on which the newspaper notice is published[242]: (a) a document describing, in outline, the nature and extent of the proposed development; (b) a location map—drawn to a scale of 1:1,000 in built-up areas, and 1:2,500 in all other areas—identifying clearly the land on which it is proposed to carry out the development; (c) drawings or particulars outlining the external appearance of any structure to be provided or extended, or, (d) where applicable, showing how the development would affect the character of a protected (or proposed protected) structure.   **8–364**

Neither the State authority nor An Bord Pleanála is required to disclose details of the internal arrangements of a development which might prejudice the internal or external security of the development or facilitate any unauthorised entrance to, or exit from, the development of any person when it is completed.[243]   **8–365**

The State authority is required to have regard to any (valid) submissions or observations made by a planning authority or any other person or body.[244] The State authority has discretion to decide whether the proposed development should be carried out—with or without variations or modifications—or refused.[245] The State authority must send notice of its decision to the planning authority, and to any person who has made submissions or observations.[246] This latter requirement is dispensed with, however, where a large number of submissions or observations have been made as part of an organised campaign, or where it is not possible to readily ascertain the name and address of those   **8–366**

---

[240] The public notice requirements are broadly similar to those governing applications for planning permission, and the discussion at para.3–03 and onwards may be of some relevance.
[241] Planning and Development Regulations 2001, art.88 (as amended by the 2006 Regulations).
[242] Planning and Development Regulations 2001, art.89 (as amended by art.22 of the 2006 Regulations).
[243] PDA 2000, s.181B(13) (as inserted by the 2006 Act).
[244] Planning and Development Regulations 2001, art.90(1).
[245] Planning and Development Regulations 2001, art.90(2).
[246] Planning and Development Regulations 2001, art.91.

persons who made submissions or observations. In such cases, the State authority may give notice to the public by some other means.

8–367 A State authority has discretion to publish notice of its decision in an approved newspaper.

3. Environmental impact assessment

8–368 State authority development which has been specified for the purposes of s.181 of the PDA 2000 is subject to environmental impact assessment where it is likely to have significant effects on the environment.[247] This assessment procedure is instead of, rather than in addition to, the public consultation procedure described above.[248]

8–369 The assessment is performed by An Bord Pleanála, and the proposed development shall not be carried out unless the board has approved it (with or without modifications).[249]

8–370 The statutory wording is somewhat unusual in that there does not appear to be any express requirement that the development be of a type prescribed under Annex I or Annex II of the EC environmental impact assessment Directive ("the EIA Directive"). Rather, it seems that any development of a type set out in art.86 of the Planning and Development Regulations 2001 is subject to assessment where it is likely to have significant effects on the environment. On this analysis, then, the requirement for an assessment under national law is far wider than that under the EIA Directive. Assessment under the Directive is confined to the development projects prescribed under Annex I and Annex II. There will be little overlap between development projects prescribed for the purposes of the Directive, and the type of development specified for the purposes of s.181(1) of the PDA 2000. A State authority is unlikely to carry out development of a type within any of the categories prescribed for the purposes of the Directive, save for the possible exception of "infrastructure projects" under Annex II.

8–371 Thus, to take a practical example, development consisting of the extension of a courthouse beyond its existing curtilage might require assessment under national law if, say, the original courthouse is a protected structure. The development could be said to be likely to have a significant effect on architectural or cultural heritage. No such assessment would be required for the purposes of the EIA Directive, however. Similarly a small-scale State authority development might require assessment under national law were it to involve excavation in an archaeologically sensitive area.

---

[247] PDA 2000, s.181A (as inserted by the 2006 Act).
[248] PDA 2000, s.181B(12) (as inserted by the 2006 Act). See also Planning and Development Regulations 2001, art.87(1)(b) (as substituted by the 2006 Regulations).
[249] PDA 2000, s.181A(2) (as inserted by the 2006 Act).

Screening

A State authority may request An Bord Pleanála to make a determination of whether development which it proposes to carry out or have carried out is likely to have significant effects on the environment.[250]   **8–372**

Scoping

A State authority may request An Bord Pleanála to give an opinion in writing on what information will be required to be contained in an environmental impact statement in relation to the proposed development.[251]   **8–373**

Pre-application consultations

A State authority shall, before making the application, enter into consultations with An Bord Pleanála in relation to the proposed development. An Bord Pleanála may give advice regarding the proposed application and, in particular, regarding (a) the procedures involved in making the application, and (b) what considerations, related to proper planning and sustainable development or the environment, may, in the opinion of the board, have a bearing on its decision.[252]   **8–374**

An Bord Pleanála is required to keep a record in writing of any such consultations, including the names of those who participated in the consultations, and a copy of such record shall be placed and kept with the documents to which any application in respect of the proposed development relates.[253]   **8–375**

Application procedure

Prior to making the application for approval to An Bord Pleanála, the State authority is required to give public notice of the proposed development.[254] Notice is to be published in one or more newspapers circulating in the area. The notice should indicate the nature and location of the proposed development; that an environmental impact statement has been prepared in respect of the proposed development; and that submissions or observations may be made to An Bord Pleanála relating to the implications of the proposed development for proper planning and sustainable development in the area concerned and its likely effects on the environment.   **8–376**

The environmental impact statement is to be available for public inspection (and for purchase) for a specified period of not less than six weeks.   **8–377**

The State authority is also required to send a copy of the application and the environmental impact statement (together with a notice stating that submissions   **8–378**

---

[250] PDA 2000, s.181C(3) (as inserted by the 2006 Act).
[251] PDA 2000, s.181C(3) (as inserted by the 2006 Act).
[252] PDA 2000, ss.181C(1) and (2) (as inserted by the 2006 Act).
[253] PDA 2000, s.181C(7) (as inserted by the 2006 Act).
[254] PDA 2000, s.181A(3) (as inserted by the 2006 Act).

or observations may be made in writing to An Bord Pleanála) to the local authority or each local authority in whose functional area the proposed development would be situate, and to any prescribed bodies.[255]

8–379 Where the proposed development is likely to have significant effects on the environment of a Member State of the European Communities or a State which is a party to the Transboundary Convention, the State authority must send a prescribed number of copies of the application and the environmental impact statement to the prescribed authority of the relevant State or States, together with a notice stating that submissions or observations may be made in writing to An Bord Pleanála.[256]

8–380 An Bord Pleanála has discretion to require the State authority to furnish to the board such further information in relation to the effects on proper planning and sustainable development or the environment of the proposed development as the board may specify.[257]

8–381 An Bord Pleanála must require the State authority to give further public notice, and give notice to the prescribed bodies, where it considers that any further information received contains "significant additional data" relating to (i) the likely effects on the environment of the proposed development, and (ii) the likely consequences for the proper planning and sustainable development in the area in which it is proposed to situate the development of such development.[258] A period of at least three weeks must be allowed for the making of submissions and observations.

Alterations to proposed development

8–382 Where An Bord Pleanála is provisionally of the view that it would be appropriate to approve the proposed development with certain alterations, it may invite the State authority to make specified alterations to the proposed development, and to furnish such information, if any, as the board may specify or, where necessary, to furnish a revised environmental impact statement.[259] If a State authority accepts an invitation to make the specified alterations, then the proposed development shall be deemed to be the development as so altered.[260] In such circumstances, An Bord Pleanála must require the State authority to give further public notice, and give notice to the prescribed bodies, of the nature of the alterations to the proposed development and, if it be the case, that information in relation to the terms of the development as so altered, or a revised environmental impact statement, has been furnished to the board.[261] A period

---

[255] PDA 2000, s.181A(3)(b) (as inserted by the 2006 Act).
[256] PDA 2000, s.181A(3)(c) (as inserted by the 2006 Act).
[257] PDA 2000, s.181A(4)(a) (as inserted by the 2006 Act).
[258] PDA 2000, s.181A(6)(a) (as inserted by the 2006 Act).
[259] PDA 2000, s.181A(4)(b) (as inserted by the 2006 Act).
[260] PDA 2000, s.181A(5) (as inserted by the 2006 Act).
[261] PDA 2000, s.181A(6)(b) (as inserted by the 2006 Act).

of a minimum of three weeks must be allowed for inspection and purchase, and for the making of submissions and observations.

Decision on environmental impact assessment

In deciding whether or not to approve the proposed development (with or without modifications), An Bord Pleanála shall have regard to the following considerations (a) the environmental impact statement itself, any submissions or observations made and any other information furnished relating to (i) the likely consequences for proper planning and sustainable development in the area in which it is proposed to situate the proposed development of such development, and (ii) the likely effects on the environment of the proposed development; and (b) where there is an oral hearing, the report and any recommendations of the person conducting the oral hearing.[262]   **8–383**

In considering information furnished relating to the likely consequences for proper planning and sustainable development of a proposed development in the area in which it is proposed to situate such development, An Bord Pleanála shall have regard to (a) the provisions of the development plan for the area; (b) the provisions of any special amenity area order relating to the area; (c) if the area or part of the area is a European site or an area prescribed for the purposes of s.10(2)(c), that fact; (d) where relevant, the matters referred to in s.143; and (e) the provisions of the PDA 2000 and Regulations thereunder where relevant.[263]   **8–384**

An Bord Pleanála has a wide discretion as to the type of decision it may make.[264] In particular, the board is not restricted to approving development in the form proposed by the State authority, but may instead grant approval for a modified form of development. An Bord Pleanála may also grant approval for the development in part only (with or without specified modifications). An Bord Pleanála may, of course, also refuse to grant approval. Where approval is granted, An Bord Pleanála may impose conditions.   **8–385**

Planning gain

Without prejudice to the generality of its power to attach conditions, An Bord Pleanála is expressly empowered to attach a condition obliging the State authority to provide a planning gain in the form of a "facility or service" which would, in the opinion of the board, constitute a substantial gain to the community. The condition may require either the construction, provision or financing—in whole or in part—of such a facility or service. This power is subject to the following limitation: such a condition shall not require such an amount of financial resources to be committed as would substantially deprive the person in whose favour the approval operates of the benefits likely to accrue from the grant of the approval.   **8–386**

---

[262] PDA 2000, s.181B(1) (as inserted by the 2006 Act).
[263] PDA 2000, s.181B(11) (as inserted by the 2006 Act).
[264] PDA 2000, s.181B(6) (as inserted by the 2006 Act).

8–387   The concerns raised at paras 10–88 to 10–90—in the context of private-sector development—as to the legality of the extraction of such a planning gain do not apply with the same force where the developer is a State authority.

4. Exemption from requirement for environmental impact assessment

An Bord Pleanála

8–388   In cases other than those where a transboundary State has indicated that it wishes to furnish views on the effects on the environment of the proposed development, An Bord Pleanála may, where it is satisfied that exceptional circumstances so warrant, exempt proposed State authority development from the requirement for environmental impact assessment.[265]

8–389   An Bord Pleanála must consider whether (a) the effects, if any, of the proposed development on the environment should be assessed in some other manner, and (b) the information arising from such an assessment should be made available to the members of the public. An Bord Pleanála may then apply alternative requirements to the proposed development.[266]

Minister for Defence

8–390   The Minister for Defence has a discretion to grant an exemption from environmental impact assessment in the case of proposed development in connection with, or for the purposes of, national defence, where the Minister is satisfied that the assessment procedure would have adverse effects on those purposes.[267]

Notice of grant of exemption

8–391   Notice of the grant of an exemption must be published in *Iris Oifigiúil* and in at least one daily newspaper published in the State. The Commission of the European Communities must also be notified of the grant of the exemption, and provided with a copy of any information made available to members of the public pursuant to any alternative procedure imposed by An Bord Pleanála.[268]

5. Major-accident hazards Directive/Seveso Directive

8–392   In the case of certain types of development, a State authority is required to notify the HSA, and to request technical advice on the effects of the proposed development on the risk or consequence of a major accident.[269] The notification

---

[265] PDA 2000, s.181B(2) (as inserted by the 2006 Act).
[266] PDA 2000, s.181B(3) (as inserted by the 2006 Act).
[267] PDA 2000, s.181B(4) (as inserted by the 2006 Act).
[268] PDA 2000, s.181B(5) (as inserted by the 2006 Act).
[269] Planning and Development Regulations 2001, art.150 (as amended by the 2006 Regulations).

requirements only apply in respect of State authority development which will be in the vicinity of an existing major-accident establishment, and thus the assumption is that it is unlikely that State authorities will carry out development involving the provision of, or modifications to, an existing establishment.

P. Compulsory Acquisition of Lands

1. Introduction

Significant amendments to compulsory purchase law were introduced under Pt XIV of the PDA 2000. The reforms include an extension of the circumstances in which a planning authority is entitled to acquire land compulsorily for planning purposes. In addition, the procedure for the confirmation of compulsory purchase orders was amended, with An Bord Pleanála succeeding to the role of confirming authority in most instances.   **8–393**

The enhanced role of planning authorities in positive or proactive planning presents difficult legal issues. As discussed below, the compulsory purchase powers of a planning authority are drawn very widely and, on a literal interpretation, land can be acquired for almost any planning purpose. The foremost issue which arises for consideration is as to how the exercise of such potentially far-reaching powers is to be policed so as to ensure the proper balance between public rights and private rights (which include not only property rights, but might also include the right to respect for the home under Art.8 of the European Convention on Human Rights). Another issue of principle presented is as to how far the concept of public interest can be stretched and, in particular, whether or not the public interest can be said to justify a planning authority using its powers of compulsory acquisition to take land from a private individual with the intention of transferring the ownership of that land to a commercial developer. It is also necessary to examine any potential conflict between the role of a planning authority in promoting development, and the exercise of its regulatory functions, in particular, its function in determining applications for planning permission.   **8–394**

Before turning to address these various matters, the nature of the statutory powers of positive planning will be summarised briefly.   **8–395**

2. Positive planning

Although utilised little, a planning authority was empowered even under the previous legislation to develop or secure the development of land.[270] The relevant provision went on, without prejudice to the general power, to list a number of specific activities which the planning authority could carry on. These   **8–396**

---

[270] Local Government (Planning & Development) Act, 1963, s.77.

included, for example, the provision of areas with roads and such services and works as may be needed for development, and securing the development of obsolete areas.

8–397 Similar powers are now provided under s.212 of the PDA 2000. The powers have, in some instances, been expanded upon. Thus, for example, a planning authority is now expressly entitled to "facilitate" the development of land. A planning authority may also secure, facilitate or carry out the development and renewal of areas in need of physical, social or economic regeneration and provide open spaces and other public amenities. Again as under the previous legislation, a planning authority is also entitled to provide sites for the establishment or relocation of industries, businesses, dwellings, offices, shops, schools, churches, leisure facilities and other community facilities. A planning authority may also provide factory buildings, office premises, shop premises, houses, amusement parks and structures for the purpose of entertainment, caravan parks, buildings for the purpose of providing accommodation, meals and refreshments, buildings for the purpose of providing trade and professional services and advertisement structures.

8–398 For these purposes, a planning authority may make and carry out arrangements or enter into agreements with any person or body for the development or management of land, and may incorporate a company for those purposes. Under s.4(1)(f), development carried out on behalf of, or jointly or in partnership with, a local authority that is a planning authority, pursuant to a contract entered into by the local authority concerned is exempted development.

8–399 In considering the provisions of Pt XIV, it is important to distinguish between those provisions which empower a planning authority to carry on particular activities, and those other provisions which might actually *confer* a statutory right to compulsorily acquire lands. The former are found mainly in s.212. Insofar as the actual power to acquire land compulsorily is concerned, it is not at all clear that Pt XIV of the PDA 2000 actually confers such a power. On one view, Pt XIV merely supplements *existing* powers of compulsory purchase, and it is, therefore, necessary to identify the source of the power to compulsorily acquire in some other piece of legislation. This was the interpretation adopted by the Supreme Court in *Clinton v An Bord Pleanála*.[271] Geoghegan J. suggested that all powers of compulsory acquisition by a local authority for any one or more of its many statutory functions derive in the first place from s.10 of the Local Government (Ireland) Act 1898 (as amended).[272]

8–400 It is at least arguable, however, that the combined effect of s.213(2) and s.213(4) of the PDA 2000 is to confer a power of compulsory acquisition. Section 213(2)

---

[271] [2007] I.E.S.C. 19; unreported, May 2, 2007.
[272] Section 10 has been amended a number of times, but in particular by s.11 of Local Government (No. 2) Act 1960.

expressly states that a local authority may acquire land compulsorily. Section 213(4) provides as follows.[273]

> "A local authority may be authorised by compulsory purchase order to acquire land for any of the purposes referred to in subsection (2) of this section and section 10 (as amended by section 86 of the Housing Act, 1966) of the Local Government (No. 2) Act, 1960, shall be construed so as to apply accordingly and the reference to 'purposes' in section 10(1)(a) of that Act shall be construed as including purposes referred to in subsection (2) of this section."

Section 212(4) provides that a planning authority may use any of the powers available to it under any enactment, including any powers in relation to the compulsory acquisition of land, in relation to its functions under s.212 and, in particular, in order to facilitate the assembly of sites for the purposes of the orderly development of land.   **8–401**

3. "Public interest"

It is well established that a power of compulsory acquisition should only be used in the public interest and that the onus of establishing that the acquisition is in the public interest lies with the acquiring authority.[274] Perhaps the greatest challenge in compulsory purchase law is working out how the general principles are to be applied to the particular facts of any case.   **8–402**

The difficulty with the extension of the powers of a planning authority, and with its becoming involved more proactively in facilitating and, indeed, in actually carrying out, development, is that it puts a strain on the traditional concept or understanding of public interest. Traditionally, powers of compulsory acquisition were employed where it was actually intended to put the acquired land to a public use. Thus, for example, land was acquired for the purposes of roads, railways or parks. Land was also acquired for the purposes of public housing. The extended powers under the PDA 2000 present the question as to whether or not it is open to a planning authority to use its powers of compulsory   **8–403**

---

[273] Section 10(1) of the Local Government (No. 2) Act 1960 (as amended by s.86 of the Housing Act 1966) reads as follows: "Where— (a) a local authority intend to acquire compulsorily any land, whether situate within or outside their functional area, for purposes* for which they are capable of being authorised by law to acquire land compulsorily, (b) those purposes are purposes other than the purposes of the Housing Act, 1966, or are purposes some only of which are purposes of that Act, and (c) the local authority consider that it would be convenient to effect the acquisition under that Act, the local authority may decide so to effect the acquisition." * "Purposes" is to be construed as including the purposes referred to in s.213(2) of the PDA 2000.

[274] See, for example, *Prest v Secretary of State for Wales* (1982) 81 L.G.R. 193; *Chesterfield Properties plc v Secretary of State for the Environment* (1997) 76 P. & C.R. 117 (substantial public interest outweighing landowner's rights); *Tesco Stores Ltd. v Secretary of State for the Environment Transport and the Regions* (2000) 80 P. & C.R. 427; *London Borough of Bexley v Secretary of State for the Environment Transport and the Regions* [2001] E.W.H.C. Admin 323; [2001] J.P.L. 1442; and *R (On the application of Clays Lane Housing Co-Operative Ltd.) v Housing Corporation* [2004] E.W.C.A. Civ 1658.

acquisition to take land from a private individual with the intention of transferring the ownership of that land to a commercial developer.

8–404 The Irish courts have considered the concept of public interest or the common good on a number of occasions in the context of the planning legislation. It appears that the concept is a fluid one and capable of expansion. Thus, objectives such as public safety,[275] the renewal or regeneration of obsolete areas,[276] and the provision of social and affordable housing[277] have all been held to justify restrictions on property rights.

8–405 It is worth considering the language used by the Supreme Court in upholding the constitutionality of a form of compulsory acquisition—as it happens with discounted compensation—for the purposes of social and affordable housing.[278]

> "In the present case, as a condition of obtaining a planning permission for the development of lands for residential purposes, the owner may be required to cede some part of the enhanced value of the land deriving both from its zoning for residential purposes and the grant of permission in order to meet what is considered by the Oireachtas to be a desirable social objective, namely the provision of affordable housing and housing for persons in the special categories and of integrated housing. Applying the tests proposed by Costello J. in *Heaney v. Ireland* [1994] 3 I.R. 593 and subsequently endorsed by this court, the court in the case of the present Bill is satisfied that the scheme passes those tests. They are rationally connected to an objective of sufficient importance to warrant interference with a constitutionally protected right and, given the serious social problems which they are designed to meet, they undoubtedly relate to concerns which, in a free and democratic society, should be regarded as pressing and substantial. At the same time, the court is satisfied that they impair those rights as little as possible and their effects on those rights are proportionate to the objectives sought to be attained."

8–406 It remains to be seen as to whether facilitating a commercial development by a private developer—even with attendant benefits in terms of employment creation and tax revenue—could ever be said to be "an objective of sufficient importance to warrant interference with a constitutionally protected right". This is especially so in cases where the lands sought to be acquired are not rundown or in need of renewal; if the proposed development is not part of some wider scheme to regenerate a deprived area, it will be more difficult to argue that the compulsory purchase order is designed to meet "serious social problems".

8–407 The United States Supreme Court—in *Kelo v City of New London*[279]—has recently had to consider whether the "public use" restriction under the Fifth

---

[275] *Liddy v Minister for Public Enterprise* [2004] 1 I.L.R.M. 9.
[276] *Central Dublin Development Association Ltd. v Attorney General* (1969) 109 I.L.T.R. 69.
[277] *In re Part V of the Planning and Development Bill, 1999* [2000] 2 I.R. 321.
[278] *In re Part V of the Planning and Development Bill, 1999* [2000] 2 I.R. 321.
[279] No. 04-109; June 23, 2005.

Amendment precludes the taking (compulsory acquisition) of private property for the purposes of economic development.

> "While the government may take their homes to build a road or a railroad or to eliminate a property use that harms the public, say petitioners, it cannot take their property for the private use of other owners simply because the new owners may make more productive use of the property."

The majority held that promoting economic development is a traditional and long accepted function of government. The majority went on to say that there was no principled way of distinguishing economic development from other public purposes.   **8–408**

The majority did, however, indicate that there were limits to the circumstances in which a taking could be justified. This point was further emphasised by Kennedy J. in a concurring opinion, where he stated that a court applying rational-basis review should strike down a taking that, by a clear showing, is intended to favour a particular private party, with only incidental or pretextual public benefits.   **8–409**

In a powerful dissent, O'Connor J. stated that, under the majority's theory, nearly all real property was susceptible to condemnation (compulsory acquisition).   **8–410**

> "Any property may now be taken for the benefit of another private party, but the fallout from this decision will not be random. The beneficiaries are likely to be those citizens with disproportionate influence and power in the political process, including large corporations and development firms. As for the victims, the government now has license to transfer property from those with fewer resources to those with more. The Founders cannot have intended this perverse result."

4. Must planning authority put forward scheme of development?

Two practical questions which arise for consideration are, first, the extent to which a planning authority is required to have formulated a particular proposal or scheme of development, and, secondly, the extent to which the basis for the making of a compulsory purchase order must have been laid down in advance in the development plan.   **8–411**

The answers to these questions turn on the extent, if any, to which An Bord Pleanála, as confirming authority, is entitled to consider in detail the intentions of the planning authority in relation to the land. As discussed presently, the response of the Irish courts to these issues is disappointing.[280] Before turning to examine that case law, however, it may be useful to consider the question from first principles.   **8–412**

---

[280] *Crosbie v Custom House Dock Development Authority* [1996] 2 I.R. 531; and *Clinton v An Bord Pleanála* [2007] I.E.S.C. 19; unreported, May 2, 2007.

8–413 There is a sliding scale. On one end, the planning authority should be required to put forward specific proposals and to demonstrate that the necessary permissions and consents will be available for the development. Indeed, there is much to be said for having the confirmation of the compulsory purchase order dealt with in tandem with either the planning application or the Pt 8 procedure. It might also be possible to deal with the question of any requisite environmental impact assessment at the same time. One oral hearing could then be held in respect of all matters.[281]

8–414 At the other end of the scale, the acquiring authority might only have to go so far as establishing that anything would be better than the current use of the land. This might most readily be understood in the context of land requiring redevelopment or regeneration. There, all that the acquiring authority would have to do is to establish that the lands were in need of regeneration.

5. Role of development plan

8–415 Again approaching the matter from first principles, one would expect that the development plan should play a pivotal role in the compulsory purchase procedure. The courts have emphasised time and time again that the development plan represents a form of environmental contract between the planning authority, developers and the public. A planning authority is generally required to disclose in its development plan its own proposals for the development of land. One would have thought, therefore, that before a planning authority resorted to the making of a compulsory purchase order it would, first, set out its policy in relation to the use of powers of compulsory acquisition and indicate that it proposed to use them in particular instances; and, secondly, would identify in its development plan the nature and extent of the particular developments in aid of which compulsory purchase powers were to be invoked.

8–416 The fact that the acquiring authority had carefully formulated an economic development plan which it believed would provide appreciable benefits to the community, including new jobs and increased tax revenue, was given particular weight by the United States Supreme Court in *Kelo v City of New London*.[282]

8–417 This first-principles analysis would appear to be borne out by the provisions of the legislation in respect of development plans. In particular, certain of the mandatory objectives under s.10 of the PDA 2000 mirror the statutory purposes under s.212. Thus, for example, a planning authority is required to include development objectives in its development plan for the development and renewal of areas in need of regeneration; this reflects the statutory function of securing facilities or carrying out the development and renewal of areas in

---

[281] *cf.* PDA 2000, s.220, which allows for the holding of concurrent hearings in respect of compulsory purchase confirmation and environmental impact assessment of local authority development.

[282] No. 04-109; June 23, 2005.

need of physical, social or economic regeneration under s.212. Moreover, under s.213(2)(a) a planning authority may for the purposes of performing any of its functions including giving effect to or facilitating the implementation of a development plan acquire land by agreement or, in certain circumstances, compulsorily.

This issue arose in *Clinton v An Bord Pleanála*. At least part of the lands the subject-matter of the impugned compulsory purchase order had been identified in an integrated area plan prepared for the purposes of the Urban Renewal Act 1998. It was a development objective of the planning authority to seek to implement the integrated area plan. **8–418**

6. Function of An Bord Pleanála

One of the greatest mysteries of compulsory purchase law is as to what precisely it is that An Bord Pleanála must be satisfied of before it confirms a compulsory purchase order. In particular, there is little guidance as to the nature and extent of the considerations which An Bord Pleanála is to take into account in reaching its decision. **8–419**

A further difficulty is that the legislation—at least as interpreted by the Supreme Court in *Clinton v An Bord Pleanála*—does not seem to require the acquiring authority to identify with any degree of specificity the purpose for which the land is to be acquired. This is a real difficulty given the fact that the powers of compulsory acquisition are so widely drawn. Whereas previously the confirmation of a compulsory purchase order would arise in the context of a proposal by the planning authority to carry out—itself—particular development; for example road construction or improvements or the provision of housing; the concept of positive planning means that the range of possibilities is far wider. In the absence of the purpose being identified, it is difficult to understand how An Bord Pleanála, as confirming authority, is expected to balance the individual rights of the landowner as against the wider public interest. **8–420**

What the case law appears to establish is that the compulsory acquisition must be necessary.[283] With respect, this formulation is largely meaningless unless there is to be some context. Necessity might mean a number of different things. The narrowest interpretation would be to say that the use of a power of compulsory acquisition must be necessary in the sense of the landowner being unwilling to sell the land to the acquiring authority voluntarily. Under this analysis, all that would need to be established is that the acquiring authority had made a *bona fide* attempt to negotiate the purchase of the property. **8–421**

---

[283] *Crosbie v Custom House Dock Development Authority* [1996] 2 I.R. 531 at 543/4 (Minister may adjudicate on claim that acquisition not necessary); and *Clinton v An Bord Pleanála* [2007] I.E.S.C. 19; unreported, May 2, 2007.

8–422   A slightly wider formulation would address the question as to whether or not a particular parcel of land was necessary to carry out the scheme of development underlying the compulsory purchase order. Thus, for example, in the context of the compulsory acquisition of land for road development, it would be a question of fact and degree as to whether or not the safe and efficient design of the road required the taking of a particular piece of land.[284] Analogous issues might arise in the case of public housing.[285]

8–423   Of course, this test only works in circumstances where it is possible to debate the appropriate footprint of the proposed development. This can readily be done in the context of road development, but if, as the Supreme Court ruled in *Clinton v An Bord Pleanála*, there is no requirement for the planning authority to put forward any specific development proposals—at least not in cases involving urban regeneration—then the test becomes largely meaningless.

8–424   A third formulation would involve a detailed consideration of proposals for the use or development of the land to be acquired. The fact that the confirming function has now been entrusted to An Bord Pleanála might be taken as suggesting that same should involve some consideration of the planning merits of the proposal.[286] Under this analysis, the test of necessity would be more than simply a one-dimensional question. Rather, the acquiring authority would be required to justify its proposal both in terms of proper planning and in economic terms. All of this would require the confirming authority to consider such alternative development proposals, if any, as might be put forward by those objecting to the compulsory purchase order. An example of the extent of the inquiry which might be required in this regard is provided by the decision of the High Court of England and Wales in *London Borough of Bexley v Secretary of State for the Environment, Transport and the Regions*; *Sainsburys Supermarkets Ltd. v Secretary of State for the Environment, Transport and the Regions*.[287]

> "I do not accept that it is necessary for the Secretary of State to set out in some formulaic way the degree to which the Safeways scheme is better than Sainsburys' scheme, the extent of interference with property rights and a conclusion on proportionality following the weighing of those factors. It is sufficient if the relevant conclusions can be determined from reading the decision letter as a whole. In this case, the Secretary of State carried out a comparative exercise between the two schemes and gave his reasons why the Safeways scheme was better than the Sainsburys scheme. He thereby indicated the extent to which one scheme was better than the other, whilst the degree of interference with Sainsburys'

---

[284] *cf. R v Secretary of State for Transport, Ex p. De Rothschild* [1989] 1 All E.R. 933; 57 P. & C.R. 330.

[285] *Coleen Properties Limited v Minister of Housing and Local Government* [1971] 1 All E.R. 1049 at 1054 (acquisition must be reasonably necessary for the satisfactory development or use under consideration).

[286] See, by analogy, *Kildare County Council v An Bord Pleanála* [2006] I.E.H.C. 173; unreported, MacMenamin J., March 10, 2006.

[287] [2001] E.W.H.C. Admin 323, [48].

rights was self-apparent. In those circumstances, he was entitled to express the conclusions in the way that he did, namely that as a matter of judgment there was a compelling case in the public interest and that a fair balance had been struck between the rights of the individual and the public interest. I do not therefore accept the submission made on behalf of the Sainsburys that the Secretary of State failed to adopt a legally correct approach to his CPO decision. I should also add that, although it was not a matter relied upon by the Secretary of State, he would in my view have been entitled to take into consideration the manner and timing of Sainsburys' acquisition of land on the Grassington Road site when weighing Sainsburys' individual rights against the public interest."

The High Court of England and Wales has indicated that the use of compulsory purchase powers can be justified in the public interest in order to achieve a scheme of development which is better than an alternative scheme (put forward by an objector) which does not require compulsory acquisition.[288] **8–425**

Any requirement for such a wide ranging review by the confirming authority has been disavowed by the Irish courts in at least two decisions. In *Crosbie v Custom House Development Authority*, Costello J. in the High Court appeared to suggest that all that was to be considered was whether the acquisition was necessary to give effect to the particular statutory purpose, without any consideration of whether the proposed development was itself desirable or necessary. **8–426**

> "[…] When deciding whether a compulsory purchase order should be confirmed or not it is not relevant for the Minister to consider (a) whether the proposed development in the planning scheme is desirable or not (b) whether development proposed by an objector in respect of his land is a preferable form of development or not."

The facts of *Crosbie* were peculiar—and hence readily distinguishable—in that the principle that the lands were in need of regeneration had been established by primary legislation. Specifically, the boundaries of the Custom House Docks area had been identified under the Urban Renewal Act 1986 and by an extension order under the Urban Renewal (Amendment) Act 1987. **8–427**

> "The making and confirming of an order compulsorily to acquire an objector's property rights results in an interference with the objector's constitutionally protected rights. Whilst it is true that the actual interference is effected by the confirmation of the compulsory purchase order it is more proper to regard the law which enables the compulsory purchase order to be made as the means by which the rights have been restricted. Here the Oireachtas, by enacting a law which (a) allows the Minister to extend the Custom House Docks Area (b) imposes a duty on the Authority to secure the redevelopment of the new extended Area (c) imposes a duty whose nature is such that in all probability it cannot be carried out unless the Authority owns all the land in the new Area and (d) gives a power to acquire compulsorily land in the new Area from landowners unwilling to convey

---

[288] *Bexley Borough Council v Secretary of State for the Environment, Transport and the Regions* [2001] E.W.H.C. Admin 323; [2001] J.P.L. 1442.

voluntarily their land, has in effect concluded that the public good which is to be achieved by urban renewal requires the limitations on the objector's constitutionally protected rights. *It is the law enacted by the Oireachtas which makes this determination, not the Minister carrying out an administrative function conferred on him by the law.*"
*Emphasis supplied.

8–428 A narrow approach to the confirming authority's function was also taken by the Supreme Court in *Clinton v An Bord Pleanála*.[289] Geoghegan J., having referred earlier to a planning authority's power under s.212 to secure, facilitate or carry out the development and renewal of areas in need of physical, social or economic regeneration, described the onus on the planning authority, as acquiring authority, in the following terms.

"The regeneration purpose, which the council had in mind when deciding to make the Compulsory Purchase Order, was expressly permitted by the Oireachtas. It cannot have been envisaged that the council would have to have a specific plan as to how the regeneration was to be carried out and would have to specify that in the CPO because, as in this case, the whole process would usually involve private developers in some form at least and plans as yet unknown which they would propose and envisage and which would eventually require planning permission. That is quite different from property required for the purposes of council offices or a public swimming pool for instance.

It was at all times perfectly clear that the property was being acquired for regeneration of O'Connell Street. In my view, it was only necessary for the council to demonstrate that a CPO was desirable in the public interest to achieve that purpose. It was not necessary to prove how exactly it would be carried out. Quite apart from the necessity to obtain planning permissions into the future, such a requirement would defeat the purpose of the power conferred by the section."

7. Test of proportionality?

8–429 One of the consequences which the European Convention on Human Rights Act 2003 may have for the confirmation of compulsory purchase orders is that An Bord Pleanála may be required to apply a test of proportionality. It seems that the test of proportionality involves a two-stage test. In particular, it seems that a distinction is to be drawn between proportionality of means and proportionality of ends.[290] Proportionality of means requires consideration of whether the objective may be achieved by means which are less interfering of an individual's rights. This seems to involve a consideration of alternative statutory powers which may be available to the decision-maker. Proportionality of ends, then, requires consideration of whether the measure will have an excessive or disproportionate effect on the interests of affected persons. In other words, even the least intrusive of a number of alternative measures may be found to be disproportionate. In *R. (On the application of Baker) v First*

---

[289] [2007] I.E.S.C. 19; unreported, May 2, 2007.
[290] *R. (On the application of Baker) v First Secretary of State* [2003] E.W.H.C. 2511(Admin); [2004] J.P.L. 729.

Secretary of State,[291] the High Court of England and Wales had to consider whether the making of a compulsory purchase order was proportionate. The facts of the case were exceptional. The lands the subject-matter of the compulsory purchase order were manifestly unfit for human habitation. The premises had been devastated by a fire and all that was left was a shell, filled with rubbish. The planning authority decided that the most satisfactory course of action to deal with the unfitness of the premises was to make a clearance order, and, subsequently, if the property could not be acquired by consent, to make a compulsory purchase order. The landowner argued, conversely, that alternative measures, less intrusive than compulsory purchase, should have been considered. The High Court held that the inspector's report provided relevant and adequate reasons to justify why a compulsory purchase order was the necessary and proportionate way of giving effect to the public interest in the case.

The requirement to apply a two-tier test—albeit in the context of compulsory **8–430** transfer of a registered social landlord's housing stock—was doubted subsequently by the Court of Appeal in *R. (On the application of Clays Lane Housing Co-Operative Ltd.) v Housing Corporation.*[292]

> "In my judgment, the task in which HC was engaged was wholly different from the task of the Secretary of State in *Samaroo*. Having lawfully decided that there would have to be a transfer, the decision was then one between two proffered alternatives. Although not in every respect the same as a planning decision, it approximated to what Keene LJ was describing in Lough (above), namely 'a situation where the essential conflict is between two or more groups of private interests'. I conclude that the appropriate test of proportionality requires a balancing exercise and a decision which is justified on the basis of a compelling case in the public interest and as being reasonably necessary but not obligatorily the least intrusive of Convention rights. That accords with Strasbourg and domestic authority. It is also consistent with sensible and practical decision-making in the public interest in this context. If 'strict necessity' were to compel the 'least intrusive' alternative, decisions which were distinctly second best or worse when tested against the performance of a regulator's statutory functions would become mandatory. A decision which was fraught with adverse consequences, would have to prevail because it was, perhaps quite marginally, the least intrusive. Whilst one can readily see why that should be so in some Convention contexts, it would be a recipe for poor public administration in the context of cases such as *Lough* and the present case."

The judgment in *Clinton v An Bord Pleanála*[293] suggests that the Supreme **8–431** Court accepts, in principle, that a more exacting standard of judicial review applies in the case of the compulsory acquisition of land.

> "I think it appropriate to make the following further observation. It is axiomatic that the making and confirming of a compulsory purchase order (CPO) to acquire

---

[291] [2003] E.W.H.C. 2511 (Admin); [2004] J.P.L. 729.
[292] [2004] E.W.C.A. Civ. 1658, [25].
[293] [2007] I.E.S.C. 19; unreported, May 2, 2007.

a person's land entails an invasion of his constitutionally protected property rights. The power conferred on an administrative body such as a local authority or An Bord Pleanála to compulsorily acquire land must be exercised in accordance with the requirements of the Constitution, including respecting the property rights of the affected landowner (East Donegal Co-Operative v. The Attorney General [1970] I.R. 317). Any decisions of such bodies are subject to judicial review. It would insufficiently protect constitutional rights if the court, hearing the judicial review application, merely had to be satisfied that the decision was not irrational or was not contrary to fundamental reason and common sense."

8–432   It has to be said, however, that the limited role ascribed in *Clinton* to the confirming authority undermines greatly the ability of an affected landowner to demonstrate—whether before the confirming authority or before the courts— that the competing rights of the public and the landowner have been properly balanced. In particular, the finding that it is sufficient that the acquiring authority identify as the "particular purpose", for which compulsory acquisition is required, one of the statutory purposes under s.212, *i.e.* urban regeneration, tends to undermine the credibility of the entire process. Further, the failure to insist that An Bord Pleanála, as confirming authority, provide other than the most perfunctory statement of reasons is also regrettable.

8. "Particular purpose"

8–433   A clear distinction is drawn under s.212 of the PDA 2000 between acquisition by agreement and acquisition compulsorily. Land may only be acquired compulsorily where it is required for a "particular purpose".[294] Moreover, if the land is not immediately required for a particular purpose, the planning authority must be of the opinion that the land will be required for that purpose in the future. Conversely, acquisition may be effected by *agreement* in respect of any land which, in the opinion of the planning authority, it will require in the future for the purposes of any of its functions, notwithstanding that the planning authority has not yet determined the manner in which or the purpose for which it will use the land.[295]

8–434   It seems, therefore, that the concept of a "particular purpose" is crucial in identifying and restricting the power of compulsory acquisition.

8–435   The High Court in its decision of first instance in *Clinton v An Bord Pleanála* held that a particular purpose could be a statutory purpose and that it would be sufficient for a planning authority merely to indicate which of the statutory

---

[294] The first paragraph of the Third Schedule of the Housing Act 1966 requires that a compulsory purchase order shall be in the prescribed form. The prescribed forms are to be found under the Housing Act 1966 (Acquisition of Land) Regulations 2000. As appears from the directions for completing Form No. 6 thereof, the purposes for which the land is required should be full and accurately stated. ('*Directions for completing this form*', No. 4).

[295] *cf. Murphy v Dublin Corporation* [1976] I.R. 143 at 151.

purposes under s.212 it sought to advance by compulsory acquisition. In *Clinton*, the compulsory purchase order as made by the planning authority had stated as its purpose "development purposes". An Bord Pleanála in confirming the order stated that it had concluded that the acquisition by the planning authority of the lands included in the order was necessary for the purposes of facilitating the implementation of the Dublin City Development Plan and that the objections made could not be sustained against the said necessity.

> "I am satisfied that the meaning to be ascribed to 'particular purpose' in section 213(3)(b) is to be found in a consideration of section 213 of the Act of 2000 as a whole. Section 213(2) contains the phrase 'for the purposes of performing any of its functions'. Section 213(4) also refers to 'purposes' in its reference to section 10(1)(a) of the Local Government (No. 2) Act 1960 section 10 as substituted by section 86 of the Housing Act 1966. 'Purposes' in section 10 as substituted is part of a phrase – 'purposes for which they are capable of being authorised by law to acquire land compulsorily'. It is clear that in section 213(1) and (4) of the 2000 Act and section 10 of the 1960 Act 'purposes' refers to statutory purposes and not as is suggested by the Applicant to a particular scheme of development intended to be pursued that is to means of achieving the statutory purpose. I can find no indication that the phrase 'particular purpose' in section 213(3) should be accorded any different meaning than statutory purpose and I am satisfied that the same refers to a particular statutory purpose. I am fortified in this view by the circumstance that section 213(3)(b) clearly distinguishes purpose and means*."
> * This appears to be a reference to the use of the words "the manner in which or the purpose for which" in s.213(3)(b).

With respect, the foregoing analysis of the provisions of s.213 is not convincing. Any statutory power of a local authority to acquire land is to be construed in accordance with s.213. The distinction drawn between acquisition by agreement and compulsory acquisition under the section becomes meaningless if all that the acquiring authority is required to do is to point, in an abstract way, to a particular statutory purpose.   **8–436**

Section 213 contrasts circumstances where the acquisition is for a "particular purpose" with those where the planning authority has not yet determined "the manner in which or the purpose for which" it will use the land. The clear implication of this is that the general power of *compulsory* acquisition is qualified and may only be exercised where the planning authority has determined the manner in which it will use the land. This interpretation sits better with the constitutional requirement that a substantial public interest outweighing the landowner's rights be demonstrated before the exercise of powers of compulsory acquisition is justified.   **8–437**

On appeal, the Supreme Court declined to overrule this aspect of the High Court judgment. Geoghegan J., while expressing some reservations as to the High Court's interpretation, stated that it was not necessary to give any final determination in respect of it. Geoghegan J. preferred to decide the case on the narrower ground that the regeneration purpose was a "particular purpose" within the meaning of s.213.   **8–438**

9. Possible conflicting roles?

8–439 The fact that planning authorities are now enabled to take a more proactive role in the development and regeneration of lands might be thought to undermine their independence as a decision-maker. One of the requirements of Art.6 of the European Convention on Human Rights is that the "determination of civil rights and obligations" be carried out by an independent and impartial tribunal. In circumstances where a planning authority is involved (whether directly or indirectly) with a proposed development, there might be a perception that it would be predisposed to grant planning permission for the development, and, possibly, to refuse planning permission for rival development.

8–440 To a certain extent, this concern is met by the existence of a statutory right of appeal to An Bord Pleanála. The adequacy of an appeal is, however, undermined insofar as the development plan enjoys a special status in the determination of an application/appeal for planning permission. The planning authority is the author of the development plan, and although An Bord Pleanála is not necessarily bound by the development plan, its discretion is fettered to some extent (especially where planning permission is refused at first instance by reference to a material contravention of the development plan). All of this leaves open the possibility of the planning authority, through the development plan, exercising some influence on the decision on appeal.

8–441 The legal position where *no* planning permission is required is more stark. As indicated earlier, development carried out on behalf of, or jointly or in partnership with, a local authority that is a planning authority is exempted development. Therefore, unless the proposed development is subject to environmental impact assessment, there will be no independent adjudication on the proposed development. This might not matter as much if the compulsory purchase confirmation procedure before An Bord Pleanála allowed for consideration of the merits of the proposed development. However, the judgment in *Clinton* suggests that An Bord Pleanála is not required to evaluate any development proposals before confirming a compulsory purchase order. All of this means that a landowner might be deprived of his or her property—and that property put to an alternative use—without there ever having been a proper determination by an independent or impartial decision-maker.

8–442 The general principle as to whether a local authority determining an application for planning permission for development promoted by it is compatible with the Convention was considered by the High Court of England and Wales in *R. (On the application of Kathro) v Rhondda Cynon Taff County Borough Council.*[296]

> "In the present case the fact that the defendant council will be deciding on its own application for planning permission in respect of a development it is promoting on its own land is plainly sufficient to establish a lack of independence

---

[296] [2002] J.P.L. 304, [16].

and impartiality for the purposes of Article 6 (and it has not been necessary to consider whether any other features of the process, *e.g.* the application of local planning policies, would also give rise to a lack of independence and impartiality). Here, too, the question is whether compliance in principle with Article 6 is achieved by the availability of judicial review."

The High Court of England and Wales concluded that judicial control via the availability of judicial review was, in principle, sufficient to overcome the seeming lack of independence. The court did indicate, however, that the limited scope to review for error of fact on judicial review might present a difficulty, but that it was premature to rule on this issue until such time as an actual decision had been made on the application for planning permission.   **8–443**

All of this might suggest that the Irish High Court will be called upon to apply a more exacting standard of review to decisions confirming compulsory purchase orders than that prescribed under *O'Keeffe v An Bord Pleanála*. Reference is made in this regard to the decision of the High Court in England and Wales in *Chesterfield Properties plc v Secretary of State for the Environment*.[297]   **8–444**

> "In summary, the position is that while the *Wednesbury* principle is the avenue for this court's approach to a judicial review of the Secretary of State's confirmation of a Compulsory Purchase Order, it must in accordance with that principle be demonstrated that in confirming it he has concluded that there exists a substantial public interest or interests outweighing the landowner's rights. The Secretary of State is the first judge whether the public interest 'decisively demands' acquisition. If he has concluded that it does, he is only to be reviewed if in the circumstances that is an irrational conclusion."

---

[297] (1997) 76 P. & C.R. 117 at 131; [1998] J.P.L. 568 at 580.

CHAPTER NINE

APPEAL ON APPLICATION FOR PLANNING PERMISSION

A. Persons Entitled to Appeal

Decisions on a planning application involve a two-tier process, with a statutory right of appeal to An Bord Pleanála from the planning authority's decision of first instance. A *locus standi* (standing) requirement for bringing an appeal has been introduced under the PDA 2000.[1] The right of appeal is now confined to the applicant for planning permission, and to any person who had made submissions or observations in writing to the planning authority in relation to the planning application. Thus, a party who did not participate at the planning authority stage of the decision-making process will not normally be allowed to make an appeal to An Bord Pleanála. There are, however, a number of exceptions to this, as follows.   **9–01**

1. Person with an interest in adjoining lands

The first exception is in favour of neighbouring landowners. Under s.37(6), a person who has an interest in adjoining lands may apply for "leave to appeal" where the nature and extent of the proposed development has been materially altered as a result of the imposition of a condition by the planning authority.[2]   **9–02**

---

[1] PDA 2000, s.37(1).
[2] PDA 2000, s.37(6) (as amended by the Planning and Development (Amendment) Act 2002).

The purpose of this exception seems to be to ensure that a neighbouring landowner is not prejudiced by a modification to the development introduced by way of planning condition. The neighbouring landowner may have had no objection to the development as initially applied for, and thus may not have bothered to make submissions or observations to the planning authority. It is only fair that such a person be afforded an opportunity to have his or her say— by way of an appeal to An Bord Pleanála—where the development as granted by the planning authority differs materially from the development as set out in the initial application.

9–03   Such a person may apply to An Bord Pleanála for leave to appeal notwithstanding the fact that he or she did not make submissions or observations to the planning authority. The application for leave to appeal must be made within four weeks of the date of the decision of the planning authority.

9–04   The following qualifications must be met before leave to appeal may be granted. First, the applicant must have an interest in adjoining land. The applicant must then show that (i) the development for which a decision to grant planning permission has been made will differ materially from the development as set out in the application for permission by reason of conditions imposed by the planning authority; and (ii) that the imposition of such conditions will materially affect the applicant's enjoyment of the land or reduce the value of the land.

9–05   Within one week from the receipt of an application for leave to appeal, An Bord Pleanála shall require, by notice in writing, the planning authority concerned to submit copies of the following materials: (i) a copy of the planning application concerned and of any drawings, maps, particulars, evidence, environmental impact statement, other written study or further information received or obtained by the planning authority from the applicant; (ii) a copy of any report prepared by or for the planning authority in relation to the planning application; and (iii) a copy of the decision of the planning authority in respect of the planning application and a copy of the notification of the decision. The planning authority is required to comply with such requirement within one week from the date of receiving the notice.

9–06   The decision on the application for leave to appeal is to be made within four weeks from the receipt of the application for leave to appeal. An Bord Pleanála shall notify in writing the applicant and the planning authority of a decision to grant or refuse an application for leave to appeal within three days from its making. A person to whom leave to appeal has been granted shall bring the appeal within two weeks from the receipt of this notification.

9–07   Where leave to appeal is granted, the (aspirational) period for the determination of the substantive appeal is reduced from eighteen weeks to fourteen weeks. The purpose of this modification seems to be to ensure that any time lost during the course of the determination of the application for leave to appeal is made up.

2. Non-Governmental Organisations ("NGOs")

In the case of appeals involving EIA development projects, certain non-governmental organisations ("NGOs") are entitled to appeal notwithstanding that they did not make a submission or observation at the planning authority stage.[3] A non-governmental organisation for this purpose is a body or organisation (not being a State authority, a public authority or a governmental body or agency) (i) the aims or objectives of which relate to the promotion of environmental protection; (ii) which has, during the period of twelve months preceding the making of the appeal, pursued those aims or objectives; and (iii) which satisfies such additional requirements (if any) as are prescribed by Minister for the Environment Heritage and Local Government.

9–08

3. Prescribed bodies not properly notified

A planning authority is required under art.28 of the Planning and Development Regulations 2001 (as substituted by the 2006 Regulations) to notify prescribed bodies of certain types of planning application. Thus, for example, the National Roads Authority ("the NRA") is to be notified where the application relates to certain types of road development, and the Irish Aviation Authority is to be notified of development which might endanger or interfere with the safe and efficient navigation of aircraft.

9–09

Occasionally, for whatever reason, a planning authority will fail to notify a prescribed body. To meet this contingency, s.37(4) of the PDA 2000 allows any prescribed body which is entitled to be notified of a planning application to appeal to An Bord Pleanála notwithstanding that it had not made any submissions or observations at the planning authority stage. An Bord Pleanála may, however, dismiss any such appeal where it considers that the body concerned was not entitled to be sent notice of the planning application in accordance with the permission Regulations.

9–10

The wording of certain of the sub-paragraphs of art.28 of the Regulations presents a potential difficulty in this regard. In many cases, the obligation to notify is qualified by the phrase "where it appears to the planning authority". To take just one example: the requirement to notify Fáilte Ireland is triggered "where it appears to the authority that the development might obstruct or detract from the value of any tourist amenity or tourist amenity works". On a literal reading, this might suggest that the obligation to notify is contingent on the *subjective* opinion of the planning authority. On this interpretation, it is not clear that An Bord Pleanála would have jurisdiction to correct a mistaken opinion, on the part of the planning authority, that the effects of a proposed development on tourist amenity were not such as to trigger the requirement to notify Fáilte Éireann.

9–11

---

[3] PDA 2000, s.37(4)(c) and (d) (as inserted by the 2006 Act).

9–12   In order to give effect to s.37(4), however, it is necessary to allow An Bord Pleanála to revisit the question of the impact of the proposed development. Otherwise the section becomes largely meaningless. One approach would be to say that because An Bord Pleanála is to determine an appeal as if the planning application had been made to it in the first instance, the references to the planning authority in art.28 can be read as references to An Bord Pleanála. An Bord Pleanála could thus substitute its opinion on the impact of the proposed development for that of the planning authority. This approach is not entirely convincing in that, if followed to its logical conclusion, it would suggest that An Bord Pleanála must replicate the art.28 notification procedure in its entirety: if one substitutes "An Bord Pleanála" for "the planning authority" throughout art.28, then An Bord Pleanála would be required to notify all of the prescribed bodies of the making of the appeal. This is not how art.28 has been interpreted in practice.

B. Time-Limits on Bringing an Appeal

9–13   There is a four week time-limit on the bringing of an appeal.[4] Where the last day falls on a weekend, a public holiday or any other day on which the offices of the board are closed, the appeal may be made on the next following day on which the offices are open.[5] The four week time period begins on the day of the decision of the planning authority; this is not necessarily the date upon which the decision is actually notified to the appellant.[6]

9–14   An appeal which is not made within time is invalid.[7] Failure to comply with the requirements as to the manner of the making of an appeal will also render the appeal invalid.[8] For example, if in lieu of posting the appeal document, the appeal document is to be delivered to the offices of the board, it is necessary that it be left with an employee of the board personally; it is not sufficient that an employee may *subsequently* come into possession of the appeal document.[9]

9–15   In *Kerry County Council v Lovett*,[10] the applicant put forward the ingenious argument that, in the case of a "Section 4 motion",[11] the time for appealing to

---

[4]   PDA 2000, s.37(1).

[5]   PDA 2000, s.141(2).

[6]   For a discussion of this distinction under the differently worded provisions of the previous legislation, namely (Local Government (Planning & Development) Act 1963, s.26(5) (as amended by the Local Government (Planning & Development) Act 1992), see *Keelgrove Properties Ltd. v An Bord Pleanála* [2000] 1 I.R. 47; [2000] 2 I.L.R.M. 168.

[7]   PDA 2000, s.127(2). See, generally, *McCann v An Bord Pleanála* [1997] 1 I.R. 264; [1997] 1 I.L.R.M. 314.

[8]   These requirements are specified under PDA 2000, s.128(5). An appeal or referral shall be made (a) by sending the appeal or referral by prepaid post to the board; (b) by leaving the appeal or referral with an employee of the board at the offices of the board during office hours (as determined by the board); or (c) by such other means as may be prescribed.

[9]   *Graves v An Bord Pleanála* [1997] 2 I.R. 205.

[10]   [2003] 2 I.R. 589; [2003] 2 I.L.R.M. 434.

[11]   The precursor to s.140 of the Local Government Act 2001.

An Bord Pleanála ran from the date of the resolution of the elected members, and not from any subsequent act on behalf of the manager giving effect to that resolution. In rejecting this argument, Keane C.J. held that the effect of a "Section 4" resolution was not to vest in the elected members the function of deciding to grant or withhold planning permission. Rather, the passing of the resolution constituted a direction by the elected members which obliged the manager to perform a particular act which he was empowered to do, *i.e.* the making of a decision to grant planning permission. It seems to follow from all of this that there is only one decision, that of the manager himself. It is from the date of this decision then that the time-limit in respect of the making of an appeal to An Bord Pleanála runs. On the facts of the case, the relevant appeal had, accordingly, been made in time.

Although not expressly referred to in the decision of the Supreme Court, this analysis would appear to be entirely consistent with the decision in *Wicklow County Council v Wicklow County Manager*.[12] This earlier judgment seems to suggest that the manager retains some autonomy in the face of a "Section 4" resolution. More specifically, the manager is entitled to decline to comply with the terms of the resolution in circumstances where he thinks that the resolution is invalid. Thus it would seem that the resolution is not self-executing, and, accordingly, time should only run from the date on which effect is actually given to same. **9–16**

C. Appeals Against Conditions Only

1. Appeal under section 138 of the PDA 2000

Under s.138, provision is made for an appeal to be brought against a condition (or conditions) only. This procedure might be attractive to a developer who has received a decision to grant permission from the planning authority, but wishes to challenge certain conditions attaching to that decision. There is a risk, however, that An Bord Pleanála may exercise its express power to re-open the *entire* planning decision rather than confine its consideration to the impugned conditions. **9–17**

Two anomalies arise from the section. First, the relevant considerations appear to be narrower than in the case of a full-blooded appeal: specifically, the board is confined to the matters set out in s.34(2)(a) of the PDA 2000, and relevant permissions; this may have the effect that the board is not entitled to have regard to government policy under the amended s.143 (as amended). Secondly, unlike the case of a conventional appeal, the decision of the board does not operate to annul the decision of the planning authority: one effect of this is that **9–18**

---

[12] Unreported, High Court, Ó Caoimh J., February 26, 2003.

as the appeal documentation does not form part of the (original) application, it cannot be called in aid in the interpretation of the determination of the board.[13]

2. Appeal against condition requiring payment of contribution

9–19   There is only a limited right of appeal to An Bord Pleanála in relation to a condition requiring a contribution to be paid in accordance with a development contribution scheme. An appeal may only be brought against such a condition where an applicant for planning permission considers that the terms of the scheme have not been properly applied in respect of any condition laid down by the planning authority.[14]

9–20   The limited nature of an appeal of this type was emphasised by the High Court in *Cork City Council v An Bord Pleanála*.[15]

> "It is clear that the function of the board in an appeal under s. 48(10) is extremely limited. It has no entitlement to consider or review the merits of the scheme under which the contribution is required. Its remit is confined solely to the question of whether or not the terms of the relevant scheme have been properly applied. The appellate jurisdiction provided under s. 48(10) is in marked contrast to the board's function in what may be described as ordinary planning appeals. In such appeals the board is obliged to consider applications for planning permission *de novo* (see s. 37(1)(b) of the Act). Such a power is not given to the board in an appeal under s. 48(10).
>
> All parties to this litigation agree that in considering an appeal under s. 48(10) the board is confined to a consideration of whether or not the terms of the relevant scheme have been properly applied."

9–21   The applicant can ensure that the commencement of development is not held up by the bringing of such an appeal by furnishing to the planning authority security for payment of the full amount of the contribution as specified in the condition. Provided that there is no other appeal pending brought by any other person, the planning authority is then required to make the grant of permission as soon as may be after the expiration of the period for the taking of an appeal. Thus by agreeing to provide security on a contingency basis, the applicant can secure a working grant of planning permission.[16]

3. Appeal against condition requiring payment of special contribution

9–22   The general power whereby An Bord Pleanála can treat an appeal against a condition only as a full review is removed in the case of an appeal against a condition of this type.[17] There is also similar provision made (in the event of

---

[13] *MCD Management Ltd. v Kildare County Council* [1995] 2 I.L.R.M. 532. *Cf. Ashbourne Holdings Ltd. v An Bord Pleanála* [2002] 1 I.L.R.M. 321 (High Court).
[14] PDA 2000, s.48(10)(a).
[15] [2006] I.E.H.C. 192; unreported, Kelly J., June 1, 2006.
[16] PDA 2000, s.48(10)(c).
[17] PDA 2000, s.48(13)(a).

there being no other appeals) for the grant of planning permission to issue in advance of the determination of the limited appeal, on the furnishing of security for payment of the full amount of the contribution as specified in the condition.[18]

D. Restriction on Making Further Planning Applications Pending Appeal

Section 37(5) of the PDA 2000 imposes a restriction on the making of further planning applications while an application in respect of the same development, or development of the same description, is the subject of an appeal pending before An Bord Pleanála.[19] One advantage of this restriction is that it avoids the potential abuse of a developer making a series of applications for planning permission of the same type in the hope that an objector might miss out on making a formal objection to one. **9–23**

Section 37(5), and, in particular, what was meant by an application which is "the subject of an appeal" was considered in detail in *Swords Cloghran Properties Ltd. v Fingal County Council*.[20] The planning authority had refused planning permission for a commercial development, and the developer sought both to appeal against this decision and to make a second application for what was described as a revised development. The developer had attempted to avoid s.37(5) by making the second application for planning permission the day before its first party appeal was lodged. The developer argued that the section did not apply on the facts as there was no appeal pending before An Bord Pleanála as of the date of the making of the second application. The developer went on to argue that the planning authority had erred in law in refusing to accept the second application, and that the failure by the planning authority to make a decision on the merits of that application within eight weeks gave rise to a default planning permission. **9–24**

Herbert J. rejected the claim for a default planning permission, holding that the decision to reject the second application was a "decision" for the purposes of s.34(8); it was thus sufficient to stop time running for the purposes of a default planning permission even if it transpired to be an invalid decision. **9–25**

Herbert J. found on the facts that the planning authority was mistaken in concluding that the second application was in respect of the "same development", but the court nevertheless went on to consider the issue of the **9–26**

---

[18] PDA 2000, s.48(13)(b).
[19] Section 37(5) provides that no application for planning permission for the same development, or for development of the same description, as an application for planning permission for development which is the subject of an appeal shall be made before (i) An Bord Pleanála has made its decision on the appeal; (ii) the appeal is withdrawn; or (iii) the appeal is dismissed.
[20] Unreported, High Court, Herbert J., June, 2006.

correct interpretation of s.37(5). Herbert J. indicated that the restrictive interpretation of the phrase an application "which is subject to an appeal to the Board" advanced by the developer was contrary to the grammatical, and therefore the literal, meaning of s.37(5)(a). Herbert J. further stated that even if the section was ambiguous—and he did not accept that it was—the narrow interpretation would defeat the manifest intention of the legislature, namely to assert the primacy of the decision of An Bord Pleanála as the appellate body and to prevent the altogether inappropriate circumstance of the same issue being considered simultaneously by the planning authority and An Bord Pleanála, with the unacceptable possibility of divergent conclusions.

9–27   Any dispute as to whether an application is for the same development or is for development of the same description as an application for permission which is the subject of an appeal to An Bord Pleanála may be referred to the board for determination. In *Swords Cloghran Properties Ltd. v Fingal County Council*, it was indicated that if the only issue between the parties was whether the development was the same or development of the same description judicial review would have been refused as a matter of discretion on the basis that An Bord Pleanála was uniquely equipped to resolve this factual issue.[21] However, as the case also raised a question of statutory interpretation, judicial review was appropriate.

E. Contents of Appeal

9–28   Under s.127(1) of the PDA 2000, an appeal must be made in writing; state the name and address of the appellant (and of any person acting on his behalf)[22]; state the subject-matter of the appeal[23]; and state in full the grounds of appeal and the reasons, considerations and arguments on which they are based.[24] In addition to the foregoing requirements, an appeal must also be accompanied by the acknowledgement by the planning authority of receipt of the submissions or observations; and be accompanied by such a fee (if any) as may be payable. An appeal shall be accompanied by such documents, particulars or other information relating to the appeal as the appellant considers necessary or to be

---

[21] Unreported, High Court, Herbert J., June, 2006.
[22] In *Kenney Construction Ltd. v An Bord Pleanála* [2005] I.E.H.C. 30; unreported, O'Neill J., February 10, 2005 the misdescription of a third party appellant (by the omission of the word "Limited") was held not render the appeal invalid.
[23] It is unclear whether or not the term "subject matter of the appeal" should be interpreted as the planning authority's decision, *i.e.* the decision under appeal, or as the proposed development. A question arises as to whether the subject matter of the appeal must be precisely the same development as that submitted to the planning authority, or if the applicant for planning permission may present revised plans to An Bord Pleanála other than pursuant to an invitation under Planning and Development Regulations 2001, art.73.
[24] In *O'Reilly (Bros) Wicklow Ltd. v An Bord Pleanála* [2006] I.E.H.C. 363; unreported, Quirke J., November 22, 2006, it was argued, unsuccessfully, that there had been a failure to comply with this requirement in the context of a section 5 reference. See para.10–11.

appropriate. These various requirements place a heavy onus on an appellant in that he or she must prepare and submit a comprehensive appeal document within a very short period of time.

An appellant will generally not be entitled to elaborate upon in writing, or **9–29** make further submissions in writing, in relation to the grounds of appeal, or to submit further grounds of appeal. Section 127(3) appears to permit of two exceptions to this. First, in the case of a notice served under s.131 requesting further submissions.[25] Secondly, in circumstances where an oral hearing is to be held.[26]

The requirement that the appeal be accompanied by the acknowledgement by **9–30** the planning authority of the receipt of the submissions or observations was held to be mandatory by the High Court in *Murphy v Cobh Town Council*.[27] On the unusual facts of the case, however, MacMenamin J. found that there had been substantial compliance with the requirement, and that the breach was *de minimis*. The appeal had been accompanied, not by the formal acknowledgement furnished by the planning authority at the time of the making of the submission or observation, but by a subsequent letter from the planning authority giving notice that an appeal (by different appellants) had been received by An Bord Pleanála. This letter did, however, make express mention of a previous communication with the planning authority, and thus it could be readily inferred that the appellant had made a submission or observation in respect of the planning application. Notwithstanding this, An Bord Pleanála had rejected the appeal as invalid. The appellant brought judicial review proceedings challenging this decision. MacMenamin J. ruled that the requirement that the appeal be accompanied by the formal acknowledgement was mandatory, and that absent the *de minimis* rule, non-compliance would render an appeal invalid. MacMenamin J. held that the planning authority had unwittingly created a trap for the unwary in that the various letters it had issued to the appellant—the acknowledgement, the notification of decision and the notification of an appeal—were all similar in layout and substance, and the date of each set out in miniscule print. The appellant had mistakenly submitted the third, rather than the first, in a series of three almost identical letters. The letter actually submitted included the relevant information necessary for An Bord Pleanála to proceed. No prejudice had occurred to the procedures save in the most

---

[25] *cf. Mulhall v An Bord Pleanála*, unreported, High Court, McCracken J., March 21, 1996 (*Irish Times* Law Report, June 10, 1996).
[26] The extent to which further grounds or arguments can be advanced at an oral hearing is unclear. PDA 2000, s.127(2)(b) indicates that the requirement as to the contents of an appeal shall apply whether or not the appellant requests, or proposes to request, an oral hearing of the appeal: the purpose of this provision would appear to be to prevent an appellant submitting a truncated appeal in writing, while reserving the right to make further submissions by way of oral hearing. PDA 2000, s.127(3) suggests, however, that in the event of an oral hearing being held, an appellant may even be permitted to make further submissions in writing.
[27] [2006] I.E.H.C. 324; unreported, MacMenamin J., October 26, 2006.

technical, and perhaps trivial, way. MacMenamin J. accordingly ruled that there had been substantial compliance and that the appeal was valid.

F. Obligations of Planning Authority in Case of Appeal

1. Submission of documents to An Bord Pleanála

9–31   Where an appeal is made to An Bord Pleanála, a planning authority is required to submit the following documents to the board within a period of two weeks beginning on the day on which a copy of the appeal is sent to the planning authority by the board: (i) a copy of the planning application concerned and of any drawings, maps, particulars, evidence, environmental impact statement, other written study or further information received or obtained by it from the applicant; (ii) a copy of any (valid) submission or observation in respect of the planning application;[28] (iii) a copy of any report prepared by or for the planning authority in relation to the planning application; and (iv) a copy of the decision of the planning authority and a copy of the notification of the decision given to the applicant.[29] The planning authority must also notify An Bord Pleanála where the development is subject to transboundary consultation under Pt 10 of the Planning and Development Regulations 2001 (as amended in 2006).[30]

9–32   The legal consequences of a failure to comply with the equivalent obligation under the previous legislation[31] were considered by the High Court in *McAnenley v An Bord Pleanála*.[32] Kelly J. held that the statutory requirements in this regard were mandatory, and, further, that on the facts of the case there had been substantial non-compliance with the obligations imposed on the planning authority. Kelly J. further held that given the lacunae identified, he was not satisfied that the appeal to An Bord Pleanála was dealt with within jurisdiction or in accordance with law, and, consequently, the determination of An Bord Pleanála was quashed. The matter was remitted to An Bord Pleanála to be dealt with afresh.

2. Public inspection and notification

9–33   A planning authority is required to make available for public inspection a copy of the appeal at its offices during the currency of the appeal.[33] Same may be

---

[28] The requirement to furnish copies of any (valid) submission or observation in respect of the planning application was introduced for the first time under the Planning and Development (Strategic Infrastructure) Act 2006.

[29] PDA 2000, s.128(1)(a) (as substituted by s.21 of the 2006 Act).

[30] Planning and Development Regulations 2001, art.127 (as substituted by the 2006 Regulations).

[31] Local Government (Planning & Development) Act 1992, s.6.

[32] [2002] 2 I.R. 763. See also *Jerry Beades Construction Ltd. v Dublin Corporation* [2005] I.E.H.C. 406; unreported, McKechnie J., September 7, 2005 (failure to transmit an earlier report prepared by a planner).

[33] Planning and Development Regulations 2001, art.68 (as amended by the 2006 Regulations).

purchased for a fee not exceeding the reasonable costs of making a copy. The planning authority is also required to notify any person who made a submission or observation in respect of the application for planning permission of the existence of the appeal.[34]

G. Submissions and Observations on Appeal

An Bord Pleanála is required to give a copy of the appeal to each other party as soon as may be after receipt of an appeal.[35] The other parties in this context are the planning authority, and the applicant for the permission.[36] Each party then has a period of four weeks, from the day on which the copy of the appeal is sent to that party, to make submissions or observations in writing to An Bord Pleanála.[37] Again, this is a strict time-limit: any submission or observation received after the expiration of the four week period shall not be considered by the board.[38]   **9–34**

In addition, other persons (hereinafter referred to as "observers") may make submissions and observations in writing within a period of four weeks beginning on the date of receipt of the (last) appeal.[39] This time period is extended, *inter alia*, in the case of development subject to environmental impact assessment, and where An Bord Pleanála directs further public notice of the appeal.[40]   **9–35**

An Bord Pleanála has a power under s.131 of the PDA 2000 to request submissions or observations in relation to any matter which has arisen in relation to an appeal. The notice must specify a period within which such submissions or observations are to be made. This period is not to be less than two weeks or more than four weeks beginning on the date of service of the notice. The consequences of a failure to comply strictly with the requirements of a similar provision under the previous legislation[41] were considered in *Hickey v An Bord Pleanála*.[42] On the facts, it was admitted that the applicant for judicial review had only been given 13 days, rather than 14 days, within which to make her submissions or observations. Smyth J. refused to quash the decision of An Bord Pleanála, ruling that there was no evidence that the applicant had sustained any prejudice as a result of the shortened time-limit: a response had actually been made by the applicant, and there was no evidence that one further day would have made any difference to the applicant's response. Smyth J. relied in   **9–36**

---

[34] Planning and Development Regulations 2001, art.69.
[35] PDA 2000, s.129.
[36] PDA 2000, s.2.
[37] PDA 2000, s.129(2).
[38] PDA 2000, s.129(2)(b).
[39] PDA 2000, s.130. A submission or observation must state in full the reasons, considerations and arguments on which same is based.
[40] PDA 2000, s.130.
[41] Local Government (Planning and Development) Act 1992, s.9.
[42] Unreported, High Court, Smyth J., June 10, 2004.

this regard on the judgment in *Ryanair Ltd. v An Bord Pleanála.*[43] In *Ryanair Ltd.* the High Court held that once the submission had been made within the statutory period the letter inviting same could not act in a manner to defeat the legal rights of the applicant.

9–37   In order to avoid the strictures of the judgment of the Supreme Court in *Monaghan UDC v Alf-a-bet Promotions Ltd.*,[44] Smyth J. held that there had been "substantial compliance" with the statutory requirements. This approach can be contrasted with that usually taken in relation to time-limits, to the effect that a time-limit is either met or it is not, and that there can be no half-way house or partial compliance.[45]

9–38   Although the legislation envisages a tight time period for the making of submissions and observations, the rules of natural and constitutional justice may, on occasion, require that further submissions be allowed,[46] and, presumably for this reason, An Bord Pleanála has been given a statutory discretion to allow submissions outside the prescribed time periods.[47] Guidance may be sought as to the manner in which this discretion might be exercised from the earlier case law which, although decided prior to the introduction of the various statutory time-limits on the making of submissions and observations, does indicate the nature of the function being exercised by An Bord Pleanála. In this regard, reference is made to the following passage from the judgment of Finlay P. in *State (Genport Ltd.) v An Bord Pleanála.*[48]

> "I am satisfied that as a matter of general law An Bord Pleanála carrying out a quasi-judicial function would have an obligation to take reasonable steps to ensure that every party interested in any particular application before it should be aware of the submissions or representations made by any other party; should have a reasonable opportunity of replying to them; and should have a general reasonable opportunity of making representations to the board."

9–39   The courts have also recognised, however, the need for finality in proceedings,[49] and have even suggested that the rights of objectors may be less than those of a developer.[50] Reference is made to the following passage from the judgment in *Finnegan v An Bord Pleanála.*[51]

---

[43] [2004] 2 I.R. 334.

[44] [1980] I.L.R.M. 64.

[45] See, for example, *McCann v An Bord Pleanála* [1997] 1 I.R. 264; [1997] 1 I.L.R.M. 314. See also *Graves v An Bord Pleanála* [1997] 2 I.R. 205.

[46] See, generally, *State (Genport Ltd.) v An Bord Pleanála* [1983] I.L.R.M. 12; *State (Boyd) v An Bord Pleanála* unreported, High Court, Murphy J., February 18, 1983; and *State (Coras Iompar Éireann) v An Bord Pleanála*, unreported, Supreme Court, December 12, 1984.

[47] *cf. Mulhall v An Bord Pleanála*, unreported, High Court, McCracken J., March 21, 1996 (Irish Times Law Report, June 10, 1996).

[48] [1983] I.L.R.M. 12 at 14.

[49] *Finnegan v An Bord Pleanála* [1979] I.L.R.M. 134.

[50] *State (Haverty) v An Bord Pleanála* [1987] I.R. 485 at 493.

[51] [1979] I.L.R.M. 134 at 137, *per* McWilliam J.

"This statement was not considered by the tribunal and, in my opinion, it would have been more satisfactory if it had been but, if it was relevant, a statement to the same effect could have been tendered at an earlier stage in the hearing as the matters being dealt with were all of a general nature, and there must be some limitation put to the indefinite extension of the hearing of an appeal or inquiry such as this. I cannot see that there was any breach of the principles of natural or constitutional justice in the conduct of the proceedings in this respect."

An Bord Pleanála is an expert body and therefore unlike a judicial body can rely on its own knowledge to inform its decisions. An Bord Pleanála must, however, inform the parties of the matters which it intends to take into account and to afford an opportunity to respond: to do otherwise is a breach of fair procedures.[52] The response, presumably, may be by way of written submission, or submission at any oral hearing. Under s.137, An Bord Pleanála has an express power to take into account matters other than those raised by the parties or by observers; the board must, however, afford an opportunity to the parties and the observers to make submissions on these matters either in writing or at any oral hearing. The statutory entitlement to make additional submissions represents an exception to the rigorous timetable provided under the legislation for the exchange of submissions, but this exception itself is hedged with time-limits, and submissions must be confined to the matters identified by An Bord Pleanála. **9–40**

H. Power to Dismiss Appeals

An Bord Pleanála is empowered under s.138 (as amended under the 2006 Act) to dismiss an appeal which is vexatious, frivolous or without substance or foundation, or is made with the sole intention of delaying the development or the intention of securing the payment of money, gifts, consideration or other inducement by any person.[53] This section makes provision for a fast track procedure whereby An Bord Pleanála can dismiss an appeal or reference. An Bord Pleanála can act of its own motion and does not have to await one of the other party's suggestion that the appeal is vexatious. Indeed, on one reading of the section, it would appear that the decision to dismiss is to be based on a consideration only of the grounds of appeal or referral, without reference to submissions made by any of the other parties. **9–41**

The fact that An Bord Pleanála must state the main reasons and considerations on which its decision was based, and the fact that there is provision for an oral hearing, indicates that the decision to dismiss attracts the rules of natural and **9–42**

---

[52] *McGoldrick v An Bord Pleanála* [1997] 1 I.R. 497; and *Stack v An Bord Pleanála*, unreported, High Court, O'Neill J., July 11, 2000. *Cf. Fairyhouse Club Ltd. v An Bord Pleanála*, unreported, High Court, Finnegan J., July 18, 2001 (no requirement to notify intention to rely on previous decision of An Bord Pleanála); and *Stack v An Bord Pleanála (No. 2)*, unreported, High Court, Ó Caoimh J., March 7, 2003.
[53] As to the dismissal of legal proceedings, see *Sean Quinn Group Ltd. v An Bord Pleanála* [2001] 1 I.R. 505; [2001] 2 I.L.R.M. 94.

constitutional justice. In *Finnegan v An Bord Pleanála*,[54] the Supreme Court held that the power under the previous legislation to dismiss an appeal as vexatious or for delay was to be read as only being exercisable after an opportunity had been afforded to the appellant to put forward his case. The decision to dismiss is open to judicial review by the High Court in the ordinary way, but absent any breach of fair procedures, it is to be expected that the High Court will show deference to the decision of An Bord Pleanála.[55]

9–43 The power to dismiss an appeal is separate from the power to declare an (abandoned) appeal as withdrawn under s.140(2).

I. Discovery/Production of Documents

9–44 Section 132 of the PDA 2000 provides that where An Bord Pleanála is of opinion that any document, particulars, or other information is or are necessary for the purpose of enabling it to determine an appeal, the board may serve on any party or any person who has made submissions or observations to the board in relation to the appeal, a notice under the section requiring the submission of such documents; the power is, however, not coercive in that the only sanction for failure to comply is that the board may determine the appeal in the absence of the documents or particulars.[56] The term "necessary" is not a synonym of "relevant": documents, particulars or other information only become necessary within the meaning of s.132 if the board cannot determine the appeal without them.[57] An Bord Pleanála also has a more radical power to order the production of documents under s.135(5).

9–45 These powers should be used sparingly: proceedings before An Bord Pleanála do not involve a *lis inter partes* in that there are no rights being determined and, accordingly, it would be inappropriate to incorporate a discovery type procedure into the appeal process. The making of an order for production represents an interference with the constitutionally protected right to privacy and should only be done where absolutely necessary to determine the appeal.

9–46 Finally, it is important to note that these powers reside with An Bord Pleanála and not with a person conducting an oral hearing, and thus it would be incorrect to seek an order against a person holding an oral hearing compelling him or her to direct the production of documents.[58] The limited powers of a person conducting an oral hearing are discussed at para.9–78 below and onwards.

---

[54] [1979] I.L.R.M. 134.
[55] See, for example, *Cablelink Ltd. v An Bord Pleanála* [1999] 1 I.R. 596; and *Ní Ghruagáin v An Bord Pleanála*, unreported, High Court, Murphy J., June 19, 2003.
[56] PDA 2000, s.133.
[57] *Huntstown Air Park Ltd. v An Bord Pleanála* [1999] 1 I.L.R.M. 281.
[58] *Huntstown Air Park Ltd. v An Bord Pleanála* [1999] 1 I.L.R.M. 281.

J. Report and Site Inspections

Under s.146 of the PDA 2000, An Bord Pleanála (or an employee of the board **9–47** duly authorised by the board) may, in connection with the performance of any of the board's functions under the PDA 2000, assign a person to report on any matter on behalf of the board. In practice, the board assigns an inspector to prepare a report in respect of almost all appeals.

A person so assigned shall make a written report on the matter to the board, **9–48** which shall include a recommendation, and the board shall consider the report and recommendation before determining the matter.[59] Such reports are to be made available—within three days—for inspection and purchase at the board's offices, and at any other place or by electronic means as the board considers appropriate.[60]

The following general principles, set out in the decision of the Supreme Court **9–49** in *Geraghty v Minister for Local Government*,[61] apply equally to reports under s.146.

> "Under each of the Acts, there are certain fundamental matters or principles which are unalterable. The first is that the Minister is the deciding authority. He cannot in any way be treated simply as an authority whose function is to review the recommendations or the opinions, if any such are made or offered, of the person holding or conducting the inquiry. The second is that the Minister is acting *ultra vires* if he comes to a conclusion or makes a decision which is not supportable upon the evidence or the materials properly before him. Thirdly, neither the Minister nor the person holding or conducting the inquiry can come to a conclusion of fact unless there is evidence upon which such a conclusion could be formed. Fourthly, if the person holding or conducting the inquiry should come to a conclusion of fact and should express it, the Minister is not bound to come to the same conclusion of fact and is quite free to form a contrary conclusion if there is evidence and materials properly before him from which he could come to such a conclusion. Fifthly, to enable the Minister to come to any decision, the person holding or conducting the inquiry must transmit to the Minister a report which fairly and accurately informs the Minister of the substance of the evidence and the arguments for or against the issues raised at the inquiry by those represented at the inquiry."

The obligations of an inspector in preparing his or her report were summarised **9–50** more recently, in *Kenney Construction Ltd. v An Bord Pleanála*, as follows.[62]

> "In essence, therefore, what is involved in giving to the Bord a fair and accurate report is one which fairly sets out and fully sets out for the benefit of the Bord the relative contentions in regard to whatever the issues are in the planning

---

[59] PDA 2000, s.146(2).
[60] PDA 2000, s.146(5) and (6) (as substituted by the 2006 Act).
[61] [1976] I.R. 153 at 168.
[62] [2005] I.E.H.C. 30; unreported, O'Neill J., February 10, 2005.

application, but bearing in mind that the Bord already have a variety of material before them, and it would be superfluous for any report to recite material which was clearly available and highlighted in other documentation. But the essence of it is that the report must present to the Bord a fair and accurate picture of the proposal and of the reasons for it and of the reasons against as made by the objectors and as made by the applicant in the planning permission."

9–51 Given the sparse nature of the reasons typically stated by An Bord Pleanála for its decisions, the focus of judicial review proceedings is often directed toward the contents of the inspector's report. In the absence of a meaningful statement of reasons, the report at least provides something concrete which might be analysed and criticised. Such an approach is, however, often fruitless in that the courts are far less keen to impute an error on the part of the inspector to the members of the board,[63] than they are to find that the members had, by implication, adopted some aspect of the report which would help shore up what would otherwise be deficient reasoning on the part of the board. An Bord Pleanála is thus permitted to approbate and reprobate insofar as the contents of reports are concerned.

9–52 An inspector's report is, of course, only a procedural step and the ultimate decision remains that of An Bord Pleanála. For this reason, then, the inspector's report is not itself susceptible to judicial review. Reference is made in this regard by analogy to the judgment in *Lord Ballyedmond v Commission for Energy Regulation*.[64] This case concerned a decision in respect of the compulsory acquisition of land under the Gas Acts. Clarke J. distinguished between a stand alone report which may have formal consequences—such as the first stage in a disciplinary procedure—and a report which is merely a step in a decision-making process. A report of the latter type is not open to judicial review.

> "I have therefore come to the view that the report of an Inspector appointed to conduct a hearing for the purposes of enabling the assembly of materials which are required to be considered by a statutory body fulfilling a role such as the Commission in this case, is not open to judicial review, notwithstanding the fact that such report may contain recommendations where those recommendations are neither binding nor give rise to any formal consequences for the process as a whole."

9–53 Under art.75 of the Planning and Development Regulations 2001, An Bord Pleanála may arrange for the carrying out of inspections in relation to, *inter alia*, an appeal, by a person appointed for that purpose by the board (whether generally or for a particular appeal). It would thus seem that the person

---

[63] For an example of an inspector's error being imputed to the members of the board, see *Cork City Council v An Bord Pleanála* [2006] I.E.H.C. 192; unreported, Kelly J., June 1, 2006 (reasonable to conclude that An Bord Pleanála adopted inspector's reasoning where it did not differ from her recommendation and in the absence of any dissent from her line of thought).

[64] [2006] I.E.H.C. 206; unreported, Clarke J., June 22, 2006.

conducting the oral hearing may carry out a site inspection in order to be in a position to understand the evidence to be given at the oral hearing. Such a person must not, however, supplement the evidence given at the oral hearing with material drawn from his own inspection of the site.[65]

K. Decision on Appeal

1. Time period for decision

The eighteen week time period provided for under s.126 of the PDA 2000 is aspirational only.[66] There is no provision for a default decision in the event of An Bord Pleanála failing to meet the four month time period, and the time period can be extended by notice to the parties (and observers) to an appeal. The general time period of eighteen weeks can be varied by the Minister for the Environment, Heritage and Local Government either generally or in respect of particular class or classes of appeal. The Minister may also give a direction that particular appeals or referrals shall be given priority.

9–54

2. Determination as if application made to An Bord Pleanála

Under s.37(1)(b), An Bord Pleanála is required to determine the application as if it had been made to it in the first instance. It seems that this means that it is determining the matter *de novo* and without regard to anything that had transpired before the planning authority.[67] It is unclear as to what are the precise effects of this. Although it is certainly the case that certain defects which occurred at the planning authority stage will not affect the jurisdiction of An Bord Pleanála,[68] other defects will subsist before An Bord Pleanála so as to invalidate its decision.[69] This issue is considered in more detail in the context of the chapter on judicial review, especially the discussion of s.50(4) and (5). See para.11–328 and onwards.

9–55

Although An Bord Pleanála is determining an appeal from the decision of the planning authority, the board would appear to enjoy the same discretion as a planning authority to grant permission for a *modified* version of the development

9–56

---

[65] *Lancefort Ltd. v An Bord Pleanála*, unreported, High Court, McGuinness J., March 12, 1998, citing with approval *Killiney and Ballybrack Development Association Ltd. v Minister for Local Government* (1974) 112 I.L.T.R. 69. See also, by analogy, *Geraghty v Minister for Local Government* [1976] I.R. 153.

[66] *cf. Dietacaron Ltd. v An Bord Pleanála* [2005] 2 I.L.R.M. 32 (no prejudice caused by the delay on the particular facts of the case).

[67] *O'Keeffe v An Bord Pleanála* [1993] 1 I.R. 39 at 52; [1992] I.L.R.M. 237 at 247, *per* Costello J.

[68] *Hynes v An Bord Pleanála (No. 2)*, unreported, High Court, McGuinness J., July, 30, 1998.

[69] *ibid.*

applied for. More specifically, s.142(2) and (3) empowers the Minister for the Environment, Heritage and Local Government to make Regulations enabling An Bord Pleanála to invite an applicant to submit revised plans or other drawings modifying, or other particulars providing for the modification of, the development to which the appeal relates, and for An Bord Pleanála to grant planning permission for the relevant development as modified by all or any of the plans, drawings or particulars. Regulations to this effect have been made under art.73 of the Planning and Development Regulations 2001.[70]

9–57   A second consequence of the appeal being as if made to An Bord Pleanála at first instance seems to be that it would represent an abdication of its responsibilities were the board to leave over matters of importance to be agreed between the developer and the planning authority.[71] (Such a condition would also be open to the objection that it frustrated the public's right to participate in the planning process.) This appears to be recognised under the PDA 2000 in that under s.34(5) it would seem that it is only matters of detail which can properly be left over to be dealt with in this way.[72]

3. Duty to state main reasons and considerations

9–58   See, generally, paras.12–119 to 12–163. An Bord Pleanála is required to state the main reasons and considerations on which the decision is based. Where conditions are imposed in relation to the grant of any permission, the decision shall state the main reasons for the imposition of any such conditions, provided that where a condition imposed is a condition described in the list of conditions under s.34(4), a reference to the paragraph of subsection (4) in which the condition is described shall be sufficient.[73]

9–59   Where the decision is different in relation to the granting or refusal of permission from the recommendation in a report of a person assigned to report on an appeal on behalf of the board, the statement of reasons must, additionally, indicate the main reasons for not accepting the recommendation in the report or reports to grant or refuse permission.[74]

9–60   Where An Bord Pleanála grants planning permission in circumstances where the planning authority, at first instance, had refused planning permission on the grounds that the development materially contravened the development plan,

---

[70] It is to be noted that the circumstances in which An Bord Pleanála may invite revised plans are less restrictive than those applying to a planning authority under art.34 of the Planning and Development Regulations 2001 (as amended by the 2006 Regulations). Specifically, there is no express requirement that An Bord Pleanála be *disposed* to grant planning permission.

[71] *Houlihan v An Bord Pleanála*, unreported, High Court, Murphy J., October 4, 1993.

[72] As to the position under the previous legislation, where there was no such express power, see, generally, *Boland v An Bord Pleanála* [1996] 3 I.R. 435.

[73] PDA 2000, s.34(10).

[74] PDA 2000, s.34(10)(b).

the board is required, in addition to the general requirements, to indicate in its decision the main reasons and considerations for contravening materially the development plan.[75]

4. Material contravention of development plan

Under the previous legislation, whereas An Bord Pleanála was required to   **9–61**
have regard to the provisions of the development plan, no particular procedure had to be observed before the board could grant planning permission in material contravention of the development plan.[76] The position is more strict under the PDA 2000. In particular, where a planning authority has decided to refuse permission on the grounds that a proposed development materially contravenes the development plan, An Bord Pleanála may only grant planning permission where it considers that (i) the proposed development is of strategic or national importance; (ii) there are conflicting objectives in the development plan or the objectives are not clearly stated insofar as the proposed development is concerned; (iii) planning permission for the proposed development should be granted having regard to regional planning guidelines for the area, statutory guidelines, statutory policy directives, the statutory obligations of any local authority in the area, and any relevant policy of the Government, the Minister for the Environment, Heritage and Local Government or any Minister of the Government; or (iv) planning permission for the proposed development should be granted having regard to the pattern of development, and permissions granted, in the area since the making of the development plan.

Where An Bord Pleanála exercises its power to grant planning permission,   **9–62**
there is also a requirement under s.37(2)(c) to give additional reasons indicating the main reasons and considerations for contravening materially the development plan.

It is to be noted that, somewhat surprisingly, these restrictions are only triggered   **9–63**
where the planning authority has decided to refuse planning permission on the grounds that a proposed development materially contravenes the development plan. Thus if the planning authority mistakenly rules that a proposed development does not involve a material contravention of the development plan, and proceeds to grant planning permission without invoking the special material contravention procedure, then it seems that An Bord Pleanála is free from the restrictions.

---

[75] PDA 2000, s.37(2)(c).
[76] Local Government (Planning & Development) Act 1976, s.14(8).

L. Costs/Expenses

9–64   Under s.145 of the PDA 2000 (as amended by the 2006 Act), An Bord Pleanála has a discretion—irrespective of the result of the appeal—to direct the planning authority to pay the expenses incurred by the appellant and/or the board.

9–65   If the decision of the planning authority is confirmed or varied and the board, in determining the appeal, does not accede in substance to the grounds of appeal, then the expenses of the planning authority, the board and the other parties, may be awarded against the appellant.

9–66   If the appeal is decided, dismissed under s.138 or withdrawn under s.140 and An Bord Pleanála, in any of those cases, considers that the appeal was made with the intention of delaying the development or securing a monetary gain by a party to the appeal or any other person, then the expenses of the planning authority, the board and the other parties, may be awarded against the appellant.

1. Measure of expenses/costs

9–67   An Bord Pleanála is stated to have an "absolute discretion" as to the sum to be paid as compensation for the expense incurred or occasioned by the planning authority, any other party or of the board itself in relation to the appeal or referral.

2. Constitutionality of power to award costs

9–68   There must be a question mark over the constitutional validity of these provisions.[77] The power to award costs or expenses against third parties is, arguably, an *indicium* of the administration of justice. The wording of s.145 (as amended) goes further and suggests that the power to direct expenses to be paid is to be used as a punitive measure. One of the circumstances in which a party may be directed to pay expenses is where the board considers that the appeal was made with the intention of delaying the development or securing a monetary gain. This requires the making of an adverse finding against a particular party. There are strong grounds for saying that the making of a such an adverse finding, followed by the imposition of a penalty—in the form of a direction to pay expenses—constitutes an administration of justice.

9–69   On a separate point, the fact that An Bord Pleanála is empowered to direct the payment of costs simply because it does not accede in substance to the grounds of appeal suggests that even a *bona fide* appellant is at risk of having a penalty imposed on him or her. This is inconsistent with the right of public participation in the planning process, and may make access to the appeal process prohibitively expensive.

---

[77] *cf. Haughey v Moriarty*, unreported, High Court, Geoghegan J., April 28, 1998.

Finally, the provisions are also open to challenge on the basis that there is no **9–70**
clear statement of principles and policies to guide the exercise of the jurisdiction
to direct the payment of costs.

3. Power of court to award costs for offence in respect of oral hearing

Section 135(7) of the PDA 2000 proscribes certain acts or omissions at an oral **9–71**
hearing. Thus, where any person (a) wilfully gives evidence which is material
to the oral hearing and which he or she knows to be false or does not believe to
be true; (b) by act or omission, obstructs or hinders the person conducting the
oral hearing in the performance of his or her functions; (c) refuses to take an
oath or to make an affirmation when legally required to do so by a person
holding the oral hearing; (d) refuses to answer any question to which the person
conducting an oral hearing may legally require an answer; or (e) does or omits
to do any other thing which, if the inquiry had been by the High Court, would
have been contempt of that court, that person shall be guilty of an offence.

Where a person is convicted, on indictment, of an offence under s.135(7), the **9–72**
court may, where it finds that the act or omission constituting the offence delayed
the conduct of the oral hearing concerned order (a) the person convicted, or
(b) any body with whose consent, connivance or approval the court is satisfied
the offence was committed, to pay to An Bord Pleanála or to any party or
person who appeared at the oral hearing such an amount as is equal to the
amount of any additional costs that it is shown to the court to have been incurred
by the board, party or person in appearing or being represented at the oral
hearing by reason of the commission of the offence.[78]

M. Oral Hearings

1. Request for oral hearing

A party to an appeal, or any person who makes a submission or observation on **9–73**
an appeal, may request an oral hearing.[79] The request should be made in writing
and accompanied by the prescribed fee. An appellant must make his or her
request within the time limited for making the appeal. An observer must make
his or her request within the time limited for making submissions and
observations.

An Bord Pleanála has an "absolute discretion" as to whether or not to hold **9–74**
such an oral hearing. It would be extremely difficult to challenge a decision of
the board not to hold an oral hearing,[80] nor does it appear that it is necessary

---

[78] PDA 2000, s.156(9) (as inserted by s.31 of the 2006 Act).
[79] PDA 2000, s.134 (as substituted under s.22 of the 2006 Act).
[80] *Hynes v An Bord Pleanála (No. 1)*, unreported, High Court, Laffoy J., December 10, 1997.

for the board to give reasons as to why it may have decided not to hold an oral hearing. An Bord Pleanála must notify its decision to all parties to the appeal and to any observers.

2. Notice of oral hearing, and adjournments

9–75   An Bord Pleanála is required to give all relevant persons and any other person or body which it considers appropriate not less than five working days' notice of the time and place of the opening of an oral hearing.[81] (A lesser period of notice may be given if accepted by all such persons or bodies.)[82] Generally three working days' notice must be given of any alteration in the time or venue.[83] The definition of "relevant person" includes the parties to the appeal,[84] and any persons who have (validly) made submissions or observations to An Bord Pleanála.[85]

9–76   An oral hearing may be adjourned from time to time, and in the event that new matters are to be considered, an oral hearing may even be re-opened.[86] It is submitted that, although the decision as to whether or not to grant an adjournment is open to review by the High Court and that the standard of review is not the attenuated standard of unreasonableness or irrationality, the decision whether or not to adjourn is first and foremost a matter for the person conducting the oral hearing.[87]

9–77   Where the report has been submitted to the members of An Bord Pleanála, an oral hearing shall not be reopened unless the board considers it expedient to do so and so directs.[88] Again, notice must be given to the relevant persons.[89]

3. Procedure at oral hearing

9–78   Under s.135 (as amended in 2006), An Bord Pleanála, or an employee of the board duly authorised by the board, may assign a person to conduct an oral hearing.[90] The person conducting the oral hearing shall have discretion as to

---

[81] Planning and Development Regulations 2001, art.76(1)(a) (as substituted by the 2006 Regulations).

[82] ibid.

[83] Planning and Development Regulations 2001, art.76(4) (as substituted by the 2006 Regulations).

[84] "Party" is defined under PDA 2000, s.2.

[85] Planning and Development Regulations 2001, art.67(1) (as substituted by the 2006 Regulations).

[86] See PDA 2000, s.137(2) and Planning and Development Regulations 2001, art.77.

[87] *London Borough of Croydon v Secretary of State for the Environment* [2000] P.L.C.R. 171. See, more generally, *O'Callaghan v Clifford* [1993] 3 I.R. 603.

[88] Planning and Development Regulations 2001, art.77.

[89] Planning and Development Regulations 2001, art.77.

[90] As to the replacement of the person appointed to conduct the oral hearing, see Planning and Development Regulations 2001, art.78.

the conduct of the hearing and shall conduct the hearing expeditiously and without undue formality.[91]

As a result of an amendment introduced under the 2006 Act, the board may give a direction to the person conducting an oral hearing that he or she shall require persons intending to appear at the hearing to submit to him or her, in writing and in advance of the hearing, the points or a summary of the arguments they propose to make at the hearing.[92] The person conducting the oral hearing can refuse to allow the making of a point or an argument if the point or a summary of the argument has not been submitted in advance to the person in accordance with such a requirement.[93]   **9–79**

The person conducting the oral hearing (a) shall decide the order of appearance of persons at the hearing; (b) shall permit any person to appear in person or to be represented by another person; (c) may limit the time within which each person may make points or arguments (including arguments in refutation of arguments made by others at the hearing), or question the evidence of others, at the hearing.[94] He or she may also refuse to allow a point or argument to be made if the point or argument is not relevant to the subject-matter of the hearing, or it is considered necessary so as to avoid undue repetition of the same point or argument.   **9–80**

The person conducting the oral hearing also has a discretion to hear a person other than a person who has made submissions or observations to An Bord Pleanála in relation to the subject-matter of the hearing if it is considered appropriate in the interests of justice to allow the person to be heard.[95]   **9–81**

An oral hearing may proceed notwithstanding that any relevant person (as defined) has failed to attend.[96]   **9–82**

A person conducting an oral hearing may require any officer of a planning authority or a local authority to give to him or her any information in relation to the appeal, application or referral which he or she reasonably requires for the purposes of the appeal, and it shall be the duty of the officer to comply with the requirement.[97]   **9–83**

---

[91] PDA 2000, s.135(2) (as substituted by the 2006 Act).

[92] PDA 2000, s.135(2A) (as substituted by the 2006 Act).

[93] PDA 2000, s.135(2B)(d) (as substituted by the 2006 Act).

[94] Prior to the introduction of an express power in this regard under the 2006 Act, the High Court had previously indicated that the person conducting an oral hearing, in the interest of justice, must be allowed a discretion in relation to the limitation or abbreviation of excessive arguments or submissions: *Keane v An Bord Pleanála*, unreported, High Court, Murphy J., June 20, 1995.

[95] The other parties and non-parties should be allowed an opportunity to respond if any new point arises, in order to ensure compliance with the rules of natural and constitutional justice. An adjournment may be necessary in some cases.

[96] Planning and Development Regulations 2001, art.77(1). "Relevant person" is defined under art.67.

[97] PDA 2000, s.135(3) (as substituted by the 2006 Act).

9–84 A person conducting an oral hearing may take evidence on oath or affirmation and for that purpose may administer oaths or affirmations, and a person giving evidence at any such hearing shall be entitled to the same immunities and privileges as if he or she were a witness before the High Court.[98]

9–85 The previous guidelines issued by An Bord Pleanála had precluded the use of stenographers, and, accordingly, the person conducting an oral hearing had been obliged to take notes by hand. To expedite the hearing, parties often prepare written submissions. An issue arises as to the extent to which an appellant may elaborate on his grounds of appeal at an oral hearing. Under s.127 an appellant may not elaborate *in writing* upon his grounds of appeal; this appears to leave open the possibility of elaboration by way of oral submission. In practice, the person conducting an oral hearing tends to allow some latitude in this connection.

9–86 Whatever may be the general position in this regard, it is submitted that if an issue is raised that goes to the *jurisdiction* of the board, submissions on the point must be entertained notwithstanding that the issue may only have been raised for the first time at the oral hearing. Following upon the decision of the Supreme Court in *Lancefort Ltd. v An Bord Pleanála*,[99] it appears that in order not to prejudice any subsequent judicial review proceedings, an objector is required to raise all legal issues at the oral hearing. This often proves unpopular with the person conducting the oral hearing, as he or she may be of the view that he or she is concerned only with the merits of the appeal, and not with legal points.

4. Supplemental powers of An Bord Pleanála re: oral hearing

9–87 In addition to the powers residing with the person conducting the oral hearing, An Bord Pleanála has supplemental powers in relation to an oral hearing. Under s.135(5), An Bord Pleanála may, in relation to an oral hearing of any appeal, by giving notice on that behalf in writing to any other person,[100] require that person to do either or both of the following: (i) to attend at such time and place as is specified in the notice to give evidence in relation to any matter in question at the hearing; and (ii) to produce any books, deeds, contracts, accounts, vouchers, maps, plans, documents or other information in his or her possession, custody or control which relate to any such matter.[101]

---

[98] PDA 2000, s.135(4). As to the limits on the privilege, see *Looney v Bank of Ireland* [1996] 1 I.R. 157.

[99] [1998] 2 I.L.R.M. 401.

[100] It may be necessary to notify other parties interested in the documents etc. See, by analogy, *Haughey v Mr Justice Moriarty* [1999] 3 I.R. 1.

[101] The power to summons a witness and/or to require the production of documents is an exceptional one. The powers of the person holding the oral hearing are much wider than those of An Bord Pleanála under PDA 2000, s.132: failure to comply with the latter is a criminal offence.

5. Further power to hold oral hearings

Under s.134A of the PDA 2000 (as inserted by the 2006 Act), An Bord Pleanála **9–88** has a general power to hold oral hearings where the board considers it necessary or expedient for the purposes of making a determination in respect of any of its statutory functions. Thus, An Bord Pleanála may decide, in its absolute discretion, to hold an oral hearing in respect of say, for example, the reference of a dispute in respect of social and affordable housing under Part V.

N. Challenges to Conduct of Oral Hearing

Occasionally an issue will arise as to the manner in which an oral hearing is **9–89** being, or is to be, conducted. More particularly, a party to the appeal may be of the view that the conduct of the oral hearing is, or will be, unsatisfactory. In the circumstances, the question arises as to whether or not such a person, in order to avoid a subsequent finding of waiver or acquiescence against him or her, must make an application for judicial review to the High Court *prior* to a decision being made by An Bord Pleanála. On one view, it might be thought that it is better that a challenge be brought as early as possible rather than embark on what may prove to be a lengthy and costly appeal procedure. Support for this approach is to be found, by analogy, in the decision of the High Court in *Cavern Systems Dublin Ltd. v Clontarf Residents Association*.[102] Costello J. in that decision held that one of the objectives of imposing a short limitation period on the taking of challenges to a decision of a planning authority was:

> "to make applicants for development permission and planning authorities aware that the legal validity of a decision was being challenged so as to give them an opportunity to apply for an adjournment of a planning appeal so as to avoid the possibility that unnecessary costs might be incurred and the time of public officials unnecessarily wasted; and to enable An Bord Pleanála to adjourn an appeal before it if it considered it appropriate to do so during the pendency of High Court proceedings."

Reference is also made to the decision in *Max Developments Ltd. v An Bord* **9–90** *Pleanála*.[103] The facts of the case were as follows. An objector to the proposed development had argued at an oral hearing that the development was of a type which was subject to environmental impact assessment. In particular, the objector had argued that the development project exceeded the relevant threshold. The inspector conducting the oral hearing advised the objector's counsel that he did not accept that an environmental impact statement was required. The inspector further advised that he would adjourn the oral hearing to permit the objector to make an application to the High Court. Following the adjournment, counsel for the objector confirmed that he did not propose to proceed with an application to the High Court at that time, and the oral hearing

---

[102] [1984] I.L.R.M. 24 at 29.
[103] [1994] 1 I.R. 121.

accordingly proceeded. Subsequently a decision was made by An Bord Pleanála to grant planning permission. This decision was then challenged by way of an application for judicial review by the objector. Flood J. refused to grant leave to apply for judicial review on the basis, in effect, that the objector was estopped from seeking to challenge the decision in circumstances where it elected to continue the oral hearing, and failed to challenge the procedure, at that time, before the High Court.[104]

1. Prematurity

9–91   As against all of this, an argument can be made, and the foregoing judgments criticised, on the basis that the bringing of a challenge directed to the oral hearing is inappropriate in that such a challenge is premature. The concept of prematurity may be analysed in a number of ways. First, the challenge may be one not properly directed at the oral hearing at all. For example, the objection raised may be one which the members of An Bord Pleanála, as opposed to the person conducting the oral hearing, are in a position to remedy. This point may be illustrated by reference to the facts of the decision in *Huntstown Air Park Ltd. v An Bord Pleanála*.[105] In that case, the objectors sought to have a statutory notice served on an observer to the appeal, requiring that person to submit to An Bord Pleanála specified documents and particulars.[106] At the oral hearing, the inspector requested the observer to produce the documents but the observer refused on grounds of commercial confidentiality. Following on the refusal, the inspector declined to make any further direction in relation to the documents and insisted on proceeding with the oral hearing. The objector brought an application for judicial review before the High Court. As part of the order granting leave to apply for judicial review, the High Court granted a stay on the oral hearing.

9–92   The application for judicial review was ultimately dismissed, however, on the basis that the statutory provision which the objector had sought to invoke in relation to the production of documents related to a power which resided in the members of An Bord Pleanála and not in the inspector conducting the oral hearing. Accordingly, the High Court held that the application for judicial review was premature: the members of An Bord Pleanála were entitled to exercise the relevant statutory power at any stage before making the final decision on the appeal and, therefore, until such time as a final decision had been made on the appeal without there having been an exercise of the statutory power to seek the production of documents, any application for judicial review was premature.

---

[104] See also *Healy v Dublin County Council*, unreported, High Court, Barron J., April 29, 1993 (applicants estopped from obtaining relief because of failure to seek to restrain third party appeals); and *Sloan v An Bord Pleanála* [2003] 2 I.L.R.M. 61.
[105] [1999] 1 I.L.R.M. 281.
[106] The relevant power was under s.10 of the Local Government (Planning & Development) Act 1992. A similar power is now to be found under PDA 2000, s.132.

Similar logic applies to a number of other potential objections which might be raised in the context of an appeal. Indeed, it is arguable that the point raised in *Max Developments Ltd. v An Bord Pleanála*, namely whether or not to require an environmental impact statement, was not a matter for the inspector conducting the oral hearing at all, in circumstances where the power to call for an environmental impact statement would appear to have resided with the members of An Bord Pleanála. **9–93**

The second sense in which the concept of prematurity might be understood is this. It is trite law that judicial review is not concerned with the substance or merits of a decision but rather with its legality. One consequence of this seems to be that, generally speaking, the High Court will not determine any facts but will, instead, merely review the findings of fact of the decision-maker.[107] Depending on the nature of the objection raised, it may be crucial that the High Court have before it the findings of fact of the decision-maker on the relevant point. To use again the example of environmental impact assessment, an argument may arise as to whether or not an environmental impact assessment should have been required in respect of a proposed development. This might require a consideration of matters such as whether or not the nature and extent of the proposed development would be such as to bring it above the specified threshold, or, more generally, as to whether the proposed development would or would not be likely to have significant effects on the environment. These are matters which might well not be fully elucidated until after an oral hearing.[108] **9–94**

The third, and broadest, sense in which prematurity might be understood is that of the application for judicial review being premature on account of the fact that the ultimate decision on the substantive appeal might be to the satisfaction of the objector. To put the matter another way, it might be thought unnecessary to embark on a possible lengthy judicial review hearing in circumstances where An Bord Pleanála might have decided, on the planning merits of the appeal, to refuse planning permission (or to modify the development so as to remove the aspects objected to). For this pragmatic reason then it might be thought that a "wait and see" attitude should be adopted and that it would only be in the event that the decision on the substance of the appeal went against the objector that he or she would be required to institute judicial review proceedings. **9–95**

In practice, it is difficult to advise an objector as to at how early a stage judicial review proceedings should be taken. The conservative view must be that once a ground of judicial review has crystallised, steps should be taken to institute judicial review proceedings in order to protect the objector's position, and, in particular, to avoid a point on delay being taken against him.[109] Once judicial review proceedings have been instituted, it may be possible to persuade the **9–96**

---

[107] See, by analogy, *R. v Association of Futures Brokers and Dealers Ltd.* [1991] 3 Admin. L.R. 254.
[108] *RGDATA v An Bord Pleanála*, unreported, High Court, Barron J., April 30, 1996.
[109] *cf. Sloan v An Bord Pleanála* [2003] 2 I.L.R.M. 61. See paras 11–55 to 11–65.

other parties, especially An Bord Pleanála, to agree to the proceedings being adjourned pending the making of a decision by An Bord Pleanála. The applicant by laying down a marker will have protected himself from any allegation of delay or waiver. The adjournment of the proceedings may represent a common sense compromise which will allow the parties to then "wait and see" what the substantive outcome of the appeal will be.

2. Staying or restraining the oral hearing

9–97   An issue closely related to that of prematurity is as to whether or not, in the event that an objector decides to bring judicial review proceedings in advance of a final decision of An Bord Pleanála, it is necessary to apply within the context of those judicial review proceedings for an interlocutory injunction restraining any oral hearing before An Bord Pleanála. If the supposed rationale of any requirement that an objector seek judicial review proceedings at an early stage (namely to avoid the incurring of unnecessary time and expense in relation to an appeal which may ultimately prove to be invalid) is to be pursued to its logical conclusion, then it would seem necessary for the objector to seek interlocutory relief.

9–98   Reference is made, by analogy, to the decision in *Broadnet Ireland Ltd. v Office of the Director of Telecommunications Regulations*.[110] In that judgment, the High Court held that the grant of leave to apply for judicial review *per se*, even without a formal order in the nature of a stay or an interlocutory injunction, could have a chilling effect on a decision-making process. Accordingly, it might be necessary to impose as a condition on the grant of, or the continuation of, leave a requirement that an applicant give an undertaking as to damages as in the case of an interlocutory injunction. Similar reasoning might be thought to apply in the context of an appeal to An Bord Pleanála, if an applicant were allowed simply to issue judicial review proceedings at an early stage without any necessity to pursue an application for an interlocutory injunction this might be thought unsatisfactory in that it would leave a question mark over the entire appeal process.

3. Application of *Campus Oil* principles

9–99   Turning now to a more detailed consideration of the principles which would be applicable to any such interlocutory injunction, the leading decision would appear to be that of *Martin v An Bord Pleanála*.[111] In that decision, O'Sullivan J. confirmed that such an application fell to be determined by reference to the general principles established in *Campus Oil Ltd. v Minister for Industry and Energy*.[112] This well-known decision posits three considerations against which

---

[110] [2000] 3 I.R. 281; [2000] 2 I.L.R.M. 241.
[111] [2002] 2 I.R. 655; [2003] 1 I.L.R.M. 257.
[112] [1983] I.R. 82.

an application for an interlocutory injunction is to be considered, as follows. First, whether or not the applicant has established a serious issue to be tried. Secondly, the adequacy of damages as a remedy. Thirdly, the balance of convenience. See, generally, para.11–264 and onwards.

The application of the first of these tests, namely whether or not the applicant has demonstrated a serious issue to be tried, does not appear to give rise to any special difficulties or peculiarities. Accordingly, it is proposed to move directly to a consideration of the second and third limbs. **9–100**

Damages

The determination of the adequacy of damages as an alternative remedy does give rise to special considerations. The first of these relates to the ability of the applicant to recover damages at all. Generally, the consideration of the adequacy of damages works on the basis that if the applicant is refused the interlocutory injunction sought, this nevertheless can be made good by a subsequent award of damages to the applicant in the event that he ultimately succeeds in his case and proves to have been right. The difficulty with the application of this principle to the present context is, of course, that an entitlement to damages does not automatically follow from a finding that a public body, such as An Bord Pleanála, has acted *ultra vires*. It is well established that in order to succeed in a claim for damages, an applicant must demonstrate an additional basis for claiming damages over and above the mere fact that the conduct complained of was unlawful.[113] Given that a consideration of the adequacy of damages is predicated on the availability of such an award of damages, it seems that this test will be of limited use in the present context. **9–101**

A second, related difficulty in relation to the consideration of the adequacy of damages is that whereas An Bord Pleanála may well be inconvenienced, and the discharge of its statutory function to determine appeals expeditiously frustrated, it would seem difficult to argue that An Bord Pleanála would suffer any monetary damages. In *Martin*, O'Sullivan J. concentrated on the fact that whilst An Bord Pleanála would not have any monetary damages in the event that the stay sought was given, the notice party developer would. In this connection, O'Sullivan J. held that the applicant would be required to give an undertaking as to damages. On the facts of the case, the applicant had not provided sufficient detail in relation to his offered undertaking as to damages so as to enable the High Court to assess whether or not it was a realistic undertaking when balanced against the prospective losses of the notice party developer. O'Sullivan J. found that he was unable to treat the applicant's undertaking as to damages as more than a *pro forma* compliance with the usual requirement. On that ground alone, O'Sullivan J. indicated that he would be prepared to refuse the application for a stay. **9–102**

---

[113] For a recent example, see the decision of the Supreme Court in *Glencar Explorations plc v Mayo County Council* [2002] 1 I.R. 84; [2002] 1 I.L.R.M. 481.

Balance of convenience

9–103   In the circumstances, it would seem that the question of the balance of convenience will assume a particular significance in any application for an interlocutory injunction in the context of an oral hearing before An Bord Pleanála. The competing considerations in this regard would seem to be as follows. On the one hand, there is the public interest in the efficient despatch by An Bord Pleanála of the appeals which come before it.[114] This public interest finds statutory expression under s.126 of the PDA 2000: it shall be the duty of An Bord Pleanála to ensure that appeals and referrals are disposed of as expeditiously as may be and, for that purpose, to take all such steps as are open to it to ensure that, insofar as is practicable, there are no avoidable delays at any stage in the determination of appeals and referrals. Various aspirational time-limits are then set out.

9–104   On the other hand, there is the potential inconvenience and loss to the applicant for judicial review in the event that he or she is required, as a result of the refusal of an interlocutory injunction, to participate before an oral hearing which he or she alleges to be unsatisfactory. In this regard, a distinction should be drawn, in considering the nature of the objection alleged, as between defects peculiar to the conduct of the oral hearing, and general defects. If the applicant for judicial review alleges that there is some matter specific to the oral hearing which is unsatisfactory (for example, in relation to a request for an adjournment, or the availability of documents, perhaps), these are matters clearly impacting on the conduct of the oral hearing *per se*, and, in the event that the applicant is correct in his objection, are such as might require that a fresh oral hearing be held. Accordingly, there might be some merit in having these matters determined prior to the (original) oral hearing. Conversely, in the case of an objection based on a more general complaint, *i.e.* one that is not related specifically to the oral hearing, it might be thought that there is no particular advantage or necessity in staying the oral hearing and that instead the applicant's objection falls to be determined in the context of the overall decision of An Bord Pleanála. (To an extent the observations made in this regard represent the obverse of the points made in relation to prematurity: if the complaint raised is one not properly directed to the oral hearing or the person conducting the oral hearing (as in *Huntstown Air Park Ltd.*, for example) this would not seem to present good grounds for restraining the oral hearing.) The facts of *Martin* to an extent involved a hybrid: whereas the objection made as to the adequacy of the legislation implementing the environmental impact assessment Directive was not one specific to the oral hearing but one which went to the very jurisdiction of An Bord Pleanála to determine the appeal at all, the applicant had sought to argue that it would have a very real impact on the conduct of the oral hearing.

---

[114] *Martin v An Bord Pleanála* [2002] 2 I.R. 655; [2003] 1 I.L.R.M. 257.

Of course, the applicant in *Martin* faced the following difficulty. His argument **9=105** was predicated on there having been a failure to implement the environmental impact assessment Directive properly into Irish law. The applicant had implicitly conceded that the procedures proposed by An Bord Pleanála were consistent with domestic legislation and it was only if he was correct in his argument that the domestic legislation itself was invalid that he could challenge the procedure before An Bord Pleanála.

O'Sullivan J. dealt with the matter as follows in *Martin*.[115] **9=106**

> "In my opinion, the balance of convenience also favours the refusal of the granting of a stay. It is clear from authority that it would take something almost overwhelming for a court to suspend the continued application of domestic law pending a trial. In *Pesca Valentia Ltd. v Minister for Fisheries* [1985] I.R. 193 the court was persuaded to temporarily suspend the law of the land because the plaintiffs would otherwise have faced criminal liability. Furthermore, the plaintiffs would have been prevented from carrying on with their livelihood pending final determination of the action. Here the boot is on the other foot. It is the notice party that seeks, if and when so authorised, to carry on a business in respect of which the applicant has asserted strong objections. The first named respondent [An Bord Pleanála] has a statutory duty not only to consider the appeals before it but to do so within a time frame identified by statute as particularly limited, in the first instance, to a period of four months. There is a public dimension to the considerations of the court on this aspect of the application = namely the interests of the public in the efficient despatch by the first named respondent of the appeals which come before it."

---

[115] [2002] 2 I.R. 655; [2003] 1 I.L.R.M. 257.

CHAPTER TEN

REFERRALS, STRATEGIC INFRASTRUCTURE AND OTHER APPEALS

A. Reference on Development or Exempted Development

1. Overview of Section 5

A procedure is provided for under s.5 of the PDA 2000 whereby any question as to what, in any particular case, is or is not development, or is or is not exempted development, may be referred to the planning authority for a declaration on that question.[1] The procedure differs significantly from that provided for under the previous legislation (coincidentally also numbered s.5), namely s.5 of the Local Government (Planning & Development) Act 1963. In particular, a reference is now made at first instance to the planning authority, with a right of review to An Bord Pleanála. Under the previous legislation, the reference was made initially to An Bord Pleanála, with a statutory right of appeal to the High Court.[2]   **10–01**

---

[1] As to whether or not such a question has arisen, see, by analogy, *Readymix (Éire) Ltd. v Dublin County Council*, unreported, Supreme Court, July 30, 1974 (injunction sought to restrain reference in context of grant of planning permission). More generally, see also *Patterson v Murphy* [1978] I.L.R.M. 85 at 103.

[2] As to the appeal procedure, see, generally, *Rehabilitation Institute v Dublin Corporation*, unreported, High Court, Barron J., January 14, 1988; *Esat Digifone Ltd. v South Dublin County Council* [2002] 3 I.R. 585; [2002] 2 I.L.R.M. 547; and *Glancré Teoranta v Cafferkey (No. 1)* [2004] 3 I.R. 401.

10-02   Other changes include the fact that it is now expressly stated that a reference may be made by any person: under the previous legislation, doubt had been expressed as to the entitlement of a third party, having no interest in the lands, to make a reference.[3]

10-03   Other aspects of the new procedure are also less satisfactory than those under the previous legislation. In particular, it seems somewhat anomalous that the reference should be made, in the first instance, to the planning authority. During the course of the exercise of its powers, a planning authority will be required, from time to time, to take a view as to whether a particular matter constitutes development or not. For example, it will have to do so in deciding whether or not to take enforcement action. The planning authority having formed such a view, as it must, it then seems somewhat artificial to suggest that the matter can subsequently be referred to the planning authority under s.5 and that the planning authority then consider the matter afresh.[4] This is especially so in circumstances where there is case law to the effect that the determination of a question of development or exempted development involves the exercise of a quasi-judicial function.[5]

10-04   Moreover, it also seems unfortunate that the statutory right of appeal to the High Court is lost. This will make it more difficult to obtain an authoritative ruling from the High Court in relation to the interpretation of the concepts of development and exempted development. In the absence of a statutory right of appeal, the only alternatives would seem to be, first, that an application be brought for judicial review; and, secondly, that An Bord Pleanála refer the matter to the High Court pursuant to s.50(1). The difficulty with the former is that the High Court is generally reluctant to interfere with the substance of a decision on an application for judicial review; the difficulty with the latter is that An Bord Pleanála very rarely refers questions of law to the High Court.

2. Scope of matters which may be referred under section 5

10-05   Section 5(1) provides that if any question arises as to what, in any particular case, is or is not development or is or is not exempted development within the meaning of the PDA 2000, any person may, on payment of the prescribed fee, request in writing from the planning authority a declaration on that question.

10-06   There had been some controversy as to whether similar wording under the previous legislation allowed questions to be referred which required the interpretation of a planning permission. On a literal reading, the statutory

---

[3]   In *Fairyhouse Club Ltd. v An Bord Pleanála*, unreported, High Court, Finnegan J., July 18, 2001, leave to challenge the determination on a reference was granted on this ground. The judicial review proceedings were ultimately discontinued, and the point was not, therefore, decided.

[4]   *cf.* PDA 2000, s.5(4) which allows for a direct referral to An Bord Pleanála.

[5]   *Central Dublin Development Association Ltd. v Attorney General* (1969) 109 I.L.T.R. 69.

wording might suggest that a reference must be confined to a question as to whether a particular activity involved "development" or "exempted development". The question as to whether the terms of an existing planning permission are wide enough to authorise a particular use or works involves a separate exercise, and requires the interpretation of the planning permission.

The point first arose in *Palmerlane Ltd. v An Bord Pleanála.*[6] A dispute had   **10–07** arisen as to whether use of a convenience store for the sale of hot food for consumption off the premises represented development, and the store owner sought to refer the matter to An Bord Pleanála under the previous s.5. An Bord Pleanála declined to entertain the reference, stating that it did not have power to decide whether or not a particular development had been carried out in accordance with a particular permission. An Bord Pleanála considered that as the sale of hot food had been part of the user of the premises from the outset, there simply was no *change* in use, the materiality of which it could assess. The board's decision in this regard was then challenged in judicial review proceedings. Having noted that An Bord Pleanála would have been prepared to entertain the reference had the use for the sale of hot food been introduced *subsequent* to the opening of the store, the High Court took the pragmatic view that the board's jurisdiction should not turn on such nice distinctions.

> "The decision of An Bord Pleanála in the instant case also, in my view, creates the somewhat anomalous and unreasonable situation that if the applicant were to select another of its 'Spar' shops, where the position was that the premises had been in use as a retail shop under an earlier planning permission and the company had subsequently embarked on the limited sale of hot food for consumption off the premises, the applicant could presumably successfully have sought a determination of a reference pursuant to section 5 of the 1963 Act. I appreciate that each determination under section 5 deals only with the particular case on its own facts. However, in a situation where a very large number of convenience stores operate in the same way as the shop in question in the instant case, it seems to me to be in accordance with reason and common sense that questions such as this should be determined on a consistent basis by those with expertise in the planning area, namely An Bord Pleanála."

This pragmatic approach evolved into a more general statement of principle   **10–08** with the judgment of the Supreme Court in *Grianán an Aileach Interpretative Centre Ltd. v Donegal County Council.*[7] This case concerned the jurisdiction of the High Court to grant declaratory relief as to the interpretation of planning permissions. The planning authority argued that it was inappropriate for the High Court to grant declarations in circumstances where the planning legislation provided for a reference procedure. In order to rule on this argument, it was necessary for the Supreme Court to examine the nature of disputes which could properly be referred under s.5. Keane C.J. concluded that a question as to whether proposed uses constitute "development" which is not authorised by

[6] [1999] 2 I.L.R.M. 514.
[7] [2004] 2 I.R. 625; [2005] 1 I.L.R.M. 106.

planning permission is one which may be determined under s.5 of the PDA 2000.

> "In the present case, the issue that has arisen between the plaintiff and the defendant is as to whether the proposed uses are authorised by the planning permission. I am satisfied, however, that, although the issue has arisen in that particular form, it necessarily requires the tribunal which determines it to come to a conclusion as to whether what is being proposed would constitute a material change in the use of the premises. If it would not, then the question as to whether the particular uses were authorised by the permission simply would not arise. In the present case, the defendant at all times has been contending, in effect, that the proposed uses would constitute a material change in use which is not authorised by the present planning permission. Equally, for its part, the plaintiff has been contending that the uses are authorised by the existing planning permission but has not contended that, if that were not the case, it would in any event be entitled to carry them out as not constituting a material change of use. It would seem to follow that the question as to whether planning permission is required in this case necessarily involves the determination of the question as to whether the proposed uses would constitute a 'development', *i.e.* a question which the planning authority and An Bord Pleanála are empowered to determine under s. 5 of the Act of 2000."

10–09 Finally, the tribunal determining a Section 5 reference—whether the planning authority, at first instance, or An Bord Pleanála—is entitled to reformulate the question posed where necessary. The High Court had ruled in the context of the previous legislation that the function of a Section 5 reference is to clarify whether particular works or use constituted development or exempted development, and that An Bord Pleanála should not be confined in some artificial way by the wording of the referred question.[8]

3. Procedure

10–10 A reference should (i) be made in writing; (ii) state the name and address of the person making the referral and of the person, if any, acting on his or her behalf; (iii) state the subject-matter of the referral; (iv) state in full the grounds of referral and the reasons, considerations and arguments on which they are based; and (iv) be accompanied by the relevant fee.[9]

10–11 In *O'Reilly (Bros) Wicklow Ltd. v An Bord Pleanála*,[10] An Bord Pleanála's decision on a reference was challenged on the basis that the initial reference had failed to state in full the grounds of referral and the reasons, considerations and arguments on which they were based. The reference had been made by Wicklow County Council. The quality of documentation submitted in support of the reference was, in the view of the High Court, deplorable. Nonetheless

---

[8] *Esat Digifone Ltd. v South Dublin County Council* [2002] 3 I.R. 585; [2002] 2 I.L.R.M. 547.
[9] PDA 2000, s.127.
[10] [2006] I.E.H.C. 363; unreported, Quirke J., November 22, 2006.

the reference was held not to have been invalid, because the reasons, considerations and arguments on which the planning authority's referral was based could, with some difficulty, be discovered within the documentation provided to An Bord Pleanála.

> "It was possible to discover the *reasons, considerations and arguments*' on which the grounds of appeal were based within the documentation submitted by the Council. That was so because the Board was prepared, patiently and conscientiously to carry out a diligent search of the 'rag-tag' bundle of documents submitted to it by the Council. It is regrettable and indeed it was discourteous and grossly unsatisfactory that any Planning Authority should refer a question to a Board pursuant to the provisions of s. 127 of the Act in such a deplorable manner."

In arguing against an unduly strict approach to procedural requirements, An **10–12** Bord Pleanála had emphasised the importance of public participation in the referral process, pointing out that members of the public, who may be unfamiliar with maps, drawings, environmental impact statements and other technical documents and terminology, have a statutory right to refer questions to the board in simple, straight forward and sensible terms.

Third parties

There is no express requirement that third parties be notified of the making of **10–13** a reference, still less that third parties should be permitted to participate in the process. Instead, the section simply provides that a planning authority may request persons to submit information in order to allow the planning authority issue a declaration. Moreover, the right of review to An Bord Pleanála is only available to the person requesting the reference. In the circumstances, it is submitted that the statutory procedure is deficient. The consequences of this are either that the planning authority must supplement the statutory procedure by reference to general concepts of fair procedures, or that the legal effect of a declaration must be severely curtailed: in particular, same cannot be binding as against third parties.

4. Precedent

An Bord Pleanála is entitled to rely on earlier decisions as precedents when **10–14** determining a Section 5 reference. There does not appear to be any obligation on the board to notify the parties in advance of an intention to rely on an earlier decision.[11] This is because previous decisions are matters of public record and are available for inspection.[12] If a party to a reference wishes, it may draw the board's attention to any previous decision of An Bord Pleanála which it considers relevant.

---

[11] *Fairyhouse Club Ltd. v An Bord Pleanála*, unreported, High Court, Finnegan P., July 18, 2001.
[12] *ibid.*

5. Decision and reasons

10–15   There is no express statutory duty on either a planning authority or An Bord Pleanála to state reasons for the determination on a Section 5 reference. This is in marked contrast to a decision on an application for planning permission. Nevertheless, there is an implied duty to give some indication of the reasoning behind the determination. The determination of a reference constitutes a quasi-judicial function, and, accordingly, triggers a requirement to state reasons. Moreover, reasons are necessary in order to facilitate the exercise of the right of review to An Bord Pleanála from the planning authority's decision, and the right to seek judicial review of the decision of either body. See, more generally, paras 12–119 to 12–163.

10–16   It appears from the judgment of the High Court in *Fairyhouse Club Ltd. v An Bord Pleanála*[13] that it may be sufficient if the reasoning is disclosed in the inspector's report, at least in circumstances where An Bord Pleanála's decision is consistent with the inspector's recommendation and adopts his or her reasoning.

6. Question of law or fact and degree?

10–17   Whether a particular act is or is not development would appear to be a question of law, rather than one of fact and degree.[14] This is because the determination involves the application of the legal concept of "development" to a particular set of facts. Similarly, the determination of whether a particular act is "exempted development" also involves the application of a legal concept.

10–18   This analysis appears to be consistent with the scheme of the Local Government (Planning & Development) Act 1963, which provided a right of appeal to the High Court against the determination of An Bord Pleanála. The statutory appeal took the form of a re-examination from the beginning on the merits of the decision appealed from, with a view if appropriate to the substitution by the High Court of its adjudication for that of An Bord Pleanála.[15] The analysis is also consistent with the approach taken in enforcement proceedings, where the High Court was prepared to decide, as a question of law, whether a particular act was development or not.[16]

---

[13] Unreported, High Court, Finnegan P., July 18, 2001.

[14] The judgment in *Central Dublin Development Association v Attorney General* (1969) 109 I.L.T.R. 69 goes so far as to suggest that the Section 5 procedure involves the administration of justice.

[15] *Glancré Teoranta v Cafferkey (No. 1)* [2004] 3 I.R. 401.

[16] See, for example, *Glancré Teoranta v Cafferkey (No. 1)* [2004] 3 I.R. 401 ("The issue as to whether development is or is not exempted is one which the legislature clearly regarded as one within the competence of the courts in enacting s. 27 of the Local Government (Planning and Development) Act 1976, where just such an issue regularly arises. To suggest otherwise in relation to s. 5 of the Local Government (Planning and Development) Act 1963 would create an inherent contradiction within the planning code [...]").

Under the newly structured Section 5 reference procedure, the statutory right **10–19** of appeal to the High Court has been removed. Instead, the jurisdiction of the High Court can only be invoked by way of an application for judicial review. This amendment removes the anomaly under the previous legislation whereby a determination on a Section 5 was, in principle, subject to both the statutory right of appeal, and judicial review under s.82(3A) & (3B) of the Local Government (Planning & Development) Act 1963. Different time-limits applied to each procedure: three months in the case of an appeal and two months in the case of judicial review.

The procedural changes in this regard should not affect the standard of review **10–20** applicable to a Section 5 determination. The determination remains a decision on a question of law, and should, therefore, still be amenable to full-blooded review before the High Court. Although judicial review is often thought of as being available only in cases of unreasonableness or irrationality, this is not accurate. Judicial review is available to correct errors of law, and thus an incorrect finding by a planning authority or An Bord Pleanála on the legal question as to whether a particular act is or is not development (or exempted development) can properly be corrected by the High Court.

7. Major-accident hazards Directive/Seveso Directive

Planning authority

Where a planning authority receives a request for a declaration under Section **10–21** 5 relating to the provision of, or modifications to, a major-accidents establishment, and in the opinion of the planning authority, the development could have significant repercussions on major-accident hazards, the planning authority is required to notify the Health and Safety Authority ("the HSA").

The notice is to issue as soon as may be following receipt of the request for a **10–22** declaration. The notice should include a copy of the relevant request for a declaration, and request technical advice on the effects of the proposed development on the risk or consequences of a major accident.

The planning authority is required to submit a copy of any relevant technical **10–23** advice received from the HSA to An Bord Pleanála in the case of a review of a determination on a Section 5 reference.

An Bord Pleanála

An Bord Pleanála has a free standing discretion to invoke the notification **10–24** procedure in circumstances where the planning authority had not already done so. This applies where An Bord Pleanála receives a referral relating to the provision of, or modifications to, an establishment, which, in the opinion of the board, could have significant repercussions on major-accident hazards.

10–25   An Bord Pleanála is to send the notice as soon as may be following the receipt of the referrals. The notice should include a copy of the relevant referral, and request technical advice on the effects of the proposed development on the risk or consequences of a major accident. The weekly list shall refer to the fact that the Section 5 reference relates to the provision of, or modifications to, an establishment.

10–26   Where a notice is required under s.142(4) of the PDA 2000 in respect of a reference under Section 5 which relates to the provision of, or modifications to, an establishment, and which, in the opinion of the board, could have significant repercussions on major-accident hazards, the notice shall indicate that fact.

8. Parallel enforcement proceedings

10–27   On occasion, the procedure under s.5 of the PDA 2000 may have been invoked in parallel with enforcement proceedings. A developer in response to the threat of enforcement action might seek to refer the matter for a determination under s.5. In particular, it seems that where it is sought to challenge an enforcement notice, the appropriate procedure may be a reference under s.5, rather than judicial review.[17]

10–28   It was well established under the previous legislation that in the context of an application for a planning injunction the court had full original jurisdiction to determine any question as to development or exempted development on the hearing of the enforcement proceedings, and that it was not necessary to adjourn those proceedings pending the outcome of a reference. The Supreme Court had indicated that the planning injunction procedure represented a summary and self-contained procedure,[18] and that the jurisdiction was not ousted by the making of a reference.[19] It is submitted that this reasoning applies *a fortiori* to the newly constituted reference procedure. This is because, as discussed above, there is no longer a right of appeal to the High Court in respect of a reference. Instead, the matter will generally rest with the determination of An Bord Pleanála (subject only to judicial review). Whereas there might have been an argument under the previous legislation that the enforcement proceedings should await the outcome of the hearing of an appeal on a reference to the High Court, there is little reason to suggest that the courts must show such diffidence to An Bord Pleanála by adjourning the enforcement proceedings pending a determination by the board.

---

[17] *O'Connor v Kerry County Council* [1988] I.L.R.M. 660.

[18] *Cork Corporation v O'Connell* [1982] I.L.R.M. 505 at 511, *per* Henchy J. See also *Patterson v Murphy* [1978] I.L.R.M. 85 at 103; *Dublin County Council v Tallaght Block Company Ltd.*, unreported, Supreme Court, May 17, 1983; [1982] I.L.R.M. 534 (High Court); *Dublin Corporation v Regan Advertising Ltd.* [1989] I.R. 61; [1986] I.R. 171 (delay by applicant); *Stafford v Roadstone Ltd.* [1980] I.L.R.M. 1 at 12–13; *Clarke v Brady*, unreported, High Court, Hamilton P., October 30, 1990; and *Cork County Council v Ardfert Quarry Product Ltd.*, unreported, High Court, Murphy J., December 7, 1982.

[19] *Cork Corporation v O'Connell* [1982] I.L.R.M. 505 at 510, *per* Griffin J.

9. Residual jurisdiction of High Court to grant declarations?

The extent to which, notwithstanding the existence of the Section 5 procedure, **10–29** the High Court retains a residual jurisdiction to grant declarations as to the correct interpretation of planning permissions was considered by the Supreme Court in *Grianán An Aileach Interpretative Centre Company Ltd. v Donegal County Council*.[20] The Supreme Court held, *per* Keane C.J., that the existence of the Section 5 reference procedure precluded the High Court from determining such issues. In this regard, it was suggested that for the High Court to retain a jurisdiction to give declaratory relief would create a danger of overlapping and unworkable jurisdictions.

> "Thus, in the present case, if the jurisdiction of the planning authority or An Bord Pleanála under s. 5 were invoked and they were invited to determine whether the uses in controversy were within the uses contemplated by the planning permission or constituted a material change of use for which a new planning permission would be required, either of those bodies might find itself in a position where it could not exercise its statutory jurisdiction without finding itself in conflict with a determination by the High Court. No doubt a person carrying out a development which he claims is not a material change of use is not obliged to refer the question to the planning authority or An Bord Pleanála and may resist enforcement proceedings subsequently brought against him by the planning authority on the ground that permission was not required. In that event, if the enforcement proceedings are brought in the High Court, that court may undoubtedly find itself having to determine whether there has been a material change of use or whether a development is sanctioned by an existing planning permission, as happened in *O'Connor v. Kerry County Council* [1988] I.L.R.M. 660. But for the High Court to determine an issue of that nature, as though it were the planning authority or An Bord Pleanála, in proceedings such as the present would seem to me to create the danger of overlapping and unworkable jurisdictions referred to by Henchy J."

It is submitted that this aspect of the judgment is incorrect and should not be **10–30** followed.[21] First, the determination as to whether or not planning permission is required is pre-eminently a question of law, and one which the High Court should have jurisdiction to determine. Secondly, in any event, both the High Court and the Circuit Court are regularly called upon to address these issues in the context of planning injunctions under s.160 of the PDA 2000. It has long since been established that, in the exercise of their jurisdiction in respect of the planning injunction (both under the present and previous legislation), the courts are not inhibited by the fact that there is a parallel procedure whereby such matters can be determined. Given the ongoing existence of this overlapping jurisdiction, it seems somewhat anomalous to suggest that the High Court's

---

[20] [2004] 2 I.R. 625; [2005] 1 I.L.R.M. 106.
[21] *cf. R. (On the application of Reprotech (Pebsham) Ltd.) v East Sussex County Council* [2003] 1 W.L.R. 348; [2002] U.K.H.L. 8; [2003] 1 P. & C.R. 5, where Lord Hoffmann doubted whether the High Court's jurisdiction to grant declarations survived the introduction of a statutory right of appeal against enforcement notices.

inherent jurisdiction to give declaratory relief is extinguished. This is especially so where there is no express suggestion to that effect under the PDA 2000.

10–31   The judgment of the Supreme Court has already given rise to confusion in practice. In *Dublin City Council v Liffeybeat Ltd.*,[22] the High Court refused relief in s.160 injunction proceedings on the basis that the planning authority had failed to adduce evidence as to what was intended by a particular planning condition. Quirke J. refused to interpret the condition as it would be understood within its ordinary meaning by members of the public without legal training, holding that it was not the function of the court to impose its view as to how the premises should be used.

B. Strategic Infrastructure Development

1. Introduction

10–32   Generally an application for planning permission is made in the first instance to the relevant planning authority, with a right of appeal thereafter to An Bord Pleanála. In the case of specified categories of infrastructure projects, however, the planning application is made directly to An Bord Pleanála. This special procedure was introduced for the first time under the Planning and Development (Strategic Infrastructure) Act 2006 ("the 2006 Act"). The commencement date was January 31, 2007.[23]

10–33   An Bord Pleanála is required to establish a special division—known as "the Strategic Infrastructure Division"—to determine any matter in relation to strategic infrastructure development.[24] The Strategic Infrastructure Division is to consist of the chairperson of An Bord Pleanála, the deputy chairperson and three other ordinary members nominated by the chairperson to be, for the time being, members of the division. The total number of board members has been increased to 10: a chairman and nine ordinary members.[25]

10–34   Either (a) the chairperson or, in his or her absence, the deputy chairperson, or (b) a person acting as chairperson of a meeting of the division, may, at any stage before a decision is made, transfer the consideration of any matter from the Strategic Infrastructure Division to a meeting of all available members of the board where he or she considers the matter to be of particular complexity or significance.

---

[22] [2005] 1 I.R. 478.
[23] Planning and Development (Strategic Infrastructure) Act 2006 (Commencement) (No. 3) Order 2006 (S.I. No. 684 of 2006). See also the Planning and Development Regulations 2006 (S.I. No. 685 of 2006).
[24] PDA 2000, s.112A (as inserted by the 2006 Act).
[25] PDA 2000, s.104(1) (as inserted by the 2006 Act).

Removal of planning authority stage

The significance of the removal of the planning authority stage is not as far **10–35**
reaching as it might first appear. The fact that under the unamended PDA 2000
the decision of the planning authority was subject to a *de novo* appeal to An
Bord Pleanála meant that, even before the 2006 Act, the final decision on most
major infrastructural developments was already being taken by An Bord
Pleanála, not by the planning authority.

Opponents of the new procedure will, of course, point to the fact that in the **10–36**
majority of cases under the previous system the decision of An Bord Pleanála
whether to grant or refuse had been the same as that of the planning authority,[26]
thus suggesting that the planning authority's decision had some influence on
the outcome of the appeal process. Such a suggestion probably proves too
much in that, from a strictly legal viewpoint, it undermines the independence
and impartiality of the appeal system to suggest that the decision of the planning
authority influences the outcome. As discussed at paras 14–114 to 14–127,
independence and impartiality are essential in order to comply with the European
Convention on Human Rights.

Again from a purely legal viewpoint, it is more satisfactory that the views of **10–37**
the planning authority are made known by way of the submission of a report
on the application—which report is to be considered along with all other
submissions—rather than by way of a formal decision which it might be
suggested should exert some subliminal influence on the outcome of the appeal.

Fair hearing

It does not appear to be a requirement of constitutional justice that decision- **10–38**
making take place in two stages, *i.e.* that there is an inherent right of appeal.
Rather, the test is whether fair procedures were available prior to a (final)
decision being made, and there is no reason in principle why this should not be
achieved in a one-stage process.[27]

Nor can a requirement for a freestanding right of appeal be inferred from the **10–39**
case law under Art.6 of the European Convention on Human Rights. Generally,
when the terms of an appeal have been examined by the ECtHR, this has been
done solely with a view to ascertaining whether a deficient first stage is remedied

---

[26] An Bord Pleanála's Annual Report (2005) indicates that the planning authority's decision
at first instance was reversed by An Bord Pleanála in only thirty per cent of cases.

[27] Of course, there are many examples of decision-making where the nature of the first stage
is such that, on its own, it would not be acceptable, but the shortcomings are remedied by
the existence of a second stage. Indeed, the current planning process itself provides an
example of this. The absence of certain of the *indicia* of a fair hearing—such as the
possibility of an oral hearing or the production of documents—is probably only acceptable
because of the existence of a second stage before An Bord Pleanála where such procedures
are, in principle, available. It does not follow, however, that there is a freestanding right to
an appeal: the significance of the procedure before An Bord Pleanála is that is supplements
deficiencies at the first stage.

by an appeal. The requirement for independence and impartiality does not necessarily have to be fulfilled at each layer of the decision-making process: it may be sufficient if it is available on appeal or on judicial review. There is no suggestion in the case law that there must always be a right of appeal.

10–40   Assuming for a moment that a third party's rights under Art.6 are engaged by a decision to grant planning permission for development in the vicinity, the next question is as to whether An Bord Pleanála constitutes an independent and impartial tribunal. The answer to this question is not entirely clear. Whereas the rules governing the appointment and conduct of the members of An Bord Pleanála are such as to guarantee its impartiality, there is a potential difficulty in terms of its independence from a strictly legal viewpoint. This is because An Bord Pleanála is required—in determining an application for strategic infrastructure development—to have regard to (a) the policies and objectives for the time being of the Government, a State authority, the Minister for Environment Heritage and Local Government, planning authorities and any other body which is a public authority whose functions have, or may have, a bearing on the proper planning and sustainable development of cities, towns or other areas, whether urban or rural; (b) the national interest and any effect the performance of the board's functions may have on issues of strategic economic or social importance to the State; and (c) the National Spatial Strategy and any regional planning guidelines for the time being in force.[28]

10–41   It could be argued that the requirement for An Bord Pleanála to have regard to, for example, government policy undermines its independence and impartiality. The strict view is that a decision-maker cannot be regarded as independent and impartial where it has a role as policy-maker. Thus, in *R. (On the application of Alconbury Developments Ltd.) v Secretary of State for the Environment Transport and the Regions*,[29] it was accepted that decision-making under the auspices of the Secretary of State was not to be regarded as meeting the requirements of Art.6(1) because of his role in setting national planning policy.[30] An Bord Pleanála does not have a formal policy-making function, but the fact that it is obliged to have regard to government policy and objectives makes it difficult to argue that it is entirely independent.

10–42   For the sake of completeness, it should be noted that the role of a planning authority in determining applications for planning permission presents even greater difficulties. First, a planning authority has a significant policy-making role as author of the development plan. This suggests that in determining an application for planning permission it cannot be regarded as an independent and impartial tribunal. Secondly, the fact that planning authorities are empowered under Pt XIV of the PDA 2000 to take a more proactive role in the development and regeneration of lands might be thought to undermine their

---

[28] PDA 2000, s.37G(2)(g) and s.143 (as inserted by the 2006 Act).
[29] [2001] U.K.H.L. 23; (2001) 82 P. & C.R. 40.
[30] See also *Bryan v United Kingdom* (1996) 21 E.H.R.R. 342.

independence as a decision-maker. In circumstances where a planning authority is involved (whether directly or indirectly) with a proposed development, there might be a perception that it would be predisposed to grant planning permission for the development, and, possibly, to refuse planning permission for rival development.

Oral hearings

Another potential deficiency in the new procedure is in relation to oral hearings. An Bord Pleanála enjoys an "absolute discretion" to hold an oral hearing.[31] The entitlement to a "public" hearing in Art.6(1) of the European Convention on Human Rights has been held to imply a right to an "oral hearing" before at least one court or tribunal. This obligation is not an absolute one, and a hearing may be dispensed with if a party unequivocally waives his or her right thereto and there are no questions of public interest making a hearing necessary. **10–43**

The Court of Appeal, in *R. (On the application of Adlard) v Secretary of State for Transport, Local Government and the Regions*,[32] reiterated that the question of whether or not Art.6(1) is satisfied falls to be considered by reference not merely to the initial decision-making process but also in the light of the High Court's review jurisdiction. The Court of Appeal rejected an argument that Art.6(1) confers an absolute right to be heard orally by the administrative decision-making body. The decision-making process had to be looked at in its entirety. Any application for judicial review would entail an oral hearing. This would normally be sufficient—in the context of the planning process—to ensure compliance with the Convention. **10–44**

In reaching its conclusions, the Court of Appeal emphasised the subject-matter of the decision-making process. The subject-matter lay "towards that end of the spectrum where judgment and discretion, rather than fact-finding, play the predominant part".[33] The Court of Appeal in an earlier judgment[34]—with regard to the homelessness legislation—had indicated that where a scheme generally or systematically requires the application of judgment or the exercise of discretion, especially if it involves weighing of policy issues and regard being had to the interests of others who are not before the decision-maker, then for the purposes of Art.6 the court will incline to be satisfied with a form of inquisition at first instance in which the decision-maker is more of an expert than a judge, and the second instance appeal is in the nature of a judicial review. The Court of Appeal in *Adlard* went on to say that if the court were satisfied that exceptionally, on the facts of any particular case, it was unfair or unreasonable to deny an objector any or any sufficient oral hearing, the court would quash the decision and require such a hearing to be given.[35] **10–45**

---

[31] PDA 2000, s.134A(1) (as substituted by s.22 of the 2006 Act).
[32] [2002] E.W.C.A. Civ. 735; [2002] 2 P. & C.R. 28; [2002] J.P.L. 1379.
[33] *ibid.*, [17] *per* Simon Brown L.J., quoting from *London Borough of Tower Hamlets v Runa Begum* [2002] E.W.C.A. Civ. 239.
[34] *London Borough of Tower Hamlets v Runa Begum* [2002] E.W.C.A. Civ. 239, [42].
[35] [2002] E.W.C.A. Civ. 735; [2002] 2 P. & C.R. 28; [2002] J.P.L. 1379, [32].

Material contravention of development plan

10–46   It should be noted that the role of the planning authority is attenuated in that the development plan—although it remains a material consideration—is not binding on An Bord Pleanála. In contrast to the position in respect of all other development, there are no qualifications on the circumstances in which An Bord Pleanála may decide to grant a permission for strategic infrastructure development, or any part thereof, which contravenes materially the development plan.[36]

10–47   Prior to the 2006 Act there were qualifications imposed on the circumstances in which An Bord Pleanála could override a decision of the planning authority to refuse planning permission on the basis of material contravention. The removal of these statutory qualifications in the case of strategic infrastructure downgrades the status of the development plan. An examination of the detail of the unamended legislation, however, indicates that this change in status is more apparent than real. An Bord Pleanála had been entitled—prior to the 2006 Act—to grant planning permission in material contravention of the development plan where the proposed development was of "strategic or national importance", or where planning permission should be granted having regard to regional planning guidelines. As discussed at para.10–49, the new procedure under the 2006 Act is only applicable to developments which meet certain qualifications: these include that the development be of strategic economic or social importance, or that the development would contribute significantly to the fulfilment of any of the objectives in the National Spatial Strategy or in any regional planning guidelines. In many cases, therefore, development of the type now subject to the new procedure would not, even under the unamended legislation, have had to be refused where it would involve a material contravention.

2. Development projects to which the procedure applies

10–48   The categories of infrastructure project are specified in the Seventh Schedule of the amended PDA 2000. They include energy infrastructure projects; transport infrastructure projects; and environmental infrastructure projects (including certain waste disposal installations). An analogous procedure is provided for the approval of electricity and gas infrastructure.[37] Strictly speaking, such approvals do not constitute planning permissions and will not be dealt with further in this book.[38]

10–49   In order for the strategic infrastructure procedure to apply, not only must the development be of a category prescribed under the Seventh Schedule, it must also meet one or more of the following criteria set out in s.37A(2).

---

[36] PDA 2000, s.37G(6) (as inserted by the 2006 Act).

[37] PDA 2000, ss.182A to 182E, PDA 2000 (as inserted by the 2006 Act).

[38] See J. Macken, "The Planning and Development (Strategic Infrastructure) Act 2006" (2006) 13 I.P.E.L.J. 139 for an overview of the procedure for the approval of electricity and gas infrastructure.

(a) the development would be of strategic economic or social importance to the State or the region in which it would be situate;

(b) the development would contribute substantially to the fulfilment of any of the objectives in the National Spatial Strategy or in any regional planning guidelines in force in respect of the area or areas in which it would be situate;

(c) the development would have a significant effect on the area of more than one planning authority.

3. Consultation with An Bord Pleanála prior to application

An applicant proposing to make an application in respect of any of the specified categories of development project must first consult with An Bord Pleanála as to whether the special procedure is to apply.[39] In any such consultation An Bord Pleanála may give advice to the prospective applicant regarding the proposed application and, in particular, regarding (a) whether the proposed development would, if carried out, fall within one or more of paragraphs (a) to (c) of s.37A(2); (b) the procedures involved in making a planning application and in considering such an application; and (c) what considerations, related to proper planning and sustainable development or the environment, may, in the opinion of the board, have a bearing on its decision in relation to the application.[40] Under the Planning and Development Regulations 2006, the board is required during the course of a pre-application consultation to indicate (a) the plans, particulars or other information which the board will require for the purposes of consideration of an application; (b) the time frames and sequencing to be applied to the application process; and (c) any other matters in relation to the application process as the board considers appropriate.[41]   **10–50**

An Bord Pleanála may, during the course of a pre-application consultation, require a prospective applicant to give notice to the public or to carry out consultations with the public in advance of an application being submitted, including (i) the erection or fixing of notice or notices on the site in a form to be specified by the board; (ii) the provision of a specific place or a specific website to make available the application, environmental impact statement and any other relevant documentation for inspection or purchase at a fee not exceeding the reasonable cost of making a copy; (iii) the use of local or national media; or (iv) the holding of meetings, with any person or body or for the public.[42]   **10–51**

---

[39] PDA 2000, s.37B(1) (as inserted by the 2006 Act).
[40] PDA 2000, s.37B(3) (as inserted by the 2006 Act).
[41] Planning and Development Regulations 2001, art.210(2) (as inserted by the 2006 Regulations).
[42] Planning and Development Regulations 2001, art.210(4) (as inserted by the 2006 Regulations).

10–52   An Bord Pleanála may also indicate to a prospective applicant which of the bodies prescribed under art.213 of the Planning and Development Regulations 2001 should, in the opinion of the board, be notified by the prospective applicant of the making of an application, and the prospective applicant shall notify those bodies.[43]

10–53   A prospective applicant shall, for the purposes of the consultation, supply to the board sufficient information in relation to the proposed development so as to enable the board to assess the proposed development.[44] An Bord Pleanála is required to keep a record in writing of any consultation, including the names of those who participated in the consultation, and a copy of such record shall be placed and kept with the documents to which any planning application in respect of the proposed development relates.[45]

10–54   An Bord Pleanála may consult with any person who may, in the opinion of the board, have information which is relevant for the purposes of such consultations.[46]

10–55   It is expressly provided that the holding of consultations shall not prejudice the performance by the board of any other of its functions under the PDA 2000 or Regulations under the Act, and cannot be relied upon in the formal planning process or in legal proceedings.[47]

10–56   Where following consultations An Bord Pleanála is of the opinion that the proposed development would, if carried out, fall within one or more of paragraphs (a) to (c) of s.37A(2), it shall serve a notice in writing on the prospective applicant stating that it is of that opinion.[48]

10–57   If, conversely, the board is of the opinion that the proposed development would not fall within any of those subparagraphs, it shall serve a notice in writing on the prospective applicant stating that it is of that opinion.[49] The notice shall include a statement that the prospective applicant's application for permission, if it is proceeded with, must be made to the appropriate planning authority.[50] An application cannot be made to a planning authority in respect of a specified category of infrastructure project unless the consultation procedure has been gone through, and An Bord Pleanála has given notice that it is not of opinion that the proposed development would, if carried out, fall within one or more of paragraphs (a) to (c) of s.37A(2), i.e. a form a negative clearance is required.[51]

---

[43] Planning and Development Regulations 2001, art.210(5) (as inserted by the 2006 Regulations).
[44] PDA 2000, s.37C(1) (as inserted by the 2006 Act).
[45] PDA 2000, s.37C(3) (as inserted by the 2006 Act).
[46] PDA 2000, s.37C(4) (as inserted by the 2006 Act).
[47] PDA 2000, s.37C(2) (as inserted by the 2006 Act).
[48] PDA 2000, s.37B(4)(a) (as inserted by the 2006 Act).
[49] PDA 2000, s.37B(4)(b) (as inserted by the 2006 Act).
[50] PDA 2000, s.37B(5) (as inserted by the 2006 Act).
[51] PDA 2000, s.37B(7) (as inserted by the 2006 Act).

4. Environmental impact assessment

Environmental impact assessment is mandatory in the case of all planning applications subject to the special procedure.[52] The planning application must be accompanied by an environmental impact statement. An Bord Pleanála may refuse to deal with any application made to it where it considers that the application for permission or the environmental impact statement is inadequate or incomplete, having regard in particular to the permission Regulations and any Regulations made under s.177 or to any consultations held. **10–58**

Scoping

A prospective applicant may request An Bord Pleanála to give to him or her an opinion in writing prepared on what information will be required to be contained in an environmental impact statement in relation to the development.[53] On receipt of such a request the board shall (a) consult with the requester and the bodies specified by the Minister for the purpose,[54] and (b) comply with the request as soon as is practicable.[55] **10–59**

The prospective applicant is required to supply to An Bord Pleanála sufficient information in relation to the proposed development so as to enable the board to assess the proposed development.[56] **10–60**

It is expressly provided that the provision of such a (scoping) opinion shall not prejudice the performance by An Bord Pleanála of any other of its functions under the PDA 2000 or Regulations under the Act, and cannot be relied upon in the formal planning process or in legal proceedings.[57] **10–61**

5. Public notice

Public notices must be published, in advance of the making of the planning application, in one or more newspapers circulating in the area or areas in which it is proposed to carry out the development.[58] The notice must indicate the nature and location of the proposed development and state that (i) the person proposes to make an application to An Bord Pleanála for permission for the proposed development; (ii) an environmental impact statement has been prepared in respect of the proposed development; and (iii) where relevant, the **10–62**

---

[52] PDA 2000, s.37E(1) (as inserted by the 2006 Act).
[53] PDA 2000, s.37D(1) (as inserted by the 2006 Act).
[54] The specified bodies under art.211 of the Planning and Development Regulations 2001 (as inserted by the 2006 Regulations) are the Minister for the Environment, Heritage and Local Government; the Environmental Protection Agency; the Minister for Communications, Marine and Natural Resources; and the relevant planning authority.
[55] PDA 2000, s.37D(2) (as inserted by the 2006 Act).
[56] PDA 2000, s.37D(3) (as inserted by the 2006 Act).
[57] PDA 2000, s.37D(4) (as inserted by the 2006 Act).
[58] PDA 2000, s.37E(3) (as inserted by the 2006 Act).

proposed development is likely to have significant effects on the environment of a Member State of the European Communities or other party to the Transboundary Convention.

10–63   The public notice must also specify the times and places at which, and the period (not being less than six weeks) during which, a copy of the application and the environmental impact statement may be inspected free of charge or purchased on payment of a specified fee (which fee shall not exceed the reasonable cost of making such copy). The public notice must also invite submissions and observations on the implications of the proposed development for proper planning and sustainable development, and the likely effects on the environment of the proposed development. Finally, the public notice should specify the types of decision which An Bord Pleanála may make.

6. Notice to planning authority and prescribed bodies

10–64   The applicant must send a prescribed number of copies of the application and the environmental impact statement to the planning authority or authorities in whose area or areas the proposed development would be situate.[59]

10–65   The applicant must also send a prescribed number of copies of the application and the environmental impact statement to the prescribed authorities[60] together with a notice stating that submissions or observations may be made in writing to An Bord Pleanála in relation to (i) the implications of the proposed development for proper planning and sustainable development, and (ii) the likely effects on the environment of the proposed development, if carried out.

10–66   Where the proposed development is likely to have significant effects on the environment of a Member State of the European Communities or a State which is a party to the Transboundary Convention, the applicant must send a prescribed number of copies of the application and the environmental impact statement to the prescribed authority of the relevant State or States together with a notice stating that submissions or observations may be made in writing to An Bord Pleanála.[61]

7. Planning authority report

10–67   The planning authority for the area (or, as the case may be, each planning authority for the areas) in which the proposed development would be situated shall, within ten weeks from the making of the application (or such longer period as may be specified by the board), prepare and submit to An Bord Pleanála a report setting out the views of the authority on the effects of the

---

[59] PDA 2000, s.37E(3)(b) and (c) (as inserted by the 2006 Act).
[60] The bodies are prescribed under art.213 of the Planning and Development Regulations 2001 (as inserted by the 2006 Regulations).
[61] PDA 2000, s.37E(3)(d) (as inserted by the 2006 Act).

proposed development on the environment and the proper planning and sustainable development of the area of the authority, having regard in particular to the matters specified in s.34(2).[62]

An Bord Pleanála may, where it considers it necessary to do so, require the relevant planning authority or authorities or any planning authority or authorities on whose area or areas it would have a significant effect to furnish to the board such *additional* information in relation to the effects of the proposed development on the proper planning and sustainable development of the area concerned and on the environment as the board may specify.[63] **10–68**

Elected members

Provision is made for the elected members to have an input into the contents of this statutory report. The manager is required to submit an advance copy of the report to the elected members and to seek their views on the proposed development.[64] The elected members may, by resolution, decide to attach recommendations specified in the resolution to the report.[65] Where this happens, those recommendations (together with the meetings administrator's record)[66] shall be attached to the report submitted to An Bord Pleanála. **10–69**

8. Further information and revised plans or particulars

An Bord Pleanála may require the applicant to submit further information, including a revised environmental impact statement.[67] It should be noted that An Bord Pleanála enjoys a *discretion* in this regard, and is not obliged to afford an applicant an opportunity to mend his hand where the environmental impact statement is inadequate: in such circumstances, An Bord Pleanála may instead simply refuse to deal with the application.[68] **10–70**

Where it is considering granting planning permission subject to the applicant submitting revised particulars, plans or drawings in relation to the development, the board may invite the submission of same.[69] **10–71**

---

[62] PDA 2000, s.37E(4) (as inserted by the 2006 Act).
[63] PDA 2000, s.37E(8) (as inserted by the 2006 Act).
[64] PDA 2000, s.37E(5) (as inserted by the 2006 Act).
[65] PDA 2000, s.37E(6) (as inserted by the 2006 Act).
[66] PDA 2000, s.37E(7) (as inserted by the 2006 Act) provides that "the meetings administrator's record" means a record prepared by the meetings administrator (within the meaning of s.46 of the Local Government Act 2001) of the views expressed by the members on the proposed development.
[67] PDA 2000, s.37F(1) (a) (as inserted by the 2006 Act).
[68] PDA 2000, s.37E(2). See, by analogy, *Kildare County Council v An Bord Pleanála* [2006] I.E.H.C. 173; unreported, MacMenamin J., March 10, 2006.
[69] PDA 2000, s.37F(1)(b) (as inserted by the 2006 Act).

Further public notice

10–72 Where an applicant submits a revised environmental impact statement or otherwise submits further information or revised particulars, plans or drawings, which, in the opinion of the board, contain "significant additional information" on the effect of the proposed development on the environment to that already submitted, the board shall (a) make the information, particulars, plans or drawings, as appropriate, available for inspection; (b) give notice that the information, particulars, plans or drawings are so available; and (c) invite further submissions or observations to be made to it within such period as it may specify.[70] By analogy with the discussion at paras 3–127 to 3–129, the determination of whether "significant additional information" is involved is probably a question of fact and degree for An Bord Pleanála.

9. Meetings

10–73 An Bord Pleanála may hold meetings with the applicant or any other person (i) where it appears to the board to be expedient for the purpose of determining the application, or (ii) where it appears to the board to be necessary or expedient for the purpose of resolving any issue with the applicant or any disagreement between the applicant and any other party, including resolving any issue or disagreement in advance of an oral hearing.[71]

10–74 The board, or an employee of the board duly authorised by the board, may appoint any person to hold such a meeting.[72] An Bord Pleanála is required to keep a written record of any such meeting, and to make that record available for inspection.[73]

10. Interaction between An Bord Pleanála and the EPA

10–75 Before making a decision in respect of proposed development comprising or for the purposes of an activity for which an integrated pollution prevention control licence or a waste licence is required, An Bord Pleanála may request the Environmental Protection Agency ("the EPA") to make observations within such period (which period shall not in any case be less than three weeks from the date of the request) as may be specified in relation to the proposed development.[74] An Bord Pleanála is required to have regard to the observations, if any, received from the EPA within time.[75] It is expressly provided that the making of observations by the EPA shall not prejudice any other function of the Agency.[76]

---

[70] PDA 2000, s.37F(2) (as inserted by the 2006 Act).
[71] PDA 2000, s.37F(1)(e) (as inserted by the 2006 Act).
[72] PDA 2000, s.37F(4) (as inserted by the 2006 Act).
[73] PDA 2000, s.37F(3) (as inserted by the 2006 Act).
[74] PDA 2000, s.37F(5) (as inserted by the 2006 Act).
[75] PDA 2000, s.37F(6) (as inserted by the 2006 Act).
[76] PDA 2000, s.37F(8) (as inserted by the 2006 Act).

Notwithstanding the licensing of the activity by the EPA, An Bord Pleanála is entitled to refuse planning permission where it considers that the development is unacceptable on environmental grounds, having regard to the proper planning and sustainable development of the area in which the development will be situated.[77] **10–76**

An Bord Pleanála shall not, where it decides to grant permission, subject that permission to conditions which are for the purposes of (a) controlling emissions from the operation of the activity, including the prevention, limitation, elimination, abatement or reduction of those emissions, or (b) controlling emissions related to or following the cessation of the operation or the activity.[78] As mitigation measures are often imposed by way of planning condition, the qualifications in this regard hamper the ability of An Bord Pleanála to fulfil one of the principal objectives of the assessment procedure, *i.e.* the imposition of mitigation measures as part of development consent. **10–77**

The statutory scheme therefore exhibits a preference that environmental controls be exercised by the EPA. The difficulty, however, is that under the legislation the primary responsibility for performing the environmental impact assessment still resides with An Bord Pleanála. Moreover, many of the impacts which must be assessed are what might be regarded as land-use matters and, accordingly, would probably be better dealt with in the context of a planning application. There is a risk that the division of function between An Bord Pleanála and the EPA may result in a failure to carry out a holistic assessment of the development project. **10–78**

11. Major-accidents Directive/Seveso Directive

Additional procedural requirements apply where the proposed development relates to the provision of, or modifications to, a major-accidents establishment, or would be in the vicinity of, or would impact on, a major-accidents establishment and be relevant to the risk or consequences of a major accident.[79] **10–79**

If the Health and Safety Authority ("the HSA") has not previously provided to An Bord Pleanála, either in relation to the proposed development or on a generic basis, relevant technical advice on the risk or consequences of a major accident, the board must notify the HSA. The notice shall include a copy of the application and environmental impact statement; identify the relevant establishment or establishments; and request technical advice on the effects of the proposed development on the risk or consequences of a major accident. **10–80**

---

[77] PDA 2000, s.37G(5) (as inserted by the 2006 Act).
[78] PDA 2000, s.37G(4) (as inserted by the 2006 Act).
[79] Planning and Development Regulations 2001, art.215 (as inserted by the 2006 Regulations).

12. Decision: relevant considerations

10–81   In deciding whether to grant or refuse planning permission, An Bord Pleanála may consider any relevant information before it or any other matter which, by virtue of the PDA 2000, it can have regard to. An Bord Pleanála is required to have regard to the following matters.

(a) the environmental impact statement; any submissions or observations made within time; the planning authority's report (and the recommendations and record, if any, attached to it); any information furnished in accordance with s.37F(1) and any other relevant information before it relating to (i) the likely consequences of the proposed development for proper planning and sustainable development in the area in which it is proposed to situate the development, and (ii) the likely effects on the environment of the proposed development;

(b) any report or recommendation prepared in relation to the application in accordance with s.146, including the report of the person conducting any oral hearing of the proposed development and the written record of any meeting referred to in s.37F(3);

(c) the provisions of the development plan or plans for the area;

(d) the provisions of any special amenity area order relating to the area,

(e) if the area or part of the area is a European site or an area prescribed for the purposes of s.10(2)(c), that fact;

(f) if the proposed development would have an effect on a European site or an area prescribed for the purposes of s.10(2)(c), that fact;

(g) the matters referred to in s.143 (as amended); and

(h) any relevant provisions of the PDA 2000 and of any Regulations made under the Act.

10–82   An Bord Pleanála may decide to grant or refuse planning permission. If An Bord Pleanála decides to grant planning permission, it is not restricted to granting planning permission for the entire of the development as applied for. Instead, An Bord Pleanála has an express power to specify modifications to the proposed development, or to grant planning permission for part only of the development (with or without specified modifications).

13. Conditions

10–83   An Bord Pleanála is empowered to attach conditions to the grant of planning permission. The power is expressed in very general terms, but must be read subject to an implied restriction that any condition must be relevant to proper planning and sustainable development.[80] Section 37G(7) of the PDA 2000 (as

---

[80] See, by analogy, *Brady v Environmental Protection Agency* [2007] I.E.H.C. 58; unreported,

inserted by the 2006 Act) goes on to enumerate, without prejudice to the general power, specific types of condition which may be attached, as follows.

(a) Conditions under s.34(4) of the PDA 2000

An Bord Pleanála may impose conditions with regard to any of the matters   **10–84** specified in s.34(4) of the PDA 2000. Thus the full range of conditions which are available in the case of a conventional planning permission are equally available in the case of strategic infrastructure development. See further paras 4–87 to 4–100.

(b) Development contributions

An Bord Pleanála may impose conditions requiring the payment of a   **10–85** contribution or contributions of the same kind as the appropriate planning authority could require to be paid under ss.48 or 49 (or both) were that authority to grant the permission. The relevant development contribution scheme is to apply to the determination of such contribution(s).

(c) Conditions requiring further information

An Bord Pleanála may impose conditions requiring the applicant to submit   **10–86** further information to it or any other local or State authority, as An Bord Pleanála may specify, before commencing development. It is not entirely clear what purpose such conditions are intended to serve. They should not, however, be used to overcome shortcomings in an environmental impact statement. The general rule is that the decision-maker should have sufficient information at the time of the giving of the development consent to allow it to assess the likely significant effects of the proposed development. It is not permissible to leave over questions which relate either (i) to the significance of the impact on the environment or (ii) to the effectiveness of any mitigation. See further paras 13–217 to 13–229.

(d) Planning gain

An Bord Pleanála is empowered to attach a condition obliging the developer   **10–87** to provide a planning gain in the form of a "facility or service" which would, in the opinion of the board, constitute a substantial gain to the community. The condition may require either the construction, provision or financing—in whole or in part—of such a facility or service. This power is subject to the following limitation: such a condition shall not require such an amount of financial resources to be committed as would substantially deprive the person in whose favour the permission operates of the benefits likely to accrue from the grant of the permission.

Charleton J., March 9, 2007; and *Hanrahan Farms Ltd. v Environmental Protection Agency*, unreported, High Court, Smyth J., July 21, 2005.

10–88   There must be a question mark over the constitutionality of this provision. Although the Supreme Court accepted, in *In re Part V of the Planning and Development Bill, 1999*,[81] that the State is entitled to recoup some part of the enhanced value of development land—whether deriving from its zoning or from the grant of planning permission—the circumstances of that case were very different from those contemplated under the amended s.37G(7)(d). The Supreme Court were concerned with a legislative scheme which was directed to an objective, namely the provision of social and affordable housing, which was pressing and substantial and, further, was clearly defined. The extent of the planning gain required—which consisted of the transfer of land at less than its open market value—was also clearly defined, and subject to a ceiling fixed by reference to the value of twenty per cent of the land within the application site. Finally, the most that a developer could be compelled to do was to transfer land in its undeveloped state.

10–89   The power under s.37G(7)(d), in contrast, is open-ended. The objective justifying the extraction of a planning gain, namely a substantial gain to the community, is vague, and is not necessarily confined to pressing or substantial social objectives such as the provision of social and affordable housing. The section might therefore have to be "read down" by applying the double-construction rule.

10–90   The extent of the planning gain is delimited only by reference to the imprecise standard that it not "substantially deprive" the applicant of the benefit of the planning permission. In the absence of a clear statement of the principle or policy in this regard, it will be almost impossible for a developer to challenge the imposition of such a condition. This offends against legal certainty, and may well render the subsection unconstitutional.

Points of detail for subsequent agreement

10–91   Section 37G(10) states that planning conditions may provide that points of detail relating to the grant of the permission may be agreed between the planning authority or authorities in whose functional area or areas the development will be situate and the person carrying out the development; if that authority or those authorities and that person cannot agree on the matter, the matter may be referred to the board for determination.

10–92   It is only points of detail which can properly be left over for agreement[82]; any matters of importance must be dealt with with particularity.[83] Further, the condition must set forth the purpose of such details; the overall objective to be achieved by the matters which have been left for agreement; state clearly the

---

[81] [2000] 2 I.R. 321; [2001] 1 I.L.R.M. 81.
[82] *Boland v An Bord Pleanála* [1996] 3 I.R. 435 at 466.
[83] *Houlihan v An Bord Pleanála*, unreported, High Court, Murphy J., October 4, 1993 (at p. 8).

reasons therefor; and lay down criteria by which the developer and the planning authority can reach agreement.[84] See further paras 4–126 to 4–134.

14. Form of decision and duty to state "main reasons and considerations"

An Bord Pleanála is required to send a copy of its decision to the applicant, to any planning authority in whose area the development would be situated and to any person who made submissions or observations on the application.

10–93

Both the decision itself and the notification of the decision shall state the main reasons and considerations on which the decision is based; and, where conditions are imposed in relation to the grant of any permission, the main reasons for the imposition of any such conditions. The decision shall also state that, in making a decision, the board has had regard to any submissions or observations received in accordance with the PDA 2000 or the Planning and Development Regulations 2001.[85] See, generally, paras 12–119 to 12–163.

10–94

15. Costs

An Bord Pleanála has jurisdiction to order the applicant for planning permission to pay a sum to the board towards its costs in determining the application.[86] An Bord Pleanála has an "absolute discretion" as to what it considers to be reasonable costs.[87] These costs should not, seemingly, duplicate costs recovered separately by the board by way of a fee charged under s.144.[88]

10–95

An Bord Pleanála may also require the applicant to pay reasonable costs to any planning authority that incurred costs during the course of consideration of the planning application, and a contribution to the costs incurred by any other person during the course of consideration of that application.[89]

10–96

The legislation is silent as to what principles should govern the exercise of the discretion to order the payment of costs. Presumably, the discretion must be exercised judicially, and the statement that An Bord Pleanála has "absolute discretion" should not be taken at face value.

10–97

An interesting question arises as to the circumstances in which it would be appropriate to order the costs of a third party to be paid. One of the objectives

10–98

---

[84] *Boland v An Bord Pleanála* [1996] 3 I.R. 435 at 467.
[85] Planning and Development Regulations 2001, art.219 (as inserted by the 2006 Regulations).
[86] PDA 2000, s.37H(2)(c) (as inserted by the 2006 Act).
[87] PDA 2000, s.37H(3) (as inserted by the 2006 Act).
[88] PDA 2000, s.37H(3) (as inserted by the 2006 Act).
[89] PDA 2000, s.37H(2)(c) (as inserted by the 2006 Act).

of environmental impact assessment is to ensure public participation in the decision-making process, and it is arguable that a member of the public who has gone to the trouble and expense of making a detailed submission to An Bord Pleanála, and has possibly participated in an oral hearing, should receive some reimbursement. This is especially so in the light of the Aarhus convention.[90] As against this, the fact that the ECJ ruled—in *Commission v Ireland*[91]—that a requirement for members of the public to *pay* a participation fee was consistent with the EIA Directive might suggest that no subsidisation is necessary.

10–99　Where the applicant fails to pay a sum in respect of costs, the board, the authority or any other person concerned (as may be appropriate) may recover the sum as a simple contract debt in any court of competent jurisdiction.[92] The planning permission shall not become operative until any requirement in relation to the payment by the applicant of a sum in respect of costs has been complied with.[93]

16. Grant of planning permission

10–100　A grant of permission under s.37G shall be made as soon as may be after the making of the relevant decision but shall not become operative until any requirement made under subsection (2)(c) in relation to the payment by the applicant of a sum in respect of costs has been complied with.

17. Time-limits for decision-making

10–101　The real grievance which developers have with the planning process is not the fact that time has to be set aside for public participation, rather it is the failure to meet the statutory time-limits for decision-making. The statutory time-limits under the PDA 2000—eight weeks for the planning authority and eighteen weeks for An Bord Pleanála—are largely meaningless. The time-limit applying to An Bord Pleanála is aspirational only and cannot be enforced. Although the planning authority stage is, in principle, policed by the availability of default planning permission, the reality is that the eight week time-limit is inevitably pushed out by the service of a request for further information, with subsequent requests for clarification.

10–102　It is not at all clear that the position will be much better under the strategic infrastructure procedure. The provisions in respect of time-limits—which are set out in detail below—are again only aspirational. It remains to be seen whether

---

[90] Convention on Access to Information, Public Participation in Decision-Making and Access to Justice in Environmental Matters (Aarhus, Denmark, June 25, 1998).
[91] (Case C–216/05); November 9, 2006.
[92] PDA 2000, s.37H(5) (as inserted by the 2006 Act).
[93] PDA 2000, s.37H(4) (as inserted by the 2006 Act).

the establishment of the Strategic Infrastructure Division within An Bord Pleanála results in faster decision-making.[94]

An Bord Pleanála is under a duty to ensure that (a) the pre-application consultations are completed, and (b) a decision on an application is made, as expeditiously as is consistent with proper planning and sustainable development. For that purpose, An Bord Pleanála is to take all such steps as are open to it to ensure that, in so far as is practicable, there are no avoidable delays at any stage in the holding of those consultations or the making of that decision. **10–103**

Without prejudice to the generality of this duty, it shall be the objective of An Bord Pleanála to ensure that a decision on an application is made (a) within a period of eighteen weeks beginning on the last day for making submissions or observations, or (b) within such other period as the Minister may prescribe either generally or in respect of a particular class or classes of matter. **10–104**

Where it appears to An Bord Pleanála that it would not be possible or appropriate, because of the particular circumstances of the matter with which the board is concerned, to determine the matter within the appropriate period, the board shall, by notice in writing served on the applicant, any planning authority involved and any other person who submitted submissions or observations in relation to the matter before the expiration of that period, inform the authority and those persons of the reasons why it would not be possible or appropriate to determine the matter within that period and shall specify the date before which the board intends that the matter shall be determined. Where such a notice has been served, the board shall take all such steps as are open to it to ensure that the matter is determined before the date specified in the notice. **10–105**

The Minister for Environment Heritage and Local Government may, by regulations, vary the period referred to in subsection (2)(a) either generally or in respect of a particular class or classes of applications, where it appears to him or her to be necessary, by virtue of exceptional circumstances, to do so and, for so long as the Regulations are in force, the section shall be construed and have effect in accordance therewith. **10–106**

Where the Minister considers it to be necessary or expedient that a certain class or classes of application that are of special strategic, economic or social importance to the State be determined as expeditiously as is consistent with proper planning and sustainable development, he or she may give a direction to the board that priority be given to the determination of applications of the class or classes concerned, and the board shall comply with such a direction. **10–107**

---

[94] PDA 2000, s.112A (as inserted by the 2006 Act).

18. Alteration of permitted strategic development

10–108　An Bord Pleanála may, on the request of any person who is carrying out or intending to carry out a strategic infrastructure development, alter the terms of the development the subject of a planning permission, approval or other consent granted under the PDA 2000.[95]

10–109　An Bord Pleanála must consider, in the first instance, whether the requested alteration would represent a "material alteration" of the terms of the development concerned. If it does represent a "material alteration", then An Bord Pleanála must go on to consider whether the alteration would be likely to have significant effects on the environment such as to trigger a requirement for environmental impact assessment.

No material alteration

10–110　If An Bord Pleanála decides that the making of the alteration would not constitute the making of a "material alteration" of the terms of the development concerned, it shall alter the planning permission accordingly. Notice of the making of the alteration is to be given to the person who made the request, and the planning authority or each planning authority for the area or areas concerned.

Material alteration

10–111　If the alteration requested does constitute a "material alteration", An Bord Pleanála has a discretion as to whether or not to make the alteration.[96] It may refuse to make any alteration, or may, instead, make a different alteration from that requested (provided that that different alteration would not represent, overall, a more significant change to the terms of the development).

Screening

10–112　An Bord Pleanála must consider whether the material alteration should be subject to environmental impact assessment. Under the terms of the EIA Directive, any change or extension of an EIA development already authorised, executed or in the process of being executed must itself be subject to assessment where it may have significant *adverse* effects on the environment.

10–113　Under s.146B(4) of the PDA 2000 (as amended by the 2006 Act), An Bord Pleanála is required to determine whether the extent and character of any alteration would be likely to have significant effects on the environment. Where An Bord Pleanála is considering making an alteration in terms different from those requested, the board must reach a final decision as to what is the extent and character of any alternative alteration which it is considering making.

10–114　In making its determination the board shall have regard to the criteria for the

---

[95] PDA 2000, s.146B(1) (as inserted by the 2006 Act).
[96] PDA 2000, s.146B(3)(b) (as inserted by the 2006 Act).

purposes of determining which classes of development are likely to have significant effects on the environment set out in any regulations made under s.176. Such criteria are currently prescribed at Sch.7 to the Planning and Development Regulations 2001. An Bord Pleanála is required to engage in a limited form of consultation before reaching its determination on whether or not the alteration would be likely to have significant effects on the environment. The consultation is to involve such person, such class of person or the public as the board considers appropriate ("the consultees"). The consultees are entitled to inspect information relating to the request for the alteration, and to make submissions or observations within such period, as the board determines.

Environmental impact assessment

Where An Bord Pleanála determines that the alteration under consideration is likely to have significant effects on the environment, it must require the requester to prepare an environmental impact statement in relation to the proposed alteration of the terms of the development concerned. The requester is also required to give public notice of the fact that an environmental impact statement has been submitted to An Bord Pleanála, that the statement is available for inspection and/or purchase, and that submissions or observations may be made within a period of not less than four weeks from the date the notice was first published. Notice must also be sent to the prescribed bodies and to each local authority in whose functional area the proposed development would be situate **10–115**

Among the considerations to be taken into account by An Bord Pleanála in deciding whether to make the alteration are, first, any social or economic benefit that would accrue to the State, a region of the State or the area were the development concerned to be carried out in the terms as they are proposed to be altered; and, secondly, commitments entered into and the stage at which the development concerned has progressed under the permission in the terms as originally granted.[97] **10–116**

C. Points of Detail Under Planning Conditions

As discussed at paras 4–126 to 4–134, provision is made under s.34(5) of the PDA 2000 (as amended) whereby a condition attached to a planning permission may provide that points of detail relating to a grant of permission be agreed between the planning authority and the person carrying out the development. If the planning authority and that person cannot agree on the matter, the matter may be referred to An Bord Pleanála for determination. The matter is thus brought before An Bord Pleanála not by way of an appeal in the ordinary way, but by way of a referral.[98] **10–117**

---

[97] PDA 2000, s.146C(6) (as inserted by the 2006 Act).
[98] See definition of "referral" under PDA 2000, s.2.

10–118   In determining such a referral An Bord Pleanála enjoys only a very limited discretion. The overall objective to be achieved by the matters which have been left for agreement, and the purpose of such details, should have been clearly stated in the condition. The condition should also have laid down criteria by which the developer and the planning authority can reach agreement.[99] In the circumstances, it is simply a matter for An Bord Pleanála to implement what has already been decided in essence. Thus, An Bord Pleanála must ascertain what is the true or correct meaning of the conditions attached to the planning permission and confine itself and the developer to such proposals as are in compliance with the conditions.[100] An Bord Pleanála does not enjoy a statutory discretion in this regard, and, accordingly, its decision is not subject to the attenuated form of review otherwise applicable under the decision in *O'Keeffe v An Bord Pleanála*.[101]

10–119   A question arises as to whether an opportunity should be allowed for the public to make submissions and representations at the agreement stage. There is no formal mechanism under the legislation for such consultation, however. The decision of Blayney J. in *Boland v An Bord Pleanála*[102] seems to suggest that having regard to the very detailed instructions set out in the conditions, and the purpose for which they were imposed, no member of the public could reasonably have objected to them and so the board in imposing the conditions was not interfering with or prejudicing any right of the public. This might be taken as suggesting that once the principle of development has been accepted, *i.e.* the objectors have been unsuccessful in their appeal, it is then in the objectors' interest that the development be regulated to the greatest possible extent, and, possibly, that an objector would not be prejudiced by being precluded from objecting to the ultimate form of the agreement. Barr J. in his decision in *McNamara v An Bord Pleanála (No. 2)*[103] considered, however, that third parties would be entitled to make representations with respect to matters left over for agreement.[104] In *Arklow Holidays Ltd. v An Bord Pleanála*,[105] Clarke J. suggested that members of the public would be entitled to challenge an agreement reached on foot of such a condition if the agreement did not comply with the criteria specified in the condition imposed by An Bord Pleanála.

---

[99]   *Boland v An Bord Pleanála* [1996] 3 I.R. 435 at 467.
[100]   *O'Connor v Dublin Corporation (No. 2)*, unreported, High Court, O'Neill J., October 3, 2000 (at p. 29).
[101]   [1993] 1 I.R. 39; [1992] I.L.R.M. 237. See *O'Connor v Dublin Corporation (No. 2)*, unreported, High Court, O'Neill J., October 3, 2000.
[102]   [1996] 3 I.R. 435.
[103]   [1996] 2 I.L.R.M. 339.
[104]   *cf. R. v Lichfield DC Ex p. Lichfield Securities Ltd.* [2000] P.C.L.R. 458.
[105]   [2006] I.E.H.C. 15; [2007] 1 I.L.R.M. 125.

D. Strategic Development Zone

As discussed at paras 8–200 to 8–202, there is a right of appeal against the **10–120** decision of a planning authority to make a planning scheme in respect of a strategic development zone. This right of appeal is confined to (i) the development agency, and (ii) any person who made submissions or observations in respect of the draft planning scheme. The reasons for the appeal must be stated.

An Bord Pleanála may, following the consideration of an appeal, approve the **10–121** making of the planning scheme, with or without modifications or it may refuse to approve it.

In considering a draft planning scheme An Bord Pleanála shall consider the **10–122** proper planning and sustainable development of the area and consider the provisions of the development plan, the provisions of the housing strategy, the provisions of any special amenity area order or the conservation and preservation of any European site and, where appropriate (a) the effect the scheme would have on any neighbouring land to the land concerned; (b) the effect the scheme would have on any place which is outside the area of the planning authority, and (c) any other consideration relating to development outside the area of the planning authority, including any area outside the State.

E. Protected Structures

As discussed at paras 8–24 to 8–34, provision is made whereby an owner or **10–123** occupier of a protected structure may make a written request to a planning authority to issue a declaration as to the type of works which it considers would or would not materially affect the character of the structure or any element of the structure.[106] A planning authority may at any time review a declaration issued but the review shall not affect any works carried out in reliance on the declaration prior to the review.[107]

A right of referral to An Bord Pleanála against both an initial declaration, and **10–124** against any review of a declaration, is introduced under the Planning and Development (Amendment) Act 2002.[108] More specifically, any person to whom a declaration or a reviewed declaration has been issued may refer the declaration for review by An Bord Pleanála within four weeks from the date of the issuing of the declaration, or the declaration as reviewed, as the case may be.[109]

---

[106] PDA 2000, s.57(2).
[107] PDA 2000, s.57(7).
[108] Planning and Development (Amendment) Act 2002, s.13.
[109] PDA 2000, s.57(8) (as amended).

F. Revocation of Planning Permission

10–125 There is a statutory right of appeal from the decision of the planning authority to An Bord Pleanála. This right of appeal may be exercised by any person served with notice under s.44(1), namely the applicant for planning permission and any other person who, in the opinion of the planning authority, will be materially affected by the revocation or modification. Somewhat surprisingly, it seems that the right of appeal might extend even to a decision *not* to revoke or modify the planning permission. An appeal must be made within four weeks of the date of the decision of the planning authority.

10–126 This right of appeal is discussed further at paras 5–94 to 5–96.

G. Removal or Alteration of Structure or Discontinuance of Use

10–127 As discussed at paras 8–210 to 8–220, a planning authority has an express power to require the removal or alteration of a structure or the discontinuance of a use.[110] There is a statutory right of appeal to An Bord Pleanála against a notice confirmed by the planning authority. Any person served with a confirmed notice may, within eight weeks of the date of service of the notice, appeal to An Bord Pleanála against the notice.

10–128 An Bord Pleanála may confirm the notice with or without modifications or annul the notice. An Bord Pleanála is required to consider the same matters as the planning authority is, namely (a) the proper planning and sustainable development of the area; (b) the provisions of the development plan; (c) the provisions of any special amenity area order, any European site or other area designated for the purposes of s.10(2)(c) relating to the area; and (d) any other relevant provision of the PDA 2000 and any Regulations made thereunder.

H. Special Planning Control Scheme

10–129 As discussed at paras 8–80 to 8–86, a notice requiring that specified measures be undertaken for either (i) the restoration, demolition, removal, alteration, replacement, maintenance, repair or cleaning of any structure; or (ii) the discontinuance of any use or the continuance of any use subject to conditions, may be served where a special planning control scheme is in force. These notices are referred to by the shorthand "Section 88 notices".

10–130 There is a right of appeal to An Bord Pleanála from a decision to confirm or amend a Section 88 notice. Any person served with a notice may within eight

---

[110] PDA 2000, s.46.

weeks from the date of notification of the confirmation or amendment of the notice appeal to An Bord Pleanála against the notice.

In determining an appeal, An Bord Pleanála is required to take into account (a) **10–131** the proper planning and sustainable development of the area; (b) the provisions of the development plan for the area; (c) any local area plan or integrated area plan (within the meaning of the Urban Renewal Act 1998) in force relating to the area to which the scheme relates, and (d) the provisions of the approved special planning control scheme.

I. Replacement of Structures Demolished or Destroyed by Fire or Otherwise

Special provision is made in respect of structures substantially replacing **10–132** structures demolished or destroyed by fire or otherwise. In very general terms: subject to certain exceptions in the case of unauthorised structures, and unlawful acts on the part of the owner, compensation is not to be excluded for the refusal of planning permission or the grant of planning permission subject to certain (onerous) conditions.[111]

Every dispute and question as to whether a new structure would or does replace **10–133** substantially a demolished or destroyed structure shall be referred to An Bord Pleanála for determination.

J. Acquisition of Land for Open Spaces

As discussed at paras 7–206 to 7–219, a special enforcement mechanism is **10–134** prescribed in respect of a breach of an obligation under planning permission to provide or maintain open space.[112] In summary, in the case of breach, a planning authority is empowered to acquire the open space land compulsorily.

Any person having an interest in the land to which an acquisition notice relates **10–135** may within the period specified in the notice appeal to An Bord Pleanála.[113] An Bord Pleanála may (a) annul the acquisition notice to which the appeal relates, or (b) confirm the acquisition notice, with or without modification, in respect of all or such part of the relevant land as An Bord Pleanála considers reasonable.

---

[111] PDA 2000, s.193.
[112] PDA 2000, s.45.
[113] PDA 2000, s.45(3).

Chapter Eleven

STATUTORY JUDICIAL REVIEW PROCEDURE

A. Overview of Statutory Judicial Review Procedure

1. General

A special judicial review procedure applies to decisions made, and acts done, by planning authorities or An Bord Pleanála in the performance (or purported performance) of a function under the PDA 2000. The procedure is set out at ss.50 and 50A of the PDA 2000, as amended by the Planning and Development (Strategic Infrastructure) Act 2006 ("the 2006 Act"). **11–01**

The statutory procedure differs in many respects from conventional judicial review. The key points of distinction are as follows. First, stricter time-limits apply to the issue and service of judicial review proceedings. Specifically, there is a general eight week time-limit, with the possibility of an extension in certain circumstances. Secondly, the application for leave to apply for judicial review is on notice to certain prescribed parties, and the criteria against which the decision to grant or to refuse leave is made are more demanding. Thirdly, the right of appeal to the Supreme Court is restricted, both in respect of the determination of an application for leave to apply for judicial review, and the determination of a substantive application for judicial review. **11–02**

2. Legislative history

11–03 Restrictions on challenges to certain decisions of planning authorities and of An Bord Pleanála had first been introduced under the Local Government (Planning & Development) Act 1976, and were considerably tightened under the Local Government (Planning & Development) Act 1992, which inserted ss.82(3A) & (3B) into the Local Government (Planning & Development) Act 1963.

11–04 A yet more restrictive procedure was prescribed under the PDA 2000 in its unamended form.[1] The principal differences between this procedure and that under the 1992 Act were as follows. The *locus standi* or standing requirement was put on a statutory footing, and the standard changed from "sufficient interest" to "substantial interest". There was also an express requirement that an applicant have previously participated in the statutory planning process. The time-limit was changed from two months to eight weeks, and a power to extend the period introduced.[2] Provision was also made whereby judicial review proceedings challenging the decision of a planning authority might be stayed in preference to a statutory appeal to An Bord Pleanála.

11–05 The judicial review procedure was further modified under the Planning and Development (Strategic Infrastructure) Act 2006 ("the 2006 Act").[3] The principal amendments are as follows. First, the circumstances in which the special judicial review procedure applies have been greatly extended: rather than being confined to certain categories of decisions, the procedure now applies to "any decision made or other act done" by a local authority, planning authority or An Bord Pleanála in the performance or purported performance of a function under the PDA 2000. Secondly, the express statutory requirement for prior participation has been removed. Thirdly, the time for the bringing of proceedings may now only be extended where the delay was as a result of circumstances outside the control of the applicant. Fourthly, certain non-governmental organisations ("NGOs") are exempted from the usual *locus standi* requirement.

11–06 Unless otherwise stated, all references to the judicial review procedure in this chapter are to that procedure as amended under the 2006 Act. Where it is necessary to refer to the procedure as it stood prior to those amendments, it will be described as "the unamended s.50 procedure" or "the original s.50 procedure".

---

[1] See, generally, G. Simons, "Special Judicial Review Procedure under the Planning and Development Act 2000" (2002) 2(1) *Judicial Studies Institute Journal* 125; and G. Simons, "Judicial Review of Planning Decisions – Section 50 Practice and Procedure" (2001) 6 *Bar Review* 449. See also G. Simons, "Judicial review under the planning legislation – The case for the abolition of the leave stage" (2001) 8 I.P.E.L.J. 55.

[2] The absolute nature of the two month time-limit under the previous legislation had been found to be unconstitutional in *White v Dublin City Council* [2004] 1 I.R. 545; [2004] 2 I.L.R.M. 509. See *Lennon v Cork City Council* [2006] I.E.H.C. 438; unreported, Smyth J., December 19, 2006 for a discussion as to whether the declaration of unconstitutionality has retrospective effect.

[3] 2006 Act, s.13.

3. Law Reform Commission Report

The effectiveness of the statutory procedure is open to serious doubt. In **11–07** particular, the combination of the requirement that the leave application be on notice and the heightened threshold of "substantial grounds" has had the result that the hearing of the leave application can take almost as much time as the hearing of a substantive application for judicial review. In cases where leave to apply is granted, this results in unnecessary duplication and, moreover, can result in delays in that it is necessary to secure not one, but two, hearing dates. The pressure on the judicial review list is such that there may well be a considerable period of time between the two.

This difficulty has attracted judicial comment. In *Arklow Holidays Ltd. v An* **11–08** *Bord Pleanála (No. 1)*,[4] Clarke J., echoing earlier comments of Kelly J. in *Mulholland v An Bord Pleanála (No. 2)*,[5] stated as follows.

"I should not leave this point without commenting that the current practice in relation to leave applications in planning matters points to a potential duplication in the work of courts which are required to hear such applications.

There can be little doubt but that the statutory requirement that leave can only be granted after an application on notice, and where a higher standard has been established, was introduced as a means of attempting to streamline challenges to planning permissions. Thus, it was hoped, insubstantial cases would be disposed of in early course. While that end has, in part, been achieved, the fact is that leave applications have now come to take on a life of their own. It is interesting to note that it is common practice for respondents and notice parties in planning leave applications to file detailed replying affidavits even though it is rare for the respondent Minister or respondent statutory bodies charged with making decisions in the immigration sphere to file any replying affidavits in the almost identical process that applies to such cases. There may, of course, be good reasons for the filing of affidavits in some cases. However the reality is that leave applications have now turned into substantial hearings themselves. On the initial date the hearing has to be adjourned from time to time to allow for the filing of further affidavits. Furthermore, in many cases, the leave application takes, as here, a number of days at hearing and thus requires to wait for a suitable place in the court list. Where leave is granted, whether on some or all grounds, a second substantive hearing then follows."

The question as to whether the leave stage should be retained in statutory judicial **11–09** review was one of the matters considered by the Law Reform Commission in its report on Judicial Review Procedure.[6] The Law Reform Commission recommended that the leave stage be retained.

---

[4] [2006] I.E.H.C. 15; [2007] 1 I.L.R.M. 125 at 134-135.
[5] [2005] I.E.H.C. 306; [2006] 1 I.R. 453 at 471; [2006] 1 I.L.R.M. 287 at 304 ("It is regrettable that having had detailed argument made to me of the type and depth that will be reproduced at the full hearing I am precluded from deciding the case. But such is the scheme of the Act.").
[6] LRC 71 – 2004 (February, 2004).

"After consideration of dispensing with the leave stage the Consultation Paper concluded that the beneficial effects of the filter stage outweigh the problems involved. While it was accepted that the leave stage may in some circumstances lead to delay and frustration, the Commission was of the view that such problems could be alleviated through reconsidering the question of notice rather than through the wholesale abandonment of a generally useful procedure. The role of the judge in balancing the interests of all parties involved was considered to be of paramount importance in achieving a fair outcome."[7]

11–10 Insofar as the mechanics of the leave application were concerned, the Law Reform Commission recommended that the current threshold of "substantial grounds" be retained, but that the judge hearing the application for leave have discretion as to whether to hear the proceedings on an *ex parte* or *inter partes* basis.

11–11 It remains the writer's view that the leave stage should be abolished.[8] It is respectfully submitted that the arguments put forward by the Law Reform Commission are unconvincing and that the leave application in its current form causes more difficulties than it resolves. The judge hearing the leave application is in an invidious position. There will ordinarily be sufficient material before the High Court at the stage of the leave application to allow the court to decide the substance of the case. The logic of ss.50 and 50A, however, of course precludes such an outcome. Thus, a judge having heard full argument must resist the temptation to decide the case, but instead grant leave in the knowledge that the case may well be unsuccessful ultimately, with further delays being suffered in the interim.

11–12 The Planning and Development (Strategic Infrastructure) Bill 2006 as published involved the removal of the requirement for an *inter partes* hearing, but same was reinserted during the Bill's passage through the Houses of the Oireachtas.

4. Transitional provisions

11–13 As the statutory judicial review procedure involves a restriction on the right of access to the courts, it would seem that its provisions may only have prospective effect.[9] As flagged above, certain amendments were introduced to the procedure under the 2006 Act, and it would seem to follow that, at the very earliest, the amended procedure can only apply in the case of "decisions" made, or "acts" done, after the commencement date of October 17, 2006.[10] This is especially so as, under the original s.50 procedure, the eight week time-limit had only

---

[7] *ibid.*, §1.12.

[8] First mooted in 2001; see G. Simons, "Judicial review under the planning legislation – The case for the abolition of the leave stage" (2001) 8 I.P.E.L.J. 55.

[9] See, by analogy, *Electricity Supply Board v Gormley* [1985] I.R. 129; [1985] I.L.R.M. 494; and *State (Pine Valley Developments Ltd.) v Dublin County Council* [1984] I.R. 407; [1982] I.L.R.M. 169.

[10] The commencement date is prescribed under the Planning and Development (Strategic Infrastructure) Act (Commencement) Order 2006 (S.I. No. 525 of 2006).

applied to certain types of "decisions". It would clearly be unfair if the time-limit were to apply retrospectively to judicial review proceedings directed to *other* types of "decisions" or "acts" which had not been subject to the time-limit at the time they were made or done.

An argument might even be made to the effect that the amended procedure should only apply to challenges in relation to decisions in respect of which the initial *application* (for planning permission or otherwise) was made after the date of commencement.[11]   **11–14**

5. Judicial review under Order 84

The full extent of the distinction between the statutory judicial review procedure and conventional judicial review remains unclear. Although s.50(2) refers to "an application for judicial review under Order 84", this is somewhat misleading in that the requirements of ss.50 and 50A work considerable changes to the conventional judicial review procedure. In particular, the threshold of "substantial grounds" for obtaining leave to apply; the more stringent *locus standi* requirement; and the fact that the application for leave is on notice, all mean that the procedure under Ord.84 could only ever apply in a modified way to an application under s.50. The full range of these modifications has not yet been chartered, however. For example, there is case law decided under ss.82(3A) & (3B) of the Local Government (Planning & Development) Act 1963 (as amended) which suggests that the provisions of Ord.84, r.23—which allow for the amendment of a statement of grounds—did not apply to the special statutory judicial review procedure.[12] In *McCarthy v An Bord Pleanála*,[13] Geoghegan J. appears to have accepted a suggestion by counsel that—in enacting the then legislation—it was not intended to introduce some new kind of judicial review application different from conventional judicial review, but instead the procedure and requirements for obtaining leave were merely altered. The question as to who were necessary notice parties fell to be determined, therefore, on an *ad hoc* basis, as in the case of conventional judicial review. (The decision was appealed to the Supreme Court, but the entire proceedings were ultimately compromised.) There are also conflicting signals as to whether the requirement under Ord.84, r.21 to move promptly might survive, or if instead an applicant is always entitled to the full reach of the statutory eight week time-limit.[14]   **11–15**

---

[11] See, by analogy, *Kenny v An Bord Pleanála (No. 1)* [2001] 1 I.R. 565.

[12] *McNamara v An Bord Pleanála (No. 2)* [1996] 2 I.L.R.M. 339 at 351–352. This decision will have to be reconsidered in view of the fact that the time-limit can now be extended. It would seem to follow that if an applicant may be permitted to issue proceedings outside the eight weeks, then, in principle, an applicant who has issued within the eight weeks should be permitted to take the lesser step of amending his statement of grounds out of time.

[13] [2000] 1 I.R 42.

[14] The decisions in *O'Connell v Environmental Protection Agency* [2001] 4 I.R. 494; [2002] 1 I.L.R.M. 1 and *Harrington v An Bord Pleanála (No. 1)* [2005] I.E.H.C. 344; [2006] 1 I.R. 388, suggest that the requirement to move promptly does survive. It is arguable that the finding in *Lancefort Ltd. v An Bord Pleanála*, unreported, High Court, Morris J., May

6. Expeditious determination

11–16   There is provision made under s.50A(10) for the expeditious determination of the application for leave, and of the substantive application for judicial review. More specifically, there is an obligation on the High Court to act as "expeditiously as possible consistent with the administration of justice". Under s.50A(11), there is a corresponding obligation on the Supreme Court in determining an appeal.

11–17   Under the procedure as amended by the 2006 Act, the obligation now applies to all applications for judicial review. Under the unamended s.50 procedure, conversely, this requirement had only applied to the following decisions: a decision of a planning authority in respect of proposed local authority development; and the decisions of An Bord Pleanála in respect of environmental impact assessment of local authority development, and in relation to the compulsory acquisition of land. The obligation also extended to decisions relating to development of a class or classes of special strategic, economic or social importance to the State, and prescribed by the Minister for the Environment Heritage and Local Government.

7. Commercial Court

11–18   Order 63A of the Rules of the Superior Courts created a special list for commercial cases.[15] The Commercial List came into operation on January 12, 2004. One of the principal benefits of the Commercial List is in terms of expedition. The list provides case management which results in the exchange of pleadings and affidavits being completed in much earlier course than is usually the position in the judicial review list. Moreover, cases can be assigned much earlier hearing dates than normal. All of this makes the Commercial List very attractive to beneficiaries of planning permissions faced with judicial review proceedings. The Commercial List provides a procedure whereby such challenges can be dealt with in short course.

11–19   There is no automatic entitlement to have any particular case admitted into the Commercial List. Rather, it is necessary to make an application, on notice to the other parties, for admission.[16] The decision to admit or not is within the discretion of the court. The term "commercial proceedings" is defined under Ord.63A, r.1. Various categories of cases are identified. The sub-category relevant to judicial review proceedings is that under para.(g). This refers to appeals from or judicial review of decisions given by a person or body authorised

---

13, 1997 that the time period expires at midnight, and that the ordinary rules as to reckoning the date of service under Ord.122 do not apply, indicates that the statutory time-limit is the only restriction on time.

[15] S.I. No. 2 of 2004. See, generally, S. Dowling, *The Commercial Court* (Thomson Round Hall, Dublin, 2007).

[16] See S. Dowling, *The Commercial Court* (Thomson Round Hall, Dublin, 2007), para.3–82.

by statute to make such decision where the judge in charge of the Commercial List considers it appropriate for entry in the list having regard to the commercial or any other aspect thereof.

The circumstances in which it is appropriate to admit judicial review proceedings challenging planning decisions to the Commercial List were considered in detail in *Mulholland v An Bord Pleanála (No. 1)*.[17] The proceedings involved a challenge under the unamended s.50 procedure to a decision of An Bord Pleanála to grant planning permission. The proceedings were taken by two local businessmen. The court found that the second named applicant was a major commercial rival of the proposed development, and noted that he himself had applied for planning permission for similar type development—a factory outlet centre—previously. In the circumstances, Kelly J. found that there were very substantial commercial aspects to the development the subject of the impugned planning permission. Kelly J. went on to comment generally, as follows.

11–20

> "It would be unwise to set out hard and fast rules as to the business which can qualify for admission to the list under Order 63A, r.1(g) particulary since the rules committee itself gave such a wide discretion to the judge in charge of the list. It would seem, however, that any case involving a statutory appeal or judicial review of the type described in Order 63A, r.1(g) should be capable of admission to the list if it can be demonstrated that a commercial development or process or substantial sums of money whether by way of profit, investment, loan or interest are likely to be jeopardised if the case is not given a speedy hearing or is denied the case management procedures which are available in the Commercial Court. This is so where one of the parties to the suit are involved in commerce, giving a broad meaning to that term. Such parties would include entities involved in commercial activities whether they be individuals, corporate bodies, semi-State bodies, State bodies or indeed the State itself in an appropriate case."

The case was, accordingly, admitted to the Commercial List.

11–21

B. Scope of Statutory Judicial Review Procedure

1. General

The circumstances in which the statutory judicial review procedure applies have been greatly extended as a result of the amendments under the 2006 Act: rather than being confined to certain categories of decisions as had been the case under the unamended s.50,[18] the procedure now applies to "any decision

11–22

---

[17] [2005] I.E.H.C. 188; [2005] 3 I.R. 1 at 8; [2005] 2 I.L.R.M. 489.

[18] The unamended procedure was confined to the following types of decisions. The decision of the planning authority (i) on an application for planning permission under Pt III of the PDA 2000; (ii) on whether or not to proceed with proposed local authority development under s.179 of the PDA 2000; and (iii) to confirm an unopposed compulsory purchase order. A decision of An Bord Pleanála (i) on any appeal or referral; (ii) in respect of environmental impact assessment of local authority development; and (iii) under Pt XIV of the PDA 2000.

made or other act done" by a planning authority, a local authority or An Bord Pleanála in the performance or purported performance of a function under the PDA 2000.

11–23   This amendment probably deserves a cautious welcome. It has the benefit of removing certain anomalies which had existed under the unamended s.50. In particular, it will no longer be possible for an applicant to avoid the statutory judicial review procedure by the expedient of moving in *advance* of a formal decision on an application or an appeal.

11–24   On a separate point, the quirk whereby, in respect of certain categories of decision, the statutory judicial review procedure applied to one, but not both, of the decisions of the planning authority or An Bord Pleanála, is removed.[19]

11–25   Other aspects of the amendment are less satisfactory. The fact that the procedure now applies to acts occurring during the course of the processing of a planning application or planning appeal may—especially in view of the amendments introduced to the reckoning of the eight week time-limit—result in an increase in the number of legal challenges. Rather than await the outcome of the planning process—which might well produce a result favourable to them—litigants may feel obliged to move for judicial review at an early stage, lest they find themselves time-barred subsequently.

11–26   The statutory procedure extends to decisions made or acts done by An Bord Pleanála in the performance or purported performance of a function transferred to it under Pt XIV of the PDA 2000. An Bord Pleanála has taken over the function of the Minister for the Environment, Heritage and Local Government in respect of the confirmation of compulsory purchase orders, and the environmental impact assessment of certain projects under the Roads Acts 1993 to 1998. The statutory procedure also applies to decisions made or acts done by a local authority in the performance or purported performance of a function conferred by an enactment specified under s.214 of the PDA 2000 relating to the compulsory acquisition of land.

2. "Shall not question validity of"

11–27   The provisions of the statutory judicial review procedure are triggered where there is a challenge to the validity of a decision or act: a person shall not question the validity of a prescribed decision or act other than by way of an

---

[19] This produced the anomalous result that the unamended s.50 procedure applied to some decisions of An Bord Pleanála in circumstances where the equivalent decision of the planning authority, at first instance, was subject to conventional judicial review. For example, in connection with the revocation of planning permission, the decision of An Bord Pleanála, on an appeal, was protected by the unamended s.50 procedure, whereas the planning authority's decision at first instance is not. The decision was not a "decision on an application for a permission". See, by analogy, *O'Connor v Dublin Corporation (No. 1)* [2000] 3 I.R. 420; [2001] 1 I.L.R.M. 58.

application for judicial review under Ord.84. This formula "shall not question the validity of" had not been discussed much in the case law in respect of the former Local Government (Planning & Development) Acts. The High Court had indicated in one judgment that it would look to the substance of the relief sought in legal proceedings, and that the fact that a formal order of *certiorari* quashing a decision was not sought did not necessarily indicate that the validity of the decision was not being questioned.[20]

The full extent to which the formula excludes collateral challenges to the validity of a decision in other proceedings remains open, however. The fact that a particular decision is challenged may carry with it the implication that another, distinct decision may also have been invalid. Two obvious examples are as follows. First, a successful challenge to the provisions of a development plan might give rise to the inference that any planning permission granted previously on the basis of the impugned provisions of the development plan was similarly vitiated. Secondly, the fact that a challenge to a decision to refuse planning permission is upheld might tend to suggest that other refusals which had relied on the same flawed reasoning were also bad.   **11–28**

Whereas it is arguable that the principal objective of ss.50 and 50A is simply to put a decision to grant planning permission—or an analogous decision—out of the reach of judicial review proceedings within a short space of time in the interests of legal certainty,[21] on a very strict interpretation each of the examples cited above might be regarded as involving a challenge to the validity of the earlier decisions.[22]   **11–29**

Similarly, it is debatable as to whether the raising of jurisdictional issues on an appeal to An Bord Pleanála is to "question the validity of" the decision of the planning authority at first instance. Whereas to appeal a decision on the merits is not to question its validity,[23] strictly speaking, any error of law goes to jurisdiction,[24] and thus if the grounds of appeal include an allegation that the planning authority erred in law, it could be argued that such a ground of appeal is inadmissible before An Bord Pleanála. The difficulty with this approach is that the Supreme Court in *Lancefort Ltd. v An Bord Pleanála*[25] appeared to suggest that in order to be entitled to pursue judicial review proceedings subsequently, an applicant should have raised the legal objection before An Bord Pleanála. It would also appear that, on one interpretation, s.50(4) and (5)   **11–30**

---

[20] *Goonery v Meath County Council*, unreported, High Court, Kelly J., 15 July 1999. See also *Lennon v Cork City Council* [2006] I.E.H.C. 438; unreported, Smyth J., December 19, 2006 (declaration refused where same would serve no useful purpose other than as stepping stone to asserting entitlement to default planning permission).
[21] *KSK Enterprises Ltd. v An Bord Pleanála* [1994] 2 I.R. 128; [1994] 2 I.L.R.M. 1.
[22] This issue was tangentially adverted to in *Liddy v Minister for Public Enterprise* [2004] 1 I.L.R.M. 9.
[23] *Cavern Systems Dublin Ltd. v Clontarf Residents Association* [1984] I.L.R.M. 24 at 28–29.
[24] *cf. Harte v Labour Court* [1996] 2 I.R. 171; [1996] 2 I.L.R.M. 450.
[25] [1999] 2 I.R. 270; [1998] 2 I.L.R.M. 401.

indicate that legal objections should be pursued in the first instance before An Bord Pleanála. See further below at paras 11–328 to 11–347. In the circumstances, it may be that notwithstanding the provisions of s.50(2), the courts will adopt the pragmatic approach of allowing the validity of the decision to be raised before An Bord Pleanála; this might be achieved by relying on the fact that the decision of An Bord Pleanála *annuls* the decision of the planning authority.[26] It would be more consistent, however, if there were no right to challenge the decision of the planning authority by way of judicial review.[27]

11–31 The peculiar position of enforcement proceedings must be considered next. An issue arises as to whether or not it is possible to challenge the validity of an earlier decision on a planning application in subsequent enforcement proceedings.[28] The most obvious example of when this might occur would be where a developer seeks to resist enforcement proceedings on the basis that a planning condition which it is sought to enforce is invalid. The wording of s.50(2) would suggest that the invalidity of the decision cannot be raised other than in judicial review proceedings; indeed, this might run counter to the perceived objective that the decision be "entirely legally protected against subsequent challenge".[29] As against this, a number of arguments can be advanced in support of allowing a collateral challenge. First, the challenge is not strictly speaking directed to the decision but rather to a condition attached thereto.[30] Secondly, the court may have discretion as to whether or not to grant relief in the enforcement proceedings[31]; it may be that as a matter of discretion the court would refuse to enforce a condition which is clearly invalid.[32]

3. Pre-emptive challenges

11–32 Prior to 2006 Act, applicants would occasionally seek to move for judicial review before the planning process had concluded, and thus in advance of a final decision having been made. The unamended s.50 procedure had only applied to a *final* decision—such as, for example, the decision to grant or to refuse planning permission—and not to interim decisions of an informal nature

---

[26] See *O'Keeffe v An Bord Pleanála* [1993] 1 I.R. 39 at 52–53; [1992] I.L.R.M. 296 at 247.

[27] *cf. Chambers v An Bord Pleanála* [1992] 1 I.R. 134; [1992] I.L.R.M. 296.

[28] In *R. v Wicks* [1998] A.C. 92, the House of Lords indicated that the accused in criminal proceedings was not entitled to raise issues as to the validity of the enforcement notice on which the prosecution was based. Questions of validity were properly a matter for a statutory appeal against the issuance of an enforcement notice, or, in exceptional cases, for judicial review. Such questions could not be raised in the context of a criminal prosecution.

[29] *KSK Enterprises Ltd. v An Bord Pleanála* [1994] 2 I.R. 128; [1994] 2 I.L.R.M. 1.

[30] *cf.* the express power to sever a decision under PDA 2000, s.50A(9) (as amended by the 2006 Act, s.13).

[31] This is certainly the case in an application for an injunction under PDA 2000, s.160 (previously, s.27 of the Local Government (Planning & Development) Act 1976 (as amended)).

[32] *cf. Dublin Corporation v Garland* [1982] I.L.R.M. 104 (cannot reopen planning matters on application under s.27 of the Local Government (Planning & Development) Act 1976 (as amended)).

which might be made in relation to any particular matter arising in the course of an appeal or application.[33] Thus, by striking before a final decision was made, an applicant could proceed by way of conventional judicial review proceedings, and seek a stay at the *ex parte* leave application restraining the decision-making process pending the determination of the judicial review proceedings.[34] In other words, not only could such an applicant avoid a contested leave hearing, he or she might also be able to secure a restraining order in the absence of the other side.

As a result of the amendments introduced under the 2006 Act, such a pre-emptive challenge would itself most likely be subject to the statutory judicial review procedure, for the following reasons. First, the procedure is no longer confined to final decisions, and thus decisions taken during the course of the planning process—such as, for example, a decision to invite revised plans—are now protected. Secondly, the procedure is not confined to "decisions", but also extends to acts done in the performance or purported performance of a function under the PDA 2000. Accordingly, the taking of, or failing to take, a particular step in the course of decision-making—even if not involving a formal "decision" as such—would also be protected under the statutory procedure. **11–33**

4. Combination of reliefs

Occasionally, an applicant for judicial review will seek a combination of reliefs, some of which are within the scope of the statutory procedure and some of which are outwith. This is likely to happen only infrequently now given the wide range of decisions and acts subject to the statutory procedure. It did, however, occur from time to time under the unamended s.50. For example, an applicant might have wished to argue that a particular objective of the development plan is invalid, and that reliance on that objective vitiated a subsequent decision to grant planning permission.[35] Under the unamended s.50 procedure, only the latter decision was subject to the statutory procedure. A question then arose as to what form the judicial review proceedings should take. **11–34**

The better view is that both categories of relief should be rolled-up in an application under ss.50 and 50A rather than two separate sets of proceedings **11–35**

---

[33] *Huntstown Airpark Ltd. v An Bord Pleanála* [1999] 1 I.L.R.M. 281 (decision of inspector to refuse to direct production of documents).

[34] A challenge to an interim decision did, of course, run the risk that it might be dismissed as being premature; *Huntstown Airpark Ltd. v An Bord Pleanála* [1999] 1 I.L.R.M. 281 *cf. Hughes v An Bord Pleanála* [2000] 1 I.L.R.M. 452. This, however, was a matter going to discretion rather than to procedure. Where a final decision was subsequently made on the matter, then it would be necessary to commence fresh proceedings; the existing proceedings could not be amended so as to include a challenge to this final decision; see *Brick v Burke* [2002] 2 I.L.R.M. 427.

[35] Failure to challenge the development plan itself might well redound against the applicant: see, for example, *Glancré Teoranta v An Bord Pleanála (No. 1)*, unreported, High Court, MacMenamin J., May 2, 2006.

issued.[36] The greater includes the lesser. The requirements of ss.50 and 50A are far more stringent than those applicable to conventional judicial review, and, therefore, it would not lie in the mouth of a respondent to complain that that part of the relief outside s.50(2) should have been sought by way of an *ex parte* application. This is entirely consistent with the legislative scheme wherein an application under s.50(2) is expressed to be an application for "judicial review under Order 84". The fact that, in respect of certain relief, an applicant has volunteered to seek leave on notice by including this relief in an application under s.50(2) does not deprive this aspect of the claim of its character as judicial review proceedings; it remains an application for judicial review under Ord.84. In deciding on whether or not to grant leave, however, the High Court should apply different tests, namely stateable or arguable case, and substantial grounds, respectively.[37]

11–36   However, where the reliefs sought involve a collateral or indirect attack on a decision protected by s.50(2) then the higher standard of "substantial grounds" will apply. This point arose on the facts of *Kinsella v Dundalk Town Council*.[38] The applicant alleged that the planning authority had acted unlawfully in its processing of an application for planning permission. In particular, it was alleged that the planning authority should have required further public notice on receipt of a response to a request for further information. It was alleged that the response contained "significant additional data" such as to trigger the statutory requirement for further public notice. The applicant sought to quash the "decision" of the planning authority not to require further public notice, and also to quash the subsequent decision to grant planning permission. On the precedent of *Huntstown Air Park Ltd. v An Bord Pleanála*,[39] only the latter decision was subject to the statutory procedure under the unamended s.50. In the circumstances, the applicant had sought to argue that he was only required to meet the lower threshold of an arguable or stateable case in respect of the challenge to the earlier "decision" of the planning authority not to require further public notice. Kelly J. rejected this submission, holding that it would serve no useful purpose to set aside this earlier decision without going on to quash the decision to grant planning permission.

> "It was suggested on the part of the applicant that whilst the application for leave to apply for *certiorari* against the decision to grant permission undoubtedly fell within the ambit of s. 50, the application for leave to apply for *certiorari* in respect of the decision of 25th June, 2004, did not. It was said that it fell to be decided by reference to ordinary judicial review principles and that the threshold

---

[36] *cf. Keane v An Bord Pleanála*, unreported, High Court, Murphy J., June 20, 1995, where conventional grounds of challenge were also put forward. *Cf. Neville v An Bord Pleanála* unreported, High Court, Ó Caoimh J., July 31, 2001 (at p. 14) and October 12, 2001.

[37] *Keane v An Bord Pleanála*, unreported, High Court, Murphy J., June 20, 1995 (at p. 21). As to the test to be applied where a constitutional challenge is involved, see *Hynes v An Bord Pleanála (No. 1)*, unreported, High Court, Laffoy J., December 10, 1997, discussed below at paras 11–37 to 11–40.

[38] Unreported, High Court, Kelly J., December 3, 2004.

[39] [1999] 1 I.L.R.M. 281.

of arguable case identified by the Supreme Court in *G. v. D.P.P.* [1994] 1 I.R. 374 was all that had to be achieved.

I rejected that submission at an early stage in the hearing for reasons which I enunciated then. I took the view that it was quite clear that the whole thrust and ambition of these proceedings was to quash the decision of 3rd August, 2004. As the applicant was quite plainly questioning the validity of the decision to grant planning permission he could not avoid or evade meeting the necessary threshold of proof required under s. 50 of the Planning and Development Act, 2000. Indeed as I pointed out in giving my ruling on this topic, if the applicant were correct in his submission in this regard an absurd result could be achieved which would be entirely contrary to the letter and intent of s. 50.

Accordingly, as I ruled at the outset it is necessary for the applicant to demonstrate substantial grounds for contending that the decisions which he impugns in these proceedings are invalid or ought to be quashed."

5. Constitutional challenges

An applicant, as part of an overall challenge to a planning decision, may seek to allege that a particular legislative provision is invalid having regard to the provisions of the Constitution. For example, the applicant company in *Lancefort Ltd. v An Bord Pleanála*[40] had initially sought leave to argue that the then legislative provision which allowed An Bord Pleanála to grant planning permission in material contravention of the development plan was invalid. Such constitutional challenges give rise to the following two procedural issues. The first issue is whether it is permissible to include a constitutional challenge as part of an application under ss.50 and 50A. This question is closely related to that considered immediately above at para.11–34 under the heading "Combination of Reliefs".   **11–37**

The better view must be that it is appropriate to include a constitutional challenge as part of the application for judicial review, rather than to bring separate plenary proceedings seeking a declaration of constitutional invalidity.[41] Such an approach is consistent with the objective of ensuring that any challenge to the validity of a planning decision is determined expeditiously. It would be inimical to this objective were the constitutional, and non-constitutional, grounds of challenge to be dealt with in separate proceedings as this would almost certainly add to delay. Two hearings would involve unnecessary duplication. This is especially so in circumstances where a constitutional challenge is often pleaded in the alternative: the applicant will often argue for a particular interpretation of a legislative provision, while reserving the right to argue that if this interpretation does not prevail, the provision is unconstitutional. Obviously, it is more convenient if these arguments are heard together in the one set of proceedings.   **11–38**

---

[40] [1997] 2 I.L.R.M. 508.
[41] See, generally, *Hynes v An Bord Pleanála (No. 1)*, unreported, High Court, Laffoy J., December 10, 1997.

11–39   The second procedural issue, then, is as to the approach to be taken by the court at the leave stage to the constitutional grounds of challenge. In particular, questions arise as to whether the standard to be met at the leave stage is that of "substantial grounds", or the lesser standard of an arguable or stateable case applicable to conventional judicial review proceedings; and as to the implications of the principle of judicial self-restraint. Some of these matters were considered by the High Court in *Hynes v An Bord Pleanála*[42] under the unamended s.50 procedure. Laffoy J. held that the High Court should address both the constitutional, and non-constitutional, grounds of challenge at the leave stage. Laffoy J. also suggested that the fact that express provision was made with respect to a constitutional challenge in the case of an appeal to the Supreme Court gave rise to an inference that the legislature envisaged that a constitutional challenge might properly be brought by way of proceedings under the statutory judicial review procedure. The absence of any special provision with respect to the leave stage in the case of a constitutional challenge indicated that constitutional grounds fell be dealt with at the leave stage in the same way as non-constitutional grounds. It is respectfully submitted that this approach is correct. The principle of judicial self-restraint simply requires that the courts do not make declarations of unconstitutionality unnecessarily in circumstances where the particular legal proceedings might have been determined on non-constitutional grounds. The principle does not extend so as to inhibit the courts from even *considering* arguments based on alleged constitutional invalidity: a finding that an applicant has raised "substantial grounds" for a constitutional challenge does not involve a final determination of constitutional invalidity and thus, it is submitted, does not offend against the principle of judicial self-restraint.

11–40   Finally it is to be noted that the statutory judicial review procedure would thus appear to impose a greater burden on an applicant seeking to raise a constitutional challenge. But for the provisions of ss.50 and 50A, such a challenge could be brought by way of conventional judicial review (in which case the applicant would simply have to demonstrate an arguable or stateable case at the leave stage), or by way of plenary proceedings (in which case there would be no requirement for leave at all).

6. Challenges to transposition of EC Directives

11–41   An approach slightly different to that which governs constitutional challenges—discussed above at paras 11–37 to 11–40—applies where the judicial review proceedings raise a challenge to the transposition of an EC Directive. In *Arklow Holidays Ltd. v An Bord Pleanála (No. 1)*,[43] Clarke J. accepted that a court should only consider whether there has been a failure to transpose a Directive in circumstances where such a determination is necessary for the purposes of

---

[42] Unreported, High Court, Laffoy J., December 10, 1997.
[43] [2006] I.E.H.C. 15; [2007] 1 I.L.R.M. 125.

resolving the litigation. Insofar as an application for leave to apply for judicial review was concerned, Clarke J. accepted that if there were circumstances in which a transposition issue might arise at the substantive hearing and if there were substantial grounds in favour of the argument on transposition, then leave should be granted to ensure that the transposition issue could be dealt with if, in the light of the views which the judge hearing the substantive case took on other issues, it became necessary so to do.

Thus far, the approach appears to mirror that in respect of constitutional **11–42** challenges. Clarke J. went on, however, to introduce the following gloss, which was said to arise from the obligation of the Irish courts to construe, where possible, national legislation in a manner consistent with EC law. Clarke J. indicated that leave to argue a transposition point should only be granted where there were substantial grounds for believing that there was no interpretation which could properly be placed on the relevant national legislation which was consistent with the proper meaning of the relevant EC Directive.

On the facts, the applicant had sought to argue that the Waste Management **11–43** Act 1996 should be interpreted as governing the proposed development; in the alternative, it was argued that if this was not the correct interpretation, then there had been a failure to transpose properly the environmental impact assessment Directive. Clarke J. ruled that there could not be "substantial grounds" for contending both that the waste management legislation could be interpreted in a manner consistent with the environmental impact assessment Directive—in support of the argument that a waste licence was required—and for saying that there had been a failure in transposition.

> "[…] it seems to me that there cannot, in principle, be substantial grounds for both of the propositions. If the argument in favour of Arklow's construction for the waste management legislation is sufficiently strong to afford substantial grounds for the proposition that the legislation should be construed as Arklow suggests then it is difficult to envisage circumstances where the legislation could not, if necessary, be construed in that fashion in circumstances where the court was required so to do so as to bring the legislation into conformity with EU law."

Clarke J. accordingly refused the applicant leave to argue the transposition **11–44** point in the alternative. With respect, this aspect of the judgment is not entirely convincing. It is quite possible that an applicant, at the leave stage, would be able to put forward substantial grounds for a particular interpretation only for those arguments to be rejected at a full hearing. In such circumstances, it would be potentially unjust, and contrary to the requirement to give effect to EC law, if the applicant were then to be shut out from raising a transposition argument in the alternative.

In a subsequent ruling, Clarke J. refused leave to appeal to the Supreme Court **11–45** on the question of whether leave should be granted on both grounds where a transposition point is raised in the alternative. Clarke J. held that the question was essentially procedural, and did not amount to a question of law of public exceptional importance.[44]

11–46 A further difficulty which an applicant raising a transposition point faces is the mistaken belief of some judges that a challenge to the implementation of a Directive may only be brought against the State in plenary proceedings, and may not be raised during the course of judicial review proceedings impugning a particular administrative decision.[45] This specific issue is discussed in some detail in the context of the EC environmental impact assessment Directive at paras 13–277 to 13–286.

7. Exclusive procedure

11–47 Where applicable, the statutory judicial review procedure is mandatory. This is in contrast with the position obtaining prior to the Local Government (Planning & Development) Act 1992, where an applicant could elect to go by way of plenary summons seeking declaratory relief instead of applying for judicial review.[46]

11–48 Where an applicant has instituted plenary proceedings seeking declaratory relief, the appropriate response on the part of a respondent or notice party is to bring an application by way of notice of motion seeking to strike out or dismiss the proceedings.[47] In the event that an applicant erroneously proceeds by way of an *ex parte* application for judicial review in respect of a matter properly within the ambit of ss.50 and 50A, it would appear that the appropriate response on the part of a respondent or notice party is to apply to set aside the grant of leave.[48] It may well then be too late for the applicant to seek to institute proceedings under ss.50 and 50A, in that the eight week time-limit may have expired.

---

[44] *Arklow Holidays Ltd. v An Bord Pleanála (No. 2)* [2006] I.E.H.C. 102; [2007] 1 I.L.R.M. 125.

[45] See *Lancefort Ltd. v An Bord Pleanála* [1997] 2 I.L.R.M. 508; and, possibly, *Cosgrave v An Bord Pleanála* [2004] 2 I.R. 435. For a discussion of the practical procedural difficulties presented by any necessity for plenary proceedings, see M. Healy Rae, "Judicial Review and the Transposition of EU Directives" (2005) 10 *Bar Review* 131.

[46] *Cavern Systems Dublin Ltd. v Clontarf Residents Association* [1984] I.L.R.M. 24. See, generally, *O'Donnell v Dun Laoghaire Corporation* [1991] I.L.R.M. 301; *Landers v Garda Síochána Complaints Board* [1997] 3 I.R. 347; and *Murphy v Wicklow County Council* unreported, High Court, O'Sullivan J., December 19, 1999.

[47] *Lennon v Limerick City Council* [2006] I.E.H.C. 112; unreported, Laffoy J., April 3, 2006.

[48] *Goonery v Meath County Council*, unreported, High Court, Kelly J., July 15, 1999.

C. Time-Limits

1. Eight week time-limit

The courts have recognised on numerous occasions that there is a need for short time-limits in respect of challenges to planning permissions.[49] Under the Local Government (Planning & Development) Acts, the time-limits were generally two months, commencing on the date on which the decision was "given". There is now a general eight week time-limit on the issuing and service of judicial review proceedings.[50]   **11–49**

In cases *other* than the compulsory acquisition of land, judicial review proceedings must be issued and served within eight weeks beginning on the date of the "decision"[51] or, as the case may be, the date of the doing of the "act" by the planning authority, local authority or An Bord Pleanála, as appropriate. In the case of a decision of An Bord Pleanála, it seems that time runs from the date the formal decision is issued or drawn up, rather than from the date of the board meeting at which the decision is reached.[52] Of course, the date on which notification of the decision is actually received may be a little later again.[53]   **11–50**

In the case of the compulsory acquisition of land, judicial review proceedings must be issued and served within eight weeks beginning on the date on which notice of the decision was first sent or first published.   **11–51**

In reckoning the time periods, the first day of the eight week period should be included, and the last day excluded.[54] The better view is that the time-limit expires on midnight of the last day.[55]   **11–52**

---

[49] See, for example, *Cavern Systems Dublin Ltd. v Clontarf Residents Association* [1984] I.L.R.M. 24; *Brady v Donegal County Council* [1989] I.L.R.M. 282; *KSK Enterprises Ltd. v An Bord Pleanála* [1994] 2 I.R. 128; [1994] 2 I.L.R.M. 1; *McCann v An Bord Pleanála* [1997] 1 I.R. 264; [1997] 1 I.L.R.M. 314; *Hynes v Wicklow County Council*, unreported, High Court, Murphy J., May 15, 2003; and *Openneer v Donegal County Council* [2005] I.E.H.C. 156; [2006] 1 I.L.R.M. 150. See also *In the matter of the Illegal Immigrants (Trafficking) Bill 1999* [2000] 2 I.R. 360 at 392.

[50] PDA 2000, s.50(6), (7) and (8) (as amended by the Planning and Development (Strategic Infrastructure) Act 2006, s.13).

[51] In the case of an application for planning permission, the date of the "decision" is not the same as the date of the "grant"; *Henry v Cavan County Council* [2001] 4 I.R. 1; [2001] 2 I.L.R.M. 161.

[52] *Friends of the Curragh Environment Ltd. v An Bord Pleanála (No. 1)* [2006] I.E.H.C. 243; unreported, Kelly J., July 14, 2006 ("The board met on 6th January, 2006 and made a decision to grant permission. The decision order was not finalised or issued until 18th January, 2006. Accordingly the 18th January, 2006, is the date of the decision of the board from the point of view of the reckoning of time. Time began to run from that date for the purposes of s. 50 of the Act.").

[53] *Keelgrove Properties Ltd. v An Bord Pleanála* [2000] 1 I.R. 47; [2000] 2 I.L.R.M. 168.

[54] Interpretation Act 1937.

[55] *Lancefort Ltd. v An Bord Pleanála*, unreported, High Court, Morris J., May 13, 1997.

11–53   In order to comply with the time-limits, it is sufficient that the proceedings be issued and served on all the statutory parties within the prescribed period[56]; it is not necessary that the application for leave to apply should actually have been moved before the High Court, or even listed for hearing, within the eight week period.[57] Partial compliance is not possible.[58]

11–54   Finally, it remains to be seen whether the time constraints imposed on an applicant for judicial review are complemented by similar expedition on the part of the courts in the despatch of judicial review proceedings. Ironically, the pressure on court lists is such that an objection that an applicant delayed by a matter of days might not be resolved by the court for many months.[59] As discussed at paras 11–16 to 11–17, there is limited provision made under s.50A for expeditious hearings.

2. Promptness

11–55   There are conflicting indications as to whether or not the requirement under Ord.84, r.21 of the Rules of the Superior Courts 1986 that an applicant move promptly survives the introduction of a statutory time-limit. The decision in *O'Connell v Environmental Protection Agency*[60] suggests that the requirement to move promptly does survive.[61] However, it is arguable that the finding in *Lancefort Ltd. v An Bord Pleanála*[62] that the time period expires at midnight, and that the ordinary rules as to reckoning the date of service under Ord.122 do not apply, indicates that the statutory time-limit is the only restriction on time.

11–56   On one view, to introduce a concept of promptness into what is already an extremely tight time-limit will only give rise to confusion, and is unnecessary. In interpreting the provisions of the previous legislation, the courts had regard to legal certainty as the touchstone by which the provisions might be construed.[63] Undoubtedly, if the only purpose of a requirement to move

---

[56] *KSK Enterprises Ltd. v An Bord Pleanála* [1994] 2 I.R. 128; [1994] 2 I.L.R.M. 1; *Keelgrove Properties Ltd. v An Bord Pleanála* [2000] 1 I.R. 47; [2000] 2 I.L.R.M. 168; and *Murray v An Bord Pleanála* [2000] 1 I.R. 58. *Cf. McCarthy v An Bord Pleanála* [2000] 1 I.R. 42.

[57] *cf. Tennyson v Dun Laoghaire Corporation* [1991] 2 I.R. 527 (conventional judicial review application).

[58] *McCann v An Bord Pleanála* [1997] 1 I.R. 264; [1997] 1 I.L.R.M. 314.

[59] Note the sequence of events in *Dekra Erin Teoranta v Minister for the Environment and Local Government* [2002] 2 I.L.R.M. 30 (High Court).

[60] [2001] 4 I.R. 494; [2002] 1 I.L.R.M. 1.

[61] See also *Harrington v An Bord Pleanála (No. 1)* [2005] I.E.H.C. 344; [2006] 1 I.R. 388, where it was suggested *obiter* that the applicant had not complied with a requirement to move promptly, having filed his papers on the last day of the eight week statutory period.

[62] Unreported, High Court, Morris J., May 13, 1997.

[63] Reference is made to *KSK Enterprises Ltd. v An Bord Pleanála* [1994] 2 I.R. 128; [1994] 2 I.L.R.M. 1; and *Keelgrove Properties Ltd. v An Bord Pleanála* [2000] 1 I.R. 47; [2000] 2 I.L.R.M. 168. In each of these cases, judgment was informed, in part at least, by a desire to promote legal certainty.

promptly was to penalise an applicant who had moved within the eight weeks, this objective would not justify the uncertainty created.

The only possible justification for the continued existence of a requirement for promptness is to address delay *prior* to the eight week period. In certain cases, the grounds of challenge will have crystallised at a time well in advance of the making of the impugned decision.[64] In some instances, the grounds of challenge will relate to an earlier step in the decision-making process, and, following the amendments under the 2006 Act, it can now be argued that the eight week time-limit runs from that date of that "decision" or "act". In other instances, however, the crystallising event will not be directly connected to the decision the subject-matter of the judicial review proceedings, and it will be necessary to rely on a requirement for promptness. For example, in *Salafia v Minister for the Environment Heritage and the Local Government*,[65] conventional judicial review proceedings were ruled to be inadmissible on grounds of delay because the applicant had failed to challenge an earlier decision of An Bord Pleanála. The case concerned the M3 motorway. The applicant had sought to challenge certain Ministerial directions issued under the national monuments legislation. The judicial review proceedings had been instituted shortly after the issuing of these directions. For the purposes of assessing delay, however, the High Court reckoned time not from the date of the Ministerial directions, but from the date of the decision of An Bord Pleanála to approve the particular road development. Smyth J. considered that whereas the proceedings were undoubtedly framed as a challenge to the Ministerial directions, in substance the proceedings involved a collateral challenge to the route selection of the M3 motorway, a decision made by An Bord Pleanála almost three years earlier. The applicant was aware of the making of An Bord Pleanála's decision, but had not challenged it before the courts.[66] Smyth J. concluded that scrutiny of unlawful practices should take place when the first questionable irregularity takes place, rather than years later, when a course of action has been embarked upon at public expense.

11–57

Analogous situations might arise under the planning legislation. For example, an applicant may seek to challenge a decision on an application for planning permission notwithstanding the fact that the legal objection now sought to be relied upon had previously arisen, but had not been pursued, in respect of an earlier planning application. The continued existence of a requirement for promptness would allow the court to penalise delay of this type. If the

11–58

---

[64] See, for example, S*loan v An Bord Pleanála* [2003] 2 I.L.R.M. 61 (grounds of complaint crystallised once inspector at oral hearing made certain rulings).

[65] Unreported, High Court, Smyth J., March 1, 2006.

[66] See, also *An Taisce v National Roads Authority*, *ex tempore*, High Court, McGovern J (*Irish Times*, April 5, 2007), where An Taisce were refused leave to challenge a tolling scheme in circumstances where the High Court found An Taisce had raised the legal objection—the absence of a statutory plan under the Roads Act, s.18—some years earlier in the context of the decision of An Bord Pleanála to approve the road development, but had not pursued a legal challenge at that time.

requirement for promptness is to remain for this purpose, proceedings issued and served within the eight weeks should not normally be defeated for delay save in circumstances where the delay relates to a period *prior* to the eight weeks.[67]

3. Awaiting the outcome of decision-making

11–59 The fact that time is now to be reckoned from the date of the doing of an "act" by the planning authority or An Bord Pleanála suggests that it might no longer be safe to await the final outcome of the administrative decision-making stage before bringing judicial review proceedings. This is because any challenge to a final decision might be time-barred if the challenge involved impugning some "act" done by a planning authority or An Bord Pleanála during the course of processing an application/appeal; for example, the service of a request for further information or the failure to call for an environmental impact statement. At the time of writing, this aspect of the amended judicial review procedure has yet to be judicially considered. There is much to be said for the position obtaining under the unamended s.50 procedure whereby a litigant would not normally be penalised for awaiting the final outcome of the administrative decision-making stage.

Case law under the unamended s.50 procedure

11–60 The judgment in *Openneer v Donegal County Council*[68] addressed—in the context of the unamended s.50 procedure—the question as to whether, in circumstances where the grounds of complaint arose during the course of the processing of a planning application, time started running prior to the date of the final decision to refuse or grant planning permission. Two applications for planning permission had been made on the one day. The applicant in the judicial review proceedings had purported to object to both planning applications: the written submission referred to both applications, but was accompanied by a fee (twenty euros) appropriate to a single application only. The planning authority returned the submission on the basis that the incorrect fee had been paid. In the judicial review proceedings, it was argued that the planning authority should have accepted at least one of the submissions, by allocating the fee to one or other of the two planning applications. There was a further suggestion that the planning authority should have notified the objector of the incorrect fee.

11–61 As the proceedings had been made well outside the eight week statutory period, it was necessary for the applicant to seek an extension of time. In resisting the application for an extension, the planning authority suggested that promptness

---

[67] See, by analogy, the judgment of Fennelly J. in *Dekra Erin Teoranta v Minister for the Environment and Local Government* [2003] 2 I.L.R.M. 210 (claim commenced within statutory period cannot normally be defeated for delay unless special factor such as prejudice to third party).

[68] [2005] I.E.H.C. 156; [2006] 1 I.L.R.M. 150.

should be reckoned from the date of the rejection of the submission, as the grounds of challenge had crystallised at that time. Macken J. rejected this argument, ruling that the fact that the applicant would have been entitled to move for judicial review at that early stage did not preclude him, for that reason alone, from seeking to challenge subsequently the decisions to grant planning permission, provided he had moved promptly and within the eight week period. It is respectfully submitted that the approach of Macken J. in this regard has much to recommend it. It would impose an unnecessary burden on the courts, and on litigants, were it necessary to move for judicial review in advance of the final decision on an application. Some of the case law in this area indicates a growing acceptance of this. Thus, for example, in *Martin v An Bord Pleanála*,[69] O'Sullivan J. cited with apparent approval a statement of Woolf L.J. to the effect that an application at the end of administrative proceedings will avoid the possibility of successive applications for judicial review, and will be more in keeping with the general principle that judicial review should be a remedy of last resort.

Reference is made, by analogy, to the decision of the House of Lords in *R. (On the application of Burkett) v Hammersmith and Fulham LBC*.[70] There, under the relevant rule, a claim form for an application for judicial review was to be filed promptly and, in any event, not later than three months after "the grounds to make the claim first arose". The issue before the House of Lords was as to whether the applicant for judicial review should have moved against a *resolution* to grant planning permission, rather than await an actual grant of planning permission. The House of Lords ruled that, in the interests of legal certainty, time should run from the latter date only.   **11–62**

> "For my part the substantive position is straightforward. The court has jurisdiction to entertain an application by a citizen for judicial review in respect of a resolution before or after its adoption. But it is a jump in legal logic to say that he *must* apply for such relief on pain of losing his right to judicial review of the actual grant of planning permission which does affect his rights. Such a view would also be in tension with the established principle that judicial review is a remedy of last resort."

The principles in *Burkett* were subsequently applied by the Court of Appeal, in *R. (On the application of Catt) v Brighton and Hove City Council*, in respect of a challenge to a planning permission based on an allegedly invalid screening decision.[71]   **11–63**

> "To deprive a citizen of the right to challenge a planning permission by way of judicial review would be a major and a retrograde step. The screening opinion certainly has a formality and status in the statutory planning scheme. It may itself

---

[69] [2002] 2 I.R. 655.
[70] [2002] U.K.H.L. 23, [42] *per* Lord Steyn; [2003] 1 P. & C.R. 3. *Cf. R. (On the application of Catt) v Brighton and Hove City Council* [2006] E.W.H.C. 1337 (Admin), where it was suggested that, notwithstanding *Burkett*, time should be taken as running from the date of a negative screening decision, not from the date of the (later) decision on the planning application.
[71] [2007] E.W.C.A. Civ 298; [2007] P. & C.R. 11, [49] *per* Pill L.J.

be challenged and that may be the appropriate course in some situations. However, the opportunity to challenge does not affect the right to challenge by judicial review a subsequent planning decision. The opinion does not create, or inevitably lead, to a planning permission and the right to challenge a subsequent planning permission relating to the same proposed development is not, in my judgment, defeated by the passage of time between the screening opinion and the planning permission. Moreover, this is not a case where the screening decision was received in silence. Its lawfulness was challenged by the appellant in a letter of 16 March 2005 and the objection was noted in the planning officer's report of 18 May. A detailed letter of objection was sent to the Council by the appellant's solicitor on 14 July."

11–64   Reference is also made, again by analogy, to the judgment of the Supreme Court in *Mulcreevy v Minister for the Environment Heritage and Local Government*.[72] This case arose in a non-planning context, and involved a challenge to an approval under the national monuments legislation ("the order"). One of the issues which arose for consideration was as to whether the application for judicial review should be refused on the basis of delay. The order had to be laid before the Houses of the Oireachtas, and would not become effective until twenty-one sitting days of both Houses without a resolution annulling the order having been passed by either House. Notwithstanding this, the State respondents had argued that the application for judicial review should have been moved as soon as the order had been made, as the grounds of challenge could be said to have arisen at that stage. It was further argued that the procedure involved in laying the order before the Houses of the Oireachtas was in no sense equivalent to an appeal: the order sought to be impugned had either been properly made or not at that stage and, if it was improperly made, the defect bringing about that result could not be cured by the absence of a parliamentary resolution annulling the order.

11–65   The Supreme Court, *per* Keane C.J., rejected this argument, holding that the applicant could not be regarded as having acted unreasonably in not instituting proceedings to challenge a statutory consent/approval which was devoid of legal effect until the relevant period had expired.

D. Extension of Time

1. Introduction

11–66   Section 50(8) empowers the High Court to extend the prescribed period.[73] This provision remedies a defect in the previous legislation: the absence of

---

[72] [2004] 1 I.R. 72; [2004] 1 I.L.R.M. 419.
[73] The precursor to this provision under the unamended s.50 procedure had been considered in a number of cases, including *Casey v An Bord Pleanála* [2004] 2 I.R. 296; [2004] 2 I.L.R.M. 296; *Marshall v Arklow Town Council* [2004] 4 I.R. 92; *Openneer v Donegal County Council* [2005] I.E.H.C. 156; [2006] 1 I.L.R.M. 150; and *Kelly v Leitrim County Council* [2005] I.E.H.C. 11; [2005] 2 I.R. 404.

any exception to the two month time-limit had led to the Supreme Court declaring the relevant part of s.82(3B) of the Local Government (Planning & Development) Act 1963 (inserted under the 1992 Act) to be unconstitutional.[74]

Section 50(8) provides that the High Court shall only extend the relevant period if it is satisfied that (a) there is "good and sufficient reason for doing so", and (b) the circumstances that resulted in the failure to make the application for leave within time were "outside the control" of the person seeking the extension. This latter requirement is new, and did not form part of the unamended s.50 procedure. **11–67**

It is important to note that what must be shown is good and sufficient reason for extending time, not simply good and sufficient reason for the delay.[75] The court is thus entitled to consider matters other than the delay *per se*. Accordingly, even if an applicant can justify his or her delay, an extension of time might nevertheless be refused. For example, the court might consider that there is no merit in the judicial review application, or that there is some aspect of the conduct of the applicant which disentitles him to an extension of time (such as, perhaps, delay at an earlier stage of the statutory process). **11–68**

It would seem that a decision on an application to extend time is not subject to the requirement under s.50A(7) to obtain leave to appeal to the Supreme Court, but may instead be appealed in the ordinary way. The Supreme Court so found in relation to the equivalent provision under the immigration legislation.[76] **11–69**

The approach to be taken to an application to extend time is as follows. First, the applicant must both explain the delay, and offer a justifiable excuse for the delay.[77] Under s.50(8)(b), the circumstances giving rise to the delay must have been "outside the control of" the applicant. Secondly, the court must then consider the issue of prejudice. It seems that prejudice is a distinct consideration, and, in particular, that the absence of prejudice cannot *per se* represent a good and sufficient reason for extending time. A third consideration then is the merits **11–70**

---

[74] *White v Dublin City Council* [2004] 1 I.R. 545; [2004] 2 I.L.R.M. 509. In *Jerry Beades Construction Ltd. v Dublin Corporation* [2005] I.E.H.C. 406; unreported, McKechnie J., September 7, 2005, the High Court fell back on the provisions of Ord.84 of the Rules of the Superior Courts 1986 in the absence of a (valid) statutory time-limit. In *Lennon v Cork City Council* [2006] I.E.H.C. 438; unreported, December 19, 2006, Smyth J. suggested that a person who had not challenged the constitutionality of the two month time-limit might not be entitled to rely on the declaration of invalidity, citing the judgment of the Supreme Court in *A v Governor of Arbour Hill Prison* [2006] 2 I.L.R.M. 481.

[75] See, by analogy, *GK v Minister for Justice Equality and Law Reform* [2002] 2 I.R. 418.

[76] *AB v Minister for Justice, Equality and Law Reform* [2002] 1 I.R. 296; [2002] 2 I.L.R.M. 161. Attention was drawn to the fact that if the decision to *refuse* to extend time were regarded as a "determination" of the application for leave this would have the anomalous and discriminatory result that the applicant would be denied a right of appeal, whereas the respondent would be entitled to appeal a decision to *allow* an extension of time.

[77] See, by analogy, *O'Donnell v Dun Laoghaire Corporation* [1991] I.L.R.M. 301, cited with approval most recently in *Dekra Erin Teoranta v Minister for the Environment and Local Government* [2003] 2 I.L.R.M. 210.

of the substantive application for judicial review. The Supreme Court has indicated in relation to the similarly worded provisions of the immigration legislation that if a claim is manifestly unarguable, then there can normally be no good or sufficient reason for permitting it to be brought, however slight the delay requiring the exercise of the court's discretion, and however understandable the delay may be in the particular circumstances.[78] The merits should not be addressed in detail but the applicant is required to demonstrate an arguable case.[79] In *O'Shea v Kerry County Council*,[80] the High Court held that, in circumstances where the applicant had failed to satisfy the court that she had established substantial grounds or that she had a substantial interest, there were not good and sufficient reasons to extend time.

2. Practice and procedure

11–71   The better view seems to be that where an extension of time is required, this should be expressly included as one of the reliefs sought in the originating notice of motion.[81] Where this is not done, the court appears to have discretion to allow the necessary amendment to the notice of motion.[82] The facts which are to be relied upon in seeking the extension of time should be set out on affidavit. The affidavit(s) should also address the substance of the judicial review application because—as discussed at para.11–70—the court is entitled to have some regard to the merits of the case in deciding whether or not to extend time.

11–72   In *Kelly v Leitrim County Council*,[83] Clarke J. suggested that the notice of motion should be accompanied by a *draft* of the statement of grounds; the usual practice, however, is to file the statement of grounds in final form. Notwithstanding the fact that the leave of the court is required to pursue the judicial review proceedings, the practice in both statutory and conventional judicial review is to file papers in the Central Office, and to obtain a record number, in advance of the hearing of the application for leave. The fact that an extension of time is sought does not appear to justify a change in this practice.

11–73   A practical issue arises as to whether the application to extend time should be dealt with as a preliminary issue in advance of hearing the application for leave proper. This is a difficult question. On the one hand, considerations of expedition might suggest that the extension of time should be dealt with on a stand-alone basis, without the necessity of an examination of the merits of the case with all the attendant delay. On the other hand, however, it appears that

---

[78] *GK v Minister for Justice Equality and Law Reform* [2002] 2 I.R. 418.
[79] *ibid.*
[80] [2003] 4 I.R. 143.
[81] *Kelly v Leitrim County Council* [2005] I.E.H.C. 11; [2005] 2 I.R. 404. See also *AB v Minister for Justice, Equality and Law Reform* [2002] 1 I.R. 296; [2002] 2 I.L.R.M. 161.
[82] *Marshall v Arklow Town Council* [2004] 4 I.R. 92.
[83] [2005] I.E.H.C. 11; [2005] 2 I.R. 404.

the test of "good and sufficient reason" may require some consideration of the merits as there is little reason to extend time for a case which is insubstantial. Further, if there are to be separate hearings in respect of each of the application to extend time, and the application for leave to apply, this may result in unnecessary delay.

In *Marshall v Arklow Town Council*,[84] Peart J. decided that it was necessary to rule on the application to extend time as a preliminary issue, in advance of hearing the application for leave to apply for judicial review.   **11–74**

> "It follows that this Court must determine first of all whether an extension is required and, if so, whether it should be granted for good and sufficient reason. A refusal of such an extension has the effect of finally determining the application from the applicants' viewpoint, in the sense that without it they cannot proceed further. To deal with the merits of the application at the same time as determining the time point would result in the Court dealing unnecessarily with the substantive merits in a case where an extension of time is found not to be merited. That consideration must outweigh any countervailing consideration such as having the entire matter aired at one sitting, rather than dealing with each aspect separately. I have therefore decided to proceed with my decision in relation to time and delay, and if finding in favour of the applicants on that issue, I will then proceed to fix as early a date as possible for the hearing of the substantive application for leave."

With respect, whereas this approach has much to recommend it, it is questionable whether it will always be appropriate. In certain cases the question of an extension of time will be inextricably linked with the substantive merits of the case. Indeed, it is arguable that this was the position on the facts of *Marshall* itself, where the principal ground put forward for challenging the validity of the planning permission, namely that a site notice was not erected and maintained in compliance with the regulations, was also the point relied upon in seeking an extension of time. In the circumstances there must be something to be said for dealing with all matters together, rather than, in effect, giving the applicants the benefit of the doubt. As it happens, the applicants in *Marshall* were ultimately successful in the substantive application for judicial review as well, but one can readily envisage cases where an extension of time might be granted—with all the attendant uncertainty and delay for the developer—only for the applicants to fail to obtain leave to apply for judicial review subsequently.   **11–75**

In *Kelly v Leitrim County Council*,[85] Clarke J. made the pragmatic suggestion that whether or not an extension of time would be dealt with on a stand-alone basis should be a matter for the election of the respondent decision-maker. Although this approach has the attraction of allowing the respondent to decide   **11–76**

---

[84] [2004] 4 I.R. 92 at 100–101. In *Openneer v Donegal County Council* [2005] I.E.H.C. 156; [2006] 1 I.L.R.M. 150, the application for an extension of time was, in effect, dealt with as a preliminary issue by the High Court. Macken J. refused to make an order extending time, and instead dismissed the application for judicial review.

[85] [2005] I.E.H.C. 11; [2005] 2 I.R. 404.

whether to run the risk of there ultimately being two separate hearings, *i.e.* if an extension is granted, then there will have to be a further hearing on the application for leave proper; the range of matters to be considered in deciding whether to extend time is such that it may be difficult to deal with as a preliminary issue, divorced from the substance of the case. Reference is made in this regard to the judgment of the Supreme Court in *BTF v Director of Public Prosecutions*.[86] There, the Supreme Court indicated—albeit in the context of conventional judicial review proceedings—that the range of matters to be considered in deciding whether to extend time is such that it was doubtful that it would normally be useful to deal with alleged applicant-delay as a preliminary issue.

3. Delay contributed to by developer

11–77 The fact that the delay on the part of the applicant has been contributed to by the developer would seem to afford a good and sufficient reason to extend time. For example, if the delay was caused by some defect in the public notices which the developer is required to publish, then it would seem equitable that the time period be extended. In *Marshall v Arklow Town Council*,[87] the High Court, in deciding to extend time, had regard to the fact that the applicants claimed not to have seen the site notice, and had moved with all reasonable haste once they learnt subsequently of the decision to grant planning permission. Similarly, if a developer makes radical amendments to the proposed development by way of the submission of modified plans without proper public notice, any delay in the institution of judicial review proceedings may be referable to the developer's own conduct.[88]

11–78 There must be a direct link between the delay and the defect complained of.[89] Thus, a delay in the erection of a site notice might not justify an extension of time in circumstances where the notice, although erected belatedly, had nevertheless been erected in sufficient time to allow submissions and observations to be made.[90]

4. Grounds of challenge belatedly disclosed

11–79 In the absence of culpability on the part of the developer or the decision-maker, one of the primary considerations must be the applicant's state of knowledge as to the making of, and the circumstances surrounding, the decision to be

---

[86] [2005] I.E.S.C. 37; [2005] 2 I.R. 559; [2005] 2 I.L.R.M. 367.

[87] [2004] 4 I.R. 92.

[88] See, for example, the facts of *White v Dublin Corporation* [2004] 1 I.R. 545; [2004] 2 I.L.R.M. 509.

[89] *O'Shea v Kerry County Council* [2003] 4 I.R. 143 (applicant had not seen site notice and thus had not been damnified by alleged defects in same).

[90] See, by analogy, the facts of *Openneer v Donegal County Council* [2005] I.E.H.C. 156; [2006] 1 I.L.R.M. 150 (site notice erected before expiration of five week period for making submissions and observations).

impugned.[91] The test for delay must be more objective in the context of the judicial review of planning decisions; those hostile to a development cannot overcome the problem of delay by finding someone ignorant of the relevant facts to mount a challenge.[92]

In most cases, any grounds of challenge will be apparent from the decision itself or from the documents on the planning file. Occasionally, however, a ground of challenge may only come to light much later. Reference is made in this regard to the case of *Jerry Beades Construction Ltd. v Dublin Corporation*.[93] The applicant sought to challenge a decision of An Bord Pleanála to refuse planning permission, on the basis that there had been serious irregularities in the manner in which officials of the planning authority had processed the application and that these irregularities had also tainted the appeal process. Approximately eleven months had elapsed between the date of the decision of An Bord Pleanála and the institution of judicial review proceedings. This case arose under the Local Government (Planning & Development) Acts, subsequent to the judgment of the Supreme Court in *White v Dublin City Council*[94] striking down the two month time-limit as unconstitutional. In the absence of a statutory time-limit, it was necessary to fall back on the general requirements in respect of time under Ord.84 of the Rules of the Superior Courts 1986, and, accordingly, the application had to be made "promptly", and, in any event, within certain outer time-limits.
11–80

In deciding to extend time under Ord.84, McKechnie J. attached weight to the following factors. First, while an applicant is not entitled to defer proceedings until he is subjectively satisfied as to his proofs, the applicant company in the present case was justified in not issuing proceedings until it had received a comprehensive account from an official of the planning authority as to the manner in which the planning application had been dealt with internally. Secondly, there were no third parties whose rights would be adversely affected. Thirdly, having regard to his findings on the substantive action—which included a finding that the planning application was not considered fairly or impartially— McKechnie J. was of the view that an enlargement of time was essential to protect justice.
11–81

In *Openneer v Donegal County Council*,[95] an extension of time was refused on the basis that the applicant had been well aware for many months that the decisions to grant planning permission had been made. Macken J. rejected a suggestion that the applicant only knew the factual position definitively on receipt of a letter from the planning authority shortly before the proceedings were issued, holding instead that the applicant was sufficiently aware both of
11–82

---

[91] *Ní Éili v Environmental Protection Agency* [1997] 2 I.L.R.M. 458 at 466; and *O'Connell v Environmental Protection Agency* [2001] 4 I.R. 494; [2002] 1 I.L.R.M. 1.
[92] *R. v North West Leicestershire District Council Ex p. Moses* [2000] 2 J.P.L. 1287.
[93] [2005] I.E.H.C. 406; unreported, McKechnie J., September 7, 2005.
[94] [2004] 1 I.R. 545; [2004] 2 I.L.R.M. 509.
[95] [2005] I.E.H.C. 156; [2006] 1 I.L.R.M. 150.

the true facts and also of the legal consequences arising from those facts for at a period of five months prior to instituting the proceedings.

5. Lack of co-operation by respondents or notice parties

11–83 The conduct of a respondent or notice party in the lead-in to the institution of the proceedings may also have contributed to delay in either issuing or serving the proceedings. Thus, for example, the fact that a party has sought to avoid service, or failed to nominate solicitors to accept service when requested, would constitute grounds for extending time.

11–84 Similarly, the failure of a respondent to reply in a timely manner to pre-litigation correspondence or to provide information or documents requested by a putative litigant might justify an extension of time.[96]

6. Delay by legal advisers

11–85 The extent to which an applicant may have any delay or inefficiency on the part of his legal advisers imputed to him is unclear,[97] and whether these can be said to be outside his or her control as required under s.50(8)(b). In *Marshall v Arklow Town Council*[98]—a case decided under the unamended s.50 procedure—the High Court held that the fact that an Easter vacation intervened and delay resulted from counsel's unavailability could not, in fairness, be laid at the applicants' door. More generally, however, it seems that where an applicant has knowledge of the making of the decision, delay on the part of his legal advisers may not be sufficient to ground an extension of time.[99] Similarly, a change of legal representation might not excuse delay.[100] Some greater leeway may be allowed where the legal issues raised by a case are complex.[101]

7. Delay pending outcome of planning process

11–86 Occasionally, a legal defect will occur at an early stage of a decision-making process, and be so fundamental that it will operate to taint the ultimate decision.

---

[96] See, for example, *R. (On the application of Rockware Glass Ltd.) v Chester CC* [2005] E.W.H.C. 2250; [2006] J.P.L. 699 (importance of statutory bodies and their advisers ensuring that all relevant non-confidential material is provided on request within a reasonable time frame).

[97] *GK v Minister for Justice Equality and Law Reform* [2002] 1 I.L.R.M. 81 (High Court); and *S v Minister for Justice Equality and Law Reform* [2002] 2 I.R. 163 (delay by legal advisers not *prima facie* a good and sufficient reason to extend time).

[98] [2004] 4 I.R. 92.

[99] See *In the matter of an application by Burkett* [2001] J.P.L. 775. See the decision of the House of Lords [2002] U.K.H.L. 23; [2003] P. & C.R. 20.

[100] *Ní Éili v Environmental Protection Agency* [1997] 2 I.L.R.M. 458 at 466.

[101] *S v Minister for Justice Equality and Law Reform* [2002] 2 I.R. 163 (extension allowed where case straddled a time of transition in the law). See also, by analogy, *O'Connell v Environmental Protection Agency* [2001] 4 I.R. 494; [2002] 1 I.L.R.M. 1.

If the legal defect is not disclosed until after the decision has been made—for example, on the making available by An Bord Pleanála of its file on a planning appeal—an applicant for judicial review cannot be criticised for not having moved earlier. If, conversely, the defect would have been evident at an earlier stage, then the eight week period might run from the date of the doing of the relevant "act" by the planning authority, local authority or An Bord Pleanála, as the case may be. An objector might wish to await the outcome of the planning process before committing him or herself to the cost of judicial review proceedings. For example, a legal defect might have occurred at an early stage in the processing of a planning appeal, and an applicant might wish to hold off issuing judicial review proceedings in the hope that the planning application might be rejected on its merits. The question which arises therefore is as to whether this might constitute a good and sufficient reason for an extension of time in the event that the ultimate decision was unfavourable.

Prior to the amendments introduced under the 2006 Act, it had been accepted **11–87** in a number of cases that there might be some justification for an applicant awaiting the outcome of the planning process before moving for judicial review. See further paras 11–60 to 11–65. Of course, these cases were decided against a statutory background where time only began running for the purpose of the eight week time-limit from the date of the formal decision. These cases may, nevertheless, provide some support for an argument that the desire to await the outcome of the statutory decision-making process might constitute a good and sufficient reason for extending time for the bringing of judicial review proceedings subsequently.

8. Length of delay

The length of the delay will obviously always be a relevant factor on an **11–88** application to extend time.[102] On the facts of *Kelly v Leitrim County Council*,[103] there had been a delay of 19 days in issuing and serving the proceedings. Clarke J., in refusing to extend time, took the view that this delay of nineteen days in relation to a period of eight weeks was significant having regard to the necessity to bring finality to all planning matters, even those that do not involve third parties. Clarke J. also attached weight to the fact that the applicant had had the benefit of expert professional advice prior to the commencement of the time running by virtue of his having engaged professionals in the planning process which led to the impugned decision.

---

[102] *GK v Minister for Justice Equality and Law Reform* [2002] 1 I.L.R.M. 81 (High Court); *S v Minister for Justice Equality and Law Reform* [2002] 2 I.R. 163 (extension allowed where short delay of matter of weeks); *Casey v An Bord Pleanála* [2004] 2 I.R. 296; [2004] 2 I.L.R.M. 296 (delay of one day; extension of time refused); and *Openneer v Donegal County Council* [2005] I.E.H.C. 156; [2006] 1 I.L.R.M. 150 (delay of some five months; extension refused). See also *de Róiste v Minister for Defence* [2001] 1 I.R. 190; [2001] 2 I.L.R.M. 241 (extremely long delay, without cogent explanation and justification, may itself represent a ground for refusing relief).

[103] [2005] I.E.H.C. 11; [2005] 2 I.R. 404.

9. Prejudice

11–89   As indicated above, it seems that even where an applicant has demonstrated good and sufficient reason, an extension of time may nevertheless be refused where same would cause prejudice. The difficulty with this is that prejudice to third parties is effectively built in to applications under ss.50 and 50A. Save in cases where the developer himself is the applicant, an application for judicial review will almost always result in prejudice in terms of blighting a planning permission. If the existence of such prejudice were to assume the same significance in the context of s.50 as in conventional judicial review, the power to extend time would be rendered nugatory as there would be very few extensions of time granted. It is submitted, therefore, that prejudice to the developer cannot be decisive. In particular, the dynamic in planning judicial review is different from that typical of conventional judicial review. More specifically, the rights of a third party objector will be joined in the balance by the community's interest in environmental matters.

11–90   In *R. (On the application of Gavin) v Haringey London Borough Council*[104] the High Court of England and Wales declined to set aside a decision to grant planning permission, on the basis of prejudice to the developer. Under the relevant statute, the court had discretion to refuse relief where it considered that there has been undue delay in making an application for judicial review if it considered that the granting of the relief sought would be likely to cause substantial hardship to, or substantially prejudice the rights of, any person or would be detrimental to good administration.

11–91   On the facts, there had been a failure, first, to advertise the planning application, and, secondly, to make a screening decision, *i.e.* to consider whether the proposed development was likely to have significant effects on the environment by virtue of factors such as its nature, size or location. There was a delay of some 32 months from the date of the grant of planning permission to the date of the commencement of proceedings. The applicant sought to explain the delay by reference to the fact that—as a result of the failure to comply with the notice requirements—the applicant had been unaware of the making of the planning application or of the grant of planning permission. The High Court concluded that the prejudice to the developer militated against setting aside the planning permission.

> "The conclusion I have reached is that I should refuse an order quashing the planning permission. It is unnecessary to repeat what I have said about each of the relevant factors. I stress that, in the claimant's favour, I attach substantial weight to the fact that the failure to comply with the publicity requirements and the EIA requirements were serious procedural errors and that the claimant has been denied an opportunity to make representations in opposition to a development that affects his home. I also bear in mind that the claimant is not to blame for the delay. But there has been undue delay within s.31(6) and it has been a very long

---

[104] [2003] E.W.H.C. 2591 (Admin); [2004] J.P.L. 785; [2004] P. & C.R. 13.

delay; and to quash the planning permission after that lapse of time and in the circumstances now existing would in my judgment cause very substantial hardship or prejudice to [the developer]. The adverse financial consequences for [the developer], even taken at their lowest, are very large and are not to be discounted by reference to the speculative possibility that the fresh application for planning permission might succeed or that full enforcement action might not be taken or that losses might be recouped by a claim in damages against the council. Even allowing for the criticisms of [the developer's] conduct, to the extent that I have accepted them, I take the view that the hardship or prejudice to [the developer] is a sufficient reason for the refusal of a quashing order. To grant such an order would also be detrimental to good administration, but in the event I do not need to rely on this as a factor tipping the balance in favour of refusal."[105]

Reference is made, by analogy, to the judgment in *Lynch v Dublin City Council*.[106] Although the judgment was given in the context of the full hearing of the judicial review proceedings, and did not concern an application to extend time, it is nevertheless of some relevance in that it indicates the attitude of the courts to prejudice caused by delay. The applicant had made a written objection to an application for planning permission. The planning authority failed to issue the requisite acknowledgement in writing. Moreover, the planning authority failed to notify the objector of the making of the decision to grant planning permission. The objector did not learn of the making of the decision until after the four week period delimited for the making of an appeal had expired. Accordingly, the objector was not in a position to make an appeal to An Bord Pleanála because, first, she did not have the necessary written acknowledgement and, secondly, she was, in any event, out of time. Ó Caoimh J. held that the requirement to furnish a written acknowledgement was mandatory in nature. It was not, in his opinion, necessary to make a decision as to whether the requirement to notify a decision was mandatory or directory. **11–92**

> "I am conscious of the fact that I have indicated that the requirement in question was mandatory, but at the same time I am not inclined to hold that the failure to comply with that requirement necessarily results in an invalidity of the decision process itself.
>
> In the instant case, as I have already indicated, the passage of time has resulted in the construction of the extension to the property owned by the notice party. While some suggestion has been made that the notice party may have proceeded with works somewhat prematurely, in the light of the decision that had been made, it is quite clear that any works that have been effected were effected in circumstances where a decision had been made to grant planning permission. No application was made to this court at any time to restrain the development in question pending the outcome of the proceedings."

Accordingly, the High Court refused to set aside the planning authority's decision. Insofar as costs were concerned, the High Court ordered that the planning authority pay the costs of the applicant. An order for the notice party's **11–93**

---

[105] *ibid.*, [90] *per* Richards J.
[106] Unreported, High Court, Ó Caoimh J., July 25, 2003.

costs was made as against the applicant, with an order over as against the planning authority.

11–94   It might be thought that a more forgiving standard should be applied in cases where the developer himself seeks to challenge the decision; the element of prejudice is obviously lessened.[107] As against this, however, there will usually be less excuse for delay on the part of the developer as he is unlikely to be unaware of the making of the impugned decision. In particular, it may be difficult for the developer to satisfy the court that the circumstances giving rise to the delay were outside his or her control as required under s.50(8)(b).

11–95   In *Kelly v Leitrim County Council*,[108] the element of third party prejudice was absent in that the decision—on a Section 5 reference—was being challenged by the developer himself. Clarke J. nevertheless, in refusing to extend time, considered that the delay of 19 days in relation to a period of eight weeks was significant having regard to the necessity to bring finality to all planning matters, even those that did not involve third parties. Earlier in the judgment, Clarke J. had summarised the position thus.

> "[…] there is nonetheless a clear legislative policy involved in all such measures which requires that, irrespective of the involvement of the rights of third parties, determinations of particular types should be rendered certain within a short period of time as part of an overall process of conferring certainty on certain categories of administrative or quasi judicial decisions. Therefore while it may well be legitimate to take into account the fact that no third party rights are involved that should not be regarded as conferring a wide or extensive jurisdiction to extend time in cases where no such rights may be affected. The overall integrity of the processes concerned is, in itself, a factor to be taken into account."

10. Conveyancing implications

11–96   Finally, the fact that the time period for the taking of judicial review proceedings can be extended may present concerns to persons purchasing land with the benefit of planning permission. Under the previous legislation prior to the judgment in *White v Dublin City Council*,[109] once the two month period had expired, the planning permission was immune from challenge. Under the new scheme, the possibility of a late challenge cannot always be ruled out. It remains to be seen how conveyancing practice adopts to this new change: a cautious purchaser may seek to protect himself by some form of indemnity from the vendor. Alternatively, a warranty might be sought to the effect that there had been compliance in respect of those aspects of the application for planning permission—for example, public notices—which might otherwise ground an application to extend time.

---

[107] The fact that the High Court is now empowered under PDA 2000, s.50A(9) to amend the planning permission and does not necessarily have to set it aside in its entirely may encourage developers to bring limited challenges to aspects of the planning permission.

[108] [2005] I.E.H.C. 11; [2005] 2 I.R. 404 at 412.

[109] [2004] 1 I.R. 545; [2004] 2 I.L.R.M. 509.

E. Notice Parties and Service

1. Notice parties

Under s.50A(2), the application for leave to apply for judicial review should **11–97** be on notice to certain prescribed parties.

In the case of a challenge to a decision or act of the planning authority on an **11–98** application for planning permission, the planning authority and the applicant for planning permission should be put on notice.[110] In the case of a challenge to a decision or act of An Bord Pleanála on an appeal or referral, An Bord Pleanála and the parties to the appeal or referral should be put on notice. The parties to an appeal or referral include, *inter alia*, the planning authority; the person making the appeal or referral; and an applicant for planning permission.[111] In the case of a challenge to a decision or act of An Bord Pleanála on application for permission or approval, An Bord Pleanála and the applicant for permission or approval should be put on notice.

Section 50A does not expressly distinguish between the concept of a respondent **11–99** and a notice party. Nor is such a distinction evident in the Rules of the Superior Courts 1986.[112] In practice, however, it is usual to name the decision-maker (whether the planning authority or An Bord Pleanála) as respondent, and the other prescribed parties as notice parties. Occasionally, if injunctive relief is sought against the developer, the applicant for planning permission will be formally joined as a respondent. In strict terms, there does not appear to be any distinction between a respondent and a notice party. Order 84, r.22(2) simply requires that the notice of motion be served on all persons directly affected. Accordingly, it would seem that in the event that a notice party wishes to oppose the application for judicial review, it would be necessary for him to file a statement of opposition as in the case of a respondent. The position with respect to costs may be different, however; this is considered further at paras 11–301 to 11–304.

The extent, if any, to which the High Court can dispense with the requirement **11–100** for service upon all the prescribed parties is unclear. On a literal interpretation of the provisions of s.50A, it is mandatory to serve each and every of the prescribed parties. Such an interpretation of the previous legislation, however,

---

[110] PDA 2000, s.50A(2)(a) (as amended).
[111] PDA 2000, s.2.
[112] In the case of conventional judicial review, there does not appear to be any distinction drawn between a notice party and a party *simpliciter*. It would seem to follow from the definition of "party" under Ord.125 that such a person is then a party to the proceedings. See also Ord.84, r.22(6) and rule 26(1). (Discussed briefly in *TDI Metro Ltd. v Delap (No.1)* [2000] 4 I.R. 337; [2001] 1 I.L.R.M. 321.) Further, the Supreme Court in its decision in *Spin Communications trading as Storm FM v IRTC*, unreported, Supreme Court, April 14, 2000 appears to have assimilated the position of a notice party to that of a respondent.

appears to have been rejected in *McCarthy v An Bord Pleanála*[113]; Geoghegan J. seems to have accepted a suggestion by counsel that in enacting the then legislation[114] it was not intended to introduce some new kind of judicial review application different from conventional judicial review but instead the procedure and requirements for obtaining leave were altered, and that the question as to who were necessary notice parties fell to be determined on an *ad hoc* basis, as in the case of conventional judicial review.[115] The facts of *McCarthy* may be distinguishable in that, unusually, there were a number of co-appellants before An Bord Pleanála and reasons of pragmatism would suggest that a multiplicity of parties might delay judicial review proceedings and defeat the purposes of the Local Government (Planning & Development) Act 1992. It would appear from the subsequent decision in *Murray v An Bord Pleanála* that whatever may be the position in respect of appellants, the planning authority[116] (and presumably the applicant for planning permission)[117] are mandatory parties.[118] It would also appear that an applicant is not absolved from the requirement to serve a mandatory party by waiver on the part of same.[119]

11–101 The High Court has an express power under s.50A(2)(e) to specify by order that notice of the proceedings be served on any other person. No guidance is given as to the exercise of this discretion, but it would appear that the provision supplements Ord.84, r.22(6), which requires that, in the case of conventional judicial review, the notice of motion must be served on all persons directly affected. In the event that the applicant, notwithstanding the imperatives of these rules, fails to serve notice of the application for leave on a person directly affected, the High Court can direct service, and, presumably, adjourn the hearing of the leave application.[120] Reference is also made to the decision in *O'Keeffe v An Bord Pleanála* (which predated the Local Government (Planning & Development) Act 1992).[121]

---

[113] [2000] 1 I.R 42. The decision was appealed to the Supreme Court but the entire proceedings were ultimately compromised.

[114] Local Government (Planning & Development) Act 1992.

[115] *cf. Spin FM v IRTC*, unreported, Supreme Court, April 14, 2000.

[116] [2000] 1 I.R. 58.

[117] See *O'Keeffe v An Bord Pleanála* [1993] 1 I.R. 39 at 78; [1992] I.L.R.M. 237 at 258.

[118] *Quaere* whether it should be necessary to join the planning authority to proceedings challenging the decision of An Bord Pleanála. See, for example, *Electricity Supply Board v Gormley* [1985] I.R. 124 at 157; [1985] I.L.R.M. 494 at 507 ("If in fact the plaintiff seeks to rely upon the grant of planning permission directly affecting the interest of the defendant and if that planning permission can be shown to have been made without authority, there does not appear to me to be any procedural requirement nor requirement of justice which would prevent the defendant from mounting successfully the challenge without adding the planning authority [...]").

[119] *Lancefort Ltd. v An Bord Pleanála*, unreported, High Court, Morris J., May 13, 1997; and *Murray v An Bord Pleanála* [2000] 1 I.R. 58.

[120] Ord.84, r.22(6). See also Ord.84, r.26(1).

[121] [1993] 1 I.R. 39 at 78; [1992] I.L.R.M. 237 at 268. See also at 68/258: "[...] they were accordingly given liberty to become a party, subject to the restriction that they should not be entitled to raise any additional ground of opposition to the plaintiff's claim which had not been raised by the defendants in the High Court." See also *TDI Metro Ltd. v Delap (No.1)* [2000] 4 I.R. 337; [2001] 1 I.L.R.M. 321.

"If application is made for liberty to issue proceedings for judicial review and the claim includes one for *certiorari* to quash the decision of a court or of an administrative decision-making authority the applicant must seek to add as a party any person whose rights would be affected by the avoidance of the decision impugned. If liberty is granted the court should except for special reasons ordinarily add such person as a party."

One obvious example of circumstances where it might be necessary to join an additional party would be where the applicant for planning permission is not the person intending to carry out the development; for example, because the property has since been sold on, or because the applicant for planning permission was never the full owner of the property. Certainly, if injunctive relief were to be sought, it would be necessary to join such a party in the proceedings.[122]   **11–102**

In *Monopower Ltd. v Monaghan County Council*,[123] the High Court had to consider two separate applications to be joined into judicial review proceedings. The proceedings involved a claim by the applicant that it was entitled to a default planning permission. The first application to be joined was made by a number of local residents. Herbert J. held that although these people might be indirectly affected if the default planning permission issued and the development was to proceed, the only party "directly affected" by the proceedings was the planning authority. The legal and factual issues arising in the proceedings were between the planning authority and the applicant for planning permission alone.   **11–103**

The second application to be joined was made by the Minister for the Environment Heritage and Local Government. The proceedings involved a collateral attack on the Regulations governing the environmental impact assessment of development projects with transboundary impacts. Somewhat surprisingly, Herbert J. ruled that the Minister was not a "person directly affected".   **11–104**

2. Mode of service

No particular mode of service is prescribed under ss.50 and 50A for the service of the notice of motion in respect of the application for leave. The more cautious approach would be to employ personal service; under Ord.9, r.16 of the Rules of Superior Courts, 1986, it is provided that Ord.9, so far as is practicable, shall apply to the originating documents in proceedings not commenced by summons and to notice in lieu of service. This would generally require the originating notice of motion to be served personally. (On one view, however, there are no proceedings in being until such time as leave to apply has been granted and thus it is arguable that Ord.9 is not necessarily applicable.)[124]   **11–105**

---

[122] See, for example, the facts of *Village Residents Association Ltd. v An Bord Pleanála (No. 3)* [2001] 1 I.R. 441.

[123] [2006] I.E.H.C. 253; unreported, Herbert J., July 10, 2006.

[124] *cf. O'Connell v Environmental Protection Agency* [2001] 4 I.R. 494; [2002] 1 I.L.R.M. 1.

11–106 An alternative mode of service is arguably provided for under s.250 of the PDA 2000. Section 250 states, *inter alia*, that where a notice is required or authorised under the PDA 2000 to be served on, or given to, a person it shall be addressed to him or her, and served in one of a number of ways prescribed under the section. These include leaving it at the address at which he or she ordinarily resides, or, where an address for service has been furnished, at that address. As the requirement that the application for leave to apply for judicial review be on notice derives solely from PDA 2000, and not from the Rules of the Superior Courts, it can be regarded as a notice within the meaning of s.250.[125]

11–107 Given the short time-limits involved, a practical approach to the issue of service would be to write to the various prescribed parties and request each to nominate a solicitor to accept service.[126] If a party failed to comply with such a request, this might be relied upon in an application to deem service good or to extend time.

11–108 An affidavit of service should be prepared, and filed in the Central Office of the High Court.

3. Deeming service good

11–109 An application to deem service good, or for substituted service, may be made pursuant to the provisions of Ord.9,[127] and Ord.10 of the Rules of the Superior Courts 1986, respectively. Given the importance attaching to time-limits under s.50, there is much to be said for making use of this procedure. The rules are silent as to whether the application to deem service good should be on notice or *ex parte*. The practice tends to be to move the application *ex parte*. This is consistent with the nature of the application, which generally only arises in circumstances where there was a difficulty in serving the initial documentation: it would be anomalous were the applicant to be required to attempt to serve the elusive party again, this time with motion papers.

---

[125] See *Lancefort Ltd. v An Bord Pleanála*, unreported, High Court, Morris J., May 13, 1997 (at p. 8), where Morris J. appears to have accepted that the equivalent provision under the Local Government (Planning & Development) Act 1963 (s.7) applied to the service of proceedings under that Act.

[126] Again, a lacuna in the Rules of the Superior Courts 1986: as there is no requirement to enter an appearance to judicial review proceedings, those rules governing an undertaking to enter an appearance are not applicable.

[127] *Lancefort Ltd. v An Bord Pleanála*, unreported, High Court, Morris J., May 13, 1997.

F. Application for Leave

1. Introduction

The application for leave to apply for judicial review under s.50A is quite **11–110** different from that in the case of conventional judicial review. As previously discussed, the application for leave is on notice to certain prescribed parties, and it is accepted practice that such parties are entitled to be heard on the application for leave,[128] and to file affidavits in reply. More importantly, however, the criteria by which the decision to grant or refuse leave is to be made are different. In conventional judicial review, five criteria were laid down by the Supreme Court in its decision in *G v Director of Public Prosecutions*,[129] only some of which are expressly derived from the provisions of Ord.84 of the Rules of the Superior Courts 1986. These may be summarised as follows: (a) that the applicant has a sufficient interest in the matter; (b) that the facts averred in the grounding affidavit, if proved, support a stateable ground for the form of relief sought; (c) that there is an arguable case in law on those facts; (d) that the application has been made promptly and in any event within the time-limits provided for under Ord.84, r.21; and (e) that judicial review is the only effective remedy, or, if there be an alternative remedy, that the application by way of judicial review is a more appropriate form of procedure.

The application for leave to apply under s.50A is, by contrast, regulated by an **11–111** embarrassment of statutory provisions. The first three of the criteria in *G v Director of Public Prosecutions* are replaced by the concepts of "substantial interest" and "substantial grounds". The fourth requirement has been modified: there is a statutory time-limit of eight weeks, with the possibility of extension, and there are conflicting signals as to whether the requirement under Ord.84 rule 21 to move promptly might survive, or if an applicant is always entitled to the full reach of the statutory eight week time-limit.[130] The time-limits have already been considered separately at paras 11–49 to 11–96, and nothing further need be said here. In connection with the fifth requirement it would seem that it still survives, and the adequacy of alternative remedies must be considered as part of the application for leave.[131] This requirement must, however, be read in conjunction with the provisions of ss.50(4) and (5); see further paras 11–328 to 11–347. It would also seem that the High Court may retain a non-

---

[128] See, by analogy, *Neville v An Bord Pleanála*, unreported, High Court, Ó Caoimh J., October 12, 2001, where the High Court rejected an argument that the parties were not entitled to be heard on an application for leave to appeal to the Supreme Court.

[129] [1994] 1 I.R. 374.

[130] *Lancefort Ltd. v An Bord Pleanála*, unreported, High Court, Morris J., May 13, 1997 (time-limit extends to midnight of the last day). *Cf. O'Connell v Environmental Protection Agency* [2001] 4 I.R. 494; [2002] 1 I.L.R.M. 1 (duty to move promptly survives).

[131] *Kennedy v South Dublin County Council* (1998) 5 I.P.E.L.J. 31; *Byrne v Wicklow County*, unreported, High Court, Keane J., November 3, 1994; and *Delgany Area Residents Association Ltd. v Wicklow County Council*, unreported, High Court, Barr J., May 28, 1998.

statutory discretion to refuse leave on the basis that judicial review is not an effective remedy, or not the most appropriate remedy.[132]

11–112 The criterion "substantial interest" appears to cede part of its natural territory to the criterion "substantial grounds". One of the reforms effected by the introduction of a test of "substantial grounds" under the previous legislation was to exclude an applicant from relying on a technical defect in the application for planning permission in circumstances where he or she was not prejudiced by same. O'Higgins J. put it in pithy terms: "The argument, in my view, is only available to somebody in the real world and not in the abstract".[133] Approached from first principles, this requirement might be thought to be an aspect of "substantial interest", whereas the case law in connection with the previous legislation appears to have treated it as part of the criterion "substantial grounds". As one of the objectives of a *locus standi* requirement, namely to exclude vexatious or meddlesome litigation, is achieved by the imposition of a requirement to demonstrate substantial grounds of challenge, it is arguable that the justification for a separate standing requirement falls away.[134] Insofar as EC law is concerned, Gordon suggests that to deny standing in a case that was less than clear would be to deprive the applicant of his right (at least ultimately) to have the legal merits of his case adjudicated upon by the ECJ, and that this would breach the principle of effectiveness.

2. Substantial grounds

11–113 Various definitions had been put forward in judgments under the previous legislation as to what the criterion "substantial grounds" entailed. For example, Egan J. put the test as follows in *Scott v An Bord Pleanála*.[135]

> "What meaning should be given to the word 'substantial'? [...] I fall back on a word which is so often used as a test in legal matters. It is the word 'reasonable' and I suggest, therefore, that the words 'substantial grounds' require that the grounds must be reasonable."

11–114 The definition most often cited is that of Carroll J. in *McNamara v An Bord Pleanála (No. 1)*,[136] which was subsequently approved by the Supreme Court.[137]

---

[132] *O'Brien v Tipperary South Riding County Council*, unreported, High Court, Ó Caoimh J., October 22, 2002.

[133] *Springview Management Co. Ltd. v Cavan Developments Ltd.* [2000] 1 I.L.R.M. 437 at 441. See also *Blessington & District Community Council Ltd. v Wicklow County Council* [1997] 1 I.R. 273. The effect of the introduction of a test of "substantial grounds" appears to have been to sweep away older cases such as *Electricity Supply Board v Gormley* [1985] I.R. 129; [1985] I.L.R.M. 494.

[134] R. Gordon, *EC Law in Judicial Review* (Oxford University Press, 2007), para.3.54.

[135] [1995] 1 I.L.R.M. 424 at 428.

[136] [1995] 2 I.L.R.M. 125 at 130.

[137] *In the matter of the Illegal Immigrants (Trafficking) Bill, 1999* [2000] 2 I.R. 360. See also *P v Minister for Justice Equality and Law Reform* [2002] 1 I.R. 164; [2002] 1 I.L.R.M. 16 (High Court, Smyth J.).

"What I have to consider is whether any of the grounds advanced by the appellant are substantial grounds for contending that the board's decision was invalid. In order for a ground to be substantial it must be reasonable, it must be arguable, it must be weighty. It must not be trivial or tenuous. However, I am not concerned with trying to ascertain what the eventual result would be. I believe I should go no further than satisfy myself that the grounds are 'substantial'. A ground that does not stand any chance of being sustained (for example, where the point has already been decided in another case) could not be said to be substantial. I draw a distinction between the grounds and the various arguments put forward in support of those grounds. I do not think I should evaluate each argument and say whether I consider it is sound or not. If I consider a ground, as such, to be substantial, I do not also have to say that the applicant is confined in his arguments at the next stage to those which I believe may have some merit."

The difficulty with these definitions is that little attempt has been made to analyse the function of the High Court at the leave stage, or to articulate how its function at the leave stage differs from that on the hearing of the substantive application for judicial review.[138] **11–115**

In the case of conventional judicial review, there is a clear distinction between the application for leave, and the substantive application. At the leave stage, the High Court is simply concerned that it should not permit proceedings which are not arguable to be pursued, but the High Court goes no further than that in the investigation it can make at that time; in particular, it is not appropriate or proper for it to express any view as to whether the case is strong or weak.[139] What is envisaged by the application for leave is a quick perusal of the material then available.[140] **11–116**

"The whole purpose of requiring that leave should first be obtained to make the application for judicial review would be defeated if the court were to go into the matter in any depth at that stage. If, on a quick perusal of the material then available, the court thinks that it discloses what might on further consideration turn out to be an arguable case in favour of granting to the applicant the relief claimed, it ought, in the exercise of a judicial discretion, to give him leave to apply for that relief. The discretion that the court is exercising at this stage is not the same as that which it is called upon to exercise when all the evidence is in and the matter has been fully argued at the hearing of the application."

In the case of ss.50 and 50A the distinction is less obvious. The High Court had indicated on a number of occasions that the statutory criterion of "substantial grounds" under the previous legislation demanded a more exacting standard than that of an arguable or stateable case.[141] Again, it is difficult to appreciate **11–117**

---

[138] See, generally, G. Simons, "Judicial review under the planning legislation – The case for the abolition of the leave stage" (2001) 8 I.P.E.L.J. 55.

[139] *O'Reilly v Cassidy* [1995] 1 I.L.R.M. 306 at 309.

[140] *R. v Inland Revenue Commissioners Ex p. National Federation of Self-Employed and Small Businesses Ltd.* [1982] A.C. 617 at 643-664 *per* Lord Diplock, cited with apparent approval by Denham J. in *G v Director of Public Prosecutions* [1994] 1 I.R. 374 at 382.

[141] *Byrne v Wicklow County Council*, unreported, High Court, Keane J., November 3, 1994; *Keane v An Bord Pleanála*, unreported, High Court, Murphy J., June 20, 1995 (at p. 21);

from the judgments just what the practical effect, if any, of the ratcheting up of the standard is. Indeed, it is perhaps ironic that the one specific example provided for in the formula in *McNamara v An Bord Pleanála (No. 1)*,[142] namely that the matter is not governed by precedent/authority, would not appear to be peculiar to s.50 but is, in fact, already encompassed in the conventional test of arguable or stateable case.

11–118 If one accepts that a higher standard is intended, this simply gives greater urgency to the question as to what then is the distinction between the function of the High Court at the leave stage, and that at the substantive hearing. It would appear that there has been a considerable narrowing of the gap between the leave stage and the substantive hearing, with the application for leave to apply for judicial review in respect of the planning legislation approximating more closely to that of the substantive hearing in conventional judicial review than to a leave application.

11–119 In order to maintain the façade of some qualitative distinction between the two hearings, the High Court has had to resort to ingenuity. In *Kenny v An Bord Pleanála (No. 1)*,[143] McKechnie J. stated that some difference in approach between an application for leave on notice, and one made *ex parte*, may be justified, and that whereas the High Court should not attempt to resolve conflicts of fact on an application for leave, nonetheless within the existing limitations an evaluation of the factual matrix should be made. McKechnie J. also stated that, at the leave stage, the High Court should, where with certainty it could, form some view of the appropriate statutory provisions and the relevant and material case law. With respect, such an approach, while involving a formalistic acknowledgement of the narrow function of the High Court on the leave application, brings the High Court at the leave stage tantalizingly close to a final determination.[144] There is an unreality in expecting the High Court at the leave stage to examine the merits of the case in considerable detail, but to refrain from progressing to a final determination at that time.

11–120 A more forthright approach to the nature of the leave application was taken by the High Court in the context of the special judicial review procedure under the Illegal Immigrants (Trafficking) Act 2000 (which is similar to that under the planning legislation). Smyth J., in the decision of *P v Minister for Justice*

Jackson Way Properties Ltd. v Minster for the Environment, unreported, High Court, Geoghegan J., July 2, 1999 (at p. 3) ("stricter criteria"); *Kenny v An Bord Pleanála (No. 1)* [2001] 1 I.R. 565 at 572 ("different and higher threshold"); and *de Faoite v An Bord Pleanála*, unreported, High Court, Laffoy J., May 2, 2000 (at p. 4) ("higher threshold"). See also *O'Brien v Dun Laoghaire Rathdown County Council* [2006] I.E.H.C. 177; unreported, O'Neill J., June 1, 2006 ("substantial" equated with a "reasonable chance of success").

[142] [1995] 2 I.L.R.M. 125.

[143] [2001] 1 I.R. 565.

[144] The temptation to proceed to a final determination exists even in respect of conventional judicial review; see *Keane v An Bord Pleanála*, unreported, High Court, Murphy J., June 20, 1995.

Equality and Law Reform,[145] indicated that it is appropriate on the leave stage to consider the prospects of success, and to grant leave only if satisfied that the applicant's case is not merely arguable but is strong; that is to say, is likely to succeed.[146]

The difficulties which arise as a result of the collapse of the distinction between **11–121** the leave stage and the substantive hearing can readily be illustrated by reference to the application of the principles established in *O'Keeffe v An Bord Pleanála*.[147] The Supreme Court decision in that case, in brief, had indicated that in order to succeed in a challenge to a planning decision on its merits, an applicant must overcome the almost insurmountable hurdle of demonstrating that the planning decision was unreasonable or irrational. Strictly speaking, it should only be necessary, at the leave stage, for an applicant to demonstrate that there are substantial grounds for arguing that the decision was unreasonable or irrational. In practice, however, leave to apply for judicial review on the grounds of unreasonableness or irrationality has been refused at the leave stage.[148] It is submitted that this is unfair in circumstances where an applicant has not had the benefit of the procedural weapons of discovery; cross-examination; or interrogatories. The failure of either An Bord Pleanála or a planning authority to provide a proper statement of reasons can, on occasion, frustrate an applicant's right to invoke the supervisory jurisdiction of the High Court, especially in terms of establishing an allegation of unreasonableness.[149]

The approach to be taken on the leave stage as to issue of facts, and, in particular, where the facts are disputed.

In the case of conventional judicial review, insofar as facts are concerned, the **11–122** High Court at the leave stage must simply be satisfied that the facts averred in the grounding affidavit would be sufficient, if proved, to support a stateable ground for the form of relief sought by way of judicial review.[150] As the application for leave under ss.50 and 50A is on notice to various parties, however, there is a real possibility that the High Court will be confronted with a conflict on the facts. This presents the following conundrum. If the special procedure for the leave application is to have any teeth, it would appear necessary that the High Court be in a position to refuse leave in cases where notwithstanding the (theoretical) merits of the legal arguments, those arguments

---

[145] [2002] 1 I.L.R.M. 16 (High Court, Smyth J.). The Supreme Court, on appeal, did not find it necessary to determine this issue: [2002] 1 I.R. 164.

[146] Following the judgment in *Gorman v Minister for the Environment (No. 1)* [2001] 1 I.R. 306, citing with approval the views of Glidewell L.J. in *Mass Energy Ltd. v Birmingham City Council* [1994] Env L.R. 298 at 307–308.

[147] [1993] 1 I.R. 39; [1992] I.L.R.M. 237.

[148] See, for example, *Village Residents Association Ltd. v An Bord Pleanála (No. 1)* [2000] 1 I.R. 65; [2000] 2 I.L.R.M. 59. See also *Irish Cement Ltd. v An Bord Pleanála*, unreported, High Court, McCracken J., February 24, 1998.

[149] See, by analogy, *State (Creedon) v Criminal Injuries Compensation Tribunal* [1988] I.R. 51 at 55; and *International Fishing Vessels Ltd. v Minister for Marine* [1989] I.R. 149.

[150] *G v Director of Public Prosecutions* [1994] 1 I.R. 374 at 378.

do not arise on the facts. This may necessitate the High Court embarking on a detailed inquiry at the leave stage; this may prolong the leave application to the extent that it matches the time required for a full hearing, and would also appear to run counter to the general reluctance of the courts to determine issues of fact or law on an interlocutory hearing.[151] The High Court is thus faced with the dilemma of performing an attenuated review of the facts at the leave stage, for reasons of expedition, or engaging in a time-consuming exercise.

11–123   The decision in *Village Residents Association Ltd. v An Bord Pleanála (No. 1)*[152] provides some support for the proposition that the High Court should not attempt at the leave stage to resolve factual disputes but, instead, the same test as applies to legal arguments, namely substantial grounds, should be applied to the factual contentions put forward by the applicant. To put the matter another way, an applicant does not have to prove facts definitively at the leave stage; the court must simply satisfy itself that the facts averred in the grounding affidavit would be sufficient, if proved, to support a stateable ground for the form of relief sought by way of judicial review. In *Village Residents Association Ltd. v An Bord Pleanála*, the applicant wished to argue that An Bord Pleanála had a special or additional duty to give reasons in circumstances where planning permission was granted in material contravention of the development plan.[153] In order to expose this legal argument, it would first be necessary for the applicant to establish that there had, in fact, been a material contravention. Geoghegan J. did not seek to determine this factual issue at the leave stage. Ultimately, the case was disposed of shortly on the basis that the applicant could not establish such a material contravention.[154]

11–124   Conversely, the decision in *Byrne v Wicklow County Council*[155] suggests that factual disputes are unlikely to occur in the context of judicial review proceedings wherein the debate will ordinarily centre on legal issues. Accordingly, it might be thought appropriate for the High Court to determine at the leave stage whether or not all facts necessary for the applicant's case to succeed have been established/proved.[156]

11–125   As a matter of practice, An Bord Pleanála, in proceedings in which it is the respondent, generally tends not to put in affidavit evidence at the leave stage. The High Court is, in effect, invited to take the applicant's case at its height for the purposes of determining whether or not to grant leave. In this regard, an analogy might be drawn with the case law on applications to strike out plenary proceedings on the basis that same are frivolous or vexatious, or disclose no cause of action. In the latter type of application, the High Court assumes for

---

[151] See, for example, *Village Residents Ltd. v An Bord Pleanála (No. 2)* [2000] 4 I.R. 321; [2001] 2 I.L.R.M. 22.
[152] [2000] 1 I.R. 65; [2000] 2 I.L.R.M. 59.
[153] See now PDA 2000, s.37(2).
[154] *Village Residents Association Ltd. v An Bord Pleanála (No. 3)* [2001] 1 I.R. 441.
[155] Unreported, High Court, Keane J., November 3, 1994.
[156] *cf. Kenny v An Bord Pleanála (No. 1)* [2001] 1 I.R. 565.

the purpose of the application that the plaintiff will be in a position to prove the facts pleaded in the statement of claim. Were such an approach to be adopted universally in the context of applications for leave under ss.50 and 50A, it would certainly have the virtue of expedition. Whether such a pragmatic solution could be reconciled with the apparent objective of ss.50 and 50A to introduce a more rigorous screening of applications for leave than obtains in respect of conventional judicial review procedure, is not certain, however.[157]

G. Substantial Interest

1. Introduction

Under the statutory judicial review procedure, an applicant is required to have **11–126** a "substantial interest" in the matter which is the subject of the judicial review application. This standard is different from that applicable in conventional judicial review proceedings, where an applicant is required under Ord.84, r.20(4) merely to demonstrate a "sufficient interest". The "substantial interest" requirement was first introduced under the PDA 2000, and continues as part of the amended procedure provided for under the Planning and Development (Strategic Infrastructure) Act 2006.[158]

There is a potential clash between the "substantial interest" requirement and **11–127** the terms of Art.10a of the amended EC Directive on environmental impact assessment ("the EIA Directive"). Article 10a only permits Member States to require an applicant to demonstrate a "sufficient interest". National law continues to recognise the concept of "sufficient interest", yet insists on a higher standard, *i.e.* that of "substantial interest", in the context of proceedings challenging decisions or acts under the planning legislation, including decisions and acts subject to the public participation provisions of the Directive. It should be noted that the difficulty in this regard will only apply to judicial review proceedings alleging a breach of the EIA Directive. This entire issue is discussed in detail at paras 13–352 to 13–358, and the balance of the present chapter is confined to the interpretation of the requirement as a matter of national law.

To the extent that the legislature chose to use different language under s.50A, **11–128**

---

[157] It appears from the decision in *O'Donnell v Dun Laoghaire Corporation* [1991] I.L.R.M. 301, that Costello J. considered an application to strike out under Ord.19 as the obverse of an application for leave to apply for conventional judicial review. If the provisions of the former s.82(3A) & (3B) of the Local Government (Planning & Development) Act 1963 (as amended), and of the PDA 2000, ss.50 and 50A, were intended to introduce a higher threshold for the grant of leave, then it would seem that the comparison with an application under Ord.19 can no longer hold good. Accordingly, the protocol whereby facts are assumed to be true must also fall. This may, however, be to attach too much significance to a decision that did not itself consider this issue.

[158] PDA 2000, s.50A(3)(b) as inserted by the Planning and Development (Strategic Infrastructure) Act 2006, s.13. The separate statutory requirement for prior participation was removed as part of the 2006 reforms. See further para.11–165.

it is to be assumed that the criterion of "substantial interest" was intended to introduce a different standard than that of "sufficient interest" under Ord.84.[159] Other than stating that a substantial interest is not limited to an interest in land or other financial interest,[160] however, the draftsman gives no indication as to what this new standard might involve. Notwithstanding this lack of direction from the legislature, the High Court, in a number of cases under the unamended s.50, had taken a very restrictive approach to the interpretation of "substantial interest".[161] Before turning to a detailed consideration of the case law in this regard, it is necessary to put the "substantial interest" requirement into context by describing briefly the previous law in relation to *locus standi*.

2. The previous requirement: "sufficient interest"

11–129 Judicial review is a public law remedy, and, traditionally, the courts had adopted a generous approach to *locus standi*. There is a public interest in upholding the rule of law,[162] and, for this reason, it was not always necessary for an applicant to demonstrate that he or she had been personally affected by an impugned administrative act or decision. A very recent example of this is provided by the judgment of the Supreme Court in *Mulcreevy v Minister for the Environment Heritage and Local Government*.[163] The case concerned a challenge to certain consents given under the national monuments legislation. The State respondents argued, unsuccessfully, that the applicant did not have the requisite interest to maintain the proceedings. The Supreme Court, *per* Keane C.J., rejected the argument in the following terms.

> "It has been made clear in decisions of the High Court and this court in recent times that it is not in the public interest that decisions by statutory bodies which are of at least questionable validity should wholly escape scrutiny because the person who seeks to invoke the jurisdiction of the court by way of judicial review cannot show that he is personally affected, in some sense peculiar to him, by the decision. It is in that sense, I think, that the requirement in O. 84, r. 20(4) of the Rules of the Superior Courts 1986 should be read."

11–130 The risk that such a generous approach to standing might be open to abuse was off-set by the discretionary nature of the judicial review remedies. The courts enjoyed a wide discretion to refuse relief where the application was brought by a stranger.[164]

---

[159] *Harrington v An Bord Pleanála (No. 1)* [2005] I.E.H.C. 344; [2006] 1 I.R. 388 ("a clearly more onerous test"); and *Friends of the Curragh Environment Ltd. v An Bord Pleanála (No. 2)* [2006] I.E.H.C. 390; [2007] 1 I.L.R.M. 386 (a "greater interest" required).

[160] PDA 2000, s.50A(4) as inserted by the Planning and Development (Strategic Infrastructure) Act 2006, s.13.

[161] These cases are discussed at paras 11-138 to 11-154.

[162] *Attorney General (Martin) v Dublin Corporation*, unreported, High Court, February 12, 1979 ("Under our constitution it is as much the duty of the State to render justice against itself in favour of citizens as it is to administer the same between private individuals.").

[163] [2004] 1 I.R. 72 at 78; [2004] 1 I.L.R.M. 419.

[164] This distinction between *locus standi* and the court's entitlement to refuse relief as a

The public interest in upholding the rule of law was recognised as being **11–131** particularly strong where planning and environmental decisions were concerned.[165] This particular public interest, which had previously been adverted to in litigation under the planning legislation, had evolved into a more concrete concept with judgments such as that of Denham J. in *Lancefort Ltd. v An Bord Pleanála*,[166] or of O'Higgins J. in *Springview Management Company Ltd. v Cavan Developments Ltd.*[167] An analogy was drawn with constitutional cases, where the courts had also accepted a move from victim related standing to one of public interest. Denham J. stated that[168]:

> "Environmental issues by their very nature affect the community as a whole in a way a breach of an individual personal right does not. Thus the public interest element must carry some weight in considering the circumstances of environmental law cases and the *locus standi* of its parties."

Although the concept had initially been put forward as part of an analysis of **11–132** the *locus standi* of limited liability companies, it was soon extended to personal litigants with the decision in *Murphy v Wicklow County Council*[169] in respect of road development at the Glen of the Downs. Kearns J. held that the applicant in that case had demonstrated a genuine interest in the matter, and was in a position to present expert evidence on a range of points, all of which were pertinent to the "huge stake" the public at large had in relation to the proper and lawful management of the Glen of the Downs.

There is even an argument to be made that in certain cases a public interest **11–133** litigant has a stronger claim to standing than a neighbour or other individual more directly affected.[170] A public interest litigant may be in a position to

---

matter of discretion where the applicant for relief had no real interest in the proceedings, and was not a person aggrieved by the decision, is emphasised in *State (Abenglen Properties Ltd.) v An Bord Pleanála* [1984] I.R. 381 at 393; [1982] I.L.R.M. 590 at 597, per O'Higgins C.J. See also *dicta* of Fennelly J. in *de Róiste v Minister for Defence* [2001] 1 I.R. 190 at 220; [2001] 2 I.L.R.M. 241 at 270. This distinction was not strictly observed by the majority of the Supreme Court in *Lancefort Ltd. v An Bord Pleanála* [1999] 2 I.R. 270; [1998] 2 I.L.R.M. 401; see G. Simons, "Lancefort Ltd. v An Bord Pleanála" (1998) 5 I.P.E.L.J. 131.

[165] *Attorney General (McGarry) v Sligo County Council* [1991] 1 I.R. 99 (doubted whether necessary for plaintiffs to seek fiat of Attorney General to bring proceedings challenging local authority development); *Murphy v Wicklow County Council*, unreported, High Court, Kearns J., March 19, 1999 (public interest in Glen of the Downs); and *Village Residents Association Ltd. v An Bord Pleanála (No. 1)* [2000] 1 I.R. 65; [2000] 2 I.L.R.M. 59 ("Planning is a matter of great public importance and it is not just of interest to the particular parties involved in a particular planning permission. A liberal view should therefore be taken to *locus standi*.").

[166] [1999] 2 I.R. 270; [1998] 2 I.L.R.M. 401. The judgment of Denham J. was a dissenting one. The majority decided the case on the narrow ground of the conduct of the (then future) promoters of the applicant company.

[167] [2000] 1 I.L.R.M. 437.

[168] *Lancefort Ltd. v An Bord Pleanála* [1999] 2 I.R. 270 at 292; [1998] 2 I.L.R.M. 401 at 420.

[169] Unreported, High Court, Kearns J., March 19, 1999.

[170] *R. v Inspectorate of Pollution Ex p. Greenpeace Ltd. (No. 2)* [1994] 4 All E.R. 329.

mount a more carefully selected, focused, relevant and well-argued challenge than a private litigant.[171] One of the objectives of a standing requirement is to avoid the crank litigant: it would seem to follow from this that the quality of presentation which a litigant is able to bring to a case should be a relevant factor in determining standing.[172] An analogy can be drawn with constitutional challenges: it appears that the inability, for pragmatic reasons, of suitably qualified plaintiffs to take an action may allow other less directly affected plaintiffs to proceed.[173]

3. The new requirement: "substantial interest"

11–134   As appears from the foregoing discussion, prior to the introduction of the "substantial interest" requirement, judicial review proceedings which raised planning and environmental issues of general importance might be brought at the suit of any person with a *bona fide* interest in such matters. The leading cases concerned major development projects which were themselves of public interest, namely a landmark building in Dublin city centre and a controversial road development through the Glen of the Downs. Presumably, however, the concept was not necessarily confined to major developments, and even smaller developments could give rise to planning issues, or indeed legal issues, of public interest. For example, important issues of principle in relation to matters such as social and affordable housing or the rights of neighbours might arise in the case of even a modest housing development.

11–135   The right of a public spirited applicant to challenge planning decisions was so well established that it would require clear statutory language to uproot it. The better view is that the introduction of the "substantial interest" requirement did not achieve this result, and that the element of *actio popularis* survives the change in the standing requirement.

11–136   Some support for this proposition is to be found in the judgment in *Friends of the Curragh Environment Ltd. v An Bord Pleanála (No. 2)*.[174] Finlay Geoghegan J. suggested that in order to construe the "substantial interest" requirement in a manner consistent with the constitutional right of access to the courts, it was necessary to have regard to the principle stated in *Lancefort Ltd. v An Bord Pleanála*[175] that the adoption of unlawful practices by public bodies should not escape scrutiny by the courts because of an absence of indisputably qualified objectors. Finlay Geoghegan J. went on to indicate that this approach required

---

[171] *ibid.*
[172] *cf. Construction Industry Federation v Dublin City Council* [2005] 2 I.R. 496; [2005] 2 I.L.R.M. 256, where a representative body was held not to have *locus standi* on the basis that a challenge should more properly be brought by an individual member directly affected. This case is discussed at paras 11–201 to 11–202.
[173] *Iarnrod Éireann v Ireland* [1996] 3 I.R. 321; [1996] 2 I.L.R.M. 161.
[174] [2006] I.E.H.C. 390; [2007] 1 I.L.R.M. 386.
[175] [1999] 2 I.R. 270; [1998] 2 I.L.R.M. 401.

the court to have some regard to the grounds on which it was being sought to challenge the planning decision.

> "In practical terms, this seems to require the court to have some regard to the grounds on which the decision is challenged when deciding whether the applicant has satisfied the standing requirement of section 50(4)(b). The wording of the section so permits. What the applicant must have is a substantial interest in 'the matter which is the subject of the application'. In a judicial review application such as this, 'the matter which is the subject of the application' is the challenge to the validity of the decision on specified grounds."

Finlay Geoghegan J. accepted that a limited liability company which had **11–137** professed an interest in the environment and had participated in the appeal before An Bord Pleanála might, in principle, have *locus standi* to maintain judicial review proceedings. The company's standing would be restricted, however, to such grounds of challenge as arose out of the content of its appeal to An Bord Pleanála. The extent to which prior participation is required in order to establish *locus standi* is examined in more detail at para.11–164 and onwards. For the purposes of the present discussion, the significance of the judgment lies in the fact that the court was prepared to accept that a company might have standing—albeit limited to certain grounds—notwithstanding the fact that no proprietary interest of the company would be affected by the proposed development. (On the particular facts of the case, the High Court ultimately ruled that the company did not have standing.)

The approach in *Friends of the Curragh Environment Ltd. v An Bord Pleanála* **11–138** *(No. 2)* is to be contrasted with the much narrower approach to standing taken in a number of earlier judgments. The gist of these judgments is that, in order to have a substantial interest, an applicant must demonstrate that he or she will be affected by the proposed development in a way which is "peculiar or personal"[176] to him or herself. As discussed at paras 11–155 to 11–162, these judgments then go on to define what constitutes a personal interest in a very restrictive way.

This approach was first heralded by the judgment in *O'Shea v Kerry County* **11–139** *Council*.[177] The High Court ruled that the applicant had failed to establish a substantial interest because she had failed to show in what manner, if any, she would be personally affected by the proposed development. A general interest in upholding the rule of law was not enough.

---

[176] *O'Brien v Dun Laoghaire Rathdown County Council* [2006] I.E.H.C. 177; unreported, O'Neill J., June 1, 2006; and *Harding v Cork County Council (No. 2)* [2006] I.E.H.C. 295; unreported, Clarke J., October 12, 2006. This phrase appears to have been used for the first time in *Harrington v An Bord Pleanála (No. 1)* [2005] I.E.H.C. 344; [2006] 1 I.R. 388, [38]. The judgment in *Harrington*, however, turned on the narrow issue of prior participation and it was in this special context that the phrase was used. See further para.11–171 and onwards.

[177] [2003] 4 I.R. 143 at 160.

"I am satisfied that the fact that a member of the public may have an interest in seeing that the law is observed is not such as to amount to the existence of a 'substantial interest' within the terms of the section."

11–140 In *O'Brien v Dun Laoghaire Rathdown County Council*,[178] a distinction was drawn between an interest in planning matters, and an interest in the subject-matter of a particular planning application. O'Neill J. ruled that in order to have a "substantial interest" a person must have an interest in the outcome of the application for planning permission which is personal or peculiar to him or her. On this analysis, even a passionate interest in planning matters would not, in the judgment of the court, suffice to establish a substantial interest in the subject-matter of a particular application as required under s.50A(3).

11–141 The High Court in *O'Brien* rejected an argument that the applicant's membership of An Taisce gave her standing. An Taisce itself has a special status as a prescribed body and it would, in the view of the court, be nonsensical if persons who were members of An Taisce could assert a separate special status simply because of their membership.

11–142 Even more alarmingly, the judgment in *O'Brien* appears to suggest that the entitlement to assert standing on the basis of a public interest might depend on whether the applicant's objectives coincide with those of the planning authority, as expressed in its development plan. Ms O'Brien had expressed a deep concern for the preservation of protected structures in order to preserve the architectural and historical amenity of the area. The High Court noted that the development plan contemplated the demolition of older structures in certain circumstances, and then went on to say that the pursuit of an objective such as the preservation from demolition in all circumstances of these older structures would be inconsistent with the development plan and, in the court's view, could not be said to, alone, form the basis of a substantial interest.

11–143 In *Harding v Cork County Council (No. 2)*,[179] the High Court again ruled that an applicant was required to have an interest peculiar or personal to him or herself. Clarke J. then went on to consider in some detail the criteria by reference to which a person without a financial or property interest at stake may be said to have a substantial interest. The criteria identified by the court are discussed at paras 11–160 to 11–162. On the facts, Clarke J. ruled that the applicant had failed to make out a "substantial interest". The High Court subsequently granted the applicant leave to appeal to the Supreme Court, certifying a point of law in respect of the interpretation of "substantial interest".

11–144 If the approach adopted by the judgments discussed above is correct, then the introduction of the "substantial interest" requirement has brought about a radical change in the law. In particular, the public interest in ensuring that the rule of

---

[178] [2006] I.E.H.C. 177; unreported, O'Neill J., June 1, 2006.
[179] [2006] I.E.H.C. 295; unreported, Clarke J., October 12, 2006.

law is upheld will have been made subservient to the objective of achieving finality in planning matters. For example, if the judgment in *Harding v Cork County Council (No. 2)* is upheld by the Supreme Court, then proceedings which involve allegations of serious breaches of the statutory public consultation procedure will be shut out simply because the particular applicant was not able to establish that he was personally affected by the proposed development.[180]

It must be doubted as to whether the wording of s.50A is competent to bring about such a radical change in the law. Had the legislature wished to impose a requirement that an applicant be affected personally or peculiarly, then a formula such as "a person aggrieved" or "a person directly affected" should have been employed. There are relevant precedents for the use of both of these phrases. The right to challenge a compulsory purchase order under the Housing Act 1966 had been couched in terms of "a person aggrieved",[181] and that phrase had been employed in other contexts under the Town and Regional Planning Act 1934. The concept of persons "directly affected" is still in use in the context of conventional judicial review proceedings under Ord.84.[182] **11–145**

Rather than adopt one of these precedents, the legislature chose instead to employ the nebulous phrase "substantial interest", together with an express proviso that same is not limited to an interest in land or other financial interest. **11–146**

The case law to date is open to the criticism that the traditional rules of statutory interpretation have not been followed. There is a constitutional right of access to the courts[183] and, accordingly, any statutory provision—such as a standing requirement—which restricts access must be interpreted strictly. Moreover, the Supreme Court had indicated that the public interest in upholding the rule of law is something which should influence the interpretation of statutory provisions regulating *locus standi*.[184] **11–147**

---

[180] Similarly, in *Harrington v An Bord Pleanála (No. 1)* [2005] I.E.H.C. 344; [2006] 1 I.R. 388, proceedings, which the High Court subsequently accepted gave rise to serious and complex issues of law of general importance—see the ruling in relation to costs: [2006] I.E.H.C. 223; unreported, July 11, 2006—had been ruled inadmissible because the applicant was found not to have a substantial interest on account of his failure to raise certain points before An Bord Pleanála.

[181] Housing Act 1966, s.78. This procedure does not apply where the compulsory purchase order has been confirmed by An Bord Pleanála; PDA 2000, s.217(7).

[182] Ord.84, r.25. See, generally, *Monopower Ltd. v Monaghan County Council* [2006] I.E.H.C. 253; unreported, Herbert J., July 10, 2006.

[183] See, for example, *White v Dublin City Council* [2004] 1 I.R. 545; [2004] 2 I.L.R.M. 509, where the time-limit under the previous legislation was held to be unconstitutional because it undermined or compromised the constitutional right of access to the courts. See also, by analogy, *Clinton v An Bord Pleanála* [2006] I.E.S.C. 58; unreported, November 1, 2006 (any legislative attempt to limit either the right or the scope of the constitutionally conferred right of appeal from the High Court to the Supreme Court must be expressed in clear and unambiguous terms).

[184] See the cases discussed at paras 11–129 to 11–133, in particular, *Mulcreevy v Minister for the Environment Heritage and Local Government* [2004] 1 I.R. 72; [2004] 1 I.L.R.M. 419.

11–148   Rather than insist that any restriction on access to the courts be spelt out in express statutory language, some of the recent judgments—in particular that of *Harrington v An Bord Pleanála (No. 1)*[185]—suggest that a "rigorous approach" to standing is justified by reference to the underlying scheme of the statutory judicial review procedure. This suggestion is based, in large part, on the following passage in *Lancefort Ltd. v An Bord Pleanála.*[186]

> "In cases where *certiorari* is sought in respect of a decision by a planning authority on an application for a permission or a decision of the first respondent on any appeal, these considerations must be given even greater weight, having regard to the policy of the Oireachtas as reflected in s. 82(3A) and (3B) of the Local Government (Planning and Development) Act, 1963, as amended by s. 19(3) of the Local Government (Planning and Development) Act, 1992. In requiring, as they do, an applicant to institute such proceedings within a strict time limit of two months, and to establish 'substantial grounds' for contending that the decision in question is invalid before leave is granted and in severely restricting the right of appeal from the decision of the High Court to this Court, the Oireachtas has made plain its concern that, given the existence of an elaborate appeals procedure which can be invoked by any member of the public and the determination of the issues by an independent board of qualified persons, the judicial review procedure should not be availed of as a form of further appeal by persons who may well be dissatisfied with the ultimate decision, but whose rights to be heard have been fully protected by the legislation. The courts are bound in their decisions to have serious regard to that concern."

11–149   With respect, this passage does not support the meaning sought to be placed on it in subsequent judgments, and, in particular, does not provide a convincing basis for saying that "substantial interest" should be interpreted restrictively. First, the judgment in *Lancefort Ltd. v An Bord Pleanála* was directed to the narrow question of prior participation. The majority of the Supreme Court held that the applicant company did not have standing because of the failure to raise before An Bord Pleanála the legal objection on which the judicial review proceedings were subsequently grounded. The promoters of the company had had an opportunity to raise their concerns before An Bord Pleanála, but failed to do so. It is in this context, then, that the reference to objectors' rights to be heard having been "fully protected by the legislation" must be understood. The majority of the Supreme Court decided that the right to rely on a point in judicial review proceedings was contingent on that point having been raised previously before An Bord Pleanála.

11–150   The *non sequitur* which bedevils later judgments is to conclude from this that the statutory rights of participation are intended to be exhaustive, with the right to seek judicial review restricted to a limited category of persons. Such an inference simply does not follow from the judgment in *Lancefort Ltd. v An Bord Pleanála*. There is a world of difference between saying that a person who fails to participate fully in the planning process will, in effect, be estopped

---

[185] [2005] I.E.H.C. 344; [2006] 1 I.R. 388.
[186] [1999] 2 I.R. 270 at 309–310; [1998] 2 I.L.R.M. 401 at 434–435.

from raising his or her concerns for the first time before the High Court, and saying that a person who has participated does not have standing to enforce his rights. The planning legislation places great emphasis on the right of public participation, and if public participation is to be excluded at the level of judicial review, one would have expected that express language would have been used.

A second reason for saying that the judgment in *Lancefort Ltd. v An Bord Pleanála* does not justify a restrictive approach to standing is that its analysis of the underlying legislative policy is suspect. The statutory judicial review procedure is directed largely to regulating the *application for leave* to apply for judicial review, and has nothing at all to say in relation to the grounds upon which judicial review is available. The legislation makes it more difficult to obtain leave: there are strict time-limits; the application for leave must be on notice; and the applicant must establish "substantial grounds" of challenge. The only aspect of the procedure which is not confined to the leave stage is the regulation of the right of appeal to the Supreme Court: this applies both to the leave stage and to the determination by the High Court of a substantive application for judicial review.   **11–151**

Insofar as the legislative intent can be divined, therefore, it is limited to ensuring that cases are determined expeditiously. More cases will be weeded out at the leave stage than in the case of conventional judicial review. Whether leave is granted or not, most cases will conclude in the High Court, with an appeal to the Supreme Court only being allowed in exceptional cases. It is difficult to understand how any of this could assist in interpreting the *locus standi* requirement, still less justify a rigorous approach. The introduction of the phrase "substantial interest" is the only aspect of the procedure which addresses *locus standi* in any way, so it must stand or fall on its own terms.   **11–152**

At least some judges are uncomfortable with the possible consequences which a restrictive approach to standing may have. Somewhat paradoxically, therefore, some of the very judgments which endorse a restrictive approach to standing go on then to articulate a concern that a lack of standing should not prevent the courts from remedying a clear abuse of process, or a serious failure to apply the law correctly.[187] These judgments suggest that the courts retain a residual discretion to entertain an application for judicial review notwithstanding the absence of a "substantial interest" on the part of the particular applicant. This approach is difficult to square with the express wording of the legislation: it is the essence of any *locus standi* requirement that what would otherwise be a good case will fail because it has been brought by the wrong person.   **11–153**

A more satisfactory approach might be for the courts to accept that the question of standing cannot be divorced from the substantive merits of an application for judicial review, and that the more serious the illegality alleged in the judicial   **11–154**

---

[187] *Harrington v An Bord Pleanála (No. 1)* [2005] I.E.H.C. 344; [2006] 1 I.R. 388; and *O'Brien v Dun Laoghaire Rathdown County Council* [2006] I.E.H.C. 177; unreported, O'Neill J., June 1, 2006.

review proceedings, the more ready the court will be to hold that a particular applicant has standing. This would necessitate the courts reassessing what is involved in the statutory concept of "substantial interest". This would result in a more flexible standing requirement, and obviate the necessity of carving out an extra-statutory jurisdiction to entertain an application for judicial review notwithstanding the absence of standing on the part of the particular applicant.

4. Applicant directly affected by development

11–155 Traditionally, the courts had regarded a person directly affected by proposed development as indisputably having a "sufficient interest" to maintain challenges to planning decisions.[188] Thus, for example, in *Seery v An Bord Pleanála*,[189] it was readily accepted that a couple who lived adjacent to development the subject-matter of the impugned planning decision had standing.

> "In the present case I am satisfied that the facts which are not in dispute clearly establish the applicants as affected by the permission granted. Their dwelling immediately adjoins the proposed development and at all times they expressed a concern about the proximity of the houses on the proposed development to their own dwelling house. They have sufficient interest and accordingly, *locus standi*."

11–156 The legal position in this regard is not changed by the ratcheting of the standard from one of "sufficient interest" to "substantial interest", and an applicant who is able to show that he or she is directly affected by proposed development has a substantial interest,[190] and thus continues to have standing to challenge a decision to grant planning permission. As discussed at para.11-138 and onwards, a number of recent judgments have suggested that an applicant will *only* ever have a substantial interest where he or she is directly affected by the proposed development. These judgments go on then to take a very narrow view of the circumstances in which an applicant will be found to be directly affected.

11–157 In *O'Shea v Kerry County Council*, an applicant who lived adjacent to the proposed development and was the owner of lands over which there was a right of way giving access to the application site was held not to have a "substantial interest".[191]

---

[188] *Chambers v An Bord Pleanála* [1992] 1 I.R. 134; [1992] I.L.R.M. 296; *Blessington Heritage Trust Ltd. v Wicklow County Council* [1999] 4 I.R. 571 (court recognised interest of ordinary members of the public who reside in the environment which is vitally affected both by overall development plans and by individual planning decisions); *Seery v An Bord Pleanála*, unreported, High Court, Finnegan J., June 2, 2000; and *O'Connell v Environmental Protection Agency* [2001] 4 I.R. 494; [2002] 1 I.L.R.M. 1. See also *Electricity Supply Board v Gormley* [1985] I.R. 139; [1985] I.L.R.M. 494 (subsequent purchaser of lands held to have a special interest).
[189] Unreported, High Court, Finnegan J., June 2, 2000 (at p. 12). See also *O'Connell v Environmental Protection Agency* [2001] 4 I.R. 494; [2002] 1 I.L.R.M. 1.
[190] See, for example, *Ryanair Ltd. v An Bord Pleanála* [2004] 2 I.R. 334 at 360; and *O'Shea v Kerry County Council* [2003] 4 I.R. 143 at 160.
[191] [2003] 4 I.R. 143 at 160-161, *per* O'Caoimh J.

"The applicant has indicated that she is the owner of the land over which a right of way exists to the golf club. No particular point has been made by the applicant showing how she will be affected by the proposed development. She has confined herself to indicating that, had she been aware of the application for planning permission, she would have objected to same and would have appealed to An Bord Pleanála, had a decision been made in favour of the grant of planning permission and had she been aware of same. I am satisfied, however, that the applicant has failed to show in what manner, if any, she will be affected by the proposed development and, in this regard, I am satisfied that she has failed to show a substantial interest in the matter."

In *O'Brien v Dun Laoghaire Rathdown County Council*,[192] a neighbouring landowner, who lived within sight of the proposed development, was held not to have a "substantial interest" because, in the opinion of the court, the proposed development would not have any "significant detrimental effect" on visual amenity. It is submitted that the judgment goes too far, and that it is quite inappropriate that a person's standing should turn on whether or not the court considers the proposed development would have an adverse impact on that person's property. Once a person has demonstrated that his or her property is sufficiently proximate to the proposed development to be affected by it, he or she is entitled to insist that any decision to grant planning permission is reached in accordance with law, if necessary by bringing judicial review proceedings. The entitlement to seek judicial review should not be short-circuited simply because a judge of the High Court makes the subjective assessment that there will be no significant detrimental effect. **11–158**

In *Moriarty v South Dublin County Council*,[193] it was suggested *obiter* that a rival retail business might not have standing to challenge a planning permission in the absence of evidence of an impact on the company's business such as would give rise to a special interest. It is submitted that these *obiter dicta* should not be followed. Businesses have a legitimate interest in ensuring that their commercial rivals comply with the requirements of the planning legislation.[194] To impose a high evidential burden on such businesses seems inappropriate, and might well involve the High Court having to adjudicate on **11–159**

---

[192] [2006] I.E.H.C. 177; unreported, O'Neill J., June 1, 2006.
[193] [2006] I.E.H.C. 109; unreported, Hanna J., November 24, 2005. See also *Ryanair Ltd. v An Bord Pleanála* [2004] 2 I.R. 334 at 360 (the fact that Ryanair Ltd. was a user of Dublin airport did not in itself indicate that it had standing to challenge a planning permission in respect of the extension of the airport).
[194] *R. (On the application of Rockware Glass Ltd.) v Chester County Council* [2005] E.W.H.C. 2250; [2006] J.P.L. 699 (company in an industrial sector with substantial investment decisions to be made on capital works had sufficient interest to seek judicial review in order to ensure that competitors are subject to the same consistency of approach in respect of environmental matters). The Court of Appeal in *R. (On the application of the Noble Organisation Ltd.) v Thanet District Council* [2005] E.W.C.A. Civ. 782; [2006] 1 P. & C.R. 13; [2006] J.P.L. 60, *per* Auld L.J., expressed concern that the remedy of judicial review might be exploited as a commercial weapon by rival potential developers to frustrate and delay their competitors' approved developments, rather than for any demonstrated concern about potential environmental or other planning harm.

matters such as market impact, in circumstances where retail impact assessment is more properly a matter for the planning bodies.

11–160   The most sophisticated analysis of what comprises a "substantial interest" to date is to be found in *Harding v Cork County Council (No. 2)*.[195] Clarke J. suggested that the court, having identified the interest which an applicant has expressed (or might be taken to have been prevented from expressing), should identify the importance of the interest by reference to criteria such as: (a) the scale of the project and the extent to which the project might be said to give rise to a significant alteration in the amenity of the area concerned (the greater the scale and the more significant the alteration in the area, then the wider range of persons who may legitimately be able to establish a substantial interest); (b) the extent of the connection of the applicant concerned to the effects of the project by particular reference to the basis of the challenge which he puts forward to the planning permission and the planning process; and (c) such other factors as may arise on the facts of an individual case.

11–161   On the facts of *Harding*, Clarke J. concluded that the applicant did not have a substantial interest. The applicant had grown up in the area of the proposed development and retained family connections with the area; he lived at Kinsale, some two to three kilometres from the headland where the proposed development was to be carried out; and visited the area on a relatively regular basis. Clarke J. accepted that Mr Harding was more than a mere bystander and that he would have had a "sufficient interest" for the purpose of conventional judicial review proceedings. In the view of the court, however, the test of "substantial interest" required more than a familial connection with an area coupled with a pattern of visiting the area as a former native and as a seafaring person.

11–162   The approach in *Harding* seems unduly restrictive. As indicated earlier, it is expressly provided under s.50A(4) that a substantial interest is not limited to an interest in land or other financial interest. Thus, an interest less than a proprietary interest must, in some circumstances, qualify. The court had accepted that Mr Harding was more than a mere bystander, and it is difficult, therefore, to understand what additional factor—short of asserting a proprietary interest—would have brought Mr Harding into the category of persons with a substantial interest.

11–163   Finally, the judgment in *Cumann Thomas Daibhis v South Dublin County Council*[196] confirms that the requirement that an interest must be "peculiar or personal" to an applicant does not mean that if some other party has the same or similar interest in the subject-matter of the application that both are thereby excluded from having a "substantial" interest. O'Neill J. stated that, in his view, what the phrase "peculiar or personal" imports is that the proposed

---

[195] [2006] I.E.H.C. 295; unreported, Clarke J., October 12, 2006.
[196] [2007] I.E.H.C. 118; unreported, O'Neill J., March 30, 2007.

development the subject-matter of the application is one which affects the applicant personally or individually in a substantial way as distinct from any interest which the wider community, not so personally and individually affected, might have in the proposed development. Thus, as in the case of a housing estate many people might be affected substantially in this way and have a "substantial interest".

5. Prior participation in planning process

It had been suggested in some judgments decided prior to the coming into force of the 2006 Act that in order to have a "substantial interest" a person must have previously participated in the planning process.[197] Thus, or so it was said, even an applicant directly affected by a proposed development may be denied standing if he or she had failed to make submissions to the planning authority or An Bord Pleanála. An exception to this requirement applied where the non-participation was as the result of some breach of procedure during the decision-making process. **11–164**

There is no express statutory basis for such a prior participation requirement. This was not always the case, and under the unamended s.50 procedure the requirement to demonstrate a "substantial interest" had been supplemented by an additional requirement as to prior participation in the planning process. Specifically, the unamended s.50(4)(c) had provided that leave to apply for judicial review should not be granted unless the applicant showed to the satisfaction of the High Court either that the applicant had made objections, submissions or observations during the planning process or that "there were good and sufficient reasons" for not making such objections, submissions or observations. The statutory requirement in this regard was removed under the Planning and Development (Strategic Infrastructure) Act 2006. **11–165**

The legislative history in this regard—involving as it does the repeal of the previous statutory requirement—indicates that prior participation should no longer be a prerequisite to standing. Such a change in the law is also entirely understandable. One of the purposes of the amendments introduced under the 2006 Act was to give effect to the provisions of the amended EC environmental impact assessment Directive. A requirement for prior participation would give rise to a potential conflict with EC law, and, in particular, with the requirement that—where permitted to do so under national law—a national court must examine *of its own motion* whether the legislative or administrative authorities of the Member State remained within the limits of their discretion under the Directive.[198] The requirement for prior participation had been interpreted as **11–166**

---

[197] *Harrington v An Bord Pleanála (No. 1)* [2005] I.E.H.C. 344; [2006] 1 I.R. 388; and *Harding v Cork County Council (No. 2)* [2006] I.E.H.C. 295; unreported, Clarke J., October 12, 2006, [3.8].

[198] *Kraaijeveld* (Case C–72/95) [1996] E.C.R. I–5403. More generally, the case law of the ECJ suggests that a national court will be required to apply EC law of its own motion unless there is some countervailing reason not to do so. See *Peterbroeck* (Case C–312/

requiring not only that the individual not only have participated in the planning process, but also that he or she have raised before the planning authority or An Bord Pleanála the point subsequently sought to be relied upon in the judicial review proceedings. The logical consequence of such a rule would, however, be that the court could not raise an issue as to compliance with the Directive if the parties had not done so previously, and hence the potential conflict with EC law.

11–167   Aside entirely from the fact that the express requirement for prior participation has now been repealed, it is difficult to understand how—applying the relevant rules of statutory interpretation—a requirement to demonstrate a "substantial interest" could ever be read as encompassing an additional requirement of prior participation. Even on the narrowest interpretation, a person directly affected by a proposed development has a "substantial interest" in the relevant planning decision. The impact of the proposed development is in no way lessened by the fact that the applicant may not have personally participated in the planning process, and thus his interest in the matter remains a substantial one. Reference is made in this regard to the judgment of the High Court of England and Wales in *R. (On the application of Edwards) v Environment Agency*.[199] There, it was held that a temporarily homeless local resident who had not participated in the statutory licensing procedures nevertheless had a "sufficient interest" to bring judicial review proceedings challenging a permit from the Environment Agency. Keith J. held that if the consultation exercise ends with a decision which affects a person's interests, that person is no less affected by that decision simply because he or she took no part in the exercise, but left it to others to do so. Keith J. indicated that a person should not be debarred from subsequently challenging the decision on the ground of inadequate consultation simply because he or she chose not to participate in the consultation exercise, provided that he or she is affected by its outcome.

---

93) [1995] E.C.R. I-4599 and *Van Schijndel and Van Veen* (Joined Cases C–430/93 and C–431/93) [1995] E.C.R. I–4705. The subject-matter of the Directive at issue is also relevant. Thus the ECJ has required national courts to set aside normal procedural rules where necessary to ensure consumer protection: see, for example, *Mostaza Claro v Centro Móvil Milenium SL* (Case C–168/05) October 26, 2006 (national court seised of an action for annulment of an arbitration award must determine whether the arbitration agreement is void and annul that award where that agreement contains an unfair term, even though the consumer had not pleaded that invalidity in the course of the arbitration proceedings). Advocate General Maduro summarised as follows in his opinion in *van der Weerd* (Joined Cases C–222/05, C–223/05, C–224/05 and C–225/05) June 7, 2006: "[…] the principle of effectiveness does not impose a duty on national courts to raise pleas based on Community law of their own motion, except in circumstances where this would be necessary in order to ensure that judicial protection is available where Community law confers a right. Therefore, national courts have a duty to intervene when it is necessary to guarantee the protection of rights granted by Community law. Yet, the principle of effectiveness does not entail a general duty for national courts to ensure, under all circumstances, the application of rules arising from the Community legal order.".

[199] [2004] E.W.H.C. 736 (Admin); [2004] 3 All E.R. 21; [2004] 2 P.& C.R. 370; [2004] J.P.L. 1691.

More generally, it is submitted that any failure on the part of an applicant for **11–168** judicial review to have participated in the planning process is something which goes to the court's discretion, and not to the question of *locus standi*. It has long been accepted that standing is something which must be capable of objective assessment and that there is, therefore, no question of a person being "granted" or "denied" *locus standi*. A person directly affected by a proposed development will always have standing to challenge the grant of planning permission; his conduct—including any failure to have participated previously—may, however, result in his being refused relief as a matter of discretion. The proper observation of this distinction between *locus standi* and discretion allows for a much more flexible approach. In some cases it may well be appropriate to refuse relief by reference to the conduct of the applicant. In other cases, however, the public interest—or the need to give effect to EC law—will dictate that the impugned decision be set aside in any event, irrespective of any shortcomings on the part of the applicant.

Finally in this regard, it is submitted that whereas a person directly affected by **11–169** a proposed development should not be denied standing on account of his or her failure to have participated in the planning process, the fact that a person not directly affected by the proposed development *did* participate may assist in establishing *locus standi*. A person who has availed of the statutory right to participate in the decision-making process should be entitled to complain to the High Court if there has been a procedural breach in the decision-making process. The right to participate must carry with it a correlative entitlement to enforce that right.[200]

Matters are complicated greatly, however, by the fact that it has been suggested **11–170** in a number of judgments that the concept of "substantial interest" carries with it an implicit requirement for prior participation. These judgments were decided under the unamended s.50, and thus may well have to be reconsidered in light of the subsequent legislative history and, in particular, the repeal of the express statutory requirement for prior participation. Indeed, it is very surprising that the High Court felt it necessary to deal with prior participation as an aspect of the "substantial interest" requirement at all, given that these cases were decided against a statutory background which included a separate and additional requirement for prior participation.

---

[200] See, by analogy, *Turner v Secretary of State for the Environment* (1973) 28 P. & C.R. 123, where it was suggested that any person who has attended and made representations at the inquiry should have the right to establish in the courts that the decision is bad in law because it is *ultra vires* or for some other good reason. The statutory requirement was that the person be a "person aggrieved". See also *Eco-Energy (GB) Ltd. v First Secretary of State* [2004] E.W.C.A. Civ. 1566; [2005] 2 P. & C.R. 5 (someone who took a sufficiently active role in the planning process, *i.e.* a substantial objector, not just somebody who objected and did no more about it, qualifies as a "person aggrieved"). See commentary at [2005] J.P.L. 554.

11–171   The first judgment is that of *Harrington v An Bord Pleanála (No. 1)*.[201] Macken J. indicated that an applicant for judicial review could only have a "substantial interest" in a matter which he had previously expressed in the course of the planning process as being peculiar or personal to him.[202]

> "It is difficult in logic to see how a ground which the applicant for leave has never, up until now, and certainly not during the course of the appeal, expressed himself to have any interest in, can thereupon form the basis for the applicant's 'substantial interest in the subject matter of the application' at the leave stage, provided it could have been raised by him during that appeal. Here it could certainly have been, but was not. In that regard, I note that the applicant has not given any indication to the court why the concerns which he now wishes to raise were nevertheless not raised by him in the course of the appeal procedure."

11–172   In reaching this conclusion, Macken J. relied upon the judgment of the Supreme Court in *Lancefort Ltd. v An Bord Pleanála*,[203] wherein it was indicated that failure to raise a ground of objection before the relevant planning body might preclude an applicant from relying on such a ground in subsequent judicial review proceedings.[204] *Lancefort Ltd.* had been decided prior to the PDA 2000, and thus the standing requirement at issue was that of "sufficient interest" under Ord.84, rule 20(4).

11–173   On the particular facts of *Harrington v An Bord Pleanála (No. 1)*, similar issues to those sought to be relied upon by Mr Harrington in the judicial review proceedings had been raised before An Bord Pleanála by another party, but not by Mr Harrington himself. Macken J. nevertheless ruled that Mr Harrington did not have standing, holding that an applicant will not, as a general rule, be entitled to invoke grounds not raised by him merely because the same, or substantially the same, grounds were presented by a third party during the course of the appeal procedure.[205]

11–174   Macken J. went on, however, to qualify this ruling by indicating that, notwithstanding the fact that a particular applicant had failed to satisfy the court that he had the requisite substantial interest, the court should not be precluded from scrutinising a (serious) failure to properly apply the law.

---

[201] [2005] I.E.H.C. 344; [2006] 1 I.R. 388.

[202] *ibid.*, [39].

[203] [1999] 2 I.R. 270; [1998] 2 I.L.R.M. 401.

[204] See also *Murphy v Wicklow County Council*, unreported, High Court, Kearns J., March 19, 1999. Kearns J. ruled that the applicant did not have *locus standi* in respect of one particular ground of challenge, namely the adequacy of an environmental impact statement, for reasons including the fact that the applicant had not participated in the statutory procedure.

[205] The approach in *Harrington* is to be contrasted with that of the High Court of England and Wales in *R. (On the application of Kides) v South Cambridgeshire District Council* [2001] E.W.H.C. Admin. 839, [108]; [2003] 1 P. & C.R. 4, where it was suggested that once standing exists in relation to the impugned decision, it would be rather exceptional for a specific ground to constitute mere meddling; such a point is more likely fairly to be dealt with as a matter of discretion.

Accordingly, the court should go on to consider whether or not there were "substantial grounds" for contending that An Bord Pleanála's decision was invalid.

This latter aspect of the judgment is hard to reconcile with the statutory language. It appears that the requirement to demonstrate a "substantial interest" is a mandatory one, and that the court has no discretion to allow an unqualified applicant to proceed. The essence of any standing requirement is that an otherwise good case will be defeated because the particular applicant lacks the necessary standing; to suggest that, if the merits of the case are strong, the standing requirement can be overlooked ignores this reality. A more satisfactory approach would have been for the court to observe the distinction which existed under the then legislation between "substantial interest" and the separate statutory requirement of prior participation. The latter requirement was subject to an express exception and, accordingly, could have provided a route out of the difficulty.   **11–175**

The judgment in *Harrington v An Bord Pleanála (No. 1)* was cited with approval in *Harding v Cork County Council (No. 2)*.[206] Again, it was suggested by the High Court that a requirement for prior participation is inherent in the concept of "substantial interest", and that an applicant for judicial review must have previously asserted his or her interest in the context of the planning process (either expressly or by implication as deriving from the case he or she makes). An exception to this requirement was said to apply where the non-participation was caused by a breach of proper process in the planning application.   **11–176**

The necessity for prior participation was also discussed in *Friends of the Curragh Environment Ltd. v An Bord Pleanála (No. 2)*.[207] The facts of that case were somewhat unusual, however, in that the applicant company staked its claim for standing, not on any alleged impact on property owned by it, but primarily by reference to its participation in the planning process and as a party to an appeal before An Bord Pleanála. Finlay Geoghegan J. held that in the circumstances the question of "substantial interest" fell to be determined by reference primarily to the interest asserted by the applicant company in its appeal—whether expressly or by implication from the nature of the appeal— and the connection between that and the grounds on which the company sought to challenge the validity of the decision.   **11–177**

As indicated above, the approach suggested by these judgments may have to be reconsidered in light of the amendments introduced under the Planning and Development (Strategic Infrastructure) Act 2006. For the sake of completeness, it is proposed to examine briefly below how any prior participation requirement which survives might operate in practice.   **11–178**

---

[206] [2006] I.E.H.C. 295; unreported, Clarke J., October 12, 2006.
[207] [2006] I.E.H.C. 390; [2007] 1 I.L.R.M. 386.

6. Extent of prior participation

11–179   The principal justification for the imposition of a requirement for prior participation is to ensure that issues of concern are raised during the administrative stage of the decision-making process, rather than raised for the first time in judicial review proceedings. If issues of concern are raised at an early stage, then it may be possible for the planning authority or An Bord Pleanála to take corrective measures, and thus to avoid any necessity for recourse to the High Court. An obvious example is provided by the facts of *Lancefort Ltd. v An Bord Pleanála.*[208] A grant of planning permission was challenged on the basis that the proposed development should have been subjected to environmental impact assessment. This point was not raised before An Bord Pleanála, however, notwithstanding the fact that An Bord Pleanála had power to call for the submission of an environmental impact statement even where the planning authority had failed to do so, and thus could have remedied any defect. In the circumstances, a majority of the Supreme Court ruled that the applicant did not have standing to raise the issue for the first time in judicial review proceedings. Keane J. suggested that it would be a significant injustice to a party in the position of the notice party developer to be asked to defend proceedings on the ground of an alleged irregularity which could have been brought to the attention of all concerned at any time prior to the granting of permission, but which was not relied on until the application was made for leave to bring the proceedings.

11–180   A further example is provided by *Ryanair Ltd. v An Bord Pleanála.*[209] This case was decided under the unamended s.50, which it will be recalled involved an express statutory requirement for prior participation. On the facts, Ó Caoimh J. held that the failure of the applicant to raise an objection to a particular aspect of the proposed development precluded it from complaining in judicial review proceedings as to how that aspect had been dealt with in the decision of An Bord Pleanála.

> "In the instant case it is clear that the applicant could have raised at the appeal stage certain of its concerns relating to the new pier itself which it did not raise until the bringing of this application. In this regard I refer to its failure to address the proposal for bridges on the southern side of the new pier. Insofar as that is the situation I am satisfied that to that extent also it lacks the necessary *locus standi* and cannot show that it has a 'substantial interest.'"

11–181   Again, the underlying rationale seems to have been that had the particular planning concern been raised before An Bord Pleanála, the board would have then had an opportunity to address the issue as necessary.

11–182   Certain defects, of course, will not come to light until after the planning decision has been made; and thus the applicant for judicial review cannot be expected

---

[208] [1999] 2 I.R. 270; [1998] 2 I.L.R.M. 401.
[209] [2004] 2 I.R. 334.

to have raised the issue in advance. An obvious example is in relation to the adequacy of the statement of the main reasons and considerations for the decision: these will not be published until after the decision is made. In other instances, a procedural error will only be discovered once the file has been made available for inspection upon the conclusion of the decision-making process.

The judgment in *Friends of the Curragh Environment Ltd. v An Bord Pleanála (No.2)*[210] appears to suggest that where an error is disclosed in the decision of the planning authority at first instance, an applicant should raise that issue with An Bord Pleanála, lest the board replicate the error. The applicant had sought to challenge the validity of certain conditions attached to the grant of planning permission. The appeal submitted by the applicant to An Bord Pleanála had not, however, made any submission as to the type of planning conditions which it might be permissible or impermissible to impose, notwithstanding the fact that the planning authority, in its decision of first instance, had included conditions of the very type sought to be criticised in the judicial review proceedings. Nor did the appeal contain any submission of substance in relation to those aspects of the development—such as archaeology—to which the impugned conditions related. In the circumstances, Finlay Geoghegan J. held that the company did not have standing to pursue this issue. **11–183**

An interesting question arises as to the extent to which an applicant for judicial review can rely on the prior participation of others in order to ground an application for judicial review. Two particular scenarios come to mind. First, where the applicant for judicial review did not personally participate in the planning process, but persons with whom he or she is associated did. Secondly, where the applicant did participate, but failed to raise the specific point sought to be argued in the judicial review proceedings, and seeks to rely instead on the fact that the point was raised by other parties to the process. **11–184**

In the first case, the applicant probably will have standing. The courts have recognised that it would be unwieldy were each and every individual objector required to make his or her own submission to the relevant planning body, and that it is reasonable to allow general representations to be made instead. Thus, for example, in *Chambers v An Bord Pleanála*,[211] Egan J. stated that it was readily understandable why, in circumstances where there were nineteen appellants, the applicants had left it to a representative body to deal with the appeal. This reasoning would seem to apply *a fortiori* to circumstances where individual objectors subsequently associate through the medium of a limited liability company for the purpose of pursuing a legal challenge.[212] The company, **11–185**

[210] [2006] I.E.H.C. 390; [2007] 1 I.L.R.M. 386.
[211] [1992] 1 I.R. 134 at 143.
[212] See, by analogy, *Chambers v An Bord Pleanála* [1992] 1 I.R. 134; [1992] I.L.R.M. 296. See also *Village Residents Association Ltd. v An Bord Pleanála (No. 1)* [2000] 1 I.R. 65 at 72; [2000] 2 I.L.R.M. 59 at 66 ("it would be unwieldy and unwise to try and mount litigation in the name of or on behalf of an unincorporated association.").

as applicant in judicial review proceedings, should be allowed point to the previous participation of its (then future) promoters in order to establish standing.[213] The position in relation to security for costs is considered separately at paras 11–313 to 11–322.

11–186 The situation where an applicant seeks to rely on submissions made by other parties to the process, with whom he or she is not associated, is more problematic. The judgment in *Harrington v An Bord Pleanála (No. 1)*—decided under the unamended legislation with its express requirement for prior participation—suggests that the applicant for judicial review must have personally raised the point sought to be relied upon in the judicial review proceedings.[214]

> "If it were the correct interpretation of Section 50 that any person who was a party to a planning appeal, who, while not raising a specific issue himself on that appeal, could nevertheless raise any number of issues raised by other parties, but abandoned by them on the decision being made by The Board, there would be in effect, an 'open season' on such appeals."

11–187 Macken J. concluded that this could not have been the intention of the Oireachtas, and, accordingly, that the applicant was not entitled to invoke grounds not raised by him merely because the same or substantially the same grounds had been raised by other parties in the course of the appeal before An Bord Pleanála.

11–188 It is respectfully submitted that no convincing reason is put forward as to why this should be the case. Whereas it is certainly conducive to good administration to require objectors to raise legal issues at as early a stage as possible—with a view to their being resolved by the statutory decision-makers—it is difficult to understand why the *identity* of the person raising the point should be critical. This is especially so where the case gave rise to issues of EC law, and, arguably, the court was not entitled to rely on a procedural rule to shut out consideration of these issues, but required to consider them of its own motion. As it happens, the court did go on to consider these matters on the basis of a residual discretion.

---

[213] *Lancefort Ltd. v An Bord Pleanála* [1999] 2 I.R. 270; [1998] 2 I.L.R.M. 401; and *R. v Hammersmith and Fulham LBC Ex p. People before Profit Ltd.* (1981) L.G.R. 322.

[214] See also *O'Brien v Dun Laoghaire Rathdown County Council* [2006] I.E.H.C. 177; unreported, O'Neill J., June 1, 2006. This case was also decided under the unamended s.50, with its express statutory requirement for prior participation. The applicant for judicial review had not personally participated in the planning process, although she was a member of An Taisce, which had made submissions on the application for planning permission. The applicant submitted that the reason she did not make a submission or observation was because of her membership of An Taisce, and that her objections at the time were expressed by the An Taisce. The High Court rejected this argument, ruling that the applicant had not demonstrated that there were good and sufficient reasons for her failure to participate personally in the planning process, and that having decided not to object in her personal capacity, but to pursue her interest through An Taisce instead, she could not now step outside it, and continue a struggle which An Taisce did not wish to pursue.

Finally in this regard, reference is made briefly to *Coll v Donegal County*   **11–189**
Council.[215] This case concerned conventional, as opposed to statutory, judicial
review proceedings. Peart J. ruled, on the facts, that the applicant did not have
the requisite sufficient interest to challenge a decision of the local authority to
extend the duration (life) of a planning permission.

> "In my view, firstly, the applicant enjoys no locus standi to seek the relief she
> seeks under this heading. Firstly, she did not participate in the planning process
> at all, but secondly and critically, the power of the planning authority to exercise
> a discretion to extend the duration of a planning permission is one which may be
> exercised appropriately without consultation with the public. It is not necessary
> under the statutory scheme to publish any notice of intention to apply for an
> extension, and neither is it necessary to erect any notice at the site of the
> development indicating an intention to apply for an extension. Under that scheme,
> as provided by s. 42 of the 2000 Act, a planning authority shall on application
> being made to it, extend the appropriate period for such additional period as it
> considers requisite to enable the development to be completed provided certain
> requirements are complied with, one of which is that referred to already, namely
> that the planning authority is satisfied that the development will be completed
> within a reasonable time. *The applicant has no entitlement to be consulted in the
> making of that decision and therefore in my view cannot be heard to raise
> objections to the decision made.* It is a matter within the discretion of the planning
> authority, and provided that the discretion is exercised in a judicial manner it is a
> decision which the planning authority may make in its discretion."
> *Emphasis supplied.

This aspect of the judgment is surprising. First, the applicant found herself in   **11–190**
a "Catch-22" situation whereby she was criticised for failing to participate in a
statutory process in which the court held she had no right to participate.
Secondly, the grounds on which an administrative decision can be challenged
are numerous, and are in no sense confined to allegations of a breach of fair
procedures. Thus, even if the process leading up to a particular decision allows
for *no* public participation, a person affected by the decision should be entitled
to challenge the legality of that decision by reference to other judicial review
grounds. Here the ground of challenge was a classic jurisdictional ground: the
applicant was alleging that one of the prerequisites to an extension of planning
permission, namely that the development would be completed within a
"reasonable time", had not been satisfied. The entitlement of a person affected
by the decision to raise such a point could not be contingent on the existence
of a general right of public participation at an earlier stage. As it happens,
Peart J. was better than his word, and went on, in any event, to address the
applicant's complaint that the planning authority could not have concluded
that the development would be completed within a reasonable period of time
as required under s.42. Peart J. ruled against the applicant, stating that the
planning authority was entitled to revisit an earlier decision not to extinguish a
right of way, and that, if the relevant right of way was extinguished, then in
those circumstances the planning authority could reasonably have formed the
view that the development would be completed in a "reasonable time".

---

[215] [2005] I.E.H.C. 231; unreported, Peart J., July 7, 2005.

7. Prior participation frustrated

11–191   Such prior participation requirement as there may be is, seemingly, subject to an exception in cases where the non-participation was caused by a breach of proper process in the planning application.[216] Thus, for example, if a newspaper notice is deficient or misleading, an applicant for judicial review should not be criticised for failing to make a submission to the planning authority or An Bord Pleanála, as the case may be.[217] The full rigour of any requirement for prior participation can, of course, only apply where the public consultation requirements have been properly observed.

11–192   Somewhat surprisingly, the logic of this self-evident proposition appears to have been lost in a number of cases concerning alleged material contraventions of development plans. Under s.34(6) of the PDA 2000, a special procedure, involving further public consultation, must be gone through before a planning authority can grant planning permission for development which would involve a material contravention.[218] Failure to observe this procedure will result in the planning permission being invalid. Of critical importance for the present discussion is the fact that an allegation that a planning authority failed to observe the material contravention procedure, if well founded, means that there has been a failure to comply with the statutory requirements in respect of public consultation. Notwithstanding this, in at least two recent judgments—*Moriarty v South Dublin County Council*[219] and *Deerland Construction Ltd. v Westmeath County Council*[220]—the High Court refused judicial review on the basis that the applicant had not participated in the planning process.

11–193   The fact that the planning authority may have engaged in a truncated form of public consultation, short of that mandated under statute, should not redound against the applicant for judicial review. Either the statutory requirements in respect of public notice have been fully observed or they have not. A planning authority should not be allowed to escape the consequences of such a breach by arguing that the applicant for judicial review should have made submissions in response to the standard public notices in respect of the application.

---

[216] *Harding v Cork County Council (No. 2)* [2006] I.E.H.C. 295; unreported, Clarke J., October 12, 2006, [3.8].

[217] It seems that the applicant must have been damnified by the procedural defect alleged. In *O'Shea v Kerry County Council* [2003] 4 I.R. 143, the applicant was found not to have standing on the basis that she had failed to advance any evidence to show or even suggest that, had the notice in question been placed closer to the boundary of the land in question, she would have observed same as no case had been made that she attended at any time at or near the boundary to the land in question.

[218] See further para.1–28.

[219] [2006] I.E.H.C. 109; unreported, Hanna J., November 24, 2005.

[220] [2006] I.E.H.C. 420; unreported, Kelly J., December 12, 2006.

8. *Jus tertii*

Strictly speaking, a distinction should be drawn between the concepts of *locus*   **11–194**
standi and *jus tertii*. The fact that an applicant has standing to challenge a
decision (*locus standi*) does not necessarily mean that he is unrestricted in the
arguments which he can make on the application (*jus tertii*). In particular, the
statutory requirement to establish "substantial grounds" of challenge may mean
that an applicant is precluded from raising technical defects in circumstances
where he was not affected by same. This latter point does not properly go to
standing at all,[221] but some decisions have conflated the concept of *locus standi*
with that of *jus tertii*. For example, in *Halpin v Wicklow County Council*,[222]
O'Sullivan J. held that an applicant affected by the impugned decision did not
have standing to raise a point against a public notice in circumstances where
he personally had not been prevented from making submissions.[223] The practical
significance of such conflation may not be great, however: even if it did not go
to the issue of *locus standi*, the fact that an applicant was not personally
prejudiced by an alleged defect would in any event be relevant to the exercise
of the High Court's discretion to withhold relief[224]; it would also go to the
statutory requirement of "substantial grounds".[225]

In *Arklow Holidays Ltd. v An Bord Pleanála (No. 2)*,[226] Clarke J. indicated   **11–195**
that the question of whether a person, who has not been personally misled, is
excluded from challenging a planning permission on the basis of a potentially
significant failure to comply with the requirements of the planning regulations,
involved a point of law of exceptional public importance, and was an issue
which could arise in a great number of cases. Clarke J. ultimately refused to

---

[221] For an example of the distinction being observed, see *Electricity Supply Board v Gormley*
[1985] I.R. 129; [1985] I.L.R.M. 494 (a member of the public with "a special interest"
(at 157/507) was permitted to raise arguments as to defects in a public notice in
circumstances where she had not been prejudiced by those defects, on the basis that the
planning permission was invalid, not by reason of prejudice or disadvantage to the person
challenging it, but by reason of a want of power and jurisdiction in the planning authority).
See also *Seery v An Bord Pleanála*, unreported, High Court, Quirke J., November 26,
2003 ("If the breach is fatal, then the breach is fatal for want of jurisdiction, and the
jurisdiction is not present, and whether or not a person is prejudiced is not, therefore,
relevant.").

[222] Unreported, High Court, O'Sullivan J., March 15, 2001. See also *O'Shea v Kerry County
Council* [2003] 4 I.R. 143.

[223] An even more dramatic example of such conflation is provided by *Lancefort Ltd. v An
Bord Pleanála* [1999] 2 I.R. 270; [1998] 2 I.L.R.M. 401. See also *Arklow Holidays Ltd.
v An Bord Pleanála (No. 1)* [2006] I.E.H.C. 15; [2007] 1 I.L.R.M. 125 (applicant did not
have standing as it was not misled by alleged error in site layout map).

[224] *Cunningham v An Bord Pleanála*, unreported, High Court, Lavan J., May 3, 1990. See
also *Dunne v An Bord Pleanála* [2006] I.E.H.C. 400; unreported, McGovern J., December
14, 2006.

[225] *Blessington & District Community Council Ltd. v Wicklow County Council* [1997] 1 I.R.
273.

[226] [2006] I.E.H.C. 102; [2007] 1 I.L.R.M. 125.

grant leave to appeal on the point, however, holding on the particular facts of the case that an appeal to the Supreme Court was not desirable in the public interest.

9. Limited liability companies

11–196 The change from "sufficient" to "substantial" does not appear to advance—by alteration or clarification—the legal position in respect of limited liability companies. The law in this regard had been clarified by decisions such as *Blessington Heritage Trust Ltd. v Wicklow County Council*[227] and *Lancefort Ltd. v An Bord Pleanála*,[228] and it is submitted that these authorities are unaffected by the change in language.

11–197 The ordinary rules in relation to standing apply, with necessary modifications, to limited liability companies. The fact that a company's property or financial interests may be affected by the planning decision being challenged would, as in the case of a natural person, appear to be sufficient to found standing.[229] It is important to note, however, that for any property interest to be relied upon, the relevant property must be held by the company itself. It is not possible for the members of a company to seek to have their own property interests imputed to the company in order to supply a "substantial interest": the fact that members of the company have property rights does not in some way afford the company a property right.[230] The legal person of the company is capable of holding property in its own right, and thus it is not necessary to have regard to the property of its members. It is only in the case of an anthropomorphism such as *bona fides* that it is necessary to look through to the members of the company.

11–198 The converse situation, whereby the shareholders of a limited liability company seek to rely on the property rights of the company in order to establish standing personally, was considered in *Moriarty v South Dublin County Council*.[231] The case concerned a challenge to a planning permission brought by the principal of a rival retail business. The proceedings were brought in the principal's own name. At the full hearing, an objection was raised to the applicant's *locus standi* on the basis that he was not the owner of the relevant lands, which lands were instead held under a lease by the limited liability company. The applicant for judicial review was a director and principal shareholder of that company. Hanna J. ruled that the applicant had failed to demonstrate a substantial interest, indicating that the applicant could not "dip in and out of corporate status".

---

[227] [1999] 4 I.R. 571.
[228] [1999] 2 I.R. 270; [1998] 2 I.L.R.M. 401.
[229] *Malahide Community Council Ltd. v Fingal County Council* [1997] 3 I.R. 383; and *Lancefort Ltd. v An Bord Pleanála* [1999] 2 I.R. 270; [1998] 2 I.L.R.M. 401.
[230] *Springview Management Company Ltd. v Cavan Developments Ltd.* [2000] 1 I.L.R.M. 437. Cf. *R. v Leicester City Council Ex p. Blackford and Boothcorpe Action Group Ltd.* [2000] J.P.L. 1266 at 1278.
[231] [2006] I.E.H.C. 109; unreported, Hanna J., November 24, 2005.

The nature of the proprietary interest which must be held by a company in   **11–199**
order to establish standing was considered in *Ballintubber Heights Ltd. v Cork
Corporation.*[232] The applicant company sought to challenge a decision of a
planning authority to grant planning permission. At the same time, a shareholder
and director of the applicant company had brought a statutory appeal to An
Bord Pleanála. The only proprietary interest which the applicant company had
which was relevant to the proposed development was an option to purchase
neighbouring lands. This option had been granted to the applicant company by
its shareholders immediately before the judicial review proceedings were issued.
Ó Caoimh J. held that the interest of the applicant company appeared to have
been created to enable the applicant to advance the proceedings, and its interest
was best described as remote. Moreover, Ó Caoimh J. held that the applicant
company was not entitled to rely on an (alleged) representation made to the
directors/shareholders of the company by the planning authority.

In circumstances where it is sought to found standing by reference to the public   **11–200**
interest, it is submitted that characteristics—such as, for example, the promoters'
commitment to environmental affairs—may be imputed to the company. The
Supreme Court in *Lancefort Ltd. v An Bord Pleanála* had recognised that there
were valid reasons for which persons concerned with planning or environmental
issues might legitimately decide to associate in the form of a limited liability
company,[233] and the fact of incorporation should not *per se* be a bar to standing.
It also appeared from the majority judgment in *Lancefort Ltd. v An Bord
Pleanála* that not even the fact that a company was incorporated *after* the
planning decision under review had been made would be fatal to standing, in
circumstances where there was an identity of interest between persons who
had objected at an earlier stage and the applicant company. The standing of the
company in such cases should then fall to be determined on the same basis as
in the case of individual litigants seeking to assert a public interest; whether or
not this might constitute a "substantial interest" has been discussed earlier at
para.11-134 and onwards.

The recent judgment of the Supreme Court in *Construction Industry Federation*   **11–201**
v Dublin City Council[234] sounds a discordant note in this regard, in that a
representative body was found not to have "sufficient interest" under Ord.84
to bring a challenge to a statutory development contribution scheme. This
represents one of the few examples in recent times of an application for judicial
review being refused on the basis that the applicant did not have a "sufficient
interest". The applicant sought to challenge the validity of a statutory
development contribution scheme, which under the unamended legislation was

---

[232] Unreported, High Court, Ó Caoimh J. June 21, 2002.
[233] See also *Village Residents Association Ltd. v An Bord Pleanála (No. 1)* [2000] 1 I.R. 65
at 72; [2000] 2 I.L.R.M. 59 at 66 ("it would be unwieldy and unwise to try and mount
litigation in the name of or on behalf of an unincorporated association."). *R. v Leicester
City Council Ex p. Blackford and Boothcorpe Action Group Ltd.* [2000] J.P.L. 1266 at
1278.
[234] [2005] 2 I.R. 496; [2005] 2 I.L.R.M. 256.

not subject to s.50. The applicant claimed to represent the interests of its members, who were involved in the construction industry and would, accordingly, be affected by the development contribution scheme. The Supreme Court ruled that, given the nature of the challenge, the applicant company did not have sufficient interest to maintain the proceedings. McCracken J. held that to allow the applicant to argue this point without relating it to any particular planning application and without showing any damage to the applicant itself, meant that the court was being asked to deal with a hypothetical situation, which was always undesirable. The Supreme Court was of the view that it was preferable that any challenge would be brought by an individual member of the applicant, related to the particular circumstances of that member.

> "The members themselves are, in many cases, very large and financially substantial companies, which are unlikely to be deterred by the financial consequences of mounting a challenge such as this. Unlike many of the cases in which parties with no personal or direct interest have been granted locus standi there is no evidence before the Court that, in the absence of the purported challenge by the Appellant, there would have been no other challenger. Indeed the evidence appears to be to the contrary. While there is no suggestion that the Appellant in the present case is in any way acting vexatiously or irresponsibly in seeking this relief, nevertheless I can see no justification for departing from the normal rule which requires that an applicant for judicial review must have a "sufficient interest" in the outcome of the application, and I cannot see any justifiable basis upon which it can be said that the Appellant has any interest other than that of its individual members. In the circumstances of this case where there is no reason why one or more of such individual members should not have made this application I would refuse to allow this application and dismiss this appeal on the basis that the Appellant does not have *locus standi*."

11–202   It is submitted that this judgment does not take cognisance of the fact that a representative body may well be in a position to present a more coherent challenge than an individual litigant. Moreover, it fails to take account of the reality that an individual developer may well not have the stomach for judicial review proceedings: the risk in terms of time and costs are such that a developer will often be reluctant to challenge conduct on the part of a planning authority. This is especially so if the bringing of judicial review proceedings would necessitate the postponement of development works pending the determination of the proceedings.

11–203   The recent judgment of the High Court in *Friends of the Curragh Environment Ltd. v An Bord Pleanála (No. 2)*[235] appears to suggest that where a company relies on the public interest to establish a "substantial interest", then its standing will be restricted by reference to the nature of its prior participation in the planning process. In particular, it was suggested that where a company (i) has no financial, property or other interests adversely affected by the challenged decision; (ii) has a general interest in the protection of the relevant environment; and (iii) primarily relies for standing upon its participation in the planning

---

[235] [2006] I.E.H.C. 390; [2007] 1 I.L.R.M. 386.

process and as a party to an appeal, then, in the absence of special circumstances, the question of "substantial interest" falls to be determined by reference primarily to the interest asserted (expressly in the appeal or by implication from the nature of the appeal) and the connection between that and the grounds on which the company has sought to challenge the validity of the decision. On the particular facts, Finlay Geoghegan J. ruled that as the company had failed to raise before An Bord Pleanála the grounds it subsequently sought to rely upon in the judicial review proceedings, it did not have a substantial interest to pursue those grounds. The substance of the matters sought to be relied upon in the judicial review proceedings had not been brought to the attention of An Bord Pleanála in the course of the appeals, and the applicant company had not demonstrated that it was prevented from doing so, nor that some special circumstances existed.

11–204 The company had sought to raise, in the judicial review proceedings, two broad heads of challenge; first, it was alleged that conditions leaving matters over for subsequent agreement were in breach of the environmental impact assessment Directive, and, secondly, an allegation of project-splitting was made. The appeal to An Bord Pleanála, however, had contained no substantive objection to the proposed development based on any specific identified adverse impact on the environment of the Curragh of Kildare. Rather, the company had argued in a general way that the appeals must be determined in accordance with law, and, in particular, with the requirements of the environmental impact assessment Directive. The appeal had made no submission as to the type of planning conditions which might be permissible or impermissible to impose, notwithstanding the fact that the planning authority, in its decision of first instance, had included conditions of the type sought to be criticised in the judicial review proceedings. Nor did the appeal contain any submission of substance in relation to those aspects of the development—such as archaeology—to which the impugned conditions related.

11–205 In reaching its conclusion on the question of standing, the High Court declined to have regard to Art.10a of the amended EC Directive on environmental impact assessment, on the basis that the question of the direct effect of Art.10a had already been concluded between the parties in *Friends of the Curragh Environment Ltd. v An Bord Pleanála (No. 1).*[236] This aspect of the judgment is discussed further at para.13–365.

Summary

11–206 It would appear to follow from all of the foregoing that the fact that individual members of a company would have standing in their own right does not necessarily indicate that the company will have standing. This depends on the basis on which standing is founded. In the case of public interest litigation, it is submitted that the interposing of a company between the individual members

---

[236] [2006] I.E.H.C. 243; unreported, Kelly J., July 14, 2006.

of the company and the court does not affect the issue of standing. Conversely, if the objective of the litigation is to protect private property interests, it would seem that the property interests engaged must be those of the company, and not of its individual members. The dividing line between private and public interest is less clear in the context of local issues.

11–207 The main distinction between a corporate litigant and an individual litigant is in relation to costs. A concern had been expressed in a number of cases that a company might be used to shield individual litigants from liability for legal costs. The Supreme Court indicated in *Lancefort Ltd. v An Bord Pleanála*[237] that this concern might be addressed by the making of an order for security for costs under s.390 of the Companies Act 1963. Laffoy J. was more explicit in *Village Residents Association Ltd. v An Bord Pleanála (No. 2)*.[238] In response to an argument that the provision of security for costs might be a *quid pro quo* for affording *locus standi*, Laffoy J. stated as follows.[239]

> "In my view, when the court is invited on a challenge to standing to infer that objectors to planning decisions have clothed themselves with limited liability for the less than pure motive of conferring immunity against costs on themselves and the challenge is successfully resisted, on a subsequent attempt to resist an application for security for costs by the company, the *bona fides* of the members of the company requires cautious consideration."

11–208 The availability of security for costs is discussed separately below at paras 11–313 to 11–322.

10. Principals and agents

11–209 The judgment in *Lennon v Limerick County Council*[240] suggests that an agent—such as a planning consultant, architect or engineer—does not have standing to bring proceedings arising out of a planning application made by his or her principal. The proceedings involved a challenge to a decision to reject a planning application as invalid. The proceedings were brought not by the applicant for planning permission, but by a member of the consulting engineers who had been retained by the applicant. It was argued that the consulting engineers had a potentially beneficial interest in the planning application because the payment of their fees and expenses was contingent on planning permission being granted.

---

[237] [1999] 2 I.R. 270; [1998] 2 I.L.R.M. 401.
[238] [2000] 4 I.R. 321; [2001] 2 I.L.R.M. 22.
[239] See also *R. v Leicester City Council Ex p. Blackford and Boothcorpe Action Group Ltd.* [2000] J.P.L. 1266 at 1278 ("The costs position can be dealt with adequately by requiring the provision of security for costs in a realistically large sum.").
[240] [2006] I.E.H.C. 112; unreported, Laffoy J., April 3, 2006, cited with approval in *John Paul Construction Ltd. v Minister for the Environment Heritage and Local Government* [2006] I.E.H.C. 255; unreported, Kelly J., August 15, 2006. See also *Lennon v Cork City Council* [2006] I.E.H.C. 438; unreported, December 19, 2006 ("In my judgment a contingent professional pecuniary interest in the outcome of a planning application by an advisor to an applicant is not what was envisaged by the statute as an interest in the property.").

Laffoy J. rejected this argument. The agent had no proprietary interest in the relevant lands and thus would not have been entitled to make a planning application in his own name, and had not, in fact, made the planning application the subject of the proceedings. Accordingly, he did not have standing to seek a declaration as to the validity of the planning application. **11–210**

11. Non-governmental organisations

Non-governmental organisations ("NGOs") are exempted from the statutory requirement to demonstrate a "substantial interest" in the matter the subject-matter of the application for judicial review.[241] This exemption applies only to EIA development. To qualify as a non-governmental organisation, the organisation must fulfil the following requirements. First, its "aims or objectives" must relate to the "promotion of the environment". Secondly, it must have, within the period of twelve months preceding the date of application, pursued those aims or objectives. Thirdly, it must satisfy such additional requirements as may be prescribed by the Minister. In this latter connection, the Minister is empowered to prescribe requirements of a general nature and for the purposes of promoting transparency and accountability in the operation of such organisations including requirements (i) in relation to its membership; (ii) that the pursuit of its aims or objectives be otherwise than for profit; (iii) in relation to the possession of a specified legal personality and the possession of a constitution or rules; (iv) that the area of environmental protection to which its aims or objectives relate is relevant to the class of matter into which the decision, the subject of the application for judicial review, falls. **11–211**

12. Stage of proceedings at which substantial interest to be determined

An interesting procedural issue has arisen as to whether an applicant's *locus standi* should be determined conclusively at the stage of the application for leave to apply for judicial review. The earlier judgment of the Supreme Court, in *Lancefort Ltd. v An Bord Pleanála*,[242] had suggested that it would be appropriate to determine the issue of *locus standi* (which in the case of conventional judicial review is normally revisited at the substantive hearing) at the leave hearing, on the basis that the hearing was *inter partes*. MacMenamin J. adopted this approach in *Murphy v Cobh County Council*,[243] suggesting that the issue of standing should be determined at the leave application and should not, absent exceptional circumstances, be revisited at the full hearing. Conversely, in *Moriarty v South Dublin County Council*,[244] Hanna J. indicated that the leave application was a filtering process only and did not determine the question of *locus standi* conclusively. **11–212**

---

[241] PDA 2000, s.50A(3)(b) (as inserted by Planning and Development (Strategic Infrastructure) Act 2006, s.13).

[242] [1999] 2 I.R. 270; [1998] 2 I.L.R.M. 401.

[243] [2006] I.E.H.C. 324; unreported, MacMenamin J., October 26, 2006.

[244] [2006] I.E.H.C. 109; unreported, Hanna J., November 24, 2005.

11–213 In *Harding v Cork County Council (No.2)*,[245] the High Court accepted, in principle, that the question as to whether an applicant had a substantial interest might be dealt with as a preliminary issue, in advance of the hearing of the leave application proper. Clarke J. added the caveat that it may be necessary, at least in some cases, to leave open the possibility of revisiting what would otherwise be a preliminary issue until after the question of whether substantial grounds have been established has been dealt with. This would be more likely to arise where there were a multiplicity of grounds advanced and, thus, a wide range of bases on which the applicant might, theoretically, be granted leave.

H. Alternative Remedies at Leave Stage

1. Introduction

11–214 The Supreme Court, in its decision in *G v Director of Public Prosecutions*,[246] had identified a further discretionary criterion (the fifth) for the grant of leave to apply, as follows.

> "That the only effective remedy, on the facts established by the applicant, which the applicant could obtain would be an order by way of judicial review or, if there be an alternative remedy, that the application by way of judicial review is, on all the facts of the case, a more appropriate method of procedure."

11–215 Although such a requirement does not find expression in the detailed provisions of ss.50 and 50A, it appears to have been well established by case law in relation to the previous legislation that such a discretion did, in fact, survive, and that leave to apply for judicial review might be refused where there was a more appropriate remedy.[247]

11–216 Under the previous legislation, there was a choice of remedies open in respect of a decision by a planning authority: a statutory appeal to An Bord Pleanála, or judicial review in the High Court. Section 82(3A) and (3B) of the Local Government (Planning & Development) Act 1963 (as substituted)[248] expressly preserved the right to proceed directly against the decision of the planning authority, by way of judicial review, notwithstanding the alternative remedy of a statutory appeal.[249] The existence of a right of appeal to An Bord Pleanála

---

[245] [2006] I.E.H.C. 295; unreported, Clarke J., October 12, 2006.

[246] [1994] 1 I.R. 374 at 378.

[247] *O'Brien v Tipperary South Riding County Council*, unreported, High Court, Ó Caoimh J., October 22, 2002. See also *Kennedy v South Dublin County Council* (1998) 5 I.P.E.L.J. 31; *Byrne v Wicklow County*, unreported, High Court, Keane J., November 3, 1994; and *Delgany Area Residents Association Ltd. v Wicklow County Council*, unreported, High Court, Barr J., May 28, 1998.

[248] Local Government (Planning & Development) Act 1992, s.19(3).

[249] See *Chambers v An Bord Pleanála* [1992] 1 I.R. 134 at 144; [1992] I.L.R.M. 296 at 302. See, to similar effect with respect to the 1976 reforms, *Cavern Systems Dublin Ltd. v Clontarf Residents Association* [1984] I.L.R.M. 24 at 28–29.

was not a bar to judicial review proceedings[250]; it was, however, a fact relevant to the exercise of the High Court's discretion to grant or refuse relief ultimately or, more recently, to grant or refuse leave to apply for judicial review.[251]

Although the Supreme Court in *State (Abenglen Properties Ltd.) v Dublin Corporation*[252] had suggested that the planning legislation represented a self-contained administrative code with limited access to the courts, subsequent decisions confirmed the right of an objector to have a decision of a planning authority quashed for want of validity,[253] even in circumstances where the applicants themselves had also sought to appeal to An Bord Pleanála.[254] **11–217**

2. Stage of proceedings at which adequacy to be considered

The assessment of the adequacy of an alternative remedy is often difficult, and in the case of conventional judicial review, the issue was typically not determined until the full hearing of the judicial review proceedings. In other words, the existence of an alternative remedy was not usually decisive at the leave stage. In circumstances where the application for leave to apply under s.50 involves an *inter partes* hearing, and the High Court generally has a fuller appreciation of the issues involved, the better view would seem to be that the issue of alternative remedies should be determined conclusively at the leave stage.[255] In *Harding v Cork County Council (No.2)*,[256] Clarke J. went further and suggested that in some cases it might be appropriate to deal with the question of the adequacy of an appeal to An Bord Pleanála as a preliminary issue, in **11–218**

---

[250] *State (Abenglen Properties Ltd.) v Dublin Corporation* [1984] I.R. 381; [1982] I.L.R.M. 590.

[251] *Kennedy v South Dublin County Council* (1998) 5 I.P.E.L.J. 31; *Byrne v Wicklow County*, unreported, High Court, Keane J., November 3, 1994; and *Delgany Area Residents Association Ltd. v Wicklow County Council*, unreported, High Court, Barr J., May 28, 1998. In *Kinsella v Dundalk Town Council*, unreported, High Court, Kelly J., December 3, 2004, the High Court indicated *obiter* that the existence of a pending appeal would justify the refusal of leave to apply for judicial review in a case based on an allegation that the planning authority had acted unlawfully in failing to direct further public notice in circumstances where a response to a request for further information contained what the applicant alleged to be "significant additional data". See also Ord.84, r.20(5), which appears to envisage a steer towards statutory appeal at an earlier stage.

[252] [1984] I.R. 381; [1982] I.L.R.M. 590.

[253] *P & F Sharpe Ltd. v Dublin City & County Manager* [1989] I.R. 701 at 721; [1989] I.L.R.M. 565 at 581. See also *Ardoyne House Management Ltd. v Dublin Corporation* [1998] 2 I.R. 147.

[254] As in the cases of *P & F Sharpe Ltd. v Dublin City & County Manager* [1989] I.R. 701; [1989] I.L.R.M. 565; *Tennyson v Dun Laoghaire Corporation* [1991] 2 I.R. 527; and *Ardoyne House Management Ltd. v Dublin Corporation* [1998] 2 I.R. 147.

[255] See, by analogy, the decision in *Lancefort Ltd. v An Bord Pleanála* [1999] 2 I.R. 270; [1998] 1 I.L.R.M. 401, where it was indicated that the issue of *locus standi* should be determined at the leave stage. It has to be admitted, however, that *locus standi* is not a discretionary issue, and therefore there are stronger grounds for saying that it should be ruled at the leave stage. See also *O'Brien v Tipperary South Riding County Council*, unreported, High Court, Ó Caoimh J., October 22, 2002.

[256] [2006] I.E.H.C. 295; unreported, Clarke J., October 12, 2006.

advance of considering whether there were "substantial grounds" of challenge. Clarke J. indicated, however, that such an approach might not be appropriate where a multiplicity of grounds were advanced.[257]

> "Where an applicant raises one or a small number of grounds, then it may be easy, in advance, to take a view as to whether those grounds, if they were found to be good grounds, could, even cumulatively, be regarded as a sufficient basis for quashing the order of a planning authority on the basis that the statutory right of appeal to the Board would be inadequate. Where, however, as here, a multiplicity of grounds are relied upon, and where it at least possible that the court may be satisfied that substantial grounds might be found to exist in respect of some but not all of those grounds, it may be that the court might have to adopt a somewhat different approach.
>
> In such circumstances it seems to me that it is likely that the court will first have to consider whether, on the assumption that all of the grounds put forward are valid, such a finding would give rise to circumstances where an appeal would nonetheless be an adequate remedy. If that be the case then there is no point in going on to consider whether substantial grounds exist for the contentions of the applicant concerned.
>
> If, however, the court takes the view that it at least possible that the cumulative effect of all of the issues complained of by the applicant might render the process before the planning authority so flawed that it would justify reaching a conclusion that an appeal would not be an adequate remedy, then it may be necessary for the court to consider each of the grounds put forward to ascertain whether there are substantial grounds for the applicants contention. In the event that the applicant succeeds in persuading the court in respect of some, but not all, of the grounds relied on, then it may be necessary to revisit the question of the adequacy or otherwise of an appeal to the Board based upon a review of those grounds in respect of which it has been successfully established that the applicant has substantial grounds for challenge."

3. Criteria against which adequacy of alternative remedy to be assessed

(i) Subsisting defect

11–219   If the invalidity alleged against the planning authority's decision subsists so as to affect An Bord Pleanála's jurisdiction, then leave to apply for judicial review should not be refused. Ordinarily a subsisting defect will involve some breach of a statutory requirement: for example, it might be alleged that the initial application for planning permission was invalid because the applicant did not have the requisite interest in the lands the subject-matter of the application.[258] In extreme cases, however, a breach of fair procedures *per se* at the planning authority stage may taint the appeal process.[259] This point is discussed in more detail at paras 3–88 to 3–92.

---

[257] *ibid.*, [2.6].

[258] *Hynes v An Bord Pleanála (No. 2)*, unreported, High Court, McGuinness J., July 30, 1998.

[259] See *Jerry Beades Construction Ltd. v Dublin Corporation* [2005] I.E.H.C. 406; unreported, McKechnie J., September 7, 2005, [72].

Given that the exercise of the planning authority's jurisdiction is hemmed in **11–220** by more restrictions and limitations than that of the board, it will often be the case that the defect is spent at the appellate stage. In other cases, An Bord Pleanála will have power to remedy an otherwise subsisting defect, and rescue its own jurisdiction (for example, by requiring an environmental impact statement).[260] This latter category presents much greater conceptual difficulties and it is submitted that an applicant should not be refused leave to apply for judicial review in such circumstances. The ability of An Bord Pleanála to rescue its own jurisdiction is examined further as part of the discussion of the stay procedure under s.50A(4) and (5) at para.11–328 and onwards.

(ii) Competence of An Bord Pleanála to determine questions of law

An Bord Pleanála does not have jurisdiction to decide other than simple **11–221** questions of law, and, accordingly, if legal issues arise, judicial review will generally be the appropriate remedy.[261] Conversely, in respect of certain issues touching on the correctness of the planning authority's decision, An Bord Pleanála will be the more appropriate decision-maker. For example, the determination of whether or not a particular application for planning permission is in respect of development which is so similar to that applied for previously, so as to be governed to a prior decision (whether by precedent or *res judicata*) is properly a matter for An Bord Pleanála.[262]

The fact that the decision of An Bord Pleanála operates to annul the decision **11–222** of the planning authority[263] has the effect that, in many cases, the invalidity alleged against the planning authority's decision will be spent by the time the matter reaches An Bord Pleanála. It has been suggested that in the circumstances it would serve no useful purpose to set aside the decision of the planning authority, which decision is sterile of legal effect.[264] The mere fact that An Bord Pleanála's jurisdiction is not tainted by the invalidity alleged does not, however, necessarily indicate that an appeal is an adequate remedy. The point may be illustrated by reference to in *Kennedy v South Dublin County Council*.[265] Mr Kennedy alleged that the proposed development involved a material contravention of the development plan, and that the planning authority had acted unlawfully in purporting to grant planning permission for the development

---

[260] Planning and Development Regulations 2001, art.109.
[261] *State (Abenglen Properties Ltd.) v An Bord Pleanála* [1984] I.R. 381 at 391; [1982] I.L.R.M. 590 at 598. Matters are complicated somewhat by the fact that An Bord Pleanála is empowered to refer a question of law to the High Court (PDA 2000, s.50(1)). This power is rarely used (see *Shannon Regional Fisheries Board v An Bord Pleanála* [1994] 3 I.R. 449), and its relevance to the issue of the adequacy of an appeal to An Bord Pleanála is uncertain.
[262] *Delgany Area Residents Association Ltd. v Wicklow County Council*, unreported, High Court, Barr J., May 28, 1998.
[263] PDA 2000, s.37. See also *O'Keeffe v An Bord Pleanála* [1993] 1 I.R. 39; [1992] I.L.R.M. 237.
[264] *Byrne v Wicklow County Council*, unreported, High Court, Keane J., November 3, 1994.
[265] Unreported, High Court, O'Sullivan J., December 17, 1997; (1998) 5 I.P.E.L.J. 31.

without complying with the material contravention procedure. An appeal was pending before An Bord Pleanála. O'Sullivan J. refused to entertain a High Court challenge on the basis that the legal issues raised would become irrelevant in the context of the appeal to An Bord Pleanála because the board could grant planning permission notwithstanding that the proposed development might constitute a material contravention.

11–223 The approach of O'Sullivan J. has the merit of being pragmatic in that it allowed the substantive merits of the planning application to be determined by An Bord Pleanála. The fact remains, however, that the legislation has placed a fetter on the power of a planning authority to permit development in material contravention of the development plan and in order to vindicate the rule of law, it is necessary that some redress be available for a breach of this restriction. The fact that An Bord Pleanála is unconcerned with the question as to whether or not there has been a material contravention is, therefore, a factor in *favour* of allowing judicial review. Given the limitations on an appeal to An Bord Pleanála, the High Court is the only forum in which the applicant can raise the legality of the planning authority's decision to grant planning permission.

(iii) Questions of EC law

11–224 A nice question arises as to the extent to which An Bord Pleanála has competence to rectify alleged breaches of EC law. As discussed above, An Bord Pleanála normally does not have jurisdiction to decide other than simple questions of law. However, as an emanation of the State, An Bord Pleanála is required to give effect to EC law. It is arguable therefore that where complaint is made that a planning authority's decision was made in breach of EC law, An Bord Pleanála should have competence to address the point.

11–225 This issue arose tangentially in *O'Brien v Tipperary South Riding County Council*.[266] The gravamen of the applicants' case was that there had been a failure to correctly implement the EC environmental impact assessment Directive. In particular, it was alleged that—under the then legislation—neither a planning authority nor An Bord Pleanála could properly assess development in respect of which there was also to be an integrated pollution control licence. Ó Caoimh J. granted leave to apply for judicial review. In so doing, Ó Caoimh J. indicated that he considered, *inter alia*, that the legal issues raised were such that An Bord Pleanála would not be in a position to determine same.

(iv) Breach of fair procedures at planning authority stage

11–226 Finally, there is the more fundamental issue as to whether or not an appeal to An Bord Pleanála can provide adequate redress for a complaint of procedural unfairness. There are strong *dicta* to the effect that a fair appeal does not necessarily cure an unfair initial hearing[267]: the structure of the administrative

---

[266] Unreported, High Court, Ó Caoimh J., October 22, 2002.
[267] See, for example, *Stefan v Minister for Justice Equality, and Law Reform* [2001] 4 I.R.

scheme may be such that a person is entitled to two proper hearings and thus even where the second hearing is unexceptionable, this may not make up for the loss of a first bite at the cherry.

The extent to which this logic might apply to the two-tier decision-making system provided for under the planning legislation is uncertain. On one view, the planning process involves a unified decision-making structure, with provision for a two-stage hearing.[268] It is a peculiar feature of the process that many of the *indicia* of fair procedures are absent from the planning authority stage.[269] For example, there is no provision for an oral hearing; the formal exchange of submissions; nor the production of documents: these are, however, available on appeal to An Bord Pleanála. The scheme is therefore to be distinguished from those where there is only a limited right of appeal, and where, for this reason, a want of fair procedures at the initial stage could not be remedied by an attenuated appeal. The opposite is true: there is a full-blooded right of appeal, with An Bord Pleanála hearing the matter *de novo*, as if the application for planning permission had been made to it in the first instance. If anything, the scheme is top heavy in that the range of procedural safeguards is far greater at the appeal stage. Accordingly, it would appear difficult to argue that, as a matter of statutory interpretation, the scheme should be analysed as providing an entitlement to two self-contained hearings. Rather, the appeal stage is integral to the process in circumstances where the procedures available at the planning authority stage are always insufficient. It would be anomalous were judicial review to lie in respect of a breach of the limited fair procedures available at the planning authority stage, whereas in the case of an inherent and arguably more fundamental defect—for example, the absence of the possibility of an oral hearing—the only remedy would be by way of appeal.

11–227

The nature of the decision-making process was recently considered by the High Court in *Harding v Cork County Council (No. 2)*.[270] Clarke J. indicated that the mere fact that an issue in respect of which complaint is made relating to the first stage of a two-stage process will not be dealt with by an appellate body dealing with the second stage does not necessarily mean that an appeal would not be an adequate remedy. The appeal is an adequate remedy if the

11–228

---

203. *Cf. Bane v Garda Representative Association* [1997] 2 I.R. 449 at 477. See also *Eircell Ltd. v Leitrim County Council* [2000] 1 I.R. 479; [2000] 2 I.L.R.M. 81; and *McGoldrick v An Bord Pleanála* [1997] 1 I.R. 497.

[268] See also *Gammell v Dublin Corporation* [1983] I.L.R.M. 413, where a distinction was drawn between an appeal against an effective decision, and a procedure whereby an aggrieved person may make submissions before a decision becomes effective. In the case of the planning legislation, it could be argued that there is only ever one effective decision in circumstances where a decision of An Bord Pleanála expressly operates to annul the decision of the planning authority, and the initial decision of the planning authority does not constitute the grant of planning permission: it is only in the case of there being no appeal (or an appeal withdrawn) that the planning authority can then proceed to make an actual grant of planning permission.

[269] See the *dicta* in *McCann v An Bord Pleanála* [1997] 1 I.R. 264 at 271; [1997] 1 I.L.R.M. 314 at 320.

[270] [2006] I.E.H.C. 295; unreported, Clarke J., October 12, 2006.

appeal body comes to a fair and proper decision considering all appropriate matters. Clarke J. went on to say that an appeal is likely to be regarded as an adequate remedy in a two-stage administrative process unless either (a) the matters complained of in respect of the first stage of the process are such that they taint the second stage or affect overall jurisdiction, or (b) the process at the first stage was so flawed that it can be reasonably be said that the person had not been afforded his or her entitlement to a proper first stage of the process in any meaningful sense.

11–229 Clarke J. then considered the specific grounds of challenge being advanced in the judicial review proceedings. The following two broad heads of complaint were of significance in assessing the adequacy of the alternative remedy of an appeal to An Bord Pleanála. First, it was alleged that the development proposal had been radically revised during the course of the application and that this had undermined the public consultation process and impaired proper consideration of the applicant's objections to the proposed development. Secondly, it was alleged that in order to retain the benefit of significant tax advantages, it was necessary that the permission (if it was to be granted) should be in respect of an application submitted before December 31, 2004, and that this consideration had led to the application being dealt with in an inappropriate way in a number of respects. Clarke J. suggested that the cumulative effect of all or most of the grounds advanced was such that, if they were to be established not just at the leave stage but at a substantive hearing, such grounds might give rise to a situation where it would be appropriate for the court to conclude that the applicant had suffered a sufficiently significant impairment of his entitlement to the proper consideration of his objection at the planning authority stage, so as to justify forming the view that an appeal would not necessarily be an adequate remedy.

4. Comparison with stay procedure under Section 50A(4) and (5)

11–230 It should be noted that the circumstances in which a discretion to refuse leave to apply for judicial review on the grounds of alternative remedies may be exercised differ from those in which a stay on judicial review proceedings may be granted under s.50(4) and (5).[271] First, the existence of a right of appeal is sufficient, there is no requirement that the appeal procedure actually have been invoked. Secondly, it is not necessary that a formal application be brought by way of notice of motion: the High Court can raise the issue of alternative remedies of its own volition.

---

[271] See paras 11–328 to 11–347 below.

I. The Extent to Which the Grant of Leave is Discretionary

1. General

Judicial review is a discretionary remedy, and the High Court may withhold **11–231** relief to an applicant for reasons relating to his or her conduct. Traditionally, the discretion only comes into play upon the conclusion of the substantive hearing; the essence of the discretion is that notwithstanding the fact that the legal merits of the case have been *determined* in favour of the applicant, relief may nevertheless be denied. In conventional judicial review there is a further practical reason as to why the exercise of the discretion is deferred. Save with the possible exception of the issue of delay,[272] or alternative remedies, the High Court will not usually have sufficient material before it on the *ex parte* application for leave to exercise its discretion.[273] It is only on the exchange of affidavits that the matters relevant to the exercise of the discretion fully crystallise.

The application for leave under ss.50 and 50A is, conversely, on notice to **11–232** other parties and this might suggest that at least some of the discretionary factors should be addressed at that stage. This argument can be supported, by analogy, by reference to the decision in *Lancefort Ltd. v An Bord Pleanála*[274] in respect of *locus standi*, although this is not a discretionary factor. More specifically, Keane J. indicated that it would be appropriate to determine the issue of *locus standi* (which in the case of conventional judicial review is normally revisited at the substantive hearing) at the leave hearing on the basis that the hearing was *inter partes*.

As against this, there are at least two factors which militate against the **11–233** introduction of discretionary factors at the leave stage. First, it is clear from the formula posited by Carroll J. in *McNamara v An Bord Pleanála (No. 1)*[275] that it is no function of the High Court on the leave application to try "to ascertain what the eventual result would be".[276] As it is at least arguable that the discretion does not properly fall to be considered until the merits of the application have been determined, it might be thought that to do so at the leave stage would offend against this principle by involving an element of second-guessing the merits.[277] Secondly, the term "substantial" in the statutory criterion "substantial grounds" suggests that at the leave stage the High Court is concerned only with the substantive merits of the applicant's case; again, the

---

[272] *O'Flynn v Mid Western Health Board* [1991] 2 I.R. 223.
[273] *cf. G v Director of Public Prosecutions* [1994] 1 I.R. 374.
[274] [1999] 2 I.R. 270; [1998] 2 I.L.R.M. 401.
[275] [1995] 2 I.L.R.M. 125.
[276] [1995] 1 I.L.R.M. 125 at 130.
[277] *cf. Bula Ltd. (in receivership) v Flynn*, unreported, High Court, McGuinness J., March 7, 2000, in which the learned judge considered the alternative remedies issue as a preliminary matter before going on to address the substance of the arguments. In the event, she refused the relief sought on substantive grounds.

essence of the discretionary nature of the judicial review remedies is that the discretion is independent of the substantive merits.[278]

2. Mootness

11–234 Judicial review proceedings will be found to be moot and to serve no useful purpose if—irrespective of the outcome of the judicial review proceedings— the ultimate decision to grant or refuse planning permission would remain the same.[279] This point arose for consideration in *Talbot v An Bord Pleanála*.[280] The applicants had sought leave to apply for judicial review of a decision to refuse planning permission. An Bord Pleanála had stated two reasons for refusal; the first related to the application of an objective of the relevant development plan restricting new residential development within a strategic greenbelt. The second reason was stated in more general terms, and involved a finding that the proposed development would constitute suburban type sprawl in a rural area and would, therefore, be contrary to the proper planning and sustainable development of the area.

11–235 The applicants sought to challenge the decision to refuse, on the basis that either An Bord Pleanála had misinterpreted the relevant provisions of the development plan, or those provisions themselves were unlawful by reference to principles of constitutional law or by reference to the European Convention on Human Rights. All of the various grounds of challenge put forward were directed to the first of the two reasons for refusal. Peart J. refused leave to apply for judicial review on discretionary grounds. Peart J. stated that the court was entitled to refuse leave to apply where it would be futile in the sense that no real benefit would accrue to the applicants even if, having been granted leave, the applicants were to be successful in the substantive hearing and the decision quashed.

> "[…] the Court should be ever watchful that cases which ought not to be permitted to take up the time of the Court in vain, should be excluded from entry into the arena at the start, where no ultimate or worthwhile benefit can result to the applicant, even if successful. There is a public interest, particularly these days when the resources of courts and court time are pushed to their limit, in ensuring that those resources are appropriately, justly and fairly preserved for worthy causes."

---

[278] In *Cumann Thomas Daibhis v South Dublin County Council* [2007] I.E.H.C. 118; unreported, O'Neill J., March 30, 2007, O'Neill J. suggested that an argument as to whether the relief sought in the judicial review proceedings would confer any practical benefit on the applicant was a matter going to the court's discretion and was not a factor which would warrant the refusal of leave.

[279] Proceedings may also be moot where the developer has secured a further planning permission in the interim: see comments in *Moriarty v South Dublin County Council* [2006] I.E.H.C. 109.

[280] [2005] I.E.H.C. 215; unreported, Peart J., June 21, 2005.

Peart J. concluded that even if the court were to find a frailty in the first ground **11–236** of refusal (the development plan point), the applicants would be left with the inevitable prospect that, in any further application for planning permission, the second ground of refusal would remain. They would therefore have gained nothing of benefit even if successful in the judicial review proceedings. The application for leave to apply for judicial review was, accordingly, refused. Peart J. did, however, subsequently grant the applicants leave to appeal to the Supreme Court.

The judgment in *Talbot* has since been cited with approval in *Kildare County* **11–237** *Council v An Bord Pleanála.*[281]

> "It is well established that the court will not act in vain. There are circumstances where a court will refuse relief otherwise available were to do so would serve no useful purpose. Thus even if a court were to fall into error regarding one of a number of grounds it could nonetheless refuse either a grant of leave or substantive judicial review were it to hold that relief should not be granted in relation to other separate or discrete determinations which would continue to provide a basis for the continuing validity of the decision impugned."

Although the approach adopted in these judgments to the issue of mootness is **11–238** superficially attractive, it is submitted that it runs counter to the general principle that a court, on an application for judicial review, is ordinarily not concerned with the substantive merits of the impugned planning decision. In order to form a view on whether the outcome of the decision-making process is likely to be different, it is necessary for the court to make some sort of evaluation of the planning merits. This is dangerous territory. Even on the facts of *Talbot* itself, it is arguable that the second of the two reasons for refusal was not entirely divorced from the issues raised in the proceedings as to the interpretation of, and validity of, the development plan. The safer course in all cases would be to remit the matter to the decision-maker so that the decision can be reconsidered in light of the judgment of the court.

On a separate point, in *Fairyhouse Club Ltd. v An Bord Pleanála,*[282] the High **11–239** Court ruled that, notwithstanding a change in the legislative regime, judicial review proceedings were not merely of academic interest but of practical benefit to the parties in that the outcome of the judicial review proceedings might still have relevance for future Section 5 references.[283]

In *Lennon v Cork City Council,*[284] the applicant sought certain declaratory **11–240** relief arising out of the processing of an application for planning permission,

---

[281] [2006] I.E.H.C. 173; unreported, MacMenamin J., March 10, 2006.
[282] Unreported, High Court, Finnegan J., July 18, 2001.
[283] See also *R. (On the application of Bushell) v Newcastle upon Tyne Licensing Justices* [2006] U.K.H.L. 7 (no rule of law or practice that the House of Lords will not proceed with an appeal because there has been a change of circumstances as a result of which the questions which remain in issue between the parties are no longer of general public importance).
[284] [2006] I.E.H.C. 438; unreported, Smyth J., December 19, 2006.

and, in particular, a requirement for further public notice. The planning authority had ultimately refused planning permission, and an appeal had been made to An Bord Pleanála, but subsequently withdrawn. Almost seven years later, judicial review proceedings were instituted. The High Court refused to grant a declaration in circumstances where no useful purpose would be served. The only practical purpose of seeking the declaration would have been a stepping stone to asserting an entitlement for a default planning permission, but the High Court found that no such entitlement arose on the facts.

J. Grant of Leave

1. Grounds on which leave granted to be identified

11–241   The High Court in granting leave to apply for judicial review is required to identify the particular grounds upon which leave is being granted. This follows as a consequence of s.50A(5), which provides that no grounds shall be relied upon in the (substantive) application for judicial review other than those determined by the court to be substantial.[285]

11–242   It is debatable whether this practice of editing the grounds of challenge is desirable. It is often the case that the application for leave will have been made in advance of discovery, and in advance of the respondent decision-maker filing evidence. In such circumstances, the applicant may be required to present a number of grounds in the alternative. This is because until discovery, and the exchange of affidavits, the precise grounds of challenge may not crystallise. Were the applicant to be tied down at the leave stage to particular grounds, this might shut him out from fully arguing his case and thus frustrate his right to invoke the supervisory jurisdiction of the High Court. Reference is made to the facts of *Village Residents Association Ltd. v An Bord Pleanála,*[286] where the applicant claimed not to be aware of the view of An Bord Pleanála on the question of whether or not there had been a material contravention of the development plan until evidence was adduced after the leave stage. If the purpose of ss.50 and 50A is to exclude trivial and tenuous challenges,[287] then once the applicant has established even one substantial ground of challenge, the threshold has been met and the applicant should, arguably, be permitted to proceed on all grounds.

11–243   A related issue is the precision with which the grounds on which relief is sought should be set out. Order 84, r.20(2)(ii) requires an applicant to state the relief sought and the grounds upon which relief is sought. The extent to which the

---

[285] Such a limitation was implicit under the unamended s.50 procedure. See, by analogy, *LR v Minister for Justice, Equality and Law Reform* [2002] 1 I.R. 260 (applicant not be permitted to reintroduce grounds in respect of which leave was refused).

[286] [2001] 1 I.R. 441.

[287] See *McNamara v An Bord Pleanála (No.1)* [1995] 1 I.L.R.M. 125 at 130. See also *Irish Cement Ltd. v An Bord Pleanála*, unreported, High Court, McCracken J., February 24, 1998.

grounds must be particularised is unclear. It is only in the case of a claim for damages that there is an express requirement to set out particulars, or an entitlement to further and better particulars.[288] This would appear to support an inference that generally there is no requirement to set out particulars. The decision in *McNamara v An Bord Pleanála (No. 2)*[289] suggests, however, that it is inappropriate to seek to rely on broad general catch-all pleas which tell the respondent little or nothing as to the actual nature and basis of the challenge and what it should do to meet the case which will be presented against it.[290] This may well be correct, but there is a danger that to impose too strict a requirement as to pleading would be unfair[291]; as stated above, until discovery, and the exchange of affidavits, the precise grounds of challenge may not crystallise, and while an applicant should make a proper attempt to set out his claim, some flexibility should be allowed.

2. Plenary summons or originating notice of motion

In granting leave to apply, the High Court must consider whether to direct that the application for judicial review be made by plenary summons, as opposed to by way of notice of motion.[292] Where a plenary summons is directed, then the action should be presented on oral evidence, unless the court directs by order a hearing on affidavit, or accepts from the parties an expressly agreed statement of facts.[293] (As discussed at paras 11–298 to 11–300, there appears to be reluctance to allow either cross-examination or oral evidence.) It would seem to follow from the mandatory requirement to bring a challenge by way of an application for judicial review that the proceedings would retain their character as judicial review proceedings.[294] **11–244**

3. Stay on proceedings

In circumstances where the High Court directs that the grant of leave is to operate as a stay pursuant to Ord.84, r.(20)(7)(a), this should be formally recorded in the order.[295] Best practice would suggest that an applicant should **11–245**

---

[288] Ord.84, r.24(2). *Quaere* whether an order can be made at a stage in the proceedings later than the grant of leave.

[289] [1996] 2 I.L.R.M. 339 at 351–352. Reference was made to an earlier *ex tempore* judgment in *Keane v An Bord Pleanála*, unreported, High Court, Murphy J., May 23, 1995.

[290] *ibid.*, at 351.

[291] See *Jackson Way Properties Ltd. v Minister for Environment and Local Government*, unreported, High Court, Geoghegan J., May 20, 1999.

[292] Ord.84, r.22(1).

[293] *O'Keeffe v An Bord Pleanála* [1993] 1 I.R. 39 at 78–79; [1992] I.L.R.M. 237 at 268.

[294] *cf. O'Leary v Minister for Transport, Energy and Communications* [2001] 1 I.L.R.M. 125. See also the order of the High Court in *Butler v Dublin Corporation* [1998] 1 I.L.R.M. 533, where declaratory relief was granted against the *applicant* in judicial review proceedings. Contrast the circumstances of Ord.84, r.22(1) with those of Ord.84, r.26(5).

[295] *Halpin v Wicklow County Council*, unreported, High Court, O'Sullivan J., March 15, 2001.

include a claim for such relief as a separate prayer in the originating notice of motion. The jurisdiction to grant a stay is examined in detail at paras 11–328 to 11–347.

4. Undertaking as to damages

11–246 Section 50(6) provides that the High Court may, as a condition for granting leave to apply for judicial review, require the applicant to give an undertaking as to damages.

11–247 There was no equivalent provision under the unamended s.50 procedure, but the High Court had accepted that it had such a jurisdiction in *Seery v An Bord Pleanála*.[296] Finnegan J. held that the grant of leave to challenge the validity of a grant of planning permission had like effect upon the notice party developers as the grant of an interlocutory injunction: it would have been "commercial folly" to embark upon the development envisaged by the planning permission while the judicial review proceedings were pending. Accordingly, Finnegan J. made it a condition of the grant of leave that the applicants provide an undertaking as to damages. In so doing, Finnegan J. relied on Ord.84, r.20(6) of the Rules of the Superior Courts 1986 which provides that if the High Court grants leave to apply for judicial review, it may impose such terms as to costs as it thinks fit, and may require an undertaking as to damages.[297]

11–248 It is unclear, therefore, whether the introduction under s.50(6) of an express power to require such an undertaking as to damages advances matters greatly. It is a pity, however, that having gone to the trouble of making express reference to undertakings as to damages, the legislature did not go on to provide guidance as to the criteria by which this discretion is to be exercised. The opportunity was also lost to clarify other procedural issues such as, for example, to which parties the undertaking need be given,[298] or as to the circumstances, if any, in which a fortified undertaking as to damages might be appropriate.

Governing principles?

11–249 It is submitted that the following principles should govern the exercise of this jurisdiction. First, an undertaking as to damages should never be required where the proceedings allege breaches of the public participation requirements of the EC environmental impact assessment Directive. It is an express requirement of Art.10a of the amended Directive that the review procedure not be prohibitively expensive, and any requirement to give an undertaking as to

---

[296] [2001] 2 I.L.R.M. 151.

[297] These provisions had been considered in detail, in the context of conventional judicial review proceedings, in *Broadnet Ireland Ltd. v Office of the Director of Telecommunications Regulation* [2000] 3 I.R. 281; [2000] 2 I.L.R.M. 241.

[298] In *O'Connell v Environmental Protection Agency* [2001] 4 I.R. 494; [2002] 1 I.L.R.M. 1, Herbert J. expressed a concern as to whether a mere notice party would be entitled to the benefit of an undertaking as to damages.

damages would be inconsistent with that. See further Chapter 13. Secondly, and more generally, an undertaking as to damages should not be required in any proceedings which raise issues of public interest. As discussed at para.11–305 and onwards, there is case law to the effect that special rules should govern the costs of such proceedings, and, by analogy, such proceedings should not be inhibited by the necessity of having to provide an undertaking as to damages. In *Coll v Donegal County Council (No. 2)*,[299] the High Court refused to order an applicant to provide an undertaking as to damages in circumstances where the proceedings raised a public law issue as to the extinguishment of a right of way. Dunne J. refused to order an undertaking as to damages notwithstanding that the applicant openly admitted that she was a "man of straw" and any undertaking as to damages would be worthless, but the judgment goes on to suggest that if a court were satisfied that the use of a particular applicant was a deliberate tactic to frustrate the possibility of an undertaking being obtained—fortified or otherwise—that could amount to an abuse of process such as to merit the requirement of an undertaking as to damages even where matters of public law were at issue.

Finally, it seems that an applicant will only be required to provide a fortified undertaking as to damages, *i.e.* an undertaking backed up by some form of security, in rare or unusual cases.[300] The fact that the potential loss to a notice party developer might exceed the ability of an applicant to make good that loss is not a basis for regarding the undertaking as worthless or an abuse of the process of the court.[301]   **11–250**

K. Interlocutory Injunctive Relief

1. Introduction

The structure of this next section is as follows. First, the implications of a stay under Ord.84, r.20(7)(a) are considered: this is a feature peculiar to judicial review proceedings. Secondly, the application of the more general principles governing the grant of interlocutory injunctions will be examined. In this regard, the position where an applicant seeks interlocutory relief *prior* to the making of a final decision will be considered only after the more usual instance, namely where the matter has proceeded as far as a final decision, has been discussed. Finally, the position in relation to an undertaking as to damages will then be addressed.   **11–251**

---

[299] Unreported, High Court, Dunne J., March 29, 2007.

[300] *O'Connell v Environmental Protection Agency* [2001] 4 I.R. 494; [2002] 1 I.L.R.M. 1; *Harding v Cork County Council (No. 1)* [2006] I.E.H.C. 80; [2006] 1 I.R. 294; [2006] 2 I.L.R.M. 392.

[301] *O'Connell v Environmental Protection Agency* [2001] 4 I.R. 494; [2002] 1 I.L.R.M. 1.

2. Stay on proceedings

11–252 In principle, applications for interlocutory injunctive relief may be brought within proceedings under ss.50 and 50A, as in the case of other forms of proceedings. Ord.84, r.25 provides that applications for interlocutory relief may be made in judicial review proceedings.[302] There is, however, one feature peculiar to the judicial review procedure, namely the availability of a stay under Ord.84, r.20(7)(a), which must be considered before turning to an examination of the application of the traditional principles governing interlocutory injunctive relief to judicial review proceedings under ss.50 and 50A.

11–253 Order 84, r.20(7)(a) provides that where leave to apply for judicial review is granted then if the relief sought is an order of prohibition or *certiorari* and the High Court so directs, the grant shall operate as a stay on the proceedings to which the application relates until the determination of the application or until the court otherwise orders.

11–254 A number of points may be made as to the wording of the sub-rule. First, the ambit of a stay turns on the interpretation of the term "proceedings". At first blush, this term would appear to envisage circumstances where the matter the subject-matter of the judicial review proceedings is still before the respondent decision-maker. An obvious example, from conventional judicial review, would be where an application for judicial review is made to prohibit criminal proceedings then pending before the District Court or Circuit Court. The term "proceedings" would not appear to be apt to embrace circumstances where An Bord Pleanála or a planning authority has determined a planning application or appeal; once its decision is made, An Bord Pleanála or the planning authority (as the case may be) is arguably *functus officio*,[303] and there are no proceedings extant before it.[304] Secondly, it is necessary to apply for an order directing a stay; the stay is not automatic.[305] The High Court has discretion as to whether or not to grant a stay.[306] Thirdly, in circumstances where a stay is granted, the default is that the stay operates until the final determination of the High Court proceedings.[307] (This provision is of greater significance in the context of conventional judicial review proceedings where the grant of leave, and any stay, will be obtained *ex parte*; a stay obtained *ex parte* may be contrasted with

---

[302] *Harding v Cork County Council (No. 1)* [2006] I.E.H.C. 80; [2006] 1 I.R. 294; [2006] 2 I.L.R.M. 392.

[303] An Bord Pleanála is required to make the grant of planning permission as soon as may be after a decision to grant: PDA 2000, s.34(11)(b).

[304] *R. v Secretary of State for Education and Science Ex p. Avon County Council* [1991] 1 Q.B. 558.

[305] Care should be taken that the terms of the order as drawn up reflect the fact that a stay was directed; see facts of *Halpin v Wicklow County Council*, unreported, High Court, O'Sullivan J., March 15, 2001. In this connection, best practice would be to include a prayer for a stay in the notice of motion and statement of grounds.

[306] *Gilligan v Ireland* [2000] 4 I.R. 579 at 585; and *McDonnell v Brady* [2001] 3 I.R. 588.

[307] cf. *Fitzpatrick v Garda Commissioner*, unreported, High Court, Kelly J., October 16, 1996, where this practice is disapproved.

an interim injunction which is usually made returnable for a date shortly thereafter. In the case of an application under ss.50 and 50A, the application for leave is on notice, and thus any order for an interlocutory injunction will only be made after an *inter partes* hearing.) Finally, it is expressly provided by Ord.84, r.20(6) that the grant of leave may be made subject to such order, including costs, as the High Court directs.[308]

It would appear that an application for a stay might be made in two principal circumstances. The first and more orthodox of these would be where a stay is sought, in the context of a challenge to a decision of first instance, to restrain the hearing of a statutory appeal against that decision. The second is where a stay is sought on the *implementation* of a planning permission or other planning decision. Each of these is considered in turn, below. **11–255**

The first example above would seem to come within the literal wording of Ord.84, r.20(7)(a). More specifically, the existence of an outstanding appeal would satisfy any requirement that there be "proceedings" in being upon which the stay could bite. Thus the court would seem to have jurisdiction to grant a stay. Approaching the matter from first principles, however, it is submitted that there would have to be some special reason demonstrated before the High Court should intervene by restraining an appeal. This is because the planning legislation provides for a self-contained administrative code,[309] and it is submitted that this should ordinarily be allowed to run its course. One possible example of a special reason would be where the ultimate decision of the High Court would provide guidance as to the proper and appropriate conduct of the appeal. In such circumstances, it might be thought more expedient to stay the appeal pending such a determination by the High Court. In the absence of a special reason or circumstance, it is submitted that a stay on an appeal should not be granted. In particular, it would seem that any nuisance or annoyance to an applicant would be far less than the disruption which would otherwise be caused by the granting of a stay.[310] **11–256**

The second instance in which a stay might be sought, namely a stay to restrain the implementation of a planning application, was considered in *Lancefort Ltd. v An Bord Pleanála*.[311] The facts were unusual in that the application for a stay was not made until the judicial review proceedings were at a very advanced stage; the substantive hearing had, in fact, taken place, and judgment had been reserved. Prior to delivery of this judgment on the substantive application for judicial review, the notice party developer commenced works. The applicant then applied to the High Court for an order restraining the works on the basis that were a listed building on the lands to be demolished, this **11–257**

---

[308] *cf. Broadnet Ltd. v Office of the Director of Telecommunications Regulation* [2000] 3 I.R. 281; [2000] 2 I.L.R.M. 241.
[309] *cf. State (Abenglen Properties Ltd.) v Dublin Corporation* [1984] I.R. 381; [1982] I.L.R.M. 590.
[310] *Martin v An Bord Pleanála* [2002] 2 I.R. 655; [2003] 1 I.L.R.M. 257.
[311] Unreported, High Court, Morris P., February 13, 1998; *Irish Times* February 14, 1998.

would render the judicial review proceedings nugatory. Morris P. granted the relief sought, and in so doing differentiated between an application for a stay pursuant to Ord.84, r.20(7)(a), and an application for an interlocutory injunction. In particular, Morris P. held that in the case of a stay, and on the particular facts of the case, an undertaking as to damages was not required.

> "[...] whereas the matter comes before me in the nature of an application for interlocutory relief based on the equitable doctrine, and in those circumstances an undertaking as to damages would be appropriate, I do not grant the relief which is sought on that basis. I grant the relief sought on the basis of the high probability that a stay would have been put on the development under Order 84, Rule 20, or on the basis that McGuinness J. would have granted the relief if application had been made to her at the conclusion of the hearing on 18th November 1997. Therefore, I do not propose to require the applicants in this case to give an undertaking as to damages."

11–258   In making his determination, Morris P. expressly relied on the fact that the promoters of the applicant company had previously demonstrated their *bona fides* to the High Court and had provided security for costs, and on the fact that were the destruction of the building to proceed, no amount of compensation could ever make good that loss.

11–259   The position adopted by Morris P. is to be contrasted with the approach taken by the Court of Appeal in England and Wales in *R. v Inspectorate of Pollution Ex p. Greenpeace*.[312] In brief, this latter case appears to suggest that where the effect of an order would impact on the beneficiary of a permission or licence, then any application to stay the implementation of the impugned decision should be treated as if an application for an interlocutory injunction.

11–260   The decision in *Lancefort Ltd. v An Bord Pleanála*,[313] and, in particular, the finding that no undertaking as to damages may be required, has radical implications. Prior to that decision, it would appear that in the absence of some form of interlocutory injunction, a developer was free to commence development works notwithstanding the existence of judicial review proceedings, albeit on hazard that the planning permission might ultimately be quashed. Neither the fact of the judicial review proceedings, nor even the grant of leave to apply for judicial review, operated to suspend the planning permission. In order to obtain an interlocutory injunction, an applicant would be required to give an undertaking as to damages in the ordinary way and this might well prove a deterrent in the context of a large-scale development where the losses incurred by any delay would be significant. Thus, a developer faced with what he regarded as an unmeritorious challenge by way of judicial review could vote with his feet and commence development. The decision in *Lancefort Ltd. v An Bord Pleanála* suggested an alternative course: an applicant could

---

[312] [1994] 1 W.L.R. 570. This judgment is discussed briefly in *Broadnet Ireland Ltd. v Office of the Director of Telecommunications Regulation* [2000] 3 I.R. 281; [2000] 2 I.L.R.M. 241.

[313] Unreported, High Court, Morris P., February 13, 1998; *Irish Times*, February 14, 1998.

apply for a stay pursuant to Ord.84, r.20(7)(a). A restraining order in this form might be available free of any requirement to provide an undertaking as to damages. It might also be the case that the standard of proof required might be different; specifically, the fact that an applicant had been granted leave to apply for judicial review (and thus, by definition, established "substantial grounds" of challenge) might be confirmatory that he had raised a fair question to be tried.[314]

In order to avoid such an outcome, there might well be a temptation in future cases to seek to distinguish the decision in *Lancefort Ltd. v An Bord Pleanála*, and to confine it to its own special facts. In particular, the irreversible nature of the development works, involving as they did the possible destruction of a listed building, and the fact that the developer had failed to signal its intention to commence development to the trial judge, might well be pointed to as distinctions.   **11–261**

The ruling in *Lancefort Ltd. v An Bord Pleanála* must be contrasted with the subsequent decision in *Seery v An Bord Pleanála*.[315] In the latter decision, the applicants had been granted leave to apply for judicial review but ultimately did not seek a stay under Ord.84, r.20(7)(a), choosing to abandon reliance on a plea in the statement of grounds seeking such relief. Finnegan J. (as he then was) nevertheless held that the grant of leave to challenge the validity of a grant of planning permission had like effect upon the notice party developers as the grant of an interlocutory injunction: it would have been commercial folly to embark upon the development envisaged by the planning permission sought to be impugned while the judicial review proceedings were pending. Accordingly, Finnegan J. made it a condition of the grant of leave that the applicants provide an undertaking as to damages. In so doing, Finnegan J. relied on Ord.84, r.20(6) of the Rules of the Superior Courts 1986 which provides that if the High Court grants leave to apply for judicial review, it may impose such terms as to costs as it thinks fit, and may require an undertaking as to damages.[316] As a result of an amendment introduced under the 2006 Act, the High Court now has an express power to require an undertaking as to damages as a condition for granting leave to apply for judicial review. This is discussed at para.11–246 and onwards.   **11–262**

The decisions in *Lancefort Ltd. v An Bord Pleanála* and *Seery v An Bord Pleanála* may possibly be reconciled on this basis. There was a public interest in the proceedings taken by Lancefort Ltd. which was lacking in the case of   **11–263**

---

[314] *cf. Martin v An Bord Pleanála* [2002] 2 I.R. 655; [2003] 1 I.L.R.M. 257 (conventional judicial review), citing with approval *Ryanair Ltd. v Aer Rianta cpt*, unreported, High Court, Kelly J., January 25, 2001 (at p. 5).

[315] [2001] 2 I.L.R.M. 151. See also *O'Connell v Environmental Protection Agency* [2001] 4 I.R. 494; [2002] 1 I.L.R.M. 1.

[316] These provisions had been considered in detail, in the context of conventional judicial review proceedings, in *Broadnet Ireland Ltd. v Office of the Director of Telecommunications Regulation* [2000] 3 I.R. 281; [2000] 2 I.L.R.M. 241.

Seery v An Bord Pleanála. Specifically, whereas the former proceedings related to a building which was arguably of historical interest, in the latter proceedings, the whole tenor of the applicants' objection to the proposed development related to a small portion of the proposed development which would overlook the applicants' own dwelling house. In the circumstances, it did not seem that the application had the necessary public nature to constitute a countervailing factor.

3. Application of *Campus Oil* principles

11–264   The test for the grant of relief by way of interlocutory injunction has been set out in the decision of the Supreme Court in *Campus Oil Ltd. v Minister for Industry and Energy*.[317] In brief, the test to be applied is whether a fair *bona fide* question has been raised by the person seeking the relief. Once such a fair question has been raised, the court should not seek to determine that question on the interlocutory application but should move to a consideration of whether damages would be an adequate remedy to either party, and of the broader balance of convenience.

11–265   These principles have been held to extend to, and to govern, applications for interlocutory injunctions in conventional judicial review.[318] There are, however, certain peculiarities of ss.50 and 50A proceedings which may suggest that the traditional principles applicable to an application for interlocutory injunctive relief may have to be modified in the context of proceedings under that section, as follows.

11–266   First, an applicant who has been granted leave to apply will, by definition, have established "substantial grounds" of challenge. Accordingly, it is submitted that the first requirement, namely a fair *bona fide* question, will have been met.[319] Secondly, as judicial review proceedings are generally heard on affidavit, the judge hearing the interlocutory application may be in nearly as good a position to assess the merits of the case as the trial judge. To put the matter another way, the gap between the interlocutory and the full hearing is narrower in judicial review proceedings than in plenary proceedings, where the trial judge will have the advantage (over the judge hearing the interlocutory application) of an oral hearing, and of pleadings. Accordingly, in judicial review proceedings it may be appropriate to apply a more rigorous test than simply a

---

[317] [1983] I.R. 88.

[318] See, for example, *Fitzpatrick v Garda Commissioner*, unreported, High Court, Kelly J., October 16, 1996; *Birmingham v Birr Urban District Council* [1998] 2 I.L.R.M. 136; *Ryanair Ltd. v Aer Rianta cpt*, unreported, High Court, Kelly J., January 25, 2001; and *Martin v An Bord Pleanála* [2002] 2 I.R. 655; [2003] 1 I.L.R.M. 257. See also *Harding v Cork County Council (No. 1)* [2006] I.E.H.C. 80; [2006] 1 I.R. 294; [2006] 2 I.L.R.M. 392.

[319] *cf. Martin v An Bord Pleanála* [2002] 2 I.R. 655; [2003] 1 I.L.R.M. 257 (conventional judicial review), citing with approval *Ryanair Ltd. v Aer Rianta cpt*, unreported, High Court, Kelly J., January 25, 2001 (at p. 5).

fair *bona fide* question.[320] Thirdly, the question of the adequacy of damages (which can be decisive in plenary proceedings) will usually not be relevant in judicial review proceedings insofar as the applicant is concerned.[321] This is because the fact that a decision is invalid does not *per se* entitle an applicant to an award of damages; it is necessary that the applicant establish some *additional* element in order to found a claim in tort (for example, for misfeasance of public office or for negligence).[322] An applicant's entitlement, if any, to damages is a matter separate from the question of whether or not the decision is invalid. Thus on the interlocutory hearing it cannot be assumed that the applicant would ever achieve an award of damages, even if his claim that the decision is *ultra vires* is well founded. In circumstances where the applicant will not be entitled, as a matter of law, to pursue a claim for damages as a substantive relief, it must be doubted that the court has any jurisdiction to enforce an undertaking as to damages against a respondent: to do otherwise, and thus permit an applicant to recover damages on an interim basis only would seem anomalous. Insofar as the respondent decision-maker is concerned, the question of the adequacy of damages is again unlikely to prove decisive. This is because other than citing the unsettling and disruptive effect of judicial review proceedings,[323] the decision-maker is unlikely to be in a position to allege any particular monetary loss or damage. Of course, a decision-maker might legitimately point to the public interest in the expeditious despatch of its business, but this is more properly a matter relevant to the third aspect of the *Campus Oil* test, namely the balance of convenience.

Balance of convenience

For the foregoing reasons then, it would seem that the balance of convenience **11–267** will assume a greater significance in judicial review proceedings under s.50 than in the case of conventional judicial review.[324] It is submitted that the nature of the considerations affecting the balance of convenience differs according to the stage of the decision-making process at which the interlocutory injunction is sought. For ease of exposition, the single example of an application for planning permission will be used throughout the following discussion. The same principles apply, however, to other decisions protected under s.50 which

---

[320] *cf. Broadnet Ireland Ltd. v Office of the Director of Telecommunications Regulation* [2000] 3 I.R. 281; [2000] 2 I.L.R.M. 241.

[321] *Dunne v Dun Laoghaire Rathdown County Council* [2003] 2 I.L.R.M. 147 ("As to adequacy of damages, I cannot see how, in a case where no damages are claimed and where the right asserted is a public right, it can be said that damages would be an adequate remedy to the plaintiffs.").

[322] See, for example, *Glencar Explorations plc v Mayo County Council* [2002] 1 I.R. 84; [2002] 1 I.L.R.M. 481.

[323] For examples of judicial acknowledgement of the unsettling and disruptive effect of judicial review proceedings, see *Dekra Erin Teoranta v Minister for the Environment and Local Government* [2003] 2 I.L.R.M. 210; or *Adams v Minister for Justice Equality and Law Reform* [2001] 3 I.R. 43; [2001] 2 I.L.R.M. 452.

[324] See, for example, *Harding v Cork County Council (No. 1)* [2006] I.E.H.C. 80; [2006] 1 I.R. 294; [2006] 2 I.L.R.M. 392.

allow development to be carried out, such as, for example, a decision by a local authority under s.179 of the PDA 2000 to proceed with local authority own development.

11–268   If the decision-making process has proceeded as far as a final decision to grant planning permission, then the principal competing considerations relevant to the balance of convenience would seem to be as follows. The fact that planning permission has been granted generally indicates that the proposed development could commence "but for" the application for an interlocutory injunction. The notice party developer will thus usually be in a position to point to a direct and immediate loss on his part. In addition to the developer's hardship, there is the public interest in ensuring that development, especially major infrastructural development, not be unnecessarily delayed. Weighing in on the other side of the balance then, there is the public interest in environmental and planning matters generally.[325] If the grounds of challenge put forward by the applicant in the judicial review proceedings are well founded, then the impugned planning permission should not have been granted. If development is allowed to commence in the interim in such circumstances, then such works as are carried out will represent unauthorised development (based as they are on an invalid decision to grant planning permission). The court may be concerned that if development works are not enjoined, the developer may subsequently seek to resist any attempt to have the structures removed on the basis that to do so would be disproportionate. In other words, the developer by literally altering the situation on the ground might be in a position to render the final outcome of the judicial review proceedings nugatory by subsequently relying on the natural reluctance of a court to direct that substantial development works be torn down. Reference is made to the judgment in *Birmingham v Birr Urban District Council*,[326] where the applicants had claimed just such a prejudice in support of their application for an interlocutory injunction. In this regard it is to be noted that the courts have indicated on a number of occasions that the desirability of preserving the *status quo ante* might well be a relevant consideration to the balance of convenience.[327]

11–269   It is submitted that the courts will still be reluctant to grant an interlocutory injunction restraining the carrying out of development and that even the desirability of preserving the *status quo ante* will not be sufficient of and in itself to overcome this. It is only in cases where there is some additional factor that there will be a reasonable prospect of obtaining an interlocutory injunction. One obvious example would be where the development would involve some irreversible act, such as, for example the demolition of a structure. Reference is made in this regard to the judgment of the Supreme Court in *Dunne v Dun*

---

[325] See, generally, *Blessington Heritage Trust Ltd. v Wicklow County Council* [1999] 4 I.R. 571 at 594–595.

[326] [1998] 2 I.L.R.M. 136.

[327] For a recent example, see *Dunne v Dun Laoghaire Rathdown County Council* [2003] 2 I.L.R.M. 147.

Laoghaire Rathdown County Council.[328] An interlocutory injunction was granted restraining the defendant from, *inter alia*, injuring or interfering with an alleged national monument.

> "The difficulty for a court in dealing with any case on an interlocutory basis is that there is an ever present risk, either in granting or in withholding relief, of doing an injustice to the party who succeeds in the end. One has to balance the risks of injustice to the respective parties. In this context it is significant that, if no relief is granted, the court will be effectively deciding the issue by inaction, since the apprehended interference with the alleged national monument will be complete long before the action can be tried."

Different considerations apply where the judicial review proceedings are taken **11–270** at an earlier stage in the decision-making process. If a final decision has not been made on the application/appeal for planning permission then the notice party developer cannot argue that "but for" the judicial review proceedings, he would be in a position to commence the development. The developer would still have to endure the lead time inherent in the statutory decision-making process irrespective of the judicial review proceedings. The prejudice suffered by the developer is thus less immediate than that obtaining in the case of an actual decision to grant planning permission; the most the developer can point to is the marginal increase in delay attributable to the judicial review proceedings. In addition to this prejudice to the developer, there is again a public interest engaged: on this occasion, the public interest in the efficient despatch of applications/appeals for planning permission.[329] The countervailing factors relevant to the balance of convenience would include the desirability of avoiding unnecessary costs and time being incurred in an abortive administrative process.[330] The thinking here being that if there is a subsisting defect which will undermine any decision subsequently reached, it may be best to have this determined at as early a stage as possible.

Absent some special reason or circumstance, it would seem that the balance of **11–271** convenience will generally indicate that an application for an interlocutory injunction during the course of the decision-making process should be refused. In particular, it would seem that any nuisance or annoyance to an applicant would be far less than the disruption which would otherwise be caused by the granting of an interlocutory injunction.[331] For example, it would seem difficult for an applicant to point to any substantive prejudice which he or she might suffer.

Finally in this regard, it is necessary to refer briefly to the position obtaining **11–272** where a legal challenge is brought to a decision at first instance, notwithstanding the fact that the matter is on appeal to An Bord Pleanála. Under the planning

---

[328] [2003] 2 I.L.R.M. 147 at 160 *per* Hardiman J.
[329] *Martin v An Bord Pleanála* [2002] 2 I.R. 655; [2003] 1 I.L.R.M. 257 (conventional judicial review).
[330] *Cavern Systems Dublin Ltd. v Clontarf Residents Association* [1984] I.L.R.M. 24.
[331] *Martin v An Bord Pleanála* [2002] 2 I.R. 655; [2003] 1 I.L.R.M. 257.

legislation, a decision of An Bord Pleanála on an appeal annuls the decision of the planning authority. The applicant for judicial review will therefore be concerned lest the making of a decision by An Bord Pleanála would render the judicial review proceedings as against the decision of the planning authority moot. However, in many cases far from being a reason to regard the judicial review proceedings as urgent, the fact that the decision of An Bord Pleanála will operate to annul the decision of the planning authority simply demonstrates the inappropriateness of seeking judicial review against the decision of the planning authority. The very fact that such proceedings are ephemeral would seem to point towards the refusal of leave to apply for judicial review, rather than justify an application for an interlocutory injunction.[332]

11–273   In *Harding v Cork County Council (No. 1)*,[333] the High Court held that the balance of convenience lay in favour of granting an interlocutory injunction restraining An Bord Pleanála from determining an appeal. The facts of the case were somewhat unusual. First, the proceedings had been admitted into the Commercial List of the High Court and hence an early hearing date would be allocated. Secondly, the judicial review proceedings alleged serious breaches of the public participation requirements and—in the event these allegations were well founded—an appeal to An Bord Pleanála would not have been an adequate alternative remedy.

4. Undertaking as to damages

11–274   The general rule seems to be that an applicant for an interlocutory injunction is required to furnish an undertaking as to damages as a *quid pro quo* for obtaining the interlocutory injunction.[334] It may be that an exception should be made to this general rule in circumstances where the applicant is pursuing public interest litigation. Reference is again made to the judgment in *Lancefort Ltd. v An Bord Pleanála*, discussed at para.11–257 above.[335] It has to be said, however, that that judgment was based on a somewhat suspect extension of the concept of a "stay" under Ord.84, r.20(7)(a). At all events, subsequent judgments have pursued a more conservative approach and an undertaking as to damages was seen as a prerequisite.

11–275   Indeed, it appears that there have been two subsequent refinements introduced which tighten the requirement further. First, it seems that in certain circumstances the courts will be prepared to assess the worth of the undertaking as to damages, and, may even insist that the undertaking be fortified (for

---

[332] *cf. O'Brien v Tipperary South Riding County Council*, unreported, High Court, Ó Caoimh J., October 22, 2002.

[333] [2006] I.E.H.C. 80; [2006] 1 I.R. 294; [2006] 2 I.L.R.M. 392.

[334] See, for example, *Martin v An Bord Pleanála* [2002] 2 I.R. 655; [2003] 1 I.L.R.M. 257; *O'Brien v Tipperary South Riding County Council*, unreported, High Court, Ó Caoimh J., October 22, 2002; and *Birmingham v Birr Urban District Council* [1998] 2 I.L.R.M. 136.

[335] Unreported, High Court, Morris P., February 13, 1998; *Irish Times*, February 14, 1998.

example, by way of the provision of security or a guarantee).[336] Thus, in *O'Connell v Environmental Protection Agency*,[337] the High Court seems to have acknowledged that it has jurisdiction to require a fortified undertaking but declined to do so on the particular facts.

> "In our system of jurisprudence, with a constitutional right of access to the courts, the occasions on which a court might properly require what is described as a 'fortified undertaking to pay damages' must be very few. This is certainly not such an occasion.
>
> In *Broadnet Ireland Ltd. v Office of the Director of Telecommunications Regulations* [2000] 3 I.R. 281 Laffoy J. held that an undertaking as to damages from that particular applicant would be worthless (see p. 304 of the report). Counsel for the applicant in my judgment correctly pointed to the very real difference between a limited liability company with no assets or capital and the applicant for whom as a person resident in the State of full age and not under any legal or other disability or incapacity and with some interest in immovable property in the State, an undertaking to pay damages was a very serious matter indeed. The fact that the potential loss to the first named notice party might exceed her ability to make good that loss is no basis for regarding her undertaking as worthless and an abuse of the process of the court."

In *Martin v An Bord Pleanála*,[338] the High Court indicated that a pro forma undertaking as to damages without sufficient detail to allow the court to assess it as a realistic undertaking when balanced against the prospective losses of the notice party developer, was not satisfactory.[339]   **11–276**

Secondly, there is now an express statutory power—under s.50(6)—to require an undertaking as to damages as a condition for granting leave to apply for judicial review. Indeed, even prior to this amendment in 2006, the courts had already determined that an undertaking as to damages might be required even in circumstances where no formal restraining order (whether a stay or an interlocutory injunction) has been granted.[340] The justification for this is that the mere existence of judicial review proceedings *per se* may exert a chilling effect: Finnegan J. put the matter pithily in *Seery v An Bord Pleanála*, suggesting that it would be "commercial folly" to proceed with the development until such time as the judicial review proceedings had been resolved.[341]   **11–277**

---

[336] See, generally, *Broadnet Ireland Ltd. v Office of the Director of Telecommunications Regulation* [2000] 3 I.R. 281; [2000] 2 I.L.R.M. 241.

[337] [2001] 4 I.R. 494 at 509, *per* Herbert J.; [2002] 1 I.L.R.M. 1. See also *Harding v Cork County Council (No. 1)* [2006] I.E.H.C. 80; [2006] 1 I.R. 294; [2006] 2 I.L.R.M. 392.

[338] [2002] 2 I.R. 655; [2003] 1 I.L.R.M. 257.

[339] *cf. O'Brien v Tipperary South Riding County Council*, unreported, High Court, Ó Caoimh J., October 22, 2002, where the decision in *Martin v An Bord Pleanála* [2002] 2 I.R. 655; [2003] 1 I.L.R.M. 257 was distinguished on the basis that the applicant was in a position to give a meaningful undertaking as to damages.

[340] See, generally, *Broadnet Ireland Ltd. v Office of the Director of Telecommunications Regulation* [2000] 3 I.R. 281; [2000] 2 I.L.R.M. 241.

[341] [2001] 2 I.L.R.M. 151. See also *O'Connell v Environmental Protection Agency* [2001] 4 I.R. 494; [2002] 1 I.L.R.M. 1.

5. Injunctive relief prior to grant of leave

11–278   The question as to whether it is possible to obtain injunctive relief prior to the grant of leave to apply for judicial review was considered by the High Court in *Harding v Cork County Council (No. 1)*.[342] Kelly J. was satisfied that the court did have jurisdiction to grant an injunction, either by reference to the provisions of Ord.84, r.25 or as part of its inherent jurisdiction. The proceedings involved a challenge to a planning authority's decision to grant planning permission. The decision had been appealed, by persons other than the applicant, to An Bord Pleanála, and the applicant was concerned lest the making of a decision by An Bord Pleanála would render his proceedings nugatory.

11–279   Kelly J. rejected the argument put forward on behalf of the notice party developer that the High Court did not have jurisdiction to grant an injunction in advance of the leave application.[343]

> "If the notice party is correct and the court does not have jurisdiction then an absurd result follows. It means that the court is empowered after a grant of leave to seek judicial review has been obtained to make an order to prevent a particular mischief, namely the doing of an act which would alter the *status quo* in such a way as to make ultimate success by the applicant hollow, but is sterile and impotent to make such an order in advance of hearing the application for leave to apply for judicial review. In my view such a situation would be absurd."

11–280   Order 84, r.25 provides that any interlocutory application may be made to the High Court in proceedings on an application for judicial review. Kelly J. held that the phrase "interlocutory application" was sufficiently wide to encompass an application for an injunction. In the alternative, Kelly J. held that the High Court had an inherent jurisdiction to preserve the *status quo* prior to leave being granted, assuming that the circumstances for such an intervention were appropriate.[344] Kelly J. went on then to state that the interlocutory injunction should be decided by reference to the well established *Campus Oil* principles, and that the burden on the applicant would be to demonstrate that there was a serious issue to be tried, rather than to establish that there were "substantial grounds" of challenge.

11–281   The existence of this pre-leave jurisdiction sits uneasily with the scheme of ss.50 and 50A, and this power should be exercised sparingly. It seems anomalous for an applicant to be permitted to secure the dramatic remedy of an injunction, without first having to satisfy the stringent requirements of the leave application, and, in particular, without having demonstrated "substantial grounds" of challenge or a "substantial interest" in the matter. In those cases where there is a genuine urgency—for example where the implementation of an impugned

---

[342] [2006] I.E.H.C. 80; [2006] 1 I.R. 294; [2006] 2 I.L.R.M. 392.

[343] *ibid.*, [15].

[344] Kelly J. cited with approval the decisions in *M v Home Office* [1994] A.C. 377; and *YD (Turkey) v Secretary of State for the Home Department* [2006] E.W.C.A. Civ. 52; [2006] 1 W.L.R. 1646.

planning permission might result in irreversible harm—it would be preferable if there could be an expedited hearing of the leave application. Unfortunately, this will often not be possible. This is because it is not unusual for a leave application to last for several days, and the High Court cannot be expected to set aside a number of hearing days at very short notice. The most that the High Court may be able to do is to make time available for a brief interlocutory hearing. The *Campus Oil* principles are designed to allow the High Court to reach a fair decision after the shortest of hearings, by allowing the court to concentrate on the balance of convenience rather than becoming embroiled in a consideration of the substantive merits of a case.

More generally, the courts should be astute lest an applicant for judicial review **11–282** rely on the existence of a parallel appeal to An Bord Pleanála to create an *artificial* sense of urgency. It does not always follow from the fact that the decision of An Bord Pleanála on the appeal will annul the decision of the planning authority that the appeal process should be stayed in preference to judicial review proceedings. Unless the grounds of challenge alleged against the decision of the planning authority equally affect An Bord Pleanála's jurisdiction, *i.e.* subsisting defects, then the appeal process will result in a valid decision by An Bord Pleanála. The fact that the grounds of challenge will be spent once the decision is made by An Bord Pleanála, far from justifying an injunction restraining the appeal process, suggests instead that judicial review proceedings were inappropriate, and that an appeal is an adequate alternative remedy. To restrain an appeal in such circumstances turns the statutory scheme on its head. On the particular facts of *Harding*, the breaches of the public consultation procedure alleged were so serious that—if well founded—an appeal to An Bord Pleanála would not be an adequate remedy.[345]

The application for leave to apply for judicial review in *Harding* was **11–283** subsequently heard by Clarke J., and leave refused.[346] Clarke J. did, however, grant leave to appeal to the Supreme Court. An application was then made to have the stay on the proceedings before An Bord Pleanála continued. Clarke J. held that just as the High Court has a jurisdiction to grant interim or interlocutory injunctions to preserve the *status quo* pending a trial, it also had, in an appropriate case, a jurisdiction to continue such injunctions (or to grant new or different injunctions) so as to preserve the *status quo* pending the hearing of the appeal.[347] Clarke J. extended the stay on the proceedings before An Bord Pleanála for a number of months, and indicated that if the Supreme Court appeal had not been determined within that time, any application to extend the stay further should be made to the Supreme Court directly.

---

[345] *Harding v Cork County Council (No. 2)* [2006] I.E.H.C. 295; unreported, Clarke J., October 12, 2006.
[346] *Harding v Cork County Council (No. 2)* [2006] I.E.H.C. 295; unreported, Clarke J., October 12, 2006.
[347] *Harding v Cork County Council (No. 4)* [2007] I.E.H.C. 31; unreported, Clarke J., January 31, 2007.

11–284   Thus on the facts of *Harding* the High Court not only granted a stay on an appeal to An Bord Pleanála in advance of the hearing of the leave application, but also extended that stay after the application for leave had been heard and leave refused.

L. Amendment of Statement of Grounds

1. Amendments and the eight week time-limit

11–285   It is not entirely clear as to whether it is permissible for an applicant under ss.50 and 50A to seek to amend his or her statement of grounds.[348] In conventional judicial review proceedings, the High Court has an express power to allow such an amendment,[349] and in principle this might extend to statutory judicial review proceedings. As against this, it can be argued that to allow amendments might undermine the effectiveness of the eight week time-limit. In *McNamara v An Bord Pleanála (No. 2)*,[350] a case decided under the Local Government (Planning & Development) Acts, the High Court had ruled that the obligation on an applicant was not merely to inform the developer within time that his planning permission was being challenged, but also to indicate the specific grounds for the proposed challenge, so as to allow the developer to know the case he has to meet.[351]

11–286   *McNamara* was decided against a statutory regime where there was an absolute two month time-limit. The fact that time can now be extended for good and sufficient reason means that the case may no longer represent good law. In particular, it would seem to follow that if an applicant may be permitted to

---

[348] In *Sweetman v An Bord Pleanála*, unreported, High Court, Clarke J., April 27, 2007, the High Court accepted, in principle, that an application to amend could be made. The applicant would, however, have to show "good and sufficient reason" for not having sought the relief within the eight week time period.

[349] Ord.84, r.23(2). See, generally, H. Delaney, "Amendments to a statement of grounds in judicial review proceedings" [2001] 3(1) P. & P. 2. Despite the elliptical wording of the rule, the application to amend can be made in advance of the hearing; *Molloy v Governor Limerick Prison*, unreported, Supreme Court, *ex tempore*, July 12, 1996 (overruling *Ahern v Minister for Industry and Commerce* [1990] 1 I.R. 55).

[350] [1996] 2 I.L.R.M. 339 at 351–352. Reference was made to an earlier *ex tempore* judgment in *Keane v An Bord Pleanála*, High Court, Murphy J., May 23, 1995. It is to be noted that the Supreme Court has not ruled on this issue; the following point was certified in *Lancefort Ltd. v An Bord Pleanála*, unreported, High Court, McGuinness J., March 31, 1998. See report of Supreme Court judgment, [1999] 2 I.R. 270 at 273–274, namely whether an applicant for judicial review pursuant to the provisions of the Local Government (Planning & Development) Act 1963 (as amended) may on the hearing of the substantive application for judicial review raise and rely upon grounds not pleaded and upon which leave to apply for judicial review was not sought nor granted before the High Court. The case was ultimately disposed of on the narrow ground of *locus standi*.

[351] See also *Ní Éili v Environmental Protection Agency* [1997] 2 I.L.R.M. 458 at 466: "To allow such a thing to occur would run counter to the statute, negative its intent, and in effect permit of no time bar at all in respect of the additional reliefs sought."

issue proceedings outside the eight weeks, then, in principle, an applicant who has issued within the eight weeks should be permitted to take the lesser step pf amending his statement of grounds out of time. The latter step is less significant in that at least the developer will have had notice of the existence of a challenge to the decision within the initial eight week period.

In the absence of an express requirement to state grounds in full with the eight week time period,[352] it is arguable that there is no room for the implication of such a requirement. The amendments introduced to the judicial review procedure under the Rules of Superior Courts 1986 were intended to do away with technical difficulties,[353] and it would be a retrograde step were they to be used to put unnecessary obstacles in the way of an applicant. Until discovery, and the exchange of affidavits, the precise grounds of challenge may not crystallise.[354]   **11–287**

2. Circumstances in which amendments might be permissible

In the event that an amendment to a statement of grounds outside time is permissible, it would seem by reference to the case law in relation to conventional judicial review proceedings that an applicant will have to demonstrate that there are special circumstances justifying the amendment.[355] In order not to compromise the requirement to extend time, the applicant should also be required to demonstrate a good and sufficient reason for the delay.[356] An example of one such special circumstance might be where facts come to light which could not have been known at the time when leave was obtained. It is submitted that this should be extended to include circumstances where factual matters are only made known to the applicant through the respondent's replying affidavits.[357] Obviously, if leave to apply for judicial review has been refused on particular grounds, an applicant should not be permitted to re-introduce   **11–288**

---

[352] The absence of any express requirement to state the grounds in full can be contrasted with the position in connection with the making of a statutory appeal to An Bord Pleanála.

[353] See, for example, the provisions of Ord.84, r.19 (interchangeability of reliefs).

[354] See *Aquatechnologie Ltd. v National Standards Authority of Ireland*, Supreme Court, unreported, July 10, 2000; and *Dooner v Garda Síochána Complaints Board*, unreported, High Court, Finnegan J., June 2, 2000, for examples of decisions where an amendment to the statement of grounds was permitted in circumstances where certain matters were disclosed to the applicant for the first time in the respondents' replying affidavits.

[355] *McCormack v Garda Síochána Complaints Board* [1997] 2 I.R. 489; [1997] 2 I.L.R.M. 321. See also *Ní Éili v Environmental Protection Agency* [1997] 2 I.L.R.M. 458, where Kelly J. indicated *obiter* that leave to amend would be refused where no satisfactory explanation had been given for the failure to apply at the leave stage for the reliefs sought to be introduced.

[356] *Sweetman v An Bord Pleanála*, unreported, Clarke J., April 27, 2007. For an example in conventional judicial review, see *Hynes v Wicklow County Council*, unreported, High Court, Murphy J., May 15, 2003 (delay of over a year in seeking amendment held to be unreasonable).

[357] *Aquatechnologie Ltd. v National Standards Authority of Ireland*, unreported, Supreme Court, July 10, 2000.

those grounds under cover of an application to amend the (redacted) statements of grounds on which leave was granted.[358]

11–289 More radically, it might be argued that the standard discussed above is too high, and that an analogy should instead be drawn with case law in respect of the Statute of Limitations.[359] It would seem from the decision in *Krops v Irish Forestry Board Ltd*[360] that, provided proceedings have been issued within the limitation period, and provided also that no new allegations of fact which might prejudice or embarrass the defendant are made, it is permissible to amend the pleadings subsequently, even in circumstances where this would introduce a new head of claim which would otherwise be statute barred.

M. Discovery and Interrogatories
Cross-Examination

1. General

11–290 The procedural weapons of discovery and interrogatories have been expressly applied to judicial review proceedings under Ord.84, r.25. The importance of discovery and interrogatories in judicial review proceedings has been recognised by the Supreme Court on a number of occasions.[361] Indeed, one of the objectives of the reforms wrought by the Rules of the Superior Courts 1986 seems to have been to harmonise the procedural rules applicable to the various public law remedies, so that discovery of documents and interrogatories should be available whatever the ultimate relief sought may be.[362] The possibility of cross-examination under Ord.39 is also expressly provided for by Ord.84, r.25.

2. Discovery

11–291 It seems that there is no difference in the principles governing an application for discovery as between judicial review proceedings and private law proceedings. The limited grounds on which judicial review is available under Irish law means, however, that the categories of documents which a court would

---

[358] *LR v Minister for Justice, Equality and Law Reform* [2002] 1 I.R. 260.
[359] See, generally, H. Delany and D. McGrath, *Civil Procedure in the Superior Courts* (2nd ed., Thomson Round Hall, Dublin).
[360] [1995] 2 I.R. 113; [1995] 2 I.L.R.M. 290.
[361] *O'Keeffe v An Bord Pleanála* [1993] 1 I.R. 39 at 79; [1992] I.L.R.M. 237 at 268; *Ambiorix Ltd. v Minister for the Environment* [1992] 1 I.R. 277 at 285; and *Aquatechnologie Ltd. v National Standards Authority of Ireland*, unreported, Supreme Court, July 10, 2000.
[362] See Law Reform Commission, "Judicial Review of Administrative Action: The Problem of Remedies" (Working Paper No. 8-1979), pp.18–19 and 32–33. This paper does observe that, historically, the Irish courts have been more liberal than their English counterparts in their attitude to the availability of discovery on applications for *certiorari* and the other prerogative remedies.

consider were necessary to be discovered will be much more confined than if the litigation related to the merits of the case.[363]

The justifications put forward for this restrictive approach include first, that discovery is not relevant to challenges based on allegations of administrative unreasonableness, and secondly, that an applicant should not be permitted to fish for information (so-called "Micawber discovery"). Both rationales are, however, suspect, for the following reasons.   **11–292**

One tenet of the concept of administrative unreasonableness is that the decision-maker must take into account all relevant considerations, and not have regard to irrelevant ones.[364] Discovery of documents would clearly be of assistance in allowing an applicant to determine what material was before the decision-maker.[365]   **11–293**

In connection with so-called Micawber discovery, the following points can be made. The concept of administrative unreasonableness is closely allied to the duty to give reasons. Specifically, the absence of reasons may give rise to an inference that the decision is unreasonable.[366] If a decision-maker fails to provide a proper statement of its reasons, and continues to do so in the face of judicial review proceedings by failing to file proper affidavits,[367] it can hardly complain if the applicant seeks to resort to an order of discovery in an attempt to reveal those reasons. (It would also seem to follow from this that where elliptical affidavits are filed in response, an applicant must be entitled to cross-examine, at the very least in relation to a deponent's means of knowledge.)   **11–294**

Provided that a respondent has been entirely up front in disclosing both its procedures and the documentation which was before it, discovery will not normally be considered necessary.[368]   **11–295**

---

[363] *Carlow Kilkenny Radio Ltd. v Broadcasting Commission of Ireland* [2003] 3 I.R. 528. See also *Shortt v Dublin City Council* [2003] 2 I.R. 69 ("I am satisfied that while the remedy of discovery is available in judicial review proceedings, the fact that the same is rare in judicial review proceedings does not relate to any restriction in the right to apply for same in judicial review proceedings, but relates to the fact that the necessity for same will be more difficult to establish in judicial review proceedings having regard to the nature of same.").

[364] Indeed, this is stated in an extreme form in *O'Keeffe v An Bord Pleanála* [1993] 1 I.R. 39; [1992] I.L.R.M. 237.

[365] *Ambiorix Ltd. v Minister for the Environment* [1992] 1 I.R. 277 at 285.

[366] *O'Keeffe v An Bord Pleanála* [1993] 1 I.R. 39; [1992] I.L.R.M. 237; *Gavin v Criminal Injuries Compensation Tribunal* [1997] 1 I.R. 132; and *McCormack v Garda Síochána Complaints Board* [1997] 1 I.R. 132.

[367] See the decisions in *Gavin v Criminal Injuries Compensation Tribunal* [1997] 1 I.R. 132; *Village Residents Association Ltd. v An Bord Pleanála (No. 3)* [2001] 1 I.R. 441; and *Dooner v Garda Síochána Complaints Board*, unreported, High Court, Finnegan J., June 2, 2000, for recent examples of respondents making unsatisfactory responses.

[368] *Carlow Kilkenny Radio Ltd. v Broadcasting Commission of Ireland* [2003] 3 I.R. 528 at 537.

"The established English and Northern Irish jurisprudence, which would seem to be in conformity with our own principles of discovery, is to the effect that discovery will not normally be regarded as necessary if the judicial review application is based on procedural impropriety as ordinarily that can be established without the benefit of discovery. Likewise, if the application for judicial review is on the basis that the decision being impugned was a wholly unreasonable one in the *Wednesbury* sense, discovery will again not normally be necessary because if the decision is clearly wrong it is not necessary to ascertain how it was arrived at. Where discovery will be necessary is where there is a clear factual dispute on the affidavits that would have to be resolved in order properly to adjudicate on the application or where there is *prima facie* evidence to the effect, either that a document which ought to have been before the deciding body was not before it or that a document which ought not to have been before the deciding body was before it."

3. Discovery prior to grant of leave

11–296 The question as to whether it is appropriate to direct the discovery of documents in advance of the grant of leave in judicial review proceedings was discussed in *Arklow Holidays Ltd. v An Bord Pleanála*.[369] Clarke J. indicated that he was not prepared to hold that the High Court had no jurisdiction to make an order for discovery at the leave stage, or that there could never be circumstances where it would be appropriate to make an order at that stage. Clarke J. went on, however, to say that the availability of discovery in judicial review proceedings is significantly more limited than in ordinary plenary proceedings, and that the circumstances in which an applicant will be entitled to discovery in aid of a leave application must necessarily be more restricted still. In particular, Clarke J. stated that it would be necessary to demonstrate that the documents concerned were required for the proper resolution of the issues that would arise at the leave stage.

11–297 Clarke J. suggested that where there is a clear factual dispute on the affidavits that dispute must, on a leave application, be resolved in favour of the applicant, who is entitled to have the question of whether he has established substantial grounds considered on the basis that any factual dispute reasonably appearing might be found on his side. Similarly, where there is *prima facie* evidence that a document which ought to have been before the deciding body was not before it, or that a document which ought not to have been before the deciding body was before it, that *prima facie* case can, without discovery, be advanced as part of the substantial grounds relied on.

4. Cross-examination

11–298 Turning now to the availability of cross-examination, there appears to be some confusion as to whether this is governed by the provisions of Ord.39, r.1, or by

---

[369] Unreported, High Court, Clarke J., August 3, 2005. See also *GS v Minister for Justice* [2004] 2 I.R. 417.

those of Ord.40, r.1. More specifically, Ord.84, r.25(1) provides, in effect, that for the purpose of that rule, an interlocutory application includes, *inter alia*, an application under Ord.39, r.1. Order 39, r.1, in turn, provides that the High Court may order that any particular fact or facts may be proved by affidavit, subject to an exception where it appears to the court that the other party *bona fide* desires the production of a witness for cross-examination, and that witness can be produced. This would appear to suggest that affidavit evidence is the exception rather than the norm. No application to compel the production of a witness for cross-examination is envisaged, as it is clear that the proviso relates to a reason for *not* acceding to an application to allow facts to be proved by affidavit at all.

Notwithstanding that it is expressly referred to in Ord.84, r.25(1), the provisions of Ord.39, r.1 would appear to have little relevance to most judicial review proceedings. In practice, judicial review proceedings tend to be pursued by way of originating notice of motion, and in this connection the provisions of Ord.40, r.1 would seem to be of more immediate relevance. More specifically, Ord.40, r.1 provides, *inter alia*, that upon any motion, evidence may be given by affidavit, but the High Court may, on the application of either party, order attendance of the person making the affidavit. This is the rule generally relied upon in practice. **11–299**

A question then arises as to the test to be applied to the determination of whether or not to allow cross-examination. In this connection, there is arguably a tension between the two rules in that Ord.39, r.1 appears to involve a presumption in favour of oral evidence whereas any such presumption is less strong in the case of Ord.40, r.1. However, any seeming tension is easily resolved. Order 40, r.1 is on its own terms wholly permissive: it confirms that evidence may in prescribed circumstances be given on affidavit, and that the High Court enjoys the power to order a deponent to attend to be cross-examined on his or her affidavit. It does not lay down the test to be applied in deciding whether or not it is appropriate to make such an order. In the circumstances, it is submitted that regard should be had to the following general principles. First, it is well established that oral evidence, tested by cross-examination, is the most effective method of resolving factual disputes (whether arising in legal or administrative proceedings).[370] Secondly, there is nothing to indicate that judicial review proceedings are in a different category from others in relation to the importance of oral testimony. It is simply a matter of empirical fact that, for the most part, judicial review proceedings tend not to involve vigorously contested factual issues. This is not because of any special restriction imposed by the Rules of the Superior Courts but rather because of the subject-matter of the proceedings, involving decisions by public bodies which are matters of record. Where, unusually, there is a dispute as between the parties as to a factual matter, it is **11–300**

---

[370] *Galvin v Chief Appeals Officer* [1997] 3 I.R. 240. See also *Gallagher v Revenue Commissioners* [1995] 1 I.R. 65; [1995] 1 I.L.R.M. 250. In the specific context of judicial review proceedings, see *O'Reilly v Mackman* [1982] 3 W.L.R. 1096.

submitted that, having regard to the importance attached to oral testimony, the court should ordinarily accede to an application for leave to cross-examine.[371]

N. Costs

1. General

11–301   The general principle is that costs follow the event,[372] and thus the unsuccessful party is usually required to pay the other side's costs. As discussed below, the multiplicity of parties may require a refinement of this.[373] The courts have, however, identified at least two circumstances in which this general rule will not be followed. The first is where, even though the applicant has been unsuccessful in the judicial review proceedings, there has been some aspect of the conduct of the decision-maker worthy of censure. For example, the decision-maker may have caused unnecessary expense and delay by refusing to admit certain matters.[374] In such circumstances, the justice of the case might more properly be met by making no order for costs in respect of the decision-maker, or, indeed, by the making of an order for costs against the decision-maker. The second instance, then, is where the proceedings raise matters of public interest. This is discussed separately at paras 11–305 to 11–311.

2. Multiplicity of parties

11–302   The fact that ss.50 and 50A requires that a number of mandatory parties be served with notice of judicial review proceedings presents difficulties in terms of any award of costs. Although, as indicated immediately above, the general principle is that costs follow the event, a judge may be reluctant to award two sets of costs (those of the respondent planning body, and of the notice party developer) against an unsuccessful applicant. Indeed, the House of Lords has indicated that the developer will not normally be entitled to his costs unless he can show that there was likely to be a separate issue in respect of which he was entitled to be heard, or unless he has an interest which requires separate representation: the mere fact that he is the developer will not of itself justify a second set of costs in every case.[375]

11–303   Even if it is the case that only one set of costs should be awarded, it does not necessarily follow that it is the respondent decision-maker, *i.e.* either the

---

[371]   See, for example, *O'Reilly v Mackman* [1982] 3 W.L.R. 1096 at 1107. *Cf. Phonographic Performance (Ireland) Ltd. v Cody* [1998] 4 I.R. 504; [1994] 2 I.L.R.M. 241 (Ord.39, r.1).

[372]   Rules of the Superior Courts 1986, Ord.99.

[373]   See paras 11–302 to 11–304.

[374]   See, for example, *McEvoy v Meath County Council (No. 2)* [2003] 1 I.R. 208 (planning authority's refusal to admit facts resulted in unnecessary discovery).

[375]   *Bolton Metropolitan District Council v Secretary of State for the Environment* [1995] 3 P.L.R. 37.

planning authority or An Bord Pleanála, who should receive costs. If the test is which person is the proper party to advance the argument, it might well be that in respect of certain arguments, the notice party developer is the *legitimus contradictor*. For example, several cases have been disposed of on the basis of procedural points in relation to time-limits, and the service of documents. As the Supreme Court has indicated in *KSK Enterprises Ltd. v An Bord Pleanála*[376] that time-limits are for the benefit of the developer, perhaps such points are more properly made by the notice party developer. More radically, it might be argued that in the case of a challenge to the validity of a decision of An Bord Pleanála, it is not necessary for the planning authority to appear at the proceedings, and if it does do so, it must bear its own costs.[377]

The judgment of the Supreme Court in *O'Connor v Nenagh Urban District Council*[378] is of note in that it confirms the entitlement of a notice party to participate in proceedings, and, where appropriate, to an award of costs. The applicant for judicial review had been unsuccessful in the High Court. The form of the proceedings was somewhat unusual in that there was no direct challenge to a planning permission, and, accordingly, the proceedings were brought by way of conventional judicial review rather than statutory judicial review. The developer was a notice party to the proceedings. The unsuccessful applicant sought to appeal to the Supreme Court against the decision of the High Court judge to award costs to the notice party developer. The Supreme Court dismissed the appeal. Denham J. held that whereas there was an element of public interest, the application as originally drafted sought specific remedies potentially detrimental to the notice party developer. The notice party, who was a necessary party, had participated fully in the trial, was an entirely innocent party and acted in good faith at all times. Accordingly, there was no compelling reason as to why, the notice party having been successful in the proceedings, costs should not follow the event. **11–304**

3. Public interest litigation

The normal rule is that costs follow the event, *i.e.* that the successful party is awarded its costs against the unsuccessful party. The courts do, however, have a discretion in this regard. One circumstance in which this discretion may be exercised is where the taking of the proceedings was, in the opinion of the court, in the public interest. This might arise where, for example, the proceedings represent a "test case", raising a point which affects a large number of pending cases.[379] Another instance might be where—as in *Curtin v Ireland*—the Supreme Court was required to address novel but crucial constitutional questions **11–305**

---

[376] [1994] 2 I.R. 128; [1994] 2 I.L.R.M. 1.

[377] For a more extreme example, prior to the Local Government (Planning & Development) Act 1992, see *Electricity Supply Board v Gormley* [1985] I.R. 124; [1985] I.L.R.M. 494 (at 157/507) ("It has not been suggested that even if the Wexford County Council had been joined it could have made any submission not made by the plaintiff.").

[378] Unreported, Supreme Court, May 16, 2002.

[379] Such as, for example, *F v Ireland*, unreported, Supreme Court, July 27, 1995.

in an uncharted constitutional terrain, and where the judgment of the Supreme Court would provide certainty and obviate the risk of later litigation.

11–306 In a number of cases, it had been suggested that if the applicant had a private interest in the outcome of the proceedings, he or she should not be regarded as a public interest litigant and, accordingly, not entitled to any special order in respect of costs.[380] This requirement that the applicant have no private interest seems to have derived from the judgment of the English High Court in *R. v Lord Chancellor Ex p. Child Poverty Action Group.*[381]

> "The essential characteristics of a public law challenge are that it raises public law issues which are of general importance, where the applicant has no private interest in the outcome of the case. It is obvious that many, indeed most judicial review challenges, do not fall into the category of public interest challenges so defined. This is because, even if they do raise issues of general importance, they are cases in which the applicant is seeking to protect some private interest of his or her own."

11–307 With respect, it is must be open to question as to whether it is correct to say that the jurisdiction is confined to litigants with no private interest in the outcome of the proceedings.[382] First, any such principle would be inconsistent with previous decisions of the Supreme Court where special costs order were made in favour persons who did have a private interest. Reference is made in this regard, by way of example, to the judgment of the Supreme Court in *F v Ireland,*[383] wherein—against the background of family law proceedings—the unsuccessful party was awarded the costs of a constitutional challenge against the State.

11–308 Secondly, to limit the availability of special costs orders to persons *without* a personal interest appears to run counter to the general requirement—of both constitutional and administrative law—that a litigant establish *locus standi* or a "sufficient interest" (to use the language of Ord.84, r.20). This normally entails demonstrating a personal interest, albeit that in certain circumstances a public interest will be sufficient. It would be anomalous if it were only persons without a private interest in the outcome of proceedings who could ever qualify for favourable treatment in relation to costs.

---

[380] *McEvoy v Meath County Council* [2003] 1 I.R. 208; and *Dunne v Minister for the Environment Heritage and Local Government* [2005] I.E.H.C. 79; March 18, 2005. See also *Friends of the Curragh Environment Ltd. v An Bord Pleanála (No. 1)* [2006] I.E.H.C. 243; unreported, Kelly J., July 14, 2006 (pre-emptive costs order).

[381] [1998] 2 All E.R. 755 at 762, *per* Dyson J.

[382] See also R. Gordon, *EC Law in Judicial Review* (Oxford University Press, 2007), para.14.88, where it is suggested that a requirement that the applicant have no private interest in the outcome of the proceedings should not apply in an EC environmental challenge, where the deterrent effect of expensive court proceedings may, in practice, operate adversely to EC environmental law objectives.

[383] Unreported, Supreme Court, July 27, 1995.

A concern as to the correctness of the requirement that a litigant have not **11–309** private interest in the outcome of the proceedings has been expressed—in the context of statutory judicial review procedure under the unamended s.50—by the High Court in *Harrington v An Bord Pleanála (No. 3).*[384]

> "While noting with great care and respect the cases cited in the judgment of Laffoy J in *Dunne v. the Minister for the Environment*, supra., I am not entirely satisfied that the wide discretion vested in the courts to grant costs is or ought to be as strictly limited as it is submitted must follow from that jurisprudence. To preclude a person who is required by statute to establish a 'substantial interest' in the very subject matter of an application for judicial review, from claiming and in an appropriate case being awarded costs, does not, in my view, seem justified on any principle of law. The judgment of Laffoy J. was not concerned with the question of judicial review applications made pursuant to the provisions of the [Planning and Development Act 2000], or to the statutory requirements imposed by that Act on applicants in respect of decisions of a planning authority or of An Bord Pleanála."

It is respectfully submitted that the approach of Macken J. is to be preferred to **11–310** that of the earlier authorities. The critical determinant of whether a special costs order is appropriate surely is that the *issues* raised in the proceedings be of public importance. The absence of a private interest is at best a neutral factor, and in many cases will actually militate against a special costs order.

One of the objectives underlying a special costs order is to ensure that points **11–311** of genuine public interest are litigated. It is implicit in this that the points be raised in proceedings where they will be properly ventilated; for example, that there is a proper factual basis for the claim. The fact that a person has no personal interest in the outcome of the proceedings may mean that he or she is not the best qualified person to bring the case. If there are other potential litigants more directly affected, then the policy should be to encourage them to bring proceedings as their personal circumstances will bring the force and urgency of reality to any test case.

4. Costs of leave application

The requirement that the application for leave to apply for judicial review be **11–312** on notice often results in lengthy hearings on the leave application. In the event that leave is granted, it might be argued that the leave should not have been opposed and that, irrespective of the outcome of the substantive application for judicial review, costs should be awarded against those parties unsuccessfully opposing the leave application. In *Usk and District Residents Association Ltd. v Environmental Protection Agency,*[385] it was suggested that it may be appropriate to award the applicant its costs of the leave application independently of the ultimate outcome of the judicial review proceedings. On

---

[384] [2006] I.E.H.C. 223; unreported, Macken J., July 11, 2006.
[385] Unreported, High Court, Finlay Geoghegan J., October 13, 2006.

the particular facts of the case, however, costs were reserved on the basis that it was not unreasonable to oppose the leave application in circumstances where leave was only granted on limited grounds: extensive grounds had been advanced in the statement of grounds, some of which were abandoned only at the commencement of the hearing and others of which were pursued but refused.

5. Security for costs

11–313 It should be noted that security for costs is generally not available in the case of a personal litigant.[386] For this reason, the balance of the discussion of security for costs is confined to the statutory entitlement to security in the case of limited liability companies. Before turning to that discussion, however, brief mention should be made of two exceptional circumstances where security may be obtained against a personal litigant. The first of these is where the individual is resident outside the jurisdiction and is not resident in a state subject to the judgments convention or regulation. The second is where the individual is an appellant before the Supreme Court. Order 58 provides that security for the costs of an appeal may be ordered, and this is not confined to limited liability companies.[387] As leave to appeal to the Supreme Court will only be granted under s.50A(7) where a point of law of exceptional public importance is involved, it may well be that security for costs will be refused as a matter of discretion. The Supreme Court will not ordinarily entertain an application for security for costs on an appeal if it is satisfied that the question at issue in the case is a question of law of public importance.[388]

Section 390 of the Companies Act 1963

11–314 Section 390 of the Companies Act 1963 provides that where a limited liability company is plaintiff in any action or other legal proceedings, any court having jurisdiction in the matter, may, if it appears by credible testimony that there is reason to believe that the company will be unable to pay the costs of the defendant if successful in his or her defence, require sufficient security to be given for those costs and may stay all proceedings until such security is given. It has been accepted in a number of judgments that judicial review proceedings constitute "other legal proceedings" for the purpose of s.390.[389] In the event that security is not provided within the time fixed, or some other reasonable time, the proceedings may be dismissed.[390]

---

[386] See, for example, *Coll v Donegal County Council (No. 2)*, unreported, High Court, Dunne J., March 29, 2007.

[387] See, for example, *Fallon v An Bord Pleanála* [1992] 2 I.R. 380.

[388] *Fallon v An Bord Pleanála* [1992] 2.I.R. 380 at 384, *per* Finlay C.J.

[389] *Lancefort Ltd. v An Bord Pleanála* [1998] 2 I.R. 511; and *Usk District Residents Association Ltd. v Environmental Protection Agency* [2006] I.E.S.C. 1; [2006] 1 I.L.R.M. 363.

[390] *Lough Neagh Explorations Ltd. v Morrice* [1999] 4 I.R. 515; [1999] 1 I.L.R.M. 62; and *Superwood Holdings Ltd. v Sun Alliance and London Insurance plc* [2004] I.E.S.C. 19; [2004] 2 I.R. 407.

The question of the applicant company's ability to pay the costs of the successful **11–315** defendants is the first matter to be addressed by the court. Thereafter, if there is inability to meet the costs, the court must consider whether there exist any special circumstances which would justify the refusal of an order for security for costs. The onus is on the respondent to establish that the applicant company would be unable to meet the costs, and on the applicant company to establish the existence of the necessary special circumstances.[391]

Timing of application for security for costs

There are a number of aspects of the statutory judicial review procedure which **11–316** give rise to special considerations on an application for security for costs, as follows. The first relates to the timing of the application. There is a general obligation on a party seeking security for costs not to delay. Given the bifurcated nature of the judicial review procedure under ss.50 and 50A, a question arises as to whether security for costs should be sought in advance of the application for leave to apply for judicial review. This question was answered in the negative in *Village Residents Association Ltd. v An Bord Pleanála (No. 2)*[392]; Laffoy J. suggested that delay is only relevant to an application for security for costs where the applicant has altered its position to its detriment by reason of the application for security not having been made earlier.

Prima facie defence

The second consideration relates to the assessment of whether the respondent **11–317** has a *prima facie* defence to proceedings. The strength or otherwise of the parties' cases is generally not an appropriate consideration in an application for security for costs, but if it can be shown that the strength of the applicant's case is such that there is no real defence to proceedings, then the application for security should be refused. Under the statutory judicial review procedure, there is, of course, the potential for separate hearings on the leave application, and—in the event that leave is granted—on the substantive application for judicial review. Even if an applicant company proves unsuccessful at the full hearing, it might nevertheless be awarded its costs of the leave application, on the basis that it was unreasonable for the respondents to have opposed leave.[393] On this analysis, it is arguable that what the respondent must show is that it has a *prima facie* defence to the application for leave.

This very issue came before the Supreme Court in *Usk District Residents* **11–318** *Association Ltd. v Environmental Protection Agency.*[394] Clarke J., giving the judgment of the court, stated that it could not be assumed that the costs of the leave application would be treated as a discrete item of costs. Further, the wording of s.390 referred to a successful defence of the proceedings. Thus, the appropriate test was whether the party seeking security could establish a

---

[391] *Irish Press plc v EM Warburg Pincus & Co.*, unreported, Supreme Court, July 29, 1998.
[392] [2000] 4 I.R. 321; [2001] 2 I.L.R.M. 22.
[393] See para.11–312.
[394] [2006] I.E.S.C. 1; [2006] 1 I.L.R.M. 363.

prima facie defence to the proceedings as a whole. For the purposes of establishing a *prima facie* defence, the party seeking security was entitled to rely on any factual matters which are properly before the court—including any matters which are contained in the substantive proceedings as opposed to in the application for security—and also to rely on any legal arguments which may be open on the basis of the facts asserted by the applicant or facts which have been prima facie established in the materials properly before the court.[395]

Special circumstances

11–319   The third issue, then, concerns one of the special circumstances which would justify not making an order to provide security. Specifically, it is now established (by analogy with the case law in respect of appeals to the Supreme Court),[396] that an order requiring the provision of security will not normally be made where the proceedings give rise to a question of law of exceptional public importance. Accordingly, in the context of judicial review proceedings under ss.50 and 50A, the court should on an application for security for costs consider whether or not the proceedings give rise to a point of law of exceptional public importance.[397] The mere fact that an applicant has established "substantial grounds" of challenge at the leave stage does not necessarily indicate that the case involves such a point of law.[398] Nor does the fact that an applicant company has established "substantial grounds" constitute a separate special circumstance; every applicant is required to overcome the statutory threshold, and, in any event, it is well settled that the strength or otherwise of a party's case is not generally an appropriate consideration on an application for security for costs, unless the case of the plaintiff or applicant is unanswerable, in which circumstances security should be refused.[399]

Sufficient security

11–320   The requirement under s.390 of the Companies Act 1963 is that "sufficient security" be given for the defendant's costs. The measure of security requires the making of a reasonable estimate or assessment of the actual costs which it is anticipated the defendant/respondent will have to meet.[400] The Supreme Court has suggested that where security is sought in advance of the application for leave to apply for judicial review, it is appropriate to limit the quantum to the costs which might reasonably be expected to arise at the leave application.[401]

---

[395]   *ibid.*, at 372.
[396]   *Lancefort Ltd. v An Bord Pleanála* [1998] 2 I.R. 511. No particular weight appears to have been attached to the fact that in the context of security for costs of an appeal to the Supreme Court, the appellant already has a finding by the High Court against him.
[397]   *Lancefort Ltd. v An Bord Pleanála* [1998] 2 I.R. 511; and *Village Residents Association Ltd. v An Bord Pleanála (No. 2)* [2000] 4 I.R. 321; [2001] 2 I.L.R.M. 22.
[398]   See, by analogy, *Kenny v An Bord Pleanála (No. 1)* [2001] 1 I.R. 565.
[399]   *Village Residents Association Ltd. v An Bord Pleanála (No. 2)* [2000] 4 I.R. 321; [2001] 2 I.L.R.M. 22.
[400]   *Lismore Homes Ltd. v Bank of Ireland Finance Ltd. (No. 3)* [2001] 3 I.R. 536; [2002] 1 I.L.R.M. 541.
[401]   *Usk District Residents Association Ltd. v Environmental Protection Agency* [2006] I.E.S.C. 1; [2006] 1 I.L.R.M. 363.

If the applicant company were required to give security for the entirety of the proceedings at that stage, *i.e.* to include the costs of a possible substantive hearing, the quantum might well significantly exceed the costs which would be ultimately be awarded in the event that the leave to apply for judicial review was refused.

Stifling effect

An allegation that the true purpose of the moving party in seeking security is to stifle the applicant company's legitimate claim would not generally, on its own, justify refusing security.[402] It is, of course, the case that any stifling effect does not follow from the making of the order for security for costs *per se*, but from the failure of the members of the applicant company to demonstrate their commitment by providing the necessary funds to support the company's application.[403]   **11–321**

Security for costs and locus standi

Finally, the question whether or not the provision of security for costs might be a *quid pro quo* for allowing *locus standi* to limited liability companies, is considered separately above at para.11–207.   **11–322**

6. Pre-emptive or protective costs order ("PCO")

Order 99, r.5 of the Rules of the Superior Courts 1986 provides that costs may be dealt with by the court at any stage of the proceedings or after the conclusion of the proceedings and that an order for the payment of costs may require the costs to be paid forthwith, notwithstanding that the proceedings have not been concluded. This rule has been interpreted in *Village Residents Association Ltd. v An Bord Pleanála (No. 2)*[404] as allowing, in principle, for the making of a pre-emptive or protective costs order. On the particular facts of the case, however, Laffoy J. refused to make such an order, for the following reasons. First, the challenge was not brought by a public interest litigant in the strict sense, in that the members of the applicant company had a private interest in the outcome of the proceedings. Secondly, any issue of public importance was not sufficiently immediate to justify a pre-emptive costs order. Thirdly, the court did not have sufficient appreciation of the merits of the application at the interlocutory stage to conclude that it would be in the public interest to make a pre-emptive costs order. The fact that the applicant had satisfied the statutory criterion of "substantial grounds" at the leave stage was not, on its own, a circumstance from which one could conclude that it was in the public interest to insulate the applicant company from a future award of costs without awaiting the outcome of the challenge. Fourthly, the applicant had sought a pre-emptive costs order against a non-public body (the notice party developer).   **11–323**

---

[402] *Village Residents Association Ltd. v An Bord Pleanála (No. 2)* [2000] 4 I.R. 321; [2001] 2 I.L.R.M. 22.
[403] *Lismore Homes Ltd. v Bank of Ireland Finance Ltd. (No. 2)* [1999] 1 I.R. 501.
[404] [2000] 4 I.R. 321; [2001] 2 I.L.R.M. 22.

11–324 The jurisdiction of the High Court to make a pre-emptive costs order was elaborated upon in *Friends of the Curragh Environment Ltd. v An Bord Pleanála (No. 1)*.[405] Kelly J. considered the judgment in *Village Residents Association Ltd. v An Bord Pleanála (No. 2)*, and the subsequent judgment of the Court of Appeal in England and Wales in *R. (On the Application of Corner House Research) v Secretary of State for Trade and Industry*.[406] The Court of Appeal had restated the circumstances in which such an order would be appropriate, as follows.

> "1. A PCO may be made at any stage of the proceedings, on such conditions as the court thinks fit, provided that the court is satisfied that: (i) The issues raised are of general public importance; (ii) The public interest requires that those issues should be resolved; (iii) The applicant has no private interest in the outcome of the case; (iv) Having regard to the financial resources of the applicant and the respondent(s) and to the amount of costs that are likely to be involved it is fair and just to make the order; (v) If the order is not made the applicant will probably discontinue the proceedings and will be acting reasonably in so doing.
> 2. If those acting for the applicant are doing so pro bono this will be likely to enhance the merits of the application for a PCO.
> 3. It is for the court, in its discretion, to decide whether it is fair and just to make the order in the light of the considerations set out above."

11–325 Kelly J. indicated that these represented the appropriate principles which courts in this jurisdiction ought to have regard to in deciding whether or not to exercise their discretion to make a PCO, and that the restated principles differed very little from those stated by Laffoy J. in *Village Residents Association Ltd. v An Bord Pleanála (No. 2)*.

11–326 The requirement that an applicant have no private interest in the outcome of the proceedings is controversial. Liberty and the Civil Rights Trust, in a recent report, have recommended that the lack of a private interest, although a relevant consideration, should not be a prerequisite for obtaining a PCO.[407]

> "Nonetheless, the Group thought that the extent and nature of an applicant's private interest is relevant to the decision whether to grant a PCO. It should not be determinative. The weight to be attached to it should be a matter for the judge considering the application. The courts can legitimately weigh the private interest against the public interest in the case; there are doubtless cases where the public interest in the case is so strong that a relatively modest private interest in the outcome on the part of the person seeking a PCO (particularly where the nature of the case is such that there is unlikely to be anyone else who could bring the case who did not have such an interest) should not prevent one being granted."

---

[405] [2006] I.E.H.C. 243; unreported, Kelly J., July 14, 2006.
[406] [2005] 4 All E.R. 1 at 23.
[407] "Litigating the Public Interest", Report of the Working Group on Facilitating Public Interest Litigation (July, 2006), at p.29.

7. Moot cases

Occasionally, for various reasons, judicial review proceedings may be rendered **11–327** moot. For example, there may have been a change in the legislation, or a developer may no longer be interested in implementing the proposed development the subject-matter of the judicial review proceedings. In such cases, the only issue outstanding between the parties may be in relation to costs. Given that court time is a scarce resource, the High Court will often be reluctant to embark on a possibly lengthy hearing in respect of a moot, and will encourage the parties to reach an accommodation on costs. In principle, however, the court retains jurisdiction to determine the legal issues, even if solely for the purpose of determining the incidence of costs.[408]

O. Stay on Judicial Review Proceedings

1. General

Sections 50(4) and (5) empower the High Court to stay judicial review **11–328** proceedings before it pending the making of a "decision" by a local authority, a planning authority or An Bord Pleanála.[409] Little direction is given under the legislation, however, as to the circumstances in which it would be appropriate to exercise this discretion; the only statutory criterion—which is apparently a condition precedent to the exercise of the power—is that the court considers that the matter is "within the jurisdiction" of the relevant decision-maker.

Although some guidance may be sought from the earlier cases in relation to **11–329** the failure to exhaust a right of appeal as a matter going to the discretionary nature of judicial review remedies, the analogy is imperfect, for the following three reasons. First, an application for a stay under ss.50(4) and (5) may arise at an earlier stage in the proceedings. In the case of conventional judicial review, the discretion generally only comes into play once the substantive merits of the case have been determined[410]; the court may nonetheless decide to withhold relief from an otherwise entitled applicant. Under ss.50(4) and (5), conversely, an application to stay can be made at any time after the bringing of the

---

[408] See, by analogy, *Smyth v Colgan* [1999] 1 I.R. 548 (enforcement proceedings). See also *R. v Holderness Borough District Council Ex p. James Robert Developments Ltd.* (1992) 66 P. & C.R. 46; and *R. (On the application of Bushell) v Newcastle upon Tyne Licensing Justices* [2006] U.K.H.L. 7, [5].

[409] This represents an advance on the little-used provisions of Ord.84, r.20(5), which allowed the High Court to adjourn an application for leave to apply for judicial review pending an appeal or the expiry of time for an appeal.

[410] *cf. G v Director of Public Prosecutions* [1994] 1 I.R. 374 at 378. See also *Kennedy v South Dublin County Council* (1998) 5 I.P.E.L.J. 31, where O'Sullivan J. appears to have refused *leave* to apply for judicial review on the discretionary ground that there was a more appropriate remedy. *Byrne v Wicklow County Council*, unreported, High Court, Keane J., November 3, 1994; and *Delgany Area Residents Association Ltd. v Wicklow County Council*, unreported, High Court, Barr J., May 28, 1998. See also Ord.84, r.20(5).

application for leave to apply for judicial review.[411] It is possible, therefore, that the application for a stay might be brought in advance of the hearing of the application for leave to apply for judicial review; that is, in advance of any consideration by the High Court of the judicial review proceedings. The legal issues, if any, arising on the proceedings may not readily be separated from the factual circumstances at such an early stage.[412] The fact that the judge hearing the application for a stay may have to anticipate the course of the judicial review proceedings runs counter to the general reluctance on the part of the High Court to determine substantive matters on an interlocutory hearing.[413]

11–330   Secondly, there is a subtle distinction in the considerations to be applied in each of the respective applications. In the case of conventional judicial review, the test is the adequacy of the alternative remedy, whereas in the case of an application under ss.50(4) and (5), the statutory criterion is whether or not the matter is within the jurisdiction of the relevant decision-maker. The concept of the adequacy of the alternative remedy is a composite one, and includes consideration, *inter alia*, of the jurisdiction of the appellate body to determine the issues raised on the appeal.[414] The statutory criterion under ss.50(4) and (5) is far less elastic: the fact that the pending "decision" is within the jurisdiction of the relevant decision-maker appears to be determinative, whereas this factor is only one of many strands in the concept of the adequacy of the alternative remedy. For example, in the context of conventional judicial review, factors such as public interest,[415] or possibly fair procedures,[416] might intrude to allow judicial review in respect of a matter properly within the jurisdiction of An Bord Pleanála.

11–331   Thirdly, it is a condition precedent to an application under ss.50(4) and (5) that a "decision" be pending, *i.e.* that there is some form of an application, appeal

---

[411] The application is "made" upon the issue and service of the notice of motion seeking leave to apply for judicial review; *KSK Enterprises Ltd. v An Bord Pleanála* [1994] 2 I.R. 128; [1994] 2 I.L.R.M. 1 It is submitted that the term "bringing" envisages a stage equivalent to, or prior to, the making of the application.

[412] See, for example, the facts of *Village Residents Association Ltd. v An Bord Pleanála (No. 1)* [2000] 1 I.R. 65; [2000] 2 I.L.R.M. 59; *Village Residents Association Ltd. v An Bord Pleanála (No. 2)* [2000] 4 I.R. 321; [2001] 2 I.L.R.M. 22.

[413] See, for example, *Broadnet Ireland Ltd. v Office of the Director of Telecommunications Regulations* [2000] 3 I.R. 281; [2000] 2 I.L.R.M. 241. See, also, *Village Residents Association Ltd. v An Bord Pleanála (No. 2)* [2000] 4 I.R. 321; [2001] 2 I.L.R.M. 22; and *McNamara v An Bord Pleanála* [1995] 2 I.L.R.M. 125 at 130 ("not concerned in trying to ascertain what the eventual result would be"). *Cf. Kenny v An Bord Pleanála (No. 1)* [2001] 1 I.R. 565; and *P v Minister for Justice, Equality and Law Reform* [2002] 1 I.L.R.M. 16 (High Court, Smyth J.).

[414] See *P & F Sharpe Ltd. v Dublin City & County Manager* [1989] I.R. 701; [1989] I.L.R.M. 565.

[415] *Eircell Ltd. v Leitrim County Council* [2000] 1 I.R. 479; [2000] 2 I.L.R.M. 81.

[416] *Jerry Beades Construction Ltd. v Dublin Corporation* [2005] I.E.H.C. 406; unreported, McKechnie J., September 7, 2005; *Bane v Garda Representative Association* [1997] 2 I.R. 449; *Eircell Ltd. v Leitrim County Council* [2000] 1 I.R. 479; [2000] 2 I.L.R.M. 81; and *Electricity Supply Board v Cork County Council*, unreported, High Court, Finnegan J., June 28, 2000.

or referral in being. Thus the fact that the applicant for judicial review arguably should have proceeded by way of statutory appeal is irrelevant if neither he nor any other person, in fact, invoked the appeal mechanism.[417]

In connection with conventional judicial review, conversely, the mere existence of a right of appeal is sufficient to permit the exercise of the discretion to withhold relief.[418] The fact, however, that the refusal of relief by way of judicial review might leave an applicant with no remedy (in circumstances where the applicant had allowed the statutory period for the bringing of an appeal to expire), may have been an unarticulated consideration in some of the conventional judicial review cases,[419] and the fact that the applicant, having not made submissions at the planning authority stage, was not entitled to appeal was expressly cited in *O'Brien v Dun Laoghaire Rathdown County Council*.[420] Obviously, no such inhibition (express or implied) operates in the case of an application for a stay under ss.50(4) and (5). Although it should be noted that the application, appeal or referral does not necessarily have to be one brought by the applicant for judicial review, nor, indeed, is it necessary even that the applicant for judicial review be a party to same. At the time of the application for a stay under ss.50(4) and (5), therefore, the applicant for judicial review might already be out of time to engage in the planning process.

11–332

In those rare cases on conventional judicial review where the fact of a *pending* appeal did inform the exercise of the court's discretion, it appears to have been treated as an additional factor to be weighed in the exercise of the discretion. In *Healy v Dublin County Council*,[421] for example, the fact that an appeal (brought by a third party) was in being appears to have tilted the balance in favour of the refusal of relief by judicial review. The more usual approach, however, seems to have been to treat the existence of an appeal as a neutral factor, even in circumstances where the applicant for judicial review himself had in tandem sought to appeal to An Bord Pleanála.[422]

11–333

---

[417] It should also be noted that the appeal does not necessarily have to be made by the applicant for judicial review, nor, indeed, is it necessary even that the applicant for judicial review be a party to the appeal.

[418] Even in circumstances where refusal of judicial review would leave the applicant without any remedy in that the time-limit for bringing an appeal would have long since expired. It is for this reason that applicants often lodge an appeal on a without prejudice basis; see, for example, *P & F Sharpe Ltd. v Dublin City & County Manager* [1989] I.R. 701; [1989] I.L.R.M. 565; and *Ardoyne House Management Ltd. v Dublin Corporation* [1998] 2 I.R. 147. Contrast with the provisions of Ord.84, r.20(5).

[419] *Dooley v Galway Corporation* [1992] 2 I.R 136. See, by analogy, *Lancefort Ltd. v An Bord Pleanála* [1997] 2 I.L.R.M. 508 at 515–516.

[420] [2006] I.E.H.C. 177; unreported, O'Neill J., June 1, 2006.

[421] Unreported, High Court, Barron J., April 29, 1993.

[422] *P & F Sharpe Ltd. v Dublin City & County Manager* [1989] I.R. 701; [1989] I.L.R.M. 565; *Ardoyne House Management Ltd. v Dublin Corporation* [1998] 2 I.R. 147; and *Tennyson v Dun Laoghaire Corporation* [1991] 1 I.R. 527. Cf. *Duff v Mangan* [1994] 1 I.L.R.M. 91; and *Buckley v Kirby* [2000] 3 I.R. 431; [2001] 2 I.L.R.M. 395.

2. Mechanics of application for stay

11–334 An application for a stay under ss.50(4) and (5) may only be made by a planning authority, a local authority or by An Bord Pleanála. The application may be brought "at any time" after the "bringing" of an application for leave to apply for judicial review. It is unclear as to whether the term "bringing" envisages a stage subsequent to the *hearing* of the application for leave to apply for judicial review, or an earlier stage in the proceedings. An application for leave to apply is *made* once the notice of motion seeking leave to apply for judicial review has been issue and served.[423] If this is sufficient to constitute the "bringing" of the application, then it would appear that an application for a stay may be made in advance of the actual hearing of the leave application. An issue would then arise as to which application should be heard first: the application for leave to apply for judicial review, or the application for the stay. On one view, if the purpose of the application for the stay is to expedite the statutory appeal process by staying any competing parallel judicial review proceedings, it would appear more effective to address the application for a stay first, rather than embark on a possibly lengthy hearing on the leave application. As against this, however, in order to identify the issues raised on the judicial review proceedings, it may be necessary to examine in some detail the grounds of challenge advanced in the statement of grounds, and, rather than replicate this exercise at a later stage (in the event of a stay not being granted), it might be more pragmatic to determine the two applications at the one hearing.[424]

11–335 The precise relationship between the considerations bearing on each of the two applications is unclear. At first blush, it would seem that they are directed to two very different issues. On an application for leave to apply for judicial review, the High Court must determine that there are "substantial grounds" for contending that the decision of the planning authority is invalid or ought to be quashed, and that the applicant has a "substantial interest" in the matter. On an application for a stay under ss.50(4) and (5), the High Court must consider whether the matter is within the jurisdiction of the relevant decision-maker. The first is not the obverse of the second: it is quite possible for the matter to be "within the jurisdiction" of the relevant decision-maker, and for there nevertheless to be substantial grounds of challenge. The logic of exhaustion of rights—and, presumably, of ss.50(4) and (5)—is that even in case of invalidity it still might be more appropriate to proceed by way of statutory appeal, rather than by way of judicial review. Accordingly, it would seem that the consideration mandated by ss.50(4) and (5) represents an additional, discrete test and one which is not concluded by a finding of "substantial grounds" and the granting of leave to apply for judicial review.[425] If this is the case, then there is little

---

[423] *KSK Enterprises Ltd. v An Bord Pleanála* [1994] 1 I.R. 124; [1994] 2 I.L.R.M. 1.

[424] A suggestion to like effect in respect of the equivalent provision of the unamended s.50 procedure was not taken up by the moving party in *Harding v Cork County Council (No. 1)* [2006] I.E.H.C. 80; [2006] 1 I.R. 294; [2006] 2 I.L.R.M. 392.

[425] An analogy might be drawn with the reasoning in *Lancefort Ltd. v An Bord Pleanála* [1999] 2 I.R. 270; [1998] 2 I.L.R.M. 401, where a not dissimilar distinction was drawn between "substantial grounds" and *locus standi*.

benefit in determining the application for leave to apply for judicial review in advance of any application for a stay under ss.50(4) and (5).

3. Matter within jurisdiction of relevant decision-maker

The statutory criterion under s.50(5) is whether or not the matter before the authority or An Bord Pleanála is "within the jurisdiction" of the relevant decision-maker. The precise meaning to be attributed to the term "matter" is unclear, and it is submitted that there are two viable interpretations, a broad one and a narrow one.

11–336

Broad interpretation

On the broad interpretation, the test would be whether or not the "application", "appeal" or "referral" (as appropriate) was properly before the authority or An Bord Pleanála ("the decision-maker"). This would require consideration of whether or not the grounds pleaded in the judicial review proceedings—if well founded—would affect the jurisdiction of the decision-maker. In some cases, the judicial review proceedings will allege a defect at an earlier stage of the decision-making process, but the effects of that defect will have been spent by the time the matter came before the relevant decision-maker. The most obvious example of where this might happen is where judicial review proceedings are directed towards the planning authority's decision on an application for planning permission, and, in parallel, the decision of the planning authority has also been appealed to An Bord Pleanála. The decision of An Bord Pleanála on appeal operates to annul the decision of the planning authority, and thus the fact that the decision of the planning authority may have been invalid does not *per se* prevent An Bord Pleanála from having jurisdiction to entertain the appeal.[426] Certain defects at the planning authority stage can, however, continue to subsist even before An Bord Pleanála,[427] and in such circumstances An Bord Pleanála does not have jurisdiction to entertain the appeal. For example, the fact that the applicant for planning permission did not have the minimum requisite interest in the lands the subject-matter of the application,[428] would render an application for planning permission invalid[429] and any decision to grant planning permission, whether by the planning authority or by An Bord Pleanála, would be voidable. Moreover, in extreme cases a breach of fair procedures at the planning authority stage may, notwithstanding the fact that a *de novo* hearing is involved, taint the appeal process.[430]

11–337

---

[426] PDA 2000, s.37(1)(b). See also *O'Keeffe v An Bord Pleanála* [1993] 1 I.R. 39 at 52; [1992] I.L.R.M. 237 at 247.

[427] *Hynes v An Bord Pleanála (No. 2)*, unreported, High Court, McGuinness J., July 30, 1998.

[428] For the requirements as to interest, see *Keane v An Bord Pleanála* [1998] 2 I.L.R.M. 241.

[429] *Hynes v An Bord Pleanála (No. 2)*, unreported, High Court, McGuinness J., July 30, 1998.

[430] See *Jerry Beades Construction Ltd. v Dublin Corporation* [2005] I.E.H.C. 406; unreported, McKechnie J., September 7, 2005, [72]; and *Harding v Cork County Council (No. 1)* [2006] I.E.H.C. 80; [2006] 1 I.R. 294; [2006] 2 I.L.R.M. 392.

11–338 For the purposes of s.50(5) then, on the broad interpretation, the High Court would simply have to consider whether the legal grounds of challenge raised in the judicial review proceedings were ones which, if well founded, would impact on the jurisdiction of An Bord Pleanála, or were ones which were spent by the time the appeal/application reached An Bord Pleanála. In many cases, the grounds of challenge would fall into the latter category,[431] and, accordingly, it would be open to the High Court to stay the judicial review proceedings on the basis that the matter was within the jurisdiction of An Bord Pleanála.

11–339 Under the unamended s.50 procedure, the power to stay judicial review proceedings was confined to situations where a matter was pending before An Bord Pleanála. Now, as a result of amendments under the 2006 Act, a stay is also available where a matter is pending before a local authority or planning authority. It is difficult, however, to think of circumstances where a defect alleged in judicial review proceedings against a local authority or planning authority would not taint the jurisdiction of the authority to make a decision in the matter. This is because the judicial review proceedings will usually involve a challenge to an act or decision at an earlier stage in the decision-making process, and—unlike the case of an appeal to An Bord Pleanála—there will have been no intervening event to break the link between the defect complained of and the final decision. For example, if the complaint made in the judicial review proceedings is that a planning authority failed to require further public notice following the receipt of a response to a request for additional information, this is a subsisting defect and one which would vitiate any decision to grant planning permission.

11–340 It is only where the authority has the ability to rescue its own jurisdiction by remedying the defect alleged in the judicial review proceedings that it would be appropriate to stay the proceedings. This might occur where the judicial review proceedings allege an identifiable legal defect, but one which is within the competence of authority to address or remedy. For example, the omission of an environmental impact statement from an application in respect of development for which an environmental impact statement is required would render a decision invalid. A planning authority is empowered—under the Planning and Development Regulations 2001—to require an environmental impact statement to be submitted in circumstances where the developer fails to submit one in the first instance.

11–341 In such cases, the answer to the question as to whether or not the matter is within the jurisdiction of the authority is contingent on the authority exercising the relevant power to remedy the defect. It may well be, however, that at the time of the application for the stay under s.50(5) the authority will not yet have

---

[431] For example, an allegation that the proposed development would involve a material contravention of the development plan, or that there had been a failure to comply with public notice requirements, would not normally affect the jurisdiction of An Bord Pleanála (*cf.* Planning and Development Act 2000, s.37(2)).

considered the exercise of such a power. It is submitted that in judicial review proceedings involving challenges of this type, a "wait and see" attitude must be adopted. The judicial review proceedings must initially be stayed as the applicant cannot, at that stage, demonstrate that it is inevitable that authority's jurisdiction is destroyed. If the authority subsequently fails to exercise the remedying power, however, then the stay on the judicial review proceedings should be lifted. The applicant for judicial review has laid down a marker as to the defect by issuing and serving the judicial review proceedings and, accordingly, is not open to the criticism that he has waived his right to object to the defect alleged.[432]

Narrow interpretation

On the narrow interpretation, the term "matter" would be read as meaning "the grounds on which the decision or act is challenged". This interpretation would require that, in addition to confirming that the appeal, referral or application itself was properly before the relevant decision-maker, the High Court would also have to consider whether the decision-maker had the competence to address the legal issues raised in the judicial review proceedings. In at least some cases, the decision-maker will be in position to determine the matter before it, without having to decide or rule on the legal issues raised in the judicial review proceedings. Under the previous legislation, this point was readily illustrated by reference to material contravention of the development plan.[433] An Bord Pleanála took free of the restrictions imposed on the planning authority in connection with granting planning permission for a development which would involve a material contravention of the development plan. Thus, An Bord Pleanála was not compelled to inquire into an allegation that the planning authority had acted *ultra vires* in granting planning permission in material contravention of the plan; the illegality, if any, was spent by the time the matter reached An Bord Pleanála. The High Court was the only forum in which this issue would have to be canvassed and, in order to vindicate the rule of law, therefore, judicial review ought to be allowed.[434]

11–342

Similarly, the relevant decision-maker may be able to make its determination on the application, appeal or referral before it without having to rule on allegations of unfair procedures at an earlier point. Again, this is more likely to occur where the complaints relate to an act on the part of a local authority or planning authority, and the matter has gone on appeal to An Bord Pleanála.

11–343

---

[432] *cf. Max Developments Ltd. v An Bord Pleanála* [1994] 2 I.R. 121. The desire to avoid such criticism gives rise to the intriguing possibility that an applicant himself might seek to stay his own judicial review proceedings.

[433] Specifically, s.26(3) of the Local Government (Planning & Development) Act 1963, and s.14(8) of the Local Government (Planning & Development) Act 1976. The position is not as clear-cut under the PDA 2000 in that under s.37(2), the issue of material contravention retains some significance before An Bord Pleanála.

[434] *Tennyson v Dun Laoghaire Corporation* [1991] 2 I.R. 527. *Cf. Kennedy v South Dublin County Council* (1998) 5 I.P.E.L.J. 31; and *Byrne v Wicklow County Council*, unreported, High Court, Keane J., November 3, 1994.

Strictly, want of fair procedures at the planning authority stage should not affect An Bord Pleanála's jurisdiction: the decision of An Bord Pleanála operates to annul the decision of the planning authority and, save in the case of a subsisting defect, this should sweep away any irregularity at the planning authority stage. Moreover, An Bord Pleanála may well have power to address the want of fair procedure alleged; for example, An Bord Pleanála has a discretion to require further public notices.[435] The question of whether or not an appeal to An Bord Pleanála provides adequate redress for a complaint of procedural unfairness has already been considered at paras 11–219 to 11–229, and will not be considered further here.

Summary

11–344   In summary, it is submitted that the narrow interpretation is to be preferred to the broad interpretation, as the one best vindicating the rule of law. There is a public interest in ensuring that the conduct of the planning authorities is kept in check.[436] In circumstances where a planning authority has breached the limitations imposed on its statutory powers, a remedy should not be denied to an applicant (who in order to obtain leave must demonstrate a "substantial interest") simply on the basis that there is an alternative forum where the planning merits of the particular decision can be appealed. As stated in *P & F Sharpe Ltd. v Dublin City & County Manager*,[437] it would not be just to deprive a party of its right to have a decision quashed for want of validity. The narrow interpretation of ss.50(4) and (5) would indicate that a stay should not be granted in circumstances where the judicial review proceedings raised issues in respect of any of the following: the legality of actions of the local authority or its officials[438]; the validity of notices served[439]; the exposition of the statutory concept of "proper planning and [sustainable] development"[440]; the interpretation of the statutory development plan[441]; or serious breaches of procedural requirements.[442]

11–345   A narrow approach to the interpretation of the equivalent subsection under the unamended s.50 procedure appears to have been favoured by the High Court in *Harding v Cork County Council (No. 1)*.[443] Kelly J. indicated that points

---

[435] Planning and Development Regulations 2001, art.113. *Quaere* whether this power is only available in respect of applications/appeals subject to environmental impact assessment.

[436] *Eircell Ltd. v Leitrim County Council* [2000] 1 I.R. 479 at 495; [2000] 2 I.L.R.M. 81 at 97.

[437] [1989] I.R. 701; [1989] I.L.R.M. 565.

[438] *P & F Sharpe Ltd. v Dublin City & County Manager* [1989] I.R. 701; [1989] I.L.R.M. 565; *Tennyson v Dun Laoghaire Corporation* [1991] 1 I.R. 527; and *Electricity Supply Board v Cork County Council*, unreported, High Court, Finnegan J., June 28, 2000.

[439] *Ardoyne House Management Ltd. v Dublin Corporation* [1998] 2 I.R. 147.

[440] *Eircell Ltd. v Leitrim County Council* [2000] 1 I.R. 479; [2000] 2 I.L.R.M. 81.

[441] *Tennyson v Dun Laoghaire Corporation* [1991] 1 I.R. 527.

[442] *Jerry Beades Construction Ltd. v Dublin Corporation* [2005] I.E.H.C. 406; unreported, McKechnie J., September 7, 2005.

[443] [2006] I.E.H.C. 80; [2006] 1 I.R. 294; [2006] 2 I.L.R.M. 392.

relating to *vires*, fair procedures and bias should properly be determined by a court rather than on appeal to An Bord Pleanála.

4. Lifting the stay

The effect of a successful application under ss.50(4) and (5) is simply to stay the judicial review proceedings, it is not equivalent to a dismissal or even to the refusal of leave to apply for judicial review. A question therefore arises as to the circumstances in which it would be appropriate to lift the stay. As discussed above, the availability of a stay is contingent merely on the matter being within the jurisdiction of the relevant decision-maker; it does not necessarily follow from this, however, that the decision-maker will in fact address the matter complained of. It might be thought that in such circumstances, an applicant should be entitled to revive his application for judicial review. In the case of an appeal to An Bord Pleanála, the fact that the decision of An Bord Pleanála operates to annul the decision of the planning authority presents the following conceptual difficulty: if An Bord Pleanála has been allowed to make a decision before the stay is lifted, then it would seem that the judicial review proceedings would have been rendered moot. Whereas the applicant might be entitled to issue and serve fresh proceedings challenging the decision of An Bord Pleanála, free from any criticism that he had waived the objection by allowing an appeal to be pursued before An Bord Pleanála, it is difficult to understand what useful purpose might be served by continuing the proceedings as against the annulled decision of the planning authority.   **11–346**

It would seem therefore that it would only be in cases where An Bord Pleanála indicated its ruling on any procedural issues concurrently raised in the judicial review proceedings, in advance of the substantive decision on the appeal, that there would be any real benefit in lifting the stay and allowing the challenge to the planning authority's decision to be pursued.   **11–347**

P. Remittal

Order 84, r.26(4) indicates that where the relief sought in judicial review proceedings is *certiorari*, and the court is satisfied that there are grounds for quashing the decision, the High Court has a discretion to remit the matter to the decision-maker with a direction to reconsider it and to reach a decision in accordance with the findings of the High Court.   **11–348**

The nature of the court's discretion is this regard was considered in detail in *Usk and District Residents Association Ltd. v An Bord Pleanála*.[444] The facts of the case were unusual, with An Bord Pleanála conceding that the absence of satisfactory records leading to a decision to grant planning permission meant   **11–349**

---

[444] Unreported, High Court, Kelly J., March 14, 2007.

that it could not establish whether conditions drafted by an inspector were ever approved at a formal board meeting. The inspector had initially recommended that planning permission be refused. The board decided that planning permission should be granted, and requested that the inspector draw up conditions in accordance with the board's determination. There was, however, no record of a subsequent meeting of the board approving the conditions as drafted. In the circumstances, the board conceded that the decision should be quashed.

11–350   There was then a dispute between the parties as to whether, on the particular facts of the case, it was appropriate to remit the matter to the board, or whether the planning permission should be quashed *simpliciter*. This latter course would have required the developer to reapply for planning permission to the planning authority, a course which the court considered would be disproportionate in the circumstances. Kelly J. ruled that the matter should instead be remitted to the board, but went on to make a number of recommendations which he considered would minimise the risk of further judicial review. These included a suggestion that it would be prudent and correct for the board to exercise its jurisdiction to reopen the oral hearing into the appeal, and that the appeal be considered and dealt with by members of the board other than those involved in the impugned decision.

Q. Appeal to Supreme Court

1. Introduction

11–351   Section 50A(7) of the PDA 2000 (as inserted under the 2006 Act) provides that the determination of the High Court on the application for leave to apply for judicial review, or on the substantive application for judicial review, shall be final, and no appeal shall lie from the decision of the High Court to the Supreme Court in respect of either decision except with the leave of the High Court. The subsection goes on to provide that leave to appeal shall only be granted where the High Court certifies that its decision involves a point of law of exceptional public importance, and that it is desirable in the public interest that an appeal should be taken to the Supreme Court.[445]

11–352   The structure of the equivalent provisions of the previous legislation was analysed by the Supreme Court in *Irish Asphalt Ltd. v An Bord Pleanála*.[446] The Supreme Court held that the provision represented an exception to the Supreme Court's appellate jurisdiction within the meaning of Article 34.4.3° of the Constitution.[447] It was further held that the subsection, having excepted

---

[445] See, generally, G. Simons, "Leave to appeal to the Supreme Court" (2002) 9 I.P.E.L.J. 3.
[446] [1996] 2 I.R. 179; [1997] 1 I.L.R.M. 81. See also *Irish Hardware v South Dublin County Council* [2001] 2 I.L.R.M. 291; and *Baby O v Minister for Justice Equality and Law Reform* [2002] 2 I.R. 169; [2003] 1 I.L.R.M. 241.
[447] In *Irish Hardware Association v South Dublin County Council* [2001] 2 I.L.R.M. 291, the provisions were characterised as a "regulation". It would appear, however, that the term "exception" may be more consistent with the analysis actually applied.

those cases from the appellate jurisdiction, goes on to create an exception to this exception: the High Court may allow an appeal if the case involves a point of law of exceptional public importance and it is in the public interest that an appeal should be taken to the Supreme Court.[448] It has also been held that it is the High Court, and that court alone, which is to grant leave for an appeal.[449] The decision of the High Court to grant or refuse leave to appeal is apparently unimpeachable, and may not itself be the subject of an appeal to the Supreme Court. This second decision, namely to grant or refuse leave to appeal, seemingly, does not represent a separate "decision" of the High Court within the meaning of Article 34.4.3° of the Constitution so as to attract the general right of appeal.

The legislative provisions in this regard are open to serious criticism, as follows. **11–353**
First, whatever may be the position in respect of the decision of the High Court on the substantive application for judicial review, it is indefensible that an applicant, on a summary hearing, may be shut out at the leave stage from even bringing judicial review proceedings on the basis of the say so of a single High Court judge. Judicial review of planning decisions can often give rise to complex legal issues, and the viability of novel points of law can often be missed on an application for leave.[450] In the circumstances, the safeguard of an appeal to

---

[448] *Irish Asphalt Ltd. v An Bord Pleanála* [1996] 2 I.R. 179 at 185; [1997] 1 I.L.R.M. 81 at 85.

[449] *Irish Hardware Association v South Dublin County Council* [2001] 2 I.L.R.M. 291. See also *Irish Asphalt Ltd. v An Bord Pleanála* [1996] 2 I.R. 179 at 186; [1997] 1 I.L.R.M. 81 at 85. Although it is idle to pursue the matter given that the Supreme Court has ruled on the point twice (see, further, *Baby O v Minister for Justice Equality and Law Reform* [2002] 2 I.R. 169; [2003] 1 I.L.R.M. 241), the analysis of the provisions is open to the following criticisms. The "exception to the exception" interpretation is highly artificial and does not appear to be correct. The decision to grant or refuse leave to appeal is distinct from the decision on the judicial review proper, and this second decision is not expressly excluded from the appellate jurisdiction. Article 34.4.3° applies to all decisions of the High Court; see, for example, *Dublin Wellwoman Centre Ltd. v Ireland* [1995] 1 I.L.R.M. 408; and *SPUC v Grogan* [1990] I.L.R.M. 350. The Supreme Court has traditionally been jealous of its appellate jurisdiction, and it is of particular concern that the Supreme Court now seeks to support its interpretation by suggesting that it would be contrary to a perceived legislative objective that there should be a greater degree of certainty and expedition in the determination of proceedings challenging planning decisions. With respect, any exclusion of appellate jurisdiction can only be achieved by express language, not by reference to some implied objective. It can also be added that it is a *non sequitur* to suggest that it follows from the fact that the intention to challenge a decision be made known within a short time period (two months/eight weeks) that those judicial review proceedings must generally be disposed of without any involvement of the Supreme Court. The Supreme Court can readily assess, on an interlocutory application, whether or not a case involves a point of law of exceptional public importance, and often does so; see, for example, the analogous jurisdiction in connection with the provision of security for costs where the Supreme Court will not require security to be provided if the case involves a point of law of exceptional public importance.

[450] See, for example, the case of *Butler v Dublin Corporation* [1999] 1 I.R. 565; [1999] 1 I.L.R.M. 481, where leave to apply for conventional judicial review was refused in the first instance by the High Court (Smyth J.). The application for judicial review was ultimately successful. In the context of an application pursuant to court's inherent

the Supreme Court is essential. Secondly, the restricted right of appeal may have the effect that the Supreme Court will precluded from ruling definitively on many important legal issues. Thirdly, the criteria for the grant of leave are cumbersome. In particular, the relationship between the two limbs, namely point of law of exceptional public importance, and public interest, is confused.[451] There is also the fact that there is no express requirement that the issue of whether or not the proposed grounds of appeal are arguable or stateable be considered.[452]

11–354   At a very minimum, the procedure should be reformed so as to allow for the application for leave to appeal to be renewed before the Supreme Court, at least in cases where leave to apply for judicial review has been refused.

2. Decisions in respect of which leave to appeal not required

General

11–355   It would seem that the requirement to obtain leave to appeal only applies in respect of the formal decision on the application for leave to apply for judicial review, or on the substantive application for judicial review. Accordingly, it is submitted that other decisions made under ss.50 and 50A—for example, a decision on an application for a stay under s.50(4), or a decision on an application to extend time under s.50(8)—are subject to an appeal in the ordinary way.[453]

Constitutional grounds of appeal

11–356   The requirement to obtain leave to appeal does not apply to a determination of the High Court insofar as it involves a question as to the validity of any law having regard to the provisions of the Constitution.[454] It would appear from the decision in *Jackson Way Properties Ltd. v Minister for Environment and Local Government*,[455] in relation to analogous provisions under the Roads Act 1993 (as amended), that even in the case of a constitutional challenge, a certificate would still be required in respect of the non-constitutional grounds of appeal.

---

jurisdiction to strike out proceedings as frivolous or vexatious, the decision in *Irish Permanent Building Society v Caldwell* [1979] I.L.R.M. 273 indicates that the jurisdiction to strike out proceedings ought not to be exercised in cases raising complex and novel issues of law.

[451] See *Kenny v An Bord Pleanála (No. 2)* [2001] 1 I.R. 704; [2002] 1 I.L.R.M. 68.

[452] cf. *Raiu v Refugee Appeals Tribunal*, unreported, High Court, Finlay Geoghegan J., February 26, 2003.

[453] In respect of this latter point, see, by analogy, *AB v Minister for Justice Equality and Law Reform* [2002] 1 I.R. 296; [2002] 2 I.L.R.M. 161.

[454] PDA 2000, s.50A(8) (as inserted under the 2006 Act).

[455] [1999] 4 I.R. 608.

3. Refusal of leave not certifiable

In *Arklow Holidays Ltd. v An Bord Pleanála (No. 3)*,[456] the High Court had to **11–357** consider whether a decision to refuse leave to appeal might itself be certified for appeal. It was argued that the initial decision to refuse leave to appeal was part of the "determination" of the High Court of the application for leave to apply for judicial review, and, as such, was itself capable of being certified for appeal. In the alternative it was said that if the refusal of leave to appeal was not part of the "determination", then there was no express prohibition on an appeal being brought to the Supreme Court without leave. Clarke J. rejected these arguments.

> "It is clear, therefore, that the proper interpretation of this section is that it, in principle, precludes any appeal to the Supreme Court in respect of planning judicial review matters. That exclusion is subject to the limited exception which derives from the certification process. However, it is clear from those determinations of the Supreme Court that the decision as to whether to grant a certificate is a matter for the High Court and for the High Court alone. I am therefore satisfied that it is not open to the High Court to certify a question as to whether there should have been a certificate in the first place as a matter for appeal to the Supreme Court."

Clarke J. went on to say that to permit an appeal of the type sought would **11–358** create the possibility of a huge multiplicity of hearings which would defeat the purpose of expedition which, it has been clearly held on many occasions, formed the policy behind the relevant provisions.

4. Two conditions for leave

Section 50A(7) requires that two conditions be fulfilled before leave to appeal **11–359** can be granted. First, that the decision of the High Court must involve a point of law of exceptional public importance. Secondly, that it is desirable in the public interest that an appeal should be taken to the Supreme Court. These requirements are cumulative[457]; it would seem to follow from this that even where a point of law of exceptional public importance is exposed, leave to appeal must nevertheless be refused unless the public interest requirement is satisfied.

5. Point of law of exceptional public importance

Leave to appeal shall only be granted where the High Court certifies that its **11–360** decision involves a point of law of exceptional public importance. Two consequences appear to flow from this. First, in determining whether or not to

---

[456] [2006] I.E.H.C. 280; unreported, Clarke J., September 8, 2006.
[457] *Kenny v An Bord Pleanála (No. 2)* [2001] 1 I.R. 704; [2002] 1 I.L.R.M. 68; and *Raiu v Refugee Appeals Tribunal*, unreported, High Court, Finlay Geoghegan J., February 26, 2003.

grant leave to appeal, regard must be had to the decision itself, and not to the merits of the arguments which resulted in that decision.[458] This would appear to suggest that the High Court should not attempt to predict what the outcome of the appeal might be; instead, it should take the appellant's case at its height and consider whether or not the point of law is of exceptional public importance.

11–361 Secondly, it is the decision of the High Court which must give rise to the point of law. Thus if the decision of the High Court was based on narrow grounds (in particular, on factual grounds), it may be that no point of law can properly be isolated.[459] To put the matter another way, it is not permissible to allow an appeal on a moot, or on theoretical points of law which might have arisen for discussion or consideration during the hearing, but which did not go to the actual determination or decision of the High Court.[460] The point of law must be "of" or in some way contained "in" the decision or determination in the first instance, and must at the same time transcend the case itself to meet the requirements of exceptional public importance and public interest.[461]

11–362 If the factual background to a case is unusual so that it would not be necessary or desirable for the Supreme Court in its judgment to address general legal principles, then this might be a reason for taking the view that a point of law of exceptional public importance does not arise.[462]

---

[458] *Lancefort Ltd. v An Bord Pleanála*, unreported, High Court, Morris J., July 23, 1997 at pp. 3–4; and *Raiu v Refugee Appeals Tribunal*, unreported, High Court, Finlay Geoghegan J., February 26, 2003.

[459] See *Lancefort Ltd. v An Bord Pleanála*, unreported, High Court, McGuinness J., March 31, 1998: "Many of the questions seem to me to be too closely connected either with the facts of the instant case or with the specific arguments made by counsel for the applicant during the hearing before me." The requirement that the point of law have immediacy also occurs in the analogous situation of security for costs or pre-emptive costs. For example, in *Village Residents Association Ltd. (No. 2)* [2000] 4 I.R. 321; [2001] 2 I.L.R.M. 22, Laffoy J. found that before the point of law relied upon in that case could actually be isolated, several controversies had to be disposed of, and the issue of general importance was not sufficiently immediate. See also *Begley v An Bord Pleanála*, unreported, High Court, Ó Caoimh J., May 23, 2003.

[460] *Ashbourne Holdings Ltd. v An Bord Pleanála (No. 3)*, unreported, High Court, Kearns J., June 19, 2001.

[461] *Ashbourne Holdings Ltd. v An Bord Pleanála (No. 3)*, unreported, High Court, Kearns J., June 19, 2001. *Quaere* what the position would be if the High Court judge were to decide the case on a narrow ground but were to go on to decide (if wrong on that point) the wider issues. Technically the second limb of the judgment would be *obiter dictum* but it might suffice for a decision to "involve" a point of law. This speculation is probably idle, however, since the course of conduct posited is usually adopted only by judges who are concerned to render their decisions appeal-proof. Since the PDA 2000 accomplishes this anyway the judge is unlikely to go further than is strictly necessary to dispose of the case and, in any event, on the suggested analysis would have quite the opposite effect from that intended.

[462] *Harding v Cork County Council (No. 3)*, unreported, High Court, Clarke J., November 30, 2006. See also *Harrington v An Bord Pleanála (No. 2)*, unreported, High Court, Macken J., March 16, 2006, where it was suggested that as the question of delay is always something to be considered in the context of a particular application, it was difficult to see how a point of exceptional public importance could arise in the absence of a finding of general application.

The requirement that the point of law must be "of" or in some way contained **11–363** "in" the decision or determination of the High Court is subject to an exception where the High Court fails, through inadvertence, to deal with a point which arose in the course of argument and which, if it be a good point, could have affected the result of the case notwithstanding the other findings made by the court and set out in the court's judgment.[463] A party who might otherwise be entitled to a certificate to appeal will not be deprived of that entitlement due to the fact that the High Court had, by inadvertence, failed to deal with an issue which was properly argued.[464]

In order to constitute a point of law of exceptional public importance, the point **11–364** must be of such gravity and importance that it transcends the interests and considerations of the parties actually before the court.[465] Moreover, the law, at the time of granting the certificate, must have remained in a state of uncertainty and it must have been in the common good that the law be clarified so as to enable the courts to administer the law not only in the instant case but in future cases.[466] Uncertainty cannot be imputed to the law by an applicant simply raising a question as to the point of law.[467]

The following are examples of some issues (in summary form) in respect of **11–365** which points of law have been certified: (i) the legality of conditions leaving matters over for agreement between the developer and the planning authority[468]; (ii) the appropriate date from which the giving of a decision by a planning authority or An Bord Pleanála is to be reckoned[469]; (iii) whether or not a planning authority, where specific statutory measures exist and are available to it for the creation of a public right of way, may nonetheless chose to impose a condition which for all practical purposes creates a public right of way but which not only avoids the usual consequences which attend the exercise of the specific

---

[463] *Harding v Cork County Council (No. 3)*, unreported, High Court, Clarke J., November 30, 2006.

[464] *ibid.* In *Power v An Bord Pleanála (No. 2)* [2006] I.E.H.C. 288; unreported, Quirke J., October 2, 2006 the High Court rejected an allegation that the judgment on the leave application—unreported, January 17, 2006—failed to address one of the applicant's principal arguments.

[465] *Lancefort Ltd. v An Bord Pleanála*, unreported, High Court, Morris J., July 23, 1997 applying the test set out in the context of an application for security for costs in *Lancefort Ltd. v An Bord Pleanála* [1998] 2 I.R. 511 at 516. The test was subsequently approved by McGuinness J. in *Lancefort Ltd. v An Bord Pleanála*, unreported, High Court, March 31, 1999. See also *Ashbourne Holdings Ltd. v An Bord Pleanála (No. 3)*, unreported, High Court, Kearns J., June 19, 2001; *Kenny v An Bord Pleanála (No. 2)* [2001] 1 I.R. 704; [2002] 1 I.L.R.M. 68; *Neville v An Bord Pleanála*, unreported, High Court, Ó Caoimh J., October 12, 2001; and *Begley v An Bord Pleanála*, unreported, High Court, Ó Caoimh J., May 23, 2003.

[466] *Lancefort Ltd. v An Bord Pleanála* [1998] 2 I.R. 511 at 517. Also approved by McGuinness J. in *Lancefort Ltd. v An Bord Pleanála*, unreported, High Court, March 31, 1999.

[467] *Glancré Teoranta v An Bord Pleanála (No. 2)* [2006] I.E.H.C. 250; unreported, MacMenamin J., July 13, 2006.

[468] *Boland v An Bord Pleanála* [1996] 3 I.R. 435. *Cf.* PDA 2000, s.34(5).

[469] *Keelgrove Properties Ltd. v An Bord Pleanála* [2000] 1 I.R. 47; [2000] 2 I.L.R.M. 168 (proceedings compromised).

statutory powers but which also imposes further attendant obligations on a developer[470]; (iv) whether an intending developer of minerals who obtains the consent of the Minister for the Environment and Local Government to his applying for planning permission has, by virtue of that consent, a sufficient interest to make a valid application[471]; (v) whether An Bord Pleanála is obliged to have regard to the provisions of Council Directive 85/337/EEC notwithstanding the (alleged) inadequate implementation of its provisions into domestic law[472]; (vi) whether in respect of below-threshold projects, An Bord Pleanála is required to consider the question as to whether the proposed development would be likely to have significant effects on the environment so as to necessitate environmental impact assessment and whether An Bord Pleanála is obliged to record its decision on such questions in a manner which is susceptible to judicial review[473]; (vii) whether a limited liability company with no material property or assets likely to be affected by the proposed development has *locus standi*[474]; (viii) whether an applicant for judicial review pursuant to the provisions of the Local Government (Planning & Development) Act 1963 (as amended) may on the hearing of the substantive application for judicial review raise and rely upon grounds not pleaded and upon which leave to apply for judicial review was not sought nor granted before the High Court[475]; (ix) the criteria for determining whether a person without a financial or property interest may be said to have a "substantial interest" in an application for leave to apply for judicial review[476]; (x) whether the State has properly transposed the environmental impact assessment Directive[477]; and (xi) whether, having regard to s.213 of the PDA 2000, An Bord Pleanála may lawfully confirm a compulsory purchase order made for "development purposes" without requiring the acquiring authority to specify the development it is proposed to carry out on the affected land and/or subjecting the said proposed development to scrutiny, at an oral hearing or otherwise, in order to ascertain whether or not it has been established that all of the land affected by the compulsory purchase order is required to carry out the proposed development.[478]

11–366   In addition, in the context of an application for security for costs, Laffoy J. in *Village Residents Association Ltd. v An Bord Pleanála (No. 2)*[479] suggested that the issue of whether An Bord Pleanála had a special or additional duty to

---

[470] *Ashbourne Holdings Ltd. v An Bord Pleanála (No. 3)*, unreported, High Court, Kearns J., June 19, 2001.

[471] *Scott v An Bord Pleanála* [1995] 1 I.L.R.M. 424 at 428.

[472] *Lancefort Ltd. v An Bord Pleanála*, unreported, High Court, Morris J., July 23, 1997.

[473] *Lancefort Ltd. v An Bord Pleanála*, unreported, High Court, McGuinness J., March 31, 1998. See report of Supreme Court judgment [1999] 2 I.R. 270 at 273–274.

[474] *ibid.*

[475] *ibid.*

[476] *Harding v Cork County Council (No. 3)*, unreported, High Court, Clarke J., November 30, 2006.

[477] *Martin v An Bord Pleanála (No. 2)*, unreported, High Court, Smyth J., November 30, 2004.

[478] *Clinton v An Bord Pleanála* [2006] I.E.S.C. 58; unreported, November 1, 2006.

[479] [2000] 4 I.R. 321 at 330–331; [2001] 2 I.L.R.M. 22 at 31.

give reasons in circumstances where planning permission was granted in material contravention of the development plan, was one of *general* public importance.[480]

6. Relationship between substantial grounds and point of law of exceptional public importance

The relationship between the test for the grant of leave to apply for judicial review ("substantial grounds") and the requirement to demonstrate a point of law of exceptional public importance must be examined. It has been held that no matter what standard is applied to the statutory criteria of "substantial grounds", it cannot be less than that applicable to establishing a point of law of exceptional public importance.[481] Two consequences would appear to flow from this, as follows.

11–367

First, the mere fact that an applicant had established "substantial grounds" of challenge at the leave stage does not necessarily mean that the case involves a point of law of exceptional public importance. Accordingly, it does not follow that in the case of an application for leave to appeal against the decision on the substantive application for judicial review, leave to appeal must necessarily be granted.[482]

11–368

Secondly, in the case of the refusal of leave to apply for judicial review, the following paradox occurs. In order to grant leave to appeal against the refusal of leave to apply for judicial review, it will be necessary for the High Court to certify that its decision involves a point of law of exceptional public importance and that it is in the public interest that an appeal should be taken to the Supreme Court. Yet it is implicit in the decision to refuse leave to apply for judicial review that the grounds of challenge put forward are insubstantial. It is difficult to understand how it can be said that within the same decision one can have, on the one hand, a failure to establish substantial grounds and yet, on the same material, have a point of law of exceptional public importance.[483] Indeed, this appears to have been the view taken by the Supreme Court in *Keane v An Bord Pleanála*[484]; the High Court had refused leave to apply for judicial review, but

11–369

---

[480] *cf.* PDA 2000, s.37.

[481] *Kenny v An Bord Pleanála (No. 2)* [2001] 1 I.R. 704 at 715–716; [2002] 1 I.L.R.M. 68 at 79.

[482] Laffoy J. considered this very issue (albeit in the context of an application for security for costs) in *Village Residents Association Ltd. v An Bord Pleanála (No. 2)* [2000] 4 I.R. 321; [2001] 2 I.L.R.M. 22. See also, by analogy, *Lancefort Ltd. v An Bord Pleanála* [1999] 2 I.R. 270; [1998] 2 I.L.R.M. 401 (substantial grounds not conclusive of *locus standi*).

[483] *Kenny v An Bord Pleanála (No. 2)* [2001] 1 I.R. 704 at 715–716; [2002] 1 I.L.R.M. 68 at 79. See also *Hodgers v Cork City Council* [2006] I.E.H.C. 139; unreported, Murphy J., May 5, 2006, where the High Court refused to certify a question as to whether it is ever possible to certify an issue to the Supreme Court where leave to seek judicial review has been refused and/or leave to amend a statement of grounds refused.

[484] Unreported, Supreme Court, *ex tempore*, March 12, 1996.

had nevertheless certified for an appeal. The Supreme Court disposed of the appeal by granting leave to apply for judicial review and thus allowed the matters to be litigated in full before the High Court.[485]

11–370 One circumstance where the paradox might be avoided, and leave to appeal properly granted notwithstanding the absence of substantial grounds of challenge, is where the point of law certified relates to the *procedure* under ss.50 and 50A.[486] The procedural point of law may be one which transcends the facts of the case. For example, an issue might arise as to the application of the time-limits under the section, or, indeed, as to the application of the test of "substantial grounds" itself. Leave to appeal has been granted on points of this type on a number of occasions in the past.[487]

11–371 In a number of these cases, the point of procedural law had been dealt with as a preliminary issue, in advance of any consideration of whether or not the applicant had established "substantial grounds" of challenge. An appeal was then allowed in respect of this preliminary issue.[488] It is debatable as to whether or not this approach is correct. It might be thought that there is little benefit in allowing an appeal in respect of a moot: if, on the facts of the case, the applicant is unable to show substantial grounds of challenge it matters not whether, for example, the proceedings were served within time, or on all necessary parties. As against this, however, it might be argued that until the procedural issue has been resolved, the High Court might not have jurisdiction to entertain the proceedings and, accordingly, should not embark on a consideration of the issue of substantial grounds.[489] Moreover, in the case of a knockout point, it may be more expeditious to allow an appeal on a net point of procedural law, rather than embark upon a possibly lengthy inquiry as to substantial grounds.

---

[485] See also the contrast in the judgments on the application for leave to apply for judicial review, and the application for leave to appeal in *Jackson Way Properties Ltd. v Minister for the Environment*, unreported, High Court, Geoghegan J., July 2, 1999 and [1999] 4 I.R. 608, respectively.

[486] See *Kenny v An Bord Pleanála (No. 2)* [2001] 1 I.R. 704 at 715–716; [2002] 1 I.L.R.M. 68 at 79.

[487] *KSK Enterprises Ltd. v An Bord Pleanála* [1994] 2 I.R. 128; [1994] 2 I.L.R.M. 1 (time-limits); *Keelgrove Properties Ltd. v An Bord Pleanála* [2000] 1 I.R. 47; [2000] 2 I.L.R.M. 168 (time-limits); and *McCarthy v An Bord Pleanála* [2000] 1 I.R. 42 (service of proceedings). In the latter two instances, the proceedings were compromised prior to the hearing of any Supreme Court appeal. See also the decision *P v Minister for Justice Equality and Law Reform* (High Court, Smyth J.) [2002] 1 I.L.R.M. 16 under the Illegal Immigrants Act 2000 (interpretation of "substantial grounds").

[488] See, for example, *Harding v Cork County Council (No. 3)*, unreported, High Court, Clarke J., November 30, 2006.

[489] *Kenny v An Bord Pleanála (No. 2)* [2001] 1 I.R. 704; [2002] 1 I.L.R.M. 68. *Cf. O'Connell v Environmental Protection Agency* [2001] 4 I.R. 494; [2002] 1 I.L.R.M. 1 (point at which judicial review proceedings "instituted"). See also *AB v Minister for Justice, Equality and Law Reform* [2002] 1 I.R. 296; [2002] 2 I.L.R.M. 161.

7. Public interest

The second limb of the statutory requirements for the grant of leave to appeal is that it be desirable in the public interest that an appeal should be taken to the Supreme Court. The legislation appears to envisage that there may be circumstances where a point of law of exceptional public importance is exposed, yet leave to appeal must nevertheless be refused because the public interest requirement is not satisfied. It is uncertain as to what additional element is involved in this requirement. Indeed, there would appear to be two competing public interests at play. First, the public interest in environmental and planning matters generally.[490] Secondly, the public interest in ensuring that administrative decisions, particularly those taken pursuant to detailed procedures laid down by law, should be capable of being applied or implemented with certainty at as early a date possible, and that any issue as to their validity should accordingly be determined as soon as possible.[491] In at least two written judgments, the High Court has refused leave to appeal by reference to the desirability of finality and of avoiding further delay.[492] Moreover, it would appear that the financial position and general interests of the beneficiary of the planning permission impugned "while not the only factor of importance [are] one[s] which [the High Court] must seriously bear in mind".[493]

11–372

It would seem that in order to prevail over the second competing objective of expedition in the interests of legal certainty, the person seeking leave to appeal must counterpoise a claim to public interest greater than that present in all judicial review proceedings. Given that a point of law of exceptional public importance is a distinct requirement, it may be that it is necessary to consider matters specific to the particular proceedings then before the High Court. In order to establish that it is in the public interest that the point of law raised should be litigated before the Supreme Court in the context of those proceedings, an applicant might be required to point to some feature of the decision being challenged which lifts it above other proceedings. For example, it may be that

11–373

---

[490] The public interest in this regard was relied on in the specific context of an application for leave to appeal in *Lancefort Ltd. v An Bord Pleanála*, unreported, High Court, McGuinness J., March 31, 1998. See more generally *Blessington Heritage Trust Ltd. v Wicklow County Council* [1999] 4 I.R. 571 at 594–595.

[491] *In the matter of the Illegal Immigrants (Trafficking) Bill, 1999* [2000] 2 I.R 360. The following decisions under the planning legislation were cited as authority for the proposition set out in the text above: *Brady v Donegal County Council* [1989] I.L.R.M. 282; *Irish Asphalt Ltd. v An Bord Pleanála* [1996] 2 I.R. 179; and *KSK Enterprises Ltd. v An Bord Pleanála* [1994] 2 I.R. 128; [1994] 2 I.L.R.M. 1. See also *Irish Cement Ltd. v An Bord Pleanála*, unreported, High Court, McCracken J., February 24, 1998; and *Irish Hardware Association v South Dublin County Council* [2001] 2 I.L.R.M. 291.

[492] *Glancré Teoranta (No. 2) v An Bord Pleanála*, unreported, High Court, MacMenamin J., July 13, 2006 (no public interest in further ventilation of applicant's concerns); and *Arklow Holidays Ltd. v An Bord Pleanála (No. 2)* [2006] I.E.H.C. 102; [2007] 1 I.L.R.M. 125 (potential consequences of further significant delay).

[493] *Lancefort Ltd. v An Bord Pleanála*, unreported, High Court, McGuinness J., March 31, 1998.

"what is at issue is a true public interest issue of general importance, perhaps a heritage protection issue or an environmental issue".[494] In this connection, reference is made to the decision on the application for leave to appeal in *Lancefort Ltd. v An Bord Pleanála.*[495]

> "[…] judicial review cannot be permitted to become what is, in essence, an appeal based on planning criteria against the decision of An Bord Pleanála. However, this court cannot be blind to the fact that the site involved is one of very great importance in the development of the City of Dublin. It is central; it adjoins the major classical buildings of College Green, Trinity College and the Bank of Ireland. A planning decision in regard to this site will not only affect the contemporary citizens of Dublin, it will for good or ill, have a major impact on future generations."

11–374   More radically, it might be argued that in order to be entitled to leave to appeal, an applicant would have to demonstrate that he was a public interest litigant, and that he had no private interest in the outcome of the proceedings. The concept of a public litigant interest litigant had been considered (in the context of an application for a pre-emptive order as to costs) in *Village Residents Association Ltd. v An Bord Pleanála (No. 2).*[496] Laffoy J. in that decision endorsed, as a broad proposition, a definition of public interest litigation put forward in *R. v Lord Chancellor Ex p. Child Poverty Action Group.*[497] Moreover, Laffoy J. appears to have accepted that the existence of a private interest in the outcome of the application would be inimical to a finding that the proceedings were a public law challenge.[498]

11–375   The extent to which the importance of the proposed development project might be considered in deciding whether or not to allow an appeal was considered in *Arklow Holidays Ltd. v An Bord Pleanála.* In his judgment on the application for leave to appeal,[499] Clarke J. had held that it would not be in the public interest to certify an appeal, by reference to the importance of the proposed development project and the consequences of the likely delay that would be incurred. Clarke J. elaborated upon this issue in a subsequent ruling.[500] In

---

[494] *Village Residents Association Ltd. v An Bord Pleanála (No. 2)* [2000] 4 I.R. 321; [2001] 2 I.L.R.M. 22.

[495] Unreported, High Court, McGuinness J., March 31, 1998.

[496] [2000] 4 I.R. 321; [2001] 2 I.L.R.M. 22.

[497] [1999] 1 W.L.R. 347; [1998] 2 All E.R. 755.

[498] [2000] 4 I.R. 321 at 328 and 330; [2001] 2 I.L.R.M. 22 at 29 and 31. See also at 330–331: "First, the challenge is not a public law challenge in the sense that that concept was explained by Dyson J. The members of the company clearly have a private interest in the outcome of the application." Such an approach would also appear to be consistent with *Seery v An Bord Pleanála (No. 2)* [2001] 2 I.L.R.M. 151, where, in the context of an application for an undertaking as to damages, Finnegan J. indicated that the private interest of the applicants meant that the proceedings did not have necessary public nature to constitute a countervailing factor.

[499] *Arklow Holidays Ltd. v An Bord Pleanála (No. 2)* [2006] I.E.H.C. 102; [2007] 1 I.L.R.M. 125.

[500] *Arklow Holidays Ltd. v An Bord Pleanála (No. 3)* [2006] I.E.H.C. 280; unreported, Clarke J., September 8, 2006.

particular, Clarke J. rejected any suggestion that the merits of the development project had been taken into account in refusing leave to appeal.

> "Nothing in the certification judgment should be taken as indicating a view as to the merits or otherwise of the project in dispute or that such merits were or could be a factor in the exercise of the court's discretion. However what the judgment does say is that an early resolution of legal questions concerning all projects is an important aspect of the statutory regime and, in my view, such a policy applies with particular force in respect of major public infrastructural projects. In those circumstances, without taking any view as to the merits or otherwise of the project itself, I took into account the undoubted major public infrastructural nature of the project involved in this case and the importance of bringing finality to the questions concerning the validity of it, as a factor to be properly taken into account and weighed against, on the facts of this case, the position of Arklow which sought to rely on what I described as a technical argument and one in respect of which Arklow had suffered no prejudice.
>
> It is therefore the fact that there is a particular public interest in the early resolution of questions which have the capacity to delay major public projects that was taken into account, not any view that the project as proposed was, necessarily, meritorious."

With respect, the approach of the High Court in this regard is not entirely **11–376** convincing. First, the fact that proceedings concern a major development project cuts both ways: contrary to what the judgment suggests, the scale and importance of the proposed development might actually tell in favour of allowing an appeal. Such projects are capable of having significant effects on the environment, and it is important, therefore, that any decision to grant planning permission have been reached properly in accordance with the law. The approach in *Arklow Holidays Ltd.* is to be contrasted with that of McGuinness J. in *Lancefort Ltd. v An Bord Pleanála*.

Secondly, insofar as Clarke J. relies on the "technical nature" of the point of **11–377** law certified as justifying the refusal of leave, there is an element of begging the question. Whether the point is a good one or a bad one is ultimately a matter for the Supreme Court, and not for the High Court in deciding whether or not to certify. Clarke J. had previously ruled that the question of whether a person is excluded from an ability to challenge a planning permission on the basis of a potentially significant failure to comply with the requirements of the planning regulations, on the basis of not having been misled, was a point of law of exceptional public importance, and was an issue which could arise in a great number of cases. It seems somewhat anomalous, therefore, for the court to then turn around and dismiss the point as a technical one.

8. Procedure

Somewhat surprisingly, there is no time-limit prescribed for the making of an **11–378** application for leave to appeal. Strictly, such an application should be made before the order of the High Court on the decision to be appealed has been perfected[501]; indeed, it is arguable that once the order has been perfected, the High Court is *functus officio*.[502] An application for leave to appeal moved some three months after the judgment was refused on the basis of delay in *Ní Ghruagáin v An Bord Pleanála*.[503]

11–379 In practice, the intention to make an application for leave to apply is usually flagged at the time of the giving of judgment; the matter is then either dealt with forthwith, or adjourned for legal argument. It is usual for counsel to formulate the points of law said to arise, and to submit these to the court. Although the section is silent on the point, it is well established in practice that the other parties to the proceedings are entitled to make submissions as to why leave to appeal should not be granted, or as to the form of the points certified.[504] There is no statutory obligation to the effect that the order must recite the point of law certified but it is desirable that it should do so.[505]

11–380 As a result of an amendment introduced under the 2006 Act,[506] the Supreme Court has jurisdiction to determine only the point of law certified by the High Court, and to make only such order in the proceedings as follows from such determination. Under the unamended s.50 procedure, an appellant was not confined to arguing the certified point, but could advance any other ground of appeal which properly arose from the decision of the High Court.[507] It behoves the High Court, in light of this limitation on the appellate jurisdiction, to ensure that the point certified is formulated in a broad way, so as to allow the Supreme Court to give an authoritative ruling which will be of general application. If the point certified is too narrow, then the ruling may of little benefit than to the immediate parties.

11–381 The question of the form of the certified point was discussed—albeit in the context of the unamended s.50 procedure—in some detail in *Harding v Cork County Council (No. 3)*.[508] In order for a point of law to be of exceptional public importance it must be capable of affecting a significant number of cases. Clarke J. suggested that in the circumstances it would be in the public interest to have "definitive clarification" of the legal principles involved from the Supreme Court.

---

[501] Were the matters to be dealt with by two separate orders, a difficulty could arise in that time would run under various time-limits (for example, as to issuing of the Notice of Motion on the substantive application for judicial review, or as to serving of any Notice of Appeal) from the date of the perfection of the substantive order in circumstances where the application for leave to appeal might not be heard and determined for some while.

[502] See, by loose analogy, *McNamara v An Bord Pleanála* [1998] 3 I.R. 453.

[503] Unreported, High Court, Murphy J., June 19, 2003.

[504] See also *Neville v An Bord Pleanála*, unreported, High Court, Ó Caoimh J., October 12, 2001 at p. 5.

[505] *Kenny v An Bord Pleanála (No. 2)* [2001] 1 I.R. 704 at 707; [2002] 1 I.L.R.M. 68 at 72.

[506] PDA 2000, s.50A(11)(a) (as inserted by the 2006 Act, s.13).

[507] *Clinton v An Bord Pleanála* [2006] I.E.S.C. 58; unreported, November 1, 2006.

[508] Unreported, High Court, Clarke J., November 30, 2006.

"It seems likely, therefore, that in many cases, there will be a broad and a narrow question. The broad question will concern general principles. The narrow, the application of those principles to the facts of the case. Where the principles by reference to which a court should approach an important aspect of planning law have not been the subject of an authoritative ruling of the Supreme Court and where exceptionally important questions are raised by the issue concerned, it may well be appropriate to express the issue arising in general terms even though the court, will, necessarily, concentrate on the application of those principles to the facts of an individual case."

In cases where the High Court has refused leave to apply for judicial review, **11–382** *i.e.* where the High Court proceedings have been disposed of at the leave stage, it is submitted that any point of law certified should be framed in terms of the test of "substantial grounds" rather than in terms of the specific grounds of challenge.[509] If the High Court proposes to certify a ground of challenge wholesale, this is, it is submitted, inconsistent with a finding that there are no substantial grounds of challenge, and is indicative that leave to apply for judicial review should actually have been granted. An example of a point of law tied into the test of "substantial grounds" might be as follows: "Is the High Court entitled on an application for leave to apply for judicial review to have any regard to the probability of the application succeeding or otherwise?"

9. Article 234 reference procedure

The requirement to obtain leave to appeal from the High Court gives rise to **11–383** potential difficulties in the context of applications for preliminary rulings from the European Court of Justice ("the ECJ"). Under Art.234 of the Treaty (formerly Art.177), a more exacting standard applies in the case of a court or tribunal against "whose decision there is no judicial remedy under national law". Such a court must bring the matter before the ECJ where a decision on the question is necessary for it to give judgment. The difficulty presented by the provisions of s.50A(7) of the PDA 2000 (as amended) is that it will not be known whether the High Court will be the final court until such time as a ruling is made on any application for leave to appeal to the Supreme Court; this will not normally occur until such time as the High Court has made its decision on either the application for leave to apply for judicial review or the substantive application for judicial review. At that stage, it might well be argued that it is too late to make a reference as judgment will have already been given.[510]

---

[509] *cf. Scott v An Bord Pleanála* [1995] 1 I.L.R.M. 424; notwithstanding the fact that the decision in this case turned primarily on the meaning of "substantial grounds", the point of law certified was actually in terms of the ground of challenge, namely whether an intending developer of minerals who obtains the consent of the Minister for the Environment to his applying for planning permission has, by virtue of that consent, a sufficient interest to make a valid application.

[510] *McNamara v An Bord Pleanála* [1998] 3 I.R. 453. A practical example of the difficulties which can arise in this regard is to be found in the judgment of the High Court in *Arklow Holidays Ltd. v Wicklow County Council*, unreported, High Court, Murphy J., February 4, 2004.

11–384   This issue came before the Supreme Court in *McNamara v An Bord Pleanála (No. 3).*[511] The facts of the case were unusual in that the application for a preliminary reference was only made for the first time *after* the High Court had delivered judgment on the substantive application for judicial review. The High Court refused to make a reference, principally on the basis that it was too late for the applicant to seek to seek a reference in that there were no longer any proceedings pending before the High Court in respect of which a reference might usefully be made.

11–385   The applicant then appealed to the Supreme Court. The Supreme Court dismissed the appeal.

> "The purpose of the procedure is to enable a national court to obtain any guidance as to European Union law which it may require in order to decide the case pending before it. When the national court has given judgment, there is no case pending in respect of which any such question can be referred. Counsel for the applicant in the present case was, understandably enough, not in a position to give any satisfactory answer to the obvious questions as to which court was now to make the reference, the High Court having found that it had no jurisdiction so to do, to which court the Court of Justice should be asked to address its 'preliminary ruling' and, in the event of that court being the High Court, what possible effect in law the ruling could have on a case already decided by the national court.
>
> As to the submission that, as counsel for the applicant put it, there was a 'window of opportunity' for an Article 177 reference for so long as the application for leave to appeal to this Court was at hearing, that also is clearly unsustainable. Whether or not the High Court decided to grant a certificate pursuant to s. 82 (3B)(b)(i), the fact remains that there was no case pending before it in respect of which a preliminary ruling could have any relevance: the only effect of granting such a certificate is to vest this Court with an appellate jurisdiction which it would otherwise lack."

11–386   The fact that the applicant had not sought the reference at an earlier stage in the proceedings meant that it was unnecessary for the Supreme Court to rule on an argument that the High Court constituted the final court, and thus was subject to an obligation to refer.

> "It might be open to a party such as the applicant in judicial review proceedings of this nature to inform the court, while the case is at hearing, that in the event of the court rejecting a submission based on European Union law which he is advancing, he would be applying for a certificate under s.82 (3B)(b)(i) and/or a reference pursuant to Article 177 for a preliminary ruling on the question of European Union law on that question. Since it is acknowledged that that course was not taken in this case, it is again unnecessary to express any concluded opinion as to whether, in the event of that course being taken while the case was at hearing, and no certificate being granted under s.82 (3B)(b)(i), the court would be obliged to refer the question of European Union law for a preliminary ruling."

---

[511] [1998] 3 I.R. 453.

In *Harrington v An Bord Pleanála (No. 2)*,[512] the High Court considered it **11–387**
was unnecessary, on the particular facts of the case, to decide whether the
High Court, having rejected an application for leave to apply for judicial review,
was nevertheless a court before which a case is pending for the purposes of
Art.234.

The question thus remains open as to whether the High Court is a court against **11–388**
"whose decision there is no judicial remedy under national law" for the purposes
of Art.234 of the Treaty. The ECJ had to consider whether a requirement for
leave to appeal constituted a lower court as a court against "whose decision
there is no judicial remedy under national law" in *Lyckeskog*.[513] The ECJ held
that the fact that an appeal to the Swedish Supreme Court was subject to a
prior declaration of admissibility by the Supreme Court did not mean that the
decision of the lower court was a final decision for the purposes of Art.234.
The ECJ went on to rule that if a question arose as to the interpretation or
validity of a rule EC law, the Swedish Supreme Court would be under an
obligation, pursuant to the third paragraph of Art.234, to refer a question to the
ECJ for a preliminary ruling either at the stage of the *examination of
admissibility*, or at a later stage.

Under Swedish law, the Supreme Court was required to grant leave to appeal— **11–389**
"declaration of admissibility"—in cases where the uniform application of the
law in that legal system was at issue. As noted by Advocate General Tizzano,
a question of interpretation of EC law would clearly fall into that category, and
thus would be subject to an appeal.

Applying these principles to the Irish procedural regime, it is submitted that in **11–390**
order to give effect to the object of Art.234, the High Court should either be
treated as a final court and thus subject to the mandatory obligation to refer in
all cases, or, alternatively, should be permitted to make a reference in the context
of a pending application for leave to appeal to the Supreme Court. As discussed
at para.11–352 above, the statutory scheme has been analysed as creating an
exception to the appellate jurisdiction of the Supreme Court, with the possibility
of leave to appeal representing an exception to this exception. The determination
of the High Court is thus normally the final decision. This is to be contrasted
with procedural regime considered by the ECJ in *Lyckeskog*, whereby it was
the appellate court who, in effect, gave leave to appeal. Moreover, the
circumstances in which the Swedish Supreme Court was required to entertain
an appeal were much wider than those contemplated under Irish law. The
concept of a point of law of exceptional importance is so tightly drawn—in
particular, the requirement that the point transcend the facts of the individual
case—that it cannot be guaranteed that an appeal would be allowed in all cases
presenting genuine issues of EC law. This would run counter to the objective

---

[512] Unreported, High Court, Macken J., March 16, 2006.
[513] (Case C–99/00); [2002] E.C.R. I-4839.

of Art.234 of preventing the emergence of a body of national case law not in accord with the rules EC law, which might jeopardise the uniform interpretation and application of EC law.

11–391 The ECJ reiterated in *Intermodal Transports BV v Staatssecretaris van Financien*[514] that the third paragraph of Art.234 must be interpreted as meaning that such courts of final instance are required, where a question of EC law is raised before them, to comply with their obligation to make a reference, unless they have established that the question raised is irrelevant or that the EC provision in question has already been interpreted by the ECJ or that the correct application of EC law is so obvious as to leave no scope for any reasonable doubt. The existence of such a possibility must be assessed in the light of the specific characteristics of EC law, the particular difficulties to which its interpretation gives rise and the risk of divergences in judicial decisions within the Community.

---

[514] (Case C–495/03); September 15, 2005.

GROUNDS OF JUDICIAL REVIEW

A. Overview

The objective of this chapter is to attempt to discuss the various grounds upon which it is possible to challenge a decision of a planning authority or of An Bord Pleanála. As will all too readily become apparent, it is very difficult to articulate any clear scheme of principles underlying the possible grounds of challenge. There are two principal reasons for this, as follows. First, the range and diversity of potential grounds of challenge is such as to make it difficult, if not impossible, to put forward a coherent set of rules which would capture even part of the spectrum. Indeed, as appears further below, any attempt even to group the grounds of challenge under broad headings causes confusion, with certain grounds straddling more than one category. Secondly, there is very little discussion in the case law as to the nature of the function being exercised by the High Court on an application for judicial review.[1] **12–01**

B. Breach of Procedures

1. General introduction

It is trite law to say that judicial review is primarily—although not exclusively—concerned not with the decision, but with the decision-making process.[2] For **12–02**

---

[1] For a notable exception see *Ashford Castle Ltd. v SIPTU* [2006] I.E.H.C. 201; unreported, Clarke J., June 21, 2006; [2006] E.L.R. 201 at 215-216.

[2] See, for example, *O'Keeffe v An Bord Pleanála* [1993] 1 I.R. 39; [1992] I.L.R.M. 237, citing with approval *R. v Chief Constable of North Wales Police Ex p. Evans* [1982] 1 W.L.R. 1155. The courts do retain, however, an exceptional jurisdiction to review the substantive merits of a decision by reference to the doctrine of administrative unreasonableness. See further paras 12–74 to 12–89.

this reason, one of the most fruitful grounds of challenge is to allege that a decision was made in breach of fair procedures. Such a procedural objection is more likely to succeed than a challenge to the substantive merits of the decision. This is because the courts place great emphasis on procedural regularity. The thinking here seems to be that compliance with proper procedures operates so as to ensure the integrity of the decision. Such an approach represents a double-edged sword for the decision-maker: if the procedures are observed during the course of the decision-making process, then the courts will show considerable deference and it will prove very difficult for an applicant to have the decision set aside. Conversely, if there has been a failure to comply with the procedures, then the courts will readily intervene and, generally, will be hostile to any defence along the lines that the alleged breach did not affect the substance of the decision (in other words, that the outcome would have been the same even had the alleged breach of procedure not occurred).[3] One consequence of all of this is that even a relatively minor or technical breach of procedure can result in a decision being set aside.

12–03   Thus far, reference has been made to the requirement to comply with fair procedures in a general sense only. In fact, a distinction must be made between those procedural requirements which are prescribed under statute (statutory procedure), and the general concept of fair procedures implied under the Constitution and under the European Convention on Human Rights Act 2003[4] (fair procedures). Under the planning legislation, detailed procedural requirements are laid down in many instances as to the process to be followed before a particular decision is made or a particular act carried out. It is important to emphasise, however, that the process which must actually be observed will often extend beyond that which has been prescribed. This is because even in circumstances where an elaborate procedure has been prescribed, it may nevertheless be necessary to supplement same by reference to more general principles of fair procedures. Moreover, it will also be necessary to have recourse to general concepts of fair procedures in circumstances where the legislation does not prescribe a procedure in respect of the making of a particular decision or the carrying out of a particular act, or where the legislation only provides for procedures in respect of some aspects of the process. The interaction between statutory procedure and fair procedures is examined in further detail below. Before turning to that task, however, it is necessary to set the scene by elaborating on what is involved in the concept of fair procedures.

---

[3] See, for example, *State (Boyd) v An Bord Pleanála*, unreported, High Court, Murphy J., February 18, 1983 (court not concerned whether making of submission would have led to different conclusion). *Cf. McBride v Galway Corporation* [1998] 1 I.R. 485; *Lancefort Ltd. v An Bord Pleanála* [1999] 2 I.R. 270; [1998] 2 I.L.R.M. 401; and *Dunne v An Bord Pleanála* [2006] I.E.H.C. 400; unreported, McGovern J., December 14, 2006 (discretion would be exercised against granting relief as final result of any renewed planning application would be the same).

[4] See, generally, Chapter 14.

Under Irish law, fair procedures are styled as natural and constitutional justice. **12–04** The requirements of natural and constitutional justice can be best analysed as forming a continuous spectrum, with the nature of the procedural requirements being determined by the gravity of the decision for the person affected. Thus, the most elaborate requirements in relation to fair procedures are to be found in the context of a criminal trial. Here an accused person is entitled to notice of the charges against him; to hear the evidence against him and to test same by way of cross-examination; to lead evidence in his defence; to make submissions in his defence; to have legal representation; and to appeal the decision. The less directly a decision affects a person, the further one moves across the spectrum, and the less comprehensive the range of procedural protections.

Applying these principles to the planning legislation, the greater procedural **12–05** protections apply to those decisions which most directly impact on property rights. Thus, for example, the owner of affected property is entitled to notice of an intention to designate a protected structure,[5] and of the making of a proposed compulsory purchase order.[6] Adjoining landowners have the benefit of a special *locus standi* rule in the case of appeals against decisions on planning applications.[7]

The matter was explained thus by Murphy J. in *State (Haverty) v An Bord* **12–06** *Pleanála*.[8]

> "The essence of natural justice is that it requires the application of broad principles of common sense and fair play to a given set of circumstances in which a person is acting judicially. What will be required must vary with the circumstances of the case. At one end of the spectrum it will be sufficient to afford a party the right to make informal observations and at the other constitutional justice may dictate that a party concerned should have the right to be provided with legal aid and to cross-examine witnesses supporting the case against him. I have no doubt that on an appeal to the planning board the rights of the objector – as distinct from a developer exercising property rights [*sic*] the requirements of natural justice fall within the former rather than the latter range of the spectrum. This flows from the nature of the interest which is being protected, the number of possible objectors, the nature of the function exercised by the planning board and the limited criteria by which appeals are required to be judged and the practical fact that in any proceedings whether oral or otherwise there must be finality. Some party must have the last word."

In very general terms, there appears to be a hierarchy of procedural rights **12–07** commencing with those which are required for even the most basic decision, and ascending to those which are only required in the most grave cases. Moreover, it seems that a less exacting standard may apply to the preliminary stages of any decision-making process, at least in circumstances where there

---

[5] PDA 2000, s.12(3).
[6] Housing Act 1966, Sch.3.
[7] PDA 2000, s.37(6).
[8] [1987] I.R. 485 at 493.

will be a sufficiency of fair procedures at a later stage. The specific example of the two-tier decision-making process in relation to an application for planning permission is dealt with at para.12–21 below. Another example is that in relation to enforcement proceedings: the fact that it is not always mandatory to give advance notice of an intention to take action can, presumably, be justified on the basis that the respondent will have an opportunity to state his case in the course of any court proceedings.[9]

12–08   As with many administrative decision-making schemes, the planning legislation provides for its own peculiar procedures. In particular, matters such as time-limits; whether the procedure be by way of oral hearing or written submission; and a right of appeal, are in certain instances prescribed. Again, as in the case of general fair procedures, it may be of help to think in terms of there being a hierarchy of procedural requirements. The greater the policy content of a decision, or the graver its impact, the more elaborate are the procedural requirements prescribed. Thus the decision to grant or refuse planning permission, which is pre-eminently a policy decision, is governed by a very detailed legislative scheme, whereas a decision which is made in the discharge of a ministerial, as opposed to a judicial, function attracts a less complicated procedure. Thus, for example, only a very simple procedure is prescribed in the case of the decision as to whether or not to extend the duration of a planning permission.

2. Interrelationship between statutory procedure and fair procedures

12–09   As indicated at the start of this chapter, there is an artificiality in attempting to separate out the infinite variety of grounds of challenge into groups or blocks. In ease of exposition, however, it is necessary to make some attempt to do so. In this regard, attention has already been drawn to the distinction between conduct involving a breach of those procedural requirements prescribed under the legislation (breach of statutory procedure), and conduct which although not involving non-compliance with any express statutory requirement, nevertheless represents a breach of fair procedures (breach of fair procedures). The question as to the interrelationship between these statutory requirements, and the inherent requirements of fair procedures, must be considered briefly. In particular, it is necessary to examine the extent, if any, to which the prescribed procedure should be regarded as definitive, even where same appears to attenuate fair procedures. It is also necessary to consider whether the statutory procedure should ever be supplemented by reference to general principles of fair procedures.

---

[9] See also *Huntsgove Developments Ltd. v Meath County Council* [1994] 2 I.L.R.M. 36, where it was held that the requirement to observe fair procedures did not apply to the initial stages of the process of making a development plan. The legislative position has since been changed under the PDA 2000.

No prescribed procedure

The legal position is relatively straightforward where no procedure is prescribed **12–10** under either the primary legislation or regulations. In such circumstances, general fair procedures are to be imported. The point may be illustrated by reference to the position obtaining under the previous legislation with respect to the revocation of planning permission. Under the previous legislation, there was no express requirement to provide advance notice of an intention to revoke a planning permission. Notwithstanding this, the High Court held in *Eircell Ltd. v Leitrim County Council*[10] that the planning authority was required to give prior notification of an intention to consider the revocation, and to afford an opportunity to make representations. In *Electricity Supply Board v Cork County Council*,[11] the gloss was added that the notice given had to be sufficiently detailed as to enable (meaningful) submissions to be made. Although the statutory requirements with respect to the revocation of planning permission have since been enhanced under the PDA 2000 (see paras 5–87 to 5–97), these judgments provide an important precedent for other decision-making under the planning legislation. For example, the prescribed procedure in respect of the determination of a reference under s.5 of the PDA 2000 is, arguably, deficient, and must be supplemented by reference to general concepts of fair procedures. (In particular, little express provision is made for third party involvement.) The necessity of resorting to general concepts is even clearer in the case of the procedure for making local area plans: the legislation provides that a planning authority shall take whatever steps it considers necessary to consult the public before preparing, amending or revoking such a plan.[12] It is submitted that a planning authority cannot be at large in this regard, and that a minimum level of fair procedures is mandatory.

Prescribed procedure

Where a procedure is prescribed under the legislation or the regulations it **12–11** should be followed, and any significant or unauthorised deviation from same will not normally be ignored by the courts.[13] In many cases the requirements of the statutory procedure and general fair procedures will be co-extensive. Indeed, some requirements of the statutory procedure can be considered as simply being declaratory of the general principles of fair procedures. This is particularly so in relation to the requirement to give advance notice of, and an opportunity to make submissions and representations in relation to, any proposed decision which might adversely affect a person's property rights. For example, it is a statutory requirement that the owner and occupier be given notice of an intention to designate a protected structure,[14] or of an intention to

---

[10] [2000] 1 I.R. 479; [2000] 2 I.L.R.M. 81.
[11] Unreported, High Court, Finnegan J., June 28, 2000.
[12] PDA 2000, s.20.
[13] *Lord Ballyedmond v Commission for Energy Regulation* [2006] I.E.H.C. 206; unreported, Clarke J., June 22, 2006.
[14] PDA 2000, s.12(3).

acquire lands by way of a compulsory purchase order.[15] It is submitted that even in the absence of any express statutory requirement, there would still be an obligation to afford such procedural protections. Reference is made in this regard to the decision of the Supreme Court in *MacPharthalain v Commissioners of Public Works in Ireland*.[16] There, a decision to designate lands as an area of scientific interest, which designation was found to have affected the rights of the owners, was held to be invalid in circumstances where the designation was made without notice, and without affording an opportunity to object.[17]

12–12   Even where a procedure is prescribed, it may be necessary to supplement same by recourse to general fair procedures. Thus, for example, in *P & F Sharpe Ltd. v Dublin City & County Manager*[18] the Supreme Court held, in the context of a proposal to grant planning permission in material contravention of the development plan, that apart from and in addition to compliance with the statutory procedure, it would also have been necessary to ensure that all persons with a potential interest in the result of the deliberations be given a fair and ample opportunity to be heard and their point of view be properly considered. In *Finnegan v An Bord Pleanála*,[19] the Supreme Court held that the power under the previous legislation to dismiss an appeal as vexatious or for delay was to be read as only being exercisable after an opportunity had been afforded to the appellant to put forward his case.

12–13   It also seems that in interpreting the legislative scheme, the courts are entitled to have regard to principles of constitutional justice as a guide to interpretation. In so doing, the courts are not necessarily *supplementing* the statutory procedure; rather recourse is being had to more general concepts in order to determine what is actually required by the legislation.

12–14   The decision of the Supreme Court in *State (Stanford) v Dun Laoghaire Corporation*[20] provides one example of the use of the principles of natural and constitutional justice as a guide to interpretation. Under the (then) regulations, there was no express entitlement on the part of a member of the public to make submissions or observations in relation to an application for planning permission. The Supreme Court determined, however, that it was an implied but essential precondition for the grant of a valid planning permission that interested persons be given a reasonable opportunity to submit written representations or objections. In identifying this implied precondition, the Supreme Court had regard, *inter alia*, to the fact that the exercise of the quasi-judicial function inherent in the determination of an application for planning permission would be flawed if the public, one of the interested parties, whose

---

[15] Housing Act 1966, Sch.3.
[16] [1994] 3 I.R. 353; [1992] 1 I.R. 111.
[17] *cf. Liddy v Minister for Public Enterprise* [2004] 1 I.L.R.M. 9.
[18] [1989] I.R. 701; [1989] I.L.R.M. 565.
[19] [1979] I.L.R.M. 134.
[20] Unreported, Supreme Court, February 20, 1981.

interests do not necessarily coincide with those of the planning authority, were to be denied the opportunity of yielding forth interested persons who could make representations or objections.

An example of a decision involving an approach closer to the actual supplanting of the statutory procedure by a more generalised notion of fair procedures is to be found in *State (Coras Iompair Eireann) v An Bord Pleanála*.[21] In that case, a party opposed to a proposed development (CIE) had not chosen not to participate in an appeal to An Bord Pleanála against the refusal of planning permission at first instance. The Supreme Court held that as a decision to grant planning permission adverse to the interests of CIE was made without first seeking to hear the views of CIE, natural justice was not observed and the decision of An Bord Pleanála was, accordingly, quashed. It has to be said that the outcome of this case is somewhat surprising, and it is unlikely that a similar result would occur under the present legislation. In particular, under the present statutory scheme, there would appear to be a much greater onus on the objector to make timely submissions. **12–15**

This approach of supplementing the prescribed procedure will also be relevant under the European Convention on Human Rights Act 2003. **12–16**

Conflict between statutory procedure and fair procedures

It is only where there is a mismatch between what the statutory procedure requires, and what would otherwise be required under general fair procedures, that real difficulties can occur. This is especially so where the statutory procedure appears to attenuate the level of procedural protection which might otherwise have applied. The question then arises as to whether, when a procedure is prescribed under statute, same prevails even where a higher level of fair procedures or protection would have been *implied* under general principles if no procedure had been prescribed. The most obvious tension between the statutory requirements, and the concepts of general fair procedures, is in relation to time-limits. The case law seems to suggest that the courts are prepared to hold that general principles of fairness will have to yield to a time-limit prescribed under statute. **12–17**

It is a feature of the planning legislation that very strict time-limits are prescribed for the doing of a host of actions. These prescribed time-limits are often much shorter than those which would be allowed by reference to general fair procedures. **12–18**

The latitude which would otherwise apply under general principles of fair procedures may be illustrated by reference to the position of appeals to An Bord Pleanála prior to the Local Government (Planning & Development) Act 1992. Before the imposition of a statutory timetable in respect of appeals, the **12–19**

---

[21] Unreported, Supreme Court, December 12, 1984.

courts had shown considerable indulgence insofar as delay was concerned. In *State (Genport Ltd.) v An Bord Pleanála*,[22] it was held that, as a matter of general law, An Bord Pleanála in carrying out a quasi-judicial function would have an obligation to take reasonable steps to ensure that every party interested in any application before it should be aware of the submissions or representations made by any other party; should have a reasonable opportunity of replying to them; and should have a reasonable opportunity of making representations to the board. Indeed, in *State (Elm Developments Ltd.) v An Bord Pleanála*,[23] the Supreme Court went so far as to hold that the requirement that an appellant should state the grounds of appeal in the written notice to An Bord Pleanála was directory, not mandatory, and that non-compliance was not fatal to the appeal.

12–20 More recent judgments indicate that the courts are prepared to uphold the stringent requirements now prescribed by statute. Thus, for example, in *McCann v An Bord Pleanála*,[24] the High Court upheld a ruling rejecting an appeal as having been made one day out of time. Similarly, in *Graves v An Bord Pleanála*,[25] the High Court upheld a decision of An Bord Pleanála to reject an appeal on the basis that the precise requirements in relation to service within the time-limit had not been observed minutely. In *Cobh Fishermen's Association Ltd. v Minister for Marine and Natural Resources*,[26] the High Court had regard to the objective of the relevant statutory scheme, *i.e.* to ensure that an application be processed with reasonable dispatch, in rejecting an argument that there was some additional extra-statutory obligation on the decision-maker to allow the making of further submissions or representations after the statutory period for the making of objections had elapsed.

Relevance of right of appeal

12–21 Once it is accepted in principle that statutory procedure may be supplemented by reference to general concepts of fair procedures, it is necessary to consider against what aspect of the statutory procedure is the measurement to take place. More specifically, certain decision-making procedures of first instance, if viewed in isolation and without reference to the concomitant appeal procedures, might arguably be found wanting in terms of fair procedures. The point may be illustrated by reference to the decision on an application for planning permission: many of the *indicia* of fair procedures are absent from the planning authority stage.[27] For example, there is no provision for an oral hearing; for the formal exchange of submissions; nor for the production of documents: these are, however, available on appeal to An Bord Pleanála. If one were to focus solely

---

[22] [1983] I.L.R.M. 12.
[23] [1981] I.L.R.M. 108.
[24] [1997] 1 I.R. 264; [1997] 1 I.L.R.M. 314.
[25] [1997] 2 I.R. 205.
[26] Unreported, High Court, O'Sullivan J., August 29, 1997.
[27] See the *dicta* in *McCann v An Bord Pleanála* [1997] 1 I.R. 264 at 271; [1997] 1 I.L.R.M. 314 at 320.

on the planning authority stage, an attractive argument might be made to the effect that it is necessary to supplement same by reference to general concepts of fair procedures. It is submitted, however, that the better view is that the planning process involves a unified decision-making structure, with provision for a two-stage hearing.[28] There is a full-blooded right of appeal, with An Bord Pleanála hearing the matter *de novo* as if the application for planning permission had been made to it in the first instance. Accordingly, it is submitted that any check for compliance with fair procedures must be made against the entirety of the two-tier process.

3. Effect of breach of statutory procedure

It is essentially a matter of statutory interpretation as to what is the effect of a breach of any particular aspect of the prescribed procedure. The position under the previous planning legislation was unsatisfactory in that, more often than not, the legislation was silent as to the effect of non-compliance. Accordingly, the courts were obliged to consider the procedural requirement in context and make an attempt to determine whether or not same was mandatory, or merely directory or permissive. In this regard, even the use of the word "shall" was not always necessarily conclusive. For example, in *State (Elm Developments Ltd.) v An Bord Pleanála*,[29] it was held that the requirement that an appellant should state the grounds of appeal in the written notice to An Bord Pleanála was directory, not mandatory, and that non-compliance was not fatal to the appeal. See now s.127 of the PDA 2000.[30]   **12–22**

In other judgments, particular procedural requirements were held to be mandatory with the result that breach of same vitiated any decision so reached. This was so even in the case of what might be regarded as a relatively minor breach. Thus, in *Dublin County Council v Marren*,[31] an application for planning permission was held to be invalid on the basis, *inter alia*, that same did not comply with the requirements of the regulations as to the form of maps and plans accompanying the application. In *Ó Nualláin v Dublin Corporation*,[32]   **12–23**

---

[28] See also *Gammell v Dublin Corporation* [1983] I.L.R.M. 413, where a distinction was drawn between an appeal against an effective decision, and a procedure whereby an aggrieved person may make submissions before a decision becomes effective. In the case of the planning legislation, it could be argued that there is only ever one effective decision in circumstances where a decision of An Bord Pleanála expressly operates to annul the decision of the planning authority, and the initial decision of the planning authority does not constitute the grant of planning permission: it is only in the case of there being no appeal (or an appeal withdrawn) that the planning authority can then proceed to make an actual grant of planning permission.

[29] [1981] I.L.R.M. 108.

[30] See *Murphy v Cobh Town Council* [2006] I.E.H.C. 324; unreported, MacMenamin J., October 26, 2006 (appeal must be accompanied by planning authority acknowledgment); and *O'Reilly (Bros) Wicklow Ltd. v An Bord Pleanála* [2006] I.E.H.C. 363; unreported, Quirke J., November 22, 2006 (mandatory that grounds of appeal be set out in full).

[31] [1985] I.L.R.M. 593.

[32] [1999] 4 I.R. 137.

the High Court held that compliance with a procedural requirement that certain specified bodies be furnished with a copy of the plans and particulars of the proposed development was mandatory, and was not of a technical or peripheral nature such as could be excused or overlooked in the instant case.

12–24   The position under the current planning legislation is clearer in that express provision is made in a number of instances as to the effect of non-compliance. Thus, for example, under art.26 of the Planning and Development Regulations 2001 an application must be returned as invalid where there has been failure to comply with certain of the prescribed procedural requirements. Elsewhere it is provided that failure to comply with other procedural aspects does not vitiate the decision reached. For example, it is expressly provided under s.12(16) of the PDA 2000 that a person shall not question the validity of the development plan by reason only that certain prescribed procedures were not completed within the time stipulated.

12–25   There still remain, however, a number of procedural requirements in respect of which no express provision is made as to the consequences of a breach thereof. To take one example. A planning authority is required to acknowledge in writing the receipt of any submission or observation validly made in respect of an application for planning permission.[33] In order to make an appeal against the decision of the planning authority, it is necessary for a third party appellant to ensure that the appeal is accompanied by the acknowledgement by the planning authority of receipt of submissions or observations.[34] Clearly, a third party would be prejudiced by the failure of the planning authority to furnish such an acknowledgement in writing. In particular, it would seem that the third party would be precluded from bringing an appeal to An Bord Pleanála. A question thus arises as to what remedy is available to that third party. The procedural defect involved is unusual in that it does not appear to impact on the *quality* of the decision of the planning authority. As discussed above, the courts will generally insist on compliance with statutory requirements in order to ensure that the integrity of the decision is protected. It is readily apparent that certain defects do impinge on the quality of the decision. For example, it is clear from the legislative scheme that the legislature think that it is conducive to good decision-making that the decision-maker have regard to submissions or observations made by third parties. If, for whatever reason, such a third party is wrongly prevented from making such a submission or observation then there is at least a risk that the decision reached is flawed. Conversely, in the case of a failure to provide a written acknowledgement, the quality of the decision of the planning authority remains unaffected. Instead, the third party suffers a different prejudice in that his or her right to appeal has been compromised.

---

[33] Planning and Development Regulations 2001, art.29(2) (as amended by the 2006 Regulations). The form is set out at Form No. 3 of Sch.3 (as amended by the 2006 Regulations).

[34] PDA 2000, s.127(1)(e).

In *Lynch v Dublin City Council*,[35] the High Court held that the requirement to furnish a written acknowledgement was mandatory in nature, but that failure to do so would not invalidate any subsequent decision to grant planning permission.

12–26

One possible means of redress for the third party might be to analyse the position as follows. Although the defect alleged has not affected the quality of the decision of the planning authority, it nevertheless remains the position that under the legislative scheme any decision of a planning authority was always to be subject to the safeguard of an appeal to An Bord Pleanála. The consequence of a failure on the part of a planning authority to provide an acknowledgement in writing is to frustrate this safeguard of the appeal and to purport to render the decision of the planning authority unimpeachable. Such an unimpeachable decision was never in the contemplation of the legislative scheme, and, accordingly is invalid on that ground.

12–27

Reference is made in this regard to the decision in *McAnenley v An Bord Pleanála*.[36] This case also related to a defect on the part of the planning authority which did not impact on the quality of its decision. Under the (then) legislation, there was a requirement that in the case of an appeal to An Bord Pleanála, the planning authority concerned submit to An Bord Pleanála certain specified documents. Kelly J. held that the legislature in setting up the statutory scheme of appeals had in mind that certain documents would be placed before An Bord Pleanála when it was called upon to exercise its *de novo* jurisdiction involving an appeal to it from a decision of a planning authority. Kelly J. further held that this requirement was mandatory and that in circumstances where there had been non-compliance the appeal was not within jurisdiction or in accordance with law. The decision of An Bord Pleanála was quashed, and the matter remitted to An Bord Pleanála to be dealt with afresh.

12–28

It should be noted that breach of even a mandatory procedural requirement is not always fatal to a decision. Although as a matter of strict law, such a decision might well be regarded as invalid, the nature of judicial review is such that in practice the decision might more accurately be regarded as voidable not void. There are at least two reasons for this. First, judicial review is pre-eminently a discretionary remedy. Thus even if breach of a mandatory requirement is demonstrated, an applicant may nevertheless be denied relief as a matter of discretion. If the breach is technical or trivial, the courts may well refuse to set aside the relevant decision.[37]

12–29

---

[35] Unreported, High Court, Ó Caoimh J., July 25, 2003.

[36] [2002] 2 I.R. 763.

[37] For a recent example, see *Hickey v An Bord Pleanála*, unreported, High Court, Smyth J., June 10, 2004, where the High Court refused to quash a decision of An Bord Pleanála, ruling that there was no evidence that the applicant had sustained any prejudice as a result of the shortened time period afforded for making submissions. See also *Murphy v Cobh Town Council* [2006] I.E.H.C. 324; unreported, MacMenamin J., October 26, 2006.

12–30   Relief may also be refused where there is some aspect of the conduct of the applicant (such as his motive) of which the court disapproves. If, however, the breach alleged involves a breach of a requirement of EC law (for example, a breach of the requirements of the environmental impact assessment Directive), then it is arguable that the court has no discretion but must instead grant relief unless, notwithstanding the breach, there has been substantial compliance with the prescribed procedure.[38] See further paras 13–345 to 13–351.

12–31   Secondly, the special statutory judicial review scheme which applies with respect to challenges to decisions of a planning authority or of An Bord Pleanála on an application for planning permission is such that an applicant might not be permitted to raise a particular ground of challenge. Under ss.50 and 50A of the PDA 2000 (as amended by the 2006 Act), an applicant is required to demonstrate a "substantial interest" in the matter which is the subject of the application, and that there are "substantial grounds" for contending that the decision is invalid or ought to be quashed. Thus, in *Blessington & District Community Council Ltd. v Wicklow County Council*,[39] the applicant company was refused leave to apply for judicial review on the basis that neither it nor its members had been prejudiced by an alleged defect in the public notice in respect of the application for planning permission.[40]

C. Procedural Requirements

12–32   For ease of exposition, in examining the various aspects of procedural requirements, it is not proposed to use separate headings in respect of statutory procedure, and fair procedures. Instead both will be considered together, with an indication given as appropriate where the source of the requirement is non-statutory.

1. Notice

12–33   Under the planning legislation, an obligation to give notice may arise in two broad categories of circumstances. The first of these is where, of its own volition, a planning authority proposes to make a decision which will affect rights and liabilities. The second is where a particular matter is referred to either a planning authority or An Bord Pleanála for adjudication. The procedure in this latter case partakes of some of the characteristics of an *inter partes* hearing.

12–34   The nature and extent of the obligation to give notice differs according to the gravity of the proposed decision. In the case of a decision affecting property

---

[38] *Berkeley v Secretary of State for the Environment* [2001] 2 A.C. 603; (2001) P. & C.R. 492.

[39] [1997] 1 I.R. 273.

[40] See also *Springview Management Ltd. v Cavan Developments Ltd.* [2000] 1 I.L.R.M. 437.

rights, the owner/occupier of the lands may be entitled to notice in either a specific or a general way. Thus, for example, if it is proposed to designate a structure as a "protected structure", then it is necessary to give the owner or occupier express notice of that intention.[41] Similarly, in the case of a compulsory purchase order, it is also necessary that express notice be served. Conversely, in the case of other, less specific, provisions of the development plan, it is sufficient to give notice in a general way; for example, by way of newspaper advertisement.

The position in relation to the making of an application for planning permission is curious in that no particular distinction in terms of the entitlement to notice is drawn between those immediately affected by the proposed development, and those with a more general interest. It is sufficient that notice is given in a general way by way of the erection of a site notice, and publication of a newspaper advertisement. There is no requirement that, for example, the owner or occupier of neighbouring premises be given express notice.[42]   **12–35**

Depending on how one characterises the entitlement of a neighbouring owner or occupier to object to a proposed development, the statutory requirements in this regard might represent an attenuation of that which would otherwise have been implied by reference to the concept of fair procedures. More specifically, certain judgments, such as that in *White v Dublin Corporation*,[43] might be taken as suggesting that the right to object forms part of the property rights of the neighbouring landowner. If this is the case, then it would seem that the position of the property owning objector should slot in closer to that of the applicant for planning permission in the spectrum of fair procedures. As against this, to the extent that decisions such as, for example, those in *State (Stanford) v Dun Laoghaire Corporation*,[44] and *Crodaun Homes Ltd. v Kildare County Council*,[45] elevate the rights of the public in general, it might be argued that there is no basis for affording any preferential treatment to adjoining landowners.   **12–36**

The procedural requirements applicable in the context of an *inter partes* process, such as, for example, an application for planning permission, present the following additional issue. Here the question is not so much the right to notice of an intention to make a decision—by definition, the applicant for planning permission having invoked the procedure will know that a decision is to be made—but the right to notice of the matters informing the making of the decision. The applicant will, for example, wish to know what objections have been made by third parties. This point is more closely allied to the right of the applicant to make meaningful submissions and is discussed at paras 12–44 to 12–49 below. A more difficult question is the extent to which the decision-   **12–37**

---

[41] PDA 2000, s.12(3).

[42] The only special protection afforded to adjoining landowners is under PDA 2000, s.37(6) (right of appeal). See further paras 9–02 to 9–07.

[43] [2004] 1 I.R. 545; [2004] 2 I.L.R.M. 509.

[44] Unreported, Supreme Court, February 20, 1981.

[45] [1983] I.L.R.M. 1.

maker is required to alert the applicant to matters of concern to it (the decision-maker). The case law suggests that in certain unusual circumstances, it will be necessary for the decision-maker to make its concerns known. Thus, in *Frenchurch Properties Ltd. v Wexford County Council*,[46] the High Court held—in the context of an application to extend the duration of a planning permission—that if there is a point on which the planning authority knows that the applicant relies to a significant extent and which the planning authority (unknown to the applicant) thinks is invalid, the planning authority should draw the applicant's attention to this point to give the applicant an opportunity of trying to persuade the planning authority that he is right and the planning authority is wrong.[47]

12–38 The judgment in *Fairyhouse Club Ltd. v An Bord Pleanála*[48] would appear to suggest that there is no requirement to bring to the express attention of a party an intention to rely on a previous decision as a precedent, at least not in circumstances where the earlier decision was publicly available.

12–39 Next, various examples of decisions in respect of which the prescribed procedure is deficient in terms of notice need to be considered. The first of these is the issuance of a declaration under s.5 of the PDA 2000. In short, this involves a planning authority making a decision as to whether a particular act involves development or not, or exempted development or not. Under the previous legislation, this function had been performed at first instance by An Bord Pleanála, with a statutory right of appeal to the High Court. The function had been characterised by the High Court as being a judicial function, involving a (limited) administration of justice.[49] Under the PDA 2000, the reference is made at first instance to a planning authority, with an appeal to An Bord Pleanála. The curious aspect is that there is no express requirement that third parties be notified of the making of a reference, still less that third parties should be permitted to participate in the process. Instead, the section simply provides that a planning authority may request persons to submit information in order to allow the planning authority issue a declaration. Moreover, the right of appeal to An Bord Pleanála is only available to the person requesting the reference. In the circumstances, it is submitted that the statutory procedure is deficient. The consequences of this are either that the planning authority must supplement the statutory procedure by reference to general concepts of fair procedures, or that the legal effect of a declaration must be severely curtailed: in particular, same cannot be binding as against third parties.

---

[46] [1992] 2 I.R. 268; [1991] I.L.R.M. 769. See also *Navan Tanker Services Ltd. v Meath County Council* [1998] 1 I.R. 166.

[47] See also *McGoldrick v An Bord Pleanála* [1997] 1 I.R. 497 (applicant not given any notice of intention to make a finding imputing dishonesty to him).

[48] Unreported, High Court, Finnegan J., July 18, 2001. See also *Stack v An Bord Pleanála (No. 2)*, unreported, High Court, Ó Caoimh J., March 7, 2003.

[49] *Central Dublin Development Association v Attorney General* (1969) 109 I.L.T.R. 69. See also *Fairyhouse Club Ltd. v An Bord Pleanála*, unreported, High Court, Finnegan J., July 18, 2001.

The second example then is that of an agreement in respect of social and **12–40** affordable housing. A planning authority and An Bord Pleanála are empowered, in certain circumstances, to attach a condition to a planning permission requiring that the applicant enter into an agreement with respect to the provision of social and affordable housing (hereinafter referred to by the shorthand a "Part V agreement" where convenient).[50] There is no statutory requirement that third parties be notified of, or otherwise permitted to participate in, the process leading to the Part V agreement. This raises the question as to whether or not this state of affairs is consistent with the general concepts of fair procedures. It is submitted that as the decision as to the nature and extent of provision to be made by one developer in respect of social and affordable housing may well have implications for that which will be required from other developers in the area, the latter should be entitled to have notice of the proposed terms of the Part V agreement.[51] Similarly, neighbouring landowners may wish to be heard.[52]

A similar argument can be made in connection with other matters which are **12–41** left over for agreement as between the developer and the planning authority. More specifically, under s.34(5) of the PDA 2000, a condition may be attached to a planning permission providing that points of detail are to be agreed; in default of agreement, the matter is to be referred to An Bord Pleanála for determination. Again, it may be argued that third parties should be allowed to participate in this process also.[53]

The notice given must be sufficient to alert interested persons to the fact that a **12–42** decision is to be made. Thus, for example, in the context of an application for planning permission, a brief description of the nature and extent of the proposed development must be accurately stated, as must the location of the proposed development. The initial notice does not, however, have to be all embracing. It is enough that the notice alert any vigilant party to what is contemplated: if such a person wishes to have further information as to precisely what is envisaged, he can then inspect the plans submitted with the application.[54] To put the matter another way, the initial notice may be in short terms provided that there is an opportunity to obtain further details and information subsequently. This aspect is considered further at para.12–45 below, under the heading the "Right to make meaningful submissions".

---

[50] PDA 2000, s.96 (as amended by the Planning and Development (Amendment) Act 2002).
[51] See, by analogy, *R. v Lichfield District Council Ex p. Lichfield Securities Ltd.* [2001] P.C.L.R. 519.
[52] *cf. Dunne v An Bord Pleanála* [2006] I.E.H.C. 400; unreported, McGovern J., December 14, 2006 (neighbouring landowners not entitled to complain as to Part V agreement involving payment to planning authority).
[53] In *Arklow Holidays Ltd. v An Bord Pleanála (No. 1)* [2006] I.E.H.C. 15; [2007] 1 I.L.R.M. 125, it was suggested that members of the public would be entitled to challenge an agreement reached on foot of such a condition if the agreement did not comply with the criteria specified in the condition imposed by An Bord Pleanála.
[54] *Blessington & District Community Council Ltd. v Wicklow County Council* [1997] 1 I.R. 273 at 287.

12–43 Finally, it seems that the requirement for notice may be largely dispensed with in situations of urgency.[55] Thus, for example, whereas it is ordinarily necessary to serve a warning letter in advance of the issue of an enforcement notice, this is obviated where urgent action is required.[56]

2. Right to make meaningful submissions

12–44 The right to notice ordinarily implies a concomitant right to make submissions. As with the right to notice itself, the nature and extent of this right to make submissions is determined by the gravity of the decision. Thus, for example, the procedure with respect to the making of a compulsory purchase order entails very extensive rights to make submissions, although an oral hearing is no longer mandatory.[57] In the case of a less direct impact, such as the effect of a decision to grant planning permission on neighbouring lands, the right to make submissions may be heavily curtailed. For example, there are very strict time-limits as to the making of such submissions. In certain situations, it would seem that there must be equality of arms as between those in favour of, and those opposing, a particular decision. Thus where those in favour of a decision are permitted to make *oral* submissions, a similar facility must be made available to opponents.

12–45 The notice given must be sufficient to allow the person affected to make a meaningful submission.[58] In the case of an application for planning permission, this is achieved by affording access to the public file.[59] (Additional material may be available under the Freedom of Information Acts 1997 to 2003.) A further safeguard is provided in that where "significant additional data" is received in respect of an application, there is a requirement that further notice be given.[60] Similarly, there is a requirement for further public notice where a planning authority proposes to grant planning permission in material contravention of the development plan.[61] Insofar as the making of the development plan is concerned, there is a requirement that same be published in draft form, and, further, that any "material alteration" to the draft must itself be notified and subject to public consultation (albeit more limited).[62]

---

[55] See, by analogy, *O'Callaghan v Commissioners of Public Works in Ireland* [1985] I.L.R.M. 364 (notice of making of preservation order not required in emergency situation created by plaintiff).

[56] PDA 2000, s.155. See also *O'Connor v Kerry County Council* [1988] I.L.R.M. 660 in relation to the previous legislation.

[57] PDA 2000, s.218 (as amended by the 2006 Act).

[58] See, for example, *State (Boyd) v An Bord Pleanála*, unreported, High Court, Murphy J., February 18, 1983 (failure to provide full copy of report to appellant); and *Electricity Supply Board v Cork County Council*, unreported, High Court, Finnegan J., June 28, 2000 (failure to provide copies or summary of materials before elected members).

[59] PDA 2000, s.38(3). *Cf. Aer Rianta cpt v An Bord Pleanála*, unreported, High Court, Kelly J., June 25, 2002.

[60] Planning and Development Regulations 2001, art.35 (as substituted by the 2006 Regulations).

[61] PDA 2000, s.34(6).

[62] PDA 2000, s.12(7). *Cf. Finn v Bray UDC* [1960] I.R. 169.

A more difficult issue is the extent to which background documentation must **12–46** be disclosed. In the case of a decision directly affecting property rights, it seems that there may well be a duty of full disclosure. Thus, in the context of a compulsory purchase order, for example, it would seem that a person affected may have the right to disclosure of relevant, non-privileged documentation. Reference is made in this regard to the judgment of the Supreme Court in *Nolan v Irish Land Commission*.[63] In the case of revocation of planning permission under the previous legislation, the High Court held that the beneficiary of the planning permission was entitled to have sight of the material circulated to the elected members, or, at the very least, to a sufficiently detailed statement of the contents thereof to allow (meaningful) submissions to be made.[64]

The question of the requirement of disclosure in the context of an appeal to An **12–47** Bord Pleanála arose tangentially in the judgment in *Huntstown Air Park Ltd. v An Bord Pleanála*.[65] The case was dismissed on the basis of prematurity, but the High Court did indicate *obiter* that the power of An Bord Pleanála to request the production of documents was limited to circumstances where same were "necessary" for the determination of the appeal. Under the PDA 2000, a distinction is drawn between the limited power of a person conducting an oral hearing to require an officer of a planning authority to give information which is reasonably required for the purposes of the appeal or referral,[66] and the powers of An Bord Pleanála, first, to direct the production of documentation, and, secondly, to request the submission of documentation.[67]

An Bord Pleanála is an expert body and therefore, unlike a judicial body, can **12–48** rely on its own knowledge to inform its decisions. An Bord Pleanála must, however, inform the parties of the matters which it intends to take into account and afford an opportunity to respond: to do otherwise is a breach of fair procedures.[68] The response, presumably, may be by way of written submission, or submission at any oral hearing. Under s.137 of the PDA 2000, An Bord Pleanála has an express power to take into account matters other than those raised by the parties or by observers; the board must, however, afford an opportunity to the parties and the observers to make submissions on these matters either in writing or at any oral hearing. The statutory entitlement to make additional submissions represents an exception to the rigorous timetable provided under the legislation for the exchange of submissions, but this

---

[63] [1981] I.R. 23.
[64] *Electricity Supply Board v Cork County Council*, unreported, High Court, Finnegan J., June 28, 2000.
[65] [1999] 1 I.L.R.M. 281.
[66] PDA 2000, s.135(3) (as amended by the 2006 Act).
[67] PDA 2000, s.135(5) (as amended by the 2006 Act) and s.132, respectively.
[68] *McGoldrick v An Bord Pleanála* [1997] 1 I.R. 497; and *Stack v An Bord Pleanála*, unreported, High Court, O'Neill J., July 11, 2000. *cf. Fairyhouse Club Ltd. v An Bord Pleanála*, unreported, High Court, Finnegan J., July 18, 2001 (no requirement to notify intention to rely on previous decision of An Bord Pleanála); and *Stack v An Bord Pleanála (No. 2)*, unreported, High Court, Ó Caoimh J., March 7, 2003.

exception itself is hedged with time-limits, and submissions must be confined to the matters identified by An Bord Pleanála.

12–49   A sufficient period of time must be allowed so as to enable a proper submission to be made.[69] It is here that the tension between the statutory procedure and the general concepts of fair procedures is at its greatest. As noted above, strict time-limits are imposed under the legislation on the performance of various acts. For example, an appeal to An Bord Pleanála must be made within four weeks of the date of the decision of the planning authority. In certain instances, however, the harshness of the time-limit is tempered by a residual discretion on the part of the decision-maker to receive submissions out of time. For example, An Bord Pleanála may request submissions on an appeal or referral notwithstanding the expiration of the normal time-limits.[70] A nice question arises as to the extent, if any, to which a decision-maker might be *compelled* to exercise its discretion. An argument might be constructed to the effect that the discretion cannot be unfettered, and, accordingly, were a decision-maker to fail to invoke its power in an obviously appropriate case, then the court could intervene. In this regard, a decision-maker is, arguably, under an obligation to take reasonable steps to ensure fair procedures,[71] and this obligation should extend to the exercise of its discretionary powers where appropriate. Moreover, it is submitted that the correct standard of review would not be to ask whether the decision-maker had acted irrationally but rather whether, objectively, the procedure was fair.[72]

3. Right to reasons

12–50   A person affected by a decision is generally entitled to a statement of the reasons therefor. This is discussed in detail at paras 12–119 to 12–163. One objective of this duty is to ensure that where an appeal lies against the decision, the person affected is provided with such information as may be necessary to enable him, first, to consider whether he has a reasonable chance of succeeding in appealing the decision, and, secondly, to enable him to arm himself for the hearing of such appeal.[73] Indeed, even where there is no right of appeal, it is submitted that such information is necessary so as not to frustrate that person in invoking the supervisory jurisdiction of the High Court by way of an

---

[69] See, for example, *State (Stanford) v Dun Laoghaire Corporation*, unreported, Supreme Court, February 20, 1982 (decision on application for planning permission made one day after further newspaper notice held to be invalid).

[70] PDA 2000, s.131. *cf. Mulhall v An Bord Pleanála*, unreported, High Court, McCracken J., March 21, 1996 (Irish Times Law Report, June 10, 1996), where the High Court appears to have mistakenly considered that the equivalent power under the previous legislation was, in fact, governed by the time-limits.

[71] See, by analogy, *State (Genport Ltd.) v An Bord Pleanála* [1983] I.L.R.M. 12.

[72] *London Borough of Croydon v Secretary of State for the Environment* [2000] P.L.C.R. 171. See, more generally, *O'Callaghan v Clifford* [1993] 3 I.R. 603.

[73] *State (Sweeney) v Minister for the Environment* [1979] I.L.R.M. 35.

application for judicial review.[74] To this extent then, the duty to give reasons might be regarded as an aspect of the right to make meaningful submissions, albeit at a subsequent stage of the decision-making process.

4. Oral hearing

Considerations of administrative convenience dictate that many decisions be made on the basis of written submissions only. It is a vexed question as to in what circumstances a person affected is entitled to an oral hearing. In certain instances it seems that an oral hearing is the only fair way of dealing with the matter. Thus, for example, in *Galvin v Minister for Social Welfare*,[75] Costello J. held that the only way in which a dispute as to the making of employee contributions could be dealt with was by way of an oral hearing. It is a peculiar feature of the planning legislation, however, that there is little provision made for the holding of an oral hearing. For example, in the context of an application for planning permission, it seems that a planning authority does not have power to hold an oral hearing: the possibility of an oral hearing only arises on appeal, and even then it is expressly provided that An Bord Pleanála enjoys an "absolute discretion".[76] (The constitutionality of a similar provision under the previous legislation was considered tangentially by the Supreme Court in *Finnegan v An Bord Pleanála*.[77])

12–51

The absence of other than a precarious opportunity of an oral hearing might possibly be justified on the basis that the decision on an application for planning permission is primarily concerned with matters of policy rather than with the determination of facts: the role of an oral hearing would obviously be more critical in connection with the latter function. As against this, it is submitted that the courts should, on an application for judicial review, be prepared to consider whether An Bord Pleanála acted unfairly in denying any or any sufficient oral hearing.[78]

12–52

The provisions of the European Convention on Human Rights Act 2003 may be relevant here. The entitlement to a "public" hearing under Art.6(1) has been held to imply a right to an "oral hearing" before at least one court or tribunal. For a detailed discussion, see para.14–128 and onwards.

12–53

---

[74] *State (Creedon) v Criminal Injuries Compensation Tribunal* [1988] I.R. 51; *International Fishing Vessels Ltd. v Minister for Marine* [1989] I.R. 149; and *McCormack v Garda Síochána Complaints Board* [1997] 2 I.R. 489; [1997] 2 I.L.R.M. 321.
[75] [1997] 3 I.R. 240.
[76] cf. *Hynes v An Bord Pleanála (No. 1)*, unreported, High Court, Laffoy J., December 10, 1997.
[77] [1979] I.L.R.M. 134.
[78] *R. (On the application of Adlard) v Secretary of State for the Environment Transport and the Regions* [2002] J.P.L. 1377.

5. Cross-examination

12–54 Closely allied to the question as to whether or not a person is entitled to an oral hearing is the question as to cross-examination. The importance of the right to cross-examination in general was recently reiterated by the Supreme Court in its decision in *Maguire v Ardagh*.[79] As to its importance in relation to compulsory purchase orders, see *Nolan v Irish Land Commission*.[80] In broad terms, it would seem that if a matter is sufficiently serious so as to justify an oral hearing, the person affected should be entitled to test evidence by way of cross-examination. In this regard, an interesting example is provided in practice as to the subtle distinction between the varying degrees of procedural rights afforded to different categories of persons: at an oral hearing, it is generally only the first party developer, and third party appellants, who will be permitted to cross-examine witnesses; such a right is not ordinarily afforded to mere observers. It is also to be noted that notwithstanding the fact that the person conducting an oral hearing has an express power to take evidence on oath or affirmation, the usual practice is to receive unsworn evidence. To this extent, it seems that the general statutory exhortation that an oral hearing be conducted without undue formality prevails: whether this represents sufficient compliance in all cases with the requirements of fair procedures remains to be tested.

12–55 The High Court has indicated that the person conducting an oral hearing, in the interests of justice, must be allowed a discretion in relation to the limitation or abbreviation of excessive arguments or submissions.[81]

6. Right of appeal

12–56 The planning legislation provides for a right of appeal against certain decisions. Thus, for example, an appeal lies to An Bord Pleanála against the following decisions of a planning authority at first instance: (i) a decision on an application for planning permission[82]; (ii) a determination on a s.5 reference[83]; (iii) a determination of points of detail left over for agreement under a condition attached to a planning permission[84]; (iv) certain decisions with respect to social and affordable housing agreements under Part V of the PDA 2000 (as amended); and (v) a declaration in respect of works to a protected structure.[85] Conversely, no appeal lies in the case of an application for planning permission in a strategic development zone.[86]

---

[79] [2002] 1 I.R. 447.
[80] [1981] I.R. 23.
[81] *Keane v An Bord Pleanála*, unreported, High Court, Murphy J., June 20, 1995.
[82] PDA 2000, s.37.
[83] PDA 2000, s.5.
[84] PDA 2000, s.34(5) (as amended in 2006).
[85] PDA 2000, s.57(8) (as inserted by the Planning and Development (Amendment) Act 2002).
[86] PDA 2000, s.170(3).

A nice question arises as to the extent, if any, to which a right of appeal might, **12–57** in certain circumstances, be regarded as being an inherent aspect of a person's entitlement to fair procedures. This is especially relevant now given the introduction of a one-stage decision-making process for strategic infrastructure development under the Planning and Development (Strategic Infrastructure) Act 2006. Subject to the caveat entered immediately below, it seems that the better view is that there is no right of appeal other than that which may be prescribed by statute, and, accordingly, a right of appeal cannot be *implied* by reference to underlying concepts of fair procedures.[87] The one proviso to this is that where the legitimacy of a decision-making process is dependent on redress for seeming deficiencies in fair procedures at the first stage being provided by the existence of a right of appeal, the right of appeal cannot be removed unless the procedures available at the first stage are enhanced.

7. Right to an impartial hearing

One of the fundamental principles of natural and constitutional justice is the **12–58** rule against bias. In short, this requires that the decision-maker should be disinterested in the outcome of the decision-making process. The rule extends not only to actual bias, but also to any reasonable apprehension or suspicion of bias. The test is objective: would a reasonable person in the circumstances have a reasonable apprehension of bias.[88]

A dramatic example of a planning decision being set aside on the grounds of **12–59** alleged bias is provided by *Jerry Beades Construction Ltd. v Dublin Corporation*.[89] The High Court found that there had been a breach of fair procedures in that an application for retention planning permission had not been considered fairly or impartially. The allegations made in the case were unusual. It had been alleged that an official of the planning authority had indicated to the principal of the applicant company that any application for retention planning permission would be treated with contempt. This allegation was then raised by the developer with a more senior planning official, which official indicated that he personally would deal with the application. This official then prepared a report, which recommended the grant of planning permission, and the report was then send forward to the "decisions' section" which would then transmit a draft manager's order to the assistant city manager for his ultimate decision. Following a meeting in the interim between the two officials and the Deputy Dublin City Planner, a (second) report, this time recommending the refusal of planning permission, was sent to the assistant county manager:

---

[87] *cf. Ni Eili v Environmental Protection Agency* [1997] 2 I.L.R.M. 458, where the applicant had sought to argue that the absence of an independent right of appeal in the context of the decision on an application for an integrated pollution control licence rendered the legislation unconstitutional. The High Court refused the applicant leave to amend her pleadings and thus the applicant was precluded from pursuing the argument.

[88] *Bula Ltd. (In receivership) v Tara Mines Ltd.* [2000] 4 I.R. 412.

[89] [2005] I.E.H.C. 406; unreported, McKechnie J., September 7, 2005.

this report had been countersigned by the Deputy Dublin City Planner. The first report was at some stage removed from the file by a person who has never been identified. Ultimately, a decision to refuse planning permission was made. This decision was then appealed by the applicant to An Bord Pleanála.

12–60 McKechnie J. held that the process and the planning authority's decision "were reached in a manner contrary to fair procedures and involved a breach of natural and constitutional justice". In particular, the decision of the assistant city manager was, according to McKechnie J., based on an incomplete version of the true circumstances. McKechnie J. further ruled that the breaches in this regard tainted the decision on the appeal to An Bord Pleanála.

Distinction between judicial and administrative functions

12–61 A distinction of sorts has been drawn in some of the case law between judicial functions and administrative functions. The precise implications of this distinction are not, however, at all clear. It may be that a lesser standard applies to administrative functions: for example, it would seem that a bias of necessity may be tolerated.[90] Thus, in *Radio One Limerick Ltd. v Independent Radio and Television Commission*,[91] the Supreme Court recognised that an administrative body exercising quasi-judicial powers may, because of the special knowledge and involvement of its members in the matters with which the body has to deal, lack the appearance of strict impartiality which would be expected of a court administering justice. Such a body should not, however, be prevented from discharging its statutory function by strict application of the requirement of impartiality, at least where, as on the facts of that case, all practical steps have been taken by the body to free itself not merely from actual bias, but from the apprehension of bias in the minds of reasonable people.[92]

12–62 This distinction between judicial functions and administrative functions was relied upon in the context of the (previous) planning legislation in *Huntsgrove Developments Ltd. v Meath County Council*.[93] There, the High Court characterised a decision to review a development plan as an administrative act, and held that in order for the applicant to succeed in its challenge, it would have to satisfy the court that as a matter of probability the respondent planning authority had acted for an indirect or improper motive; *i.e.* the applicant was required to establish a real likelihood of *actual* bias.

---

[90] See *O'Brien v An Bord na Mona* [1983] I.R. 255 at 282. *Cf. Kingsley v United Kingdom* (2002) 34 E.H.R.R. 52, [58], which was cited with approval by Hardiman J. in his dissenting judgment in *O'Callaghan v Judge Mahon* [2007] I.E.S.C. 17; unreported, March 30, 2007.

[91] [1997] 2 I.R. 291.

[92] *ibid.* See also *Usk and District Residents Association Ltd. v An Bord Pleanála*; unreported, High Court, Kelly J., March 14, 2007, where the High Court recommended, when remitting a planning decision for further consideration, that the matter be considered by a differently constituted division of the board.

[93] [1994] 2 I.L.R.M. 36.

Bias must arise from factors external to the decision-making process

The manner in which the decision-making process has been conducted may **12–63** give rise to a concern on the part of one of the parties that the decision-maker is biased. However, the Supreme Court has indicated in a number of recent judgments that should an adjudicator pursue a line of enquiry concerning a matter relevant to the decision to be made in a tendentious or unfair manner, this did not in itself permit, as a matter of law, the decision to be impugned on the grounds of bias, but rather it fell to be reviewed in accordance with the requirements of fair procedures or natural justice.[94] The test to be applied in determining whether there is objective bias is whether a reasonable person, with full knowledge of the circumstances, would consider that there are external factors which would cause the decision-maker to make a particular decision, or would inhibit him from making a decision impartially, as would give rise to a reasonable apprehension of bias.[95]

Institutional or structural bias

There are certain aspects of the decision-making procedures under the planning **12–64** legislation which might give rise to institutional or structural bias. The first two of these relate to the role of the planning authority. In addition to its function as decision-maker of first instance with respect to an application for planning permission, a planning authority has a function in relation to facilitating, and, indeed, in relation to the carrying out of, development. This latter function may well give rise to a seeming conflict with the former adjudicatory function. For example, under Pt XIV of the PDA 2000, a planning authority may, *inter alia*, secure, facilitate or carry out the development and renewal of areas in need of physical, social or economic regeneration, and in this connection may enter into agreements with any person for the development of land.[96] One can readily envisage circumstances where a planning authority will be required to determine an application for planning permission in respect of development, its support for which it will have already signalled by the entering into of such an agreement. This might well lead to an allegation of bias by way of prejudgment. The provisions of s.47 are interesting in this regard. Section 47 enables a planning authority to enter into an agreement with a person interested in land for the purpose of restricting or regulating the development of land. It is expressly provided that nothing in the section, or any agreement made thereunder, shall be construed as restricting the exercise of statutory powers so long as those powers are not exercised to materially contravene the provisions of the development plan. The implication of this seems to be that by entering into such an agreement, a planning authority is allowed to fetter its discretion,

---

[94] See *Orange Communications Ltd. v Director of Telecommunications Regulation* [2000] 4 I.R. 159; *Spin Communications Ltd. v Independent Radio and Television Commission* [2001] 4 I.R. 411; and *O'Callaghan v Judge Mahon* [2007] I.E.S.C. 17; unreported, March 30, 2007.

[95] *O'Callaghan v Judge Mahon* [2007] I.E.S.C. 17; unreported, March 30, 2007, *per* Denham J.

[96] PDA 2000, s.212.

subject only to the proviso that the development plan must be complied with. Although the provisions of s.47 are only available where the other person has an interest in land in the area, it does seem to suggest a certain tolerance for bias by way of prejudgment.

12–65 A second example of possible institutional bias is of more general application. It relates to the dual function of a planning authority as both adjudicator and policy-maker. More specifically, a planning authority is required to formulate planning policy and to include same in the development plan. The objection can therefore be made that the planning authority is not impartial in that it will be predisposed towards upholding its own policies. A similar objection has been raised before the courts of England and Wales in the context of the Human Rights Act 1998. More specifically, in *R. (On the application of Alconbury Developments Ltd.) v Secretary of State for the Environment, Transport and the Regions*,[97] it appears to have been accepted that the Secretary of State would not represent an independent and impartial tribunal because of his role as policy-maker. The decision-making scheme as a whole was, however, held to be compliant with the human rights legislation in that the possibility of judicial review did ensure the necessary independence and impartiality. The House of Lords ruled that there was no requirement that the judicial review involve a full rehearing: given the policy content of the decision, there was no necessity that the court should be able to substitute its decision for that of the administrative authority.

12–66 This reasoning would seem to apply equally under Irish law. In particular, the sentiment of leaving over a considerable margin of appreciation or discretion to a statutory decision-maker in respect of matters of planning expertise sits comfortably with the doctrine of administrative unreasonableness. See, generally, para.12–74 below and onwards. Moreover, under Irish law there is the possibility that the existence of an independent appeal's board, namely An Bord Pleanála, would be sufficient, even without recourse to judicial review, to comply with any requirement for an impartial hearing. In other words, even if a very strict definition of impartiality is applied such as to disqualify the planning authority on the basis of its role as policy-maker, it may be that the existence of a right of appeal to An Bord Pleanála meets the concerns in this regard.

12–67 In this connection, it is relevant to note that a number of safeguards are built into the legislation so as to ensure the impartiality of An Bord Pleanála. For example, under Pt VII of the PDA 2000 there is a requirement, *inter alia*, that members of the board disclose any pecuniary or other beneficial interest in, or which is material to, any appeal, contribution, question, determination or dispute which falls to be decided or determined by An Bord Pleanála.[98] Under s.114, there is a prohibition on certain communications in relation to an appeal.

---

[97] [2001] U.K.H.L. 23; (2001) 82 P. & C.R. 40.
[98] PDA 2000, s.148.

There are, however, at least two aspects of the composition and role of the   **12–68**
board which may undermine any claim that it has a genuinely independent
status. First, there is provision for the appointment of persons to the board on
a *temporary* basis.[99] This is open to criticism on the ground that security of
tenure is usually considered to be one of the principal desiderata of independent
decision-making. Secondly, An Bord Pleanála is required to have regard to,
inter alia, the policies and objectives for the time being of the Government.[100]

8. Right to judicial review

The planning legislation is unusual in that a special judicial review procedure   **12–69**
is prescribed. More specifically under ss.50 and 50A of the PDA 2000 (as
amended under the 2006 Act), challenges to certain decisions and acts of a
local authority, planning authority and of An Bord Pleanála, may only be brought
pursuant to the prescribed procedure. Typically, the stipulation of such a special
judicial review procedure is seen as a protection for decision-makers against
unmeritorious challenges, achieved by way of the imposition of limitations on
the bringing of legal proceedings. What is not often considered, however, is
the extent to which the existence of a *right* to judicial review may represent an
indispensable underpinning to the legitimacy of the decision-making process.
It is at least arguable that certain decisions made under the planning legislation
involve the determination of legal rights and liabilities. Although the courts
have shied away from categorising such decisions as involving the
administration of justice,[101] they have gone as far as describing certain functions
as being quasi-judicial.[102] It is only a short step from this to say that the
availability of judicial review represents a necessary *quid pro quo* for allowing
such significant powers to a non-judicial body.

A right to judicial review may also be a requirement of EC law, and of the   **12–70**
European Convention on Human Rights ("the Convention"). As discussed in
detail in Chapter 13, it is a requirement of Art.10a of the amended environmental
impact assessment Directive that Member States provide a "review procedure"
to challenge the substantive or procedural legality of decisions, acts or omissions

---

[99] PDA 2000, s.104.
[100] PDA 2000, s.143 (as amended by the 2006 Act). The obligation under the previous
legislation to keep informed of government policy was interpreted as entailing an
obligation on the part of the decision-maker to take those policies and objectives into
account in discharging its statutory duty. *Keane v An Bord Pleanála* [1998] 2 I.L.R.M.
241.
[101] *cf. Central Dublin Development Association v Attorney General* (1969) 109 I.L.T.R. 69
(determination of reference under s.5 of the Local Government (Planning & Development)
Act 1963 an administration of justice).
[102] See, for example, *State (Stanford) v Dun Laoghaire Corporation*, unreported, Supreme
Court, February 20, 1981 ("quasi-judicial function"); *State (Abenglen Properties Ltd.) v
Dublin Corporation* [1984] I.R. 381; [1982] I.L.R.M. 590 ("self-contained and quasi-
judicial scheme"); and *P & F Sharpe Ltd. v Dublin City and County Manager* [1989]
I.R. 701; [1989] I.L.R.M. 565 ("judicial manner").

subject to the public participation provisions of the Directive.[103] Insofar as the Convention is concerned, in certain instances the availability of judicial review is essential to ensure that decision-making procedures are compliant with the Convention.

12–71   At all events, as matters currently stand there is an express statutory entitlement under national law to challenge certain decisions by way of an application for judicial review.[104] Whereas it is open to the legislature to stipulate that the procedure by which such a challenge may be brought is to be more exacting than that for conventional judicial review, it would not be open to remove entirely the right to challenge such decisions.

9. Right to timely decision-making

12–72   Article 6(1) of the Convention requires a determination to be made with in a "reasonable time". This aspect has been interpreted by the ECtHR as imposing a duty on the contracting States to organise their judicial systems in such a way that their courts can meet each of its requirements, including the obligation to hear cases within a reasonable time.[105] These principles apply to the determination of planning matters.[106]

12–73   There is only limited provision made under the PDA 2000 to police timely decision-making. Although aspirational time-limits are prescribed for various decisions—for example, An Bord Pleanála is to determine appeals "as expeditiously as may be"— it is only in the case of delay at the planning authority stage of an application for planning permission that there is an actual sanction imposed. As it happens, that sanction, namely default planning permission, may itself be incompatible with the Convention for other reasons. See further Chapter 14, paras 14–189 to 14–193.

D. Doctrine of Administrative Unreasonableness

1. Introduction

12–74   The concept of administrative unreasonableness represents a gloss on, or exception to, the general rule that a court on an application for judicial review is never concerned with the merits of the impugned decision. What the concept of administrative unreasonableness allows for is just such a consideration by a court of the *merits* of the decision of the inferior body, albeit only in

---

[103] See, generally, *Sweetman v An Bord Pleanála*, unreported, High Court, Clarke J., April 27, 2007.

[104] See *Chambers v An Bord Pleanála* [1992] 1 I.R. 134; [1992] I.L.R.M. 296 (statutory scheme contemplates challenge in the courts).

[105] See, for example, *Frydlender v France* (2001) 31 E.H.R.R. 52, [45].

[106] *Morscher v Austria* [2004] E.C.H.R. 54039/00 (delay of up to six years in final determination of planning permission unreasonable).

circumstances where the decision-maker is shown to have disregarded fundamental reason and common sense in reaching a decision. Sight is often lost, however, of the fact that the doctrine is actually in ease of an applicant. This is due in no small part to the fact that the threshold to be met by an applicant before a decision may be set aside as unreasonable is so high. This has tended to create the mistaken impression that the rule is one for the protection of decision-makers.

The doctrine of unreasonableness is based on the very simple premise that no statutory discretionary power is unreviewable. Reference is made in this regard to the judgments of the Supreme Court in *State (Lynch) v Cooney*.[107] In particular, reference is made to the following passage from the judgment of Henchy J.   **12–75**

> "I conceive the present state of evolution of administrative law in the Courts on this topic to be that when a statute confers on a nonjudicial person or body a decision-making power affecting personal rights, conditional on that person or body reaching a prescribed opinion or conclusion based on subjective assessment, a person who shows that a personal right of his has been breached or is liable to be breached by a decision purporting to be made in exercise of that power has standing to seek, and the High Court has jurisdiction to give, a ruling as to whether the pre-condition for the valid exercise of the power has been complied with in a way that brings the decision within the express, or necessarily implied, range of the power conferred by the statute. It is to be presumed that, when it conferred the power, Parliament intended the power to be exercised only in a manner that would be in conformity with the Constitution and within the limitations of the power as they are to be gathered from the statutory scheme or design. This means, amongst other things, not only that the power must be exercised in good faith but that the opinion or other subjective conclusion set as a precondition for the valid exercise of the power must be reached by a route that does not make the exercise unlawful — such as by misinterpreting the law, or by misapplying it through taking into consideration irrelevant matters of fact, or through ignoring relevant matters. Otherwise, the exercise of the power will be held to be invalid for being *ultra vires*."

Accordingly, even the broadest discretion afforded under statute is subject to the: **12–76**

> "necessarily implied constitutional limitation of jurisdiction in all decision-making which affects rights or duties requires, *inter alia*, that the decision-maker must not flagrantly reject or disregard fundamental reason or common sense in reaching his decision".[108]

The courts thus reserve unto themselves an exceptional power to set aside, in rare and limited circumstances, a decision on its substantive merits. One of the very few examples of the High Court interfering to set aside a planning decision on the grounds of reasonableness was in the case of *Ashbourne Holdings Ltd.*   **12–77**

---

[107] [1982] I.R. 337 at 380–381.
[108] *State (Keegan) v Stardust Victims' Compensation Tribunal* [1986] I.R. 642 at 658.

v An Bord Pleanála.[109] Kearns J. held that certain conditions attached to a planning permission were invalid as unreasonable. In particular, the conditions (requiring public access) had the capacity to frustrate and/or render inoperable the use of the relevant lands as a golf course. Kearns J. indicated that it could hardly be said that a peripheral condition which had such damaging implications for the development as a whole could be fairly or reasonably related to the development.

12–78 The courts have been at pains to emphasise that the power to intervene on the basis that a decision is unreasonable or irrational is an exceptional one, and one which is to be used sparingly. To this end, the threshold to be met by an applicant seeking to challenge a decision on the basis of unreasonableness is extraordinarily high. The applicant must demonstrate that the decision is fundamentally at variance with reason and common sense; that the decision is indefensible for being in the teeth of plain reason and common sense; and that the decision-maker has flagrantly rejected reason or disregarded fundamental reason or common sense in reaching his decision.[110] A court cannot interfere with a decision of an administrative decision-maker merely on the grounds that (a) it is satisfied on the facts as found, it would have raised different inferences and conclusions, or (b) it is satisfied that the case against the decision is stronger than the case for it.[111]

12–79 In effect, it is necessary for the applicant to establish to the satisfaction of the court that the decision-maker had before it no relevant evidence or material which would support its decision.[112] The volume of such evidence is, seemingly, irrelevant: there does not have to be anything approaching abundant, substantial or irrefutable evidence, it is sufficient that there be some evidence, even conflicting evidence.[113]

12–80 More recently, the High Court, in *Aer Rianta cpt v Commissioner for Aviation Regulation,*[114] sought to restate the principle. In this judgment, O'Sullivan J. drew a distinction between error and invalidity. O'Sullivan J. held that a decision is not invalid because it is wrong nor is it invalid because it is very wrong, fundamentally wrong or even absolutely wrong.

---

[109] [2002] 2 I.L.R.M. 321 (High Court). This matter was not considered in the same detail by the Supreme Court: [2003] 2 I.R. 114; [2003] 2 I.L.R.M. 446.

[110] *State (Keegan) v Stardust Victims' Compensation Tribunal* [1986] I.R. 642, cited with approval in *O'Keeffe v An Bord Pleanála* [1993] 1 I.R. 39; [1992] I.L.R.M. 237.

[111] *O'Keeffe v An Bord Pleanála* [1993] 1 I.R. 39; [1992] I.L.R.M. 237.

[112] *O'Keeffe v An Bord Pleanála* [1993] 1 I.R. 39; [1992] I.L.R.M. 237.

[113] *MA Ryan & Sons Ltd. v An Bord Pleanála*, unreported, High Court, Peart J., February 6, 2003 (at p.39). See also *Lord Ballyedmond v Commission for Energy Regulation* [2006] I.E.H.C. 206; unreported, June 22, 2006.

[114] Unreported, High Court, O'Sullivan J., January 16, 2003 (at p.48), cited with approval in *Kildare County Council v An Bord Pleanála* [2006] I.E.H.C. 173; unreported, MacMenamin J., March 10, 2006, [78].

"The type of grievous error so reviewable is of a completely different order. It is not reached by the extension of the line on which are to be found mere errors, serious errors, multiple errors and fundamental errors because that is a line of rationale attempt no matter how misguided the outcome. But the kind of error that produces invalidity is one which no rational or sane decision-maker, no matter how misguided, could essay. To be reviewable [as] irrational, it is not sufficient that a decision-maker goes wrong or even hopelessly and fundamentally wrong: he must have gone completely and inexplicably mad; taken leave of his senses and come to an absurd conclusion. It is only when this last situation arises or something akin to it that a court will review the decision for irrationality."

This judgment is open to the criticism that it overstates the position in relation **12–81** to the doctrine of unreasonableness. The nature and extent of the discretion afforded under any particular statute is ultimately a matter of statutory interpretation. In some cases, it may well be that a decision-maker is entrusted by legislation with a very broad discretion and the courts quite properly should be reluctant to interfere. In other circumstances, however, the courts must be prepared to apply a more exacting standard of review. This is especially so where the decision affects constitutional rights. Further, there may be some particular aspect of the legislation which indicates that a higher or lower standard of review applies. For example, if the legislation itself provides an alternative remedy whereby any breach on the part of the decision-maker might be remedied, this would tell against there being other than a limited right of review.

2. Standard of review

As intimated above, the doctrine of unreasonableness is rooted in statutory **12–82** interpretation. The principal aspect of this is that even the broadest discretion afforded under legislation is subject to the necessarily implied constitutional limitation that the decision-maker must not flagrantly reject or disregard fundamental reason or common sense in reaching his decision.[115] In addition to this general consideration, however, the courts must also examine the governing legislation so as to identify any further factors, peculiar to that legislation, which indicate that a more exacting standard of review should apply. First and foremost of these is, it is submitted, the nature of the discretion being exercised by the decision-maker. The greater the policy content of the decision, the less searching the review must be. The decision being challenged in *O'Keeffe v An Bord Pleanála*[116] was one which involved the exercise of a discretionary power *par excellence*. The decision to grant or refuse planning permission is pre-eminently a policy matter which has been entrusted under the legislation

---

[115] See *State (Keegan) v Stardust Victims' Compensation Tribunal* [1986] I.R. 642. See also comments of Fennelly J. in *O'Brien v Moriarty* [2006] I.E.S.C. 6; [2006] 2 I.R. 415 at 469–470 ("The courts will, of course, always have regard to the context of a decision, the statutory purpose of the body concerned and its duties and, where appropriate, the need to have regard to the rights or interests of individuals or categories of individuals, whose interests it is the object of legislation to protect.").

[116] [1993] 1 I.R. 39; [1992] I.L.R.M. 237.

to the planning authorities and An Bord Pleanála. In other circumstances, however, the decision under review although still technically one made in the exercise of a discretion should, it is submitted, be more susceptible to challenge.

12–83 The point may be illustrated by reference to the judgment of the High Court in *McEvoy v Meath County Council*.[117] This case concerned a challenge to a decision to make a development plan. The applicants sought to argue that the respondent planning authority had not had proper regard to the statutory regional planning guidelines. Quirke J. held that although the nature and extent of the consideration given by the elected members to the regional guidelines gave rise to concern (and indeed unease), he was not satisfied that the evidence adduced had established that the planning authority had failed to "have regard to" the regional guidelines. In this connection, Quirke J. expressly relied upon the principles in *O'Keeffe v An Bord Pleanála*.[118]

12–84 Although a planning authority clearly has some freedom in relation to the making of its development plan, it is submitted that this discretion is hedged in by the requirement to have regard to matters such as the statutory guidelines. If the obligation to have regard to the statutory guidelines is to have any meaning, then it would seem that a heightened standard of review should apply. At the very least, it might be expected that the courts would require more by way of objective justification: if a planning authority is to depart from the guidelines, it should be evident from the face of its decision as to why it has adopted this course. Moreover, the fact that the development plan, on its face, appeared to be inconsistent would strongly suggest that whatever statutory discretion was enjoyed by the planning authority had been abused in the sense of an arbitrary or unreasoned decision having been produced.

12–85 The second consideration which should influence the standard of review is the impact of the decision on personal rights. In particular, a decision which adversely affects an individual's property rights or other personal rights should be subject to more anxious scrutiny. Reference is made in this connection to the decision of the High Court in *Bailey v Mr Justice Flood*.[119] The argument had been made that there should be a different standard of review applicable to decisions involving constitutional rights. In this regard, the applicants relied upon the decision of the Court of Appeal in *R. v Lord Saville Ex p. A*.[120] Having referred to the authorities, Morris P. indicated that he was prepared to accept the following as a correct statement of the test which the court ought to apply when reviewing a decision that impinges on constitutionally guaranteed rights.

---

[117] [2003] 1 I.R. 208; [2003] 1 I.L.R.M. 431.

[118] [1993] 1 I.R. 39; [1992] I.L.R.M. 237.

[119] Unreported, High Court, Morris P., March 6, 2000. This decision was subsequently affirmed on narrower grounds by the Supreme Court: unreported, April 14, 2000. See also *VZ v Minister for Justice Equality and Law Reform* [2002] 2 I.R. 135, where the question of a heightened standard applying in the context of immigration cases was canvassed.

[120] [1999] 4 All E.R. 860.

"The court may not interfere with the exercise of an administrative discretion on substantive grounds save where the court is satisfied [...] that it is beyond the range of responses open to a reasonable decision-maker. But in judging whether the decision-maker has exceeded this margin of appreciation the human rights context is important. The more substantial the interference with human rights, the more the court will require by way of justification before it is satisfied that the decision is reasonable in the sense outlined above."

Morris P. went on to find on the facts that, seemingly even under this formulation, the applicants had failed to demonstrate that the impugned decision was unreasonable. **12–86**

The suggestion that a heightened standard of review should apply where the decision impacts on constitutional rights obviously has a particular resonance in the context of the planning legislation. More specifically, certain decisions impact directly on constitutionally protected property rights. This is especially so in relation to the compulsory purchase of lands, and, to a lesser extent, in relation to the decision on an application for planning permission. In the circumstances, it is at least arguable that the standard of review posited by *O'Keeffe v An Bord Pleanála* is inappropriate. **12–87**

Such an approach has recently been endorsed by the Supreme Court in *Clinton v An Bord Pleanála*.[121] Geoghegan J. having stated that it was axiomatic that the making and confirming of a compulsory purchase order entails an invasion of constitutionally protected property rights, went on to suggest that it would insufficiently protect constitutional rights if the court, hearing a judicial review application, merely had to be satisfied that the decision was not irrational or was not contrary to fundamental reason and common sense. **12–88**

A third factor then is whether or not the legislation prescribes an alternative enforcement mechanism. Just as an order of mandamus may be withheld in circumstances where the legislation prescribes some other procedure by which a breach of statutory duty may be enforced, it is submitted that the existence of an alternative solution might relieve the courts from engaging in a more rigorous review of an impugned decision. Thus, in the context of the making of a development plan, for example, it would seem relevant that the Minister for the Environment, Heritage and Local Government has certain powers which would allow him to police the duties of the planning authorities.[122] **12–89**

---

[121] [2007] I.E.S.C. 19; unreported, May 2, 2007.
[122] *cf. McEvoy v Meath County Council* [2003] 1 I.R. 208; [2003] 1 I.L.R.M. 431.

E. Over-Application of Doctrine of Unreasonableness

1. Introduction

12–90   One of the most serious criticisms of the doctrine of unreasonableness is that it is being over applied.[123] In order to understand this criticism, it is necessary to rehearse briefly the rationale of the doctrine. As discussed at para.12-75 and onwards, recourse to the doctrine allows the courts an exceptional power to review the substance or merits of a decision. Such a power is at odds with the general principle that judicial review is concerned with the decision-making process and not with the decision. For this reason, the courts are reluctant to employ the power, and accordingly same is used only sparingly. In particular, and again as discussed above, the courts have posited a very high threshold for its exercise.

12–91   Difficulties can and do arise, however, where sight is lost of the precept that the doctrine of unreasonableness only applies in respect of the exercise of a statutory *discretion*. What the doctrine does is to ensure that even in the context of the exercise of a discretion, the courts have an exceptional jurisdiction to intervene and set aside the decision. In other words, notwithstanding the fact that the legislation has entrusted a particular matter to a statutory decision-maker, the High Court nevertheless has a supervisory role albeit one that it is reluctant to invoke. This is to be contrasted with the position where a decision-maker is required, out of necessity, to take a "view" (to use a neutral term) on a matter which is outside the scope of its statutory discretion. To elaborate: during the course of its decision-making, a decision-maker may well have to take a view on various matters which although relevant to its decision may not necessarily come within the four corners of its statutory discretion. The view that the decision-maker takes on such collateral matters is not deserving of the same deference which the courts show towards a matter within the four corners of the statutory discretion. Rather, this aspect of the decision-making process will be subject to full-blooded review by the High Court. This is because the fact that the matter is outwith the statutory discretion means, by definition, that it is not a matter which has been *entrusted* under the legislation to the decision-maker. Indeed, as discussed below by reference to the example of material contravention of the development plan, the collateral matter may well entail a fetter or limitation on the exercise of the statutory discretion.

12–92   For ease of reference, the shorthand "question of fact and degree" will be used to describe the type of decision which has been entrusted to a decision-maker under legislation and is accordingly reviewable only under the doctrine of unreasonableness. The shorthand "question of law" will be used to describe matters which are subject to full-blooded review by the High Court. This distinction is of much more than academic importance in that the demarcation

---

[123]   See, generally, G. Simons, "The unreasonable planning authority, Parts I and II" (2000) 7 I.P.E.L.J. 164; (2001) 8 I.P.E.L.J. 26.

will often seal the fate of a challenge to a decision. If the challenge is to a question of fact and degree, then it will not be enough to demonstrate that the decision was wrong[124]; rather, for the challenge to succeed it will have to be shown that the decision was unreasonable or irrational. If, conversely, the challenge is to a question of law, then it is sufficient to demonstrate that the decision was wrong.

2. Example: material contravention of development plan

The point may be illustrated, by example, by reference to the concept of material contravention of the development plan. Section 178 of the PDA 2000, in brief, precludes a planning authority from carrying out development which would involve a material contravention of its development plan. Local authority development is generally exempted development under the planning legislation,[125] and thus the prohibition under s.178 represents one of the few controls on a local authority's own development.

12–93

Before embarking on development, a local authority should, therefore, address its mind to the question as to whether or not the particular development represents a material contravention of the development plan. Presumably no responsible local authority would proceed with the development unless it was satisfied that there was no material contravention involved, and thus it would seem that a decision to proceed with a particular development should, by definition, indicate that the local authority was of the view that there was no material contravention. Suppose then that the conduct of the local authority is challenged by an objector by way of an application for judicial review. The principal matter which the High Court will have to determine is, obviously, whether or not there is a material contravention of the development plan. If not, then the challenge must fail. The local authority may well seek to argue that the question of whether there is a material contravention or not is a planning-type question, and one in respect of which the High Court should defer to its expertise. In other words, the planning authority may well urge that the "decision" which it has taken (to the effect that there is no material contravention) is one in respect of which the High Court could only properly intervene were the decision to be shown to be unreasonable or irrational. Although the argument is superficially attractive, recent judgments of the High Court have rejected such an approach.[126] This is because the concept of "material contravention"—when properly understood—far from being a matter

12–94

---

[124] See, for example, *Bailey v Mr Justice Flood*, unreported, High Court, Morris P., March 6, 2000 ("The freedom to exercise a discretion necessarily entails the freedom to get it wrong; this does not make the decision unlawful.").

[125] PDA 2000, s.4.

[126] See, for example, the decision in *Wicklow Heritage Trust Ltd. v Wicklow County Council*, unreported, High Court, McGuinness J., February 5, 1998. In *Cork City Council v An Bord Pleanála* [2006] I.E.H.C. 192; unreported, Kelly J., June 1, 2006, the High Court ruled that the interpretation of a development contribution scheme involved a question of law.

which has been entrusted under the legislation to a local authority, actually represents a fetter on the powers of a local authority. More specifically, the competence of a local authority to carry out development without planning permission is expressly limited to circumstances where same does not involve a material contravention of the development plan. Were a local authority to be allowed determine this issue conclusively, this would set the limitation at naught. To put the matter in blunt terms, it would not make much sense to impose a restriction on a local authority, and then to allow the local authority an almost unreviewable discretion to determine the parameters of that restriction. Accordingly, the question of whether a material contravention is involved is a question of law to be determined by the High Court without the necessity of showing any particular deference to the initial "view" taken by the local authority.

3. Question of law

12–95   It must be conceded that the use of the shorthand "question of law" may give rise to some confusion. In particular, its use may create the impression that a planning authority has no entitlement to ever consider a matter which involves a question of law. Thus, in the example immediately above at para.12-93, it might mistakenly be thought that it would be necessary for a planning authority to apply to the High Court each and every time a question arose as to whether or not a particular development represented a material contravention of the development plan. This is, of course, not the legal position. What the use of the term "question of law" is intended to signify is simply the standard of review which would be applicable in the event of judicial review proceedings, and, in particular, the extent to which the High Court should defer to the opinion of the planning authority on the particular issue. The use of the term "question of law" does not indicate that a planning authority is not entitled to have an *opinion* on the particular matter: it can and must. The practical reality is that a planning authority should take a view on whether or not there is a material contravention prior to making a decision to proceed with particular development. This view will obviously be known to the High Court in the event that judicial review proceedings are taken. All that the attribution of the term "question of law" does is to indicate that the view of the planning authority on the question of material contravention or not is subject to full-blooded review by the High Court. In other words, the court will not ask whether the planning authority was unreasonable in thinking that there was no material contravention, but rather will assess objectively whether or not there was a material contravention.

4. Designation as question of law, or question of fact and degree

12–96   Ultimately, the determination of which matters have been entrusted under legislation to a decision-maker is an exercise in statutory interpretation. There are, however, a number of presumptions which may assist in this task. It should be emphasised that these are presumptions only, and the legislation in each case will have to be considered on its own terms.

The first presumption is that, generally speaking, questions involving the interpretation of law will not have been entrusted to an administrative decision-maker.[127] More typically, the types of matters which will have been entrusted to an administrative decision-maker will be matters of policy, or will involve the determination of facts. Thus, for example, questions of planning policy in the context of an application for planning permission are entrusted to a planning authority and to An Bord Pleanála. In certain cases, however, the determination of even legal issues may have been entrusted by legislation to an administrative decision-maker. One such example is in the case of the Labour Court. The High Court in *Harte v Labour Court*[128] held that the Oireachtas had vested in the Labour Court the power to decide, not merely questions of fact, but also mixed questions of fact and law. Under the planning legislation, it is arguable that the function of determining whether a particular matter involves development or not, or exempted development or not—now consigned to the planning authorities and An Bord Pleanála under the modified s.5 procedure—involves them in determining legal issues.[129] This point is discussed further at paras 10–17 to 10–20.

12–97

The second presumption is that if a particular matter operates so as to limit or fetter the exercise of a statutory power, the decision-maker will not be permitted to determine that matter conclusively. This has already been illustrated at paras 12–93 to 12–94 above by reference to the significance of the concept of material contravention of the development plan in the context of local authority own development. The concept of material contravention also has significance in the context of an application for planning permission[130]: where such a material contravention is involved, the planning authority is required to undertake special procedures before it can grant planning permission. These special procedures involve, *inter alia*, the giving of public notice, and a requirement for a special voting procedure. The effect of all of this is to make it more difficult for a planning authority to grant planning permission for development in material contravention than in the case of ordinary development. The concept of material contravention, accordingly, operates as a fetter on the planning authority's power in this context also.

12–98

A third presumption, albeit one put forward on a tentative basis only, is that where the matter relates to the requirements of fair procedures, the court is entitled to subject the conduct of the planning authority to full-blooded

12–99

---

[127] For a trenchant statement to this effect, see *Tennyson v Dun Laoghaire Corporation* [1991] 2 I.R. 527. See also *Lambert v An tArd Chláraitheoir* [1995] 2 I.R. 372.
[128] [1996] 2 I.R. 171; [1996] 2 I.L.R.M. 450.
[129] *cf. Central Dublin Development Association v Attorney General* (1969) 109 I.L.T.R. 69.
[130] See, generally, *Tennyson v Dun Laoghaire Corporation* [1991] 2 I.R. 527.

review.[131] The reason this presumption is only put forward on a tentative basis is that the issue does not appear to have been considered in any detail in the Irish case law. The judgments in connection with the environmental impact assessment Directive are of interest in that they suggest that whereas any question as to the adequacy or quality of an environmental impact statement is a matter for the statutory bodies,[132] the requirement in the first instance that a particular development be subject to environmental impact assessment is a question of law for the courts. This might be taken as indicating that the courts will carefully scrutinise decisions affecting rights of public participation. To be frank, however, the case law in this regard is more heavily influenced by the consideration that environmental impact assessment is a requirement of EC law.

12–100   Two recent judgments have suggested that the determination of whether a statutory requirement for further public consultation has been triggered is a question of fact and degree. The first, *Dietacaron Ltd. v An Bord Pleanála*,[133] concerned revised plans. An Bord Pleanála had exercised its power to invite an applicant for planning permission to submit revised plans. An Bord Pleanála indicated that the revised plans would be circulated to the parties to the appeal, and those parties would be given a further opportunity to make submissions and observations in relation thereto. One of the parties to the appeal argued that the nature and extent of the revisions sought by An Bord Pleanála went beyond mere modifications and, in fact, so radically altered the development as to comprise a new development requiring a fresh application for planning permission.

12–101   One of the preliminary issues to be determined by the High Court was as to the standard of review to apply. Quirke J. held that the decision fell to be reviewed against the standard of administrative unreasonableness. On the facts, Quirke J. held that the decision of An Bord Pleanála to invite revisions of the type sought was not unreasonable.

12–102   The second case, *Kinsella v Dundalk Town Council*,[134] involved a response to a request for further information. It was alleged that the planning authority should have required further public notice on receipt of the response. Specifically, it was said that the response contained "significant additional data" such as to trigger the statutory requirement for further public notice. Kelly J. ruled that the task of assessing whether the response contained "significant additional data" involved the exercise of planning expertise and judgment which the High Court did not have, and was precisely the kind of question which falls within the competence of an expert decision-maker. The

---

[131]   *R. (On the application of Adlard) v Secretary of State for the Environment Transport and the Regions* [2002] J.P.L. 1377.
[132]   See, in particular, *Kenny v An Bord Pleanála (No. 1)* [2001] 1 I.R. 565.
[133]   [2005] 2 I.L.R.M. 32.
[134]   Unreported, High Court, Kelly J., December 3, 2004.

planning authority's decision was, therefore, only subject to review on grounds of unreasonableness.

In each of these cases, the High Court considered that the *content* of the decision under review was such that it would be difficult for the court to second-guess the view of An Bord Pleanála, and of the planning authority, respectively. An alternative approach would be to look to the *objective* of the relevant statutory requirements. Once the relevant statutory test is triggered, it becomes mandatory for An Bord Pleanála or the planning authority to engage in further public consultation. It is at least arguable that the courts should be prepared to police, by way of full-blooded review, these mandatory requirements.

12–103

This issue has yet to be fully considered by the Supreme Court. A public notice case, *White v Dublin City Council*,[135] was certified for appeal, but the Supreme Court resolved it on the basis that the relevant official of the planning authority had, in effect, asked himself the wrong question in deciding whether to require further public notice. The case concerned an application for planning permission for proposed residential development. A similar application had been refused previously by the planning authority. In the course of processing the subsequent application—the subject-matter of the judicial review proceedings—the planning authority exercised its powers under the regulations to invite the applicant to submit revised plans. The effect of the revised plans was to radically alter the nature of the proposed development. The planning authority did not, however, exercise its discretion to require further public notice.

12–104

The Supreme Court ruled that, in deciding whether to require further public notice, the proper test was whether, in the circumstances of the application before the planning authority, some members of the public might reasonably wish to object to the plans as modified. Instead, the relevant official in deciding not to require further public notice had acted as if he was deciding whether or not planning permission should be granted. The Supreme Court held that not to require further public notice was unreasonable and irrational in the circumstances.

12–105

5. Examples of over-application

Returning now to the initial criticism, namely that the courts have on occasion over applied the doctrine of unreasonableness, the following are submitted as examples of judgments in which the concept has mistakenly been extended.[136] The first example arises in the context of the interpretation of the development plan itself. Although it appears now to be accepted that for the purposes of local authority own development the assessment of whether or not there has

12–106

---

[135] [2004] 1 I.R. 545; [2004] 2 I.L.R.M. 509.
[136] See, generally, G. Simons, "The unreasonable planning authority, Parts I and II" (2000) 7 I.P.E.L.J. 164; (2001) 8 I.P.E.L.J. 26.

been a material contravention is a question of law for the courts,[137] the position obtaining in the case of an application for planning permission is less clear. The better view is that as the concept of material contravention represents a fetter in this context too (triggering a special statutory procedure), the matter is still a question of law.[138] In a number of judgments, however, the opposite conclusion has been suggested, namely that the matter is a question of fact and degree.[139]

12–107   The second example also relates to the development plan. Under the previous legislation, there was a statutory requirement to undertake a further round of public consultation in circumstances where an amendment was proposed to a draft development plan which amendment represented a "material alteration". Notwithstanding the fact that the criteria of "material alteration" represented an apparent fetter on the freedom of a planning authority to modify the draft development plan, the High Court in *Keogh v Galway Corporation (No. 2)*[140] seems to have suggested that where the planning authority had actually addressed its mind to the issue, the courts should only intervene if the "decision" of the planning authority was shown to be unreasonable or irrational.

12–108   The last example involves the requirement under EC law that certain development projects be subject to environmental impact assessment. See, generally, Chapter 13, paras 13–154 to 13–164. A distinction is drawn under the EIA Directive between Annex I projects and Annex II projects. Insofar as Annex I projects and above-threshold Annex II projects are concerned, the question as to whether or not there should be an environmental impact assessment is a question of law and one in respect of which the court need show no special deference to the views of the planning authorities or An Bord Pleanála. The position with respect to sub-threshold Annex II projects is more complicated in that a planning authority and An Bord Pleanála do enjoy some measure of discretion under statute in this regard. The decision in *Ó Nualláin v Dublin Corporation*[141] would appear to suggest, however, that the question of whether or not a proposed development will have significant effects on the environment is one capable of objective assessment and, accordingly, one in respect of which the High Court might be entitled to substitute its views for those of the planning authority. Somewhat surprisingly then, the decision of the High Court in *Max Developments Ltd. v An Bord Pleanála*[142] suggests the precise opposite, namely that the determination of whether or not environmental impact assessment is required is actually a question of fact and degree. It is submitted that where mandated under the legislation, an environmental impact statement is a condition precedent to the jurisdiction to entertain the application

---

[137] *cf. O'Reilly v O'Sullivan*, unreported, High Court, Laffoy J., July 25, 1996.
[138] *Tennyson v Dun Laoghaire Corporation* [1991] 2 I.R. 527.
[139] See, for example, *Healy v Dublin County Council*, unreported, High Court, Barron J., April 29, 1993.
[140] [1995] 3 I.R. 457.
[141] [1999] 4 I.R. 137.
[142] [1994] 2 I.R. 121.

for planning permission, and that, by definition, neither a planning authority nor An Bord Pleanála can be allowed to determine conclusively such an issue collateral to jurisdiction. The fact that review of a particular type of decision might necessitate the High Court examining broad factual issues (on the facts of *Max Developments Ltd.*, whether the proposed development came within an existing urban area or an extended urban area) cannot *per se* indicate that the matter should only be open to limited review.

Finally, reference is made to the judgment in *O'Connor v Dublin Corporation* **12–109** *(No. 2)*[143] for a dramatic example of an attempt by a planning authority to invoke the protection of the doctrine of administrative unreasonableness in entirely inappropriate circumstances. The case involved a challenge, by way of an application for judicial review, to the manner in which the respondent planning authority had dealt with certain matters which had been left over, by condition attached to a planning permission, for agreement. The applicant for judicial review alleged that the matters agreed by the respondent planning authority materially altered the development in respect of which An Bord Pleanála had granted planning permission, and were not a faithful implementation of the conditions attached to that planning permission. In the course of its judgment, the High Court rejected a submission on behalf of the respondent planning authority and notice party developer to the effect that the "decision" fell to be assessed by reference to the doctrine of administrative unreasonableness. O'Neill J. ruled that what was required of the planning authority was no more than faithful implementation of the decision of An Bord Pleanála, and that the planning authority's jurisdiction was "a very limited one and of a ministerial nature".[144] The function of the planning authority in this regard was to be contrasted with that involved in an adjudication on an application for planning permission; the latter function was clearly of a judicial nature and involved the planning authority drawing on its resources of expertise in planning matters in exercising an extensive discretion.

The judgment in *O'Connor* was cited with approval in *Cork City Council v An* **12–110** *Bord Pleanála*.[145] Kelly J. ruled that the interpretation of a statutory development contribution scheme was a question of law.

6. Material error of fact

The terms of the judgment of the High Court in *Aer Rianta cpt v Commissioner* **12–111** *for Aviation Regulation*[146] would appear to extend the doctrine of administrative unreasonableness to errors of fact. Earlier judgments had, however, suggested that an administrative decision might be set aside on judicial review where

---

[143] Unreported, High Court, O'Neill J., October 3, 2000. *Cf. McNamara v An Bord Pleanála (No. 2)* [1996] 2 I.L.R.M. 339 at 361.
[144] Unreported, High Court, O'Neill J., October 3, 2000 (at p. 29).
[145] [2006] I.E.H.C. 192; unreported, Kelly J., June 1, 2006.
[146] Unreported, High Court, O'Sullivan J., January 16, 2003.

there was a material error of fact. The thinking here seems to have been that it is a condition precedent to the exercise of a statutory discretion that the decision-maker have had a proper understanding of the facts. To put the matter in crude terms, provided the decision-maker had correctly understand the facts of say, for example, a planning appeal, its decision on the application of planning policy to those facts was virtually unreviewable. Conversely, if the decision-maker misunderstood those facts, then the decision was liable to be set aside.[147]

12–112   The point may be illustrated by reference to the facts of *Seery v An Bord Pleanála*.[148] The applicants sought to challenge a decision to grant planning permission for residential development on lands adjacent to their own. One of the principal issues on the appeal related to the extent to which the proposed development would overlook the applicants' own dwelling. The applicants alleged that An Bord Pleanála's inspector had overestimated the separation distance between the proposed development and the existing property (the alleged overestimation was in the order of approximately fourteen metres). The applicants further sought to argue that the error had crept in as a result of an inaccuracy in a map or plan accompanying the application for planning permission. The High Court ruled that the application had not been made in accordance with the regulations, and, accordingly, set aside the decision to grant planning permission.

12–113   Reference is also made to the judgment in *Mulhall v An Bord Pleanála*.[149] Again, it was alleged that an error of fact in the inspector's report vitiated the subsequent decision of An Bord Pleanála. McCracken J. found that in the particular circumstances of the case, there was no evidence that An Bord Pleanála had been misled by the alleged error, and that the error was immaterial. The judgment appears to accept, however, that it would be possible, in principle, to challenge a decision on the basis of a material error of fact.

12–114   Approaching the matter from first principles, there would appear to be something to be said for allowing material error of fact as a ground of review. In particular, it might be argued that in circumstances where the courts allow decision-makers considerable latitude in the exercise of their statutory discretion, it is vital that the courts are vigilant in the review of matters outside the statutory discretion. A proper understanding of the facts might well be regarded as a condition precedent to the decision-maker's jurisdiction. In practice, however, there would be very real difficulty in distinguishing between facts and matters of inference. Whereas it is easy enough to detect an error in relation to basic matters such as separation distances, or the scale of a development, there are other matters which might be less clear-cut. To take one obvious example, traffic is often an important issue in an application for

[147] *cf. Geraghty v Minister for Local Government* [1976] I.R. 153.
[148] Unreported, High Court, Quirke J., November 26, 2003.
[149] Unreported, High Court, McCracken J., March 21, 1996 (Irish Times Law Report, June 10, 1996).

planning permission. In the case of major development, the developer may well be relying on predictions of future traffic. In the event that An Bord Pleanála takes a particular view of predicted traffic, should the disappointed party be allowed to argue that this is an error of fact, amenable to review?

No evidence rule

Ironically, the attenuated standard of review applicable under the formula in **12–115** *O'Keeffe v An Bord Pleanála*[150] might be regarded as giving some support to the argument in favour of a jurisdiction to review for factual error. The Supreme Court appeared to indicate that the substantive merits of a decision reached in the exercise of a statutory discretion would only be open to review where there was no material before the decision-maker capable of supporting the decision. The volume of such evidence is, seemingly, irrelevant: there does not have to be anything approaching abundant, substantial or irrefutable evidence, it is sufficient that there be some evidence, even conflicting evidence.[151]

This suggests that to make a decision on the basis of no evidence represents an **12–116** error of law. It seems only a short step to argue that to make a decision on the basis of an erroneous understanding of the evidence should also constitute a reviewable error of law.

More recently, the High Court has sought to articulate a distinction between **12–117** fact-finding and the reaching of decisions on matters of policy or expertise. In *Ashford Castle Ltd. v SIPTU*,[152] Clarke J. observed that the tasks which administrative bodies have been given under statute vary significantly. At one end of the spectrum are issues which involve the same sort of mixed questions of law and fact with which the courts are frequently faced; Clarke J. gave as an example the question of the entitlement of a person to social welfare benefit.[153] At the other end of the spectrum, Clarke J. noted that expert bodies may be required to bring a great deal of their own expertise in relation to matters which involve the exercise of expert judgment, citing the example of planning decisions.

> "Bodies charged with, for example, roles in the planning process are required to exercise a judgment as to what might be the proper planning and development of an area. Obviously in coming to such a view the relevant bodies are required to have regard to the matters which the law specifies (such as, for example, a development plan). However a great deal of the expertise of the body will be concerned with exercising a planning judgment independent of questions of disputed fact. In such cases the underlying facts are normally not in dispute. Questions of expert opinion (such as the likely effect of a proposed development)

---

[150] [1993] 1 I.R. 39; [1992] I.L.R.M. 237.
[151] *MA Ryan & Sons Ltd. v An Bord Pleanála*, unreported, High Court, Peart J., February 6, 2003 (at p.39).
[152] [2006] I.E.H.C. 201; [2006] E.L.R. 201 at 215–216.
[153] An example which proved to be prescient given the subsequent judgment of the ECtHR in *Tsfayo v United Kingdom* Application No. 60860/00; November 14, 2006; [2007] H.L.R. 19.

may well be in dispute and may be resolved, in a manner similar to the way in which similar issues would be resolved in the courts, by hearing and, if necessary, testing competing expert evidence. However above and beyond the resolution of any such issue of expert fact, the authority concerned will also have to bring to bear its own expertise on what is the proper planning and development of an area."

12–118 Clarke J. went on to say that where decisions fell towards the expert end of the spectrum, language such as "evidence" and "findings of fact" had, in his view, a capacity to mislead and that it might be more appropriate to talk of "materials" rather than "evidence", and more appropriate to talk of "conclusions" than of "findings of fact".[154]

F. Reasons and Main Considerations

1. Introduction

12–119 A person affected by a decision is generally entitled to a statement of reasons.[155] One objective of this is to ensure that, where an appeal lies against the decision, the person affected is provided with such information as may be necessary to enable him, first, to consider whether he has a reasonable chance of succeeding in appealing the decision, and, secondly, to enable him to arm himself for the hearing of such appeal.[156] Even where there is no right of appeal, such information is still necessary in order to allow the supervisory jurisdiction of the High Court to be invoked by way of an application for judicial review.[157]

12–120 In the case of a number of decision-making functions, planning authorities and An Bord Pleanála are under an *express* obligation to state reasons. The most obvious example is in respect of the decision on an application for planning permission. Under s.34(10) of the PDA 2000, a planning authority, and An Bord Pleanála on appeal, are required to state the "main reasons and considerations" on which the decision is based. Another example occurs in the context of the variation of a development plan. Under s.13(3) of the PDA 2000, a planning authority is required to state the reason or reasons for the

---

[154] See also *Lord Ballyedmond v Commission for Energy Regulation* [2006] I.E.H.C. 206; unreported, June 22, 2006 (Commission for Energy Regulation, when exercising its remit in relation to decisions concerning the grant of consent to the construction of a pipeline and the making of acquisition orders necessary for the construction of such a pipeline, expected to bring to bear, in reaching its conclusions, its own expertise on the issues concerned).

[155] For the duty to give reasons for administrative decisions generally, see *State (Creedon) v Criminal Injuries Compensation Tribunal* [1988] I.R. 51; *International Fishing Vessels Ltd. v Minister for Marine* [1989] I.R. 149; and *McCormack v Garda Síochána Complaints Board* [1997] 2 I.R. 489; [1997] 2 I.L.R.M. 321.

[156] *State (Sweeney) v Minister for the Environment* [1979] I.L.R.M. 35.

[157] *Mulholland v An Bord Pleanála (No. 2)* [2005] I.E.H.C. 306; [2006] 1 I.R. 453; [2006] 1 I.L.R.M. 287.

proposed variation. The objective is to put the public on notice of matters likely to interest those concerned and to do so in such a way that any member of the public who informatively considers the notice will recognise the essentials of the proposal.[158] Other examples of decisions in respect of which reasons must be stated include a declaration on a Section 5 reference; the revocation or modification of a planning permission; or the dismissal of an appeal as vexatious.

It has been suggested by the High Court, in *Sandyford Environmental Planning and Road Safety Group Ltd. v Dun Laoghaire Rathdown County Council*,[159] that the standard of reasons required in any particular instance will depend on the type of decision in question and on the aim and objective of the reasons requirement. On the particular facts of the case before him, McKechnie J. indicated that the reasons given for a proposal to vary a development plan need not be extensive. The variation of the development plan could only be made after a statutory process and procedure had been complied with, and McKechnie J. contrasted the proposal with other decisions which could have "profound and immediate consequences for those affected".   **12–121**

In the discussion which follows, the obligation to state the main reasons and considerations for a decision on a planning application will be examined in detail. The principles discussed will be of some relevance to the duty to give reasons in other contexts. In light of the comments of McKechnie J. in *Sandyford Environmental Planning and Road Safety Group Ltd. v Dun Laoghaire Rathdown County Council*, however, it should be borne in mind that the reasoning requirement is probably at its height in the context of a decision on a planning application, and less extensive reasons may be acceptable in other contexts.   **12–122**

Finally, it should be noted that there may be an enhanced duty to give reasons in the context of development projects which are subject to the EC environmental impact assessment Directive.[160] See further paras 13–238 to 13–244.   **12–123**

---

[158] *Sandyford Environmental Planning and Road Safety Group Ltd. v Dun Laoghaire Rathdown County Council*, unreported, High Court, McKechnie J., June 30, 2004, [45].

[159] Unreported, High Court, McKechnie J., June 30, 2004, [44]–[45]. See also, by analogy, *McCormack v Garda Síochána Complaints Board* [1997] 2 I.R. 489 ("Where a claim is made that a breach of a constitutional duty to apply fair procedures has occurred by a failure to state reasons for an administrative decision the court will be required to consider (a) the nature of the statutory function which the decision-maker is carrying out, (b) the statutory framework in which it is to be found and (c) the possible detriment the complainant may suffer arising from the failure to state reasons. To give an example of a possible detriment; if a statute permitted an appeal to the court from the decision of an administrative authority on a point of law, the failure to give reasons for a decision may well amount to a breach of a duty to apply fair procedures, if it could be shown that their absence rendered ineffectual a statutory right of appeal.").

[160] See also R. Gordon, *EC Law in Judicial Review* (Oxford University Press, 2007), para.10.54, where it is stated that the general principle of effectiveness requires the giving of reasons in respect of decisions which adversely affect EC law rights.

2. Decision on planning application

12–124   Under s.34(10) of the PDA 2000, a planning authority, and An Bord Pleanála on appeal, are required to state the "main reasons and considerations" on which the decision is based. The statutory obligations in this regard are replicated under the Planning and Development Regulations 2001 (as substituted by the 2006 Regulations).[161] There is an additional requirement under the Regulations to specify that, in deciding a planning application, the planning authority or An Bord Pleanála in accordance with s.34(3) of the PDA 2000 "has regard to submissions or observations" received by it.[162]

12–125   The obligation under s.34(10) is more exacting than that which had applied under the Local Government (Planning & Development) Acts. The new requirement is to state the "main reasons and considerations" on which the decision is based, rather than simply the "reasons" for the decision. The new wording replicates that found under the amended EC environmental impact assessment Directive: see further para.13–238.

12–126   Prior to the amendments, the reasons given for planning decisions tended to be formulaic, and in many cases involved little more than a recital of stock phrases such as that the proposed development would be "in accordance with proper planning and development" or "would not seriously injure amenities". Whereas the standard set for reasons was notionally high, in practice the courts were prepared to accept as adequate the most perfunctory of reasons. The new wording should result in more informative decisions.

3. The old requirement: "reasons"

12–127   The case law prior to the PDA 2000 suggests that the adequacy of a statement of reasons is to be assessed by reference to its intended function. The reasons furnished must be sufficient, first, to enable the courts to review the decision, and, secondly, to satisfy the persons having recourse to the tribunal that it has directed its mind adequately to the issues before it.[163] The reasons should indicate that the decision-maker has addressed its mind to the substantive issues before it.[164] The position was summarised thus in *O'Donoghue v An Bord Pleanála*.[165]

---

[161] Planning and Development Regulations 2001, arts 31(f) and (l) (planning authority) and arts 74(2)(f) and (k) (An Bord Pleanála) (as substituted by the 2006 Regulations).

[162] Planning and Development Regulations 2001, art.31(g) (planning authority) and art.74(2)(j) (An Bord Pleanála) (as substituted by the 2006 Regulations).

[163] *O'Donoghue v An Bord Pleanála* [1991] I.L.R.M. 750 at 757.

[164] *ibid.* See also *Ní Éili v Environmental Protection Agency*, unreported, Supreme Court, July 30, 1999 ("Those who have gone to the trouble and expense of formulating and presenting serious objections on a matter of intense public interest must be entitled to obtain an explanation as to why their submissions were rejected.").

[165] [1991] I.L.R.M. 750 at 757.

"It has never been suggested that an administrative body is bound to provide a discursive judgment as a result of its deliberations but on the other hand the need for providing the grounds of the decision as outlined by the Chief Justice could not be satisfied by recourse to an uninformative if technically correct formula. For example it could hardly be regarded as acceptable for the bord to reverse the decision of a planning authority stating only that 'they considered the application to accord with the proper planning and development of the authority'. It seems to me that in the nature of problems as defined by the Chief Justice it would be necessary for the administrative tribunal to indicate in its decision that it had addressed its mind to the substantive issue which had led the planning authority to believe that the permission would have an adverse effect on the planning and development of the area."

The test to be applied is what an intelligent person who had taken part in the appeal, or had been appraised of the broad issues which had arisen, would understand from the decision, the conditions and the reasons.[166]   **12–128**

In the case of a decision of a planning authority, the statement of reasons, in addition to enabling the courts to exercise their supervisory jurisdiction, should also provide such information as may be necessary and appropriate for the applicant, first, to consider whether he has a reasonable chance of succeeding in appealing against the decision of the planning authority to An Bord Pleanála, and, secondly, to enable him to arm himself for the hearing of such an appeal.[167]   **12–129**

Thus far, the courts' approach to the assessment of the adequacy of reasons is unexceptionable. Where the case law is open to real criticism, however, is in respect of the application of these principles in practice. In a number of cases, the courts have accepted, as adequate, reasons which consisted of little more than the "uninformative if technically correct formula" deprecated in *O'Donoghue v An Bord Pleanála*.[168]   **12–130**

This approach is illustrated by the facts of *Aer Rianta cpt v An Bord Pleanála*,[169] a case involving a challenge to a decision of An Bord Pleanála to grant planning permission. The permitted development consisted of the provision of a car park with 3,500 car parking spaces, together with associated facilities. The development was to be located in proximity to the southern end of runway 16/34 at Dublin airport, lying about 300 metres from the end of that runway.   **12–131**

The then operator of Dublin airport, Aer Rianta, had objected to the development on the basis that the development presented an unacceptable risk to safety, arguing that the application site was within a red (safety) area. A red (safety) area is the area at the end of a runway strip where development is restricted in the interest of the safety of aircraft passengers and the public.   **12–132**

---

[166] *O'Keeffe v An Bord Pleanála* [1993] 1 I.R. 39; [1992] I.L.R.M. 237; and *Village Residents Association Ltd. v An Bord Pleanála (No. 3)* [2001] 1 I.R. 441.
[167] *State (Sweeney) v Minister for the Environment* [1979] I.L.R.M. 35.
[168] *O'Donoghue v An Bord Pleanála* [1991] I.L.R.M. 750 at 757.
[169] Unreported, High Court, Kelly J., June 25, 2002.

12–133   The decision of An Bord Pleanála to grant planning permission recited the following reason(s) for the grant of planning permission.

> "Having regard to the nature and location of the proposed long-term car park in close proximity to the airport, it is considered that, subject to compliance with the conditions set out in the Second Schedule, the proposed development would be acceptable in terms of traffic safety and convenience and would be in accordance with the proper planning and development of the area."

12–134   One of the substantive issues raised on the appeal by Aer Rianta had been the issue of public safety, both in terms of the safety of the occupants of aircraft, and of persons on the ground using the proposed car park. There was no reference in the statement of reasons, however, to the issue of public safety. Nor was there any reference in the second schedule of the decision—which contained the conditions and reasons therefor—to ground safety issues.

12–135   The fact that the only specific planning issue referred to in the reasons is "traffic safety and convenience" might suggest that An Bord Pleanála had confined its assessment to traffic issues, and that in this narrow context the proximity to the airport was, in fact, an advantage. There is nothing on the face of the decision to suggest that An Bord Pleanála had addressed its mind to the wider issue of public safety or as to the appropriateness of locating a car park within a red (safety) area.

12–136   The wording employed by An Bord Pleanála in its decision is to be contrasted with that recommended by its inspector in his report, as follows.

> "Having regard to the location of the proposed long term car park in close proximity to the airport which it is to serve, it is considered that it would not materially contravene the County Development Plan and, subject to the conditions below, would not constitute a hazard to aircraft or to the public."

12–137   Had An Bord Pleanála similarly made express reference to "hazard to aircraft or to the public" it would have at least confirmed that the board members had regard to these wider issues. Of course, even this form of wording would not be adequate in that it simply states a conclusion, *i.e.* that the proposed development would not constitute a hazard to aircraft or to the public, but does not disclose the reasoning by which that conclusion was reached.

12–138   Aer Rianta had been given leave to argue that An Bord Pleanála had failed to have regard to the status of red (safety) areas under the development plan, or to the requirement to have regard to the observations of the airport operator under the plan, and that An Bord Pleanála erred in failing to give reasons for departure from the provisions of the development plan and/or granting planning permission in material contravention of the development plan. At the full hearing of the application for judicial review, the High Court rejected these arguments, holding that Aer Rianta had not made out a case demonstrating that there had been a material contravention of the development plan. In the circumstances, it was unnecessary for the High Court to consider the specific complaint that reasons were not given for such alleged departure from the plan and the granting of permission in material contravention of it. Rather the court assessed the decision by reference to the general duty to give reasons. Kelly J. concluded that the reasons, when considered in light of the documents—including the inspector's report and the board's direction—were adequate and sufficient.

4. The new requirement: "main reasons and considerations"

The requirement under s.34(10) of the PDA to state the main reasons and considerations for the decision has been considered in a number of cases.[170] The most detailed discussion of the general principles applicable to the new requirement is to be found in *Mulholland v An Bord Pleanála (No. 2)*.[171] Kelly J. recognised that the statutory obligation to state reasons had been expanded, but went on to suggest that the legislature had made no attempt under the PDA 2000 to alter the existing jurisprudence as to the adequacy of reasons. The existing case law, therefore, in the court's opinion continued to apply.

12–139

Kelly J. went on to endorse a functional test: a statement of "reasons" and "considerations" must give an applicant such information as may be necessary and appropriate for him to consider whether he has a reasonable chance of succeeding in appealing or judicially reviewing the decision (and allow him to arm himself for such hearing or review); and to know if the decision-maker has directed its mind adequately to the issues which it has considered or is obliged to consider. It must also enable the courts to review the decision.

12–140

There is a danger of reading too much into the judgment in *Mulholland*. The proceedings were at the leave stage, and it was unnecessary for Kelly J. to decide whether the statement of reasons and considerations was adequate, in circumstances where he intended to grant leave to apply for judicial review. It would be up to the judge hearing the substantive application for judicial review to elaborate upon the general principles stated by Kelly J. For the purposes of a leave application, it was enough to say that a statement of reasons and considerations must be sufficient to allow the decision to be subject to judicial review.

12–141

In the events that transpired, the proceedings were ultimately compromised and no judgment was ever delivered on the substantive application. In the absence of a definitive ruling by the Irish courts in this regard, it is submitted that some useful guidance may be had from the ruling of the House of Lords in *South Bucks District Council v Porter (No. 2)*.[172]

12–142

---

[170] *Ryanair Ltd. v An Bord Pleanála* [2004] 2 I.R. 334; *Mulholland v An Bord Pleanála (No. 2)* [2005] I.E.H.C. 306; [2006] 1 I.R. 453; [2006] 1 I.L.R.M. 287; *Grealish v An Bord Pleanála (No. 2)* [2006] I.E.H.C. 310; unreported, O'Neill J., October 24, 2006; and *Dunne v An Bord Pleanála* [2006] I.E.H.C. 400; unreported, McGovern J., December 14, 2006.

[171] [2005] I.E.H.C. 306; [2006] 1 I.R. 453; [2006] 1 I.L.R.M. 287.

[172] [2004] U.K.H.L. 33, [36].

"The reasons for a decision must be intelligible and they must be adequate. They must enable the reader to understand why the matter was decided as it was and what conclusions were reached on the 'principal important controversial issues', disclosing how any issue of law or fact was resolved. Reasons can be briefly stated, the degree of particularity required depending entirely on the nature of the issues falling for decision. The reasoning must not give rise to a substantial doubt as to whether the decision-maker erred in law, for example by misunderstanding some relevant policy or some other important matter or by failing to reach a rational decision on relevant grounds. But such adverse inference will not readily be drawn. The reasons need refer only to the main issues in the dispute, not to every material consideration. They should enable disappointed developers to assess their prospects of obtaining some alternative development permission, or, as the case may be, their unsuccessful opponents to understand how the policy or approach underlying the grant of permission may impact upon future such applications. Decision letters must be read in a straightforward manner, recognising that they are addressed to parties well aware of the issues involved and the arguments advanced."[173]

12–143 The test put forward by the House of Lords is more elaborate than that in *Mulholland*. This is no criticism of the latter judgment, as a judgment on a leave application *Mulholland* is more than ample. Previous case law indicates, however, that the devil is in the detail when it comes to the application of general principles to the actual reasons given for any particular planning decision. It is thus necessary to breakdown the general requirement that the reasons should allow an applicant to know whether he or she has grounds for judicial review into a series of specific requirements including, for example, that the decision discloses not only the conclusions on the principal issues, but also how any issue of law or fact was resolved. Too often what were put forward as "reasons" under the previous legislation consisted of little more than a statement of conclusions—such as that the proposed development was in accordance with proper planning and development, or would not give rise to serious pollution—without any indication being given as to the *reasoning* by which these conclusions were reached.

12–144 Moreover, even as a statement of conclusions, many decisions were inadequate in that same were framed in generic terms without any specific reference to the facts of the planning application. Objectors and developers alike were required to engage in a form of parlour game whereby the use of stock phrases—such as "traffic hazard" or "amenities of the area"—were to be read as ciphers for the actual planning issues raised. Thus an objector who complained that his detailed submissions on the impact of the proposed development on his property were not properly considered would be expected to accept a generic reference

---

[173] The final sentence of the passage quoted reads as follows: "A reasons challenge will only succeed if the party aggrieved can satisfy the court that he has genuinely been substantially prejudiced by the failure to provide an adequately reasoned decision." The terms "party aggrieved" and "substantially prejudiced" stem from the statutory wording of s.288 of the Town and Country Planning Act 1990, and thus these requirements are not necessarily relevant to Irish law.

in the decision to the "amenities of the area" as confirmation that same had been properly adjudicated upon.

The point made in *Porter* that the reasoning should disclose how any issue of law was resolved is worth emphasising. Legal issues, especially in respect of EC law, regularly arise on planning applications and appeals. Planning authorities and An Bord Pleanála, as emanations of the State, are required to give effect to EC law, and it is important that the conclusions reached on legal issues should be set out clearly in the decision. Failure to do so frustrates the supervisory jurisdiction of the High Court. Such a failure can only be properly policed by way of an order setting aside the decision, and remitting the matter for further consideration. It is in the interest of all parties, therefore, that the decision-maker ensures that its conclusions on legal issues are clearly set out. Not only will this avoid decisions being set aside on the basis of inadequate reasons, it may actually reduce the number of judicial review applications to the High Court. If the parties are satisfied that the planning authority or An Bord Pleanála, as the case may be, has had regard to the proper legal principles in reaching its decision, they may be more willing to accept its findings on the planning issues.

12–145

5. Judgments since *Mulholland v An Bord Pleanála (No.2)*

Kelly J.'s judgment in *Mulholland v An Bord Pleanála (No. 2)*[174] has been cited with approval in at least two subsequent written judgments. In the first case, *Grealish v An Bord Pleanála (No. 2)*,[175] the High Court ruled that the statement of reasons and considerations given for the impugned decision were inadequate. The facts of *Grealish* were unusual. An Bord Pleanála had granted, on two consecutive occasions, temporary planning permissions for development consisting of a tri-vision rotating advertising sign. In each instance, the reason for granting only temporary planning permission was stated in terms of allowing an assessment of the effects or impact of the development. Following the expiration of the second of these two temporary planning permissions, a further application for planning permission was made. The application was refused, at first instance, by the planning authority, and an appeal was brought to An Bord Pleanála. An Bord Pleanála's inspector recommended that planning permission be granted subject to conditions reducing the size of the advertising structure. An Bord Pleanála made a decision to refuse planning permission.

12–146

In its first two decisions, An Bord Pleanála had concluded that the advertising structure would not seriously injure the visual amenities of the area, and would not be contrary to the proper planning and development of the area. In the impugned decision, An Bord Pleanála concluded that the very same advertising structure would seriously injure the visual amenities of the area and would be contrary to the proper planning and sustainable development of the area. The

12–147

---

[174] [2005] I.E.H.C. 306; [2006] 1 I.R. 453; [2006] 1 I.L.R.M. 287.
[175] [2006] I.E.H.C. 310; unreported, O'Neill J., October 24, 2006.

High Court found as a fact that that there was no material change whatsoever in the physical environment of the development between the date of the second and the third decision.

12–148   The applicant sought judicial review of An Bord Pleanála's third decision. It was argued that there had been no change in the prevailing circumstances between the dates of the two earlier decisions to grant planning permission and the date of the instant decision. It was also argued that An Bord Pleanála had failed to give adequate reasons for its decision insofar as it was (i) contrary to its previous decisions and (ii) a departure from the recommendation of the inspector.

12–149   O'Neill J. held that the decision failed to satisfy the criteria identified in *Mulholland v An Bord Pleanála (No. 2)*.

> "As set out above the legal obligation resting on the respondents to explain their decisions is a very light one, one could even say almost minimal. It is well settled that they do not have to give a discursive judgment. They do however as set out in the judgment of Kelly J., have to provide sufficient information to enable somebody in the position of the applicant in this case to consider whether he has a reasonable chance of succeeding in judicially reviewing the decision, can arm himself for such a review; can know if the respondent has directed its mind adequately to the issues it has to consider; and finally give sufficient information to enable the court to review the decision. Insofar as two of the main elements of the decision in this case are concerned i.e. reasons and considerations based on scale and non-integration, the decision fails on every aspect of the foregoing test. There is literally nothing there to explain why a different conclusion is reached on these issues to that in 1990 or 1997.
>
> If one were to assume that the decision somehow explained itself this court would inexorably have to reach the conclusion that the decision was vitiated by irrationality on the basis that there was no material supporting the reversal of the conclusion reached in 1990 and 1997, as per *O'Keeffe v An Bord Pleanála* [1993] 1 I.R. 39."

12–150   O'Neill J. went on to examine the third planning issue which had arisen on the appeal, namely a change in the development plan. O'Neill J. indicated that if the change in the development plan had been the main reason and consideration for An Bord Pleanála's conclusion, then a short and simple statement to that effect should have been included in the decision.

> "Neither this Court, nor the applicant, nor the world at large should have to, make assumptions, as to what the main reasons or considerations were, when that would be wholly unnecessary, if the minimal statement required to make these things clear, was included in the statement of reasons and considerations in the decision.
>
> In an age of near universal literacy one can but observe, that such omission represents a standard of literary communication which is very low and in my opinion fails to satisfy the legal requirement, of stating the main reasons and considerations, for its change of stance, in deciding to refuse permission in 2003."

In *Dunne v An Bord Pleanála*,[176] planning permission had been sought for the **12–151**
demolition of existing buildings, and the erection of seven apartments in a
two- and three-storey building over basement car parking at the former Chester
Beatty Library, Shrewsbury Road, Dublin. The inspector had recommended
that planning permission be refused, principally on the basis that the residential
nature of the proposed development and its proximity to the boundaries of the
Royal Dublin Society grounds ("the RDS") might give rise to levels of complaint
which would jeopardise the continuation of activities at the grounds. An Bord
Pleanála decided to grant planning permission, and the following reasons and
considerations were stated for its decision.

> "Having regard to the planning history relating to the site and the provisions of
> the current development plan for the area, the location of the site in a Residential
> Conservation Area and the pattern of new and existing development in the vicinity,
> it is considered that, subject to compliance with the conditions set out below, the
> proposed development would not seriously injure the amenities of the area or of
> property in the vicinity, would be acceptable in terms of traffic safety and
> convenience and would be in accordance with the proper planning and sustainable
> development of the area.
>
> In deciding not to accept the Inspector's recommendation to refuse permission,
> the Board had particular regard to the planning history relating to the site and
> considered that the development, as proposed, would not jeopardise the
> continuation of activities at the grounds of the Royal Dublin Society. In arriving
> at its decision, the Board generally concurred with the decision of the planning
> authority."

The High Court held that the statement complied with the statutory requirements **12–152**
under s.34(10).

> "Having considered the submissions and the Act, the Regulations and the legal
> authorities, I am satisfied that the first respondent did address adequately, in its
> statement of reasons, the substantive issues in the appeal and in particular the
> suitability of the proposed development. It took into account all the relevant
> criteria such as the current development plan, the planning history in relation to
> the site, the fact that it was in a Residential Conservation Area and the pattern of
> new and existing development in the vicinity. It considered the impact of the
> proposed development on the adjoining properties and the immediate area and
> this is clear from the conditions which attach to the grant of permission. In
> considering the planning history of the area it is impossible to ignore the fact that
> several earlier applications had been made and these had been scaled down by
> the first respondent to the point where the only permitted development would be
> seven apartments. The second named respondent had originally applied for thirteen
> apartments and at one point had been granted permission for ten by the local
> authority. I reject the applicants' claim that insufficient reasons and considerations
> were given for the decision which is the subject matter of either the first application
> or the second application."

It is difficult to predict on the basis of either of these judgments whether the **12–153**
introduction of the requirement to state the "main reasons and considerations"

---

[176] [2006] I.E.H.C. 400; unreported, McGovern J., December 14, 2006.

has produced any significant improvement in the law. This is because each case turned largely on its own facts. Thus, whereas the judgment in *Grealish*, at first blush, appears to involve a more exacting standard for reasons than had previously applied, it may be that this standard only applies where an apparent inconsistency in decision-making needs explanation. Similarly, it may have been that the perfunctory statement of reasons and considerations in *Dunne* only passed muster because there was a long history of applications on the site which appeared to establish the principle of residential development.

6. The role of the inspector's or planning officer's report

12–154   One device often employed by the courts to overcome the paucity of reasoning in the formal statement of reasons was to supplement same by reference to the planning officer's, or the inspector's, internal report ("planning reports"). The reasoning contained in the report would, in effect, be imputed to the planning authority or An Bord Pleanála. With respect, this practice is undesirable and, hopefully, will not survive the amendments introduced under s.34(10). The statutory requirement is that the decision *itself* state the main reasons and considerations on which it is based. The report is not part of the decision, and thus no matter how detailed the reasons contained therein, it cannot be regarded as fulfilling the statutory requirement. This will be the position even were the formal decision to include an express cross-reference to the report, such as "the board decided to grant planning permission in accordance with the inspector's recommendations". The decision itself must state the main reasons and considerations.[177]

12–155   If, contrary to what is suggested above, it is acceptable to supplement the formal decision by reference to the contents of the planning report(s), this should only be done where the formal decision expressly adopts the recommendations, findings and conclusions of the inspector or planning officer.[178] One of the more questionable aspects of the earlier case law was the eagerness with which the courts were prepared to *assume* that the members of the board were in full agreement with the inspector.[179]

---

[177]   See, by analogy, *Ní Éili v Environmental Protection Agency*, unreported, Supreme Court, July 30, 1999 (desirable that reasons for the decision should be readily available without the necessity of excessive research or inquiry; incorporation by reference only acceptable in very complex cases).

[178]   *cf. Ní Éili v Environmental Protection Agency*, unreported, Supreme Court, July 30, 1999 ("Perhaps it might have been more appropriate for the Agency to say (and for the secretary to record) that the Board accepted not merely the recommendation but also the findings and conclusions of the Hearing Officer. On the other hand it seems that the acceptance of the recommendations necessarily implied the acceptance of the conclusions on which they were based.").

[179]   See, for example, *Ryanair Ltd. v An Bord Pleanála* [2004] I.E.H.C. 52; [2004] 2 I.R. 334 at 357 (could be inferred that An Bord Pleanála accepted the report of its inspector to the extent that it did not depart from his recommendations). See also *Fairyhouse Club Ltd. v An Bord Pleanála*, unreported, High Court, Finnegan J., July 18 , 2001; and *Aer Rianta v An Bord Pleanála*, unreported, High Court, Kelly J., June 25, 2002 (court

Failure to follow inspector's recommendation

Where the decision by the planning authority or An Bord Pleanála is different, **12–156** in relation to the granting or refusal of planning permission, from the recommendation in the planning reports, the statement of reasons must indicate the main reasons for not accepting the recommendation in the report or reports to grant or refuse permission.[180] The term "recommendation" has been interpreted in *Dunne v An Bord Pleanála*[181] as being confined to the recommendation to grant or refuse planning permission *simpliciter*, as opposed to a recommendation that a particular type of planning condition be imposed. McGovern J. concluded that there is no obligation on the members of An Bord Pleanála to give reasons for not imposing a planning condition recommended by the inspector.

The requirements in this regard are more full than those under the previous **12–157** legislation. In particular, under the previous legislation there was no *express* requirement to give special or additional reasons in circumstances where the planning authority or An Bord Pleanála did not accept the recommendation in the planning reports. Whereas the Supreme Court, in *O'Keeffe v An Bord Pleanála*,[182] had intimated that there was no obligation on An Bord Pleanála to follow the recommendation of its inspector, subsequent decisions had accepted that there might be substantial grounds for arguing that a duty to give additional or special reasons arose in the circumstances: see, in particular, the decision of the High Court on the application for leave to apply for judicial review in *Stack v An Bord Pleanála*.[183]

The amendment will have significant consequences in terms of the standard of **12–158** reasons required in circumstances where the members of An Bord Pleanála have not followed the inspector's recommendation. An Bord Pleanála will not have the luxury of a complementary report by reference to which it might bolster otherwise deficient reasoning. The members of An Bord Pleanála will not be able to argue, for example, that the reasoning of the inspector should be imputed to them. Nor will they be able to rely on the detail of the report to decipher the vague generalities of the stated reasons. Instead, the decision itself will have to set out the findings and conclusions of An Bord Pleanála on the principal issues arising on the appeal.

7. Elaboration upon reasons post-decision

Finlay C.J. in *O'Keeffe v An Bord Pleanála* said that it was of importance, **12–159** though not necessarily vital, to his decision on the adequacy of reasons that no

---

attached no weight to significant differences between wording recommended by inspector and that ultimately employed by An Bord Pleanála).
[180] PDA 2000, s.34(10)(b).
[181] [2006] I.E.H.C. 400; unreported, McGovern J., December 14, 2006.
[182] [1993] 1 I.R. 39; [1992] I.L.R.M. 237.
[183] Unreported, High Court, O'Neill J., July 11, 2000. *Cf. Stack v An Bord Pleanála (No. 2)*, unreported, High Court, Ó Caoimh J., March 7, 2003.

request had been made for the elaboration of, or explanation of, the reasons as stated. This comment might be taken as suggesting that an applicant should first seek an elaboration or explanation of the stated reasons before instituting judicial review proceedings. This suggestion is surprising on a number of grounds. First, given that the statutory obligation is to state the main reasons and considerations as part of the decision, it is difficult to understand what legal significance reasons furnished subsequently could have.[184] Secondly, there is a risk that the decision-maker may engage in an *ex post facto* rationalisation of the decision. The dangers of relying on reasons furnished subsequently, and, in particular, in response to litigation are discussed in detail in *R. (On the application of Hereford Waste Watchers Ltd.) v Hereford Council*.[185]

> "[...] any supplementary reasons must elucidate or explain and not contradict the written reasons. It will be rare indeed for an inconsistent explanation, given in the course of the judicial review proceedings, to be accepted as the true reason for the decision.
>
> This is in accordance with basic principles of fairness. Plainly the courts must be alive to ensure that there is no rewriting of history, even subconsciously. Self deception runs deep in the human psyche; the truth can become refracted, even in the case of honest witnesses, through the prism of self justification. There will be a particular reluctance to permit a defendant to rely on subsequent reasons where they appear to cut against the grain of the original reasons."

12–160   To date, the Irish courts have shown little enthusiasm for the provision of supplementary reasons. In a number of judgments, affidavit evidence in this regard has been ruled inadmissible because the deponent failed to establish that he or she had participated in the deliberation process.[186]

8. Remedy

12–161   Some confusion has arisen in the case law as to whether a failure to state reasons may be remedied by the giving of proper reasons subsequently. This point is of vital importance in that if it is sufficient to give proper reasons subsequently, then the relief available in judicial review proceedings should not be an order quashing the decision but rather an order of mandamus directing that proper reasons be stated.

---

[184] See *Village Residents Association Ltd. v An Bord Pleanála (No. 3)* [2001] 1 I.R. 441 ("A curious feature of the passage from the judgment of the Supreme Court in *O'Keeffe v An Bord Pleanála* [1993] 1 I.R. 39 which I have quoted above is that it seems to envisage the first respondent elaborating on or explaining its reasons on request from an interested party, notwithstanding that it is quite clear that the obligation under s. 26(8) and under reg. 65 is to give reasons contemporaneous with the decision, in fact, in the decision itself and in the notification of it.").

[185] [2005] E.W.H.C. 191, [47]–[48]; [2005] Env. L.R. 29.

[186] *Village Residents Association Ltd. v An Bord Pleanála (No. 3)* [2001] 1 I.R. 441; and *Grealish v An Bord Pleanála (No. 2)* [2006] I.E.H.C. 310; unreported, O'Neill J., October 24, 2006.

In *R. (On the application of Richardson) v North Yorkshire County Council*,[187] **12–162** the Court of Appeal in England and Wales ruled that a breach of the obligation to state the main reasons and considerations should be capable, in principle, of being remedied, and the legislative purpose achieved, by a mandatory order requiring the planning authority to make available *ex post facto* a statement containing the specified information. In deciding that the failure to state the reasons and main considerations should not necessarily lead to the planning permission being quashed, the Court of Appeal emphasised the fact that the requirement under the EIA Directive focuses on the availability of information for public inspection *after* the decision has been made, rather than on the decision-making process.

The better view, however, is that a failure to state reasons at the time of the **12–163** decision invalidates the decision under Irish law, and same should be set aside in judicial review proceedings. The statutory obligation is to give reasons contemporaneous with the decision, both in the decision itself and in the notification of it, and cannot therefore be satisfied by the giving of reasons subsequently.[188] One of the objectives of the duty to give reasons is to facilitate a challenge to the decision, whether by way of statutory appeal or by way of an application for judicial review. The bringing of such a challenge is subject to very tight statutory time-limits, and the failure to give reasons at the time of the decision would frustrate the preparation of a focused challenge within time.[189]

G. Legitimate Expectation and Estoppel

The fact that a planning authority has adopted a particular practice or policy in **12–164** the past may give rise to an expectation on the part of others that this practice or policy will be continued. For example, a planning authority may have a practice of issuing letters of compliance confirming conditions attached to a planning permission have been complied with.[190] Similarly, the officials of a planning authority by their conduct may have led a developer to think that planning permission was not required for a particular activity,[191] or that compliance with a condition or conditions attached to a planning permission might be waived.

---

[187] [2003] EWCA Civ 1860, [50]; [2004] 2 P. & C.R. 15; [2004] J.P.L. 911.

[188] See *Village Residents Association Ltd. v An Bord Pleanála (No. 3)* [2001] 1 I.R. 441.

[189] See, by analogy, *McCormack v Garda Síochána Complaints Board* [1997] 2 I.R. 489 (if a statute permitted an appeal to the court from the decision of an administrative authority on a point of law, the failure to give reasons for a decision may well amount to a breach of a duty to apply fair procedures if it could be shown that their absence rendered ineffectual a statutory right of appeal).

[190] See, for example, *Glenkerrin Homes v Dun Laoghaire Rathdown County Council*, unreported, High Court, Clarke J., April 27, 2007.

[191] See, for example, *Dublin Corporation v McGrath* [1978] I.L.R.M. 208 (representation by planning inspector that he would look after the matter of planning permission); and *Dublin City Council v Eircom plc* [2002] 3 I.R. 237 (mistaken suggestion that part of development exempted).

12–165 The extent to which a planning authority should be held to a previous practice or policy, or bound by representations made by its officials, is a matter of controversy. On the one hand, it might be thought unfair to allow a planning authority to resile from a previous practice or policy, or from a representation, especially in circumstances where a person has acted to his detriment on the strength of it. On the other hand, however, planning policy must be flexible so as to respond to the evolving needs of an area in terms of proper planning and sustainable development. Moreover, the public's right of participation in the planning process might be undermined if too much weight were given to informal practices and statements.

12–166 Consistency in formal planning decisions is ensured by the doctrine of *res judicata*, and this is discussed at paras 4–18 to 4–21. The discussion below is directed to how the doctrine of legitimate expectation regulates matters of policy and representations.

1. Legitimate expectation

12–167 The Irish courts have accepted on a number of occasions that it may be unfair for a public body to resile from a representation made by or on its behalf.[192] The precise basis for this proposition is unclear. In *Webb v Ireland*, it was suggested that the doctrine of legitimate expectation was but an aspect of the well recognised equitable concept of promissory estoppel.[193] Later cases, however, indicate that there are important distinctions between the two concepts. Promissory estoppel was traditionally regarded as being defensive in nature— a shield and not a sword—whereas a breach of legitimate expectation gives a cause of action. Moreover, it is not necessary in the context of legitimate expectation to demonstrate that the individual acted to his detriment in reliance on the practice or representation.[194]

> "An expectation may be legitimate and cognisable by the courts even in the absence of the sort of action to the claimant's detriment that forms part of the law of estoppel. On the other hand, I would not accept that the mere fact of an expectation can suffice without some context relevant to fairness in the exercise of legal or administrative powers. Those who come within the ambit of an

---

[192] See, for example, *Webb v Ireland* [1988] I.R. 353 (promise or representation as to intention may in certain circumstances be held to be binding); *Duggan v An Taoiseach* [1989] I.L.R.M. 710 (courts will protect legitimate expectation of receiving a privilege or benefit); *Philips v Medical Council* [1991] 2 I.R. 115 (unfair to allow rules to be rescinded when application for full registration as medical doctor pending); *Kavanagh v Governor of Mountjoy Prison* [2002] 3 I.R. 97 (decision-makers should not be allowed to disappoint expectations which they have themselves created and which are reasonably entertained by those within the purview of the powers they exercise); and *Power v Minister for Social and Family Affairs* [2006] I.E.H.C. 170; [2007] 1 I.L.R.M. 109 (unjust to permit amendment of extra-statutory scheme where applicant had committed to following a course of third level education on foot of representations).

[193] [1988] I.R. 353 at 384.

[194] *Daly v Minister for the Marine* [2001] 3 I.R. 513 at 528, *per* Fennelly J.

administrative or regulatory regime may be able to establish that it would be unfair, discriminatory or unjust to permit the body exercising a power to change a policy or a set of existing rules, or depart from an undertaking or promise without taking account of the legitimate expectations created by them. However, the very notion of fairness has within it an idea that there is an existing relationship which it would be unfair to alter."

The House of Lords has recently suggested that it is unhelpful to introduce private law concepts of estoppel into planning law, and that public law has already absorbed what is useful from the moral values which underlie the private law concept of estoppel.[195] There are competing policy issues at play here in that the desirability of holding a planning authority to a representation made by or on its behalf has to be balanced against the wider public interest. The planning process is not simply a bilateral one involving the planning authority and the developer, but rather one in which the public has statutory (and constitutional) rights of participation. **12–168**

The Supreme Court in *Fingal County Council v William P Keeling & Sons Ltd.*[196] expressly left open the general question of whether, and to what extent, the doctrine of estoppel has a role to play in the field of the relations in public law between an individual and a planning authority. On the particular facts of the case, the Supreme Court ruled that an owner of land could not be estopped from arguing that particular development was exempted development merely by reason of the fact, and by nothing more, that he or she had made a perfectly proper and lawful application for planning permission.[197] **12–169**

More recent case law suggests that the true basis for holding a public body to its representations may simply be that to permit a public body—in the absence of countervailing reasons—to resile from a previous representation is unfair and represents an abuse of power.[198] **12–170**

---

[195] *R. (On the application of Reprotech (Pebsham) Ltd.) v East Sussex County Council* [2002] U.K.H.L. 8; [2003] 1 P. & C.R. 5, cited with approval in *Illium Properties Ltd. v An Bord Pleanála* [2004] I.E.H.C. 403; unreported, Smyth J., December 16, 2004.

[196] [2005] I.E.S.C. 55; [2005] 2 I.R. 108.

[197] See also *Ashbourne Holdings Ltd. v An Bord Pleanála* [2003] 2 I.R. 114; [2003] 2 I.L.R.M. 446, where the Supreme Court held that an applicant for planning permission was not estopped from challenging conditions notwithstanding an alleged failure to challenge similar conditions in the past ("I would not refuse relief in the exercise of discretion in the circumstances of the present case. First, the impugned conditions are ultra vires and against that most radical form of invalidity estoppel, acquiescence or consent does not avail. It is just that this should be so, in the case of a condition, which however invalid will run with the land. Secondly, it is particularly important that this principle be maintained in the public interest, so as to assert the principle of fairness as between one applicant for an identical or analogous permission and another, and so as to safeguard the integrity and transparency of the administration of the planning code.").

[198] See, for example, *Power v Minister for Social and Family Affairs* [2006] I.E.H.C. 170; [2007] 1 I.L.R.M. 109.

2. Planning authority must have made statement or representation

12–171   In order for a legitimate expectation to have arisen, the planning authority must have made a statement or adopted a position amounting to a promise or representation, express or implied, as to how it would act in respect of an identifiable area of its activity. The representation must be addressed or conveyed either directly or indirectly to an identifiable person or group of persons, affected actually or potentially, in such a way that it forms part of a transaction definitively entered into or a relationship between that person or group and the public authority or that the person or group has acted on the faith of the representation.[199]

12–172   In *Glenkerrin Homes v Dun Laoghaire Rathdown County Council*,[200] the High Court held that the fact that the relevant local authority, together with most other local authorities, had permitted a practice to evolve whereby so-called "certificates of compliance" or "letters of compliance" had come to be regarded as quasi-documents of title in relation to newly built houses gave rise to a legitimate expectation that the existing practice would not be terminated without reasonable notice. Reasonable notice in this context would include giving general public notice sufficient to give a reasonable opportunity to those involved in conveyancing (and, in particular, the relevant conveyancing committee of the Law Society) to consider and make recommendations as to the manner in which conveyancing issues arising in relation to newly built homes should be dealt with in the absence of such certificates or letters of compliance.

12–173   A further example of an informal practice giving rise to a legitimate expectation is to be found in the decision of the High Court of England and Wales in *R. (On the application of Rubin) v First Secretary of State*.[201] Although there was no statutory requirement to do so, the relevant planning authority's practice was to give notice of proposed appeal hearings to all parties who had previously been notified of the original planning application. A neighbour affected by proposed development sought to rely on this practice. The Secretary of State argued that there could be no legitimate expectation because there was no written policy and no course of dealing between the planning authority and the neighbour in which notice of appeal hearings had been given. The High Court was nevertheless prepared to hold that the neighbour was entitled to rely on the general practice, and that, even though there was no promise to notify him, there was an established practice.

12–174   This case suggests that a planning authority which has gone beyond the minimum procedural requirements required by statute—for example, by

---

[199] *Glencar Explorations plc v Mayo County Council (No. 2)* [2002] 1 I.R. 84, *per* Fennelly J.
[200] Unreported, High Court, Clarke J., April 27, 2007.
[201] [2004] E.W.H.C. 266; [2005] J.P.L. 234.

engaging in more extensive public consultation that strictly required—may find itself bound to comply with those extra-statutory procedures.[202]

The representation or statement must be to the effect that a person or class of persons would obtain some specific benefit, whether procedural or substantive. Thus, in *Glencar Explorations plc v Mayo County Council*,[203] the Supreme Court rejected a claim for damages for breach of legitimate expectation in circumstances where the evidence established no more than that the developer had a legitimate expectation that the planning authority would act properly and lawfully. It was never represented to the developer that it would obtain planning permission. Fennelly J. observed that every citizen could assert an expectation that public authorities would act within the law, but that was clearly not enough to found a successful claim for legitimate expectation. If it were, the doctrine would be almost meaningless and would duplicate the ordinary right, for example, to seek judicial review of administrative action. Similarly, the High Court ruled that the grant of a *temporary* planning permission did not give rise to any express or implied representation that a further planning permission would be forthcoming.[204]   **12–175**

An interesting question arises as to whether a statement of policy in a statutory development plan or a local area plan could ever give rise to a legitimate expectation. Approaching the matter from first principles, it might be argued that it is capable of so doing, as it represents a public statement of the planning authority's policy on a particular issue. As against this, policies and objectives in a development plan are rarely expressed in unequivocal terms, and, moreover, the terms of a development plan are not self-executing, but contingent on some further step. Even the zoning of land for a particular purpose does not amount to a "representation" or "promise" that planning permission will be granted for conforming development: it is still necessary to make an application for planning permission even for development which conforms with the necessary zoning, and that application falls to be determined on its own merits. A development plan is also addressed to the public in general, rather than to a particular class of persons such as, for example, landowners.[205] In all the circumstances, it is unlikely that a statement of policy in a development plan meets the criteria necessary to give rise to an actionable expectation.   **12–176**

---

[202] See, for example, *Aughey Enterprises Ltd. v Monaghan County Council* [2005] I.E.H.C. 191; unreported, Macken J., June 15, 2005, where the High Court granted leave to an applicant company to argue that it had a legitimate expectation that it would be consulted on, and have opportunity to contest, any change to proposed local authority development.

[203] [2002] 1 I.R. 84.

[204] *Grealish v An Bord Pleanála (No. 1)* [2005] I.E.H.C. 24; [2006] 1 I.L.R.M. 140.

[205] *Glencar Explorations plc v Mayo County Council (No. 2)* [2002] 1 I.R. 84 at 127, *per* Keane C.J. ("The decision by the respondent to include the mining ban constituted the purported exercise by it of a power vested in it by law for the benefit of the public in general. It was not the fulfilment by it of a duty imposed by statute for the specific protection of particular categories of persons, the breach of which may lead to an action for damages.").

12–177 As it happens, an attempt has been made in the PDA 2000 to preclude zoning objectives from giving rise to a legitimate expectation. Section 10(8) provides that there shall be no presumption in law that any land zoned in a particular development plan (including a development plan which has been varied) shall remain so zoned in any subsequent development plan. Whether this section achieves its intended effect of defeating a legitimate expectation remains to be seen. By definition, the type of representations which give rise to a legitimate expectation are often non-statutory, and thus to provide that there is no "presumption in law" does not necessarily preclude a landowner from arguing that there was nevertheless an implied representation.

3. Expectation must be legitimate or reasonable

12–178 Any representation must be such as to create an expectation reasonably entertained that the public authority will abide by the representation to the extent that it would be unjust to permit the public authority to resile from it.[206]

12–179 Some of the earlier case law also suggested that a legitimate expectation would not be enforced in respect of a substantive, as opposed to a procedural, benefit. A number of more recent decisions of the High Court indicate that an expectation is capable of being enforced even in respect of a *substantive* benefit.[207]

12–180 The circumstances in which a court will enforce a legitimate expectation are heavily qualified by considerations of the wider public interest. In the context of planning law, three particular countervailing interests are as follows.

(i) Planning authority cannot act ultra vires

12–181 The earlier case law emphasised that—with the possible exception of mere irregularity of procedure—a plea of estoppel of any kind could not prevail as an answer to a well founded claim that something done by a public body in breach of a statutory duty or limitation of function is *ultra vires*.[208] More recently, the usefulness of the doctrine of *ultra vires* as a touchstone seems to have lessened: as discussed below, the principal concern now appears to be the impact on the public's rights of participation. Obviously, if a particular course

---

[206] *Glencar Explorations plc v Mayo County Council (No. 2)* [2002] 1 I.R. 84, *per* Fennelly J.

[207] See, in particular, *Power v Minister for Social and Family Affairs* [2006] I.E.H.C. 170; [2007] 1 I.L.R.M. 109. In *Dunleavy v Dun Laoghaire Rathdown County Council* [2005] I.E.H.C. 381; unreported, Macken J., November 5, 2005, the High Court appears to have accepted that an expectation to purchase a maisonette at a particular price could be enforced against a local authority as a legitimate expectation, but went on to hold that, in any event, same was enforceable by dint of promissory estoppel. In *Glenkerrin Homes v Dun Laoghaire Rathdown County Council*, unreported, High Court, Clarke J., April 27, 2007, a legitimate expectation arose in respect of letters of compliance.

[208] *In re Green Dale Building Co. Ltd.* [1977] I.R. 256 (invalid notice to treat).

of conduct is found to undermine public participation it might be said that it is *ultra vires*, but the case law tends not to emphasise this aspect.

The judgment of the ECtHR in *Stretch v United Kingdom*[209] suggests that an **12–182** absolute rule that a legitimate expectation cannot prevail against *ultra vires* action may not be compliant with the European Convention on Human Rights. On the facts, the applicant had the benefit of a lease, together with an option to renew, from a local authority. The applicant erected a number of buildings for light industrial use on the land. When the applicant came to exercise his option to renew, however, the local authority argued that the option had been granted *ultra vires* in that a local authority's statutory power to let land did not extend to the grant of an option. The local authority's objection in this regard was upheld subsequently by the Court of Appeal.

The ECtHR held that this amounted to a violation of Art.1 of the First Protocol. **12–183** The court considered that the option to renew had been an important part of the lease for a person undertaking building obligations and who otherwise would have had a limited period in which to recoup his expenditure.

Whereas the court did not dispute the purpose or usefulness of the doctrine of **12–184** *ultra vires*—as an important safeguard against abuse of power by local or statutory authorities—it held that the application to the facts was disproportionate.[210]

> "The Court observes that local authorities inevitably enter into many agreements of a private law nature with ordinary citizens in the pursuance of their functions, not all of which however will concern matters of vital public concern. In the present case, the local authority entered in a lease and was unaware that its powers to do so did not include the possibility of agreeing to an option for renewal of the lease. It nonetheless obtained the agreed rent for the lease and, on exercise of the renewal of the option, had the possibility of negotiating an increase in ground rent. There is no issue that the local authority acted against the public interest in the way in which it disposed of the property under its control or that any third party interests or the pursuit of any other statutory function would have been prejudiced by giving effect to the renewal option. The subsequent statutory amendments further illustrate that there was nothing per se objectionable or inappropriate in a local authority including such a term in lease agreements (see para.26)."

In reaching its conclusion, the ECtHR rejected the suggestion that the applicant **12–185** had some form of constructive knowledge that the local authority lacked the legal capacity to grant renewal options. The court stated that since the local authority itself considered that it had the power to grant an option, it was not unreasonable that the applicant and his legal advisers entertained the same belief.

---

[209] (2004) 38 E.H.R.R. 12.
[210] *ibid.*, [39].

(ii) Rights of public participation must not be defeated

12–186   The courts will not normally hold a planning authority to an informal representation where this would result in a formal statutory procedure, involving public participation, being by-passed. Reference is made, by analogy, to the decision of the House of Lords in *R. v East Sussex County Council Ex p. Reprotech (Pebsham) Ltd.*[211] One of the issues raised in those proceedings was as to whether or not a purchaser of lands was entitled to rely on an indication by the county planning officer that planning permission would not be required for a particular activity (involving the use of waste to generate electricity). The House of Lords found that the opinion of the county planning officer could not reasonably have been taken as a binding representation that no planning permission was required. In reaching this conclusion, the House of Lords attached great significance to the fact that a statutory procedure was provided for whereby any person could apply for a "certificate of lawful use". The House of Lords indicated that whereas planning officers are generally helpful in offering opinions on whether or not planning permission is required, everyone knew that if a binding determination was required, a formal application had to be made under the relevant section.

12–187   It is submitted that similar considerations should apply under Irish planning law, given the existence of the Section 5 reference procedure. This procedure is discussed in detail at paras 10–01 to 10–31, but, in brief, it allows any question as to what, in any particular case, is or is not development or is or is not exempted development to be referred to the planning authority. The planning authority is empowered to make a declaration, which is to be entered in the planning register. There is a right to have the planning authority's declaration reviewed by An Bord Pleanála. It would clearly be incompatible with the statutory intent were the courts to uphold a parallel, informal procedure whereby representations made by officials of the planning authority outside the context of a Section 5 reference were held to be binding. The Section 5 procedure allows for certainty in that any declaration affecting land can be inspected on the planning register. This is in contrast to any *ad hoc* representation made by officials of the planning authority.

12–188   Although there is no express provision made for public participation in a Section 5 reference, it is arguable that the courts would be prepared to imply, in at least some circumstances, that affected members of the public could participate. Moreover, it could be argued that a third party member of the public would be entitled to appeal to An Bord Pleanála in relation to a planning authority's declaration.

12–189   Similar considerations apply in respect of the waiver of planning conditions. The Court of Appeal of England and Wales has indicated in *Henry Boot Homes*

---

[211] [2002] U.K.H.L. 8; [2002] J.P.L. 821.

Ltd. v Bassetlaw District Council[212] that scope for waiver by non-statutory means of the need to comply with a planning condition must be extremely limited. It is important to emphasise, however, that the judgment of the Court of Appeal was given against a statutory background whereby a special statutory procedure is provided for the making of an application to have, in effect, a condition modified. A planning condition could only be modified by the appropriate statutory procedure, which involved an application for planning permission. If such procedures were not followed, interested third parties would be unable to make representations against the grant of planning permission and have those representations taken into account. Although there had been a similar provision under Irish law under s.28(4) of the Local Government (Planning and Development) Act 1963, there is no equivalent express provision provided for under the PDA 2000.

(iii) Freedom to exercise properly a statutory power must be respected

The extent to which the making of a representation can trammel the subsequent exercise of a statutory discretion is not entirely clear. The earlier case law suggests that the exercise of a discretion should not be fettered, and that in cases involving the exercise of a discretionary statutory power the only legitimate expectation relating to the conferring of a benefit is a conditional one, namely that a benefit will be conferred provided that at the time the decision-maker considers that it is a proper exercise of the statutory power in the light of current policy to grant it. Such a conditional expectation cannot give rise to an enforceable right to the benefit should it later be refused in the public interest.[213]   **12–190**

The position was summarised thus by McCracken J. in *Abrahamson v Law Society of Ireland*.[214]   **12–191**

> "Where a Minister or a public body is given by statute or statutory instrument a discretion or a power to make regulations for the good of the public or of a specific section of the public, the court will not interfere with the exercise of such discretion or power, as to do so would be tantamount to the court usurping that discretion or power to itself, and would be an undue interference by the court in the affairs of the persons or bodies to whom or to which such discretion or power was given by the legislature."

---

[212] [2002] E.W.C.A. Civ. 983; [2003] 1 P. & C.R. 23. See also *R. v Leicester City Council Ex p. Powergen United Kingdom plc* [1999] 4 P.L.R. 91 (Dyson J.); [2000] J.P.L. 1037 (Court of Appeal); *R. (On the application of Wandsworth BC) v Secretary of State for Environment, Transport and the Regions;* [2003] E.W.C.A. 622 Admin; and *Coghurst Wood Leisure Park Ltd. v Secretary of State of Transport, Local Government and the Regions* [2003] J.P.L. 206. See, generally, Ellis and Thomas "Putting the Boot into Development Control: A User's Guide to Recent Case Law. [2005] J.P.L. 735.

[213] *Tara Prospecting Ltd. v Minister for Energy* [1993] I.L.R.M. 771. See also *Hempenstall v Minister for the Environment* [1994] 2 I.R. 20 (regulation of hackney cabs).

[214] [1996] 1 I.R. 403 at 423.

12–192 It seems that even in the case of discretionary powers or functions a public authority may find itself restricted—albeit to a very limited extent—by its previous policy or practice. More specifically, the public authority may be required to give reasonable notice of its change of policy or practice, or to afford interested persons an opportunity to make submissions as to why the policy or practice should not change.

12–193 Thus, for example, on the facts of *Glenkerrin Homes v Dun Laoghaire Rathdown County Council*,[215] the High Court held that the relevant local authority could not terminate an existing practice of issuing so-called "certificates of compliance" or "letters of compliance" without reasonable notice.

H. Summary of Some Other Possible Grounds of Challenge

1. Relevant and irrelevant considerations

12–194 This category of ground of review is intended to cover the situation where a decision-maker has either failed to have regard to a relevant consideration, or had regard to an irrelevant consideration. In most cases in which a statutory discretion is conferred, some indication will be given in the legislation as to the matters which are to inform the exercise of that discretion. Perhaps the most comprehensive scheme is to be found in relation to the planning legislation itself. There, in deciding to grant or refuse planning permission, a planning authority or An Bord Pleanála shall consider the proper planning and sustainable development of the area. In addition, regard is to be had to a number of matters including, for example, the development plan.

12–195 In a number of cases, a decision to grant or refuse planning permission was set aside on the basis that the decision-maker took into account irrelevant considerations such as, for example, the personal circumstances of the applicant,[216] or the existence of the structure in the context of an application for retention planning permission.[217]

12–196 Interestingly a number of these cases arose in the context of the decision on the application for planning permission being made by the elected members of the planning authority. The public nature of the discussions where a decision is being made by the elected members means that potential grounds of review may well be more readily exposed than where the decision is, in effect, made in private by the executive.

---

[215] Unreported, High Court, Clarke J., April 27, 2007.

[216] *Flanagan v Galway City and County Manager* [1990] 2 I.R. 66; and *Griffin v Galway City and County Manager*, unreported, High Court, Blayney J., October 31, 1990. *Cf. Great Portland Estates v Westminster City Council* [1985] A.C. 661.

[217] *State (FitzGerald) v An Bord Pleanála* [1985] I.L.R.M. 117. See also *Village Residents Association Ltd. v An Bord Pleanála (No. 2)* [2000] 4 I.R. 321; [2001] 2 I.L.R.M. 22.

The statement of reasons for a decision may indicate that an irrelevant **12–197** consideration has been taken into account. Of course, the fact that the courts have not, to date, insisted on a very full statement of reasons weakens the importance of this. See para.12–119 and onwards.

2. Improper purpose

A decision may be open to challenge on the basis that the decision-maker has **12–198** exercised the power for an improper purpose. Although this might be regarded as a subset of the category discussed immediately above at paras 12–194 to 12–197, in that the improper purpose would presumably involve the taking into account of an irrelevant consideration, it is convenient to consider this separately.

This ground of challenge arises most commonly in the context of conditions **12–199** attached to a planning permission. The fact that the conditions appear on the face of the decision will make any improper purpose easier to detect than in the case of other more inscrutable decisions. The leading judgment is that of the Supreme Court in *Ashbourne Holdings Ltd. v An Bord Pleanála*.[218] See, generally, paras 4–29 to 4–32.

In *McDowell v Roscommon County Council*,[219] the High Court held that it **12–200** was improper for a planning authority to use the occasion of an application for an extension to prevent the completion of what the planning authority regarded as an unauthorised development, in circumstances where the planning authority had available to it a range of enforcement mechanisms under Pt VIII of the PDA 2000.

> "In this case I am satisfied that the primary object of section 42 of the Act of 2000 is to enable a development already commenced to which a planning permission relates to be completed: it is not permissible to use the section to prevent the completion of a development to which the planning permission relates which the Planning Authority has concluded does not comply fully with that permission. What the Planning Authority must consider is whether the development relates to the permission and not whether it is in full compliance with the same. It is not permissible to use a statutory power conferred for a particular purpose for some other purpose."

For the reasons set out at paras 5–61 to 5–63, it is submitted that the finding of **12–201** an improper purpose was incorrect.

---

[218] [2003] 2 I.R. 114; [2003] 2 I.L.R.M. 446.
[219] [2004] I.E.H.C. 396; unreported, Finnegan P., December 21, 2004.

3. Unlawful delegation

12–202 Occasionally it may be possible to challenge a decision on the basis that the designated decision-maker improperly delegated his or her function to another. A straightforward example is provided on the facts of *Ó Nualláin v Dublin Corporation*.[220] There the decision as to the form of procedure to apply to a proposed local authority development (the spire in O'Connell Street, Dublin) was taken by an official to whom that function had not been properly delegated.

12–203 Although the argument normally arises in the context of a failure to duly delegate a function to a particular officer, similar principles apply where the decision-maker abdicates its decision-making function to another body.[221] For example, it might be argued that were An Bord Pleanála to leave over, by way of condition, matters central to an appeal for agreement between a planning authority and the developer this would represent an improper delegation of the appellate function to the planning authority. Under the legislation, it is An Bord Pleanála which must determine an appeal, and this requires that all matters of substance be determined by the board itself.[222]

12–204 A variation of this theme arose in the case of *Aer Rianta cpt v An Bord Pleanála*.[223] There, the applicant company argued (unsuccessfully) that An Bord Pleanála had failed to address the public safety issues arising on an appeal in respect of development in the vicinity of an active airport runway, by abdicating this aspect of its function to the Irish Aviation Authority.

4. Breach of limitation or fetter on jurisdiction

12–205 In addition to prescribing various procedural requirements, the PDA 2000 imposes other more substantive requirements. Failure to comply with these substantive requirements might well give rise to grounds for judicial review. A straightforward example arises in the context of local authority development. As discussed at paras 1–10 to 1–20, under s.178 of the PDA 2000 a local authority is prohibited from effecting any development in its functional area which contravenes materially its development plan. Failure to observe this limitation is actionable.

---

[220] [1999] 4 I.R. 137.
[221] *H. Lavender and Son Ltd. v Minister of Housing and Local Government* [1970] 1 W.L.R. 1231.
[222] *Houlihan v An Bord Pleanála*, unreported, High Court, Murphy J., October 4, 1993. *Cf. Boland v An Bord Pleanála* [1996] 3 I.R. 435.
[223] Unreported, High Court, Kelly J., June 25, 2002.

CHAPTER THIRTEEN

ENVIRONMENTAL IMPACT ASSESSMENT

A. Introduction

It is a requirement of both European Community law and national law that an **13–01** environmental impact assessment ("EIA") procedure be carried out before a development consent may be granted in respect of certain development projects. As will all too readily become apparent, nothing about the issue of environmental impact assessment is straightforward, and this area has given rise to an enormous amount of litigation. It is very difficult to state the law in this regard with any confidence. Even the simple statement in the opening sentence of this chapter is not uncontroversial, in that the respective definitions of a "development consent" and "project" have themselves been the subject of hard fought litigation.[1]

---

[1] See, for example, *Dunne v Minister for the Environment Heritage and Local Government (No. 2)* [2006] I.E.S.C. 49; [2007] 1 I.L.R.M. 264 ("development consent"); and *R. (On the application of Candlish) v Hastings Borough Council* [2005] E.W.H.C. 1539 (Admin); [2006] J.P.L. 22 ("project").

13–02 Scannell provides an excellent discussion of the law in respect of environmental impact assessment in *Environmental and Land Use Law*,[2] and readers are encouraged to consult that text. The treatment here is narrower, and the principal focus of this chapter will be directed to how the environmental impact assessment requirements affect the decision-making process in respect of applications for planning permission. However, in order to put this into context it will also be necessary to discuss various legal concepts under the EIA Directive. This chapter will, in addition, briefly examine the implications of environmental impact assessment for local authority and State authority development. The assessment of local authority and State authority development is also considered at paras 8–316 to 8–348, and at paras 8–368 to 8–392, respectively.

13–03 In brief terms, what the environmental impact assessment process requires is that the main effects on the environment (both adverse and beneficial) which a development project is likely to have, be identified and assessed, and the public consulted, before any decision on a development consent is made.

13–04 The requirement for environmental impact assessment changes the manner in which an application for planning permission is dealt with. First, the information which must be before the decision-maker is far more extensive than that which would be necessary for an ordinary application for planning permission. Secondly, the range of considerations which the decision-maker is required to take into account is greater; for example, consideration must be given to alternatives, and to the impact of the development when cumulated with other development projects. Thirdly, there is an express requirement to address mitigation measures. Fourthly, the public is afforded enhanced rights of participation. Thus, for example, the fact that a proposed development is subject to environmental impact assessment must be expressly referred to in the public notices,[3] and copies of the environmental impact statement must be available for inspection and purchase. There is also an express right of access to a review procedure before a court of law, or another independent and impartial body established by law, to challenge the substantive or procedural legality of decisions, acts or omissions subject to the public participation provisions of the Directive.[4] Finally, the statement of the reasons and considerations underlying the decision may have to be fuller than in the case of an ordinary application for planning permission.[5]

13–05 To an extent, there is some overlap between the procedural requirements arising under the EIA Directive and those governing any application for planning permission. Thus, for example, even in the case of ordinary development there are generous rights of public participation, and the concept of "proper planning

[2] Thomson Round Hall, Dublin, 2006, Chapter 5.
[3] Planning and Development Regulations 2001, art.98 (planning authority stage) and art.112 (as amended by the 2006 Regulations) (appeal to An Bord Pleanála).
[4] Directive 85/337/EEC, Art.10a (inserted by Directive 2003/35/EC).
[5] See Directive 85/337/EEC, Art.9 (inserted by Directive 2003/35/EC).

and sustainable development" encompasses environmental issues. Notwithstanding this overlap, however, the better view is that the procedural requirements of environmental impact assessment are sufficiently different that a failure to carry out a formal environmental impact assessment, in the case of development to which the Directive applies, could not be overlooked on the basis that the ordinary planning procedure constitutes a surrogate form of environmental impact assessment. Insofar as the judgment in *Browne v An Bord Pleanála* appears to suggest the contrary, it is submitted that it is wrong and should not be followed.[6]

A similar point came before the House of Lords in *Berkeley v Secretary of State for the Environment*.[7] In the leading speech, Lord Hoffmann identified the directly enforceable right under the Directive as not merely a right to a fully informed decision on the substantive planning issues, but as requiring the inclusive and democratic procedure prescribed by the Directive in which the public, however misguided or wrongheaded its views may be, is given an opportunity to express its opinion on the environmental issues. Lord Hoffmann stated that the Directive contemplated an environmental statement constituting a single and accessible compilation, produced by the applicant at the very start of the application process, of the relevant environmental information and a summary in non-technical language. The paper chase produced on the facts of the case could not be treated as its equivalent. Lord Hoffmann went on to make the further point that a court should not ordinarily be willing to validate a failure to comply with national legislation transposing a Directive on the ground that a different form of transposing legislation—allowing an environmental statement to take the composite form put forward in that case— might possibly have also satisfied the terms of the Directive. **13–06**

To this can be added the point that, under Irish law at least, the Directive extends the range of relevant considerations to be taken into account by the decision-maker, and thus even if the procedures were fortuitously replicated under the ordinary planning process, this would not be enough. **13–07**

B. An Overview of the Environmental Impact Assessment Directive

1. The amended Directive

The starting point for any discussion of environmental impact assessment has to be the relevant European Community Directives. The principal Directive is **13–08**

---

[6] [1991] 2 I.R. 209; [1989] I.L.R.M. 865. Barron J. had stated as follows: "It is clear therefore that if the directive had been brought into force within the State, nevertheless the planning procedures which were followed both before the planning authority and on appeal would have been a sufficient compliance with the provisions thereof intended to protect the public."
[7] [2001] 2 A.C. 603; (2001) P. & C.R. 492.

Council Directive 85/337/EEC of June 27, 1985 on the assessment of the effects of certain public and private projects on the environment.[8] This Directive has been amended on a number of occasions, and, in particular, by Council Directive 97/11/EC,[9] and Directive 2003/35/EC of the European Parliament and of the Council of May 26, 2003 providing for public participation in respect of the drawing up of certain plans and programmes relating to the environment and amending with regard to public participation and access to justice Council Directives 85/337/EEC and 96/61/EC.[10] Unless otherwise indicated, all references hereinafter to "the Directive" or to "the EIA Directive" will be to Council Directive 85/337/EEC as amended.

13–09   A form of environmental assessment has been introduced for certain plans and programmes on the environment under Directive 2001/42/EC of the European Council and Parliament.[11] This Directive has been implemented into Irish law principally through the EC (Environmental Assessment of Certain Plans and Programmes) Regulations 2004.[12] Insofar as development plans, local area plans and regional planning guidelines are concerned, additional procedural requirements have been imposed under the Planning and Development (Strategic Assessment) Regulations 2004.[13] More detailed reference is made to same in the context of the general discussion of development plans and local area plans in Chapter 1, and, in particular, at paras 1–106 to 1–113.

13–10   The objective of the EIA Directive is to ensure that certain categories of "projects" which are likely to have significant effects on the environment should be subject to environmental impact assessment prior to any decision being made to grant "development consent".[14]

2. Annex I and Annex II projects

13–11   A distinction is drawn under the EIA Directive between two types of projects: Annex I projects and Annex II projects. In the case of Annex I projects, an environmental impact assessment is mandatory.[15] The position in relation to Annex II projects is more complicated.[16]

13–12   Annex II projects are of a type which may or may not have a significant effect on the environment. Member States may establish criteria and/or thresholds to assist in determining whether a particular project within the classes listed in Annex II is to be subject to environmental impact assessment.

---

[8] [1985] O.J. L175/40.
[9] [1997] O.J. L73/5.
[10] [2003] O.J. L156/17.
[11] [2001] O.J. L197/30.
[12] S.I. No. 435 of 2004.
[13] S.I. No. 436 of 2004.
[14] See, generally, *World Wildlife Fund v Autonome Provinz Bozen* (Case C–435/97) [1999] E.C.R. I–5613, [45].
[15] See paras 13–41 and onwards for a more detailed discussion.
[16] See discussion following, and, for a more detailed discussion, paras 13–46 and onwards.

The implementation method chosen by Ireland relies heavily on the use of   **13–13**
such thresholds. These thresholds are set out at Pt 2 of Sch.5 of the Planning
and Development Regulations 2001. Thresholds relate to matters such as the
area of the development; the number of units involved; or, in the case of
agricultural development, the number of animals involved. For example,
development consisting of the construction of more than 500 dwelling units
requires an environmental impact assessment, as does development consisting
of installations for intensive rearing of poultry which would have more than
40,000 places for poultry.

It is important to note that, as discussed at para.13–46 and onwards, a Member   **13–14**
State is not entitled to rely solely on thresholds which take account only of the
size of the project without also taking the nature and location of the project
into consideration. Thus, Ireland was found to be in breach of its obligations
under the Directive by the ECJ in its judgment in *Commission v Ireland*.[17] The
absolute nature of the threshold applicable under the (then) national legislation
to certain peat extraction projects was held to be unlawful, in that it excluded
consideration of the nature and location of the projects in deciding whether or
not to require an environmental impact assessment. (The relevant threshold
was confined to peat extraction projects over a particular acreage.)

3. Information to be provided

Article 3 of the Directive provides that the environmental impact assessment   **13–15**
shall identify, describe and assess in an appropriate manner, in the light of
each individual case, the direct and indirect effects of a project on the following
factors[18]:

    (i)   human beings, fauna and flora;
    (ii) soil, water, air, climate and the landscape;
    (iii) material assets and the cultural heritage; and
    (iv) the interaction between the factors mentioned at (i), (ii) and (iii).

Member States are required—under Art.5—to adopt the necessary measures   **13–16**
to ensure that the developer supplies in an appropriate form the information
specified in Annex IV inasmuch as (a) the Member States consider that the
information is relevant to a given stage of the consent procedure and to the
specific characteristics of a particular project or type of project and of the
environmental features likely to be affected; and (b) the Member States consider
that a developer may reasonably be required to compile this information having
regard, *inter alia*, to current knowledge and methods of assessment. Thus, it
will be seen that the requirement to provide information is qualified.

---

[17] (Case C–392/96) [1999] E.C.R. 5901.
[18] Art.3 (as substituted by Directive 97/11/EC).

4. Public participation

13–17   Public participation is an essential element of environmental impact assessment. It is important to note that the latitude allowed to Member States in this regard has been greatly reduced as a result of amendments to Art.6 introduced under Directive 2003/35/EC. The emphasis now is on ensuring that public consultation occurs early in the environmental decision-making procedures. Under Art.6(4), the public concerned shall be given early and effective opportunities to participate in the decision-making procedure and shall, for that purpose, be entitled to express comments and opinions when all options are open to the competent authority or authorities before the decision on the request for development consent is taken. This requirement that public consultation occur when "all options are open" is one which is not always satisfied under Irish law. In at least some instances the form of development—for example, the particular route of a road—is presented as a *fait accompli*, with alternative options having been discounted by the time the environmental impact statement is published. In such circumstances, the ultimate development consent may be open to challenge on the basis that the requirements of Art.6 have not been met.

13–18   Under Art.6(6), reasonable time-frames for the different phases are to be provided, allowing sufficient time for informing the public, and for the public concerned to prepare and participate effectively in the environmental decision-making. It must be open to question as to whether the very strict time-limits on the making of submissions under the PDA 2000 would be regarded as "reasonable" in this regard. This is discussed further at paras 13–166 to 13–168.

13–19   Under Art.6(5), the detailed arrangements for informing the public (for example, by bill posting within a certain radius or publication in local newspapers) and for consulting the public concerned (for example by written submissions or by way of a public inquiry) shall be determined by the Member States.

13–20   Special procedural requirements apply—under Art.7 of the Directive—where a project is likely to have significant effects on *another* Member State. These requirements are triggered either where the first Member State is aware that a project is likely to have significant effects on the environment in another Member State, or where that second Member State so requests. See further paras 13–408 to 13–425.

13–21   The results of consultations and the information gathered pursuant to Arts 5, 6 and 7 must be taken into consideration in the development consent procedure.[19]

---

[19] Art.8 (as substituted by Directive 97/11/EC).

5. Decision

When a decision to grant or refuse development consent has been taken, the **13–22** competent authority or authorities shall inform the public thereof in accordance with the appropriate procedures and shall make available to the public the following information[20]:

— the content of the decision and any conditions attached thereto;
— having examined the concerns and opinions expressed by the public concerned, the main reasons and considerations on which the decision is based, including information about the public participation process;
— a description, where necessary, of the main measures to avoid, reduce and, if possible, offset the major adverse effects.

The competent authority or authorities are also required to inform any Member **13–23** State which has been consulted, pursuant to Art.7, of the decision, forwarding to it the information referred to above.

Under Art.10a, members of the public affected have a right of access to a **13–24** review procedure before a court of law or another independent and impartial body established by law to challenge the substantive or procedural legality of decisions, acts or omissions subject to the public participation provisions of the Directive. This is discussed in detail at paras 13–316 to 13–407.

C. Transitional: So-Called Pipeline Projects

The deadline for the implementation of the original EIA Directive was July 3, **13–25** 1988. More recently, Member States were required to bring into force the laws, regulations and administrative provisions necessary to comply with Directive 2003/35/EC by June 25, 2005 at the latest.[21] It seems to follow from the case law discussed below that any application for a development consent made after that date will be subject to the new procedural requirements under the amended Directive, even if national law has not been updated.

The position of so-called pipeline projects, *i.e.* projects in respect of which the **13–26** consent procedure was initiated before July 3, 1988 and which were still in progress on that date, had been considered by ECJ in *Commission v Germany*.[22] In the absence of any transitional rules under the Directive covering so-called pipeline projects, the ECJ appeared to accept that the requirements of the Directive might not apply where the application for consent was formally lodged *before* July 3, 1988. On the particular facts of the case, the application for

---

[20] Art.9(1) (as substituted by Directive 2003/35/EC).
[21] Ireland was criticised by the High Court in *Friends of the Curragh Environment Ltd. v An Bord Pleanála* [2006] I.E.H.C. 243; unreported, Kelly J., July 14, 2006 for failing to implement the amendments in time.
[22] (Case C–431/92) [1995] E.C.R. I–2189, [32]. See also *Burgemeester en wethouders van Haarlemmerliede en Spaarnwoude v Gedeputeerde Staten van Noord-Holland* (Case C–81/96) [1998] E.C.R. I–3923, [23].

consent had not been made until after that date. The ECJ held that a formal application was required: it was not sufficient that informal contacts and meetings between the competent authority and the developer, relating to the content and proposal to lodge an application for consent for a project, had occurred prior to July 3, 1988.

13–27 The rationale of the ECJ was that as the Directive is primarily designed to cover large-scale projects, which will most often require a long time to complete, it would not be appropriate to make the procedure more cumbersome and time-consuming by applying the requirements of the Directive to consent procedures which were formally initiated prior to the date of the expiry of the period for transposing the Directive.[23] These considerations did not apply, however, where a *fresh* consent procedure was formally initiated after July 3, 1988.[24]

13–28 More generally, it has to be said that the treatment of pipeline projects under Irish law is not always consistent with the jurisprudence of the ECJ. In particular, it seems that the favourable treatment previously afforded to peat extraction under national law was almost certainly in breach of the requirements of the Directive. Until 2005, peat extraction was exempted development where the drainage of the bogland commenced prior to January 21, 2002, *i.e.* the relevant commencement date under the Planning and Development Regulations 2001. The choice of this date was, in terms of the Directive, entirely arbitrary. The Directive had first come into effect on July 3, 1988. Whereas it could be argued—assuming for a moment that drainage and peat extraction could properly be regard as a unitary act of development—that peat extraction based on drainage works commenced prior to July 3, 1988 was not caught by the Directive, there was simply no basis for employing a date in 2002 as the cut-off point.

13–29 The illegality in this regard has since been rectified, to some extent at least, under the Planning and Development Regulations 2005. Although the date of January 21, 2002 is again improperly employed as a cut-off date, the exemption is now expressly qualified, and, in summary, is not available where the peat extraction would be likely to have significant effects on the environment by reference to the criteria set out in Sch.7 of the 2001 Regulations.

13–30 The position of quarries is addressed separately at paras 8–118 to 8–175.

D. Overview of the Implementation of Directive into Irish Law

1. General

13–31 The EIA Directive has been implemented into Irish law principally through the planning legislation. As discussed in detail by Scannell, the requirement

---

[23] *Burgemeester* (Case C–81/96) [1998] E.C.R. I–3923, [24].
[24] *ibid.*, [28].

for environmental impact assessment does occasionally also arise under other legislation, for example, under the Foreshore Acts or the Gas Acts.[25] In many instances, however, the requirement for environmental impact assessment will derive solely from the PDA 2000, and the focus of this chapter is confined to such circumstances.

Under the PDA 2000, the requirements of the Directive have been grafted onto the conventional planning application procedure. Thus, in the case of prescribed development, special provision has been made for screening, *i.e.* deciding whether sub-threshold development is nevertheless likely to have a significant effect on the environment; the submission of an environmental impact statement; scoping; additional rights of public participation; extended time-limits; the consideration of the adequacy of the environmental impact statement; the taking into account of additional considerations by the decision-maker; and the form of the decision. **13–32**

Annexes I and II; Annex III and Annex IV of the Directive have, more or less, been replicated in Scheds 5, 6 and 7 of the Planning and Development Regulations 2001. **13–33**

The employment of the planning legislation as the principal vehicle through which to implement the Directive is not entirely satisfactory. If, for whatever reason, planning permission is not required in respect of a particular project, there is a risk that that project will not then be assessed. More specifically, there is a risk that, as certain development is exempted from the requirement to obtain planning permission, it will thus avoid scrutiny for the purposes of deciding whether or not there should be an environmental impact statement.[26] The principal classes of exempted development are provided for under s.4 of the PDA 2000, and under the Planning and Development Regulations 2001. See, generally, Chapter 2. **13–34**

Certain classes of exempted development overlap with categories prescribed under the Directive. To take an example: the use of uncultivated land or semi-agricultural areas for intensive agricultural purposes is exempted development provided that the area involved is less than 100 hectares.[27] This coincides with one of the categories of project prescribed for the purposes of Annex II, *i.e.* the use of uncultivated land or semi-natural areas for intensive agricultural purposes. **13–35**

The same figure of 100 hectares has been fixed—under the Planning and Development Regulations 2001—as the threshold for environmental impact assessment purposes. The use of such thresholds is, of course, only lawful **13–36**

---

[25] Y. Scannell, *Environmental and Land Use Law* (Thomson Round Hall, Dublin, 2006), para.5–159 and onwards.

[26] This entire issue is the subject of infringement proceedings being pursued against Ireland by the Commission: Case C-66/06 [2006] O.J. C108/1.

[27] Planning and Development Regulations 2001, Sch.2, Pt 2, Class 14.

provided that the possibility of environmental impact assessment in respect of a sub-threshold project exists. This presents no concerns where the development exceeds 100 hectares, in such cases (i) the benefit of exempted development will not be available, and (ii) assessment will be mandatory. A potential difficulty does arise, however, in the case of sub-threshold development. Such development is *prima facie* exempt from the requirement to obtain planning permission, and there is no formal procedure under national law whereby it is *mandatory* for a developer to seek a screening decision in advance of purporting to rely on a class of exempted development. Thus, unless the farmer volunteers to make a Section 5 reference, the question of whether or not an intensive agricultural use involving an area of less than 100 hectares is likely to have significant effects on the environment will not necessarily come before the planning bodies prior to the commencement of development. The farmer might, instead, seek unilaterally to rely on the benefit of the exempted development.

13–37　The concerns in this regard are, to some extent at least, off-set by the provisions of art.9 of the Planning and Development Regulations 2001. Article 9 imposes a number of general restrictions on the availability of exempted development. Certain of these restrictions are apt to capture development of a type which is likely, by reference to its location or characteristics, to have significant effects on the environment, and, accordingly, it will be necessary to apply for planning permission in respect of such development, and screening can then be carried out in the ordinary way. For example, where development will involve the excavation, alteration or demolition of various places or objects of, *inter alia*, archaeological or historical interest, the benefit of exempted development is unavailable. This restriction applies where it is an objective of the development plan or draft development plan to preserve the relevant feature. Under s.10 of the PDA 2000 it is mandatory for a planning authority to include objectives, *inter alia*, for the conservation and protection of the environment including, in particular, the archaeological and natural heritage and the conservation and protection of European sites.

13–38　There is a more general restriction provided for under art.9(1)(c) where the development is one to which Pt 10 of the Planning and Development Regulations 2001 applies. Part 10 deals with environmental impact assessment. Accordingly, on one view, the benefit of exempted development is never available in respect of development which is of a type which should be subject to environmental impact assessment. This applies even to sub-threshold development.

2. Environmental Protection Agency

13–39　The Environmental Protection Agency ("the EPA") performs a licensing function in respect of, *inter alia*, waste management licences and integrated pollution prevention and control licences under the Waste Management Acts 1996 to 2003, and the Environmental Protection Agency Acts 1992 to 2003, respectively. The role of the EPA in respect of environmental impact assessment is somewhat ambivalent. Although the EPA does have a function in carrying out an assessment, it does not have the power to call for an environmental impact statement, but is instead dependent on such a statement having been sought as part of the planning process. This can present difficulties in practice. It is quite possible that a project which is likely to have significant effects on the environment may have evaded any requirement for environmental impact assessment under the planning legislation. This might occur where the development is exempted development and thus no planning permission is required. It could also occur, in the case of sub-threshold development, were the planning authority to make an erroneous screening decision and fail to call for the submission of an environmental impact statement.

There is no provision made under national legislation whereby the EPA can **13–40** exercise an independent discretion so as to require an environmental impact statement in the circumstances outlined above. It may be, however, that the deficiencies of the national legislation in this regard can be made good by reliance directly on the Directive. The better view must be that the decision on either an integrated pollution prevention and control licence or a waste licence—whether in its own right or in conjunction with a planning permission—represents "development consent" within the meaning of the Directive. The EPA, as an emanation of the State, is obliged to give effect to the Directive. Accordingly, it must ensure that a project has been subject to environmental impact assessment before it can grant a licence. Normally, the EPA will be entitled to take cognisance of the fact that there will have been some form of assessment carried out in the context of an application for planning permission. Where this has not happened, however, it is submitted that the EPA must take whatever steps are necessary to ensure that a proper assessment will be performed. This might involve the EPA itself calling for the submission of an environmental impact statement. It may also require the EPA to undertake full assessment; in the absence of a proper assessment by the planning bodies, the EPA cannot rely on the fact that assessment of planning issues has already been carried out and confine its own assessment to environmental issues. Rather, the EPA must itself address all of the Art.3 matters. This entire issue is discussed in greater detail at paras 13–293 to 13–315 onwards.

E. Annex I Projects

Environmental impact assessment is mandatory in respect of Annex I projects. **13–41** A wide range of development projects are included, some of which are defined by reference to thresholds. Examples of Annex I projects include waste disposal installations for the incineration, chemical treatment or landfill of hazardous waste; pipelines for the transport of gas, oil or chemicals with a diameter of more than 800mm and a length of more than 40km; and installations for the reprocessing of irradiated nuclear fuel.

13–42   Agricultural development coming within Annex I obviously cannot benefit from the general exemption under s.4(1)(a) of the PDA 2000 in favour of the use of land for the purpose of agriculture.[28]

13–43   The High Court of England and Wales had to consider what was meant by the phrase "intensive agricultural purposes" in the context of Annex I of the EIA Directive in *Department for Environment, Food and Rural Affairs v Alford*.[29] The facts of the case were unusual. Certain land had been abandoned to nature for decades without the application of fertilizer. The new owner then applied farmyard manure and calcified seaweed to the lands. The effect of this was to bring land back to a normal level of agricultural productivity. In a literal sense, however, the works had *intensified* the agricultural usefulness of the lands. The question for the court was whether this was sufficient to trigger the requirement for an environmental impact assessment. In effect, the court was being asked to decide whether the test was a subjective one (whether the use of particular lands had been intensified) or an objective one (had the use intensified to above a particular threshold). The court held that the Directive was not intended to catch a project that was concerned only to bring land back to a normal level of agricultural productivity.

13–44   Reference is also made to the following types of infrastructural development for which environmental impact assessment is mandatory under Annex I.

> "7. (a) Construction of lines for long-distance railway traffic and of airports with a basic runway length of 2,100 m or more;
>   (b) Construction of motorways and express roads;
>   (c) Construction of a new road of four or more lanes, or realignment and/or widening of an existing road of two lanes or less so as to provide four or more lanes, where such new road, or realigned and/or widened section of road would be 10 km or more in a continuous length."

13–45   Road development by roads authorities in their own functional area is usually exempted from the requirement to obtain planning permission. Such development may, however, be subject to environmental impact assessment under Roads Act 1993 (as amended).

F. Annex II Projects

13–46   The legal position in respect of Annex II projects which are below threshold is more complicated. Unlike Annex I projects, an environmental impact assessment is not always mandatory in respect of Annex II projects. The objective of the Directive is to ensure that development projects which are likely to have significant effects on the environment should be subject to

---

[28] There appears to be a lacuna in the planning legislation in that the benefit of exempted development under s.4 of the PDA 2000 is not expressly disapplied in the case of EIA development projects.
[29] [2005] E.W.H.C. 808 (Admin); [2006] J.P.L 44.

environmental impact assessment prior to any decision being made to grant development consent.[30] The Community legislature is, seemingly, of the view that the various types of development project under Annex II may possibly have significant effects on the environment depending on the characteristics exhibited by individual projects.[31] Accordingly, the Member States must take steps to require environmental impact assessment where appropriate.

Members States are to determine—through either (a) a case-by-case examination **13–47** or (b) thresholds or criteria set by the Member State—whether the project should be subject to environmental impact assessment. The Directive requires that the relevant selection criteria set out in Annex III of the Directive shall be taken into account when a case-by-case examination is carried out or thresholds or criteria are set for this purpose.

Thus, under Art.4(2) of the Directive, Member States have a measure of **13–48** discretion to specify certain types of Annex II projects which are to be subject to an assessment or to establish the criteria or thresholds applicable. The ECJ has made it clear on a number of occasions, however, that there are limits on the Member States' discretion in this regard,[32] and that the limits of that discretion lie in the obligation set out in Art.2(1) that projects likely, by virtue, *inter alia*, of their nature, size or location, to have significant effects on the environment are to be subject to an impact assessment. The ECJ has also ruled that the criteria and/or thresholds mentioned in Art.4(2) are designed to facilitate the examination of the actual characteristics exhibited by a given project, in order to determine whether it is subject to the requirement to carry out an assessment, and not to exempt in advance from that obligation certain whole classes of projects (including modifications to those projects)[33] listed in Annex II which may be envisaged in the territory of a Member State.[34] Thus, Flemish legislation which excluded certain classes of projects mentioned in Annex II totally and definitively from environmental impact assessment was found to be in breach of the Directive in *Commission v Belgium*.[35] The ECJ noted that the Community legislature itself considered that all the classes of projects listed in Annex II may possibly have significant effects on the environment (depending

---

[30] See, generally, *World Wildlife Fund v Autonome Provinz Bozen* (Case C–435/97) [1999] E.C.R. I–5613, [45].

[31] *Commission v Belgium* (Case C–133/94) [1996] E.C.R. I–2323, [41].

[32] *Aannemersbedrijf P.K. Kraaijeveld BV v Gedeputeerde Staten van Zuid-Holland* (Case C–72/95) [1996] E.C.R. I–5403; see also *Commission v Ireland* (Case C–392/96) [1999] E.C.R. 5901.

[33] The reference to modifications of Annex II projects derives from *World Wildlife Fund v Autonome Provinz Bozen* (Case C–435/97) [1999] E.C.R. I–5613.

[34] *Commission v Belgium* (Case C–133/94) [1996] E.C.R. I–2323, [42]; *Aannemersbedrijf P.K. Kraaijeveld BV v Gedeputeerde Staten van Zuid-Holland* (Case C–72/95) [1996] E.C.R. I–5403, [51]; and *Commission v Germany* (Case C–301/95) [1998] E.C.R. I–6135, [45].

[35] (Case C–133/94) [1996] E.C.R. I–2323. See also *Commission v Ireland* (Case C–66/06), where the transposition of other categories of agricultural projects has been challenged on the basis that the relevant thresholds do not take into account factors other than size.

on the characteristics exhibited by those projects).[36] Any blanket rule which effectively exempted an entire class would be contrary to this legislative intent.[37]

13–49   The term "classes" in this context does not refer simply to the categories of project listed in Annex II, but to all the projects listed, under different letters of the alphabet, as subdivisions of those categories. The ECJ has held that any other interpretation would negate the effectiveness of the requirement that projects likely to have significant effects on the environment are to be made subject to an environmental impact assessment, and would leave Member States free to apply Annex II as they saw fit.[38] Consequently, a Member State fails to fulfil its obligations under Arts 2(1) and 4(2) of the Directive if it does not include in the scope of its implementing legislation *all* the subdivisions listed in Annex II to the Directive (thereby excluding in advance from the environmental impact assessment requirement whole classes of projects).[39]

13–50   Whatever the method adopted by a Member State to determine whether or not a specific project needs to be assessed, be it by legislative designation or following an individual examination of the project, the method adopted must not undermine the objective of the Directive, which is that no project likely to have significant effects on the environment, within the meaning of the Directive, should be exempt from assessment, unless the specific project excluded could, on the basis of a comprehensive assessment, be regarded as not being likely to have such effects.[40]

13–51   In *Kraaijeveld*, environmental impact assessment was not required under the relevant Dutch legislation in respect of the construction of a dyke unless the dyke was 5km or more in length, with a cross-section of at least 250 metres squared.[41] The ECJ held that the question whether, in laying down such criteria, the Member State went beyond the limits of its discretion could not be determined in relation to the characteristics of a *single* project. Rather, it depended on an overall assessment of the characteristics of projects of that nature which could be envisaged in the Member State. Thus a Member State which established criteria or thresholds at a level such that, in practice, all projects relating to dykes would be exempted in advance from the requirement of an impact assessment would exceed the limits of its discretion under Art.2(1) and Art.4(2) of the Directive, unless all projects excluded could, when viewed as a whole, be regarded as not being likely to have significant effects on the environment.

---

[36] *Commission v Belgium* (Case C–133/94) [1996] E.C.R. I–2323, [41].
[37] Unless all projects excluded could, when viewed as a whole, be regarded as not being likely to have significant effects on the environment.
[38] *Commission v Germany* (Case C–301/95) [1998] E.C.R. I–6135.
[39] *Commission v Germany* (Case C–301/95) [1998] E.C.R. I–6135.
[40] *World Wildlife Fund v Autonome Provinz Bozen* (Case C–435/97) [1999] E.C.R. I–5613, [45].
[41] *Aannemersbedrijf P.K. Kraaijeveld BV v Gedeputeerde Staten van Zuid-Holland* (Case C–72/95) [1996] E.C.R. I–5403.

In *Commission v Ireland*,[42] the Commission successfully argued that Ireland **13–52** had transposed Art.4(2) incorrectly by setting absolute thresholds for the following Annex II projects: use of uncultivated land or semi-natural areas for intensive agricultural purposes; initial afforestation/land reclamation; and extraction of peat. The ECJ ruled that Ireland had exceeded its discretion, and was in breach of its obligations under the Directive, in establishing criteria or thresholds taking account only of the size of projects, without also taking their nature and location into consideration. The ECJ held that even a small-scale project can have significant effects on the environment if it is in a location where the environmental factors set out in Art.3 of the Directive, such as fauna and flora, soil, water, climate or cultural heritage, are sensitive to the slightest alteration.[43] Similarly, a project was likely to have significant effects where, by reason of its nature, there is a risk that it will cause a substantial or irreversible change in those environmental factors, irrespective of its size. The ECJ also criticised the relevant Irish legislation for its failure to take into account the cumulative effects of projects.[44]

The judgment in *Commission v Ireland* is also of interest insofar as the ECJ **13–53** ruled that, in order to prove that the transposition of a Directive is insufficient or inadequate, it was not necessary to establish the actual effects of the legislation transposing the Directive into national law where it was the wording of the legislation itself which harboured the insufficiencies or defects of transposition.[45] There was, therefore, nothing to prevent the Commission from demonstrating that transposing legislation was *ex facie* defective or insufficient without waiting for the application of the transposing legislation to produce harmful effects. This judgment should be read in light of the more recent judgment in *Commission v United Kingdom*,[46] where it was held that the Commission cannot limit itself to general assertions by, for example, merely pointing out that the information provided shows that the project in question is located in a highly sensitive area, without presenting specific evidence to demonstrate that the national authorities concerned made a manifest error of assessment in their screening decision. The Commission must furnish at least some evidence of the effects that the project is likely to have on the environment.

Similarly the restriction—under Spanish law—of environmental impact **13–54** assessment to Annex II projects affecting special areas of conservation established under the Habitats Directive was considered by the ECJ to have

---

[42] (Case C–392/96) [1999] E.C.R. 5901.
[43] *cf. Howard v Commissioners of Public Works* (High Court) [1994] 1 I.R. 101 at 121, where Costello J. incorrectly suggested—in the context of a development in the Burren, Co. Clare—that the Directive would only apply to "major installations of a very large size". This suggestion is incorrect because it fails to take into account that even small-scale development may have significant effects on the environment where it is located in a sensitive area.
[44] *Commission v Ireland* (Case C–392/96) [1999] E.C.R. 5901, [76].
[45] *ibid.*, [60].
[46] (Case C–508/03); May 4, 2006, [91]. See also *Commission v Portugal* (Case C–117/02) [2004] E.C.R. I-5517.

the impermissible effect of excluding a considerable number of projects, situated outside those areas, which were likely to have significant effects on the environment.[47] The choice of such a criterion, which precluded generally the taking into account of criteria and/or thresholds relating to the size and nature of projects, was held to exceed the limits of the Member States' discretion.

13–55   In *Commission v Spain*,[48] the ECJ confirmed that similar principles continue to apply to the EIA Directive as amended by Directive 97/11/EC. The amended provisions were held to have, in essence, the same scope as that of Art.4(2) of Directive 85/337/EEC in its original version. The amended provisions do not vary the general rule, set out in Art.2(1) of that Directive, that projects likely to have significant effects on the environment, by virtue, *inter alia*, of their nature, size or location, are to be made subject to an assessment of their effects on the environment.

13–56   One theme which emerges from the ECJ case law is that only limited reliance may be placed on thresholds and criteria.[49] Ultimately, any development project which is likely to have significant effects on the environment must be subject to environmental impact assessment. In many of the cases referred to above, a Member State had prescribed absolute thresholds or criteria which had the practical effect of wrongfully excluding certain development projects from assessment. It seems that the safest course is only to employ thresholds and criteria in conjunction with a case-by-case analysis. It is only where thresholds or criteria are set at such a level that *no* development project below that level— irrespective of its location or cumulative impact with other development— could be said to be likely to have significant effects on the environment that it would be safe to dispense with a case-by-case analysis.[50] In practical terms, this probably requires some form of screening as part of the planning application process.

13–57   It is also evident from the case law that the ECJ expects the national courts to take an active role in ensuring that any development project which is likely to have significant effects on the environment is assessed. At the very least, this will involve examining the terms of the national legislation to ensure that

---

[47] *Commission v Spain* (Case C–474/99) [2002] E.C.R. I–5293.

[48] (Case C–121/03), September 8, 2005.

[49] See Advocate General Geelhoeld in *Commission v Spain* (Case C–474/99) [2002] E.C.R. I–5293 for a useful summary of the case law regarding Art.4(2).

[50] See also Lord Hoffmann in *Berkeley v Secretary of State for the Environment* [2001] 2 A.C. 603; (2001) P. & C.R. 492 ("The primary obligation under the Directive, under article 2(1), is for a member state to require an EIA before consent is given in every case in which the project is likely to have significant effects on the environment. But the decision as to whether an Annex II project is likely to have such effects is left to the member state. It depends, as article 4(2) says, on whether the member states 'consider' that the characteristics of the project so require. This must mean that in Annex II cases the member states are under an obligation to consider whether or not an EIA is required. If this were not so, a member state could in practice restrict the scope of the Directive to Annex I cases simply by failing to consider whether in any other case an EIA was required or not.").

thresholds and criteria have not been set at such a level as to wrongfully exclude from assessment some development projects which are likely to have significant effects on the environment. In this regard, it will not be sufficient to address the appropriateness of the threshold or criteria by reference to the characteristics of a *single* project, rather it will be necessary to engage in an overall assessment of the characteristics of projects of that nature which could be envisaged in the Member State.[51] Similarly, the national court will have to consider whether the national legislation protects against project-splitting (sometimes referred to as "salami-slicing"). The cumulative effect of a number of projects—none of which on its own might have a significant effect—might be likely to have significant effects on the environment.[52]

More controversially, national courts are required to consider not just the terms **13–58** of national legislation, but also, on occasion, the terms of a particular screening decision, *i.e.* the national court may be required to review a decision of the relevant competent authority not to subject a particular development project to environmental impact assessment. This follows both from the finding that the Directive has direct effect and from the provisions of Art.10a of the Directive. In *World Wildlife Fund v Autonome Provinz Bozen*,[53] the ECJ reiterated that, whatever the method adopted by a Member State to determine whether or not a specific project needs to be assessed, be it by legislative designation or following an individual examination of the project, the method adopted must not undermine the objective of the Directive.[54]

Bozen had come before the ECJ by way of a preliminary reference from a **13–59** national court. The ECJ indicated in its response that it was for the national court to review whether, on the basis of the individual examination carried out by the competent authorities which resulted in the exclusion of the specific project from assessment, those authorities correctly assessed, in accordance with the Directive, the significance of the effects of that project on the environment.[55] This might be taken as suggesting that the national court had to examine in detail the screening decision. The obvious question which arises is as to how searching any such examination must be. Traditionally the Irish courts have shown a marked reluctance to second-guess decisions of planning authorities or An Bord Pleanála. The content of such decisions is normally only subject to review on unreasonableness or irrationality grounds. It seems to have been suggested in *Waddington v An Bord Pleanála*[56] that a decision on

---

[51] *Aannemersbedrijf P.K. Kraaijeveld BV v Gedeputeerde Staten van Zuid-Holland* (Case C–72/95) [1996] E.C.R. I–5403.

[52] See, for example, *Commission v Ireland* (Case C–392/96) [1999] E.C.R. 5901, [76].

[53] (Case C–435/97) [1999] E.C.R. I–5613.

[54] (Case C–435/97) [1999] E.C.R. I–5613, [45].

[55] See also *Commission of the European Communities v Italian Republic* (Case C–87/02) [2004] E.C.R. I–5975, [49] ("It must be observed that a decision by which the national competent authority takes the view that a project's characteristics do not require it to be subjected to an assessment of its effects on the environment must contain or be accompanied by all the information that makes it possible to check that it is based on adequate screening, carried out in accordance with the requirements of Directive 85/337.").

[56] Unreported, High Court, Butler J., December 21, 2000.

whether sub-threshold development is likely to have significant effects on the environment, *i.e.* a screening decision, was subject to the principles in *O'Keeffe v An Bord Pleanála*. *Quaere* whether such a deferential standard of review is sufficient in light of Art.10a of the Directive. This is discussed in detail at para.13–387 and onwards.

G. Definition of Project

1. Introduction

13–60   The concept of "project" is central to the EIA Directive. It is the effects of the project which are to be considered in deciding whether or not to insist on an environmental impact assessment, and which are to be described in any environmental impact statement. If a particular project is drawn too narrowly, this may give rise to project-splitting.

2. Purposive interpretation

13–61   The ECJ has indicated in *Kraaijeveld* that, in interpreting the various classes of project, the national courts should have regard to the purpose and general scheme of the Directive.[57] This case concerned the interpretation of Annex II, and, in particular, whether the expression "canalization and flood-relief works" in point 10(e) of Annex II was to be interpreted as including certain types of work on a dyke running alongside waterways. The ECJ held that, given the divergence in the various language versions of the Directive, it was necessary to go to the purpose and general scheme of the Directive. The ECJ ruled that the wording of the Directive—in particular, the definition of "project", and the fact that the Directive was aimed at "projects likely to have significant effects on the environment by virtue, *inter alia*, of their nature, size or location"— indicated that it has a wide scope and a broad purpose, and that that observation alone should suffice to interpret point 10(e) of Annex II as encompassing all works for retaining water and preventing floods—and therefore dyke works— even if not all the linguistic versions were so precise.

13–62   In *Commission v Spain*,[58] it was held that point 7 of Annex I to Directive 85/ 337—which referred, among other projects, to construction of "lines for long-distance railway traffic"—must be understood to include the doubling of an already existing railway track.

13–63   The Spanish Government had sought to argue that the Directive was not applicable since the work undertaken merely consisted of improving an already existing railway line by doubling the original single *track*, and did not involve

---

[57] *Aannemersbedrijf P.K. Kraaijeveld BV v Gedeputeerde Staten van Zuid-Holland* (Case C–72/95) [1996] E.C.R. I–5403.
[58] (Case C–227/01) [2004] E.C.R. I– 8253.

constructing a new railway line. The ECJ rejected this argument on the basis that the objective of the Directive would be seriously undermined if the construction of new railway track, albeit parallel to existing track, could be excluded from the obligation to carry out an assessment. A project of that sort could not be considered a mere modification to an earlier project within the meaning of point 12 of Annex II to the Directive. That conclusion was, the ECJ held, all the more obvious when the execution of the project at issue involves a new track route, even if that applies only to part of the project. Such a construction project is by its nature likely to have significant effects on the environment within the meaning of the Directive. As discussed further at para.13–93, *Commission v Spain* also addresses the issue of project-splitting.

The Irish High Court in *Shannon Regional Fisheries Board v An Bord Pleanála*,[59] and in *Maher v An Bord Pleanála*,[60] has endorsed the view that, in interpreting the national legislation implementing the Directive, a purposive approach to the interpretation of the various classes of projects should be adopted. A purposive approach may be contrasted with a literal approach: the principal distinction being that the former approach requires a consideration of the purpose or objective of the legislation. To illustrate by way of example. *Maher v An Bord Pleanála* concerned the interpretation of the term "pig". Under the then national regulations, the relevant threshold for pig-rearing installations was stated in terms of units, with a pig being reckoned as one unit and a sow as ten units. The separate identification of "sows" from "pigs" by the regulations, and the attribution to them of ten units rather than one unit, was a clear acknowledgement that at least some of the sow's progeny must have been taken into account in attributing ten units to its capacity. The question before the High Court was as to whether it was only piglets were to be so reckoned, with weaners and finishers being regarded as individual units in their own right. **13–64**

On a literal interpretation, the term "pig" would cover boars, weaners, finishers and piglets. Kelly J. considered that such a literal approach would not give effect to the real intention of the legislature. Kelly J. stated that, in his view, the resolution of this question was best achieved by resorting to a teleological or purposive approach to interpretation. **13–65**

> "It seems to me that the intention of the regulations in attributing 10 units to a sow was intended to take account of the polluting impact of her litter before weaning. At that time the piglets are dependant on their mother and whilst on a literal construction are pigs, the effluent discharged by them would be of such a quantity as to be captured within the 10 units assigned to the mother. When however they move on from being dependant upon her and are producing an ever greater quantity of effluent as they develop I cannot see any merit in the argument advanced by the Board that they should still be reckoned as falling within the 10 units assigned to the mother. I do not find any sound basis for the

---

[59] [1994] 3 I.R. 449.
[60] [1999] 2 I.L.R.M. 198 at 214.

argument that the units accorded to the sow are intended to account for the environmental impact of that sow and her progeny right up to slaughter."

13–66 Kelly J. concluded that weaners and finishers should have been regarded as pigs in their own right and ought to have been reckoned as attracting one point each.

3. "Project" and "development"

13–67 A "project" is defined under Art.1(2) of the Directive as:

— the execution of construction works or of other installations or schemes;
— other interventions in the natural surroundings and landscape including those involving the extracting of mineral resources.

13–68 The concept of a "project" under EC law is, on a literal view, narrower than the national law concept of "development" under the PDA 2000. In particular, the definition of "project" appears to be directed more to physical works, rather than to uses or processes. Thus, a "project" approximates more closely to development works than to development by way of material change in use or an "activity" licensable under the Environmental Protection Agency Acts 1992 to 2003. It is surprising that the definition of "project" should be so confined, given the fact that in most instances the Annex I and Annex II projects are directed principally to processes, rather than the erection of structures.

13–69 The discrepancy between project and development will have its most serious repercussions in the context of development which involves simply a material change in use, without any development works. One example is where waste is introduced as a fuel in an existing industrial process without there being any necessity for facilitating works to the existing structure or plant. As discussed at paras 2–46 to 2–47, the introduction of waste disposal or waste recovery activities may represent a material change in use such as to trigger a requirement to obtain planning permission. The more difficult question is as to whether a change of use *per se* constitutes a project for the purposes of the Directive. In *R. (On the application of Edwards) v Environment Agency*,[61] the High Court of England and Wales suggested that some physical work has to be done if a scheme is to be a project. The Court of Appeal, conversely, indicated that a "project" was not confined to the construction of undertakings, but would also include the operation of undertakings of various sorts, or changes falling short of a material change of use that may have significant adverse effects on the environment.[62]

13–70 The case concerned the introduction of disused or unsuitable vehicle tyres as a fuel in a cement-making works. Previously the kiln at the works had burned coal and petcoke. The change in fuel did not require any construction works or

---

[61] [2005] E.W.H.C. 657 (Admin); [2005] J.P.L. 1576; [2006] E.W.C.A. Civ. 877; [2007] Env. L.R. 9.
[62] [2006] E.W.C.A. Civ. 877, [38].

installation to be executed. In the High Court, Lindsay J. stated that the reference in the definition of "project" to "other interventions in the natural surroundings and landscape", and the specific inclusion of interventions involving extraction of mineral resources, suggested that some physical work has to be done if a scheme is to be a project. The judge did not consider that a change in the fuel used in the kiln at the works could itself be a "project". Lindsay J. went on to state that if a mere change in the fuel consumed was intended to be a project then one might reasonably expect provisions amplifying what sort of degree of change would be required in order that a project should emerge. The judge then posed a number of rhetorical questions such as whether either a change from part coal, part petcoke to wholly petcoke, or a change from coal and petcoke to oil, would of itself amount to a project, and whether it would be a project if the proportion of one fuel burned to another, where more than one fuel was burned, was changed. His conclusion was that a continuation of existing operations with a change in fuel did not amount to a project.

The Court of Appeal approached the matter slightly differently, placing **13–71** emphasis on the unchallenged finding of fact that the introduction of vehicle tyres as a fuel in the cement-making works would itself have no significant adverse effects on the environment. In the circumstances, the Court of Appeal considered that the proposed change did not come within either of the two sub-categories of project sought to be relied upon. The introduction of the new fuel did not, in the opinion of the Court of Appeal, constitute the cement-making works an installation for the disposal of waste within the meaning of para.11(b) of Annex II. The essential purpose and process of the plant remained that of the manufacture of cement, not the disposal by incineration of waste tyres, which was simply ancillary to that purpose and process.[63]

The Court of Appeal reached a similar conclusion in respect of the argument **13–72** that the requirement for an assessment was triggered under Class 13, Annex II, *i.e.* as a change to or an extension of an existing project which might have significant adverse effects on the environment.

It is unclear as to how an Irish court might resolve the tension between **13–73** development and project in this context. It is submitted that where—as a matter of national law—a change which results in the use of land for the disposal or recovery of waste requires planning permission, then consideration should be given as to whether the proposed change in use is likely to have significant effects on the environment. It is further submitted that, notwithstanding the literal definition of "project", this should be done irrespective of whether the change of use necessitates any facilitating works.

Finally in this regard, it is to be noted that the High Court in *Edwards* emphasised **13–74** the general distinction under EC environmental law as between the "disposal" and "recovery" of waste, and held that the incineration of waste as a fuel (*a*

---

[63] [2006] E.W.C.A. Civ. 877, [48].

fortiori when it is not the only or even the principal fuel) could not properly be regarded as waste disposal for the purposes of the EIA Directive. The Court of Appeal, *per* Auld L.J., did not find it necessary to determine this issue, but did offer the following observations.[64]

> "[…] I do not need to express a concluded view on Mr Elvin's and Mr Pleming's alternative submission that, in any event, paragraph 11(b) of Annex II is not a candidate for reliance upon the EIA Directive because it is concerned with waste recovery, not waste disposal, a distinction which, as I have noted, is drawn elsewhere in EU environmental law, notably and expressly in the Air Framework Directive. However, it may be of assistance to say that, notwithstanding that that Directive, unlike the EIA Directive, provided separately for cement production plants and waste incineration plants, a commonsense as well as purposive interpretation of the latter points in the same direction, subject to the same or similar reasoning exhibited in Gibson and Lowther as to the relationship and relative significance, one with another, of the uses in question."

4. Project and EPA licensing

13–75   The definition of "project" also presents a potential difficulty in the case of developments subject to licensing by the Environmental Protection Agency ("the EPA"). The difficulty arises because the concept of "development consent" is dependent on the definition of "project". As discussed in more detail at paras 13–230 to 13–237, where development is subject to licensing by the EPA, the assessment function is carried out both by the planning bodies and by the EPA. The theory is that, between them, the planning bodies and the EPA will ensure that all aspects of the development are properly assessed. Thus, by the time planning permission and the relevant licence have been granted, the requirements of the Directive will have been met. If, however, a narrow view is taken of what constitutes a "project", *i.e.* if one confines it to physical works, then it is the grant of planning permission *per se* which authorises the development to proceed. If this is correct, then it is the planning permission alone which represents the "development consent". On this analysis, then, it is possible—as a result of there being no restrictions on the sequence on which the respective applications for planning permission and an EPA licence are either made or determined—that planning permission might be granted in advance of the EPA having carried out its part of the assessment function. This would arguably represent a breach of the Directive in that a development consent, *i.e.* planning permission, would have been granted without there having been a full assessment.

13–76   A similar argument had been raised, in the context of the previous legislation, in *Martin v An Bord Pleanála (No. 2)*.[65] The case involved a challenge to a decision to grant planning permission for development consisting of, *inter alia*, a waste incinerator. The impugned decision had been made under the previous legislation, with its strict division of the assessment function between An Bord

---

[64] [2006] E.W.C.A. Civ. 877, [53]; [2007] Env. L.R. 9.
[65] [2007] I.E.S.C. 23; unreported, Supreme Court, May 10, 2007.

Pleanála and the EPA. Under this statutory regime, An Bord Pleanála was precluded from considering matters of "environmental pollution", these matters being within the exclusive remit of the EPA. As of the time An Bord Pleanála made its decision to grant planning permission, the EPA had not yet granted a waste licence. Thus, there had been no assessment of "environmental pollution" prior to the grant of the planning permission.

It was urged on behalf of Mr Martin that the "project" was the construction of the physical structure of the proposed waste incinerator and, further, that as the grant of planning permission authorised construction works, it represented the development consent for the purposes of the Directive. As the decision to grant planning permission had been made without any consideration of "environmental pollution", it was submitted that there had been a clear failure to comply with the requirements of the Directive in that a development consent had been granted on the basis of only a partial assessment.   **13–77**

The Supreme Court rejected these arguments, holding that development consent for the waste incinerator would only be in place when both planning permission and a waste licence had been granted. The two decisions—those of An Bord Pleanála and the Environmental Protection Agency, respectively—were complementary and together represented a single development consent.   **13–78**

> "It seems to me wholly artificial and unreal to seek to divide the development in this case into two, as the appellant seeks to do, thus requiring two development consents. To regard it as two projects would do violence to ordinary language. It is manifestly clear that the project in this case is for a '*waste installation*'. Its consent to proceed depends on planning permission in the first instance and a waste licence in the second instance. In the circumstances I think it would be absurd to consider that planning permission on its own constitutes '*development consent*'."

Murray C.J. expressly distinguished the case from those involving a principal and subsidiary consent.   **13–79**

> "The process which arises under Irish law in the context of this case does not in any sense involve '*a principal decision*' followed by '*an implementing decision which cannot extend beyond the parameters set by the principal decision*'. As a matter of Irish law the decision of An Bord Pleanála could not be characterised as a '*principal decision*' in the sense of the *Wells* decision nor any decision of the EPA on a licence an '*implementing decision*'. On the contrary a refusal to grant a licence by the EPA would mean that there was no consent to the project and it would not proceed. Alternatively, the EPA could impose conditions which reduced substantially the scope or size of the project allowed to proceed. I would also note, as the respondents have pointed out, in any given case concerning a project of this nature a waste licence could be granted before a planning application is decided ... In short, all of the factors referred to in Article 3 of the Directive, and the interaction between them, are examined as required by the Directive and the interaction between them at each stage of the consent process by the relevant competent authority namely the Board and the EPA respectively. The Board carries out an '*integrated assessment*' insofar as the construction of the project is concerned and the EPA carries out an '*integrated assessment*' insofar as the activity stemming from theoperation of the plant is concerned."

743

13–80   The Supreme Court has thus resolved the discord between the definitions of "development" and "project". On a literal reading of the Directive, the planning permission did authorise the execution of construction works, and thus, arguably, was a development consent. Moreover, again on a literal interpretation, there was nothing under national law precluding the commencement of development works as soon as planning permission was granted, notwithstanding that the Annex II use or process, *i.e.* the incineration of waste, itself could not be carried on until such time, if any, as the requisite licence was granted by the EPA. A licence from the EPA is only required in respect of the "activity" (which approximates to user in planning terms) and thus, in principle, a developer is legally entitled to commence to construct the relevant structure (development works) as soon as planning permission is granted, notwithstanding that a licence will have to be in place before the activity itself can start.

13–81   If this literal interpretation had prevailed, it would probably have necessitated a finding that the (then) national legislation failed to implement properly the Directive. Of course, national courts are obliged, in interpreting a provision of national law designed to implement the provisions of a Directive, to interpret national law in the light of the wording and the purpose of the Directive in order to achieve the result envisaged by the Directive.[66] Accordingly, an implied restriction must be read into the planning legislation to the effect that no development works should be commenced until such time as the requisite licence is granted by the EPA.

13–82   An amended scheme for environmental impact assessment has since been introduced under the PDA 2000[67] and, in particular, the rigid division of function as between An Bord Pleanála and the EPA has now been abandoned. See further paras 13–230 to 13–237. The judgment of the Supreme Court in *Martin v An Bord Pleanála (No. 2)* is nonetheless still of relevance. It has particular relevance in the context of multiple consents and this is discussed further at para.13–114 and onwards. Insofar as the concept of "project" is concerned, it suggests that "unauthorised development" may have a special meaning in the context of Directive-projects. In particular, the commencement of construction works in the case of Directive-projects will not be authorised until such time as the relevant EPA licence has been secured.

13–83   The judgment of the Supreme Court is also of relevance in that it confirms the legitimacy of having an assessment carried out by more than one decision-maker. The Supreme Court confirmed that both An Bord Pleanála and the EPA had a function in assessing the proposed development, and that there was nothing in the EIA Directive which precluded such a division of function. In

---

[66] *Nathan v Bailey Gibson Ltd.* [1998] 2 I.R. 162 at 174, *per* Hamilton C.J. See also *O'Connell v Environmental Protection Agency* [2003] 1 I.R. 530 at 555; and *Maher v An Bord Pleanála* [1999] 2 I.L.R.M. 198, where a purposive approach to interpretation was taken in the specific context of the EIA Directive. See also *Arklow Holidays Ltd. v An Bord Pleanála* [2006] I.E.H.C. 15; [2007] 1 I.L.R.M. 125 (legislation to be construed where possible in a manner consistent with EC law).
[67] PDA 2000, ss.256 and 257.

particular, the Supreme Court rejected the suggestion that a division of function offended against the general requirement that the assessment be carried out at the earliest possible stage of the decision-making process, or that the division of function precluded an integrated assessment of the development project.

5. Project-Splitting

It is important that the full extent of a project be properly identified. If a project is identified in a restricted way, this may result in the evasion of the obligation for environmental impact assessment. For example, if what is, in reality, only one project is artificially presented as a series of separate projects it may be that none of these on its own will trigger an environmental impact assessment. This practice is known as "project-splitting" (sometimes also referred to as "salami-slicing"). In other instances, the failure to identify correctly the entire project can result in only a partial assessment. Development at one location may also involve development at another location, for example, the development of a power station might necessitate peat extraction elsewhere. If the assessment process is to be meaningful, both aspects should be examined together. As it happens, the knock-on effect on the other location should have been assessed in any event—as part of the consideration of cumulative effects—even if not identified as part of the project. Unfortunately, this does not always occur in practice and it is for this reason that it is more satisfactory to insist that the entire project is properly delineated from the very outset. **13–84**

In *Dunne v Minister for the Environment Heritage and Local Government (No. 2)*,[68] the extent of the "project" involved in road development was addressed briefly. The Supreme Court suggested that a road project did not necessarily extend to archaeological excavation works carried out pursuant to Ministerial directions. This aspect of the judgment may be open to question. Whereas it is perfectly legitimate to say that the Ministerial directions did not constitute part of the "development consent" for the project—the Minister was not empowered to modify the road development—it may go too far to say that impacts on archaeology were not part of the overall "project". **13–85**

In most cases, the full extent of the project will be readily identifiable. The regulatory authorities should be vigilant, however, so as to ensure that, where separate applications for development consent are made, in quick succession, by the same person or body, a project is not being artificially divided. This is especially so where the use of separate applications results in the individual development consents coming in sub-threshold. **13–86**

The case of *R. (On the application of Candlish) v Hastings Borough Council*[69] involved an allegation of project-splitting. An application was made for planning **13–87**

---

[68] [2006] I.E.S.C. 49; [2007] 1 I.L.R.M. 264.
[69] [2005] E.W.H.C. 1539 (Admin); [2006] J.P.L. 22.

permission for certain infrastructural works (a spine road and associated mini-roundabout, and surface water attenuation works). The application itself indicated that it represented the first of two intended applications, the second application to be for development consisting of, *inter alia*, residential development. It was argued that the first application should have been subject to environmental impact assessment, and that the "project" consisted not just of the infrastructural works, but rather also included the proposed residential development.

13–88   The High Court of England and Wales rejected this argument, holding that the relevant assessment of whether a development is likely to have significant effects on the environment, *i.e.* the screening decision, was to be made by reference to the application for planning permission made. The court considered that, if it were otherwise, there could be difficulties in any given case in assessing just what project might be involved or, even if there was some wider project in mind, just what form it might take. With respect, whereas such difficulties might well arise on occasion, the particular facts of the case were straightforward and the development was clearly intended as part of a wider project. It seems therefore that the cumulative effect should have been considered as part of the screening decision. Reference is made in this regard to *BAA plc v Secretary of State for Transport, Local Government and the Regions*.[70] The High Court of England and Wales held that two separate applications in respect of the construction of a link development were part of a single development and hence the combined effect of both should have been considered when deciding whether or not an environmental impact assessment should have been carried out. Turner J. cited with approval the passage in *R. v Swale Borough Council Ex p. Royal Society for the Protection of Birds*[71] to the effect that a proposal should not be considered in isolation if, in reality, it should properly be regarded as an integral part of an inevitably more substantial development.

13–89   In *Arklow Holidays Ltd. v An Bord Pleanála*,[72] Clarke J. granted leave to apply for judicial review on the ground, *inter alia*, that An Bord Pleanála may have erred in failing to assess certain aspects of the proposed development. The project consisted of a wastewater treatment plant. The inspector, and by inference An Bord Pleanála, appear to have taken the view that it was unnecessary to assess the impact of those aspects of the development outside the wastewater treatment plant itself. Clarke J. held that it was arguable, for the purposes of a leave application, that aspects of a project, which themselves might not have impacts which would be significant, when taken on a cumulative basis and added to the impacts of other aspects of the same project might have significant environmental effects.

---

[70] [2003] J.P.L. 610.
[71] [1991] J.P.L. 39. As the reporter notes, other aspects of this judgment must now be viewed with suspicion: [2003] J.P.L. 610 at 628.
[72] [2006] I.E.H.C. 15; [2007] 1 I.L.R.M. 125.

Theoretical difficulties are presented by some types of infrastructural **13–90** development. In particular, it can be difficult to say what defines the start and end points for major road projects. For logistical reasons, such development is often carried out as a series of separate steps, occasionally by different bodies. For example, individual roads authorities are often responsible for so much of a national or regional road project as is within their functional area. Different budgetary considerations and timescales may apply to these individual sections, notwithstanding the fact that same will ultimately form part of the one regional or national road project.

This issue was considered briefly by Advocate General Gulmann in *Bund* **13–91** *Naturschutz in Bayern BV v Freistaat Bayern*.[73] The Advocate General agreed with a submission that it was not possible to interpret the Directive to the effect that it makes an environmental impact assessment mandatory for anything other than the *specific* projects submitted by developers to the competent authorities in order to obtain authorisation, even if the actual application related to only one part of a longer road link which was to be constructed in stages. The Advocate General went on to suggest that it must be self-evident that the Directive cannot indirectly have the effect of forcing the Member States to depart from the normal practice according to which long road links are executed by constructing sections over staggered periods.[74] The Advocate General also noted that difficulties could arise in laying down what comprises an "entire project" when that concept is not the same as "a specific project in respect of which an application has been submitted".

Strictly speaking, the above comments were *obiter* in that the ECJ ultimately **13–92** decided the case on other grounds. However, the approach suggested by the Advocate General, which concentrates on the extent of the development consent being sought, may well find favour with the Irish courts. In *O'Connell v O'Connell*,[75] Finnegan J. (as he then was) indicated that an inspector conducting an oral hearing was confined to an inquiry into matters relating to the scheme the subject-matter of the application for approval. The inspector was not required to inquire into the impacts of a possible further extension of the road, which extension would itself be the subject-matter of a separate inquiry. It should be emphasised that the decision in *O'Connell* was given in the context of a procedural application to amend pleadings only (as opposed to on a full hearing). It was, however, cited with approval by Kearns J. in *Sloan v An Bord Pleanála*.[76]

In *Commission v Spain*,[77] the ECJ rejected an argument that the construction **13–93** of a 13.2km section of railway between two neighbouring towns did not relate

---

[73] [1994] E.C.R. I–3717.
[74] [1994] E.C.R. I–3717, [69].
[75] Unreported, High Court, Finnegan J., March 29, 2001. See also *R. (On the application of Candlish) v Hastings Borough Council* [2005] E.W.H.C. 1539 (Admin); [2006] J.P.L. 22 (relevant assessment is to be made by reference to the application for planning permission).
[76] [2003] 2 I.L.R.M. 61.
[77] (Case C–227/01) [2004] E.C.R. I–8253.

to "long-distance railway traffic". The ECJ identified the project in question as being part of a 251km long railway line between Valencia and Tarragona, which formed part of the project known as "the Mediterranean corridor", linking the Spanish region of Levante to Catalonia and the French border. The ECJ added that if the argument of the Spanish Government to the contrary were upheld, the effectiveness of the Directive could be seriously compromised, since the national authorities concerned would need only to split up a long-distance project into successive shorter sections in order to exclude from the requirements of the Directive both the project as a whole and the sections resulting from that division.

13–94   In conclusion, it is submitted that it is legitimate to seek a series of development consents where major road development is involved, and for there to be a series of separate environmental impact assessments in this regard.[78] Of course, each individual environmental impact statement would have to include some information on the cumulative effect of the project with other projects. The mischief of project-splitting really only arises where development is carved up in such a way as to avoid *any* requirement for environmental impact assessment; for example, application might be made for a series of sub-threshold development consents. Provided that all of the road development is ultimately subject to environmental impact assessment, it is submitted that it is appropriate to present a series of separate applications for development consent. To seek to deal with road development by way of a single environmental impact assessment would be unwieldy, and, indeed, might undermine public participation in the process because it would be difficult for individuals—in the context of an omnibus environmental impact statement—to readily identify the information relevant to their area. Moreover, it must follow, almost by definition, that an assessment purporting to cover a very lengthy road route would contain so many imponderables and contingencies as to undermine the usefulness of the exercise.

6. Quarries

13–95   A practical issue arises as to the application of the concept of a "project" to quarries. The excavation of many quarries will have commenced prior to the coming into force and effect of the Directive in July 1988. Such quarries might be regarded as "pipeline" projects and, as such, not subject to assessment. Indeed, in the case of some quarries the initial excavation may even predate the introduction of the requirement to obtain planning permission in its modern form: the commencement date for the Local Government (Planning & Development) Act 1963 was October 1, 1964. Of course, the mere fact that limited quarrying activities commenced before a particular date cannot mean that the quarry activities can be extended indefinitely, without the necessity for

---

[78] See also, Y. Scannell, *Environmental and Land Use Law* (Thomson Round Hall, Dublin, 2006), paras 5–61 to 5–64.

planning permission. Clearly some limit has to be imposed, and the question which arises, therefore, is as to what area of lands should be regarded as being encompassed in the original quarry. In this regard, it is to be noted that quarry projects are prescribed under Annex I of the Directive where the surface area exceeds 25 hectares. The gradual extension of an established quarry might well result in the quarry ultimately exceeding this threshold, and it would undermine the objective of the Directive if same were to escape assessment simply on the basis that the initial excavation commenced prior to October 1964.

A similar issue arose in the context of the concept of established use under the previous planning legislation. Reference is made in this regard to the judgment of the Supreme Court in *Waterford County Council v John A. Wood Ltd.*[79] The case concerned the correct interpretation of s.24 of the Local Government (Planning & Development) Act 1963, which had provided that planning permission would not be required in respect of development which had commenced before the appointed day, *i.e.* October 1, 1964, the date on which the statutory requirement to obtain planning permission in its modern form was introduced. **13–96**

The Supreme Court indicated that the benefit of the exclusion from the requirement to obtain planning permission necessarily permitted the *continuation* of excavation works, even where this involved a material change in the user of adjoining ground. The Supreme Court, *per* Murphy J., suggested that had the planning legislation not contained a provision so as to exclude existing uses and works from the requirement to obtain planning permission "serious and perhaps unconstitutional injustice might have been imposed upon those who had invested time, money and resources in such developments". **13–97**

The right to continue works commenced before the appointed day did not, however, give to the developer an unrestricted right to engage in activities of the nature commenced before the relevant date. Rather, the relevant section merely permitted the continuation to completion of the particular works commenced before the appointed day at an identified location. It is a question of fact and degree as to what was or might reasonably have been anticipated in October 1964 as having been involved in the works then taking place. Relevant factors would include the extent of any land acquisitions as of that date, and the extent of the ore body. If work had commenced on the extraction of ore from a small ore body, the fullest extent of the rights preserved would be the extraction of that ore body; it could not be argued successfully that work on a different ore body had been commenced prior to October 1964. **13–98**

It might be argued that similar principles should apply in the case of extraction works commenced prior to the coming into force of the EIA Directive, and **13–99**

---

[79] [1999] 1 I.R. 556.

that quarry projects commenced prior to July 1988 should be allowed to extend without the necessity for assessment. Certainly, there are some parallels between the reasoning of the Supreme Court in *Waterford County Council v John A. Wood Ltd.* and that of the ECJ in *Commission v Germany.*[80] The ECJ, in ruling that the requirements of the Directive did not apply where the application for consent was formally lodged *before* July 3, 1988, emphasised the fact that as the Directive is primarily designed to cover large-scale projects, which will most often require a long time to complete, it would not be appropriate to make the procedure more cumbersome and time-consuming by applying the requirements of the Directive to consent procedures which were formally initiated prior to the date of the expiry of the period for transposing the Directive.[81]

13–100 Having said this, however, the better view is that the test for deciding whether a particular quarry project is caught by the Directive will be much more stringent than that governing whether the quarry can properly be regarded as an established pre-1964 development. The objectives of the Directive would be undermined if quarry projects were allowed to extend without assessment simply because the initial quarrying activity commenced at a date prior to July 1988. For this reason, then, the scope or area of the initial quarry project is likely to be interpreted narrowly, with an assessment required in respect of any extension. This result might be achieved either by taking a purposive approach to the interpretation of a quarry project, or by holding that an extension of a "pipeline" quarry project is caught in any event under Class 13 of Annex II, *i.e.* as a change or extension of a project already authorised, executed or in the process of being executed which may have adverse effects on the environment.

13–101 Finally, it should be noted that special controls have been introduced under national law in respect of quarries and these are discussed in detail at paras 8–118 to 8–175.

H. Modifications and Extensions of Projects

1. General

13–102 Class 22 of Annex I applies to any change or extension of projects listed in that annex where such a change or extension in itself meets the thresholds, if any, set out in that annex.[82] Class 13 of Annex II applies to any change or extension of projects listed in Annex I or Annex II, already authorised, executed or in the process of being executed, which may have significant adverse effects

---

[80] (Case C–431/92) [1995] E.C.R. I–2189, [32]. See also *Burgemeester en wethouders van Haarlemmerliede en Spaarnwoude v Gedeputeerde Staten van Noord-Holland* (Case C–81/96) [1998] E.C.R. I–3923, [23].
[81] *Burgemeester* (Case C–81/96) [1998] E.C.R. I–3923, [24].
[82] Added by Directive 2003/35/EC, Art.8.

on the environment (change or extension not included in Annex I).[83] Class 13 also applies to projects in Annex I undertaken exclusively or mainly for the development and testing of new methods or products and not used for more than two years.

Class 13 of Annex II has been implemented at para.13 of Pt 2 of Sch.5 of the **13–103** Planning and Development Regulations 2001. A gloss has been introduced, however, in that—rather than refer to "significant adverse effects on the environment"—a form of threshold is introduced, where the change or extension results in an increase in size greater than either 25 per cent or an amount equal to 50 per cent of the appropriate threshold.

2. Planning and Development (Strategic Infrastructure) Act 2006

A procedure whereby existing planning permissions may be amended has been **13–104** introduced under the Planning and Development (Strategic Infrastructure) Act 2006. This is discussed in detail at paras 10–108 to 10–116.

I. Development Consent

1. General

Development of the type subject to environmental impact assessment will often **13–105** require other permits and licences in addition to planning permission. In many instances a licence will be required from the Environmental Protection Agency. Occasionally, licences or permits may also be required, for example, under the national monuments legislation. Even in the context of a planning permission, it may be necessary to seek the further agreement of the planning authority pursuant to conditions attached to the planning permission.[84]

The question arises as to which, if any, of these various permits or licences **13–106** constitute "development consents" for the purposes of the Directive. The question is not just of academic interest; it assumes a real significance in at least two circumstances, as follows. First, where two or more decisions together constitute a development consent, any deficiencies in the assessment, at the earlier stage, of the environmental impacts may have to be remedied before the final decision is given.[85] This may be so even where the national legislation intended the formal environmental impact assessment to be carried out at the

---

[83] Words in parentheses added by Directive 2003/35/EC, Art.9.
[84] cf. *O'Connor v Dublin Corporation*, unreported, High Court, O'Neill J., October 3, 2000 (at 43), where the High Court held that the compliance procedure did not constitute a "development consent" as it merely involved the implementation of a condition attached to the planning permission.
[85] *R. (On the application of Barker) v London Borough of Bromley* (Case C–290/03); May 4, 2006, [49].

earlier stage. See para.13–293 and onwards. Secondly, where planning permission does not itself constitute the full development consent, it may be that no steps can be taken to implement a planning permission until all components of the development consent are in place. See para.13–82.

13–107   "Development consent" is defined for the purposes of the Directive as "the decision of the competent authority or authorities which entitles the developer to proceed with the project".

13–108   On a literal reading, the definition suggests some sort of "but for" test. If a development project cannot proceed without a particular permit or licence, then that permit or licence must be part of the "development consent": the development could not proceed but for the permit or licence. The difficulty with such a test is that it might result in permits or licences unrelated to the environmental impacts of the development being categorised as part of the development consent. As discussed further below, the definition of "development consent" must therefore be read subject to the qualification that the particular permit or licence must regulate environmental matters.

13–109   The leading Irish judgment is that of the Supreme Court in *Dunne v Minister for the Environment Heritage and Local Government (No. 2)*.[86] The case concerned a road development being carried out at Carrickmines. The road development was authorised pursuant to approvals granted under the Roads Acts 1993 to 1998. Some years after those approvals had been granted, an issue arose as to whether an additional consent might be required pursuant to the national monuments legislation. This question was itself the subject of earlier litigation,[87] and, ultimately, the national monuments legislation was amended with the result that what was now required were Ministerial directions. The question before the Supreme Court in *Dunne (No. 2)* was as to whether the Ministerial directions constituted part of the development consent for the road development, so as to attract the requirement for environmental impact assessment.

13–110   The Supreme Court held that Ministerial directions regulating archaeological works did not form part of the development consent for a road development. Rather, there was a single development consent, the statutory approval under the Roads Acts, and the subsequent Ministerial directions merely involved the regulation of activities for which the principal consent, raising the substantial environmental issues, had already been given.

> "The Court is satisfied for the following reasons that the Ministerial directions under s. 8 do not fulfil any of the requirements necessary to constitute a *'development consent'*:—
> (a)   Firstly, the Minister does not have power under s. 8 to embark upon a

---

[86] [2006] I.E.S.C. 49; [2007] 1 I.L.R.M. 264.
[87] *Dunne v Minister for the Environment Heritage and Local Government (No. 1)* [2003] 1 I.R. 567.

reconsideration of the environmental issues arising for the road development, and, more importantly, does not have power to modify the road development. All that is left for the Minister is a power to regulate the manner in which the works which are necessary to allow the road to proceed are carried out.

(b) Secondly, the project is prescribed for the purposes of the environmental impact assessment Directive as the road development, the subject matter of the 1998 consent. Excavation works of the type the subject matter of the Ministerial directions under s. 8 are not a prescribed project."

It seems to follow from the Supreme Court judgment that in order to constitute a "development consent" the relevant decision must allow for the consideration of, and regulation of, environmental impacts. **13–111**

In analysing a series of consents, therefore, it seems that a "but for" test cannot be conclusive. In other words, the mere fact that development cannot be completed without a particular consent cannot, without more, mean that that consent must be a development consent. Thus, for example, a fire safety certificate, even if a prerequisite to the carrying on of a particular activity, would not constitute a "development consent". The test is more sophisticated. The question to be asked is the extent to which, in reaching the decision on whether or not to grant the consent, the decision-maker is entitled to take into account environmental impacts. Where environmental impacts are to be taken into account in any particular decision-making process, the resulting consent probably constitutes development consent. **13–112**

Critics might argue that the above analysis is flawed in that it is based on a circular argument. The relevance of whether a particular decision is part of a multi-stage development consent is that if it is, then the relevant decision-maker is required to address his or her mind to environmental impacts. There is an element of begging the question if the test to be employed in determining whether a particular decision is a development consent is whether the decision-maker is entitled to take into account environmental impacts. As discussed immediately below, it is precisely this sort of dubious reasoning that produced a sharp contrast in the respective approaches of the House of Lords and the ECJ to the question of whether the approval of reserved matters subsequent to outline planning permission constituted development consent. **13–113**

2. Principal and ancillary decisions

The initial approach of the courts of England and Wales had been to seek to impose a further qualification on the definition of "development consent", and to exclude what were described as ancillary or implementing decisions. The Directive, or so it was suggested, did not apply to decisions which involved merely the detailed regulation of activities for which the principal consent, raising the substantial environmental issues, has already been given.[88] Thus, the Court of Appeal suggested—incorrectly as it transpires—that the approval **13–114**

---

[88] *R. v North Yorkshire County Council Ex p. Brown* [2000] 1 A.C. 397.

of reserved matters pursuant to an outline planning permission was not part of the development consent.[89]

13–115 This case law will have to be reassessed now in light of recent judgments by the ECJ.[90] Whereas the ECJ does recognise a distinction between principal or ancillary decisions, its view of the consequences of this distinction is vastly different. The ECJ—while accepting that it will generally be appropriate to carry out the environmental impact assessment at the stage of the principal consent—regards even an ancillary decision as forming part of the development consent.

13–116 The leading judgment of the ECJ is that in *R. (On the application of Wells) v Secretary of State for Transport, Local Government and the Regions.*[91] The factual background to *Wells* involved an old mineral planning permission. Under the relevant national legislation, an application had to be made to register such planning permissions. In the case of a dormant planning permission, an application had to be made to have the conditions, to which the resumption of quarrying activities was to be subject, determined.

13–117 The initial planning permission in *Wells* had been granted at a time far in advance of the EIA Directive. The questions referred by the national court to the ECJ concerned the requirement, if any, to carry out an assessment either on the occasion of the approval of a new scheme of conditions, or, following such approval, the approval of further matters required under the new scheme of conditions.

13–118 As a preliminary point, the ECJ ruled that the term "development consent" should be given an autonomous and uniform interpretation throughout the Community, which interpretation should take into account the context of the provision and the purpose of the Directive. Accordingly, the interpretation of the meaning and scope of "development consent" was a matter of Community, not national, law.[92]

13–119 The ECJ drew a distinction between two different types of consent which might arise where national law provided for the consent procedure to be carried out in several stages, namely, principal decisions and implementing decisions. An implementing decision was described in terms of a decision which cannot extend beyond the parameters set by the principal decision. The ECJ indicated that,

---

[89] *R. (On the application of Barker) v London Borough of Bromley* [2001] E.W.C.A. Civ. 1766.
[90] *R. (On the application of Wells) v Secretary of State for Transport, Local Government and the Regions* (Case C–201/02); [2004] E.C.R. I–723; and *Commission v United Kingdom* (Case C–508/03); May 4, 2006. See, generally, G. Simons, "Development Consents and the EIA directive" (2006) 12 *Bar Review* 129.
[91] (Case C–201/02) [2004] E.C.R. I–723.
[92] See also *R. (On the application of Barker) v London Borough of Bromley* (Case C–290/03); May 4, 2006, [40]–[41].

generally, the effects which the project may have on the environment must be identified and assessed at the time of the procedure relating to the principal decision. The ECJ went on, however, to state an exception: where the effects are not identifiable until the time of the procedure relating to the implementing decision, then the assessment should be carried out in the course of that procedure. The ramifications of this are discussed at para.13–293 and onwards.

The ECJ concluded that the approval of a new scheme of conditions, and, following such approval, the approval of further matters required under the new scheme of conditions, constituted development consents, and hence environmental impact assessment was required.[93]   **13–120**

> "Without new decisions such as those referred to in the previous paragraph, there would no longer have been 'consent', within the meaning of art 2(1) of Directive 85/337, to work the quarry.
>
> It would undermine the effectiveness of that directive to regard as mere modification of an existing 'consent' the adoption of decisions which, in circumstances such as those of the main proceedings, replace not only the terms but the very substance of a prior consent, such as the old mining permission.
>
> Accordingly, decisions such as the decision determining new conditions and the decision approving matters reserved by the new conditions for the working of Conygar Quarry must be considered to constitute, as a whole, a new 'consent' within the meaning of Article 2(1) of the directive, read in conjunction with Article 1(2) thereof."

The ECJ regarded the decision determining new conditions and the decision approving matters reserved by the new conditions as representing principal consents. With respect, this must be correct: it would have been artificial to suggest—in circumstances where the previous planning permission would have lapsed but for the application for registration and the determination of the new conditions, and where the very substance of the old planning permission was replaced—that the more recent decisions were merely ancillary to the old planning permission. A similar conclusion had been reached earlier by the House of Lords in *R. v North Yorkshire County Council Ex p. Brown*.[94] Where the House of Lords and the ECJ parted company, however, was in their analysis of how the Directive applied to ancillary or implementing decisions.   **13–121**

Brown—like *Wells*—concerned old mining planning permissions. Again, the initial planning permission had been obtained at a time well in advance of the Directive. The local authority was of the view that this earlier permission represented the development consent, and that there was, therefore, no requirement to carry out a formal environmental impact assessment at the time of the subsequent application for registration. The local authority determined the conditions to be imposed on the continued operation of the mine without an environmental impact assessment. This determination was challenged by a local objector.   **13–122**

---

[93] (Case C–201/02); [2004] E.C.R. I–723, [45]–[47].
[94] [2000] 1 A.C. 397.

13–123   The House of Lords, *per* Lord Hoffmann, considered that the purpose of the procedure applicable under national law to old mining planning permissions was to give the relevant planning authority a power to assess the likely environmental effects of such permissions which had been granted without, to modern ways of thinking, any serious consideration of the environment at all. Notwithstanding that the power to deal with these effects was limited to the imposition of conditions, rather than complete prohibition, the procedure was nevertheless a "new and freestanding examination" of the environmental issues. It was therefore a "development consent" within the meaning of the Directive.

> "Can it therefore be said that the decision imposing the conditions is a 'decision of the competent authority or authorities which entitles the developer to proceed with the project' - the definition of a 'development consent' in the Directive? The imposition of conditions is not a decision *that* the developer shall be entitled to proceed. Mr. Straker, who appeared for the authority, was quite right in saying that the source of the developer's right to proceed with the project was and remained the planning permission of 1947, even after conditions had been imposed. Section 22(2) expressly says that the effect of the registration of conditions is that the old mining permission has effect as if granted subject to the conditions. On the other hand, the developer cannot proceed unless the planning authority has determined (or is deemed to have determined: paragraph 2(6)(b)) the appropriate conditions. So that although the determination does not decide *whether* the developer may proceed but only the manner in which he may proceed, it is nevertheless a necessary condition for his being entitled to proceed at all.
>
> Is this sufficient to bring it within the European concept of a development consent? I think it is. The purpose of the Directive, as I have said, is to ensure that planning decisions which may affect the environment are made on the basis of full information. In *Aannemersbedrijf P.K. Kraaijeveld BV v. Gedeputeerde Staten van Zuid-Holland* (Case I-72/95) [1996] E.C.R. I-5403, 5444, para. 31 the European Court of Justice said that 'the wording of the Directive indicates that it has a wide scope and a broad purpose.' A decision as to the conditions under which a quarry may be operated may have a very important effect on the environment. It can protect it by imposing limits on noise, vibration and dust, requiring the preservation of important natural habitats or the reinstatement of damage to the landscape and in many other ways. Without such conditions, the unrestricted operation of the quarry might well have a significant effect on the environment. It cannot therefore be said that the environmental effect of the quarry was determined once and for all in 1947. One of the purposes of the Act of 1991 was to allow mineral planning authorities to assess those effects in the light of modern conditions."

13–124   During the course of his speech, Lord Hoffmann distinguished between principal and subsidiary consents, suggesting that the Directive does not apply to decisions which involve merely the detailed regulation of activities for which the principal consent, raising the substantial environmental issues, had already been given.

13–125   This suggestion will have to be reconsidered in light of the subsequent case law of the ECJ, in particular the judgment in *Wells*. The ECJ is of the view that an ancillary or implementing decision represents a stage of a multi-stage development consent, but that the effects which the project may have on the environment must be identified and assessed at the time of the procedure relating to the principal decision.[95] It is only if those effects are not identifiable until the time of the procedure relating to the implementing decision that the assessment should be carried out in the course of that procedure.[96]

The divergence between the approach adopted by the House of Lords in *Brown* **13–126** and that of the ECJ is not merely semantic. Although both approaches indicate that the environmental impact assessment should generally be carried out at the time of the principal consent, the ECJ's analysis makes contingency for a deficient assessment at that stage, by requiring that a proper assessment be carried out where necessary at the time of the second decision. Conversely, on the House of Lords' analysis, the ancillary or implementing decision is not subject to the Directive at all, and thus the possibility of a remedial assessment at that stage is not contemplated. It was the absence of such a possibility that led the ECJ to rule that the outline planning permission/approval of reserved matters procedure was inconsistent with the requirements of the Directive in *Commission v United Kingdom*.[97]

The judgment in *Commission v United Kingdom* concerned the application of **13–127** the concept of "development consent" to outline planning permission. Under the then English legislation, outline planning permission could be granted subject to a requirement to obtain the subsequent approval of reserved matters. (Unlike the position under Irish law, it was possible to apply for outline planning permission in respect of development projects subject to the Directive.)[98] In the case of such development, any environmental impact assessment was to be carried out at the time of the application for the outline planning permission. Screening of sub-threshold development was similarly to be performed at the time of the initial application.

The ECJ held that the two decisions together constituted a multi-stage **13–128** development consent, and, further, considered that the failure to provide for the possibility of assessment at the stage of the approval of reserved matters meant that the legislative scheme was not consistent with the requirements of the Directive.[99] The fact that the development project could not proceed "but for" the approval of the reserved matters was sufficient to constitute same as part of the development consent.

> "In the present case, it is common ground that, under national law, a developer cannot commence works in implementation of his project until he has obtained reserved matters approval. Until such approval has been granted, the development in question is still not (entirely) authorised.

[95] *R. (On the application of Wells) v Secretary of State for Transport, Local Government and the Regions* (Case C–201/02); [2004] E.C.R. I–723, [52].
[96] *ibid.*
[97] (Case C–508/03) May 4, 2006.
[98] Planning and Development Regulations 2001, art.96.
[99] (Case C–508/03); May 4, 2006, [101]–[102]; [2007] Env. L.R. 1.

Therefore, the two decisions provided for by the rules at issue in the present case, namely outline planning permission and the decision approving reserved matters, must be considered to constitute, as a whole, a (multi-stage) 'development consent' within the meaning of Article 1(2) of Directive 85/337, as amended."

3. Decision not to take enforcement action

13–129   In *R. (On the application of Prokopp) v London Underground Ltd.*,[100] the Court of Appeal concluded that the failure to take enforcement action against development being carried out pursuant to an expired planning permission did not represent a "development consent". In reaching their conclusion, the members of the Court of Appeal gave considerable weight to factors such as (i) the absence of any formal application for any consent; (ii) the fact that the environmental impact of the development had been assessed at the time of the grant of the planning permission; and (iii) the fact that the planning authorities remained entitled to serve enforcement notices should they so wish and they had not promised not to do so in the future.

13–130   Buxton L.J. stated that the fact that, by a rule of the domestic law of a particular Member State, further permission is required in the course of a project, though for reasons unconnected with its environmental impact, does not mean that the granting of such permission must be treated as a "development consent". Buxton L.J. then went on to suggest that it was even less likely that a failure to interrupt a project—as opposed to a formal permission in the course of the project—would constitute a development consent. The failure to take enforcement action did not entitle the developer to proceed, but merely left him to proceed at his peril.

13–131   It is important to note that the Court of Appeal, *per* Schiemann L.J., accepted for the purposes of the case that if a project which falls within the Directive went ahead without there having been an environmental impact assessment and the national authorities simply stand by and do nothing, then this might well amount to a breach of the obligations under the Directive.

J. Local Authority and State Authority Development

1. Local authority development

13–132   The requirement to carry out an environmental impact assessment is not confined to private-sector development, but also applies to development by a local authority or by a State authority. Generally, local authority development in its own functional area is exempted development and does not require planning permission. The EIA Directive thus has added significance in the context of such development in that in many cases this development might

---

[100] [2003] E.W.C.A. Civ. 961; [2004] J.P.L. 44.

otherwise be free from any requirement for public consultation, or for any independent approval. In the case of local authority development, the assessment is performed by An Bord Pleanála under s.176 of the PDA 2000 (as amended by the 2006 Act). Certain aspects of the procedure are broadly similar to those governing an application for planning permission. Thus, provision is made for the submission of an environmental impact statement; public participation (including the possibility of an oral hearing); the consideration of the adequacy of the environmental impact statement; the considerations to be taken into account by An Bord Pleanála; and the form of the decision.[101] These requirements are discussed in detail at paras 8–316 to 8–348.

2. State authority development

As discussed at para.8–357, certain specified classes of State authority development are excepted from the requirement to obtain planning permission. Prior to the Planning and Development (Strategic Infrastructure) Act 2006, no provision was made under the planning legislation for the carrying out of an environmental impact assessment in respect of such State authority development. This represented a possible lacuna in the transposition of the EIA Directive.

13–133

The classes of State authority development prescribed included development of a type which might come within Annex I or Annex II of the Directive. For example, "premises or installations (including airfields and naval yards)" used for the purposes of, or in connection with, the operations of the Defence Forces should trigger assessment if an airport with a basic runway length of 2,100 metres or more is involved. More radically, it might be argued that the construction of a significant public building such as a courthouse might constitute an "urban development" project. This is not as far-fetched as it first might sound, when one considers that the High Court in *Ó Nualláin v Dublin Corporation* ruled that a monument on O'Connell Street constituted an urban development project.[102]

13–134

As discussed at paras 8–368 to 8–392 provision has now been made for the assessment of such State authority development.

13–135

There is provision made under Art.1(4) of the Directive for Member States to decide, on a case-by-case basis if so provided by national law, not to apply the Directive to projects serving national defence purposes, if they deem that such application would have an adverse effect on those purposes. The ECJ has ruled in *Bozen* that, as Art.1(4) introduces an exception to the general rule that environmental effects are to be assessed in advance, it must accordingly be

13–136

---

[101] PDA 2000, s.175 (as amended by the Planning and Development (Strategic Infrastructure) Act 2006).
[102] [1999] 4 I.R. 137 at 148.

interpreted restrictively.[103] Only projects which mainly serve national defence purposes may therefore be excluded from the assessment obligation. The exception was held not to cover the project at issue in the national proceedings in *Bozen*: the principal objective of restructuring the airport was in order for it to be capable of commercial use, even though it might also be used for military purposes.

K. Triggering Environmental Impact Assessment

1. Screening

13–137 The requirement for environmental impact assessment has been grafted onto the conventional planning application procedure.[104] The first step involves the planning authority addressing its mind to whether the proposed development should be subject to environmental impact assessment ("screening").

13–138 A planning authority has—under art.103 of the Planning and Development Regulations 2001 (as amended in 2006)—a power to require the submission of an environmental impact statement where a planning application has not been accompanied by one. Assessment will be mandatory in the case of Annex I projects. In the case of sub-threshold Annex II projects, the planning authority is required to consider whether the proposed development is likely to have significant effects on the environment. In deciding whether a proposed development would or would not be likely to have significant effects on the environment, a planning authority is to have regard to the criteria set out in Sch.7 of the Planning and Development Regulations 2001.

13–139 Under art.103 of the Planning and Development Regulations 2001 (as amended under the 2006 Regulations), a planning authority is under an *express* duty to "decide" whether sub-threshold development would be likely to have significant effects on the environment in the case of European sites and land subject to specified designations under the Wildlife (Amendment) Act 2000.[105] In all other cases, an environmental impact statement is to be required where the planning authority "considers" that the development would be likely to have significant effects on the environment. Presumably, this carries with it an *implied* duty to address its mind to, and reach a conclusion on, this question.[106]

13–140 It is not at all clear why an *express* obligation to consider the question of whether sub-threshold development would be likely to have significant effects was not imposed in all cases.

---

[103] *World Wildlife Fund v Autonome Provinz Bozen* (Case C–435/97) [1999] E.C.R. I–5613.
[104] See, generally, PDA 2000, s.172, and Planning and Development Regulations 2001, Pt 10.
[105] Planning and Development Regulations 2001, art.103(2).
[106] See, by analogy, *Berkeley v Secretary of State for the Environment* [2001] 2 A.C. 603; (2001) P. & C.R. 492.

In all cases the planning authority's decision, including the main reasons and **13–141** considerations on which it is based, must be placed and kept with the documents relating to the planning application.[107]

These obligations stem from Art.4(4) of the Directive, which requires that **13–142** screening determinations made by the competent authorities be made available to the public. The ECJ in *Commission v Italian Republic*[108] held that a decision by which the national competent authority takes the view that a project's characteristics do not require it to be subjected to an assessment must contain or be accompanied by all the information that makes it possible to check that it is based on adequate screening, carried out in accordance with the requirements of the Directive.

It is submitted that insofar as the High Court of England and Wales has suggested **13–143** that it is sufficient for the decision-maker to state that it is satisfied that the proposed development is unlikely to cause significant effects on the environment, without the necessity of giving further reasons, its judgment is inconsistent with the requirements of the Directive.[109]

An Bord Pleanála, in exercising its appellate jurisdiction, is under obligations **13–144** similar to those of the planning authorities to consider whether to call for an environmental impact statement.[110]

2. Can mitigation measures be taken into account?

Ordinarily the decision-maker must call for an environmental impact statement **13–145** in the case of sub-threshold development where it is of the view that the proposed development is likely to have significant effects on the environment. In a borderline case, however, the decision-maker might be prepared to forgo the requirement for an environmental impact statement provided that some safeguard (in the form of a planning condition) was put in place to cover the contingency that the development did, in fact, give rise to some unanticipated impact. One obvious example is in relation to archaeological impact: the proposed development might be located in an area where no significant archaeological impacts were expected, and the planning authority or An Bord Pleanála might well be minded to grant planning permission without insisting on the submission of an environmental impact statement. A condition might instead be attached to the planning permission requiring further archaeological assessment of the development. A different situation would arise where it was clear, or at least established as probable, that there would be significant

---

[107] Planning and Development Regulations 2001, art.103(5) (as amended by art.26 of the 2006 Regulations).
[108] (Case C–87/02) [2004] E.C.R. I–5975.
[109] *Gillespie v First Secretary of State* [2003] E.W.H.C. Admin 8, [91]; [2003] 1 P. & C.R. 30
[110] Planning and Development Regulations 2001, art.109.

archaeological material which needed to be addressed in the course of the development.[111]

13–146   This issue has been discussed in a number of cases from England and Wales. These cases suggest that it is necessary, in the context of a screening decision, to distinguish between the (unmitigated) environmental impacts of the proposed development, and the separate issue of whether those impacts might be avoided, reduced or remedied by remediation measures. It is not appropriate for a person charged with making a screening decision to start from the premise that, although there may be significant impacts, these can be reduced to insignificance as a result of the implementation of mitigation conditions of various kinds. Rather, the appropriate course in such a case is to require an environmental statement setting out the significant impacts and the measures which it is said will reduce their significance.[112]

13–147   The appropriate question to be addressed, therefore, is: what are the likely environmental impacts of the proposed development in the *absence* of mitigation measures?

13–148   In *British Telecommunications plc v Gloucester City Council*,[113] the planning authority, in deciding that an environmental impact statement was not required, had relied on the fact that a mitigation strategy was to be put in place in relation to the effect on archaeology. The High Court of England and Wales held that it was clear that there would be potentially highly significant effects on archaeology unless measures were taken to eliminate them.

> "I confess to having had some difficulty initially with this point. There is no doubt that it is for the planning authority to decide in the first instance whether or not there are likely to be significant effects on the environment such as to warrant an environmental statement. Can they conclude that there would be significant effects, save for the fact that they have required (or at least will require) the developer to take mitigating steps whose effect is to render such effects insignificant? In my judgment they cannot. Paragraph 3 of Schedule 2, which sets out the information required (and in turn reflects Article 5 of the Directive read with Appendix IV) requires amongst other things that there is a description of the measures envisaged to 'avoid, reduce and if possible' remedy adverse effects. The purpose is surely to enable public discussion to take place about whether the measures will be successful, or perhaps whether more effective measures can be taken than those proposed to ameliorate the anticipated harm. In my opinion, therefore, the question whether or not there are likely to be significant environmental effects should be approached by asking whether these would be likely to result, absent some specific measures being taken to ameliorate or reduce them. If they would, the environmental statement is required and the mitigating measures must be identified in it."

---

[111] *Arklow Holidays Ltd. v An Bord Pleanála* [2006] I.E.H.C. 15; [2007] 1 I.L.R.M. 125.

[112] *R. (On the application of Lebus) v South Cambridgeshire DC* [2002] E.W.H.C. Admin 2009; [2003] 2 P. & C.R. 5; [2003] J.P.L. 446 (planning authority in error in taking into account pollution control measures in deciding whether environmental impact statement required).

[113] [2001] E.W.H.C. Admin 1001; [2002] 2 P. & C.R. 33; [2002] J.P.L. 993.

The planning authority had, accordingly, erred in law in taking the mitigation **13–149** measures into account in deciding that no significant effects were likely. Similarly, in *Gillespie v First Secretary of State*,[114] the High Court of England and Wales held—in the context of contaminated land—that the Secretary of State had erred in taking special and elaborate remediation measures into account in deciding whether the development was likely to give rise to significant environmental effects.[115]

The Court of Appeal of England and Wales has suggested that the decision- **13–150** maker is not obliged to shut his eyes to the remedial measures submitted as part of the planning proposal.[116] In some cases the remedial measures will be so modest in scope, or so plainly and easily achievable, that it might be proper to hold that the development project would not be likely to have significant effects on the environment even though, in the absence of the proposed remedial measures, it would be likely to have such effects.[117] Where the measures are controversial, however, an environmental impact assessment will be required.

> "Where the Secretary of State is contemplating an application for planning permission for development which, but for remedial measures, may or will have significant environmental effects, I do not say that he must inevitably cause an EIA to be conducted. Prospective remedial measures may have been put before him whose nature, availability and effectiveness are already plainly established and plainly uncontroversial; though I should have thought there is little likelihood of such a state of affairs in relation to a development of any complexity. But if prospective remedial measures are not plainly established and not plainly uncontroversial, then as it seems to me the case calls for an EIA. If then the Secretary of State were to decline to conduct an EIA, as it seems to me he would pre-empt the very form of enquiry contemplated by the Directive and Regulations; and to that extent he would frustrate the purpose of the legislation."[118]

In the later case of *R. (On the application of Jones) v Mansfield District* **13–151** *Council*,[119] the Court of Appeal held that a planning authority cannot rely on conditions and undertakings as a surrogate for the environmental impact assessment process. A planning authority cannot conclude that a development is unlikely to have significant effects on the environment simply because all such effects are likely to be eliminated by measures that will be carried out by the developer pursuant to conditions and/or undertakings. But the question whether a project is likely to have significant effects on the environment is one of degree which calls for the exercise of judgment. Thus, remedial measures contemplated by conditions and/or undertakings can be taken into account to a

---

[114] [2003] E.W.H.C. Admin 8; [2003] 1 P. & C.R. 30.
[115] This judgment was upheld, on slightly different grounds, in *Bellway Urban Renewal Southern Ltd. v Gillespie* [2003] E.W.C.A. Civ. 400; [2003] 2 P. & C.R. 16.
[116] *Bellway Urban Renewal Southern Ltd. v Gillespie* [2003] E.W.C.A. Civ. 400, [36]; [2003] 2 P. & C.R. 16. See also *R. (On the application of Catt) v Brighton and Hove City Council* [2007] E.W.C.A. Civ. 298.
[117] *Bellway Urban Renewal Southern Ltd. v Gillespie* [2003] E.W.C.A. Civ. 400, [37].
[118] *ibid.*, [46].
[119] [2003] E.W.C.A. Civ. 1408; [2004] 2 P. & C.R. 14.

certain extent. The effect on the environment must be "significant". Significance in this context is not a hard-edged concept: the assessment of what is significant involves the exercise of judgment.

13–152 The Court of Appeal went on to state that the planning authority must have sufficient information about the impact of the project to be able to make an informed judgment as to whether it is likely to have a significant effect on the environment. But this does not mean that all uncertainties have to be resolved or that a decision that an environmental impact assessment is not required can only be made after a detailed and comprehensive assessment has been made of every aspect of the matter. The uncertainties may or may not make it impossible reasonably to conclude that there is no likelihood of significant environmental effect. It is possible in principle to have sufficient information to enable a decision reasonably to be made as to the likelihood of significant environmental effects even if certain details are not known and further surveys are to be undertaken. Everything depends on the circumstances of the individual case.

13–153 On the facts of *Jones*, it was held by the Court of Appeal that there was no inconsistency between the planning authority deciding that the development was not likely to have significant effects on wildlife (specifically, golden plovers and bats), and the acceptance of undertakings and the imposition of conditions requiring further survey work. Having regard to the information already available, it was reasonable for the planning authority to decide that the development would be unlikely to have significant effects in relation to birds and bats, and it did not rely on the conditions and undertaking in order to arrive at its conclusion that the development was unlikely to have an environmental effect in relation to bats, golden plovers or birds generally.

3. Mixed questions of law and of fact

13–154 The decision whether a proposed development should be subject to environmental impact assessment might best be described as involving mixed questions of law and of fact. The meaning to be attributed to the various categories of projects under Annex I and Annex II is a question of law, involving statutory interpretation, and thus a matter for the courts. The question as to whether a particular development is likely to have significant effects on the environment, on the other hand, is a question of fact and degree. The case law in this regard is summarised below.

13–155 In *Shannon Regional Fisheries Board v An Bord Pleanála*,[120] an issue arose as to the correct interpretation of the term "sow" for the purposes of determining whether or not an environmental impact assessment was required. It was urged on behalf of An Bord Pleanála that it was not for the High Court to arrive at its own definition of "sow" within the meaning of the Regulations, as this was a

---

[120] [1994] 3 I.R. 449. Similar sentiments were expressed in the decision in *Maher v An Bord Pleanála* [1999] 2 I.L.R.M. 198 (interpretation of term "pig").

matter solely within the competence of the planning authority and An Bord Pleanála, and that the court ought not to interfere unless it concluded that the definition adopted was wholly irrational. Barr J. rejected this argument.

> "I reject this proposition. Statutory interpretation is solely a matter for the courts and no other body has authority to usurp the power of the court in performing that function. However, this does not imply that a competent body, such as a local planning authority, is not entitled to determine whether, for example, a certain aspect of a proposed development conforms to a statutory requirement. In such a case, where the statutory obligation is clear, the issue is whether the development conforms to it. That is a matter which is peculiarly within the competence of the planning authority and the court ought not to interfere unless there is no reasonable basis on which the decision of the authority might be upheld. In the present case the meaning of 'sow' in the context of paragraph 1(e) of Part II of the First Schedule to the European Communities (Environmental Impact Assessment) Regulations, 1989, is not free from doubt and, therefore, it is a matter for the court to interpret the regulation."

Similarly, in *Maher v An Bord Pleanála*,[121] Kelly J. held that the question of the proper interpretation of the national regulations was a matter of law to be decided on the judicial review application, with the previous approach of An Bord Pleanála not being directly relevant. **13–156**

In *R. (On the application of Goodman) v Lewisham LBC*,[122] the Court of Appeal of England and Wales held that the interpretation of the various categories of project under the environmental impact assessment Regulations will generally be a matter for the courts. The Court of Appeal went on to say, however, that in some instances the meaning in law may itself be sufficiently imprecise that in applying it to the facts, as opposed to determining what the meaning was in the first place, a range of different conclusions may legitimately be available. On the facts of *Goodman*, it was held that the planning authority had erred in finding that a storage and distribution facility was not an "infrastructure project" or "urban development project". **13–157**

It seems to follow from the foregoing cases that insofar as any screening decision involves the interpretation of the various categories of project, same will be subject to full-blooded review before the courts. In other words, the courts will show no particular deference to the view taken by the planning bodies as to the question of interpretation. The gloss introduced by *R. (On the application of Goodman) v Lewisham LBC*—to the effect that some margin of appreciation may have to be shown to the decision-maker—should be treated with caution. As stated in *Shannon Regional Fisheries Board*, statutory interpretation is solely a matter for the courts and no other body has authority to usurp the power of the court in performing that function. The national courts are required to give effect to the objectives of the Directive, and it is submitted that this requires careful scrutiny of any decision which purports to exempt a project from environmental impact assessment. **13–158**

---

[121] [1999] 2 I.L.R.M. 198 at 206.
[122] [2003] E.W.C.A. Civ. 140; [2003] 2 P. & C.R. 18.

13–159   When one moves on from the interpretation of the Directive to the question of its application to any given project, the respective roles to be played by the planning bodies and the courts are less clear-cut. In this regard, it seems necessary to distinguish between development which either comes within Annex I or exceeds the thresholds under Annex II, on the one hand, and development which is of a type prescribed under Annex II but which does not exceed the relevant threshold, *i.e.* sub-threshold development, on the other. The reason for making this distinction is that, in the case of the first grouping, it will be a relatively straightforward matter to confirm that the development does, in fact, exceed the relevant threshold, and is a project of the type prescribed. The matter is thus capable of objective determination and should be amenable to full-blooded review by the courts. In the case of sub-threshold development, conversely, the test ultimately resolves itself to whether the given development is likely to have significant effects on the environment. This is obviously more subjective. A nice question arises as to the extent of the discretion enjoyed by a planning authority or An Bord Pleanála in this regard, and, in particular, as to the circumstances in which same might be set aside on judicial review.

13–160   Approaching the issue purely as a matter of national law, one might be tempted to characterise the question as one of fact and degree, and in respect of which the courts should show deference to the planning bodies. This might be said to follow from the wording of the relevant articles of the Planning and Development Regulations 2001 (as amended by the 2006 Regulations) which suggests that planning authorities and An Bord Pleanála enjoy a *discretion* as to whether to require an applicant to submit an environmental impact statement in respect of sub-threshold development. Traditionally, where a matter has been entrusted to the discretion of an expert body, the substance of the decision will only be subject to judicial review by reference to the principles in *O'Keeffe v An Bord Pleanála*.[123]

13–161   A similar approach was taken by the Court of Appeal of England and Wales in *R. (On the application of Jones) v Mansfield District Council*.[124]

---

[123] See, for example, *Max Developments Ltd. v An Bord Pleanála* [1994] 2 I.R. 121 (question of whether proposed development located in an existing urban area or a new and extended urban area a matter within the jurisdiction of An Bord Pleanála); or *Waddington v An Bord Pleanála*, unreported, High Court, Butler J., December 21, 2000 (suggestion that decision on whether sub-threshold development is likely to have significant effects on the environment, *i.e.* a screening decision, was subject to the principles in *O'Keeffe v An Bord Pleanála*).

[124] [2003] E.W.C.A. Civ. 1408; [2004] 2 P. & C.R. 14. See Carnwath L.J. in the same case at [61] ("Quite apart from the legal analysis, that view clearly makes practical sense. It enables an authoritative decision as to the procedure to be made at the outset, without risk of subsequent challenge except on legal grounds. Furthermore, the word 'significant' does not lay down a precise legal test. It requires the exercise of judgment, on technical or other planning grounds, and consistency in the exercise of that judgment in different cases. That is a function for which the courts are ill-equipped, but which is well-suited to the familiar role of local planning authorities, under the guidance of the Secretary of State."). See also *R. (On the application of the Noble Organisation Ltd) v Thanet District Council* [2005] E.W.C.A. Civ. 782, [30]; [2006] 1 P. & C.R. 13; [2006] J.P.L. 60 ("It is

"Whether a proposed development is likely to have significant effects on the environment involves an exercise of judgment or opinion. It is not a question of hard fact to which there can only be one possible correct answer in any given case. The use of the word 'opinion' in reg 2(2) is, therefore, entirely apt. In my view, that is in itself a sufficient reason for concluding that the role of the court should be limited to one of review on *Wednesbury* grounds."[125]

As against this, the judgment of the Irish High Court in *Ó Nualláin v Dublin Corporation*[126] would appear to suggest that the question of whether or not a proposed development will have significant effects on the environment is one capable of objective assessment and, accordingly, one in respect of which the High Court might be entitled to substitute its views for those of the planning authority. It has to be said, however, that the facts of that case were somewhat unusual in that the question of whether or not there should have been an environmental impact assessment had not been considered by the planning authority, or at least not considered by a person to whom that function had been properly delegated. Further, the judgment was given in the context of the previous legislation. Accordingly, it may well be that there are good grounds for distinguishing the case.

13–162

A stronger argument in favour of a more exacting standard of review might be derived from the case law of the ECJ. In particular, the judgment in *Bozen* indicated that it was for the national court to review whether the competent authorities had correctly assessed, in accordance with the Directive, the significance of the effects of the particular project on the environment.[127] This might be taken as suggesting that full-blooded judicial review should be available. Similarly, insofar as the judgment in *Commission v Italian Republic*[128] indicated that a screening decision by the national competent authority must contain or be accompanied by all the information that makes it possible to check that it is based on adequate screening, carried out in accordance with the requirements of the Directive, it might be read as suggesting that a full review is to be available.

13–163

Moreover, it is arguable that any attenuated standard of review would not be consistent with the express right of access under Art.10a of the Directive to a review procedure before a court of law or another independent and impartial body established by law to challenge the substantive or procedural legality of

13–164

---

a matter of planning judgment of a planning authority, challengeable only on grounds of unreasonableness, whether it has sufficient material before it at the *outline* planning stage to decide whether a proposed development would be likely to have such significant effects on the environment as to require an environmental impact assessment."). See also *R. (On the application of Catt) v Brighton and Hove City Council* [2006] E.W.H.C. 1337 (Admin). Under Irish law, outline planning permission is not available in respect of development subject to environmental impact assessment.

[125] *ibid.*, [17].
[126] [1999] 4 I.R. 137.
[127] *World Wildlife Fund v Autonome Provinz Bozen* (Case C–435/97) [1999] E.C.R. I–5613, [48].
[128] (Case C–87/02) [2004] E.C.R. I–5975.

decisions, acts or omissions subject to the public participation provisions of the Directive.[129] This is discussed generally at paras 13–387 to 13–407.

L. Public Notice and Consultation

1. Planning authority stage

13–165 The fact that a planning application is accompanied by an environmental impact statement must be stated in both the site notice and the newspaper notice in respect of the application.[130] Where the initial application is not accompanied by an environmental impact statement, but the planning authority call for one to be submitted, further public notice must be given not more than two weeks before the submission of the environmental impact statement.[131]

13–166 The period for the making of submissions and observations by members of the public is the standard five weeks beginning on the date of the receipt of the application.[132] Where the initial application is not accompanied by an environmental impact statement, but the planning authority call for one to be submitted, the application shall be deemed to be made on the date of receipt by the planning authority of the environmental impact statement.[133]

13–167 A question arises as to whether this five week period can be said to be a reasonable time-frame within the meaning of Art.6(6) of the Directive. Under this article, reasonable time-frames for the different phases are to be provided, allowing sufficient time for informing the public and for the public concerned to prepare and participate effectively in the environmental decision-making.

13–168 During the course of an application for planning permission, further information and evidence or revised plans, drawings or particulars may be received by the planning authority. It would seem to follow from the tenor of the Directive that members of the public must be consulted in respect of any additional material which relates to the environmental impact of the proposed development. Under art.35 of the Planning and Development Regulations 2001 (as substituted under the 2006 Regulations), the planning authority is required to engage in further consultation where it considers that further information, evidence, revised plans, drawings or particulars received contain "significant additional data, including information relating to the effects on the environment". See further paras 3–119 to 3–129. In the case of EIA development, the period within which the submissions or observations are to be made is five weeks.

---

[129] Directive 85/337/EEC, Art.10a (inserted by Directive 2003/35/EC).
[130] Planning and Development Regulations 2001, art.98.
[131] Planning and Development Regulations 2001, art.105 (as amended by the 2006 Regulations).
[132] Planning and Development Regulations 2001, art.29 (as substituted by the 2006 Regulations).
[133] Planning and Development Regulations 2001, art.103(4).

The planning authority enjoys discretion as to whether or not to seek further **13–169** information from the developer. It is not obliged to do so, but is instead entitled—according to the seriousness of the deficiencies—to reject the application as invalid, or to refuse planning permission on the basis that the environmental impact statement is inadequate.[134]

The maximum period allowed for the determination of an application subject **13–170** to environmental impact assessment is eight weeks beginning on the date of receipt of a valid application, or, in cases where a request for further information has been served, eight weeks of the notice being complied with.[135]

2. Appeal to An Bord Pleanála

An Bord Pleanála has a power, under art.109 of the 2001 Regulations, to require **13–171** the submission of an environmental impact statement where one had not been submitted to the planning authority. This is a very important provision in that it ensures that An Bord Pleanála is empowered to remedy any failure to carry out an assessment at the planning authority stage. It also suggests that the appropriate response, where an objector thinks that development should have been subject to environmental impact assessment, is to appeal to An Bord Pleanála, rather than to seek judicial review of the planning authority's decision.

Under art.112 of the Planning and Development Regulations 2001 (as amended **13–172** by the 2006 Regulations), An Bord Pleanála is required to publish, in at least one approved newspaper, notice of any appeal in respect of which it has *requested* and received an environmental impact statement. In other words, the obligation only applies where no environmental impact statement had been received at the planning authority stage.

An environmental impact statement received by An Bord Pleanála in connection **13–173** with an appeal shall, as soon as possible following its receipt, be made available for inspection or purchase at a fee not exceeding the reasonable cost of making a copy.[136] This is to be done at the offices of An Bord Pleanála or such other convenient place as the board may specify.

The environmental impact statement should also be available for inspection or **13–174** purchase at the offices of the planning authority during the currency of the appeal.[137]

Generally members of the public may participate in an appeal before An Bord **13–175** Pleanála in one of two ways. First, any person who made submissions or

---

[134] See, by analogy, *Kildare County Council v An Bord Pleanála* [2006] I.E.H.C. 173; unreported, MacMenamin J., March 10, 2006.
[135] PDA 2000, s.34(8)(c).
[136] Planning and Development Regulations 2001, art.114.
[137] Planning and Development Regulations 2001, art.115.

observations at the planning authority stage is entitled to appeal to An Bord Pleanála.[138] Such a person is referred to as a "party" to the appeal. An appeal must be made within four weeks of the date of the decision of the planning authority. Secondly, non-parties may make submissions or observations to An Bord Pleanála within a period of four weeks from the date of publication of any notice required under regulation or, where no such notice is required, within the period of four weeks beginning on the day of receipt by An Bord Pleanála of the (last) appeal.[139] It seems that the right to make submissions or observations is not conditional on that person having previously participated at the planning authority stage.

13–176   Where An Bord Pleanála considers that any submission, observation, document, particulars or other information submitted to it in response to a request or requirement of the board contains "significant additional information on the effects on the environment" of the proposed development, the board is required to engage in further public consultation. It would appear to follow from the judgment in *Kinsella v Dundalk Town Council*[140] that whether information on the environment is "significant"—so as to trigger the requirement for further public consultation—is a question of fact and degree, not a question of law.

13–177   One peculiar aspect of the Planning and Development Regulations 2001 is that no minimum period is specified within which the submissions or observations on the additional information are to be made. Instead, An Bord Pleanála has discretion to prescribe a period, which must be notified to the various parties. It is submitted—in reliance on Art.6 of the Directive—that sufficient time must be allowed. The time required will vary depending on the nature of the information received, but less than three weeks will rarely be sufficient.

13–178   An Bord Pleanála enjoys a discretion as to whether or not to seek further information from the developer. It is not obliged to do so, but is instead entitled—according to the seriousness of the deficiencies—to reject the application as invalid, or to refuse planning permission on the basis that the environmental impact statement is inadequate.[141]

3. Requirement to pay participation fee

13–179   Generally a person making a submission or observation at the planning authority stage of the decision-making process is required to pay a fee of €20.[142] There is a similar requirement in the case of a submission to An Bord Pleanála (€50).

---

[138] PDA 2000, s.37.
[139] PDA 2000, s.130.
[140] Unreported, High Court, Kelly J., December 3, 2004.
[141] See, by analogy, *Kildare County Council v An Bord Pleanála* [2006] I.E.H.C. 173; unreported, MacMenamin J., March 10, 2006.
[142] Planning and Development Regulations, art.29 (as substituted by the 2006 Regulations).

The introduction of this requirement to pay a participation fee was controversial. Ryall, for example, had argued that the imposition of the requirement is inconsistent with the Directive.[143]

> "Creating an economic obstacle to participation appears to be fundamentally at odds with the underlying objective of the EIA directive to ensure that decisions are taken 'in full-knowledge' of the likely environmental impacts. In light of the Court's consistently robust and purposive approach to the core requirements of the EIA directive, and in the absence of an express provision authorising the levying of a charge, the legality of the fee under EC law is doubtful."

This issue was ultimately the subject of infringement proceedings brought against Ireland by the Commission of the European Community.[144] The Commission argued, *inter alia*, that the requirement to pay a participation fee might have the effect of dissuading members of the public, one of the principal sources of information, from participating in the decision-making process, or the effect of making their participation more difficult; and that Ireland had exceeded its discretion under the terms of the Directive. **13–180**

The ECJ rejected the Commission's claim, ruling that the wording of the Directive gave Member States a "wide discretion" in the determination of the detailed arrangements for public consultation. When determining the arrangements, the Member States were, in principle, free to impose a participation fee, provided that it is not such as to constitute an obstacle to the exercise of the rights of participation conferred by Art.6 of Directive. The amount of the fees at issue, could not, in the judgment of the Court, be regarded as constituting an obstacle to the exercise of the rights of participation. Nor had the Commission succeeded in refuting Ireland's argument that the level of the fees was justified in the light of the administrative costs involved in processing the observations received from persons concerned. **13–181**

M. Scoping

Under Art.5(2) of the Directive, Member States shall take the necessary measures to ensure that, if the developer so requests before submitting an application for development consent, the competent authority shall give an opinion on the information to be supplied by the developer. This procedure is colloquially referred to as "scoping" in that the applicant seeks guidance as to the "scope" or ambit of matters to be addressed in the environmental impact statement. The fact that the authority has given an opinion does not preclude it from subsequently requiring the developer to submit further information. **13–182**

---

[143] A. Ryall, "The EIA Directive and the Irish Planning Participation Fee" (2002) 14 *Journal of Environmental Law* 317.
[144] *Commission v Ireland* (Case C–216/05), November 9, 2006.

1. Planning authority

13–183   These requirements have been implemented into Irish law as follows. Under s.135 of the PDA 2000 (as amended under the 2006 Act), an applicant or a person intending to apply for permission may request the planning authority concerned to give a written opinion on the information to be contained in an environmental impact statement. The form of the request is prescribed under art.95 of the Planning and Development Regulations 2001 (as amended by the 2006 Regulations). The planning authority is required to notify, and to invite submissions or observations from, An Bord Pleanála, the Minister for the Environment Heritage and Local Government, the Minister for Communications, Marine and Natural Resources, and from any other body which would be entitled to notice of the application for planning permission under art.28 of the Planning and Development Regulations (as substituted by the 2006 Regulations).[145] The (scoping) opinion should be given before the submission by that person of an application for the grant of planning permission. This should be done not later than three weeks after either the expiration of the period for consultation with the prescribed bodies, or the expiration of the period specified for complying with a request for further information.[146]

2. An Bord Pleanála

13–184   In cases where an environmental impact statement has to be submitted to An Bord Pleanála, the board may similarly be requested to provide a scoping opinion.[147]

3. Power to request further information on planning application not prejudiced

13–185   It is expressly stated that the giving of a (scoping) opinion shall not prejudice the exercise by the planning authority concerned or An Bord Pleanála of its powers under the PDA 2000, or any Regulations made thereunder, to require the person who made the request to submit further information regarding the application concerned or, as the case may be, any appeal.

---

[145] Planning and Development Regulations 2001, art.95(2) (as substituted by the 2006 Regulations).
[146] Planning and Development Regulations 2001, art.95(4).
[147] PDA 2000, s.173(3); and art.95 of the Planning and Development Regulations (as amended under the 2006 Regulations).

N. Information to be Contained in
Environmental Impact Statement

A distinction of sorts is drawn under the Directive as between what is involved   **13–186**
in the *assessment* (Art.3), on the one hand, and the *information* which the
developer is to provide (Art.5 and Annex IV), on the other.

This distinction is not observed under national law. Article 94 of the Planning   **13–187**
and Development Regulations 2001 prescribes the content of an environmental
impact statement by reference to Sch.6 of the Regulations. Schedule 6 replicates,
with some discrepancies, the provisions of both Art.3 and Annex IV of the
Directive.

Article 3 provides as follows.[148]   **13–188**

> "The environmental impact assessment shall identify, describe and assess in an
> appropriate manner, in the light of each individual case and in accordance with
> Articles 4 to 11, the direct and indirect effects of a project on the following
> factors:
> (i)   human beings, fauna and flora;
> (ii) soil, water, air, climate and the landscape;
> (iii) material assets and the cultural heritage;
> (iv) the interaction between the factors mentioned at (i), (ii) and (iii)."

An indication should be given of any difficulties (technical deficiencies or   **13–189**
lack of know-how) encountered by the developer in compiling the required
information.

Member States are afforded some discretion under Art.5 of the Directive as to   **13–190**
precisely what information is to be provided by the developer. The minimum
requirements are prescribed under Art.5(3). Thereafter, the Member States shall
adopt the necessary measures to ensure that the developer supplies in an
appropriate form the information under Annex IV inasmuch as:

(a)   the Member States consider that the information is relevant to a given stage
      of the consent procedure and to the specific characteristics of a particular
      project or type and of the environmental features likely to be affected, and
(b)   the Member States consider that a developer may reasonably be required to
      compile this information having regard *inter alia* to current knowledge and
      methods of assessment.

Schedule 6 of the Planning and Development Regulations 2001 is divided into   **13–191**
two paragraphs. It is mandatory—under art.94(a)—to include the information
specified in para.1. This largely coincides with the information specified in
Art.5(3) of the Directive; the requirement for a non-technical summary is to be
found in art.94(c).

---

[148] Art.3 (as substituted by Directive 97/11/EC).

13–192   Article 5(3) of the Directive provides as follows.

> "The information to be provided by the developer include at least:
>
> (i)   a description of the project comprising information on the site, design and size of the project;
>
> (ii) a description of the measures envisaged in order to avoid, reduce and, if possible, remedy significant adverse effects;
>
> (iii) the data required to identify and assess the main effects which the project is likely to have on the environment;
>
> (iv) an outline of the main alternatives studied by the developer and an indication of the main reasons for his choice, taking into account the environmental effects,
>
> (v)   a non-technical summary of the information mentioned in the previous indents."

13–193   The information specified under para.2 of Sch.6 consists of further information, by way of elaboration or amplification of the information referred to in para.1. Rather unhelpfully Art.94(b) simply paraphrases the two subparagraphs of Art.5(1) of the Directive set out above. In other words, Ireland has made no attempt to provide any guidance in the regulations as to what sort of information is relevant or is reasonable having regard to current knowledge and methods of assessment. It is doubtful whether this represents an adequate transposition of the Directive.

13–194   The information specified under Annex IV is set out under a number of main headings, as follows.

1. Description of the project

13–195   The description should cover the direct effects and any indirect, secondary, cumulative, short-, medium- and long-term, permanent and temporary, positive and negative effects of the project.

13–196   The obligation to describe the proposed development project applies both to its construction and operational stages. The physical characteristics of the whole project and the land use requirements during the construction and operational phases should be described. The obligation also extends to a description of the main characteristics of the production processes, for instance, nature and quantity of the materials used, and an estimate, by type and quantity, of expected residues and emissions (water, air and soil pollution, noise, vibration, light, heat, radiation, etc.) resulting from the operation of the proposed project.

13–197   It is not entirely clear from the wording of the Directive as to what level of detail is required in terms of the description of the proposed development. Under Irish law, it is not possible to apply for *outline* planning permission where the development is subject to environmental impact assessment,[149] and

---

[149] Planning and Development Regulations 2001, art.96.

thus the plans and particulars submitted with the application will have to comply with the requirements of arts 22 and 23 of the Planning and Development Regulations 2001 (as substituted by the 2006 Regulations). Disputes may still arise in practice as to whether a proposed development project has been described in sufficient detail. There is an obvious tension between the desire of the developer to maintain some degree of flexibility as to the final design of the development, and the need to assess the project properly. Almost by definition, development subject to environmental impact assessment will be of a type which will take some time to construct, and a developer will want to leave his options open in order to respond to any changes in market demand in the interim.

Reference is made in this regard to the judgment of the High Court of England and Wales in *R. v Rochdale Metropolitan Borough Council Ex p. Milne*.[150]   **13–198**

> "Since the 'description of the project' required by art 5(2) is a means to that end, in that it provides the starting point for the assessment process, there is no reason to believe that the directive was seeking to be unduly prescriptive as to what would amount to an appropriate description of a particular project. The requirement in art 5(2) (see page 89C to E) to provide 'information on the site, design and size of the project' is, and is intended to be, sufficiently flexible to accommodate the particular characteristics of the different types of project listed in annexes I and II (Schs 1 and 2 to the assessment regulations). It may be possible to provide more or less information on site, design and size, depending on the nature of the project to be assessed.
>
> If a particular kind of project, such as an industrial estate development project (or perhaps an urban development project) is, by its very nature, not fixed at the outset, but is expected to evolve over a number of years depending on market demand, there is no reason why 'a description of the project' for the purposes of the directive should not recognise that reality. What is important is that the environmental assessment process should then take full account at the outset of the implications for the environment of this need for an element of flexibility. The assessment process may well be easier in the case of projects which are 'fixed' in every detail from the outset, but the difficulty of assessing projects which do require a degree of flexibility is not a reason for frustrating their implementation. It is for the authority responsible for granting the development consent (in England the local planning authority or the Secretary of State) to decide whether the difficulties and uncertainties are such that the proposed degree of flexibility is not acceptable in terms of its potential effect on the environment."[151]

It seems that, in considering the effect of the proposed development on *future* development, regard should be had to development objectives under the development plan. In *O'Mahony v An Bord Pleanála*,[152] O'Neill J. indicated   **13–199**

---

[150] [2001] J.P.L. 470. This judgment was subsequently upheld by the Court of Appeal on December 20, 2000. See also the judgment of the Court of Appeal in *R. (On the application of Barker) v London Borough of Bromley* [2001] E.W.C.A. Civ. 1766.

[151] *ibid.*, [89] and [90].

[152] [2005] I.E.H.C. 39; unreported, O'Neill J., February 18, 2005.

that to ignore the likelihood of "zoned development" would be a significant deficiency in an environmental impact statement and a failure to comply with the Directive. The case concerned a challenge to a proposed road scheme under the Roads Acts. Part of the land take under a compulsory purchase order included lands zoned for mid-density residential development. The applicant argued that the impact of the road scheme on any future residential development—in terms of noise, air quality and vehicular access—had not been properly considered.

13–200   O'Neill J. held that, in circumstances where zoning on the land indicates that, within the lifetime of the development plan, development of a particular kind may take place, same should have been addressed in the environmental impact statement, notwithstanding that there was as yet no grant of planning permission in existence. On the facts, however, O'Neill J. concluded that the complaint was tenuous in nature and lacked the kind of weight or substance necessary to justify leave to apply for judicial review. The applicant had failed to raise any concerns as to noise or air quality (as opposed to vehicular access) during the course of the statutory procedures.

2. Main alternatives

13–201   An outline of the main alternatives studied by the developer is to be provided, together with an indication of the main reasons for this choice, taking into account the environmental effects. Again, it is not entirely clear as to what precisely is required in this regard. In particular, the extent, if any, to which the developer is required to identify, and give reasons for discounting, alternative sites is unclear. There is a certain artificiality in that in many instances the site (and indeed the scale of the development) will have been dictated by the fact that the applicant owns certain lands. Thus, unless a developer had formulated a development proposal prior to purchasing land, alternative sites are unlikely to have been considered in any detail. Of course, the question of alternative sites will have a particular relevance in the context of the exercise by a local authority of its powers of compulsory acquisition, and the acquiring authority should be required to justify its selection of the particular lands to be acquired.

3. Environment likely to be significantly affected

13–202   A description should be provided of the aspects of the environment likely to be significantly affected by the proposed project, including, in particular, population, fauna, flora, soil, water, air, climatic factors, material assets, including the architectural and archaeological heritage, landscape and the inter-relationship between the above factors.

4. Likely significant effects

13–203   The likely significant effects of the proposed project on the environment resulting from (i) the existence of the project, (ii) the use of natural resources, and (iii) the emission of pollutants, the creation of nuisances and the elimination of waste should be described. In addition, the description by the developer of the forecasting methods used to assess the effects on the environment should also be given.

It is well established that the requirement to describe the likely significant **13–204** effects of a proposed development is not confined to adverse effects but extends to include even beneficial effects.[153] In *British Telecommunications plc v Gloucester City Council*,[154] the High Court of England and Wales stated that if "effects" had meant simply "adverse effects", there would be no purpose in specifying that details of mitigation measures had to be given in respect of adverse effects. The reference to "adverse" would be wholly otiose.

> "In my judgment an important feature of this democratic process, as the part of the government publication which I have emphasised notes, is that individuals 'should form their own judgments on the significance of the environmental issues raised by the project.' This involves a recognition that it is not always clear whether an impact is beneficial or not. In particular, where the development sites of historic or architectural interest are concerned, there will generally be a range of views held about the artistic and aesthetic features of the scheme and whether they best preserve the true character of the area which is the subject of the development. It would frustrate the process of debate about the merits of such a development if the planning authority could determine that the impact was beneficial and as a consequence rule that no environmental statement was needed. In this context benefit, like beauty, is in the eye of the beholder. Moreover, as Lord Hoffmann points out in his judgment, even the wrongheaded and misguided are entitled to express their views."

5. Mitigation measures

A description of the measures envisaged to prevent, reduce and where possible **13–205** offset any significant adverse effects on the environment should be provided. This express obligation to address mitigation measures is one of the distinguishing features between a conventional application for planning permission and one subject to environmental impact assessment.

O. Adequacy of Environmental Impact Statement

1. General

Under the terms of the Planning and Development Regulations 2001, the **13–206** adequacy of an environmental impact statement is, in the first instance, a matter for the planning bodies. The planning authorities and An Bord Pleanála are required to consider whether an environmental impact statement complies with

---

[153] *Ó Nualláin v Dublin Corporation* [1999] 4 I.R. 137 at 148.
[154] [2002] J.P.L. 993, [69].

the requirements of the Regulations, or of any scoping opinion.[155] Where it is decided that the environmental impact statement is not compliant, further information should be sought. Presumably, however, if the environmental impact statement was wholly inadequate, the planning bodies would be entitled to treat the application as invalid.[156]

13–207　An "environmental impact statement" is defined as meaning a statement of the effects, if any, which the proposed development, if carried out, would have on the environment.[157] Thus, in addressing the adequacy of the statement, what is to be examined is not just the initial documentation submitted at the outset with an application for planning permission, but also any supplementary information furnished.[158]

13–208　Reference is made in this regard to the judgment of the High Court of England and Wales in *R. (On the application of Blewett) v Derbyshire County Council*.[159]

> "In an imperfect world it is an unrealistic counsel of perfection to expect that an applicant's environmental statement will always contain the 'full information' about the environmental impact of a project. The regulations are not based upon such an unrealistic expectation. They recognise that an environmental statement may well be deficient and made provision through the publicity and consultation processes for any deficiencies to be identified so that the resulting 'environmental information' provides the local planning authority with as full a picture as possible."

13–209　If the information ultimately provided is inadequate, this may lead to the grant of a development consent being ruled invalid. For example, in *R. (On the application of Hereford Waste Watchers Ltd.) v Hereford Council*,[160] a planning permission—for a waste and recycling facility—was set aside on the basis that certain information which the planning authority required, and which it had stipulated by way of planning condition should be made available prior to the development commencing, should have been made available prior to the planning permission being granted.

13–210　The High Court inferred from the fact of the imposition of conditions—requiring the agreement in advance of development of certain matters relating to emissions—that the officials of the planning authority were of the view that

---

[155] Planning and Development Regulations 2001, arts 108 and 111, respectively.
[156] See *Kildare County Council v An Bord Pleanála* [2006] I.E.H.C. 173, [66]; unreported, MacMenamin J., March 10, 2006. See also, by analogy, *R. (On the application of Blewett) v Derbyshire County Council* [2004] J.P.L. 751, [41] (a document purporting to be an environmental statement may be so deficient that it could not reasonably be described as an environmental statement).
[157] PDA 2000, s.2.
[158] See also PDA 2000, s.173.
[159] [2004] J.P.L. 751, [41]. The subsequent decision of the Court of Appeal turned on a different point, namely an allegation that the County Council had failed to consider the best practicable environmental option: [2004] E.W.C.A. Civ. 1508.
[160] [2005] E.W.H.C. 191 (Admin).

the emissions could have significant effects on the environment, and that the information sought by the conditions was not merely for the purposes of monitoring what the planning authority regarded as insignificant emissions.

2. Standard of review

Traditionally, where a matter has been entrusted to the discretion of an expert body, the substance of the decision will only be subject to judicial review by reference to the principles in *O'Keeffe v An Bord Pleanála*. Certainly the approach of the Irish courts to date has been to regard any examination of the quality of an environmental impact statement as principally being a matter for the planning bodies. McKechnie J. stated as follows in *Kenny v An Bord Pleanála (No. 1)*.[161] **13–211**

> "Once the statutory requirements have been satisfied I should not concern myself with the *qualitative nature* of the environmental impact study or the debate on it had before the inspector. *These are not matters of concern to this court.* The fourth notice party and the respondent, as these bodies must under the regulations, were satisfied as to the environmental impact statement, with the inspector and the respondent also being satisfied with the evidence, both documentary and oral, produced at the oral hearing. That in my view, concludes the matter." *Emphasis supplied.

Similarly, in *Kildare County Council v An Bord Pleanála*,[162] MacMenamin J. held as follows. **13–212**

> "Under the statutory regime the respondent is entrusted with considering the adequacy of the EIS. It is the exercise of the statutory discretion which the applicants now seek to challenge. A challenge can only be mounted on contention that the decision of the Board was unreasonable or irrational and that the well established principles laid down in *O'Keeffe v. An Bord Pleanála* [1993] 1 I.R. 39 therefore apply."

The approach of the Irish High Court to date is consistent with that of the courts of England and Wales. Reference is made in this regard to the decision in *R. v Rochdale Metropolitan Borough Council Ex p. Milne*.[163] **13–213**

> "It is for the local planning authority to decide whether it has sufficient information in respect of the material considerations. Its decision is subject to review by the courts, but the courts will defer to the local planning authority's judgment in that

---

[161] [2001] 1 I.R. 565 at 578. See also *Murphy v Wicklow County Council*, unreported, High Court, Kearns J., March 19, 1999. Ryall has criticised the judgment in *Kenny*, suggesting that the entrenched deferential attitude towards decisions of specialists tribunals, in particular, planning authorities and An Bord Pleanála, must be revisited and revised in light of the clear mandate from the ECJ to enforce environmental impact assessment law locally; see A. Ryall, "Judicial Review and the Adequacy of the EIS: Kenny v. An Bord Pleanála" (2002) 9 I.P.E.L.J. 20.

[162] [2006] I.E.H.C. 173, [73]; unreported, March 10, 2006.

[163] (2001) 81 P. & C.R. 27, [108]–[110].

matter in all but the most extreme cases. Regulation 4(2) re-enforces this general obligation to have regard to all material considerations in a case of a particularly material consideration: 'environmental information' which has been provided pursuant to the assessment regulations.

There is no reason why the adequacy of this information, which includes the sufficiency of information about the site design, size and scale of development should not be determined by the local planning authority: see paragraph 48 of Circular 2/99 above.

The question whether such information does provide a sufficient 'description of the development proposed' for the purposes of the assessment regulations is, in any event, not a question of primary fact, which the court might be well equipped to answer. It is pre-eminently a question of planning and judgment, highly dependent on a detailed knowledge of the locality, of local planning policies and the essential characteristics of the various kinds of development project that have to be assessed."

13–214 The decision of the High Court of England and Wales in this regard was subsequently upheld by the Court of Appeal.[164]

"In my judgment what is sufficient is a matter of fact and degree. There is no blueprint which requires a particular amount of information to be supplied. What is necessary depends on the nature of the project and whether, given the wording of [Article 2] of the Directive, enough information is supplied to enable the decision-making body to assess the effect of the particular project on the environment. I agree with Sullivan J. that the court cannot place itself in the position of re-considering the detailed factual matters considered by the local planning authority. Equally I accept that the court does have a role and there may be cases where the court can and should intervene and hold that no reasonable local authority could have been satisfied with the amount of information with which it was supplied in the circumstances of the particular case."

13–215 More recently, the High Court of England and Wales in *R. (On the application of Kent) v First Secretary of State*[165] summarised the effect of the case law thus.

"The authorities show that, whilst the environmental statement must contain sufficient information to enable the decision maker to make an informed judgment as to whether the development is likely to have a significant effect on the environment, it is for the decision maker to decide whether the information contained in the document is sufficient to meet the definition of an environmental statement in reg.2 of the EIA Regulations, subject only to review on *Wednesbury* grounds, whilst also bearing in mind that the document does not have to contain information about all the effects, only the 'main effects' or 'the likely significant effects'."

13–216 It must be open to question as to whether or not this deferential approach on the part of the courts is consistent with EC law. Whereas one can readily appreciate and empathise with the reluctance on the part of the courts to become

---

[164] Unreported, Pill and Chadwick L.JJ., December 21, 2000, [33] *per* Pill L.J.
[165] [2004] E.W.H.C. 2953 (Admin), [76]; [2005] 2 P. & C.R. 16; [2005] J.P.L. 951.

involved in a qualitative assessment of the adequacy of an environmental impact statement, it may be that the standard of review posited by the test of unreasonableness or irrationality allows too much latitude to the regulatory bodies in this regard. In particular, as discussed further at para.13–387 and onwards, the attenuated standard of review may not be compatible with the obligations imposed under Art.10a of the Directive. Scannell suggests, however, that there are ample opportunities to address an inadequate environmental impact statement during the course of the decision-making process—including the ability of a planning authority or An Bord Pleanála to request further information—and consequently that the likelihood of an environmental impact statement being declared inadequate in judicial review proceedings must be very rare.[166]

P. Planning Conditions and Environmental Impact Assessment

Difficult questions arise as to the extent, if any, to which concerns as to the environmental impacts of a development can be hived off to planning conditions. This arises most starkly in the case of planning permission granted in respect of sub-threshold development without any environmental impact assessment having been carried out. Whether a decision not to require the submission of an environmental impact statement may be justified on the basis that the environmental impacts have been mitigated by way of planning condition has been considered in detail at paras 13–145 to 13–153.   **13–217**

Even where an environmental impact statement has been submitted, issues can arise as to the legitimacy of conditions which require further investigations to be carried out, or leave over remediation measures to be agreed between the developer and the planning authority. By definition, conditions of this type are deferring consideration of certain matters until *after* the relevant development consent, namely the planning permission, has been granted. It is necessary to consider whether this approach is compatible with the requirements of the Directive.   **13–218**

The general rule is that the decision-maker should have sufficient information at the time of the giving of the development consent to allow it to assess the likely significant effects of the proposed development. It is not permissible to leave over questions which relate either (i) to the significance of the impact on the environment or (ii) to the effectiveness of any mitigation.[167]   **13–219**

Thus, if a planning authority considers that a process or activity will have significant environmental effects then the environmental impact statement needs to include the details of the measures envisaged in order to avoid, reduce and,   **13–220**

---

[166] Y. Scannell, *Environmental and Land Use Law* (Thomson Round Hall, Dublin, 2006), para.5–105.

[167] *Smith v Secretary of State for the Environment Transport and the Regions* [2003] E.W.C.A. Civ. 262, [27]; [2003] 2 P. & C.R. 11.

if possible, remedy the significant adverse effects. The planning authority cannot leave the matter over for subsequent agreement. Even if that might otherwise be a satisfactory way of dealing with the problem, it frustrates the democratic purpose of the consultation process.[168]

13–221 In *Sweetman v An Bord Pleanála*, the High Court upheld the validity of a condition requiring ground water monitoring to be carried out along the route of the permitted road to establish ground water levels and quality ground water flow patterns. The condition required that the monitoring continue for a period of three years following the completion of the proposed road. The stated reason for the condition was to ensure adequate monitoring of potential impacts on a candidate Special Area of Conservation ("cSAC"). The condition had been recommended by An Bord Pleanála's inspector, and accepted by the members of the board.

> "It would, therefore, appear to be appropriate to characterise the decision of the Inspector as amounting to a decision that the risk of any adverse consequences was so small that it did not warrant refusing the application but that, for an abundance of caution, it was appropriate to impose a monitoring requirement so that, not only the local authority but the public generally, could be made immediately aware of any unexpected consequences. Of course at a time when any such adverse consequences occurred the road would in fact have been built and could not, in all probability, be undone. Therefore the judgment as to whether the project was to go ahead at all necessarily involved assessing the level of risk of adverse consequences. It would appear that the risk was found to be extremely small and thus not such as would have justified refusing the project. In those circumstances it seems to me that the question of whether any additional measures were required on top of the monitoring was more than within the technical judgment of the Inspector and An Bord Pleanála who came to consider his report and the other materials in the case. It does not seem to me that it could be said that the Inspector considered any inappropriate factors, failed to consider any appropriate factors, or came to an unreasonable decision on the materials. Likewise the same applies to the Board. Even applying a more stringent test (if it be so required) of a manifest error it is difficult to see how the decision could be said to show a manifest error."

13–222 A distinction should be drawn between those cases where the proposed condition is intended to elicit further information (for example, a condition requiring further surveys or investigations), and those where the condition seeks to leave over, for further agreement with the planning authority, the detail of the measures to be taken to remedy known environmental impacts. Conditions of the former type suggest that there is not sufficient information before the decision-maker to allow it to make a proper determination of the likely environmental impacts of the development.[169] In such cases, it is inappropriate

---

[168] R. *(On the application of Hereford Waste Watchers Ltd.) v Hereford Council* [2005] E.W.H.C. 191 (Admin), [25].

[169] Whether sufficient information is available to enable a judgment to be made as to the likelihood of significant effects is, seemingly, primarily a matter for the decision-maker subject to review on grounds of rationality. See *British Telecommunications plc v*

either to conclude that an environmental impact statement is not necessary, or, where an environmental impact statement has been submitted, to proceed to grant planning permission without further investigation.

Conditions of the latter type (conditions seeking to regulate *known* **13–223** environmental impacts) may be acceptable where an environmental impact statement has been submitted: whereas it is improper to decide that an environmental impact statement is not necessary by reference to the mitigated effects of the proposed development, it may be lawful to leave over matters to planning conditions provided that the decision-maker is satisfied that even on a worst case scenario there will be no *unanticipated* environmental impacts.[170] Thus, in *R. (On the application of PPG11 Ltd.) v Dorset County Council*,[171] the High Court of England and Wales upheld conditions which required further surveys and the identification of mitigation measures in respect of badgers and reptiles prior to the commencement of land filling, tree felling or clearance of scrub and vegetation. There was material before the planning authority which allowed it to conclude that there was unlikely to be a significant adverse effect on the relevant ecology resulting from the development project. To the extent that this conclusion was supported by the remedial proposals, the planning authority was not relying on or influenced by anything that could be described as non-modest, complicated or controversial. What was contemplated involved well-understood techniques of survey, and, possibly, translocation on what was likely to be a very limited scale.

In *R. v Cornwall Council Ex p. Hardy*, an environmental impact statement had **13–224** been submitted.[172] The planning authority had purported to grant outline planning permission subject to a condition that further surveys should be carried out to ensure that a protected species (bats) would not be adversely affected by the proposed development. The High Court of England and Wales held that, having decided that the surveys were necessary, it was incumbent on the planning authority to await the results of the surveys before deciding whether to grant planning permission so as to ensure that the full environmental information was available.[173]

> "Moreover, it is clear from the comprehensive list of likely significant effects in paragraph 3, and the reference to mitigation measures in paragraph 2(d), that it is intended that in accordance with the objectives of the Directive, the information

---

Gloucester City Council [2001] E.W.H.C. Admin 1001, [78]; *Gillespie v First Secretary of State* [2003] E.W.H.C. Admin 8, [83]; [2003] 1 P. & C.R. 30; *R. (On the application for Jones) v Mansfield DC* [2003] E.W.H.C. Admin 7; [2003] 1 P. & C.R. 31; [2003] E.W.C.A. Civ. 1408; [2004] 2 P. & C.R. 14; and *R. (On the application of Hereford Waste Watchers Ltd.) v Hereford Council* [2005] E.W.H.C. 191 (Admin), [26].

[170] See, by analogy, *Gillespie v First Secretary of State* [2003] E.W.H.C. Admin 8, [87]; [2003] 1 P. & C.R. 30 (no environmental impact statement required).

[171] [2003] E.W.H.C. 1311; [2004] 1 P. & C.R. 16.

[172] [2001] Env. L.R. 25, [41], cited with approval by the Court of Appeal in *Smith v Secretary of State for the Environment Transport and the Regions* [2003] E.W.C.A. Civ. 262; [2003] 2 P. & C.R. 11.

[173] *ibid.*

contained in the environmental statement should be both comprehensive and systematic, so that a decision to grant planning permission is taken 'in full knowledge' of the project's likely significant effects on the environment. If consideration of some of the environmental impacts and mitigation measures is effectively postponed until the reserved matters stage, the decision to grant planning permission would have been taken with only a partial rather than a 'full knowledge' of the project's likely significant effects of the project. That is not to suggest that full knowledge requires an environmental statement to contain every conceivable scrap of environmental information about a particular project. The Directive and the Assessment Regulations require likely significant effects to be assessed. It will be for the local planning authority to decide whether a particular effect is significant but a decision to defer a description of a likely significant adverse effect and any measures to avoid, reduce or remedy it to a later stage would not be in accordance with the terms of Schedule 3, would conflict with the public's right to make an input into the environmental information and would therefore conflict with the underlying purpose of the Directive."

13–225   A further example of a planning permission being set aside on the basis that development consent had been granted in the absence of sufficient information is found in *R. (On the application of Hereford Waste Watchers Ltd.) v Hereford Council.*[174] Planning permission had been sought for a waste and recycling facility. A series of conditions had been attached to the grant of planning permission. These included a number of conditions in respect of emissions, as follows.

> "No development shall take place until proposals for the location and construction of the areas and means of:
> [...] a report specifying the levels of all pollutants (including dust and odour) within the steam/emissions from the autoclaves and process building and the predicted emission level of these from the discharged point to atmosphere, based on the analysis of captured autoclave or stack emissions have been submitted to and agreed in writing by the local planning authority"

> "The general building structure and ventilation shall be designed to contain fugitive emissions and ensure containment of steam, odorous air and dust within the building. To achieve this, the ventilation system shall be suitable and sufficient, so as to maintain negative pressure at all times when processing or when steam, odours or dust are likely to be present within the building."

> "Prior to the discharge of process air from the building, suitable and sufficient abatement plant shall be installed to abate dust and odour (and any other pollutant identified) prior to its release to atmosphere. Details of these plant shall be submitted to Herefordshire Council for approval, and shall not be installed until they have expressed their satisfaction in writing."

13–226   The High Court inferred from the fact of the imposition of these conditions that the officials of the planning authority were of the view that the emissions could have significant effects on the environment, and that the information

---

[174] [2005] E.W.H.C. 191 (Admin); [2005] Env. L.R. 29.

sought by the conditions was not merely for the purposes of monitoring what the planning authority regarded as insignificant emissions.

The planning permission was, accordingly, set aside on the basis that certain information which the planning authority required, and which it had stipulated by way of planning condition should be made available prior to the development commencing, should have been made available prior to the planning permission being granted. **13–227**

Conditions leaving matters over for agreement will be subject to the usual constraints applying to conditions under s.34(5) of the PDA 2000. Thus, for example, the conditions will have to set out the parameters within which the various matters are to be agreed.[175] In addition, the conditions must not allow for the introduction of new, or for the aggravation of existing, environmental impacts, where such impacts had not been assessed at the time of the grant of the planning permission.[176] If necessary, the conditions should be interpreted narrowly so as to avoid such a result.[177] **13–228**

The Directive requires not only that the decision-maker be informed as to the likely significant effects, but also that the public be consulted in relation to the mitigation measures to be taken. If the mitigation measures are left over for subsequent agreement between the developer and the planning authority by way of a condition under s.34(5), this may well frustrate public consultation and participation. There is no express provision for any public participation in the process of reaching agreement under s.34(5). In *Arklow Holidays Ltd. v An Bord Pleanála*,[178] Clarke J. suggested that if the prescribed criteria were impermissibly wide, it might well be arguable that the public was excluded from appropriate consultation, as required by the Directive, in relation to the final determination of the matters subject to the condition. On the particular facts, however, Clarke J. held that An Bord Pleanála had imposed sufficiently detailed criteria as a result of a process involving public engagement. **13–229**

Q. Interaction of Planning Permission and Pollution Control

A related issue is as to the extent to which a planning authority or An Bord Pleanála may have regard to the fact that controls will be exercised by the Environmental Protection Agency ("the EPA"), under other legislation, in respect of the proposed development. The Court of Appeal in England and Wales has suggested that the planning decision-maker is not entitled to leave the assessment of likely impacts to a future occasion simply because it **13–230**

---

[175] See further paras 4–126 to 4–134.
[176] See, by analogy, *Smith v Secretary of State for the Environment Transport and the Regions* [2003] E.W.C.A. Civ. 262, [33]; [2003] 2 P. & C.R. 11.
[177] See discussion by Sedley L.J. in *Smith v Secretary of State for the Environment Transport and the Regions* [2003] E.W.C.A. Civ. 262, [55]; [2003] 2 P. & C.R. 11.
[178] [2006] I.E.H.C. 15; [2007] 1 I.L.R.M. 125.

contemplates that some other agency will act competently.[179] Constraints must be placed on the planning permission within which future details can be worked out, and the decision-maker must form a view about the likely details and their impact on the environment.

13–231 The position under Irish law is more complicated in that there is an inherent inconsistency in the statutory scheme. Notwithstanding the fact that the role of performing an environmental impact assessment resides principally with the planning authorities and An Bord Pleanála, the powers of the planning bodies are qualified in cases where the development is also subject to control by the EPA.[180] In particular, there is a limit on the types of conditions which may be imposed on a planning permission in such circumstances. Specifically, there is a prohibition on the attachment of conditions for the purposes of (a) controlling emissions from the operation of the activity, including the prevention, limitation, elimination, abatement or reduction of those emissions, or (b) controlling emissions related to or following the cessation of the operation of the activity. As mitigation measures are often imposed by way of planning condition, the qualifications in this regard hamper the ability of the planning bodies to fulfil one of the principal objectives of the assessment procedure, *i.e.* the imposition of mitigation measures as part of a development consent.

13–232 The statutory scheme therefore exhibits a preference that environmental controls be exercised by the EPA. The difficulty, however, is that under national law the primary responsibility for performing the environmental impact assessment still resides with the planning bodies. Moreover, many of the impacts which must be assessed are what might be regarded as land-use matters and, accordingly, would probably be better dealt with in the context of a planning application. There is a risk that the division of function between An Bord Pleanála and the EPA may result in a failure to carry out a holistic assessment of the development project.

---

[179] *Smith v Secretary of State for the Environment Transport and the Regions* [2003] E.W.C.A. Civ. 262, [33]; [2003] 2 P. & C.R. 11. See also *R. (On the application of Kent) v First Secretary of State* [2004] E.W.H.C. 2953 (Admin), [78]; [2005] 2 P. & C.R. 16; [2005] J.P.L. 951 (decision-maker in the planning process must set the parameters within which the likely significant effects of the development can be assessed, but within those parameters is entitled to take into account that there are matters which can properly be left for subsequent consideration and determination, whether it be by way of a planning condition or in the pollution control permit process). See also *R. (On the application of Hereford Waste Watchers Ltd.) v Hereford Council* [2005] E.W.H.C. 191 (Admin), [33] ("[…] The primary obligation to ensure that the environmental safeguards are complied with rests with the planning authority and they cannot abdicate responsibility by relying upon other enforcement agencies to make good their failings. They can, however, assume that if a system is in principle capable of operating without creating significant environmental effects, or if the details of the project are left to be determined with an input from other agencies, it should be assumed that the relevant enforcement agencies will operate competently to ensure that the system will operate as it should. Even if the system would have significant effects if not competently regulated, the authority should not act on the premise that this may occur.").

[180] See Environmental Protection Agency Act 1992, s.98 (as amended by PDA 2000, s.256), and Waste Management Act 1996, s.54 (as amended by the PDA 2000, s.257).

The position was even less satisfactory under the previous legislation. Under **13–233** s.98 of the Environmental Protection Agency Act 1992—prior to its amendment under s.256 of the PDA 2000—a planning authority and An Bord Pleanála were precluded from having regard to the risk from "environmental pollution" in determining an application for planning permission. More specifically, neither a planning authority nor An Bord Pleanála could decide to refuse planning permission for the reason that the development would cause environmental pollution, or decide to grant planning permission subject to conditions which were for the purposes of prevention, limitation, elimination, abatement or reduction of environmental pollution from the activity. To put the matter another way, where the proposed development would require both planning permission, and an integrated pollution control licence, the consideration of "environmental pollution" was removed from the planning process. Similar provision had been made—again prior to the PDA 2000—in relation to development which was to be the subject-matter of both a waste licence, under the Waste Management Acts 1996 to 2001, and a planning permission.

The legislation in this regard has since been amended under the PDA 2000.[181] **13–234** The present position is that planning permission may be refused where a planning authority or An Bord Pleanála considers the development, notwithstanding the licensing of the activity under either the Environmental Protection Agency Act 1992 or the Waste Management Acts 1996 to 2001, is unacceptable on environmental grounds, having regard to the proper planning and sustainable development of the area in which the development is or will be situate.

The appropriateness of the division of function under the previous legislation **13–235** had been challenged in numerous judicial review proceedings. In somewhat over-simplified terms, the argument seems to have been this. The prohibition on a planning authority or An Bord Pleanála having regard to environmental pollution was matched by an obverse prohibition on the EPA having regard to matters *other than* environmental pollution in determining either an application for an integrated pollution control licence or a waste licence. A concern was therefore expressed that there might be a blind spot between the two decision-making processes with the (alleged) result that no one decision-maker would be in a position to assess the development as a whole and, in particular, to assess the interaction of the various aspects of the development. The textbook example was of a chimney stack. It would seem that there is an optimum height for a chimney stack, involving a trade-off between the desire to reduce emissions, and the question of visual amenity. On one reading of the previous legislation, An Bord Pleanála would have jurisdiction in respect of visual amenity, and the EPA jurisdiction in relation to emissions, with neither body being entitled to make an overall assessment of the development, nor to attempt to strike the correct balance as between the visual amenity considerations and environmental pollution considerations (in the narrow sense).

---

[181] PDA 2000, ss.256 and 257.

13–236   The division of function between An Bord Pleanála and the EPA was addressed in detail by the Supreme Court in *Martin v An Bord Pleanála (No. 2)*.[182] The argument that this division of function prevented there being an integrated assessment of development projects was roundly rejected. Murray C.J. noted that nowhere in the EIA Directive was it suggested that one competent body must carry out a "global assessment" nor a "single assessment" of the relevant environmental factors and the interaction between them. Murray C.J. went on to observe that the Directive specifically envisaged that more than one authority may be responsible for exercising obligations arising from the Directive. It was manifestly clear therefore that the Directive did not envisage that the interaction between the various factors identified at Art.3 of the Directive could only be carried out by one competent authority with global responsibility.

> "It seems to me that it would be absurd to interpret the Directive so as to suggest that in permitting two or more competent bodies to carry out an EIA of the factors referred to in Article 3, including the interaction between them, by each body at the relevant stage of the process with which it was concerned, that nonetheless it was intended that there must be one body only that carries out an assessment of all the factors as if there was only one stage in the process and it was the only body making the assessment. This would run contrary to the plain meaning of the provisions and scheme of the Directive."

13–237   By way of an aside, it has to be said that it is an indictment of the Irish legal system that it took years before this issue—which was of fundamental importance and had implications for numerous developments—was finally ruled upon definitively. This was so notwithstanding the fact that the argument or variants of it had been raised in numerous cases. The sensible and efficient course would have been for a test case to have been fast-tracked and brought before the Supreme Court. This would have allowed the issue to be decided—one way or another—at an early stage. This would have provided certainty, and avoided the incurring of unnecessary legal costs. Instead, there was seemingly endless litigation, with tangential aspects of the argument dealt with periodically in various judgments.[183] All the while large-scale developments were stalled. It was not until the judgment of the High Court in *Martin v An Bord Pleanála (No. 2)* that the gravamen of the objection was finally addressed. Thereafter, further delay ensued: the matter was appealed to the Supreme Court and judgment was not delivered for the best part of two years.[184]

---

[182] Unreported, Supreme Court, May 10, 2007; [2007] I.E.S.C. 23.

[183] *O'Connell v Environmental Protection Agency* [2003] 1 I.R. 530; *Martin v An Bord Pleanála (No. 1)* [2002] 2 I.R. 665; and *O'Brien v Tipperary South Riding County Council*, unreported, High Court, October 22, 2002.

[184] Unreported, Supreme Court, May 10, 2007; [2007] I.E.S.C. 23.

R. Decision on Development Consent

It is a requirement under Art.9(1) of the Directive[185] that, when a decision to grant or refuse development consent has been taken, the competent authority or authorities shall inform the public thereof in accordance with the appropriate procedures and shall make available to the public the following information:

13–238

— the content of the decision and any conditions attached thereto;
— having examined the concerns and opinions expressed by the public concerned, the main reasons and considerations on which the decision is based, including information about the public participation process; and
— a description, where necessary, of the main measures to avoid, reduce and, if possible, offset the major adverse effects.

The relevant provisions of the PDA 2000 are not as forthright in their terms. There, the requirement is to state the main reasons and considerations on which the decision is based, and, where conditions are imposed, to state the main reasons for the imposition of any such conditions.[186] The duty to give reasons is discussed generally at paras 12–119 to 12–163. The form of notification of a decision on a planning application is prescribed under art.31 of the Planning and Development Regulations 2001 (as substituted by the 2006 Regulations). The 2006 Regulations introduce a new requirement to specify that in deciding the application the planning authority or An Bord Pleanála "has regard to submissions or observations received" in accordance with the Planning and Development Regulations.[187] Explanatory notes produced by the Department of the Environment Heritage and Local Government suggest that this amendment is as a consequence of the obligation under the amended EIA Directive "to include reference to the public participation process and that the fact that the concerns and opinions expressed by the public have been examined".

13–239

It is submitted that these provisions of national law will now have to be interpreted in the light of the requirements of the amended Directive. In particular, it seems that the reasons and considerations will have to be much fuller than has previously been the case, and should address the principal issues of concern raised in the public participation process. The general practice of An Bord Pleanála has been to provide a very terse statement of reasons and considerations. It is very unusual for express reference to be made in the board's decision to concerns and opinions expressed during the course of the appeal process, rather the decisions tend to contain generic references to matters such as "traffic safety", "public health and safety" or "injury to amenities".

13–240

---

[185] (As substituted by Directive 2003/35/EC).
[186] PDA 2000, s.34(10). See, generally, *Mulholland v An Bord Pleanála (No. 2)* [2005] I.E.H.C. 306; [2006] 1 I.L.R.M. 287; and *Kildare County Council v An Bord Pleanála* [2006] I.E.H.C. 173; unreported, MacMenamin J., March 10, 2006.
[187] Planning and Development Regulations 2001, art.31(g) (planning authorities) and art.74(2)(j) (An Bord Pleanála) (as substituted by the 2006 Regulations).

13–241 It is unlikely that such a perfunctory approach to the giving of reasons will pass muster under the amended Art.9 of the Directive. A more discursive decision will be required, making reference in specific terms to the principal concerns raised by the public concerned. The newly introduced requirement under the Planning and Development Regulations 2006 to specify that in deciding the application the planning authority or An Bord Pleanála "has regard to submissions or observations received" is risible. Such a bald statement is meaningless without reference to the specific concerns raised on the particular planning application.

13–242 It also seems that An Bord Pleanála will not be allowed to rely to the same extent as previously on inspectors' reports. Until now it was necessary, in almost every case, to read the inspector's report in order to gain any understanding of the issues arising on an appeal. The courts had for a long time condoned this practice, ruling that in considering the adequacy of the board's decision, regard was to be had to the inspector's report.[188] All of this will now have to be reassessed. In particular, what Art.9 requires is that the decision itself set out, not only the reasons, but also the considerations underlying the decision.

13–243 (In *O'Mahony v An Bord Pleanála*,[189] O'Neill J. had rejected an argument that the duty to carry out this assessment lies solely with the members of An Bord Pleanála—not the inspector—and must be recorded in its decision. This may no longer represent good law.)

13–244 In *R. (On the application of Richardson) v North Yorkshire County Council*,[190] the Court of Appeal in England and Wales ruled that a breach of the obligation to state the main reasons and considerations should be capable, in principle, of being remedied, and the legislative purpose achieved, by a mandatory order requiring the planning authority to make available *ex post facto* a statement containing the specified information. In deciding that the failure to state the reasons and main considerations should not necessarily lead to the planning permission being quashed, the Court of Appeal emphasised the fact that the requirement focuses on the availability of information for public inspection *after* the decision has been made, rather than on the decision-making process.

---

[188] *O'Keeffe v An Bord Pleanála* [1993] 1 I.R. 39; *Village Residents Association Ltd. v An Bord Pleanála* [2001] 1 I.R. 441; *Aer Rianta v An Bord Pleanála*, unreported, High Court, Kelly J., June 25, 2002; and *Fairyhouse Club Ltd. v An Bord Pleanála*, unreported, High Court, Finnegan J., July 18, 2001.

[189] [2005] I.E.H.C. 39; unreported, O'Neill J., February 18, 2005.

[190] [2003] E.W.C.A. Civ. 1860, [50]; [2004] 2 P. & C.R. 15; [2004] J.P.L. 911.

S. Remedies for Breach of Directive

1. Introduction

We turn now to examine the nature of the remedies available in the event of a   **13–245**
breach of the requirements of the Directive. Two points must be emphasised
from the outset. First, certain provisions of the EIA Directive have been held
to have direct effect. See further para.13–259 and onwards. The significance
of this is that the Directive confers rights which can be invoked, not just before
the national courts, but also before a planning authority or An Bord Pleanála
(as emanations of the State). Secondly, there is now an express right, under
Art.10a of the Directive, to access to a review procedure before a court of law
(or another independent and impartial body established by law) to challenge
the substantive or procedural legality of decisions, acts or omissions subject to
the public participation provisions of the Directive. All of this means that—
even where there is no allegation that there has been a failure to transpose the
Directive properly into Irish legislation—a breach of the Directive is never
simply a matter of Irish law, but rather has an EC law aspect.

The EIA Directive thus gives rise to enforceable procedural rights whereby   **13–246**
members of the public are entitled to be consulted in advance of the making of
decisions to grant development consent for certain development projects. These
procedural rights extend to a right to make submissions or observations, and a
right to a statement of the main reasons and considerations for decisions.

It is possible to imagine many circumstances which would give rise to a breach   **13–247**
of these rights. These range from where there has been a failure to subject a
particular development to environmental impact assessment at all, to where
there has been some deficiency in the procedure followed; for example, proper
public notice of the application may not have been given or mitigation measures
may not have been dealt with in advance of the grant of the development consent.

In some instances, the breach will have arisen as a result of the failure to   **13–248**
implement the Directive properly; in others, the difficulty will have arisen, not
because of any deficiency in transposition, but rather as a result of the
misapplication of the provisions of national law in the case of a particular
development. In either event, it is open to the complainant to make reference
to the provisions of the Directive. This is so even where there is no allegation
that the national implementing law is defective: the complainant is entitled to
rely on the Directive in arguing that the national legislation is being
misapplied.[191]

Even before the introduction of Art.10a, the Directive could be raised before   **13–249**
the Irish courts, both as an aid to the interpretation of national legislation, and
by reference to its direct effect. It is important to note, however, that there were

---

[191] See, by analogy, *Marks & Spencers plc v Customs and Excise Commissioners* (Case C–
62/00) [2002] E.C.R. I-6325.

limitations in this regard. In particular, the rules of court practice and procedure remained a matter of national law. Thus, a litigant alleging that there has been a failure to comply with the Directive might find his proceedings ruled inadmissible on the basis of a failure to comply with some procedural requirement—such as a time-limit or a *locus standi* requirement—imposed under Irish law. Provided that the requirements of equivalence and effectiveness were met, the national procedural rule could be applied even if it resulted in an alleged breach of the Directive going unexamined. The intriguing prospect presented by Art.10a is that some national procedural rules might now have to be disapplied. This is discussed in detail at paras 13–336 to 13–407.

2. National law and the EIA Directive

13–250   Ireland has, to a large extent, properly transposed the requirements of the EIA Directive into national law. Consequently, in any particular instance, a breach of the procedural requirements of the Directive will simultaneously represent a breach of national law. Thus, for example, it is a requirement of national law that a planning application for development of a type prescribed under Sch.5, Pt I of the Planning and Development Regulations 2001 be accompanied by an environmental impact statement. Schedule 5, Pt I corresponds closely to Annex I of the Directive. The failure to submit an environmental impact statement will therefore also represent a breach of national law. In such cases, it can be argued that any resulting decision is invalid by reference to national law.

13–251   An objector would, however, be well advised not to confine himself to national law, but to emphasise that a breach of the Directive is also involved. This is because certain procedural obstacles—such as a time-limit or a *locus standi* requirement—which would otherwise apply might have to be disapplied in the case of a breach of the Directive. This is discussed below at para.13–336 and onwards.

13–252   It is worth reiterating that it is permissible to have regard to the provisions of the Directive even where there is no allegation that the Directive has not been properly implemented. In this regard, reference is made, by analogy, to the judgment of the ECJ in *Marks & Spencers plc v Customs and Excise Commissioners*.[192]

> "Consequently, the adoption of national measures correctly implementing a directive does not exhaust the effects of the directive. Member States remain bound actually to ensure full application of the directive even after the adoption of those measures. Individuals are therefore entitled to rely before national courts, against the State, on the provisions of a directive which appear, so far as their subject-matter is concerned, to be unconditional and sufficiently precise whenever the full application of the directive is not in fact secured, that is to say, not only

---

[192] (Case C–62/00) [2002] E.C.R. I-6325, [27].

where the directive has not been implemented or has been implemented incorrectly, but also where the national measures correctly implementing the directive are not being applied in such a way as to achieve the result sought by it."

The suggestion of the High Court of England and Wales in *R. v London Borough of Hammersmith and Fulham Ex p. CPRE (London Branch)*[193] to the contrary is wrong and should not be followed.[194]   **13–253**

A second reason for which an objector would be well advised to make reference to the Directive is that this may result in a purposive interpretation of the national legislation. In a number of cases, applicants have successfully argued that the Irish courts should have regard to the purpose of the Directive in interpreting national law.[195]   **13–254**

In other instances, there may be some deficiency in the manner in which the Directive has been implemented into Irish law. For example, for a long time it was alleged that the division of the assessment function as between the Environmental Protection Agency and An Bord Pleanála under the previous legislation did not comply with the Directive.[196] Examples of other possible deficiencies include the fact that certain development projects—notably certain peat extraction projects—sometimes improperly avoid environmental impact assessment.[197] Similarly, the application of the Directive to local authority and State authority development is haphazard. There may thus be some daylight between the provisions of the implementing legislation and the provisions of the Directive.   **13–255**

Any such deficiencies might, in principle, be made good by the adoption of a purposive approach to the interpretation of the national legislation. It is well established that national courts and administrative bodies, in interpreting a provision of national law designed to implement the provisions of a Directive, should interpret their national law in the light of the wording and the purpose of the Directive in order to achieve the result envisaged by the Directive.[198] In *O'Connell v Environmental Protection Agency*,[199] the Supreme Court took a   **13–256**

---

[193] (2001) 81 P. & C.R. 6.
[194] "In my view, once the directive is correctly transposed into the national law, an individual cannot continue to assert rights in the national courts under the directive. In this case, Directive 85/337/EEC, having been correctly transposed into national law by the 1988 Regulations, the applicant cannot rely on a Community law right derived from it in support of its case." at [35].
[195] See, for example, *Shannon Regional Fisheries Board v An Bord Pleanála* [1994] 3 I.R. 449; *Maher v An Bord Pleanála* [1999] 2 I.L.R.M. 198; *O'Connell v Environmental Protection Agency* [2003] 1 I.R. 530; and *Arklow Holidays Ltd. v An Bord Pleanála* [2006] I.E.H.C. 15; [2007] 1 I.L.R.M. 125.
[196] See further para.13–235.
[197] See further para.13–28.
[198] *Nathan v Bailey Gibson Ltd.* [1998] 2 I.R. 162 at 174, *per* Hamilton C.J.
[199] [2003] 1 I.R. 530 at 555. See also *Arklow Holidays Ltd. v An Bord Pleanála* [2006] I.E.H.C. 15; [2007] 1 I.L.R.M. 125 (legislation to be construed where possible in a manner consistent with EC law).

purposive approach—in the specific context of the EIA Directive—to the interpretation of (since amended) provisions of the Environmental Protection Agency Act 1992.

> "When applying national law, whether adopted before or after the Directive, the national court called upon to interpret that law must do so, as far as possible, in the light of the wording and the purpose of the directive so as to achieve the result which it has in view (see, for example *Dorsch Consult* (Case C-54/96) [1997] E.C.R. I-4961). It is more natural to interpret an existing provision of the law, even in the event of ambiguity, so as to make that meaning conform to Community law than to insert a provision into a particular national law so as to give it a meaning it does not naturally bear."

13–257 The adoption of a purposive approach to interpretation might well overcome some minor discrepancies in the implementation of the Directive. It might be possible to imply into the national legislation certain requirements to make good possible deficiencies. An obvious example is in relation to local authority development. An Bord Pleanála has jurisdiction to determine whether sub-threshold development should be subject to environmental impact assessment, but there is no corresponding obligation on the local authority to refer the matter to An Bord Pleanála. Thus, whereas An Bord Pleanála has power to make a screening decision, there is no formal procedure whereby An Bord Pleanála is notified in advance of proposed local authority development. Rather, it is up to each local authority to refer individual projects for a screening decision on an ad hoc basis. It is arguable, by analogy with the decision of the House of Lords in *Berkeley v Secretary of State for the Environment*,[200] that a duty to refer can be implied.

13–258 In other cases, however, even a purposive interpretation will not be sufficient to close the gap between the national law and the requirements of the Directive. In such cases it will be necessary to rely on the direct effect of the Directive. This is discussed next.

3. Direct effect

13–259 The ECJ has consistently held that whenever the provisions of a Directive appear, so far as their subject-matter is concerned, to be unconditional and sufficiently precise, they may be relied on before the national courts by individuals against the State where the latter has failed to implement the Directive in domestic law by the end of the period prescribed or where it has failed to implement the Directive correctly.[201] In *World Wildlife Fund v Autonome Provinz Bozen*,[202] the ECJ ruled that Arts 4(2) and 2(1) of the EIA

---

[200] [2001] 2 A.C. 603; (2001) P. & C.R. 492.

[201] See, for example, *Becker v Finanzamt Münster-Innenstadt* (Case 8/81) [1982] E.C.R. 53, [25]; *Flli Costanzo SpA v Comune di Milano* (Case 103/88) [1989] E.C.R. 1839, [29]; and *Criminal proceedings against Kortas* (Case C–319/97) [1999] E.C.R. I–3143, [21].

[202] (Case C–435/97) [1999] E.C.R. I–5613.

Directive were to be interpreted as meaning that, where the discretion conferred by those provisions has been exceeded by the legislative or administrative authorities of a Member State, individuals may rely on those provisions before a court of that Member State against the national authorities and thus obtain from the latter the *setting aside* of the national rules or measures incompatible with those provisions. In such a case, it is for the authorities of the Member State to take, according to their relevant powers, all the general or particular measures necessary to ensure that projects are examined in order to determine whether they are likely to have significant effects on the environment and, if so, to ensure that they are subject to an impact assessment.[203] The ECJ subsequently confirmed, in *R. (On the application of Wells) v Secretary of State for Transport, Local Government and the Regions*,[204] that the obligation of the Member States extends, subject to the limits laid down by the principle of procedural autonomy of the Member States, to the revocation or suspension of a consent already granted.

The judgment in *Bozen* had been to a large extent foreshadowed by that in **13–260** *Kraaijeveld*.[205] Although there had been no express finding in *Kraaijeveld* that the Directive had direct effect, it is arguable that this was implicit in the judgment. In particular, the ruling that the competent authorities of a Member State were obliged to take, within the sphere of their competence, all the general or particular measures necessary to ensure that projects are examined in order to determine whether they are likely to have significant effects on the environment and, if so, to ensure that they are subject to an impact assessment, must surely have been predicated on Arts 2 and 4 of the Directive having direct effect.

The House of Lords accepted in *Berkeley v Secretary of State for the* **13–261** *Environment*[206] that the Directive has direct effect. Lord Hoffmann described the nature of the directly enforceable right in the following terms.

> "The directly enforceable right of a citizen which is accorded by the Directive is not merely a right to a fully informed decision on the substantive issue. It must have been adopted on an appropriate basis and that requires the inclusive and democratic procedure prescribed by the Directive in which the public, however misguided or wrongheaded its views may be, is given an opportunity to express its opinion on the environmental issues."

To some extent the finding that the Directive has direct effect has been overtaken **13–262** by the subsequent introduction of Art.10a. This article confers on qualified members of the public a right of access to a review procedure before a court of law or another independent and impartial body established by law to challenge the substantive or procedural legality of decisions, acts or omissions subject to

---

[203] See also *Luxemburg v Linster* (Case C–287/98).
[204] (Case C–201/02) [2004] E.C.R. I–723.
[205] (Case C–72/95) [1996] E.C.R. I–5403.
[206] [2001] 2 A.C. 603 at 615; (2001) 81 P. & C.R. 492 at 501.

the public participation provisions of the Directive. It follows as a corollary of the creation of such a remedy that members of the public enjoy "rights" under the Directive. This may help overcome certain theoretical difficulties which might otherwise arise in applying the concept of direct effect to a Directive which is arguably somewhat vague in its application.

13–263   The initial approach of the Irish courts had been hostile to the notion of the Directive having direct effect. In *McBride v Galway Corporation*, the High Court—at a time prior to the judgment of the ECJ in *World Wildlife Fund v Autonome Provinz Bozen*[207]—had suggested that it was impossible to interpret the obligation to subject Annex II projects to environmental impact assessment as being so unconditional and sufficiently precise as to be capable of being relied upon by an individual against the State where the latter has failed to implement the Directive in its national law by the end of the prescribed period.[208] Whereas this suggestion cannot withstand the judgment in *Bozen*, it does serve to emphasise the practical difficulties in interpreting the somewhat vague wording of the EIA Directive as having direct effect. On appeal, the Supreme Court, *per* Keane J. (as he then was), suggested that the obligation to ensure that development was subject to environmental impact assessment lay with the Member States alone, and, therefore, the respondent decision-maker, although undoubtedly an organ of administration, could not be regarded as being in breach of any requirement of the Directive during the relevant period. This suggestion is clearly wrong and it is difficult to understand how it came to have been made in circumstances where the judgment of the ECJ in *Kraaijeveld*[209] had been opened to the court. A similar misconception underlies the much earlier judgment of the High Court in *Browne v An Bord Pleanála*.[210]

13–264   A related heresy is found in the judgment on the leave application in the *Lancefort Ltd.* saga.[211] Morris J. appeared to suggest that relief by way of judicial review was only available where the decision-maker had breached national law; this suggestion seems to have been based on the mistaken assumption that An Bord Pleanála was only required to apply national law.

13–265   It does not appear that the question of direct effect has come squarely before the Irish courts since the judgment in *World Wildlife Fund v Autonome Provinz Bozen*.[212] The issue did arise tangentially in *Cosgrave v An Bord Pleanála*, in that it was alleged that the (then) national legislation failed to implement the Directive properly insofar as the assessment function was split in some cases as between An Bord Pleanála and the Environmental Protection Agency. As discussed below at para.13–280, the High Court ultimately disposed of the case on narrow procedural grounds. The distinct question as to whether Art.10a

---

[207] (Case C–435/97) [1999] E.C.R. I–5613.
[208] *McBride v Galway Corporation* [1998] 1 I.R. 485 at 509.
[209] (Case C–72/95) [1996] E.C.R. I–5403.
[210] [1991] 2 I.R. 209; [1989] I.L.R.M. 865.
[211] *Lancefort Ltd. v An Bord Pleanála* [1997] 2 I.L.R.M. 508.
[212] (Case C–435/97) [1999] E.C.R. I–5613.

has direct effect was addressed in *Friends of the Curragh Environment Ltd. v An Bord Pleanála (No. 1)*,[213] and this is discussed further at para.13–326.

4. Direct effect and private developers

The direct effect of the EIA Directive gives rise to some interesting theoretical issues as to the rights of affected developers. Generally a Directive may only be relied upon directly as against the national authorities of a Member State ("emanations of the State"). This is sometimes referred to as "vertical direct effect". An unimplemented Directive may not normally be relied upon as against private individuals or companies. There are two aspects to this, first, where one individual seeks to rely on a Directive against another individual ("horizontal direct effect"), and, secondly, where an emanation of the State seeks to rely on the Directive against an individual ("descending vertical direct effect" or "inverse direct effect"). The term "direct effect" in this context refers to the situation where the terms of the Directive are relied upon directly in legal proceedings, in distinction to the situation where a provision of national legislation is *interpreted* in a particular way so as to give effect to the objectives of the Directive. This latter phenomenon—whereby the interpretation of national legislation is coloured by the Directive—is sometimes referred to as "indirect direct effect". **13–266**

On one view, this distinction between horizontal and vertical direct effects is not always observed in the case law on the EIA Directive. The facts of many of the cases involve a private developer losing the benefit of a planning permission, the relevant court having found that the requirements of the Directive were not met and the planning permission therefore invalid. Whereas the relevant decision-maker is—as an emanation of the State—clearly bound to give effect to the Directive, the question can legitimately be asked as to whether the forfeit suffered by the developer might not be regarded as an impermissible inverse direct effect. **13–267**

This issue has been considered by the courts on a number of occasions. The Court of Appeal of England and Wales carried out a very thoughtful analysis of the issue in *R. v Durham County Council Ex p. Huddlestone*.[214] The Court of Appeal ultimately concluded that enforcement of a Directive by an individual against the State is not rendered inadmissible solely by its consequential effect on other individuals. **13–268**

The case concerned an old mining planning permission. The relevant planning authority had failed to determine the application for conditions within time, and, accordingly, as a matter of national law, there was a deemed determination and the conditions set out in the application applied. A local resident sought to have the deemed determination set aside on judicial review. **13–269**

---

[213] [2006] I.E.H.C. 243; unreported, Kelly J., July 14, 2006.
[214] [2000] 1 W.L.R. 1484; [2000] J.P.L. 1125.

13–270   At first instance, the High Court refused the relief sought. The High Court considered that to hold that no deemed determination could arise by reliance on the Directive would involve the relevant planning authority relying on the Directive as overriding the rights conferred on the developer by national law, *i.e.* an impermissible descending vertical direct effect.[215]

> "In my judgment the key to the issue lies in the fact that, in order to succeed, the applicant must show that [the planning authority] was required as a matter of European law to disregard the deeming provision contained in the 1991 Act and to apply the remaining statutory procedures as if the deeming provision were ineffective. So long as the deeming provision had legal effect, there was nothing left for [the planning authority] to do: it could not insist on the provision of an environmental statement before reaching a determination, since by virtue of the statute it was already deemed to have made a determination. The reason why this seems to me to be the key to the issue is that, in order to disregard the statutory deeming provision, [the planning authority] would have had to rely on the directive as overriding the rights conferred on [the developer] by national law. That would have involved [the planning authority], an emanation of the State, relying on the Directive as against [the developer], an individual. In my judgment that would be contrary to the principles laid down by the European Court of Justice concerning the direct effect of directives. An individual may rely on the direct effect of a directive as against the State so as to have inconsistent national law disapplied; but the State which has defaulted in its implementation of the directive cannot rely on the direct effect of the directive as against an individual so as to disregard inconsistent national law or have it disapplied. If [the planning authority] was unable to rely on the Directive as against [the developer], then it seems to me to follow that the applicant cannot show that [the planning authority] erred in law or otherwise acted unlawfully in failing to disregard the deeming provision or to apply the remaining statutory procedures as if the deeming provision was ineffective. The fact that an application for judicial review is brought by an individual against a State authority cannot confer on that authority rights that it would not otherwise enjoy or impose on it obligations to which it would not otherwise be subject."

13–271   On appeal, the Court of Appeal reversed the decision of the High Court. Sedley L.J. placed emphasis on the distinction between private law and public law. The applicant for judicial review was not seeking to assert a private law right as against the developer, but rather was seeking to assert his rights under the Directive.

> "In doing so he was neither having [the developer] criminalised nor securing some change in his own relationship with them: he was seeking, in the commentators' jargon, to give the Directive a vertical effect which would clothe [the planning authority] with the powers it ought to have had. This would of course subject [the developer] to more onerous conditions for the grant of permission (though by their counsel they have disavowed any desire to go on regardless of the effect on the environment, and although they have in fact now produced an environmental impact assessment); but to do this is not, in my

---

[215] *ibid.*, [39].

judgment, to impose an obligation in the objectionable sense identified in the court's jurisprudence – that is to say, to interpose a new obligation in the relations between individuals or retrospectively to criminalise the activity of one of them. It is to prevent the state, when asked by a citizen to give effect to the unambiguous requirements of a directive, from taking refuge in its own neglect to transpose them into national law."[216]

The question of inverse direct effect ultimately came before the ECJ in *R. (On the application of Wells) v Secretary of State for Transport, Local Government and the Regions.*[217] The ECJ rejected an argument that the Directive could not be invoked against a particular "development consent" as this would otherwise involve inverse direct effect.[218]   **13–272**

> "According to the United Kingdom Government, acceptance that an individual is entitled to invoke Article 2(1) of Directive 85/337, read in conjunction with Articles 1(2) and 4(2) thereof, would amount to inverse direct effect directly obliging the Member State concerned, at the request of an individual, such as Mrs Wells, to deprive another individual or individuals, such as the owners of Conygar Quarry, of their rights.
>
> As to that submission, the principle of legal certainty prevents directives from creating obligations for individuals. For them, the provisions of a directive can only create rights (see Case 152/84 *Marshall* [1986] ECR 723, paragraph 48). Consequently, an individual may not rely on a directive against a Member State where it is a matter of a State obligation directly linked to the performance of another obligation falling, pursuant to that directive, on a third party (see, to this effect, Case C-221/88 *Busseni* [1990] ECR I-495, paragraphs 23 to 26, and Case C-97/96 *Daihatsu Deutschland* [1997] ECR I-6843, paragraphs 24 and 26).
>
> On the other hand, mere adverse repercussions on the rights of third parties, even if the repercussions are certain, do not justify preventing an individual from invoking the provisions of a directive against the Member State concerned (see to this effect, in particular, Case 103/88 *Fratelli Costanzo* [1989] ECR 1839, paragraphs 28 to 33, *WWF and Others*, cited above, paragraphs 69 and 71, Case C-194/94 *CIA Security International* [1996] ECR I-2201, paragraphs 40 to 55, Case C-201/94 *Smith & Nephew and Primecrown* [1996] ECR I-5819, paragraphs 33 to 39, and Case C-443/98 *Unilever* [2000] ECR I-7535, paragraphs 45 to 52).
>
> In the main proceedings, the obligation of the Member State concerned to ensure that the competent authorities carry out an assessment of the environmental effects of the working of the quarry is not directly linked to the performance of any obligation which would fall, pursuant to Directive 85/337, on the quarry owners. The fact that the mining operations must be halted to await the assessment is admittedly the consequence of the belated performance of the State's obligations. Such a consequence cannot, however, as the United Kingdom claims, be described an inverse direct effect of the provisions of that directive in relation to quarry owners."

It has to be said that the reasoning of the judgment is somewhat spare, and, in particular, tends to gloss over the conceptual difficulties involved in a finding   **13–273**

---

[216] *ibid.*, [25].
[217] (Case C–201/02) [2004] E.C.R. I–723.
[218] *ibid.*, [55]–[58].

that a private developer can suffer a forfeit in terms of the loss of a planning permission. The reasoning of the Advocate General is more cogent. The Advocate General, in his opinion, identified two principles which might possibly have militated against a finding that a planning permission should be set aside, as follows. First, the prohibition on horizontal direct effect, *i.e.* an unimplemented Directive cannot be invoked as such by an individual in proceedings against another individual. Secondly, the prohibition on what was described as "descending vertical direct effect", *i.e.* a national authority may not rely, as against an individual, upon a provision of a Directive whose implementation in national law has not yet taken place.

13–274   The Advocate General concluded that neither of these principles would be offended against by a finding that the relevant planning permission could be set aside. No horizontal direct effect was involved because the proceedings were not as between two private individuals, but between the applicant and an emanation of the State, *i.e.* the relevant planning authority. Insofar as descending vertical effect was concerned, the Advocate General considered that this principle could not constitute an obstacle to performance, by the national authorities, of their obligation to nullify the consequences of breach of a Directive's provisions, first, by setting aside the national measures incompatible with those provisions and, second, by taking the measures necessary in order for the requirements contained therein to be implemented. In such a case the State did not impose obligations on an individual to its own advantage on the basis of an untransposed Directive, but adopted all the measures necessary for implementing that Directive.

13–275   The Advocate General went on to suggest that a contrary interpretation of the principle that Directives do not have descending vertical direct effect would, without a doubt, undermine the principle of the primacy of Community law.

13–276   Notwithstanding the judgment of the ECJ in *Wells*, the Court of Appeal in England and Wales recently suggested *obiter* in *Wirral BC v Brock plc*[219] that it may still be impermissible to rely on the Directive in declaratory proceedings as between a developer and a planning authority. The case concerned a claim for a deemed decision in respect of an old mineral planning permission. On the facts, the Court of Appeal found that the time for the determination of the application had actually been extended by agreement, and, consequently, a deemed decision did not arise. Aldous L.J. went on, however, to address briefly the alternative argument that the planning authority itself could not rely on the Directive as against a developer (descending vertical effect), and suggested that whereas the Directive could be enforced at the suit of an individual against the planning authority, and therefore indirectly against the developer, direct enforcement of the Directive by the planning authority might be impermissible.

---

[219] [2004] E.W.C.A. Civ. 1611, [48]; [2005] 2 P. & C.R. 18.

To date, the Irish courts have not squarely addressed the question of horizontal **13–277** and vertical direct effect. The High Court has, however, on at least two occasions suggested that even if Ireland had not adopted all measures to ensure that all projects likely to have significant effects on the environment are subject to environmental impact assessment, this fact would not entitle an objector to seek relief which would result in condemning a decision legitimately reached in accordance with national legislation.[220] The judgments do not articulate any concern as to indirect direct effect—such as had been worrying the courts of England and Wales—but rather appear to be based on narrower considerations.

In the first of the two judgments, the leave application in the *Lancefort Ltd.* **13–278** proceedings,[221] Morris J. appeared to suggest that relief by way of judicial review was only available where the decision-maker had breached national law. This suggestion seems to have been based on the mistaken assumption that An Bord Pleanála was only required to apply national law; of course, An Bord Pleanála, as an emanation of the State, is obliged to take all the general or particular measures necessary to ensure that projects are examined in order to determine whether they are likely to have significant effects on the environment and, if so, to ensure that they are subject to an impact assessment.[222] Whereas prior to *Wells* there might be some room for debate as to the *form* of relief which should be granted in the event of a finding that An Bord Pleanála had acted in breach of EC law, it was simply incorrect to suggest that the claim must fail *in limine*.

The implication of the judgment in *Lancefort Ltd.* is that a challenge to the **13–279** implementation of a Directive should properly be brought against the State in plenary proceedings, and not raised during the course of judicial review proceedings impugning a particular administrative decision.[223] This point does not, however, appear to have been discussed in any detail again until the judgment in *Cosgrave v An Bord Pleanála*.[224]

It was argued on behalf of the State and the notice party developer in *Cosgrave* **13–280** that the remedies available to the applicant by way of judicial review were limited to the decision-making process, and the applicant was not permitted to use those proceedings to challenge the implementation by the State of the Directive. Somewhat surprisingly, the judgment of the ECJ in *Wells* does not seem to have been opened to the court.

---

[220] *Lancefort Ltd. v An Bord Pleanála* [1997] 2 I.L.R.M. 508; and *Cosgrave v An Bord Pleanála* [2004] 2 I.R. 435.
[221] *Lancefort Ltd. v An Bord Pleanála* [1997] 2 I.L.R.M. 508.
[222] (Case C–72/95) [1996] E.C.R. I–5403.
[223] For a discussion of the practical procedural difficulties presented by any necessity for plenary proceedings, see M. Healy Rae "Judicial Review and the Transposition of EU Directives" (2005) 10 *Bar Review* 131.
[224] [2004] 2 I.R. 435.

13–281   Kelly J. upheld the objection.[225]

> "I have to say, having had the opportunity to read all the affidavit material, that the complaints which are made in that regard are rather generic in nature and they are not dependent upon any particular alleged deficiency in the transposition which has been effected and do not impact upon how the first respondent dealt with the appeal made to it in this particular case, having regard to the legislation that is in force.
>
> It seems to me, therefore, that the views of Morris P. in *Lancefort Ltd. v. An Bord Pleanála* [1997] 2 I.L.R.M. 508 apply with equal force here. The relief which is sought in respect of the transposition of the directives does not relate to the particular decision of the first respondent that is sought to be challenged in these proceedings. It does not seem to me that it is open, having regard to that decision, which I follow, to permit a judicial review application to be made on this basis. In essence what is being said is that the existing legislation and which regulated the appeal which was dealt with by the first respondent, was defective. That is not a view which is accepted, for detailed reasons which were gone into both by the first notice party and the third and fourth respondents.
>
> Even if there is force in the applicant's contention in that regard, it does not, it appears to me, entitle the applicant to have the decision of the first respondent quashed, and that is the primary relief sought and what this judicial review application is really all about."

13–282   The rationale of *Cosgrave* appears to be narrower than that in *Lancefort Ltd.* In particular, Kelly J. made specific reference to the fact that the complaints made by the applicant were generic in nature, and this peculiarity may provide the true *ratio* of the ruling.

13–283   In any event, it is submitted that it would be unsafe to regard *Cosgrave* as authority for any wider proposition. First, as the judgment of the ECJ in *Wells* was not opened to the court, any general ruling as to the nature of the judicial review remedy would have been made *per incuriam*. Secondly, the State subsequently disavowed reliance on the self-same procedural objection in the later case of *Martin v An Bord Pleanála (No. 2)*,[226] thus at least tacitly acknowledging the weaknesses in the argument.

13–284   It is unfortunate that this entire issue of the implications of direct effect for private-sector developers has not, to date, received a fuller consideration from the Irish courts. There is an obvious tension between the goal of ensuring that all developments which should be subject to the Directive are appropriately assessed, on the one hand, and the hardship which might be suffered by a developer who, through no fault of his own, has a grant of planning permission subsequently set aside, on the other. A developer may well find himself in a Kafkaesque situation whereby he does not know what it is that he must do to ensure that his planning permission survives scrutiny; in particular, he may not

---

[225] *ibid.*, [12]–[14].
[226] Unreported, High Court, Smyth J., November 30, 2004. This procedural issue was not discussed by the Supreme Court in its judgment: unreported, May 10, 2007; [2007] I.E.S.C 23.

be able to rely on the fact that he has fully complied with the provisions of national law lest it subsequently transpire that the national law itself is deficient.

Scannell suggests that, in such situations, the courts should not set aside the **13–285** planning permission unless and until a remedy is provided for third parties who suffer from the State's culpable failure to transpose Directives properly.[227] One possible mechanism for achieving this result is that the court—instead of quashing the planning permission directly—might order the relevant planning authority to exercise its statutory power to revoke the planning permission; this would then attract the payment of statutory compensation.[228] This is precisely the type of issue which needs to be considered before any definitive ruling can be made as to the circumstances, if any, in which a court should decline to set aside a planning permission granted in breach of the requirements of the Directive. As indicated above, this whole area has not yet been teased out in the Irish case law.

In conclusion, therefore, it seems that the better view is that where planning **13–286** permission has been granted in breach of the requirements of the Directive, the courts have a jurisdiction to set aside the grant. This should be so irrespective of whether the decision-making procedure may have been fully in accordance with the requirements of national law. An Bord Pleanála and the planning authorities are, as emanations of the State, obliged to give effect to the Directive, if necessary by disapplying provisions of national law. If they fail to do so, their decisions are liable to be set aside. The ECJ has ruled in *Wells* that this is so notwithstanding the fact that this may impact on developers. The ECJ expressly rejected an argument that this involved an impermissible inverse direct effect. It remains to be seen whether the Irish courts will nonetheless assert a discretion to refuse to set aside a planning permission in some cases, and as to how the tension between the potential hardship to developers, and the detriment to good public administration which would arise in the case of a decision reached pursuant to a deficient procedure, is to be resolved.

T. Non-Judicial Remedies

1. General

The tendency, when talking of remedies for breach of rights, is to think almost **13–287** exclusively in terms of judicial remedies. Thus if planning permission is granted in breach of some procedural requirement of national law, the first remedy which springs to mind is judicial review proceedings seeking to set aside the decision.

---

[227] Y. Scannell, *Environmental and Land Use Law* (Thomson Round Hall, Dublin, 2006), para.5–18.
[228] See the Court of Appeal judgment in *R. (On the application of Barker) v London Borough of Bromley* [2001] E.W.C.A. Civ. 1766, [45], where, in a different context and prior to the ruling of the ECJ on the preliminary reference, attention was drawn to the statutory power to revoke planning permission.

13–288 In the case of a breach of the requirements of the Directive, however, there are various non-judicial remedies which may be available. The planning process is an iterative one, with members of the public entitled to make submissions in advance of the making of decisions. This admits of the possibility of procedural mishaps being remedied during the course of the process, in advance of a final decision being made to grant planning permission. The existence of a statutory right of appeal to An Bord Pleanála—involving as it does a *de novo* hearing—is of particular importance in this connection.

13–289 Thus, for example, if a member of the public thinks that a particular development should be subject to environmental impact assessment, he should request the planning authority to require the submission of an environmental impact statement where one was not submitted with the initial application for planning permission. If the planning authority does not accede to this request, the matter can be pursued again on appeal before An Bord Pleanála. An Bord Pleanála has a freestanding discretion to require the submission of an environmental impact statement.[229] Similarly if a member of the public thinks that the environmental information submitted is not adequate, he should address this concern to the planning bodies.

13–290 It should be emphasised that planning authorities and An Bord Pleanála are obliged to take all the general or particular measures necessary to ensure that projects are examined in order to determine whether they are likely to have significant effects on the environment and, if so, to ensure that they are subject to an impact assessment.[230] Thus, it may be necessary on occasion for a planning authority or An Bord Pleanála either to supplement or disapply national law, so as to ensure compliance with the requirements of the Directive. For example, if it is some rule of national law which is preventing a particular project being subjected to an environmental impact assessment, this rule may have to be disregarded by An Bord Pleanála or the relevant planning authority.

13–291 Regrettably, it has to be said that, to date, An Bord Pleanála has not shown any great vigilance in this regard. Far too often where a legal objection is raised before An Bord Pleanála, it has simply indicated that this is a matter for the courts and not engaged with the issue itself.[231] (More accurately, the inspector dealing with the appeal will have dismissed the matter thus in his report; An Bord Pleanála rarely addresses legal points in any way in its formal statement of reasons.) With respect, such an approach is inconsistent with its obligations under the Directive.

13–292 A rare example of An Bord Pleanála (through its inspector) taking actual steps to supplement possible deficiencies in national legislation is provided by a

---

[229] Planning and Development Regulations 2001, art.109.

[230] See, for example, *R. (On the application of Wells) v Secretary of State for the Environment* (Case C–201/02) [2004] E.C.R. I–723.

[231] See, for example, the summary of the submission of An Bord Pleanála in *O'Brien v Tipperary South Riding County Council*, unreported, High Court, October 22, 2002.

decision of March 2003 in respect of the South Eastern motorway/M50.[232] Variations had been proposed—in the context of a previously approved road development—to an interchange at Carrickmines. An objector argued that these changes should themselves be subject to environmental impact assessment, and sought to refer the matter to An Bord Pleanála. Although An Bord Pleanála did have a statutory function in deciding whether certain sub-threshold road development should be assessed, the relevant statutory provisions did not specifically refer to changes to projects already authorised, executed or in the process of being executed. Notwithstanding this apparent omission from the then national legislation, the inspector, having referred to Class 13 of Annex II, recommended—having regard to An Bord Pleanála's functions in terms of approving or refusing to approve proposed road developments and directing road authorities in relation to sub-threshold developments—that it would be reasonable for the board to consider this issue and to accept jurisdiction in the absence of an alternative forum.

2. Second or subsequent development consent

Thus far the discussion has centred on steps which might be taken during the course of the decision-making process so as to ensure that that particular decision is reached in accordance with the requirements of the Directive. More radically, however, it may be that the planning authorities and An Bord Pleanála may have to take measures to remedy a deficiency in an *earlier* decision-making process. Where a particular development consent has been granted improperly because of the failure to carry out any, or any adequate, environmental impact assessment, a subsequent regulatory body may be obliged to remedy this by requiring an environmental impact assessment at the stage of a second or subsequent development consent.   **13–293**

In *R. (On the application of Barker) v London Borough of Bromley*, the ECJ held that[233]:   **13–294**

> "[…] Articles 2(1) and 4(2) of Directive 85/337 are to be interpreted as requiring an environmental impact assessment to be carried out if, in the case of grant of consent comprising more than one stage, it becomes apparent, in the course of the second stage, that the project is likely to have significant effects on the environment by virtue inter alia of its nature, size or location."

This assessment must be of a comprehensive nature, so as to relate to all the aspects of the project which have not yet been assessed or which require a fresh assessment.[234]   **13–295**

This requirement arises from the obligation on the national competent authorities to give effect to the provisions of the Directive. Reference is made in this   **13–296**

---

[232] An Bord Pleanála Reference ED2024; March 21, 2003.
[233] (Case C–290/03); May 4, 2006, [49].
[234] *ibid.*, [48].

regard to the judgment of the ECJ in *R. (On the application of Wells) v Secretary of State for Transport, Local Government Regions.*[235]

> "[…] it is clear from settled case-law that under the principle of cooperation in good faith laid down in Article 10 EC the Member States are required to nullify the unlawful consequences of a breach of Community law (see, in particular, Case 6/60 *Humblet* [1960] ECR 559, at 569, and Joined Cases C-6/90 and C-9/90 *Francovich and Others* [1991] ECR I-5357, paragraph 36). Such an obligation is owed, within the sphere of its competence, by every organ of the Member State concerned (see, to this effect, Case C-8/88 *Germany* v *Commission* [1990] ECR I-2321, paragraph 13).
>
> Thus, it is for the competent authorities of a Member State to take, within the sphere of their competence, all the general or particular measures necessary to ensure that projects are examined in order to determine whether they are likely to have significant effects on the environment and, if so, to ensure that they are subject to an impact assessment (see, to this effect, Case C-72/95 *Kraaijeveld and Others* [1996] ECR I-5403, paragraph 61, and *WWF and Others*, cited above, paragraph 70). Such particular measures include, subject to the limits laid down by the principle of procedural autonomy of the Member States, the revocation or suspension of a consent already granted, in order to carry out an assessment of the environmental effects of the project in question as provided for by Directive 85/337.
>
> The Member State is likewise required to make good any harm caused by the failure to carry out an environmental impact assessment."[236]

13-297   On the facts of *Wells*, by the time the legal proceedings had issued, the second consent had already been granted without there having been an environmental impact assessment. The issue in the legal proceedings, therefore, was whether that consent should be revoked or set aside. However, the wording of the judgment—and, in particular, the emphasis placed on the obligation of all competent authorities to take *all* measures to ensure compliance with the Directive—is such to support an inference that the (second) decision-maker should undertake the environmental impact assessment where this has not happened at an earlier stage of the decision-making process.

13-298   Reference is also made to the judgment in *Commission v United Kingdom.*[237] This case concerned the then English legislation in respect of outline planning permissions. Unlike *Barker*—which was decided on the same day—the impugned legislation was looked at in the abstract. The legislation seems to have been found deficient by the ECJ on the basis that it did not allow for remediation at the second stage, *i.e.* the English legislation precluded the possibility of any assessment at the reserved matters stage.[238]

---

[235] (Case C–201/02) [2004] E.C.R. I–723.

[236] (Case C–201/02) [2004] E.C.R. I–723, [64]–[66].

[237] (Case C–508/03); May 4, 2006.

[238] See the judgment of the Court of Appeal in *R. (On the application of Barker) v London Borough of Bromley* [2001] E.W.C.A. Civ. 1766, [27] ("There is no doubt that the effect of these legislative provisions is that in domestic law, an EA can only be required where outline planning permission is sought, at the time the application for that permission is under consideration. There is equally no doubt, again in domestic law, that the grant of

"In those circumstances, it is clear from Article 2(1) of Directive 85/337, as amended, that projects likely to have significant effects on the environment, as referred to in Article 4 of the directive read in conjunction with Annexes I and II thereto, must be made subject to an assessment with regard to their effects before (multi-stage) development consent is given (see, to that effect, Case C-201/02 *Wells* [2004] ECR I-723, paragraph 42).

In that regard, the Court stated in *Wells*, at paragraph 52, that where national law provides for a consent procedure comprising more than one stage, one involving a principal decision and the other involving an implementing decision which cannot extend beyond the parameters set by the principal decision, the effects which a project may have on the environment must be identified and assessed at the time of the procedure relating to the principal decision. It is only if those effects are not identifiable until the time of the procedure relating to the implementing decision that the assessment should be carried out in the course of that procedure.

In the present case, the rules at issue provide that an environmental impact assessment in respect of a project may be carried out only at the initial outline planning permission stage, and not at the later reserved matters stage.

Those rules are therefore contrary to Articles 2(1) and 4(2) of Directive 85/337, as amended. The United Kingdom has thus failed to fulfil its obligation to transpose those provisions into domestic law."

13–299 Although the meaning and intent of this judgment is less clear than that in either *Barker* or *Wells*, it is nevertheless submitted that the inference is that, in a multi-stage decision-making process, there is an ongoing obligation to ensure that development consent in its final form is not granted for development likely to have significant effects on the environment unless the necessary assessment has been carried out.

13–300 This obligation may arise even in circumstances where there is no requirement under national law, still less a prescribed procedure, for environmental impact assessment at the stage of the later decision. To put the matter another way, the happenstance of an application subsequently for some form of consent or approval might well trigger a requirement to make good the failure to have had any, or any adequate, environmental impact assessment at an earlier stage. It is only where—as in the case of the then English legislation in respect of outline planning permissions—the relevant legislation simply does not allow for the possibility of an assessment that same cannot be carried out.

13–301 An obvious example of where this might arise is in circumstances where no environmental impact statement was required as part of the planning process, and the development is also subject to licensing by the Environmental Protection Agency ("the EPA"). It is arguable that the EPA may be obliged to call for an

---

outline permission gives to the developer a right to develop in accordance with the conditions attached to the permission, and subject to consideration of reserved matters, which cannot be used by a planning authority to frustrate that right. The authority is bound to act in accordance with the principle of development already established by the grant.").

environmental impact statement even though there is no formal procedure under national law whereby this might be done.

13–302 Another possible example where a similar result might arise is where an application is made to extend the duration of a planning permission. Ordinarily, a planning authority enjoys only a very limited discretion—confined to ensuring that the various statutory criteria under s.42 of the PDA 2000 have been satisfied—and is not entitled to reconsider the planning merits of the permitted development. On one view, however, it is arguable that if the initial decision to grant planning permission was deficient on account of there being no proper environmental impact assessment, then the planning authority would not be entitled to extend the duration of the planning permission without an environmental impact assessment being undertaken at that stage. In reality, it would probably be simpler for the planning authority to refuse to grant the extension, in that it would be impracticable to attempt to perform an extra-statutory form of environmental impact assessment within the confines of the s.42 procedure.

13–303 The availability of this—admittedly innovative—remedy is dependent on the later decision constituting a "development consent" within the meaning of the Directive. The concept of a development consent has been discussed in detail at paras 13–105 to 13–131 and the discussion will not be repeated here.

13–304 One potential obstacle to the availability of this remedy is the prohibition under s.50 of the PDA 2000 (as amended by s.13 of the Planning and Development (Strategic Infrastructure) Act 2006) on "questioning the validity" of the decision on, *inter alia*, an application for planning permission other than by way of judicial review proceedings.

13–305 As the requirement for an extra-statutory environmental impact assessment in the case of a second or subsequent development consent can—by definition—only arise because of a deficiency at the first stage of decision-making, it might be said that to demand an environmental impact assessment is to call into question the validity of the first decision. This collateral attack might be brought months, or even years, after the expiration of the statutory time-limit under s.50 for challenging the decision on an application for planning permission.

13–306 A similar issue was considered in general terms by the High Court of England and Wales and the Court of Appeal in *R. (On the application of The Noble Organisation Ltd.) v Thanet District Council*.[239] Outline planning permission had been granted for a business park. A second outline planning permission was subsequently granted for a plot within the business park. The case was unusual in that—notwithstanding that there was no requirement to do so under the national legislation—the relevant planning authority had decided, at the

---

[239] [2004] E.W.H.C. 2576 (Admin); [2005] 1 P. & C.R. 27; [2005] E.W.C.A. Civ. 782; [2006] 1 P. & C.R. 13; [2006] J.P.L. 60.

reserved matters stage, to consider whether or not to call for an environmental impact statement. (Under the relevant English legislation, the need for an environmental impact statement fell to be considered only at the outline planning permission stage, and did not arise for reconsideration at the reserved matters stage.) Presumably this was done out of caution, in circumstances where the House of Lords in *Barker* had previously referred questions as to the compatibility of the one-off procedure to the ECJ, and that reference was, at that time, still pending.

In deciding at the reserved matters stage whether or not an environmental impact assessment was required, the planning authority relied on the fact that it had previously decided at the time of the application for the second outline planning permission that the characteristics and location of the development were not such as to require an environmental impact assessment. The applicant for judicial review had sought to criticise this approach, arguing that it was almost a contradiction in terms to enquire whether the effects of the reserved matters were likely to be significantly different from those considered at the outline planning permission stage: reserved matters must fall within the scope of the outline planning permission. The argument continued that if consideration is to be given to an environmental impact assessment at the reserved matters stage, the only proper question must be whether the development *per se* was likely to give rise to significant environmental effects. That was a fresh factual question. The formal validity of earlier planning permissions was not an answer to it.

13–307

The High Court of England and Wales rejected these arguments, holding that the earlier decisions formed part of the legal and factual context within which the need for an environmental impact assessment at the reserved matters stage fell to be assessed.[240]

13–308

> "There is a real artificiality in the very nature of the EIA exercise undertaken by the council at the reserved matters stage in this case, given that (i) a considered decision was taken at the outline planning permission stage that an EIA was not needed, and (ii) reserved matters should not have materially greater effects if they are to fall within the scope of the outline planning permission at all. In a case where, as here, the need for an EIA had been considered and rejected in a reasoned decision at the outline planning permission stage, and no challenge had been brought to that decision, I would be surprised if the law required further consideration to be given to the question of an EIA at the reserved matters stage. *Barker* might be considered a more problematic case on its facts since in that case there was no clear evidence that the need for an EIA had been considered at all by the decision-maker at the outline planning permission stage (see the judgment of the Court of Appeal [2001] EWCA Civ 1766, at para 6). I recognise, however, that one cannot reliably predict either the outcome of the reference in *Barker* or its implications for a case such as the present. In the state of uncertainty created by *Barker*, it is entirely understandable that the council saw fit, as a precautionary measure, to give further consideration to the question of an EIA at

---

[240] [2004] E.W.H.C. 2576 (Admin), [39]-[40]; [2005] 1 P. & C.R. 27.

the reserved matters stage. By following that course it cannot be taken to have been impliedly accepting that its consideration of the EIA issue at the outline planning permission stage was in some way defective. There is no foundation at all for such an inference. The only inference that can reasonably be drawn is that the council was doing the best it could to cover all eventualities in an uncertain legal position.

I do not accept that, if such an exercise was to be carried out at all in this rather unsatisfactory situation, it had to be carried out as a fresh exercise without reference back to the earlier decisions. Those earlier decisions formed part of the legal and factual context within which the need for an EIA at the reserved matters stage fell to be assessed."

13–309 It had also been argued that the initial decision that the development was not likely to have significant effects on the environment, *i.e.* the decision made at the time of the application for outline planning permission, had not, in any event, been properly made. In particular, it was argued that the planning authority had insufficient information before it to reach a lawful decision that significant environmental effects were not likely: in this regard, it was argued that the application was for development of indeterminate scale and the outline planning permission was not constrained by conditions which could ensure that significant environmental effects were not likely to occur.

13–310 Richards J. rejected this argument as involving an impermissible collateral challenge to the earlier decisions.[241]

"That brings me to Mr Phillips's [counsel for the applicant's] submission that, although the question of an EIA was expressly considered at the stage of the leisure outline planning permission, any comparison with it was still flawed because the consideration given to the question at the outline stage was inadequate and the decision not to require an EIA was defective: the information available was insufficient for the purposes of proper consideration of the EIA issue and/or the decision itself was based in turn on an inappropriate comparison with the development permitted by the business park outline planning permission. In my judgment, that line of argument constitutes a naked, if indirect, challenge to the validity of the leisure outline planning permission and the related screening decision. On normal domestic law principles, as discussed above, such a challenge to the validity of an earlier decision is impermissible. I see nothing in the EIA regime that subverts the normal position. What the Court said in *Wells* about the obligation to nullify the consequences of a breach of the Directive is not to be taken as calling into question the validity of earlier decisions which are no longer open to challenge under domestic law. The obligation was expressed to be subject to national procedural rules (with a standard proviso concerning the principles of equivalence and effectiveness). The particular issue in Wells was whether an earlier permission could be revoked or modified, rather than whether it could be treated as invalid; and even that particular issue was clearly stated to be a matter for determination by the national court applying national procedural rules. If, moreover, it were possible to mount indirect challenges of this kind to the validity of earlier EIA decisions, that would be destructive of legal certainty, which is as much a principle of EC law as of domestic law."

---

[241] *ibid.*, [48].

The question as to the extent to which it was permissible to criticise (to use a **13–311** neutral term) previous decisions in the context of a challenge to a more recent decision was to the fore when the matter was appealed to the Court of Appeal.[242] It was urged on behalf of the applicant for judicial review that unlawful reasoning in one planning decision may vitiate a later planning decision reliant upon the same reasoning, notwithstanding the formal validity of the earlier decision. It was argued in the alternative and in any event that—irrespective of the position under domestic law—the formal validity of the earlier decisions could not be a defence to a challenge to a later decision, as this would conflict with the principle of effectiveness of EC law.

The Court of Appeal held that—as a matter of domestic law—the applicant **13–312** was not entitled to challenge directly or indirectly the previous decisions to grant planning permission, nor the screening decision in respect of the second planning permission. The challenge to the decision (at the approval of reserved matters stage) not to require an environmental impact assessment was, in effect, an impermissible collateral challenge to those decisions. The Court of Appeal did accept that there was a difference between a challenge to the validity of an earlier decision, and a subsequent challenge to the *reasoning* underlying it, but considered that this did not advance the applicant's case. The relevance of the previous decisions was that they would have certain effects, and the planning authority in its screening exercise at the approval of the reserved matters stage was entitled to conclude that those matters were unlikely to have any greater significant environmental impact than already the consequence of the outline permission.

Turning now to the Court of Appeal's treatment of the argument based on the **13–313** effectiveness of EC law. The applicant had argued that an unlawful failure to undertake an environmental impact assessment at the outline planning permission stage triggered a remedial obligation at the approval of reserved matters stage, having regard to the proposition in *R. (On the application of Wells) v Secretary of State for Transport, Local Government and the Regions*[243] that an environmental impact assessment should be conducted at the earliest possible stage for identifying and assessing all the effects which the project may have on the environment. This was so notwithstanding the formal validity of the previous planning permission. The Court of Appeal rejected this argument, emphasising that there was a clear domestic remedy available, if exercised promptly, for quashing the previous decisions. The Court of Appeal found that the domestic requirement of promptness in the exercise of the remedy struck a reasonable balance between the need to provide a remedy and, in this instance, the public interest in the effective administration of planning controls and legal certainty. In the circumstances, it could not be said that it was contrary to EC law to allow reliance to be placed on the formal validity of the earlier decisions.

---

[242] [2005] E.W.C.A. Civ. 782; [2006] 1 P. & C.R. 13; [2006] J.P.L. 60.
[243] (Case C–201/02) [2004] E.C.R. I–723.

13–314   The Court of Appeal noted that the ECJ had upheld the importance of giving certainty to public decisions by holding that the application of reasonable time-limits for challenging them does not infringe the principle of effectiveness; express reference was made in this regard to the case of *Rewe v Landwirtschaftskammer Saarland*.[244] The Court of Appeal also emphasised that the ECJ in *Wells* had held that detailed procedural rules are a matter for the domestic legal order of each Member State, under the principle of procedural autonomy of the Member States, provided that such rules are not less favourable than those governing similar domestic situations (principle of equivalence) and that they do not render impossible in practice or excessively difficult the exercise of rights conferred by the Community legal order (principle of effectiveness).

> "Applying those principles to the facts of this case, if either of the two outline planning permissions required and/or were not the subject of valid screening exercise, there was a clear domestic remedy, if exercised promptly, for quashing either of them and/or the screening opinion at the leisure park outline permission stage. The domestic requirement of promptness in the exercise of the remedy, as Miss Robinson observed, strikes a reasonable balance between the need to provide a remedy and, in this instance, the public interest in the effective administration of planning controls and legal certainty. Accordingly, in my view, this challenge to the reserved matters screening opinion was not deprived of effect by the Council's reliance on the formal validity of the outline permissions and the screening opinion in relation to the latter, since they had been challengeable by judicial review, if sought promptly - a sufficient remedy as a matter of community law."[245]

13–315   With respect, the approach of the Court of Appeal is not entirely convincing. First, the logic of the judgment in *Wells*—and of the subsequent judgments in *Barker* and *Commission v United Kingdom*—is that a failure to have any or any adequate environmental impact assessment at an earlier stage is something which should be remedied on the occasion of a subsequent application for a development consent. This logic would be entirely undermined if it was always an answer to say that environmental impact assessment could not be carried out in the context of the application for the later development consent because this might cast aspersions on the earlier decision. Indeed the requirement for the environmental impact assessment will, by definition, only have arisen precisely because there was some mishap at the stage of the decision on the earlier development consent. Secondly, is it not sufficient for the purposes of legal certainty that the earlier decision is not set aside; is it not going too far to say that one cannot even call into question the correctness of that decision whilst leaving its formal validity intact?

---

[244] (Case 33/76) [1976] E.C.R. 1989.
[245] [2005] E.W.C.A. Civ. 782; [2006] 1 P. & C.R. 13; [2006] J.P.L. 60, [61].

U. Judicial Review and Article 10a

1. Article 10a

Article 10a, as inserted by Directive 2003/35/EC, provides as follows.   **13–316**

> "Member states shall ensure that, in accordance with the relevant national legal system, members of the public concerned,
>   (a) having a sufficient interest, or alternatively,
>   (b) maintaining the impairment of a right, where administrative procedural law of a Member State requires this as a precondition,
> have access to a review procedure before a court of law or another independent and impartial body established by law to challenge the substantive or procedural legality of decisions, acts or omissions subject to the public participation provisions of this Directive.
>   Member states shall determine at what stage the decision, acts or omissions may be challenged.
>   What constitutes a sufficient interest and impairment of a right shall be determined by the Member States consistently with the objective of giving the public concerned wide access to justice. To this end, the interest of any non-governmental organisation meeting the requirement referred to in Article 1(2), shall be deemed sufficient for the purpose of subparagraph (a) of this Article. Such organisations shall also be deemed to have rights capable of being impaired for the purpose of subparagraph (b) of this Article.
>   The provisions of the Article shall not exclude the possibility of a preliminary review procedure before an administrative authority and shall not affect the requirement of exhaustion of administrative review procedures prior to recourse to judicial review procedures, where such a requirement exists under national law.
>   Any such procedure shall be fair, equitable, timely and not prohibitively expensive.
>   In order to further the effectiveness of the provisions of this article, Member States shall ensure that practical information is made available to the public on access to administrative and judicial review procedures."

Under the amended Art.1(2) of the Directive, "the public concerned" is defined   **13–317** as the public affected or likely to be affected by or having an interest in, the environmental decision-making procedures. For the purposes of the definition, non-governmental organisations promoting environmental protection and meeting any requirements under national law shall be deemed to have an interest.

The Member States were required to bring into force the laws, regulations and   **13–318** administrative provisions necessary to comply with the amended Directive by June 25, 2005 at the latest. When Member States adopt these measures, they shall contain a reference to Directive 2003/35/EC or shall be accompanied by such a reference on the occasion of their official publication. The methods of making such a reference shall be laid down by Member States.

2. Transposition of Article 10a into Irish law

13–319   The European Commission has threatened to refer Ireland to the ECJ for failing to adopt and provide correct information on measures to give effect to Directive 2003/35/EC.[246] At the time of writing, there is some confusion as to what measures Ireland intends to rely on as transposing Art.10a into national law. One would have assumed that Ireland would rely on the existing judicial review process, making whatever modifications were necessary to ensure compliance with Art.10a. The Irish courts have exercised a supervisory jurisdiction, by way of judicial review, over planning decisions for decades now, and the procedure might readily be adjusted so as to accommodate the Art.10a review procedure. Indeed, Ireland had—belatedly—introduced certain amendments to the planning legislation which seemed to be intended to transpose Art.10a. These included exempting, in the context of EIA development, non-governmental organisations ("NGOs") from the requirement to demonstrate a "substantial interest" in judicial review proceedings.[247]

13–320   The requirement that national implementing measures contain a reference to Directive 2003/35/EC, or be accompanied by such a reference on the occasion of their official publication, does not appear to have been complied with. This has led to some confusion in practice, and in at least one case, it was suggested that the Art.10a review procedure might be available by way of an appeal to An Bord Pleanála. More specifically, in *Friends of the Curragh Environment Ltd. v An Bord Pleanála (No. 1)*,[248] Kelly J. observed as follows.

> "The board is an independent and impartial body which is established by statute. It is empowered to hear challenges, both substantive and procedural. It conducts a *de novo* consideration of the application for planning permission.
>
>   Whilst there is a right of redress on a limited basis to the courts by means of judicial review, it is not clear that it is covered by the Directive. It is just as arguable that the Directive covers an appeal to the board."

13–321   With respect, it is submitted that this suggestion, which was strictly speaking *obiter*, is not correct. First, although An Bord Pleanála has an appellate function in relation to planning authorities' decisions, it does not carry out a "review procedure" within the meaning of Art.10a. Rather, An Bord Pleanála is *part* of the public participation process required by the Directive, and, as such, its "decisions, acts or omissions" must themselves be subject to review. As discussed at paras 3–88 to 3–92, the decision-making in respect of planning permissions, although carried out in two stages, is, in effect, a unitary procedure. In particular, what might otherwise be deficiencies in public participation

---

[246] See Press Release IP/07/391 of March 22, 2007.

[247] NGOs are also entitled to appeal a decision on an application in respect of EIA development to An Bord Pleanála free from the usual requirement of having to have made submissions and observations at the planning authority stage. This is presumably explicable by reference to the requirement to exhaust administrative procedures.

[248] [2006] I.E.H.C. 243; unreported, Kelly J., July 14, 2006.

occurring at the planning authority stage—notably the absence of any possibility for an oral hearing—are made good by the existence of a right of appeal to An Bord Pleanála. What Art.10a requires, however, is that a review procedure be provided extrinsic to the development consent procedure.

Secondly, an appeal to An Bord Pleanála involves a *de novo* hearing, with An Bord Pleanála determining the application as if it had been made to it in the first instance. Moreover, as the decision of An Bord Pleanála annuls the decision of the planning authority, the board does not, as a matter of practice, usually concern itself with any alleged irregularities at the planning authority stage. It is difficult, therefore, to say that An Bord Pleanála reviews the "substantive or procedural legality" of the planning authority's decision.　**13–322**

Thirdly, Art.10a itself appears to distinguish between "administrative review", and an independent and impartial review. An Bord Pleanála has traditionally been regarded as part of a self-contained administrative code, and the concept of an "independent and impartial review" would appear to more closely resemble the supervisory jurisdiction exercised by the High Court by way of judicial review than the appellate function of An Bord Pleanála. Indeed, it could be argued that the requirement under s.143 of the PDA 2000 (as amended) for An Bord Pleanála to have regard to Government policy undermines its independence and impartiality. See further paras 14–114 to 14–127.　**13–323**

Fourthly, the intent of the legislature itself seems to be that the review procedure is to be provided by way of judicial review. As discussed at para.13–319, special provision has been made under the amended s.50 for the standing (*locus standi*) of non-governmental organisations in judicial review proceedings. Insofar as these amendments appear to have been prompted by the amended Directive, and, in particular, the obligation on Member States to ensure access to the review procedure by non-governmental organisations, this tends to suggest that the legislature regard judicial review as constituting the Art.10a review procedure.　**13–324**

Finally, it should be borne in mind that in many contexts An Bord Pleanála is the decision-maker of first instance. This is the position, for example, in relation to local authority own development, and strategic infrastructure development under the Planning and Development (Strategic Infrastructure) Act 2006. It would create a surprising anomaly were An Bord Pleanála to be a review body in some instances and not others.　**13–325**

3. Is Article 10a directly applicable in national law?

The question as to whether the Art.10a review procedure is directly applicable in national law came up for consideration in *Friends of the Curragh Environment Ltd. v An Bord Pleanála (No. 1)*.[249] Given the confusion—as of　**13–326**

---

[249] [2006] I.E.H.C. 243; unreported, Kelly J., July 14, 2006.

the time of writing in June 2007—as to the measures by which Ireland says it has transposed Art.10a, this question is obviously of some significance.

13–327   The applicant company sought to challenge a decision by An Bord Pleanála to grant planning permission. The proceedings were brought by way of an application for judicial review, pursuant to the unamended s.50 procedure. The applicant company sought what was described as a "protective costs order" ("PCO"). In effect, the applicant company requested the High Court to grant it, at the outset of the proceedings, immunity from any liability for the legal costs of the other parties. The applicant company similarly sought immunity from having to furnish security for costs, or having to provide an undertaking as to damages. This application was dealt with as a preliminary issue in advance of any hearing on the application for leave to apply for judicial review.

13–328   The sequence in which the High Court dealt with the national law, and EC law, issues arising was somewhat unusual. First, the entitlement, if any, of the applicant company to a protective costs order was dealt with as a matter of national law, without any reference to the provisions of Art.10a. In this regard, the High Court applied the test set down in *Village Residents Association Ltd. v An Bord Pleanála (No. 2)*.[250] Having concluded that the applicant company was not entitled under national law to the orders sought, the High Court then went on to consider, as a separate issue, whether Art.10a might have direct effect.

13–329   At no stage did the High Court attempt to apply a purposive approach to national law, *i.e.* to interpret national law, so far as possible, in the light of the wording and the purpose of the Directive in order to achieve the result sought by the Directive.[251] Such an approach to the interpretation and application of national law in respect of protective costs orders might well have allowed the High Court to ensure compliance with the amended Directive. As Ward explains, a finding that a Directive has direct effect is only one of a number of tools for the enforcement of a Directive in national law.[252] Ward goes on to suggest that there is a discernible trend towards application of sympathetic interpretation as a first line of inquiry.[253]

13–330   As discussed at paras 13–389 to 13–390, the High Court also failed to apply a purposive approach to interpretation when discussing the standard of judicial review applicable. Such a purposive approach was adopted by Clarke J. in the subsequent judgment in *Sweetman v An Bord Pleanála*.[254] The judgment in *Sweetman* is discussed at paras 13–400 to 13–401, but for present purposes it

---

[250] [2000] 4 I.R. 321; [2001] 2 I.L.R.M. 22.
[251] See, for example, *Marleasing* (Case C–106/89); [1990] E.C.R. I–4135.
[252] A. Ward, *Judicial Review and the Rights of Private Parties in EU Law* (Oxford University Press, 2007), pp.31–35.
[253] *ibid.*, p.51.
[254] Unreported, High Court, Clarke J., April 27, 2007.

is sufficient to note that Clarke J. applied a sympathetic interpretation in analysing the judicial review procedure available under national law. In particular, Clarke J. indicated that if it should prove to be necessary, on the facts of any individual case, to give a more generous interpretation to the "substantial interest" requirement under ss.50 and 50A so as to meet the "wide access to justice" criteria set out in Art.10a, then there would be no difficulty in construing the term "substantial interest" in an appropriate manner.

The High Court in *Friends of the Curragh Environment Ltd. v An Bord Pleanála (No.1)* ruled that the provisions of Art.10a were not sufficiently clear, precise and unconditional as to have direct effect. In particular, Kelly J. considered that the requirement that the review procedure not be "prohibitively expensive" was imprecise. **13–331**

> "Even if the Directive can be taken to applying to judicial review applications the question arises as to what the words 'prohibitively expensive' refer to. It is not clear whether this refers to court fees which are chargeable by the State or to legal costs which are not. If it is court fees then access is available to any person on paying a modest court fee. It is particularly modest in the case of judicial review proceedings in planning matters where the originating document is a notice of motion carrying a fee which is a fraction of the fee payable for the issue of a plenary summons. If the Directive is dealing only with fees then it has no application whatsoever in the case of a PCO [pre-emptive costs order]."

With respect, it must be doubtful whether the ECJ would agree that Art.10a does not have direct effect.[255] As discussed earlier at para.13–259 and onwards, the ECJ has taken a very robust attitude to the EIA Directive and has ruled that the requirement to carry out an assessment has direct effect. This was so notwithstanding the vague wording of the Directive in this regard. The introduction of a remedies element to the Directive under Art.10a was self-evidently intended to enhance the rights of the public under the Directive: it would be ironic if this aspect of the Directive alone were found not to have direct effect. **13–332**

The reasons put forward by the High Court in support of its finding that Art.10a does not have direct effect are not convincing, and overstate the extent of the discretion left over to the Member States under Art.10a. In this regard, it is submitted that there is an important distinction between terms of a Directive which are merely ambiguous, and those which afford a genuine discretion to the Member States. Prechal refers to the existence of a distinction between "indefinite legal concepts" and discretion.[256] **13–333**

---

[255] The Commission has decided to refer Ireland to the ECJ for failing to adopt and provide correct information on measures to give effect to Directive 2003/35/EC, citing the judgment in *Friends of the Curragh Environment Ltd. v An Bord Pleanála (No. 1)*. See Press Release IP/07/391 of March 22, 2007.

[256] S. Prechal, *Directives in EC Law* (2nd ed., Oxford University Press, 2005), p.248. Prechal cites Kapteyn and VerLoren van Themaat (ed. Gormley), *Introduction to the Law of the European Communities* (Kluwer, 1998).

"The question as to whether or not discretion is left to the Member State is a matter of interpretation of the relevant provision or set of provisions. Sometimes matters may be quite straightforward. In other cases, however, things are less certain. In particular, provisions using vague concepts which have to be substantiated in the light of the facts of the case are notoriously difficult. A theoretical distinction often referred to in this respect is that between indefinite legal concepts and discretion. The former imply that there are several possible views as to their interpretation but only one is right; discretion means not only that a choice of different views is possible but also that it is lawful to follow any of them. It is only the latter form, which some call 'real discretion', which seems to preclude direct effect."

13–334   Whereas certain terms under Art.10a—"timeliness" or "prohibitively expensive"—are arguably vague, it does not necessarily follow that the Member States enjoy a discretion in this regard. It would seem to follow, by analogy with the approach taken by the ECJ in respect of the term "development consent", that these terms must be given an autonomous and uniform interpretation throughout the Community, which interpretation should take into account the context of the provision and the purpose of the Directive. Indeed, the fact that the terms have their origins in the Aarhus Convention[257] reinforces the case for an autonomous and uniform interpretation.

13–335   It is submitted, therefore, that the mere fact that some of its terms may be ambiguous does not preclude Art.10a from having direct effect. As Prechal observes, problems of ambiguity and lack of clarity can be resolved by interpretation by the courts and, where necessary, by the ECJ on a preliminary reference.[258] To take an example: one of the concerns raised by the High Court in *Friends of the Curragh Environment Ltd.* was that it was unclear as to whether the notion of "prohibitively expensive" extended to lawyers' fees, or was confined to court fees. This is a fair point: the wording is ambiguous. However, it is submitted that it would be a mistake to draw any inference that the Member States consequently enjoy a discretion in this regard, or that it is a matter for the individual Member States to decide whether to confine Art.10a to court fees. Rather, it is submitted that even this aspect of Art.10a must be capable of definition and that a minimum standard has been laid down one way or the other. If the High Court considered that, even having regard to the objectives of the Directive as previously identified by the ECJ and to the origins of the amendments in the Aarhus Convention, it was not in a position to interpret the provision itself, the matter could have been dealt with by way of a preliminary reference to the ECJ.

4. Procedural rules

13–336   Prior to the introduction of Art.10a, it seems that the detailed procedural rules

---

[257] Convention on Access to Information, Public Participation in Decision-making and Access to Justice in Environmental Matters (1998).

[258] S. Prechal, *Directives in EC Law* (2nd ed., Oxford University Press, 2005), at p.244.

applicable to Directive-cases were a matter for the domestic legal order of each Member State provided that the rules were not less favourable than those governing similar domestic situations (principle of equivalence), and that they did not render impossible in practice or excessively difficult the exercise of rights conferred under EC law (principle of effectiveness).[259]

The approach of the Irish courts in this regard had been somewhat confused. The majority judgment, *per* Keane J. (as he then was), of the Supreme Court in *Lancefort Ltd. v An Bord Pleanála*[260] had suggested that the requirements of national law as to standing (*locus standi*) might in some instances have to yield to the paramount obligation on national courts to uphold the law of the European Union. In support of this, Keane J. cited the judgment of the ECJ in *Kraaijeveld*.[261] In that case the ECJ had confirmed that where, as a matter of national law, a national court had jurisdiction to raise of its own motion pleas in law based on a binding national rule which were not put forward by the parties, it also had to examine of its own motion whether the legislative or administrative authorities of the Member State remained within the limits of their discretion under Arts 2(1) and 4(2) of the Directive. As discussed below, it is not entirely clear that the judgment in *Kraaijeveld* actually went as far as suggested by Keane J.   **13–337**

The majority of the Supreme Court considered that the Directive had been properly transposed into Irish law, and that what was involved in *Lancefort Ltd.* was simply an allegation that An Bord Pleanála had failed to apply properly the national implementing legislation. Accordingly, the majority considered that no adjustment was required on account of EC law to the ordinary rules of standing. The implication seems to have been that once the Directive had been properly transposed, its application thereafter was purely a matter of national law. Of course, the correct legal position, as explained in cases such as *Marks & Spencers plc v Customs and Excise Commissioners*,[262] is that Member States remain bound to ensure full application of the Directive even after the adoption of implementing measures, and individuals are allowed to rely on the provisions of a Directive before the national courts for this purpose.   **13–338**

As it happens, the judgment in *Kraaijeveld* may not have gone as far as Keane J. suggested. On one view, the ECJ was simply reiterating the requirement for equivalence, *i.e.* that remedies for the breach of EC law should not be less favourable than those available for a breach of national law.[263] In particular,   **13–339**

---

[259] *R. (On the application of Wells) v Secretary of State for Transport, Local Government and the Regions* (Case C–201/02) [2004] E.C.R. I–723.
[260] [1999] 2 I.R. 270.
[261] (Case C–72/95) [1996] E.C.R. I–5403.
[262] (Case C–62/00) [2002] E.C.R. I-6325.
[263] See also *R. v London Borough of Hammersmith and Fulham Ex p. CPRE London Branch* (2001) 81 P. & C.R. 6 ("I see nothing in Kraaijveld that would deprive the Court of its discretion in relation to time limits. The fact that there exists an arguable breach of Community law does not mean that normal procedural safeguards, including those that

the obligation on a national court to raise of its own motion issues in respect of the implementation of the Directive only applied where, as a matter of *national* procedural law, the court had jurisdiction to raise pleas not raised by the parties. If this is the *ratio*, then even in the case of an improper transposition, it might not have been necessary to adjust the Irish rules in respect of *locus standi*. It is only since Art.10a was enacted that an explicit standing requirement is provided for under the EIA Directive.

13–340   At all events, having decided—for the wrong reasons—that it was not obliged to make any adjustment to national procedural law, the majority in *Lancefort Ltd.* then went on to refuse relief on the basis that the applicant company did not have standing to bring a challenge to the planning permission, principally because its future promoters had failed to make an objection before An Bord Pleanála to the effect that the proposed development should have been subject to environmental impact assessment.

13–341   It is meaningful that the Supreme Court treated this failure to raise the objection before An Bord Pleanála as going to the issue of *locus standi*. Prior to *Lancefort Ltd.*, a failure to raise an objection at an earlier stage of a decision-making process had been regarded as a matter which might be taken into account by the court in the exercise of its discretion to withhold relief, rather than as going to the issue of *locus standi*. Thus, in *Chambers v An Bord Pleanála*,[264] the Supreme Court had distinguished between the issue of standing and discretion: the fact that the court might ultimately exercise its discretion against the applicant on the basis of his failure to participate in the appeal before An Bord Pleanála did not affect the standing of the applicant to bring the proceedings in the first instance. A cynical observer might suggest that the characterisation of the issue in *Lancefort Ltd.* as one of standing was intended to avoid any possible argument that a national court would not be entitled to exercise its discretion in such a way as to refuse to remedy a breach of EC law. The same cynical observer might also suggest that the treatment of the issue as one of standing also allowed the court to side-step the prescription of the ECJ in *Kraaijeveld*[265] to the effect that—where permitted to do so under national law—a national court had to examine *of its own motion* whether the legislative or administrative authorities of the Member State remained within the limits of their discretion under Arts 2(1) and 4(2) of the Directive. Under Irish law, courts are entitled to raise issues of their own motion. By definition, therefore, the fact that the question of environmental impact assessment had not been raised before An Bord Pleanála could not have been decisive in this context.

13–342   In the later case of *Martin v An Bord Pleanála (No. 1)*,[266] the High Court took a more *communautaire* approach. O'Sullivan J. suggested that if the only thing preventing the application of EC law with direct effect in this jurisdiction was

---

are there to protect legal certainty, have to be thrown out the window.").
[264] [1992] 1 I.R. 134.
[265] (Case C–72/95) [1996] E.C.R. I–5403.
[266] [2002] 2 I.R. 665 at 662.

a rule or procedure in domestic law, then the court should set aside the latter to ensure application of the former. O'Sullivan J. went on, then, to state that at the stage of an application for an interlocutory injunction, however, there was no question of the application of EC law being frustrated in this way.

This formulation might put the matter a little too strongly. As indicated above— prior to Art.10a—rules of national procedural law were subject only to the principles of equivalence and effectiveness. Thus the national rule would not automatically have to be set aside.   **13–343**

It is proposed to discuss next the possible ramifications of Art.10a. This will be done under a number of subheadings. In order to put this discussion in context, the previous legal position will also be examined.   **13–344**

(i) Discretion

Judicial review is traditionally a discretionary remedy. Relief may be withheld from an otherwise entitled applicant by reference to various factors such as delay, lack of personal prejudice, or hardship to third parties. Even prior to Art.10a coming into force, there had been some suggestion in the case law from England and Wales that, where a breach of the EIA Directive is involved, such discretion may be more limited than usual. The speech of Lord Hoffmann in *Berkeley v Secretary of State for the Environment*[267] probably represents the high-water mark in this regard. Lord Hoffmann doubted whether, consistently with its obligations under European law, a court might exercise its statutory discretion to uphold a planning permission which has been granted contrary to the provisions of the Directive, saying that to do so would seem to conflict with the duty of the court under Art.10 of the EC Treaty to ensure fulfilment of the United Kingdom's obligations under the Treaty. It was only in circumstances where there was a failure to observe some procedural step which was clearly superfluous to the requirements of the Directive that it would be possible to exercise a discretion not to quash the planning permission.   **13–345**

It is uncertain as to whether Art.10a will have any great effect in this regard. On the one hand, it can be argued that to allow relief to be withheld as a matter of discretion undermines the effectiveness of the review procedure. On the other hand, it might be said that whereas Art.10a gives a right of access to a review procedure, it does not necessarily guarantee the outcome of that procedure. It is expressly provided that the procedure is to be fair and equitable. The retention of a measure of discretion might be justified as being necessary to ensure such fairness and equity; an inflexible procedure which mandated the setting aside of a planning permission in every case—without any reference to the hardship to the developer or to the conduct of the applicant—might be thought to be inequitable.   **13–346**

In a number of decisions subsequent to *Berkeley*, but prior to the coming into   **13–347**

---

[267] [2001] 2 A.C. 603; (2001) P. & C.R. 492.

force of Art.10a, it had been suggested that the courts still retain a discretion even where breaches of the Directive are involved. For example, in *R. (On the application of Jones) v Mansfield District Council*,[268] Carnwath L.J. reiterated comments he had made in an earlier case (involving the Birds Directive) to the effect that care was needed in applying the principles in *Berkeley* to other circumstances such as where there was clear evidence of a pressing public need for the impugned scheme of development. The point was made that the developer had not been represented before the House of Lords in *Berkeley*, and that there was no reference in that case to any evidence of actual prejudice to his, or any other, interest. The implication being that if such factors arose in other cases, they might represent appropriate grounds for refusing to set aside a planning permission.

13–348 The decision of the Court of Appeal in *Younger Homes (Northern) Ltd. v First Secretary of State*[269] demonstrates a high level of indulgence on the part of the courts to procedural irregularities by a planning authority. Article 4(4) of the Directive requires that screening determinations made by the competent authorities be made available to the public. Provision had been made under national regulations whereby a planning authority could provide a screening opinion as to whether or not an environmental impact assessment was necessary in respect of a proposed development. In breach of the regulations, and in breach of the Directive, the planning authority had failed to place the screening opinion on the register. The Court of Appeal did not regard this as a ground for setting aside the decision to grant planning permission.[270]

13–349 Similarly in *R. (On the application of Gavin) v Haringey London Borough Council*[271] the High Court of England and Wales suggested that there was no reason in principle as to why the exercise of a statutory discretion to refuse relief by way of judicial review where there had been undue delay should give rise to a problem under EC law.

> "To entertain a claim outside the normal time limit but at the same time to take into account the consequences of that delay for third parties and good administration does not render it impossible or excessively difficult to enforce EU rights, or involve any denial of effective protection, or otherwise offend general principles of EU law."[272]

13–350 In *R. (On the application of Richardson) v North Yorkshire County Council*,[273] the Court of Appeal declined to quash a decision to grant planning permission notwithstanding the fact that a proper statement of the main reasons and considerations for the decision had not been provided at the time of the decision.

[268] [2003] E.W.C.A. Civ. 1408; [2004] 2 P. & C.R. 14.
[269] [2004] E.W.C.A. Civ. 1060; [2005] 1 P. & C.R. 14; [2005] J.P.L. 354.
[270] See also *R. (On the application of Wembley Filed Ltd.) v Chancerygate Group Ltd.* [2005] E.W.C.A. 2978 (Admin) (planning decision made before twenty-one minimum period had expired: relief refused as a matter of discretion).
[271] [2003] E.W.H.C. 2591 (Admin), [41]; [2004] J.P.L. 785.
[272] *ibid.*, [41].
[273] [2003] E.W.C.A. Civ. 1860, [50]; [2004] 2 P. & C.R. 15; [2004] J.P.L. 911.

Berkeley was distinguished on the basis that it involved a failure in the decision-making process, *i.e.* the failure to consider whether there should have been an environmental impact assessment, whereas the instant case related to a requirement arising *after* the making of the decision.

To date, the Irish courts have had little cause to examine whether a more limited discretion might apply in the case of a breach of the EIA Directive. This is largely because there have been very few cases where applicants have succeeded in persuading a court that a breach of the Directive has actually occurred. Obviously, the question of discretion only properly arises where an applicant has succeeded on the substance of his claim. In one of the few cases where the question of discretion was addressed—*McBride v Galway Corporation*[274]— the Supreme Court suggested *obiter* that even had the applicant been successful, the court would have exercised its discretion to withhold relief, on the basis that the preparation of a further environmental impact statement, the notification of the public and of interested parties, etc., would not merely be a redundant exercise, since those procedures had already been gone through, but would also delay further the provision of a comprehensive system of drainage for Galway City and its environs, with the resultant continuing pollution of the Galway Bay area. Keane J. (as he then was) stated that that could hardly be regarded as upholding the primary objective of the EIA Directive of preventing the creation of pollution or nuisances at source, rather than subsequently trying to counteract their effects. **13–351**

(ii) Locus standi

Under Art.10a, the Member States retain a discretion to impose a *locus standi* requirement. It seems that, as a matter of EC law, access to the review procedure can be limited to those members of the public affected who either have a "sufficient interest" or, alternatively, maintain the impairment of a right (where administrative procedural law of a Member State requires this as a precondition). It is not certain as to what exactly is meant by the phrase "impairment of a right"; for example, would it be permissible as a matter of EC law to limit access to the review procedure to persons whose property rights might be affected by the proposed development? **13–352**

Under Irish law, the requirement for a person seeking conventional judicial review is to demonstrate a "sufficient interest". However, under s.50A(3) of the PDA 2000 (as amended), an applicant is required under the special statutory judicial review procedure to demonstrate a "substantial interest" in the subject-matter of the application. It is expressly provided that a substantial interest is not limited to an interest in land or other financial interest.[275] **13–353**

---

[274] [1998] 1 I.R. 517.
[275] PDA 2000, s.50A(4) (as amended by the Planning and Development (Strategic Infrastructure) Act 2006, s.13).

13–354   There is a possible conflict, therefore, between national law and the requirements of the Directive. Article 10a only permits Member States to require an applicant to demonstrate a "sufficient interest". National law continues to recognise the concept of "sufficient interest", yet insists on a higher standard, *i.e.* that of "substantial interest", in the context of proceedings challenging decisions or acts under the planning legislation, including decisions and acts subject to the public participation provisions of the Directive. It is arguable therefore that Ireland has exceeded its discretion under the Directive by imposing a standard other than permitted under Art.10a, *i.e.* that of "sufficient interest". Under national law, the term "substantial interest" is not synonymous with "sufficient interest", but rather was specifically intended to impose a "more onerous test".[276]

13–355   An argument that the imposition of the "substantial interest" requirement was in breach of the terms of Art.10a was rejected by the High Court in *Sweetman v An Bord Pleanála*.[277] Clarke J. held that the term "sufficient interest" under the EIA Directive could not have been intended as a reference to that term as understood under Irish law, but referred instead to the interest which the particular Member State determines, subject only to the requirement that it afford "wide access to justice". That latter requirement had, in the judgment of Clarke J., to be seen in the context that the EIA Directive expressly permits the confining of a right of challenge to those who are able to demonstrate an "impairment of a right".

> "In all those circumstances it does not seem to me that the existence of the 'substantial interest' test can be said to give rise to a situation where judicial review, as it is available in Ireland, fails to meet the requirements of the directive. If it should prove to be necessary, on the facts of any individual case, to give a more generous interpretation of the requirement of 'substantial interest' so as to meet the 'wide access to justice' criteria set out in Article 10a then there would be no difficulty in construing the term 'substantial interest' in an appropriate manner. It seems to me that it follows, therefore, that the term 'substantial interest' needs to be construed having regard to the requirement that Article 10a, in the cases to which it applies, such as this, and having regard to the requirement that there be wide access to justice. I propose considering the application of the substantial interest test in this case on that basis. In those circumstances it does not seem to me that there can be said to be any failure to transpose properly on those grounds."

13–356   Clarke J. went on to hold on the facts that Mr Sweetman met the substantial interest requirement: the case concerned a candidate Special Area of Conservation ("cSAC"). Clarke J. held that, having regard to the obligation under the Directive to allow wide access to justice and the application of that principle to the necessity to afford a reasonably wide range of people an opportunity to have their concerns dealt with in relation to sensitive areas, Mr Sweetman had standing.

---

[276] *Harrington v An Bord Pleanála (No. 1)* [2005] I.E.H.C. 344; [2006] 1 I.R. 388.
[277] [2007] 2 I.L.R.M. 328; unreported, High Court, Clarke J., April 27, 2007.

It is arguable that the imposition of the "substantial interest" requirement offends **13–357** against the principle of equivalence, *i.e.* that procedural rules governing the enforcement of EC law are not less favourable than those governing similar domestic situations.[278] National law imposes differing *locus standi* requirements depending on the type of judicial review proceedings involved—conventional or statutory—and the higher of the two standards, *i.e.* the "substantial interest" requirement, extends to proceedings alleging breaches of the EIA Directive. This would appear to involve a breach of the principle of equivalence. The only possible defence Ireland could offer is to argue that the higher standard is not confined to proceedings arising out of the EIA Directive, but applies to *all* decisions or acts under the planning legislation. Such an argument is unlikely to be accepted by the ECJ. The opinion of the Advocate General in *Commission v Ireland* suggests that the appropriate comparison is with the procedures governing administrative law challenges generally, rather than being confined to those applicable to challenges under the planning legislation.[279] Thus, the fact that a "sufficient interest" is generally enough to maintain a challenge to a decision on domestic law grounds means that a challenge based on the Directive is treated less favourably.

For these reasons, then, it is submitted that an Irish court when faced with **13–358** proceedings alleging a breach of the public participation provisions of the EIA Directive must set aside the "substantial interest" requirement.[280] In order to ensure compliance with the Directive, the court should only require an applicant to meet the lesser standard of "sufficient interest". Article 10a indicates that the determination of what constitutes a "sufficient interest" should be consistent with the objective of giving the public concerned wide access to justice. The case law in relation to the "sufficient interest" requirement under Irish law has been discussed in detail at paras 11–129 to 11–133, and suggests that it is not necessary for an applicant to demonstrate that he or she would be personally affected by the proposed development. Such a requirement would probably be inconsistent with the rights afforded to the public in general under the EIA Directive, or with the notion of "wide access" to justice. There is nothing in the Directive which suggests that the right to be consulted and to participate is limited to those persons who will be directly affected by the proposed development.

---

[278] See, for example, *R. (On the application of Wells) v Secretary of State for Transport, Local Government and the Regions* (Case C–201/02) [2004] E.C.R. I–723, [67].

[279] (Case C–216/05). The Advocate General, in concluding that the provisions of Irish planning law governing public consultation pursuant to Art.6(2) of the EIA Directive did not offend against the principle of equivalence, carried out a comparison with other national administrative procedures.

[280] The jurisdiction of a national court to disapply national law which is inconsistent with EC law is well established; see, for example, *Simmenthal* (Case 106/77); [1978] E.C.R. 629. For an example of the application of this jurisdiction in the specific context of the EIA Directive, see *Aannemersbedrijf P.K. Kraaijeveld BV v Gedeputeerde Staten van Zuid-Holland* (Case C–72/95); [1996] E.C.R. I–5403.

Prior participation

13–359 As a result of amendments made under the Planning and Development (Strategic Infrastructure) Act 2006, there is no longer any *express* requirement that an applicant for judicial review have previously participated in the planning process. However, as discussed in detail at paras 11–164 to 11–178, it has been suggested in a number of judgments that such a requirement may be implicit in the "substantial interest" requirement. In *Harrington v An Bord Pleanála (No. 1)*,[281] the High Court went so far as to suggest that an applicant for judicial review will normally be required to have *personally* raised, before the decision-maker, the legal objection subsequently sought to be relied upon in the judicial review proceedings. This case is discussed in more detail at paras 11–171 to 11–175, and it is suggested there that the judgment goes too far.

13–360 It is uncertain as to whether a prior participation requirement is compatible with Art.10a of the Directive. On one view, it can be argued that such a requirement undermines the effectiveness of the review procedure in that a court would be precluded from addressing an alleged breach of the Directive simply because the point had not been raised earlier. Ever before Art.10a came into force, the ECJ had ruled that—where permitted to do so under national law—a national court must examine *of its own motion* whether the legislative or administrative authorities of the Member State remained within the limits of their discretion under the Directive.[282] Now that the amended Directive expressly provides for a review procedure it might be thought anomalous were a Member State entitled to maintain such a rule.

13–361 On another view, however, it might be said that the imposition of a prior participation requirement is something which falls squarely within a Member State's discretion. Article 10a expressly states that its provisions shall not affect any national law requirement to exhaust administrative review procedures prior to recourse to judicial review procedures. It can be argued that a person who has failed to raise an objection before the planning authority or An Bord Pleanála has failed to exhaust his remedies at the administrative stage, and, as a result, might legitimately be precluded from bringing judicial review proceedings.

13–362 There is certainly much to be said for encouraging the raising of concerns before the decision-making bodies—rather than waiting until judicial review proceedings—with a view to the concern being rectified at as early a stage as possible.[283] Both a planning authority and An Bord Pleanála have wide powers, including the power to disapply conflicting provisions of national law, and might well be in a position to provide an adequate remedy.

---

[281] [2005] I.E.H.C. 344; [2006] 1 I.R. 388.

[282] *Kraaijeveld* (Case C–72/95) [1996] E.C.R. I–5403.

[283] cf. *Gwennap Parish Council v Cornwall County Council* [2003] J.P.L. 105 (not acceptable to challenge a decision, then when the decision is quashed, raise further concerns that could have been raised at an earlier hearing).

However, it seems unduly harsh to exclude from the review procedure a person   **13–363**
who is directly affected by the proposed development simply because he
personally had not raised an issue before the planning authority or An Bord
Pleanála. This is especially so where, as in *Harrington v An Bord Pleanála
(No. 1)*, the ground of complaint had, in fact, been raised by other parties.

Reference is made in this regard to the decision of the High Court of England   **13–364**
and Wales in *R. (On the application of Edwards) v Environment Agency*.[284]
There, it was held that a temporarily homeless local resident who had not
participated in the statutory licensing procedures nevertheless had a "sufficient
interest" to bring judicial review proceedings challenging a permit from the
Environment Agency. Keith J. held that if the consultation exercise ends with
a decision which affects a person's interests, that person is no less affected by
that decision simply because he or she took no part in the exercise but left it to
others to do so. A person should not be debarred from subsequently challenging
the decision on the ground of inadequate consultation simply because he or
she chose not to participate in the consultation exercise, provided that he or
she is affected by its outcome.

As of the time of writing, it appears that there has been little or no discussion   **13–365**
in Irish case law as to the implications, if any, of Art.10a for the prior
participation requirement. The point arose tangentially in *Friends of the Curragh
Environment Ltd. v An Bord Pleanála (No. 2)*,[285] but the High Court considered
that the question of Art.10a having direct effect was *res judicata* following an
earlier judgment in the proceedings.[286] It must be doubtful as to whether this
conclusion was justified on the facts. The earlier judgment, *Friends of the
Curragh Environment Ltd. v An Bord Pleanála (No. 1)*,[287] concerned a different
aspect of Art.10a, namely the requirement that the review procedure not be
prohibitively expensive. It is difficult to understand how a ruling on this issue
could be determinative of the distinct issue of *locus standi*. This is especially
so where the earlier ruling was based to a large extent on what the High Court
perceived to be the ambiguous nature of the term "prohibitively expensive".
Similar difficulties should not have arisen in the case of "sufficient interest", a

---

[284] [2004] E.W.H.C. 736 (Admin); [2004] 3 All E.R. 21; [2004] 2 P.& C.R. 370; [2004] J.P.L. 1691.

[285] [2006] I.E.H.C. 390; [2007] 1 I.L.R.M. 386.

[286] An interesting question arises as to the extent to which a national court may—by reference to the principle of *res judicata*—rely on an earlier mistaken ruling so as to exclude a party invoking a right under EC law. The ECJ in *Kapferer v Schlank & Schick GmbH* (Case C–234/04) [2006] E.C.R. 2585 has indicated that the principle of co-operation under Art.10 of the EC Treaty does not require a national court to disapply its internal rules of procedure in order to review and set aside a final judicial decision if that decision should be contrary to Community law. Whether the ruling on the preliminary application for a pre-emptive costs order in *Friends of the Curragh Environment Ltd.* constituted a final decision must be open to doubt, especially as it is not clear whether the High Court constituted a court or tribunal against "whose decision there is no judicial remedy under national law" for the purposes of Art.234 of the EC Treaty.

[287] [2006] I.E.H.C. 243; unreported, Kelly J., July 14, 2006.

concept more familiar to the common law. Even if the terms of the earlier judgment did conclude the question as to whether Art.10a had direct effect, the obligation on the High Court to interpret national legislation, so far as possible, in the light of the wording and the purpose of the EIA Directive in order to achieve the result sought by the Directive remained.[288] This obligation applies irrespective of whether a Directive has direct effect. Accordingly, the High Court in construing the "substantial interest" requirement should have had regard to the objective of giving the public concerned wide access to justice. This was the approach subsequently adopted by the High Court in *Sweetman v An Bord Pleanála*.[289]

Non-governmental organisations

13–366 Special provision is made under Art.10a for the position of non-governmental organisations ("NGOs"). Under Art.1(2) of the amended Directive, NGOs promoting environmental protection and meeting any requirements under national law are deemed to have an interest for the purposes of the definition of the "public concerned". Under Art.10a itself, the interest of any non-governmental organisation meeting the requirement referred to in Art.1(2) shall be deemed sufficient for the purpose of subparagraph (a) of Art.10a. Such organisations shall also be deemed to have rights capable of being impaired for the purpose of subparagraph (b) of Art.10a.

13–367 Non-governmental organisations are now exempt from the statutory requirement to demonstrate a "substantial interest" in the matter the subject-matter of the application for judicial review.[290] This exemption applies only to EIA development. To qualify as a non-governmental organisation, the organisation must fulfil the following requirements. First, its "aims or objectives" must relate to the "promotion of the environment". Secondly, it must have, within the period of twelve months preceding the date of application, pursued those aims or objectives. Thirdly, it must satisfy such additional requirements as may be prescribed by the Minister. In this latter connection, the Minister is empowered to prescribe requirements of a general nature and for the purposes of promoting transparency and accountability in the operation of such organisations, including requirements (i) in relation to its membership; (ii) that the pursuit of its aims or objectives be otherwise than for profit; (iii) in relation to the possession of a specified legal personality and the possession of a constitution or rules; (iv) that the area of environmental protection to which its aims or objectives relate is relevant to the class of matter into which the decision, the subject of the application for judicial review, falls.[291]

---

[288] See, for example, *Marleasing* (Case C–106/89) [1990] E.C.R. I–4135.
[289] Unreported, High Court, Clarke J., April 27, 2007.
[290] PDA 2000, s.50A(3)(b) (as inserted by Planning and Development (Strategic Infrastructure) Act 2006, s.13).
[291] PDA 2000, s.50A(3)(k)(ii) (as inserted by the Planning and Development (Strategic Infrastructure) Act 2006, s.10).

(iv) Time-limits

There is a general eight week time-limit on the taking of judicial review   **13–368**
proceedings under s.50 of the PDA 2000 (as amended). The High Court has a
jurisdiction to extend time where there is "good and sufficient" reason for so
doing, and where the circumstances which resulted in the failure to apply in
time were outside the control of the applicant for judicial review. Prior to the
coming into force of Art.10a, the Irish Supreme Court had indicated in
McNamara v An Bord Pleanála[292] that the imposition of a time-limit on the
taking of proceedings was not incompatible with EC law as it did not render
the assertion of EC law rights virtually impossible or excessively difficult.
This case concerned the two month time-limit under the previous legislation,
but the principles would seem to apply equally to the s.50 time-limit.

> "The time limit imposed by s. 82(3A) of the Act of 1963, as amended by s. 19(3)
> of the Act of 1992, is applicable to all proceedings in which a person seeks to
> question the validity of decisions to grant planning permissions, whether the
> challenge is based on domestic law or European Union law or a combination of
> both. Cases involving questions of European Union law are thus not treated in
> any sense less favourably and, while the time limit applicable is undoubtedly
> inflexible, it cannot be seriously contended that it renders the assertion of rights
> under European Union law 'virtually impossible' or 'excessively difficult'."

Reference is also made to the judgment of the Court of Appeal of England and   **13–369**
Wales in *R. v North West Leicestershire District Council Ex p. Moses*.[293] A
renewed application for leave to apply for judicial review was dismissed on
the basis of delay. The proceedings sought to impugn a decision to grant
planning permission. It was alleged that the planning authority had failed to
properly consider whether the proposed development was likely to have
significant effects on the environment. A period of almost five years had elapsed
between the date of the grant of planning permission and the judicial review
proceedings. The Court of Appeal, *per* Simon Brown L.J., ruled that the long
delay in the case was plainly inexcusable.

The Court of Appeal rejected an argument to the effect that as the planning   **13–370**
authority was under a continuing duty in EC law to ensure that the development
was subject to environmental impact assessment, it could not rely on delay to
resist the challenge. Simon Brown L.J. stated that the delay and prejudice in
the case were enormous and that there could be no argument but that the English
court was entitled to apply the time-limit even in the case of an alleged breach
of EC law.

---

[292] [1998] 3 I.R. 453.
[293] [2000] J.P.L. 1287. It should be noted that this judgment was decided before the rulings
of the House of Lords in *R. (On the application of Burkett) v Hammersmith and Fulham
LBC* [2002] U.K.H.L. 23; [2003] 1 P.& C.R. 3; [2002] J.P.L. 1346; and in *Berkeley v
Secretary of State for the Environment* [2001] 2 A.C. 603; (2001) 81 P. & C.R. 35;
accordingly some of the comments in the judgment may now have to be reappraised.

13–371   Simon Brown L.J. also suggested that there came a point when the EC principles of legal certainty and proportionality supported the rejection, rather than the admission, of long delayed challenges where third parties have acted in reliance on apparently valid decisions.

13–372   Similarly, in *R. (On the application of Gavin) v Haringey London Borough Council*,[294] the High Court of England and Wales ruled that there was no reason in principle as to why the exercise of a statutory discretion to refuse relief by way of judicial review should give rise to a problem under EC law. The case concerned an admitted failure on the part of the local planning authority to make a screening decision, *i.e.* to consider whether the proposed development was likely to have significant effects on the environment by virtue of factors such as its nature, size or location. On the facts, relief was refused on the basis that there had been undue delay. The court did not consider that a jurisdiction to entertain a claim outside the normal time-limit, which allowed the court to take into account the consequences of that delay for third parties and good administration, rendered it impossible or excessively difficult to enforce EC law rights, or involved any denial of effective protection, or otherwise offended general principles of EC law.

13–373   A recent example of an applicant being shut out from raising a complaint based on the Directive is to be found in the case of *Derrybrien Cooperative Society Ltd. v Saorgus Energy Ltd.*[295] Three separate planning permissions had been granted in respect of development consisting of a wind farm with wind turbines. It was alleged that planning permission had not been obtained for the removal of trees. It was argued that this aspect of the development represented "deforestation" for the purposes of the Directive, and should have been the subject of an application for planning permission. The point being that, as the area of land involved was greater than 70 hectares, this aspect of the development was not exempted development.[296]

13–374   The High Court indicated that such arguments were precluded by virtue of the statutory time-limit.

> "If there was a deficiency either in the earlier environmental impact assessment or the environmental statement prepared in respect of the later application for planning permission it would have been open to the applicant's predecessor and indeed to any of the local residents to object to the planning permission sought on that ground. If, notwithstanding any objection that could have been made, planning permission had been granted then it would have been open to the applicant or its predecessors or any of the residents to judicially review the decision by which planning permission was granted. This did not happen. I have come to

---

[294] [2003] E.W.H.C. 2591 (Admin), [41]; [2004] J.P.L. 785. See also the judgment of the Court of Appeal in *R. (On the application of the Noble Organisation Ltd.) v Thanet District Council* [2005] E.W.C.A. Civ. 782; [2006] 1 P. & C.R. 13; [2006] J.P.L. 60.

[295] Unreported, High Court, Dunne J., June 3, 2005.

[296] See now Sch.5 of the Planning and Development Regulations 2001, Pt 2, subpara.1(d).

the conclusion that in questioning the validity of the environment impact statement and environmental assessment as it is referred to in respect of the 00/4581 planning permission that the applicant herein is in effect attempting to retrospectively object to the planning permission or, perhaps more accurately, seeking to challenge the validity of the permissions granted. Clearly this cannot be done now. The time for making such a challenge to the validity of the permission has long since passed."

The question arises as to whether different considerations must now apply in the light of Art.10a of the Directive. Again, there is a balance to be struck between ensuring compliance with the procedural requirements of the Directive, on the one hand, and competing considerations such as legal certainty and fairness to developers who have relied on an unchallenged planning permission, on the other. It is expressly provided under Art.10a that the review procedure is to be fair and equitable. The imposition of a reasonable time-limit, with provision for its extension for good and sufficient reason, might be thought to strike the correct balance in ensuring fairness and equity. An inflexible procedure which mandated the setting aside of a planning permission in every case, without any reference to the hardship to the developer or any delay on the part of the applicant, might be thought to be inequitable. The legislative scheme under s.50 might just pass muster, although it has to be said that the eight week time-limit is very tight. It is essential, therefore, that when it comes to the exercise of their discretion to extend time, the courts have regard to Art.10a. In particular, in interpreting the phrase "good and sufficient" reason under ss.50 and 50A, the courts should have cognisance of the fact that there is a *right* of review and that this right must be weighed against the competing rights of the developer. The case law on extension of time is discussed generally at para.11–66 and onwards.

13–375

The requirement—introduced under the Planning and Development (Strategic Infrastructure) Act 2006—that the delay must have been outside the control of the applicant may not be compatible with Art.10a. A breach of the Directive should normally be rectified. This principle may have to yield to considerations of fairness to the developer, and thus, in some cases of delay, it would be inequitable to allow a late challenge to be brought to a planning permission. The requirement that the delay have been outside the control of the applicant is too blunt: it might result in judicial review proceedings being barred in circumstances where there would, in fact, be no prejudice to the developer.

13–376

A further difficulty now arises as a result of the amendments introduced under the 2006 Act. As discussed in detail at paras 11–59 to 11–65, the fact that time is now to be reckoned from the date of the doing of an "act" by the planning authority or An Bord Pleanála suggests that it might no longer be safe to await the final outcome of a planning application before bringing judicial review proceedings. This is because any challenge to a final decision might be time-barred if the challenge involved impugning some "act" done by a planning authority or An Bord Pleanála during the course of processing an application/appeal; for example, the failure to call for an environmental impact statement

13–377

where one is necessary. On a literal reading of the amended s.50, it is arguable that time is to be calculated from the date of the negative screening decision, rather than from the (later) date of the decision on the application. It must be doubtful whether such a strict regime would be compatible with Art.10a. As discussed above, absent some countervailing factor, such as prejudice to the developer, a breach of the Directive should normally be remedied. A developer is not entitled to carry out works until such time as a final decision is made on the planning application, and provided any challenge is brought within eight weeks of that date it is submitted that the correct balance between the need to enforce the Directive and to ensure fairness to the developer is struck.[297] To preclude a challenge to a defective planning permission simply because proceedings were not issued in advance of the final decision seems unnecessarily harsh, and would undermine the effectiveness of the Art.10a remedy.

13–378 There is, probably, at least one aspect of current national law which may need to be reconsidered in the light of Art.10a. Under s.50 of the PDA 2000 (as amended), there is a prohibition on questioning the validity of a decision on a planning application other than by way of judicial review. This has been discussed at para.13–304 and onwards. On one view, this prohibition goes too far and would shut out any proceedings which would involve any insinuation that an earlier decision had been reached unlawfully, even where no formal order is sought setting aside that previous planning permission. This would seem to be disproportionate. It should be sufficient protection to allow a developer to retain the benefit of a deficient planning permission where no timely challenge has been brought; it seems unnecessary to shut off an objector from other forms of relief which might be of assistance to him simply because this would involve, in some abstract way, calling into doubt the previous planning decision. Take the example of consecutive applications for planning permission. It sometimes happens that a developer is not able to implement a planning permission within time, and might therefore decide to reapply. Similarly, a developer might seek a second planning permission for a modified version of development. The first planning permission may have been granted without there having been any environmental impact assessment. If, on the occasion of the second application, the objection is made that the development should be subject to environmental impact assessment, this in a literal sense involves questioning the validity of the first decision, in that the logic of saying that the development should be subject to environmental impact assessment must have applied equally to the first planning application. It is submitted that this objection should nevertheless be allowed, and that the phrase "shall not question the validity" should be interpreted narrowly. See further para.13–304.

---

[297] *cf. R. (On the application of Catt) v Brighton and Hove City Council* [2006] E.W.H.C. 1337 (Admin), where it was suggested that, notwithstanding *Burkett* [2002] UKHL 23, [42]; [2003] 1 P. & C.R. 3, time should be taken as running from the date of a negative screening decision, not from the date of the (later) decision on the planning application.

(iv) Not prohibitively expensive

The review procedure to be provided by the Member States pursuant to Art.10a must not be "prohibitively expensive". The issue of the costs of judicial review proceedings generally is examined at paras 11–301 to 11–327.   **13–379**

There are two aspects to the expense of legal proceedings: court fees and lawyers' fees. It is not entirely clear as to whether the requirements of Art.10a apply only to the former, *i.e.* the nominal fee payable on the institution of legal proceedings together with the fees payable on the filing of various court documents. Court fees for judicial review proceedings are very modest, and, accordingly, if Art.10a is confined to court fees, no procedural changes are required in that it cannot realistically be argued that the current level of court fees are prohibitively expensive. If, conversely, Art.10a extends to lawyers' fees then procedural changes may be required.   **13–380**

It is submitted that there are strong grounds for saying that Art.10a does extend to lawyers' fees. The risk of incurring liability for the other side's costs is one of the principal deterrents to the bringing of judicial review proceedings, and it would, therefore, be artificial to exclude lawyers' fees from a Directive which seeks to regulate access to justice in environmental matters. Insofar as there may be any ambiguity in the wording of Art.10a, it is submitted that it must be resolved in favour of an interpretation which includes lawyers' fees.   **13–381**

If one assumes that Art.10a is to be so interpreted, the next question to be considered is as to the changes necessary to national procedural law. A balance has to be struck between ensuring that the review procedure is not prohibitively expensive, on the one hand, and considerations of fairness and equity and the need to prevent an abuse of the court process, on the other. The matter might be best examined in two stages. First, the question arises as to in what circumstances, if any, it would be appropriate to order an unsuccessful applicant to pay the costs of any or all of the respondents. At present, the risk of incurring liability to pay the other side's costs is a very real deterrent to bringing judicial review proceedings. One extreme solution would be to say that no order for costs should ever be made against an applicant in proceedings alleging a breach of the EIA Directive. This solution has an obvious disadvantage in that it leaves no sanction against bringing frivolous or vexatious proceedings. The threat of an adverse costs order does have a disciplining effect, and the challenge is to formulate a rule which maintains this benefit without creating an obstacle for genuine cases. A compromise, therefore, would be to say that costs should only be awarded against an applicant who was refused leave to apply for judicial review. In other words, other applicants, who obtained leave only to fail at the full hearing, would not be at risk of an adverse costs order. This difference in treatment might be justified by saying that proceedings which passed the first hurdle of the leave application, by definition, could not be frivolous or vexatious. Of course, it might well be argued that the requirement under s.50 (as amended) that an applicant establish "substantial grounds" and demonstrate a "substantial interest" provides sufficient protection against frivolous or vexatious   **13–382** proceedings, and that, consequently, there is no need for an additional safeguard in terms of the threat of adverse costs orders.

13–383 An alternative solution would be to insist on some additional factor before a special rule in relation to costs would apply. For example, the ordinary rule that costs follow the event might only be disapplied where the case raised a public law issue of general importance or met some other criterion. There is already a body of case law in relation to public interest litigation—discussed at paras 11–305 to 11–311—and this might be applied by analogy. Proponents of a more generous rule on costs might argue, however, that the implication of Art.10a is that cases alleging a breach of the Directive, almost by definition, raise issues of public importance and there is, therefore, no basis for imposing a further qualifying requirement under national law.

13–384 The second stage of the analysis, then, is in respect of the applicant's own legal costs, and, in particular, as to the circumstances, if any, in which an unsuccessful applicant should not only avoid liability for the other side's costs, but actually receive a contribution—whether in whole or in part—in respect of his own costs. It is submitted that the case for such an order is very weak. One of the objectives of Art.10a is to ensure that there is effective access to the review procedure. As matters currently stand, the only real deterrent is the risk of incurring liability for the other side's costs. In terms of funding one's own legal team, anecdotal evidence would suggest that there is an ample number of lawyers prepared to take on such cases—whether on a *pro bono* basis or in the hope that the case may succeed and the applicant then receive an award of costs in his favour—so as to ensure that cases can be brought.

13–385 As discussed at para.13–326 and onwards, the High Court, in *Friends of the Curragh Environment Ltd. v An Bord Pleanála (No. 1)*,[298] considered that the requirement that the review procedure not be "prohibitively expensive" was too imprecise to have direct effect. In *Sweetman v An Bord Pleanála*,[299] the High Court held that Art.10a was not intended (nor were there substantial grounds for arguing to the contrary) to cover the exposure of a party to reasonable legal costs in judicial review proceedings. The High Court has thus purported to interpret definitively the term "prohibitively expensive" under Art.10a in circumstances where the High Court itself had previously ruled that the self-same term was ambiguous. Moreover, in reaching this conclusion, the High Court relied on the text of an extraneous document, the Aarhus Convention, in interpreting the provisions of an EC Directive. With respect, it is submitted that such an approach to the interpretation of EC Directives is liable to give rise to inconsistent application of EC law. There are strong grounds for saying that the Irish High Court should have referred the question of the interpretation of Art.10a to the ECJ under Art.234 of the EC Treaty.

---

[298] [2006] I.E.H.C. 243; unreported, Kelly J., July 14, 2006.
[299] Unreported, High Court, Clarke J., April 27, 2007.

The High Court may well have been acting as a court of final instance for the **13–386** purposes of Art.234 in that leave to appeal to the Supreme Court is required before the matter can be pursued before that court. The ECJ, in *Intermodal Transports BV v Staatssecretaris van Financien*,[300] emphasised that the third paragraph of Art.234 must be interpreted as meaning that such courts of final instance are required, where a question of EC law is raised before them, to comply with their obligation to make a reference, unless they have established that the question raised is irrelevant, or that the EC provision in question has already been interpreted by the ECJ or that the correct application of EC law is so obvious as to leave no scope for any reasonable doubt. The existence of such a possibility must be assessed in the light of the specific characteristics of EC law, the particular difficulties to which its interpretation gives rise and the risk of divergences in judicial decisions within the Community.

(v) Standard of review

The right under Art.10a is of access to a review procedure to challenge the **13–387** "substantive or procedural legality" of decisions, acts or omissions subject to the public participation provisions of the EIA Directive. The requirement to review substantive legality may well have ramifications for the approach adopted by the Irish courts. As discussed in Chapter 12, at para.12–02 in particular, judicial review under Irish law is primarily—although not exclusively— concerned with the decision-making process, *i.e.* the procedural legality of the decision. The substance or merits of a decision are only subject to review by reference to the attenuated standard of unreasonableness or irrationality. Thus the courts would only accede to a merits-challenge where the applicant could demonstrate that the decision was "fundamentally at variance with reason and common sense" or "indefensible for being in the teeth of plain reason and common sense".[301]

It has been intimated in a number of judgments that such an attenuated standard **13–388** of review applies to various aspects of the environmental impact assessment procedure. Thus, in *Kenny v An Bord Pleanála (No. 1)*,[302] the High Court held—in the context of a challenge to the adequacy of the environmental information submitted with a planning application—that the quality of the information was a matter for An Bord Pleanála. Similarly, it seems to have

---

[300] (Case C–495/03); September 15, 2005.
[301] *O'Keeffe v An Bord Pleanála* [1992] 1 I.R. 39 at 70, *per* Finlay C.J., citing *State (Keegan) v Stardust Compensation Tribunal* [1986] I.R. 642.
[302] [2001] 1 I.R. 565 at 578, cited with approval in *Kildare County Council v An Bord Pleanála* [2006] I.E.H.C. 173; unreported, MacMenamin J., March 10, 2006. See also *Murphy v Wicklow County Council*, unreported, High Court, Kearns J., March 19, 1999. Ryall has criticised the judgment in *Kenny v An Bord Pleanála*, suggesting that the entrenched deferential attitude towards decisions of specialists tribunals, in particular, planning authorities and An Bord Pleanála, must be revisited and revised in light of the clear mandate from the ECJ to enforce environmental impact assessment law locally; see A. Ryall, "Judicial Review and the Adequacy of the EIS: Kenny v. An Bord Pleanála" (2002) 9 I.P.E.L.J. 20.

been suggested in *Waddington v An Bord Pleanála*[303] that a decision on whether sub-threshold development is likely to have significant effects on the environment, *i.e.* a screening decision, was subject to the principles in *O'Keeffe v An Bord Pleanála*.

13–389 Perhaps the most dramatic example is provided by the judgment in *Friends of the Curragh Environment Ltd. v An Bord Pleanála (No. 1)*.[304] As discussed at paras 13–326 to 13–335, the High Court—in determining an application for a protective costs order—concluded that Art.10a did not have direct effect. In this connection, Kelly J. stated that it was questionable whether Art.10a applied to judicial review proceedings at all, given the limited grounds of review available under national law.

> "Indeed it is also questionable as to whether the Article applies to court proceedings at all in the Irish context. It must be remembered that Irish court proceedings in questions of this type do not permit of a substantive review. The only form of review is a judicial review which does not address the merits of the case. Thus, it is doubtful if the Directive applies at all."

13–390 With respect, this judgment does not appear to give sufficient weight to the obligation on the High Court to interpret national legislation, so far as possible, in the light of the wording and the purpose of the EIA Directive in order to achieve the result sought by the Directive.[305] If—as contended for below—Art.10a requires a more exacting standard of review than before, then national law will have to be "read up" so as to meet that standard. This was the approach adopted by the High Court in *Sweetman v An Bord Pleanála*,[306] where Clarke J. held—to the extent that it may be necessary to allow, in certain circumstances, for a review which goes beyond the existing parameters of Irish judicial review law—that Irish law was more than capable of being adapted by the courts to accommodate such a requirement.

13–391 The usual justification given for the traditional deferential standard of review applied to planning matters is that the particular matter has been entrusted under legislation to the relevant decision-maker, and the courts should respect the legislature's choice in this regard. Finlay C.J. formulated it thus in *O'Keeffe v An Bord Pleanála*.

> "Under the provisions of the Planning Acts the legislature has unequivocally and firmly placed questions of planning, questions of the balance between development and the environment and the proper convenience and amenities of an area within the jurisdiction of the planning authorities and the Board which are expected to have special skill, competence and experience in planning questions. The court is not vested with that jurisdiction, nor is it expected to, nor can it, exercise discretion with regard to planning matters."

[303] Unreported, High Court, Butler J., December 21, 2000.
[304] [2006] I.E.H.C. 243; unreported, Kelly J., July 14, 2006.
[305] See, for example, *Marleasing* (Case C–106/89) [1990] E.C.R. I–4135.
[306] Unreported, High Court, Clarke J., April 27, 2007.

Unfortunately, there has been little analysis in the subsequent case law as to **13–392** why it is that the attenuated standard of review is being applied to more and more circumstances. The judgment in *O'Keeffe v An Bord Pleanála* concerned a challenge to a decision on an application for planning permission, a decision which was pre-eminently a matter of planning policy. Before the principles are applied to other types of decision, a check should be made to ensure that it is appropriate to do so. In practice, this does not often happen. Instead, there has been a regrettable tendency in the more recent jurisprudence simply to focus on the practical difficulties which would be involved for the court were it to attempt to weigh in on planning matters, rather than on any principled reason as to why the court should show deference. Expediency triumphs over principle.

Even prior to Art.10a, it was arguable that the *O'Keeffe* principles were being **13–393** applied too extensively.[307] For example, the question as to whether a particular development is likely to have significant effects on the environment is a lot less subjective than the question as to whether a particular development should be granted planning permission. The ECJ has made it clear on a number of occasions that the competent authorities of a Member State are to take, within the sphere of their competence, all the general or particular measures necessary to ensure that projects are examined in order to determine whether they are likely to have significant effects on the environment and, if so, to ensure that they are subject to an impact assessment.[308] This obligation extends to the national courts, and it is difficult to reconcile the courts' obligations in this regard with the taking of such a deferential approach to the views of the planning authorities and An Bord Pleanála.

The approach taken in *O'Keeffe* was justified by reference to legislative intent. **13–394** The Supreme Court read the then planning legislation as entrusting questions of planning; questions of the balance between development and the environment; and the proper convenience and amenities of an area, to the planning authorities and An Bord Pleanála. The exercise of such a statutorily conferred discretion was, quite properly, subject to only limited merits-based review by the courts. The same conclusion does not necessarily follow from the legislative scheme in respect of environmental impact assessment. Although it might be argued that—on a literal interpretation—the planning bodies enjoy a discretion in deciding matters such as screening decisions or in examining the adequacy of an environmental impact statement, it is submitted that these are not true discretionary powers. Rather, these are matters which the planning bodies are required to consider and, if the relevant circumstances are met, to act in a particular way, for example, by calling for an environmental impact statement or by requesting further information to remedy inadequacies.

---

[307] See, generally, paras 12–90 to 12–118.
[308] *Aannemersbedrijf P.K. Kraaijeveld BV v Gedeputeerde Staten van Zuid-Holland* (Case C–72/95) [1996] E.C.R. I–5403; and *R. (On the application of Wells) v Secretary of State for Transport, Local Government and the Regions* (Case C–201/02) [2004] E.C.R. I–723.

13–395   Even if national law should—contrary to what is submitted above—be interpreted as allowing a discretion, same has to be read and interpreted in the light of the obligation imposed under the Directive on competent authorities to ensure that projects are examined in order to determine whether they are likely to have significant effects on the environment and, if so, to ensure that they are subject to an impact assessment.

13–396   The introduction of Art.10a adds further support to the argument that the courts must play a more active role than that stipulated under the *O'Keeffe* principles. The procedure envisaged under Art.10a extends not only to the procedural aspects of, but also to the substance of, the reviewable decisions.

13–397   It is not clear from Art.10a as to the extent of the discretion which has been left to the Member States in this regard. Traditionally, in the absence of Community rules governing the matter, Member States were not required to provide an extensive judicial review procedure. Even in cases involving alleged breaches of EC law rights, a judicial review procedure which was confined to grounds such as manifest error or a misuse of powers would be sufficient.[309]

13–398   More recent judgments had emphasised, however, that limited judicial review was only compatible with EC law on condition that the national procedure for judicial review enabled the court to apply the relevant principles and rules of EC law when reviewing the legality of the impugned decision.[310] Even without reference to Art.10a, it is arguable that judicial review under Irish law failed to meet this standard. In particular, the *O'Keeffe* principles meant that the standard of review applied under Irish law to the exercise of the "discretion" to require an environmental impact assessment in the case of sub-threshold development was far less exacting than that exercised by the ECJ itself. See para.13–58.

13–399   The fact that the review procedure is now subject to express regulation under Art.10a suggests that the standard of review required will be higher again. In this regard, a loose analogy might be drawn with the legal position obtaining in respect of public procurement as discussed by the Supreme Court in *SIAC Construction Ltd. v Mayo County Council*.[311] Under the relevant Directives, Member States were required, *inter alia*, to ensure that decisions taken by contracting authorities could be "reviewed effectively". The Supreme Court, *per* Fennelly J., indicated that this might require some adjustment to the standard of review, with a more exacting standard applicable than that under the *O'Keeffe* principles.

> "I do not think, however, that the test of manifest error is to be equated with the test adopted by the trial judge, namely that, in order to qualify for quashing, a decision must 'plainly and unambiguously fly in the face of fundamental reason and common sense.' It cannot be ignored that the Advocate General thought the

---

[309] *Upjohn Ltd.* (Case C–120/97) [1999] E.C.R. I–223.
[310] *HLH Warenvertriebs GmbH* (Case C–211/03); June 9, 2005.
[311] [2002] 3 I.R. 148.

test should be 'rather less extreme.' Such a formulation of the test would run the risk of not offering what the Remedies Directive clearly mandates, namely a judicial remedy which will be effective in the protection of the interests of disappointed tenderers. It is significant, I think, that member states are required to make available, where appropriate and necessary, measures of interim relief (*i.e.*, potentially halting the public procurement procedure) and damages.

The courts must be ready, in general, to render effective the general principles of the public procurement, already discussed. Where a failure to respect the principles of equality, transparency or objectivity is clearly made out, there is, of course, no question of permitting a margin of discretion. Equally, where the tender is on the basis of the lowest price (first indent of art. 29(1)), the courts must be ready to restrain any breach. Even in cases of the most economically advantageous contract, it is clear that unlimited discretion cannot be permitted. The margin of discretion enjoyed by the awarding authority does not absolve it from explaining a choice, such as was made in the present case, of a tender other than the lowest."

This theme was taken up by Clarke J. in *Sweetman v An Bord Pleanála*.[312]   **13–400**

"It is important to note that what the Directive allows persons to challenge is 'the substantive or procedural legality of decisions'. While it is clear that Irish judicial review law allows an extensive review of the procedural legality of decisions, it is important to note that the Directive does not require that there be a judicial review of the substance of the decision itself but rather the 'substantive legality' of the decision. It seems clear therefore (and indeed it was not otherwise argued on behalf of Mr. Sweetman) that the Directive does not require a complete appeal on the merits. In addition to a review of the procedures followed, to determine whether they were in accordance with law, it is also necessary that there be a review of the 'substantive legality' of the decision. It seems to me that current Irish judicial review law goes a long way towards (and indeed may well meet) that requirement. Judicial review proceedings can review whether it was, as a matter of law, open to the decision-maker to come to the decision taken. It can review whether all proper matters were taken into account and no improper matters taken into account. The limitation on the review is that the court is not permitted to 'second guess' a judgment made by the decision-maker on the basis of materials which could allow such a judgment to be reached."

Clarke J. went on to reject the contention that the requirement that there be a   **13–401**
judicial review of the substantive legality of a decision in the environmental field goes beyond the test of "manifest error" analysed by Fennelly J. in *SIAC Construction Ltd.*

In conclusion, therefore, the question as to the standard of review to be applied   **13–402**
to decisions reviewable under Art.10a is a perplexing one. The temptation for the courts will be to continue to defer to the views of the planning authorities and An Bord Pleanála. To do otherwise, and to engage in a fuller review, will impose a greater strain on scarce judicial resources; hearings will take longer with the need for more detailed evidence and legal submissions. Moreover, the possibility of full-blooded review may excite more litigation. The threshold

---

[312] [2007] 2 I.L.R.M. 328; unreported, High Court, Clarke J., April 27, 2007.

imposed by the *O'Keeffe* principles is set so high that it discourages merits-challenges; any recalibration of the standard of review may have the opposite effect.

13–403 Notwithstanding these considerations, it will probably be necessary for the courts to make material adjustments to the standard of review. Whereas it may still be permissible to have some regard to the fact that the planning bodies have specialist expertise, the standard set by *O'Keeffe* attaches far too much weight to the role of the planning authorities and An Bord Pleanála. In effect, it resolves itself to a no-evidence rule, whereby a decision cannot be overturned unless it can be demonstrated that there was no material—however weak—before the decision-maker which would justify the decision. Such a deferential approach is likely on occasion to undermine the application of the Directive, and is contrary to the previous jurisprudence of the ECJ and to the terms of Art.10a.

13–404 There is likely to be a marked reluctance, or even hostility, on the part of the courts to any extension of the principles on which merits-based review will be allowed. This is, perhaps, odd, given that the judgment in *O'Keeffe v An Bord Pleanála* was based on statutory interpretation: if, as a result of the coming into force and effect of Art.10a, the statutory background has changed and a more exacting standard of review is required, there should be no objection to adjusting the principles of review accordingly.

13–405 An issue related to the standard of review is as to where the onus of proof lies. In a number of judgments it has been suggested that the onus is on an applicant to demonstrate that there has been a failure on the part of the relevant decision-maker to comply with the requirements of the Directive. Thus, McGuinness J., in *Lancefort Ltd. v An Bord Pleanála*,[313] ruled that the onus of proof in establishing that An Bord Pleanála did not consider the question of environmental impact assessment lay squarely with the applicant company. McGuinness J. further ruled that the applicant company had failed to discharge fully this burden; this finding was made notwithstanding the fact that the board failed to adduce any positive evidence that it had considered the possible requirement for an environmental impact statement. Similarly, in *Boyne Valley and Newgrange Environmental Protection League Ltd. v Environmental Protection Agency*,[314] Ó Caoimh J. held—in response to an allegation that no proper assessment had been carried out—that the onus rested on the applicant to show that the Environmental Protection Agency had acted in excess of its jurisdiction or in essential disregard of its obligations, and that the mere fact that the public file did not record in any particular form how the assessment was carried out did not entitle one to conclude that no such assessment was in fact carried out.

---

[313] Unreported, High Court, McGuinness J., March 12, 1998. The Supreme Court ultimately disposed of the case on the narrower issue of *locus standi*.

[314] Unreported, High Court, Ó Caoimh J., April 17, 2002.

It is submitted that the burden imposed in these cases is unfair, and would now **13–406** be contrary to Art.10a. In effect, applicants were required to prove a negative. There is now an obligation on decision-makers to state reasons for screening decisions (para.13–142), and to refer in the decision on a development consent to the assessment carried out (para.13–240). Accordingly, it is no longer sufficient for a decision-maker to maintain a sphinx-like silence, and, in the event of a legal challenge, the court must consider whether the stated reasons justify the decision taken, rather than throwing the onus on the applicant.

It is further submitted that the *O'Keeffe* principles operate, in effect, as a defence **13–407** and, accordingly, the onus of establishing the factual basis for such a defence should be on the respondent decision-maker, as it is a matter peculiarly within its knowledge. In the absence of such evidence, an applicant should be entitled to draw any reasonable inference. McCarthy J. expressly recognised in *O'Keeffe* that a stage may be reached where the onus of proof in judicial review proceedings may *shift* to the administrative body concerned. Such a shift in the onus of proof would be entirely consistent with the requirement on a decision-maker to maintain some record (although not necessarily in the form of minutes of meetings) of the material considered by it, in order to allow the High Court exercise its supervisory jurisdiction; see, for example, *P. & F. Sharpe Ltd. v Dublin City and County Manager*[315]; and the judgment in *O'Keeffe* itself. It would also be consistent with the duty under Art.9 of the Directive to state the reasons and considerations for the decision on an application for a development consent. The existence of such a duty indicates that there may be an onus on an administrative body to justify its decisions.

V. Transboundary Effects

1. Article 7 of the EIA Directive

Special procedural requirements apply—under Art.7 of the Directive—where **13–408** a project is likely to have significant effects on *another* Member State. These requirements are triggered either where the first Member State is aware that a project is likely to have significant effects on the environment in another Member State, or where that second Member State so requests.

The first procedural step involves the sending to the affected Member State of **13–409** information including (a) a description of the project, together with any available information on its possible transboundary impact; and (b) information on the nature of the decision which may be taken. The affected Member State is then to have a reasonable period of time in which to indicate whether it wishes to participate in the environmental decision-making procedures. If the affected Member State does decide to participate, then it is to be sent the Art.6 information.

---

[315] [1989] I.R. 701.

13–410   Under Art.7(5), the detailed arrangements for the implementation of the consultation are to be determined by the Member States concerned. The arrangements shall be such as to enable the public concerned in the territory of the affected Member State to participate effectively in the environmental decision-making procedures.

2. Planning and Development Regulations 2001 (as amended)

13–411   These requirements have been implemented principally under Part 10, chapter 5 of the Planning and Development Regulations 2001 (as substituted by the 2006 Regulations).[316] The procedure applies not only to applications for planning permission, but also to applications in respect of strategic infrastructure and to applications for the approval/assessment of local authority, and State authority, development.[317]

13–412   The procedure applies not only to another Member State, but also to a State which is a party to the Transboundary Convention.

Notification and furnishing of information to the Minister

13–413   A planning authority is required to notify the Minister for the Environment Heritage and Local Government, as soon as may be after receipt, of any planning application, where, in its opinion, the proposed development to which the application relates would be likely to have significant effects on the environment in a transboundary State.[318]

13–414   An Bord Pleanála has a similar obligation in the case of any appeal, any application for strategic infrastructure development, and any application for approval/assessment of local authority or State authority development.[319] Of course, in the case of an application for strategic infrastructure development or a request to alter strategic infrastructure development, the applicant or requester is under an obligation to notify the transboundary State.[320] An Bord Pleanála must notify the Minister of these cases also.[321]

---

[316] Planning and Development Regulations 2001, arts 124–132 (as substituted by the 2006 Regulations). The Regulations are made pursuant to s.174 of the PDA 2000.

[317] See art.92 of the Planning and Development Regulations 2001 (as amended by art.23 of the 2006 Regulations).

[318] Planning and Development Regulations 2001, art.124(1)(a) (as inserted by the 2006 Regulations).

[319] Planning and Development Regulations 2001, art.124(1)(b) (as inserted by the 2006 Regulations).

[320] PDA 2000, s.37E(3)(d) and s.146C(4)(d) (as inserted by the 2006 Act). An Bord Pleanála may indicate to the prospective applicant which States should be notified: see art.210(3) and art.221(1) of the Planning and Development Regulations 2001 (as substituted by the 2006 Regulations).

[321] Planning and Development Regulations 2001, art.124(1)(b)(ii) (as substituted by the 2006 Regulations).

Where the Minister is notified, he or she shall consult with the relevant planning **13–415** authority or An Bord Pleanála as appropriate in relation to the proposed development.

In addition, the Minister has a freestanding power to require a planning authority **13–416** or An Bord Pleanála, as appropriate, to furnish him or her with such details, information or documents as he or she may specify in relation to any application, appeal or application for approval. This power arises where either (a) the development, in the Minister's opinion, would be likely to have significant effects on the environment in a transboundary State, or (b) where a transboundary State considers that the development would be likely to have such effects and has requested that it be provided with information on the proposed development.[322]

Transboundary consultation

The relevant planning authority or An Bord Pleanála, as appropriate, is required **13–417** to provide the following information to the transboundary State concerned (except where this information has already been provided to the transboundary State by the applicant or requester in the case of an application for strategic infrastructure or a request for an alteration to strategic infrastructure development).

(a) a description of the project, together with any available information on its possible transboundary impact;
(b) an indication that the project is subject to an environmental impact assessment procedure;
(c) an indication that the planning authority or the board, as the case may be, is the competent authority responsible for taking the decision;
(d) an indication of the types of decision the planning authority or the board, as the case may be, may make in relation to the application, appeal, application for approval or application for strategic infrastructure;
(e) an indication that a decision will not be taken on the proposed development until the views, if any, of the transboundary State have been received or the consultations are otherwise completed;
(f) an indication that where the transboundary State indicates that it wishes to take part in the decision-making procedures in relation to the proposed development, a copy of the environmental impact statement will be sent to it.

The planning authority or An Bord Pleanála, as appropriate, is then required to **13–418** enter into consultations with that State in relation to the potential transboundary effects of the proposed development. The other parties to the application or appeal are to be notified of this fact.

---

[322] Planning and Development Regulations 2001, art.125 (as substituted by the 2006 Regulations).

Request for further information

13–419 Special rules apply in respect of requests for further information. The usual rule—under art.33(3) of the Planning and Development Regulations 2001—to the effect that only one request for further information can be made seems to be disapplied. The planning authority has discretion, having regard to the views of a transboundary State, to require an applicant for planning permission to submit further information or evidence.[323] The planning authority may require the applicant to give further public notice, and to send a copy of the further information to the prescribed bodies, the Minister and the transboundary State, where the response to a request for further information contains "significant additional data" on the effects on the environment of the proposed development.[324] Notice of the receipt of the response must be send to any person who had made submissions or observations on the planning application.

13–420 Submissions and observations on the further information or evidence may be made within a period of four weeks.

13–421 Where an applicant fails to comply with such a request for further information or evidence, the planning application shall be declared to be withdrawn after six months has elapsed from the date of the request.[325]

13–422 An Bord Pleanála similarly has a power to request the submission of further information or evidence in respect of an appeal, an application for strategic infrastructure development or an application for approval/assessment of local authority, or State authority, development.[326] An Bord Pleanála is also required to notify the Minister and the transboundary State where it considers that any submission, observation, document, particulars or other information submitted to it in response contains "significant additional data" on the effects on the environment of the proposed development.

13–423 These powers to request further information or evidence are in addition to the *general* powers which planning authorities and An Bord Pleanála enjoy to request further information or evidence. Where a response to a request for further information or evidence made pursuant to the general power contains significant additional data, the Minister and the transboundary State are to be send a copy of the response.[327]

---

[323] Planning and Development Regulations 2001, art.128(1) (as substituted by the 2006 Regulations).
[324] Planning and Development Regulations 2001, art.128(2) (as substituted by the 2006 Regulations).
[325] Planning and Development Regulations 2001, art.128(4) (as substituted by the 2006 Regulations).
[326] Planning and Development Regulations 2001, arts 128(5) to (7).
[327] Planning and Development Regulations 2001, art.129 (as substituted by the 2006 Regulations).

Time period for determining planning application

The time period within which a decision on an application for planning **13–424** permission must be made is extended in the case of transboundary development until after (a) the views, if any, of any relevant transboundary State have been received in response to consultations under art.126(1), or (b) the consultations are otherwise completed. The legality of this extension of time, and the implications for default planning permissions, have been raised in proceedings entitled *Monopower Ltd. v Monaghan County Council.*

Notice of the decision on the application, appeal or application for approval, **13–425** as the case may be, must be sent to the Minister, and to any relevant transboundary State.[328]

Procedure where Ireland affected by transboundary development

Where the Minister receives information from a transboundary State in respect **13–426** of any development which is subject to the EIA Directive or the Transboundary Convention, which is likely to have significant effects on the environment, the Minister shall, as soon as may be following receipt of such information, notify any planning authority likely to be affected by the proposed development and send a copy of the information to any such authority.[329]

The planning authority is then required to give public notice, and notice to the **13–427** prescribed bodies under art.28 of the Planning and Development Regulations 2001. The notice shall contain the following information.

(i)   that information has been received in relation to the proposed development in such transboundary State;
(ii) the nature of the information received;
(iii) that the proposed development is subject to an environmental impact assessment procedure and has potential transboundary effects;
(iv) the nature of possible decision, or where there is one, the draft decision;
(v)   that the information is available for inspection, or purchase at a fee not exceeding the reasonable cost of making a copy, during office hours at the offices of the authority;
(vi) that a submission or observation in relation to the proposed development may be made in writing to the authority within a specified period.

The planning authority is required to consult with the Minister as soon as may **13–428** be following receipt of any submission or observation.[330] The planning authority is then to enter into consultations with the transboundary State in relation to the potential transboundary effects of the proposed development.[331]

---

[328] Planning and Development Regulations 2001, art.131 (as substituted by the 2006 Regulations).
[329] Planning and Development Regulations 2001, art.132(1) (as substituted by the 2006 Regulations).
[330] Planning and Development Regulations 2001, art.132(4) (as substituted by the 2006 Regulations).
[331] Planning and Development Regulations 2001, art.132(5) (as substituted by the 2006 Regulations).

13–429 Where the Minister receives information from a transboundary State in relation to a decision to grant or refuse the relevant development, the Minister shall, as soon as may be following receipt of such information, send such information to any planning authority likely to be affected by the decision.[332]

13–430 The planning authority is required, as soon as may be after receipt of the information, to publish a notice in an approved newspaper stating: (a) that it has received information on a decision taken by a transboundary State; (b) the nature of the decision; and (c) that the information is available for inspection or purchase at a fee not exceeding the reasonable cost of making a copy during office hours at the offices of the planning authority.[333]

W. Environmental Impact Assessment by Legislative Act

13–431 Article 1(5) provides that the Directive is not to apply to projects the details of which are adopted by a specific act of national legislation, since the objectives of the Directive, including that of supplying information, are achieved through the legislative process. The ECJ indicated, in *World Wildlife Fund v Autonome Provinz Bozen*,[334] that the availability of this exemption was subject to two conditions. The first required the details of the project to be adopted by a specific legislative act; under the second, the objectives of the Directive, including that of supplying information, must be achieved through the legislative process. Therefore, if it is a legislative act, instead of a decision of the competent authorities, which grants the developer the right to carry out the project, that act must be specific and display the same characteristics as the development consent specified in Art.1(2) of the Directive. If the specific legislative act by which a particular project is adopted, and therefore authorised, does not include the elements of the specific project which may be relevant to the assessment of its impact on the environment, the objectives of the Directive would be undermined, because a project could be granted consent without prior assessment of its environmental effects even though they might be significant.

13–432 An example of the level of detail which will be required of a legislative act before it can justify the exemption under Art.1(5) is provided by *Luxemburg v Linster*. The ECJ ruled that, on a proper construction of Art.1(5) of the Directive, a measure adopted by a parliament after public parliamentary debate constitutes a specific act of national legislation within the meaning of that provision where the legislative process has enabled the objectives pursued by the Directive, including that of supplying information, to be achieved, and the information available to the parliament at the time when the details of the project were

---

[332] Planning and Development Regulations 2001, art.132(6) (as substituted by the 2006 Regulations).
[333] Planning and Development Regulations 2001, art.132(7) (as substituted by the 2006 Regulations).
[334] (Case C–435/97) [1999] E.C.R. I–5613.

adopted was equivalent to that which would have been submitted to the competent authority in an ordinary procedure for granting consent for a project.

Thus, in the case of a motorway project, it seems that information as to the environmental impact of the route of the motorway should be assessed as part of the legislative process. If the route of a planned motorway has not been laid down in the legislative act, then it seems Art.1(5) would only apply where several alternative routes had been studied in detail and those alternatives were recognised by the legislature as having an equivalent environmental impact.

13–433

CHAPTER FOURTEEN

EUROPEAN CONVENTION ON HUMAN RIGHTS ACT 2003

A. Introduction

The provisions of the European Convention on Human Rights ("the **14–01** Convention") have been given limited effect under national law by the European Convention on Human Rights Act 2003 (hereinafter "the ECHR Act 2003" or "the 2003 Act" where convenient).[1]

The ECHR Act 2003 has the potential to affect both the manner in which **14–02** planning authorities and An Bord Pleanála carry out their statutory functions, and the manner in which the courts will interpret the legislation giving rise to those functions. In some instances it may affect the standard of judicial review to be applied to decision-making.

The principal provisions of the Convention which impact on planning are as **14–03** follows.[2]

   (i) Article 6(1), insofar as relevant, provides that in the determination of his civil rights and obligations everyone is entitled to a fair and public hearing within a reasonable time by an independent and impartial tribunal established by law. Many of the decision-making functions carried out by the planning

---

[1] See, generally, *ECHR and Irish Law* (Kilkelly ed., Jordans, Bristol, 2004); P. McGarry, "The European Convention on Human Rights Act 2003: Implications for Local Planning and Housing Authorities" (2006) 13 I.P.E.L.J. 3; and A. Lowry, "Practice and Procedure under the European Convention on Human Rights Act 2003" (2003) 8 *Bar Review* 183.

[2] For a discussion of additional provisions of the Convention which may impact on planning and environmental law, see Y. Scannell, *Environmental and Land Use Law* (Thomson Round Hall, Dublin, 2006), para.13–78 and onwards.

authorities and An Bord Pleanála come within the scope of Art.6(1). As discussed presently, current procedures and practices may have to modified to ensure that the requirements for timeliness; for a public hearing; and for independence, are met.[3]

(ii) Article 8 provides that a person has a right to respect for his private and family life, his home and correspondence. This article has been interpreted as involving both a negative and a positive duty: the former precludes arbitrary interference by public authorities, the latter requires a State to take reasonable and appropriate measures to secure the rights under Art.8(1). Article 8 may be engaged where enforcement action is taken against an existing home, or where a decision on an application for planning permission—whether to grant or refuse—affects an existing home.

(iii) Article 1 of the First Protocol provides that every person is entitled to the peaceful enjoyment of his possessions, and, further, that no one shall be deprived of his possessions except in the public interest and subject to the conditions provided for by law and by the general principles of international law. The principal impact of this provision will be on the exercise of powers of compulsory purchase. It may also be relevant in deciding whether compensation is necessary where the refusal of planning permission reduces the value of land, or where the development of land has been put on hold for a lengthy period pending the final determination of planning policies; for example, where land is subject to a road reservation ("planning blight").

14–04 The discussion in this chapter is structured as follows. First, an overview of the scheme of the ECHR Act 2003 will be provided. Secondly, the interaction between constitutional rights and Convention rights will be examined. Thirdly, the nature of the substantive rights protected under Art.8 and Art.1 of the First Protocol, and the procedural rights under Art.6(1), will be discussed. Finally, an attempt will then be made to chart the implications of the ECHR Act 2003 for specimen functions under the PDA 2000.

B. Scheme of the ECHR Act 2003

14–05 The ECHR Act 2003 does not incorporate the Convention directly into Irish national law. Rather, the scheme of the Act involves (1) the imposition of a general requirement on organs of the State to perform their functions in a manner compatible with the Convention; (2) the introduction of a special rule of statutory interpretation; and (3) the creation of new statutory remedies. Each of these aspects is examined further below.

1. Performance of functions

14–06 Under s.3 of the ECHR Act 2003, every organ of the State is, subject to any statutory provision or rule of law, required to perform its functions in a manner compatible with the State's obligations under the Convention. The definition of an "organ of the State" under s.1 is apt to include planning authorities and An Bord Pleanála.

---

[3] See below, para.14–98 and onwards.

Thus, in exercising their various statutory powers, planning authorities and **14–07** An Bord Pleanála are required to act in a manner compatible with the Convention. The various consequences of this are discussed in detail later, but the following general observation should be made from the outset. In order to ensure that decision-making is compatible with the Convention, a significant change in mindset will be required on the part of planning authorities and An Bord Pleanála. In particular, the quality of the reasons stated for decisions will have to be improved greatly. The relevant decision-maker will have to address, where material, any Convention right issue which arises during the course of an application or appeal.

2. Statutory interpretation

Under s.2 of the ECHR Act 2003, a court in interpreting and applying any **14–08** statutory provision and rule of law is required, insofar as possible subject to the rules of law relating to such interpretation, to do so in a manner compatible with the State's obligations under the Convention. The precise implications of this, and, in particular, the extent to which a court is entitled to move away from a literal interpretation, are unclear. Traditionally, the courts had tended to apply the so-called literal rule, interpreting legislation by reference to its ordinary and natural meaning. It is only where the literal rule produces an absurd result which is pointless and which negates the intention of the legislature that a court may be prepared to adopt a purposive approach to interpretation.[4]

The strictness of the literal rule has recently been tempered to some degree by **14–09** the Interpretation Act 2005.[5] In particular, where a literal interpretation would be "absurd" or would "fail to reflect the plain intention" of the Oireachtas or parliament, the provision is to be given a construction that best reflects the plain intention where that intention can be ascertained from the relevant Act as a whole.[6] The latter qualification, namely that a literal interpretation would fail to reflect the plain [parliamentary] intention, would appear to involve a less stiff test than absurdity, and should, accordingly, be available in a greater number of instances. More generally, it seems that the burden of proving that a literal interpretation would be absurd, or would fail to reflect the intention of the Oireachtas or parliament, lies with the party so asserting.[7]

---

[4] *DPP (Invers) v Murphy* [1999] 1 I.L.R.M. 46 at 46, *per* Denham J. *Cf. Howard v Commissioners of Public Works* [1994] 1 I.R. 91 (clear and unequivocal statutory language must be enforced however harsh or absurd or contrary to reason the result might be).

[5] See, generally, P. O'Rourke, "The Interpretation Act 2005: Key Features" Bar Council Continuing Professional Development, May 22, 2006; and G. Hogan, "The Rise of the Purposive Approach to Statutory Interpretation and Its Limitations" Bar Council Continuing Professional Development, May 22, 2006.

[6] Interpretation Act 2005, s.5. For one of the first examples of use being made of s.5, see *Minister for Finance v Civil and Public Service Union* [2006] I.E.H.C. 145; unreported, Laffoy J., May 11, 2006.

[7] *Kelly v Roscommon County Council* [2006] I.E.H.C. 197; unreported, McGovern J., June 20, 2006.

14–10 The precise relationship between the literal rule and the more purposive approach allowed for under s.2 of the ECHR Act 2003 is not entirely clear. In particular, whereas s.2 appears to herald a new approach to statutory interpretation, it is expressly stated to be subject to the rules of law relating to such interpretation. This presents little difficulty where the wording of a statute is ambiguous. If a provision is open to various interpretations, then there can be no objection that—in electing for the one which best serves the needs of the Convention—the court is encroaching on the legislative role of the Oireachtas. A loose analogy might be drawn with the so-called "double construction" rule in constitutional law. In brief, this rule requires that if, in respect of any provision or provisions of a post-1937 Act, two or more constructions are reasonably open, one of which is constitutional and the other or others are unconstitutional, it must be presumed that the Oireachtas intended only the constitutional construction, and a court called upon to adjudicate upon the constitutionality of the statutory provision should uphold the constitutional construction. It is only when there is no construction reasonably open which is not repugnant to the Constitution that the provision should be held to be repugnant.[8]

14–11 The position where a provision is not ambiguous is different. If effect is to be given to the Convention, then this may require a straining of, or even a departure from, the literal meaning. Under the Interpretation Act 2005, however, it seems that—where a provision is unambiguous—a departure from the literal interpretation is only permissible in cases where a literal interpretation would be "absurd" or would "fail to reflect the plain intention" of the Oireachtas or parliament. It would represent a significant change in the law in this regard if, in addition to the foregoing circumstances, the literal rule is also to be disapplied in wider circumstances in the case of Convention rights. As indicated earlier, s.2 of the ECHR Act 2003 expressly states that its terms are "subject to the rules of law relating to such interpretation and application", and this seems to suggest that the literal rule—as modified by the Interpretation Act 2005—is to prevail in the event of any tension between a literal interpretation and the giving of effect to the Convention. It might be possible to harmonise the two rules by saying that the Oireachtas is to be presumed to have intended to comply with the Convention and, accordingly, a literal interpretation which would result in a breach is one which would "fail to reflect the plain intention" of the Oireachtas or parliament. Of course, in many cases the relevant legislation will predate the enactment of the ECHR Act 2003, and thus it would be somewhat artificial to impute an intention to comply with the Convention.

14–12 The literal rule is not the only rule of interpretation which might restrict the scope of s.2. In a number of planning cases, the courts have had recourse to two other rules of interpretation. First, that the courts should favour an interpretation which provides certainty. Thus, in *KSK Enterprises Ltd. v An Bord Pleanála* the Supreme Court, *per* Finlay C.J., held—in the context of the

---

[8] *McDonald v Bord na gCon* [1965] I.R. 217 at 239, *per* Walsh J. See also *East Donegal Co-Operative Society Ltd. v Attorney General* [1970] I.R. 317.

calculation of time-limits—that where a restriction is being imposed upon the exercise of a right in a statute it is desirable, to the extent of being almost imperative, that it should be capable of being construed, and should be construed, in a clear and definite fashion.

The second rule of interpretation commonly relied upon is that—at least in the case of ambiguous statutory provisions—any interference with property rights should be given a restrictive interpretation. Thus, in *In re Viscount Securities*,[9] the High Court held that if the legislature had intended to restrict the development of land *without* the payment of compensation, it was a necessary principle of construction that it should have "expressly and unambiguously so provided". Similarly, in the much later case of *Hoburn Homes Ltd. v An Bord Pleanála*,[10] the High Court, in interpreting another statutory provision excluding compensation, was again influenced by the fact that compensation was a statutory right and should only be removed in "clear and precise" cases.[11]   **14–13**

There is an obvious tension between these established rules of interpretation and the more flexible approach which might otherwise flow from the s.2 rule. In order to read a statutory provision in a Convention-compliant manner it may be necessary to strain the wording actually employed by the draftsman. Whereas this has the benefit of ensuring that the rights under the Convention are respected, it arguably undermines legal certainty. This might be considered a small price to pay, and that whereas certainty is a good thing, justice is better. However, the scheme of s.2 appears to give priority to existing rules of interpretation and suggests that these are to prevail.   **14–14**

Contrast with position in England and Wales

The legal position is dramatically different in England and Wales. There, the House of Lords has indicated, in cases such as *Ghaidan v Mendoza*,[12] that the Human Rights Act 1998 is apt to require a court to read in words which change the meaning of the enacted legislation, so as to make it Convention-compliant.   **14–15**

Under the Humans Rights Act 1998, the requirement to interpret legislation in a Convention-compliant manner is subject to the express limitation "in so far as it is possible to do so". The House of Lords accepted that Parliament had thus expressly envisaged that not all legislation would be capable of being made Convention-compliant; the question was as to what test was to be applied, as Lord Nicholls of Birkenhead put it, "in separating the sheep from the goats".[13]   **14–16**

---

[9] (1976) 112 I.L.T.R. 17.
[10] [1993] I.L.R.M. 368.
[11] *cf. Ebonwood Ltd. v Meath County Council* [2004] 3 I.R. 34; [2004] 1 I.L.R.M. 305 ("common sense" approach taken to interpretation of provisions restricting entitlement to statutory compensation).
[12] [2004] U.K.H.L. 30; [2004] 2 A.C. 557.
[13] *ibid.*, [27].

14–17   Lord Nicholls of Birkenhead suggested that it cannot have been the intention that the operation of the new rule of interpretation should depend critically upon the particular form of words adopted by the parliamentary draftsman in the statutory provision under consideration, as that would make the application of the rule something of a semantic lottery.[14] Rather, the limitation was that in the discharge of this extended interpretative function the courts should not adopt "a meaning inconsistent with a fundamental feature of legislation".[15] The interpretation must be compatible with the underlying thrust of the legislation being construed.

14–18   Lord Rodger of Earlsferry also emphasised that the language employed in the relevant legislation was not critical, and that it was permissible to read words in provided that same were not inconsistent with the scheme of the legislation.[16]

> "[...] it is possible for the courts to supply by implication words that are appropriate to ensure that legislation is read in a way which is compatible with convention rights. When the court spells out the words that are to be implied, it may look as if it is 'amending' the legislation, but that is not the case. If the court implies words that are consistent with the scheme of the legislation but necessary to make it compatible with convention rights, it is simply performing the duty which Parliament has imposed on it and on others. It is reading the legislation in a way that draws out the full implications of its terms and of the Convention rights. And, by its very nature, an implication will go with the grain of the legislation. By contrast, using a convention right to read in words that are inconsistent with the scheme of the legislation or with its essential principles as disclosed by its provisions does not involve any form of interpretation, by implication or otherwise. It falls on the wrong side of the boundary between interpretation and amendment of the statute."

14–19   Under the Irish ECHR Act 2003, by contrast, the interpretative function is not only qualified by the phrase "in so far as is possible", but is also subject to the "rules of law" relating to statutory interpretation. As discussed earlier, these rules include the literal rule, as modified by the Interpretation Act 2005, and thus the entitlement to depart from the language of the legislation being interpreted will be much more limited than appears to be the position in England and Wales.

14–20   The difference in approach between the two jurisdictions may have as much do to with the remedies available as with the manner in which the interpretive function is phrased. There are very real limitations on the usefulness of the alternative remedy of a declaration of incompatibility, and for this reason Lord Steyn emphasised that interpretation is the prime remedial remedy and that resort to declarations of incompatibility must always be an exceptional course.[17]

---

[14] *ibid.*, [31].
[15] *ibid.*, [33].
[16] *ibid.*, [121].
[17] [2004] U.K.H.L. 30, [50]; [2004] 2 A.C. 557.

The fact that the Irish courts already enjoy the much more powerful jurisdiction **14–21** to review the *constitutionality* of legislation may well lessen the significance of the remedies under the ECHR Act 2003. Hogan suggests that it is unlikely that the Irish courts will strain the language of a statute beyond that which it could reasonably bear, but rather will elect in such circumstances to declare the legislation invalid by reference to the Constitution.[18]

> "[…] It may be anticipated that, in practice, the Supreme Court when faced with such a problem will simply elect to declare the legislation unconstitutional. In other words, the Court, asked to find that particular legislation is either unconstitutional or incompatible with the ECHR and, finding itself unable to strain the construction of the statutory language in order to make the statute ECHR-compatible, will again simply tire of the whole rigmarole and declare the law invalid on ordinary constitutional grounds. To that extent, just as with the declaration of incompatibility, the adoption of the interpretation model is likely to have a distorting effect in some instances on the development of constitutional law and what we might term domestic ECHR law."

This entire question of the relationship between Convention rights and **14–22** constitutional rights, and, in particular, the concerns raised by Hogan, will be examined in greater detail presently at paras 14–29 to 14–38.

3. Remedies under ECHR Act 2003

Section 5 of the ECHR Act 2003 confers a jurisdiction on the High Court, and **14–23** the Supreme Court when exercising its appellate jurisdiction, to make a declaration that a statutory provision or rule of law is incompatible with the State's obligations under the Convention. This remedy is only open where "no other legal remedy is adequate and available".

A declaration of incompatibility is not self-executing: it is expressly provided **14–24** under s.5(2) that a declaration of incompatibility—

(a) shall not affect the validity, continuing operation or enforcement of the statutory provision or rule of law in respect of which it is made, and

(b) shall not prevent a party to the proceedings concerned from making submissions or representations in relation to those matters to which the declaration relates in any proceedings before the European Court of Human Rights.

The Taoiseach is required to cause a copy of any order containing a declaration **14–25** of incompatibility to be laid before each House of the Oireachtas within the next twenty-one days on which that House has sat. Presumably, the purpose of this exercise is to allow the legislature to consider the introduction of amendments to remedy the statutory provision or rule of law which has been found to be non-compliant with the Convention. There is, however, no express *obligation* in this regard.

---

[18] G. Hogan, "Incorporation of the ECHR: Some Issues of Methodology and Process" in *ECHR and Irish Law* (Kilkelly ed., Jordans, Bristol, 2004), para.2.66.

14–26   The making of a declaration of incompatibility also opens up the possibility of the making of an *ex gratia* payment under s.5(4).

14–27   A statutory remedy of damages is created under s.3(2). More specifically, if no other proceedings to recover damages are available, a person who has suffered injury, loss or damage as a result of a contravention of the duty of an organ of the States to perform its functions in a manner compatible with the State's obligations under the Convention provisions can institute proceedings to recover damages under s.3. As indicated above, s.3 of the ECHR Act 2003 provides that, subject to any statutory provisions (other than that Act) or rule of law, every organ of the State shall perform its functions in a manner compatible with the State's obligations under the Convention provisions.

14–28   It seems that the statutory right to damages under s.3 only arises where the underlying legislation itself was compliant with the Convention. In particular, it seems that an organ of the State is only required to perform its functions in accordance with national law (where necessary as read in the light of s.2), and is not required to disapply national law where same is non-compliant. In circumstances where national law cannot—given the limitations of the interpretation rule under s.2—be read in a manner consistent with the Convention, then its seems that the appropriate remedy is confined to a declaration of incompatibility under s.5.[19]

C. Convention Rights and Constitutional Rights

14–29   To a large extent, the sentiments of the Convention already find expression under the Irish Constitution. For example, property rights are expressly recognised under the Constitution, and the right to fair procedures is recognised as having a constitutional aspect. Under Art.40.5, the dwelling of every citizen is inviolable and shall not be forcibly entered save in accordance with law. Thus protections of a type afforded under Arts 6 and 8 of the Convention, and Art.1 of the First Protocol, already exist under the Constitution. There are, however, subtle distinctions in the nature and extent of the rights afforded as between the Constitution and the Convention, and it may well be that the scope of the rights under the Convention is, in a small number of specific instances, greater.

14–30   The remedies provided for under the ECHR Act 2003, however, are vastly inferior to those available where the High Court exercises its jurisdiction to review the constitutionality of legislation. If a statutory provision or rule of law cannot be interpreted in a Convention-compliant manner, then the principal remedy available under the ECHR Act 2003 is a declaration of incompatibility. This will be of little practical benefit to the individual litigant, because a

---

[19] See also A. Lowry, "Practice and Procedure under the European Convention on Human Rights Act 2003" (2003) 8 *Bar Review* 183 at 185.

declaration of incompatibility is not self-executing. Even if—the declaration of incompatibility having been laid before it—the legislature responds by amending or repealing the offending legislation, it may well take some considerable period of time before this happens, and even then the changes might not be retrospective in nature.

Contrast this with the position where a statute is found to be invalid having regard to the provisions of the Constitution. A declaration of unconstitutionality will result in the offending legislation being set aside forthwith. This will result in an immediate benefit to the litigant involved.[20]   **14–31**

Against this background, then, a litigant would be well advised to pursue a constitutional challenge in preference to a claim under the ECHR Act 2003. Given the very real limitations of the declaration of incompatibility, it is submitted that the ECHR Act 2003 is only of assistance where the particular right sought to be asserted cannot be grounded in the Constitution, but only in the Convention.   **14–32**

All of this presents difficulties in terms of how a case should be pleaded. A lawyer faced with a statutory provision or rule of law which—even when interpreted in a purposive way—is alleged to breach his or her client's rights must decide whether to seek relief by way of a declaration of incompatibility, or a declaration of constitutional invalidity. A cautious approach might suggest that both should be pleaded. There is, however, a risk that if this is done, a court will feel compelled to defer any consideration of the constitutional claim until after determination of the Convention claim. Ironically, the danger here is that the claim under the ECHR Act 2003 might be *successful*, and that the court might then decide that this is sufficient to dispose of the case and accordingly not address the constitutional argument. This would leave the applicant with the unsatisfactory remedy of a declaration of incompatibility. In such circumstances, the lawyer might have wished that he had simply omitted the claim under the ECHR Act 2003 and, instead, gone for gold by aiming for the declaration of constitutional invalidity.   **14–33**

In deciding how to plead a case therefore it will be necessary to know in what sequence a court will take any competing Convention and constitutional claims. The judgment in *Carmody v Minister for Justice, Equality and Law Reform*[21] indicates that the court will address the Convention point first. Laffoy J.   **14–34**

---

[20] It appears from the recent judgment of the Supreme Court in *A v Governor of Arbour Hill Prison* [2006] I.E.S.C. 45; [2006] 2 I.L.R.M. 481 that there is no principle that a declaration of unconstitutionality has retrospective application outside the particular parties of a case or litigants specifically named by the court, *per* Denham J. (at 525). Murray C.J. stated that final decisions in judicial proceedings, civil or criminal, which have been decided on foot of an Act of the Oireachtas (which has been relied upon by parties because of its status as a law considered or presumed to be constitutional), should not be set aside by reason *solely* of a subsequent decision declaring the Act constitutionally invalid (at 511).

[21] Unreported, High Court, Laffoy J., January 21, 2005.

suggested that this approach would be consistent with the general principle of judicial self-restraint which indicates that a court should only embark on a constitutional challenge where a case cannot be resolved on non-constitutional grounds.

14–35 Hogan has criticised this aspect of the judgment as being incorrect for several reasons.[22] In particular, he points out that judicial self-restraint is but a rule of judicial practice which would, in any event, have to yield to statute. A declaration of incompatibility is only available where "no other legal remedy is adequate and available". Hogan suggests that this is the clearest possible legislative signal that constitutional issues should be exhausted first, with the declaration of incompatibility as a form of long stop.

14–36 Hogan goes on to make the further point that a favourable finding on a claim for a declaration of incompatibility is unlikely to dispose of the proceedings in that "[I]n practically every case the litigant would then surely insist on a sort of legal run-off competition so that they could be in line for the first prize of a declaration of unconstitutionality [...]". Hogan suggests that if the court is going to be required to address the constitutional issue anyway, then the entire basis of the application of the rule of judicial self-restraint disappears.

14–37 Hogan also expresses a concern that, if the sequence in *Carmody* were to stand, a point might be reached whereby the Convention would *de facto* have replaced the Constitution so far as the protection of fundamental rights is concerned. He suggests that this could scarcely have been the intention of the Oireachtas in enacting the ECHR Act 2003, and that such a construction would equally be unconstitutional.

14–38 As of the time of writing in June 2007, it remains to be seen whether the judgment in *Carmody* can withstand the criticisms made above. Until the matter is resolved, one way or another, it leaves the lawyer drafting pleadings with a dilemma: to plead the Convention or to go for the gold of a declaration of constitutional invalidity.

D. Article 8

1. Introduction

14–39 Under Art.8 of the Convention every person has a right to respect for, *inter alia*, his home, family and private life. This right is, however, qualified under Art.8(2), as follows.

---

[22] G. Hogan "Some Thoughts on the Relationship between the ECHR Act 2003 and the Constitution in the light of Dublin City Council v. Fennell and Carmody v. Minister for Justice, Equality and Law Reform", paper delivered at the Bar Council Conference on Human Rights, December 2005.

"There shall be no interference by a public authority with the exercise of this right except such as is in accordance with the law and is necessary in a democratic society in the interests of national security, public safety or the economic well-being of the country, for the prevention of disorder or crime, for the protection of health or morals, or for the protection of the rights and freedoms of others."

Article 8 has been successfully invoked before the European Court of Human Rights ("the ECtHR") in various cases involving environmental concerns. The ECtHR has made it clear, however, that Art.8 is not violated every time that environmental deterioration occurs. Article 8 is not specifically designed to provide general protection of the environment as such.[23] Moreover, the ECtHR has stated that whereas environmental protection should be taken into consideration by States in acting within their margin of appreciation, and by the ECtHR in its review of that margin, it would not be appropriate for the ECtHR to adopt a special approach in this respect by reference to a special status of environmental human rights.[24] **14–40**

Article 8 is only engaged where the interference complained of directly affects the applicant's home, family or private life. Breaches of the right to respect for the home are not confined to concrete or physical breaches, such as unauthorised entry into a person's home, but also include those that are not concrete or physical, such as noise, emissions, smells or other forms of interference.[25] **14–41**

The ECtHR has further pointed out that the adverse effects of environmental pollution must attain a certain minimum level if they are to fall within the scope of Art.8.[26] The assessment of that minimum is relative, and depends on all the circumstances of the case, such as the intensity and duration of the nuisance, or its physical or mental effects. In this regard, it is to be noted that it is not only polluting industries which are capable of interfering with Art.8 rights: impacts such as overshadowing might, in principle at least, equally give rise to an actionable interference.[27] The general environmental context should also be taken into account. In *Fadeyeva v Russia*, the court stated that there would be no arguable claim under Art.8 if the detriment complained of was negligible in comparison to the environmental hazards inherent to life in every modern city.[28] **14–42**

Thus, in order for a complaint relating to environmental nuisance to fall within Art.8, it is necessary to show, first, that there was an actual interference with the applicant's private sphere, and, second, that a level of severity was attained. **14–43**

---

[23] *Kyrtatos v Greece* (2005) 40 E.H.R.R. 16, [52]–[53] (animal well-being not with art.8).
[24] *Hatton v United Kingdom* (2003) 37 E.H.R.R. 28, [122].
[25] *Giacomelli v Italy* Application No. 59909/00; November 2, 2006, [76].
[26] *López Ostra v Spain* (1995) 20 E.H.R.R. 277, [51]; and *Hatton v United Kingdom* (2003) 37 E.H.R.R. 28, [118].
[27] See, for example, *R. (On the application of Malster) v Ipswich Borough Council* [2001] E.W.C.A. Civ. 1715.
[28] [2007] 45 E.H.R.R. 10, [69].

Positive duty to secure Art.8 rights

14–44   A violation of Art.8 occurs not only where a State is directly responsible for the interference with a person's home, family or private life complained of, but may also arise from a failure to regulate private industry.[29] Although the object of Art.8 is essentially that of protecting the individual against arbitrary interference by public authorities, it does not merely compel the State to abstain from such interference.[30] There is also a positive duty on a State to take reasonable and appropriate measures to secure the rights under Art.8(1).[31] The test in this regard seems to be whether the State could reasonably be expected to act so as to prevent or put an end to the alleged infringement of an applicant's rights.[32]

14–45   At its most basic, this will presumably require a contracting State to enact legislation regulating development which is likely to have the level of severity of environmental effect necessary to trigger Art.8. Thus, for example, a contracting State will probably be in compliance with the positive duty flowing from Art.8 if it demonstrates that it has introduced a statutory scheme for the licensing of polluting development. Such legislation must be effective however. In particular, provision must be made for ensuring that Art.8 rights are considered and weighed in the decision-making process. Moreover, it seems that proper provision must be made for enforcement, and that, where appropriate, enforcement action must actually be taken against development in breach of national law requirements.

14–46   In *Moreno Gómez v Spain*,[33] the ECtHR found that there had been a violation of Art.8 in circumstances where the relevant city council had tolerated, and thus contributed to, the repeated flouting of the rules about noise pollution which it itself had established. The ECtHR reiterated that regulations to protect guaranteed rights serve little purpose if they are not duly enforced, and that the Convention was intended to protect effective rights, not illusory ones. The ECtHR held, on the facts, that the applicant had suffered a serious infringement of her right to respect for her home as a result of the authorities' failure to take action to deal with the night-time disturbances.

14–47   Interestingly, in the leading cases where a violation of Art.8 has been found by the ECtHR, the violation was "predicated on a failure by the national authorities to comply with some aspect of the domestic legal regime".[34] Thus, in *López*

---

[29] *Hatton v United Kingdom* (2003) 37 E.H.R.R. 28, [98]. See also *Giacomelli v Italy* Application No. 59909/00; November 2, 2006, [78] ("Article 8 may apply in environmental cases whether the pollution is directly caused by the State or whether State responsibility arises from the failure to regulate private-sector activities properly.").

[30] *Guerra v Italy* (1998) 26 E.H.R.R. 357, [58].

[31] *Powell v United Kingdom* (1990) 12 E.H.R.R. 355, [41]; and *Guerra v Italy* (1998) 26 E.H.R.R. 357, [58].

[32] *Fadeyeva v Russia* [2007] 45 E.H.R.R. 10, [89].

[33] Application No. 4143/02; November 16, 2004.

[34] *Fadeyeva v Russia* Application No. 55723/00; June 9, 2005, [97].

Ostra v Spain, there had been a failure to take measures against an unauthorised waste treatment plant: the waste-treatment plant at issue was illegal in that it operated without the necessary licence, and it was eventually closed down. In *Guerra v Italy*, the breach of Art.8 consisted of a failure under national law to make available to the applicants essential information that would have enabled them to assess the risks they and their families might run if they continued to live in a town particularly exposed to danger in the event of an accident at the relevant factory. In *Giacomelli v Italy*,[35] a facility for the treatment of harmful and toxic waste was permitted to continue operating notwithstanding a finding of an administrative court that the facility's operation had no legal basis and should therefore be suspended with immediate effect.

Insofar as there is a positive duty on a State to take reasonable and appropriate measures to secure Art.8 rights, the Irish legislation probably provides an adequate scheme to ensure compliance with the Convention. Most private-sector "development" of a type which might be said to interfere with Art.8 rights will be subject to a requirement to obtain planning permission and/or some form of licence from the Environmental Protection Agency. Thus the Irish State has enacted a decision-making scheme within which the competing private and public interests can be balanced. In order to comply with the Convention, however, it is essential that effective enforcement action be taken where development is carried out or continued in breach of national law.   **14–48**

There is a potential difficulty in respect of certain public-sector development. In particular, the exemption from the requirement to obtain planning permission afforded to local authority development (which extends to local authority development carried out jointly with the private sector) should not be used for any development which might interfere with Art.8 rights. Local authorities on occasion carry out major schemes of development, and in order to comply with Art.8 (and Art.6), these should be subject to control by an independent and impartial decision-maker.   **14–49**

2. Whether interference justified

Where an interference with Art.8 rights has been established, it is necessary to consider whether this interference is justified. In the case of direct interference by the State, any justification will have to be by reference to the provisions of Art.8(2). There are a number of aspects to this. First, the interference must be "in accordance with the law". Secondly, the interference must pursue one of the prescribed legitimate aims of national security, public safety or the economic well-being of the country, be for the prevention of disorder or crime, for the protection of health or morals, or for the protection of the rights and freedoms of others. Thus, in *Hatton v United Kingdom*, it was legitimate for the respondent State, in regulating night flights, to balance "the economic interests of the operators of airlines and other enterprises as well as their clients, but also, and   **14–50**

---

[35] Application No. 59909/00; November 2, 2006.

above all, to the economic interests of the country as a whole" against the rights of individuals living in the flight path of Heathrow airport.[36] Thirdly, the interference must be "necessary in a democratic society". An interference will be considered "necessary in a democratic society" for a legitimate aim if it answers a pressing social need and, in particular, if it is proportionate to the legitimate aim pursued.[37]

14–51   Although Art.8(2) is, strictly speaking, only applicable to direct interference, *i.e.* the negative obligations flowing from Art.8(1), rather than to an alleged breach of the positive duty on the State to take reasonable and appropriate measures to secure rights under Art.8(1), the ECtHR has held that the aims under Art.8(2) may nevertheless be relevant in the latter context also.[38]

14–52   It seems, therefore, that the analysis to be applied differs little between (i) cases where it is alleged that there has been a failure to fulfil the positive duty on the State to take reasonable and appropriate measures to secure an applicant's rights under Art.8(1), and (ii) cases where the State or a public authority is directly responsible for the pollution or other interference complained of. In each case, a fair balance has to be struck between the competing interests of the individual and of the community as a whole.[39]

14–53   One point of distinction is that a breach of *national* law will be less significant in the case of an alleged breach of the positive duty. Whereas direct interference by the State with the exercise of Art.8 rights will not be compatible with Art.8(2) unless it is "in accordance with the law"—and thus a breach of national law would necessarily lead to a finding of a violation—the choice of means where the positive duty is asserted is in principle a matter that falls within the contracting States' margin of appreciation.[40] There are different avenues to ensure "respect for private life", and even if the State has failed to apply one particular measure provided by national law, it may still fulfil its positive duty by other means.

3. Proportionality

14–54   It is inherent in the striking of a "fair balance" between private and public interests, and in the requirement that the interference be "necessary in a democratic society", that the interference with the Art.8 rights must be proportionate: not only must the interference pursue, on the facts as well as in principle, a legitimate aim, but there must also be a reasonable relation of proportionality between the means employed and the aim sought to be realised by any measures applied by the State.

---

[36] *Hatton v United Kingdom* (2003) 37 E.H.R.R. 28, [121].

[37] See, for example, *Connors v United Kingdom* (2005) 40 E.H.R.R. 9, [81].

[38] *Fadeyeva v Russia* [2007] 45 E.H.R.R. 10, [99].

[39] *López Ostra v Spain* (1995) 20 E.H.R.R. 277, [51]. See also *Giacomelli v Italy* Application No. 59909/00; November 2, 2006, [78].

[40] *Fadeyeva v Russia* [2007] 45 E.H.R.R. 10, [96].

The concept of proportionality is of more immediate relevance in cases where   **14–55**
the State has *directly* interfered with a Convention right, than in cases of a
breach of the positive duty to secure Art.8 rights. Thus it features more
prominently in the context of enforcement action against a person's home, or
the refusal of planning permission to retain a home, than it does in cases where
planning permission affects the rights of third parties in the vicinity. More
generally it also arises in the context of the protection of property rights under
Art.1 of the First Protocol. This is discussed at para.14–78.

A test of proportionality has been formulated in various different ways. The   **14–56**
formula approved of by the Irish Supreme Court in *In re Planning and
Development Bill 1999*[41] runs along the following lines. The means chosen
must (a) be rationally connected to the objective and not be arbitrary, unfair or
based on irrational considerations; (b) impair the right as little as possible; and
(c) be such that their effects on rights are proportional to the objective. As
discussed presently at paras 14–169 and onwards, just how exactly a test of
proportionality works in the context of an application for planning permission
is a matter of controversy.

4. Margin of appreciation

The ECtHR has consistently stated that a margin of appreciation must be allowed   **14–57**
to the national authorities, who are in principle better placed than an international
court to evaluate local needs and conditions. However, while it is for the national
authorities to make the initial assessment of "necessity", the final evaluation
as to whether the justification given by the State is relevant and sufficient
remains subject to review by the ECtHR.

As the ECtHR reiterated in *Fadeyeva v Russia*, there are limits to this margin   **14–58**
of appreciation.[42]

> "It remains open to the Court to conclude that there has been a manifest error of
> appreciation by the national authorities in striking a fair balance between the
> competing interests of different private actors in this sphere. However, the
> complexity of the issues involved with regard to environmental protection renders
> the Court's role primarily a subsidiary one. The Court must first examine whether
> the decision-making process was fair and such as to afford due respect to the
> interests safeguarded to the individual by art 8 (see *Buckley v UK* (1997) 23
> E.H.R.R. 101), and only in exceptional circumstances may it go beyond this line
> and revise the material conclusions of the domestic authorities (see *Taskin and
> Others v Turkey* (2006) 42 E.H.R.R. 50)."

There are two aspects to the inquiry which may be carried out by the ECtHR.   **14–59**
First, the court may assess the substantive merits of the relevant government's
decision to ensure that it is compatible with Art.8. Secondly, it may scrutinise

---

[41] [2000] 2 I.R. 321; [2001] 1 I.L.R.M. 81.
[42] [2007] 45 E.H.R.R. 10, [105].

the decision-making process to ensure that due weight has been accorded to the interests of the individual.[43] In scrutinising the procedural element, the ECtHR is required to consider all the procedural aspects, including the type of policy or decision involved, the extent to which the views of individuals were taken into account throughout the decision-making procedure, and the procedural safeguards available.[44] Whilst Art.8 contains no explicit procedural requirements, the decision-making process leading to measures of interference must be fair and such as to afford due respect to the interests safeguarded to the individual by Art.8.[45]

14–60 Reference is made in this regard to the judgment of the ECtHR in *Connors v United Kingdom*.[46] There, the court found a summary eviction procedure represented a breach of Art.8 as it was not attended by the requisite procedural safeguards. A distinction was drawn under the relevant English legislation as between the protection afforded to occupiers of caravans on privately owned residential sites and certain local authority sites, on the one hand, and the occupiers of land run by a local authority as a caravan site for gypsies, on the other. In the case of the former, a person who lived in a caravan or mobile home as his only or main residence could not be evicted save by court order. This protection did not apply to caravan sites for gypsies.

14–61 The ECtHR held that the existence of procedural safeguards was a crucial consideration in the assessment of the proportionality of the Art.8 interference. The court did not think that the possibility of judicial review was sufficient in circumstances where the applicant sought to dispute the factual basis on which the local authority sought to evict him and his family. The local authority was not required as a matter of national law to establish any substantive justification for evicting him, and on this point judicial review could not provide any opportunity for an examination of the facts in dispute between the parties.

14–62 The ECtHR stated that, even allowing for the margin of appreciation which is to be afforded to the State in such circumstances, the court was not persuaded that the necessity for a statutory scheme which permitted the summary eviction of the applicant and his family has been sufficiently demonstrated by the Government. The power to evict without the burden of giving reasons liable to be examined as to their merits by an independent tribunal had not been convincingly shown to respond to any specific goal or to provide any specific benefit to members of the gypsy community.

---

[43] *Hatton v United Kingdom* (2003) 37 E.H.R.R. 28, [99]; and *Taskin v Turkey* (2006) 42 E.H.R.R. 50, [115].

[44] *Hatton v United Kingdom* (2003) 37 E.H.R.R. 28, [104].

[45] *McMichael v United Kingdom* (1995) 20 E.H.R.R. 205, [87]; *Buckley v United Kingdom* (1997) 23 E.H.R.R. 101, [76]; and *Taskin v Turkey* (2006) 42 E.H.R.R. 50, [118].

[46] (2005) 40 E.H.R.R. 9.

5. Planning decisions engaging Article 8 rights

There is some controversy as to whether or not the refusal of planning **14–63** permission for the retention of an existing home, and subsequent pursuit of enforcement action, *per se* represents an interference with Art.8 rights. In *Chichester DC v First Secretary of State*,[47] Auld L.J., in a dissenting judgment, suggested that a three-stage test is involved. First, is Art.8 "engaged" in the sense that a person's right to respect for his or her home is an issue? Secondly, has there been an "interference" with the right to respect to a home? Thirdly, is the interference justified by reference to Art.8(2)? Auld L.J. seemed to suggest that it did not automatically follow that the pursuit of enforcement action gave rise to an "interference". The implication here seems to be that the right under Art.8(1) is a limited one.

The majority in *Chichester DC v First Secretary of State* considered, conversely, **14–64** that the refusal of planning permission and subsequent pursuit of enforcement action did give rise to an interference. This interference was capable of justification, however, under Art.8(2). The appropriate test was whether the interference was necessary for any of the legitimate aims, and, if so, whether the enforcement action was a proportionate response to the identified objective.

It might be thought that the debate in this regard may be academic in that the **14–65** same result may follow whether one regards the Art.8(1) right as a very limited one which is not interfered with, or whether one finds that there has been an interference, but that same is justified under Art.8(2). The distinction does, however, have the following significance. If the Art.8(1) right is drawn narrowly, so that there is no interference in particular circumstances, it will not be necessary for any balancing exercise to be performed. This would then leave the way open for enforcement action to be taken summarily. Thus, for example, it might not be necessary for the personal circumstances of the person alleged to be in breach of planning control to be considered in the context of a s.160 injunction.

The better view is probably that, howsoever a decision to refuse planning **14–66** permission should be categorised, the pursuit of enforcement action does give rise to an interference with Art.8 rights.

What, then, are the legal consequences if a particular decision does engage **14–67** Art.8? The principal consequence seems to be that the relevant decision-maker must have addressed his mind, first, to the question of whether the proposed decision involves interference with respect to a home, and, if so, secondly, to the question as to whether this interference is justified by reference to the requirements of Art.8(2). In general terms, the decision-maker will have to demonstrate that he engaged in some sort of balancing exercise between the competing rights of the respect for the affected person's home and one of the public rights identified under Art.8(2).

---

[47] [2004] E.W.C.A. Civ. 1248; [2005] J.P.L. 1029.

E. Article 1 of the First Protocol

1. Introduction

14–68   Article 1 of the First Protocol provides as follows.

> "Every natural or legal person is entitled to the peaceful enjoyment of his possessions. No one shall be deprived of his possessions except in the public interest and subject to the conditions provided for by law and by the general principles of international law.
>
> The preceding provisions shall not, however, in any way impair the right of a State to enforce such laws as it deems necessary to control the use of property in accordance with the general interest or to secure the payment of taxes or other contributions or penalties."

14–69   The ECtHR has held that Art.1 of the First Protocol comprises three distinct rules.[48] The first rule, set out in the first sentence of the first paragraph, is of a general nature and enunciates the principle of the peaceful enjoyment of property. The second rule, contained in the second sentence of the same paragraph, covers deprivation of possessions and makes it subject to certain conditions. The third rule, stated in the second paragraph, recognises that contracting States are entitled, amongst other things, to control the use of property in accordance with the general interest.

14–70   The three rules are not distinct in the sense of being unconnected: the second and third rules are concerned with particular instances of interference with the right to the peaceful enjoyment of property, and should therefore be construed in the light of the general principle enunciated in the first rule, and must comply with the principle of lawfulness and pursue a legitimate aim by means reasonably proportionate to the aim sought to be realised.[49]

14–71   The requirement that any deprivation of possessions must be subject to the conditions provided for by law has been held by the ECtHR to presuppose that the applicable provisions of domestic law are sufficiently accessible, precise and foreseeable in their application.

2. Public interest

14–72   Article 1 requires that no one shall be deprived of his possessions "save in the public interest". The ECtHR has ruled that the notion of "public interest" in the second sentence of the first paragraph is necessarily extensive. In particular, the decision to enact property laws will commonly involve consideration of political, economic and social issues. The taking of property in pursuance of

---

[48] See *Sporrong and Lönnroth v Sweden* (1983) 5 E.H.R.R. 35; and *Jacobson (Allan) v Sweden* (1989) 12 E.H.R.R. 56.

[49] See, for example, *Beyeler v Italy* [2000] E.C.H.R. 33202/96 [108]–[114].

legitimate social, economic or other policies may be in the public interest even if the community at large has no direct use or enjoyment of the property.[50]

The ECtHR held in *James v United Kingdom*[51] that whereas a deprivation of property effected for no reason other than to confer a private benefit on a private party cannot be "in the public interest", nonetheless, the compulsory transfer of property from one individual to another may, depending upon the circumstances, constitute a legitimate means for promoting the public interest. **14–73**

> "The taking of property in pursuance of a policy calculated to enhance social justice within the community can properly be described as being 'in the public interest.' In particular, the fairness of a system of law governing the contractual or property rights of private parties is a matter of public concern and therefore legislative measures intended to bring about such fairness are capable of being 'in the public interest,' even if they involve the compulsory transfer of property from one individual to another."[52]

Thus, it seems that in certain circumstances, the transfer of property from one person to another for the latter's private benefit alone could be "in the public interest" within the meaning of the second sentence of Art.1, even if the community at large has no direct use or enjoyment of the property taken. **14–74**

In *James v United Kingdom*, the ECtHR indicated that there was nothing in the third rule that precludes a State from implementing a policy of ensuring the equitable distribution of economic advantages by resort to deprivation of property, as opposed to by way of taxation. **14–75**

As in the case of Art.8, the ECtHR has indicated that a wide margin of appreciation must be allowed to the contracting States in implementing social and economic policies. The national authorities are in principle better placed than the international judge to appreciate what is in "the public interest". The ECtHR will respect the legislature's judgment as to what is in the public interest unless that judgment is manifestly without foundation.[53] Provided that the legislature remains within the bounds of its margin of appreciation, it is not for the ECtHR to say whether the legislation represented the best solution for dealing with the problem or whether the legislature's discretion should have been exercised in another way.[54] **14–76**

The concept of public interest is wide enough to cover legislation aimed at securing greater social justice in the sphere of housing, even where such legislation interferes with existing contractual relations between private parties, and confers no direct benefit on the State or the community at large. Thus, in **14–77**

[50] *JA Pye (Oxford) Ltd v United Kingdom* (2006) 43 E.H.R.R. 3, [43].
[51] (1986) 8 E.H.R.R. 123.
[52] *James v United Kingdom* (1986) 8 E.H.R.R. 123, [41].
[53] *James v United Kingdom* (1986) 8 E.H.R.R. 123, [46]; and *JA Pye (Oxford) Ltd v United Kingdom* (2006) 43 E.H.R.R. 3, [44].
[54] *James v United Kingdom* (1986) 8 E.H.R.R. 123, [51].

James v United Kingdom,[55] the ECtHR held that the aim pursued by leasehold enfranchisement legislation was a legitimate one.[56] Similarly, in *Mellacher v Austria*,[57] the court upheld rent control legislation. In *Jacobsson v Sweden*,[58] the ECtHR held town planning to be a legitimate aim.[59]

14–78 Any interference with the peaceful enjoyment of possessions must nevertheless strike a "fair balance" between the demands of the public or general interest of the community, and the requirements for the protection of the individual's fundamental rights. In particular, there must be a reasonable relationship of proportionality between the means employed and the aim sought to be realised by any measure depriving a person of his possessions or controlling their use.[60] The requisite balance will not have been struck if the person concerned has had to bear "an individual and excessive burden".[61]

3. Compensation

14–79 The ECtHR has indicated that the taking of property in the public interest without payment of compensation reasonably related to its value is justifiable only in exceptional circumstances.[62] This principle is not confined to the taking of property for public purposes, but is equally applicable to the compulsory transfer of property from one individual to another. Compensation terms are material to the assessment of whether contested legislation respects a fair balance between the various interests at stake and, notably, whether it imposes a disproportionate burden on certain individuals.

14–80 Article 1 does not, however, guarantee a right to full compensation in all circumstances.[63] Legitimate objectives of "public interest" such as pursued in measures of economic reform or measures designed to achieve greater social justice, may call for less than reimbursement of the full market value. Thus, in *James v United Kingdom*,[64] the ECtHR upheld leasehold enfranchisement legislation which it has been argued provided for only limited compensation.

[55] (1986) 8 E.H.R.R. 123.
[56] See *Shirley v A O'Gorman & Company Ltd.* [2006] I.E.H.C. 27; unreported, Peart J., January 31, 2006, where *James v United Kingdom* (1986) 8 E.H.R.R. 123 was applied by the High Court in the context of a constitutional challenge to leasehold enfranchisement legislation under Irish law.
[57] (1990) 12 E.H.R.R. 391.
[58] (1990) 12 E.H.R.R. 56, [63].
[59] See also *Skibinscy v Poland* (Application No. 52589/99); November 14, 2006 (securing land in connection with the implementation of the local land-development plan a legitimate aim).
[60] *Sporrong and Lönnroth v Sweden* (1983) 5 E.H.R.R. 35, [69]; *JA Pye (Oxford) Ltd v United Kingdom* (2006) 43 E.H.R.R. 3, [46]; and *Hutten-Czapska v Poland* (35014/97), [150].
[61] *Sporrong and Lönnroth v Sweden* (1983) 5 E.H.R.R. 35, [69].
[62] *James v United Kingdom* (1986) 8 E.H.R.R. 123, [54].
[63] See, for example, *Papachelas v Greece* (2000) 30 E.H.R.R. 923, [48].
[64] (1986) 8 E.H.R.R. 123.

The Irish Supreme Court cited the judgment in *James v United Kingdom* with **14–81** approval in assessing the constitutionality of the provision in respect of social and affordable housing. The Supreme Court found the payment of only limited compensation—at less than market value—to be constitutional. See further Chapter 15.

4. Deprivation or control?

A distinction is drawn under the terms of Art.1 between the deprivation **14–82** (expropriation) of possessions and the control of the use of property. The principal significance of the distinction lies in whether the payment of compensation will be required.

As discussed above at para.14–79, the deprivation or taking of property in the **14–83** public interest without payment of compensation reasonably related to its value is justifiable only in exceptional circumstances. It seems, however, that different considerations apply to controls on the use of property. The Court of Appeal in England and Wales appeared to suggest in *R. (On the application of Trailer & Marina (Leven) Ltd.) v Secretary of State for the Environment, Food and Rural Affairs*[65] that whereas in assessing the proportionality of the regulation in question it will be of relevance whether compensation is payable, there may be less call for the payment of compensation than in the case of a taking. As the Court of Appeal itself noted, however, any difference in this regard has not been made explicit by the ECtHR.

At all events, the ECtHR has emphasised that the requirement for proportionality **14–84** applies similarly to the regulation of the use of land as it does to its expropriation. The ECtHR has also been astute to detect *de facto* expropriations, and even in the absence of a formal expropriation it will look behind appearances and investigate the realities of the situation.

In *Fredin v Sweden*,[66] the ECtHR held that the revocation of an extraction **14–85** permit (which authorised the extraction of gravel) did not constitute a deprivation or expropriation of property, but rather fell to be considered as a control of use of property within the scope of the second paragraph of Art.1. The interference with the general property right was held not to be disproportionate. The developers had only initiated their investments seven years after the relevant legislation had been amended to allow for the potential revocation of existing permits. They must therefore reasonably have been aware of the possibility that they might lose their permit after a particular date. In addition, it was clear that the authorities had not given the developers any assurances that they would be allowed to continue to extract gravel after this date. Accordingly, when embarking on their investments, the developers could

---

[65] [2004] E.W.C.A. Civ. 1580; [2005] 1 P. & C.R. 28.
[66] (1991) 13 E.H.R.R. 784.

have relied only on the authorities' obligation, when taking decisions relating to nature conservation, to take due account of their interests. This obligation could not, at the time the developers had made their investments, reasonably have founded any legitimate expectation on their part of being able to continue exploitation for a long period of time.

14–86 In *Pine Valley Developments Ltd v Ireland*,[67] the ECtHR accepted that the annulment of the grant of outline planning permission constituted an interference with property rights. Prior to the annulment, the applicants had at least a legitimate expectation of being able to carry out their proposed development and this had to be regarded, for the purposes of Art.1, as a component part of the property in question.[68] The ECtHR went on to hold that the interference was justified without the payment of compensation, as it was designed and served to ensure that the relevant planning legislation was correctly applied. The court emphasised that the applicants were engaged on a commercial venture which, by its very nature, involved an element of risk, and that they were aware not only of the terms of the development plan—which designated the lands as a green belt—but also of the opposition of the planning authority to any departure from it. (A breach of Art.14 was held to have occurred as a result of the fact that the developer was, seemingly, excluded from the benefit of consequential remedial legislation.)

5. Planning "blight" as an interference with property rights

14–87 The ECtHR has confirmed that the "blighting" of land can, in certain circumstances, constitute a violation of Art.1. In *Sporring & Lönnroth v Sweden*,[69] the applicants' lands were the subject of expropriation permits. The expropriation permits were not self-executing: the issue of a permit simply entitled a given public authority (or, in exceptional cases, a private individual or a company) to effect the acquisition if necessary by initiating judicial proceedings for the fixing of compensation. The landowner was free to deal with the land—whether by sale, lease or mortgage—in the interim. The permits were generally limited for a period of five years, after the expiration of which they lapsed. In the case of the applicants' lands, however, the expropriation permits had been extended from time to time. Separately, the applicants' lands were also subject to prohibitions on construction.

14–88 The applicants complained that the expropriation permits and the prohibitions on construction had been maintained in force for a lengthy period (23 and eight years for the permits; 25 and 12 years for the prohibitions). It was urged on their behalf that the combination of the expropriation permits and prohibition on construction had adverse effects on their property rights. It was contended that they had lost the possibility of selling their properties at normal market

---

[67] (1992) 14 E.H.R.R. 319.
[68] *ibid.*, [51].
[69] (1985) 5 E.H.R.R. 35.

prices; that they had encountered difficulties in obtaining mortgages; and that they would have run too great a risk had they incurred expenditure on their properties.

The ECtHR, by a majority, held that although the actions did not assimilate to an actual deprivation of property, they nevertheless amounted to an interference with the peaceful enjoyment of possessions within the meaning of the first sentence of Art.1. The combined effect of the expropriation permits and prohibition on construction created a situation which upset the fair balance which should be struck between the protection of the individual's property rights and the requirements of the general interest. The majority of the court held that the applicants bore an individual and excessive burden which could have been tendered legitimate only if they had had the possibility of seeking a reduction of the time-limits or of claiming compensation.[70]   **14–89**

The facts of *Sporring & Lönnroth v Sweden* were distinguished in *Jacobsson (Allan) v Sweden*.[71] There, the applicant complained of the effect on his property of local building prohibitions, which were renewed from time to time. The ECtHR found that the applicant's right of property was never rendered precarious by the issuing of any expropriation permit, and that the interference at issue, being the result of a control of use of property, fell to be examined under the third rule of Art.1. The court also placed emphasis on the fact that the applicant had purchased the land with notice of the restrictions, and that the existing use had not been interfered with.   **14–90**

The court concluded, albeit expressing concern as to the long duration of the impugned prohibitions, that same could not be considered disproportionate to the requirements of the municipality's legitimate aim of planning the area.   **14–91**

More recently, in *Skibinscy v Poland*,[72] the ECtHR ruled that the prolonged designation of land for expropriation at some undetermined future date gave rise to a breach of the first sentence of Art.1. Part of the applicants' lands had been designated under a land-development plan for use for the construction of a major roadway. This resulted in the applicants being denied the opportunity to develop their lands for a period of approximately 10 years, between 1994 and 2003. This was so notwithstanding that the local investment plan did not provide for the construction of the road to begin before 2010. The designation eventually expired at the end of 2003, and was not renewed.   **14–92**

Although the designation had neither amounted to a *de facto* expropriation nor to control of use of property, the ECtHR held that there was nevertheless an interference with the peaceful enjoyment of the applicants' possessions.[73]   **14–93**

---

[70] The majority also held that there was a breach of art.6, finding that the expropriation permits affecting the applicants' properties related to a "civil" right and, as regards their period of validity, gave rise to a "dispute" within the meaning of art.6(1).

[71] (1989) 12 E.H.R.R. 56.

[72] Application No. 52589/99; November 14, 2006.

[73] *ibid.*, [80].

14–94 In reaching its conclusion, the ECtHR emphasised that the applicants were negatively affected not so much by the mere prospect of expropriation, but by the fact that this future expropriation was to be carried out at an undetermined point in time and in the absence of any indication, even approximate, as to its future date.

> "To sum up, the measures complained of, taken as a whole, although in law they left intact the applicants' right to continue to use and dispose of their possessions, nevertheless in practice they significantly reduced the effective exercise of that right. Not only were the applicants prevented from bringing their construction projects to fruition, their property was also to be expropriated at some undetermined future date, without there being any provision for immediate compensation under the applicable laws. The applicants' right of property thus became precarious and defeasible (*mutatis mutandis, Sporrong and Lönnroth v. Sweden*, judgment of 23 September 1982, Series A no. 52, §§ 58-60)."

14–95 The ECtHR found that the interference with the applicants' property rights was disproportionate. The land had been blighted for a prolonged period of time—for almost ten years—and, at the time when the applicants' request to obtain final building permission was pending, there were no good grounds on which to believe that the relevant development plan would be implemented promptly. As a result, the *de facto* blocking of any construction on the applicants' property did not serve any immediate or medium-term purpose in the interest of the community. In the Court's view, given that it was uncertain whether the development plans would be implemented in the reasonably near future, this state of affairs disclosed a lack of sufficient diligence in weighing the interests of the owners against the planning needs of the municipality.

6. Procedural requirements

14–96 Although Art.1 of the First Protocol contains no explicit procedural requirements, the ECtHR has held that the affected individual must be afforded a reasonable opportunity of putting his or her case to the responsible authorities for the purpose of effectively challenging the measures interfering with his property rights. In ascertaining whether this requirement has been satisfied, a comprehensive view must be taken of the applicable procedures.[74] The lack of procedural protections was considered significant by the ECtHR in reaching its finding that limitation periods giving rise to adverse possession of registered land violated Art.1.[75]

14–97 Similarly an inflexible system of compensation which fails to take into account the diverse circumstances of property owners may not be compliant. Thus, in *Tsomtsos v Greece*,[76] the ECtHR held—in the context of the expropriation of

---

[74] *Jokela v Finland* [2002] E.C.H.R. 28856/95, [45].

[75] *JA Pye (Oxford) Ltd v United Kingdom* (2006) 43 E.H.R.R. 3. See N. Buckley, "Calling Time on Adverse Possession?" (2006) 11 *Bar Review* 32.

[76] (2001) 32 E.H.R.R. 6. See further *Efstahiou v Greece* (2006) 43 E.H.R.R. 24.

land for road development—that a system which did not allow the owners concerned to argue that in reality the effect of the works concerned either has been of no benefit, or less benefit, to them or had caused them to sustain varying degrees of loss, was "manifestly without reasonable foundation". The offending national legislation deemed adjoining landowners, *i.e.* those whose properties fronted the newly built road, to have derived a benefit from the construction road. The deemed benefit was then to be set-off against the compensation payable in respect of expropriated land.

F. Article 6

1. Introduction

Article 6(1) insofar as relevant provides as follows.   **14–98**

> "In the determination of his civil rights and obligations or any criminal charge against him, everyone is entitled to a fair and public hearing within a reasonable time by an independent and impartial tribunal established by law."

It is proposed to consider first the concepts of "civil rights and obligations"   **14–99** and of "an independent and impartial tribunal", before turning to a more general discussion as to the possible implications of Art.6 for planning law.

2. "Civil rights and obligations"

Article 6(1) extends only to disputes over "civil rights and obligations". It is   **14–100** important to note that Art.6(1) does not itself confer substantive rights, *i.e.* it does not guarantee any particular content for "civil rights and obligations" in the substantive law of the contracting States. Article 6(1) is not aimed at creating new substantive rights, but rather at providing procedural protection for rights already recognised under national law. Therefore in order to invoke Art.6(1) an applicant must be able to point to a substantive right which can be said, at least on arguable grounds, to be recognised under national law, and to demonstrate that this right is of a "civil" character.

The procedural protections under Art.6(1) apply to the "determination" of a   **14–101** civil right. In this regard, the ECtHR has indicated that there must be a dispute in existence: the dispute must be genuine and serious; it may relate not only to the actual existence of a right, but also to its scope and the manner of its exercise. The outcome of the proceedings must be directly decisive for the right in question. Article 6(1) is not confined solely to proceedings which are already in progress: it may also be relied on by anyone who considers that an interference with the exercise of one of his civil rights is unlawful, and complains that he has not had the possibility of submitting that claim to a tribunal meeting the requirements of Art.6(1).[77]

---

[77] *Sporrong and Lönnroth v Sweden* (1983) 5 E.H.R.R. 35, [80].

14–102 In an early judgment—*Ringeisen v Austria*[78]—the ECtHR rejected an argument that it was necessary that the dispute be between private parties, holding that it covered all proceedings the result of which is decisive for private rights and obligations. Thus Art.6(1) can apply to disputes between a private individual and a public body exercising regulatory functions. Various regulatory decisions and actions can be said to determine civil rights.

14–103 The fact that a decision-maker has a broad discretion does not preclude a finding of there being a dispute: unless the decision-maker has an unfettered discretion, there can be a dispute as to whether the relevant decision conflicted with national law administrative principles.[79]

14–104 Where an administrative decision or action is directed towards particular property, the owner of that property will normally be able to invoke Art.6(1). Thus, the ECtHR has confirmed that the following were all directly decisive of a civil right: the issue of an expropriation permit[80]; the refusal to grant an exemption from a municipal building plan[81]; the amendment of a municipal building plan[82]; an appeal against an enforcement notice[83]; the refusal of planning permission[84]; the revocation of an extraction licence[85]; and the designation of land as a protected nature site (the legal consequences of designation were that the owner was no longer free to cultivate his land as he saw fit and was required to seek authorisation for various activities).[86]

14–105 The requirement that the outcome be "directly decisive" has, however, presented difficulties for third parties seeking to rely on Art.6. In particular, in a number of judgments the ECtHR has found, on the facts, that the connection between the substantive national-law right being relied upon and the administrative decision being challenged was too tenuous or the consequences too remote.

14–106 Thus, in *Balmer-Schafroth v Switzerland*,[87] an attempt to invoke Art.6 was unsuccessful. The applicants had sought to rely on their right under national law to have their physical integrity adequately protected. The ECtHR held that the applicants had failed to establish a direct link between the operating conditions of the relevant power station and their right to protection of their physical integrity, as they failed to show that the operation of the power station

---

[78] (1971) 1 E.H.R.R. 455.
[79] *Skarby v Sweden* (1991) 13 E.H.R.R. 90, [28].
[80] *Bodin v Sweden* (1988) 10 E.H.R.R. 367.
[81] *Skarby v Sweden* (1991) 13 E.H.R.R. 90.
[82] *Jacobsson (Mats) v Sweden* (1991) 13 E.H.R.R. 79, [33]–[34].
[83] *Bryan v United Kingdom* (1996) 21 E.H.R.R. 342 (the United Kingdom Government did not contest that the impugned planning proceedings involved a determination of the applicant's civil rights).
[84] *Jaccobson (Allan) v Sweden* (1990) 12 E.H.R.R. 56 (disputed right to build on land).
[85] *Fredin v Sweden* (1991) 13 E.H.R.R. 784.
[86] *Oerlemans v Netherlands* (1991) 15 E.H.R.R. 561. See also *R. (On the application of Aggregates Industries UK Ltd.) v English Nature* [2002] E.W.H.C. 908.
[87] (1998) 25 E.H.R.R. 598.

exposed them personally to a danger that was not only serious but also specific and, above all, imminent. Similarly, in *Athanassoglou v Switzerland*,[88] the ECtHR held that the connection between the impugned decision and the domestic law rights invoked was too tenuous and remote. Significantly, in neither case had the applicants claimed to have suffered any loss—economic or otherwise—for which they intended to seek compensation.

Conversely, in *Okyay v Turkey*,[89] the applicants successfully argued that their right under the Turkish constitution to live in a healthy and balanced environment represented a civil right within Art.6. This was so notwithstanding the fact that the applicants lived a distance of some 250km from the thermal-power plants in issue. Article 6(1) was found to apply because, although the applicants could not point to any serious, specific or imminent risk to their physical integrity, they had standing under Turkish law to ask the administrative courts to issue injunctions for the suspension of the power plants' environmentally hazardous activities, and to set aside the administrative authorities' decision to continue to operate them.[90]   **14–107**

In *Okyay v Turkey*, the applicants successfully translated a substantive national-law right into Art.6 procedural rights. An interesting question arises as to whether it is possible to rely on a procedural right under national law for the purposes of Art.6(1)? This question is especially meaningful in the context of the PDA 2000 where statutory rights to participate in the planning process are, in many instances, afforded to all, irrespective of whether a person is affected by the proposed development.   **14–108**

Reference is made in this regard to the judgment of the ECtHR in *Ortenberg v Austria*.[91] The applicant had objected to the grant of building permits on land adjoining her property. Under Austrian law, a neighbour had a statutory right to make objections to a grant of planning permission on the ground that the proposed development would infringe personal rights derived from either private law (private-law objections) or public law (public-law objections).   **14–109**

The Austrian government argued that Art.6(1) did not apply, saying that the right of neighbours to object was essentially a public-law right designed to ensure compliance with legal provisions, in particular those for the protection of the environment. It was submitted further that a grant of planning permission concerned the relationship between a public authority and an individual; it did not directly affect the owner of adjacent land.   **14–110**

---

[88] (2001) 31 E.H.R.R. 13.
[89] (2006) 43 E.H.R.R. 37.
[90] *cf. R. (On the application of Vetterlein) v Hampshire County Council* [2001] E.W.H.C. 560 Admin; [2002] 1 P. & C.R. 31 (grant of planning permission not directly decisive of a third party's rights); and *Gwennap Parish Council v Cornwall County Council* [2003] J.P.L. 105.
[91] (1995) 19 E.H.R.R. 524.

14–111   The ECtHR rejected these arguments, having regard to the close link between the national law proceedings and the consequences of their outcome for the applicant's property. Although the applicant had relied on public law objections, in so doing she nonetheless wished to avoid any infringement of her pecuniary rights, because she considered that the works on the land adjoining her property would jeopardise her enjoyment of it and would reduce its market value.

14–112   What is interesting about the judgment in *Ortenberg v Austria* is that it suggests that the combination of a national-law procedural right with a pecuniary or property interest may be sufficient to engage Art.6(1). This would obviously provide a much more direct route to the procedural protections under Art.6(1), and would avoid the requirement, laid down in cases such as *Balmer-Schafroth v Switzerland*, to demonstrate a direct impact from the impugned development.

14–113   If this is so, then circumstances which will trigger Art.6 will be far, far wider than those covered by Art.8 or by Art.1 of the First Protocol. A third party can only assert Art.8 rights, for example, in the context of an application for planning permission where the adverse impacts of the proposed development cross a certain threshold of severity. Insofar as Art.6(1) is concerned, however, it may be that the grant of planning permission constitutes a determination of "civil rights", and thus a third party who is able to point to a pecuniary or proprietary interest may be in a position to invoke the Art.6(1) procedural requirements.[92]

3. "Independent and impartial tribunal established by law"

14–114   In order to establish whether a tribunal can be considered "independent" for the purposes of Art.6(1), regard must be had, *inter alia*, to the manner of appointment of its members and their term of office; the existence of safeguards against outside pressures; and the question whether the tribunal presents an appearance of independence.

14–115   The distinct requirement for "impartiality" has two aspects. First, the tribunal must be subjectively free of personal prejudice or bias. Secondly, it must also be impartial from an objective viewpoint, that is, it must offer sufficient guarantees to exclude any legitimate doubt in this respect. Here, even appearances may be of a certain importance. What is at stake is the confidence which the courts in a democratic society must inspire in the public and above all in the parties to proceedings.[93] In deciding whether in a given case there is a legitimate reason to fear that these requirements are not met, the standpoint

---

[92] In *R. (On the application of Bushell) v Newcastle Licensing Justices* [2003] E.H.W.C. 1937 [Admin]; [2004] J.P.L. 805, the High Court of England and Wales held that a decision to commit the special removal of an old on-licence to other premises engaged art.6(1). In *British Telecommunications plc v Gloucester City Council* [2001] E.W.H.C. Admin 1001; [2002] 2 P. & C.R. 33, the High Court of England and Wales held that the securing of planning permission over another's lands engaged art.6(1). See *contra* the cases cited at fn.90.

[93] See, for example, *Morris v United Kingdom* (2002) 34 E.H.R.R. 52, [58].

of a party is important but not decisive. What is decisive is whether this fear can be held to be objectively justified.[94]

It appears from judgments such as that in *Kingsley v United Kingdom*[95] that the ECtHR is less forgiving of so-called bias of necessity than the Irish courts might be. The ECtHR considers that it is generally inherent in the notion of judicial review that, if a ground of challenge is upheld, the reviewing court has power to quash the impugned decision, and that either the decision will then be taken by the review court, or the case will be remitted for a fresh decision by the same or a different body. Thus, where complaint is made of a lack of impartiality on the part of the decision-making body, the concept of "full jurisdiction" involves that the reviewing court not only considers the complaint, but has the ability to quash the impugned decision and to remit the case for a new decision by an impartial body.[96] On the facts, the courts of England and Wales had declined to quash the impugned decision on the basis of bias of necessity.

14–116

The consecutive exercise of advisory and judicial functions within one body may, in certain circumstances, raise an issue as regards the impartiality of the body seen from the objective viewpoint.[97] It is interesting to note that such conclusions are, seemingly, not based on the separation of powers, nor on any theoretical constitutional concepts regarding the permissible limits of the powers' interaction.[98]

14–117

The ECtHR held in *McGonnell v United Kingdom*[99] that "any direct involvement in the passage of legislation, or of executive rules, is likely to be sufficient to cast doubt on the judicial impartiality of a person subsequently called on to determine a dispute over whether reasons exist to permit a variation from the wording of the legislation or rules at issue".[100] The court held that the fact that the Bailiff who presided over an appeal against the refusal of planning permission had previously presided over the legislative body that adopted the relevant development plan was capable of casting doubt on his impartiality.

14–118

Similarly, it seems that where it has a role in setting policy, a decision-maker cannot be regarded as independent and impartial in disputes involving the application of that policy. Reference is again made in this regard to *Bryan v United Kingdom*.

14–119

---

[94] See, for example, *Hauschildt v Denmark* [1989] E.C.H.R. 10486/83 [48].
[95] (2002) 34 E.H.R.R. 52, [58]. This case was cited with approval by Hardiman J. in his dissenting judgment in *O'Callaghan v Mahon* [2007] I.E.S.C. 17; unreported, March 30, 2007.
[96] *cf. Usk and District Residents Association Ltd. v An Bord Pleanála*, unreported, High Court, Kelly J., March 14, 2007 (High Court remitted planning appeal to An Bord Pleanála with recommendation that it be considered by a differently constituted division of the board).
[97] *Procola v Luxembourg* (1996) 22 E.H.R.R. 193.
[98] *Kleyn v Netherlands* [2003] E.C.H.R. 46664/99.
[99] *McGonnell v United Kingdom* [2000] E.C.H.R. 28488/95.
[100] Application No. 28488/95; September 28, 1999, [55].

14–120   In *R. (On the application of Alconbury Developments Ltd.) v Secretary of State for the Environment Transport and the Regions*,[101] it was accepted that decision-making under the auspices of the Secretary of State was not to be regarded as meeting the requirements of Art.6(1) because of his role in setting national planning policy.

14–121   Certain decision-making by planning authorities under the PDA 2000 must be suspect in terms of Art.6(1). The role of a planning authority in authorising its own development under s.179 of the PDA 2000 is in clear breach of Art.6(1). Local authority development in its own functional area is exempt from the requirement to obtain planning permission, but certain prescribed development is subject to a form of public consultation under s.179 and Pt 8 of Planning and Development Regulations 2001. There is a clear lack of independence and impartiality.

14–122   Moreover, the role of a planning authority in determining applications for planning permission also presents difficulties. First, a planning authority has a significant policy-making role as author of the development plan. This suggests that in determining an application for planning permission it cannot be regarded as an independent and impartial tribunal. Secondly, the fact that planning authorities are empowered under Pt XIV of the PDA 2000 to take a more proactive role in the development and regeneration of lands might be thought to undermine their independence as decision-makers. In circumstances where a planning authority is involved—whether directly or indirectly—with a proposed development, there might be a perception that it would be predisposed to grant planning permission for the development, and, possibly, to refuse planning permission for rival development.

14–123   The general principle as to whether a local authority determining an application for planning permission for development promoted by it is compatible with the Convention was considered by the High Court of England and Wales in *R. (On the application of Kathro) v Rhondda Cynon Taff County Borough Council.*[102]

> "In the present case the fact that the defendant council will be deciding on its own application for planning permission in respect of development which it is promoting on its own land is plainly sufficient to establish a lack of independence and impartiality for the purposes of Article 6 (and it has not been necessary to consider whether any other features of the process, *e.g.* the application of local planning policies, would also give rise to a lack of independence and impartiality). Here, too, the question is whether compliance in principle with Article 6 is achieved by the availability of judicial review."

14–124   The High Court of England and Wales concluded that judicial control via the availability of judicial review was, in principle, sufficient to overcome the

[101] [2001] U.K.H.L. 23; (2001) 82 P. & C.R. 40.
[102] [2002] J.P.L. 304, [16].

seeming lack of independence. The court did indicate, however, that the limited scope to review for error of fact on judicial review might present a difficulty, but that it was premature to rule on this issue until such time as an actual decision had been made on the application for planning permission.

These concerns are met, to some extent, under Irish law by the existence of a right of appeal to An Bord Pleanála. An Bord Pleanála has no policy-making role. The right of appeal may not provide a complete answer, however, in that although An Bord Pleanála is not necessarily bound by the development plan, its discretion is fettered to some extent (especially where planning permission is refused at first instance by reference to a material contravention of the development plan). All of this leaves open the possibility of the planning authority, through the development plan, exercising some residual influence on the decision on appeal. Moreover, insofar as An Bord Pleanála is required under s.143 of the PDA 2000 (as amended)[103] to have regard to government policies and objectives it might be thought that this undermines its independence and impartiality.   **14–125**

It follows from this that certain aspects of the planning process are *prima facie* not compliant with the Art.6(1) requirement for independence and impartiality. It may be, however, that any seeming breach in this regard is remedied by the availability of judicial review. The ECtHR has stated—in *Albert and Le Compte v Belgium*[104]—that even where an adjudicatory body determining disputes over "civil rights and obligations" does not comply with Art.6(1) in some respect, no violation of the Convention will be found if the proceedings before that body are subject to subsequent control by a judicial body that has "full jurisdiction" and does provide the guarantees of Art.6(1).   **14–126**

Thus, the requirement for independence and impartiality does not necessarily have to be fulfilled at each layer of the decision-making process: it may be sufficient if it is available on appeal or on judicial review. The decision-making process must, therefore, be looked at in its entirety. The question of whether the limited judicial review allowed for under Irish law is sufficient in this regard is addressed at paras 14–136 to 14–157.   **14–127**

4. Procedural requirements under Article 6(1)

We turn now to consider briefly the extent to which Art.6(1) may impose procedural requirements over and above those already required under national law. With two possible exceptions—in respect of oral hearings and delay—the existing procedural requirements are probably sufficient to meet Art.6(1). This is because the notion of fair procedures is already deeply ingrained in the planning process. In many instances the PDA 2000 itself imposes detailed   **14–128**

---

[103] Planning and Development (Strategic Infrastructure) Act 2006, s.26.
[104] (1983) 5 E.H.R.R. 533, [29].

procedural requirements: where these are insufficient, these statutory procedures will—as discussed in Chapter 12—be supplemented where necessary to ensure fair procedures. The national law concept of natural and constitutional justice parallels, to a large degree, the concept of a "fair" hearing under Art.6(1).

14–129 One possible area where Art.6(1) may have implications is in relation to the requirement for an oral hearing.[105] The entitlement to a "public" hearing in Art.6(1) has been held to imply a right to an "oral hearing" before at least one court or tribunal. This obligation is not an absolute one, and a hearing may be dispensed with if a party unequivocally waives his or her right thereto, and there are no questions of public interest making a hearing necessary. A waiver can be made explicitly or tacitly; in the latter case, for example, by refraining from submitting or maintaining a request for a hearing.[106]

14–130 Under the PDA 2000, there is no provision for an oral hearing at the planning authority stage of an application for planning permission, and An Bord Pleanála has an "absolute" discretion as to whether to hold an oral hearing on appeal. There is no provision at all for an oral hearing in respect of the decision of a planning authority to serve an enforcement notice. Insofar as objections to compulsory purchase orders are concerned, an oral hearing is no longer mandatory as a result of amendments introduced under the Planning and Development (Strategic Infrastructure) Act 2006.[107]

14–131 The Court of Appeal, in *R. (On the application of Adlard) v Secretary of State for Transport, Local Government and the Regions*,[108] reiterated that the question of whether or not Art.6(1) is satisfied falls to be considered by reference not merely to the initial decision-making process, but also in the light of the High Court's review jurisdiction. The Court of Appeal rejected an argument that Art.6(1) confers an absolute right to be heard orally by the administrative decision-making body. The decision-making process had to be looked at in its entirety. Any application for judicial review would entail an oral hearing. This would normally be sufficient—in the context of the planning process—to ensure compliance with the Convention.

14–132 In reaching its conclusions, the Court of Appeal emphasised the subject-matter of the decision-making process. The subject-matter lay "towards that end of the spectrum where judgment and discretion, rather than fact-finding, play the

---

[105] See further W. McKechnie, "Article 6 of the European Convention on Human Rights, Administrative Tribunals and Judicial Review" (2002) 7 *Bar Review* 333 and 364.

[106] Note the requirement to make an express request for an oral hearing in the case of an appeal to An Bord Pleanála imposed under the Planning and Development (Strategic Infrastructure) Act 2006, s.22.

[107] PDA 2000, s.218 (as amended by s.39 of the Planning and Development (Strategic Infrastructure) Act 2006).

[108] [2002] E.W.C.A. Civ. 735; [2002] 2 P. & C.R. 28; [2002] J.P.L. 1379.

predominant part".[109] The Court of Appeal in an earlier judgment[110]—with regard to the homelessness legislation—had indicated that where a scheme generally or systematically requires the application of judgment or the exercise of discretion, especially if it involves weighing of policy issues and regard being had to the interests of others who are not before the decision-maker, then for the purposes of Art.6 the court will incline to be satisfied with a form of inquisition at first instance in which the decision-maker is more of an expert than a judge, and the second instance appeal is in the nature of a judicial review.

The Court of Appeal in *Adlard* went on to say that if the court were satisfied that exceptionally, on the facts of any particular case, it was unfair or unreasonable to deny an objector any or any sufficient oral hearing, the court would quash the decision and require such a hearing to be given.[111]   **14–133**

Another area where Art.6(1) may have repercussions is in relation to delay. Article 6(1) requires a determination to be made with a "reasonable time". This aspect has been interpreted by the ECtHR as imposing a duty on the contracting States to organise their judicial systems in such a way that their courts can meet each of its requirements, including the obligation to hear cases within a reasonable time.[112] These principles apply to the determination of planning matters.[113]   **14–134**

There is only limited provision made under the PDA 2000 to police timely decision-making. Although aspirational time-limits are prescribed for various decisions—for example, An Bord Pleanála is to determine appeals "as expeditiously as may be"— it is only in the case of delay at the planning authority stage of an application for planning permission that there is an actual sanction imposed. As it happens, that sanction, namely default planning permission, may itself be incompatible with the Convention for other reasons. See paras 14–189 to 14–193.   **14–135**

G. "Full Jurisdiction" and Judicial Review

1. General

In certain instances, what might otherwise represent shortcomings in compliance with the Convention might be made good by the availability of a remedy by way of judicial review. In particular, where—as discussed above at para.14–126—the requirement for independence and impartiality is not met at the   **14–136**

---

[109] *ibid.*, [17] *per* Simon Brown L.J., quoting from *London Borough of Tower Hamlets v Runa Begum* [2002] E.W.C.A. Civ. 239.
[110] *London Borough of Tower Hamlets v Runa Begum* [2002] E.W.C.A. Civ. 239, [42].
[111] [2002] E.W.C.A. Civ. 735; [2002] 2 P. & C.R. 28; [2002] J.P.L. 1379, [32].
[112] See, for example, *Frydlender v France* (2001) 31 E.H.R.R. 52, [45].
[113] *Morscher v Austria* [2004] E.C.H.R. 54039/00 (delay of up to six years in final determination of planning permission unreasonable).

administrative stage of decision-making, it may be sufficient if that decision is subject to subsequent control by a judicial body that has "full jurisdiction" and does provide the guarantees of Art.6(1).

14–137 It must be doubtful as to whether judicial review can ever do more than redress a lack of independence and impartiality at the first stage; in particular, it is unlikely that other inherent deficiencies in the administrative decision-making stage—for example, the absence of a right to make meaningful submissions—could be made good on judicial review. This issue is discussed further in the specific context of enforcement notices at paras 14–228 to 14–236.

14–138 Under Irish law, various decisions of the planning authorities and An Bord Pleanála are amenable to judicial review, in most instances pursuant to the special judicial review procedure prescribed under ss.50 and 50A of the PDA 2000 (as amended).[114] There is no doubt that the High Court meets the Art.6(1) requirement of independence and impartiality. What is questionable, however, is whether, given the limited nature of judicial review allowed for under Irish law, it can be said that the High Court has "full jurisdiction".

14–139 The concept of "full jurisdiction" is a nebulous one. The ECtHR has suggested that the tribunal must be competent to determine all aspects of the matter.[115] However, it seems that a full rehearing is not necessarily required, and that the intensity of review required will differ according to the subject-matter of the impugned decision. The greater the policy content of the decision, the less searching the review must be. Thus, the ECtHR has indicated that a deferential standard of review is sufficient in the context of specialist decision-making such as that involved in town planning. This proposition must be treated with caution, however, in that not every decision made by a planning authority or An Bord Pleanála can properly be said to be a policy decision. For example, the decision-making process on a Section 5 reference involves legal issues, *i.e.* the interpretation and application of the statutory concepts of development and exempted development. It must follow as a corollary from the propositions discussed above that the greater the *legal* content of a decision, the more searching the review must be.

14–140 The adequacy of review available under English planning law was considered by the ECtHR in *Bryan v United Kingdom*.[116] The case concerned an appeal against an enforcement notice. The relevant legislation provided for a statutory right of appeal to the High Court on prescribed grounds. The appeal against the enforcement notice had raised two distinct issues. First, whether planning permission should have been granted for the development sought to be enforced against. Secondly, whether or not the impugned development was unauthorised. Whereas the former is a policy decision, the latter arguably involves the

---

[114] Planning and Development (Strategic Infrastructure) Act 2006, s.13.
[115] *Sporrong and Lönnroth v Sweden* (1983) 5 E.H.R.R. 35, [87].
[116] (1996) 21 E.H.R.R. 342.

determination of questions of law. As it happens, the appeal against the finding that the development was unauthorised was not pursued as the applicant had been advised by counsel that an invitation to the High Court to substitute its own findings for those of the inspector would fail. It should be noted that there was no dispute as to the primary facts, nor, following the withdrawal of the second ground of appeal, as to the factual inferences drawn by the inspector. As the ECtHR subsequently put it in its recent judgment in *Tsfayo v United Kingdom*,[117] whereas the inspector's decision that there had been a breach of planning control involved some fact-finding, namely that the buildings which Mr Bryan had erected had the appearance of residential houses rather than agricultural barns, the inspector was also called upon to exercise his discretion on a wide range of policy matters involving development in a green belt and conservation area, and it was these policy judgments, rather than the findings of primary fact, which Mr Bryan challenged in the High Court.

The inspector was not considered to be independent within the meaning of Art.6 because the Secretary of State could at any time, even during the course of proceedings which were in progress, issue a direction to revoke the power of an inspector to decide an appeal. The ECtHR considered that, in the context of planning appeals, the very existence of this power available to the executive, whose own policies may be in issue, was enough to deprive the inspector of the requisite appearance of independence, notwithstanding the limited exercise of the power in practice as described by the Government, and irrespective of whether its exercise was or could have been in issue in the present case. **14–141**

It was argued that the limited scope of judicial review meant that it did not remedy the deficiencies at the administrative stage. The ECtHR considered, however, that the availability of a statutory appeal to the High Court rendered the procedure compliant with Art.6. The court indicated that, in assessing the sufficiency of the review available on appeal to the High Court, it was necessary to have regard to matters such as (i) the subject-matter of the decision appealed against; (ii) the manner in which that decision was arrived at; and (iii) the content of the dispute, including the desired and actual grounds of appeal. **14–142**

The ECtHR drew attention to the specialist subject-matter of the decision-making process. The appeal against the refusal of planning permission involved policy matters such as development plans, and the fact that the property was situated in a green belt and a conservation area. The subject-matter of the contested decision by the inspector was, according to the court, therefore a typical example of the exercise of discretionary judgment in the regulation of citizens' conduct in the sphere of town and country planning. In such circumstances, the court did not consider that limited judicial review was insufficient. **14–143**

---

[117] Application No. 60860/00; November 14, 2006; [2007] H.L.R. 19.

14–144   Insofar as the abandoned appeal against the finding that the development was unauthorised was concerned, the ECtHR noted that, while the High Court could not have substituted its own findings of fact for those of the inspector, it would have had the power to satisfy itself that the inspector's findings of fact or the inferences based on them were neither perverse nor irrational.

> "Such an approach by an appeal tribunal on questions of fact can reasonably be expected in specialised areas of the law such as the one at issue, particularly where the facts have already been established in the course of a quasi-judicial procedure governed by many of the safeguards required by Article 6(1)."

14–145   The ECtHR emphasised the manner in which the decision was reached, referring to the safeguards attending the procedure before the inspector: the quasi-judicial character of the decision-making process; the duty incumbent on each inspector to exercise independent judgment; the requirement that inspectors must not be subject to any improper influence; and the stated mission of the inspectorate to uphold the principles of openness, fairness and impartiality.

14–146   The court placed particular emphasis on the jurisdiction of the High Court to quash the inspector's decision if it had been made by reference to irrelevant factors or without regard to relevant factors; or if the evidence relied on by the inspector was not capable of supporting a finding of fact; or if the decision was based on an inference from facts which was perverse or irrational in the sense that no inspector properly directing himself would have drawn such an inference.

14–147   The implications of the judgment in *Bryan v United Kingdom* were considered in detail by the House of Lords in *R. (On the application of Alconbury Developments Ltd.) v Secretary of State for the Environment Transport and the Regions*.[118] Lord Hoffmann sought to introduce a gloss to the judgment in *Bryan*, suggesting that where the subject-matter of the dispute is one of policy or expediency, the procedural safeguards were irrelevant. It was only where one comes to a finding of fact, or the evaluation of facts, such as arise on whether there has been a breach of planning control, that the safeguards are essential to the acceptability of a limited review of fact by the appellate tribunal.[119]

14–148   In its judgment in *Chapman v United Kingdom*,[120] the ECtHR again emphasised—albeit in the context of Art.8 rights—the specialised subject-matter of town planning in accepting the limited judicial review.[121]

> "The court recalls that in the case of *Bryan v UK* [1995] ECHR 19178/91 at paras 34-47 it held that in the specialised area of town planning law full review of the facts may not be required by art 6 of the Convention. It finds in this case

---

[118] [2001] U.K.H.L. 23; (2001) 82 P. & C.R. 40.
[119] *ibid.*, [117].
[120] (2001) 33 E.H.R.R. 18.
[121] *ibid.*, [124].

that the scope of review of the High Court, which was available to the applicant after a public procedure before an inspector, was sufficient in this case to comply with art 6(1). It enabled a decision to be challenged on the basis that it was perverse, irrational, had no basis on the evidence or had been made with reference to irrelevant factors or without regard to relevant factors. This may be regarded as affording adequate judicial control of the administrative decisions in issue."

Two recent judgments of the ECtHR serve to emphasise that where decision-making involves an adjudication on contested factual matters, then a more searching standard of judicial review will be necessary to remedy any deficiencies at the administrative stage of the decision-making process. Judicial review was found to be inadequate in *Connors v United Kingdom*,[122] a case concerning Art.8 rights. The ECtHR found a summary eviction procedure represented a breach of Art.8, as it was not attended by the requisite procedural safeguards. The Court did not accept that the possibility of judicial review was sufficient in circumstances where the applicant sought to dispute the factual basis on which the local authority sought to evict him and his family. The local authority was not required as a matter of national law to establish any substantive justification for evicting him, and on this point judicial review could not provide any opportunity for an examination of the facts in dispute between the parties.   **14–149**

Similarly, in *Tsfayo v United Kingdom*,[123] the ECtHR again held that judicial review was inadequate to remedy a lack of independence at the administrative decision-making stage. The proceedings arose in the context of a claim for housing benefit, and concerned the question as to whether a claimant had shown "good cause" for her delay in maintaining a claim. The decision-maker of first instance was held not to be independent and impartial within the meaning of Art.6.   **14–150**

The ECtHR considered that the decision to reject the claim for housing benefit turned essentially on the assessment of the claimant's credibility. No specialist expertise was required to determine that issue. The previous case law in respect of town planning decisions was distinguished, on the basis that the factual findings in the present case could not be said to be merely incidental to the reaching of broader judgments of policy or expediency which it was for the democratically accountable authority to take.   **14–151**

The ECtHR held that judicial review was inadequate in the circumstances, in that the High Court did not have jurisdiction to rehear the evidence or substitute its own views as to credibility. Thus, in the view of the ECtHR, there was never the possibility that the central issue would be determined by a tribunal that was independent of one of the parties to the dispute, and, accordingly, there was a violation of Art.6.   **14–152**

---

[122] (2005) 40 E.H.R.R. 9.
[123] Application No. 60860/00; November 14, 2006; [2007] H.L.R. 19.

14–153   This distinction between fact-finding and the exercise of specialist expertise has recently been considered by the Irish High Court in *Ashford Castle Ltd. v SIPTU*.[124] Clarke J. observed that the tasks which administrative bodies have been given under statute vary significantly. At one end of the spectrum are issues which involve the same sort of mixed questions of law and fact with which the courts are frequently faced; Clarke J. gave as an example the question of the entitlement of a person to social welfare benefit. At the other end of the spectrum, Clarke J. noted that expert bodies may be required to bring a great deal of their own expertise in relation to matters which involve the exercise of expert judgment, citing the example of planning decisions.

> "Bodies charged with, for example, roles in the planning process are required to exercise a judgment as to what might be the proper planning and development of an area. Obviously in coming to such a view the relevant bodies are required to have regard to the matters which the law specifies (such as, for example, a development plan). However a great deal of the expertise of the body will be concerned with exercising a planning judgment independent of questions of disputed fact. In such cases the underlying facts are normally not in dispute. Questions of expert opinion (such as the likely effect of a proposed development) may well be in dispute and may be resolved, in a manner similar to the way in which similar issues would be resolved in the courts, by hearing and, if necessary, testing competing expert evidence. However above and beyond the resolution of any such issue of expert fact, the authority concerned will also have to bring to bear its own expertise on what is the proper planning and development of an area."

14–154   Clarke J. went on to say that where decisions fell towards the expert end of the spectrum, language such as "evidence" and "findings of fact" had, in his view, a capacity to mislead, and that it might be more appropriate to talk of "materials" rather than "evidence", and more appropriate to talk of "conclusions" than of "findings of fact".[125]

2. Judicial review under Irish law

14–155   Notwithstanding the judgments in *Bryan v United Kingdom* and *Chapman v United Kingdom*, it should not be too readily assumed that availability of judicial review ensures that the decision-making processes of the planning authorities and An Bord Pleanála are compliant with the Convention. The principal reason for this is that the grounds on which judicial review are available under Irish law are so limited that it cannot be said that the requirement under Art.6(1) for subsequent control by a judicial body that has "full jurisdiction" is met. The

---

[124] [2006] I.E.H.C. 201; unreported, Clarke J., June 21, 2006; [2006] E.L.R. 201 at 215–216.

[125] See also *Lord Ballyedmond v Commission for Energy Regulation* [2006] I.E.H.C. 206; unreported, Clarke J., June 22, 2006 (Commission for Energy Regulation, when exercising its remit in relation to decisions concerning the grant of consent to the construction of a pipeline and the making of acquisition orders necessary for the construction of such a pipeline, expected to bring to bear, in reaching its conclusions, its own expertise on the issues concerned).

grounds of review under Irish law are much more limited than those available on a statutory appeal to the High Court under the relevant English legislation. For example, in *Bryan* the ECtHR emphasised that even findings of fact by the inspector were subject to review in certain circumstances. Regrettably, the test under Irish law—as formulated in *O'Keeffe v An Bord Pleanála*—effectively forecloses review on this basis. Scannell suggests that the "extraordinary high thresholds" set for those seeking to challenge the unreasonableness of administrative decisions must surely compromise the potential of judicial review to ensure respect for Convention rights.[126]

There are other reasons for saying that judicial review under Irish law falls short of the mark set by the ECtHR. In particular, the rigorous procedural requirements emphasised in *Bryan* are absent. First, the administrative decision-making stage rarely involves any oral hearing, still less the formal inquiry featuring in *Bryan*. Secondly, the poor quality of stated reasons for decisions makes it very difficult to ascertain whether the decision-maker had regard to all relevant considerations and disregarded irrelevant ones. Finally, in certain instances—notably the decision to issue an enforcement notice or in the case of local authority own development under s.179—there is no appeal to An Bord Pleanála. A planning authority does not even have the semblance of independence exhibited by the planning inspectorate in *Bryan*.   **14–156**

Judicial review is all the more inadequate where non-policy decisions are concerned. It is to be recalled that the decision impugned in *Bryan*—whether to grant planning permission on appeal from an enforcement notice—was a policy decision *par excellence*. Conversely, the subject-matter of many of the decisions made by the planning authorities and An Bord Pleanála—for example, a decision as to the existence of unauthorised development—are closer to the legal than to the discretionary end of the spectrum, and there is considerably less justification for deference to expert bodies. Moreover, such decisions involve fact-finding and thus there is a necessity for a more exacting standard of review. The limitations of judicial review in the particular context of enforcement notices are discussed further at para.14–228 and onwards.   **14–157**

H. Decision-Making in Respect of Planning Applications

1. Introduction

We move now to consider the practical implications of the Convention, starting with the implications for applications for planning permission. The determination of a planning application normally involves a determination of "civil rights"—those of the landowner, and possibly of neighbouring property owners—and thus will usually attract the procedural requirements of Art.6.   **14–158**

---

[126] Y. Scannell, *Environmental and Land Use Law* (Thomson Round Hall, Dublin, 2006), para.13–95.

Moreover in some instances Art.8 may also be engaged. Whilst Art.8 contains no explicit procedural requirements, the ECtHR has consistently ruled that the decision-making process leading to measures of interference must be fair and such as to afford due respect to the interests safeguarded to the individual by Art.8.[127] It seems to follow from this that, where Art.8 is applicable, the decision-making process must allow for the balancing of the Art.8 rights of any affected persons against the wider public interest. Similarly, consideration may also have to be given to property rights under Art.1 of the First Protocol.

14–159 For the purposes of the discussion following it is proposed to distinguish between decisions to grant planning permission which affect third parties, on the one hand, and decisions to refuse planning permission which affect existing homes, on the other.

2. Grant of planning permission affecting third parties

14–160 The grant of planning permission will only engage the Art.8 rights of third parties, resident in the vicinity, where the adverse effects of the development attain a certain minimum level of severity. The assessment of that minimum is relative and depends on all the circumstances of the case, such as the intensity and duration of the nuisance, and its physical or mental effects. Examples of activities which have been held to interfere with Art.8 rights include the operation of a steel plant[128]; noise from nightclubs[129]; night flights to and from an airport[130]; the operation of a chemical factory[131]; and the emission of smells, noise and polluting fumes from a plant for the treatment of liquid and solid waste.[132]

14–161 In *R. (On the application of Bushell) v Newcastle Licensing Justices*,[133] the High Court of England and Wales held that a decision to permit the special removal of an old on-licence to other premises was capable of resulting in an infringement of rights under Art.8.

14–162 The Court of Appeal in England and Wales appears to have accepted that overshadowing of a person's home might, in principle, constitute an interference under Art.8, but found on the particular facts that the "threshold level of impact would not be reached as a result of the proposed development".[134]

---

[127] *McMichael v United Kingdom* (1995) 20 E.H.R.R. 205, [87]; *Buckley v United Kingdom* (1997) 23 E.H.R.R. 101, [76]; and *Taskin v Turkey* (2006) 42 E.H.R.R. 50, [118].
[128] *Fadeyeva v Russia* (2007) 45 E.H.R.R. 10
[129] *Moreno Gómez v Spain* Application No. 4143/02; November 16, 2004.
[130] *Hatton v United Kingdom* (2003) 37 E.H.R.R. 28.
[131] *Guerra v Italy* (1998) 26 E.H.R.R. 357.
[132] *López Ostra v Spain* (1995) 20 E.H.R.R. 277.
[133] [2003] E.H.W.C. 1937 [Admin]; [2004] J.P.L. 805.
[134] *Lough v First Secretary of State* [2004] E.W.C.A. Civ. 905, [54] *per* Keene L.J.; [2005] 1 P. & C.R. 5; [2005] J.P.L. 208.

In *R. (On the application of Vetterlein) v Hampshire County Council*,[135] the **14–163** High Court of England and Wales held that generalised concerns as to the effect of an incinerator in terms of increased nitrogen dioxide emissions were not sufficient to engage Art.8.

As discussed at paras 14–50 to 14–53, a proposed development which appears **14–164** to interfere with Art.8 rights, may nevertheless be justified under Art.8(2). In summary, the interference must be in accordance with law; pursue one of the legitimate aims under Art.8(2); and be necessary in a democratic society. The first requirement, *i.e.* that the interference be in accordance with law, will, presumably, be met if the proposed development is carried out in accordance with the terms and conditions of a planning permission and any applicable licence from the Environmental Protection Agency. The latter two requirements merit further consideration.

The legitimate aims under Art.8(2) include, *inter alia*, the interests of the **14–165** economic well-being of the country and the protection of the rights and freedoms of others. Thus, in *Hatton v United Kingdom*, it was legitimate for the respondent State, in regulating night flights, to balance "the economic interests of the operators of airlines and other enterprises as well as their clients, but also, and above all, to the economic interests of the country as a whole" against the rights of individuals living in the flight path of Heathrow airport.[136] Similarly, in *Fadeyeva v Russia*,[137] the fact that the continuing operation of a steel-plant contributed to the economic system of the region was something which could be weighed in the balance.

In broad terms, then, the objective of the decision-making process is to strike a **14–166** fair balance between the various conflicting interests at stake in determining issues of environmental and economic policy. (As discussed below at para.14–169, there is some controversy as to the extent to which the test of proportionality applies.)

It seems to follow from this that while it is not necessary that "comprehensive **14–167** and measurable data are available in relation to each and every aspect of the matter to be decided", the decision-making process must involve appropriate investigations and studies in order to allow the prediction and evaluation in advance of the effects of those activities which might damage the environment and infringe individuals' rights.[138]

It also seems that there is an implicit right of public access to the conclusions **14–168** of such studies, and to information which would enable members of the public to assess the danger to which they are exposed.[139] The individuals concerned

---

[135] [2001] E.W.H.C. Admin 560; [2002] 1 P. & C.R. 31.
[136] *Hatton v United Kingdom* (2003) 37 E.H.R.R. 28, [121].
[137] (2007) 45 E.H.R.R. 10.
[138] *Taskin v Turkey* (2006) 42 E.H.R.R. 50, [119].
[139] *ibid*, [119].

must also be able to appeal to the courts against any decision, act or omission where they consider that their interests or their comments have not been given sufficient weight in the decision-making process.[140]

14–169 There has been some controversy before the courts of England and Wales as to the extent, if any, to which the principle of proportionality applies in the context of an application for planning permission. The concern seems to be that the test for proportionality only properly applies where there is a straight contest between private rights and public rights, whereas a planning application also involves the competing rights of the developer.[141]

14–170 In its classic form, the application of the principle of proportionality requires a two-stage test.[142] At the first stage, the question is: can the objective of the measure be achieved by means which are less interfering of an individual's rights? The essential purpose of this stage of the inquiry is to see whether the legitimate aim can be achieved by means that do not interfere, or interfere so much, with a person's rights under the Convention.

14–171 At the second stage, it is assumed that the means employed to achieve the legitimate aim are necessary, in the sense that they are the least intrusive of Convention rights that can be devised in order to achieve the aim. The question at this stage of the consideration is: does the measure have an excessive or disproportionate effect on the interests of affected persons?

14–172 The difficulty with the application of this two-stage approach to planning permission is that the requirement to consider—at the first stage—whether the objective might be achieved by means which are less interfering of an individual's rights might suggest that great weight must be given to whether a particular type of desirable development might be located elsewhere. To put the matter another way, it might not be sufficient for the decision-maker to say that the benefits of the proposed development outweigh the impact on third parties, and thus justify any interference with Art.8 rights. There might be an additional requirement to consider whether the benefits achieved by the grant of planning permission could have been achieved in some other way or on some other site.

14–173 The Court of Appeal has indicated, in *Lough v First Secretary of State*,[143] that the two-stage approach is not wholly appropriate to decision-making in the context of an application for planning permission, in that it does not take into account the right of a landowner to make use of his land. There was, according

---

[140] *ibid*, [119].

[141] See *Lough v First Secretary of State* [2004] E.W.C.A. Civ. 905, [49] *per* Pill L.J.; [2005] 1 P. & C.R. 5; [2005] J.P.L. 208 (right of landowner to make use of his land).

[142] See, for example, *R. (Daly) v Secretary of State for the Home Department* [2001] U.K.H.L. 26; [2001] 3 All E.R. 433; [2001] 2 W.L.R. 1622; and *R. (On the application of Samaroo) v Secretary of State for the Home Department* [2001] E.W.C.A. Civ. 1139.

[143] [2004] E.W.C.A. Civ. 905; [2005] 1 P. & C.R. 5; [2005] J.P.L. 208.

to Pill L.J., no requirement that, before any development of land is permitted, it must be established that the objectives of the development cannot be achieved in some other way or on some other site.[144]

More generally, the Court of Appeal in *Lough* suggested that the concept of proportionality was inherent in decision-making under the national legislation and that Art.8 did not achieve a "radical change in planning law". The court did caution, however, that Art.8 should be considered as an integral part of the decision-maker's approach to material considerations and not as a footnote.[145]   **14–174**

> "Recognition must be given to the fact that art 8 and art 1 of the First Protocol are part of the law of England and Wales. That being so, art 8 should in my view normally be considered as an integral part of the decision maker's approach to material considerations and not, as happened in this case, in effect as a footnote. The different approaches will often, as in my judgment in the present case, produce the same answer but if true integration is to be achieved, the provisions of the Convention should inform the decision maker's approach to the entire issue. There will be cases where the jurisprudence under art 8, and the standards it sets, will be an important factor in considering the legality of a planning decision or process. Since the exercise conducted by the Inspector, and his conclusion, were comfortably within the margin of appreciation provided by art 8 in circumstances such as the present, however, the decision is not invalidated by the process followed by the Inspector in reaching his conclusion. Moreover, any criticism by the Appellants of the Inspector on this ground would be ill-founded because he dealt with the Appellants' submissions in the order in which they had been made to him."

In *Cranage Parish Council v First Secretary of State*,[146] the High Court of England and Wales confirmed—following *Lough*—that the failure to expressly use the term "proportionality" did not, of itself, render a decision liable to be quashed. On the facts, Davis J. found that the relevant considerations had been assessed and weighed and a conclusion accordingly reached in a way and by a procedure which was compliant with Art.8.   **14–175**

What then are the implications of all of this for An Bord Pleanála and the planning authorities here? It is submitted that the relevant decision-maker must, first, consider whether the impact of the proposed development is of a severity to give rise to an interference with Art.8 rights, and, if so, to balance the rights of the individual affected against other considerations. As it is a requirement of the Convention that the justification of the interference with Art.8 rights be subject to judicial review—albeit with a significant margin of appreciation—it would seem to follow that the terms of the decision should disclose that the Art.8 issue was properly considered. This will require a change from current practice in that the quality of the stated reasons will have to improve vastly.   **14–176**

---

[144] *ibid.*, [49].
[145] *ibid.*, [48].
[146] [2004] E.W.H.C. 2949, [90]; [2005] J.P.L. 1176.

3. Decisions to refuse planning permission which affect existing homes

14–177　As discussed at paras 14–63 to 14–66, there is some controversy as to whether the refusal of planning permission for the retention of an existing home "engages" Art.8 rights. The better view seems to be that it does. Accordingly, a decision to refuse planning permission in such circumstances may require to be justified by reference to Art.8(2). In this regard, planning control has been held by the ECtHR to pursue the legitimate aim of protecting the "rights of others" through the preservation of the environment.[147]

14–178　What approach then should a decision-maker take to an application for planning permission in respect of the retention of an existing home? The case law from England and Wales indicates that the first matter to be addressed is the identification of the relevant planning policies and, in particular, the circumstances in which development will be permitted. For example, the relevant lands might be designated as a green belt, with a restriction on development save in special or exceptional circumstances.

14–179　Next, if the development is inappropriate, regard should be had to whether the personal circumstances of the applicant might nevertheless militate against the refusal of planning permission. The decision-maker should consider whether the development is appropriate. Auld L.J. suggested in *Chichester DC v First Secretary of State* that where the planning harm caused by the development is said to be weak, and the countervailing material considerations—including personal circumstances of the applicants—are said to be strong, recourse to Art.8 may add little but unnecessary complication to the balancing exercise required for a planning decision under the national provisions.[148]

14–180　Finally, the reasons stated for the decision must disclose that the requisite balancing exercise was carried out. In *R. (On the application of Gosbee) v First Secretary of State*,[149] Elias J. stated that it is the duty of the court to be satisfied that the inspector has given careful consideration ("anxious scrutiny") to ensure that the relevant considerations bearing on the human rights issues have been properly weighed. Elias J. went on to say that questions of proportionality are highly facts-sensitive and it is necessary that there should be an intense scrutiny of the material facts in order for the balancing exercised to be carried out.[150]

14–181　Personal circumstances which have been found to be relevant and to be weighed in the balance include the following: age; health; and educational needs.

14–182　The absence of alternative accommodation elsewhere is relevant, but the mere fact that there is no identified alternative site does not necessarily mean that it

---

[147] *Chapman v United Kingdom* (2001) 33 E.H.R.R. 18, [82].
[148] [2004] E.W.C.A. Civ. 1248, [63]; [2005] J.P.L. 1029.
[149] [2003] E.W.H.C. 770; [2003] J.P.L. 1467.
[150] *ibid.*, [23].

is disproportionate to require the land to be vacated.[151] Somewhat controversially, a majority of the Court of Appeal in *Chichester DC v First Secretary of State* accepted that the failure of the relevant local authority to recognise and provide for the needs of gypsies in the district was a relevant consideration in deciding to grant planning permission. This was so notwithstanding the fact that the ECtHR itself has emphasised that Art.8 does not extend to a right to be provided with a home, and that whether a contracting State provides funds to enable everyone to have a home is a matter for political and not judicial decision.[152]

The significance of a "home" having been established unlawfully was considered in *South Bucks DC v Porter (No. 2)*.[153] The House of Lords, *per* Lord Brown of Eaton-under-Heywood, did not accept that the unlawfulness of development could never properly militate against the retrospective grant of planning permission. Lord Brown made the further point that there was a distinction between a development without planning permission, and one which has been persisted in for many years despite being enforced against. **14–183**

In considering whether the interference is disproportionate, it may be appropriate for the decision-maker to address his mind to whether planning permission might be granted on a *temporary* basis.[154] It is probably incumbent on the applicant for planning permission to canvass the possibility of a temporary planning permission.[155] **14–184**

In *R. (On the application of Chelmsford BC) v First Secretary of State*,[156] the High Court of England and Wales held that the relevant decision-maker had acted unreasonably in concluding that the educational needs of the gypsy's children represented a "very special circumstance" within the meaning of the relevant planning policy. There was no evidence that the children had special educational needs that were being met at a local school with particular expertise in meeting those needs, nor was there evidence that having to move schools would be particularly disruptive to the child's education because, for example, of the child's physical or mental health or the stage reached in the educational curriculum. On the facts, Sullivan J. considered the educational needs—both in terms of the number of children involved and in terms of their individual needs—to be entirely normal. **14–185**

---

[151] *Egan v Secretary of State for Transport Local Government and the Regions* [2002] E.W.H.C. 389.

[152] See, for example, *Chapman v United Kingdom* (2001) 33 E.H.R.R. 18, [99].

[153] [2004] U.K.H.L. 33.

[154] *Lee v First Secretary of State* [2003] E.W.H.C. Admin 3235. *Cf. Woods v First Secretary of State* [2004] E.W.H.C. 456.

[155] *Ayres v Secretary of State for the Environment Transport and the Regions* [2002] E.W.H.C. 295.

[156] [2003] E.W.H.C. 2978; [2004] 2 P. & C.R. 34. See also *Doncaster MBC v Secretary of State for the Environment Transport and the Regions* [2002] E.W.H.C. 808.

Standard of judicial review

14–186   It seems that the requirement to perform the necessary Art.8 balancing exercise resides principally with the planning bodies, and that this is subject only to limited judicial review. This would seem to follow, by analogy, from the approach taken by the ECtHR to the margin of appreciation to be shown to the contracting States in the context of planning and environmental controls. Reference is made in this regard to the judgment in *Chapman v United Kingdom*.[157]

> "The judgment in any particular case by the national authorities that there are legitimate planning objections to a particular use of a site is one which the court is not well equipped to challenge. It cannot visit each site to assess the impact of a particular proposal on a particular area in terms of impact on beauty, traffic conditions, sewerage and water facilities, educational facilities, medical facilities, employment opportunities and so on. Because planning inspectors visit the site, hear the arguments on all sides and allow examination of witnesses, they are better situated than the court to weigh the arguments. Hence, as the court observed in *Buckley v UK* [1996] ECHR 20348/92 at para 75, 'in so far as the exercise of discretion involving a multitude of local factors is inherent in the choice and implementation of planning policies, the national authorities in principle enjoy a wide margin of appreciation', although it remains open to the court to conclude that there has been a manifest error of appreciation by the national authorities. In these circumstances, the procedural safeguards available to the individual applicant will be especially material in determining whether the respondent state has, when fixing the regulatory framework, remained within its margin of appreciation. In particular, it must examine whether the decision-making process leading to measures of interference was fair and such as to afford due respect to the interests safeguarded to the individual by art 8 (see *Buckley v UK* (1997) 23 E.H.R.R. 101)."

14–187   The High Court of England and Wales has suggested, in *Buckland v Secretary of State for the Environment Transport and the Regions*,[158] that many of the same arguments as articulated in *Chapman* apply to the High Court's ability to review planning decisions.[159] On judicial review, the court was not required to satisfy itself that the relevant decision-maker had struck the right balance between planning policy and the applicants' Art.8 rights. Striking that balance was, according to Sullivan J., a matter for the decision-maker, using his own planning expertise in the light of all the evidence, including, most importantly in so many planning cases, the site visit.

14–188   The High Court of England and Wales also rejected a similar argument that where Art.8 is engaged the court, on an application for judicial review, should apply a heightened standard of review, in *R. (On the application of Evans) v First Secretary of State*.[160]

---

[157] *ibid.*, [92].
[158] [2001] E.W.C.A. Admin 524; [2002] J.P.L. 570.
[159] See, generally, Maurici "Gypsy planning challenges in the High Court" [2004] J.P.L. 1654.
[160] [2005] E.W.H.C. Admin 149; [2005] J.P.L. 1343.

I. Default Planning Permission

As discussed above, the adjudication on an application for planning permission **14–189** involves a "determination" of civil rights within the meaning of Art.6(1). Moreover, it may also engage property rights under Art.1 of the First Protocol, and, in some cases, Art.8 rights.

It is submitted that the requirement for a fair hearing, and, in the case of Art.8 **14–190** and Art.1 of the First Protocol, the requirement for some form of balancing exercise to be carried out, entail an implicit proscription on default or deemed decisions. Accordingly, it is submitted that the provision under s.34(8)(f) of the PDA 2000, whereby a decision to grant planning permission is to be regarded as having been given where a planning authority fails to make a decision within time, is incompatible with the Convention.

By definition, a default decision to grant planning permission involves no **14–191** consideration of the planning merits of the application. Accordingly, there is a clear breach of Art.6 in that there is no hearing, still less a fair and public hearing.

Insofar as Art.8 rights are concerned, there is no balancing of the rights of **14–192** third parties whose homes may be adversely affected by the permitted development. This is especially so as a default planning permission is not subject to any conditions. Thus whereas it might have been legitimate, having performed the necessary balancing test and attached suitable conditions, to permit, for example, industrial development adjacent to existing homes, the grant by default of an unconditional planning permission might well involve an unjustifiable interference with Art.8 rights.

Moreover, the provision for default planning permission can be said to be **14–193** disproportionate. The mischief to be remedied is that of planning authorities delaying in adjudicating on planning applications. Arguably a lengthy delay in this regard would constitute a breach of the developer's rights under Art.6 (and possibly his rights under Art.1 of the First Protocol). The provision for default planning permission goes too far the other way, however, in that it does not properly observe the Art.8 rights of neighbouring third parties. A more proportionate approach would be to provide that a decision to *refuse* planning permission should be deemed to have been made where the planning authority fails to make a decision within time. The developer would then be able to appeal the decision to An Bord Pleanála.

J. Planning Injunction

1. General

14–194 A court enjoys a wide discretion in deciding whether or not to grant a planning injunction under s.160 of the PDA 2000. The nature and extent of this discretion is discussed in Chapter 7, at paras 7–166 to 7–195. The discussion in the present chapter is confined to the question as to whether in deciding to grant or refuse an injunction, the court may have to apply a test of proportionality.

14–195 In certain instances the effect of an order under s.160 will be to require the discontinuance of the use (and possibly the removal) of an existing home, and thus may engage Art.8 rights.[161] Even where an existing home is not involved, an order may affect the property rights of the landowner—for example, by requiring the demolition of existing buildings—and thus engage Art.1 of the First Protocol. A question arises, therefore, as to whether the previous practice of the Irish courts needs to be modified, in light of s.2 of the ECHR Act 2003, so as to ensure that the s.160 procedure is compatible with the Convention. As appears from the discussion which follows, the short answer to this question is that some changes will be required, and, in particular, the courts will need to make express reference to the concept of "proportionality".[162]

14–196 It is well established that the court enjoys a wide discretion under s.160. Ever before the ECHR Act 2003, a court had been entitled to take into account hardship to the respondent in deciding whether or not to grant relief. Thus for example, where an injunction was sought against travellers, the court had been entitled to take into account any breach of relevant local authority's statutory duty to provide halting sites, seemingly even where this might prejudice third party landowners.[163]

14–197 The requirements of the Convention, and, in particular, the requirement to consider the proportionality of the enforcement measures, probably adds little more than emphasis in this respect.[164] The reality is that the Irish courts, although not using the term "proportionality", were already having regard to the personal circumstances of respondents in deciding whether or not to grant planning

---

[161] See, generally, paras 14–63 to 14–66.

[162] See, for example, *Coates v South Buckinghamshire District Council* [2004] E.W.C.A. 1378; [2005] J.P.L. 668, [7].

[163] See, for example, *County Meath V.E.C. v Joyce* [1994] 2 I.L.R.M. 210, where the immediate relief sought was apparently denied to the applicant, who was a neighbouring landowner.

[164] See *South Bucks District Council v Porter (No. 1)* [2003] U.K.H.L. 26; [2003] A.C. 558; [2003] J.P.L. 1412, where Lord Bingham of Cornhill suggested that when asked to grant injunctive relief the court must consider whether, on the facts of the case, such relief is proportionate in the Convention sense, and grant relief only if it judges it to be so. His Lordship went on to suggest that this was in all essentials the task which the court was in any event required by national law to carry out, notwithstanding that national law was expressed in terms of justice and convenience rather than proportionality.

injunctions. This exercise will, however, have to be placed on a more formal footing in light of the ECHR Act 2003. In particular, the court should make it clear when ruling on a s.160 application that it has considered the issue of proportionality.

> "The judge's reasons should make clear to the parties why he has reached his decision. Where he has had to balance competing factors it will usually be possible to explain why he has concluded that some have outweighed others. Even where the competition is so unequal that the factors speak for themselves it is desirable to say so."[165]

2. Personal circumstances

In very broad terms, a court will be required to decide whether the considerations in favour of granting the injunction outweigh the interference with the right to respect for a person's home or property. Obviously, this will be a question of fact and degree in each case. The principal factor which may weigh against the grant of an injunction will be the personal circumstances of the respondents. For example, if a particular respondent suffers from ill-health, this may well tell against the grant of an injunction.[166] The fact that the respondents may have links with the local area—in particular in terms of the education of children—may also be relevant. The grant of an injunction might, for example, result in the family having to move far away from the children's current school.[167]

14–198

The fact that the respondents may have no alternative accommodation available to them should also be given some weight, especially where there is a suggestion that the relevant local authority has failed to discharge a statutory obligation to provide such accommodation.

14–199

3. Prospect of planning permission being secured

The House of Lords indicated in *South Bucks District Council v Porter (No. 1)*[168] that the prospect of planning permission being secured is another matter which may point against the grant of an injunction. Indeed, in the events that transpired, a number of the respondents in *Porter* did subsequently obtain planning permission. The courts of England and Wales are, therefore, entitled to have regard to the likelihood of a pending or prospective planning application succeeding, and would be entitled to grant an injunction where the previous

14–200

---

[165] *Coates v South Buckinghamshire District Council* [2004] E.W.C.A. 1378, [7]; [2005] J.P.L. 668.

[166] *South Bucks District Council v Porter (No. 1)* [2003] U.K.H.L. 26; [2003] A.C. 558; [2003] J.P.L. 1412.

[167] *cf. South Bucks District Council v Smith* [2006] E.W.H.C. 281; [2006] J.P.L. 1519 (evidence suggested that family would not have to move far).

[168] [2003] U.K.H.L. 26; [2003] A.C. 558; [2003] J.P.L. 1412.

planning history indicated that there was no "real prospect" that planning permission would be granted.[169]

14–201   The extent to which this may be a legitimate consideration under Irish law is uncertain. Section 162(3) of the PDA 2000 (as amended) indicates that enforcement proceedings are not to be stayed or withdrawn by reason of an application for retention planning permission. See, generally, paras 7–08 to 7–11.

4. Public interest in planning control

14–202   Thus far, the discussion has focussed on the rights of the respondents and, in particular, the need to take their personal circumstances into account in deciding whether or not to grant an injunction. Of course, the concept of proportionality involves the balancing of competing rights, and it is important therefore that the countervailing public interest in enforcing planning law not be lost sight of. In *South Bucks District Council v Porter*, Lord Bingham of Cornhill stated that where it appears that a breach or apprehended breach will continue or occur unless and until effectively restrained by law, and that nothing short of an injunction will provide effective restraint, this will point strongly towards the grant of an injunction.[170] Similarly, a history of unsuccessful enforcement and persistent non-compliance will also point towards the grant of an injunction.

14–203   The impetus to grant an injunction will be even greater where the unauthorised development has been carried out in breach of an existing court order. In *Mid-Bedfordshire DC v Brown*,[171] gypsies had breached an earlier court order and brought further caravans onto a site. The Court of Appeal overturned the decision of the High Court to suspend the injunction pending the determination of a planning application, on the basis that that decision did not take proper account of "the vital role of the court in upholding the important principle that the orders of the court are meant to be obeyed and not to be ignored with impunity".

> "The practical effect of suspending the injunction has been to allow the defendants to change the use of the land and to retain the benefit of occupation of the land with caravans for residential purposes. This was in defiance of a court order properly served on them and correctly explained to them. In those circumstances there is a real risk that the suspension of the injunction would be perceived as condoning the breach. This would send out the wrong signal, both to others tempted to do the same and to law-abiding members of the public. The message would be that the court is prepared to tolerate contempt of its orders and to permit those who break them to profit from their contempt.

---

[169] *South Cambridgeshire District Council v Flynn* [2006] E.W.H.C. 1320 ("real prospect"). *Cf. South Bucks District Council v Smith* [2006] E.W.H.C. 281; [2006] J.P.L. 1519 (injunction refused while there remained "a real, even if not a good, chance" that in due course planning permission might be obtained).
[170] [2003] U.K.H.L. 26; [2003] A.C. 558; [2003] J.P.L. 1412, [29].
[171] [2004] E.W.C.A. Civ. 1709; [2005] J.P.L. 1060.

The effect of that message would be to diminish respect for court orders, to undermine the authority of the court and to subvert the rule of law. In our judgment, those overarching public interest considerations far outweigh the factors which favour a suspension of the injunction so as to allow the defendants to keep their caravans on the land and to continue to reside there in breach of planning control."[172]

An interesting example of the divergent views which can be taken on the application of the test proportionality in this context is to be found in the judgments of the Court of Appeal of England and Wales in *Coates v South Buckinghamshire District Council*.[173] The issue before the Court of Appeal was as to whether an obligation to comply with an injunction should be stayed pending the determination of a proposed application for planning permission. The relevant lands were being used as an unauthorised halting site. The unchallenged evidence was that the lands were located in a particularly sensitive greenbelt area. There was a history of planning refusals on the site.

14–204

The majority of the Court of Appeal took the view that the operation of the injunction should not be stayed pending the determination of any application for planning permission. Lord Phillips M.R. put the matter thus.[174]

14–205

"[...] The plight of Gypsies or others who travel in caravans with no permanent place to rest in is an unhappy one. They can rightly complain that their plight reflects a failure on the part of some authorities to comply with their statutory duty to provide sites for such travellers. That cannot, however, entitle them to stop wherever they choose and contend that their rights under Art. 8 entitles them to remain. The other factors that I have outlined make the overall picture particularly unattractive. The site chosen was a very sensitive part of the greenbelt. It was a site where Gypsies had already fought and lost a lengthy planning battle. It was, to their knowledge, subject to an enforcement notice. Some person or persons was or were conducting a commercial adventure, involving bulldozing the site and selling off plots, knowing that this was unlawful. The court orders were flouted. If the appellants are permitted to remain on the site, despite such conduct this is likely to be seen as an open invitation to similar lawlessness. These are the considerations that weight most with me. This is a case where the legitimate aim of maintaining a planning regime really does not make it necessary to interfere with the Art. 8 rights of the appellants. Added to this is the fact that the prospect of planning permission ever being granted for this site is remote."

Sedley L.J. dissented on the facts.[175]

14–206

"The strong arguments for immediate eviction is the disgraceful history, spelt out by the Judge and summarised by Lord Philips M.R., of outright defiance of two orders of the court as well as the legitimate enforcement action by the Council – not so much by staying put as by bringing more and more caravans and dwellers on the land. But this seems to me to be the crux of the proportionality issue: is

---

[172] *ibid.*, [26]–[27].
[173] [2004] E.W.C.A. Civ. 1378; [2005] J.P.L. 668.
[174] *ibid.*, [24].
[175] *ibid.*, [36].

immediate eviction irrelevant and necessary response to this contumacious conduct, or is it a punishment – mass punishment, in fact – which relates less to the rights and freedoms of others or to the prevention of disorder or crime (the material Art.8(2) factors) than to the need of the court to vindicate its own authority? The latter is a proper and entirely legitimate imperative which in equity may often be sufficient to justify an order which would not otherwise be justified. But the Convention rights do not necessarily fall out in the same way. It does not appear to me, with great respect, that either the judgment below or the other judgments in this court address this essential issue."

14–207 Sedley L.J. went on then to state that there were other ways in which a court could deal with contumacious defiance of orders, citing fines on those directly responsible, imprisonment or penal awards of costs. Sedley L.J. concluded that if the consequence is that the travellers remained where they were until the next summer, it was "not the end of the world".

14–208 In *Bromley London Borough Council v Maughan*,[176] an injunction had been granted restraining the stationing or causing to be stationed any caravans on certain lands. The order was made against persons unknown in the sense that the defendants were identified only as "the owners" of the relevant lands. The order provided that an application to vary or discharge the order could be made on notice to the local authority's solicitor. Mrs Maughan purchased, and moved caravans onto, the lands *after* the planning injunction had been granted. Committal proceedings were brought against Mrs Maughan and others, and they were found to be in breach of the order and in contempt of court. It was argued before the Court of Appeal that the court below should have had regard, in the context of that committal proceedings, to her Art.8 rights and to ought to have engaged in the requisite balancing exercise.

14–209 The Court of Appeal distinguished the decision in *South Bucks District Council v Porter (No. 1)*[177] on the basis that in *Porter* each of the respondents had been in occupation of the lands at the time the injunction had been granted. In the instant appeals, each of the gypsies became an occupier of the land after the injunction was granted.[178]

> "By the time of the committal proceedings, in each case the Appellant was a defendant to the proceedings, was in breach of the injunction and, given her state of knowledge, was in contempt of court. Those conclusions follow in each case from the terms of the injunction, the actions of the Appellant and the state of knowledge of the Appellant. The conclusions do not depend upon any judicial decision involving the exercise of any discretion or balance on the part of a judge. The exercise of such a discretion or balance only arises on an original application by a claimant for an injunction against a named party, on any subsequent application to vary or discharge by a person named as a defendant, and affected by the injunction, and to some extent at least in the course of a sentencing exercise."

---

[176] [2005] E.W.C.A. Civ. 1429.
[177] [2003] U.K.H.L. 26; [2003] A.C. 558; [2003] J.P.L. 1412.
[178] [2005] E.W.C.A. Civ. 1429, [33].

The Court of Appeal went out to explain that a person who takes action in **14–210** breach of the injunction in the knowledge that he is in breach may apply to the court to vary the injunction for the future. He should acknowledge that he is in breach and explain why he took the action knowing of the injunction. The court will then take account of all the circumstances of the case, including the reasons for the injunction, the reasons for the breach and the applicant's personal circumstances, in deciding whether to vary the injunction for the future and in deciding what, if any, penalty the court should impose for a contempt committed when he took the action in breach of the injunction.

5. Respective roles of court and planning authority

The extent to which a court should defer to the views of the planning authority **14–211** when deciding to grant or refuse a planning injunction has been examined in some detail by the House of Lords in *South Bucks District Council v Porter (No. 1)*.[179] The relevant planning authorities had argued that it was for the planning authority to determine whether an injunction was appropriate, and for the court, exercising a limited review jurisdiction, to grant an injunction in terms suited to restraining the relevant breach. The Convention, or so it was said, did not require the court to consider for itself matters of policy or expediency, or to decide where the balance lay between the interests of the respondent and the wider interests of the community.

The House of Lords rejected these submissions. The House of Lords ruled that **14–212** the jurisdiction to grant an injunction was an original, not a supervisory, jurisdiction. Thus, a respondent seeking to defend an application for an injunction was not restricted to grounds which would found an application for judicial review.[180] A court was not obliged to grant an injunction because a local authority considers it necessary or expedient for any actual or apprehended breach of planning control to be restricted by an injunction and makes application to the court.[181] A court hearing an application for an injunction was entitled to take into account factors such as the personal circumstances of, and hardship to, the respondent.[182]

In attempting to demark the respective roles of the courts and the planning **14–213** authorities, the House of Lords sought to draw a distinction between the decision of the local authority to seek to take enforcement action (which decision was not binding on the court) and other decisions—for example, in terms of previous refusals of planning permission or the policies of the relevant development plan—which normally should be accorded some respect by the court. Thus, whereas it would never be appropriate for a court to hold that planning permission should not have been refused, a court was not precluded from

---

[179] [2003] U.K.H.L. 26; [2003] A.C. 558; [2003] J.P.L. 1412.
[180] [2003] U.K.H.L. 26, [27]; [2003] 2 A.C. 558.
[181] *ibid.*, [28].
[182] *ibid.*, [31], [73] and [83].

entertaining issues not related to planning policy or judgment, such as the visibility of a development from a given position or the width of a road.

14–214 Lord Hutton suggested that a court is as well placed as a planning authority to decide whether considerations relating to the human factor outweigh purely planning considerations, and that the weight to be attached to the personal circumstances of a defendant in deciding whether a coercive order should be made against him is a task which is constantly performed by the courts.[183]

14–215 Lord Clyde suggested that the enforcement of planning decisions which have been reached by planning authorities did not strictly involve the exercise of a planning judgment.

14–216 Injunctive relief was ultimately refused in *South Bucks District Council* on the particular facts. Whereas the lands were located within a green belt, there was no suggestion that there was any urgent environmental problem. Factors pointing against the grant of an injunction included problems of health and the lack of alternative accommodation. Some weight was also attached to the fact that the case for the grant of planning permission were far from hopeless on the merits.

K. Enforcement Notices

1. General

14–217 There must be very real doubts as to whether the enforcement notice procedure is compliant with the Convention. The principal concern is that a planning authority is afforded Draconian powers without there being any necessity for court approval. The effect of the service of an enforcement notice is to authorise a planning authority, following the expiration of the period allowed under the notice, to enter onto land and take such steps as are specified in the notice. This may involve the demolition of structures and the restoration of land. It is only if the planning authority wishes to pursue a criminal prosecution for failure to comply with the notice that it is necessary to bring the matter before the court: the power to enter and carry on works is self-executing.

14–218 Given its role in policy-making—in particular, as author of the development plan—a planning authority does not meet the Art.6(1) requirement of independence and impartiality. Moreover, the procedural safeguards leading up to a decision to issue an enforcement notice are deficient. There is only a limited opportunity for the alleged developer to make submissions, and there is no provision for an oral hearing. As discussed presently, judicial review does not provide an effective remedy in this regard.

---

[183] *ibid*, [86].

The legitimacy of the procedure is further undermined by the following. There **14–219** are no principles and policies set out under the PDA 2000 as to in what circumstances enforcement action is justified, nor as to what considerations a planning authority is to take into account in deciding whether to issue an enforcement notice. For example, it is not clear whether an enforcement notice may only be served where the development is objectionable in planning terms and any application for planning permission would inevitably be refused, or whether the planning authority may decide to penalise a regulatory breach, *i.e.* the failure to apply for planning permission in advance of development, by requiring the removal of development which is not objectionable *per se*.

An attempt had been made by the High Court in the context of the previous **14–220** planning legislation—in advance of the ECHR Act 2003—to redress the balance in favour of the recipient of an enforcement notice. In his judgment in *Dublin Corporation v O'Callaghan*,[184] Herbert J. stated that the making of a decision that it was expedient to serve an enforcement notice must be attended by some formality, by some recording of the fact that a decision to serve such a notice had been taken and the basis upon which it had been determined that it was expedient so to do. (It had been an express requirement of the previous legislation that the planning authority decide that it was "expedient" to serve an enforcement notice.)

Even if a similar obligation is read into Pt VIII of the PDA 2000, and a planning **14–221** authority does disclose its thinking, the difficulty still remains that, in the absence of any statement of principles and policies, it is simply not possible to say what are relevant and what are irrelevant considerations. This standardless delegation means that the discretion of the planning authority is effectively unreviewable.

Article 6

The procedure falls to be analysed in Convention terms as follows. The **14–222** administrative decision-making stage is *prima facie* in breach of Art.6(1). The effects of an enforcement notice are so serious that there can be no doubt that the decision to issue one involves a "determination" of the affected landowner's rights. The planning authority is not independent and impartial. Thus unless there is sufficient review of the planning authority's actions available elsewhere, there is a breach of Art.6(1).

There is no statutory appeal against an enforcement notice and thus judicial **14–223** review is the only other "stage" of the decision-making process. As the availability of judicial review has some relevance—albeit to a much lesser extent—in the context of Art.8 and Art.1 of the First Protocol, a detailed discussion of same will be deferred until we have briefly considered these other two articles. The discussion of judicial review begins at para.14–228.

---

[184] Unreported, High Court, Herbert J., February 13, 2001.

Article 1 of the First Protocol

14–224 Turning now to Art.1 of the First Protocol, it is submitted that the enforcement notice procedure breaches both the requirement for proportionality, and the implicit requirement that the affected individual must be afforded a reasonable opportunity of putting his or her case to the responsible authorities for the purpose of effectively challenging the measures interfering with his property rights.

14–225 To allow a planning authority to enter onto lands and to carry out works which might include the demolition of valuable structures represents an interference with property rights. Such interference would undoubtedly be disproportionate unless there were strong planning reasons justifying the demolition.[185] Yet on one view, discussed above at para.14–219, the purpose of an enforcement notice may be regulatory in the sense of penalising failure to apply for planning permission in advance of development. If this is correct, then on a literal reading of the legislation a planning authority is perfectly entitled, as a matter of national law, to issue an enforcement irregardless of such considerations.

14–226 Moreover, the absence of proper procedural safeguards, and the lack of any coherent statement of principles and policies under Pt VIII of the PDA 2000, offends against the implicit requirement under the Convention that the applicable provisions of national law are sufficiently accessible, precise and foreseeable in their application.

Article 8

14–227 Moving on to Art.8, the service of an enforcement notice is capable of engaging Art.8 rights where the notice purports to require the removal of an existing home. The enforcement notice procedure is deficient in that there is no requirement for the planning authority to weigh up Art.8 rights, and there is only limited opportunity afforded to an affected party to make submissions to the planning authority in advance of a decision to issue and serve an enforcement notice.

2. Judicial review

14–228 As appears from the foregoing, the enforcement notice procedure is suspect. It should be recalled, however, that the ECtHR has indicated that in assessing procedural safeguards—especially in the context of Art.6(1)—it is necessary to examine the entire of the decision-making process. In principle, a decision of a planning authority to issue an enforcement notice is subject to judicial

---

[185] In *R. v Leominster District Council, Ex p. Pothecary* [1998] J.P.L. 335, the Court of Appeal *per* Schiemann L.J. suggested that there would be situations where the planning authority would not have given permission for the development if asked for permission for precisely that which had been built, but the development would not so be objectionable that it would be reasonable to require it to be pulled down.

review, and therefore, again in principle, it may be that some of the concerns identified above are made good by the availability of judicial review. The test in this regard is whether the High Court can be said to have "full jurisdiction".

As discussed above at para.14–139, the intensity of review required before a tribunal or court can be said to have "full jurisdiction" depends, *inter alia*, on the subject-matter of the impugned decision, and the manner in which the first-instance decision was arrived at. In the context of the enforcement notice procedure, both of these aspects indicate that an exacting standard of review is required. **14–229**

First, the decision whether or not to take enforcement action is not simply one of planning judgment. The decision involves the consideration of a range of matters, both legal and factual. Thus the subject-matter is not such as to justify a deferential standard of review. For example, there may be a dispute as to whether the development is unauthorised, in which case the statutory concepts of "development" and "exempted development" will have to be interpreted and applied. The subject-matter of the decision is thus to be contrasted with, for example, the decision to refuse or grant planning permission, which requires the subjective assessment of planning policy, and consequently a more deferential standard of review ("margin of appreciation") will be justified. Moreover, a decision on whether to take enforcement action may require the resolution of factual disputes ("findings of fact"), a task alien to most other forms of decision-making under the planning legislation. **14–230**

Secondly, the marked absence of procedural safeguards at the planning authority stage means that there is a significant gap to be bridged before it can be said that the requirement for a fair and public hearing has been met. Thus, in order to have "full jurisdiction", the High Court would have to provide an opportunity to the alleged developer to make submissions and to challenge findings of fact by the planning authority. The position is to be contrasted with that obtaining in *Bryan v United Kingdom*,[186] where the limited nature of review of facts was held to be justified because the facts had already been established in the course of a quasi-judicial procedure governed by many of the safeguards required by Art.6(1).[187] The ECtHR had placed particular emphasis on the safeguards attending the procedure before the inspector: the quasi-judicial character of the decision-making process; the duty incumbent on each inspector to exercise independent judgment; the requirement that inspectors must not be subject to any improper influence; and the stated mission of the inspectorate to uphold the principles of openness, fairness and impartiality. **14–231**

The grounds on which judicial review is available under existing Irish law simply do not allow for any meaningful review of the substance or merits of decisions of a planning authority. Yet, in Convention terms, the shortcomings **14–232**

---

[186] (1996) 21 E.H.R.R. 342.
[187] *ibid.*, [47].

of the enforcement notice procedure can only be remedied by allowing the developer to make arguments before the High Court addressed to the merits of the decision to take enforcement action. This is the only way in which the lack of independence and impartiality and absence of fair procedures can be made good. Such a hands-on approach is likely to prove an anathema to the Irish High Court.

14–233 The real stumbling block is the judgment of the Supreme Court in *O'Keeffe v An Bord Pleanála*. As discussed in Chapter 12, this judgment effectively precludes any challenge to the merits of decisions by the planning authorities or An Bord Pleanála. For the reasons already discussed at para.14–230, it is submitted that such a deferential standard of review is inappropriate in the context of a decision to issue an enforcement notice. Notwithstanding this it seems almost inevitable that the *O'Keeffe* principles would be applied to a decision to issue an enforcement notice. Although there is no judgment directly on point in the context of enforcement notices, the recent judgment of the Supreme Court in *Grianán an Aileach Interpretative Centre Company Ltd v Donegal County Council*[188] suggests that the deferential standard of review is—unjustifiably—being extended to decisions reached by the planning bodies on non-policy matters. See further paras 10–29 to 10–31.

14–234 The limited grounds on which judicial review is available under Irish law also present difficulties in the context of Art.8. It will be recalled that amongst the grounds suggested earlier for saying that the enforcement notice procedure is not compliant with the Convention is that there is no requirement to consider, on the facts, whether the removal of structures is disproportionate.

14–235 It seems unlikely that this defect is capable of being remedied by judicial review. Under Irish law, judicial review is principally concerned with the procedural aspects of the decision-making process. Thus, the court will examine matters such as whether the prescribed procedures have been followed, or whether the decision-maker has taken into account irrelevant considerations or failed to have regard to relevant ones. These traditional grounds of review are next to worthless in the absence of a clear statement of principles and polices under Pt VIII of the PDA 2000. To put the matter another way, judicial review is only as good as the underlying legislation: if that legislation fails to lay down principles and policies, then it will be difficult, if not impossible, to say whether the planning authority has confined itself to relevant considerations.

14–236 Reference is made to the judgment of the ECtHR in *Connors v United Kingdom*.[189] Judicial review was held not to be sufficient to make good the absence of procedural safeguards in a summary eviction procedure. Judicial review could only hold the local authority to the statutory scheme, and that statutory scheme had been interpreted by the national courts as not requiring

---

[188] [2004] 2 I.R. 625.
[189] (2005) 40 E.H.R.R. 9.

the local authority to establish any substantive justification for eviction. It is submitted that, similarly, the failure under Pt VIII to require a planning authority to justify the issuing of an enforcement undermines the utility of judicial review in this context also.

3. Analogy with case law from England and Wales

An analogy can be drawn with recent case law from England and Wales. In *R. (On the application of O'Brien) v Basildon District Council*,[190] it was argued that it was disproportionate for a planning authority to take direct action pursuant to an enforcement notice. The planning authority had served enforcement notices in respect of unauthorised halting sites. The planning authority then decided to take steps to remove the caravans so as to enforce compliance with the enforcement notices ("direct action"). The travellers challenged that decision by way of judicial review proceedings. **14–237**

In summary, the High Court upheld the right in principle of the planning authority to take direct action to remove the unauthorised caravans without any necessity for a court application, but found on the facts that the planning authority had not given proper consideration to the personal circumstances of the gypsies in reaching the decision to take direct action. **14–238**

The High Court emphasised the procedural protections available before an enforcement notice becomes effective. **14–239**

> "[…] The enforcement process envisages a decision to issue an enforcement notice, an appeal, appeal rights against that enforcement notice (the grounds for which can cover planning merits, including individual circumstances) lesser measures than the removal of the caravans to remedy the harm, and time in which to comply with the requirements of the enforcement notice."[191]

The judgment goes on to indicate that the question of any interference with Art.8 rights is properly considered at this planning merits stage. **14–240**

> "I see that decision making structure as generally demonstrative of proportionality in both the consideration of individual cases, balancing their needs against policies reflective of the wider public interest and in the framework of decision making, which includes appeal against the steps required and the time allowed for compliance. The grant of a temporary or permanent planning permission has always been an option available for argument through an appeal."[192]

The High Court rejected an argument that a decision to take direct action was necessarily unlawful and disproportionate because it involved a residential eviction. There was no requirement under the relevant legislation for a [further] procedural safeguard of civil proceedings or the interposition of the court **14–241**

---

[190] [2006] E.W.H.C. 1346 (Admin); [2007] 1 P. & C.R. 16.
[191] *ibid.*, [145].
[192] *ibid.*, [150].

between the planning authority and those to be removed. The judgment goes on to note that the claimants had actual notice of the decision to take direct action, and they had sufficient time to enable them to challenge the lawfulness of that decision. The High Court considered that judicial review, with whatever intensity of review is appropriate for the decision, coupled with the procedures for substantive decision-making, which the planning system involves, provided all the procedural protection necessary for interference by direct action with Art. 8 rights to be proportionate.

14–242 On the particular facts, however, the High Court found that the planning authority had failed to have regard to all relevant considerations in reaching its decision to take direct action. In particular, the planning authority had failed to assess the claimants' prospects of success in their appeal against the refusal of planning permission. It was not necessarily sufficient, and certainly not in a residential eviction case, for the planning authority to say that all that matters is the determination of which is the swiftest and most effective remedy available.

> "The power given by s 178, when used as I conclude the Act permits, for residential eviction is a drastic power. Even when notice is given, as here, of the decision and of the actual taking of the action (steps likely to be necessary for this mode of action to be proportionate), s 178 remains a drastic step in these circumstances.
>
> It is in my view necessary for a local planning authority in deciding whether to use s 178 to consider and weigh various factors: the degree of harm done to the interests protected by planning control; the need for a swift or urgent remedy; the need to uphold and enforce planning control embodied in an effective enforcement notice and the criminal law; the personal circumstances and impact on the individuals of removal."[193]

14–243 It appears from the later judgment in *R. (On the application of Smith) v South Norfolk Council*[194] that the role of a court in reviewing a decision to take direct action is different from that involved where it is exercising its discretionary jurisdiction in deciding whether or not to grant a planning injunction.

> "First, the court is still reviewing the lawfulness of the decision; it is not taking a decision itself as to whether it would use s 178 powers, nor is it asking whether it would grant an injunction. The review is undertaken with the degree of intensity appropriate to the fact that the interference with art 8 rights would leave a group of people with children and who have particular needs, to camp by the roadside, or being moved on to other equally unsatisfactory locations. There is still scope for a discretionary area of judgment to be accorded not just to planners on areas of planning evaluation which the court is less well placed to judge, but also to the views of those who have local responsibilities, know their area and have had to consider the issues, including the need for effective enforcement, with the expertise and experience which they have. The court does not have full merits appeal before it."

---

[193] *ibid.*, [183]–[184].
[194] [2006] E.W.H.C. 2772 (Admin), [62].

Relevance for Irish law

These two judgments emphasise the necessity that Art.8 rights be considered **14–244** before the "drastic power" of direct action pursuant to an enforcement notice is exercised. These cases were decided against a statutory background which provides procedural protection at the stage of the service of an enforcement notice. There is a statutory right of appeal against an enforcement notice, and the making of an appeal has the effect of suspending the effect of the notice until the final determination of the appeal. The High Court envisaged a further layer of protection at the stage of the decision to take direct action, with the planning authority being required to consider whether the taking of such action would be proportionate in the circumstances.

It was only against this background of comprehensive procedural safeguards **14–245** that the taking of direct action without the necessity of prior court approval was found to be acceptable in principle. The absence of equivalent procedural safeguards under the Irish planning legislation suggests that our enforcement notice procedure is in breach of the Convention.

CHAPTER FIFTEEN

SOCIAL AND AFFORDABLE HOUSING

A. Overview of Part V

Part V of the PDA 2000 (as amended)[1] establishes the provision of social and **15–01** affordable housing as an objective of the planning legislation, and introduces a mechanism whereby the developers of residential development may be required either to cede land at its "existing use" value to the planning authority for the purposes of social and affordable housing, or to make alternative provision equivalent in monetary terms to the value of the land which the planning authority would otherwise have received.

Under s.96 (as amended), it is mandatory to impose a special type of condition **15–02** on certain residential planning permissions. Such conditions require the applicant for planning permission, or any other person with an interest in the land, to enter into an "agreement" with the planning authority for the provision of social and affordable housing.

---

[1] Part V of the PDA 2000 was significantly amended by the Planning and Development (Amendment) Act 2002. The commencement date for Pt V was November 1, 2000 (Planning and Development Act 2000 (Commencement) Order 2000 (S.I. No. 349 of 2000)). The Minister for the Environment and Local Government issued statutory guidelines for planning authorities pursuant to PDA 2000, s.28 in or about December, 2000. A number of circulars have been issued since then, and these are discussed presently.

15–03   In its mandatory form, a Part V agreement will simply involve the transfer of land in its undeveloped state. Some flexibility is allowed for, however, in that the developer may, as an alternative to this, volunteer to make provision for social and affordable housing in other ways. The range of potential options includes the transfer to the planning authority of the ownership of any other land within the functional area of the planning authority; and the transfer of built houses and/or serviced sites (again, not necessarily on the land the subject-matter of the application for planning permission). Moreover, a Part V agreement might provide simply for the payment of monies to the planning authority.

15–04   Save in the exceptional circumstances discussed immediately below at para.15–05, the transfer of undeveloped land is the only one of the various options which a developer can be *compelled* to accept.[2] None of the other options—such as the transfer of built houses or serviced sites—can be imposed unilaterally on the developer: the developer must, in effect, indicate his willingness to meet the requirements of Part V in one of these ways. This should be done at the time of the making of the application for planning permission, in accordance with the obligation on the developer to specify the manner in which he or she proposes to comply with a condition in respect of social and affordable housing.[3] Applicants should be wary in that, once such proposals are made, it may be difficult to resile from them thereafter.

15–05   If a developer commences development prior to reaching an agreement with the planning authority as to the method by which he or she is to comply with Part V, he or she runs the risk that he or she may subsequently be required to transfer built houses to the planning authority. This is so notwithstanding the fact that generally the transfer of undeveloped land is the only one of the various options which a developer can be *compelled* to accept. By implementing the planning permission, the developer may bring about a situation whereby the default option is no longer available in that the application site will have been developed in full. The High Court has indicated that in such circumstances the developer may be required to transfer built houses to the planning authority.[4]

15–06   The mechanics of Part V are unusual in that matters of basic detail (including the very identity of any land to be transferred) are not specified by way of condition attached to the planning permission, but rather are left over for subsequent agreement. This has the effect that final decisions as to the logistics

---

[2]   This follows from s.96(3)(g) (as inserted by the Planning and Development (Amendment) Act 2002). Section 96(3)(g) provides that nothing in subs.(3) shall be construed as requiring the applicant or any other person (other than the planning authority) to enter into an agreement under paragraph (b) instead of an agreement under paragraph (a).

[3]   PDA 2000, s.96(4) (as inserted by the Planning and Development (Amendment) Act 2002). See also art.22(1)(e) of the Planning and Development Regulations 2001 (as substituted by the 2006 Regulations).

[4]   *Glenkerrin Homes v Dun Laoghaire Rathdown County Council*, unreported, High Court, Clarke J., April 27, 2007.

are postponed; planning permission is granted in principle, in the first instance, subject to a condition requiring that the developer enter into an agreement. It also has the result that the public are excluded: the agreement process is not subject to public scrutiny nor can a member of the public appeal the terms of an agreement to An Bord Pleanála.[5] Finally, the fact that such a condition leaves over significant matters for agreement with the planning authority represents an exception to the principle that the decision of An Bord Pleanála, on appeal, concludes all substantial issues raised on the application.[6] (In default of agreement, certain aspects of an agreement can be referred to An Bord Pleanála subsequently for determination.)

Certain safeguards are built into the legislation for the benefit of the owner of **15–07** the land. For example, pending the provision of social and affordable housing, the planning authority is required to maintain the land or sites in a manner which does not detract, and is not likely to detract, to a material degree from the amenity, character or appearance of the land or houses in the neighbourhood of the land or sites.

B. Position under the Previous Legislation

Under the Local Government (Planning & Development) Acts 1963 to 1999, a **15–08** planning authority was not entitled to impose conditions on residential development which would require a developer to take on at his own expense the duty of a local authority as housing authority.[7] Thus a condition which required a developer to make houses available at a reduced price, or which restricted occupation of those houses to persons on the local authority's housing list, would be invalid.

---

[5] In *Dunne v An Bord Pleanála* [2006] I.E.H.C. 400; unreported, McGovern J., December 14, 2006, the High Court suggested that it was a matter between the developer and the planning authority as to how the developer's obligations under Part V would be complied with. The applicants for judicial review were held not to be prejudiced because the only option which was ever proposed and considered was the payment of a sum of money in lieu of housing within the application site. See also *R. (On the application of Kides) v South Cambridgeshire District Council* [2001] E.W.H.C. Admin. 839, [108]; [2003] 1 P. & C.R. 4, where it was held that the applicant for judicial review had no interest in social housing and was attempting to seize adventitiously on the point to make difficulties.

[6] *cf.* s.34(5); *Boland v An Bord Pleanála* [1996] 3 I.R. 435; *McNamara v An Bord Pleanála* [1996] 2 I.L.R.M. 339; and *Houlihan v An Bord Pleanála* unreported, High Court, Murphy J., October 4, 1993.

[7] See, for example, *R. v Hillingdon London Borough Council Ex p. Royco Homes Ltd.* [1974] 1 Q.B. 720. See also, by analogy, *Westminster Rensdale Ltd. v Secretary of State for the Environment* (1983) P. & C.R. 255; and *Ashbourne Holdings Ltd. v An Bord Pleanála* [2003] 2 I.R. 114; [2003] 2 I.L.R.M. 446.

C. Definition of "Social and Affordable Housing"

15–09   Although a housing strategy is directed towards housing for the existing and future population *in general* of the area,[8] the power to require a Part V agreement is directed to the provision of social and affordable housing. The term "social housing" is not actually defined in the Act but is rather a convenient shorthand. The Act involves a cross-reference to s.9(2) of the Housing Act 1988 which identifies the need for housing of a number of classes of persons. The list includes, *inter alia*, persons who are homeless; persons who are living in accommodation that is unfit for human habitation or is materially unsuitable for their adequate housing; persons who are living in overcrowded accommodation; and persons who traditionally pursue or have pursued a nomadic way of life.[9]

15–10   The concept of "affordable housing" is defined under the Act in terms of an "eligible person", as follows. A person who is in need of accommodation and whose income would not be adequate to meet the payments on a mortgage for a purchase of a house to meet his or her accommodation needs because the payments calculated over the course of a year would exceed 35 per cent of that person's annual income (net of income tax and pay related social insurance). Criteria for the determination of "accommodation needs" have been prescribed under art.50 of the Planning and Development Regulations 2001 (as amended in 2003).[10]

15–11   A planning authority has a discretion under s.95 as to the percentage of land zoned for residential use (or a mixture of residential use and other uses) to be *reserved* for the provision of social and affordable housing, subject to a maximum ceiling of 20 per cent. In particular, a planning authority may indicate specific objectives in respect of each area zoned for residential use, and may indicate in respect of any particular area that there is *no requirement* for social and affordable housing, in order to counteract undue segregation.

D. Development to Which Part V Applies

15–12   A number of prerequisites must be fulfilled before the provisions of Part V are triggered.[11] First, the application must be for the "development of houses", or a mixed development with a residential element. Secondly, the relevant land must be zoned for residential use (or for a mixture of residential and other uses). Thirdly, the land must be subject to a development plan objective which

---

[8]   PDA 2000, s.94.

[9]   Housing Act 1988, s.13 (as substituted by the Housing (Traveller Accommodation) Act 1998, s.29).

[10]   Amended by the Planning and Development Regulations 2003 (S.I. No. 90 of 2003).

[11]   PDA 2000, s.96(1) (as amended by the Planning and Development (Amendment) Act 2002).

requires that a specified percentage of any land zoned solely for residential use (or for a mixture of residential and other uses) be made available for social and affordable housing. The first of these prerequisites should present little difficulty in practice. The second and third may prove more problematic.

1. "Development of houses"

"House" is defined under s.2 of the PDA 2000 as meaning a building or part of a building which is being or has been occupied as a dwelling or was provided for use as a dwelling but has not been occupied, and where appropriate, includes a building which was designed for use as two or more dwellings or a flat, an apartment or other dwelling within such a building.   **15–13**

The question as to whether the provisions of Part V apply to the development of holiday homes remains unresolved. As appears from the general definition of "house", one of the key concepts is that of a "dwelling". The issue which arises for consideration, therefore, is as to whether a holiday home can be said to be a "dwelling". Reference is made by analogy to the judgment of the Supreme Court in *Kerry County Council v Kerins*.[12] This case arose in the context of rating and valuation. A "domestic hereditament" was defined as any hereditament which consists wholly or partly of premises used as a dwelling and which is not a mixed hereditament. The question before the Supreme Court was as to whether holiday chalets constituted dwellings. The Supreme Court held that they did.   **15–14**

2. Zoning for "residential use" and "mixture of residential and other uses"

It will be relatively straightforward to say whether or not particular land is zoned for "residential use". The much more difficult question is as to what is meant by zoning for a "mixture of residential and other uses"? In particular, does the fact that residential development might be permitted in even limited circumstances under the relevant zoning mean that "residential" is one of the "mix" of zoned uses? To take an extreme example, houses will sometimes be permitted in green belt zones in exceptional circumstances: is this enough to allow one to say that the green belt land is "zoned" for a "mixture of residential and other uses"?   **15–15**

In the absence of decided case law directly on point, it is simply not possible to give a definitive answer to these questions. The most that can be done is to state a number of general propositions, as follows.   **15–16**

The introduction of a qualifying zoning indicates that the requirements of Part V were not intended to apply to *all* residential developments. If it were   **15–17**

---

[12] [1996] 3 I.R. 493.

otherwise, the reference to zoning in s.96(1) would be unnecessary. It must be possible, therefore, to identify circumstances where planning permission for residential development could properly be granted, but nevertheless the land cannot be said to be zoned for a "a mixture of residential and other uses".

15–18 One possible interpretation would be to say that it is only where residential development, even on a limited scale, would constitute a *material contravention* of the development plan that Part V is avoided. Thus unless a particular zoning— for example, commercial—precluded the possibility of any residential development in any circumstances, then Part V will apply. On this interpretation, Part V will apply to a wide variety of zoning objectives.

15–19 An alternative interpretation would be to say that there is a half-way house, and that before land should be regarded as zoned for a particular use (even as part of a mixture of uses) that use would have to be one of the "primary" uses permitted. On this analysis, it would not be enough that housing might be permitted in very limited circumstances. In support of this interpretation, one might argue that "zoning" is a term of art, and that when reading the provisions of s.96(1) it is appropriate to have regard to the wording of s.10, and, in particular, to the use of the phrase "solely or primarily".

15–20 A further argument in support of the interpretation at para.15–19 above is as follows. One purpose of a housing strategy is to ensure that provision is made for the housing of the existing and future population of the area in the manner set out in the strategy. A planning authority is required to ensure that sufficient and suitable land is zoned for residential use, or for a mixture of residential and other uses, to meet the requirements of the housing strategy and to ensure that a scarcity of such land does not occur at any time during the period of the development plan. All of this seems to suggest that, before land could be said to have the qualifying zoning, same would have to have been earmarked as intended to meet part of the demand for housing. Thus, if only a *limited* amount of housing is ever permissible under a particular zoning, an argument can certainly be made to the effect that land so designated was never seriously intended to contribute towards meeting the demand for housing identified under the housing strategy.

3. Social and affordable housing zoning objective

15–21 The planning application must relate to land subject to an objective under the development plan that a certain percentage of the land be made available for social and affordable housing.[13] Accordingly, an applicant for planning permission should ascertain whether or not the land the subject-matter of the application is subject to a zoning objective in respect of social and affordable

---

[13] PDA 2000, s.96(1) (as amended by the Planning and Development (Amendment) Act 2002). Note that the original wording of s.96 was not necessarily restricted to lands which were themselves subject to a specific zoning objective.

housing. If not, it is suggested that best practice would be to state this fact expressly in the planning application.

In this regard, it is important to note that there can be considerable variation in **15–22** the development plan as to the requirements in respect of social and affordable housing. It is expressly provided under s.95(1)(c) that different specific objectives may be indicated in respect of different areas. Thus, for example, the planning authority may indicate in respect of a particular area that there is no requirement for social and affordable housing, or that a lower percentage may instead be required, in order to counteract undue segregation in housing between persons of different social backgrounds. Nothing in s.95 shall prevent any land being developed *exclusively* for social and affordable housing.[14] Section 94(4)(d) provides that the ceiling of 20 per cent does not operate to prevent any person (including a local authority) from using *more* than 20 per cent of land zoned for residential use, or for a mixture of residential and other uses, for the provision of social and affordable housing.

Material contravention

Ironically, the fact that the statutory requirements in respect of social and **15–23** affordable housing are tied-in to zoning objectives would appear to have the result that these requirements are avoided entirely where the proposed development represents a material contravention of the development plan.

E. Exemptions from the Requirements of Part V

1. Section 96(13)

Under s.96(13) (as amended), the requirements in respect of social and **15–24** affordable housing do not apply in respect of, *inter alia*, the conversion of an existing building or the reconstruction of a building to create one or more dwellings, provided that 50 per cent or more of the existing external fabric of the building is retained; nor to the carrying out of works to an existing house. Exemptions are also provided under s.96(13) (as amended) for development consisting of the provision of houses by an approved body, and for the development of houses pursuant to an agreement in respect of social and affordable housing.

2. Section 97

Further exemptions are provided for under s.97 (as amended) in respect of **15–25** certain minor developments: specifically, development consisting of the

---

[14] PDA 2000, s. 95(2) (as amended by the Planning and Development (Amendment) Act 2002).

provision of four or fewer houses, or for housing on land of 0.1 hectares or less.[15]

15–26 Where it is sought to rely on these exemptions, it is necessary to make a formal application in that regard to the planning authority for a certificate stating that s.96 shall not apply to a grant of planning permission in respect of the development concerned. The application for this certificate should be made *before* the application for planning permission proper. The legislation contains anti-avoidance provisions designed to ensure that the requirements in respect of social and affordable housing cannot be by-passed by the ready expedient of making a series of sub-threshold applications. To this end, the applicant for a certificate is required to furnish a statutory declaration giving particulars, *inter alia*, of any interest that the applicant has or has had in any land in the immediate vicinity, and of any interest that any person with whom the applicant is acting in concert has, or has had, in any land in the immediate vicinity. Land in the "immediate vicinity" of other land shall be deemed in any particular case not to include land that is more than 400 metres from that other land.

15–27 The planning authority is, generally, required to make a decision on an application for a certificate within a period of four weeks from the later of the date of the making of the application, or the date any request for information or documentation has been complied with. In default of the making of a decision, the planning authority is deemed to have granted a certificate to the applicant concerned on the expiry of the relevant period. In case of the refusal of a certificate, the applicant has a right of appeal to the Circuit Court.

15–28 It is to be noted that it is a criminal offence to make a statutory declaration or provide information or documentation that is false or misleading in a material respect.

F. Planning Application Procedure

1. Pre-application consultation

15–29 The Ministerial guidelines issued to planning authorities in November 2006 encourage applicants to avail of pre-application consultations under s.247 of the PDA 2000. The guidelines go on to suggest that an agreement in principle should normally be reached prior to submission of a planning application on the measures necessary to comply with Part V.

---

[15] Reduced from 0.2 hectares under s.5 of the Planning and Development (Amendment) Act 2002.

2. Planning application must specify proposals

If an application for planning permission is subject to the requirements of social **15–30** and affordable housing, then the applicant for planning permission is required to specify the manner in which he or she proposes to comply with a condition in respect of social and affordable housing.[16]

The Ministerial guidelines of November 2006 make a number of **15–31** recommendations as to the form of the proposals, as follows.

> "Where the option proposed is land on-site or off-site, this should be clearly identified on an accompanying separate map. Where units or sites are proposed on-site or off-site, the applicant must indicate in writing either the number of units, including types and sizes, to be transferred or the number of sites. In all instances the applicant must indicate the location within the application lands or off-site lands, as appropriate."

The suggestion that the applicant should indicate the *number* of units or sites **15–32** should be treated with caution. As discussed presently at para.15–76 and onwards, the number of houses or sites to be transferred is determined by reference to the equivalent monetary value requirement. At the time of making the planning application, it is unlikely that an applicant will know the precise number of houses or sites which he or she may be required to transfer. There is a risk, therefore, that if the applicant indicates a particular number, the planning authority might attempt to hold him or her to that number subsequently, even if a lesser number would have been required under equivalent monetary value formula.

A recent decision of An Bord Pleanála on a reference pursuant to s.96(5) **15–33** suggests that it may not be open to an applicant for planning permission to seek to amend the proposals subsequently.[17] On the facts, the developer had proposed that a number of dwelling units would be transferred to the planning authority in order to satisfy the requirements of Part V. A condition was attached to the grant of planning permission requiring the developer to enter into an agreement with the planning authority, prior to commencement of development, providing for the transfer of land, or houses, or partially or fully serviced sites. Subsequently the developer sought to meet the requirements of Part V by making a payment in lieu of transferring the dwelling units. The dispute was then referred to An Bord Pleanála. In its determination, An Bord Pleanála appears to have agreed with its inspector that it would undermine the requirement to indicate proposals at the time of the application for planning permission to allow these to be changed afterwards. The inspector dealt with the matter as follows.

---

[16] PDA 2000, s.96(4) (as amended by the Planning and Development (Amendment) Act 2002). See also art.22(1)(e) of the Planning and Development Regulations 2001 (as substituted by the 2006 Regulations).

[17] An Bord Pleanála, Referral Reference No. 04.RH2003, January 20, 2005.

"There would appear to be little point in requiring a developer to make specific proposals in a planning application or for requiring a planning authority to take the developer's specific proposals into account in making its decision if the specific proposals have no relevance or may be totally replaced at a later time. There is also the issue of third party rights. The public have a right to know the details of the Part V proposals when the application is made. To subsequently fundamentally alter the nature of the specific proposals after the grant of permission would deny third parties access to the planning process including an appeal. While I accept that there is no provision in the legislation prohibiting the submission of a new Part V specific proposal following the grant of permission, such a procedure would seem to me to be contrary to the spirit and intention of the Act."

G. Assessment of Applicant's Proposals

1. Method of compliance should be determined prior to grant

15–34   The planning authority is required to assess the applicant's proposals as part of the planning application process. Ideally, the method by which the developer is to comply with Part V should be determined conclusively prior to the grant of planning permission, and should be specified in the relevant planning condition. Thus, for example, if the developer is to comply with Part V by the transfer of built houses, the condition should state this. If the design of the houses needs to be modified so as to meet the housing requirements of the planning authority, e.g. in terms of the number of bedrooms, then this too should be dealt with by way of planning condition.

15–35   Equally, if the developer is to comply with Part V by the transfer of undeveloped land within the application site, this too should be stated in the planning permission. It may also be necessary to impose conditions requiring the omission of some houses so as to ensure that there is a sufficient area of undeveloped land reserved for the planning authority.

15–36   Regrettably, the practice of many planning authorities had been to impose a condition in general terms only, with no indication being given as to the method by which the developer was to comply with Part V. Nor were any consequential modifications made to the proposed development, whether in terms of house design or the layout of the development. The result of all of this was that by the time the planning authority finally got around to negotiating the terms of an agreement with the developer, its options had narrowed considerably.[18] The default option of the transfer of undeveloped land within the application site had been lost in that the full of the site had long since been developed and built upon. The planning authority was therefore required either to take houses within the application site, in circumstances where the design of those houses might not be suitable for its housing requirements, or to accept a financial payment.

---

[18] See, for example, the facts of *Glenkerrin Homes v Dun Laoghaire Rathdown County Council*, unreported, High Court, Clarke J., April 27, 2007.

The Ministerial guidelines of November 2006 are intended to ensure that the **15–37** decision in principle as to by which method a developer is to comply with Part V will be made prior to the grant of planning permission.

2. Request for further information or for revised plans

A planning authority has a general discretion to seek further information from **15–38** an applicant.[19] It also has discretion to invite revised plans or other drawings modifying, or other particulars providing for the modification of, the proposed development.[20]

A planning authority is not, however, entitled to use the occasion of either a **15–39** request for further information or an invitation to submit revised plans etc. to attempt to coerce the applicant into changing his proposals. The transfer of undeveloped land is the only one of the various options which a developer can be compelled to accept. The applicant is entitled to stand on his rights in this regard, and to refuse to put forward proposals involving, for example, the transfer of built houses within the application site. If the planning authority is dissatisfied with the proposals made by the applicant, the only proper response is to resort to the default option of the transfer of undeveloped land. A condition to this effect should be imposed as part of the decision, and any necessary adjustments to the layout of the development should be made. For example, it may be necessary to impose a condition requiring the omission of a number of houses so as to free up (undeveloped) land for transfer to the planning authority.

For similar reasons, it would be unlawful for a planning authority to refuse **15–40** planning permission on the basis that the applicant's proposals were not acceptable to it. As indicated above, the developer is not required to put forward proposals involving, for example, the transfer of built houses or serviced sites. It is not open to a planning authority to seek to bully developers into making such proposals by adopting a policy of refusing planning permission in all cases where such proposals are not forthcoming.

3. Criteria against which proposals to be assessed

The criteria against which the applicant's proposals are to be assessed are set **15–41** out at s.96(3)(c) (as amended). Here it is indicated that in considering whether to enter into an agreement which involves a method of compliance other than the default option of the transfer of undeveloped land, the planning authority is to consider five matters. Each of these five matters is discussed presently at paras 15–44 to 15–48.

---

[19] Planning and Development Regulations 2001, art.33 (as substituted by the 2006 Regulations).
[20] Planning and Development Regulations 2001, art.34 (as substituted by the 2006 Regulations).

15–42 The scheme of the legislation is somewhat confusing, however, in that a further set of criteria is prescribed at s.96(3)(h) (as amended). A planning authority is required to consider these criteria "for the purposes of an agreement" under s.96(3). It is not immediately apparent as to why it was thought necessary to distinguish between the two sets of criteria. One possible explanation is to say that the first set govern the making of the decision in principle as to by which method a developer is to comply with Part V; and that the second set are to be taken into consideration when drawing up the terms of the agreement subsequently. There is, however, a large measure of overlap between the two sets of criteria.

15–43 A further criticism of the drafting is that there is no express guidance as to what considerations An Bord Pleanála is to take into account in circumstances where a dispute is referred to it: the legislation simply identifies matters which a "planning authority" is to take into account. Presumably, An Bord Pleanála is to take the same matters into account, but it would have been more helpful if the legislation had made this clear, rather than leaving it to be implied.

(i) Effectiveness and efficiency

15–44 The planning authority must consider whether the agreement will contribute effectively and efficiently to the achievement of the objectives of the housing strategy.[21] This criterion would appear to be most relevant in circumstances where the applicant's proposals allow the planning authority the option of taking serviced sites or built houses. In such circumstances, the planning authority will have to consider whether it is more effective and efficient to accept serviced sites or built houses directly from the developer, than to provide houses in some other way. Such alternative options might, for example, involve using a financial payment from the developer to purchase houses elsewhere or to defray costs incurred by the planning authority in constructing houses itself. Presumably, one of the key issues will be in terms of the likely timescale for the delivery of social and affordable housing under the various competing options. For example, the developer may be in a position to construct houses faster that the planning authority.

(ii) Best use of resources and financial implications

15–45 A planning authority is required to consider whether the agreement will constitute the best use of the resources available to it to ensure an adequate supply of housing and any financial implications of the agreement for its functions as a housing authority.[22] It is unclear as to how this criterion adds to the other statutory criteria. It is a mandatory requirement of the legislation that whatever package of measures is put forward must be equivalent in monetary

---

[21] PDA 2000, s.96(3)(c)(i) (as amended by the Planning and Development (Amendment) Act 2002).

[22] PDA 2000, s.96(3)(c)(ii) (as amended by the Planning and Development (Amendment) Act 2002).

value to the land which would otherwise have been transferred to the planning authority in the event of the default option, *i.e.* the transfer of undeveloped land. Given this mandatory requirement for monetary equivalence, it is difficult to understand in what way the "financial implications" of one form of agreement might be different from those of another. It is also difficult to know in what respect consideration of the "best use of the resources" differs from the test of effectiveness and efficiency under s.96(3)(c)(i).

(iii) Counteract undue segregation

Perhaps the most controversial criterion is that to be found at s.96(3)(iii) (as amended), namely the need to counteract undue segregation in housing between persons of different social background in the area of the authority. It is difficult to square this objective with the fact that, as a result of the amendments under the Planning and Development (Amendment) Act 2002, it is now possible for a developer to meet his or her obligations in respect of social and affordable housing in a number of different ways, many of which do not relate to the land the subject-matter of the application for planning permission. Under the original wording of Part V, the normal requirement had been that provision be made for social and affordable housing within the application site. **15–46**

(iv) Provisions of the development plan

The planning authority is required to consider whether the agreement is in accordance with the provisions of the development plan.[23] Obviously, the significance of this consideration will vary depending on the level of detail set out in the development plan and the housing strategy. In practice, this issue of the manner in which provision is to be made for social and affordable housing has not been addressed in detail by many planning authorities in their housing strategies. Often, there is simply a statement that the planning authority will seek a particular percentage of social housing in the development. **15–47**

(v) Timing

The time within which social and affordable housing is likely to be provided as a consequence of the agreement is a relevant consideration under s.96(3)(c)(v) (as amended). **15–48**

H. Appeal to An Bord Pleanála

Where a condition in respect of social and affordable housing has been attached to the decision of the planning authority at first instance, the question of a first party appeal against that condition to An Bord Pleanála must be considered. It is important to note that as it is mandatory to attach a condition in respect of social and affordable housing where Part V applies, there would seem to be **15–49**

---

[23] PDA 2000, s.96(3)(c)(iv) (as amended by the Planning and Development (Amendment) Act 2002).

little point in appealing against the imposition of a condition *per se* unless there are strong grounds for saying that the planning authority misinterpreted the development plan and that the land is not actually subject to a specific zoning objective in respect of social and affordable housing.

15–50 Nonetheless, there may be some merit in appealing against the *form of wording* used by the planning authority. It is to the applicant's advantage to attempt to determine the parameters of the requirements in respect of social and affordable housing at as early a stage as possible. To this end, there is some attraction in having the condition attached to the planning permission give an indication of the method by which the requirements in respect of social and affordable housing are to be met. For example, the condition might indicate that provision is to be made by way of a financial payment to the planning authority. If this issue can be nailed down at the stage of the decision of An Bord Pleanála, this may expedite subsequent dealings with the planning authority at the stage of the entering into of the agreement. Obviously, this may represent a double-edged sword in that the more specific the condition is as to the method by which the requirements of Part V are to be met, the less discretion An Bord Pleanála or the property arbitrator will have in the event of a dispute being referred to them. See further paras 15–67 to 15–70.

15–51 An appeal will also be appropriate where the wording of the condition seeks to impose a time-limit within which the Part V agreement is to be concluded. Certain planning authorities had in the past purported to require that a Part V agreement be entered into within eight weeks of the date of the decision. This is unlawful. The dispute resolution mechanisms provided for under Part V— by way of reference to An Bord Pleanála or the property arbitrator—are only available after the expiration of a period of eight weeks. Any condition which required that the agreement be entered into prior to eight weeks would involve an unlawful attempt to cut the developer off from the statutory dispute resolution mechanisms.

I. Judicial Review

15–52 An applicant may also wish to consider the possibility of seeking judicial review of the decision of either a planning authority or An Bord Pleanála in respect of a condition requiring social and affordable housing. There is generally an eight-week time-limit on the bringing of any challenge to the validity of a decision on an application for planning permission.[24] Accordingly, unless judicial review proceedings have been brought within this period, it will not generally be open to an applicant or, indeed, to a subsequent owner of the land, to challenge the validity of a condition attached to a planning permission requiring social and affordable housing. In particular, it will probably not be possible to avoid the entry into of an agreement on the basis that the condition requiring social and affordable housing should not have been imposed in the first instance.

---

[24] PDA 2000, ss.50 and 50A (as substituted by the 2006 Act).

J. The Part V Agreement

The mechanics of Part V are unusual in that the logistics are not dealt with as **15–53** part of the planning permission proper but are, instead, left over for subsequent agreement between the developer and the planning authority. In many instances, the planning permission will simply contain a broad formula to the effect that an agreement in respect of social and affordable housing is to be entered into. It would be unwise for the developer to progress the implementation of the planning permission to any great degree before finalising the Part V agreement. To do otherwise, and to delay in this regard, leaves the developer in a vulnerable position. In particular, prospective purchasers are likely to insist on proof of compliance with Part V. Indeed, in addition to seeking sight of proof of compliance from the planning authority, such purchasers may also seek information as to precisely where it is that any social and affordable housing units are to be located. A developer who has failed to enter into an agreement with the planning authority prior to the first sales of the balance of the houses may well find himself under pressure to conclude an agreement with the planning authority and thus not be in a very strong negotiating position.

For these reasons, then, it is suggested that the developer should seek to enter **15–54** into the agreement with the planning authority *prior* to the commencement of development. Indeed, in many instances this will be expressly required by the terms of the condition in any event. There is a very short lead time after which any dispute can then be referred to An Bord Pleanála or the property arbitrator, as appropriate. More specifically, under s.96(8) (as amended) a dispute may be referred to An Bord Pleanála or the property arbitrator, as appropriate, if an agreement has not been entered into before the expiration of eight weeks from the date of the grant of the planning permission.

The planning authority is required to indicate to the applicant its intention, **15–55** insofar as same is known at the time of the agreement, in relation to the provision of housing on the land to be transferred. The planning authority's intention should then be recited in the agreement.

A planning authority is required to consider the following criteria "for the **15–56** purposes of an agreement" under s.96(3).[25]

(i) Proper planning and sustainable development

The planning authority is required to consider the proper planning and **15–57** sustainable development of the area. Given the amplitude of the other express statutory criteria, this requirement will probably add nothing in most cases. It is to be noted, however, that it may be important in some instances in that it is the only criterion which is not tied down to the concept of social and affordable

---

[25] PDA 2000, s.96(3)(h) (as amended by the Planning and Development (Amendment) Act 2002).

housing, and thus may allow the planning authority to have regard to wider considerations.

(ii) The housing strategy

15–58 Section 96(3)(h)(ii) (as amended) requires the planning authority to consider the housing strategy and the specific objectives of the development plan which relate to the implementation of the strategy. This criterion is repeated, in part, under s.96(3)(c)(iv) (as amended) which requires the planning authority to consider whether an agreement is in accordance with the provisions of the development plan when deciding to enter into an agreement.

(iii) Overall coherence of the development

15–59 The planning authority is required to consider the need to ensure the overall coherence of the development to which the application relates, where appropriate. The "Part V of the Planning and Development Act, 2000 as amended Planning and Development (Amendment) Act 2002 – Further Guidance on Implementation Issues" issued by the Department of the Environment, Heritage and Local Government in August 2003 cites matters such as phasing, building and marketing as being relevant here.

(iv) Views of the applicant

15–60 The planning authority is required to consider the views of the applicant in relation to the impact of the agreement on the development. As part of the application for planning permission, the developer will have specified the manner in which he or she proposes to comply with a condition in respect of social and affordable housing.[26] Accordingly, it would seem that what is to be considered here is the *detail* of the implementation of such proposals. A developer will probably not be permitted to attempt to resile from the principle of the initial proposals, by arguing belatedly that, for example, the provision of social and affordable housing on-site will have an adverse impact on the development.

K. Dispute Resolution Mechanisms

15–61 In the event that a developer and a planning authority are unable to reach an agreement, provision is made for the referral of the dispute to either An Bord Pleanála or the property arbitrator. The reference can be made by either party after the expiration of a period of eight weeks from the date of the grant of planning permission.[27] The respective jurisdictions of An Bord Pleanála and the property arbitrator are demarked as follows.

---

[26] PDA 2000, s.96(4) (as amended by the Planning and Development (Amendment) Act 2002). See also Planning and Development Regulations 2001, art.22(2)(e) (as substituted by the 2006 Regulations).

[27] Any condition which purports to require that the agreement be entered into earlier than eight weeks would be unlawful. See para.15–51.

1. Property arbitrator

The property arbitrator has jurisdiction over matters which entail valuation, **15–62** namely the number and price of houses to be transferred, the number and price of sites to be transferred or the amount of any monetary payment to be made. In *Glenkerrin Homes v Dun Laoghaire Rathdown County Council*,[28] the High Court held that the property arbitrator has an implied jurisdiction to identify, in the case of dispute, which units should in fact be transferred where there is a material difference between individual units, *e.g.* in terms of size or location. Clarke J. ruled that the identification of the units to be transferred was so inextricably linked to the question of the number and price of the units to be transferred, that a jurisdiction on the part of the property arbitrator to determine those matters must necessarily be implied. If the identification of the units could only be the subject of an agreement with the planning authority, or be determined on a reference to An Bord Pleanála, then there would be the potential for stalemate or for a whole series of separate dispute resolution hearings, with a potential for circularity.

Clarke J. emphasised that where the dispute between the parties was not **15–63** confined to the identification of the units to be transferred, but instead went to the question of principle as to by which method a developer was to comply with Part V, then in the absence of agreement the matter could only be resolved by An Bord Pleanála.

Procedure before the property arbitrator

The procedure before the property arbitrator is unusual in a number of respects. **15–64** First, it appears that the High Court's supervisory jurisdiction is only exercisable by way of the case stated procedure, and that the property arbitrator is not subject to judicial review.[29] Thus, the parties to the arbitration must decide *in advance* of the award whether or not they wish to pursue the matter before the High Court. If they do, then they must request the property arbitrator to state a case to the High Court. It will be too late to do so once the award has been made.

Secondly, the property arbitrators' previous practice of not normally stating **15–65** reasons for their awards is not acceptable in the context of Part V.[30] The arbitration involves a determination of the developer's civil rights, and accordingly attracts the protections of Art.6 of the European Convention on

---

[28] Unreported, High Court, Clarke J., April 27, 2007.
[29] This follows from the fact that, under s.6 of the Acquisition of Land (Assessment of Compensation) Act 1919, the decision of a property arbitrator upon any question shall be final and binding on the parties. *Cf. Manning v Shackleton* [1996] 3 I.R. 85, where a property arbitrator's award was subject to judicial review without any discussion of the appropriateness of the remedy.
[30] See *Manning v Shackleton* [1996] 3 I.R. 85, where the Supreme Court held that a property arbitrator was not required to state reasons for his award. With respect, this judgment would not appear to be consistent with the European Convention on Human Rights.

Human Rights. Article 6(1), insofar as relevant, provides that in the determination of his civil rights and obligations everyone is entitled to a fair and public hearing within a reasonable time by an independent and impartial tribunal established by law. The right to a statement of reasons forms part of a "fair and public hearing". The fact that the property arbitrators did not previously publish their awards also presents difficulties.

2. An Bord Pleanála

15–66   An Bord Pleanála has jurisdiction over all other disputes. Generally, An Bord Pleanála will be required to exercise judgment on matters of planning policy. Although it is not expressly stated in the legislation, it is to be presumed that An Bord Pleanála is to have regard to the same criteria as the planning authority is. These criteria are discussed in detail at paras 15–56 to 15–60.

Wording of condition

15–67   The wording of the condition imposing the requirement to enter into the agreement will obviously be critical in determining any dispute as to the terms of the agreement. Until recently, the approach of most planning authorities was to impose a condition in very general terms, without any indication as to the manner in which the developer was to comply with Part V.

15–68   The more specific the condition is as to the method by which the requirements of Part V are to be met, the less discretion An Bord Pleanála will have. The condition might limit the manner in which the requirements of Part V are to be met to one or two specific options; for example, it might specify that the developer is to transfer built houses or serviced sites within the application site. In such circumstances, it seems that An Bord Pleanála takes the view that it is bound by the terms of the condition and may not put forward an alternative mechanism for meeting the requirements of Part V.

15–69   The requirements of the particular condition may thus be more exacting than the general position under the legislation. As discussed earlier, the transfer of undeveloped land is the only one of the various options which a developer can be *compelled* to accept. None of the other options—such as the transfer of built houses or serviced sites—can be imposed unilaterally on the developer. It seems, however, that if the developer indicates his willingness to meet the requirements of Part V in one of these ways at the time of the making of the application for planning permission, the developer may be locked into this by virtue of the wording of the condition. To put the matter another way, the default option of transferring undeveloped land will have been lost and cannot be revived even in the context of a reference to An Bord Pleanála.

15–70   If, conversely, the wording of the condition allows for the possibility of the transfer of undeveloped land within the application site, then the better view must be that the developer is entitled to insist on an agreement in this form. The developer would argue that if An Bord Pleanála is not prepared to accede to some other form of agreement acceptable to the developer (and within the wording of the condition), the board must determine that the agreement be in the form of a transfer of undeveloped land. The basis of this argument is that no other form of agreement can unilaterally be imposed on the developer and that the default option is therefore always open to the developer, save in circumstances where this has, in effect, been conditioned out, *i.e.* the wording of the condition excludes the possibility of the transfer of undeveloped land within the application site. A condition in general terms or a condition which expressly refers to the transfer of undeveloped land cannot be said to have excluded the default option and, accordingly, the developer retains his right to insist on same.

If a developer commences development prior to reaching an agreement with the planning authority as to the method by which he or she is to comply with Part V, he or she runs the risk that he or she may subsequently be required to transfer built houses to the planning authority. This is so notwithstanding the fact that generally the transfer of undeveloped land is the only one of the various options which a developer can be *compelled* to accept. By implementing the planning permission, the developer may bring about a situation whereby the default option is no longer available in that the application site will have been developed in full. The High Court has indicated that in such circumstances the developer may be required to transfer built houses to the planning authority.[31]   **15–71**

3. Practical difficulties arising from division of jurisdiction

In at least some cases, it will be necessary to make a reference to An Bord Pleanála and the property arbitrator in turn. First, it will be necessary to make a reference to An Bord Pleanála in order that the principle of the agreement may be determined: for example, whether the developer is to transfer built houses to the planning authority. Thereafter, it may be necessary to make a subsequent reference to the property arbitrator in order that the details—for example, in terms of identity, number and prices of built houses—can be determined.   **15–72**

The division of jurisdiction as between An Bord Pleanála and the property arbitrator may present difficulties in practice, especially in cases where the developer proposes to employ a number of different methods to meet the requirements of Part V. The difficulties arise because the assessment of a combination of methods arguably requires the decision-maker to make an *overall* assessment of the package of measures, whereas under the legislation, An Bord Pleanála is precluded from considering matters such as the number and price of houses to be transferred, the number and price of sites to be transferred or the amount of any monetary payment to be made.   **15–73**

---

[31] *Glenkerrin Homes v Dun Laoghaire Rathdown County Council*, unreported, High Court, Clarke J., April 27, 2007.

15–74 This point is probably best illustrated by example. A developer proposes to meet his obligations under Part V by transferring a number of built houses together with the making of a monetary payment. A proper assessment of this proposal requires consideration of the number and price of houses to be transferred and consideration of the amount of the monetary payment. For example, An Bord Pleanála might consider that the transfer of built houses is the option which would best ensure the timely delivery of social and affordable housing. In such circumstances, An Bord Pleanála would, presumably, be anxious to ensure that the package was weighted towards the provision of built houses, rather than towards the financial payment.[32] To put the matter another way, notwithstanding the fact that, whatever its make-up, the package must always be of the same monetary value, An Bord Pleanála may have a bias towards a particular mechanism over another. The details in this regard are, however, matters within the jurisdiction of the property arbitrator and not of An Bord Pleanála.

15–75 More generally, it is arguable that at least one of the statutory criteria under s.96(3) requires consideration of details which are more properly within the property arbitrator's competence. Under s.96(3)(c)(ii), a planning authority is required to consider whether the agreement will constitute the best use of the resources available to it to ensure an adequate supply of housing and any financial implications of the agreement for its functions as a housing authority. The point has been made by one of An Bord Pleanála's own inspectors that such considerations may stray beyond purely planning matters.[33]

> "The Board would not be in a position to determine the best use of a planning authority's financial resources and the financial implications for the housing authority as such an examination could enter into areas of a purely financial nature that are within the preserve of the public auditor and the property arbitrator. It appears to me that the planning authority is uniquely in a position to determine their resources and financial limitations."

L. Equivalent Monetary Value

1. Introduction

15–76 Whatever package of measures is put forward, it seems that it must be equivalent in monetary value to the land which would otherwise have been transferred to the planning authority in the event of the default option, *i.e.* the transfer of

---

[32] It is an interesting question as to whether An Bord Pleanála would be entitled to plump entirely for the transfer of built houses in circumstances where the developer's proposal was for a combination of the transfer of houses and the making of a monetary payment. It is submitted that as the default option is the transfer of undeveloped land and that the developer cannot be compelled to do other than this, An Bord Pleanála must either work within the principles of the developer's proposals or revert to the default option of the transfer of undeveloped land.

[33] An Bord Pleanála, Referral Reference No. 04.RH2003, January 20, 2005.

undeveloped land.[34] This requirement finds expression in the amended s.96(3)(b), as follows.

> "[...] subject, in every case, to the provision that is made under this paragraph resulting in the aggregate monetary value of the property or amounts or both, as the case may be, transferred or paid by virtue of the agreement being equivalent to the monetary value of the land that the planning authority would receive if the agreement solely provided for a transfer of land under paragraph (a)."

As discussed immediately below, it is not at all certain what the concept of equivalent monetary value actually entails. **15–77**

In its default form, an agreement under Part V will simply require the transfer **15–78** to the planning authority of the relevant percentage of the land in an undeveloped state. Presumably what was intended under s.96(3)(b) (above) was that any alternative package of measures would be equivalent to the planning gain which would have arisen in the event of a straightforward transfer of undeveloped land.[35] This planning gain consists of the notional saving arising from the fact that the planning authority is entitled to acquire land at a discount: the notional saving is the difference between what it would cost to purchase the land on the open market, and the actual sum payable by the planning authority under the statutory concept of "existing use" value. Normally the existing use value of the land will be considerably less than the open market value of the land, as the open market value will usually reflect the development potential of the land.

Unhappily, as with much of Part V, the wording of the legislation in this regard **15–79** is unsatisfactory. Three particular difficulties arise in practice as follows. First, the phrase "monetary value of the land" seems inapt in that it, arguably, denotes the open market value of the land *simpliciter* rather than the value of the *planning gain* which accrues to the planning authority in the case of the transfer of undeveloped land. This is discussed at paras 15–80 to 15–92. Secondly, it is not at all clear as to how statutory compensation is to be factored in when reckoning monetary value. This is discussed at paras 15–93 to 15–100. Thirdly, the manner in which the "existing use" value of land is defined produces the anomalous result that there is little or no planning gain in the case of the transfer of built houses. This may have a knock-on effect for reckoning monetary value for the purposes of s.96(3)(b). This is discussed at paras 15–101 to 15–102.

---

[34] For a detailed discussion see E. Galligan, "The equivalent monetary value principle in social housing" (2005) 12 I.P.E.L.J. 116.

[35] Departmental Circular HMS 4/04 of April 6, 2004 suggests that "[T]he equivalent monetary value is calculated by subtracting what the planning authority would have paid for the land (existing use value, or for land purchased prior to 25 August, 1999, the price paid for the land) from the market value of the land with planning permission (development value)." See also Circular Letter PD 2/2003 of March 11, 2003.

2. Monetary value of the land

15–80 It is unclear as to what meaning the phrase "monetary value" is to bear. Insofar as the draftsman has chosen not to use one of the other terms employed elsewhere under Part V—such as "price" or "compensation"—or, indeed, to use the concept of "open market" value as *per* the Acquisition of Land (Assessment of Compensation) Act 1919, it is to be assumed that this was deliberate and that the phrase "monetary value" is intended to mean something different. In this regard, it is submitted that there are, in theory at least, three possible meanings which might be ascribed.

(i) Does monetary value mean planning gain?

15–81 The first would be to say that what was intended was a reference to the value, *i.e.* the planning gain, to the planning authority. The benchmark, then, against which all alternative packages would fall to be measured is the notional saving resulting from the fact that the planning authority is entitled to acquire undeveloped land at a discount, *i.e.* existing use value, rather than at its open market value (which would reflect the land's development potential). This is the interpretation seemingly favoured by the Department of the Environment Heritage and Local Government.[36]

15–82 It has to be said, however, that to construe "monetary value" as meaning "planning gain" necessitates a very strained interpretation of the statutory wording. In particular, the phrase "monetary value of the land" suggests that it is the value of the land *simpliciter* which is involved, rather than some notional saving to the planning authority. In this regard, it is noteworthy that a different formula for equivalence had been used under the original s.96. There, provision had been made for a planning authority to take a financial payment in lieu of a land transfer where, for reasons of the size, shape or other attribute of the site, a Part V agreement would have been impractical. The payment to the planning authority was to be of "an amount equivalent in value to the transfer of land". A similar reference to the value of the *transfer* of the land, as opposed to the value of the land *simpliciter*, should have been made under the amended s.96(3)(b) if it was intended to describe planning gain.

15–83 The difficulties with interpreting "monetary value" as planning gain are compounded when one considers the other side of the equation, where it is the aggregate monetary value "of the property", *i.e.* built houses or serviced sites, or of the "amounts", *i.e.* financial payment, which is to satisfy the equivalence test. It is difficult to understand how the monetary value of, say, a financial payment, could mean other than its value *simpliciter*.

---

[36] Departmental Circular HMS 4/04 of April 6, 2004 suggests that "[T]he equivalent monetary value is calculated by subtracting what the planning authority would have paid for the land (existing use value, or for land purchased prior to 25 August, 1999, the price paid for the land) from the market value of the land with planning permission (development value)." See also Circular Letter PD 2/2003 of March 11, 2003.

(ii) Does monetary value mean open market value?

The second possible interpretation would be to say that "monetary value" refers **15–84** to the open market value of the land *simpliciter*.[37]

Although this interpretation sits more comfortably with the literal wording of **15–85** s.96(3)(b) than that put forward at (i) above, it is almost impossible to reconcile with the general scheme of Part V (as amended). The open market value basis of assessment which normally governs claims for statutory compensation is expressly disapplied under s.96(7)(b).[38]

> "For the purposes of paragraph (a), section 2(2) of the Acquisition of Land (Assessment of Compensation) Act, 1919, shall not apply and the value of the land shall be calculated on the assumption that it was at that time and would remain unlawful to carry out any development in relation to the land other than exempted development."

In circumstances where the "open market" value basis of assessment under the **15–86** Acquisition of Land (Assessment of Compensation) Act 1919 is disapplied, it might be argued that it is not open to the property arbitrator to go beyond the existing use value basis of assessment, even in the context of assessing "monetary value".[39]

Unless, therefore, some basis can be found for saying that the phrase "the **15–87** value of the land" in s.96(7)(b) refers to something different and distinct from "the monetary value of the land" under s.96(3)(b), "monetary value" cannot be construed as meaning "open market" value.

Finally, it should also be noted that this interpretation would give rise to the **15–88** following anomaly. The value of any alternative package would have to be equivalent to the *gross* open market value of the (default) land, rather than simply the *net* difference between the open market value and existing use value. This would mean that any alternative package would, in fact, be more valuable

---

[37] In order to make this interpretation workable, however, it is probably necessary to add the following refinement: the planning authority must be absolved from any requirement to make a payment—whether described as compensation, price or otherwise—in respect of the transfer of serviced sites or built houses. This latter point will be discussed in detail at paras 15–93 to 15–100, when the entire question as to whether, in cases other than the default option of the transfer of undeveloped land, the planning authority is required to make an actual payment of some form of "compensation" is examined.

[38] PDA 2000, s.96(7)(b) (as substituted by the Planning and Development (Amendment) Act 2002).

[39] It has to be said that a similar difficulty would arise, albeit to a much lesser extent, if "monetary value" is interpreted as "planning gain" as suggested at (i) above. This is because the calculation of the planning gain, by necessity, requires the assessment of the open market value of the land; the planning gain is the difference between this figure and the existing use value of the land. A distinguishing feature, however, may be that, in this context, the attribution of a figure to open market value is only a step in the process, rather than an end in itself.

to the planning authority than a straightforward transfer of undeveloped land, *i.e.* no allowance would be made for the fact that some compensation would have been payable by the planning authority in the event of the transfer of undeveloped land. Thus, for example, if the developer is to discharge his Part V obligations by the making of a financial payment, the sum payable will be greater than the notional planning gain otherwise arising on the transfer of undeveloped land.

(iii) Does monetary value mean the "existing use" value of the land?

15–89 This, then, brings us to the third possible interpretation of "monetary value" which is that it means the existing use value of the land. Under this interpretation, the monetary value of the land is to be assessed by the same formula which governs the determination of the statutory compensation the planning authority is required to pay on the transfer of undeveloped land, *i.e.* the monetary value of the land is to be calculated on the assumption that it was at that time and would remain unlawful to carry out development other than exempted development.[40]

15–90 This approach avoids any necessity to assess the open market value of the land, consideration of which is apparently precluded by the provisions of s.96(7)(b),[41] and thus does not suffer from the difficulties discussed at paras 15–85 to 15–87 above.

15–91 The weakness of this approach, however, is that if it applies, then the benchmark of the monetary value of the land—against which any alternative package is to be compared—would be fixed at the very low level of the existing use value of the land. Thus no recognition would be given for the fact that the planning authority normally achieves a planning gain in the event of the transfer of undeveloped land under the existing use formula, and any alternative package will thus almost always be less attractive than the default option. The point may be illustrated by the following example. If the planning authority goes for the default option, and takes a transfer of undeveloped land with an existing agricultural value, then it achieves a significant planning gain in that it avoids having to pay residential value for the land. If the planning authority had decided instead to take a financial payment in lieu of a transfer of land, then—under this interpretation of "monetary value"—the developer would only be required to make a financial payment which reflected the agricultural value of the land, *i.e.* a much smaller sum.

---

[40] PDA 2000, s.96(6) (as amended by the Planning and Development (Amendment) Act 2002).

[41] PDA 2000, s.96(7)(b) (as amended by the Planning and Development (Amendment) Act 2002).

Summary

As appears from the foregoing discussion, none of the three possible **15–92** interpretations of the phrase "monetary value of the land" is entirely satisfactory. Thus, it is difficult to say how precisely the benchmark, against which all alternative packages fall to be measured, is to be calculated. The uncertainty in this regard is to be deprecated, and is causing unnecessary confusion and delay in practice.

3. How is statutory compensation to be factored in?

Things become even more confusing when one focuses on the other side of the **15–93** equation, and considers how the aggregate monetary value of any alternative package of measures put forward by a developer is to be quantified. In particular, it is unclear from the legislation as to whether statutory compensation is to be factored into the calculation.

In the case of the default option, namely the transfer of undeveloped land, **15–94** there is a two-way transaction. The developer transfers the requisite percentage of the land; the planning authority makes a payment of compensation, albeit usually discounted by reference to the existing use value of the land. Of course, the transaction is artificial, involving an unequal bargain, in that although consideration (in the form of the payment of statutory compensation) nominally passes from the planning authority, the real benefit of the transaction accrues to the planning authority in that it secures residential land for a payment far less than open market value.

In principle, a similar artificial transaction might be carried out in the case of **15–95** the transfer of built houses or serviced sites, with the planning authority again making a nominal payment to the developer. It might be more realistic, however, if the planning authority made no payment, and the developer instead simply transferred a *smaller* number of built houses or serviced sites to the planning authority. Smaller, because there will be no payment from the planning authority to set-off against the monetary value of the built houses or serviced sites. The *entire* monetary value of each unit will, therefore, be reckoned in calculating the aggregate monetary value of the built houses/serviced sites, and the target (equivalent monetary value) will be reached with a smaller number of units.

Although there is practical merit in saying that the artificiality of the planning **15–96** authority making a payment should be avoided, such a result may be difficult to reconcile with the wording of the legislation, and, in particular, with the provision made under s.96(3)(d) for the determination of the "price" to be paid for houses or sites to be transferred pursuant to a Part V agreement.

> "(d) Where houses or sites are to be transferred to the planning authority in accordance with an agreement under paragraph (b), the price of such houses or sites shall be determined on the basis of — (i) the site cost of the houses or the cost of the sites (calculated in accordance with subsection (6)), and (ii) the building

and attributable development costs as agreed between the authority and the developer, including profit on the costs."

15–97　The fact that express provision is made for the determination of prices is strongly indicative of the existence of an obligation on the planning authority to make payments in respect of the houses or sites transferred. This tends to be confirmed by the fact that s.96(6)—by which site cost is to be determined—refers to the payment of "compensation". As against this, it might be said that the determination of "price" is simply part of the process of assessing the monetary value of the built houses for the equivalence test, and was never intended to suggest that a payment in the form of a purchase price was to be made to the developer.

15–98　On balance, the better view is probably that the wording of the legislation requires compensation to be paid. If this is the position, then it may render an interpretation of "monetary value" as open market value unworkable. A requirement to pay statutory compensation would eat into the planning authority's planning gain, and thus even if the formal statutory benchmark is open market value, the reality is that a planning authority will never choose to accept built houses or serviced sites because the planning gain will almost always be less than in the case of the transfer of undeveloped land. The planning authority is required to consider matters such as whether the form of the Part V agreement will constitute the best use of the resources available to it, and thus could not ignore the fact that the planning gain would be much less in the case of the transfer of built houses/serviced sites, even if the formal requirement of equivalence had been met. This point is elaborated upon immediately below.

15–99　Monetary value must mean the same thing on both sides of the equation. Thus, if the benchmark—against which the alternative package is to be measured—is to be open market value, then this applies equally to the assessment of the monetary value of the built houses or serviced sites. One therefore determines what the open market value of the requisite percentage of undeveloped land would be, and then requires the developer to transfer built houses and serviced sites to the same value. The acreage of developed land to be transferred will be smaller because the open market value of land with a house built on it will, naturally, be greater than the same area of undeveloped land. If a requirement to pay statutory compensation is then superimposed, the planning authority will be at a loss in that the value to it of the built houses and serviced sites will have been reduced significantly, i.e. by the amount of statutory compensation payable.[42] On this analysis, a planning authority, given a choice between taking undeveloped land or built houses/serviced sites, will always have to choose the former because the planning gain will be greater. The formula for calculating building and attributable development costs (including profit on the costs) is such that there is little, if any, planning gain on same. The planning gain is thus

---

[42] The loss will be even greater if the existing use formula has the limitations discussed at paras 15–101 to 15–102.

largely confined to the site cost, and there would be a lesser planning gain were the planning authority to accept a smaller area of built houses in preference to the requisite percentage of undeveloped land.

If there is a statutory requirement to pay compensation, then planning gain **15–100** represents a much more logical benchmark. The formula for calculating planning gain is such that it will automatically adjust so as to reflect the fact that compensation is payable. Conversely, because the open market value of land is a given/datum, and the open market value of the built houses and serviced sites remains unaffected by whether the planning authority makes a payment or not, open market value results in a reduction in the acreage of land to be transferred, without making any allowance for planning gain/statutory compensation.

4. "Existing use" formula and built houses

The peculiar definition of "existing use" appears to produce a startling result **15–101** in the case of the transfer of built houses. As elaborated upon below, this occurs because the valuation date appears to be the date of transfer to the planning authority.

In the case of the transfer of built houses, the compensation payable—under **15–102** s.96(3)(d)—is the site cost, plus the building and attributable development costs. Unlike the position in the case of undeveloped land, however, the site cost may not necessarily be discounted by reference to existing use value. This is because all that the rules require is that *future* development be disregarded. In the case of built houses, the development will, by definition, have already taken place at the date of transfer and this existing development will have to be taken into account in assessing the site cost. Thus, the statutory compensation payable may well be close to market value. This may mean, in effect, that the planning authority achieves no planning gain: the price it pays for the transferred houses is open market value. Under such an analysis, it will always be more attractive for the planning authority either to take a transfer of undeveloped land or to accept a financial contribution.

5. Worked-out examples

The foregoing discussion has—as a result of the tortuous wording of the **15–103** legislation—been convoluted. I thought it might assist in making matters a little clearer were I to provide worked-out examples of how the competing interpretations might operate in practice.

Worked-out example No.1: Planning gain

This first example is based on the assumption that "monetary value" should be **15–104** interpreted as meaning "planning gain".

15–105 The benchmark—against which the alternative package falls to be assessed—would be the difference between the open market value of the land, and the compensation which would be payable in the event of the planning authority accepting a straightforward transfer of undeveloped land.

15–106 The calculation of the monetary value of the alternative package will differ according to whether statutory compensation is payable. If compensation is payable, then the monetary value is the difference between the open market value of the built house or serviced site, and the sum of (i) the site cost calculated by reference to the existing use formula, and (ii) the building and attributable development costs (including profit on those costs). As the statutory formula under s.96(3)(d) allows for little or no planning gain on the building and attributable development cost of the houses, this should mean that the developer would have to transfer an acreage of houses equivalent to the requisite area of undeveloped land. In other words, because any planning gain is on the site cost alone, and not on the building and attributable development cost of the houses, the actual land take will not be reduced.

15–107 If the existing use formula has the limitations discussed earlier at para.15–102, *i.e.* if it does not result in a discounting of the site cost in the case of land containing built houses on the date of transfer, then there will never be any planning gain in the case of the transfer of built houses and, accordingly, the mandatory requirement of monetary equivalence will never be satisfied. No quantity of houses would ever be enough to match the planning gain otherwise arising on the transfer of undeveloped land.

15–108 If, contrary to the assumption underlying paras 15–106 to 15–107, statutory compensation is not payable, then the area of land to be transferred to the planning authority will be smaller than the requisite percentage of undeveloped land. Smaller, because as there will be no payment from the planning authority to set-off against the monetary value of the built houses or serviced sites, the planning gain in the case of each unit will be its open market value. The target (equivalent monetary value) will be reached with a smaller area of land.

Worked-out example No.2: Open market value

15–109 The second example is based on the assumption that "monetary value" should be interpreted as meaning "open market value".

15–110 The benchmark—against which the alternative package falls to be assessed—would be the open market value of the land.

15–111 If equivalent monetary value simply requires that the value of the alternative package be equivalent to the open market value of the default land, *i.e.* a value which reflects the development potential of that land, then, as Galligan points out,[43] the percentage of housing units to be transferred will always be *less*

---

[43] E. Galligan, "The equivalent monetary value principle in social housing" (2005) 12 I.P.E.L.J. 116.

than the requisite percentage of undeveloped land. This is because the open market value of the houses will already include the open market value of the site. A developed site will have a greater value than an undeveloped one, hence a lesser acreage of built houses will match in value a greater area of undeveloped land. Accordingly, the land-take of the planning authority will always be diminished in the case of the transfer of built houses.

M. Restriction on Compensation

The default option is for a developer to transfer to the planning authority part **15–112** of the land the subject-matter of the application for planning permission. This represents a form of compulsory acquisition of lands, and in the ordinary course one would have expected that the planning authority would be required to pay compensation equivalent to market value to the affected landowner. One of the remarkable features of Part V, however, is that the planning authority need only pay compensation in the lesser sum of the "existing use" value of the land. As explained at paras 15–119 to 15–126, the concept of "existing use" is an artificial one and requires the property arbitrator to disregard the development potential or "hope" value of the land.

The calculation of compensation differs depending on whether or not the land **15–113** was purchased before or after August 25, 1999 (that is, before or after the publication of the Bill).[44] Further special rules apply in the case of land acquired by gift or inheritance.

1. Constitutionality of limited compensation

The constitutionality of making only limited provision for the payment of **15–114** compensation was considered by the Supreme Court in its decision in *In the matter of Part V of the Planning and Development Bill, 1999*.[45] Article 34.3.3° of the Constitution provides, *inter alia*, that no court shall have jurisdiction to question the validity of any provision of a law, the Bill for which shall have been referred to the Supreme Court under Article 26. Accordingly, whereas challenges may be made to the implementation of the procedures under Part V of the PDA 2000, the constitutionality of same is probably unimpeachable.[46]

---

[44] The constitutionality of this alleged retrospective effect was upheld by the Supreme Court in *In the matter of Part V of the Planning and Development Bill, 1999* [2000] 2 I.R. 321; [2001] 1 I.L.R.M. 81.

[45] [2000] 2 I.R. 321; [2001] 1 I.L.R.M. 81.

[46] *Quaere* the effect of s.96 having been substituted wholesale under the Planning and Development (Amendment) Act 2002.

2. Land purchased before August 25, 1999

15–115   The compensation payable is the price paid for the land together with such sum in respect of interest thereon (including, in circumstances where there is a mortgage on the land, interest paid in respect of the mortgage) as may be determined by the property arbitrator.[47]

3. Land purchased after August 25, 1999

15–116   In the case of land purchased after August 25, 1999, the compensation payable is the value of the land calculated by reference to its "existing use" on the date of the transfer of ownership, on the basis that on that date it would have been, and would thereafter have continued to be, unlawful to carry out any development in relation to that land other than exempted development.

4. Building and attributable development costs

15–117   In circumstances where the Part V agreement provides for the transfer of built houses or serviced sites, it appears—as discussed at para.15–98—that an additional sum must also be paid in respect of the building and/or attributable development costs.[48] It is important to note that it is expressly provided that this additional sum is to include "profit" on the building and/or attributable development costs. To put the matter another way, whereas the planning authority is only required to pay the statutory compensation in respect of the acquisition of the land itself (site cost), commercial market rates must be paid in respect of the actual development works or services. The number and price of houses and/or sites to be transferred is to be fixed by the property arbitrator in default of agreement.[49]

5. Affordable housing units

15–118   It is to be regretted that some confusion has arisen in practice as to the correct measure of compensation in the case of affordable housing units. In particular, it seems that some planning authorities are acting on the fallacy that compensation need only be paid in the amount that the individual purchasing the house will ultimately pay. With respect, this is to confuse the two quite separate issues of the acquisition cost to the planning authority, and the sale price to an eligible purchaser. Eligibility for affordable (as opposed to social) housing is defined primarily in terms of the ratio between an individual's income,

---

[47] PDA 2000, s.96(6)(a)(i)(I) (as substituted by the Planning and Development (Amendment) Act 2002).

[48] PDA 2000, s.96(3)(d) (as substituted by the Planning and Development (Amendment) Act 2002).

[49] PDA 2000, s.96(7) (as substituted by the Planning and Development (Amendment) Act 2002).

and the mortgage payments which would arise on the purchase of a house to meet his or her accommodation needs. In terms of the compensation payable to the developer, however, there is no distinction drawn between social housing and affordable housing. In particular, where the developer provides built houses, the compensation will include, *inter alia*, profit on the building and/or attributable development costs. The fact that the compensation payable may be greater than the price the planning authority may receive from the ultimate purchaser of the house is irrelevant for this purpose. Any shortfall must be borne by the planning authority, and cannot be avoided by paying the developer a sum less than his statutory entitlement.

N. "Existing use" value

In the case of most other compulsory acquisitions, the usual basis for the assessment of compensation is the open market value of the land. Section 2 of the Acquisition of Land (Assessment of Compensation) Act 1919 specifies a series of rules for the assessment of compensation. These rules were subsequently added to by virtue of the Local Government (Planning & Development) Act 1963.[50]   **15–119**

Rule 2 is in the following terms.   **15–120**

> "The value of land shall, subject as hereinafter provided, be taken to be the amount which the land if sold in the open market by a willing seller might be expected to realise: provided always that the arbitrator shall be entitled to consider all returns and assessments of capital value for taxation made or acquiesced in by the claimant."

In the ordinary course, the open market value of the land would include an element which reflected any development potential or "hope" value of the land. Thus, for example, agricultural land might well have a higher value if there was any prospect of the land subsequently being available for development purposes.   **15–121**

A different approach is taken under Part V of the PDA 2000 (as amended), and an attempt has been made to exclude development potential. The drafting in this regard is clumsy, however: rather than simply exclude development potential as a head of claim, the entire of Rule 2 of the Acquisition of Land (Assessment of Compensation) Act 1919 (open market value) is disapplied, and the concept of existing use value is introduced.[51] Thus the multi-faceted concept of open market value has been replaced with the single-issue concept of existing use value. This outcome is unsatisfactory. The concept of open   **15–122**

---

[50] See the saver at PDA 2000, s.265(3) and also under the Planning and Development (Strategic Infrastructure) Act 2006, s.46.
[51] PDA 2000, s.96(7) (as substituted by the Planning and Development (Amendment) Act 2002).

market value had been fleshed out by case law and was well established; development potential was but one aspect of many embraced by it. It would have been more sensible to have retained the open market value basis of assessment, and to have simply excluded development potential as a head of claim. Instead, there is an element of throwing the baby out with the bath water in the approach actually adopted under the legislation.

15–123   Section 96(7)(b) provides that:

> "[…] the value of the land shall be calculated on the assumption that it was at that time and would remain unlawful to carry out any development in relation to the land other than exempted development."

15–124   The effect of this provision is that the development potential or "hope" value of the land is to be excluded. The exclusion only applies to *subsequent* development of the land. This is made clear by the provisions of s.96(6)(b) as follows.

> "The value of the land calculated by reference to its existing use on the *date of transfer* of ownership of the land to the planning authority concerned on the basis that *on that date* it would have been, and would *thereafter* have continued to be, unlawful to carry out any development in relation to that land other than exempted development."
> *Emphasis supplied.

15–125   In the case of land which remains undeveloped as of the date of its transfer, these rules will result in compensation being payable in a very much reduced sum only. The position was summarised thus by the Supreme Court in *In the matter of Part V of the Planning & Development Bill, 1999.*[52]

> "That statutory scheme has been fully explained in the earlier part of this judgment. It clearly envisages that a landowner who develops his property for housing and who is not exempted by other provisions of Part V will in general be required to cede up to 20% of the land to the housing authority for the provision of houses at a price which reflects the existing use of the land (normally agricultural value) and which, accordingly, will be significantly below the market value of the land, if by market value is meant the price which the property might be expected to fetch if sold on the open market enjoying the same right to develop as that enjoyed by the landowner in respect of the remaining 80% or more of the lands in question. Compensation will, accordingly, be paid for the undoubted restriction on the exercise by the landowner of his property rights, but it will in that sense be compensation at a level significantly short of its market value."

15–126   The wording of the legislation is such, however, that in the case of the transfer of built houses the compensation payable for the site cost will not be reduced. This is because all that the rules require is that *future* development be disregarded. In the case of built houses, the development will, by definition, have already taken place at the date of transfer and the arbitrator will be required

---

[52] [2000] 2 I.R. 321 at 349.

to take this existing development into account in assessing the value of the land. It is submitted that the effect of all of this is that the property arbitrator is entitled to have regard to the fact that the land has the benefit of planning permission, and has been used for the development of houses. This result might appear anomalous but the fact that the legislation impacts on constitutionally protected rights demands that a strict interpretation be given to the legislation.

O. Levy

Under the PDA 2000, as initially enacted, withering provisions had applied to planning permissions granted in respect of an application made after August 25, 1999.[53] The legal position has been changed radically under the Planning and Development (Amendment) Act 2002. The amendments in this regard are achieved in a somewhat awkward manner. First, the ordinary provisions as to the life of a planning permission (in particular, as to the entitlement of a developer to apply to have the life of a planning permission extended in circumstances where he or she had carried out "substantial works" within the life of the planning permission) are expressly applied to applications made after August 25, 1999, to which the provisions in respect of social and affordable housing would have otherwise applied if the application for planning permission had been made after the inclusion of a housing strategy in the development plan. Thus, the very real difficulties as to interpretation which had arisen in respect of s.96(15) of the PDA 2000 are recreated.   **15–127**

Secondly, and as a *quid pro quo* for this release from the withering provisions, the amendments go on then to impose a requirement for the payment of a levy. More specifically, a condition is deemed to be attached to the planning permission providing for the payment of a levy.[54] In very broad terms, the levy is to be based on either the actual consideration paid (in the case of a sale at arm's length) or otherwise on the market value. If the market value/consideration paid exceeds €270,000, then the levy is to be one per cent; if less than the figure of €270,000, one half per cent.   **15–128**

The payment of the levy is to be made at such time as the planning authority specifies. It is important to note that the planning authority may specify that the payment be made *before* the date on which the disposal/sale concerned of the relevant house is effected. In other words, it would seem that a developer might be required to make a payment in advance of the actual sale.   **15–129**

Finally in this regard, there are comprehensive anti-avoidance provisions which are designed to prevent the developer passing on the cost of the levy to the purchaser. Various transactions in this regard are stated to be void. Furthermore,   **15–130**

---

[53] PDA 2000, s.96(15) (as unamended).
[54] PDA 2000, s.96B(2) (as inserted by s.4 of the Planning and Development (Amendment) Act 2002).

provision is made whereby any monies paid in this regard by the purchaser (or other person obtaining the house) are to be paid back by the developer.

1. Which planning permissions are affected?

15–131   Under s.96A, the requirement to pay a levy applies to planning permissions granted pursuant to an application made after August 25, 1999 to which Part V "would have applied if the application for permission had been made after the inclusion of a housing strategy in the development plan under section 94(1)".

15–132   Section 96(1) as originally enacted had provided, *inter alia*, that the section apply to an application for planning permission for the development of houses, or where an application related to a mixture of developments, to that *part* of the application which related to the development of houses. In other words, it would seem that Part V applied to *any* application in respect of residential development.[55] Of course, given the fact that a housing strategy may specify different percentages for different areas of land zoned residential, and, indeed, may indicate in respect of a particular area that there is *no* requirement for social and affordable housing, it does not necessarily follow that every application for planning permission in respect of residential development will be subject to social and affordable housing. Section 96A does not appear to be sufficiently flexible, however, to tolerate this fact. Accordingly, it would seem that the withering provisions might have applied to an application for planning permission in respect of land which would not, in any event, have been subject to a requirement to provide social and affordable housing under Part V (because of the contents of the housing strategy). This would produce the anomalous result that notwithstanding the fact that no benefit arose from the timing of the application for planning permission in such circumstances (in that the contents of the housing strategy had the effect that no requirement for social and affordable housing would have been imposed in any event), such a planning permission was nevertheless subject to the withering provisions.

2. Levy does not necessarily apply to all houses

15–133   The requirement to pay the levy does not necessarily apply to all of the houses under the planning permission. Again, the legislative provisions in this regard are cumbersome, and require consideration of the repealed s.96(15). Under s.96(15), a withering planning permission would, on its expiration, cease to have effect as regards any portion of the development consisting of buildings

---

[55] The deficiencies in the drafting in this regard have been tacitly acknowledged by the legislature by its action in subsequently modifying the wording under the Planning and Development (Amendment) Act 2002. The amended s.96(1) now includes the additional, qualifying words, "on land to which such an objective applies". Regrettably, this subsequent qualification of the wording is probably of no benefit in the present context in that the provisions in respect of the levy are predicated on the wording of the original, unamended s.96.

the external walls of which had not been completed. The requirement to pay a levy under s.96B only applies to those (individual) houses, permission for which would have ceased to have effect or have expired but for s.4 of the Planning and Development (Amendment) Act 2002. Thus, it would seem that the requirement to pay the levy only applies to those (individual) houses the external walls of which had not been completed by the date on which the planning permission would otherwise have expired under the withering provisions. To put the matter another way, the levy only applies to those houses which are completed (external walls) more than two years from the date of the grant of the planning permission (or after December 31, 2002 if later).

3. Criticisms

Approaching the matter from first principles, one would have thought that the following would have to be attended to in drafting the anti-avoidance provisions. First, the type of planning permission affected would be identified precisely. Secondly, provision would then have been made to disapply the requirement to pay the levy in the event that, for whatever reason, a condition requiring social and affordable housing was, in fact, applied to a planning permission notwithstanding the fact that the application had been made in the interim period. Unfortunately the provisions of s.96A do not succeed in either of these respects.

15–134

The type of planning permission to which the levy applies is defined only in terms of the timing of the making of the application for planning permission. More specifically, s.96A refers to an application made after August 25, 1999 and to which Part V would have applied if the application for planning permission had been made after the inclusion of a housing strategy in the development plan. The most obvious criticism of this aspect of the provision is, of course, that on a literal interpretation the levy applies not only to those applications which took free of any requirement to provide social and affordable housing (on account of their being applied for prior to the coming into full force and effect of Part V), but also to all planning permissions since then which were, in fact, subject to a requirement to make provision for social and affordable housing. If the seeming objective of the levy, namely to target opportunistic planning permissions, is to be achieved, a more appropriate form of wording would be as follows: "to which Part V would *otherwise* have applied if the application for planning permission had been made after the inclusion of a housing strategy in the development plan *but did not apply*".

15–135

On a literal interpretation of s.96A the levy applies even to those planning permissions in respect of which a housing condition was attached under s.96 (following the coming into full force and effect of the requirement to make provision for social and affordable housing). Even were the courts to steer away from such a literal interpretation, and instead were to interpret the section in such a way as not to apply to planning permissions of this type, a difficulty may nevertheless still remain in relation to other (earlier) planning permissions.

15–136

In particular, it seems that even prior to the coming into full force and effect of Part V it was open to an applicant for planning permission to *volunteer* to provide social and affordable housing. In practice therefore there will be certain planning permissions which notwithstanding the fact that they were granted prior to the coming into full force and effect of s.96 will nevertheless provide for social and affordable housing. It would seem quite unfair, and entirely inconsistent with the apparent rationale, to require the payment of a levy in respect of such a planning permission. Yet this is what the effect of s.96A appears to be.

P. Glenkerrin Homes Judgment

15–137   Subsequent to this book being sent for typesetting, the High Court delivered a landmark judgment in respect of Part V. Two cases were heard together, and Clarke J. delivered an omnibus judgment on the matter on July 19, 2007.[56] A summary of the principal conclusions are set out below. Obviously, due to constraints of time and space, it is only possible, at this late stage in the publishing process, to set these out in short form, and readers are urged to review the judgment in its entirety.

15–138   The first issue of principle addressed by Clarke J. was as to the interpretation of the terms "monetary value" and "aggregate monetary value". Clarke J. held that the terms should be interpreted as referring to the net benefit to the planning authority of the particular transaction, rather than to the gross or open market value of the land, house or serviced site (as the case may be). Thus, the "monetary value" of the default option of the transfer of undeveloped land consists of the difference between the open market value of the land and the statutory compensation which a planning authority would be required to pay under the existing use formula.

15–139   The next issue of principle addressed by Clarke J. was as to how the "existing use" formula operates in the case of the transfer of built houses. As discussed above at para.15–126, on one view of the legislation the existing use of the land in the case of a transfer of a house is a residential use, *i.e.* its existing use value will coincide with its open market value. On this interpretation, there would be no planning gain to the planning authority in that the existing use formula would not produce any discount on the open market value. Clarke J. rejected an argument that the legislation should be construed in this way, saying that, because the planning gain only ever arises on the site cost, an interpretation of existing use value which treated the existing use as residential would be unworkable.

---

[56] *Cork County Council v Shackleton* and *Dun Laoghaire Rathdown County Council v Glenkerrin Homes*, unreported, High Court, Clarke J., July 19, 2007.

Insofar as the calculation of the site cost of apartments is concerned, Clarke J. held that the approach to be adopted is as follows. The area of each apartment is to be calculated as a proportion of the overall apartment block. The relevant proportion of the site cost of the footprint of the apartment block is then to be attributed to the individual apartments accordingly. **15–140**

Clarke J. also addressed the question as to whether a planning authority is required to pay statutory compensation in the case of the transfer of houses. Clarke J. interpreted the legislation as requiring such a payment. First, the court accepted the argument made on behalf of the planning authorities that the use of the term "price" in s.96(3)(d) implied that such a sum was, in fact, to be paid by the planning authority, rather than being notionally included in a calculation of the number of units to be transferred. To put the matter another way, the use of the term "price" suggested that a "purchase price" had to be paid by the planning authority. Secondly, Clarke J. held that this interpretation best provided for legal certainty in that it provided a clear formula for calculating the number of houses to be transferred. **15–141**

INDEX

Planning conditions—*contd.*
occupancy conditions, 4–102—
4–108, 8–256
open spaces, 4–96
opening hours of business premises,
4–100
points of detail, 4–126—4–134,
10–117—10–119
precision, 4–82—4–83
prior to commencement of
development, 4–85,
7–19—7–30
protected structure, 4–100
public rights of way, 4–136—4–138
reasonableness, 4–84
reasons for imposing, 3–179—3–180
reinstatement of land, 4–100
relevance to planning, 4–80
removal of structures, 4–100
restoration of land, 4–139—4–141
roads, drains, car parks etc, 4–99
security for satisfactory completion,
4–98
sequence and timing of works, 4–99
social and affordable housing,
4–120—4–125 *see also* **Social
and affordable housing**
special development contributions,
4–118—4–119
statutory provisions, 4–59—4–62
strategic infrastructure development,
10–83—10–92
time limit for completion of work,
4–97
transboundary effects, 4–135
trees, shrubs etc, 4–97
use conditions, 4–101, 5–03
waste collection and recycling, 4–99
waste management licence, and,
4–86
Planning decision
appeal against *see* **Appeal to An
Bord Pleanála**
availability of documents for
inspection and purchase,
3–230
compensation for adverse decision
see **Compensation**
conditions attached to grant of
permission *see* **Planning
conditions**
default planning permission *see*
Default planning permission

Planning decision—*contd.*
development plan, duty to have
regard to, 1–21—1–26,
4–44—4–49
elected members, limited powers,
3–163—3–169
executive function, 3–163
form and contents, 3–170—3–172
hierarchy of matters to be considered,
4–41
improper purpose, 12–198—12–201
irrelevant considerations
exclusion of compensation, 4–35,
6–17
ground of judicial review,
12–194—12–197
personal circumstances,
4–39—4–40
pre-existing works in application
for retention planning
permission, 4–36—4–38
judicial review *see* **Judicial review**
maximum periods, 3–184—3–185
environmental impact statement,
request for information or
evidence, 3–190—3–192
major accident hazard, 3–194
material contravention procedure,
3–193
request for further information or
evidence, 3–186—3–189
notification requirements,
3–170—3–172
other matters to have regard to,
4–41—4–43
architectural conservation area,
4–66, 8–62
development plan, 1–21—1–26,
4–44—4–49
environmental impact assessment,
4–70
European site etc, 4–54—4–55
government policy etc,
4–56—4–58, 4–71—4–73
integrated pollution prevention
and control licence, 4–74
local area plan, 4–63
ministerial guidelines and
directives, 4–77—4–78
place of worship, 4–65, 8–36
planning conditions, 4–59—4–62
protected structures, 4–64, 8–35

Public safety development
environmental impact assessment,
13–133—13–136
exempted development, 8–357,
8–359—8–360
public consultation, 8–361—8–367
Purposive interpretation
environmental impact assessment
directive, 13–61—13–66,
13–254—13–258,
13–329—13–330
European Convention on Human
Rights Act 2003,
14–08—14–10, 14–33

Quarry
definition, 8–130
environmental impact assessment,
8–121—8–127,
13–95—13–100
pre-1964 quarry, 8–122—8–127
renewed control condition,
8–155—8–156
seven-year time limit, and, 8–175
size thresholds, 8–121
existing quarries, regulation of,
8–128—8–130
conditions, by way of *see*
**renewed control by way of
conditions** *below*
planning permission, requirement
for *see* **planning
permission** *below*
integrated pollution prevention and
control licence, effect of, 8–
145, 8–150
intensification of development *see*
**Intensification of
development**
overview of planning controls,
8–118—8–120
planning permission
compensation, 8–160
failure to apply for, 8–163—8–
164
planning authority's failure to
comply with time limits,
8–165—8–168
pre-1964 quarry, 8–159
requirement to apply for,
8–157—8–159
status pending determination of
application, 8–161—8–162

Quarry—*contd.*
registration
area registrable, 8–135
duty to register, 8–131
effect, 8–136—8–137
failure to register or submit
further information,
8–138—8–140
further information,
8–133—8–134
information required, 8–132
procedure following,
8–141—8–143
renewed control by way of
conditions
environmental impact assessment,
8–155—8–156
established pre-1964 use,
8–144—8–147
nature of conditions,
8–153—8–154
old planning permission,
8–148—8–152
planning authority's failure to
comply with time limits,
8–165—8–168
restoration condition, 4–139—4–141
unauthorised development
deeming provisions,
8–138, 8–163
enforcement action,
8–169—8–174
seven-year time limit for
enforcement action,
8–139—8–140, 8–164
whether works or material change in
use, 2–81
quia timet, 7–111, 7–159

Railway route selection corridor,
1–82—1–83, 6–38—6–41
Reasons and main considerations
additional reasons in subsequent
decisions, 3–177—3–178
conditions, decision to impose,
3–179—3–180
decision on planning application,
3–173—3–176,
12–124—12–126
duty to state, 3–173—3–176,
12–119—12–123
elaboration upon, post-decision,
12–159—12–160

Reasons and main considerations— *contd.*
environmental impact assessment, project subject to, 13–238—13–244
failure to state, as ground of judicial review, 12–50, 12–161—12–163
Mulholland criteria, 12–139—12–141
new requirement, 12–139—12–145
old requirement, 12–127—12–138
planning appeal, decision on, 9–58—9–60
planning reports
failure to follow inspector's recommendation, 12–156—12–158
reference to, 12–154—12–155
post-*Mulholland* case law, 12–146—12–153
remedy for failure to state, 12–161—12–163
revocation of planning permission, 5–91—5–92
section 5 reference, 10–15—10–16
standard required, 12–121
strategic infrastructure development, 10–94
variation of development plan, 1–155—1–158
Red line, 3–50—03–52
Reference on development or exempted development *see* **Section 5 reference**
Regional planning guidelines
duty to have regard to, 1–173—1–178
objective, 1–168
regional planning authorities, 1–167
scope, 1–169
strategic environmental assessment, 1–170—1–172
variation of development plan where, 1–150
Remittal of matter to decision-maker, 11–348—11–350
Removal of structure
appeal to An Bord Pleanála, 8–216—8–217, 10–127—10–128
compensation, 6–98—6–100, 8–218—8–219

Removal of structure—*contd.*
default powers of planning authority, 8–215
enforcement 8–214—8–215
entries in statutory register, 8–213
exceptional power where development not unauthorised, 7–03, 8–210
expenses reasonably incurred, 8–220
failure to comply with notice, 8–214
notice procedure, 6–98, 8–211
relevant considerations, 8–212
withdrawal of notice, 8–213
res judicata, 4–18—4–21
Restoration notice
access to lands, 8–47
appeal to District Court, 8–43—8–44
endangerment notice distinguished, 8–41
failure to comply, 8–46
protected structure, works restoring, 8–40
representations to planning authority, 8–42
Restoration of land
planning condition, 4–100, 4–139—4–141
planning injunction, 7–161
Restrictive covenant, 7–221, 8–257
Retail Planning Guidelines, 4–27
Retention planning permission
criminal proceedings, and, 7–108
demolition of buildings, 5–40
dual role of planning authority, 5–42—5–43
enforcement action, and, 5–39, 7–08—7–11
estoppel not applicable, 7–14—7–15
exception to five-year rule, 5–47—5–48
planning injunction, and, 7–196—7–198
pre-existing works, irrelevant planning consideration, 4–36—4–38, 5–39
refusal
exclusion of compensation, 5–41, 6–16
existing home, Convention rights, 14–63—14–67, 14–177—14–188
statutory provisions, 5–38

983

Urgent enforcement action—*contd.*
warning letter, dispensing with,
7–53, 7–64
Urgent works
local authority, by, 8–308—8–309
protected structure, 8–39
State authority, by, 8–355
temporary structures for national
security purposes, 8–361
Use
definition, 2–07—2–10
discontinuance *see* **Discontinuance of use**
extinguishment, 2–85—2–86
material change in *see* **Material change in use**
planning conditions, 4–101, 5–03

Vibrations, 4–95
View or prospect of special amenity value
exclusion of compensation, 6–44
exempted development, restriction,
2–114
planning consideration, 4–08

Warning letter
contents, 7–55
decision to issue enforcement notice,
7–52
discretion of planning authority,
7–54
duty to investigate unauthorised
development, 7–52
legal effect, 7–53
limitation period, 7–38—7–39
time for issuing, 7–52
Waste disposal or recovery
emission of smells etc from treatment
plant, 14–160
environmental impact assessment,
13–41
exempted development, 2–48—2–51,
2–123
incineration, 13–41, 13–71, 13–74,
13–76—13–81, 14–163
material change in use, 2–46—2–47
material contravention of
development plan, 1–50
planning conditions, 4–99

Waste management licence
environmental impact assessment,
and, 13–39—13–40, 13–75—
13–83, 13–230—13–237
planning conditions, and, 4–86
planning consideration, 4–75
Waste management plan
development plan, inclusion in,
1–100
material contravention of
development plan, 3–140—
3–143, 4–50—4–52, 8–352—
8–353
Weekly list of planning applications,
3–66—3–69
Words and phrases
advertisement, 2–36
agriculture, 2–91
audience, 8–266
curtilage, 2–103
default planning permission, 3–199
development, 2–05—2–10
development agency, 8–176
development consent, 13–105—
13–113
development objectives, 1–68—1–76
environmental impact statement,
13–207
establishment, 8–229—8–240
event, 8–265
funfair, 8–292
house, 2–104, 15–13
material contravention, 1–47—1–49
monetary value of land, 15–80—
15–92
project, 13–60—13–101
proper planning and sustainable
development, 4–01—4–04
protected structure, 8–03—8–05,
8–50
public infrastructure and facilities,
1–221, 4–110
public infrastructure project or
service, 1–222, 4–111
quarry, 8–130
question of law, 12–95
shall not question the validity of,
11–27—11–31
significant additional data, 3–127—
3–129

Words and phrases—*contd.*
social and affordable housing,
15–09—15–11
statutory undertaker, 2–94
substantial works, 5–53—5–63
unauthorised development, 7–94,
7–131, 7–155
use, 2–07—2–10
works, 2–06
zoning objective, 1–81—1–83,
6–37—6–41

Works
definition, 2–06
development, constituting, 2–05
material change in use distinguished,
2–11
compensation payment,
2–12—2–13
diminished importance of
distinction, 2–15—2–16
exempted development, 2–14

Zoning objectives
meaning, 1–81—1–83, 6–37—6–41
development plan, contained in,
1–77—1–78
exclusion of compensation by
reference to, 1–79—1–80
current position, 6–34—6–36
previous legislation, 6–32—6–33
legitimate expectation arising from,
12–176—12–177
mandatory, whether, 1–84
matrix or table of uses, 1–86
no special voting required for
rezoning, 1–87
railway route selection corridor,
1–82—1–83, 6–38—6–41
social and affordable housing, 1–
95—1–99, 15–21—15–23
"special village status", 1–81